D1452806

INDEX
TO THE FINAL ROLLS OF THE
FIVE CIVILIZED TRIBES IN INDIAN TERRITORY

INDEX

TO

THE FINAL ROLLS

OF

Citizens and Freedmen

OF THE

FIVE CIVILIZED TRIBES
IN INDIAN TERRITORY

———

PREPARED BY

THE COMMISSION AND COMMISSIONER
TO THE FIVE CIVILIZED TRIBES

AND APPROVED BY

THE SECRETARY OF THE INTERIOR
ON OR PRIOR TO MARCH 4, 1907

———

COMPILED AND PRINTED
Under Authority Conferred by the Act of Congress
Approved June 21, 1906 (34 Stat. L. 325).

GENEALOGICAL PUBLISHING CO., INC. • BALTIMORE

Originally published: Washington, D.C., 1907
Reprinted: Genealogical Publishing Co., Inc., 2003
1001 N. Calvert St., Baltimore, Md. 21202
Library of Congress Catalogue Card Number: 2002117832
International Standard Book Number: 0-8063-1740-X
ISBN Set Number: 0-8063-1731-0
Made in the United States of America

Contents

INDEX TO
FINAL ROLL CHOCTAWS BY BLOOD

Name.	Roll No.	Name.	Roll No.
Ainsworth, Ella M.	7793	Alley, Elsie	12718
Ainsworth, Jesse B.	8151	Amos, Anthony	1607
Ainsworth, Clifford	8152	Amos, Allen	1608
Ainsworth, Chester	8153	Amos, Minnie	1609
Ainsworth, Alice	8154	Amos, Mary J.	1610
Ainsworth, Napoleon B.	8938	Amos, Evelina	1611
Ainsworth, Ben P.	8939	Amos, Kelisin	1688
Ainsworth, Helen	8940	Amos, Eni	1689
Ainsworth, Agnes „	8941	Amos, Hickman	2200
Ala-ho-nubbi	1447	Amos, Eastman	2978
Ala-ho-nubbi, Louisiana	1448	Amos, Nellis	2979
Alemohtubbi, Israel	3363	Amos, Ainsworth	3109
Alemohtubbi, Leon	3364	Amos, William	3308
Alemohtubbi, Elus	3365	Amos, Amancy	3310
Alemohtubbi, Litty	3366	Amos, Lena	8646
Alemohtubbi, Ilas	3368	Amos, Allen Wesley	8649
Alemohtubbi, David	3414	Amos, Sidney	8931
Alemohtubbi, Inez	3415	Amos, Tecumseh	8933
Alemohtubbi, Steson	3416	Amos, Emily	8937
Alemohtubbi, Emma	3417	Amos, Ann	13112
Alemohtubbi, Ina	3418	Amos, John	13113
Alemohtubbi, Sidney	15975	Amos, Eastman	13114
Allen, Nicey	1708	Amos, Kana	14648
Allen, Salina	1709	Anderson, Lizzie	58
Allen, Tensey	1710	Anderson, Reuben	59
Allen, Joe	3899	Anderson, Margaret	60
Allen, David	5422	Anderson, Elsie	61
Allen, Rufus	5424	Anderson, Mack	75
Allen, Isom	5425	Anderson, Ella Fry	76
Allen, John	5426	Anderson, Nora	77
Allen, John	5960	Anderson, Samuel	78
Allen, Sam	6828	Anderson, Rogers M.	79
Allen, Kate	7261	Anderson, Amanda	703
Allen, Chester L.	7262	Anderson, Luella	704
Allen, Hughgo	7263	Anderson, Wilson	705
Allen, William	7675	Anderson, Minnie	706
Allen, John K.	7676	Anderson, Ainie	707
Allen, Callie	8131	Anderson, Andel	725
Allen, Maud	8132	Anderson, Laura	727
Allen, William	8133	Anderson, Minnie	728
Allen, David	8134	Anderson, Buster	765
Allen, May	8135	Anderson, Ebel	855
Allen, Walter	8136	Anderson, Colbert	1082
Allen, Benjamin	9881	Anderson, Maggie	1083
Allen, Frank	9882	Anderson, Noel	1084
Allen, George	9885	Anderson, Mary	1085
Allen, Adaline	13904	Anderson, Lucy	1086
Allen, Cora E.	15057	Anderson, Nellie	1087
Allen, Emmerson A.	15491	Anderson, William	1485
Allen, Mary I.	15640	Anderson, Tobias	2359
Allen, Evi Catherine	15641	Anderson, Alex	2463
Allen, Jesse Edger	15642	Anderson, Byington	2464
Allen, Randel M.	15643	Anderson, Silas	2496
Allen, Rovilla	16064	Anderson, Jinsey	2497
Allen, Elizabeth	16103	Anderson, Moses	2499
Alexander, Henry	3159	Anderson, Rachel	2600
Alexander, Ellen	3162	Anderson, Louis	2700
Alexander, Alex	3923	Anderson, Louisa	2701
Alexander, Lucy	3924	Anderson, Roberson	2702
Alexander, Isaac	4626	Anderson, Jimmie	2703
Alexander, Eastman	4665	Anderson, Sillean	2704
Alexander, Lila	4666	Anderson, Eliza	2705
Alexander, Ned	5669	Anderson, Wicey	2706
Alexander, Henry	5915	Anderson, John	2781
Alexander, Sarah	5916	Anderson, Wysie	2782
Alexander, Enoch	5917	Anderson, Lasen	2784
Alexander, Eastman	5082	Anderson, Daniel	2808
Alexander, John C.	6954	Anderson, Wright	3047
Alexander, Jane	12407	Anderson, Winey	3480
Alexander, Patsy	12408	Anderson, Isaac	3482
Alexander, Sophia	12409	Anderson, Joe	4048
Alexander, Eliza	14250	Anderson, Nancy	4049
Alexander, Mattie	14251	Anderson, Isaac	4829
Alexander, Reder	14252	Anderson, George	4830
Alexander, Mamie	14253	Anderson, Impson	4831
Alexander, William,	14665	Anderson, McCasson	5076
Alexander, Belle	14713	Anderson, Watson	5301
Alfred, Morris	3946	Anderson, Lucinda	5302
Alfred, Maggie	3947	Anderson, Reason	5303
Allison, Calvin	11918	Anderson, Hattie	5304
Allison, Sallie	11919	Anderson, Lonzo W.	5305
Allison, Sarah	11920	Anderson, Minerva	5306
Allison, Agnes	11921	Anderson, James H.	5307
Allison, Lea	12106	Anderson, Emily	5308
Albright, Lewis	12585	Anderson, Barnabas	5309
		Anderson, Calvin	5318

Name.	Roll No.	Name.	Roll No.
Anderson, Zona	5319	Anderson, Luella	13065
Anderson, Jackson	5320	Anderson, Mamie	13068
Anderson, Lavisa	5368	Anderson, Lizzie	13071
Anderson, Jackman	5372	Anderson, Mollie	13084
Anderson, Josephine	5377	Anderson, Gibson	13085
Anderson, Nora	5378	Anderson, Emeline	13389
Anderson, Hickman	5385	Anderson, Sampson	13592
Anderson, Lucy A.	5392	Anderson, William B.	13593
Anderson, Elum	5394	Anderson, Bessie	13595
Anderson, Charles	5434	Anderson, Rogers	13600
Anderson, Eva	5435	Anderson, Raynie	13601
Anderson, Lillie	5436	Anderson, Freeman	13602
Anderson, Crawford J.	5489	Anderson, Willie	13603
Anderson, Esther L.	5490	Anderson, Osborne	13604
Anderson, Alice M.	5491	Anderson, Tandy	13727
Anderson, Bethel E.	5492	Anderson, Ida	13728
Anderson, Myrtle	5493	Anderson, Clarence J.	13729
Anderson, Nettie	5495	Anderson, Rhoda	13764
Anderson, Wesley	5496	Anderson, Dora	13765
Anderson, Park J.	5498	Anderson, Zadick	13735
Anderson, Emma	5519	Anderson, Norton	13930
Anderson, Nona	5520	Anderson, Missie	13931
Anderson, Alice	5521	Anderson, Robert	13334
Anderson, Mary	5530	Anderson, Emmett	13335
Anderson, Maggie	5531	Anderson, Alfred	13336
Anderson, Lejah	5533	Anderson, Margaret	14303
Anderson, Virgil	5546	Anderson, Albert Loray	14304
Anderson, Edmond	5677	Anderson, Willis Elyot	14305
Anderson, Nancy	5678	Anderson, Burney Etta	14306
Anderson, Millie	5686	Anderson, Manly Marlin	14307
Anderson, James R.	5688	Anderson, Joseph Kyle	14308
Anderson, Peter M.	5689	Anderson, Cynthia Pay-	
Anderson, James D.	5692	nel	14309
Anderson, Colbert	5696	Anderson, Maxey Over-	
Anderson, Lizzie	5697	ton	14310
Anderson, Lyles	5703	Anderson, Hazel	14311
Anderson, Bedford	5705	Anderson, Tom	14342
Anderson, Levina	5819	Anderson, Mary Jane	14344
Anderson, Houston D.	6192	Anderson, Graham	14345
Anderson, Joshua	6193	Anderson, Bradley	14396
Anderson, David	6195	Anderson, Jackman	15395
Anderson, James	6196	Anna, Lucy	1295
Anderson, Allen	6239	Anna, Santa	2952
Anderson, Levicey	6240	Anna, Liswe	2953
Anderson, Dixon	6241	Anna, Melville	2954
Anderson, Jincy	6242	Anna, Kolisten	2955
Anderson, Nicey	6243	Anna, Mary	2956
Anderson, Parker	6244	Anna, Tecumseh	2957
Anderson, Auda	6246	Anna, Thompson	2958
Anderson, James	6266	Anna, Sylvanie	16047
Anderson, Lizzie	6277	Anukwiatubbee, Mattie	4289
Anderson, Annie	6774	Anotubbee, Simon	4364
Anderson, David	7922	Anchahubbi, David	4486
Anderson, Levisey	7924	Anchahubbi, Aaron	4487
Anderson, Newman	7925	Anchahubbi, Sampson	4488
Anderson, Lucy A.	8521	Anowatubbi, Stephenson	4983
Anderson, Ola May	9051	Anowatubbi, Sissy	4984
Anderson, Noel	9224	Ansley, William	9162
Anderson, Joel	9286	Ansley, Joseph	9163
Anderson, Susan	9287	Ansley, Gilbert	12515
Anderson, Edward	9288	Ansley, Henry Ray	12516
Anderson, William P.	9464	Ansley, William H.	12771
Anderson, Robert	9507	Anolatubbi, Lizzie	9425
Anderson, Gibbie	10517	Andrews, Maggie	11391
Anderson, Robinson D.	10586	Andrews, Marie	11392
Anderson, Frank	10587	Anglin, Mary	14115
Anderson, Gilbert	10588	Apototubi, Jefferson	2279
Anderson, Nancy	10589	Apototubi, Soki	2280
Anderson, Lita	10591	Apototubi, Greek	2281
Anderson, Elsie	10811	Apototubi, Judy	2282
Anderson, Tandy Lee	10812	A-pis-an-tona	2396
Anderson, Willie E.	10855	Apala, Isabelle	14899
Anderson, Sarah	10856	Archer, Mary A.	4913
Anderson, Walter	10857	Armstrong, Noel	6211
Anderson, John	11349	Armstrong, Estella	10050
Anderson, Tennessee	11462	Armstrong, Willie	10051
Anderson, Willie	11477	Armstrong, Moses	10561
Anderson, Sila	11478	Armstrong, Eliza	11421
Anderson, Eden	11695	Armstrong, Edmond	11424
Anderson, David	12601	Armstrong, Nicy	11444
Anderson, Siney	12602	Armstrong, Ellis	11445
Anderson, Hampton W.	12603	Armstrong, Enoch	11446
Anderson, Houston Jas-		Armstrong, Murrow	11943
per	12604	Armstrong, Annie	11944
Anderson, William	13063	Armstrong, Mary	11945
Anderson, Margaret	13064	Armstrong, Sofa	11946

Name.	Roll No.	Name.	Roll No.
Armstrong, Lewis	12179	Atwood, Ambrosia	9454
Armstrong, Joseph	12753	Atkins, John E.	9758
Armstrong, Wallace	13992	Atkins, Thomas D.	9759
Armby, Hodges	7669	Atkins, Willie E.	9760
Armby, Selina	7670	Atkins, Tannie Lee	9761
Armby, Charles M.	9532	Atkinson, Ella	9839
Armby, Betsy	9533	Atkinson, Josie	9840
Armby, Wesley	9535	Atkinson, Jesse J.	9841
Armby, Simpson	10708	Atkinson, Mary	14362
Armby, Martha	10709	Atkinson, Lizzie	14363
Armby, Dora	10710	Atkinson, Rosa	14364
Artice, Mary	12583	Atkinson, Nora L.	14365
Arndt, Mary E.	12797	Atkinson, Bessie Ger-	
Arndt, Samuel F.	12798	trude	14366
Arndt, Myrtle M.	12799	Atohko, Simon	13964
Arndt, Fannie J.	12800	Atohko, Sarphin	13965
Arndt, William F.	12801	Atukko, Winnie	14755
Arndt, Fred C.	12802	Atukko, Vina	14756
Arndt, Aran L.	12803	Autry, Edgar	14919
Argo, Louis	13007	Autry, Emma	285
Archibald, Mary, A.	13102	Autry, Alvah	286
Archibald, Ella	13103	Autry, Lexter	287
Archibald, Maggie	13104	Autry, Tams	14486
Archibald, David	13105	Autrey, Anna B.	12689
Archibald, Henry	13106	Autrey, Goaly	12690
Arnote, Annie T.	13140	Austin, Minerva	1142
Arnote, William T.	13142	Austin, Narcissa	1144
Arnote, Dorothy V.	13143	Austin, Ida	1145
Arbuckle, Carrie	14514	Austin, Samuel	1145
Arbuckle, Winnie	14515	Austin, Nellie	1147
Arbuckle, Leatler	14516	Austin, David	1226
Arbuckle, Juanita	14517	Austin, Emily	1227
Arbuckle, Fulsom	14518	Austin, Simon	1228
Arbuckle, Tessie	14519	Austin, Rosa	1229
Arbuckle, Verdy	14520	Austin, William	1231
Ashshalintubbi, Kale	2094	Austin, Willis	1304
Ashshalintubbi, Elsey	2095	Austin, Sillis	1305
Ashshalintubbi, Inis	2096	Austin, Ellis	1306
Ashshalintubbi, Eben	2097	Austin, Felker	1308
Ashshalintubbi, Isaac	2098	Austin, Lina	1658
Ashshalintubbi, Quitman	2983	Austin, Iyers	1845
Ashshalintubbi, Craven	2984	Austin, Lila	1846
Ashford, Thomas	4997	Austin, Alice	2294
Ashford, Elizabeth	4998	Austin, Susan	2543
Ashford, Dora M.	5000	Austin, George	2544
Ashford, Sim	5001	Austin, Benjamin	3275
Ashford, James D.	15066	Austin, Louie	3277
Ashford, Bertie M.	15067	Austin, Pauline	3278
Ashford, Florence Lela	15068	Austin, Legion	3736
Askew, B. B.	14215	Austin, Molsey	3737
Askew, Bolden	14216	Austin, Lizzie	3738
Askew, Shelton	14217	Austin, Adline	3740
Askew, Porter	14218	Austin, Ellen	4710
Askew, Edna	14219	Austin, Charles	9024
Askew, Willis	14220	Austin, Lena	14004
Askew, Hubert	14221	Austin, John	15761
Askew, Rual	14222	Battiest, Willy	1001
Askew, Suepery	14223	Battiest, Sophia	1005
Askew, Tom V.	14230	Battiest, Annie	1006
Askew, Orbra	14231	Battiest, Lawson	1129
Askew, Irene	14232	Battiest, Polly	1130
Askew, Dulsa	14233	Battiest, Wilsey	1131
Askew, Em	14240	Battiest, Marlis	1132
Askew, Lee	14241	Battiest, Kisson	1133
Askew, Dora	14243	Battiest, Enettie	1164
Askew, Roscoe	14244	Battiest, Ella	1166
Askew, Julius	14245	Battiest, Selin	1459
Askew, Callie	14246	Battiest, Nicy	1498
Askew, Willie	14247	Battiest, Wade	2125
Askew, Jewell	14249	Battiest, Sina	2126
Askew, Daniel B.	14272	Battiest, Silean	2127
Askew, Bee	14273	Battiest, Nelly	2128
Askew, Oscar	14274	Battiest, Viney	2129
Askew, Luther	14275	Battiest, Mary	2258
Askew, Cleveland	14277	Battiest, Agnes	2259
Askew, Edward A.	14278	Battiest, Johnnie	2260
Askew, Julius	14367	Battiest, Joel	2334
Askew, Floyd	14368	Battiest, Melvina	2335
Askew, Minnie Holder	15644	Battiest, Sina	2336
Atwood, Patsy N.	9447	Battiest, Loren	2361
Atwood, Ottie	9448	Battiest, Colbert	2487
Atwood, Arra	9449	Battiest, Frances	3439
Atwood, Benjamin	9450	Battiest, Aaron	3440
Atwood, Ollie	9451	Battiest, William	4362
Atwood, Coleman	9452	Battiest, Solomon	4605
Atwood, Lizzie	9453	Battiest, Winnie	4606

Name.	Roll No.	Name.	Roll No.
Battiest, John	4607	Baker, Lillie	3774
Battiest, Osborne	4632	Baker, Becky	3775
Battiest, Louisa	4633	Baker, Ida	3776
Battiest, Ratio	4682	Baker, Jackson	5273
Battiest, Josiah	4719	Baker, Rosa	7428
Battiest, Melissa	4720	Baker, Houston	8487
Battiest, Martha	4721	Baker, Elizabeth	8488
Battiest, Mary	4722	Baker, Elum	8489
Battiest, Lewis G.	5291	Baker, Louis	8490
Battiest, Lewis G., Jr.	5292	Baker, Robert	8491
Battiest, Doyle	5293	Baker, Milan	8492
Battiest, Henry Lloyd	5294	Baker, Emeline	8493
Battiest, Silas	5402	Baker, Sillin	8764
Battiest, Frances	5413	Baker, Elliott	8765
Battiest, Milton	5418	Baker, Francis	8766
Battiest, Franseway	5472	Baker, Annie	8781
Battiest, Elizabeth	5633	Baker, Sallie	8782
Battiest, Mila	5637	Baker, Lucy	8895
Battiest, Houston	5645	Baker, Noel	8897
Battiest, Lena	5646	Baker, Mattie	8898
Battiest, Sema	5647	Baker, Mary	8901
Battiest, Stephen	5710	Baker, Oscar	8902
Battiest, Morris	7159	Baker, Logan	9348
Battiest, Silway	5391	Baker, Mary A.	9349
Battiest, Nicholas	10153	Baker, Siney	9351
Battiest, Gibson	8409	Baker, Annie	9352
Battiest, Eliza	8410	Baker, Jane	9353
Battiest, Andrew	8411	Baker, Lena	9354
Battiest, Frank	10239	Baker, Winnie	9355
Battiest, Benjamin	10240	Baker, Emma	9356
Battiest, Kizzie	10332	Baker, Solomon	9359
Battiest, Turner	10334	Baker, John	9647
Battiest, Steven	10335	Baker, Allington	9948
Battiest, Lela	10336	Baker, Johnson	10809
Battiest, Frank	10389	Baker, Lottie	10810
Battiest, Mary	10390	Baker, Benjamin	11806
Battiest, Cain	13433	Baker, Selina	11807
Battiest, Allen	13434	Baker, Charles	11808
Battiest, Larence	14582	Baker, Lena	11809
Battiest, Davis	14688	Baker, Benjamin F.	11820
Battiest, Eunice	15946	Baker, Annie	11821
Battiest, Leandes	15955	Baker, Julia	11822
Battiest, Allittie	15968	Baker, Alexander	11823
Battiest, Morris	16061	Baker, Sarah	14798
Battice, Thompson	1369	Baker, Rose	14799
Battice, Sallie	1370	Baker, Ella	15759
Battice, Lena	1371	Baken, Morris	2243
Battice, Byington	5326	Baken, Lyman	1358
Battice, Lizzie	5327	Baken, Winnie	1359
Battice, Marcus	10558	Baken, Carsey	1360
Battice, William	14571	Bacon, Brazil	1843
Bathest, Pitchlynn	3521	Bacon, Ike	1844
Bathest, Allington	3552	Bacon, Silas	2373
Bathest, Samblin	3553	Bacon, Sallie	2374
Baker, Elizabeth	1079	Bacon, Joseph	2375
Baker, Rena	1081	Bacon, Johnson	2376
Baker, Coleman	1163	Bacon, Susan	2377
Baker, Malin	1165	Bacon, Susan	3841
Baker, Isham	1473	Bacon, Ellen	4019
Baker, Davis	1474	Bacon, Solomon	4055
Baker, Robinson	1475	Bacon, Sinie	4056
Baker, Charles	1476	Bacon, Devenworth	4057
Baker, Emma	1477	Bacon, Isabelle	4058
Baker, Morris	1636	Bacon, Eliza	4059
Baker, Sissie	1637	Bacon, Silas	4060
Baker, Fannie	1638	Bacon, David	4142
Baker, Nancy	1642	Bacon, Mame	4143
Baker, Wesley	1849	Bacon, Elner	4144
Baker, Judy	1850	Bacon, Bob	4145
Baker, Solomon	1851	Bacon, Pearlie	4146
Baker, Graham	1852	Bacon, Phoebe	4147
Baker, Nettie	1853	Bacon, Solomon	4148
Baker, Simpson	1854	Bacon, Mittie Belle	4149
Baker, Grace	1855	Bacon, Silas	4344
Baker, Noel	1860	Bacon, Eliza	4345
Baker, Phelan	2036	Bacon, Eliza	4402
Baker, Charkesie	2037	Bacon, Mary	4403
Baker, Olarney	2038	Bacon, Simon	5213
Baker, Chimon	2039	Bacon, Sora	5339
Baker, Ida	2040	Bacon, Esias	5554
Baker, Somis	2041	Bacon, George	5715
Baker, Joseph	2042	Bacon, Judith A.	5728
Baker, Hodgen	3770	Bacon, Allen	5782
Baker, Lecy Anna	3771	Bacon, Sibbie	5783
Baker, Noel	3772	Bacon, Odie	5784
Baker, Annie	3773	Bacon, Rosa	5785

Name.	Roll No.	Name.	Roll No.
Bacon, Jefferson.	6123	Battles, George W.	9193
Bacon, Melvina	6124	Battles, Ermer E. L.	9194
Bacon, Charles E.	6126	Battles, Jimmie	9195
Bacon, Elmira G.	6127	Battles, Lester	9196
Bacon, Ellis	6226	Battles, Pearlie	9197
Bacon, Colton	6238	Battles, William E.	13375
Bacon, Mollie	8400	Battles, Henry Franklin	13376
Bacon, Reuben J.	8401	Barker, Julius A.	8992
Bacon, Elizabeth	12682	Barker, Elizabeth A.	8993
Bacon, Daniel	13490	Barker, John	9028
Bacon, Lizzie A.	13491	Barker, Sukey	9029
Bacon, Elias	13492	Barker, Jimmie	9030
Bacon, Ed	13493	Barker, Dora E.	12275
Barney, Joseph	1411	Barker, James F. H.	12280
Banabbe	3450	Barker, Arthur L. H. A.	12281
Baxter, William	4589	Barnhill, Emma	9242
Baxter, Caroline	15465	Barnhill, Gladice	9247
Baxter, Granville	15466	Barnice, Frances	9916
Baxter, Walter W.	15467	Ballew, Ella J.	10004
Baxter, Daisy	15468	Ballew, Henry C.	10005
Baxter, Graynell	15469	Ballew, Ella	10006
Baxter, Charles E.	15470	Ballew, Lela B.	10007
Baldwin, George W.	4778	Bates, Christina A.	10358
Baldwin, Selina	4779	Barnes, Robert J.	11037
Baldwin, Mary	4781	Barnes, Cornelius	11038
Baldwin, Jesse	4782	Barnes, Alice	11043
Baldwin, Eliza	15412	Bays, Emma	11363
Barnett, Edward	7037	Bays, John Henry	11365
Barnett, Sarah	7183	Banks, Edith	11758
Barnett, Amanda	7184	Banks, Ida M.	11759
Barnett, Martha	7185	Bassett, Louisanna	12234
Barnett, Israel	7186	Bassett, Clara	12235
Barnett, Thompson	7187	Bassett, Mamie	12236
Barnett, Levicey	7188	Bassett, Leroy	12237
Barnett, Alexander Sr.	7236	Ball, Salena	12247
Barnett, Susan	7237	Baum, Hester	12462
Barnett, Alexander, Jr.	7238	Babb, Belzora	12611
Barnett, Mary	7239	Babb, Ocial	12613
Barnett, Ella	7690	Bailey, Ida L.	15018
Barnett, Ervin W.	7691	Bailey, Tobias J.	15019
Barnett, Hattie	7692	Bailey, Viola	15020
Barnett, Girtrude M.	7693	Bailey, Clementine M.	15220
Barnett, Franklin L.	7694	Bailey, Emma	15221
Barnett, William W.	9570	Bailey, Boone	15222
Barnett, Ella	9571	Bailey, Gould	15223
Barnett, Ettie	9572	Bell, Rebecca	1
Barnett, Effie	9573	Bell, Zola Alice	2
Barnett, Edna	9574	Bell, Thetas Lee	3
Barnett, Jackson B.	9581	Bell, Elsie A.	5494
Barnett, Walter J.	9582	Bell, Silas	5549
Barnett, William J.	9583	Bell, Martha	5550
Barnett, Edgar James	9584	Bell, Davis Jr.	6811
Barnett, Elizabeth J.	11666	Bell, Malinda	6816
Barnett, Levi	11669	Bell, Jinson E.	7420
Barnett, James	11670	Bell, Alice	8317
Barnett, Jesse	11671	Bell, Amon	8318
Barnett, Viola	11672	Bell, Agnes	8319
Barnett, Liddie E.	11673	Bell, Wilson	8668
Barnett, Bessie	11674	Bell, Robert E.	10551
Barnett, Amelia	12825	Bell, Sarah A.	12240
Barnet, Charles	7478	Bell, Hattie	12241
Barnet, Dallas	7479	Bell, Thomas D., Jr.	12242
Barnet, Lucille	7480	Bell, Wilber R.	12243
Barnet, August	7481	Bell, Ward H.	12244
Barnet, Rosa	7482	Bell, Thomas W.	12917
Bascom, Alice	7272	Bell, Robert W.	12918
Bascom, Charlotte	7273	Bell, Nancy F.	12919
Bascom, Oscar	8320	Bell, Eliza	13627
Bascom, John	8635	Bell, Emma O.	13629
Bascom, Charles	10554	Bell, Delila Lucinda	13631
Bascomb, Jincy	13873	Bell, Grant	13632
Bascomb, Lena	13878	Bell, Malena	13935
Baggett, Mattie	7274	Bell, Alice Vagina	13936
Baggett, William	7275	Bell, Henry Stephen	13937
Baggett, Gracie	7276	Bell, Daniel	15796
Baggett, Ida J.	7277	Bell, Eliza	15797
Baggett, Maudie E.	7278	Bell, Frances	15798
Baggett, Samuel A.	7279	Berry, Nancy	21
Baggett, Lenard B.	7280	Berry, Turner	22
Barbour, Hester A.	8126	Berry, Roscoe	23
Barbour, James William	8127	Berry, Walter Milburn	24
Barbour, David Preston	8128	Berry, Jesse	14473
Battles, Mattie E.	8285	Berry, Dina	14528
Battles, Susan	9190	Berry, Roy	14529
Battles, Finis M.	9191	Berry, May	14530
Battles, John	9192	Berry, Gipson	14531

Name.	Roll No.	Name.	Roll No.
Benton, Julia	462	Benjamin, Josephine	11395
Benton, Elmer	463	Benjamin, Simeon	11492
Benton, Osa	464	Benjamin, Katie	11493
Benton, Effie	465	Benjamin, Betsy	11494
Benton, Manda	468	Benjamin, Sampson	11495
Benton, Ola May	469	Bearden, Bessie	4020
Benton, Emerson	5311	Bearden, Flora O.	4021
Benton, Nellie	5312	Bearden, Oscar Payton	4022
Benton, Clara Mabel	5313	Bearden, Florence Es-	
Benton, George	6141	ther	4023
Benton, Eliza	6142	Bedford, Florence	4941
Benton, Amanda	6144	Bedford, Thelma Ellen	4942
Benton, Jacob	6209	Bedford, Raymond B.	1943
Benton, Eliza	6210	Beams, Seon	6217
Benton, Nelson	6247	Beams, Littie	6218
Benton, Phoebe	6248	Beams, Susan	6219
Benton, Lillie	6249	Beams, Carrie Sockey	6220
Benton, Wesley	6363	Beams, Patterson	6257
Benton, Helen	6364	Beams, Nancy	6259
Benton, Abner	6365	Beams, Wallace	6272
Benton, Robert	6515	Beams, Emiline	6273
Benton, Jane	6516	Beams, Mary	6274
Benton, Edward	6662	Beams, John	6275
Benton, Elie	8924	Beams, Syrena	6278
Benton, James	8934	Beams, Sampson	6396
Benton, Jacob	8935	Beams, Nancy	6397
Benton, James	10732	Beams, Sophia	6398
Benton, Edgar	10733	Beams, Ephraim	6399
Benton, Theodore	10829	Beams, Jesse	6700
Benton, John	12282	Beams, James	9762
Benton, Willie	13901	Beams, Isham	9763
Benton, Everidge	13902	Beams, Edmond	9764
Benton, Margaret	13903	Beams, Myrtle Emma	9765
Benton, George	13905	Beams, William	10145
Bench, Nancy	583	Beams, John D.	10146
Bench, Clay	585	Beams, Susan E.	10147
Bench, Edna May	586	Beams, Charles C.	10148
Bench, John	4224	Beams, Annie M.	10149
Bench, Sam	4659	Beams, Samuel S.	10150
Bench, Mollie	4660	Beams, Thomas J.	10151
Bench, Lydia M.	7429	Beams, Amy	10152
Bench, Noah L.	7430	Beams, Calvin S.	10424
Bench, Bettie	7048	Beams, Eliza	11282
Bench, Matilda	8860	Beams, Simon	11332
Bench, Isaac	8861	Beams, Elsie	11333
Bench, Daniel	10177	Beams, George W.	12909
Bench, Emmett C.	10178	Beams, Edna M.	12910
Bench, Agnes Alma	10179	Beams, Edgar A.	12911
Bench, Sallie	12897	Beams, Charles	12913
Bench, Ruth E.	14329	Beams, Ephraim W.	13137
Bench, Sue D.	14330	Beams, John J.	15511
Ben, John	1417	Beams, William T.	15512
Ben, Emily	1418	Beams, Viola Victoria	15515
Ben, Louisa	2977	Beames, Arthur G.	10656
Ben, Elias	2982	Beames, Arther W.	10657
Ben, Joe	2985	Beames, Josiah	10891
Ben, Henry	5369	Beames, Lenora I.	10892
Ben, Sillis	5370	Beames, David W.	10893
Ben, Sibbie	5390	Beames, Henry C.	10894
Ben, Lucy	5543	Beames, Levi L.	10895
Ben, Malena	5544	Beames, George W.	10896
Ben, Amy	5545	Beard, Julia Ann	6473
Ben, Lina	5609	Beard, Ada M.	6474
Ben, Salina	5610	Beard, Buchanan	6475
Ben, Elem	5611	Beard, Amos S.	6476
Ben, Byington	5701	Beard, Matthew	6477
Ben, Sophia	5731	Beard, Sillen	6637
Ben, McKinney B.	5732	Beard, Eric C.	6638
Ben, James	13401	Beard, Lucy A.	11031
Ben, Lewis	14598	Beard, Luther C.	11032
Benn, Simon	1962	Beard, Claudie	11033
Benn, Lula	1963	Beard, Ruthie M.	11034
Benn, Louis	1986	Beard, Levi Lee	11035
Benn, Eveline	1988	Beard, Mary Jane	14512
Benn, Jackson	1989	Beller, Ida	7659
Benjamin, Nelly	2116	Beller, Virginia	7660
Benjamin, Mina	2117	Beller, Ola May	7661
Benjamin, Narsie	2118	Belvin, Lucinda	8592
Benjamin, Rosa	2119	Belvin, Annie	8743
Benjamin, Joe	2120	Belvin, Watson	9793
Benjamin, Sokke	2121	Belvin, Harry J. W.	9794
Benjamin, Wallace	5227	Belvin, Solomon	10120
Benjamin, Winey	5228	Belvin, Nash	10121
Benjamin, Ben	5713	Belvin, Margaret	10122
Benjamin, Charlie	11394		

Name.	Roll No.	Name.	Roll No.
Belvin, Craven N.	10366	Betts, Charlie Walker	12267
Belvin, Eliza	10367	Betts, William W.	12315
Belvin, Thomas	10368	Betts, Claude	12316
Belvin, Abel	10369	Betts, Clyde	12318
Belvin, Ella	10370	Betts, Cordie Lee	12319
Belvin, Lamos	10372	Betts, James D.	14963
Belvin, Sis	10373	Betts, Selina E.	14964
Belvin, Moses	10377	Beck, Frances	12787
Belvin, Phoebe	10378	Beck, John	12788
Belvin, Robert	10425	Beck, Oliver	12789
Belvin, Johnson	10538	Beck, Samuel	12790
Belvin, Elisha	10539	Beck, Tandy	12791
Belvin, James	10721	Beck, Gilbert	12792
Belvin, Silway	10722	Beck, Wallace	12793
Belvin, John	10723	Beck, Joanna	13251
Belvin, Stephen M.	11479	Beck, Milo	13252
Belvin, Elsie	11480	Beck, Delora	13253
Belvin, Annie B.	11481	Beck, Grover	13254
Belvin, Easter	11482	Beck, Joseph D.	13255
Belvin, Robinson	11734	Beck, Green Taylor	13256
Belvin, Lizzie	11871	Beck, Nannie	14978
Belvin, Sallie	11874	Beck, Sutt	14979
Belvin, Melissa	13884	Beck, Benjamin	14980
Belvin, Lizzy	14809	Beck, Barton	14981
Belvin, Silwe	14898	Beck, Phoeba A.	14982
Belvin, Wilson	15052	Bedingfield, Mollie	15138
Bee, William	9136	Bedingfield, Mary F.	15139
Bee, Fannie	9138	Bedingfield, Clyde	15140
Bee, Annie	9139	Bedingfield, Laura M.	15141
Bee, Bessie B.	9140	Bedingfield, Claude A.	15142
Beal, Pinkney	9931	Bedingfield, Nona Thelma	15143
Beal, Wilson J.	9932		
Beal, Pinkney Jr.	9933	Benson, Eugene S.	9893
Beal, Poley	9934	Benson, Ellen L.	9894
Beal, Thomas T.	9935	Benson, Elizabeth A.	9895
Beal, Annie M.	9936	Bevill, Alice	13038
Beal, Myrtle O.	9937	Bevill, Jay	13039
Beal, James	9938	Bevill, Abbie	13051
Beal, William	9939	Bevill, Roy	13042
Beal, William C.	9954	Bevill, Ray	13043
Beal, Mahala	9955	Billis, Jackson	670
Beal, John	9956	Billis, Silvey	11888
Beal, Minnie Viola	9957	Billis, William	12112
Beal, Andrew P.	10095	Billis, Louvina	13710
Beal, Mary M.	10096	Billy, Witson	1522
Beal, Martha J.	10097	Billy, James	1524
Beal, Charles R.	10098	Billy, Daniel	2031
Beal, Hugh L.	10099	Billy, Delilah	2033
Beal, John Wesley	10100	Billy, Calvin	2034
Beal, George	15716	Billy, Nelly	2198
Beal, Millie Levana	15717	Billy, Sias	2229
Beal, William Albert	15718	Billy, Ben	2230
Beal, Samantha	15719	Billy, Loli	2231
Beal, Bulah	15720	Billy, Lyman	2503
Beal, William D.	15721	Billy, Susan	2504
Beal, Reuben Jr.	15725	Billy, Wilmon	2666
Beal, Cora	15726	Billy, Lisiana	2667
Beal, Benj.Lee	15727	Billy, Simon	2668
Beal, Arthur	15728	Billy, Naswis	2669
Beal, Johnnie	15729	Billy, Nelis	2670
Beal, John Peler	15730	Billy, Salisa	2671
Beal, Pony	15731	Billy, Easton	2673
Beal, Roy May	15732	Billy, Watson	2674
Beal, Annie	15734	Billy, Linda	2675
Beal, William T.	15736	Billy, Always	2764
Beal, Jesse B.	15747	Billy, Easter	2803
Beall, Reuben	9635	Billy, Selin	2807
Beall, Mary	9636	Billy, Frances	2989
Beall, Ida	9637	Billy, Sophina	2990
Beall, Henry	9638	Billy, Robert	2991
Belt, Malinda	11255	Billy, Marry	3165
Bentley, Lucy	11385	Billy, John	3187
Bentley,John W. E.	11386	Billy, Sallie	3188
Bentley, Ellis LeFlore	11387	Billy, Wilkin	3189
Bennett, Lucy E.	11408	Billy, Siney	3190
Bennett, William T.	11409	Billy, David	3219
Bennett, Joseph C.	11410	Billy, Frances	3320
Bennett, Margaret V.	11411	Billy, Ellen	3370
Bennett, Walter Lee	14866	Billy, Nora	3371
Betts, Ramsey D.	12191	Billy, Austin	3629
Betts, Emeline	12192	Billy, Eliza	3630
Betts, Charlie A.	12193	Billy, Simon	3645
Betts, David C.	12264	Billy, Pikey	3646
Betts, Bethel L.	12265	Billy, James	3647
Betts, Ada M. B.	12266	Billy, George	3648

Name.	Roll No.	Name.	Roll No.
Billy, Elens	3649	Billy, Winnissie	14631
Billy, Lena	3653	Billy, William	14644
Billy, Johnson	4450	Billy, Wesley	15042
Billy, John	4534	Billy, Nancy Mintubbe	15510
Billy, Louisiana	4535	Billy, Rossie	15851
Billy, Isabelle	4536	Billy, Levisie	15933
Billy, Jimanna	4537	Billy, Josiah	15976
Billy, Agnes	5035	Billie, Simon	13435
Billy, Siney	5104	Billie, Nancy	13436
Billy, Emma	5106	Birlew, Albert	3349
Billy, Isaac A.	5238	Birlew, Filena	3350
Billy, Emily	5239	Bishop, Mary	6262
Billy, Annie	5241	Bishop, Berry	6263
Billy, Susan	5242	Bishop, Irene Belle	6264
Billy, William L.	5243	Bishop, Eunice	15870
Billy, Anganora	5244	Bishop, Fannie Lundie	15871
Billy, Isom	5386	Bird, Billy	6890
Billy, John F.	5457	Bickle, Susan	8616
Billy, Melvina	5473	Bickle, Lula	8618
Billy, Helen	5479	Bickle, Lona	8619
Billy, Austin	5993	Bickle, Scott	8620
Billy, Susan	5994	Bickle, Jack	8621
Billy, Louisa	5995	Bickle, Roxy	8622
Billy, Alice	5996	Bickle, Greenwood	8623
Billy, Charles	6034	Bickle, Fannie	8624
Billy, Delilah	6055	Bilbo, Charles A.	10354
Billy, Ephriam	6026	Bilbo, Charles C.	10355
Billy, Israel	6037	Bilbo, Cecil A.	10356
Billy, Lucinda	6039	Bilbo, William W.	10357
Billy, Maggie	6187	Bills, Sarah	13857
Billy, Levi	6188	Blankenship, Winnie	4188
Billy, Sophia	6189	Blake, Lillie A.	6550
Billy, Josiah	6254	Blake, Robert W.	6552
Billy, Winnie	6255	Blaylock, Ruth A.	7540
Billy, Nancy	6256	Blaylock, Louella	7541
Billy, Jullus	6279	Blaylock, Willis Henry	7542
Billy, Nancy	6280	Blaylock, David Solo-	
Billy, Lymon	6281	mon	14765
Billy, Frances	6282	Blalack, Ida B.	9256
Billy, Rosie	6595	Blalack, Sallie J.	9257
Billy, Tyles	6783	Blue, Willy	8816
Billy, Marlin	6784	Blue, Melvina	8817
Billy, Jackson	6785	Blue, Daniel	8818
Billy, Watson	6786	Blue, Eli	8819
Billy, Simon	6798	Blue, William	8949
Billy, Albert	6799	Blue, George	8950
Billy, Dennis	6800	Blinche, Osborne	9661
Billy, Gilbert	6801	Blinche, Melvina	9662
Billy, Sissy	7225	Bledsoe, May	10171
Billy, Ally	7732	Bledsoe, Claude C.	10172
Billy, Dixon	8555	Black, Maggie E.	11752
Billy, Lita	8556	Black, Sylvanus	11753
Billy, Bicy	8557	Black, John	11754
Billy, Cephus	8558	Black, Willie	11755
Billy, Eliza	8559	Black, Clara	11756
Billy, Jennie	8561	Blakely, Perry H.	14296
Billy, Bicey	9514	Blakely, Emmet	14297
Billy, Lucy A.	9515	Blundell, Patsey	14542
Billy, Albert	9550	Blundell, Earl	14543
Billy, Walton	9863	Blundell, Thomas Clyde	14545
Billy, Phoebe	9864	Blooser, Pansy	14944
Billy, Isaac	9865	Blevins, James	15892
Billy, Willie	10636	Bonner, Salina Y.	415
Billy, Esther	10637	Bonner, Frank A.	416
Billy, Lita	11131	Bonner, William T.	417
Billy, Mary	11303	Bonner, Wellington Fol-	
Billy, Salena	11305	som	14511
Billy, Edmund	11434	Bogle, Mary C.	511
Billy, Rebecca	11435	Bogle, John D.	512
Billy, Louvisa	11436	Bogle, David H.	9641
Billy, Simon	11437	Bogle, Uple	9642
Billy, Rhoda	11438	Bourne, Maud	578
Billy, Nicholas	11590	Bourne, Annie	579
Billy, Elizabeth	11591	Bourne, Hattie	580
Billy, Wesley	11737	Bond, Lizzie	621
Billy, Elsie	11738	Bond, Alice	622
Billy, Ida	11739	Bond, Alphaeus	623
Billy, McKinley	11740	Bond, Wachit	988
Billy, Daniel	11741	Bond, Martha	989
Billy, Harlie	11891	Bond, Byington	1029
Billy, Alfred	12308	Bond, Moses	1030
Billy, Elizabeth	13044	Bond, Simmons	1031
Billy, Williamson	13045	Bond, Allen	1032
Billy, Martha	13046	Bond, Eliza	2010
Billy, Susan	13949		

Name.	Roll No.	Name.	Roll No.
Bond, Emma	2424	Bohanan, Laurina	1634
Bond, Ida	4209	Bohanan, Emma	1635
Bond, Redmond	5052	Bohanan, Benjamin	1940
Bond, David	5359	Bohanan, Timesy	1941
Bond, Silvey	5360	Bohanan, Maley	1942
Bond, Jesse	5433	Bohanan, Sillis	1943
Bond, Lizzie	5441	Bohanan, Lucy	1944
Bond, Eliza	5534	Bohanan, Elizabeth	1945
Bond, Ashford	5639	Bohanan, Williston	1946
Bond, Hoppen	5640	Bohanan, Jesse	2017
Bond, Johnson	6535	Bohanan, Sophia	2018
Bond, Sarbale	6536	Bohanan, Lucy	2019
Bond, William	7127	Bohanan, Listie	2020
Bond, Selina	7128	Bohanan, Richard	2021
Bond, Elum	7155	Bohanan, Wilson	2022
Bond, Mary J.	7156	Bohanan, Liza	2023
Bond, Susan	7218	Bohanan, Elizabeth	2024
Bond, Besssie	7219	Bohanan, Wismon	2036
Bond, Dessie Ray	7220	Bohanan, Sallie	2077
Bond, Lolin	7397	Bohanan, Sianer	2078
Bond, Eliza	7398	Bohanan, Amy	2079
Bond, Susan	7399	Bohanan, Laymon	2080
Bond, Malissa	7400	Bohanan, Stewart	2081
Bond, Luke	7401	Bohanan, Jonas	3790
Bond, Lizzie	8606	Bohanan, Lucinda	3791
Bond, Lizzie	8686	Bohanan, Impson	3793
Bond, Cynthie Renie	8687	Bohanan, Agnes	3840
Bond, Mary	8963	Bohanan, Minnie	4348
Bond, Sallie	10798	Bohanan, Dave	4349
Bond, Marvin	10800	Bohanan, Harmon J.	4462
Bond, Reed	11159	Bohanan, James	4463
Bond, Davis	11185	Bohanan, Lillie	4464
Bond, Moses	11330	Bohanan, Andrew	4592
Bond, Eastman S.	11483	Bohanan, Thomas B.	4616
Bond, Susie A.	11484	Bohanan, Bertha M.	4617
Bond, Albert	16116	Bohanan, Harmon J.	4618
Bond, Reason	11643	Bohanan, Anthony	4653
Bond, Edna	11644	Bohanan, Lizzie	4654
Bond, Salema	11660	Bohanan, Elsie	4655
Bond, Ida	11661	Bohanan, Frances	4656
Bond, Simeon	11814	Bohanan, Eli	5048
Bond, Silway	11815	Bohanan, Nicholas	5443
Bond, Eleas	11816	Bohanan, Simpson	5461
Bond, Mila S.	11817	Bohanan, Sinie	5462
Bond, Derias	11819	Bohanan, John	5463
Bond, Daniel A.	12473	Bohanan, Ellis	5511
Bond, Cillin	12474	Bohanan, Susan	5512
Bond, Yimmetonah	12479	Bohanan, Green	5513
Bond, Rhoda	12480	Bohanan, Dora	5514
Bond, Edmund M.	12724	Bohanan, Kitty	5515
Bond, Rex	12726	Bohanan, Wilson	5516
Bond, William W.	12727	Bohanan, Wesley	5517
Bond, Benjamin F.	12728	Bohanan, Anna B.	5518
Bond, Rebecca A.	12729	Bohanan, Cleopatra	5523
Bond, Sina	12740	Bohanan, Catherine	5551
Bond, Florence	12741	Bohanan, Narcissa	5584
Bond, May	12742	Bohanan, Wade	5586
Bond, Bennett F.	12743	Bohanan, Martin	5588
Bond, Wallace	12744	Bohanan, Watson	5595
Bond, Sidney	12745	Bohanan, Eliza	5596
Bond, Green M.	12746	Bohanan, Nicey	5597
Bond, Beulah	12805	Bohanan, Samuel H.	5722
Bond, Alice	13620	Bohanan, Margaret S.	5723
Bond, Jesse	13621	Bohanan, Julius H.	5725
Bond, Henry J.	13687	Bohanan, Minnie A.	5726
Bond, Mary	13688	Bohanan, Florence A.	5727
Bond, Cornelius	13689	Bohanan, Reed	5780
Bond, Eliza	13690	Bohanan, Viney	5781
Bond, Sallie Ann	13691	Bohanan, Elizabeth	5888
Bond, Emeline	13692	Bohanan, Stayman	5918
Bond, Esther	13693	Bohanan, Silas	5919
Bond, Calvin	13719	Bohanan, Impson	5920
Bond, Harrison	13361	Bohanan, Melvin	5921
Bond, Sampson	14576	Bohanan, Lartin S.	5931
Bond, Richard C.	14827	Bohanan, Sallie Ann	5932
Bohanon, Robert	760	Bohanan, Annie	5933
Bohanon, Sam	13975	Bohanan, Frances	5934
Bohanon, Vina	13976	Bohanan, Minnie	5935
Bohanon, Elsie	13977	Bohanan, Missie	5936
Bohanan, Sampson	1526	Bohanan, William J.	6160
Bohanan, John	1528	Bohanan, Emiline	6161
Bohanan, Elsey	1529	Bohanan, Eli	6163
Bohanan, Emily	1530	Bohanan, Pearl	6164
Bohanan, Lena	1531	Bohanan, Margaret	6165
Bohanan, Milwee	1632	Bohanan, Beulah	6166

Name.	Roll No.	Name.	Roll No.
Bohanan, Joshua D.	6167	Boatwright, Lonnie E.	14435
Bohanan, Levi W.	6212	Boatwright, Edith	14436
Bohanan, Harriet	6213	Boatwright, James Granville	14437
Bohanan, Thomas	6377	Boerner, Mattie	9767
Bohanan, Lizzie	6378	Boerner, Charles E.	9768
Bohanan, Dave	6379	Boerner, Wesley L.	9769
Bohanan, Bertha C.	6380	Bouton, William I.	10359
Bohanan, Levina	6381	Boydstun, John F.	10463
Bohanan, Isabelle	6382	Boydstun, Alfred E.	10464
Bohanan, Jackson	6541	Boydstun, Ellis M.	10465
Bohanan, Samuel	6542	Boydstun, Robert	10466
Bohanan, Fannie	6543	Boydstun, Ada	10467
Bohanan, Mary	7785	Boydstun, Ethel	10468
Bohanan, James W.	8069	Boydstun, John Francis	15841
Bohanan, Elmer Wear	8070	Boland, James	10994
Bohanan, Joseph	8345	Boland, Arizona	10995
Bohanan, Brazil	2609	Boland, Sallie	10996
Bohanan, Lucy	9755	Bonaparte, Simpson	12476
Bohanan, Gertrude	9756	Bonaparte, Jacob	12477
Bohanan, Minnie	9897	Bonaparte, Nabert	12481
Bohanan, Lula	9898	Bonaparte, Wynie	13393
Bohanan, Beulah	9899	Bonaparte, Oscar	13397
Bohanan, Birdie	9900	Bowers, Susan	13216
Bohanan, Mary	13683	Bowers, Rubie	13223
Bohanan, Wysie	13345	Bohree, Susan	14340
Bohanan, Silas W.	13684	Bohree, Henry	14341
Bohanan, Dennis	14332	Bohree, Addison	14342
Bohanan, Luther	14333	Bohree, Alfred	14343
Bohanan, Phoebe	14578	Bohree, Sula	14344
Bohanan, Nicholas	14600	Booker, Lizzie	15265
Bohanan, Sophia	14703	Booker, Carroll,	15270
Bohanan, Lyman	14768	Bounds, Young Walker	15630
Bohanan, Emma	14839	Bounds, James, Jr.	15681
Bohanan, Emiziah	14838	Boswell, Frank	15895
Bohanan, Sissie	15825	Bryant, Mary	41
Bohannan, Lucy	13473	Bryant, Amy	42
Boyd, Rosa	1668	Bryant, Willie Lillian	43
Boyd, Jacob	2837	Bryant, Frank Thomas	44
Boyd, May E.	15492	Bryant, Raymond	5361
Boyd, Lillie M.	15496	Bryant, Jesse	5362
Boyd, John T.	15553	Bryant, Jimmie	5363
Boyd, Louis H.	15556	Bryant, Laura	5364
Bobb, Joseph	1879	Bryant, Ora	5365
Bobb, Atkin	1880	Bryant, Bertha	5366
Bobb, Sophie	3090	Bryant, Dave	5367
Bobb, Johnson	3514	Bryant, Lucy	5690
Bobb, Mitchell	3581	Bryant, Mamie	5691
Bob, Wilson	5218	Bryant, Daniel	5747
Bob, Bensie	5221	Bryant, Napoleon	9696
Bob, Tillis	5222	Bryant, Alfred	9857
Bob, Lina	5223	Bryant, Julia	9858
Boling, Billy	3422	Bryant, Florence	9859
Bolling, John F.	11466	Bryant, Calvin	9860
Bolling, Walter C.	11467	Bryant, Minnie M.	11760
Bowlin, Susa	9429	Bryant, Bert	14697
Bowlin, Edna	9430	Brown, Agnes	1372
Boatman, Simon	4685	Brown, Grayson	1373
Boatman, Sibbie	4686	Brown, Mary	1374
Boatman, Abraham	4687	Brown, Austin	1375
Boyken, Amelia	7176	Brown, James	1985
Bower, Mary A.	7294	Brown, Michael J.	2205
Bower, James	7296	Brown, Susan	2206
Bower, Bessie	7297	Brown, Rachael	2207
Bower, Mary K.	7298	Brown, Hinmon	2208
Bower, Ernestine H.	15425	Brown, Leila	2209
Bowman, Caroline	7520	Brown, Harriet	2211
Bowman, Edward S.	7522	Brown, Sarah	3194
Bowman, Gertrude	7523	Brown, Adolphus	3195
Bowman, Euwela E.	7524	Brown, Willard	3250
Bowman, Edward G.	7525	Brown, Victor	3251
Boatright, Joseph	8095	Brown, Ephraim	3252
Boatright, Ruth I.	8096	Brown, Chloe	3253
Boatright, Viola M.	8097	Brown, Seldon	3325
Boatright, Eva J.	8098	Brown, Eastman	3588
Boatright, Robert E. W.	8099	Brown, Arnes	3590
Boatright, Martha Louzena	8100	Brown, Kitsie	3591
Boatwright, James H.	12507	Brown, Elias	3592
Boatwright, Ida M.	12508	Brown, Frank	3593
Boatwright, Ada I.	12509	Brown, Minnie	3594
Boatwright, David W.	12510	Brown, Nicholas	3595
Boatwright, Edward R.	12542	Brown, Bicey	3598
Boatwright, Thomas J.	14432	Brown, Josephine	3599
Boatwright, Ruthie L.	14433	Brown, Frances	4222
Boatwright, Thomas D.	14434	Brown, Ella May	4223

Name.	Roll No.
Brown, Mary E.	5266
Brown, Lucy	5267
Brown, Emma	5268
Brown, Charles A.	5269
Brown, Anna May	5270
Brown, John Thomas	5271
Brown, Permelia	6740
Brown, Judy	6741
Brown, Pink	6742
Brown, Mary	7463
Brown, Janie	7464
Brown, Isaiah Vasco	7465
Brown, Annie	7536
Brown, Turner	7539
Brown, Tecumseh	8048
Brown, Robert	8049
Brown, Shorty	8050
Brown, Lant	8193
Brown, Agnes	9017
Brown, Mary	9018
Brown, Wesley	9019
Brown, Milton	9033
Brown, John J.	9148
Brown, Margaret	9149
Brown, Hattie	9152
Brown, Tandy	9153
Brown, Rector	9154
Brown, Abel	9302
Brown, William	9303
Brown, Celia	11145
Brown, Melvina	11605
Brown, Rosa E.	11606
Brown, Milton	11726
Brown, Jay G.	11727
Brown, Cyrus	11728
Brown, Lorenzo	11729
Brown, Beulah	11730
Brown, Ida A.	11731
Brown, Mary A.	11757
Brown, Moses	11831
Brown, Mila	11832
Brown, David	11833
Brown, Elijah	11854
Brown, Jack	12075
Brown, Minnie	12722
Brown, Eliza	14128
Brown, Ida	14646
Brown, Belle	14790
Brown, Wesley Ann	14791
Brown, Lula May	14792
Brown, Kitty Pearl	14819
Brown, Ida F.	15513
Brown, Hettie A.	15514
Brown, Pearlie Catherine	15516
Brewer, Ellis	1455
Brewer, Agnes	1456
Brewer, Annie	1457
Brewer, Raymus	1458
Brewer, Albert	9663
Brewer, Minnie	10478
Brady, Clarence	1907
Brady, Arthur	1908
Brady, Selina	15159
Brady, Bruce M.	15160
Brady, Robert Golston	15161
Brashears, George	4170
Brashears, Edward	4172
Brashears, Mary J.	7357
Brashears, Tobias	7358
Brashears, William J.	7361
Brashears, Benjamin	7450
Brashears, Mary Estella	7451
Brashears, Johnie Tobias	7452
Brashears, Tola	7453
Brashears, John	8856
Brashears, Turner	8961
Brashears, George W.	9171
Brashears, Julia F.	9172
Brashears, Ivey	9173
Brashears, Joseph	9908
Britton, Mary	6508
Britton, Samuel	6509
Britton, Margaret	6510
Britton, James	6511

Name.	Roll No.
Britton, Myrtle	6513
Britton, Owen Columbus	6514
Brandy, Cornelius	7007
Brandy, Betsy	8454
Brandy, Fulsom	14934
Brandy, Sampson	14935
Brandy, Robert A.	14936
Briggs, Jennie	7352
Briggs, Mary	7353
Briggs, Riley	7354
Briggs, Marion Alvin	7365
Briggs, Ernest	15767
Brimage, Jennie	7572
Brimage, George	7573
Brimage, Jeff	7574
Brimage, Minerva	14450
Brimage, Josephine	14451
Brimage, Nancy	14452
Brimage, Emma	14453
Breedlove, Margaret E.	8772
Breedlove, James	8773
Breedlove, Josephine	14409
Breedlove, Bertha	14410
Breedlove, Besssie	14411
Breedlove, Pearl	14412
Breedlove, Susan	13284
Breedlove, Myrtle	14413
Breedlove, Wilson R.	14414
Brians, Mary M.	9546
Brians, Hugh E.	9547
Brackett, Laura A.	10847
Brackett, Myrtle M.	10848
Brackett, Daniel M.	10849
Brackett, Phidelia A.	10850
Brackett, Cora Lee	10851
Brackett, Margaret	11058
Brackett, Fannie	11059
Brackett, Lennie	11060
Brackett, Susan	11061
Brooks, Susie	11634
Brinkley, Robert B.	12361
Brinkley, Benjamin	15942
Brock, Minnie L.	12667
Brock, Juanita M.	12668
Brock, Clifton Rex	12669
Brock, August C.	14825
Bruner, Rosa	13249
Burris, Hampton	181
Burris, Odie	182
Burris, Isham	5381
Burris, Caroline	5382
Burris, Middleton W.	12043
Burris, Lee	12700
Burris, Sydney	13971
Burris, Berthena	15748
Burris, Samuel Sydney	16059
Burris, Hyman H.	16060
Burnett, Catherine C.	216
Burnitt, William	1401
Burnitt, Chubby	1402
Burnitt, Frances	14574
Butterly, Fannie H.	336
Butterly, John	337
Butterly, Everett	338
Butterly, Ellen	339
Butterly, Rhoda	340
Butterly, William	341
Bunce, Jerry	1866
Bunce, Aly	1867
Bunce, Bond	1869
Bunce, Vicey	1870
Bunce, Susan	2327
Bunce, Dyer	2329
Bunnup, William	2253
Bunnup, Wisey	2256
Butter, Abel	2945
Butter, Aly	2946
Butter, Silas	2947
Butter, Dwight	2948
Butter, Ellis	2949
Burney, Charles	5977
Burney, Alfred	6013
Burney, Abigail	6129
Burney, Mary R.	6131
Burney, Sarah	6366

Name.	Roll No.	Name.	Roll No.
Burney, George	10064	Buckholts, Adelbert Lorenzo	15218
Burney, John L.	12670		
Burney, Clara May	14892	Buckholts, William	15234
Bustin, Ophelia P.	7118	Buckholts, Robert E. L.	15242
Bustin, John T.	7119	Buckholts, Ennis E.	15243
Bustin, Levi	7120	Buckholts, Ida	15244
Bustin, William H.	7121	Buckholts, Rhoda	15245
Bustin, Geoorge A.	7122	Buckholts, Rebecca	15246
Burns, Joseph	7485	Buckholts, James M.	15247
Burns, Mabel	7487	Buckholts, Edward E.	15264
Burns, Alexander	7502	Bullock, Lola	15339
Burns, Jackson	7503	Bullock, Emma	15340
Burns, Lizzie	7504	Bullock, Beatrice	15341
Burns, Alice	7505	Bullock, Olive	15342
Burns, William	7506	Bullock, Jonathan	15343
Burns, Lester	7507	Bullock, J. D. Jr.	15344
Burns, Jack	7794	Byfoord, Ellen	263
Burns, Nancy	7795	Byington, Emma	771
Burns, William	8793	Byington, Emmerson	772
Burns, Jane	8794	Byington, Malissa	773
Burns, Alphy	8795	Byington, Winnie	774
Burns, Henry F.	8872	Byington, Lutie	775
Burns, Jane	8873	Byington, Thomas A.	2212
Burns, George Dewey	8875	Byington, Frances	2565
Burns, Robert Lee	14787	Byington, Zona	2754
Burns, Lawrence B.	15431	Byington, Simeon	2755
Burs, Isaac	8549	Byington, Elizabeth	2950
Burties, Rhoda	8113	Byington, Moody	3321
Burgevin, Frances H.	8208	Byington, Annie	3322
Burgevin, Edmond A.	8209	Byington, Sibbie	3323
Burgevin, Henry A.	8210	Byington, Alfred	3435
Burgevin, Julia G.	8211	Byington, Phillis	3436
Burgevin, Josephine	13737	Byington, Israel	3577
Burgevin, Agnes Elberta	13738	Byington, Davis	3687
		Byington, Wycie	8005
Burgevin, Herbert Spencer	13739	Byington, Henry	8006
		Byington, Lizzie	8007
Bullard, Villey M.	8689	Byington, Joseph	8309
Bullard, Pocahontas	8690	Byington, Alonzo	9686
Bullard, Lu Orenia	8691	Byington, Josephine	9929
Bullard, Susan F.	12779	Byington, Julia	9930
Bullard, Clarence R.	12781	Byington, Culberson	9980
Buell, Rosa L.	9770	Byington, Sarah	9981
Buell, Gladys	9771	Byington, Allen	9982
Buell, Glennie Lynne	9772	Byington, David	9983
Butler, Lizzie	10386	Byington, Sampson	9984
Butler, Abbie	10387	Byington, Cyrus	10347
Bully, Anderson	10832	Byington, Sophia	10348
Bully, Sibbie	10833	Byington, Albert	10349
Bugg, Narcissa	11010	Byington, Zue	10350
Bugg, Benjamin F.	11011	Byington, Nancy	10674
Burks, Lucinda	11046	Byington, Rufas	10675
Burks, Minnie M.	11047	Byington, Elizabeth	10781
Burks, Willie E.	11048	Byington, Thompson	10782
Burks, Marvin F.	11049	Byington, Peter	10793
Burks, Odra May	11050	Byington, Eliza	11268
Burkes, John G.	14173	Byington, Simpson	11272
Burkes, John G., Jr.	14174	Byington, Annie	11293
Burkes, Lillie B.	14176	Byington, Silas	11294
Burkes, Myrtle J.	14177	Byington, Jackson	11295
Burkes, Lelia A.	14178	Byington, Cilian	11298
Burkes, Mary Ellis	14179	Byington, Mary A.	11348
Burkes, Ben Ager	14180	Byington, Jesse	11351
Burkes, Maudie Vanita	14181	Byington, Julius	11442
Burkes, Charley McClellan	14182	Byington, Robinson	11443
		Byington, Amos	11520
Burkes, William M.	14210	Byington, Lefus	11640
Buck, Sophia A.	12545	Byington, Annie	11641
Buck, Charles A.	12546	Byington, Agnes	11642
Bumgarner, Susan	13287	Byington, Henry	11850
Bumgarner, Samuel W.	13288	Byington, Lorena	11851
Bumgarner, George A.	16112	Byington, Philip J.	11852
Busby, Biddie Caroline	13978	Byington, David J.	12981
Burch, Raymond G.	14194	Byington, Winnie E.	12982
Buckholts, George W.	15188	Byington, Rosa	12983
Buckholts, Lillie May	15189	Byington, Simon W.	12984
Buckholts, Willie Ann	15190	Byington, Melina	13424
Buckholts, John M.	15209	Byington, Benjamin	13425
Buckholts, Everett	15210	Byington, Nancy	13807
Buckholts, William Lee	15211	Byington, Joel	14002
Buckholts, Fannie Olive	15212	Byington, Maxwell	14540
Buckholts, John B. Jr.	15213	Byington, David	14645
Buckholts, Eley	15215	Byington, Francis	14650
Buckholts, William L.	15216	Byington, Richard H.	15475
Buckholts, William E.	15217	Byram, Susie W.	2595

Name.	Roll No.	Name.	Roll No.
Carnes, Molsie	720	Carshall, Simon	8703
Carnes, Evangeline	721	Cass, Robert	7020
Carnes, Elsie	722	Cass, Melissa	7021
Carnes, Selina	5371	Cass, Daniel	7022
Carnes, Sophia	5373	Cass, Clifton	7023
Carnes, Adeline	5374	Cass, Peter	7024
Carnes, Harriet	5375	Cass, Myrtle	7025
Carnes, Dora	5376	Cass, Maurice N.	7086
Carnes, James A.	5720	Cass, Amy N.	7087
Carnes, Minnie	10217	Cass, Billy N.	7088
Carnes, Willie	10751	Cass, N. Osborne	7194
Carnes, Ellen	10858	Cass, Eliza	7195
Carnes, James	10859	Cass, Jefferson	7196
Carnes, Andrew J.	10899	Cass, Florence	7797
Carnes, Charles A.	10900	Cass, Lewis	8829
Carnes, Odee	10901	Cass, Annie	5424
Carnes, Ellen	11112	Casey, Eliza	7029
Carnes, Eliza	11113	Casey, J. Sumler	7036
Carnes, Annie	11361	Casey, Julia Ann W.	15562
Carnes, Malina	11362	Casey, Pushamataha	15563
Carnes, Willie	11784	Carter, Susie	7049
Carnes, Incy	11812	Carter, Robert S.	7056
Carnes, Anderson	11982	Carter, Rosa	9235
Carnes, John	12119	Carter, Fannie	9336
Carnes, Benjamin B.	12169	Carter, Julia	9337
Carnes, Ellis	12197	Carter, Charlie	9338
Carnes, Serena	12198	Carter, Frances	13324
Carnes, Nicey	12199	Carter, Ada	13328
Carnes, Louis	12201	Carter, Nellie	13079
Carnes, Lyon	12214	Cartwright, Hannah	8026
Carnes, Phillis	12215	Cargill, Lucinda	8669
Carnes, Isaac	12228	Case, Lucy	9471
Carnes, Sam	12268	Case, Lillie M.	9472
Carnes, Melina	13081	Case, Emma	9473
Carnes, Melvin C.	13762	Case, Joseph H.	9474
Carnes, Amanda	13867	Caudill, Bertha	9896
Carnes, Lewis	13972	Cabe, Rebecca W.	11126
Carnes, Jackson	13993	Camden, Ida B.	11526
Carnes, Cillin Bertha Bell	14532	Catlin, Claude M.	12186
		Catlin, Charles W.	12187
Carnes, John	14900	Cartlidge, Minnie M.	13050
Carnes, Silvey	14941	Cartlidge, Mary E.	13051
Carnes, Lizzie	15793	Cartlidge, Richard	13052
Carnes, Mary Ann	15941	Cartlidge, Edward Jr.	13053
Carns, Solomon	5295	Cartlidge, Margaret J.	13054
Carn, Elias	2785	Cartlidge, Guy	13055
Carn, Lena	2786	Cartledge, Nancy	13293
Carn, Harlis	2882	Cartledge, Bessie	13294
Carn, Lucky	3834	Cartledge, Cecil	13295
Carn, Jackson	5280	Cassell, Serena	13485
Carn, Rufus	5281	Cassell, Leathie	13487
Carterby, Siglon	1467	Capin, Silwee	13895
Carterby, Tillis	1468	Cann, George	15803
Carterby, Moses	1469	Cannedy, Georgia	15804
Carterby, Maleum	1470	Cannedy, Earl	15807
Carterby, John	1471	Cannedy, Roy	15808
Carterby, Susan	1777	Cannedy, Irma	15809
Carterby, Salinsie	1778	Cealey, Susan	671
Carterby, Eben	2043	Cephus, Timothy	1862
Carterby, Isabelle	2044	Cephus, Henry	1864
Carterby, Ben	2045	Cephus, Wilbon	2482
Carterby, Almon	2293	Cephus, Elmesa	2483
Caldwell, Willie	2719	Cephus, Minnie	2484
Caldwell, Mary Ann	2720	Cephus, Jemima	12526
Caldwell, Clarissa	2721	Cephus, Sampson	12527
Caldwell, Mycle	2723	Chandler, Nettie	45
Caldwell, Molcy	2724	Chandler, William T.	46
Caldwell, Maria	14415	Chandler, James E.	47
Caldwell, Thomas	14416	Chandler, Lory Elvy	48
Caldwell, Marlon L.	14417	Chandler, Iva Ethel	49
Caldwell, Margaret	14418	Childs, Newton Nelson	370
Cash, Wallace	2871	Childs, Mina Adelia	371
Cash, Sophia	2872	Christy, Charley	1184
Carby, Eli	3493	Christy, Amanda	1185
Carlister, Annie	3925	Christy, Harmon	1186
Calister, James	4711	Christy, Emily	1254
Cartubbee, Frank	4786	Christy, Dallas	1263
Campala, Julius	6268	Christy, Elzire	1264
Campala, Hanna	6269	Christy, Lula	1265
Campala, Jency	6270	Christy, Francis	1266
Campala, Hewitt	14721	Christy, Janattie C.	1267
Carshall, Zack T.	6932	Christy, James	7011
Carshall, Simon	6951	Christy, Betsy	7012
Carshall, Frances	6952	Christy, Joshua	7013
Carshall, Susan	8702	Christy, Sally	7014

Name.	Roll No.	Name.	Roll No.
Christy, Wilson	7015	Choate, George R.	13200
Christy, Gibson	7149	Choate, Lydie E.	13201
Christy, Tobias	7150	Choate, Geo. W.	13202
Christy, Harriet	7151	Choate, Eliza	13203
Christy, Betsy	7152	Choate, Jefferson	13247
Christy, Aliam M.	7153	Choate, James H.	13304
Christy, Hakin	14749	Choate, Corneal	13305
Christie, Caroline	1194	Choate, Leslie R.	13306
Christie, Gilbert	1366	Choate, Lois B.	13307
Christie, Emiline	1368	Choate, Roberson	13505
Christie, Moses	1403	Choate, Jimmie	13804
Christie, Blance	1404	Choate, Mary	13805
Christie, Michael	1405	Chinka, Annie	2623
Christie, Dukes	1409	Chapman, Kate .K.	3778
Christie, Aifred	2011	Chapman, James Emery	3781
Christie, Mary	2012	Chronic, Emma	4704
Christie, David	2013	Chubbe, Miney	7016
Christie Emma	2014	Chubbee, Austin	7604
Christie, Moses	2015	Chubbee, Lila	7605
Christie, Peter	2016	Chubbee, Willis	7606
Christie, Tennessee	2159	Chubbee, Lucinda	7607
Christie, Jesse L.	3180	Chubbee, Sampson	7608
Christie, Nelson	3181	Chubbee, Lamon	10328
Christie, Adeline	3182	Chubbee, Isabelle	10329
Christie, Isaac	3206	Chubbee, Robert	10330
Christie, Edward	3719	Chubbee, Moses	11301
Christie, Sim	4498	Chubbee, Louisa	11890
Christie, Lottie	4499	Chamberlain, Fannie	9779
Christie, Amanda	5274	Chamberlain, Mariana	9780
Christie, Louvina	5275	Chateau, Martin	10796
Christie, Adam	11299	Chatau, George	15888
Christie, Isham	13131	Charleston, Martin	11787
Christie, Edward	13132	Charleston, Susan	11788
Christie, Andrew	13133	Charleston, Marion	11789
Christie, Catharine	14682	Charleston, Timothy P.	11790
Christie, Ellis	14912	Charleston, Simeon M.	11791
Christie, Annie	15935	Christian, Emma	12635
Charley, Netsie	1775	Christian, Nona A.	12636
Charley, Eliston	1776	Christian, Delilah F.	12637
Charley, Ester	2462	Christian, Elmer Lee	12643
Charley, Mary	2502	Christian, Emma Levy	12644
Charley, Sina	2860	Chunn, William R.	12733
Charley, Elam	2861	Chunn, William C.	12734
Charley, Mary	13437	Chunn, Mattie	12758
Charley, Michal	13438	Chunn, Oscar Jr.	12759
Charley, David	15795	Cheadle, Lucy B.	13694
Charles, William	3142	Cheadle, James Pushma-	
Charles, Email	13573	taha	13695
Charles, Sally	15969	Cheadle, Mary Almeda	13696
Charles, Martin	15970	Cheadle, Martin Douglas	13697
Choate, Robert	2005	Cheadle, George Rector	13698
Choate, Gilbert	2052	Cheadle, Kiska Harkins	13699
Choate, Sophia	2053	Churchman, Lizzie	13888
Choate, Sopha	2870	Churchman, Mertie May	13889
Choate, Louie	2876	Chastain, Lina M.	14793
Choate, Jency	2877	Chastain, Garvin D.	14794
Choate, Sallie	2881	Chastain, Rosa B.	14795
Choate, Dwight	3077	Chastain, Clarence C.	14796
Choate, Maud	3078	Chivers, Maud A.	15505
Choate, Green M.	3079	Chivers, Jennie A.	15506
Choate, Ben	3080	Chivers, Charles Eynon	15507
Choate, Ida	3081	Clay, Simpson	927
Choate, Patsy	4596	Clay, Wysa	928
Choate, Alexsie	5395	Clay, Lizzie	929
Choate, Elsie	5396	Clay, Betsy	930
Choate, Lummy	5612	Clay, Abner H.	1026
Choate, Millie	5614	Clay, Abner Henry	1027
Choate, Stephen	5615	Clay, Mattie Lorena	1028
Choate, William	7192	Clay, Wilsey	1552
Choate, Sillen	7193	Clay, Ida	1553
Choate, Abbie	7652	Clay, Betsy	3345
Choate, Talce	7653	Clay, Calvin	3346
Choate, Isabelle	7654	Clay, Bycey	3347
Choate, John,	7943	Clay, Andrew	5340
Choate, Jincy	8715	Clay, Gibson	5341
Choate, David	9443	Clay, Jincey	5342
Choate, William D.	9444	Clay, Sallie	5343
Choate, Joseph E.	9445	Clay, Lizzie	5344
Choate, Naoma Adilira	9446	Clay, Kizzie	5345
Choate, Christopher C.	12750	Clay, Solomon	10556
Choate, Lewis E.	12751	Clay, Louisa	13730
Choate, Jacob G.	12752	Clay, Myrtle Eugenia	14562
Choate, Walter	12756	Claxton, Arizona	4247
Choate, William F.	13198	Clark, Ella	4597
Choate, Edgar E.	13199	Clark, Josephine	5734

Name.	Roll No.	Name.	Roll No.
Clark, Flossie May	5736	Colbert, Lena	10043
Clark, Fannie	9990	Colbert, Vera	10044
Clark, Edward	10510	Colbert, Clarence, Jr.	10045
Clark, Edwin	13030	Colbert, Minnie Belle	10046
Clark, Burnetta A.	13847	Colbert, Gaines	10555
Clark, Juston T.	13849	Colbert, Aaron	11896
Cleaveland, Mollie	7810	Colbert, Eliza	11397
Cleaveland, Letetia	7814	Colbert, Charlie	11586
Cline, Lizzie	12076	Colbert, Allison	12091
Cline, John T.	12077	Colbert, Jasper	12289
Cline, Joseph V.	12078	Colbert, Sam	12609
Cline, Edward Milton	12079	Colbert, Sam	13522
Clower, Sallie M.	12253	Colbert, Edmund	13587
Clower, Joe E.	12254	Colbert, Lily	13803
Clower, Walter G.	12255	Colbert, Willie	13806
Clower, Anna H.	12256	Colbert, Ben	13872
Clower, Olivia M.	12257	Colbert, Ely	13879
Clover, R. L.	14312	Colbert, Emily	13880
Cloud, Bradda	14259	Colbert, Sallie	13900
Colbert, Mary E.	96	Colbert, Elias	13906
Colbert, Theodore W. Jr.	97	Colbert, Malissa	13952
Colbert, Nelma	98	Colbert, Sukey	13953
Colbert, Martha	758	Colbert, Annie	13954
Colbert, John	759	Colbert, Agnes	13955
Colbert, Alexander	761	Colbert, Joe	13956
Colbert, Winey	1168	Colbert, Gill	13957
Colbert, Amos	1187	Colbert, Martha	13979
Colbert, Sampson	1189	Colbert, Levi	13338
Colbert, John	1190	Colbert, Winnie	13339
Colbert, Nancy	1199	Colbert, Sina	13340
Colbert, Josie	1200	Colbert, Sillen	13341
Colbert, Joel	1201	Colbert, Philliston	13342
Colbert, Tobias	1202	Colbert, Lena	13352
Colbert, Noel	1614	Colbert, Charley	14634
Colbert, Sampson	1791	Colbert, Jincy	14698
Colbert, Sean	1792	Colbert, Webster	14702
Colbert, Reason	1793	Colbert, Aaron	14913
Colbert, Sylwid	1794	Colbert, Elijah Ruben	15603
Colbert, Davison	2026	Colbert, Margaret	15820
Colbert, Daviney	2027	Colbert, Salina	15859
Colbert, Dickson	2028	Colbert, Susan	16063
Colbert, Emiline	2029	Cobb, Maud O.	197
Colbert, Marswes	2030	Cobb, Mary Eiline	198
Colbert, Simpson	2266	Cobb, Lois	199
Colbert, Milly	2269	Cobb, Maude	200
Colbert, Osborne	2270	Cobb, Gibson	1323
Colbert, Jesse	2271	Cobb, Bettie	1325
Colbert, Golton	2272	Cobb, Sophie	1326
Colbert, Charles	2787	Cobb, Sampson	1716
Colbert, Julia Anna	2788	Cobb, Sophie	1717
Colbert, Frances	2789	Cobb, Simon	1718
Colbert, Herndon	2790	Cobb, Aaron	1719
Colbert, Acy	2791	Cobb, Sillan	1720
Colbert, William J.	3338	Cobb, Albert	1721
Colbert, Sinie	3339	Cobb, Sam	1772
Colbert, Sam	3966	Cobb, Sophia	2591
Colbert, Eliza	3967	Cobb, Selena	2710
Colbert, Frank	3968	Cobb, Keener B.	3938
Colbert, Jimmy	3970	Cobb, Frank	6021
Colbert, Nick	4443	Cobb, Lewis W.	6663
Colbert, Suckey	4820	Cobb, Sam	6968
Colbert, Vina	5059	Cobb, Loren	7850
Colbert, Washington	5537	Cobb, Micy	11277
Colbert, Johnson	5578	Cobb, Frances	13941
Colbert, Sinie	5579	Cobb, Annie	13942
Colbert, Charlie	5580	Cobb, Clarance	13943
Colbert, Bessie	5581	Cobb, Edward	13944
Colbert, John	5599	Cobb, Silas	13356
Colbert, Ellis	5641	Cobb, Rosie	14580
Colbert, Simon	6121	Cobb, Armas	14769
Colbert, Sam	6791	Cobb, Thomas	14770
Colbert, Jasper	7926	Cooper, Mary Emaline	201
Colbert, Siney	8348	Cooper, Israel	613
Colbert, Edward	8349	Cooper, Lorinda	614
Colbert, Thomas	8350	Cooper, Edmund	615
Colbert, Cornelia	8351	Cooper, Sam	616
Colbert, Dave	8750	Cooper, Sisty	2980
Colbert, Selena	8881	Cooper, Johnny	3734
Colbert, Sim	9015	Cooper, Martin	3745
Colbert, Elba	9016	Cooper, Susan	3746
Colbert, Athenius M.	9632	Cooper, Edward	3747
Colbert, Agnes J. Fisher	9633	Cooper, Lucy	3748
Colbert, Benjamin H. Jr.	9634	Cooper, Lena	3749
Colbert, Clarence	10041	Cooper, Jinsy	3752
Colbert, Lewis C.	10042	Cooper, Sina	3760

Name.	Roll No.	Name.	Roll No.
Cooper, Columbus	5146	Cochran, Joseph John	806
Cooper, Cornelius	5573	Cochran, Dan Bailey	807
Cooper, Lucy	5574	Cochran, Grover	808
Cooper, Ellen	5575	Cochran, Nellie Viola	809
Cooper, Allen	5576	Cochran, Elizabeth	11190
Cooper, Jane	5617	Cope, John B.	879
Cooper, Lucy	4261	Cope, Harry A.	880
Cooper, Sampson	4262	Cope, Mamie	881
Cooper, Nelson	4263	Cope, Pearl	882
Cooper, Mary	4264	Costilow, Jennie	1016
Cooper, Henry	5618	Costilow, Lena	1017
Cooper, George	5643	Costilow, Henretta	1019
Cooper, Abel	7306	Costilow, Laura B.	1021
Cooper, Lucy	7307	Costilow, Charles G.	1022
Cooper, Edgar	7308	Costilow, Ida Daisey	1023
Cooper, Oscar	7310	Cornelius, John	1506
Cooper, Daniel	7311	Cornelius, Elum	1507
Cooper, James	7329	Cornelius, Elizabeth	1508
Cooper, Tory	7330	Cornelius, Martha	2850
Cooper, Lester M.	7331	Cornelius, Ella M.	4761
Cooper, Herbert	7332	Cornelius, Anna M.	4762
Cooper, David	7646	Cornelius, Emmet D.	4763
Cooper, Adam	7739	Cornelius, Lorenzo F.	4764
Cooper, John	7740	Cornelius, Willie M.	4765
Cooper, Henry	8253	Cornelius, Bessie I.	4766
Cooper, Maud S.	8254	Cornelius, Jesse P.	4767
Cooper, Willie Vera	8255	Cornelius, Oliver H.	4768
Cooper, Clara	8274	Columbus, Melwissie	1758
Cooper, Doughlas	8276	Columbus, Silas	1759
Cooper, Charles	8292	Columbus, Nicholas	1978
Cooper, Joseph C.	8293	Columbus, Celin	1991
Cooper, Maggie Jane	8294	Cogswell, Ida	2836
Cooper, Andrew J.	8382	Cogswell, Herndon	2840
Cooper, Mattie	8383	Coxwell, Johnson	3575
Cooper, Stephen	8384	Coxwell, Loston	3721
Cooper, Austin Albro	8385	Coxwell, Lonie	14661
Cooper, Kirby	8541	Collin, Bittie	2934
Cooper, Dora	8542	Collin, Annie	2935
Cooper, Stephen	9253	Collin, Ed	2937
Cooper, Mattie	11861	Collin, Esther	2938
Cooper, Minnie	12044	Collin, Abel	5140
Cooper, Willis	13374	Collin, Stephen	6458
Cooper, Thomas	13403	Collin, Noah	6459
Cooper, Emily	13404	Collin, Annie	6518
Cooper, Becky	13681	Collin, Hagin	6519
Cooper, Robert	13682	Collin, Jesse	6523
Cooper, Norris	13685	Collin, Martha	6524
Cooper, Maude	13686	Collin, Lena	8579
Cooper, Jeff D.	13925	Collin, Sena	8580
Cooper, Sina	14039	Collin, Wesley Ann	6936
Cooper, Phebe	14662	Collin, Webster	6937
Cooper, Nora	14704	Collin, Phelin	6960
Cooper, Mary Belle	14779	Collin, Sibbel	6961
Cooper, Frances	14949	Collin, Moses	6962
Cooper, Henry E.	15596	Collin, Sampson	6965
Conner, Effie May	264	Collin, Buckner	6966
Conner, Alberta	265	Collins, Andrew	7972
Conner, Henry Merle	266	Collins, Claudie C.	7973
Connors, Aran	13265	Collins, Andrew L.	7974
Connors, William J. B.	13266	Collins, Nellie	7975
Connors, Annie	13267	Collins, Thomas Hugh	7976
Connors, Edward	13268	Collins, Miles S.	8221
Connors, Daniel	13269	Collins, Stella	8222
Connors, Cora	13270	Collins, Mary A.	8223
Connors, Fannie	13271	Collins, Mamie A.	8224
Connors, Patrick	13273	Collins, Miles Ricker	8225
Connors, Michael	13274	Collins, John F.	8230
Cook, Lucy Garland	412	Collins, Foly D.	8231
Cook, Will Poland	414	Collins, Elijah A.	8232
Cook, Myrtle Lee	858	Collins, Clara May	8233
Cook, Anna Bessie	859	Collins, Louisa	9281
Cook, Lizzie	13272	Collins, Nona M.	9282
Cook, Jennie Donnie	14553	Collins, Joseph	11792
Cook, Lucy J.	15683	Collins, Emily	11875
Cook, Thomas W.	15684	Collins, Elsie	12008
Cotten, Pink	561	Collins, Edmund	12010
Cotten, Pinkie	562	Collins, Joseph	14858
Cotten, Hester	14260	Collins, Charles	14859
Cotten, David Oscar	14585	Cole, Isaac	3897
Cotten, Fay	14586	Cole, Sarah	3898
Cotten, Maude	14587	Cole, Minnie	4061
Cotten, Robert L.	14997	Cole, Joseph	4601
Cotten, E. W.	15557	Cole, Willy	4613
Cochran, Viola	804	Cole, Missie	4614
Cochran, Lula Inez	805	Cole, Wilson	4795

Name.	Roll No.	Name.	Roll No.
Cole,. Titus	4797	Coleman, Dixie	13553
Cole, Louisiana	4799	Coleman, Oscar M.	13554
Cole, Amy	4800	Coleman, Arian	13647
Cole, Anice	4801	Coleman, Bertha Marie	13648
Cole, Silas E.	4821	Coleman, Bessie Neva	13649
Cole, Missie	4822	Coleman, Ola Gladys	13650
Cole, Amanda	4823	Coleman, Sarah Gaddy	13651
Cole, Eastman	4824	Coleman, Riley Buford	13652
Cole, Suaan	4825	Coleman, Donnie B.	13654
Cole, James	4987	Coleman, Roby Almedia	13655
Cole, Allen	5055	Cowen, Frances	5108
Cole, Peter	5057	Cowen, Charles	5109
Cole, Eligh	5058	Cowen, Susan	9284
Cole, John	5100	Cowen, Joseph Lee	9285
Cole, Turner	5113	Cowan, Sarah	7717
Cole, Elizabeth	5114	Cowan, Lemuel O.	7715
Cole, Eliza A.	5115	Cowan, Iman Lee	7716
Cole, Jensie	5116	Coff, Arbis	5985
Cole, Isabelle	5117	Coff, Noel	5987
Cole, Bob	5118	Coff, Martha	5988
Cole, Charley	5119	Coff, Edwin	5989
Cole, James	5120	Conser, Peter	6603
Cole, Simeon	5121	Conser, Mary A.	6604
Cole, Eliza A.	5122	Conser, Susie	6605
Cole, Susie	5123	Conser, Lue	6606
Cole, Sampson	5144	Conser, Julius	6607
Cole, Morgan	5158	Conser, Alice	6608
Cole, Mary J.	5159	Conser, Ada	6609
Cole, Forbis	5160	Conser, Simeon	6610
Cole, Anderson	5182	Cox, Letha	7937
Cole, Sissie	5183	Cox, Joseph	7938
Cole, Logan	5235	Cox, Joseph R.	7939
Cole, Emily F.	7299	Cox, Charles	7940
Cole, Ida May	7300	Cox, John	7941
Cole, Campbell	9697	Cox, Mary Melzona	7942
Cole, Mary	9698	Cox, Matilda	15678
Cole, Semus	9743	Cox, Ona Leo	15833
Cole, Israel	9744	Cox, Constant E.	15839
Cole, Jimson	11583	Coley, Anderson	8300
Cole, Lucy	11584	Coley, Biney	8301
Cole, Selina	11894	Coley, Wilburn	8302
Cole, Elfa	12007	Coley, Edward	8303
Cole, Bonnie M.	14445	Coley, Edmond	8304
Cole, Rogers L.	14446	Coley, Johnson	8305
Cole, Nelson	14686	Coley, Caldwell	8306
Cole, Susan	14687	Coley, Ella	8307
Cole, Laura	14828	Coley, Sophia	8972
Cole, Preslie L.	14829	Coley, Frank	8973
Cole, Caroline	14890	Coley, Cicero	8974
Cole, Edward	4701	Coley, Sillen	8975
Combs, Sarah	3939	Coley, Nora J.	8976
Combs, Claude W.	3940	Coley, David	12537
Combs, Buster	3942	Coley, Lovina	12538
Combs, Jesse J.	3943	Coley, Joseph Ed	12539
Combs, Cora E.	3944	Coley, Dora May	12540
Combs, John	3945	Coffman, Sarah E.	8965
Coone, Viney	4001	Coffman, Melvin	8966
Coone, Charlie	4002	Coffman, George Dewey	8967
Coone, Willie May	4003	Coffman, Elizabeth P.	8968
Coone, David	4004	Coats, Mary	9499
Coone, Emma	15782	Coats, Annie	9504
Coon, Rhoda	12129	Coats, Lola	9505
Coleman, Bond	4545	Compton, Sarah	9639
Coleman, Sukey	4546	Compton, James H.	9640
Coleman, Emily	4547	Cochnauer, Lon	9914
Coleman, Silwee	4548	Cochnauer, David W.	10113
Coleman, Thompson	4551	Cochnauer, Rhoda	10114
Coleman, Jimmie	4552	Cochnauer, Louisa P.	10115
Coleman, Emma	4553	Cochnauer, Ethel	10116
Coleman, William	4554	Cochnauer, Nicholas	10834
Coleman, Louisa	4623	Cochnauer, Bettie	10835
Coleman, Thomas	4671	Cochnauer, William	10836
Coleman, Susie	7231	Cochnauer, Melvina	10837
Coleman, Columbus G.	7232	Cochnauer, Mary C.	10838
Coleman, Henry H.	7233	Cochnauer, Zenie J.	10839
Coleman, John F. W.	7234	Cochnauer, Turner	11488
Coleman, Rosy Elizabeth	7235	Cochnauer, Rena	11489
Coleman, Norman	10715	Cochnauer, Sophia	11490
Coleman, Daly	10716	Cochnauer, Nicholas	11491
Coleman, Tennessee	10717	Cochneuer, David J.	10077
Coleman, Lou Anna	13548	Cochneuer, Nicholas F.	10078
Coleman, Romie	13549	Cochneuer, James H.	10079
Coleman, Eddy	13550	Cochneuer, Ella E.	10081
Coleman, Nellie	13551	Cochneuer, Marion McC	10082
Coleman, Tallie	13552	Conlan, Czarina	11325

Name.	Roll No.	Name.	Roll No.
Conlan, Lottie A.	11326	Crowder, Elizabeth	13589
Collier, Martha	12372	Crowder, Mary S.	14169
Collier, Oma	12378	Crowder, Laura	14170
Correll, Ella	12612	Crowder, John	14171
Compelube, Columbus	12861	Crowder, John Richard	14667
Compelube, Nicholas	12862	Crowder, Bolden	15400
Compelube, Henry	12863	Crowder, William T.	15401
Compelube, Joshua	12864	Crowder, Silvey. E.	15402
Compelube, Martin	12865	Crowder, Allie Bama	15403
Compelube, Nellie	12867	Crowder, George	15405
Compelube, Bittie	12868	Crowder, Ida	15546
Compelube, Martha	12872	Crowder, Maud May	1249
Courts, Grace	13099	Crittenden, Johnny	4372
Coston, Lina	4123	Crittenden, Sissa	4390
Conn, Minnie J.	14062	Crittenden, Isabelle	4391
Conn, Agnes	14063	Crittenden, Carrie	4392
Conn, Edna	14066	Crittenden, Herold	4393
Conn, Mary E..	14067	Crittendon, Annie	4394
Coffee, Laura	14454	Crittenden, Mary	4395
Coffee, Edwin	14455	Cravette, Amy	5460
Coffee, Ada	14456	Cravatt, Ward	11304
Coffee, Ruby Addie	14457	Cravatt, Mitchell	11432
Coy, Milton	14847	Cravatt, Isabelle	11433
Coy, Nora	14848	Cravatt, Johnson	11953
Coy, Frank	14849	Cravatt, Elma Pearl	11954
Coy Oscar	14850	Cricklin, Wilson	6837
Cooksey, William Earnest	15219	Cricklin, Fred	14734
Cowling, John A.	15963	Crawford, Charles	6883
Cowling, A. D.	15964	Crawford, Jessie	6884
Cowling, Ora Mittie	15965	Crawford, Ben	6885
Cross, A. G.	421	Crawford, Minnie	9834
Cross, Cordey Belle	422	Crawford, Gus	14369
Cross, Geo. Washington	423	Crawford, Barnett	14370
Cross, Ethel Lee	424	Crawford, Marvin	14371
Cross, George W.	425	Crawford, Pearl	14372
Cross, Elva Corintha	426	Crawford, Alice	14373
Crosby, Wallace	2341	Crawford, Ollie	14374
Crosby, Licksie	2342	Crawford, Flora May	14375
Crosby, Ida	2348	Crawford, George	15789
Crosby, Josiah	2349	Cravens, Maggie	7432
Crosby, Sissy	2350	Crowley, Nannie	7245
Crosby, Susan	2351	Crowley, Narne	11364
Crosby, Seanis	2352	Cromwell, Carrie	7473
Crosby, Davis	2353	Cromwell, Laura B.	7475
Crosby, Bettie	2354	Cromwell, Indiola	7476
Crosby, Paul	2355	Crabtree, Georgia A.	9609
Crosby, Leslan	2356	Crabtree, Wyley E. E.	9610
Crosby, Lucie	2357	Crabtree, Early	9611
Crosby, Sarah	2465	Crabtree, Edna M.	9612
Crosby, Leander	4575	Crabtree, Elmer L.	9613
Crowder, Mary A.	3994	Creecy, Ula L.	10280
Crowder, Mary M.	3997	Creecy, John Dow	10281
Crowder, John J.	3998	Crutchfield, Gertrude	11018
Crowder, Richard	4034	Crutchfield, Ida	16105
Crowder, Mary	4043	Crutchfield, Everet	16106
Crowder, Martin B.	4044	Crutchfield, Ima	16107
Crowder, Bessie L.	4045	Crutchfield, Louvinia	16108
Crowder, Ophelia L.	4046	Crutchfield, William	16109
Crowder, Bunny F.	4047	Crutchfield, Loutitia	16110
Crowder, Thomas C.	4062	Crutchfield, George W.	16111
Crowder, Green	4063	Crisp, Ella M.	11552
Crowder, Emma	4064	Cruttes, Anna B.	13358
Crowder, Jesse	4068	Crow, Mable	15484
Crowder, Louisa	4069	Crow, Andrew Dow	15486
Crowder, Alice	4070	Critz, Olive B.	16213
Crowder, Eli	4447	Critz, Elizabeth E.	16214
Crowder, Maggie	7432	Cushman, Artie M.	113
Crowder, Rebecca	9754	Cushman, Earnest	116
Crowder, Mary C.	9757	Cushman, Elvira	117
Crowder, Loran F.	10065	Cushman, Glenn	118
Crowder, John H.	10066	Cummings, Minnie Lee	441
Crowder, Harvey	10067	Cummings, Vera	442
Crowder, Thompson	10069	Cummings, Lodeva	443
Crowder, Martin S.	10201	Cummings, Dawes Bixby	444
Crowder, Emily	10202	Cummings, Erner Van	445
Crowder, Perry	10203	Curry, Clara	584
Crowder Margaret	10204	Curry, Howard F.	588
Crowder, Sibbey	10205	Culberson, Eliza	738
Crowder, Flora	10206	Culberson, James	6722
Crowder, Sallie	10207	Culberson, Sophia	6723
Crowder, Flossie L.	10841	Culberson, Johanna	6725
Crowder, Juanita H.	13182	Culberson, James Matthew	6726
Crowder, Robert S.	13183	Culberson, Elijah	7829
Crowder, Edwin McC	13184	Culberson. Sarah E.	7830

Name.	Roll No.
Culberson, Georgia C.	7831
Culberson, Ida E.	7832
Culberson, Nellie Luvinia	7833
Culberson, Josiah	15379
Culbertson, Sophia A.	12120
Culbertson, Charlie E., Jr.	12121
Culbertson, Chloe	12122
Culbertson, Lois	12123
Culbertson, Mary B.	12124
Culbertson, Zelma	12125
Culbertson, Lucile	12126
Culbertson, William F.	12127
Culbertson, Katie	13015
Culbertson, Theophelos P.	13016
Culbertson, Clyde W.	13017
Culbertson, Cornelius M.	13018
Cusher, Ellis	1958
Cusher, Elias	14592
Cusher, Simeon	14593
Cusher, Peter	14594
Cusher, Mary	14595
Cusher, Harris	14596
Curtis, Luvicey	6617
Curtis, Larabelle	6619
Curtis, Johnnie	6620
Curtis, Homer	6621
Curtis, Ella	6757
Curtis, Willie C.	6764
Curley, Rhoda	6839
Curley, Annie	6840
Curley, Arizona	6841
Cunnish, Martha	9465
Cunnish, Joel	9466
Cunnish, Webster	11373
Cunningham, Martha J.	12591
Cunningham, Alfred H., Jr.	12592
Cunningham, James W.	12593
Cunningham, Augustus	12594
Cunningham, Walter	12595
Cunningham, John W.	12596
Cunningham, Hazel Ellen	12597
Cunningham, West L.	14484
Cunningham, Sarah Ella	14485
Davis, John C.	845
Davis, Theodore H.	846
Davis, Roxie G.	847
Davis, Mabel I.	848
Davis, Joel Nail	849
Davis, Alekton	1362
Davis, Martha	1363
Davis, Eliza	1364
Davis, Viney	2777
Davis, Sylvester	2809
Davis, Louisa	2810
Davis, Delilah F.	3895
Davis, Jefferson	4474
Davis, Susan	4475
Davis, Sissy	4476
Davis, Annie	6970
Davis, Victor	6971
Davis, Emma	6972
Davis, Lou	6973
Davis, Oscar	6976
Davis, Emiline	6977
Davis, Maggie	8295
Davis, Letha	8296
Davis, Lennie	8297
Davis, Bertie Lorena	8298
Davis, Eva	3299
Davis, Minnie	9323
Davis, James	9924
Davis, Alfred	10198
Davis, Ira Cecil	10199
Davis, Mary E.	10200
Davis, George	10386
Davis, Henry Carl	12004
Davis, Etta R.	12005
Davis, Reggie Ruth	12006
Davis, Lorena	12321
Davis, Alice A.	12322
Davis, Carrie J.	12323

Name.	Roll No.
Davis, Royal E.	12324
Davis, Winnie H.	12325
Davis, Jefferson Harris	12326
Davis, Annie	12586
Davis, James G.	12587
Davis, Geo. T.	12588
Davis, Lillie G.	12589
Davis, Joseph L.	12590
Davis, William H.	12823
Davis, Eugene	12824
Davis, Riley	13028
Davis, Annie	13029
Davis, Mary E.	13599
Davis, Tom	13364
Davis, Sim	14747
Davis, Joe	15597
Davis, Charley L.	15600
Davis, Marshall A.	15610
Davis, William Z.	15611
Davis, Oria	15612
Davis, Marshall Joseph	15613
Davis, Burk	15614
Davis, Lillie M.	15615
Davis, Vinan J.	15616
Davis, Mary J.	15617
Davis, John R.	15618
Davis, Sherm Henry	15619
Davis, Albert	15814
Davis, Zachary T.	15864
Davis, Buford	15865
Davis, Anis	15866
Davis, Seemenigh	15867
Davis, Sherwood	15868
Davis, Theodore Winston	15869
David, Wister	3529
David, Viney	3896
Daniel, John	1478
Daniel, Mary	1479
Daniel, Sillian	1481
Daniel, Frances	1657
Daniel, Esias	2624
Daniel, Moses	7166
Daniel, Malissa	7167
Daniel, Sallie	7168
Daniel, Elizabeth	7169
Daniel, Mack	9007
Daniel, Zora	14405
Daniel, Sidney T.	14406
Daniel, Lela May	14407
Daniel, Eunice B.	14408
Daniel, Beatrice	14421
Daniel, William Wilson	14426
Daniels, Joe D.	7537
Daniels, Alfred P.	7538
Daniels, Turner	7771
Daniels, Rebecca	7773
Daniels, Turner, Jr.	7774
Daniels, Ida	7775
Daniels, Otto	7776
Daniels, Lottie	7777
Daniels, Mattie	7778
Daniels, Minnie	7779
Daniels, Green	8110
Daniels, Thelma	8112
Davenport, George	5002
Davenport, Eliza	5003
Davenport, Pearlie	5004
Davenport, Vena	5005
Davenport, Mack Arthur	5009
Davenport, Rebecca	5011
Davenport, Joe	5012
Davenport, Jimpson	5053
Davenport, Lina	5054
Davenport, Francis	15353
Davenport, John	15354
Davenport, Clarence G.	15355
Davenport, Arthur	15356
Davenport, Robert	15357
Davenport, Florence S.	15358
Davenport, Leslie	15359
Davenport, Ida Myrtle	15360
Daney, Perry	6041
Daney, Daniel	6198
Daney, Rebecca	6199

Name.	Roll No.
Daney, Solomon	6200
Daney, Gilbert	6201
Daney, Joel	6202
Daney, Malinda	6203
Daney, Benjamin	6204
Daney, Harris	6205
Daney, Joseph	6206
Dana, Charles A.	10647
Dana, Eliza	10648
Dana, Wilburn	10550
Dana, Rosie	10651
Dana, Henrietta	10652
Dana, Massey	10653
Daugherty, Matilda	7342
Daugherty, Charles L.	7344
Daugherty, John F.	7346
Daugherty, Mary M.	7347
Daugherty, Alica	7348
Daugherty, Myrtle	11103
Daugherty, Elvin H.	11127
Darneal, James	7751
Darneal, Sallie	7752
Darneal, Betsy	7753
Darneal, Zibbie	7754
Darneal, Adam	7755
Darneal, Frank	7756
Darneal, Emma	7757
Darneal, Anselom	7758
Darneal, Katie	7759
Darneal, Silas	7861
Darneal, Elijah	7862
Darneal, Dallas	7863
Darneal, Ida M.	7864
Darneal, Emma E.	7865
Darneal, Stephen	8145
Darneal, James	8146
Darneal, Elias	8147
Darneal, William	8148
Darneal, Henry	8149
Darneal, Fred S.	8150
Daggs, William W.	8137
Daggs, Leonidas	8138
Daggs, John C.	8139
Daggs, James W.	8140
Daggs, Sarah E.	8141
Damron, Amanda	10188
Damron, Lola	10189
Damron, Lula	10190
Danenhour, Fannie	11762
Danenhour, Hettie	11763
Danenhour, George	11764
Danenhour, Annie	11765
Danenhour, Frank	11766
Dawson, Lelan E.	12437
Dawson, Effie	12438
Dawson, Aurelia	12439
Darden, William	14104
Darden, Minnie	14105
Darden, Charley	14106
Dennis, Josie Juanita	5
Dennis, Harriet	6
Dennis, Thompson	2457
Dennis, Silway	2458
Dennis, Simpson	2912
Dennis, Sophie	2914
Deal, Ida Isabelle	206
Deal, Faye	300
Denison, Mary	2655
Denison, Henry C.	2656
Denison, Sanford	2657
Denison, Lewie	2658
Davenport, Narcissa S.	4973
Devenport, Henry E.	4975
Devenport, Lena O.	4976
DeLoach, Annie	8027
DeLoach, William	8028
DeLoach, Josie	8029
Derryberry, Emma R.	8077
Derryberry, Brandon B.	8078
Denton, Ada	8286
Denton, John	8287
Denton, Emma	8288
Denton, James L.	8289
Denton, Nancy I.	8290
Denson, Lula	13577

Name.	Roll No.
Denson, Ruel Hopkins	13578
Dendy, Annie L.	15528
Dendy, Samuel M.	15529
Dendy, Minnie I.	15530
Dendy, James L.	15531
Dendy, Ozella	15754
Dillard, Hamilton	568
Dillard, Lee Hamilton	569
Dillard, Joseph Carpenter	570
Dillard, Willam Guy	571
Dillard, Minnie Victoria	572
Dillard, Bula Mamie	573
Dillard, Cubby Fowler	574
Dillard, Floyd	575
Dillard, Vella	576
Dillard, Douglas H.	577
Dillard, Joseph George	593
Dillard, Jesse	594
Dillard, Julius C.	595
Dillard, Ed Russell	596
Dillard, Gill	10767
Dillard, Bessie	10768
Dillard, Grover	10769
Dillard, Clara E.	10770
Dillard, Velma	10771
Dillard, Malcolm C.	10772
Dillard, Tandy W.	10984
Dillard, Vera	10985
Dillard, Rice	10986
Dillard, Jewel	10987
Dillard, Virgie M.	10988
Dillard, Tandy Russell	10989
Dillard, LeFlore	11027
Dillard, Willie May	11028
Dillard, Walter	14513
Dilllard, John L.	14817
Dickson, Minerva	3509
Dixon, Billy	7954
Dixon, Lilly	7956
Dixon, Mamie	7957
Dixon, Joseph	7958
Dixon, Susan	7959
Dizon, Jesse	8720
Dixon, Bertha M.	8721
Dixon, Clyde	8722
Dixon, Eliza	12898
Dixon, Wallace	12899
Dixon, Albert	12900
Dickerson, Arthur T.	9786
Dickerson, Guy B.	9787
Dickerson, Rebecca R.	9788
Dickerson, William E. S.	9789
Dickerson, Rosa E.	12693
Dickerson, Bulah	12696
Dillon, Susan	11504
Dillon, Thomas	11505
Dillon, Richard	11506
Dillon, Angie	11507
Dick, Martin	12074
Dick, Thomas	13714
Dick, Elizabeth	13715
Dick, Sampson	13946
Dick, Taylor	13947
Dick, Malina	13948
Dickey, Earnest G.	15319
Dilbeck, Alverado	12253
Dilbeck, Bessie G.	12354
Dilbeck, Benjamin H.	15476
Dibrell, Charles	15336
Dibrell, Carl Washington	15337
Dibrell, Clyde B.	15338
Dibrell, James	15381
Dills, Rosa	15722
Dills, Nora M.	15723
Dills, Lether Lee	15724
Dowland, Mattie	4067
Doctor, Frances	5745
Doctor, Simon	5746
Doctor, Levina	9350
Doctor, Rosa	9357
Donald, Lavinia	7063
Donald, Bennie	7069
Dobson, Laura	7394
Dobson, Thomas M.	7395

Name.	Roll No.	Name.	Roll No.
Dobson, Oldia	7396	Durant, Nellie	9070
Dobson, William T.	13526	Durant, Pier	9766
Dobson, Jewel Sumpter	13527	Durant, John W.	9775
Dobson, Leonidas	13539	Durant, Lou E.	9781
Dodson, Emma	7930	Durant, Wm. A.	9782
Dodson, Sudie	7931	Durant, William E. L.	9783
Dodson, Willie E.	7932	Durant, James G.	9784
Dodson, Elisha Thomas	7933	Durant, Dixon	9811
Dodson, Charlie	7934	Durant, Jesse	10011
Dodson, Mary J.	10052	Durant, Ora	10012
Dodson, Winnie	10058	Durant, Elizabetn	10109
Dodson, Elizabeth	13186	Durant, Sealey	10245
Dodson, Ella M.	13188	Durant, Joseph S.	10596
Dobbs, Pushmataha	15627	Durant, Martha	10598
Dobyns, Joanna	11023	Durant, Rena	10599
Dobyns, Clifford	11024	Durant, Hattie	10600
Dobyns, Oscar, Jr.	11025	Durant, Mollie	10601
Dobyns, Alice	11026	Durant, Austin	10602
Donaghey, Frances A.	9516	Durant, B.	10603
Donaghey, Lula B.	9517	Durant, Mary	10604
Donaghey, Roy C.	9518	Durant, Sophia	10605
Donaghey, Walter G.	9519	Durant, Frank	10688
Donaghey, Samuel C.	9520	Durant, Eliza	10689
Donaghey, Mordecia B.		Durant, Maggie	10690
Jr.	9521	Durant, Sampson	10691
Donaghey, Golder G.	9522	Durant, Lizzie	10692
Downing, Sam	14068	Durant, Willie	10693
Downing, George Todd	14069	Durant, Allen	10694
Dorset, John	14377	Durant, Jackson	11441
Drake, Rosa	8746	Durant, Taylor	11463
Drake, John E.	8856	Durant, Nancy	11465
Drake, George W.	15483	Durant, Reuben	11732
Drake, John W.	15485	Durant, Sealy	11733
Drew, Daniel	4887	Durant, Sammie	11761
Drew, Susan	4888	Durant, Rhoda	11836
Drew, Sallie A.	11300	Durant, Wesley	12287
Dunn, Salina	212	Durant, Albert	12288
Dunn, Jane	10346	Durant, Wallace	12735
Dunn, William M.	12167	Durant, Gaines	12736
Dunn, Josephine	12381	Durant, Etta	12737
Dunn, Tabitha J.	12382	Durant, Green	12738
Dunn, Fannie M.	12383	Durant, James	13124
Dunn, James William	12384	Durant, Susan	13125
Dunn, Ellen	12385	Durant, Melvina	13839
Dunn, Annie	14972	Durant, Lena	13840
Dunn, Lillian G.	14973	Durant, Ethelbert	13841
Dunn, Emma Brazelia	14974	Durant, Martha	13842
Dunn, William Alfred	14975	Durant, Juanita	13843
Dunn, Arthur Ward	14976	Durant, Clint	13844
Dunn, Allen Yates	14977	Durant, Florence	13845
Durant, William A.	1555	Durant, Sophia	13846
Durant, Laura	1556	Durant, Zozare	13848
Durant, Gibby	1557	Durant, Albert T.	13853
Durant, Eddie	1558	Durant, Morgan J.	13854
Durant, Louie	1559	Durant, Ulmont U.	13855
Durant, Amy	1732	Durant, Oliver H.	13856
Durant, Eastman	1733	Durant, Fannie	14677
Durant, Betsy	2083	Durant, Amanda	14789
Durant, Lizzie	2580	Durant, Walter N.	14855
Durant, Jane	2844	Durant, Rina J.	14856
Durant, Alexander R.	3871	Durant, John K.	14857
Durant, Annie L.	3872	Durant, Lyazien	14889
Durant, Etna R.	3873	Durant, Sophia	14893
Durant, Rias	4306	Dukes, Loren D.	6369
Durant, Hannah	4307	Dukes, Stella	6370
Durant, George	4308	Dukes, J. Herbert Hinds	6371
Durant, Sarah	4309	Dukes, Gilbert W.	6386
Durant, Wilson	4700	Dukes, Isabelle	6387
Durant, Edward	4701	Dukes, Joseph A.	6388
Durant, Bessie	4702	Dukes, Edwin	6389
Durant, Rachel	4703	Dukes, Josephine	6390
Durant, Sallie	4802	Dukes, Minerva	6391
Durant, Ellis	4838	Dukes, Leetta E.	6392
Durant, Gleason	4959	Dukes, D. H.	6393
Durant, Levi	5130	Dukes, Henry	6400
Durant, John	6403	Dukes, LeRoy	6401
Durant, Louisa	6404	Dukes, James Bohanan	16118
Durant, Lizzie	6405	Dunlap, Rena G.	8692
Durant, Sarah	6407	Dunlap, Kitty I.	8693
Durant, Isaac	6983	Dunlap, Susie E.	8694
Durant, Permelia	6984	Dunlap, Susan L.	8981
Durant, Griggs	7079	Dunlap, Ruth	8982
Durant, Jonas	7081	Dunlap, Sibyl	8983
Durant, Susan	7082	Duer, Frances	9729
Durant, Eliza	7083	Duer, Ephriham	9730

Name.	Roll No.	Name.	Roll No.
Duer, David	9731	Eaves, Burk Henry	9804
Duer, Ella	9732	Eastes, John L.	13094
Duer, Mark	9733	Earnest, George	16119
Duer, Birdie	9734	Earnest, Willie	16120
Duer, Una Irene	9735	Eba-ho-tubbe, Ellis	1882
Duer, Isaac	10101	Eba-ho-tubbe, Charles	1884
Duer, Thomas William	10102	Eba-ho-tubbe, Sukey	1885
Duncan, Henry	10344	Ebahotubbi, Davis	2196
Duncan, Charlie	10345	Ebahotubbi, Sallie	2197
Dunagan, Willie N.	9667	Ebahotubbi, Aaron	14602
Dunagan, Lula	12488	Ebahotubbi, Nancy	14863
Dunagan, Thomas C.	12489	E-ba-ho-tubbi	2362
Dunagan, Mildred A.	12490	E-ba-ho-tubbi, Kizzie A.	2363
Dunagan, Maggie G.	12491	E-ba-ho-tubbi, Moffin	2364
Dulaney, Belle	12168	E-ba-ho-tubbi, Elliston	2365
Duford, Willie	12442	E-ba-ho-tubbi, Graven	2366
Duford, Albert	12443	E-ba-ho-tubbi, Minnie	2367
Duford, Roxy	12445	E-ba-ho-tubbi, Nicey	2368
Duford, Frankie	12446	E-ba-ho-tubbi, Fannie	2369
Dunford, Turner	13938	E-ba-ho-tubbi, Abner	2370
Dwight, Levi	998	Ebafokka, Simeon	2545
Dwight, Sarah	999	Eb-an-ow-a-tubbe, Si-	
Dwight, Edward	5231	mon	13074
Dwight, Winnie	5232	Eb-an-ow-a-tubbe, Ber-	
Dwight, Lizzie	5233	tie	13075
Dwight, Dickson	5234	Edward, Moses	2274
Dwight, George	6789	Edward, Susan	2275
Dwight, Sallie	6790	Edward, Lena	2738
Dwight, Susan	6793	Edward, Jimpson	2739
Dwight, Edward	6963	Edward, May Estell	2740
Dwight, Betsy	6964	Edward, Wesley	5135
Dwight, Albert	7898	Edward, Cely	5136
Dwight, Benjamin	9615	Edward,,Eliza A.	5137
Dwight, Edwin	10181	Edward, Salena	5138
Dwight, Emma	10182	Edward, John	5139
Dwight, Thomas L.	10183	Edward, Isaac	5148
Dwight, Simon	10184	Edward, Allington	5458
Dwight, Edwin B.	10185	Edward, Sissie	5459
Dwight, Minerva	10186	Edwards, Morton	2303
Dwight, Jeremiah	10187	Edwards, Sallie	2306
Dwight, Joseph E.	10683	Edwards, Maneffie	2307
Dwight, Solomon	11302	Edwards, Silway	2308
Dwight, Bicey	14695	Edwards, Louisa	2309
Dwight, Allie	15233	Edwards, Ebenezer	2310
Dyer, James	1151	Edwards, Betsy	2313
Dyer, Adeline	1152	Edwards, William	4050
Dyer, James Jr.	1153	Edwards, Vinson	4051
Dyer, Aaron	1154	Edwards, Benjamin	4453
Dyer, Willy	1155	Edwards, Tobias	5760
Dyer, Pearly	1156	Edwards, Lucy	5761
Dyer, Nellie May	1157	Edwards, Eli	12958
Dyer, Elliston E.	1259	Edwards, Isaac	12959
Dyer, Flordelle	1262	Edwards, Rufus M.	15701
Dyer, Artie	1605	Edwards, Emma	15702
Dyer, David	1625	Edwards, Kate	15704
Dyer, Celia	1626	Edwards, Ada	15705
Dyer, Eliza	1627	Edwards, Thomas B.	15755
Dyer, Smallwood	1628	Edwards, Emma	15878
Dyer, Wilsey	1629	Edwards, Mary L.	15994
Dyer, Johanna	1630	Edwin, Eliza	6045
Dyer, Joel	2760	Edmonds, Martha J.	12739
Dyer, Mary	2761	Eddy, Ida O.	13771
Dyer, Israel	2763	Eddy, Elsie O.	13772
Dyer, Louis	3186	Edgar, Rhoda M.	15740
Dyer, Sallie	3237	Edgar, Earnest	15741
Dyer, David Jr.	3731	Edgar, Sarah Ettie	15742
Dyer, Sam	9920	Edens, Ari Anna F.	15816
Dyer, Sarah	9921	Edens, John J.	15818
Dyer, Sampson	9922	Edens, Hester Lorine	15819
Dyer, Emma	9923	Eeds, Anna B.	7095
Dyer, Nicholas	12747	Eeds, Hazel	7096
Dyer, Granson	14649	Elliott, Anderson	1872
Dyer, Lorena A.	14867	Elliott, Eliza	1873
Dyer, Joseph A.	14868	Elliott, Coleman	1875
Dyer, Mary	14869	Elliott, Abbott	1876
Dyer, Jessie	14870	Elliott, Mollie	1877
Dyer, James R.	14871	Elliott, Aleta	1878
Dyer, Fannie	14872	Elliott, Amanda	8997
Dyer, Mamie	14873	Elliott, Ivory	8998
Dyer, Susan	14874	Elliott, Thomas	9003
Eaton, Belle	178	Elachetubbi, Liney	4445
Eaton, Ruby Pearl	179	Elachetubbi, Similly	4446
Eaton, Simmie	180	Ellis, Anna S.	7289
Eaves, Rosa	9802	Ellis, Bryan	7290
Eaves, Bessie B.	9803	Ellis, Zerena	10339

Name.	Roll No.	Name.	Roll No.
Ellis, Mary	11499	Everidge, Floyd Wesley	16062
Ellis, Gracie	12103	Evans, Susan L.	7404
Ellis, George	12225	Evans, Agnes	7410
Ellis, Isabelle	12226	Evans, Lee	7945
Ellis, Elizabeth	12227	Evans, Lizzie	7946
Elapashabbe, Barnett	13405	Evans, Edmond	7947
Emeyabbi, Forbis	990	Evans, Jesse	7948
Emeyabbi, Isham	2104	Evans, Rufus	7949
Emeyabbi, Lucen	2105	Evans, Simpson	7950
Emeyabbi, Crosby	2106	Evans, Tandy	7951
Emeyabbi, Abina	15937	Evans, Annie	16211
Emer, Stewick	5166	Evans, Marie	16212
Emer, Charlico	5167	Eyachabbe, Emily	5322
Emerson, Jackson	10037	Eyachabbe, Lizzie	5323
England, Hannah	127	Eyachabbe, Colbert	5324
Ennis, Maggie F.	4900	Eyachabbe, Thompson	5649
Ennis, Mary L.	4901	Farver, Peru	1024
Ennis, Henry D.	4902	Farver, William	1025
Enloe, Wade	15104	Falsom, Jackson L.	6461
Enloe, Maye	15105	Falconer, William C.	7211
Ervin, John N.	3892	Falconer, Henry	7212
Ervin, Edgar	3993	Fannin, Mary B.	7312
Ervin, Columbus C.	3974	Fannin, Hamilton	7313
Ervin, Lizzie H.	3975	Fannin, Hugh W.	7314
Ervin, Joel E.	3976	Fannin, Harlin J.	7315
Ervin, Myrtle M.	3977	Fannin, Johanna	8155
Ervin, Walter P.	3978	Fannin, Henry	8156
Ervin, Abraham A.	3979	Fannin, Pauline	8157
Ervin, Turner L.	3980	Fannin, Fredrica	8158
Ervin, Emmet	3981	Fannin, Georgina	8159
Ervin, Harriet N.	3982	Fannin, Myrtle I.	8160
Ervin, Mark H.	3983	Fannin, Madaline F.	8161
Ervin, Laura	3984	Fannin, Johanna F.	8162
Ervin, Archer Roy	3985	Fannin, Mella Belle	8163
Ervin, Nellie	4115	Fannin, Allice	14773
Ervin, James	4116	Farmer, Fannie	7325
Ervin, Mary	4117	Farmer, Edna L.	7326
Ervin, Rudy	4320	Farmer, Clinton L.,	7327
Ervin, Lizzie	4321	Farmer, Eugene F.	7328
Ervin, Willie M.	4322	Faudree, Dora	10620
Ervin, David	4323	Faudree, Thomas R.	10623
Ervin, Louie	4324	Faudree, Annie L.	15007
Ervin, Florence	4325	Faudree, Lola P.	15008
Ervin, Viola	4326	Faudree, Rosa Howard	15009
Ervin, William L.	12045	Fairlie, Elizabeth	12816
Ervin, Columbus	12046	Fairlie, Minta M.	12817
Ervin, Edward	12047	Fairlie, Mamie	12818
Ervin, Pearl	12048	Fairlie, Nettie	13290
Ervin, Alphonso	12049	Fairlie, John T.	13291
Ervin, Calvin	12050	Farr, Arthur T.	14313
Ervin, Minnie	12051	Farr, George C.	14314
Ervin, Emma	12052	Farr, Inez E.	14315
Ervin, Ben	12053	Farr, Estelle M.	14316
Estes, Lorena	9568	Farr, John G., Jr.	14317
Estes, Hugh David	9569	Farr, Arthur G.	14318
Estes, Perry	14544	Fargo, Emily	14386
Eubanks, Ernest	15432	Fargo, Isaac	15447
Eubanks, Ella	15954	Fargo, Robert L.	15788
Everidge, Thomas W.	4028	Farrill, Theodosia	15666
Everidge, Joseph W.	4290	Farrill, Gertrude	15667
Everidge, Josie M.	4291	Farrill, Eunice	15668
Everidge, Governor J.	4292	Farrill, John Raymond	15669
Everidge, Ophelia	4293	Farrill, Harriett	15674
Everidge, Tommie	4294	Farrill, Zelma Lee	15675
Everidge, Lydia Gertrude	4295	Felihkatabbee, Sallie	5092
Everidge, Robbie	4296	Felihkatabbee, Vina	5094
Everidge, Susan L.	4297	Felihkatabbee, Johnson	5095
Everidge, Robert T.	4365	Felihkatabbee, Gilbert	5176
Everidge, Edward M.	4366	Felihkatabbee, Lizzie	5178
Everidge, Clara W.	4367	Felihkatabbee, Lewie	5179
Everidge, David M. H.	4369	Felihkatabbee, Alexander	5180
Everidge, Effie	4370	Fennel, Louisa	8543
Everidge, Eva Laura	4371	Featherston, Mittie A.	9313
Everidge, Martin V.	4568	Featherston, Charles C.	9314
Everidge, David C.	4570	Featherston, Willis F.	9315
Everidge, Susan F.	5008	Featherston, Lucius C. Jr.	9316
Everidge, Edward M.	5017	Featherston, Henry B.	9317
Everidge, Ezra Dora	5018	Featherston, James T.	9318
Everidge, Joel	5019	Featherston, Edward M.	9319
Everidge, Edgar	5050	Fetter, Abigail	9379
Everidge, Earl	5051	Fetter, Emma Pocahontus	9380
Everidge, Harvey	13486	Fetter, Nora Cecilia	9381
Everidge, Joseph H.	13571	Ferrante, Isabinda	11196
Everidge, Helen Blanche	13572	Ferrante, Otha	11197

Name.	Roll No.
Ferrante, John	11198
Felma, Molsey	11699
Felma, Micy	11700
Felton, Clarence	14172
Ferguson, Margaret Jane	14258
Fisher, Emma	362
Fisher, Walter Van	363
Fisher, Elizabeth Ellen	364
Fisher, Altha Frances	368
Fisher, Emmett Van	369
Fisher, Blanche	648
Fisher, Thomas	1343
Fisher, Anias	1396
Fisher, Sibbel	2717
Fisher, Winston	3236
Fisher, Hicks	3342
Fisher, Elizabeth	3343
Fisher, Robert	3344
Fisher, Viney	3609
Fisher, Susan	3610
Fisher, Morris H.	4159
Fisher, Sillian	4160
Fisher, Robert	4161
Fisher, Willie	4162
Fisher, Thomas	4163
Fisher, Frank	4164
Fisher, George	4165
Fisher, Mary	7378
Fisher, Lyda	12084
Fisher, Daniel	12085
Fisher, Sallie	12086
Fisher, Absolam	12087
Fisher, John	12088
Fisher, Joanna	12089
Fisher, Mary	12090
Fisher, Sillin	15799
Fisher, George	15800
Finch, Iola	700
Finch, Burton	701
Filemontubbee, Joel	1674
Fitzer, Lourinda	7359
Fitzer, Benjamin F.	7360
Fitzer, Frances	7362
Fitzer, Pearl B.	7363
Fitzer, Jewel L. B.	7364
Fitzer, Harvey Preston	7365
Finley, Joe	9523
Finley, Melvina	9524
Finley, Abner	9525
Finley, Benjamin	9526
Filmore, Gibson	10662
Filmore, Sukey	10663
Florence, Mary Jane	222
Florence, Charley	223
Florence, Zach A.	224
Florence, Lena	225
Florence, Fannie	226
Flint, Delilah J.	549
Flint, Robert	12142
Fletcher, Mary	2737
Fletcher, Eliza	4945
Fletcher, Emiline	4946
Fletcher, Tillis	4947
Fletcher, Emma	4948
Fletcher, Amos	4949
Fletcher, Jim	4950
Fletcher, Melvina	10574
Fletcher, Sophia	10577
Fletcher, Hannah	10649
Floyd, Eliza	15016
Floyd, Huddleston	15017
Flinchum, Julia A.	9488
Flinchum, Columbus	9489
Flinchum, James M.	9490
Flinchum, Leroy	9491
Flinchum, Mary A. K.	9492
Flinchum, Nora E.	9493
Flinchum, John B.	9494
Flinchum, Samma R.	9495
Flinchum, William	13538
Fox, Angie	15
Fox, Clarence	16
Fox, Edith	17
Fox, Vera	18
Fox, Ethel	19

Name.	Roll No.
Fox, William A.	20
Fox, John R.	6422
Fox, Edie M. J.	6423
Fox, Emry Lee	6424
Folsom, Ethel	31
Folsom, Charles	605
Folsom, Andreth	606
Folsom, Charlotte	608
Folsom, Blanche	609
Folsom, Bertha	610
Folsom, Edwin Lee	611
Folsom, Ervin Moore	612
Folsom, William Lee	617
Folsom, McKee	618
Folsom, Ora	619
Folsom, Velda	620
Folsom, Alfred Wright	730
Folsom, Alfred Emerson	767
Folsom, Ollie	768
Folsom, Emis	769
Folsom, Wade	869
Folsom, Guy Vann	870
Folsom, Ellina	871
Folsom, Bertha Bell	873
Folsom, Grover C.	3843
Folsom, Sim	4438
Folsom, Joe	4439
Folsom, Frank	4440
Folsom, Jerry	6438
Folsom, Amanda	6439
Folsom, Peter	6440
Folsom, Maud	6441
Folsom, Dora	6442
Folsom, Davis	6443
Folsom, Eugne	6444
Folsom, Jincy	6485
Folsom, Maud	6486
Folsom, Emma	6487
Folsom, Pearl M.	6488
Folsom, Sidney L.	6489
Folsom, Ruth	6492
Folsom, Sidney J.	6505
Folsom, Peter R.	6508
Folsom, Loren S. W.	6507
Folsom, Noel	6568
Folsom, Sarah	6569
Folsom, Moses	6570
Folsom, Ben	6597
Folsom, Frank D.	6671
Folsom, Augusta Victoria	6672
Folsom, Amanda	6851
Folsom, Sweny	6897
Folsom, Julia	6898
Folsom, Carrie L.	6899
Folsom, Israel	6928
Folsom, Ida	6939
Folsom, Elias	7046
Folsom, Nancy	7047
Folsom, Louisa	7050
Folsom, Cornelia	7051
Folsom, Saul	7052
Folsom, Sampson	7053
Folsom, Annie	7054
Folsom, Caroline	7055
Folsom, Saul	7214
Folsom, Jane	7215
Folsom, Rufus	7216
Folsom, Cornelia	7217
Folsom, Josephine	7320
Folsom, Sampson	7380
Folsom, John	7446
Folsom, Louis L.	7447
Folsom, Artela	7448
Folsom, Jerry	7472
Folsom, Charlotte	7508
Folsom, David	7518
Folsom, Mary	7519
Folsom, Ida	8001
Folsom, Charlotte	8002
Folsom, Isreal	8003
Folsom, Annie	8085
Folsom, Walker	8094
Folsom, Albert	8115
Folsom, Susie K.	8116

Name.	Roll No.
Folsom, Claude C.	8117
Folsom, David W.	8118
Folsom, Allie M.	8119
Folsom, Ollie E.	8120
Folsom, Joseph S.	8121
Folsom, Susie Irene	8122
Folsom, Alfred	8177
Folsom, John	8180
Folsom, Robert	8185
Folsom, Robbie	8186
Folsom, George D.	8187
Folsom, James W.	8413
Folsom, Ara D.	8414
Folsom, Alexander	8723
Folsom, Rhoda	9540
Folsom, Jacob	9541
Folsom, Edith	9542
Folsom, Effie	9543
Folsom, Leonidas	9544
Folsom, Loren S. W.	10246
Folsom, Bessie	10247
Folsom, Irene	10248
Folsom, Victor	10249
Folsom, Finis E.	10470
Folsom, Mollie	10471
Folsom, Ewing	10472
Folsom, Columbus	10473
Folsom, Carril	10474
Folsom, Irmer	10475
Folsom, Jewell L.	10476
Folsom, Push-ma-ta-ha	10477
Folsom, Joseph	10511
Folsom, Sissie	10512
Folsom, Wilson	10513
Folsom, Louie	10514
Folsom, Saul	10515
Folsom, Alfred	10516
Folsom, Alice	10569
Folsom, Tandy	10570
Folsom, Annie	10571
Folsom, Oscar	10572
Folsom, Junior	10573
Folsom, John N.	10645
Folsom, Jacob	10737
Folsom, Agnes L.	10738
Folsom, William E.	10739
Folsom, George N.	10740
Folsom, Uliss C.	10741
Folsom, Ora P.	10742
Folsom, John H.	11091
Folsom, Julius C.	11099
Folsom, Tephi	11100
Folsom, Orilla	11101
Folsom, Adam	11249
Folsom, Julius, Jr.	11102
Folsom, Felix	11248
Folsom, Don J.	11374
Folsom, Daphne	11375
Folsom, Robinson	11376
Folsom, Ethel	11377
Folsom, Blanche	11378
Folsom, Henry H.	11379
Folsom, Alice	11380
Folsom, Ruth	11381
Folsom, Adelaide	11382
Folsom, Christine	11383
Folsom, Charey	11723
Folsom, Jincy	11724
Folsom, Simon	11767
Folsom, Robert	11768
Folsom, Solomon	11780
Folsom, Forbis	11824
Folsom, Czarina	11825
Folsom, Smallwood	11895
Folsom, Sina	11896
Folsom, Silas	11897
Folsom, Edward	11898
Folsom, Lizzie	11899
Folsom, Sarah	11900
Folsom, Isaac	11901
Folsom, Lee	12022
Folsom, William W.	12286
Folsom, Jefferson G.	12520
Folsom, Davis L.	12521
Folsom, Mattie	12522

Name.	Roll No.
Folsom, Alice	12523
Folsom, Jessie N.	12524
Folsom, Eunice	12525
Folsom, Ellie	12541
Folsom, Wm. S.	12614
Folsom, Ophelia P.	12615
Folsom, Aurora A.	12616
Folsom, Chlora A.	12618
Folsom, William W.	12619
Folsom, Alexander H.	12620
Folsom, Rodolph D.	12621
Folsom, Odus W.	12622
Folsom, Lillie P.	12623
Folsom, Edgar R.	12624
Folsom, George R.	12625
Folsom, Oura P.	12626
Folsom, Peter W.	12631
Folsom, Robt.	12674
Folsom, Sampson	12681
Folsom, Starns W.	12915
Folsom, Martha M.	12916
Folsom, Simpson	12942
Folsom, Daniel	12952
Folsom, Mabel	12953
Folsom, Iva L.	12954
Folsom, Elias Smedley	12955
Folsom, Zora E.	12956
Folsom, Joseph	13097
Folsom, Jincy	13098
Folsom, Levi F.	13417
Folsom, John	13503
Folsom, Arnold	13636
Folsom, Clarence	13637
Folsom, Cleveland	13638
Folsom, Prudence	13639
Folsom, Lewis F.	13640
Folsom, Walter W.	13645
Folsom, Lloyd Ray	13646
Folsom, Nathan	13657
Folsom, Elias	13667
Folsom, Irene	13668
Folsom, Willis	13669
Folsom, Dennis	13670
Folsom, Frank	13671
Folsom, Levina C.	13775
Folsom, Lewis L.	13776
Folsom, Robert E.	13777
Folsom, Nannie A.	13778
Folsom, Maud H.	13779
Folsom, Ava V.	13780
Folsom, Roy E.	13781
Folsom, Alfred W.	13799
Folsom, Silas D.	13928
Folsom, Levina	13929
Folsom, Ida	13990
Folsom, Nellie	13991
Folsom, Bacey	14805
Folsom, Myrta Lee	15632
Folsom, Lillie	16205
Folsome, I. W.	546
Folsome, Emma Pearl	547
Folsome, Wirt Telle	548
Fobb, Simon	1209
Fobb, Adeline	1210
Fobb, Edmond	1211
Fobb, Eaton	1612
Fobb, Hate	1613
Fobb, Sien	2100
Fobb, Carson	2101
Fobb, Solomon	2102
Fobb, Louisa	2103
Fobb, Simeon	2285
Fobb, Vicey	2567
Fobb, Oracy	2839
Fobb, Willie	3170
Fobb, Watkin	3372
Fobb, Lucy	3374
Fobb, Frances	3545
Fobb, Rhoda	3546
Fobb, Lee	3582
Fobb, Phillis	3583
Fobb, Jenkin	3584
Fobb, Robert	3585
Fobb, Impson	3661
Fobb, Eastman	3664

Name.	Roll No.
Fobb, Silas	3750
Fobb, Benjamin	4652
Fobb, Emma	6011
Fobb, Joseph	9965
Fobb, Incy	9966
Fobb, Fearl	9967
Fobb, Emma	9968
Fobb, Lawson	14567
Fobb, Louisa	14700
Fobb, Lily	14701
Fobb, Eliza	15750
Forbis, Alfred	1859
Forbis, Nancy	2340
Forbis, William Eddie	15069
Forbit, Singlynn	5827
Forbit, Cillen	5828
Forbit, Henry	5829
Fowler, Jane	2261
Fowler, Willie	2262
Fowler, Louella	2263
Fowler, Mary E.	2264
Fowler, Lena J.	2265
Fowler, Emma	14861
Fowler, Charlie	14862
Fowler, Josephine	15533
Fowler, John	15534
Fowler, David	15535
Fowler, Moses	15536
Fowler, Sarah	15537
Fowler, Rosetta	15538
Forrest, Sallie Ann	4923
Forrest, Joseph S.	7283
Forrest, Mamie Z.	7284
Forrest, Clifton R. H.	7285
Forrest, Minnie O.	7286
Forrest, Lena V.	7287
Forrest, Cornelia Josephine	7288
Forrest, Annie	7388
Forrest, Minnie	7389
Forrest, Alice	7390
Forrest, Mitchell	7391
Forrest, Lucy	7392
Forrest, Bertha	7393
Forrest, Joseph Smedley	14757
Foster, Wash	6271
Foster, Mamie	7304
Foster, Josiah Edwin	7305
Foster, Mary A.	7689
Foster, Betsy	9225
Foster, Addie B.	9226
Foster, Billy	9228
Foster, Louisa	9692
Foster, Sidney	9693
Foster, Albert	9694
Foster, Moses	10127
Foster, Joseph	10699
Foster, Sarah	11429
Foster, Abel	11742
Foster, Joel	11743
Foster, Daniel	11744
Foster, Thomas	11855
Foster, Solomon	11950
Foster, Sallie	13591
Foster, Ephraim	15075
Foster, W. F.	15078
Foster, John A.	15079
Foster, Robert E.	15080
Foster, Maud E.	15081
Foster, Claude F.	15082
Foster, James O.	15083
Foster, Ida O.	15084
Foster, Martin T.	15085
Foster, Earl Clyde	15086
Foster, John Abe	15087
Foster, John Wesley	15088
Foster, William Thomas	15089
Foster, Eva May	15090
Foster, Samuel	15109
Foster, William F.	15110
Foster, E. A.	15134
Foster, Roy	15135
Foster, Dewey F.	15136
Foster, Ruth Adella	15137
Foley, Lucy	7027

Name.	Roll No.
Ford, William W.	8259
Ford, Wm. A.	12641
Foreman, Fannie	8418
Foreman, Josephine	8420
Foreman, Ben G.	8421
Foreman, Simon L.	9560
Foreman, William	15926
Fout, Susan	7684
Fout, Luevina E.	7685
Fout, Sallie Jane	7686
Follis, Silway	10452
Follis, Sila	10453
Follis, Stephen	10454
Follis, Jincy	10460
Follis, Lymsia	10461
Follis, Jacob	10462
Folota, Betsy	11735
Folota, Martin	13402
Forbes, Nellie Ida	14577
Forbes, Melvina	16065
Frazier, Solomon	62
Frazier, Minnie	1390
Frazier, Robert S.	1803
Frazier, Narcissa	1804
Frazier, Noah	1805
Frazier, Julius	1806
Frazier, Emiline	1807
Frazier, Maggie M.	1808
Frazier, Wilson T.	1809
Frazier, Mary E.	1810
Frazier, Moseller E.	1811
Frazier, Samuel	1812
Frazier, Josephine	1813
Frazier, Jesse	1814
Frazier, Willie	1815
Frazier, Lewie	1816
Frazier, Bengiman	1817
Frazier, Reason	1821
Frazier, Susan	1822
Frazier, Tobias	1823
Frazier, Rhody	1825
Frazier, Doror	1826
Frazier, Dwight	1912
Frazier, Edward	2073
Frazier, Wisey	2074
Frazier, Susan	2075
Frazier, Wilson E.	2192
Frazier, Mollie	2193
Frazier, Cornelius	2194
Frazier, Cornelia	2195
Frazier, Cordelia	2504
Frazier, Susan	3152
Frazier, Davis	3155
Frazier, Billy	3156
Frazier, Lizzie	3157
Frazier, James	3158
Frazier, Frances	3230
Frazier, Martha	3534
Frazier, Betsie	3535
Frazier, Rebecca	3536
Frazier, Loren	3741
Frazier, James	4221
Frazier, Kizzie	4257
Frazier, Siney	4259
Frazier, Kelley	4356
Frazier, Ellen	4357
Frazier, Harris	4723
Frazier, Sweny	4872
Frazier, Cillen	4873
Frazier, Sibble	4874
Frazier, Sam	4933
Frazier, Mike	5060
Frazier, Sukie	5129
Frazier, Simeon	5190
Frazier, Jacob	5192
Frazier, Mack	5199
Frazier, Louisa	5200
Frazier, Sissy	5201
Frazier, Edmond	5202
Frazier, Sophia	5203
Frazier, Agnes	5204
Frazier, Dixon	5236
Frazier, Magdalene	5237
Frazier, Simon	5314
Frazier, Sissy	5315
Frazier, John	5316

Name.	Roll No.	Name.	Roll No.
Frazier, Melvina	5317	Frazier, Wilson	13450
Frazier, Jackson	5446	Frazier, Lucy	13451
Frazier, Lizzie	5541	Frazier, Adline	13621
Frazier, Rhoda	5571	Frazier, Kiliza	13596
Frazier, Ben	5572	Frazier, Rosa	13885
Frazier, Sumplin	5589	Frazier, William	13891
Frazier, Jacob	5762	Frazier, Joanna	14030
Frazier, Mary A.	5763	Frazier, Clara	14031
Frazier, Hannah	5786	Frazier, Edmund	14126
Frazier, Thomas H.	5787	Frazier, Sarah	14693
Frazier, Newton	5788	Frazier, Minnie	14722
Frazier, Verina	5789	Frazier, Harriet	14816
Frazier, Smallwood	5865	Frazier, Misson	14883
Frazier, Aben	5867	Frazier, Susan	15053
Frazier, Lucy Ann	5868	Frazier, Louisa	15061
Frazier, Lean	5869	Frazier, Louisa	15623
Frazier, Caldwell	9075	Frazier, Harriet	15784
Frazier, Ned	9209	Frazier, Eli	15824
Frazier, David	9211	Frazier, Silly	15829
Frazier, Martha	9212	Frazier, Sammy	15945
Frazier, Amanda	9396	Freeny, Ben	245
Frazier, Thompson	9397	Freeny, Lonnie Clay	246
Frazier, Impson	9398	Freeny, John W.	10501
Frazier, Susan	9399	Freeny, Malina	10624
Frazier, Annie	9412	Freeny, Ida M.	10627
Frazier, Lona	9416	Freeny, Robert C.	10961
Frazier, Lula	9419	Freeny, Ella B.	10963
Frazier, Johnson	9424	Freeny, Robert C. Jr.	10964
Frazier, Ross	9913	Freeny, Ellis D.	10965
Frazier, Mary	9917	Freeny, John W.	10966
Frazier, Louisa	9918	Freeny, Homer M.	10967
Frazier, Ella	9919	Freeny, Carrie Ida	10968
Frazier, Rogers	9925	Freeny, Arlington H.	10970
Frazier, Lizian	10221	Freeny, Jasper D.	11076
Frazier, Eliza A.	10241	Freeny, Robert L.	11077
Frazier, Wallace	10242	Freeny, Rueben	11202
Frazier, Harriet	10243	Freeny, Robert	11203
Frazier, Simon	10244	Freeny, Mary	11204
Frazier, Dixon	10253	Freeny, Reuben Jr.	11205
Frazier, Loring W.	10313	Freeny, Belle	11206
Frazier, Emma	10314	Freeny, Pearl	11207
Frazier, Lena	10315	Freeny, Chock	11208
Frazier, Emily	10331	Freeny, Chick	11209
Frazier, Jackson	10340	Freeny, Leota	11210
Frazier, James	10341	Freeny, Tokowa	11211
Frazier, Sallie A.	10422	Freeny, Indi Olla	11212
Frazier, Frances	10423	Freeny, Robert	14480
Frazier, David	10426	Freeney, Susie Ann	288
Frazier, Josephine	10427	Freeney, Henry C.	9142
Frazier, Elizabeth	10428	Freeney, Edna M.	9143
Frazier, Robert	10429	Freeney, Buena Vesta	9144
Frazier, Louisa	10519	Freeney, Benj. Andrew	15551
Frazier, Sarah	10520	Freeney, Martha Eliza-	
Frazier, John	10581	beth	15552
Frazier, Mary	10582	Freeney, Mary Ada	15553
Frazier, Virgie	10583	Frost, Belle	538
Frazier, Ben	10584	Frost, Ruth	539
Frazier, Emma	10585	Franklin, Harkins	2712
Frazier, Osborne	10638	Franklin, Susan	3094
Frazier, Sophia	10639	Franklin, Allen	3095
Frazier, Sweeney	10640	Franklin, Lizzie	6938
Frazier, Sidney	10641	Franklin, James	7114
Frazier, Fisher	10654	Franklin, Ben	7993
Frazier, Sarah	10655	Franklin, John W.	7995
Frazier, Louisa	10758	Franklin, Crosby	11475
Frazier, Thomas	10852	Franklin, Esau	11476
Frazier, Serena	10863	Franklin, Nicholas	13208
Frazier, Thompson	10864	Franklin, Houston	13224
Frazier, Mary	10865	Franklin, Green	14730
Frazier, Lymon	11186	Frederick, Mary E.	4077
Frazier, Caroline	11187	Frederick, Nola	4078
Frazier, Nicholas	11200	Frederick, Elbert	4081
Frazier, Lina	11201	Fry, Samuel	4118
Frazier, Betsy	11284	Fry, Sophia	4119
Frazier, Sweeney	11285	Fry, Joseph	4120
Frazier, Mary	11389	Fry, Cornelia	4121
Frazier, Smallwood	11613	Fry, William	9869
Frazier, Louisa	11614	Fry, Thomas	9871
Frazier, Hudson	11845	Fry, Billy	10492
Frazier, Martha	11846	Fry, Vicey	10493
Frazier, Winnie	11848	Fry, Lena	10494
Frazier, Adeline	11872	Fry, Robert	10495
Frazier, Noah	11986	Fry, Allington	10496
Frazier, Amziah	12960	Fry, Emma	10497
Frazier, Lou	12961	Fry, Natt	10498
Frazier, Salena	13117		

Name.	Roll No.
Fry, James	10499
Fry, Edmond	10500
Fry, Frederick	13035
Fry, Fannie	15437
Fry, Daniel W.	15438
Fry, Everett	15439
Fry, Henrietta	15440
Frye, Lewis	12908
Frye, Betcy	15585
Free, Rosetta	6758
Free, Lonnie	6759
Free, Maudie	6760
Free, William	6761
Free, Zona	6762
Free, Nettie	6763
Freeman, George	6787
Freeman, Memiss	6788
Freeman, John	8251
Freeman, Maria J.	12855
Freeman, Ada M.	12856
Freeman, Alexander J.	12858
Freeman, George	15889
Freeman, John	15890
Freeman, William	15966
Freeman, James Richard	15967
Fryer, Adeline	10826
Fryer, Edith	10827
Fryer, Oliver B.	10828
Fryer, Annie L.	10939
Fryer, Lurinda L.	10941
Fryer, Ella	14774
Frinzell, John	13982
Frinzell, Lena	13983
Fronterhouse, Dick	14070
Fronterhouse, Addie	14072
Fronterhouse, Willie	14073
Fronterhouse, Ward	14074
Fulsome, David McC.	537
Fulsom, Lewis G.	4017
Fulsom, Ellis	4485
Fulsom, Johnson	4885
Fulsom, Robert	10550
Fulsom, Catherine	13443
Fulton, Jeff	3884
Fulton, Susan	3885
Fulton, Edgar	3886
Fulton, Nancy	3887
Fulton, Robert	3888
Fulton, Arthur Daniel	3889
Fulton, William	4571
Fulton, Eliza	12887
Fulton, Leona S.	13236
Fulton, Alice Maurine	13237
Fulton, Norma E.	13238
Fulton, Catherine	13296
Fulton, John R.	13297
Fulton, Aurilla	13299
Fulton, Jackson	13300
Fulton, Newton	13301
Fulton, Tilda	13302
Fulton, Rilda	14689
Fullomme,, Gibson	10905
Gallamore, Eva P.	25
Gallamore, Cecil	26
Gallamore, Zada	27
Gallamore, Lucile	28
Gardner, Zachariah	148
Gardner, Levina	149
Gardner, James W.	191
Gardner, James Dolphin	192
Gardner, Benkamin	305
Gardner, Robert	715
Gardner, William Dempsey	716
Gardner, Mary	752
Gardner, Margaret Frances	753
Gardner, Roy	754
Gardner, Jefferson	1243
Gardner, Judy	1244
Gardner, Emma	1246
Gardner, Scott	1247
Gardner, Agnes	1248
Gardner, Zachariah	1249

Name.	Roll No.
Gardner, Jefferson, Jr.	1250
Gardner, Carrie	2587
Gardner, Wyles	3093
Gardner, Edmond	3549
Gardner, Lela	3550
Gardner, Alfred	3572
Gardner, Rena M.	3574
Gardner, Wilkin	3710
Gardner, Nancy	3711
Gardner, Wilson	3713
Gardner, Anderson	3751
Gardner, Edmund	3989
Gardner, Nicey	3990
Gardner, Israel	4005
Gardner, Rosa	4007
Gardner, Zachariah	4082
Gardner, Basil L.	9657
Gardner, Mary A.	9658
Gardner, Edmond	9659
Gardner, Jefferson	9660
Gardner, Georgia Ann	9719
Gardner, Jesse J.	9753
Gardner, Mary	9852
Gardner, William	9853
Gardner, Jincey	9907
Gardner, Alfred W.	10035
Gardner, Rodolphus C.	10084
Gardner, Irena	10085
Gardner, Amelia	10086
Gardner, Rodolphus C. Jr.	10087
Gardner, Sallie A.	10088
Gardner, Roscoe C.	10089
Gardner, Nora L.	10090
Gardner, Walter T.	10091
Gardner, Junia E.	10092
Gardner, Morgan M.	10093
Gardner, Oddie Myrtle	10094
Gardner, Raymon R.	10469
Gardner, Samuel G.	10658
Gardner, Willie	10659
Gardner, Martin L.	10660
Gardner, Leroy	10661
Gardner, Daniel H.	10743
Gardner, Othena	10744
Gardner, Arabella C.	10745
Gardner, Robert L.	10746
Gardner, Wellington L.	10747
Gardner, Dona S.	10748
Gardner, Bessie A.	10749
Gardner, Jesse G.	10750
Gardner, Edward N.	10752
Gardner, Iona	10753
Gardner, Dona Lee	10754
Gardner, Critten A.	13162
Gardner, Winnie J.	13163
Gardner, Josiah	13322
Gardner, Sallie	13323
Gardner, Jefferson	13325
Gardner, Rena	13326
Gardner, Castine	13327
Gardner, Lydia	14654
Gardner, Alfred	14801
Gardner, Mary	14802
Gardner, Dodie	15070
Gay, Caroline	154
Gay, Sylvia Katy	155
Gay, Press Clifton	14475
Garvin, Susan	250
Garvin, John	251
Garvin, Vivian	253
Garvin, Louis	8803
Garvin, Sopha	8804
Garvin, Simpson	8805
Garvin, Robert H.	9426
Garvin, Vashti	9427
Garvin, Robert H., Jr.	9428
Garvin, Lewis	13418
Gazaway, Cornelia	491
Gazaway, Marshal Lee	499
Gates, Gaines	669
Gann, Walter Marion	857
Gamm, Leathia	9000
Gamm, Lina F. E.	9002
Garland, John A.	1487

Name.	Roll No.	Name.	Roll No.
Garland, Garrett Arthor	1488	Gage, Cornelia	7569
Garland, John Spencer	1489	Gaines, Thomas	8910
Garland, Sarah	1496	Gaines, Wesley	8912
Garland, Mary J.	1497	Gaines, Israel	8913
Garland, Osborne	4018	Gaines, William	8914
Garland, Thomas	5256	Gaither, Lula	8991
Garland, Leonidas	5257	Garner, Alice	12387
Garland, Margaret	5258	Garner, Gladys G.	12388
Garland, Ellen	5259	Garner, Roy James	12389
Garland, Simon	5356	Garrett, Leroy B.	14724
Garland, Lucy	5357	German, Rena	7894
Garland, Minnie	5358	Ghoing, Martha	2592
Garland, William	5561	Gibson, Nicey	151
Garland, Delilah	5562	Gibson, Silas	153
Garland, Summer	5565	Gibson, Dixon W.	481
Garland, Rachel	5566	Gibson, Dicey	482
Garland, Rebecca	5569	Gibson, Sammie	483
Garland, Samuel A.	6495	Gibson, Lucinda	484
Garland, Gilbert W.	6496	Gibson, Amos	485
Garland, Jackson	6497	Gibson, Charley	486
Garland, Della M.	6498	Gibson, Annie	487
Garland, Joseph, Sr.	7061	Gibson, Isaac	488
Garland, Malissa	7062	Gibson, Joseph	862
Garland, Frank	7064	Gibson, Thomas	1660
Garland, Janie	7065	Gibson, Amanda	1661
Garland, Stella V.	7066	Gibson, Wilmon	1662
Garland, Lena May	7067	Gibson, Hettie	1672
Garland, Ward	7070	Gibson, Liza Ann	1673
Garland, Sophina	7071	Gibson, Jane	3506
Garland, Davis	7072	Gibson, Peter	3507
Garland, Columbus	7073	Gibson, Willie E.	4217
Garland, Ward Jr.	7074	Gibson, Siney	4218
Garland, Peggy	7075	Gibson, Elias	4219
Garland, Isaac	7123	Gibson, Isaac	4220
Garland, Louisa	7124	Gibson, Morris	4886
Garland, Presley I.	7125	Gibson, Ellis	4919
Garland, Arnet	7126	Gibson, Martha	4921
Garland, Joseph Jr.	7197	Gibson, Lena	4922
Garland, Zoula	7198	Gibson, John	4938
Garland, Zodah	7199	Gibson, Melissa	4939
Garland, Zona	7200	Gibson, Ella	4940
Garland, Beulah	7201	Gibson, Harrison	4966
Garland, Zenas W.	7202	Gibson, Emma	4967
Garland, Sarah	7253	Gibson, Tina	4968
Garländ, Denver	7255	Gibson, Ida	4969
Garland, Peter	7256	Gibson, Edmun	4970
Garland, Margaret	7257	Gibson, Laymon	5044
Garland, Sibbie	7258	Gibson, Sulena	5107
Garland, Josiah	7259	Gibson, Josiah	9594
Garland, Josephine	7260	Gibson, Wilson	10213
Garland, William G.	7592	Gibson, Wesley	11289
Garland, Joseph G.	7593	Gibson, Peter	11290
Garland, James C.	7594	Gibson, Molly	11291
Garland, Raymond	7595	Gibson, Cillin	13189
Garland, Louviana	7596	Gibson, Thenton	13190
Garland, Myrtle	7597	Gibson, Samuel	13191
Garland, Grace	7598	Gibson, Emily	13192
Garland, Joel	8394	Gibson, Charlotte Susan	13193
Garland, James	10759	Gibson, Johnie	13623
Garland, Aurilla	10760	Gibson, Louisa	13624
Garland, Simpson	12630	Gibson, Douglas	13630
Garland, Jack	13542	Gibson, Thomas	14078
Garland, Harriet	14131	Gibson, Ada	14079
Garland, Louisa	14132	Gibson, Jesse	14081
Garland, Louena	14133	Gibson, Etta	14082
Garland, Henry	14134	Gipson, James	2185
Garland, Inez	14549	Gipson, Elizabeth	2186
Garland, Ollie Lou	14550	Gipson, Simon	2187
Garland, Allison Nelson	14551	Gipson, Lula	2188
Garland, Mary	14552	Gipson, Stephen	2757
Garland, Bertha	15835	Gipson, Jincey	2758
Garrison, Effie M.	2467	Gipson, Charley	2759
Garrison, David C.	2468	Gipson, John	11216
Garrison, Isabelle Pernell	15028	Gipson, Cephus	12209
		Gipson, Caroline	12210
Garrison, Mina Marina	15029	Gipson, James	12211
Gabel, William	2494	Gipson, Sibbie	12212
Gabel, Jincie	14885	Gipson, Eunice	12213
Gage, Harry	7562	Gipson, Jincey	15845
Gage, Nancy	7563	Gilmon, Leonard	6901
Gage, Sallie	7564	Gillum, Emeline	9510
Gage, Israel	7565	Gillum, Albert	9511
Gage, Marlow	7566	Gillum, Authur E.	9512
Gage, Rachael	7567	Gillum, Samantha L. E.	9513
Gage, Lucy	7568	Gillum, Liman P.	14800

Name.	Roll No.	Name.	Roll No.
Gills, Lillie B.	12066	Goode, James	10877
Gibbs, Isaam	14616	Goode, David	10879
Gilstrap, Ida	14991	Goode, Minnie	10880
Gilstrap, Clara	14992	Goode, Willie F.	10881
Gilstrap, Wheeler	14993	Gotcher, Susan E.	12831
Gilstrap, Luke	14994	Gotcher, Clarence E.	12832
Glover, Samuel	4286	Gotcher, Horace E.	12833
Glenn, Ida B.	11881	Gotcher, Elizabeth E.	12834
Glenn, Mary Virginia	11887	Goddard, Felicia	14385
Goodson, John J.	10	Goodman, Ida	14467
Goodson, John J., Jr.	11	Goodman, Clyde	14468
Goer, William	95	Goodman, Willis O.	14469
Goer, Mary	13612	Goodman, Ruth	14470
Goer, Simon	13613	Grant, Thomas Jr.	215
Goer, Angeline	13614	Grant, Charley M.	282
Goer, Doney	13615	Grant, Mary E.	11677
Goer, Henderson	13616	Grant, Margaret	14482
Goer, Elmarina	13617	Grant, Aima	14483
Gore, John	13496	Gray, James	255
Gore, Minnie L.	13497	Gray, Nora	256
Goforth, Andrew	673	Gray, William	257
Goforth, Cordelia	15898	Gray, Gideon	258
Goldston, Estella	684	Gray, Rosa	259
Going, Peter	1088	Gray, Minnie	466
Going, Gibson	1091	Gray, Willie	467
Going, Sophia	1092	Gray, Cordelia	13850
Going, Osborne	1093	Gray, Roy	13851
Going, Vinson	1094	Gray, Ollie Bernetta	13852
Going, Salina	1095	Gray, Ellen	15345
Going, Rayson	1096	Gray, Ella	15346
Going, Imahoke	1441	Gray, Laura	15347
Going, Mina	1603	Gray, Pearl	15348
Going, John	2981	Gray, Elmer	15349
Going, Alfred	3024	Gray, Clifford	15350
Going, Ben	3026	Gray, Charles E.	15351
Going, Ellen	3028	Griggs, Thomas L.	874
Going, Sissy	3029	Griggs, Willy	14010
Going, Semiya	3525	Griggs, Mary	14011
Going, James	4083	Griggs, Joel	14012
Going, Frances	4084	Griggs, Wilson N.	14013
Going, Rosie	4085	Griggs, Pate 'J.	14014
Going, Jim	4086	Griggs, Thomas	14089
Going, David	4087	Greenwood, Hall	4630
Going, Thomas	4088	Greenwood, Hattie	4817
Going, Frank	4090	Greenwood, Allen	4818
Going, Lizzie	5967	Greenwood, Myatt	4819
Going, Lesine	5973	Grubbs, George	4705
Going, Lilly	8892	Grubbs, William	11078
Going, Zara Belle	15399	Grubbs, Benj. F.	12564
Goings, Nicholas	10273	Grubbs, Eli	12565
Goings, Ally Modena	10274	Grubbs, Mary V.	12566
Goings, Susan	11341	Grubbs, Robert	12567
Goings, James	11342	Grubbs, William	12568
Goings, John L.	11343	Grubbs, Addie M.	12569
Goings, Rena	11344	Grubbs, Benj., Jr.	12570
Goings, Mike	11345	Grubbs, Frank	12571
Goings, Elizabeth	10111	Grubbs, Minnie	12572
Goen, Jefferson	6384	Grubbs, Forbis L.	12579
Goen, Jimmie	6385	Grubbs, Vernon L.	12580
Goins, William	7425	Grubbs, Osborn L.	12581
Goins, Roy C.	7427	Grubbs, Leroy	12582
Goins, Hampton	10110	Grubbs, John	13570
Gooding, Osborne A.	4126	Graman, Jackson	4787
Gooding, Fannie B.	4127	Graman, Sallie	4788
Gooding, Charles H.	4128	Graman, Emerson	4789
Gooding, Louie	4129	Graman, Agnes	4790
Gooding, Josie	4130	Graman, Molsy	4791
Gooding, Henry	4131	Graman, Petross	4792
Gooding, Lettie Lee	4132	Graman, Levicey	4793
Gooding, Basil L.	4558	Graman, Gibson	4794
Gooding, Fannie	4559	Green, Ohoyona	5147
Gooding, Jesse	4560	Green, Joe	5653
Gooding, Never	4562	Green, Morris	8494
Gooding, Virginia L.	9587	Green, Daniel	8495
Gooding, Rosa A.	9588	Green, Sophie	8496
Gollihare, Harriet C.	7458	Green, Charlie	11191
Gollihare, James Henry	7459	Green, Rosa B.	11192
Goodnight, Emma	7497	Green, Ida	15002
Goodnight, Edmond	7498	Green, Robert	15003
Gouger, Estelle	8060	Graham, David	5450
Gouger, Frank	8061	Graham, Charles	6005
Gouger, Julia	8062	Graham, Ellis	6006
Gouger, Lazona	14807	Graham, Simon	6007
Gouger, Zelina	14808	Graham, George	6008
Gordon, Myrtle	9150	Graham, Thomas	6106

Name.	Roll No.
Graham, Motsey	6107
Graham, Eliza	6109
Graham, Sina	6110
Graham, Martha	6114
Graham, Emma E.	9382
Graham, Artemissa	9383
Graham, Bessie Cicilia	9384
Griffith, Ida L.	6669
Gregory, Mary E.	7546
Gregory, Enoch B.	7547
Gregory, Azalia	7548
Gregory, Willie Lee	7549
Gregory, Hazle Edna	7550
Gregory, Edwin S.	7551
Gregory, Eric G.	7552
Gregory, Mary E.	7553
Gregory, Myrtle G.	7554
Grady, Fannie E.	8130
Greyton, Lillith	8204
Gryson, John	9168
Gryson, Sina	9169
Gravitt, Maggie	9748
Gravitt, Edna	9749
Gravitt, Mary	9750
Gravitt, Johnnie	9751
Gravitt, Maggie Idell	9752
Gravitt, Willie	15680
Gravitt, Phelan	15681
Gravitt, Andy	15682
Greer, Robinson	11705
Greer, Lowena	11706
Greer, Eleas	15059
Guynes, William	73
Guynes, Thomas	11797
Guynes, James H.	11798
Guynes, William J.	11799
Guynes, Ishmael W.	11800
Guynes, Rosa L.	11801
Guynes, Lorena	11802
Guynes, Dora	11803
Guess, Amelia	4191
Guess, Henry	4195
Guess, Rhoda	9846
Guess, Jefferson P.	9847
Guess, Lillie M.	9848
Guess, Emanuel P.	9849
Guess, Jessie M.	9850
Guess, Joseph J.	9851
Guess, John	11063
Guess, Ruthie	11064
Guess, Rosa	14672
Gulley, Cora	9483
Gulley, Lillie O.	9484
Gulley, Tandy F.	9485
Gulley, Theodore	9486
Gulley, Jewell H.	9487
Gunter, Mary J.	10008
Gunter, Emma M.	10009
Gunter, Thelma	10010
Gunter, Luther W.	10013
Guthrie, Rebecca	14195
Guthrie, Susie	14196
Guthrie, Charley	14197
Guthrie, Rachel	14198
Guthrie, Edgar	14583
Guthrie, Mattie	14584
Harris, Rosa L.	213
Harris, Alred M.	214
Harris, Willie	394
Harris, John G.	1830
Harris, Nela	1831
Harris, Ernest	1832
Harris, Carl	1833
Harris, George T.	1834
Harris, Virginia	1835
Harris, Thomas P.	1836
Harris, Emma M.	1837
Harris, Arthur F.	1838
Harris, Adam	2132
Harris, Alfred	2135
Harris, Isnie	2136
Harris, Mary	2550
Harris, Mary Lottie	2551
Harris, J. Emmett	2849
Harris, Walter C.	2903
Harris, Henry C.	2904

Name.	Roll No.
Harris, Maggie E.	2905
Harirs, William	2906
Harris, Mattie M.	2907
Harris, Bessie L.	2908
Harris, Nettie Ella	2909
Harris, Jack	2992
Harris, Lena J.	2993
Harris, Frank	2994
Harris, Dewy Lee	2995
Harris, Paul C.	5045
Harris, Susie	5046
Harris, Emma	5047
Harris, Robert L.	5048
Harris, Elizabeth M.	5049
Harris, Gilbert	5790
Harris, Jincey	5791
Harris, Lucy Ann	5792
Harris, Kissey	5793
Harris, Nicey	5794
Harris, Albert	5848
Harris, Betsy	5850
Harris, Abel	6582
Harris, Henry	6583
Harris, William	6584
Harris, Thomas	6586
Harris, Zado	6587
Harris, James	6588
Harris, Elizabeth	6589
Harris, Everette J.	6590
Harris, Lena	6691
Harris, Elisha	12306
Harris, Mattie	6692
Harris, Mitchell	6693
Harris, Josie	6694
Harris, Aaron	6906
Harris, Ida	6907
Harris, Sillin	6953
Harris, Daniel	6956
Harris, Emily	8422
Harris, Rose B.	8423
Harris, Daniel	8424
Harris, Albert	8615
Harris, Nellie H.	8837
Harris, Lilly E.	8843
Harris, Ramsey	9267
Harris, Thompson	9646
Harris, Susan	10036
Harris, Jincy	10180
Harris, Amelia	11019
Harris, Thelma	11020
Harris, Fayne	11021
Harris, Kathleen	11022
Harris, Jimson	11188
Harris, Martha	11189
Harris, Elias	11223
Harris, Eastman	11521
Harris, Allen	11522
Harris, Solomon	11523
Harris, Minnie	11524
Harris, Blannie	11627
Harris, Osborne	11628
Harris, Agnes	11629
Harris, Nathan	12111
Harris, Evelina	12307
Harris, Blanche Adeline	12575
Harris, Samuel	12576
Harris, Joseph	12577
Harris, Willey	12578
Harris, Simpson	13453
Harris, Emeline	13454
Harris, Robert	13455
Harris, Bert Starr	15025
Harris, Buddy	15045
Harris, William	15415
Harris, Annie	15602
Harris, John E.	15752
Harris, Susan	15861
Harris, Millie	15957
Harris, Maria	15958
Harris, Paul	15959
Hays, Henry	316
Hays, Thomas	13858
Hays, Annetta	13859
Hays, Jennetta	13860
Hays, Andrew	14199

Name.	Roll No.
Hays, John	14201
Hays, William	14202
Hayes, Jesse	2626
Hayes, Rhoda	2627
Hayes, Mary	2628
Hayes, Eliza	3557
Hayes, Viney	3558
Hayes, Lucy	4107
Hayes, Forbis	4373
Hayes, Millie	4374
Hayes, John	4375
Hayes, Sam	4538
Hayes, Cornelius	10061
Hayes, Laurena	10062
Hayes, Sophia	10063
Hayes, Watson	10083
Hayes, Ellis	10548
Hayes, Henry B.	10801
Hayes, Edmond A.	10802
Hayes, Susan	10803
Hayes, Cornelia	10804
Hayes, Greenwood	11108
Hayes, Mary	11118
Hayes, Mary	11269
Hayes, Sallie	11270
Hayes, Nellie	11271
Hayes, Picken	11869
Hayes, Josephus	12435
Hayes, James Elmer	12436
Hayes, Thomas	13027
Hayes, Edward	13511
Hayes, Josephine	14684
Hayes, Addie F.	15860
Harrison, Lewis H.	785
Harrison, Emmet E.	786
Harrison, Cassie M.	787
Harrison, William Doyle	788
Harrison, Cevera L.	789
Harrison, Ziad	1886
Harrison, Insey	1887
Harrison, Eliza	1888
Harrison, Silas	1889
Harrison, Calvin	2113
Harrison, Sim	4511
Harrison, James H.	4513
Harrison, Thomas	4852
Harrison, Louisa	4853
Harrison, Sophie	5567
Harrison, Lymon	6094
Harrison, Amanda	6095
Harrison, Benjamin	6096
Harrison, Thomas	6599
Harrison, Della	6729
Harrison, William C. E.	6730
Harrison, Clarence	6731
Harrison, Walter Hamlet	6732
Harrison, Louisa	7662
Harrison, William H.	7663
Harrison, Albert	7664
Harrison, Louie	7665
Harrison, Benjamin	7971
Harrison, Golden	8104
Harrison, Albert	8339
Harrison, Charlie	8752
Harrison, Hilburn	9536
Harrison, Elizabeth	9724
Harrison, James D.	10590
Harrison, Margaret	10840
Harrison, Benjamin W.	10842
Harrison, William H.	10843
Harrison, Neter L.	10844
Harrison, Mary V.	10845
Harrison, Fannie R.	10846
Harrison, John M.	11155
Harrison, Rufus	10904
Harrison, William H.	11525
Harrison, Cora	11156
Harrison, Etta	11527
Harrison, Ada	11528
Harrison, Mabel	11529
Harrison, William H. Jr.	11530
Harrison, Guy	11531
Harrison, Victor V.	11532
Harrison, Ina	11736

Name.	Roll No.
Harrison, Zadoc	12173
Harrison, Robert	12172
Harrison, Claude	12174
Harrison, Robert Jr.	12175
Harrison, Theodore R.	12176
Harrison, Missie	12369
Harrison, Benj. F.	13966
Harrison, Joseph Colbert	13967
Harrison, Charles Colbert	13968
Harrison, Rutha	14015
Harrison, Solomon	14016
Harrison, Sinie	14017
Harrison, Awachima	14780
Harrison, Cillin	15421
Harrison, Susan	15422
Harrison, Mitchell	15671
Harrison, Milo H.	15672
Harkins, John G.	800
Harkins, Isaac	1148
Harkins, George	1149
Harkins, Arasona	1150
Harkins, Elsy	2084
Harkins, James	4198
Harkins, Silas	4199
Harkins, Mary	7085
Harkins, Lena	4200
Harkins, Novey	4201
Harkins, Susie	4202
Harkins, Carry	4203
Harkins, Sallie	6043
Harkins, John	6044
Harkins, Benjamin	6073
Harkins, Panson	6075
Harkins, Simpson	6309
Harkins, Edward	7828
Harkins, Sillen	8751
Harkins, George W.	10403
Harkins, Pike	10404
Harkins, Elizabeth	10405
Harkins, Willy	10406
Harkins, Memory	10407
Harkins, Lorena	10408
Harkins, Organ Carnelias	10409
Harkins, Giles W.	11235
Harkins, Charley C.	11236
Harkins, Allington T.	11237
Harkins, Erle	11238
Harkins, Willis	11275
Harkins, William	11829
Harkins, Sillen	11830
Harkins, Nelson	11856
Harkins, Levi	11860
Harkins, Stephen	11965
Harkins, Elsie	11966
Harkins, Lafayette C.	12195
Harkins, Annie A.	12196
Harkins, William M.	12360
Harkins, Alonzo J.	12968
Harkins, Nancy J.	12969
Harkins, Edward S.	12970
Harkins, Annie	13700
Harkins, Willis	13701
Harkins, Clara	13702
Harkins, Lillie	13703
Harkins, Lee	13704
Harkins, Sophie	13716
Harkins, Leonie	14565
Harkins, Cornelia	14716
Harkins, Adam	14772
Harkins, Ada	15939
Harkin, William	4930
Harkin, Betsy	4931
Hampton, Benjamin	850
Hampton, Phoebe	851
Hampton, Perry	852
Hampton, Howard	853
Hampton, Edward Ray	854
Hampton, Carrre	1910
Hampton, Bennie	3564
Hampton, Wilburn William	9831
Hampton, Johnson	4839

Name.	Roll No.	Name.	Roll No.
Hampton, Frances	4840	Hall, George B.	8448
Hampton, Josephine	4841	Hall, Ada V.	8449
Hampton, William	4845	Hall, Eliza	10778
Hampton, Josephine R.	5409	Hall, Roberson	10780
Hampton, Cornelius	5420	Hall, Allington	11587
Hampton, Mary	5421	Hall, Melissa	11588
Hampton, Aaron	5591	Hall, Dickerson	11589
Hampton, Henry	5592	Hall, William	13501
Hampton, Timothy	5594	Hall, Caroline	13502
Hampton, Susan	5644	Hall, Nicholas	13512
Hampton, Wilmon	5648	Hall, Siney	13513
Hampton, Watson	6122	Hall, Dora	13514
Hampton, Grant	9117	Hall, David	13515
Hampton, Sweeney	9155	Hall, Joseph	14601
Hampton, Elizabeth	9156	Hall, Daisy C.	15670
Hampton, Charlotte	9157	Hall, Leo Bennett	15672
Hampton, Perry	9158	Hardy, Laisie	1454
Hampton, Julius	9159	Hardy, Thomas	5538
Hampton, Dewey	9160	Hardy, Emily	5539
Hampton, William	9161	Hardy, Dickey	5540
Hampton, John L.	9828	Hardy, Emily	5620
Hampton, Jefferson	9829	Hardy, Nellie	5621
Hampton, Esther	9830	Hardy, Washington	5622
Hampton, Julius C.	10128	Hardy, Annie	5623
Hampton, Frances	10129	Hardy, Polina	5624
Hampton, Leroy	10130	Hardy, Elesine	5625
Hampton, Eagle L.	10131	Hardy, Kennedy	5626
Hampton, Leonard	10132	Hardy, Meliney	5627
Hampton, Pearl	10133	Hardy, Rogers	5629
Hampton, Alice	10134	Hardy, Delphi	14699
Hampton, Wilburn W.	10322	Harley, Silvey	1570
Hampton, Susan	10323	Harley, Monford	2988
Hampton, Joe	10611	Harley, Michael	3129
Hampton, Ellen	10612	Harley, Salena	3130
Hampton, Isaac	10613	Harley, Florence	3131
Hampton, Alex	10615	Harley, Ansie	3150
Hampton, Bennie	10617	Harley, Stiles	3254
Hampton, Alice	10618	Harley, Sissy	3255
Hampton, Michael	10619	Harley, Preston	3256
Hampton, Flossie	10621	Harley, Jane	3307
Hampton, Julius C.	10622	Harley, Maggie	3312
Hampton, Isaac D.	10958	Harley, Mary Ann	3723
Hampton, Willie	10959	Harley, Folsom	3827
Hampton, Sealy A.	11579	Harley, Efrena	10700
Hampton, Elizabeth	11810	Harley, Wysie	10701
Hampton, Jackson	12063	Harley, Mattie	14647
Hampton, Ben V.	12156	Harlin, Bency	2583
Hampton, Nellie	12475	Harlen, Logan	8600
Hampton, Nancy	12632	Harlen, Amey	8601
Hampton, Lillie E.	12633	Harlen, Sila	13959
Hampton, Susan	13408	Harlen, Edmund	13960
Hampton, Ettaline	14032	Harlen, Daniel	13961
Hampton, Walton	14955	Harlan, Sarah A	12757
Hampton, Jene	14956	Harlan, Aaron	13258
Haiakonubbee, Mary	1075	Harlan, Willie Louisa	13259
Haiakonubbee, Albert	1078	Harland, Raybin	3531
Haiakonobi, Wilson	1106	Harland, Jennie	3532
Haiakonobi, Sillis	1107	Harland, Agnes	3533
Haiakonobi, Maike	1108	Harner, Loring	3060
Haiakonobi, Adeline	1109	Harner, Sallie Ann	3061
Haiakonobi, Mary	1110	Hankins, Sarah	4153
Haiakanubbi, Hamplin	3326	Hankins, Henry	4154
Haiakanubbi, Lucy Ann	3327	Hankins, Granderson	4156
Haiakanubbi, Wellington	3328	Hankins, Charley	14670
Haiakanubbi, Jonas	3756	Hart, Eastman H.	4249
Haiakanubbi, Sissy	3757	Hart, Pearl	4251
Haiakanubbi, Colbert	3758	Hart, Eastman Jr.	4252
Hayakonubbi, Osborn	1433	Hart, John M.	4253
Hayakonubbi, Elizabeth	1434	Hart, Lula	4254
Hahklotubbee, Adeline	13923	Hart, Gertrude	4255
Hahklotubbe, Garrett	13934	Hancock, Sikey	6112
Haklochi, Johnson	7094	Hancock, Annie	7221
Hale, Elizabeth	1296	Hancock, Betsy	8526
Hale, Stephen A.	16222	Hancock, Clayton	8527
Hail, Nettie V.	11689	Hancock, Willis	8554
Hail, Laura Rachel	11690	Hancock, Israel	8644
Hall, Sampson	1327	Hancock, Albert	9320
Hall, Siney	1329	Hancock, Doy Lee	9321
Hall, Joshua	1330	Hancock, William J. Bry-	
Hall, Ellis	1331	an	9322
Hall, Jonas	1332	Hancock, Loran	9343
Hall, Lucy A.	7701	Hancock, Solomon	12484
Hall, Jeneva	7702	Hancock, Susan	12485
Hall, Cecil C.	7703	Hancock, William	12486

Name.	Roll No.
Hancock, Jefferson Lee	12487
Hancock, Lewis	13118
Hancock, Betsy	13119
Hancock, Cornelia	13120
Hancock, Simon M.	13121
Hancock, Jincey	14053
Hancock, Amanda	14054
Hancock, Aaron	14055
Hancock, Rhoda	14056
Hancock, Bazada	14057
Hancock, Corah	14058
Hancock, Isaac	14059
Hamlin, Israel	6553
Hamlin, Sallie	6554
Harrell, Matilda	7383
Harrell, Lemon	7384
Harrell, James	7385
Harrell, Eva	7386
Harrell, Leona	7387
Harrell, Selina	11148
Harrell, Pinkey	11149
Hartshorne, David C.	8123
Hartshorne, Edward D.	8124
Hartshorne, Jane E.	8125
Hardaway, Jesse H.	8430
Hardaway, John R.	8431
Hardaway, Julia	8432
Hardaway, Julius	8433
Hardaway, Edgar	8434
Hattensty, Phoebe	9180
Hattensty, Jesse	9181
Hattensty, Paul	9182
Hattensty, Noga	9183
Hattensty, Mary	9184
Hattensty, Belle	9185
Hattensty, Lela	9186
Harmby, Anderson	9358
Harmby, Wilsie	10725
Harmby, Thompson	10726
Harmby, Sophina	10727
Harmby, Wesley	13076
Harvey, Green	9361
Harvey, Willy	9362
Harvey, Jonas	9363
Harvey, Sissie	9364
Harvey, Beard	9365
Harvey, Gladys	9366
Harvey, Vicy	11283
Hallmark, Sarah	9455
Hallmark, Mary M.	9456
Hallmark, Jennie	9457
Hallmark, Uriah	9458
Hallmark, Samuel	9459
Hallmark, Lillie	9460
Hallmark, John F.	9461
Hallmark, Ottie	9462
Hallmark, Henry	9463
Hallmark, Lulu	15076
Hallmark, Ervin A.	15077
Hardage, Sarah A.	9664
Hardage, William W.	9665
Hardage, John D.	9666
Hatchett, Meta B.	9960
Hatcher, William	14931
Hawkins, Milton	10487
Hawkins, Lucinda	12291
Hawkins, Loman A.	12292
Hawkins, Stella	12293
Halpin, Margaret	10579
Halpin, Oscar	10580
Hamilton, Mamie	11139
Hamilton, Alonzo F.	11140
Hamilton, Lorena H.	11141
Hamilton, Lora Williams	11142
Hamilton, Douglas	12695
Hamilton, Alexander B. Jr.	12719
Hamilton, Frances	12720
Hamilton, Walter L.	12721
Hamilton, Rebecca	12259
Hamilton, Mary M.	15260
Hamilton, Vercy	15261
Hamilton, Rufus	15262
Hattox, Stella	11220

Name.	Roll No.
Hattox, Azile	11221
Hattox, Francis Cleo	11222
Harper, Maggie E.	12553
Hazel, Seth T.	12691
Hazel, Jinnie	12692
Hazel, Jonathan	14204
Hazel, Caroline M.	14205
Hazel, Arthur	14206
Hazel, Alberta	14207
Hazel, Lemar	14208
Hazel, George	14209
Hailey, Helen M.	12809
Hailey, Edward S.	12810
Hailey, Walter P.	12811
Hailey, Hattie	12812
Hailey, William D.	12813
Haight, Nancy B.	13161
Haight, Dora Viola	13164
Hammons, Lizzie	13275
Hammons, Cecil Emery	13276
Hammons, Czarina	15548
Hamm, Ella Camp	14505
Harkreader, Lucy A.	14824
Hammit, Wilkie	15817
Hensley, Elzira	156
Hensley, Columbus	157
Hensley, Willie	159
Hensley, Ida	160
Hensley, Guss	161
Hensley, Walter	162
Hensley, Rosabelle Lee	14476
Hermon, Cillen	1317
Henderson, Martha	1486
Henderson, Abel	2681
Henderson, Mary	2682
Henderson, George W.	4279
Henderson, Thomas E.	4287
Henderson Lucy	4288
Henderson, Ida	5694
Henderson, Stanford M.	5695
Henderson, Amanda	7172
Henderson, Olla	7173
Henderson, Joanna	7174
Henderson, Ida B.	7175
Henderson, John T.	7177
Henderson, Edna E.	12309
Henderson, Willie M.	12310
Henderson, Leonidas W.	12311
Henderson, Viola B.	12312
Henderson, Mattie	12313
Henderson, Robert David	12314
Henderson, Roy	12405
Henderson, Lena	13427
Henderson, Emily	14298
Henderson, Mollie	14299
Henderson, Rosa	14300
Henderson, Ashley	14301
Henderson, Floyd	14302
Herndon, Emma J.	2213
Herndon, Arthur S.	2214
Herndon, Bertha M.	2215
Herndon, Elmer	2216
Herndon, Claude D.	2217
Herndon, Clide H.	2218
Herndon, Lucy	2219
Herndon, Alice	2220
Herndon, Harrison	2221
Herndon, James	2227
Herndon, Isabelle	3387
Herndon, Lottie	4197
Herndon, Rosa	14603
Herndon, May	14604
Herndon, Edna	14605
Herndon, Wilma	14606
Herndon, Henry E.	14607
Herndon, Mayo	14608
Herndon, Raphiel	14609
Heath, Catherine	5903
Heath, Archibald	5904
Heath, Aribella	5905
Heavener, Tobitha	6413
Heavener, Joseph Jr.	6414
Heavener, Mary	6415
Heavener, Matthew	6416

Name.	Roll No.
Hekia, Sibby	7210
Herron, Lula	7448
Henry, Matthew	7555
Henry, Lina	7556
Henry, Amos	8365
Henry, Arian	8366
Henry, Wilburn	8367
Henry, Alexander	8368
Henry, Roosevelt	8369
Henry, Woodson	12417
Henry, Jesse P.	12650
Henry, Briton	12651
Hepsin, Adam	7735
Hepsin, Selma	7736
Hepsin, John	7737
Heflin, Lena L.	10960
Hendrickson, Clara E.	9035
Hendrickson, Aleta E.	9036
Hendrickson, Willie T.	9037
Hendricks, John	15665
Hendrix, Edy	14261
Hendrix, Clemmie	14262
Hendrix, Belle	14399
Hendrix, James	14400
Hendrix, Brit	14401
Hendrix, Birtie	14402
Hendrix, Emmet	14403
Hendrix, Elmer	14404
Hendrix, William	14447
Hendrix, Jennie F.	14448
Hendrix, Lily Bell	14449
Hembree, Amy	9467
Hembree, Edward	9468
Hembree, Lucy	9469
Hembree, Elmer	9470
Hewitt, Edna	11160
Hewitt, Mamie	11161
Hewitt, Phena	11162
Hewitt, Julia	11163
Hewitt, Minnie	11164
Hewitt, May	11165
Hewitt, Joseph G.	11166
Hewitt, Edna Jr.	11167
Hewitt, Esther	11168
Hewitt, George W.	11169
Hewitt, Lelah	15389
Hewlett, Sarah C.	15599
Hebert, Alice	12238
Hebert, Czarina	12239
Henson, Lena	12406
Henson, Mary M.	12410
Henson, Sarah Elzada	12411
Heskett, Henry	13261
Heskett, Wesley	13262
Heskett, Inez O.	13263
Henley, Edna A.	15102
Henley, Frank	15103
Hibdon, Fannie	168
Hibdon, Henry	170
Hibdon, Jesse	14183
Hibdon, Charlie	14184
Hickaly, Eli	1419
Hickaly, Litie	1420
Hickaly, Emiline	1421
Hickaly, Adeline	1422
Hickman, Simeon	1861
Hickman, Little	2646
Hickman, Wilson	2647
Hickman, Thompson	2648
Hickman, Winie	2683
Hickman, Joseph	2686
Hickman, Cephus	2858
Hickman, James	3231
Hickman, Emma P.	3837
Hickman, Sarah	4895
Hickman, Taylor	4897
Hickman, Nancy	4898
Hickman, Mary	4899
Hickman, Betsy	6562
Hickman, Nancy M.	6563
Hickman, Atchison	6564
Hickman, Samuel	6565
Hickman, Austin	6567
Hickman, Sandy	6824

Name.	Roll No.
Hickman, Lizzie A.	7834
Hickman, Hugh R.	7835
Hickman, Della Josephine	7836
Hickman, Lawrence Quinton	7837
Hickman, Minnie	8370
Hickman, Jesse J.	8371
Hickman, Cornelius P.	8927
Hickman, Eliza A.	8928
Hickman, Jeff	8929
Hickman, Ernest	8930
Hickman, Lucy	13672
Hickman, Chester	13673
Hickman, Gertie	13674
Hickman, Manie	13675
Hickman, Willis	13676
Hickman, Hester	13677
Hickman, Lucy	13678
Hickman, Edwin L.	13679
Hickman, Frankie	13680
Hickman, Lizzie	14617
Hickman, William	15571
Hicks, Holton	2239
Hicks, Cephus	2509
Hicks, Jefferson	2813
Hicks, William	3636
Hicks, Smith M.	9360
Hicks, Simeon	13479
Hicks, Jobe	15391
Hinson, David	2676
Hinson, Sina	2677
Hinson, Nicy	15762
Hibben, Mary	3930
Hibben, Ethel	3931
Hibben, Sophia J	3932
Hibben, Samuel L.	3933
Hibben, Eliza	3934
Hibben, William T.	3935
Hibben, Frances H.	3936
Hibben, George Wellington	3937
Hitcher, Catherine	6151
Hitcher, Thompson	6152
Hitcher, Eddie	6153
Hitcher, Dicey	6910
Hitcher, William	6911
Hitcher, Harrison	13921
Hitcher, Henry	13924
Hitcher, Jackson	14050
Hill, Izora	6479
Hill, Horace C.	6480
Hill, Orval Q.	6481
Hill, Elba N.	6482
Hill, Louisa A	6483
Hill, Easter	6633
Hill, Sissie	6634
Hill, Winno	6635
Hill, Emma	6636
Hill, Jennie	7250
Hill, Nancy A.	13048
Hill, Edgar	13049
Hill, Nellie B.	13126
Hill, J. B.	13127
Hill, Harry F.	13128
Hill, Mabel Lucell	13129
Hill, Houston E.	13130
Hill, Zoe	15296
Hill, Arthur G.	15297
Hill, Lonnie B.	15298
Hill, Bessie M.	15299
Hill, Vera	15300
Harker, Frank R.	7648
Harker, Henry	7649
Harker, Jane Ethel	7650
Hischa, Houston	8479
Hischa, Lillie	8480
Hischa, Sampson	9342
Hicker, Edward	8572
Hicker, Edmund	9231
Hicker, Ellen	9232
Hicker, Benny	9233
Hiberd, Willie P.	9687
Hiberd, Claude	9688
Hiberd, Homer	9689

Name.	Roll No.
Hiberd, Granville	9690
Hiberd, Clarence O.	9691
Hilseweck, Alice E.	12080
Hilseweck, Lethia E.	12081
Hilseweck, Dorothy Jane	12082
Hilseweck, Lewis	
Hodges	12083
Hightower, Madora E.	13226
Hightower, Mary A.	13227
Hines, Oma	15322
Hinchey, Lula C.	15240
Hinchey, Ora Luraney	15241
Hleotambi	3358
Hleohtambi, Esias	3361
Hleohtambi, Olacie	3362
Hleohtambi, Charley	3406
Hleohtambi, Eliona	3407
Hleohtambi, Selile	3408
Howell, Thomas P.	217
Howell, Thomas P., Jr.	218
Howell, Laura	219
Howell, Vivian	220
Howell, Gladys	221
Howell, Rhoda	342
Howell, Calvin	896
Hoover, Rosa Camp	283
Hoover, Thelma	284
Holson, John B.	645
Holson, Noel J.	8330
Holson, Lizzie	8331
Holson, Ada	8332
Holson, Boyd	8333
Holson, Clara	8334
Holson, Amanda	8396
Holson, Rebecca	8398
Holson, Charles R.	8917
Holson, James L.	8918
Holson, Julia	13881
Holson, Ida May	15542
Holson, Lula Belle	15543
Holson, William H. H.	15544
Holson, Sampson S. N.	15545
Howze, Sophronia	810
Howze, Bessie	811
Howze, Jeff	812
Hoyopatubbi, Stanley	1294
Hoyopatubbi, Wash	3000
Hoyopatubbi, Lettie	3002
Hoyopatubbi, Jincy	3003
Holman, Sally	1322
Holman, Sallie	2160
Holman, Ellen	2402
Holman, Alfred	2558
Holman, Eliza A.	2559
Holman, Nelly	2560
Holman, Gillum	2561
Holman, Martain	2562
Holman, Simon	2563
Holman, Sarah	3432
Holman, Mattie	5674
Holman, Aline	5675
Holman, Gladys	5676
Holleman, Gilley A.	12468
Holleman, Gracie R. A.	12469
Holleman, Thomas C.	12470
Holleman, Juanita M.	12471
Holleman, William Givens	12472
Hol-ba-ti-ma.	1437
Hopayashubbi, Harmon	1577
Hopayashubbi, Sophie	1578
Hopayashubbi, Tamby	1583
Hopayashubbi, Eatima	1584
Hotinlubbee, Sena	1780
Hotinlubbee, Alfred	1781
Hotinlubbee, Loring	1782
Hotinlubbee, Lena	1783
Hotinlobi, Joe	3386
Hotinlobi, Lasin	3387
Hotinlobi, Liney	4258
Ho-tambi, Louisin	2397
Hotubbi, Salina	2801
Hotubbi, Elam	2802
Hotubbi, Kissy	2804
Hotubbi, Salean	2805

Name.	Roll No.
Hotubbi, Mary	2806
Hotubbee, Joseph	5702
Hotubbee, Asie	5704
Hokubbi, Robert	5216
Hokubbi, Sisley	10924
Hokubbi, Silmy	10925
Hokubbi, Peter	11750
Ho-k-abe, Sallie	3283
Hopakonobi, Elizabeth	3319
Hoklotubbe, Ben	5679
Hoklotubbe, George	5680
Hoklotubbe, Standley	5681
Hoklotubbe, Joe	5682
Hoteyabi, Ben	6842
Hoteyabi, Sillis	6843
Hoteyabi, Lou	6844
Ho-yubbee	7110
Hoyobbee, Isabelle	11428
Honubbee, Nancy	7161
Honubbee, Frances	7162
Honubbee, Sidney	7163
Honubbee, Melvina	7164
Hoparkentubbi, Eastman	10593
Hoparkentubbi, Wesley	10594
Hoparkentubbi, Isabelle	14810
Homma, Simeon	1449
Homma, Isabel	1632
Homma, Annie	4036
Homma, Mary	4150
Homma, Joe	4451
Homma, Nancy	4452
Homma, Tecumseh	5181
Homma, Paul	5184
Homma, Wilson	5186
Homma, Reuben	5187
Homma, Siney	5188
Homma, Davis	5189
Homma, Georgian	13523
Homma, Jincy	14655
Homma, Flora	14657
Homa, Anson	2762
Homa, Franklin	3062
Homa, Louisa	3063
Homa, Elijah	3566
Homer, Edmon	1590
Homer, Silwe	1591
Homer, Sosephine	1975
Homer, Elliot	1976
Homer, Pierce	2145
Homer, Limer	2146
Homer, Arbit	2147
Homer, Emiline	2148
Homer, Mary	2589
Homer, Eden	2590
Homer, Sopha	3104
Homer, Wilson	3105
Homer, Byington	3821
Homer, Silan	4095
Homer, Laura	4433
Homer, Mayles	4918
Homer, Aaron H.	5229
Homer, Maria	5230
Homer, Edward	5707
Homer, Davis	7191
Homer, Solomon	9909
Homer, Asa J.	9973
Homer, Kizzie	9974
Homer, Dana	9976
Homer, Soloman J.	10228
Homer, St. Clair	10229
Homer, Enoch	11725
Homer, Jacob	11864
Homer, Czarina	11865
Homer, Joseph	11908
Homer, LaFayette	11909
Homer, Ella	11910
Homer, Katie	11911
Homer, Josiah	11972
Homer, Sophia	11973
Homer, Oceana	11974
Homer, Silvey	12019
Homer, Davis A.	12114
Homer, Annie	12115
Homer, Mary	12116

Name.	Roll No.	Name.	Roll No.
Homer, Aaron	12117	Hopkins, Nova V.	12231
Homer, Ida	12118	Hopkins, Edward H.	12232
Homer, Peter	12258	Hopkins, Wallace C.	12233
Homer, Ellen	13939	Hops, Louisa	15060
Homer, Soloman	14668	Holly, Frances E.	15062
Homer, Weycia	14714	Holb, Carrie M.	15164
Homer, Isaac	14832	Holb, Alice	15165
Homer, Sissy	16204	Holb, Collomer	15166
Houston, Emma	1911	Holb, Charley	15167
Houston, Isaac	2910	Holb, Lee	15168
Houston, Emma	2911	Hoyt, Milo A.	15434
Houston, Davison	3606	Hoyt, Flossie L.	15435
Houston, Sophia	3607	Hoyt, Homer	15436
Houston, Louie	3688	Hoyt, Emma	15490
Houston, Benjamin	9643	Houghton, Luther	15586
Houston, Crena	10351	Hudson, Roar	1617
Houston, Cicily	10595	Hudson, Jimmie	1618
Holt, Seley	2164	Hudson, Sophie	1619
Holt, Silin	2165	Hudson, Caroline	1622
Holt, Houston	2166	Hudson, George	1623
Holt, Mary A.	15441	Hudson, Leuvina	1797
Holt, John W.	15442	Hudson, Leeana	1798
Hopson, Reason	2488	Hudson, Enoch	1799
Hopson, Cornelius	2489	Hudson, Willis	1800
Hopson, Julius	2490	Hudson, Isham	1801
Hopson, Martha	2491	Hudson, Inis	2597
Hopson, Johney	15567	Hudson, Evelina	2598
Holmes, Archibald	2917	Hudson, Jackson	2601
Holmes, Mima	2918	Hudson, Ishtema	2602
Holmes, Little	2919	Hudson, Culberson J.	4870
Holmes, Came	2920	Hudson, Mary	4871
Holmes, Sissy	3178	Hudson, Peter J.	5483
Holmes, Betsy	8386	Hudson, Amanda	5484
Holmes, Johnson	11575	Hudson, Helen	5485
Holmes, Joseph	11576	Hudson, Preston	5486
Holmes, Allen	11577	Hudson, Irene	5487
Holmes, Sampson	11578	Hudson, Nathan Hale	5488
Holmes, Aaron	13499	Hudson, Peter W.	5673
Holmes, Mary	13500	Hudson, Rufus	5938
Hotema, Solomon	4037	Hudson, Artimissie	5939
Hotema, Nancy	4038	Hudson, Charley	6383
Hotema, Cornelia	4039	Hudson, Henry	8814
Hotema, Frank	4040	Hudson, Irie	8815
Howard, Rhoda	4041	Hudson, Rosa	8953
Howard, Selma	4042	Hudson, Adeline	1621
Holton, Sally	4642	Hutcherson, Estella	2586
Holton, Selina	9683	Hutchinson, Louis S.	9777
Holton, Gooding	9684	Hutchinson, Ollie	9778
Holton, Anderson	10907	Hutchinson, Clara Gertrue	15940
Holder, Catherine	7431	Hunter, Silas	3084
Holder, Opal Gertrude	7434	Hunter, Siney	3085
Holloway, John	8738	Hunter, Cicilia	9373
Holloway, Frank A.	12605	Hunter, Pearly J.	9376
Holloway, Rebecca	12606	Hunter, Pernina	9377
Holloway, Fannie	12607	Hunter, Clayton W.	9378
Holloway, William	12608	Hunter, Andel	9478
Holloway, Ivy Amelia	12610	Hunter, Tandy	9479
Hooe, Mattie	9013	Hunter, George	9616
Hooe, William Jennings	9014	Hunter, Thomas	9629
Holden, Siabe	9668	Hunter, Junia	9630
Holden, Jefferson	9669	Hunter, Silas	9682
Holden, Thomas	9670	Hunter, Lou	9681
Holden, Charles	9671	Huland, Isabelle	4241
Holden, Henry	9672	Huland, Amanda	4242
Hogan, Sidney	9874	Huland, Mattie	4243
Hogan, Wesley	9875	Hutchings, Willie L.	4569
Hogan, Julius	9876	Hunt, Williamson	7090
Hogan, Wilburn	10667	Hunt, Louisa	7091
Hobart, Emma	9890	Hunt, James	7092
Hooper, Agnes	10222	Hunt, Siney	7093
Hokey, Eliza	14830	Hulsey, Louvisa	8188
Honey, Simon	11350	Hulsey, May	8189
Hodges, Joseph J.	11996	Hulsey, Henry	8190
Hodges, Henry	11997	Hulsey, Walter	8191
Hodges, Henrietta	11998	Hulsey, Mary A.	8724
Hodges, Mary P.	11999	Hulsey, Lora B.	8725
Hodges, Jennie G.	12000	Hulsey, Willard E.	8726
Hodges, Joseph T.	12001	Hulsey, Alonzo L.	8727
Hodges, John M.	12060	Hulsey, Lemuel V.	8728
Hodges, Ozie T.	12061	Hulsey, Claude M.	8729
Hodges, Joseph M.	12062	Hulsey, Oral Clarence	8731
Hodges, Myrtle	12130	Hurt, Annie	9068
Hodges, David W.	12205	Hurt, Susan	9069
Hodges, Claude A.	12206	Hughes, Belle	9958
Hodges, John W.	12207	Hull, Lena B.	10909
Hodges, Elisha	15482		

Name.	Roll No.
Hull, Luther S.	10910
Hull, Loda L.	10911
Hull, Vivia B.	10912
Hull, Gussie V.	10913
Huggins, Lula E.	10932
Huggins, Ollie	10933
Huggins, Oscar	10934
Huggins, Oliver	10935
Hughart, Clarence C.	12893
Hughart, Levi	12894
Hughart, Birdie E.	12895
Hughart, Boyd	12896
Hughart, Odie	14905
Huddleston, Frank	15011
Huddleston, Sophia	15012
Huddleston, Lucy J.	15013
Huddleston, Walter J.	15014
Huddleston, May	15015
Human, John B.	15283
Human, Pearl	15284
Human, Floy	15285
Human, Myrtle Ola	15286
Human, Winona	15287
Human, Jesse M.	15301
Human, Jesse S.	15302
Human, Matabel	15303
Human, Julia May	15304
Human, George Lafayette	15305
Human, Robert W.	15633
Husbands, Thomas J.	16223
Husbands, Johnie M.	16224
Husbands, James Alexander	16225
Husbands, Sarah Malissa	16226
Hynson, Perry	4355
Hyden, Whit W.	14149
Hyden, Leonard	14150
Hyden, Whit	14152
Hyden, Ella	14153
Hyden, Cleveland	14154
Hyden, Benjamin	14155
Hyden, Rufe	14156
Hyden, Frank S.	15169
Hyden, Ahpalahona	15170
Hyden, Maude	15634
Hyden, Eva Marguerite	16102
Hybarger, Mollie M.	15406
Hybarger, Eva L.	15407
Hybarger, Charlie	15408
Hybarger, Willie R.	15409
Hybarger, Ruby M.	15410
Ilapotubbee, Susan	5085
Ilapotubbee, Sallie	5086
Ilapotubbee, Lubbin	5087
Impson, Isaac	659
Impson, Isaac J.	883
Impson, Daniel	4978
Impson, Sokey	4979
Impson, Sophia	4980
Impson, Minerva	4981
Impson, William C.	4986
Impson, William	5193
Impson, Liddy	5194
Impson, Jincy	5195
Impson, Albert	5196
Impson, Louis	5197
Impson, Morris	5198
Impson, Dennis	5225
Impson, Elizabeth	5226
Impson, Ellis	5482
Impson, William D.	10137
Impson, William C.	10138
Impson, Sallie E.	10139
Impson, Lillie A.	10140
Impson, David D.	10141
Impson, Dona A.	10142
Impson, Middleton M.	10393
Impson, Hiram W. C.	10394
Impson, Robert E. L.	10395
Impson, John A. M.	10396
Impson, LaFayette	10625
Impson, Thompson J.	10626

Name.	Roll No.
Impson, William	13248
Impson, Melvina	13460
Impson, Harriet	13461
Impson, Ammizon B.	13462
Impson, Louisa	13726
Impson, Cleveland C.	14897
Impson, Susie Burris	15785
Impalumbi, Lowinie	2168
Impalumbi, Josephine	2169
Impalumbi, Abbester	2170
Impalumbi, Sylvester	2171
Impalumbi, Ennis	2172
Ingram, Mary A.	7441
Ingram, Claude H.	7442
Ingram, Annie A.	7443
Ingram, Lillia E.	7444
Ingram, Mary M.	9527
Ingram, Lulu M.	9528
Ingram, James Hall	9529
Ingram, Nellie	10038
Ingram, Christine O.	10039
Ingra n, C. T. Bouton	10040
Ingram, Leona	12190
Intolabbee, Colbert	9842
Ireton, Henry	306
Ireton, Cleopatra O.	308
Ireton, Mary J.	821
Ireton, David R.	822
Ireton, Ben	824
Ireton, Joel	825
Ireton, Mamie	827
Ireton, Joseph Francis	828
Ireton, Juley	829
Ireton, Thomas V.	830
Ireton, Hattie E.	831
Ishteka, Elizabeth	1424
Ishteka, Watkin	1426
Ishteka, Sillin	1427
Ishcomer, Adam	2295
Ishcomer, Betsy	2296
Ishcomer, Hudson	2297
Ishcomer, Wilton	2298
Ishcomer, Joshua	2299
Ishcomer, Colberson	2300
Ishcomer, Sinsie	2301
Ishcomer, Phillip N.	3224
Ishcomer, Nicie	3225
Ischomer, Monroe	3209
Ischcomer, Lincoln N.	2769
Ischcomer, Meson	2770
Ischcomer, Kensie	2771
Ischcomer, Mary J.	2772
Ischcomer, Kaler	2773
Ischcomer, Jeulus	2774
Ischcomer, Eve	2987
Ishtonake, Gibson	3183
Ishtonake, Sis	3184
Ishtiahonobbe, Hettie	3378
Isherwood, Josephine R.	5468
Isherwood, Lillie I.	5469
Isherwood, Pearl I.	5471
Isaac, Simon	7723
Isaac, Eliza	7724
Isaac, Kizzie	7725
Isaac, James	7726
Isaac, Alice	7727
Isaac, Ida	7728
Isaac, William	8899
Isaac, Lela	8900
Isaac, George	14593
Isaac, Ben	16206
Isbell, Belle Paul	15093
Isbell, Charles George	15094
Ishtimonehoke, .	15566
Izard, John C.	10276
Izard, Sherley B.	10277
Izard, Biddy C.	10279
Izard, Silas P.	10282
Izard, Leona P.	10283
Izard, Roy P.	10284
Izard, William Leslie	10285
Izard, Sarah Ethel	10286
Jackson, Abby	50
Jackson, Adeline	51

Name.	Roll No.	Name.	Roll No.
Jackson, Louina	1690	James, Henry C.	74
Jackson, Litle	2003	James, Silas	642
Jackson, Anderson	2009	James, Orina	643
Jackson, Silas	2241	James, Silas Jackson	644
Jackson, Lizzie	2460	James, Walton	765
Jackson, Albert	2461	James, Rogers	817
Jackson, Isabel	2570	James, Sarah A.	818
Jackson, Jesse	2655	James, Jesse Earnest	819
Jackson, Susan	2658	James, Estie Lee	820
Jackson, Moses	2915	James, Silley	1051
Jackson, Narcissa	2916	James, Sarah	1052
Jackson, Semean	2959	James, Levi	1292
Jackson, Toto	2960	James, Elizabeth	1293
Jackson, Salim	2997	James, Thomas	1480
Jackson, Nicholas	2998	James, Rhoda	1481
Jackson, Susan	3046	James, Williamson	1482
Jackson, Lester	3076	James, Sibbie	1483
Jackson, Wilson	3208	James, Geon	1713
Jackson, George	5210	James, Lita	1714
Jackson, Patsy	5211	James, Davis	1715
Jackson, Sissie	5335	James, Lucy	2055
Jackson, Grace	5771	James, Reuben	2056
Jackson, Silmon	5852	James, Lina	2057
Jackson, Mary	5853	James, Cornelia S.	2150
Jackson, Loyd	5854	James, William	2151
Jackson, Melvina	6650	James, Josiah	2152
Jackson, Mila	6692	James, Frances	2153
Jackson, William B.	6821	James, Nancy	2154
Jackson, Joseph	6822	James, Raphael	2155
Jackson, Rosie	6823	James, Louella	2156
Jackson, Robert	6826	James, Betsey	2157
Jackson, Emiline	6903	James, Dallas	2158
Jackson, Henry	6904	James, Watson	2232
Jackson, Jacob, Jr.	7063	James, Winey	2233
Jackson, David	7104	James, Moses	2234
Jackson, Joseph	7105	James, Dixon	2235
Jackson, Caroline	7106	James, Allen	2287
Jackson, Cooper	7107	James, Fillis	2288
Jackson, Phenie	7108	James, Willie	2289
Jackson, Mary	7109	James, Kitsie	2290
Jackson, Annie	7526	James, Sarah	2291
Jackson, Jacob B.	7628	James, Lucy	2292
Jackson, Saran	7640	James, Milan	2459
Jackson, Lorena	7647	James, Lottie	2568
Jackson, Susie Ann	7960	James, Mary Ann	2593
Jackson, Ben	8207	James, Davis	3048
Jackson, Willis	8876	James, Mary	3141
Jackson, Robin	8877	James, Mimey	3144
Jackson, Winey	8878	James, Charlison	3146
Jackson, Joseph	8879	James, Mary	3147
Jackson, Arthur	8880	James, Lena	3148
Jackson, John	9905	James, Calvin	3382
Jackson, Billy	9906	James, Janey	3383
Jackson, Phoebe	10227	James, Shub.	3385
Jackson, Freeman	10560	James, Charles	3543
Jackson, Sampson	10695	James, Narcy	3544
Jackson, Robert	10696	James, Margaret	3547
Jackson, Sila	10697	James, Jones	3548
Jackson, Micy	11062	James, Joe	3568
Jackson, Lena	11717	James, Marswis	3570
Jackson, Davis	12011	James, Simeon	3571
Jackson, Willis	12012	James, Aaron	3580
Jackson, Mary	12014	James, Sarah	3792
Jackson, Sam	12015	James, Johnny	40b3
Jackson, Folsom	12016	James, Charles	4615
Jackson, Lamar	12017	James, Benjamin	4620
Jackson, Edmund	12158	James, Winnie	4621
Jackson, Rebecca	12259	James, Sophia	4880
Jackson, Greenwood	12260	James, Noah	4881
Jackson, Leona	12261	James, Cornelius	5110
Jackson, Cora	12262	James, Elsie	5111
Jackson, Alfred	12263	James, Frances	5112
Jackson, Laura A.	12478	James, Katie	5380
Jackson, Amanda	13457	James, Emma	5384
Jackson, Asie	13520	James, Betsy	5563
Jackson, Elum	13950	James, Melvina	5570
Jackson, Jonas	13980	James, Benjamin	5737
Jackson, Louisa E. F.	14599	James, Campbell	5738
Jackson, Silas	14746	Jamess, Dock	5739
Jackson, Jack	14940	Jame, William	5774
Jackson, Virgil	15577	James, Allen W.	5950
Jackson, Winnie	15691	James, Agnes	5952
Jackson, Annie N.	15934	James, Silas	6169
Jackson, Learner	15934	James, Mary	6170
Jackson, Mary	16002	James, Delia	6171

Name.	Roll No.
James, Patterson	6221
James, Sarah	6222
James, Caroline	6223
James, Ida	6224
James, Wallace	6225
James, Mary	6284
James, Noel	6285
James, Davis	6286
James, Robinson	6287
James, Anna	6288
James, Silan	6289
James, Eastman	6290
James, Jefferson	6314
James, Selina	6315
James, Caroline	6349
James, Austin	6409
James, Plannie	6410
James, Elie	6411
James, Joshua	6412
James, Isadora	6478
James, Wesley W.	6695
James, Clarice	6696
James, Elissie	6802
James, Wilburn	7158
James, Charles M.	7291
James, Willie E.	7292
James, Allize	7333
James, Malinda	7334
James, Eve	7335
James, Abel	7602
James, Mary J.	7603
James, Silas W.	7667
James, Mary M.	7668
James, Sarah E.	7890
James, Cornelius	7891
James, Jacob J.	7892
James, Noel	7952
James, Malissa	7953
James, Ben	7962
James, Rhoda	7963
James, Susan	7964
James, Louisa	7965
James, Jane	7967
James, Warren	7996
James, Emeline	7997
James, Selina	7998
James, Jackson	7999
James, Ella	8000
James, George	8004
James, Adam	8010
James, Ticey	8011
James, Isaac	8012
James, Frank	8013
James, Emily	8014
James, Allen	8016
James, Jesse	8017
James, Etha M.	8073
James, Walton D.	8074
James, Davis	8075
James, Dennis	8076
James, Solomon	8206
James, Eltis	8245
James, Sealy	8246
James, Amanda	8247
James, Bennie	8248
James, Mary	8249
James, Selina	8250
James, Levi	8252
James, Eli	8340
James, Lena	8341
James, Harris	8426
James, Cornelia	8427
James, Louisa	8428
James, Joseph	8636
James, Nellie	8637
James, Collin	8638
James, William	8639
James, Dallas	8641
James, Vina	8642
James, Elmer	8643
James, Jackson	9200
James, Wysie	9201
James, Joshua	9202
James, Sissy	9203
James, Anna	9204
James, Isaac	
James, Lylus	
James, Jensie	
James, Frank	
James, Rufu	
James, Jess	
James, Will	
James, Gaines	
James, Mary A.	
James, William S.	
James, Samuel M.	
James, Yancey L.	
James, George G.	
James, Katy	
James, Clementine	9533
James, Martha S.	9534
James, Pearl Deldy	9535
James, Lewis	9861
James, Isabelle	9862
James, Clayburn, W.	10117
James, Acie W.	10118
James, Cora Ethel	10119
James, Ben	10271
James, Seborn	10272
James, Laura A.	10455
James, Juanita	10456
James, Columbus	10457
James, Mary	10484
James, Edward	10485
James, Jasper	10486
James, Walton	10980
James, Julia	10981
James, Vinnie M.	10982
James, Frank	10983
James, Edward	11218
James, Cephus	11339
James, Louisiana	11340
James, Louisiana	11371
James, Sampson	11439
James, Zona	11440
James, Logan	11707
James, Silas	12138
James, Crecy I.	12139
James, Doll	12140
James, Jacob	12655
James, Fred	12870
James, Willie C.	13597
James, Lorinda	13598
James, Lewis	13896
James, Watkins	13962
James, Elizabeth	13969
James, John	14123
James, John B.	14339
James, Ada	14612
James, Cinci	14615
James, Campbell M.	14709
James, Aaron	14727
James, Levinie	14758
James, Nancy	14759
James, Daniel W.	14760
James, Ellen	15380
James, Sallissie	15638
James, Sillian	15823
James, Imy	15828
James, Joseph	15879
James, Jesse Albert	15947
James, Sealy	15991
James, Minnie	15992
James, George W.	16208
Jacob, Simeon	1220
Jacob, Sophie	1221
Jacob, Grayson	1222
Jacob, Daniel	1223
Jacob, James	1225
Jacob, Eastman	1238
Jacob, Elizabeth	1239
Jacob, Emily	1240
Jacob, Robert	1241
Jacob, Ednie	1242
Jacob, Nancy	1646
Jacob, Eli	2173
Jacob, Milin	2174
Jacob, Soffin	2175
Jacob, Isaac	2238
Jacob, Houston B.	2845
Jacob, Emma	2999

Name.	Roll No.	Name.	Roll No.
Jackson, Louina	1690	James, Henry C.	74
Jackson, Litie	2003	James, Silas	642
Jackson, Anderson	2009	James, Orina	643
Jackson, Silas	2241	James, Silas Jackson	644
Jackson, Lizzie	2460	James, Walton	755
Jackson, Albert	2461	James, Rogers	317
Jackson, Isabel	2570	James, Sarah A.	818
Jackson, Jesse	2685	James, Jesse Earnest	819
Jackson, Susan	2688	James, Estie Lee	820
Jackson, Moses	2889	James, Silley	1051
Jackson, Narcissa	2915	James, Sarah	1052
Jackson, Semean	2916	James, Levi	1292
Jackson, Toto	2959	James, Elizabeth	1293
Jackson, Salim	2960	James, Thomas	1386
Jackson, Nicholas	2997	James, Rhoda	1388
Jackson, Susan	2998	James, Williamson	1391
Jackson, Lester	3046	James, Sibbie	1394
Jackson, Wilson	3075	James, Geor	1711
Jackson, George	3208	James, Lita	1714
Jackson, Patsy	5210	James, Davis	1715
Jackson, Sissie	5211	James, Lucy	2055
Jackson, Grace	5389	James, Reuben	2056
Jackson, Silmon	5773	James, Lina	2057
Jackson, Mary	5852	James, Cornelia S.	2150
Jackson, Loyd	5853	James, William	2151
Jackson, Melvina	5854	James, Josiah	2152
Jackson, Mila	6650	James, Frances	2153
Jackson, William B.	6692	James, Nancy	2154
Jackson, Joseph	6821	James, Raphael	2155
Jackson, Rosie	6822	James, Louella	2156
Jackson, Robert	6823	James, Betsey	2157
Jackson, Emiline	6826	James, Dallas	2158
Jackson, Henry	6903	James, Watson	2232
Jackson, Jacob, Jr.	6904	James, Winey	2233
Jackson, David	7063	James, Moses	2234
Jackson, Joseph	7104	James, Dixon	2235
Jackson, Caroline	7105	James, Allen	2237
Jackson, Cooper	7106	James, Fillis	2238
Jackson, Phenie	7107	James, Willie	2239
Jackson, Mary	7108	James, Kitsie	2290
Jackson, Annie	7109	James, Sarah	2291
Jackson, Jacob B.	7526	James, Lucy	2292
Jackson, Sarah	7628	James, Milan	2459
Jackson, Lorena	7640	James, Lottie	2568
Jackson, Susie Ann	7647	James, Mary Ann	2693
Jackson, Ben	7960	James, Davis	3048
Jackson, Willis	8207	James, Mary	3141
Jackson, Robin	8876	James, Mimey	3144
Jackson, Winey	8877	James, Charlison	3146
Jackson, Joseph	8878	James, Mary	3147
Jackson, Arthur	8879	James, Lena	3148
Jackson, John	8880	James, Calvin	3382
Jackson, Billy	9905	James, Janey	3383
Jackson, Phoebe	9906	James, Shub.	3385
Jackson, Freeman	10227	James, Charles	3543
Jackson, Sampson	10560	James, Narcy	3544
Jackson, Robert	10695	James, Margaret	3547
Jackson, Sila	10696	James, Jones	3548
Jackson, Micy	10697	James, Joe	3568
Jackson, Lena	11062	James, Marswis	3570
Jackson, Davis	11717	James, Simeon	3571
Jackson, Willis	12011	James, Aaron	3580
Jackson, Mary	12012	James, Sarah	3792
Jackson, Sam	12014	James, Johnny	40b3
Jackson, Folsom	12015	James, Charles	4615
Jackson, Lamar	12016	James, Benjamin	4620
Jackson, Edmund	12017	James, Winnie	4621
Jackson, Rebecca	12158	James, Sophia	4880
Jackson, Greenwood	12259	James, Noah	4881
Jackson, Leona	12260	James, Cornelius	5110
Jackson, Cora	12261	James, Elsie	5111
Jackson, Alfred	12262	James, Frances	5112
Jackson, Laura A.	12263	James, Katie	5380
Jackson, Amanda	12478	James, Emma	5384
Jackson, Asie	13457	James, Betsy	5563
Jackson, Elum	13520	James, Melvina	5570
Jackson, Jonas	13950	James, Benjamin	5737
Jackson, Louisa E. F.	13980	James, Campbell	5738
Jackson, Silas	14599	Jamess, Dock	5739
Jackson, Jack	14746	Jame, William	5774
Jackson, Virgil	14940	James, Allen W.	5950
Jackson, Winnie	15577	James, Agnes	5952
Jackson, Annie N.	15691	James, Silas	6169
Jackson, Learner	15934	James, Mary	6170
Jackson, Mary	16002	James, Delia	6171

Name.	Roll No.
James, Patterson	6221
James, Sarah	6222
James, Caroline	6223
James, Ida	6224
James, Wallace	6225
James, Mary	6284
James, Noel	6285
James, Davis	6286
James, Robinson	6287
James, Anna	6288
James, Silan	6289
James, Eastman	6290
James, Jefferson	6314
James, Selina	6315
James, Caroline	6349
James, Austin	6409
James, Plannie	6410
James, Elie	6411
James, Joshua	6412
James, Isadora	6478
James, Wesley W.	6695
James, Clarice	6696
James, Elissie	6802
James, Wilburn	7158
James, Charles M.	7291
James, Willie E.	7292
James, Allize	7333
James, Malinda	7334
James, Eve	7335
James, Abel	7602
James, Mary J.	7603
James, Silas W.	7667
James, Mary M.	7668
James, Sarah E.	7890
James, Cornelius	7891
James, Jacob J.	7892
James, Noel	7952
James, Malissa	7953
James, Ben	7962
James, Rhoda	7963
James, Susan	7964
James, Louisa	7965
James, Jane	7967
James, Warren	7996
James, Emeline	7997
James, Selina	7998
James, Jackson	7999
James, Ella	8000
James, George	8004
James, Adam	8010
James, Ticey	8011
James, Isaac	8012
James, Frank	8013
James, Emily	8014
James, Allen	8016
James, Jesse	8017
James, Etha M.	8073
James, Walton D.	8074
James, Davis	8075
James, Dennis	8076
James, Solomon	8206
James, Elfis	8245
James, Sealy	8246
James, Amanda	8247
James, Bennie	8248
James, Mary	8249
James, Selina	8250
James, Levi	8252
James, Eli	8340
James, Lena	8341
James, Harris	8426
James, Cornelia	8427
James, Louisa	8428
James, Joseph	8636
James, Nellie	8637
James, Collin	8638
James, William	8639
James, Dallas	8641
James, Vina	8642
James, Elmer	8643
James, Jackson	9200
James, Wysie	9201
James, Joshua	9202
James, Sissy	9203
James, Anna	9204

Name.	Roll No.
James, Isaac	9208
James, Lylus	9215
James, Jensie	9216
James, Frank	9276
James, Rufus	9277
James, Jesse	9278
James, Willie D .	9279
James, Gaines	9306
James, Mary A.	9391
James, William S.	9392
James, Samuel M.	9393
James, Yancey L.	9394
James, George G.	9395
James, Katy	9532
James, Clementine	9533
James, Martha S.	9534
James, Pearl Deldy	9535
James, Lewis	9861
James, Isabelle	9862
James, Clayburn, W.	10117
James, Acie W.	10118
James, Cora Ethel	10119
James, Ben	10271
James, Seborn	10272
James, Laura A.	10455
James, Juanita	10456
James, Columbus	10457
James, Mary	10484
James, Edward	10485
James, Jasper	10486
James, Walton	10980
James, Julia	10981
James, Vinnie M.	10982
James, Frank	10983
James, Edward	11218
James, Cephus	11339
James, Louisiana	11340
James, Louisiana	11371
James, Sampson	11439
James, Zona	11440
James, Logan	11707
James, Silas	12138
James, Crecy I.	12139
James, Doll	12140
James, Jacob	12655
James, Fred	12870
James, Willie C.	13597
James, Lorinda	13598
James, Lewis	13896
James, Watkins	13962
James, Elizabeth	13969
James, John	14123
James, John B.	14339
James, Ada	14612
James, Cinci	14615
James, Campbell M.	14709
James, Aaron	14727
James, Levinie	14758
James, Nancy	14759
James, Daniel W.	14760
James, Ellen	15380
James, Sallissie	15638
James, Sillian	15823
James, Imy	15828
James, Joseph	15879
James, Jesse Albert	15947
James, Sealy	15991
James, Minnie	15992
James, George W.	16208
Jacob, Simeon	1220
Jacob, Sophie	1221
Jacob, Grayson	1222
Jacob, Daniel	1223
Jacob, James	1225
Jacob, Eastman	1238
Jacob, Elizabeth	1239
Jacob, Emily	1240
Jacob, Robert	1241
Jacob, Ednie	1242
Jacob, Nancy	1646
Jacob, Eli	2173
Jacob, Milin	2174
Jacob, Soffin	2175
Jacob, Isaac	2238
Jacob, Houston B.	2845
Jacob, Emma	2999

Name.	Roll No.	Name.	Roll No.
Jacob, Elias	4489	Jefferson, Loston	3222
Jacob, Cordelia	4490	Jefferson, Julius	3259
Jacob, Margaret	4492	Jefferson, Winnie	3260
Jacob, Joseph	4493	Jefferson, Maggie	3261
Jacob, Roxie	4494	Jefferson, Catharine	3262
Jacob, Forbis	7089	Jefferson, Anna	3264
Jacob, Lizzie	8789	Jefferson, Mahaley	3567
Jacob, Avey	11278	Jefferson, Cornelius	3586
Jacob, Austin	11418	Jefferson, Daniel	3654
Jacob, Eastman	11419	Jefferson, Josephus	3656
Jacob, Nelson	11420	Jefferson, Anna	4317
Jacob, Wilson	11422	Jefferson, Malinda	4318
Jacob, Sillen	11423	Jefferson, Henry	4884
Jacob, Sina	11447	Jefferson, Mary	5089
Jacob, Fulsom	11448	Jefferson, Benjamin	5090
Jacob, Sarah	11450	Jefferson, Wallace	5276
Jacob, Elsey	11454	Jefferson, Charles	5277
Jacob, Harriet	13470	Jefferson, Gilbert	5285
Jacob, Melissa	13351	Jefferson, Bessie	5286
Jacob, Sila	14906	Jefferson, Eliza	6351
Jacob, Johnson	15508	Jefferson, Zonie	6631
Jacobs, Rhoda	3274	Jefferson, Edna	6632
Jacobs, Colman	3276	Jefferson, Israel	6683
Jacobs, Isaac A.	15700	Jefferson, Frazen	6924
Jack, Loman	6775	Jefferson, Nancy	6925
Jack, Hama	6776	Jefferson, Thomas	6926
Jack, Martin	8883	Jefferson, Calvin	7227
Jack, George	8887	Jefferson, Sillen	7228
Jack, Winnie	8893	Jefferson, Douglas	7229
Jarrel, Lula E.	10075	Jefferson, Stephen	8336
Jarrel, Mary Elizabeth	10076	Jefferson, Layson	8338
Jenkins, Mary	172	Jefferson, Mary	8444
Jenkins, John Leonard	173	Jefferson, Mary	8466
Jenkins, Seth	174	Jefferson, Mollie	8467
Jenkins, Claude	175	Jefferson, Alfred	8476
Jenkins, Lee	176	Jefferson, Benjamin	8478
Jenkins, Clarance	177	Jefferson, Thomas	8498
Jenkins, Albert	8999	Jefferson, Vicey	8499
Jenkins, John	9001	Jefferson, Lena	8500
Jelks, Julia	373	Jefferson, Ada	8501
Jelks, Marietta	374	Jefferson, Benjamin	8502
Jelks, Almus T.	375	Jefferson, Allen	8504
Jefferson, Hickson	944	Jefferson, Sackey	8550
Jefferson, Adeline	945	Jefferson, Sampson	8551
Jefferson, Samuel	946	Jefferson, Eli	8552
Jefferson, Alliston	947	Jefferson, Joseph	8553
Jefferson, Lenie	948	Jefferson, Eastman	8562
Jefferson, Simeon	949	Jefferson, Lena	8577
Jefferson, Saikom	950	Jefferson, Smallwood	8774
Jefferson, Austin	996	Jefferson, Mary	8775
Jefferson, Margaret W.	997	Jefferson, Eliza	8776
Jefferson, Chisney	1000	Jefferson, Sam	8806
Jefferson, Sweny	1258	Jefferson, Lizzie	9087
Jefferson, Stewart	1532	Jefferson, Betsy	9137
Jefferson, Betsy	1533	Jefferson, Ellis	9476
Jefferson, Sarah	1534	Jefferson, Mollie	11346
Jefferson, Nancy	1535	Jefferson, Abraham	11347
Jefferon, Minie Raner	1701	Jefferson, Sweeny	12554
Jefferson, Sampson	1890	Jefferson, Dora	12656
Jefferson, Hoteya	1891	Jefferson, Joseph	13069
Jefferson, Wilton	1892	Jefferson, Frances	13070
Jefferson, Sophie	1893	Jefferson, Sarah	13122
Jefferson. Tennessee	1930	Jefferson, Bessie	13123
Jefferson, Fannie	2070	Jefferson, Mary	13579
Jefferson, Wellington	2071	Jefferson, Wallace	13580
Jefferson, Nina	2072	Jefferson, Rosa	13581
Jefferson, Watkin	2137	Jefferson, Sweeney	13582
Jefferson, Edson	2180	Jefferson, Kitsie	13586
Jefferson, Sealy	2181	Jefferson, Rosa	13594
Jefferson, Madison	2182	Jefferson, Thomas	13963
Jefferson, Nicholas	2183	Jefferson, Jane	14051
Jefferson, Esean	2184	Jefferson, Wallace	14052
Jefferson, Simeon	2507	Jefferson, Ellen	14569
Jefferson, Elliston	2508	Jefferson, Sissie	1457b
Jefferson, Ellis	2629	Jefferson, Laura	14579
Jefferson, Davis	2630	Jefferson, Missie	15578
Jefferson, Jacob	2631	Jefferson, Phoebe	15588
Jefferson, Mollie	2678	Jefferson, Emiline	15589
Jefferson, Pikey	2734	Jefferson, Simpson	15639
Jefferson, Sissy	2735	Jefferson, Levicy	15826
Jefferson, Emily	2736	Jeter, Sarah E.	4174
Jefferson, Madison E.	2811	Jeter, Gertrude	4175
Jefferson, Sukey	2812	Jeter, Hattie	4176
Jefferson, Hogan	3143	Jeter, James T.	4177
Jefferson, Jincy	3221	Jeter, William W.	4178
		Jeter, Olive M.	4179

Name.	Roll No.
Jerry, David	11912
Jennings, Richard P.	13144
Jennings, Nathaniel F.	13467
Jennings, Georgia D.	15493
Jennings, Arthur C.	15494
Jennings, Lilburn L.	15495
Jennings, Noah	15769
Jennings, Martha J.	15770
Jennings, James C.	15893
Jennings, Donnie May	15894
Jeflow, Maulsie	13897
Jeflow, Jane	13898
Jesse, Eastman	13983
Jessie, Buster	14116
Johnston, Jane	32
Johnston, Albert	33
Johnston, Edmund H.	34
Johnston, Allie	36
Johnston, Myrtle	38
Johnston, Lucretia	81
Johnston, George W.	82
Johnston, Myrtle Belle	84
Johnston, Amelia May	85
Johnston, Arthur	12573
Johnston, John	12574
Johnson, Frances	432
Johnson, Maude L.	676
Johnson, Victor M.	677
Johnson, Tennie	678
Johnson, Frances	956
Johnson, Cora	960
Johnson, Billis	1392
Johnson, Anthony	1393
Johnson, Hilton	1395
Johnson, Elsie	1548
Johnson, Edmond	1549
Johnson, Elam J.	1593
Johnson, Annie	1594
Johnson, Dora	1595
Johnson, Wilmon J.	1596
Johnson, Carrie	1598
Johnson, Lizzie	1599
Johnson, Lucy Ann	1676
Johnson, Sophy	1895
Johnson, Dan	1896
Johnson, Richard	1897
Johnson, Henry	1898
Johnson, James	1899
Johnson, Laura May	1901
Johnson, Louis	1931
Johnson, Lila	1932
Johnson, Irene	1933
Johnson, Bobb	1934
Johnson, Elean	1977
Johnson, Nelis	2190
Johnson, Elsie	3279
Johnson, Isabel	3578
Johnson, Joseph	3794
Johnson, Adeline	3795
Johnson, Noel	3796
Johnson, Aggie	3798
Johnson, Huston	3800
Johnson, Abner	5330
Johnson, Henry	5855
Johnson, Eliza	5856
Johnson, Hickman	5857
Johnson, Peter	5884
Johnson, Lucy	5885
Johnson, Samuel	5886
Johnson, Milsy Ann	5887
Johnson, Aribella	6038
Johnson, Hagan	6076
Johnson, Rhoda	6077
Johnson, Laura	6078
Johnson, Lorena	6079
Johnson, Adeline	6207
Johnson, Ella	6208
Johnson, McGee	6310
Johnson, Belle	6311
Johnson, Andrew	6312
Johnson, Alfred	6313
Johnson, Martha	6920
Johnson, Deller	6921
Johnson, William E.	6922
Johnson, Lynard	6923

Name.	Roll No.
Johnson, Ida	7570
Johnson, Emmitt	7571
Johnson, Maud	8030
Johnson, Ola	8031
Johnson, Sarah	8032
Johnson, Arbin	8481
Johnson, Lula	8482
Johnson, Lizzie	8483
Johnson, Susan	8484
Johnson, Simon	8672
Johnson, Levina	8673
Johnson, Alexander	8732
Johnson, Emiline	9093
Johnson, Perry F.	9094
Johnson, Daniel E.	9145
Johnson, Lillie	9146
Johnson, Belvina	9147
Johnson, Eliza A.	9170
Johnson, Simeon	9901
Johnson, Esias	9902
Johnson, Sallie	9903
Johnson, Daniel	9904
Johnson, Thomas	9910
Johnson, Lizzie	9911
Johnson, Eunice	9912
Johnson, Philip	10230
Johnson, Frances	10231
Johnson, Moses	10232
Johnson, Mary	10233
Johnson, Henry	10234
Johnson, Pearl	10235
Johnson, Missie	10236
Johnson, Eliza	10257
Johnson, Bankston	10483
Johnson, Agnes	10578
Johnson, Sealy	11012
Johnson, Carrie	11013
Johnson, Umpson	11014
Johnson, Elizabeth	12453
Johnson, John S.	12455
Johnson, Riley	13072
Johnson, Zeno	13285
Johnson, Fount	13286
Johnson, Leolena	13363
Johnson, Malvina	14471
Johnson, Robert	14472
Johnson, Sylvester	14591
Johnson, Frances	15006
Johnson, Thomas	15896
Jones, Pearl	100
Jones, Charles R.	101
Jones, C. J.	449
Jones, Gracie V.	450
Jones, Vera	473
Jones, Oma	474
Jones, Thelma Vivian	475
Jones, Sim	884
Jones, Joseph	967
Jones, George	1111
Jones, Lienda	1112
Jones, Elson	1113
Jones, Miston	1114
Jones, Liney,	1116
Jones, Louiston	1117
Jones, Wilson	1118
Jones, Agnes	1285
Jones, Isaac	1286
Jones, Jeffrey	1287
Jones, James Jr.	1288
Jones, Mahaley	1357
Jones, Quitman	1525
Jones, Betsy	1729
Jones, Mulsie	1730
Jones, Frances	1731
Jones, Hannah	2251
Jones, Solomon	2276
Jones, Lottie	2566
Jones, Cora	2588
Jones, Frances	2851
Jones, Edward	3004
Jones, Winsey	3005
Jones, Nellis	3006
Jones, Sibbie	3007
Jones, Ensie	3010
Jones, Eastman	3054

Name.	Roll No.	Name.	Roll No.
Jones, Eliza Ann	3055	Jones, Caroline	9675
Jones, Lettie	3119	Jones, Joseph	9676
Jones, Grayson	32\1	Jones, Willie	9677
Jones, Isham	3256	Jones, Jacob	9678
Jones, Sillis	3257	Jones, Sampson	9679
Jones, Thomas	3385	Jones, Robert	9680
Jones, Amos	3289	Jones, Jackson N.	10014
Jones, Sylvester	3290	Jones, Theresa	10015
Jones, Eastman	3291	Jones, Geneva	10016
Jones, Jimmie	3469	Jones, Brutus Costillo	10017
Jones, Jesse	3820	Jones, Wallace	10170
Jones, John G.	3986	Jones, Jincey	10287
Jones, Margaret A.	3987	Jones, Zack	10380
Jones, Katie B.	3988	Jones, Ellis	10381
Jones, Lena	4404	Jones, Amelia	10382
Jones, Isaac	4405	Jones, John	10383
Jones, David	4406	Jones, Misssie	10384
Jones, George	4549	Jones, Phoebe	10388
Jones, Frances	4550	Jones, Henry	10430
Jones, Sam	4572	Jones, Susan	10431
Jones, Edward	4573	Jones, Reason	10432
Jones, Willis	4803	Jones, Robert Hender-	
Jones, Louisa	4804	son	10433
Jones, Cornelius	4891	Jones, Allington	10633
Jones, Harrison	5015	Jones, Betsy	10634
Jones, Wilson	5069	Jones, Virginia	10878
Jones, Wesley	5175	Jones, Osborn Allen	10883
Jones, Almeda	5207	Jones, Jacob	10972
Jones, Ida M.	5208	Jones, Sibby	11044
Jones, Samantha	5209	Jones, Mary. B.	11045
Jones, Wilson	5212	Jones, Mary J.	11081
Jones, Rodgers	5454	Jones, William C.	11082
Jones, Charley	5655	Jones, Luella	11083
Jones, Laymon	5870	Jones, Pearly	11084
Jones, Robinson	5997	Jones, Joseph L.	11085
Jones, Nancy	5998	Jones, Lena L.	11086
Jones, Artimissa	5999	Jones, Eula A.	11087
Jones, Silsainey	6000	Jones, Allie C.	11088
Jones, Rennie	6001	Jones, Cornelius A.	11229
Jones, Silway	6002	Jones, Dora	11338
Jones, Rosanna	6003	Jones, Grayson	11369
Jones, Alfred	6100	Jones, Noel	11412
Jones, Nora	6101	Jones, Edward	11414
Jones, Melvina	6251	Jones, Israel	11415
Jones, Morris	6294	Jones, Edmond	11565
Jones, Charley	6520	Jones, Alice	11566
Jones, William P.	6623	Jones, Joseph	11567
Jones, Myrtle L.	6624	Jones, Emma	11568
Jones, Joseph	6767	Jones, Peter	11569
Jones, Sallie	6768	Jones, Amanda	11570
Jones, Sam	7371	Jones, Davis	11637
Jones, John	7372	Jones, Arthur L.	11678
Jones, Keziah	7477	Jones, William F.	11679
Jones, Sophia K.	7483	Jones, Maggie B.	11680
Jones, Eliza Caroline	7484	Jones, Wyatt M.	11681
Jones, Mike	7961	Jones, Jesse E.	11682
Jones, Edward	8275	Jones, Ida K.	11683
Jones, Emma	8328	Jones, Frank Pierce	11684
Jones, Willis	8603	Jones, Amanda	11716
Jones, Mary	8604	Jones, Suky	11793
Jones, Marteson	8777	Jones, Solomon	11795
Jones, Wilson	8779	Jones, Sam	11951
Jones, Mary	8780	Jones, Martha A.	11952
Jones, Israel	8801	Jones, Andrew	11959
Jones, James	8807	Jones, Robert M., Jr.	11960
Jones, Selissa	8808	Jones, Abagail	11961
Jones, Kitzie	8809	Jones, Jasper	11962
Jones, Morrow	8810	Jones, Impson	11963
Jones, Benjamin	8846	Jones, Mary	11964
Jones, Henry	8847	Jones, Nancy	11989
Jones, Moltsey	8848	Jones, Jonas	12025
Jones, James	8849	Jones, Sophia	12026
Jones, Ellen	8850	Jones, Joshua	12027
Jones, Frank	8952	Jones, Sophia, Jr.	12028
Jones, Willie	9040	Jones, Frances	12029
Jones, Douglas	9041	Jones, Elsie	12108
Jones, Eliza	9042	Jones, Louisa	12412
Jones, George	9043	Jones, Zenobia V.	12617
Jones, Impson	9059	Jones, Ester Gray	12627
Jones, Billy	9024	Jones, Melvina	12648
Jones, Frank	9625	Jones, James	12649
Jones, Samuel	9626	Jones, Benjamin F.	12853
Jones, Cornelius H.	9673	Jones, William F.	12854
Jones, Sophia	9674	Jones, Mary Ann	13108

Name.	Roll No.	Name.	Roll No.
Jones, Berty Lee	13109	Jones, Liddy Josephine	15699
Jones, William Edward	13110	Jones, Alfus	15779
Jones, Lou	13209	Jones, Missie	15852
Jones, Andrew	13210	Jones, Minnie	15853
Jones, Nina	13211	Jones, Annie	15956
Jones, Eva	13212	John, Cephus	1063
Jones, Harry Dewitt	13213	John, Bessie	1064
Jones, Samuel	13380	John, Felesten	1065
Jones, Rebecca	13381	John, Wynie	1066
Jones, Robert	13382	John, Narie	1067
Jones, Edmund	13383	John, Loite	1068
Jones, Willis	13478	John, Matsy	1251
Jones, Frank	13494	John, Rayson	1273
Jones, Lucetta	13557	John, Mary	1274
Jones, Frank W.	13558	John, Mattie	1275
Jones, Floyd	13559	John, Gabriel	1276
Jones, Nat	13927	John, Esa	1564
Jones, Ellen	13994	John, Wilson	1568
Jones, Osborne	13995	John, Agnes	2564
Jones, Billy	13996	John, Albert	2635
Jones, Minnie	13997	John, Elizabeth	2636
Jones, John	13998	John, Watson	2637
Jones, Pearl	13999	John, Quintus	2639
Jones, Josephine	14144	John, Isaac	2640
Jones, William B.	14147	John, Norris	2835
Jones, Capitola	14148	John, Carney	2868
Jones, Una May	14203	John, Burris	2869
Jones, Salina Izzard	14488	John, Museton	2873
Jones, Effie	14489	John, Lena	2874
Jones, Georgia	14490	John, Rencey	2875
Jones, Burr	14491	John, Morris	3031
Jones, Della	14492	John, Eliza	3032
Jones, Sadie	14493	John, James	3033
Jones, Bertie Page	14494	John, Amos	3024
Jones, Henry B.	14495	John, Edna	3036
Jones, Liman	14705	John, Israel	3037
Jones, Judea	14706	John, Sophina	3038
Jones, Elsie	14725	John, Henry	3039
Jones, Alexander	14983	John, Hagan	3375
Jones, Vergia Ellen	14984	John, Lena	3376
Jones, Maggie	15132	John. Dickson	5079
Jones, Ernest E.	15133	John, Sophia	5080
Jones, John Robert	15182	John, George	5081
Jones, Sophronia Eliza-		John, Paul	5082
beth	15183	John, Helen	5083
Jones, William M.	15184	John, Robert	5465
Jones, May Cordelia	15185	John, Emerson	5466
Jones, Walter A.	15186	John, Mary	5467
Jones, Samuel C.	15187	John, Silmon	8919
Jones, Perry	15202	John, Ellen	8920
Jones, Benjamin	15203	John, Sissie	8921
Jones, Florence	15204	John, Fannie	8922
Jones, Forbes	15205	John, Nora	8925
Jones, Everett	15206	John, Sim	11691
Jones, Lele	15207	John, Malissa	11692
Jones, Ethel	15208	John, Edward	11693
Jones, James F.	15229	John, Jimmie	11694
Jones, Cordelia C.	15230	John, Susin	11696
Jones, James O.	15231	John, Jaslin	14637
Jones, Henry P.	15232	Johns, Henry A.	11703
Jones, Lorena Elizabeth	15235	Johns, Eva	11704
Jones, Thomas J.	15236	Joel, Hampton	1217
Jones, Marens A.	15237	Joel, Solomon	4876
Jones, Rodham F.	13238	Joel, Henry	8947
Jones, Elbert M.	15239	Joel, Sillis	8948
Jones, Francis M.	15248	Joel, Lee	13362
Jones, Lenora M.	15249	Joseph, George	1218
Jones, Robert M.	15250	Joseph, Lottie	1219
Jones, Jesse F.	15251	Joseph, William	1600
Jones, Walter A.	15252	Joseph, Louisa	1601
Jones, Alfred L.	15253	Joseph, Inis	1602
Jones, Claude O.	15254	Joseph, John	1764
Jones, Roy D.	15255	Joseph, Ellissie	1765
Jones, William T.	15263	Joseph, Gibson	1766
Jones, Mary	15420	Joseph, Meta	1767
Jones, Julia	15473	Joseph, Sillian	1769
Jones, John F.	15606	Joseph, Wicy	15658
Jones, Loney Ann	15607	Joe, Sim	3971
Jones, Lafayette	15608	Joe, Visey	3972
Jones, Josephine	15609	Joe, Agnes	3973
Jones, Mary Ellen	15695	Joe, Sampson	4828
Jones, Mabel	15696	Joe, Sophia	8267
Jones, Henry Wilson	15697	Joe, Adam	13115
Jones, Ellen	15698	Joe, Ellen	13116
		Johnico, John H.	6145

Name.	Roll No.	Name.	Roll No.
Johnico, Annie	6146	Kelly, Isaac	3902
Johnico, Grant	6147	Kelly, Selina J.	3926
Johnico, Aaron	6148	Kelly, Louis V.	3928
Johnico, Caroline	6162	Kelly, James	7780
Johnico, Aline	6168	Kelly, Gilburt	7783
Johnico, John	7738	Kelly, Emmet J.	10823
Johnico, Lucy	7781	Kelly, Viola A.	10824
Josey, Malinda	11572	Kelly, John	12188
Josey, Susan	11573	Kelly, Henry	12189
Josey, Isabelle	11574	Kelly, William W.	12245
Juzan, Emma	2574	Kelly, DeWitt C.	12246
Juzan, Philliston	2575	Kelly, Lorena	13036
Juzan, Tennessee	2576	Kelly, Faye L.	13037
Juzan, Jacoway	2577	Kelly, Mary	14007
Juzan, Hannah	2578	Kelly, Dovey	14008
Juzan, Sela	3235	Kelly, Mahala	14009
Juzan, Sattie	3657	Kelly, Laura	14815
Juzan, Isaac	3660	Keltner, Mattie A.	893
Justice, Bettie M.	6426	Keltner, Sylvester G.	894
Justice, Lela V.	6427	Keltner, Neroli	895
Julius, Solomon	10540	Kendrick, Martha	3910
Julius, Serena	10541	Kendrick, William W.	3911
Julius, Eli	10542	Kendrick, Annie M.	3912
Julius, Jane	10543	Kendrick, Henry L.	3913
Julius, Sallie	10544	Kendrick, Lelia J.	3914
Julius, Rosa	10545	Kendrick, John G.	3915
Julius, Gilbert	10546	Kendrick, Emma E.	3916
Julius, Adam	10547	Kendrick, Mamie H.	3917
Juniper, Lester	15443	Kendrick, Mary Stokes	3918
Kanimaya, Hodges	1057	Kennady, Mary	6456
Kanimaya, Jennie	1058	Key, Ambrose	6781
Kanimaya, James	1059	Key, Lula	14276
Kaniatubbee, Rosa	1060	Key, Clauda	14279
Kanitobe, Gibson	2815	Keys, Sampson	14803
Kanitobe, Sely	2816	Keys, Joseph	14804
Kanitobe, Sissie	2817	Keys, Clarence	15051
Kanitobe, Annie	2818	Keel, Charlie	11239
Kanitobe, Sidney	2819	Keel, Sumela	11240
Kanitobe, Walter	2820	Keel, Josiah	11241
Kanitobe, Wilburn	2827	Keel, Annie	11242
Kanitobe, Sam	3317	Keel, Arfus	11243
Kanitobe, Sallie	3118	Keel, Charley	11245
Kanitobe, Davis	3825	Kendle, Etta	12331
Kanitobe, Ellen	3826	Kellogg, Carlton B.	12827
Ka-nim-ubbe, Mollie	2493	Kelton, Lizzie S.	13059
Kanashambe, Forbis	3241	Kelton, Russ	13060
Kanashambe, Basin	3242	Ketcham, Thomas S.	14914
Kanashambe, Israel	3475	Kirkland, Rebecca	860
Kanashambe, Chostin	3476	Kirkland, Lulu May	861
Kanashambe, Malissa	3477	King, Margaret	1774
Kanashambia, Stephen	3257	King, Allington	2829
Kaneubbe, Moses	4434	King, Mary	2830
Kaneubbe, Betsy	4435	King, Isa	2831
Kaneubbe, Hampton	4436	King, Easton	2832
Kaneubbe, Thomas	4437	King, Hinson	2833
Kaneubbe, Eliza	14678	King, Stalen	2834
Kayser, Lula V.	7413	King, Simpson	3051
Kayser, Nola A.	7414	King, Petty	3052
Kayser, Lucile	7415	King, Missey	3057
Kayser, William G., Jr.	7416	King, Robin	3058
Kanehta, Morris	8468	King, Semia	3127
Kanehta, David	8469	King, Lina	3202
Kanehta, Annette	8470	King, Jenney	3204
Katiotubbi, Milton	11639	King, Harris	3234
Katiotubbi, Phoebe	11698	King, Arlington	3273
Katiotubbi, Johnson	11868	King, Anna	3619
Kampelubbi, Rhoda	11697	King, Elsie	3620
Karl, Viola	12440	King, Wicklis	3621
Karl, Earnest Harlan	12441	King, Bessie	3622
Kate, John	13474	King, Emily	3623
Kate, Mealey	13475	King, Charlisson Isac	3624
Kaniotubbe, Mitchell	14135	King, Sophia	5693
Kanahima,	3448	King, Adaline	6176
Kemp, Sophia Virginia	80	King, William	6372
Kemp, Nelson	3192	King, Lillie	6373
Kemp, Warren	9249	King, Charles	6374
Kemp, Ansie	9251	King, Emma	6375
Kemp, Stebbin	9252	King, George William	6376
Kemp, Joanna	12137	King, Nicodemus	7181
Kemp, Martin	12686	King, Letitia	7808
Kemp, Stanton	13135	King, Abel	8515
Kemp, Bennett	15498	King, Leonidas	8969
Kemp, Sinie	15499	King, Rachael	8970
Kemp, Lena	15591	King, Ada	8971
Kelly, Joe J.	844	King, Isaac	9291
Kelly, Judia	3901		

Name.	Roll No.	Name.	Roll No.
King, Ida	9292	Klugh, Eliza	9086
King, Mary J.	9614	Koozer, Charles H.	3744
King, Sealy	10646	Krebbs, Peter B.	7609
King, Jesse	10778	Krebbs, Milton A.	7610
King, Mitchell	11104	Krebbs, Pearl M.	7611
King, Emma	11105	Krebbs, John W.	14387
King, Silas	11106	Krebbs, Benjamin	14388
King, Anderson	11334	Krebbs, May	14389
King, Louvina	11335	Krebbs, John Odus	14390
King, McGee	11336	Krebbs, John	14391
King, Anderson Jr.	11337	Krebbs, Hubert	15844
King, Lucinda	11357	Krebs, Edmund H.	14438
King, Nelson	11358	Krebs, Minnie L.	14459
King, Anderson	12483	Krebs, Tisha V.	14440
King, William	12531	Krebs, Edna L.	15626
King, Charles	12880	Krebbe, Oscar	8212
King, Harris	12881	Krieger, Margaret A.	12985
King, Martha C.	12882	Krieger, Chrystal E.	12986
King, Mary E.	12883	Krieger, William E.	12987
Kng, Russell	12884	Krieger, Estelle L.	12988
King, William S.	12885	Krieger, Ethel L.	12989
King, Eva Ethel	12886	Krieger, Clarence S.	12990
King, Mack	12977	Krieger, Henry	12991
King, Lizzie	12978	Krieger, Jesse L.	12992
King, Josephine	12979	Krieger, Mary D.	12993
King, John	13077	Krieger, Karl E.	12994
King, Frances	13078	Krieger, Catherine M.	12995
King, Alice	13321	Krieger, Rosa E.	12996
King, Elie	13415	Krieger, Arthur B.	12997
King, Levenia	13430	Krieger, Charles F.	12998
King, Charles	13506	Krieger, Irena	12999
King, Calvin	13507	Krieger, Dee S.	13000
King, Susan	13583	Krieger, Mattie E.	13001
King, Mary A.	13893	Krieger, Frances L.	13002
King, Louisa	13894	Lawrence, S. S.	99
King, Hayes	13917	Lawrence, Osborne S.	9406
King, Robert	14045	Lawrence, Pikey	9407
King, Osie	14046	Lawrence, Green D.	9408
King, Willis	14047	Lawrence, Gilbert M.	9409
King, Gilbert	14048	Lawrence, Rosa	9410
King, Oscar	14049	Lawrence, Frank	9411
King, Sibbie	13353	Lawrence, Dave	9431
King, Jackson	13354	Lawrence, Emma	9537
King, Joel	13355	Lawrence, Lora K.	9538
King, Rady	15850	Lawrence, Henry	9539
Kincade, Sissie	2581	Lawrence, Frank T.	10397
Kincade, George	2718	Lawrence, Joseph R.	10398
Kincade, Anna	5659	Lawrence, Thelma Anna	10401
Kincade, Mary	6526	Lawrence, Canady	10997
Kincade, Lela M.	6902	Lawrence, Lucy	10998
Kincade, Robert	7866	Lawrence, William	10999
Kincade, Addie	7867	Lawrence, Osborne	11000
Kincade, George	7868	Lawrence, Betsy	11001
Kincade, Emerine F.	7869	Lawrence, Annie	11002
Kincade, Levina	7966	Lawrence, Silas	11096
Kincade, Alice	8798	Lawrence, Rosa A.	11097
Kincade, Kizzie	8799	Lawrence, Louis	11109
Kincade, Tennessee	12482	Lawrence, Edna	11110
Kirby, Ed	2996	Lawrence, Adam	12009
Kirby, Robert	3020	Lawrence, Azzie Anna	13628
Kirby, Kate	3021	Lawrence, J. R.	14500
Kirby, Murtie	3642	Lawrence, Joseph	14818
Kirby, Alice	3643	Lawechobe, Hopewell	1926
Kirkpatrick, Rena	3908	Lawechobe, Abner	1927
Kirkpatrick, Dewey M.	3909	Lawechobe, Gertrude	1928
Killingsworth, Edward	6326	LaFlore, Osborne	2064
Killingsworth, Rosanna	6327	LaFlore, Daniel	2065
Killingsworth, Serena B.	6328	Laflore, Bensey	14950
Killingsworth, Elenora	6329	Labor, Parmelia	3066
Kinslow, Jenison T.	6466	Labor, Alexander	3067
Kinslow, Magnettie	6467	Labor, Elliston	3068
Kinslow, Nellie	6468	Labor, Sarah J.	3069
Kinslow, Levergie	6469	Labor, Ida	3070
Kinches, William	7005	Labor, Phoebe	3071
Kinches, Winnie	7006	Labor, Ellen	3072
Kimmel, Robert	7445	Labor, Willie	3073
Kirkendall, Jane	15148	Labor, Annie	9745
Kirkendall, Sarah Amanda	15149	Labor, Ethel M.	9746
		Labor, Caroline	9747
Kirkendall, William Edward	15150	Labor, Phoebe	11003
		Labor, Henry	11005
Kirkendall, Willie Inez	15812	Labor, Rena M.	11006
Kirkendall, Ada Lee	15813	Labor, Virgie	11007
Kingsbury, Cyrus H.	15679	Labor, Alzona	11008

Name.	Roll No.
Labor, Namelia A.	11009
Labor, Victoria	15843
Lawitaya, Hodges	3455
Lawitaya, John	3457
Lawitaya, Isabel	3458
Latimer, Josephine B.	4024
Latimer, Mattie A.	4025
Latimer, Ruby N.	4026
Latimer, Osborn W.	4027
Latimer, Lula	11193
Latimer, Joseph B.	11194
Latimer, Lulu Mattie	11195
Latimer, Allie B.	14345
Latimer, Winifred	14346
Latimer, Alvin	14347
Law, Cora L.	4327
LaForce, Monte	6522
Lane, Allie	7204
Lane, Nicey E.	7206
Lane, Myrtle Catherine	7207
Lane, Frances	10502
Lane, Edward	10503
Lane, Bartholomew, Jr.	10504
Lane, Rosa	10505
Lane, Daisy	10506
Ladd, Susan	7575
Ladd, Bertha	7576
Ladd, Carrie	7577
Lanier, Edward	7838
Lanier, Rebecca	7839
Lanier, Edward Jr.	7840
Lanier, Susan	7841
Lanier, Jane	7842
Lanier, Henry B.	15433
Lankford, Mary	9440
Lankford, William F.	9441
Lankford, Lucretia Bell	9442
Lankford, Bertha M.	12092
Lankford, Oliver H.	12093
Lancaster, Isiah	9652
Lancaster, Bicey	9653
Lancaster, Johnny	9654
Lancaster, Sallie	9655
Lancaster, Ida	9656
Lauchner, Lela V.	10105
Lauchner, Fannie M.	10607
Lauchner, Fidelia E.	10608
Lanz, Lina	12671
Lanz, Annie M.	12672
Lanz, Benjamin	12673
Landis, Clara A.	12709
Landis, Wm. H.	12710
Landis, Joseph E.	12711
Landis, Syrena M.	12712
Landis, Harry Edmon	12713
Landis, Carrie Ann	12714
Lauderdale, Eliza	13136
Lauderdale, William T.	13138
Lawachubbee, Sallie	4533
Langley, Calcie Lee	14622
Langley, Matilda Sarah	14629
Land, Addie	14985
Lacey, Frank	15595
Landram, Janie	16044
Landram, Lola May	16045
Landram, Beulah Addison	16046
Latta, Thomas	10107
Latta, Alvis S.	10108
Leader, Morris	128
Leader, Louis	11611
Leader, Joel	11969
Leader, Icey	11970
Leader, James	11971
Leader, J. M.	12161
Leader, Mary A.	12236
Leader, Isabinda	13605
Leader, Odis	13606
Leader, Aaron	13607
Leader, Jim	13608
Leader, Alice	13609
Leader, Melinda	13610
Leader, Mary	13611
Leader, Silas	13866
Leewright, Fidy	165

Name.	Roll No.
Leewright, Pearl	166
Leewright, Lizzie	167
Leslie, W. J.	436
Leslie, Clifford	437
Leslie, Robert E.	438
Leslie, Beatrice	440
Lemon, John	905
Lemon, Salina	906
Lemon, Sarah	907
Lemon, Hudson	908
Lemon, Adaline	909
Lemon, Ida	14860
Lewis, Lucy	931
Lewis, David	932
Lewis, James	933
Lewis, Gaines	934
Lewis, Wattis	935
Lewis, Listie	936
Lewis, Wilson	940
Lewis, Cissy	941
Lewis, James	1213
Lewis, Beckie	1214
Lewis, Silvy	1669
Lewis, Littie	1967
Lewis, Wilson	1972
Lewis, Simmon	2115
Lewis, Nancy	3513
Lewis, Barefield	4846
Lewis, Susan	4847
Lewis, Sampson	4848
Lewis, John	4850
Lewis, Susianna	4851
Lewis, Nancy	4926
Lewis, Johnson	4982
Lewis, Isom	5099
Lewis, Mary	5152
Lewis, William	5155
Lewis, Simeon	5598
Lewis, Josiah	5700
Lewis, Marsie	5796
Lewis, Jamison	5797
Lewis, Henry	5798
Lewis, Renda	5799
Lewis, Arrenie	5800
Lewis, Rhoda	6084
Lewis, Catherine	6085
Lewis, Silas	6191
Lewis, Seas	6435
Lewis, Dixon	6437
Lewis, Carrie	6572
Lewis, Frank	7986
Lewis, Belle	7987
Lewis, Annie	7988
Lewis, Curtis	7989
Lewis, Alice	7990
Lewis, Winnie	7991
Lewis, Wallis G.	7992
Lewis, Alexander J.	8700
Lewis, Israel	8744
Lewis, Elizabeth	8745
Lewis, Artemissa	8851
Lewis, Cyrus	8853
Lewis, Easter	8854
Lewis, Woodson	8857
Lewis, Selina	8858
Lewis, Howard	8904
Lewis, Marie	8905
Lewis, William J.	8906
Lewis, Eden	8907
Lewis, Sallie	8946
Lewis, Lena	8956
Lewis, Judie	8960
Lewis, Anderson	9189
Lewis, Overton A.	9239
Lewis, Frank	9243
Lewis, Sullivan	9244
Lewis, Loren	9245
Lewis, Harriet	9373
Lewis, George	9401
Lewis, Nancy	9402
Lewis, Houston	9403
Lewis, Ben	9405
Lewis, Josiah	9644
Lewis, Johnson A.	9645
Lewis, Charles S.	9950

Name.	Roll No.	Name.	Roll No.
Lewis, Florence E.	10565	LeFlore, Mary	7141
Lewis, Rush C.	10566	LeFlore, Columbus	7143
Lewis, Dora L.	10567	LeFlore, Forbis	7178
Lewis, James W.	10568	LeFlore, Edna	7179
Lewis, Joslin	10575	LeFlore, Robert	7180
Lewis, Peter	10576	LeFlore, Artemissa	7251
Lewis, Gipson	10671	LeFlore, Nancy	7252
Lewis, Agnes	10672	LeFlore, Lillie	7295
Lewis, Lenn	10673	LeFlore, Felix	7543
Lewis, John	10761	LeFlore, Joe	7544
Lewis, Silas	10773	LeFlore, Campbell	7545
Lewis, Silvy	10774	LeFlore, John W.	7622
Lewis, Jiman	10799	LeFlore, Turner	7623
Lewis, Bacey	10922	LeFlore, Joseph	7624
Lewis, Rachael	10923	LeFlore, Myrtle	7625
Lewis, Emma	10956	LeFlore, Viola	7626
Lewis, Sophia	11090	LeFlore, Cyrus B.	7627
Lewis, Culberson	11276	LeFlore, Noel	7671
Lewis, Mulbert	13940	LeFlore, Louie	7695
Lewis, Levi	11451	LeFlore, Margaret	7848
Lewis, Jesse	11452	LeFlore, William	7849
Lewis, Atoka	11453	LeFlore, F. Greenwood	8023
Lewis, William	11839	LeFlore, Leona A.	8024
Lewis, Phoebe	11840	LeFlore, Florence L.	8025
Lewis, Israel	11925	LeFlore, Frank T.	8173
Lewis, Sarah	11926	LeFlore, Arizona	8260
Lewis, Joseph	11947	LeFlore, Selena	8563
Lewis, Eliza	11948	LeFlore, McAlester	8564
Lewis, Sallie	11981	LeFlore, Joseph Jr.	8565
Lewis, Sampson	11983	LeFlore, Minerva	8566
Lewis, Eliza	11984	LeFlore, Polina	8567
Lewis, John	11985	LeFlore, Wilmond	8736
Lewis, Simon E.	13009	LeFlore, Mack H.	8821
Lewis, Simon F.	13010	LeFlore, Sallie	8822
Lewis, George C.	13011	LeFlore, Matt H.	8824
Lewis, Ruth	13013	LeFlore, Ethel W.	8825
Lewis, John Calvin	13014	LeFlore, Virginia	8826
Lewis, Easter	13019	LeFlore, Willie J.	8827
Lewis, Evelena	13020	LeFlore, Mary	8915
Lewis, Thompson	13625	LeFlore, Malina	9975
Lewis, Dickson	13626	LeFlore, William	10169
Lewis, Emily	13808	LeFlore, Sophia	10173
Lewis, Ruthie	14355	LeFlore, Minerva	10174
Lewis, Dora	14356	LeFlore, Earnestine	10175
Lewis, Minnie	14776	LeFlore, Geneva	10176
Lewis, Abeline	8951	LeFlore, Moses	10252
Lewis, Simon	15048	LeFlore, Charles	10291
Lewis, Joseph	15171	LeFlore, Susanna	10292
Lewis, Elmer L.	15472	LeFlore, Mary	10293
Lewis, Johnson	16117	LeFlore, Lucy	10294
Lewis, Kitsy	16203	LeFlore, Jerry	10295
LeFlore, Joel	1700	LeFlore, Clemon	10391
LeFlore, Louie N.	2249	LeFlore, Mollie	10392
LeFlore, Salena	2250	LeFlore, Ezekiel	10635
LeFlore, Henry	2398	LeFlore, Forbis F.	10763
LeFlore, Minnie	2399	LeFlore, Loraine	10764
LeFlore, Levina	2400	LeFlore, Dreda	10765
LeFlore, Mitchell	2401	LeFlore, Forbis E.	10766
LeFlore, Nancy	2403	LeFlore, Jincy	11079
LeFlore, Johnny	2404	LeFlore, Henry C.	11177
LeFlore, James	2775	LeFlore, Ruby	11178
LeFlore, Miky	2776	LeFlore, Greenwood	11352
LeFlore, Carrie	4182	LeFlore, Nola	11353
LeFlore, Basil L.	4183	LeFlore, Louie	11354
LeFlore, Rosanna	4184	LeFlore, Corrinn	11355
LeFlore, Osborne	4185	LeFlore, James	11356
LeFlore, Laudry G.	4186	LeFlore, Charles	11388
LeFlore, Susie	4187	LeFlore, Joshua	11714
LeFlore, Isaac	4281	LeFlore, Louie	11715
LeFlore, Sophia	4409	LeFlore, Abel	11837
LeFlore, Isaac	4410	LeFlore, Moses	11838
LeFlore, Susan	4411	LeFlore, Mary	11866
LeFlore, Hattie	4413	LeFlore, Lucy A.	11867
LeFlore, Jesse	4414	LeFlore, Sina	11902
LeFlore, Frank	4415	LeFlore, Michael	12020
LeFlore, Carrie	4416	LeFlore, James	13086
LeFlore, Ada	4417	LeFlore, James Jr.	13087
LeFlore, Watson	5350	LeFlore, Charley	13088
LeFlore, Elizabeth	5351	LeFlore, Campbell	13089
LeFlore, Davis	5352	LeFlore, Ethel	13090
LeFlore, Wesley	5353	LeFlore, Luther	13091
LeFlore, Silwee	5354	LeFlore, Mathias C.	13092
LeFlore, Ida	6974	LeFlore, Lucius C.	13093
LeFlore, Cora	6975	LeFlore, Mary May	13095

Name.	Roll No.
LeFlore, Lucy	13419
LeFlore, Alexander	13420
LeFlore, Watson	13421
LeFlore, Cornelia	13422
LeFlore, Allen	13532
LeFlore, Ethel	13533
LeFlore, Viola	13534
LeFlore, Michael W.	13826
LeFlore, Rosanna	13827
LeFlore, William W.	13828
LeFlore, Jincey	13829
LeFlore, Jorilla	13830
LeFlore, Josephine	13831
LeFlore, David A.	13832
LeFlore, Thomas J.	13833
LeFlore, Joseph	13951
LeFlore, Louisa	13347
LeFlore, Louis C.	14378
LeFlore, Rosa	14379
LeFlore, Michael	14380
LeFlore, Josephine	14381
LeFlore, Helen	14382
LeFlore, Campbell	14383
LeFlore, Abbott	14384
LeFlore, Morris	14641
LeFlore, Wilburn	14642
LeFlore, Forbis	14643
LeFlore, Jefferson	14674
LeFlore, Flora	14753
LeFlore, Greenwood	14771
LeFlore, Chester H.	15604
LeFlore, Chester H. Jr.	15605
LeFlore, Louis	15660
LeFlore, Irene C.	15661
LeFlore, LeRoy C.	15662
LeFlore, Bensey	14950
LeFlore, Sarah	15842
LeFlore, Isaac	15948
LeFlore, Jincy	15949
LeFlore, Wicy	15950
Leflore, Narcissa	2846
Leflore, Ada	2848
Lee, John M.	3948
Lee, Ella M.	3949
Lee, Mack	9575
Lee, Minnie	9576
Lee, Clarence	9577
Lee, Sophie	9578
Lee, Beatrice	9579
Lee, Osborne	9580
Lee, Thomas D.	14969
Lee, Willie H.	14970
Lee, Mamie A.	14971
Lenox, Lena	4657
Lenox, Wilson	4658
Leard, Cora	7704
Leard, Joseph N.	7705
Leard, Walter F.	7707
Leard, James A.	7708
Leard, Cora H.	7709
Leard, Robert R.	7710
Leard, Terry T.	7711
Leard, Laura A.	7712
Leard, Wheeler R.	7713
Ledou, Annie	9187
Ledou, Eudith E.	9188
Lester, Alice	14140
Lester, McCurtain	14141
Lester, Lucile	14142
Lester, Wynema	14143
Lester, Louise A.	14145
Lester, Preston S., Jr.	14146
Levi, Simeon	9880
Leeper, Grace Olive	14212
Leeper, Myrtle	14213
Leeper, Roy Davis	14214
Little, Lucy Wadkins	145
Little, Moma	146
Little, Frederick T.	147
Lindsay, Juanita	347
Lindsay, Tessie	348
Lindsay, Fannie	349
Lindsay, John	350
Lindsay, Guy	351

Name.	Roll No.
Lindsay, Mamie	353
Lindsey, Nina	15361
Lindsey, Quintella	15362
Lindsey, Benj. B.	15363
Lindsey, Mattie M.	15364
Lindsey, Ethel	15365
Lindsey, Guy	15366
Lindsey, Eva	15367
Lindsey, Zona	15368
Litrell, Joseph J.	3074
Litrell, Mary A.	3075
Link, Ida	12346
Link, Minnie G.	12347
Link, Edna M.	12348
Link, Arthur C.	12349
Link, Ada B.	12350
Link, Myrtle A.	12351
Link, Bertha J.	12352
Littlepage, Lucy E.	15629
Lloyd, Ida	13815
Lloyd, Anneta	13816
Lloyd, Charley	13817
Lloyd, William Gregg	13818
Lloyd, Russell	13819
Lowery, George L.	489
Lowery, Josephine	492
Lowery, Olive	493
Lowery, Choctaw	494
Lowery, Coleman	495
Lowery, Renia	496
Lowery, Goldie Lee	498
Lowery, Cordelia	7008
Lowery, Goldie L.	7009
Lowery, Samuel S.	7010
Lowery, Thomas M. Sr.	10866
Lowery, Thomas M. Jr.	10867
Lowery, Effie A.	10868
Lowery, Nevada	10869
Lowery, Joseph H.	10870
Lowery, Miller Emmett	10871
Lowery, Benjamin H.	11224
Lowery, Franklin	11225
Lowery, Ida M.	11226
Lowery, Myrtle	11227
Lowery, Ola	11228
Locke, Josie	885
Locke, Jimmie Susan	886
Locke, Victor M. Jr.,	4912
Locke, Ben D.	4914
Locke, Jesse N.	4915
Locke, Edwin S.	4916
Locke, Curtis	4917
Locke, James S.	4958
Locke, Jane	13406
Locke, Bertie	13407
Locke, Jesse	13409
Locke, Wilson	13918
Locke, Marion	13919
Locke, Mary Jane	13920
Locke, Sina J.	14032
Locke, Mattie P.	14033
Locke, Victor B.	14034
Locke, Elisha	14833
Locke, Mary	14834
Locke, Nellie	15500
Logan, Adeline	1297
Logan, Thompson	1335
Logan, Bias	1336
Logan, Sam	1337
Logan, Lina	2828
Logan, Calvin	3220
Logan, Joel	3227
Logan, Nancy	11783
Logan, Clemiake	13384
Logan, Loman	15396
Louis, Jesse	1309
Louis, Empsie	1310
Louis, Williamson	1311
Louis, Wilbert	1312
Louis, Bond	1753
Louis, Ellen	1754
Louis, Solomon	1755
Louis, Silas	1756
Louis, Liza	2690

Name.	Roll No.	Name.	Roll No.
Louis, Mary	3238	Long, Charles Henry	15708
Louis, Winey	3239	Long, Celeste	15710
Louis, Louisa	3240	Loving, John D.	6421
Louis, Johnson	3587	Loving, Sampson	8437
Louis, Gilbert	14611	Lofton, Charles W.	6721
Louis, Jefferson	15047	Lomby, Lucy	8335
Louis, Ada	15575	Low, Emanuel H.	12761
Louis, Katie	15576	Low, Nelia J.	12762
Loman, Bessie	1503	Low, Frances L. M.	12763
Loman, Samwell	1504	Low, Hugh S.	12764
Loman, Lowina	1505	Low, Anna E.	12765
Loman, Greek L.	1954	Lowe, Ella I.	14175
Loman, Emiline	1955	Lowe, Minnie	15517
Loman, Malsie	1956	Lowe, George	15518
Loman, Roxie	1957	Love, Robert M.	14458
Loman, Sarah	2326	Love, Elma E.	14459
Loman, Mary Jane	2573	Love, Arthur	14460
Loman, Willie	2725	Love, Sidney	14461
Loman, Sissy	2900	Love, Harry	14462
Loman, Burt	2901	Love, Robert M., Jr.	14463
Loman, Siah	2902	Lockley, Sillian	14748
Loman, Elizabeth	2922	Lomer, Mary	15756
Loman, Agnes	2923	Lucas, Luvicey	1141
Loman, Lucy Ann	2963	Lucas, Phoebe	1143
Loman, Lena	2965	Lucas, Joshua	7905
Loman, Thomas	3380	Lucas, Jennie	7906
Loman, Oscar	3381	Lucas, Frank	7907
Loman, Frank	3628	Lucas, Johnson	9792
Loman, Narcissy	3698	Lucas, Adam	10553
Loman, Peter	3699	Lucas, Johnson	11042
Loman, Clay	4524	Lucas, Susan	13431
Loman, Sillen	4525	Luce, Lefen	2358
Loman, Wilken	4526	Luce, Solomon	4729
Loman, Eliza	5020	Luce, Selina	7222
Loman, Annie	5038	Luce, Elbert	7223
Loman, William	6664	Luce, Tom	7373
Loman, Kizzie	8598	Luce, Selina	7374
Loman, Sillis	8891	Luce, Lita	15751
Loman, Charles	11580	Ludlow, Willis	5808
Loman, Kitise	11581	Ludlow, Emma	5809
Loman, Stephen	11582	Ludlow, Meton	5810
Loman, Gilliam	14632	Ludlow, Watkins	5811
Loman, Annie	14925	Ludlow, Anis	5812
Lowman, Elias	1565	Ludlow, Caroline	5813
Lowman, Lartie	1566	Ludlow, Austin	5895
Lowman, Moses	1786	Ludlow, Payson	5981
Lowman, Itie	1848	Ludlow, Sina	5982
Lowman, Ellis	2741	Ludlow, Nicey	5983
Lowman, Lista	2742	Ludlow, Esbie	5984
Lowman, Sallie	2743	Ludlow, Henry J.	6062
Lowman, Robert	2744	Ludlow, Mason	6063
Lowman, Davis	2745	Ludlow, Linsey	6064
Lowman, Keith	2746	Ludlow, Lisarney	6065
Lowman, Leviah	14633	Ludlow, Silward	6066
Loma, Thomas	1921	Ludlow, Marsey	6067
Loma, Annie	1922	Ludlow, Marlie	6068
Loma, James	14590	Ludlow, Anna W.	9088
Lo-ma	1925	Ludlow, Lillie	14715
Louie, Ennis	2391	Ludlow, John	14718
Loyd, Sarah	2604	Ludlow, Ellis	14719
Loud, Melissa	2847	Luke, Emma	8497
Loring, William H.	4594	Luke, David	14136
Loring, Solomon	4889	Luttrel, Ida	14392
Loring, Thomas	4890	Luttrel, Dexter	14393
Loring, Sibby	11892	Luttrel, Jessie	14394
Loring, Edmond	13892	Lucy, Harry J.	15827
Loring, Naomi	15411	Luckly, Louvinia	16227
Long, Rhoda	5753	Lynn, Ida Belle	396
Long, Julia May	5754	Lynn, Wyley Ulysses	397
Long, Effie	5756	Lynn, Will Andrew	398
Long, Frost	5757	Lynn, Worlie	399
Long, Willie A.	5758	Lynn, Laura Belle	400
Long, Wilson James	5759	Lynn, Pearlie Huston	401
Long, Rowena	7687	Lynn, E. E.	402
Long, Beatrice	7688	Lynn, Ada Winnie	403
Long, Flaurah B.	7854	Lynn, Laura	433
Long, Beulah Olena	7860	Lynn, Tamsberry	434
Long, Jesse	8196	Lynn, Maggie Tammie	435
Long, Lucy	11272	Lynn, Elsie L.	513
Long, Letitia C.	12530	Lynn, Lena B.	514
Long, Martha	13987	Lynn, Mary Cordelia	516
Long, LeRoy D.	13988	Lynn, Durley Elvie	14499
Long, Wendell McLean	13989	Lyle, Lula	794
Long, Ida	15703	Lyle, Ada	795

Name.	Roll No.	Name.	Roll No.
Lyle, Daisy	796	Martin, Canzada	13521
Lyle, Mabel	797	Martin, Howard Lee	13525
Lyle, Cleo	798	Martin, Sam	14995
Lyle, Robert Clifford	799	Martin, Willie	14996
Lyles, Hermon P.	6891	Martin, Oscar	15927
Lyles, William A.	7629	Makintubbee, Douglas	5733
Lyles, Lorenzo	7630	Matthews, Rosa	6323
Lyles, Eugene	7631	Matthews, Atha	6324
Lyles, Myrtle	7632	Matthews, Dero	6325
Lyles, Luther	7633	Mathews, Sarah E.	10919
Lyles, Cleland	7634	Mathews, Eliza	10920
Lyles, Dewey Y.	7635	Mathews, Annie	10921
Lyles, Hallie	7636	Mathews, Fannie A.	15354
Mays, Birdy	252	Mathews, Harvey A.	15355
Mays, S. J.	254	Mathews, Augustus F.	15356
Mays, James L.	686	Mathews, Alma Lee	15357
Mays, Ida Preston	687	Mathews, Aroma B.	15358
Mays, John Edward	688	Maxwell, Ida	7241
Mays, William Phillip	689	Maxwell, Lela L.	7242
Mackey, E. M.	277	Maxwell, Ida Lee	7243
Mackey, Missouri Lee	278	Maxwell, Sidney C.	7244
Mackey, Louis	279	Mason, Susan	7579
Mackey, Elum	280	Mason, Grant	7587
Mackey, Dolph	281	Marcum, Rosa	9413
Mackey, Forbis	6544	Marcum, Henry Clay	9414
Mackey, Eli	6546	Marcum, Cordelia	15711
Mackey, Solomon H.	12920	Marcum, Jesse	15712
Mackey, Elizabeth H.	12921	Marcum, Claudie	15713
Mackey, David M.	12922	Marcum, Clarence	15714
Mackey, Benjamin P.	12923	Marcum, Lulu	15715
Mackey, Willis W.	12924	Manning, Nannie H.	10400
Mackey, Beulah A.	12925	Manning, Jennie E.	10402
Mackey, Solomon H. Jr.	12926	Manning, Forbis	10533
Mackey, Narcissa E.	12927	Manning, Lizzie	10534
Mackey, Malina A.	12928	Manning, Edgar	10535
Mackey, Ouida L.	12929	Manning, Eula	10536
Mauldin, Betsie	506	Manning, Matilda	11015
Mauldin, Emma E.	507	Manning, Thomas J.	11016
Mauldin, Minnie M.	508	Manning, Arthur F.	11017
Mauldin, Gertie Arizona	509	May, Abner	10682
Mauldin, Josephine	5346	Matoy, Mary A.	10884
Mauldin, Joseph Q.	5347	Matoy, Ora	10886
Mauldin, Alberta P.	5348	Matoy, Albert	10888
Mauldin, Gertrude	5349	Mayo, Tabitha A.	11133
Maytobe, Rayburn	1376	Mayo, Leonard	11134
Maytobe, Nancy	1377	Mayo, Edna	11135
Maytobe, Benson	1378	Mayo, Albert	11136
Maytobe, Samaie	1379	Mayo, Lula	11137
Maytobe, Selin	1380	Mayo, John	11138
Maytobe, Harrison	1381	Maurer, Mary	11170
Maytobe, Mattie	1384	Maurer, Leonidas M.	11172
Maytobe, Armstead	1385	Mann, Stella	11323
Maytobe, Annie	2713	Marshal, Alwilda H.	12128
Maytobe, Lazin	2714	Marshal, Gracie	12131
Maytobe, Quintus	14572	Marshal, Richard L.	12132
Makatobe, Sarly	1499	Marshal, Delilah M.	12133
Makatobe, Seely	1500	Marshal, Joseph E.	12134
Makatobe, David	1501	Marshal, Chock	12135
Mambi, Williamson	1516	Marshall, Belle	12177
Mambi, Ellen	1517	Marshall, Henry	12273
Mambi, Stile	1518	Marshall, Ludie Paul	15095
Mambi, Wattis	1519	Marshall, Osburn Gil-	
Mambi, Norman	1520	bert	15096
Mambi, Jennie	1592	Marshall, Robert L.	15690
Mambi, Ramus	2386	Marshall, William Hen-	
Martin, Lizzie	2599	ry	15757
Martin, Rogers	4106	Marshall, William Hen-	
Martin, Bennett	6436	ry, Jr.	15758
Martin, Anna	7375	Marston, Bulah	12230
Martin, William	7376	Marston, Willie	15790
Martin, Isabella	7377	Marston, Johnnie	15791
Martin, William	7637	Mattix, Harriet	12543
Martin, Kizzie	7638	Mathis, Mary J.	12904
Martin, James	7639	Mathis, Eliza	12905
Martin, Turner	7641	Mathis, Susan F.	12906
Martin, Elsie	7642	Mathis, Josephine	12907
Martin, Bettie	7643	Manners, Eva	13169
Martin, Lela	7644	Massey, William W.	14419
Martin, Hubert	7645	Massey, Oliver	14420
Martin, Sillen	13145	Massey, Edmund	14422
Martin, Gertrude	13146	Massey, Benjamin H.	14423
Martin, Edmund	13147	Massey, Jessie	14424
Martin, Tandy W.	13148	Massey, Earnest E.	14425
Martin, Mary	13377	Massey, Reby Louise	14427

Name.	Roll No.
Massey, William W. Jr.	14820
Marlow, Crawford	15685
Marlow, Reuben F.	15686
Marlow, William J.	15687
Marlow, George	15688
Marlow, Ola	15689
Meshontambi, Louisa	125
Meshontambi, Frances	126
Meshaya, James	3285
Meashintubby, Silman	5892
Meashintubby, Nancy	5893
Meashintubby, Eastman	5894
Meashintubby, Julius	6009
Meashintubby, Nancy	6010
Meashintubby, Ida	6012
Meashintubby, Jackson	6028
Meashintubby, Lizzie	6029
Meashintubby, Missie	6030
Meashintubby, William	6322
Meashintubby, Frances	6346
Meashintubby, Susan	6356
Merryman, James F.	7895
Merryman, Earl Q.	7896
Merryman, Lillian Jo-anna	7897
Merryman, William B.	8168
Merryman, William H.	8169
Merryman, Frank S.	8170
Merryman, Nancy J.	8171
Merryman, Ezra Ruben	8172
Merryman, Leonidas	8181
Merryman, Daniel W.	8182
Merryman, Lee Roy	8183
Merryman, Theodore	8184
Merryman, John S.	8235
Merryman, Belva	8237
Merryman, John Q.	8238
Merryman, Roscoe C.	8239
Merryman, Ophelia	8240
Merryman, Minnie I.	8241
Merryman, Erie V.	8242
Merryman, Theodore Scott	8243
Merryman, Frances	8321
Merryman, David C.	8455
Merryman, Abraham	8456
Merryman, Mary J. F.	8457
Merryman, William H.	8458
Merryman, Leo E.	8459
Merryman, Walter G.	8460
Merryman, John D.	8461
Merryman, Zado C.	8462
Merryman, Izora Lula	8463
Merryman, Gabe	8464
Merryman, Gipson B.	8513
Merryman, Agnes	8514
Meshemahtubbee, Se-melian	8436
Medell, Susan	10950
Medell, William O.	10951
Medell, Lela May	10952
Medell, Lula	12194
Merrill, Elinor A.	12251
Merrill, Soulie Miriam	12252
Merrill, Anna	12395
Meadows, Laura	13024
Meadows, Leslie	13025
Meadows, Sherman A.	13026
Meggs, Jesse	13568
Meggs, Elijah	13569
Merry, Bessie	15526
Merry, Ida May	15527
Meek, Jacob	15737
Meek, James H.	15738
Meek, Calvin W.	15739
Milton, Silon	1387
Milton, Sylon	6057
Milton, George	6058
Milton, Malinda	6059
Milton, Lacin	6060
Milton, Lymon	6061
Milton, Mila	6594
Milton, Mary	6596
Mishaia, Rhoda	1547

Name.	Roll No.
Mitchell, Annie	1694
Mitchell, Elcie	3481
Mitchell, Jane	5735
Mitchell, Ely E.	7097
Mitchell, Mattie B.	7098
Mitchell, Ely S., Jr.	7100
Mitchell, Mary	7101
Mitchell, Sarah	7102
Mitchell, William F.	9586
Mitchell, William L.	9940
Mitchell, William L. Jr.	9941
Mitchell, Emily Y.	9942
Mitchell, Missouri	10070
Mitchell, Sallie	10684
Mitchell, Isaac	10685
Mitchell, Alice	10686
Mitchell, Ida	14151
Mitchell, Jose V.	14502
Mitchell, Bernice	14503
Mitchell, Mary	14561
Mitchell, Elmira	14943
Mitchell, John Allen	15654
Mitchell, Emma	15655
Mitchell, Allen Yates	15656
Mitchell, Willie	15657
Mintihaya, Silmy	2687
Miller, Henry	4190
Miller, Sophia	4192
Miller, Frances	4193
Miller, Ida	4194
Miller, Daniel	4953
Miller, Sallie	4954
Miller, Davis	4955
Miller, Lizzie	4956
Miller, Caroline	4957
Miller, Fannie	4987
Miller, Leo Victor	4988
Miller, Edgar P.	11876
Miller, Ruby Marie	11877
Miller, Samuel G.	11880
Miller, William W.	11882
Miller, James H. Jr.	11883
Miller, Ella J.	11879
Miller, Ruby C.	11884
Miller, Edith R.	11885
Miller, Frank Wright	11886
Miller, Serena J.	12715
Miller, Alta M.	12716
Miller, Joseph J.	12717
Miller, Rena P.	14036
Miller, Myrtle	14037
Miller, Stephen	14533
Miller, Lucretia R.	14901
Miller, Andrew B.	15840
Mihyachubbee, Joseph	4455
Mihyachubbee, Lizzie	4456
Minehart, Walter K.	7509
Minehart, Myrtle	7510
Minehart, John	7512
Minehart, Mary M.	7513
Minehart, Eva	7515
Minehart, George	7516
Minehart, Lorena	7517
Minton, Barney	8194
Miyabe, Esias	8977
Miyabe, Clara	8979
Mishamahtubbee, Lena	9050
Mishamahtubbee, Davis	9054
Mishamahtubbee, Wynie	9055
Mishamahtubbee, Lizzie	9056
Mishamahtubbee, Alice	9057
Mishontambi, Betsy	9415
Mishontambi, Daniel	9417
Mishontambi, Loman	9418
Mishontambi, Bency	15918
Middleton, Agnes	10143
Middleton, Eva	10144
Mitts, Lucinda	10324
Mitts, Dora E.	10325
Mitts, Dolly M.	10326
Mitts, Dovey	10327
Miashaya, Rinda	11862
Miashaya, Adeline	11863
Miashintube, Silbina	13428

Name.	Roll No.	Name.	Roll No.
Miashintube, Martha	13429	Moore, Sealy	3601
Morse, Mabel	275	Moore, Linnie	3602
Morris, Rhoda Folsom	427	Moore, Ainsworth	3603
Morris, Joel	770	Moore, Sarlin	3605
Morris, Charles	1044	Moore, Frances	3720
Morris, Rhoda	1045	Moore, Allie	3722
Morris, George	1053	Moore, Thomas G	4893
Morris, David	1054	Moore, John R.	4894
Morris, Betsy	1055	Moore, Iva	5420
Morris, Forbis	1056	Moore, Etna	5224
Morris, Solon	2967	Moore, Lena	5529
Morris, Almer	2968	Moore, Thompson	6681
Morris, Gilbert	4631	Moore, William	6847
Morris, Lucy	5063	Moore, Ellen	6949
Morris, Emma	5064	Moore, Sopha	6949
Morris, Joseph	5065	Moore, Lime	6950
Morris, Abner	5066	Moore, Edgar A.	7421
Morris, Winnie	5067	Moore, Jessie M.	7422
Morris, Simeon	5411	Moore, Pauline	7423
Morris, Polly	5412	Moore, Alvin Custer	7424
Morris, Minnie	5414	Moore, Fannie E.	7843
Morris, Sidney	5415	Moore, Lyman R.	7844
Morris, Cowdy	5417	Moore, Herbert M.	7845
Morris, Isham	5568	Moore, Napoleon B.	7846
Morris, Silas	5668	Moore, Lena B.	7847
Morris, Sibbie	5666	Moore, David A.	8055
Morris, Esias	5889	Moore, Stacy	8056
Morris, Robert	6600	Moore, Thomas	8057
Morris, William G.	5601	Moore, Cecil	8058
Morris, Robert H.	6602	Moore, Ira May	8059
Morris, Lee	6896	Moore, Andrew J	8079
Morris, Nelson	7368	Moore, Laura	8080
Morris, Arian	7578	Moore, Gertrude	8082
Morris, Robert	7580	Moore, Beuna	8083
Morris, Eddie	7581	Moore, Elsie	8685
Morris, Abbie	7582	Moore, Joseph	9044
Morris, Cora	7583	Moore, Selina	9052
Morris, Alice	7584	Moore, Willis	10562
Morris, Gus	7585	Moore, Elie	10668
Morris, Jane	7586	Moore, Sophina	10669
Morris, Alfred	10730	Moore, Loring	10718
Morris, Allington	11653	Moore, Serena	10719
Morris, Emma	11654	Moore, Suffee	10720
Morris, Temelius	11655	Moore, Rosa	10821
Morris, Forbis	11656	Moore, John E.	10825
Morris, Malinda	11657	Moore, Annie	11464
Morris, William	11658	Mooer, Fannie	11794
Morris, Peter	11659	Moore, Ida	11796
Morris, Rhoda S.	13504	Moore, Joseph R.	12002
Morris, Lorin Folsom	14254	Moore, Samuel	12136
Morris, Edward P.	14255	Moore, Alice M.	12204
Morris, Walter H.	14256	Moore, Olive M.	12356
Morris, McKinly S.	15413	Moore, James H.	12357
Morris, Agnes	15760	Moore, Lucile	12358
Morris, Artiamissia	15786	Moore, Selma	12359
Moore, Alice Camp	479	Moore, Angeline	12528
Moore, Bradford C.	480	Moore, Henry	12782
Moore, Jesse L.	624	Moore, Virgil	12783
Moore, Rosie Jessie	625	Moore, Mattie	12784
Moore, Joseph Hillary	626	Moore, Susan	12785
Moore, Ivy	627	Moore, Ella	12786
Moore, Sylvia	628	Moore, John H.	13005
Moore, Samuel	629	Moore, Oscar	13006
Moore, William H.	630	Moore, Robert	13047
Moore, Mary Cordella	631	Moore, James E.	13633
Moore, Martha Ann	632	Moore, Nancy C.	13634
Moore, Janie Lizzie	633	Moore, Mary Jennie	13635
Moore, Onie Hester	634	Moore, Austin	13759
Moore, William Lyles	635	Moore, Joseph	13802
Moore, Olley Robert	636	Moore, Nathaniel	13899
Moore, Ira Tabitha	637	Moore, Christopher D.	13945
Moore, Preston	946	Moore, Gertie	14127
Moore, Thomas	693	Moore, Maude	14257
Moore, Mary J.	694	Moore, Will McClain	14506
Moore, Elizabeth	695	Moore, Frank	14534
Moore, Robert Thomas	696	Moore, Mattie	14915
Moore, Benjamin O.	697	Moore, Levi L.	14916
Moore, Henrietta	698	Moore, Joe J.	14917
Moore, Lily	717	Moore, Susie O.	14918
Moore, Mary	734	Moore, Ben	15398
Moore, Dora	735	Moore, Maud	15676
Moore, Sampson	737	Moore, Malinda	15677
Moore, Emily	3208	Moore, Ada Bell	15733
Moore, John	3600	Moore, Roy L.	15735

Name.	Roll No.
Moore, Floyd S.	15836
Moore, Maud Alleen	15837
Mouser, Robert B.	699
Moss, Lurinda	781
Moss, Lue Willie	14541
Moss, Dora May	782
Moncrief, William	835
Moncrief, Jeff	836
Moncrief, James	837
Moncrief, Wallace	838
Moncrief, Lulu	839
Moncrief, John	840
Moncrief, William Jr.	841
Moncrief, Tolbert	842
Moncrief, Mary M.	843
Moncrief, Cap R.	12652
Moncrief, Ester	12653
Moncrief, George	13235
Moncrief, Byron	13242
Moncrief, Margaret	14548
Morrison, Charles W.	903
Morrison, Sarah	904
Morrison, Aleus	1696
Morrison, Lizzie	1697
Morrison, Paul St.	1698
Morrison, Hannibal E.	13187
Monintubbi, Sampson	3690
Mowdy, Caroline	3724
Mowdy, Elsie E.	3725
Mowdy, Margaret I.	3726
Mowdy, Lola O.	3727
Mowdy, Dieta	3728
Mowdy, Delena	3729
Mowdy, Nora Clemintine	3730
Mowdy, Viola	12099
Mowdy, John E.	12100
Mowdy, Ollie L.	12101
Mowdy, Claude	12102
Mowdy, Clide	12104
Mowdy, Lesley Lenton	12105
Monkus, Samuel	4152
Moyer, Mary J.	5246
Moyer, Grove S.	5248
Moyer, James C.	5249
Monroe, Milton	6829
Monroe, Annie	6830
Monroe, Millie	6831
Monroe, Bennett	6832
Monroe, Carrie	6833
Mote, Letha A.	7336
Motes, Levina	9506
Motes, Jefferson	9508
Motes, Dora Ann	9509
Morgan, Lorena M.	9648
Morgan, Floyd E.	9649
Morgan, Lottie V.	9650
Morgan, Doris	9651
Morgan, Stella	11534
Morgan, Reginal M.	11538
Morgan, Alice	13706
Morgan, Helen Lee	13707
Morgan, William Allen	13708
Moses, Daniel	9866
Moses, Lorena	9867
Moses, Elias	9868
Moses, Charles	12178
Moran, Daniel S.	10441
Moran, Marmaduke L.	10442
Moran, Emet B.	10443
Moran, Ova S.	10444
Moran, Elizabeth	10445
Moran, Charles H.	10446
Moran, John B.	10447
Moran, Charles	10449
Moran, Robert R.	10450
Moran, John W.	11232
Moran, Thomas	11233
Moran, Anna Laura	11234
Moran, Marmaduke Y.	15151
Moran, George M.	15152
Moran, Charles W.	15155
Moran, Bertie	15156
Moran, Cora	15157
Moran, Bessie Lee	15158

Name.	Roll No.
Moran, James E.	15743
Moran, Maude, Ola	15744
Moran, Georgia Elnora	15745
Montague, Lottie Marie	8109
Moseley, Charles S.	10644
Moseley, Wilson	10914
Mosely, William	11250
Mosely, Ida	13886
Mozley, Laura E.	15477
Mozley, Lena B.	15478
Mozley, Warren M.	15479
Mozley, Karl C.	15480
Mozley, Lois	15481
Monds, Richard	11623
Monds, Minda L.	11624
Monds, Farris	11625
Monds, Josie Lee	11626
Morrell, Sophia	12533
Morrell, Lee T.	13250
Murray, Alzira	129
Murray, Erin	130
Murray, Lula	131
Murray, Rebecca	4397
Murray, Ida	14321
Murray, Belle	14846
Murray, Arthur	14851
Murray, Heward	14852
Murray, Liddie	14853
Murray, Aldie L.	14854
Muncrief, Sam	267
Muncrief, Walter L.	268
Muncrief, Georgia	269
Muncrief, Sammie Myrtle	270
Muncrief, Linney	14191
Muncrief, Gracie	14481
Muldrow, Mary Daisy	647
Muldrow, Osborn Fisher	649
Murphy, Joe	3340
Murphy, Molsey	3341
Murphy, Jane	5735
Murphy, Robinson	13385
Murphy, Burly Sedalia	15214
Murphy, Trase	16052
Mullin, Morris	9074
Mullin, Sallie	11549
Mullin, Celie	13432
Mullen, Ada	11171
Mullen, Joseph S., Jr.	11173
Mullens, Tempy	13835
Mullens, Lewis	13836
Mullens, Claude	13837
Mullens, Marvin Allen	13838
Mugler, Theodocia	10953
Mugler, Delphine	10954
Munkus, Lewie	13330
Munkus, Ether	13331
Munkus, Joseph G.	13332
Munkus, Estell D.	13333
Myer, Lucy A.	10319
Myer, Harriet	10320
Myer, Eleat	10321
Myer, Linda	10705
McAlester, Wallace	1277
McAlester, Nancy	1278
McAlester, Aves	1279
McAlester, James	1280
McAlester, Ellen	1282
McAlister, William	4896
McAfee, Allen	2444
McAfee, Netsey	2445
McAfee, Josephine	2864
McAfee, Alice	2865
McAfee, Selina	2866
McAfee, Wilmon	2867
McAfee, Frank	2886
McAfee, Selina	2887
McAfee, Josephine	2888
McAfee, Jackson	11720
McAfee, Molsey	11721
McAfee, Hettie	14636
McAlvain, Polk	6445
McAlvain, Stonewall J.	6446
McAlvain, Robert	6447

Name.	Roll No.	Name.	Roll No.
McAlvain, Louis Riley	6448	McCoy, Freeman	1997
McAlvain, John W.	6449	McCoy, Moses	1995
McAlvain, William R.	6450	McCoy, Louisa	1998
McAlvain, Thomas J.	6451	McCoy, Ellas	2000
McAlvain, Florence	6452	McCoy, Sallie	2001
McAlvain, David W.	6453	McCoy, Alson	2002
McAlvain, Andy C.	6454	McCoy, Sam	2004
McAlvain, Odus	6455	McCoy, Wickits	2177
McAlvain, Orin Earle	14723	McCoy, Sillan	2178
McBride, Florence V.	4329	McCoy, Semencie	2179
McBride, Winnie	12013	McCoy, Alice	2603
McBride, Philip P.	15471	McCoy, Hilbon M	3818
McBee, Ella	12444	McCoy, Mullein	3819
McBee, Pryor Edward	12447	McCoy, Reuben	3919
McBrayer, Eddie	7600	McCoy, Sophia	3920
McClung, Wm. Oscar	103	McCoy, Alex	4080
McClung, Clarence M.	105	McCoy, John	4662
McClung, Fannie Dell	106	McCoy, Lillian	5979
McClung, Emma	601	McCoy, Layzinta	5980
McClung, George	602	McCoy, Wisey	6190
McClung, Eddie	603	McCoy, Georgia L.	10123
McClung, Arto	604	McCoy, Estella C.	10124
McCurtain, Allen C.	783	McCoy, Clarence B.	10125
McCurtain, Rebecca	784	McCoy, Isaac C.	10126
McCurtain, Jane F.	5404	McCoy, Hannah	11811
McCurtain, Eliza A.	5405	McCoy, Ellas	12021
McCurtain, Lucinda S.	5406	McCoy, Simon	15594
McCurtain, Ida N.	5407	McCoy, Claud E.	15998
McCurtain, Lizzie D.	5408	McClure, Preeman J.	1158
McCurtain, Cleopatra A.	5410	McClure, Laura	1159
McCurtain, Jackson	6050	McClure, Ida	1160
McCurtain, Allen	6051	McClure, Sarah Arte-	
McCurtain, Ruthie	6585	missa	1161
McCurtain, Ada	6591	McClure, Peter	1749
McCurtain, Edmond	6598	McClure, Lefina	1750
McCurtain, Mack	6679	McClure, Levisa	1751
McCurtain, Houston	6688	McClure, Leunie	1752
McCurtain, Mary V. J.	6689	McClure, Elliston	2929
McCurtain, Mollie	6733	McClure, Gibson	2931
McCurtain, Elum	6886	McClure, Minnie	2932
McCurtain, Nail P.	6887	McClure, Sam	2939
McCurtain, Zack T.	6888	McClure, Selfin	3009
McCurtain, Green	6889	McClure, Louie	3149
McCurtain, Joel	6935	McClure, Dixon	3243
McCurtain, Winnie	8391	McClure, Betsy	3244
McCurtain, Mitchell	8392	McClure, Walter	3245
McCurtain, Osborne	8393	McClure, Mary Belle	3247
McCurtain, Thomas	8485	McClure, Jourdan	3248
McCurtain, Minnie	8486	McClure, Reuben	3459
McCurtain, Green	8535	McClure, Ellen	3460
McCurtain, Katie	8536	McClure, Fannie	3461
McCurtain, Lena	8537	McClure, Jennie	3462
McCurtain, Cora	8538	McClure, Newton	3463
McCurtain, Bertha	8539	McClure, Oscar	3464
McCurtain, Lester	8540	McClure, Mollis	3465
McCurtain, Siley	8611	McClure, Isabel	3466
McCurtain, Thomas	8612	McClure, Stephen	3631
McCurtain, Martha	8613	McClure, Lena	3632
McCurtain, Mary	8614	McClure, Alex	3633
McCurtain, Bicey	8676	McClure, Josephine	3635
McCurtain, David C.	8942	McClure, Freeman	3636
McCurtain, Kate N.	8943	McClure, Gleason	3637
McCurtain, Ewart P.	8944	McClure, Absolom	3658
McCurtain, Juanita		McClure, Willis	5542
Jeanetta	8945	McClure, Biza	6625
McCurtain, Ben	13665	McClure, Nellie C.	6626
McCurtain, Randolph	13666	McClure, Jesse W.	6627
McCurtain, Joshua	14118	McClure, Rufus R.	6628
McCurtain, Cornelius	14775	McClure, Thomas M.	6629
McCurtain, Silas	14788	McClure, Bertha	6630
McCaughey, Emmet	134	McClure, Garret T.	6643
McCaughey, John	135	McClure, Albert J.	6644
McCaughey, Ethel	136	McClure, Albert W.	6645
McCuaghey, Leliah	137	McClure, Artemissa	6646
McCuaghey, Sophia	138	McClure, Josephine	6647
McCuaghey, Emmet, Jr.	139	McClure, Walter L.	6754
McCuaghey, Annie	140	McClure, Mary A.	6765
McCuaghey, Loraine	141	McClure, Isaac W.	6766
McCuaghey, Claude E.	142	McClure, Harry	6836
McCuaghey, J. C.	164	McClure, Betsy	7208
McCoy, Iston	1119	McClure, Louisa	7209
McCoy, Annie	1120	McClure, Ida	6613
McCoy, Holman	1993	McClure, Mary E.	8588
McCoy, Sillis	1994	McClure, Margaret S.	8589

Name.	Roll No.	Name.	Roll No.
McClure, Sudye J.	8590	McClendon, Eva R.	10049
McClure, Newton	9600	McClendon, Tryphenia	10052
McClure, Laura	9601	McClendon, Kate	13003
McClure, Lyda	9602	McClard, Myrtle	10434
McClure, William	9776	McCaull, Ada	12932
McClure, Napoleon B.	10135	McCaull, John S.	12933
McClure, Bunn H.	10136	McCaull, Mary A.	12934
McClure, Nicey	11114	McCaull, Ida	12935
McClure, Douglas C.	11115	McCaull, Margaret L.	12936
McClure, Lorena B.	11116	McCaull, Leonora	12937
McClure, Benjamin	11117	McCulic, Vivian. M.	13041
McClure, Gipson	11427	McDaniel, Lucetta	86
McClure, Elizabeth	12109	McDaniel, Laura	87
McClure, Alfred W.	13031	McDaniel, Alice	88
McClure, Henry E.	13032	McDaniel, Robert	89
McClure, Eunice	13033	McDaniel, William	90
McClure, Benjamin B.	13034	McDaniel, Jesse	91
McClure, Anna Dora	14581	McDaniel, Annie	92
McClure, Acy	14658	McDaniel, Lula	94
McClure, Wesley	14659	McDaniel, Leonadus	301
McClure, Lottie	14660	McDaniel, Ed	607
McCann, Ben	4346	McDaniel, Thomas	5890
McCann, Sam	4481	McDaniel, Albert	6132
McCann, Sallie	4482	McDaniel, Sam	7466
McCann, Wallace	4483	McDaniel, Louisa	7467
McCann, Willie	4484	McDaniel, Irene	7468
McCann, Philip	8201	McDaniel, Edmond	7469
McCann, Joseph	8312	McDaniel, Bailey	7470
McCann, Betsy	8313	McDaniel, James Rumley	7471
McCann, Alexander	8315	McDaniel, Nicholas	10532
McCann, Cornelius	8695	McDaniel, Mary	13658
McCann, Isophine	8697	McDaniel, Thomas	13659
McCann, Julia	8698	McDaniel, Marvin	13660
McCann, William B.	8699	McDaniel, James	13661
McCann, Nealy	9060	McDaniel, Mitchell	13662
McCann, Loli	11652	McDaniel, Ruth	13663
McCann, Austin	14129	McDaniel, Lula	13664
McCann, Julia	14130	McDaniel, Melvina	14717
McCann, Edna Algia	14777	McDaniels, Jennette	526
McCann, Thelmer	14778	McDaniels, Tenny	527
McCann, Jane	15593	McDaniels, James	528
McCann, Melissa	15794	McDonald, Lucy E.	692
McCasson, Samuel	6547	McDonald, Conales	833
McCasson, Enos F.	6549	McDonald, Muir	834
McCasson, Sam R.	6551	McDonald, Eli Jackson	11257
McCartney, Elsie	6795	McDonald, Minnie	11261
McCartney, Argie	6796	McDonald, Ada L.	11262
McCartney, Elvia	6797	McDonald, Alice M.	11263
McCarty, Mary A.	7521	McDonald, William A.	11264
McCarty, John W.	7696	McDonald, Nora Bell	11265
McCarty, Malachia	7697	McDonald, John	16053
McCarty, Robert	7698	McDuff, Charles J.	13225
McCarty, Oscar	7699	McDuff, Mary M.	14986
McCarty, Artie	7700	McDuff, Charles L.	14987
McCarty, Robert L.	7825	McDuff, Emma	14988
McCarty, Claude A.	7826	McDuff, Robert L.	14989
McCarty, Lloyd S.	7827	McDuff, Andrew J.	14990
McCarty, Mary A.	15971	McElroy, Jeff J.	6537
McCarter, Mattie	11308	McElroy, Malinda	6538
McCarter, Elmer W.	11309	McElroy, Alice	6540
McCarter, Emmet P.	11310	McFarland, Abbie	2432
McCarter, Ethel B.	11311	McFarland, John E.	3638
McCarter, Edgar C.	11312	McFarland, Anna L.	3640
McClain, Mary I.	7137	McFarland, Ina Juanita	3641
McClain, Annie P.	7138	McFarland, Daniel Zac	3644
McClain, La Rene	7139	McFarland, Willie	5284
McClain, George	7402	McFarland, Israel	5556
McClain, James T.	7403	McFarland, Polly	5557
McClain, Annie E.	7405	McFarland, Mary	5558
McClain, Sallie F.	7406	McFarland, Florence	5559
McClain, Georgia B.	7407	McFarland, Andrew	5560
McClain, John Q.	7408	McFarland, Silas	5670
McClain, Jessie W.	7409	McFarland, Susan	5671
McClain, Sophia	7411	McFarland, Alexander	6180
McClish, Lorden	9031	McFarland, Benjamin	14821
McClish, Ross	9032	McFerran, Isabelle	8217
McClish, Buddie	9234	McGee, David	764
McClish, Rena	9235	McGee, Sophia	766
McClish, Phelin	9236	McGee, Elizabeth	2961
McClish, Susan	9237	McGee, Jesse	2970
McClish, Walton	9238	McGee, Licksey	2971
McCollum, Clara L.	9585	McGee, Ennie	2972
McClendon, Annie	10047	McGee, Wattie	2973
McClendon, Posey	10048	McGee, Josie	2974

Name.	Roll No.	Name.	Roll No.
McGee, Sissy	2975	McKinney, Charley	597
McGee, Linney	2976	McKinney, Ruby May	598
McGee, Austin	3351	McKinney, Chester Cecil	599
McGee, Lizzie	3353	McKinney, Bessie Jewell	600
McGee, Lillie J.	5748	McKinney, Frances	1255
McGee, Edgar	5749	McKinney, Samuel	2046
McGee, Lillie B.	5750	McKinney, Robinson	2048
McGee, William F.	5751	McKinney, Mana	2049
McGee, Effie	5752	McKinney, Ida	2050
McGee, Sissie	5876	McKinney, John	2051
McGee, Ellen	5877	McKinney, Jamison	2066
McGee, Harris	5878	McKinney, David	2067
McGee, Arsehill	5879	McKinney, Jackson	2068
McGee, Caroline	5880	McKinney, Susan	2069
McGee, Mack	5881	McKinney, Jackson	2433
McGee, Silas	5382	McKinney, Cistin	2434
McGee, Sweeny	7113	McKinney, Green	2435
McGee, Martha	10224	McKinney, Joseph	2436
McGee, Thomas	11191	McKinney, Minerva	3027
McGee, Sim	13584	McKinney, Paul	3030
McGee, Ellis	13750	McKinney, McGowan	3102
McGee, Sol	13751	McKinney, Watson	3106
McGee, Esau	13752	McKinney, Betsy	3107
McGee, Isom	13753	McKinney, Linnie	3108
McGee, Mary M.	13754	McKinney, Ephraim	3226
McGee, Ora May	14710	McKinney, John	3332
McGee, Selin	15570	McKinney, Ishlea	3333
McGee, Henry	16209	McKinney, Simmie	3334
McGahey, John H.	5070	McKinney, Martha	4672
McGahey, Alexander J.	5071	McKinney, Laura E.	4674
McGahey, Luther L.	5072	McKinney, Sallie	4675
McGahey, Martha	5073	McKinney, Ida	4676
McGahey, Florence	5074	McKinney, Joseph	4677
McGahey, Frances	5075	McKinney, Isaac	4679
McGahey, Arthur D.	12276	McKinney, Silas	5547
McGahey, Elijah J.	12277	McKinney, Nancy	5548
McGahey, Effie	12278	McKinney, Egtill B.	5706
McGahey, Joel J.	12279	McKinney, Sweny	5990
McGahey, George F.	13495	McKinney, Sissy	5991
McGilberry, Nicholas	7043	McKinney, James J.	5992
McGilberry, Katie	7240	McKinney, Adam	7935
McGilberry, Martha	7369	McKinney, Richard	7970
McGilberry, Sibby	7379	McKinney, Alexander	9205
McGilberry, Solomon	7382	McKinney, Baxter	9206
McGilberry, Abel	9324	McKinney, Louisa	9207
McGilberry, Charlie	9325	McKinney, Hulda	10027
McGilberry, Pearl E.	9326	McKinney, George	10028
McGilberry, Simpson	9327	McKinney, Frank	10029
McGilberry, Turner	13061	McKinney, Elijah	10030
McGilberry, Osborne	13100	McKinney, Lillie E.	10031
McGinty, Ida L.	14335	McKinney, Edward L.	10032
McGinty, Lucretia	14336	McKinney, Maggie	10033
McGinty, Burney W.	14337	McKinney, Richard M.	10034
McGinty, Lois Lucile	14338	McKinney, Sampson C.	10296
McGuire, Carrie Whittle	15650	McKinney, Mattie	10297
McGuire, Isie May	15651	McKinney, Gladys	10298
McGuire, Emery Willis	15652	McKinney, Irvine	10229
McGuire, John Lewis	15653	McKinney, William H.	11904
McIntire, Belshazzar	4000	McKinney, Phoebe	11905
McIntyre, Onie	7457	McKinney, John	12229
McIntyre, Preston	14763	McKinney, Calvin	13021
McIntyre, Burle	14764	McKinney, Henry	13022
McIntosh, Silvey	4637	McKinney, Isabella	13023
McIntosh, John G.	4638	McKinney, Sampson	13516
McIntosh, Alexander	4639	McKinney, Elmer	13517
McIntosh, William R.	4640	McKinney, Clara Louisa	13747
McIntosh, Rutha	4641	McKinney, Ben A.	13748
McIntosh, Carrie M.	5777	McKinney, Mattie	13749
McIntosh, Jane	5897	McKinney, Susan	15044
McIntosh, Alexander	5898	McKinney, Milen	15392
McIntosh, Andrew	5899	McKee, Mary A.	4737
McIntosh, Annie	5900	McKee, Mary L.	4738
McIntosh, Cornelius	5902	McKee, Martin	4739
McIntosh, Jackman	11296	McKee, George	4740
McIntosh, Chostin	11297	McKee, Andrew J.	4741
McIntosh, Catherine	12418	McKee, Lula	4742
McIntosh, George	12419	McKee, John D.	4743
McIntosh, Turner	12420	McKee, Isaac	4744
McIntosh, Jonah	12421	McKinzie, Mack	5093
McIntosh, Arthur	12422	McKinzie, Goodman	5398
McIntosh, Amos	12423	McKinzie, Viney	5399
McIntosh, Nancy	12424	McKinzie, May Lina	5403
McIntosh, Lona	12425	McKinzie, Kimpsey	5603
McIntosh, Elias Thomas	12426	McKenzie, Dora	14280
		McKenzie, Claudie	14281

Name.	Roll No.
McKenzie, Leonard	14282
McKenzie, Pearl	14283
McKenzie, William	14284
McKenzie, Arnold	14285
McKasson, Mary J.	12557
McKasson, John L.	12558
McKasson, Mary E.	12559
McKasson, James C.	12560
McKasson, Laura I.	12561
McKasson, Thadeus E.	12562
McKasson, Emuel O.	12563
McKinnon, Lula	15290
McKinnon, Myrtle L.	15291
McKinnon, William A.	15292
McKinnon, George W.	15293
McKinnon, Joseph E.	15294
McKinnon, Ethel May	15295
McLain, William A.	9082
McLain, Addie	9083
McLain, George W.	9084
McLain, Wilmer Z.	9085
McLish, John E.	13798
McLaughlin, George W.	15037
McLaughlin, Sampson	15038
McLaughlin, Walter	15039
McLellan, James A.	15306
McLellan, John F.	15307
McLellan, James C.	15308
McLellan, Robert D.	15009
McLellan, Levi	15310
McLellan, Samuel J.	15311
McLellan, Edmund	15312
McLellan, Mary	15313
McLellan, Samuel	15314
McLellan, Ollie	15315
McLellan, George	15316
McLellan, Susan	15317
McLellan, Orville D.	15318
McLellan, Franklin B.	15320
McLellan, Abner, D.	15321
McLellan, Wade H.	15323
McLellan, Joseph M.	15324
McLellan, John F.	15325
McLellan, Hattie	15326
McLellan, Abner D.	15327
McLellan, Adeline	15328
McLellan, Dolly	15329
McLellan, Wade	15330
McLellan, Monroe H.	15753
McMenamin, F. P.	183
McMenamin, Michael McK	14477
McMenamin, Mary Elizabeth	14478
McMenamin, Roy Francis	14479
McMurtrey, Mattie J.	6339
McMurtrey, Joseph B.	6341
McMurtrey, Amelia	13981
McMurtrey, Irene	13984
McMurtrey, Clyde	13985
McMurtrey, Glenn	13986
McMurtry, Jerry J.	6995
McMurtry, Jerry Jr.	6996
McMurtry, Atha W.	6997
McMurtry, Clyde	6998
McMurtry, Nettie M.	6999
McMurtry, John W.	9274
McMurtry, Jessie	9275
McMurtry, Thelma	9280
McMurtry, Nettie P.	15448
McMurtry, Martha E.	15449
McMahan, Cornelia	8195
McMurry, Rebecca	13289
McMurry, Edie	13292
McNoel, Joel	6727
McNoel, Sap	6728
McNoel, Eastman	6941
McNoel, Missouri	6942
McNeely, Ellen	13560
McNeely, Julia F.	13561
McNeely, Edna	13562
Nale, Robert	813
Nale, Joel	814
Nale, Ella Toil	816
Nale, John	13277

Name.	Roll No.
Nale, Benjamin C.	13278
Nale, Joseph S.	13279
Nale, Elsie M.	13280
Nale, Daniel J.	13281
Nale, KateyGertrue	13282
Nale, William Lee	13283
Nale, Willie George	14547
Nail, Sophronia E.	889
Nail, Phoebe	2879
Nail, Simeon	2880
Nail, Joe	4266
Nail, Mary	4267
Nail, Susan	4268
Nail, Minnie	4269
Nail, Charles C.	4270
Nail, Edward	7038
Nail, Minnie	7039
Nail, West	7041
Nail, Elvira	7254
Nail, Louvina E.	7301
Nail, Jeff	8314
Nail, Richard	8359
Nail, Nelson	8360
Nail, Greenwood	8361
Nail, William	8363
Nail, Maggie	8364
Nail, Nicholas	9076
Nail, Amy	9077
Nail, Lucy	9078
Nail, Nelson	9695
Nail, Jesse	10059
Nail, Edward J.	10071
Nail, Robert W.	10072
Nail, Rennie	10073
Nail, Edward L.	10074
Nail, Peter	11906
Nail, Wilson	11907
Nail, Joel W.	12849
Nail, Jincy	13082
Nail, Jimmie	13083
Nail, Joel H.	13439
Nail, Ishtoyapi	134⬛ 442
Nail, David Oscar	13458
Nail, Claude B.	13459
Nail, Salina	13368
Nail, Mary	13369
Nail, Amanda	13370
Nail, Eliza	15050
Nail, Eva	15579
Naknitaya, Mollie	1365
Naknitaya, Reuben	1923
Naknitaya, Pisona	1924
Nakishi, Alfred	2841
Nakishi, Selina	2842
Nakishi, Osborne	2843
Nakishi, David	3232
Nakishi, Mary	3233
Nakishi, Watson	3817
Narlett, Sissie	2385
Narlett, Ellen	5833
Narlett, Adam	5834
Narlett, Emma	5835
Narlett, Carbin	5837
Narlett, Amanda	14933
Nanomantube, Solomon	2748
Nanomontube, Louisa	2750
Nanomantube, Dennie	2751
Nanomantube, Jacob	2752
Nanomantube, Wilmon	3166
Nanomantube, Lucinda	3167
Nanomantube, Jonathan	3168
Nanomantube, Sylvester	2169
Nanomantube, Mary	3523
Nanonantabbe, Adam	4014
Napier, Lucinda	5096
Napier, Wyly	5097
Napier, Fannie	5098
Napier, Mary	5101
Naylor, Ida	7677
Naylor, Zona	7678
Naylor, Mary	7679
Naylor, Lee	7680
Naylor, Hester	7681
Nelson, Sim	372
Nelson, Eliza	1663
Nelson, Alvin	1665

Name.	Roll No.	Name.	Roll No.
Nelson, Abel	1666	Nelson, Mabel	15960
Nelson, Bettie	3205	Nehka, Solomon	2371
Nelson, Fannie L.	3952	Nehka, Mintihona	2372
Nelson, Albert J.	3953	Nehka, Farris	2405
Nelson, Louise B.	3954	Nehka, Amy	2406
Nelson, Florence	3955	Nehka, Noel	2407
Nelson, William D.	3956	Nehka, Sam	2479
Nelson, Isaac	4420	Nehka, Simon	2480
Nelson, Emma	4421	Nehka, Lena	2481
Nelson, Georgie A.	4422	Nehka, Robert	2510
Nelson, Allington T.	4423	Nehka, Elizabeth	2511
Nelson, Leo. B.	4424	Newson, Sophia	6227
Nelson, Grace M.	4425	Newson, Martha	6228
Nelson, Tatsy	4426	Newson, Henry	6229
Nelson, Annie	4427	Newson, Simon L.	6231
Nelson, Cole E.	4428	Newson, Idey E.	6232
Nelson, Gabriel	4429	Needham, Nettie H.	4340
Nelson, Willy	4431	Nessmith, Mary V.	8202
Nelson, Wilson	4432	Nessmith, Frank	8203
Nelson, Silvey	4469	Nessmith, Robert P.	8205
Nelson, Simon	4470	Neely, Allen	10053
Nelson, George	4471	Neely, Joseph	10055
Nelson, Elsie	4472	Neely, Mary	10056
Nelson, Joe	4527	Neely, Ward	10057
Nelson, Stephen	4749	Neal, Annie	11804
Nelson, Lula	4750	Neal, Nancy L.	11805
Nelson, James	4751	Neal, Minnie	11990
Nelson, Cole	4752	Neal, Calvin Hicks	11994
Nelson, Eden	4754	Neal, Susan	13364
Nelson, Sisty	4756	Neal, Ira	13365
Nelson, Eden	4805	Neal, Green	13366
Nelson, Laura	4806	Neal, Mamie	13367
Nelson, Isham	4807	Neill, Dolly	12804
Nelson, Gooding	4808	Neill, Ola	12806
Nelson, Osborne	4809	Neill, Ottice Emmett	12807
Nelson, Jerusha	4810	Newton, Katie	13214
Nelson, David	4811	Newton, Robert	13215
Nelson, Maulsey	4832	Newton, Joseph	13217
Nelson, Isham	4929	Newton, Lucinda	13218
Nelson, Ellen	5010	Newton, Mada	13219
Nelson, Ellis H.	5168	Newton, Ernest	13220
Nelson, Implin	5169	Newton, Bessie	13221
Nelson, Eslin	5171	Newton, Claudie V.	13222
Nelson, Solomon	5172	Nero, Jane	13308
Nelson, Isham	5173	Nero, Henry	13309
Nelson, Jerusha	5174	Nero, Delia	13310
Nelson, Jonas	8524	Nero, Hallie	13311
Nelson, Daniel	8525	Nevins, Floyd	15010
Nelson, Houston	8994	Nichols, Emma	3133
Nelson, Rhoda	8995	Nichols, Unie	3134
Nelson, Josephine	9012	Nichols, Roy	3135
Nelson, Smallwood W.	9020	Nichols, Buel	3136
Nelson, Sarah	9021	Nichols, Ben B.	3903
Nelson, Jane	9022	Nichols, Ella	6295
Nelson, Mary A.	9053	Nichols, Sam	6296
Nelson, Eastman	9061	Nichols, Hampy H.	6297
Nelson, Melvina	9062	Nicholas, Wilson	6053
Nelson, Isaac	9063	Nicholas, Elissie	6054
Nelson, Salina	9064	Nicholas, Rosie	6087
Nelson, Jackson F.	9385	Nicholas, William	9790
Nelson, Emma C.	9386	Nicholas, Elizabeth	9791
Nelson, Richard	9387	Nicholas, David	9836
Nelson, Alice	9388	Nicholas, Alice	9837
Nelson, Adolphus B.	9389	Nicholas, Emily	9838
Nelson, Andrew J.	9390	Nicholas, Rayson	10211
Nelson, Joseph E.	9699	Nicholas, Hannah	10212
Nelson, Jennie	9700	Nicholas, Isias W.	10254
Nelson, John	9703	Nicholas, Sealy	10255
Nelson, Solomon	9704	Nicholas, Isaac	10256
Nelson, Harriet	9705	Nicholas, Amy	10308
Nelson, Isaac	9706	Nicholas, Lina	10309
Nelson, Simon J.	9707	Nicholas, Wilburn	10310
Nelson, Joseph E. Jr.	9708	Nicholas, Lucy	10311
Nelson, John Garret	9709	Nicholas, Elizabeth	10312
Nelson, Gilbert	9810	Nicholas, Wade	10664
Nelson, Martha	9928	Nicholas, Sina	10665
Nelson, Eli	12269	Nicholas, Roy	10666
Nelson, George	12448	Nicholson, Mamie E.	10399
Nelson, Beatrice	12449	Nix, Amy	7116
Nelson, George Jr.	12450	Nix, Jonathan	7117
Nelson, Osborne M.	12451	Nix, Lucinda E.	15153
Nelson, Clarissa	13585	Nix, Mabel C.	15154
Nelson, Susan	15043	Ninas, Tennessee	11092
Nelson, Garret E.	15580	Ninas, Alice	11093
Nelson, Roy M.	15581	Ninas, Flora B.	11094
Nelson, Rebecca	15929	Ninas, Josephine	11095

Name.	Roll No.	Name.	Roll No.
Nicar, Ola P.	12760	Nowahina, Esean	2619
Nicar, Grace M.	12766	Nowahina, Hitty	2620
Noah, Wilmon	977	Nohio, Thompson	4530
Noah, Salenna	978	Nohio, Sarah	4531
Noah, Marcus	979	Nohio, Harrison	4532
Noah, Reed	980	Noatabbe, Grant	5430
Noah, Agnes	981	Noatabbe, Antlin	5431
Noah, Newman	983	Noatabbe, Felix	5432
Noah, Sis	984	Norman, Houston	6138
Noah, William	985	Norman, Malinda	6139
Noah, Binsey	986	Norman, Sarah J.	6425
Noah, Lila	987	Norman, Lue M.	6428
Noah, Pearl	992	Norman, Arzena	6429
Noah, Lizzie	993	Norman, Laura B.	7944
Noah, Sillis	995	Norman, Eliza	14664
Noah, Nellis	1069	Norman, Ida	15374
Noah, Elensie	1070	Norman, Alvy	15375
Noah, Harrison	1639	Norman, Clayton	15376
Noah, Simeon	1640	Norman, Raymond	15377
Noah, Susan	1641	Norman, Oren	15777
Noah, Charles	1644	Norman, Byron	15778
Noah, Elizabeth	1695	Nolen, Thomas	6420
Noah, Frances	1699	Nolen, Thomas, Jr.	6871
Noah, John	1722	Nolen, Cephus	6872
Noah, Brazil	1953	Nowabbi, Charlie	11273
Noah, Johnson	2412	Nowabbi, Listqn	11646
Noah, Esian	2413	Nowabbi, Mary	11647
Noah, Joseph	2414	Nowabbi, James	11648
Noah, Colbertson	2415	Nowabbi, Alfred	11649
Noah, Littie	2416	Nowabbi, Jincy	11650
Noah, Mary	2417	Nowabbi, Amy	11651
Noah, Magdalene	2418	Nowabbi, Hannah	11854
Noah, Christopher	2419	Noley, Lucy	13318
Noah, Foster	2439	Noel, Ben	13800
Noah, Rogers	4746	Noel, Edward	13801
Noah, Selina	4747	Noel, Robert	14121
Noah, Abel	4961	Noel, Edmund	14122
Noah, Bessie	4962	Noel, Luena	14726
Noah, Alexander	4968	Noel, Natsy	14840
Noah, Louisa	4964	Noel, Georgia Ann	14841
Noah, Joses	4965	Noel, Ellen	15062
Noah, Ebenezer	5630	Noel, Jennie	15497
Noah, Ellen	5631	Null, John	15191
Noah, Maggie	5632	Null, Fannie	15192
Noah, Ellias	5634	Null, Robert Henry	15193
Noah, Rogers	5635	Null, Bessie	15194
Noah, Storden	5683	Null, Leota	15195
Noah, Summie	5684	Oliver, Marietta E.	4
Noah, Isom	5688	Oliver, Thomas J.	7
Noah, Davis S.	5906	Oliver, Reita Maud	8
Noah, Margaret	5907	Oliver, William Roose-	
Noah, Alfred	5908	velt	9
Noah, Isabelie	5909	Oliver, Ella	790
Noah, Irena E.	5910	Oliver, Josephine	4134
Noah, Sophia	5911	Ott, Carney	123
Noah, Webster M.	5912	Ott, Alfred	9100
Noah, Seth D.	5913	Ott, Lizzie	9101
Noah, Robert Lee	5914	Ott, Sam	9102
Noah, Sarah	11281	Ott, Mitchell	9103
Noah, Alfred	11455	Ott, Sallie	9104
Noah, Isabinda	11456	Ott, Solomon	9105
Noah, Esias	11457	Ott, Winema	9106
Noah, Jackson	11458	Ott, Josephine	9107
Noah, Mary	11459	Ott, Emma	9108
Noah, Lottie	11460	Ott, Stephen	9266
Noah, Salena	11461	Ott, John	11128
Noah, Irvin	11545	Ott, Fannie	11129
Noah, Sibbey	11546	Ott, Gilldm	11130
Noah, Aurora	11547	Ott, Dora	11132
Noah, Annie	13720	Ott, Samuel A.	11246
Noah, Rindie	13721	Ott, Rhoda	11247
Noah, Robert	13722	Ott, Johnson	11594
Noah, Reuben	13723	Ott, Bicey	11595
Noah, Mulsey	15848	Ott, Joe	13767
Noah, Emma	15974	Ott, Simeon	13768
Noahobi, Liksi	1561	Ott, Sallie	13769
Noahobi, Mila	1562	Ott, Sam	13770
Noahobi, Mitsie	1563	Overstreet, Jane B.	195
Noahobi, Williamson	2318	Overstreet, Minnie	196
Noahobi, Semy	2319	Overstreet, James	7809
Noahobi, Easter	2320	Overstreet, August	7811
Noahobi, Laymus	2321	Overstreet, Riley	7812
Noahobi, Jamyson	2322	Overstreet, Lemuel	7813
Noahobi, Sophia	2814	Overstreet, Elizabeth	7815

Name.	Roll No.	Name.	Roll No.
Overstreet, Clayton N.	7816	Olson, Rebecca	11071
Overstreet, Charles A.	7817	Oshter, Lake	11430
Overstreet, Dora F.	7818	Oshter, Sibble	11431
Overstreet, John T.	7819	Oshter, Byington	11496
Overstreet, Minnie	7820	Oshter, Isham	11893
Overstreet, Lela	7821	Oshter, Bakie	16051
Overstreet, Maggie M.	7822	Orr, Catherine	12327
Overstreet, Russell	7823	Orr, Ella	12328
Overstreet, Clayton Sen-		Orr, Etta	12329
gal	7824	Orr, George	12330
Overstreet, Addie	10448	Owens, Susie	18040
Overstreet, Nora May	10451	Owens, John	14357
Ontahyabbi, Louie	2360	Owens, Mattie	14358
Ontontabi, Isin	2440	Owens, Mary E.	14359
Onchili, Bicey	2613	Owens, Frony	14360
Ontaiyabi, Stephen	3356	Owens, William S.	14361
Ontaiyabi, Netsie	3357	Owens, Mary L.	14395
Oklahambi, Mary	3388	Owens, Cordelia B.	14396
Oklahambi, Joseph	3389	Owens, Patti	14397
Obannon, Isabel	3495	Owens, Robert Erskine	14398
Oakes, Lemuel W.	4071	Osborne, Nancy	14001
Oakes, Clarence A.	4072	Ormsby, Lena	14504
Oakes, Frank	4073	On-na-ti-ma	14573
Oakes, Mattie	4074	Okchaya, Solomon	14942
Oakes, Nola	4075	Onahabbee, Silena	15780
Oakes, Nona M.	4076	Orndorff, John	15821
Oakes, Thomas E.	4097	O'Riley, Catherine	9814
Oakes, Margaret J.	4098	O'Riley, Lester	9816
Oakes, Daniel W.	4099	O'Riley, Zula	9817
Oakes, Thomas J.	4100	O'Riley, Lula	9818
Oakes, Susan	4101	O'Riley, Lela	9819
Oakes, Rosa	4102	O'Riley, Ora	9820
Oakes, Edgar O.	4103	O'Riley, Zelma	9821
Oakes, Susan M.	4104	O'Dea, Mary E.	10944
Oakes, Harriet N.	4105	O'Dea, Anna T.	10945
Oakes, George W.	4244	O'Dea, Cora E.	10946
Oakes, Aurilla G.	4245	O'Dea, Katie E.	10947
Oakes, David F.	4246	O'Dea, Thomas J.	10948
Oakes, Pearl B.	4248	Parrish, Lillie Josephine	801
Oakes, Joel	4328	Parrish, Jewel Lorena	803
Oakes, Lizzie	4330	Parrish, Belhena	11004
Oakes, Bertie	4331	Parish, Eliza	4772
Oakes, Effie	4332	Parish, Eli	4774
Oakes, Sarah E.	4333	Parish, Elias	4835
Oakes, Elizabeth	4334	Parish, Robert	4836
Oakes, Charles D.	4502	Parish, Rosie	4837
Oakes, Christopher	4503	Parish, John	5145
Oakes, Annie M.	4504	Parish, Hattie	14691
Oakes, William W.	4505	Parker, Dixon	937
Oakes, Henry F.	4506	Parker, Betsy	938
Oakes, Levana F.	4507	Parker, Hafis	939
Oakes, Laura B.	4508	Parker, Lizzie	1014
Oakes, Hamet	4509	Parker, Moses	1015
Oakes, Albert O.	4510	Parker, Dennis	1333
Oakes, George W.	4514	Parker, Lena	1334
Oakes, Beulah B.	4515	Parker, Stephen	2641
Oakes, John E.	4516	Parker, Lena	2642
Oakes, Thomas C.	4517	Parker, Edwin	2543
Oakes, Susan M.	4518	Parker, Emerson	2644
Oakes, Nora M.	4519	Parker, Grabriel E.	4608
Oakes, Emma M.	4520	Parker, James W.	4609
Oakes, Samuel L.	4566	Parker, Lue	4610
Oakes, Tommie	4567	Parker, Cora	4611
Oakes, Mary A.	10962	Parker, Georgia O.	4612
Oakes, Thomas Clay	10969	Parker, Johnson	13101
Oakes, James G.	14685	Parker, Simeon	14558
Oakes, Malcolm Chris-		Payne, Mattie	1818
tian	16215	Payne, Ella	1819
Odelle, Ada	4238	Payne, Nebus	1913
Odelle, Pearl	4239	Pain, James	11548
Odelle, Willie	4240	Paine, Annie	11686
Odelle, Girtie	14673	Parsons, Susan	3102
Odell, Gilbert W.	10103	Parsons, Mary	4563
Odell, William R.	10104	Parsons, John	4564
Odell, Mary	10731	Parsons, Daniel	4565
Oklabbi, Davis	4539	Patterson, Thomas	4389
Oklabbi, Lena	4540	Patterson, James	5205
Oklabbi, Listie	4541	Patterson, James	5272
Oxford, Josephine	4717	Patterson, Walton	8403
Onubby, Robert L.	4748	Patterson, Maggie	8404
Onahantubbee, Joseph	9915	Patterson, Green	8405
Olson, Sarah	11068	Patterson, Pearl A.	8406
Olson, Thomas	11069	Patterson, Kittie J.	8407
Olson, Loftess	11070	Patterson, Ethel	8408

Name.	Roll No.	Name.	Roll No.
Patterson, Aman	9886	Payton, Laura	11719
Patterson, Adeline	9887	Pate, Ada	9812
Patterson, John	9888	Pate, Lula.	9813
Patterson, Mary A.	11372	Pate, Soulie L.	12249
Patterson, James	12943	Pate, Lavinia W.	12250
Patterson, Robert	12944	Pate, Josie L.	12283
Patterson, Jesse J.	12945	Pate, Arden	12284
Patterson, Luke	12946	Pate, Milton	12285
Patterson, Oscar	12947	Padier, Elizabeth	10111
Patterson, Lewis	12948	Paul, Solomon	10250
Patterson, Edmund	12949	Paul, Eliza	10251
Patterson, Green	12950	Paul, Delia	15091
Patterson, Simon L.	12951	Paul, Claude	15092
Patterson, John	13416	Pace, Harriet	10411
Patterson, Isabelle	14738	Paddock, William A.	10489
Patterson, James Oscar	14739	Paddock, Lydia	10490
Palmer, Katie	5153	Paddock, Florence	10491
Palmer, Annie	5154	Paddock, Reuben W.	10926
Palmer, Lubbin	11515	Paddock, John S.	10927
Palmer, Lina	11516	Paddock, Annie E.	10929
Palmer, Watson	11517	Paddock, James L.	10974
Palmer, Hicks	11518	Paddock, William H.	10975
Palmer, Castin	11519	Paddock, Jesse	10976
Palmer, Myrtle.	13813	Paddock, Rosa L.	10977
Palmer, Benjamin Cleve-		Paddock, Johnie R.	10978
land	13814	Paddock, Claude	10979
Paxton, Hettie	6023	Payte, Nettie W.	11535
Paxton, Minerva J.	6024	Parshall, Lula	15004
Paxton, Ivaline.	6025	Park, Ida M.	15111
Paxton, Alismon	6026	Park, Edgar Lee	15112
Paxton, Flora	6027	Park, Mary Blanche	15113
Paxton, Gabrial	6080	Perkins, Albert	124
Paxton, Eli	6172	Perkins, Elizabeth	5013
Paxton, Lizzie.	6173	Perkins, Pauline	9530
Paxton, Missie	6174	Perkins, Robert L.	9531
Paxton, Lymon	6175	Perkins, Noah	9720
Paxton, Susan	6250	Perkins, Nellie	9721
Paxton, Selina	6253	Perkins, Nora	9722
Paxton, Dora	8586	Perkins, Joana	9723
Paxton, Philip	9065	Perkins, Eli	10275
Paxton, Cholina	9066	Perkins, Simon H.	10479
Paxton, Islan	9332	Perkins, William H.	10480
Paxton, Calvin	9551	Perkins, David A.	10481
Paxton, Walter	9552	Perkins, Lavena H.	10482
Paxton, Angeline	9553	Perkins, Cornelius E.	10483
Paxton, Pearl	9554	Perkins, Shelby	10670
Paxton, Norris	14720	Perkins, George G.	10734
Parnell, Haywood P.	6115	Perkins, Maud A.	10735
Parnell, Jesse H.	6116	Perkins, Lucy	10736
Parnell, Thomas O.	6117	Perkins, Serena	11359
Parnell, Eliza E.	6118	Perkins, Lyman H.	12701
Parnell, Hoyt	15549	Perkins, Cora	12702
Parnell, Ewing	15550	Perkins, Hugh H.	12703
Page, Robert	6528	Perkins, Albert T.	12704
Page, Edward E.	6529	Perkins, Hattie A.	12705
Page, Robert N.	6530	Perkins, Dora M.	12706
Page, William C.	6655	Perkins, Pearly Lee	12707
Page, Ella L.	6656	Perkins, William Alfred	12708
Page, Nellie F.	6657	Perkins, Ethel	13441
Page, Allen W.	6658	Perkins, Nathaniel A.	15462
Page, William B.	6659	Perkins, John A.	15463
Page, Joseph M.	6660	Pernell, Henry	318
Page, Edmund Monroe	6661	Pernell, Thomas	319
Page, Jane F.	7044	Peter, Stephen	691
Page, Joshua S.	7045	Peter, Sina	917
Page, Lewis	13711	Peter, Hodges	918
Page, Benson	13712	Peter, Pitman	1012
Page, Alice	13713	Peter, Davis	1979
Patton, Prosper J.	7461	Peter, Samuel	1981
Patton, Eva E.	7462	Peter, Lillie	1983
Patton, Moses	11857	Peter, Simon	2420
Patton, Simon	15858	Peter, Salena	2421
Payton, Mary	8261	Peter, Mary	2422
Payton, Philip	8262	Peter, Sarah	2423
Payton, Mary A.	9985	Peter, Lina	2438
Payton, Noah	9986	Peter, Simon J.	2695
Payton, Andrew	9987	Peter, Sibbie	2697
Payton, Daniel	10225	Peter, Lyda	2698
Payton, Susan	10226	Peter, Sibbie	3114
Payton, Ned	10702	Peter, Gooden	3337
Payton, Josephine	10703	Peter, Lucy	4628
Payton, Harry	10704	Peter, Edward	4629
Payton, William	11718	Peter, John	5141
		Peter, Osborn	5474

Name.	Roll No.	Name.	Roll No.
Peter, Jacob	5475	Perry, Leo	7904
Peter, Caroline	5476	Perry, Wicy	8063
Peter, Billy	5477	Perry, Edna	8064
Peter, James	5478	Perry, Jonas	8065
Peter, Barnabas	6418	Perry, Gilbert	8066
Peter, Ollie	6462	Perry, Albert	8067
Peter, Lela	6463	Perry, Jennie	8269
Peter, James	6464	Perry, Stephen	8311
Peter, Davis	6734	Perry, Jane	9049
Peter, Mary Ann	6735	Perry, Emiline	9126
Peter, Larly	6736	Perry, Daniel	9254
Peter, Wynie	6737	Perry, Jane	9255
Peter, Callis	6738	Perry, Calvin C.	9420
Peter, Emiline	6835	Perry, Phoebe	9421
Peter, Minnie	6838	Perry, Calvin C., Jr.	9422
Peter, John	8962	Perry, Carrie M.	11384
Peter, William	11251	Perry, Frank	12362
Peter, Elizabeth	11259	Perry, Sally	12363
Peter, Ellis	11260	Perry, Davis	12364
Peter, Sarah	11286	Perry, Gilbert	12365
Peter, Simon	11288	Perry, Isham	12366
Peter, Thompson	11543	Perry, Mary	12367
Peter, William	11544	Perry, Louis	12368
Peter, Salena	11585	Perry, Edmund	13111
Peter, Esias	11636	Perry, Coleman	13756
Peter, Davis	11843	Perry, Jefferson	13757
Peter, Susan	11844	Perry, Becky	13758
Peter, Alexander	13883	Perry, Sydney	15423
Peter, Abbie	14597	Perryman, Rachel	7077
Peter, Arthur	11923	Perryman, Jonas	7078
Peter, Lela	14924	Pearson, Joseph	8474
Peter, Levicy	15474	Pearson, Robert T.	13155
Peters, Elisha	10839	Pearson, Walter R.	13156
Peters, William T.	10831	Pearson, Laura B.	13157
Pebsworth, Sam	1490	Pearson, Hazel F.	13158
Pebsworth, Robert L.	1491	Pearson, Paul E.	13159
Pebsworth, Hugh	1492	Pearson, James C.	13160
Pebsworth, James	1493	Pearse, George	8625
Pebsworth, John	1494	Pearce, John M.	10361
Pebsworth, Louis	1495	Pearce, Helen M.	10362
Pebsworth, James L.	10971	Pearce, Lillian	10363
Pebsworth, Vivian	3512	Pearce, James E.	13563
Pebsworth, Elmo	14743	Perteet, Lizzie	12889
Pebworth, Henry	9258	Perteet, Clarence	12892
Pebworth, Dora E.	9259	Peabody, Jonas	13463
Pebworth, Elum N.	9260	Peabody, Sallie	13464
Pebworth, Lela M.	9261	Peabody, Frank	13466
Pebworth, Etta	9262	Penny, Annie	13535
Pebworth, Preston	9263	Penny, Oran Seldon	13536
Pebworth, Thomas J.	9264	Penny, Katherine S.	13537
Pebworth, Joseph	13528	Percer, Walter	15371
Pebworth, John L.	13529	Percer, Wiley	15372
Pebworth, Frank	13530	Percer, Ludenna	15373
Pebworth, Marguerite	13531	Phillips, Selena	2582
Peeler, Valley	4214	Phillips, Sissie	3082
Peeler, Mary	4215	Phillips, Michael R.	3086
Perry, Selina	4826	Phillips, Lizer	3087
Perry, Israel M.	5455	Phillips, Annie	3267
Perry, Susan	5456	Phillips, Julia Margaret	3268
Perry, Robinson	6592	ett	
Perry, Larsin	6593	Phillips, Jefie J.	3269
Perry, Nail	6352	Phillips, Dora	3270
Perry, Matilda	6853	Phillips, Rosey	4133
Perry, Hampton	6864	Phillips, Vivian	14888
Perry, Daniel	6866	Phillips, Annie	15587
Perry, Jonas	6867	Philip, Jacob	5552
Perry, Edward	6868	Philip, Winnie	5553
Perry, Gilbert	6869	Pharis, Walter	3957
Perry, Harriet	6870	Pharis, Turner	3958
Perry, Dixon	6909	Pickens, Isom	742
Perry, Charles T.	6912	Pickens, Louisa	2555
Perry, Martha	6913	Pickens, Paulie	4706
Perry, Myrtle	6914	Pickens, Frances	4707
Perry, Maud	6915	Pickens, Sallie	4708
Perry, Charles Raymond	6916	Pickens, Johnson	4709
Perry, Siney	7057	Pickens, Edmond	6711
Perry, Elizabeth	7058	Pickens, William	6712
Perry, Levina	7059	Pickens, Nellie	6713
Perry, Annie	7060	Pickens, Dewitt	6714
Perry, Eastman	7899	Pickens, Coleman	6715
Perry, Eve	7900	Pickens, Edna	8836
Perry, Campbell	7901	Pickens, Melvina	9127
Perry, Caroline	7902	Pickens, Eve	9141
Perry, Joseph	7903	Pickens, Austin	10642

Name.	Roll No.	Name.	Roll No.
Pickens, Jefferson	10643	Plato, Charles	12544
Pickens, Gilbert	13426	Plato, Clementine	15224
Pickens, Margaret	15444	Plato, Waity Lee	15225
Pickens, Nelson	15801	Plato, William Ward	15226
Pickens, Malinda	16058	Plato, Pearl Myrtle	15227
Pisahakubbi, Malwit	2316	Plato, Arthur Herbert	15228
Pisahakubbi, Sallie	2317	Poff, Patsey	315
Pislin, Suelis	3336	Powers, Maide	365
Pisachubbi, Case	3470	Powers, Vesta	366
Pisachubbi, Sarah	3471	Powell, Julia A.	409
Pisachubbi, Sebit	3472	Powell, Ernest	6794
Pisachubbi, Nancy	3474	Powell, Susan E.	7488
Pisachubbe, Eunice	4465	Powell, Hubbard	7489
Pisachubbe, William H.	4466	Powell, Myrtle G.	7490
Pisachubbe, Robert	4467	Powell, Turner	7491
Pisachubbe, Edward	4468	Powell, Beulah A.	7492
Pisahambe, David	3505	Powell, Rufus A.	7493
Pibsworth, Vivian	3512	Powell, Key	7494
Pistokcha, Wilburn	4576	Powell, Keener	7495
Pistokache, Cornelius	10762	Powell, Edgar L.	7496
Pistokache, Adeline	10794	Powell, Joseph Lewis	15663
Pistokache, William		Poland, William P.	410
Pain	10795	Poland, Robert P.	411
Pitchlynn, Agnes	6099	Poland, Raymond G.	413
Pitchlynn, Sissie	6102	Poland, Dan Grigsby	14501
Pitchlynn, Peter	6150	Pool, Summie B.	5535
Pitchlynn, Ellington P.	6267	Pool, Ike	5536
Pitchlynn, Amy	6291	Potts, Mary	5891
Pitchlynn, Jincy	6292	Potts, Watson	6134
Pitchlynn, Alexander	6352	Potts, William	6234
Pitchlynn, Malissa	6353	Potts, Susanna	6235
Pitchlynn, Agnes	6354	Potts, Simon	6236
Pitchlynn, Louisa	14043	Potts, Davis	6265
Pitchlynn, Livingston	14044	Potts, Jesse	6316
Pitchlynn, Edward E.	14376	Potts, Forbis	6908
Pitchlynn, William B.	14441	Potts, Judy	14157
Pitchlynn, Priscilla	14442	Potts, Sarah	14158
Pitchlynn, Ida	14443	Potts, Joshua	14159
Pitchlynn, Leona	14444	Potts, Allie	14160
Pitchlynn, Lee	15064	Potts, Willie	14161
Pitchlynn, Sophia	15065	Potts, Lillie	14162
Pitchlynn, Paul P.	15071	Potts, Eli	14163
Pitchlynn, Earnest L.	15072	Potts, Horace, Jr.	14164
Pitchlynn, Garland A.	15073	Potts, Laura	14165
Pitchlynn, Carlisle M.	15074	Potts, Rebecca	14166
Pike, James	6929	Potts, Margaret Susan	14167
Pike, Emiline	6930	Potts, Florence	14735
Pike, Alfred	6931	Potts, Willie Arthur	14736
Pike, Marion	14740	Potts, Alfred	15833
Piears, Joseph	8737	Porch, Mary.	7666
Pisachabe, Harrison	10559	Pope, Lucy	8626
Piepgrass, Agnes	12796	Pope, Winnie	8629
Pisamotubby, Frances	13480	Pope, Battiest	8630
Pierce, Ed	13786	Pope, Tecumseh	8748
Pierce, Belle	13787	Pope, Noel	9004
Pierce, Hattie	13788	Pope, Lizzie	9005
Pierce, Alice	13789	Pope, Gilbert	14120
Pierce, Siney	13790	Pope, Mitchell	15792
Pierce, Susan J.	13791	Pope, Judy	15962
Pierce, Robert L.	13792	Polk, Mary	10852
Pierce, Henry C.	13793	Polk, Loren	10853
Pierce, Ella May	13794	Polk, Joseph	10854
Pigott, Annie	14428	Prudhume, Charles J.	2924
Pigott, Mary A.	14429	Prudhume, Mary	2925
Plank, Rosanna A.	3882	Pritchard, Lizzie	4210
Plank, Inez	3883	Pritchard, Cora	4211
Platt, Elizabeth F.	5250	Pritchard, Frank	4212
Platt, Mary E.	5253	Pritchard, Lewie G.	4216
Platt, Gracie Jewel	5254	Pritchard, Jane	14806
Platt, James O.	5255	Price, Cora May	9439
Plummer, Charles W.	11182	Pruden, Tecumseh	10530
Plummer, Kittie E.	11183	Primer, Moses	14537
Plummer, Mary Chris-		Push, Solomon	5804
tina	11184	Push, Louisa	5805
Plummer, Raymond	11318	Push, Califlin	5806
Plummer, Joe R.	11319	Push, Betsie	5807
Plummer, Frank E.	11320	Push, Dallas	5923
Plummer, Dawes R.	11321	Push, Elias	5925
Plummer, Joseph R.	11327	Push, Falis	5926
Plummer, John E.	11328	Push, Simpson	5927
Plummer, Walter G.	11533	Push, Harris	5928
Plummer, Archie F.	11536	Push, Williamson	5930
Plummer, Walter		Push, Susan	6049
George	11537	Push, Alice	6052

Name.	Roll No.
Push, Sylvester T.	6055
Push, Annie	15832
Pusley, Jane	9133
Pusley, Simon	9174
Pusley, Betsy	9175
Pusley, Rhoda	9176
Pusley, Lillie	9177
Pusley, William	9178
Pusley, Joshua	9198
Pusley, Silas	9220
Pusley, Nancy	9221
Pusley, Anna	9222
Pusley, Dora	9223
Pusley, Jane	9289
Pusley, Mary	9290
Pusley, Edward	9293
Pusley, Elizabeth	9368
Pusley, Murtie	9369
Pusley, George	9370
Pusley, Cornelia	9371
Pusley, Lou	9374
Pusley, Lyman	9433
Pusley, Lizzie	9424
Pusley, Ida	9435
Pusley, Evalena	9436
Pusley, Osborne	9437
Pusley, Bertha Audre	9438
Pusley, Susan	9475
Pusley, Jack	9548
Pusley, Willie	9549
Pusley, John	9562
Pusley, Will	9563
Pusley, Juanita	9564
Pusley, Ingres	9565
Pusley, Maudie May	9567
Pusley, Abner	9618
Pusley, Sedalia	9619
Pusley, Dave	9620
Pusley, Ablena	9621
Pusley, Calvin Dawes	9622
Pusley, Minnie May	9623
Pusley, McAlester	12773
Pusley, Sallie	12866
Pusley, Nancy	12869
Pusley, Nancy Jr.	12871
Pusley, William W.	12930
Pusley, Collins G.	12931
Pusley, Susan	13622
Pusley, Alinton	15639
Pulcher, John	9230
Pulcher, Ella B.	12072
Pulcher, Sarah	13809
Pulcher, Belle	13810
Pulcher, Alice	13811
Pulcher, Osborn	13812
Puckett, William	10942
Puckett, Edna C.	10943
Putman, Susan	11089
Quincy, Melvina	660
Quincy, Jerome Ervin	661
Quincy, Magdelene	662
Quincy, Martha	663
Quincy, Erasmus	664
Quincy, Vada	665
Quincy, Alice	666
Quincy, Julia	667
Quincy, Wm. Warren	668
Quincy, Jefferson	6576
Quincy, Robert Lee	6577
Quincy, Fred Ross	12687
Quincy, Nanna Pearl	12689
Quinn, Eastman	6717
Quinn, Thomas	6718
Quinn, James	6720
Quinn, Lila	7413
Quinton, Elizabeth	8769
Quinton, Samuel	8770
Quinton, Charles	8771
Quinton, Joel	8783
Quinton, Elizabeth	8784
Quinton, Edward	8785
Quinton, Lillie	8787
Quinton, James	8862
Quinton, Avery	14735
Quinton, Myrtle	14895
Randolph, Minnie	202

Randolph, Wirt Aubrey	203
Randolph, Anna E.	15522
Randolph, Lee	15523
Randolph, Leonard	15524
Randolph, Oda Olline	15525
Ramseyer, Edward	712
Ratliff, Sophia	4066
Randell, Mattie	4166
Randell, Ruth	4167
Randell, Lazerus	4168
Randell, Willie	4169
Randell, Elizabeth L.	14921
Randell, Robert J.	14922
Raulston, Arabella M.	4336
Raulston, Martin V.	4337
Raulston, Nora D.	4338
Raulston, Anna L.	4339
Raulston, John F.	4340
Raulston, Sophia	4341
Raulston, Robert E.	4342
Rail, Mary	6430
Rail, William A.	6431
Rail, Fannie	6432
Rabon, Ora	8081
Rabon, Ethel M.	8278
Rabon, Floyd	8279
Rabon, Hazel	8280
Rabon, Curtis	8281
Rabon, Cora E.	8378
Rabon, Eunice	8380
Rabon, Lee Ora	8381
Rabon, Judith M. E.	9097
Rabon, Aline May	9080
Rabon, Sudie Marie	9081
Ramsey, Ellen	10238
Ramsey, Ellis	10379
Ramsey, Lena	10678
Ramsey, Turner Munroe	10681
Ramsey, Mary N.	11036
Ray, Benton	11500
Ray, Theresa	11501
Ray, Ralph	11502
Ray, Alta	11503
Ralls, Eva A.	12180
Ralls, Sarah	12181
Ralls, Eva Claude	12182
Ralls, Joseph G. Jr.	12183
Ralls, Thomas S.	12184
Ralls, Lewis Henry	12185
Rainey, Gertrude	12333
Rainey, William Franklin	12334
Rainey, Joseph Aloyious	12335
Rexroat, Estelle Belle	490
Rexroat, Phoebe	497
Rector, Ozious James P.	791
Rector, Mary Delilah	792
Rector, Emma F.	793
Reed, Alexander H.	2091
Reed, Michael	2093
Reed, Winey	9122
Reed, Melvina	9123
Reed, Raymond	9124
Reed, Joe	9125
Reed, Arlee	9815
Reed, Jack	11074
Reed, Maggie	12808
Reed, George	13932
Reed, Seborn	14938
Reed, Chicago	15572
Read, Lizzie	5379
Reid, Archie	9822
Reid, Charles	9823
Reid, Cadmus	9824
Reid, Arthur	9825
Reid, Roy	9826
Reid, Marion V.	9827
Reeves, Rachel	3219
Reynolds, Eliza	5217
Reynolds, Inis U.	10278
Reynolds, Ada	12794
Reynolds, Ruford I.	12796
Reynolds, Charles	13907
Reynolds, Felicity L.	14319
Reynolds, James T.	14320
Reynolds, Hugh A.	14322

Name.	Roll No.
Reynolds, Alta G.	14323
Reynolds, Felicity L. Jr.	14324
Reynolds, Earl V.	14325
Reynolds, William Jackson	15831
Reichert, Josephine	6812
Reichert, William W.	6813
Reichert, Johanna Marie	6814
Reichert, Ottilie Josephine	6815
Reagan, Phoebe A.	7455
Reagan, Gertrude A.	7456
Reagan, Mary G.	11322
Reagan, Thomas B.	11324
Reese, Mollie	9725
Reese, Basil	9726
Reese, David D.	9727
Reese, John T.	9728
Redpath, Sula L.	12835
Redpath, Lula	12836
Repath, Willie	12837
Redpath, Roy Cecil	12838
Redpath, Ruth	12839
Reel, Jennie	13062
Rhea, Eugenie	15031
Rhea, Willie	15032
Rhea, Elizabeth	15033
Riley, Joanna	102
Riddle, William	184
Riddle, Ella	185
Riddle, Mary Belle	186
Riddle, Arthur Lee	187
Riddle, Robert	188
Riddle, Jesse	7790
Riddle, Lorin A.	8916
Riddle, George W.	8984
Riddle, Edmond K.	8985
Riddle, Melinee	8986
Riddle, Samuel L.	8987
Riddle, Eureka J.	8988
Riddle, Thomas J.	8989
Riddle, Richard R.	9071
Riddle, Shingo, L.	9072
Riddle, Daisy K.	9073
Riddle, Mary A.	10755
Riddle, Thelma D.	10756
Riddle, Bartis G.	10757
Riddle, Dolphus A.	10915
Riddle, Oscar	10916
Riddle, Jesse G.	10917
Riddle, Siney	11828
Riddle, Sam	12767
Riddle, Cephus	12768
Riddle, Cillin	12769
Riddle, Georgian	12770
Riddle, Sallie	12957
Riddle, Coleman	13056
Riddle, Nancy	13057
Riddle, Lucinda	14831
Riddle, John W.	15049
Riddle, Susan	15694
Riggan, Edith	291
Riggan, Vada	292
Riggan, Burniece	293
Ritchey, Mamie W.	404
Ritchey, Vera	405
Ritchey, Cora	406
Ritchey, Jennie	407
Ripley, Dixon	8609
Risener, Lillian	9854
Risener, Emery	9855
Risener, Vinnie	9856
Risener, Lucy	10258
Risener, Lizzie	10259
Risener, Elmira	10260
Risener, George	10261
Risener, Eliza	10262
Risener, Henry	10263
Risener, Jessie	10264
Risener, Jack	10265
Risener, Tryfenia	10410
Risener, Adelaide	10412
Risener, Benjamin	10413
Risener, Rufus	10414
Risener, Vivian	10415
Richards, Cornelia	10949

Name.	Roll No.
Richards, Clara E.	11157
Richards, Harriet C.	11158
Richards, Irena A.	12517
Richards, Clifton L.	12518
Richards, Oscar Horton	12519
Ridgeway, Sarah E.	11630
Ridgeway, Annie	11631
Ridgeway, Mary L.	11632
Ridgeway, William L.	11633
Ridgeway, Henry E.	11635
Riggs, Samuel	12901
Riggs, Lee	12902
Riggs, Wilson	12903
Richerson, Maggie F.	14286
Richerson, Bertha Etta	14287
Richerson, John L.	14293
Richardson, Lucinda Cordelia	15176
Richardson, Fannie Elizabeth	15177
Richardson, Panola	15178
Richardson, Nietie Jones	15179
Richardson, Lela Buford	15180
Richardson, Robert Devotie	15181
Ridley, William Munroe	14881
Ritter, David	16104
Roff, Andrew V.	70
Roff, William D.	72
Ross, Daniel	395
Ross, William T.	7761
Ross, Katie	7762
Ross, A. Frank Jr.	7763
Ross, James K.	7764
Ross, Alta	7765
Ross, Henry G.	7766
Ross, Willie	7767
Ross, Gladys	7768
Ross, Dwight M.	7769
Ross, Louis	7770
Ross, Aaron F.	9738
Ross, Samuel B.	9739
Ross, Hallie	9740
Ross, Winema	9741
Ross, Ione	9742
Robinson, Emeline E.	743
Robinson, Alex	863
Robinson, Emely F.	864
Robinson, Ida M.	865
Robinson, Birdie E.	866
Robinson, James B.	867
Robinson, Ollie Fay	868
Robinson, Amy	943
Robinson, Emma	2387
Robinson, James	2388
Robinson, Phebe	2389
Robinson, Mary	3735
Robinson, Amsiah	5966
Robinson, Elsie	5968
Robinson, Jane	5969
Robinson, Lyman	5970
Robinson, Moses	5971
Robinson, John	5972
Robinson, Frank	7316
Robinson, Ellen	7317
Robinson, Calvin	7318
Robinson, Green	7319
Robinson, Mirtle	7321
Robinson, Clisto C.	10191
Robinson, Loring	10628
Robinson, Betsy	10629
Robinson, Raymond	10630
Robinson, Sallie	10631
Robinson, Wallace	10775
Robinson, Sina	10776
Robinson, Stulger E.	10777
Robinson, Lewis	10797
Robinson, David	10813
Robinson, Jessie M.	10814
Robinson, Jerome	10815
Robinson, Edward	10816
Robinson, George	10918
Robinson, Lina	11266
Robinson, Peter	12113
Robinson, William	12200

Name.	Roll No.	Name.	Roll No.
Robinson, Lourena L.	13149	Robert, James	12064
Robinson, Coleman	13150	Robert, Malinda	12065
Robinson, Carrie A.	13151	Rosenthal, Ernestine	3845
Robinson, Nannie B.	13152	Rosenthal, Jacob	3846
Robinson, Ella L.	13153	Rosenthal, Maggie	3847
Robinson, McKee F.	13154	Rosenthal, Parker	3848
Robinson, Cyrus	13313	Rosenthal, Ally Pate	3849
Robinson, Newton	13315	Roebuck, Isabella	3900
Robinson, Joel	13316	Roebuck, Cephas	3904
Robinson, Willie May	13317	Roebuck, William	4052
Robinson, Jesse	13445	Roebuck, Malina	4092
Robinson, Finnie	13446	Roebuck, Willie	4093
Robinson, Walter	13447	Roebuck, Zack	4094
Robinson, William	13834	Roebuck, David B.	4256
Robinson, Lee	14061	Roebuck, Edward	4350
Robinson, James	14064	Roebuck, Betsy	4351
Robinson, Billy	14065	Roebuck, Percy L.	4352
Robinson, William	13348	Roebuck, Henry	4353
Robinson, Jane	14348	Roebuck, Ben	4377
Robinson, Minnie	14349	Roebuck, Edward	4378
Robinson, Josiah	14350	Roebuck, Oscar	4379
Robinson, Teresa	14351	Roebuck, Oliver	4380
Robinson, Charles J.	14352	Roebuck, Elmira	4381
Robinson, Rosa A.	14353	Roebuck, Isabelle	4382
Robinson, Mary Esther	14354	Roebuck, Ettie	4383
Robinson, Sam	14928	Roebuck, Ulyssus	4384
Robinson, Mary	14929	Roebuck, Susan	4385
Robinson, Julius	14930	Roebuck, Clarissy M.	4386
Robinson, Cora	15172	Roebuck, William	4727
Robinson, Delany	15173	Roebuck, David E.	4728
Robinson, Minnie	15174	Roebuck, Carrie	5014
Robinson, Pearl	15175	Roberson, Lymon	4302
Robinson, Mary	15573	Roberson, Sophia	4303
Robinson, Rose Ella	15873	Roberson, Tobias	4304
Robinson, Matie Lillian	15876	Roberson, Aurilla	4305
Robinson, Maudie E.	15877	Roberson, James	8594
Roberts, Myrtle	744	Roberson, Pollie	8595
Roberts, Maud	745	Roberson, Gibson	8596
Roberts, Minnie	746	Roberson, Caldwell	8597
Roberts, Mamie	747	Roberson, Margaret	10609
Roberts, Ethel	750	Roberson, Ruth	10610
Roberts, Mildred	751	Roberson, Reola	12657
Roberts, Mollie	4108	Roberson, Elbert W.	12658
Roberts, Beulah May	4109	Roberson, Alfred W.	12659
Roberts, Susan	4180	Roberson, Arthur L.	12660
Roberts, Daniel	4299	Roberson, Gertie	12661
Roberts, Eliza	4301	Robertson, Irene	8107
Roberts, Moses	4315	Robertson, Vivia	13440
Roberts, Eastman	4712	Robertson, Wesley L.	13444
Roberts, Ella	4713	Rogers, Mary M.	4989
Roberts, Benjamin J.	9943	Rogers, Mary I.	4990
Roberts, Jesse	9944	Rogers, Isaac L.	4991
Roberts, Cordelia	9945	Rogers, William F.	5030
Roberts, Solomon	9946	Rogers, William F. Jr.	5031
Roberts, Hidalgo J.	9947	Rogers, Florence May	5032
Roberts, Georgiana	11425	Rogers, Alice	12401
Roberts, Emeline	11426	Rogers, Mary E.	12555
Roberts, Laymon	11485	Rogers, John M.	12556
Roberts, Susan	11486	Rogers, George	14967
Roberts, Rebecca	11487	Rogers, Cowee	14968
Roberts, Sampson	11813	Robbins, David	6618
Roberts, Ramsey	11841	Rowe, Charles H.	7337
Roberts, Elias	11842	Rose, Annie	7717
Roberts, Henry	12024	Rose, Dallas M.	7718
Roberts, Betsey	13448	Rose, Grover C.	7719
Roberts, Sloan	13890	Rose, Norman C.	7720
Roberts, Josephine	15030	Rose, William M.	7721
Roberts, Emely F.	15041	Rose, Bertie E.	7722
Roberts, Estola	15583	Rose, Wilmon	8372
Roberts, Myrtle M.	15582	Rose, Jincy	8373
Roberts, Mary E.	15584	Rose, John	8376
Roberts, Vicey	15846	Rose, Martha	8377
Roberts, Thomas	15847	Rose, Nettie	12143
Roberts, Carrie	15872	Rose, Charles C.	12144
Robert, Semiton,	1089	Rose, Della	12145
Robert, Watkin	1090	Rose, Otto	12146
Robert, Mollie	1397	Rose, Osceola	12147
Robert, David	3313	Rose, Robert F.	12148
Robert, Silas	3554	Rose, Earnest	12149
Robert, Sarah	3555	Rose, Pearl	15891
Robert, Ben	3811	Rockman, Lizzie	8046
Robert, Daniel	5769	Rockman, William H.	8047
Robert, Wynie	5770	Rockman, Leona May	8051
Robert, Raymond D.	5771	Robeson, Joe	9432
Robert, Litsey	5772	Robb, Czarena	11143
Robert, Artie	5978	Roark, Lucy A.	12094

Name.	Roll No.	Name.	Roll No.
Rowley, Harry G.	12202	Sampson, Peter	3126
Roach, Joanna	12339	Sampson, Silena	3128
Roach, Jewel I.	12340	Sampson, Malissa	4542
Roach, Ruby W.	12341	Sampson, Joseph	4543
Roach, Vinnie O.	12342	Sampson, Angeline	9423
Roach, Garnet	12343	Sampson, Marsell	14920
Roach, Onyx	12344	Samuel, Nellie	1550
Roach, Diamond	12345	Samuel, Noel	1551
Rozel, Lucy	12548	Samuel, Louisa	1647
Rozel, Harvey	12549	Samuel, Willie C.	1648
Rozel, Edward	12550	Samuel, Sampson	5821
Rozel, Lizzie	12551	Samuel, Artie	5822
Rozel, Susan	12552	Samuel, Silas	5823
Rozel, John Newton	14823	Samuel, Jerry H.	5824
Rockett, Ida M.	15792	Samuel, Emiline	5825
Rockett, Louis Henry	16216	Samuel, Joel	5826
Rockett, Ross Lee	16217	Samuel, Austin C.	5872
Rockett, Francis Mar-		Samuel, Silesie	5873
ion	16218	Samuel, Cillen	5874
Russell, Margaret W.	452	Samuel, Sophvin	5875
Russell, John	453	Samuel, Siceley	6069
Russell, Clabon	454	Samuel, Esther	6070
Russell, William	455	Samuel, Lillie	6071
Russell, Ellen	456	Samuel, Lymon	6072
Russell, Rhoda	457	Samuel, Louie	11621
Russell, Ruthie	458	Samuel, Annie	11622
Russell, Moses C.	459	Samuel, Timothy	15855
Russell, Perry Wright	460	Sanguin, Thomas	3850
Russell, Matt	461	Sanguin, Clyde	3851
Russell, Emma	4225	Sanguin, Charles A.	3853
Russell, Nettie	4226	Sanguin, Henry	3890
Russell, Etta	4227	Sanguin, Lena V.	3891
Russell, Ethen	4228	Sanguin, William M.	4181
Russell, James	4335	Salter, Hattie	3941
Russell, Robert	8018	Sauls, Triffinnie	4577
Russell, Eva	8019	Sauls, Wilson	4578
Russell, Mary A.	8101	Sauls, Oscar	4579
Russell, Mary	8102	Sauls, Benjamin	4580
Russell, Margaret	8103	Sauls, Bertha	4581
Russell, William M.	13230	Sage, Jane F.	6521
Russell, Lula Myrtle	13232	Sage, Sidney	6648
Russell, Bertha Viola	13233	Sage, Woody	6649
Russell, Lota Orin	13234	Sage, Cora E.	6650
Russell, Dan	13590	Sage, John	6651
Russell, Minnie	15540	Sage, Myrtle	6652
Russell, Maggie M.	13231	Sage, Maude	6653
Runton, Carnolie	6804	Sage, Eugene	6654
Runton, Wilson E.	6805	Sam, Elizabeth	6771
Runton, Burton	6806	Sam, Stanford	8716
Runton, Bertha	6807	Sam, Susan	8717
Runton, Bessie May	6808	Sam, Sallie	8718
Rucker, Willie	7656	Sam, Silas	8719
Rucker, Lawrence	15664	Sam, Morris	8767
Rushing, Caroline	13618	Sam, Sophia	8768
Rushing, Chas. William	13619	Sam, Fannie	12888
Rubottom, Matilda E.	14620	Sam, Eliza A.	12890
Rubottom, Matilda P.	14630	Sam, Ace	12891
Rubottom, Rosabelle	14623	Sam, Ann	14741
Rubottom, Ruthie Ruer	14624	Sam, Emma	14742
Rubottom, Minnie Viola	14625	Sam, Clifford	14781
Rubottom, Jesse An-		Sam, Nancy	14782
drew	14626	Sam, James	14783
Rubottom, Ella Evelyn	14627	Sanders, Nona	8544
Ryan, Theron J.	12492	Sanders, Newton	8545
Ryan, Annie	12493	Sanders, William	10192
Ryan, Louisa B.	12494	Sanders, George	10193
Ryan, Lola E.	12495	Sanders, Rhoda	10194
Ryan, Roy C.	12496	Sanders, Dot	10195
Ryan, Willamette	12497	Sanders, Amy	10196
Samis, Lyman	971	Sanders, Jewel	10197
Samis, Susan	972	Sanders, Robert	10902
Samis, Frank	973	Sanders, Frances	10903
Samis, Annie	974	Sanders, Solomon	15768
Samis, Lyda	975	Savage, Ida May	9095
Samis, Noah	976	Savage, Nettie P.	9096
Sampson, William	1391	Savage, Thelma M.	9097
Sampson, Lisean	2711	Savage, Claude C.	9098
Sampson, Thomas	2821	Savage, Willie May	9099
Sampson, Colbert	2824	Sadler, Mettie	12850
Sampson, Mary	2825	Sadler, Alex Matthew	12851
Sampson, Levi	3049	Sadler, Gracie Ellen	12852
Sampson, Eyahoke	3050	Samples, Maud R.	13107
Sampson, Noel	3124	Sacra, Clemmie G.	14185
Sampson, Lucy	3125	Sacra, Bettie	14186

Name.	Roll No.	Name.	Roll No.
Sacra, Lucy	14187	Sexton, Benjamin F.	7264
Sacra, John	4188	Sexton, Bryant	7265
Sacra, Agnes	14189	Sexton, Otto T.	7266
Sacra, Clemmie	14190	Sexton, Lella Lois	7267
Sanner, Willie	14288	Sexton, Mary	8322
Sanner, Louie	14289	Sexton, David	8323
Sanner, Jesse	14290	Sexton, Cora	8324
Sanner, Arie L.	14291	Sexton, Gilbert	8325
Sanner, George	14292	Sexton, Claracy	8326
Sanner, Lenna Etta	14294	Sexton, Charles D.	8838
Sanner, Walter	14295	Sexton, Joseph R.	8839
Satterfield, Drusilla	15620	Sexton, Berta M.	8840
Satterfield, James	15621	Sexton, Irene J.	8841
Satterfield, Idella	15622	Sexton, Lela J.	8842
Satterfield, Bennie	15623	Sexton, Melvina	8908
Satterfield, Ida	15624	Sexton, Martin	11147
Satterfield, Walter	15625	Sexton, Eliza A.	11468
Satterfield, Rufus	15930	Sexton, Shepard	11469
Scroggins, Geo.Thomas	40	Sexton, Susie A.	11470
Scroggins, Lee	13543	Sexton, Elsie	11471
Scroggins, Columbus	13544	Sexton, Nellie	11472
Scroggins, Annie Bell	13545	Sexton, David Jr.	11473
Scroggins, John F.	13546	Sexton, Dixon	11987
Scroggins, May	13547	Sexton, Susan	11988
Scroggins, Lucinda	14071	Sexton, Ella	11991
Scroggins, Alvin	14075	Sexton, Iwana	11992
Scott, Phoebe Ethel	685	Sexton, Alexander	11993
Scott, Lorena	690	Sexton, Willis	11995
Scott, Cephus	7017	Sexton, Jonas	12828
Scott, Daniel	7927	Sexton, Mary	13498
Scott, Phoebe	7928	Sexton, Annie	13973
Scott, Alice	8342	Sexton, Mandy	13974
Scott, Clifford B.	8344	Sexton, Minnie	15574
Scott, Willie	9110	Sealy	2878
Scott, Elizabeth	9111	Seeley, Alfred	9118
Scott, Isabelle	9112	Seeley, Missy	9119
Scott, Mary	9113	Seeley, Lona B.	9120
Scott, Dixon	9114	Seeley, Ona J.	9121
Scott, Sissy	9116	Seeley, Birdie	10020
Scott, Alexander	9227	Seeley, Gabe Horatio	10026
Scott, Sampson	10257	Self, Annie	4204
Scott, Jeremiah	10342	Self, William P.	4205
Scott, Aaron	10364	Self, Harvey E.	4206
Scott, Sila	10365	Self, James E.	4207
Scott, John	10458	Self, William O.	4208
Scott, Sibby	10459	Self, Ida	6744
Scott, Salina	10537	Self, Eula	6746
Scott, Cephus	11967	Self, Estella	6747
Scott, Refina E.	12054	Self, Earl	6748
Scott, Gladys M.	12055	Self, Leona	12070
Scott, Johnnie C.	12059	Self, William	12071
Scott, Emily E.	12390	Self, Viva Lulu	12073
Scott, Viola M.	12391	Self, Lillian O.	12216
Scott, Claude	12392	Self, Martha G.	12217
Scott, Elbert	12393	Self, Ruth	12218
Scott, Willie	12394	Self, Joseph Manning	12219
Scott, George W.	13709	Self, Earl	12220
Scott, Phoebe	13822	Secor, William H.	9589
Scott, John	13823	Secor, Cecil R.	9590
Scott, Laura	13824	Secor, Rufinia M.	9591
Scott, Lula Elizabeth	13825	Secor, Sillin	9592
Scott, George	14903	Secor, Willie Beatrice	9593
Scott, Ina	14904	Seldner, Olive C.	9805
Scantlen, Laurena	14750	Seldner, Ruby A.	9806
Scantlen, Jennings M.	14751	Seldner, Delorus V.	9807
Scantlen, Leona	14752	Seldner, Oscar A.	9808
Schrock, Frances	15501	Seldner, Marcus O.	9809
Schrock, Arthur Lee	15502	Semple, Minnie	10162
See, Hibernia	204	Semple, William F.	10163
See, Lula	210	Semple, Charles C.	10164
See, Ollie	211	Semple, Rettie	10165
Sexton, Emmerson	757	Semple, Julia	10166
Sexton, Charles	6394	Semple, Abby	10167
Sexton, Thomas J.	6531	Semple, Annie	10168
Sexton, Ralph H.	6532	Semple, Frank P.	13540
Sexton, Roberta	6533	Semple, Alta Roberta	13541
Sexton, William Earl	6534	Senter, Lavinia S.	10564
Sexton, Henry	6803	Selsor, Agnes	11557
Sexton, George	6855	Selsor, Joe A.	11558
Sexton, Lillie A.	6856	Selsor, Ela R.	11559
Sexton, Henry Jr.	6857	Selsor, Ida S.	11560
Sexton, Mary J.	6858	Selsor, Arthur A.	11561
Sexton, Etha M.	6859	Selsor, Leona G.	11562
Sexton, Theodore Floyd	6860	Selsor, Lee Nora	11563

Name.	Roll No.	Name.	Roll No.
Selsor, Bernice	11564	Simpson, Walter	7929
Seco, Angie	12058	Simpson, Nettie R.	8164
Seago, Addie A.	14957	Simpson, Edward R.	8165
Seago, John T.	14958	Simpson, William N.	8166
Seago, David E.	14959	Simpson, Marion	8167
Seago, Charles W., Jr.	14960	Simpson, Elizabeth H.	10973
Seago, William F.	14961	Simpson, John	12465
Seago, Ramsey D.	14962	Simpson, Mima	12466
Seago, Ida May	14965	Simmons, James	2161
Seaboit, Mollie Ann	15541	Simmons, Viney	2162
Shelby, Rebecca	57	Simmons, Irvin	2163
Shi, Isaac Garvin	290	Simmons, John	9045
Shults, Effie	529	Simmons, Fred	9046
Shults, Jennette	530	Simmons, Gracy	9047
Shults, Winnie	11258	Simmons, Joshua	9048
Shults, John	12221	Simmons, Eliza E.	10928
Shults, James	12222	Simmons, Minnie May	10930
Shults, Ollie	12223	Simmons, Charley L.	10931
Shults, Verner	12224	Simmons, Matilda E.	15256
Shults, Sophia	12962	Simmons, Viola May	15257
Sheegog, Myrtie	679	Simmons, Nathaniel	
Sheegog, May Eula	680	Roddom	15258
Sheegog, James Bland	681	Simmons, Maude B.	15558
Sheegog, Maggie Lillie	682	Simmons, Fay	15559
Shotube, Dickson	1650	Simmons, Wallace	15560
Shotube, Jane	1651	Simmon, Willie	6905
Shotube, Louie	1654	Simpty, Lafit	5026
Shoney, Wilson	1726	Simpty, Narcissa	5027
Shoney, Phelena	1727	Simpty, Cillin	5034
Sheaheke, Washington	1881	Sims, Lula	6817
Shaw, Collin	3559	Sims, Elam A.	6818
Shaw, Bessie	3560	Sims, Mary Ann	6819
Shaw, Keith	3561	Silmon, Jennie	8627
Shaw, Samuel	3562	Silmon, Lee	12819
Shaw, David	3563	Silmon, Millie	12820
Shelton, James	4690	Silmon, Ike	12821
Sherred, Becky	4816	Silmon, Jefferson	12822
Sherred, Wesley	4934	Sirmans, Elsie	12400
Sherred, Martha	4935	Sirmans, Linnie	12402
Sherred, Ida	4936	SirmansGelia	12403
Sherred, Josephus	5077	Sittel, Malvina	13908
Sherred, Emma	14035	Sittel, Edward	13909
Sherred, Shub	14038	Sittel, William B.	13910
Shoat, Julius	5716	Sittel, Myrtle	13911
Shoat, Lucy	5717	Sittel, Lottie	13912
Shoat, Louie	5719	Sittel, Josie	13913
Shoat, Agnes	15830	Sittel, Fritz, Jr.	13914
Shirey, Edmond F.	6419	Sittel, Farris G.	13915
Shropshire, Susan	8105	Sittel, Melven Cornish	13916
Shropshire, Adolph	8106	Skelton, Alexander	4624
Shwinogee, Lucinda	8591	Skelton, Mollie	4625
Sharkey, Impson	10416	Skelton, Noel	4669
Sharkey, Elsie	10417	Skelton, Jincy	4670
Sharkey, Emma	10418	Skelton, James	4690
Sharkey, Israel	10889	Slaton, Mary Jane	832
Sharkey, Louisa	10890	Slaughter, Florence	6490
Shannon, Rennie	11054	Slaughter, John	6491
Shannon, Anna	11055	Slinker, Lizzie	12162
Shannon, Orrick L.	11056	Slinker, Thomas Dewey	12163
Shannon, Edfred L.	11057	Slinker, Hellen	12164
Shockley, Mary	11230	Sloan, Edward P.	12830
Shockley, Lemuel G.	11231	Sloan, Lizzie	12829
Shinn, Mary	11404	Smith, Elizabeth	329
Shinn, Rena E.	11405	Smith, Lois Hazel	330
Shinn, Charley	11406	Smith, Jane	4684
Shinn, Henry	11407	Smith, Sallie	5590
Shield, Nancy	11936	Smith, Mary A.	6159
Shield, Sarah	11937	Smith, Emma	6578
Shield, Israel	11938	Smith, Willy	6579
Shield, Jonas	11939	Smith, Fred	6580
Shield, Lurena	11940	Smith, Theodore	6581
Shield, Hattie	11941	Smith, George L.	7786
Shield, Classie	11942	Smith, Hermon E.	7787
Shipman, Ella	13861	Smith, Claude R.	7788
Shipman, Buck	13863	Smith, Ora G.	7789
Shipman, Kieth	13864	Smith, Letha	7936
Sharp, Elba	14076	Smith, Cora	8226
Sharp, Leo C.	14077	Smith, Mary F.	8227
Shoemake, Alma	14619	Smith, Robert F.	8229
Simpson, Siney	1514	Smith, Milton,	8560
Simpson, Isaac	4757	Smith, Jackson	9058
Simpson, Sarah	4758	Smith, Morris S.	10435
Simpson, John	4759	Smith, Caroline	10436
Simpson, Sally Ann	6933	Smith, Ruth	10437

Name.	Roll No.
Smith, George G.	10438
Smith, Geo. Homer Colbert	10439
Smith, Louvina	10507
Smith, Ella L.	10508
Smith, Claude	10509
Smith, Kittie	11051
Smith, Wesley	12467
Smith, Willie V. L.	12512
Smith, Jesse M.	12513
Smith, Hill T.	12514
Smith, Sibbie	13066
Smith, Jacob	13067
Smith, Hervey R.	13194
Smith, Elmore	13195
Smith, Freeman R.	13207
Smith, Eliza A.	13260
Smith, Sim	14023
Smith, Fred	14024
Smith, Ray	14025
Smith, Eric	14026
Smith, Pearl	14027
Smith, Annie	14028
Smith, Phoebe	14029
Smith, Alex	14728
Smith, Anna	15274
Smith, Napoleon Bonaparte	15280
Smith, Nellie	15281
Smith, Martha Virginia	15282
Smith, Orlean	15519
Smith, Frances	15520
Smith, Fulton	15521
Smith, Mary E.	16197
Smith, Mary D.	16198
Smith, Margurite	16199
Smith, George	16200
Smallwood, Narcissa	4396
Smallwood, Mary	4395
Smallwood, William Jr.	4399
Smallwood, Martha	4400
Smallwood, Robert	5078
Smallwood, Lena	10306
Smallwood, Daniel	10860
Smallwood, Benjamin	10861
Smallwood, Minnie	11073
Smallwood, Annie	11497
Smallwood, Ada	11498
Smallwood, Lorenzo	12248
Smallwood, Ruthie	12290
Smallwood, Lizzie	13588
Smallfield, Ellen	11254
Smallfield, John	11256
Smiser, Norma E.	11509
Smiser, Norma E., Jr.	11510
Smiser, Butler S., Jr.	11511
Smiser, Ira M.	11512
Smiser, Garnett S.	11513
Smiser, Posey B.	11514
Smart, Annie	13177
Smart, Hazel	13178
Smart, Herbert	13179
Smart, Leroy	13180
Smart, Claud	13181
Snead, Thomas K.	2058
Snead, Edward P.	2059
Snead, Susan J.	2060
Snead, Ruberta	2061
Snead, John G.	2062
Snead, Louis	3526
Snead, Emiline	3527
Snead, Josephine	3528
Snead, Dewey	3530
Snider, Annis	6777
Snider, Beatrice	6782
Snider, Nettie	9240
Snider, Beulah	9246
Solomon, Cephus	2427
Solomon, Criston	2428
Solomon, Willie	2429
Solomon, Dickson	2430
Solomon, Thompson	2431
Sockey, Robert	6111
Sockey, William	6113
Sockey, Rhoda	6233

Name.	Roll No.
Sockey, Moses	6237
Sockey, Richard	6979
Sockey, Thomas	7130
Sockey, Lewis	7132
Sockey, Robert	7133
Sockey, Cleveland	7134
Sockey, Dora	7135
Sockey, Edward	7136
Sockey, Eve	7370
Sockey, Lula	8257
Sockey, Salina	8258
Sockey, Josephine	8397
Sockey, Emmit	8402
Sockey, Ben	8678
Sockey, Elizabeth	8679
Sockey, Davis	8680
Sockey, Melvin	8681
Sockey, Martha	8682
Sockey, John	8684
Sockey, Ned	8828
Sockey, Malinda	8829
Sockey, Mary	8830
Sockey, Eli	8831
Sockey, Myrtle	8832
Sockey, Irene Maree	8833
Sockey, James	14767
Sockey, Willie	14894
Sockey, Louvicy	15834
Sorrells, Catherine	9555
Sorrells, Ada	9556
Sorrells, Dora	9557
Sorrells, Irma	9558
Sorrells, Minnie	9559
Sorrells, George Carson	9561
Sorrells, Mary Frances	14621
Sorrells, Ethel Lee	14628
Southard, Ida M.	15880
Southard, Engle	15881
Spain, Thomas G.	237
Spain, Thomas H.	238
Spain, Sidney B.	239
Spain, Elizabeth	240
Spain, Emma P.	241
Spain, Nellie May	242
Spain, Agnes	652
Spain, James R.	243
Spain, Jubilee	289
Spain, S. Beauregard	309
Spain, Ollie Lee	310
Spain, Maudie	311
Spain, Dora	312
Spain, Georgie D.	313
Spain, Mary Ann	314
Spain, Frank	343
Spain, Ruby M.	344
Spain, Leah Ima	346
Spain, Granger	650
Spain, Annie M.	651
Spain, Andrew	9736
Spain, Jesse Lee	9737
Spain, Franklin G.	14498
Spain, David M.	15564
Sperling, Henrietta W	376
Sperling, Charles A.	377
Sperling, Carrie	378
Sperling, Gertie	379
Sperling, Clabe	380
Sperling, Christina	381
Sperling, Nathie Jewell	382
Sperling, Margret Henrietta	383
Spicer, Julia Ann Margaret	638
Spicer, Nancy Belle	639
Spicer, Harmon Custer	640
Spicer, Joseph C.	641
Spring, William	3854
Spring, John	3855
Spring, Nancy	3856
Spring, Eli	3857
Spring, Isaac	3858
Spring, Melinda	3859
Spring, Christopher	3860
Spring, John Jr.	3861
Spring, Jackson	3862
Spring, Bunny	3863

Name.	Roll No.	Name.	Roll No.
Spring, Levi	3864	Stewart, John B.	15771
Spring, Sophia	3865.	Stewart, John D.	15772
Spring, David	3866	Stewart, Stella May	15773
Spring, Sarah	3867	Stewart, George E.	15774
Spring, Franklin	3868	Stewart, Wynona	
Spring, Jesse	3869	Elizabeth	15775
Spring, Simeon	3870	Stewart, Knox	15776
Spring, Joel	3874	Steward, Vicey	887
Spring, Winnie R.	3875	Steward, Carrie B.	888
Spring, Joel Jr.	3876	Steward, Robert Lee	890
Spring, Lawrence E.	3877	Steward, Benjamin	
Spring, Jesse H.	3878	Layfett	891
Spring, Winnie	3879	Steward, Lige	15035
Spring, Dewey L.	3880	Stevenson, Rosa	353
Spring, Robert Murry	3881	Stowers, Laura	517
Spring, Ida E.	3927	Stowers, Richard Henry	518
Spring, Edith Gayzelle	3929	Stowers, Lou	519
Spring, James F.	3995	Stowers, Cordelia	520
Spring, Zeno	3996	Stowers, Melvina	521
Spring, Louis	4029	Stowers, Mattie	522
Spring, Lillie	4030	Stowers, Amos Henry	523
Spring, Clarence E.	4031	Stowers, John Rally	525
Spring, Etha May	4032	Stowers, David Sidney	14507
Spring, Essie M.	4033	Stidham, Zachariah	531
Spring, Walter	4158	Stidham, Marion	532
Spring, Willie	4229	Stidham, Lillie P.	534
Spring, Laura D.	4230	Stidham, Ada	535
Spring, Granville L.	4231	Stidham, Johnathan S.	536
Spring, Nannie	4232	Stidham, Jesse	589
Spring, Lillie M.	4233	Stidham, Walter Marion	590
Spring, William B.	4234	Stidham, Jessie May	591
Spring, Carrie H.	4235	Stidham, Nettie Anna	
Spring, Baziel	4236	Bell	592
Spring, Hazel Edna	4237	Stidham, Frank R.	14557
Spring, Lula M.	4298	Stidham, Pearl	16202
Spring, Mollie	4491	Stephen, Granson	1071
Spring, Joshuaway	4496	Stephen, Sarah	1072
Spring, Samuel B.	4663	Stephen, Louis	1438
Spring, Ethel	4664	Stephen, Agnes	1439
Spring, Willie	5383	Stephen, Paul	1723
Spring, Solomon	5427	Stephen, Bicey	1724
Spring, Siney	5437	Stephen, Arion	1725
Spring, Winnie	5438	Stephen, Nancy	1734
Spring, Nancy	5439	Stephen, Simmie	2107
Spring, Rebecca	5440	Stephen, Lemus	2130
Spring, David J.	5524	Stephen, Melissa	2131
Spring, Ada	5525	Stephen, Julious	14618
Spring, Levena	5526	Stephen, Linas	14651
Spring, Daisy	5527	Stephen, Crety	14652
Spring, Benjamin J.	7230	Stephens, Bynum	2087
Spring, Joseph B.	11878	Stephens, Elsy	2088
Spring, Ida	13371	Stephens, Minnie	2089
Spring, Fatie	13372	Stephens, Martha	6877
Speaker, Millie	4312	Stephens, Charley	6878
Speaker, Martin	4418	Stephens, Roscoe	6879
Speaker, Sophia	4419	Stephens, Catherine	6880
Speegle, Lucy P. M.	5039	Stephens, Indianola	6881
Speegle, John F.	5041	Stephens, Ida M.	6882
Speegle, Lion E.	5042	Stephens, Nellie	7268
Spann, Freeman R.	8568	Stephens, Magnita	7269
Spann, John H.	8569	Stephens, James R.	7270
Spann, Claud E.	8570	Steven, Tom	2114
Spann, Carrel M.	8571	Stevens, Ellen	14083
Sparks, Cornelia Maye	9241	Stevens, Samuel	14084
Sparks, Wilford	9248	Stevens, Eva	14085
Spears, Julia Ann	13773	Stevens, Mary	14086
Sturdivant, Sallie	13	Stevens, Martha	14087
Sturdivant, Claud Osa	14	Stevens, John D.	14088
Stewart, Charles F.	193	Stanley, Salena	1350
Stewart, Nancy	194	Stanley, James W.	1351
Stewart, Siney	2278	Stanley, Ada N.	1352
Stewart, Semie	2448	Stanley, Samuel M.	1353
Stewart, Rise	2449	Stanley, Helen A.	1354
Stewart, Levi	2450	Stanley, Bettie J.	1355
Stewart, Ilis	2451	Stanley, William R.	1356
Stewart, Silison	2452	Standley, James S.	7454
Stewart, Nancy E.	9265	Standley, Marie S.	11508
Stewart, Mary	9283	Standley, James W.	14334
Stewart, Minnie B.	10783	Standley, Nannie	15288
Stewart, Samuel E.	10784	Standley, Gertrude	15289
Stewart, Wicy	11306	Standley, Eugene	15331
Stewart, Nancy	14675	Standley, Clarence	15332
Stewart, Bailey	15021	Standley, Mattie Etna	15333
Stewart, James	15022	Standley, Frederick	
Stewart, Newton	15023	Washington	15334
Stewart, Bonny	15024		

Name.	Roll No.	Name.	Roll No.
Standley, Mabel	15483	Suckkey, Julia	1675
Standley, Inez	15489	Suckky, Bettie	1680
Standley, James Frank-		Suckky, Cillissie	1681
lin	15598	Sunney, James	4604
Standley, Albert	16210	Sunny, Amy	11111
Stechi, Solomon	1707	Sunny, Dora	11287
Stechi, Eliza	15936	Surratt, Fena	7969
Stalard, Jimmy	3896	Surratt, Cooper	12493
Stacy, Andrew J.	7918	Surratt, Irene	15445
Stacy, Henry J.	7919	Surratt, Annie	15446
Stacy, William F.	7920	Sutherland, Lena D.	10360
Stallaby, James	8753	Sutherland, Valeria E.	15026
Stallaby, Sallie	8754	Sumter, Emma	12584
Stallaby, Robert	8755	Swarm, Inez	3822
Stallaby, Selaney	8756	Swarm, Nova Belle	3834
Stallaby, Hattie	8757	Swink, Lena B.	4992
Stallaby, Tennis	8758	Swink, Florence	4993
Stallaby, Dukes	8759	Swink, Henry D.	4994
Stallaby, James N.	8760	Swink, Bert R.	4995
Stallaby, Forbis	8761	Swink, J. W.	4996
Stallaby, Nannie	8762	Swink, Nannie	15706
Stallaby, Lizzie	8763	Swink, William E.	15707
Stallaby, Thomas	15993	Swink, Ida May	15709
Sterrett, Susan	9151	Swink, Inez	15854
Stallings, Carrie M.	9339	Swinney, Lola	14211
Stallings, Isabelle	9340	Taylor, John	112
Strickland, Arcola	9951	Taylor, Nettie	144
Strickland, Florence		Taylor, Carroll	446
Edna	9952	Taylor, William A.	447
Strickland, Meadie		Taylor, Pearlie May	448
Blanch	9953	Taylor, Zuleika	477
Strickland, Alfred	10898	Taylor, Johnie Rowena	478
Strickland, David E.	15919	Taylor, Lousina J.	653
Strickland, Mertie P.	15920	Taylor, Ruel Fenton	654
Starks, Thomas	10288	Taylor, Sallie	655
Starks, Lillie	10289	Taylor, Lurel E.	656
Starks, Robert Ernest	10290	Taylor, Carrie D.	657
Stanford, Rebecca	11244	Taylor, Wayne Oscar	658
Stanford, Sallie	13555	Taylor, Oliver	875
Stanford, Mary	13556	Taylor, Lonnie W.	876
Steel, Thomas	11858	Taylor, Mabel	877
Steel, Andrew	11859	Taylor, John	897
Stanton, William H.	12456	Taylor, Catherine	898
Stanton, Serena P.	12457	Taylor, Mary	899
Stanton, Arthur G.	12458	Taylor, Joseph	900
Stanton, Lettie I.	12459	Taylor, Jonas	901
Stanton, Lola Blanch	12460	Taylor, Johnson	902
Stanton, Rudolph J.	12628	Taylor, Alex	910
Stanton, Clyde E.	12629	Taylor, Yimmihona	911
Stanton, Arthur	12778	Taylor, Sibby	912
Stanton, Katie C.	12780	Taylor, Salina	913
Staton, Susan J.	12731	Taylor, Emma	914
Staton, William F.	12732	Taylor, David	915
Strong, Bridget	12754	Taylor, Robert	916
Strong, William H.	12755	Taylor, Sarah	1687
Stone, Agnes	13257	Taylor, Impson	1779
Stigler, Mary	13641	Taylor, Nancy J.	1790
Stigler, Edward Buck-		Taylor, Ellis	1856
ley	13642	Taylor, Lila	1857
Stigler, Willie Grady	13643	Taylor, Agnes	1858
Stigler, Hettie Lee	13644	Taylor, Charles J.	1959
Starritt, Mattie	14234	Taylor, Sarfin	1960
Starritt, Steadman	14235	Taylor, Simpson	1961
Starritt, Clemmy	14236	Taylor, Robert	2471
Starritt, Sidney	14237	Taylor, Bicey	2472
Starritt, Charles	14238	Taylor, Elsie	2473
Starritt, Thomas B.	14239	Taylor, Sylvester	2474
Stockman, Emely Eliza-		Taylor, Rosa	2475
beth	14522	Taylor, Icy	2476
Stockman, Jesse L.	14523	Taylor, Ben	2501
Stockman, Joseph Ven-		Taylor, Simon	2512
gel	14524	Taylor, Melvina	2513
Stealey, Lloyd G. B.	14945	Taylor, Frances	2514
Stealey, Lorenzo P.	14946	Taylor, John	2707
Stealey, Knoxa K.	14947	Taylor, Margaret	2708
Suddath, Elizabeth Roff	67	Taylor, Selin	2709
Suddath, Ralph M.	68	Taylor, John	2726
Suddath, Pauline	69	Taylor, Eliza	2727
Suddith, Ben	15601	Taylor, Levi	2728
Summer, Amanda L. M.	731	Taylor, Harriet	2729
Summer, Minnie	732	Taylor, Robinson	2730
Summer, Mertle May	15822	Taylor, Elizabeth	2731
Summers, Joseph	12003	Taylor, Susanna	2732
Suckky, Abel	1677	Taylor, Latis	3473

Name.	Roll No.	Name.	Roll No.
Taylor, Johnson	3542	Taliaferro, Janie Madison	15199
Taylor, Bicey	3703		
Taylor, Ellen	3704	Taliaferro, Henry Buford	15200
Taylor, Josiah Impson	3705		
Taylor, Becky	3706	Taliaferro, Robert Dorsey	15201
Taylor, Mary Jane	3707		
Taylor, Millie Jane	3708	Taliaferro, Nora	15382
Taylor, Summie	3709	Taliaferro, Eliza	15383
Taylor, Solomon	5814	Talvatona	3421
Taylor, Semie	5815	Talbert, Nicholas	10711
Taylor, Josephine	5816	Talbert, Victoria	10712
Taylor, Rhoda Ann	5817	Talbert, Arthur	10713
Taylor, Solomon Jr.	5818	Talbert, Katie Cristenia	10714
Taylor, Benjamin	5860	Tashka, Wallace	2314
Taylor, Alixen	5864	Tashka, Levi	2649
Taylor, Phelen	5871	Takalitubbi	3634
Taylor, Archibald	5883	Tanitubbi, Johnson	3905
Taylor, Thomas J.	5937	Tanitubbi, Lucy	3906
Taylor, Thompson	5941	Tanitubbi, James	3907
Taylor, Mary	5942	Tanitubbi, Charles	4649
Taylor, John	5943	Tanitubbi, Amelia	4650
Taylor, Sarah	5944	Tanitubbi, Allen	4689
Taylor, Battice	5945	Tanitubbi, Jennie	14690
Taylor, Joanna	5948	Taaffe, Maud	5131
Taylor, Fannie	6573	Taaffe, Jennie	5132
Taylor, Emiline	6639	Taaffe, Joseph	5133
Taylor, Phoebe	6640	Taaffe, May	5134
Taylor, Alice	6641	Taaffe, Francis	12332
Taylor, Charles	6642	Taaffe, Hollis	14694
Taylor, James	7338	Tanohubbie	7042
Taylor, Pettis	7339	Tanohubbie, Jincy	14745
Taylor, Willie M.	7340	Tarby, William	7981
Taylor, Pearl	7341	Tarney, Stephen	15783
Taylor, John	8277	Tadlock, Lou	9681
Taylor, Leitha	8415	Tanehill, Mintie	12598
Taylor, Tishy	8416	Tanehill, Edgar P.	12599
Taylor, Mamie	8417	Tanehill, Francis Ward	12600
Taylor, John	8859	Tekobbe, Bob	3813
Taylor, Wilburn	9229	Tekobbe, Susianna	3815
Taylor, Wilkin	9307	Tekobbe, Sam	15693
Taylor, Malinda	9308	Terry, Josephine	3836
Taylor, Mary	9310	Terry, James Auther	3838
Taylor, Elum	9311	Terry, Louis Victor	3839
Taylor, Johnson	9312	Terry, Edna	9843
Taylor, Charley	9328	Terry, Clarance Enoch	9844
Taylor, Rosa	9329	Takkubbee, Anna	8652
Taylor, Ben	9330	Takkubbee, Susanna	8653
Taylor, Jacob	9331	Takkubbee, Artemissa	8654
Taylor, Thomas	9333	Takkubbee, Ida	8655
Taylor, Tennessee	9334	Terry, Alice	11065
Taylor, Talitha	12547	Terry, Letha M.	11066
Taylor, James	13386	Terry, Ethel L.	11067
Taylor, Susan	13387	Tecumseh, Houston	7165
Taylor, Lillie	13390	Tecumseh, Jesse	7734
Taylor, Frances	13392	Tecumseh, Ida	7870
Taylor, Mary H.	14224	Tecumseh, Baker	7877
Taylor, Vera	14225	Terrell, Solomon	7977
Taylor, Juanita	14226	Terrell, Emiline	7978
Taylor, Lela	14227	Terrell, Daniel	7979
Taylor, John Davenport	14228	Terrell, Sillen	7980
Taylor, Sue Corine	14229	Terrell, Houston	8054
Taylor, Pelina	5947	Terrell, Louanna Smith	16201
Taylor, Lucy	14263	Tehomba, Annis	10906
Taylor, Henry	14264	Telle, Alinton	12337
Taylor, Ella	14265	Telle, Alinton R.	12338
Taylor, George	14266	Tennant, Emma H.	12662
Taylor, Lilly	14267	Tennant, Carrie E.	12663
Taylor, Frances	14268	Tennant, Wm. J. R.	12664
Taylor, Tracy	14797	Tennant, Robert B.	12665
Taylor, Bynie	14884	Tennant, Mattie K.	12666
Taylor, Ellis	14891	Thornton, Sylvia	672
Taylor, Patsey	15378	Thornton, Luther	674
Taylor, Josephine	16115	Thornton, Sallie	2796
Taylor, Nancy H.	16219	Thornton, Van	2797
Taylor, Willie B.	16220	Thornton, Anna	2798
Taylor, Sarah E.	16221	Thornton, Dovie May	2800
Taliaferro, Minnie	418	Thornton, Jhonnie A.	8084
Taliaferro, John C.	419	Thornton, Paralee	8086
Taliaferro, Gertrude	420	Thornton, John V.	8087
Taliaferro, Mary Estella	15196	Thornton, Beulah	8088
		Thornton, Maud	8089
Taliaferro, Eliza Mabel	15197	Thornton, Frederick	8090
Taliaferro, John Ambrose	15198	Thornton, Eureka	8091
		Thornton, Jessie W.	8092

Name.	Roll No.	Name.	Roll No.
Thomas, Della	709	Thomas, Ethel	15108
Thomas, Annie Jeanetta	710	Thompson, Lucy	723
Thomas, James M.	711	Thompson, Onatambe	1212
Thomas, Daniel	1047	Thompson, Wash	1268
Thomas, Cillen	1048	Thompson, Josephine	1269
Thomas, Missie	1050	Thompson, Clayton	1270
Thomas, Silwie	1413	Thompson, Nela	1271
Thomas, Sopha	1414	Thompson, William	
Thomas, Charley	1415	McKinley	1272
Thomas, Moses	1416	Thompson, Frances	1616
Thomas, James	1829	Thompson, Lucy	1624
Thomas, William	2123	Thompson, Peter	2108
Thomas, Melena	2199	Thompson, Rhoda	2109
Thomas, Joseph	2453	Thompson, Simeon	2110
Thomas, Sinie	2454	Thompson, Sena	3064
Thomas, Russell W.	2529	Thompson, Craymon	3419
Thomas, Lucy	2530	Thompson, Henry W.	3486
Thomas, Hampton	2531	Thompson, Joseph P.	3487
Thomas, Mahlone	2605	Thompson, Betsy	3488
Thomas, Emma	2606	Thompson, Alexander B.	3489
Thomas, Moses	2607	Thompson, Joel J.	3490
Thomas, Ben W.	2691	Thompson, Peter P.	3491
Thomas, Edna	2692	Thompson, Simon	3492
Thomas, Lena	2693	Thompson, Illie	3504
Thomas, Webster	2694	Thompson, Hampton	3508
Thomas, Louisa	2986	Thompson, Wincey	3665
Thomas, Phoeba	3023	Thompson, Lena	3666
Thomas, Josiah	3196	Thompson, Emma	3667
Thomas, Elbina	3197	Thompson, Robert	3668
Thomas, Lixan	3198	Thompson, George	3673
Thomas, Impson	3199	Thompson, James	3675
Thomas, Joe	3200	Thompson, Joe	3691
Thomas, Hudson	3280	Thompson, Phillis	3692
Thomas, Philiston	3314	Thompson, Jefferson	3693
Thomas, Sallie	3315	Thompson, Rosa	3696
Thomas, Benson	4598	Thompson, James	4272
Thomas, Minnie	4600	Thompson, Eliza	4273
Thomas, William T.	4718	Thompson, Simon	4275
Thomas, Dave	5740	Thompson, James E.	4387
Thomas, Elsie	5741	Thompson, Elizabeth	4388
Thomas, Mary	5742	Thompson, Cephus	4977
Thomas, Lilian G.	5743	Thompson, Melissa	5163
Thomas, Sim	5830	Thompson, John	5164
Thomas, Susan R.	6333	Thompson, Ellis	5165
Thomas, Cleo	6334	Thompson, Gilbert' W.	5296
Thomas, Leo M.	6335	Thompson, Isabel	5297
Thomas, DeGrace	6336	Thompson, Ellis W.	5298
Thomas, Florence H.	6337	Thompson, Harris J.	5299
Thomas, John Jay, Jr.	6338	Thompson, Susie E.	5300
Thomas, Loman	7878	Thompson, Josephine	6090
Thomas, Sikey	7879	Thompson, Louvina	6091
Thomas, Isaac	7880	Thompson, Robert	6332
Thomas, Sweeny	7882	Thompson, Vina	6358
Thomas, Siney	7883	Thompson, Mary	6359
Thomas, Mary	7884	Thompson, Emiline	6360
Thomas, Louisa	7886	Thompson, Susie	6361
Thomas, Joseph	7887	Thompson, Charles	6367
Thomas, Elias	8516	Thompson, Jincy	6368
Thomas, Alice	8517	Thompson, Simpson	6571
Thomas, Minnie	8518	Thompson, Benjamin	6575
Thomas, Stephen	8519	Thompson, Webster	6755
Thomas, Wilson	8520	Thompson, Miston	6834
Thomas, Lorinda	8664	Thompson, Reuben	7001
Thomas, Robert	8665	Thompson, Becky	7002
Thomas, Wicey	8666	Thompson, Ada	7003
Thomas, Mollie M.	11119	Thompson, Josephine	7004
Thomas, Mary L.	11120	Thompson, Minnie	7248
Thomas, Minnie A.	11121	Thompson, Bessie	7249
Thomas, William	11122	Thompson, James	8283
Thomas, Ethel	11123	Thompson, Bicey	8310
Thomas, John A.	11124	Thompson, Elizabeth	8346
Thomas, Burtie	11125	Thompson, Elizabeth	8347
Thomas, Hannah	11751	Thompson, Jimpson	8389
Thomas, Oliver G.	12056	Thompson, Joanna	8441
Thomas, Georgia P.	12057	Thompson, Julia	8442
Thomas, Edward G.	12814	Thompson, Nelson	8657
Thomas, Jennie I.	12815	Thompson, Malinda	8658
Thomas, Jimmie	14041	Thompson, Rosa	8659
Thomas, Cornelius	14563	Thompson, Grace	8660
Thomas, Harrison J.	14613	Thompson, Billy	8739
Thomas, Susan	14679	Thompson, Elizabeth	8740
Thomas, Isom Perry	14681	Thompson, Isom	8741
Thomas, Alice	15106	Thompson, Zelia	9009
Thomas, Jesse W.	15107	Thompson, Robert B.	9109

Name.	Roll No.
Thompson, Philip	9135
Thompson, Ellen	9217
Thompson, Harris	9309
Thompson, Willie	9785
Thompson, Green	9801
Thompson, Jacob	10990
Thompson, Minnie	10991
Thompson, Allen W.	11080
Thompson, Bun	11393
Thompson, Marful	11398
Thompson, Sissy	11399
Thompson, Lucy	11722
Thompson, Wallace	11785
Thompson, Elias	11786
Thompson, Wilburn	11976
Thompson, Malinda	11977
Thompson, Philip	11978
Thompson, Alfred	11979
Thompson, David	11980
Thompson, Gertrude	12398
Thompson, Eva	12399
Thompson, Nettie	12404
Thompson, Lucinda	13139
Thompson, William C.	13731
Thompson, Ella	13732
Thompson, Lewis	13733
Thompson, Burney	13734
Thompson, Leo Edward	13736
Thompson, Cyrus R.	13740
Thompson, Valley	13741
Thompson, Preemon C.	13742
Thompson, Cyrus Waverly	13743
Thompson, James H.	13744
Thompson, Joseph B.	13745
Thompson, Robert H.	13746
Thompson, Dora Ellen	13744
Thompson, Mattie	14090
Thompson, Juanita	14091
Thompson, Eugene	14092
Thompson, Edgar	14093
Thompson, Daisy	14094
Thompson, Grace	14095
Thompson, Atwood	14096
Thompson, Georgie	14097
Thompson, Jincy	11400
Thompson, Arre Bella	14570
Thompson, Sarah	15162
Thompson, George L.	15163
Thompson, Robert E. L.	15554
Thompson, Cornelius	15749
Thompson, Charles	15805
Thompson, Beulah	15806
Thompson, Eddy A.	15882
Thompson, Callie	15883
Thompson, James L.	15884
Thompson, Viola	15885
Thompson, Albert	15886
Thompson, Emma	15887
Thorpe, Grover	4714
Thorpe, Leta	4715
Thrasher, Ellen	13196
Thrasher, Benjamin M.	13197
Thurlow, Joseph	13868
Thurlow, Josephine	13869
Thurlow, Louisa	13870
Thurlow, Sylvina E.	13871
Tims, James B.	1035
Tims, Mary J.	1036
Tims, Evelyn	1037
Tims, Dixon	1038
Tims, Rufus	1039
Tims, Lowie	1041
Tims, Emiline	1947
Tims, Johnny	1948
Tims, Calvin	1949
Tims, Robert	2085
Tims, Fannie	2086
Tims, Mitchell	2201
Tims, Mildred	2202
Tims, Egnes E.	2203
Tims, Columbus	3355
Tims, Willie	3441
Tims, Mary	3442
Tims, Roberson	3443
Tims, Edward W.	4009

Name.	Roll No.
Tims, Lucy	4010
Tims, Minnie J.	4011
Tims, Edmond	4012
Tims, Benjamin W.	4013
Tims, Mertle	4015
Tims, Abel E.	4016
Tillis, Jim	1536
Tillis, Mila	1537
Tillis, William	1649
Tikubbi, Levi	1757
Tikebatubbi, Isin	2665
Tikbombe, Henry	2699
Tisho, Fliston	2343
Tisho, George	2344
Tisho, Lincie	2345
Tisho, Wesley	2346
Tisho, Rogers	2347
Tisho, Ida	6739
Tickness, Tillian	8198
Tickness, Frances	8199
Tickness, Frank	8200
Tiner, Francis M.	9603
Tiner, John L.	9604
Tiner, Edna M.	9605
Tiner, William T.	9606
Tiner, Myrtle	9607
Tiner, Mable	9608
Tiner, Newton	12432
Tiner, Bertha	12433
Tiner, Thomas	12432
Tigert, Benjamin Franklin	10680
Tigert, Julis A.	10676
Tindell, Amanda	10955
Tilly, Ada A.	15487
Tobby, Willis	1236
Tobby, Kitty	1237
Tonihka, Sinie	1428
Tonihka, Bitty	1429
Tonihka, Adeline	1430
Tonihka, Artie	1431
Tonihka, Phoebe	1442
Tonihka, Dickson	1443
Tonihka, Lina	1444
Tonihka, Charles	2328
Tonihka, Otson	2392
Tonihka, Salean	2393
Tonihka, Richmond	2394
Tonihka, Susan	2408
Tonihka, Sylvester	2409
Tonihka, Sallie	2410
Tonihka, Ensie	2411
Tonihka, Calvin	2548
Tonihka, George	2614
Tonihka, Jowicks	2615
Tonihka, Gissel	2616
Tonihka, Willie	2617
Tonihka, Silas	2621
Tonihka, John	2792
Tonihka, Betsy	2793
Tonihka, Rogers	2794
Tonihka, Waston	13477
Tohkubbi, Cephus	1703
Tohkubbi, Seon	1704
Tohkubbi, Marina	1705
Tohkubbi, Alphus	1706
Tontubbee, Patsy	1787
Tontubbee, Enos	1788
Tontubbee, Sophy	1789
Townsend, Charles J.	2222
Townsend, Sarah	2223
Townsend, Susan	2224
Townsend, Clark	2225
Townsend, Benjamin	2226
Tom, Morris	2425
Tom, Sally	3517
Tom, Jesse	3519
Tom, Sarah	3520
Tom, Montuna	4863
Tom, Simeon	4864
Tom, Simon	7733
Tom, Ebenezer	8033
Tom, Bicy	8034
Tom, Elsie	8035
Tonihka, Norris	2795
Tom, John	8036

Name.	Roll No.	Name.	Roll No.
Tom, Simeon	8037	Travis, Robbie	15635
Tom, Mandy	8038	Travis, William	15636
Tom, Levi	8039	Travis, Marie	15637
Tom, Albert	8040	Tucker, William	540
Tom, Benjamin	8041	Tucker, Georgia Ethel	541
Tom, Elias	8042	Tucker, Pearl	542
Tom, Wilson	8043	Tucker, Charles Edward	543
Tom, Esias	8044	Tucker, Joell Shelton	545
Tom, Gency	8045	Tucker, Zona	6665
Tom, Thomas	8068	Tucker, Ethel	6666
Tom, Bynie	9304	Tucker, Simmal C.	6667
Tom, Renie	9305	Tucker, Edith	6668
Tokabe, Lena	3191	Tucker, Hilda	6670
Totubbi, Battiest	3467	Tucker, Anna N.	6673
Totubbi, Kissie	3468	Tucker, Ida M.	6674
Tonitubbi, Sam	4310	Tucker, Ulysses G.	6675
Tonitubbi, Elsie	4311	Tucker, Sestos	6676
Town, Winchester	6046	Tucker, Chester	6677
Town, Missie	6047	Tucker, McCurtain	6678
Town, Harry Dukes	6048	Tucker, Martha M.	6992
Tomlis, Sibbail	6186	Tucker, Herman	6993
Tonler, Ellis	7672	Tucker, Ben	6994
Tonler, Margaret	7673	Tucker, Romulus	10872
Tonler, Rhoda	14766	Tucker, Sissie	10873
Tobley, Sam	8445	Tucker, Minnie	10874
Tolbert, Washington	8452	Tucker, Jane	10875
Tolbert, Rufus	14966	Tucker, Betsie	10876
Tomlinson, Harriet	12157	Tucker, John E.	12030
Tomlinson, Melvina	12159	Tucker, Susan	12031
Tomlinson, Sarah	12160	Tucker, John Hampton	12032
Towry, Juanita	12776	Tucker, Lewis	12033
Towry, Cecil McK.	12777	Tucker, Earnest	12034
Toole, John O.	13228	Tucker, Willie	12035
Toole, Mary A.	13229	Tucker, Mary	12037
Toole, Joseph Y.	13239	Tucker, Ethel	12038
Toole, May Elizabeth	13240	Tucker, Leonidas	12039
Toole, Helen	13241	Tucker, Virgie	12040
Tonahka, Wilson	13320	Tucker, Martha Belle	14732
Tobly, Sampson	14882	Tucker, Oscar McK.	14733
Tokobbe, Sam	15693	Tucker, Beulah A.	14744
Trueblood, Mary J.	271	Tubbee, Silwee	4867
Trueblood, Sam Muncrief	272	Tubbee, Emeline	4868
Trueblood, Albert H., Jr.	273	Tubbee, Levina	4869
Trueblood, Pauline	274	Turnbull, Emma	702
Trueblood, Roy G.	14192	Turnbull, Sam	733
Trueblood, Bryan Sewell	14193	Turnbull, Thomas	6846
Traylor, Jincy	4276	Turnbull, Inez	10677
Traylor, Maudie M.	4277	Turnbull, Simeon	10679
Traylor, Willie Everett	4278	Turnbull, Turner B.	10785
Trout, John R.	6778	Turnbull, Adeline D.	10786
Trout, Lillie V.	6779	Turnbull, Elizabeth	10787
Trout, Katie M.	6780	Turnbull, Timothy	10788
Trahern, Roy D.	7356	Turnbull, Walter J.	10789
Trahern, Joseph	7435	Turnbull, Charles C.	10790
Trahern, Joel P.	7436	Turnbull, William P.	10791
Trahern, Louis	7499	Turnbull, Jane L.	10792
Trahern, Willie M.	7500	Turnbull, Robert	10820
Trahern, James W.	7501	Turnbull, Eddie	10822
Trahern, Howard	7682	Turnbull, George W.	13724
Trahern, James	7683	Turnbull, Jesse James	13725
Trahern, William	7873	Tushka, Laisa s	1432
Trahern, Martha	7874	Tushka, Lena	1436
Trahern, Docia	8072	Tushka, Silvie	2524
Trahern, Lysander	8215	Tushka, Eliza	2526
Trahern, Martha	13749	Tushka, Ida	2528
Trahern, Douglas	12748	Tushka, Impson W.	3011
Trahern, Walter	14937	Tushka, Nellie	3012
Triplett, Harriet	7588	Tushka, Alfred	3013
Triplett, Oscar	7589	Tushka, Isaac	3016
Triplett, Celestine	7590	Tushka, Lowie	3017
Triplett, Mattie	7591	Tushka, Mary	3018
Truitt, Alice	9795	Tushka, Benjamin	3019
Truitt, Henry	9796	Tushka, Lizzie	3118
Truitt, Lige	9797	Tushka, Salite	3120
Tracey, John H.	10552	Tushka, Silas	3121
Traut, Minnie	12971	Tushka, Willis	3122
Traut, Minnie, Jr.	12972	Tushki, Levi	3412
Traut, Mary	12973	Tushka, Kissie	3413
Traut, Frank	12974	Tushka, Sophy	14683
Traut, John	12975	Turner, James	4769
Traut, Charley	12976	Turner, Tina	4770
Trohbe, M. L. Elizabeth	13298	Turner, Silas	4771
Trohbe, Charles Lewis	13303	Turner, Hattie	4844
		Turner, Ida F.	12725

Name.	Roll No.	Name.	Roll No.
Turner, Yulee	12730	Veach, Columbus	10095
Turner, Jackson	12857	Vincent, Lena	228
Turner, James A	12912	Vincent, Nona	229
Turner, Robert F.	13167	Vincent, Mahautie	230
Turner, Olga T.	13168	Vincent, Monnie	231
Turner, Leona	13170	Victor, Charlie	1909
Turner, James	13171	Victor, George	3065
Turner, Benjamin	13172	Victor, Alfred W.	8218
Turner, Apubkshun-		Victor, Ether M.	8219
nubbe	13173	Victor, Ida E.	8220
Turner, Nora F.	13174	Victor, John	14826
Turner, Robert S.	13185	Victor, Alfred	15034
Turner, Albert P.	15503	Vick, Lillie	7655
Turner, Charles M.	15504	Vick, Leslie	7657
Tupper, Thomas	5662	Vinson, Charles S.	11401
Tupper, Alfred	5663	Vinson, Mary A.	11402
Tupper, Jolum	5664	Vinson, Rhoda	11403
Tupper, Bartemus	14837	Vice, Robert	11675
Tupper, Louvicey	14864	Vieux, Minerva	12396
Tupper, Hobson	14865	Vieux, Louis	12397
Turley, Sissie B.	10333	Wade, Icey	119
Turley, Linsey	10337	Wade, Susanna	952
Tully, Jincy	11366	Wade, Maggie	953
Tully, Molsey	11367	Wade, Mistwright	954
Tully, Canada	11368	Wade, Emiline	1682
Tully, Emma	11370	Wade, Sylvania	1683
Tutt, Isabelle	11853	Wade, Robinson	1736
Tumbler, Willie	11922	Wade, Mary	1737
Tumbler, Annie	11924	Wade, Susan	2747
Tumbler, Maggie	11923	Wade, Nancy	2926
Tullihela, Willie	13476	Wade, Sissy	2927
Tubby, William	14331	Wade, Sarbit	3008
Tyree, Adeline	9774	Wade, Esickey	3091
Tyree, Robert Franklin	9775	Wade, Barnet	3395
Underwood, Thomas	262	Wade, Formy	3396
Underwood, Watkin	4730	Wade, Bitny	3397
Underwood, Isabella	4731	Wade, Frances	3399
Underwood, Aby	4776	Wade, Ben	3444
Underwood, John	4777	Wade, Louina	3445
Underwood, Kennedy	4903	Wade, Leasin	3446
Underwood, Alexander	4905	Wade, Sissy	3447
Underwood, Silas	4906	Wade, Gilbert	3922
Underwood, Ella	4907	Wade, Daniel F.	4359
Underwood, Jesse	4908	Wade, Malinda	4360
Underwood, Elizabeth	4910	Wade, Emerson	4361
Underwood, Sweeny	4911	Wade, Vicey	4363
Underwood, Julia V.	7213	Wade, Julia	4528
Underwood, Ruth Cleo	11708	Wade, Alberta	4529
Underwood, Harrison C.	11903	Wade, Ben	4699
Usray, Lizzie	4591	Wade, Alex	5260
Vaughn, Ellis	5964	Wade, Agnes	5261
Vaughn, George	6103	Wade, Anna	5262
Vaughn, Larkin	6104	Wade, Josephine	5263
Vaughn, Sarah E.	6105	Wade, Sissy	5264
Vaughn, Loren	6119	Wade, Mary	5265
Vaughn, Elsie	6120	Wade, Cyrus B.	5953
Vance, Clarissa	8835	Wade, Ira R.	5954
Vawter, Martha A.	9270	Wade, Ivan S.	5955
Vawter, Eula J.	9271	Wade, Nathaniel D.	5956
Vawter, Eunice E.	9272	Wade, Malcolm D.	5957
Vawter, Ethel M.	9273	Wade, Della E.	5958
Van Zant, Minnie	9988	Wade, Nellie May	5959
Van Zant, Henry Alex	9989	Wade, Nicholas	6494
Vail, Frances	12294	Wade, Stanford	6555
Vail, James T.	12295	Wade, Viola	6556
Vail, William E.	12296	Wade, William	6557
Vail, Charles E.	12297	Wade, Sarah	6558
Vail, Mary M.	12298	Wade, Noah	6559
Vail, Junior E.	12299	Wade, Charles H.	6560
Vail, Lois M.	12300	Wade, Picken	7612
Vail, Eunice	12301	Wade, Allen	7614
Vail, Ruth	12302	Wade, James	7615
Vail, Olive	12303	Wade, Jane	7616
Vail, Sophia	14168	Wade, Emma	7617
Verner, Nettie	6873	Wade, Byington	7618
Verner, Richard	6874	Wade, Lela	7619
Verner, Rody Maree	6875	Wade, Jonas	7620
Verner, Walter Green	6876	Wade, Alice	7621
Veach, Sophina	10018	Wade, Sampson	8472
Veach, Calvin	10019	Wade, Phoebe	8473
Veach, Walter	10021	Wade, Dennis	8709
Veach, Lottie	10022	Wade, Elizabeth	8710
Veach, Standley	10023	Wade, Bessie	8714
Veach, Frances	10024	Wade, Eastman	9025

Name.	Roll No.	Name.	Roll No.
Wade, Ellen	9026	Watkins, Sina	4314
Wade, Ellis	9027	Watkins, Lena	5029
Wade, Kennedy	10518	Watkins, Isam E.	7741
Wade, Abel	10521	Watkins, Henry I.	7742
Wade, Agnes	10522	Watkins, Ethel	7743
Wade, Elsie	10523	Watkins, Lochie	7744
Wade, Jefferson	10524	Watkins, Dora	7745
Wade, Sarah	10525	Watkins, Mary	7746
Wade, Lena	10526	Watkins, Fannie	7747
Wade, Sam	10527	Watkins, Wesley	7748
Wade, Thomas	10528	Watkins, Lula	7749
Wade, Dora	10529	Ward, Aaron	11599
Wade, Wicy	11179	Ward, Ira	11600
Wade, Eliza	11180	Ward, Charles O.	11601
Wade, Sissie	11181	Ward, Henry Lee	11602
Wade, Ransom	11217	Ward, Adah	11688
Wade, Allington	11592	Ward, Joseph L.	11927
Wade, Piley	11593	Ward, Coleman J.	11928
Wade, Kingsberry	11662	Ward, Lucy E.	11929
Wade, Jennie	11663	Ward, Robb D.	11930
Wade, Sarlin	11665	Ward, Henry J.	11931
Wade, Molsey	11777	Ward, Warren G.	11932
Wade, Manassas S. G.	11779	Ward, George H.	11933
Wade, Joseph	12023	Ward, Bryant G.	11934
Wade, Simon	12873	Ward, Hazle May	11935
Wade, Sally	12874	Ward, Henry	12203
Wade, Louena	12875	Ward, Edward A.	12320
Wade, David	13468	Ward, Silas	12774
Wade, Mamie	13469	Ward, Mary	12775
Wade, Bible	13471	Ward, Adeline	13312
Wade, Eli	13488	Ward, Henry	13400
Wade, Alemos F.	13820	Ward, Ida	14018
Wade, Thomas	13887	Ward, Eastman	14019
Wade, Nicey	13472	Ward, Sampson	14020
Wade, Willis	13359	Ward, Samuel	14021
Wade, Chiffie	14639	Ward, Harvey	14022
Wade, Esther	14712	Ward, John Harris	14117
Wade, Simeon	14907	Ward, Charles	14124
Wade, Amy	14908	Ward, Mary	14200
Wade, Esiah	14909	Ward, Pienna	14554
Wade, Rhoda	14910	Ward, Gilbert	14666
Wade, Sampson	15931	Ward, Jimmie	14731
Wade, Byington	15932	Ward, Joseph M.	14999
Wade, Henry	15943	Ward, Alice	15000
Wade, Louisa	15944	Ward, Martha	15001
Watkins, Frederick	163	Ward, Timothy L.	15054
Watkins, Joseph	961	Ward, Charles A.	15055
Watkins, Eliza	962	Ward, Daisy	15056
Watkins, Louisiana	964	Ward, William H.	15058
Watkins, Johnson	965	Ward, Annie	15746
Watkins, Mealey	966	Ward, Mary Margaret	15849
Watkins, Eastman	968	Wallace, Amos	1232
Watkins, Wynie	969	Wallace, Bessie	1233
Watkins, Austin	970	Wallace, Salie	1234
Watkins, Hoppen	1002	Wallace, Agnes	1235
Watkins, Sinsie	1003	Wallace, Sam	1283
Watkins, Sealney	1004	Wallace, Loston	1711
Watkins, Nicholas	1169	Wallace, Enissa	1712
Watkins, Ennissie	1170	Wallace, Serena	3213
Watkins, Hickman	1171	Wallace, Sweny	3214
Watkins, Zona	1172	Wallace, Ida	3215
Watkins, Davis	1173	Wallace, Lina	3216
Watkins, Lowiney	1174	Wallace, Charlie	3217
Watkins, Millawit	1175	Wallace, Jesse	5838
Watkins, Sealy	1176	Wallace, Amanda	5839
Watkins, Elam	1215	Wallace, Willy	7729
Watkins, Susan	1216	Wallace, Lytie	7730
Watkins, Stephen	1255	Wallace, Frank	7731
Watkins, Emma	1256	Wallace, Myrtle	9341
Watkins, Mattie	1257	Wallace, Minerva J.	11313
Watkins, Gustava	1408	Wallace, Mattie M.	11314
Watkins, J J.	1760	Wallace, Clarence E.	11315
Watkins, Melinda	1761	Wallace, May M.	11316
Watkins, Emma	1762	Wallace, Viola G.	11317
Watkins, Anna	1763	Wallace, Mary	11615
Watkins, Wesley	2273	Wallace, Jean	11616
Watkins, Susan	2466	Wallace, Robert A.	11617
Watkins, Ben	2715	Wallace, Nellie	11618
Watkins, Silva	2716	Wallace, Anna	11619
Watkins, Gibson	3282	Wallace, David	11620
Watkins, Mollie	3516	Wallace, Fannie	14951
Watkins, Cora C.	3779	Wallace, Dora	14952
Watkins, Waldo E	3780	Wallace, Caldonia	14953
Watkins, Jonas	4313	Wallace, Leona	14954
		Washington, Sally	1571

Name.	Roll No.	Name.	Roll No.
Washington, Benson	1572	Walker, Beatrice	7438
Washington, Sarah	1573	Walker, Rosa	7439
Washington, George L.	1585	Walker, Edgar	7440
Washington, Ben	1691	Walker, K. Tandy	8129
Washington, Salis	1692	Walker, Oscar W.	8546
Washington, Esias	1693	Walker, D. Clifton	8547
Washington, Isham	3516	Walker, Jesse A.	8548
Washington, Losan	6827	Walker, Malinda	10316
Washington, John	6861	Walker, Minnie	10317
Washington, Levi	6862	Waiker, Rhoda	11144
Washington, George	6863	Walker, Lindy	12680
Washington, Albert	10419	Walker, Eliza A.	12683
Washington, Edward	10420	Walker, George W	12684
Washington, Asie	10421	Walker, Charles	12685
Washington, Marcus	10531	Walker, Ada	12694
Washington, Ellen	11847	Walker, George	12697
Washington, Ida	11849	Walker, William T	13165
Washington, Nelson	14887	Walker, Elsie Louisa	13166
Wakaya, Simon	2505	Walker, Cora L. R.	13175
Wakaya, Nancy	2506	Walker, Arthur L	13176
Walters, Isabel	4724	Walker, Laura E.	14496
Wallen, Thompson	7144	Walker, Clara B.	14497
Wallen, Watson	7145	Walker, Sophie E.	14521
Wallen, Ellen	7146	Walker, Jane	14525
Wallen, John	7147	Walker, Thomas	14526
Wallen, Elish	7148	Walker, Benjamin	14527
Wallen, Sim	8008	Walker, Solen	14663
Wallen, Reubin	14754	Walker, Pauline	14762
Wadley, Beulah	7558	Walker, Willie	15592
Wadley, Beulah M.	7559	Walker, Cynthia	15862
Wadley, William H.	7560	Walker, Rose	15863
Wadley, Nellie Beatrice	7561	Wachubbe, Willie	892
Wadley, Juanita Grace	15046	Wachubbe, Lewis	13449
Walton, Nancy	9400	Watson, Thomas	919
Walden, Lizzie	9798	Watson, George	921
Walden, Winnie	9799	Watson, Sam	922
Walden, Lucile	9800	Watson, Silas	923
Walley, Eliza	9969	Watson, Insie	924
Walley Johnson	9978	Watson, Caston	925
Walley, Sinnie	9979	Watson, Agnes	926
Walley, Sillen	9991	Watson, Bernis	957
Walley, Milton	9992	Watson, Jincy	958
Walley, Jacob	9993	Watson, Ann	959
Wacome, Burney	10106	Watson, Ben J.	1450
Waichebbee, Levi	10209	Watson, Margaret	1451
Waichebbee, Ellen	10210	Watson, Lorin	1453
Walls, Thomas J. Sr.	12371	Watson, Ananias	1460
Walls, Jincy	12373	Watson, Semie	1461
Walls, Pearl	12374	Watson, John	1462
Walls, Guy	12375	Watson, Robert	1464
Walls, Annie	12376	Watson, Billy	1465
Walls, Cassie R.	12377	Watson, Rosie	1569
Watkins, Lula	7749	Watson, Artie Ann	1784
Watkins, Isam Eldrid	7750	Watson, Nicey	1785
Watkins, Wingenon	7798	Watson, Rampsey	1964
Watkins, Isadora	7799	Watson, Amy	1965
Watkins, Wingenon Jr.	7800	Watson, Larsen	1966
Watkins, Charlotte L.	7801	Watson, Sally Ann	1968
Watkins, Charlie	7802	Watson, Lena	1969
Watkins, Frank	7803	Watson, Clistie	1970
Watkins, Sallie	13456	Watson, Sophie	1971
Watkins, Sinsie J.	14588	Watson, Allen T.	2338
Watkins, Allen	14589	Watson, Minerva	2339
Waide, Helen E.	295	Watson, Betsy	3137
Waide, Harrold L.	299	Watson, Sanders	3138
Walker, Willie	327	Watson, Thomas	3478
Walker, Edna May	328	Watson, Nicie	3479
Walker, Lorinzy	1728	Watson, Julius J.	5419
Walker, Isham	2753	Watson, Calvin	6097
Walker, Semie	3828	Watson, Amanda	6098
Walker, Denison	3829	Watson, Podenie	6214
Walker, Johnson	3830	Watson, Mary	6215
Walker, Joe	3831	Watson, Isic	6216
Walker, Loston	3833	Watson, William	6772
Walker, Green	4582	Watson, Betsy	6773
Walker, Clarissa	4583	Watson, Mary	6917
Walker, Wilson	4584	Watson, Beulah M.	6919
Walker, Green Jr.	4585	Watson, Adam	11975
Walker, Martin	4586	Watson, Robinson	12095
Walker, Jesse	4587	Watson, Narcissa	12096
Walker, Clarissa	4588	Watson, Willis	12097
Walker, David	5142	Watson, Richardson	12098
Walker, Edward E.	6934	Watson, Frances M.	12964
Walker, Rebecca	7417	Watson, Mary R.	12965
Walker, Cornelia	7418	Watson, Amasa H.	12966
Walker, Laura	7437	Watson, Sudie F.	12967

Name.	Roll No.	Name.	Roll No.
Watson, Edna	13717	Ward, Simon	3299
Watson, Ida	13821	Ward, Harris	3300
Watson, Thomas	13865	Ward, Mary	3301
Watson, Jonas J .	13718	Ward, Lorancy	3302
Watson, Magdenlena	14737	Ward, Robert	3303
Watson, Martin	15417	Ward, Amy	3449
Watson, Wilburn	15565	Ward, Eastman	3777
Wall, Wilkin	1191	Ward, George	3950
Wall, Nelson	1193	Ward, Lucinda	3951
Wall, Samuel	1203	Ward, Allington	4544
Wall, William	1204	Ward, Bicey	5836
Wall, Noel	1205	Ward, Achafatubbe	5840
Wall, Chubby	1206	Ward, Sealy	5841
Wall, Nancy	1207	Ward, Minnie	5842
Wall, Frances	1208	Ward, Elias C.	5843
Wall, Lina	1937	Ward, Sina	5844
Wall, Joe	1938	Ward, Henry E.	5845
Wall, Nicy	2822	Ward, Cornelius E.	5846
Wall, Abel	5387	Ward, Celestie	5847
Wall, Phoebe	5388	Ward, David	6417
Wall, Edwin	5499	Ward, Joseph R. H.	7028
Wall, Agnes	5500	Ward, Rebecca	7031
Wall, Tandy	5501	Ward, Laura	7032
Wall, Thomas	5502	Ward, Sampson	7033
Wall, Sinie	5503	Ward, Willis	7034
Wall, Columbus	5504	Ward, Lula May	7035
Wall, Delilah	5505	Ward, Jefferson D.	7170
Wall, Margaret	5506	Ward, Maud Helene	7171
Wall, Emiline	5507	Ward, Eliza	7281
Wall, Peter	5508	Ward, Susie	7282
Wall, Laura	5509	Ward, Robert J.	7528
Wall, Victor R.	5510	Ward, Robert J. Jr.	7529
Wall, Sam	5661	Ward, Ada B.	7530
Wall, Phoebe A.	5724	Ward, Irene C.	7531
Wall, Clarance H.	5729	Ward, Frederick G.	7532
Wall, Thomas J.	6611	Ward, Gertrude B.	7533
Wall, Elizabeth R.	6612	Ward, Frank J.	7534
Wall, Thomas B.	6614	Ward, Cyrus B.	7851
Wall, Eva B.	6615	Ward, David R.	7853
Wall, Ella M.	6616	Ward, Edward O.	7855
Wall, William W.	8270	Ward, Jerry D.	7856
Wall, Lillie D.	8271	Ward, Campbell L.	7857
Wall, Czrena B.	8272	Ward, Allie	7858
Wall, Roena Estell	8273	Ward, Cyrus D.	7859
Wall, Walter T.	8352	Ward, Emma	10352
Wall, Jesse E.	8353	Ward, Mitchell	10353
Wall, Ellis W.	8354	Ward, Joel	11039
Wall, Cervera M.	8355	Ward, William G.	11053
Wall, Benjamin F.	8357	Ward, John S.	11150
Wall, Abigail E.	8358	Ward, Rachel A.	11151
Wall, Emiline	8576	Ward, Henry P.	11551
Wall, Gibson	8587	Ward, Bessie E.	11553
Wall, Jefferson	8670	Ward, William D.	11554
Wall, Johnson	8671	Ward, Naomi P.	11555
Wall, Winnie	8844	Ward, Herbert S.	11556
Wall, Delilah	14108	Ward, Charles	11596
Wall, Sarah C.	14109	Ward, Benjamin F.	11597
Wall, Pearl	14110	Ward, William A.	11598
Wall, James H.	14111	Walls, Cecil Evert	12380
Wall, Benjamin F.	14112	Walls, Jesse	12427
Wall, Mary D.	14113	Walls, Bertha	12428
Wall, Charles C.	14114	Walls, Elizabeth	12429
Wall, Lickton	14625	Walls, Edward	12430
Wall, Sibbel	14708	Walls, Lila	12431
Ward, Alfred	1196	Walls, Thomas J., Jr.	12379
Ward, Morris	1509	Watts, Israel	12386
Ward, Beckie	1510	Watts, Lillie	13653
Ward, Bensie	1511	Watts, Carrie P.	13656
Ward, Wilmon	1538	Walcott, Lutie Mary	14269
Ward, Siwen	1539	Walcott, Helen Haley	14270
Ward, Winney	1540	Walcott, Marjorie N.	14271
Ward, Henry	1541	Waldron, Eddie	14430
Ward, Cillin	1542	Wallaer, Rena	15787
Ward, Elam M.	1574	West, Robert	39
Ward, Sophie	1575	West, Allen	52
Ward, Classy	1576	West, Mary Etta	53
Ward, Casie	1586	West, Albert Harley	54
Ward, Maggie	2554	West, Pearly	55
Ward, Cornelia	2571	West, James	56
Ward, Lucinda	2625	West, Rhoda	6502
Ward, William S.	3293	West, Kenneth Fevirson	6503
Ward, Cillan	3294	West, Orvil Fitzroy	6504
Ward, Moses	3295	West, Josephine Per-	
Ward, Silena	3296	cella	14546
Ward, Sissy	3297	Wesley, Tecumseh	1121
Ward, Reed	3298		

Name.	Roll No.	Name.	Roll No.
Wesley, Louisa	1122	Webster, Lucy	4644
Wesley, Emerson	1123	Webster, Shingo	6527
Wesley, Martha	1124	Webster, Thomas	8263
Wesley, James	1125	Webster, Albert	8265
Wesley, Rayson	1126	Webster, Minnie	8266
Wesley, Sophy	1137	Webster, Wallen	8888
Wesley, Minnie	1128	Webster, Daniel	8890
Wesley, Lizzie	1581	Webster, Roy Lee	9617
Wesley, Willis	1582	Webster, Ward	9883
Wesley, Eliza	1951	Webster, Lila	9884
Wesley, Eben	1952	Webster, Julius	11213
Wesley, Winnie	2090	Webster, Susanna	11214
Wesley, Colbert	2441	Webster, Ella	11215
Wesley, Johnson	2622	Webster, Rena	11609
Wesley, Joseph	3110	Webster, Summie	11610
Wesley, Eliza	3111	Weaver, Mary	4784
Wesley, Charlie	3112	Weaver, Emily	9498
Wesley, Jackson	3115	Weaver, Zeno	9501
Wesley, James	3116	Weaver, Martha	9502
Wesley, Edward	3330	Weaver, Manda	9503
Wesley, Elias	3390	Wells, Alfred	6252
Wesley, Bettie	3391	Welch, Beatrice R.	6298
Wesley, Malissy	3392	Welch, Jefferson D.	6980
Wesley, Lucy	3393	Welch, Irving	6981
Wesley, John	3394	Welch, A. C. Earnest	6982
Wesley, Lenas	3400	Welch, Robert A.	7302
Wesley, Elsey	3401	Welch, James R.	7303
Wesley, Bicey	3524	Welch, Frances	11390
Wesley, Ben	4441	Weston, Mitchell	7140
Wesley, Viney	4442	Weston, Julius	7142
Wesley, Edmond	4733	Weston, Elsie	7367
Wesley, Rhoda	4734	Weston, Lorena	7381
Wesley, Edith	4735	Wechel, Mary E.	10060
Wesley, Thompson	4736	Weeden, Agnes	11667
Wesley, Davis	4843	Weeden, Maggie E.	11668
Wesley, Silvie	4892	Weeden, Buddy Lee	11676
Wesley, Thomas	5125	Westbrook, Mattie	12676
Wesley, Martha	5126	Westbrook, Edna	12677
Wesley, Silas	5127	Westbrook, Joe	12678
Wesley, Simeon	5287	Westbrook, Phena Ellen	12679
Wesley, Mary	5288	Whittle, Sarah	500
Wesley, Isaac	5289	Whittle, Napoleon	501
Wesley, Clarame	5290	Whittle, John	502
Wesley, Harris	8412	Whittle, Madge L.	504
Wesley, Charles	8573	Whittle, Susan C.	505
Wesley, Ickney	9067	Whittle, Arthur	15040
Wesley, Lucy Ann	9294	White, Eddie	748
Wesley, Henry	9295	White, Willie	749
Wesley, Millie	9296	White, Lena	1902
Wesley, Jane	9297	White, Julius	1903
Wesley, Lucy	10300	White, May	1904
Wesley, Johnson	10301	White, Olla	1905
Wesley, Elizabeth	10302	White, Tuck S.	1906
Wesley, Willie	10303	White, Arten	5332
Wesley, Davis	10908	White, Hettie	5333
Wesley, Betsy	11685	White, Ancey	5334
Wesley, Melvina	11781	White, Robert	5600
Wesley, Sealey	11782	White, Jincy	5601
Wesley, Nelson	11913	White, Sampson	5604
Wesley, Sillen	11914	White, Willis	5605
Wesley, Moses	11915	White, Susan	5654
Wesley, Emma	11916	White, Jency	5858
Wesley, Melissa	11917	White, Luther	5859
Wesley, Green	12208	White, Louis	6178
Wesley, Standley	12529	White, Elsie	6179
Wesley, Eliza	13319	White, Jerry	6299
Wesley, Elias	13795	White, Delilah	6300
Wesley, Siley	14535	White, Benjamin	6302
Wesley, Selin	14536	White, Amy	6433
Wesley, Stephen	14538	White, Cane	6434
Wesley, Silas	14539	White, Osborne	6697
Wesley, Moses	14614	White, Malsey	6698
Wesley, Joshua	14902	White, Alzira J.	6699
Wesley, James	15464	White, Livingston B.	6985
Wesley, Thomas	15897	White, Robert J.	6986
Webster, Daniel	2890	White, Eliza A.	6988
Webster, Lizzie	2891	White, Nancy B.	6989
Webster, Robert	2892	White, Roxey A. T.	6990
Webster, Josiah	2893	White, Sanson G.	6991
Webster, Maggie	2894	White, Edmond	9164
Webster, Ida May	2895	White, Sidney	9165
Webster, Woodkirk	2896	White, Lizzie	9166
Webster, Michael	3324	White, John	9268
Webster, Daniel	4643	White, Rosa M.	12067

Name.	Roll No.	Name.	Roll No.
White, Lillie O.	12068	Williams, Billy	2518
White, Oliver E.	12069	Williams, Mike	2519
White, Ellen	15144	Williams, Osby	2520
White, James Edward Jr.	15145	Williams, Louena	2521
		Williams, Levicy	2522
White, Ratie	15146	Williams, Emma	2552
White, Esther	15147	Williams, Nora	2553
Whiteman, Mattie J.	2883	Williams, Michael	3304
Whiteman, Maggie E.	2884	Williams, Sillan	3305
Whiteman, Mary Lena	2885	Williams, Dennis	3329
Whartner, Sophia	5840	Williams, Charles	3717
Whale, Armis	5778	Williams, James	3718
Whale, Martha	5779	Williams, Isabel	3991
Whale, David	5974	Williams, Enos	3992
Whale, Angeline J.	5975	Williams, Lena	4035
Whale, Edmon	5976	Williams, Winey	4112
Whale, Elmira	15414	Williams, Jincy	4113
Whistler, Ellis	6749	Williams, Eli	4114
Whistler, Allie	6750	Williams, Isham	4135
Whistler, Belle	6751	Williams, Fannie	4136
Whistler, Lillie M.	6752	Williams, William A.	4137
Whistler, Ada	6753	Williams, Mary C.	4138
Whistler, Neoma	6756	Williams, Alma	4139
Whistler, Sukey	7271	Williams, George C.	4140
Whistler, Martin	8020	Williams, Oscar R.	4141
Whistler, Nancy	8021	Williams, Israel	4282
Whistler, Etna	8022	Williams, Sealy	4283
Whistler, Robinson	12675	Williams, Stephen	4284
Whistler, Dora	13760	Williams, Pearl Myrtle	4285
Whistler, Mamie	13763	Williams, Emma	4500
Whitson, Rena	7099	Williams, Maxey	4501
Whitson, Marguerite	7103	Williams, Forbis	4695
Whitlock, Narcissa	7349	Williams, Melissa	4696
Whitlock, Robert R.	7350	Williams, Henry	4726
Whitlock, Mala	7351	Williams, Louisiana	4951
Whitlock, Isabelle	11107	Williams, Betsy	5447
Wheeler, Louisa	8435	Williams, Jack	5528
Wheeler, Rhoda	8436	Williams, Joe B.	5606
Wheeler, Eva L.	11603	Williams, Eastman	5607
Wheeler, Jessie	11604	Williams, Harris	5672
Wheeler, Erna	12035	Williams, Abel	5851
Wheeler, Irma	12041	Williams, Joseph	5961
Wheeler, Florence	12042	Williams, Motsy	5962
Wheeler, George W.	15335	Williams, Abel	5965
Wheat, James B.	9545	Williams, Sallie Ann	6088
Wheat, Agnes	12511	Williams, Ada	6499
Wheat, Alice	12534	Williams, Elsie	6500
Wheat, Rebecca L.	12535	Williams, John	6501
Wheat, Rena	12536	Williams, Alexander S.	6957
Whitten, Annie B.	10343	Williams, Sillis	6958
Whitner, Lizzie	14508	Williams, Florence	6959
Whitner, Annie	14509	Williams, John	7018
Whitner, James Henry	14510	Williams, Henry	7019
Williams, America	12	Williams, Turner	7658
Williams, Newt	143	Williams, Ida	7982
Williams, Georgianna N.	232	Williams, Melvina	7983
Williams, Walter K.	233	Williams, Mary	7984
Williams, Lorena	234	Williams, Senora W.	8052
Williams, Mamie	235	Williams, Forrest	8438
Williams, Leona M.	236	Williams, Jincy	8439
Williams, Emma Lee	302	Williams, Leona	8440
Williams, Ethel Lorraine	303	Williams, Freman	8443
Williams, Benjamin D.	304	Williams, George	8528
Williams, Watt	1134	Williams, Joel	8529
Williams, Eliza	1135	Williams, Phoebe	8530
Williams, Byington	1136	Williams, Hickman	8531
Williams, Abner	1137	Williams, Emeline	8532
Williams, Wacy	1138	Williams, Mattie B.	8533
Williams, Levicey	1139	Williams, Mollie	8534
Williams, Phillis	1140	Williams, Eli	8791
Williams, Louie	1289	Williams, Eddie	8792
Williams, Frances	1290	Williams, Amos	9167
Williams, Jonas	1315	Williams, Agnes	9214
Williams, Phoebe	1316	Williams, Luena	9685
Williams, Elizabeth	1318	Williams, Coleman	9701
Williams, Sibbie	1319	Williams, George	9702
Williams, Agnes	1320	Williams, Jefferson	9971
Williams, Tonsie	1321	Williams, Eliza	9972
Williams, Morris	1466	Williams, Galloway	10214
Williams, Wycie	2237	Williams, Lyless	10215
Williams, Adeline	2242	Williams, George	10216
Williams, Thomas	2515	Williams, Incy	10371
Williams, Lucy	2516	Williams, Daniel	10557
Williams, Edward	2517	Williams, Sallie	11146

Name.	Roll No.	Name.	Roll No.
Williams, Austin	11252	Willis, Irena	4124
Williams, Wycey	11253	Willis, Jimmy	4125
Williams, Mucktila	11474	Willis, Reuben	4521
Williams, Eastman	11778	Willis, Ben	4877
Williams, Rachel	11873	Willis, Sallie	4878
Williams, Willy S.	12110	Willis, John	4879
Williams, Sophia	12170	Willis, Susan	5021
Williams, Mack	12171	Willis, Lymon	5022
Williams, Warneth F.	12270	Willis, William	5036
Williams, Jesse F.	12271	Willis, Emily	5037
Williams, Effie H.	12272	Willis, Albert	5730
Williams, Molsey	12654	Willis, Rosa	5820
Williams, Mary E.	12876	Willis, James	6133
Williams, Darthula	12377	Willis, Cillen	6134
Williams, Aurelia	12878	Willis, Dixon	6135
Williams, Leo McC.	12879	Willis, Ennet	6136
Williams, Frank	12939	Willis, Allie	6137
Williams, Wilson	12940	Willis, Mary	6140
Williams, Joe	12941	Willis, Chester	6184
Williams, Julia A.	13012	Willis, Benjamin	6304
Williams, Luena	13394	Willis, Rosa	6305
Williams, Lizzie	13395	Willis, Minnie	6306
Williams, Susan	13296	Willis, Brit	6457
Williams, Alonzo D.	14431	Willis, Josiah	6943
Williams, Amanda	14707	Willis, Winnie	6944
Williams, Robert	15005	Willis, Martha	6946
Williams, Mollie E.	15097	Willis, David	6947
Williams, Lula	15098	Willis, Nellie	6948
Williams, Ollie	15099	Willis, Lou	6949
Williams, Athel	15100	Willis, Bennie	6950
Williams, Lottie	15101	Willis, Eastman	7674
Williams, Kelsey	15426	Willis, Moses	9010
Williams, Travis	15427	Willis, Mary	9011
Williams, Annie F.	15428	Willis, Abner W.	9872
Williams, Boyd	15429	Willis, Frances	9873
Williams, Royal	15430	Willis, Howard	9877
Williams, Amos	15763	Willis, Sammie	9878
Wllams, Ora	15764	Willis, Jincy	11307
Williams, Clarence	15765	Willis, Simpson	11539
Williams, Dona	15766	Willis, Phoebe	11540
Williams, Loving	15802	Willis, Josiah	11541
Winters, Clifton E.	276	Willis, Eastman	11607
Winters, Daisy L.	8142	Willis, Bicy	11608
Winters, Walter B.	8143	Willis, Isaac	11612
Winters, Amanda	8144	Willis, Siney	11968
Willis, Edward	510	Willis, Perry M.	12638
Willis, Louis	1043	Willis, Clarence L.	12639
Willis, John	1344	Willis, Florence	12640
Willis, Betty	1345	Willis, Joe	12646
Willis, Nancy	1346	Willis, Frank	12647
Willis, Frances	1347	Willis, Lee	13008
Willis, Georgiana	1348	Willis, William	13337
Willis, Tahobbe	1483	Willis, Selena	14638
Willis, Willie	1588	Willis, Thomas	14669
Willis, Denison	1589	Willis, Doda C.	15874
Willis, Martha	2007	Willis, Ethel V.	15875
Willis, Emma	2236	Wilson, Anderson	1007
Willis, Rayson	2244	Wilson, Lens	1008
Willis, Dicey	2246	Wilson, Dwight	1009
Willis, Silen	2247	Wilson, Alden	1010
Willis, Synwell	2248	Wilson, Florence	1011
Willis, Bicy	2277	Wilson, David	1100
Willis, Louisa	2469	Wilson, Wicy	1101
Willis, Kitsy	2470	Wilson, Helen	1102
Willis, Edmond P.	2532	Wilson, Lucy	1103
Willis, Liza	2533	Wilson, Mikey	1104
Willis, Harriet	2534	Wilson, Lena	1105
Willis, Nelson	2535	Wilson, Nannie	1138
Willis, Sampson	2633	Wilson, Rufus L.	1339
Willis, Emma	2634	Wilson, Cleopatra	1340
Willis, Allen	2765	Wilson, Edward O.	1341
Willis, Sistie	2766	Wilson, Isaac	1740
Willis, Matsie	2767	Wilson, Molsy	1741
Willis, Eastman H.	2940	Wilson, John	1742
Willis, Frances	2942	Wilson, Lucy	1743
Willis, Robinson	2943	Wilson, Robert	1744
Willis, Rotey	2944	Wilson, Sophie	1745
Willis, Garven	3088	Wilson, Wade	1746
Willis, Tom H.	3132	Wilson, Lilly	1747
Willis, Soys	3139	Wilson, Osborne	1748
Willis, Jones	3316	Wilson, Sarah	1894
Willis, Wallace	3404	Wilson, Raymond	1914
Willis, Emerson D.	3700	Wilson, Evadne	1915
Willis, Elmira	4122	Wilson, Dukes	1916

Name.	Roll No.	Name.	Roll No.
Wilson, Ethelind	1917	Wilson, Philip	3650
Wilson, Alexander	1918	Wilson, Caesar	3652
Wilson, Liza	1919	Wilson, Thomas	3669
Wilson, Jennie	2140	Wilson, Ilantima	3670
Wilson, Willie	2141	Wilson, Bessie Ann	3671
Wilson, Standley	2142	Wilson, Nelson	3672
Wilson, Littie	2283	Wilson, Cole	3782
Wilson, Lena	2284	Wilson, Viney	3783
Wilson, Esey	2323	Wilson, Frances	3788
Wilson, Jimison	2324	Wilson, Iden	3789
Wilson, Allington	2325	Wilson, Charles	3801
Wilson, Norwood	2378	Wilson, Lucinda	3802
Wilson, Taby	2379	Wilson, Sherman	3803
Wilson, Sina	2380	Wilson, Milton	3804
Wilson, Johnnie	2381	Wilson, Brown	3805
Wilson, Willie	2382	Wilson, Florence B.	3959
Wilson, Minnie	2383	Wilson, John L.	3960
Wilson, Anney	2384	Wilson, William E.	3961
Wilson, Willie	2527	Wilson, Hattie I.	3962
Wilson, Witkin	2556	Wilson, Bessie B.	3963
Wilson, Susanna	2557	Wilson, Curtis B.	3964
Wilson, Emma J.	2608	Wilson, Alice M.	4354
Wilson, Tom	2610	Wilson, Daniel	4448
Wilson, Raphael L.	2611	Wilson, Susan	4449
Wilson, Minnie	2652	Wilson, Brown	5149
Wilson, Bob	2653	Wilson, Malena	5151
Wilson, Stevison	2654	Wilson, Simpson	5831
Wilson, Bolin	2659	Wilson, Sallie	5832
Wilson, Lucy Ann	2660	Wilson, Ada	6330
Wilson, Angeline	2661	Wilson, Mary J.	6331
Wilson, Marcus	2662	Wilson, Archey	6716
Wilson, Raymond	2663	Wilson, Josephine	6892
Wilson, Ailin	2664	Wilson, Dora	6893
Wilson, Douglas	2779	Wilson, Luella	6894
Wilson, Tom	2780	Wilson Ed	6895
Wilson, Willis	3040	Wilson, Frank	7804
Wilson, Anna	3041	Wilson, Clayton	7805
Wilson, Martha	3042	Wilson, Minnie	7806
Wilson, Darius	3043	Wilson, Walter	7807
Wilson, Sillis	3044	Wilson, Allington	8475
Wilson, Jubel	3045	Wilson, Jerry	9034
Wilson, Michael	3100	Wilson, Sarah	9298
Wilson, Carlo A.	3171	Wilson, Mary	9299
Wilson, Margaret	3172	Wilson, Eva	9300
Wilson, Thompson	3173	Wilson, Horace	9301
Wilson, Noah	3174	Wilson, Fannie	9496
Wilson, Gardner	3175	Wilson, Eddie	9497
Wilson, Eve	3176	Wilson, Henry	9631
Wilson, Abbott	3177	Wilson, Eliza	9892
Wilson, Greenwood	3179	Wilson, Wallace	9970
Wilson, Rhoda	3258	Wilson, Allington	10374
Wilson, Willie	3265	Wilson, Becky	10375
Wilson, Willie	3266	Wilson, Henry	10376
Wilson, Ward	3402	Wilson, Reason	10706
Wilson, Sarphin	3403	Wilson, Sarah	10707
Wilson, Wiley	3410	Wilson, Abel	10805
Wilson, Mamie	3411	Wilson, Mary	10806
Wilson, Tobias	3423	Wilson, Rosa	10807
Wilson, Tom	3424	Wilson, Isaac	10808
Wilson, William P.	3425	Wilson, Louis	10992
Wilson, Jacob	3426	Wilson, Tennessee	11040
Wilson, Isabelle	3427	Wilson, Elzara	11041
Wilson, Mary	3428	Wilson, Lucy	11280
Wilson, Frank	3429	Wilson, Charles	11329
Wilson, Easter	3430	Wilson, Marcus	11360
Wilson, Walter	3431	Wilson, Narcissa	11413
Wilson, Joe	3437	Wilson, Clarence Monroe	11416
Wilson, James	3483	Wilson, Walter Green	11417
Wilson, Rosanna	3484	Wilson, Kitsy	11542
Wilson, Islan	3485	Wilson, Joseph	11638
Wilson, Emma	3496	Wilson, Elizabeth	11701
Wilson, Edward	3497	Wilson, Wauneta	11702
Wilson, James	3498	Wilson, Lane	11709
Wilson, Alma	3499	Wilson, Bicy	11710
Wilson, J. Dace	3500	Wilson, Peter	11711
Wilson, Willie H.	3501	Wilson, Levi	11712
Wilson, Frank	3510	Wilson, Agnes	11713
Wilson, Eva	3511	Wilson, Henry C.	11769
Wilson, John	3611	Wilson, Lizzie	11770
Wilson, Foston	3613	Wilson, Robinson	11771
Wilson, James	3614	Wilson, Addie	11772
Wilson, Frances	3615	Wilson, Hugo	11773
Wilson, Roah	3616	Wilson, William	11774
Wilson, Seme	3617		

Name.	Roll No.
Wilson, Leighton	11775
Wilson, Theodore R.	11776
Wilson, Josiah	11818
Wilson, Sallie	12914
Wilson, Emma	13004
Wilson, John D.	13883
Wilson, Edward	14003
Wilson, John	14006
Wilson, Jeff	14040
Wilson, Jane	14098
Wilson, Raphael F.	14099
Wilson, W. W.	14100
Wilson, Lizzie	14242
Wilson, Reuben Ray	14248
Wilson, Nancy	14560
Wilson, Cabin	14564
Wilson, Charley	14640
Wilson, Fannie Florence	14676
Wilson, Edmund	14811
Wilson, Sillena	15397
Wilson, Cillin	15509
Wilson, Stephen	15810
Wilson, Robert	15811
Wilson, George	15539
Williston, Tobia	1061
Williston, John	1073
Williston, Annie	1074
Williston, Jane	1076
Williston, Denison	1077
Williston, Joseph	1080
Williston, Silas	1671
Williston, Jacob	1684
Williston, Impson	1686
Williston, Frances	2838
Winship, Simeon	1177
Winship, Lela	1178
Winship, Virginia	1179
Winship, Andy	1180
Winship, Buddy	1181
Winship, Tobias	1182
Winship, Mitchell	1183
Winship, Ennittie	1643
Winship, Ena	1645
Winship, Stewart	3161
Winship, Sampson	9218
Winship, Seyon	9219
Winship, Isaac	13452
Winship, Rafy	14566
Winship, Riley	16114
Winship, Cornelius	15447
William, Sampson	1839
William, Moses	1840
William, Thomas	1842
William, Johnson	3625
William, James	3701
William, Levina	4773
William, Jincy	4862
William, Sarah	14559
Willie, William A.	2442
Willie, Sina	2443
Willie, Hodges	2446
Willie, Thomas	2447
Willie, Leonidas	3742
Willie, Sayanis	13481
Willie, Willis	13483
Willie, Esias	13484
Winston, Charles K.	4280
Wiltsey, Annie	4697
Wiltsey, Mary E.	4698
Wilkin, John	5335
Wilkin, Levi	5336
Wilkin, Laymon	5337
Wilkin, John	5338
Wilkin, Delia	5801
Wilkin, Lucy	5803
Wilkin, Josephine	6081
Wilkin, John	6092
Wilkin, Raymond	6093
Wilkin, Melvina	15416
Wilkin, Alfred	15418
Wilkin, Henry	15419
Willy, Joe	6408
Wilburn, Martha	6701

Name.	Roll No.
Wilburn, Lizzie N.	6702
Wilburn, Charles S.	6703
Wilburn, Blanche	6704
Wilburn, John C.	6705
Wilburn, Sarah	6706
Wilburn, Annie	6707
Wilburn, Estella	6708
Wilburn, Jesse H.	6709
Wilburn, Frederick	6710
Wilkins, Adam	7917
Wilkins, Sallie	13398
Wilkins, John	13399
Wilkins, Micey	13411
Wilkins, Henry	13412
Winlock, Lavina	8178
Winlock, Charlotte	8179
Winlock, Wattie	8704
Winlock, Johnny	8707
Winlock, Ellis	8708
Winlock, Brazil	8796
Winloch, Cora	9269
Winloch, Rufus	12452
Winloch, Bennie	12454
Winloch, Bettie	14822
Wishock, Cora	8648
Wilmoth, Kizzie	10957
Witcher, Fannie	12645
Wiley, Robert	13926
Witt, Peggy	14101
Witt, Mary A.	14102
Witt, John	14103
Witt, Fannie	14107
Wilkinson, Ada	14137
Wilkinson, Durward Arthur	14139
Worley, Annie	169
Worley, Floyd Lonzo	171
Womack, Ida	393
Wommack, George	7246
Wommack, Cubbee	7247
Wolf, Ellen	563
Wolf, Amelia	564
Wolf, Fannie	565
Wolf, Kochantubbi	566
Wolf, Matt	567
Wolf, Benjamin F.	12413
Wolf, Fannie	12414
Wolf, Lillie M.	12415
Wolf, Ida	12416
Wolfe, Rachel	14474
Wood, Leanie	2337
Wood, Levi	2536
Wood, Sean	2537
Wood, Stella	2538
Wood, Sampson	2539
Wood, Salom	2540
Wood, Amanda R.	4457
Wood, Edgar	4458
Wood, George H.	4459
Wood, Thomas L.	4460
Wood, Robert Dewey	4461
Wood, Ellis	4522
Wood, Edgar	4523
Wood, Sarah	11174
Wood, Benjamin	11175
Wood, Mary	11176
Wood, Harrison	11955
Wood, Ella	11956
Wood, Priscilla C.	12826
Wood, Minnie	15405
Woods, Emily	4692
Woods, Cyrus	4693
Woods, Elijah	4971
Woods, Samuel	4972
Woods, Henry	5776
Woods, Stephen	6014
Woods, Kizzie	6015
Woods, Martin	6016
Woods, Homer	6017
Woods, Benjamin James	6019
Woods, Florence Elizabeth	6020
Woods, John	6031
Woods, Sarah	6032
Woods, Cyrus	6033

Name.	Roll No.	Name.	Roll No.
Woods, Simon	6155	Wright, Ransis	5279
Woods, Nancy	6156	Wright, Allen	5660
Woods, Stephen A.	6157	Wright, Ellen	6318
Woods, Gilbert	6177	Wright, Josephine	6319
Woods, Wesley	6185	Wright, Watson	6321
Woods, Lizzie E.	6194	Wright, Louisa	6967
Woods, Josie Lou	6197	Wright, Sina	7527
Woods, Benjamin J.	6342	Wright, Steward	8599
Woods, Josephine	6343	Wright, Emeline	8674
Woods, Harriet	6344	Wright, George Simon	8675
Woods, Nancy B.	6345	Wright, Sampson	8903
Woods, Martha	6395	Wright, Islin	8957
Woods, Susan	8174	Wright, Carrie	8959
Woods, George	8175	Wright, Kate	9089
Woods, Louis	8176	Wright, Frank H.	9090
Woods, Hattie	9344	Wright, Gladys	9091
Woods, Willie M.	9346	Wright, Frank H. Jr.	9092
Woods, Edgar	9347	Wright, Louisa	10632
Woods, Sadie	9628	Wright, Milton	10817
Woods, Abner	11745	Wright, Fannie	10818
Woods, McGee	11746	Wright, Edna	10819
Woods, Willie	11747	Wright, Eliphalet N.	11152
Woods, Louisa	11748	Wright, Muriel H.	11153
Woods, Nancy	11749	Wright, Gertrude I.	11154
Woods, Mary A.	13782	Wright, Sarah	11274
Woods, Lillie May	13783	Wright, Allen	12840
Woods, Arthur	13784	Wright, James B.	12841
Woods, Ida Belle	13785	Wright, Eslam	12859
Woods, Jane	14125	Wright, Cephus	12860
Woods, Minnie	15815	Wright, Peter	13362
Woolery, Nancy	3761	Wright, Leslie	14610
Woolery, James	3762	Wright, Joseph	14812
Woolery, Walker	3763	Wright, Mary	14813
Woolery, Annie	3764	Wright, Daniel	14814
Woolery, Julia	3765	Wright, Winnie	16207
Woolery, John, Jr.	3766	Wyatt, Ed J.	776
Woolery, Carlston	3767	Wyatt, Roxsie	777
Woolery, Rhoda	3768	Wyatt, Ed J., Jr.	778
Woolery, Gilbert	3769	Wyatt, Mary	779
Woolery, Susan Anna	14926	Wyatt, Ernest Mont-	
Wooley, Samuel L.	9596	gomery	780
Wooley, Catherine	9597	Wyatt, Celie	13922
Wooley, Irene	9598	Wyatt, Maud Lee	13923
Wooley, Clara	9599	Wyatt, Lourena	13373
Woodward, Annie M.	9710	Wyers, Irene	7908
Woodward, Myrtle	9711	Wyers, Belle	7909
Woodward, Miriam S.	9712	Wyers, Bailey	7910
Woodward, Helen D.	9713	Wyers, Effie	7911
Woodward, Laclair	9714	Wyers, John N.	7912
Woodward, Emily E.	9715	Wyers, Pearl	7913
Woodward, Charles A. Jr.	9716	Wyers, Sampson	7914
Woodward, Gaston M.	9717	Wyers, Lorena	7915
Woodward, Annie Frank	9718	Wyers, Edna	7916
Woolridge, Nicholas	12500	Yale, Amos	3565
Woolridge, Adeline	12501	Yarborough, Belle	9959
Woolridge, Siney	12502	Yarborough, Emma E.	9961
Woolridge, Martha	12503	Yarborough, Clarence	9962
Woolridge, William	12504	Yarborough, Eunice	9963
Woolridge, Agnes	12505	Yarborough, John C.	9964
Woolridge, Flora		Yarbrough, Annie	9994
Lizzie	12506	Yarbrough, Steve	9995
Worcestor, Alfred	14948	Yarbrough, LaVere	9996
Wright, Frances	120	Yarbrough, Julian	9997
Wright, Palmar	121	Yandell, Dora	10304
Wright, Mary	122	Yandell, John	10305
Wright, John W.	227	Yandell, George	
Wright, Calvin C.	354	William	10307
Wright, Fannie	355	Yarhamby, Charles	12018
Wright, Mary	356	Yarharmby, Sin	13489
Wright, Arthur	357	Yates, Laura	15561
Wright, Nettie	358	Yotah, Joshua	5448
Wright, Edward	359	Yota, Dave	8631
Wright, Eula	360	Yota, Calvin	8633
Wright, Vallie R.	361	Yota, Adam	8964
Wright, Sarah	533	Yota, Levi	8990
Wright, Abbie	581	Young, Jeff	8864
Wright, Bicy	1099	Young, William B.	8865
Wright, Thomas	2330	Young, Eli D.	8866
Wright, Elsie	2331	Young, Robert	8867
Wright, Andy	2333	Young, Matilda E.	8868
Wright, Crockett	2523	Young, Levi	8869
Wright, John	2897	Young, Lizzie	8870
Wright, Surena	2898	Young, Jesse	8871
Wright, Hampton	3092	Young, Emma	13243
Wright, Jackson	5156	Young, Vivian	13244
Wright, Victor	5157	Young, Lois	13245

Name.	Roll No.	Name.	Roll No.
Young, Dollie	14786	York, Sarah	14939
Young, Nancy	11550	York, Roscoe	15455
York, Sampson	12842	York, John	15456
York, Sebian	12843	Zanola, Mildred	12150
York, Levi	12844	Zanola, Angestine	12151
York, Rosa	12845	Zanola, Annie	12152
York, Minnie	12846	Zanola, Hester	12153
York, Mina	12847	Zanola, Noah	12154
York, Lillie	12848	Zanola, Wavely	12155
York, Clinton J.	13204	Zion, Susan	10885
York, Myrtle A.	13205	Zion, Earie	10887
York, Mary Allice	13206		

INDEX TO
NEW BORN CHOCTAWS BY BLOOD

Name.	Roll No.
Bennett, Crecia Ann	1087
Belvin, Henry Harrison J.	1344
Belvin, Jodie	1582
Ben, Saleyan	1548
Billy, Alice Gertrude	67
Billy, Maggie	116
Billy, Edwin	883
Billy, James	945
Billy, Joseph	964
Billy, Crawford	1351
Bickle, Jessie James	940
Bird, L. B.	1317
Blundell, Emmet Grady	90
Blakely, Frederick C.	95
Blake, Beulah Jane	123
Blake, James Monroe	124
Blaylock, George Washington	173
Blue, Levenia	1042
Black, Preston Lee	1464
Bohanan, David	68
Bohanan, Thomas Briggin	38
Bohanan, Dorothy Nona	39
Bohanan, Sidney	750
Bohanan, Matilda	775
Bohanan, Andrew	776
Bohanan, Chester G.	794
Bohanan, Ethel	863
Bohanan, William J.	888
Bohanan, Harmon J. Jr.	1057
Bohanan, Sim	1238
Bohanan, Victoria May	1272
Bohanan. Selina	1345
Bohanan, Somlin	1378
Bohanan, Willis	1394
Boatright, Milton Elias	166
Bond, Clarence	193
Bond, George M.	358
Bond, Rex Abbott	359
Bond, Richard S.	512
Bond, Alice	513
Bond, Ridgely Jr.	645
Bond, Sampson	1455
Bond, Sam	1540
Bolling, Frank Alfred	198
Bolling, Louis Layfayett	199
Bolling, Octavia Belle	280
Bolling, Theodore Dixon	281
Boling, Evinie	1468
Bogle, Henry Carl	446
Bowers, Luther	578
Bowman, Lois Annie	603
Booker, Max Leo	1102
Bowlin, Gracie Marie	1447
Bridges, Elisha Paul	10
Broaddus, James Swope	14
Broaddus, Effie Lenore	15
Brown, Horace	36
Brown, Ollie	37
Brown, John R., Jr.	536
Brown, Stephen	403
Brown, Alfred Earl	716
Brown, Maud Mahalie	725
Brown, Clarice Mawrine	790
Brown, Pearl	1432
Brock,Ina M.	329
Braine, Gilbert Tennent	570
Brains, Wilbert N.	664
Brashears, Buster	677
Brashears, Viola	678
Brashears, Isa May	711
Brackett, David A.	717
Brackeen. Roseta	1472
Bryant, Nelson	1347
Brandy, Oscar	1445
Brady, Joanna	1483
Briggs, Minnie	1222
Burks, Burton Oran	746
Burks, Ora Velma	747
Bush, Daniel	800
Buckholts, Walter Howel	879
Burney, Leroy	896
Buell. June Durant	917
Buckholts, Betha C.	50
Buckholts, Bessie Lee	51

Name.	Roll No.
Burkes, Ella Jewel	83
Burns, Mable	171
Burns, Willie Jewell	998
Burns, William	1056
Burgevin, Elizabeth Mary	392
Bully, James Anderson	428
Bully, John	429
Bullard, Andrew L.	561
Bullard, Roy E.	1023
Bullard, Elmer D.	1505
Burton, Frederick Arthur	562
Burnside, Gladys	587
Butler, Rosey	1431
Butler, Henry C.	1341
Butler, Pearl	595
Butter, David	1552
Byington, Gilbert	452
Byington, Lydia	315
Byington, Sallie	1144
Byington, Lillie	1542
Bybee, Ellis	1054
Casey, Jaunita	1
Casey, Jack C.	2
Casey, Duel Joe	161
Carney, Albert	99
Carney, Agnes	456
Carney, Al	992
Carney, Joseph	1140
Carney, Noma	1295
Carney, Timothy	1387
Carney, Edward	1567
Case, Addie F.	227
Carnes, Sinie	282
Carnes, Jimmie	781
Catlin, James Darrah, Jr.	307
Campbell, Frank Hazel	406
Campbell, Marshal A.	407
Campbell, Ella Angelina	408
Campbell, Thomas E.	657
Campbell, Mildred	1372
Campbell, Dorothy Jessie	1373
Campbell, Johnnie	1583
Caldwell, Wilson	418
Camp, Lillie May	454
Camp, Catherine	890
Carr, Julia	485
Carr, Johny	1254
Carr, Jessie Redmond	708
Carpenter, Joseph	724
Cartledge, John Thomas	784
Callaway, Ruby May	959
Camden, Leroy H.	988
Cassell, Myrtle Parks	1051
Carroll, Mary E.	1065
Carter, Christanie Bell	1161
Carter, Gertie Allie	1262
Carter, Minnie Elsie	1517
Carterby, Ballied	1396
Carterby, Dora	1397
Caudill, Clarence Edward	1340
Cass. Norris	1176
Cann, Lindsy	1570
Cephus. Ellistan	667
Chandler, Orpheas Hercules	5
Chauteau, Rosa Angelina	254
Choate, Benjamin Paul	372
Choate, James H. Jr.	631
Choate, James Luke	653
Choate, Mary I.	654
Chivers, Margaret	396
Chilton, Jim	504
Christy, Adam	682
Christie, Carlison	1117
Charles, Lucy	884
Chunn, May	360
Clark, Nealie Belle	114
Clark, Virgia Lucile	930
Clark, Ella Louise	1079
Clower. Fleming P.	309
Clay, Phoebe	804
Clay, Henry	805
Clay, Mary Lyda	832
Clay, Calvin Ballaid	882
Cleaveland, Edmon Ree	715
Colbert, Harlod W.	73

Name.	Roll No.
Colbert, Harriet	206
Colbert, Lylie	852
Colbert, Clarence	956
Colbert, Sam	1311
Colbert, Fannie	1364
Colbert, Sampson	1389
Colbert, Eliza	1418
Colbert, Susie May	1419
Colbert, Julia Ann	1443
Coleman, Frank	106
Coleman, William J. P.	731
Coleman, Phoebe	1243
Coleman, Belle	1303
Cox, Eunice	133
Cox, Roland	182
Coker, Paulina T.	169
Coker, Willie R. E.	1465
Coffman, Joseph Osborn	207
Cochnauer, Henry Clay	264
Cochnauer, Nicholas Alexander	265
Cochnauer, Don W.	841
Cochneuer, Robert L.	1411
Compelube, Ellen	370
Conn, John R.	397
Conn, Leona	1306
Coon, Vernon Aldin	438
Coone, Jimmey	557
Cotton, Waneta Jeanna	458
Cotton, Oscar	703
Cotton, Nellie	704
Cooper, Sister	480
Cooper, Corine	647
Cole, Wesley Anderson	577
Cole, Elizabeth	1500
Collins, Henry Monroe	604
Collins, Ollie Belle	605
Collins, Lemuel Henry	1035
Collin, Jane	955
Cowan, Ira Lee Riley	662
Cowen, Myrtle Susie	770
Cowen, Dorsey Edmond	1139
Coley, Charles	690
Coley, Ranes M.	911
Coley, Nora	1211
Costilow, Lula Bell	811
Compton, Elisabeth	842
Cook, Lucie Garret	907
Combs, Thomas L. E.	978
Council, Howard Jacob	1071
Connors, Aram, Jr.	1080
Collier, Thomas Scruggs	1178
Coplen, Ollie May	1191
Cobb, Sinie	1334
Cobb, Louena	1461
Cromwell, Verna T.	170
Crowder, Walter L.	616
Crowder, Lisabeth	683
Crowder, Willie Uel	792
Crowder, Lena Bell	1248
Crowder, Maud May	1249
Crabtree, Edgar G.	893
Crawford, Coleman	941
Crawford, Willie Arthur	1415
Crawford, Ruby Gertrude	1529
Crutchfield, Evelynn	1120
Creecy, Douglas D.	1282
Cunningham, Alexander Evart	64
Cunningham, Mary Ethel	65
Cunningham, Clara Belle	325
Culbertson, Katherine	347
Culbertson, Ida J.	751
Culbertson, Bengamon F.	752
Culberson, Mary Catherine	718
Cushman, Charles L.	354
Curtis, Harry Edward	721
Curtis, Nealy Clarance	726
Curry, Clorine	887
Cullan, Georgia E.	1041
Curley, Lewie	1175
Cunnish, Rena	1250

Name.	Roll No.
Davis, Daisy Dean	97
Davis, Susie	200
Davis, Ruby Watson	410
Davis, Goldie Loma	714
Davis, Ella	748
Davis, Henry Russell	1288
Damron, Ethel	252
Daniels, Willis Thomas	475
Daniels, John Thomas	1182
Daniel, Walter Monroe	549
Darneal, Tandy	502
Darneal, Bennie Alfred	694
Dandridge, Martha	736
Daney, Arthur Lee	782
Daney, Allie	1365
Danna, Vester M.	1188
Daffern, Leo	1067
Daugherty, Beuna	1145
Daugherty, Beulah	1146
Daggs, Opal	1469
Denison, Stephen	19
Denison, David	20
Denison, Harry L.	881
Deal, Johnece	632
Denson, Orren Farver	870
Dendy, Herbert	878
Devenport, Wyle E.	1158
Dibrell, Erin	91
Dibrell, Louise	484
Dilbeck, Martha Iler	228
Dilbeck, John L., Jr.	730
Dilbeck, William M.	1348
Dickey, Alton H.	270
Dickerson, Ada	332
Dickinson, Emma	933
Dillard, Kermit	927
Dillard, Marie	1111
Dillard, Hellen D.	1350
Dills, Lonnie Burton	989
Dixon, Ruth May	381
Dobson, Dewey Dewitt	378
Dobson, Albert D.	688
Dobson, Goldie Ruth	915
Dobyns, Ethel	567
Dobyns, Annie Belle	568
Doshier, Pauline	624
Doctor, Wilkin	783
Downing, Ruth Shields	898
Dowland, Myrtle Lee	1036
Dodson, Loise Louisa	1084
Dorset, Carrie	1327
Donegay, Annie	1467
Dunlap, Wallace Green McCurtain	209
Duer, Ada Arlee	229
Duer, William Andrew	230
Duer, Valley May	1160
Dunn, Annie Jane	333
Dukes, Mabel	745
Dwight, Hunter	251
Dyer, Winston	814
Dyer, Winnona	1122
Dyer, Dixon	1201
Dyer, Minnie	1391
Drake, Edith M.	1518
Edwards, Lottie Loudella	305
Edwards, David Jonathan	306
Edwards, Everette	1534
Edwards, Ruth	1535
Edward, Emeline	1121
Eeds, Helen	127
Elliott, Leonard	210
Elliott, Gertrude Irine	443
Elliott, Eveline	877
Ellis, Mitchell	761
Ellis, William Leo	836
Ellis, Pushmataha F.	1123
Elapashabbe, Jency	1224
Emeyabbi, Martha	1526
Ennis, James S.	70
Enloe, Lucius Hampton	1105
Ervin, Rena Pauline	646

Name.	Roll No.
Ervin, Emma May	1059
Estes, Alfred Henry	221
Everidge, Sophiraan	710
Everidge, Joseph Woods	953
Everidge, Thomas Dudley	954
Everidge, Edgar	1058
Evans, Ethel O.	1069
Farrill, Sue Constance	507
Farrill, Walter Edwin	508
Farrill, Burnice	509
Farmer, Samuel Arnold	515
Farr, Texanna	1110
Fairlie, Ethel	365
Falconer, John Henry	563
Featherston, William A.	560
Fennel, Vannie Elizabeth	1186
Fetter, Amanda May	225
Fetter, Nina Belle	226
Ferrante, Charley	273
Fisher, Roy	71
Fisher, Hester V.	574
Fitzer, Ivery Elen D.	157
Fitzer, Raymon W.	158
Fitzer, Gracie May	481
Fitzgerald, Mable	727
Fields, Brady Efflet	1169
Floyd, Jewel	401
Flinchum, Eller Cessie	445
Flower, Lillian B.	995
Fowler, Raphael F.	33
Folsom, Maud	196
Folsom, Unis Fay	391
Folsom, Joe Mitchell	569
Folsom, Frank Davis	599
Folsom, Fletcher Daniel	600
Folsom, Oslin	606
Folsom, Rossie Glover	788
Folsom, Henry C.	916
Folsom, Eula	952
Folsom, Sweeny	976
Folsom, William E.	1437
Folsom, Cletus A.	1438
Folsom, Anus Earl	1484
Folsom, Pat It.	120
Folsom, Dora Eunice	809
Folsom, Junier Wade	810
Folsom, Fannie P.	1076
Foster, Raymond Booth	405
Foster, Bonnie B.	771
Fobb, Acy	837
Fobb, Nellis	1544
Fobb, Insey	1199
Freeny, Ada	7
Freeny, Alfred Lorraine	297
Freeny, Wilson R.	298
Freeny, Benjamin Baxter	1361
Freeny, Lee	274
Fryar, Thomas Francis	13
Frazier, Ella	261
Frazier, Julia	621
Frazier, Benjamin	1216
Frazier, Ruth	1558
Frazier, Mattie	1553
Frazier, Mary Jane	100
Frazier, Martha	101
Freeman, Pearlie M.	1297
Fulton, Catherine Jr.	375
Fulton, Florence	1299
Gardner, Sarah	48
Gardner, Hellena Lausyann	537
Gardner, Gladys Aridell	793
Gardner, Susie M.	985
Gardner, Stella	1124
Gardner, Elmer	1125
Gardner, Jack Griffin	1126
Garland, Virginia	189
Garland, Joseph Mansfield	576
Garland, Herman Newton	614
Garland, Clara Stirling	615

Name.	Roll No.
Garland, Louise	637
Garland, Sarah Annie	684
Garland, Leo	1420
Gabbert, Cyril	414
Gasaway, Jessie Jerome	505
Garrison, Catherine Isabelle	937
Garrison, Sarah E. T.	826
Gabel, Hutson	1559
Gibson, William	607
Gibson, Sallie Ann	1106
Gibson, Earnest J.	1127
Gibson, Motsy	1474
Gibson, Willie	1577
Gibson, Claude	722
Gibbs, Ollie Lee	827
Glenn, Marguerite	317
Gooding, Theodore	53
Gooding, Larence Bobbit	105
Goodson, Joel James	58
Gouger, Tokie	235
Gorman, Ora T.	338
Gotcher, Elbert Hubbard	369
Goings, Zora	692
Goodman, Lora	844
Going, Robinson	849
Going, Edith	871
Going, Earl	944
Going, Abner	1379
Going, Florence	1402
Goldston, Viola Bell	1159
Gollihare, Harvey Andrew	601
Gollihare, Hurbert	602
Gray, Dorris	167
Gray, Archie M.	1107
Gregory, Lillie M.	174
Griffith, Ula H.	400
Grant, Tom S.	497
Grant, Charlie W.	498
Grant, Charleyne	1426
Grant, George J.	1367
Graham, Lawrence	572
Graham, Willie S.	1072
Graham, Mary Ann	1546
Grubbs, Pearl	1017
Grubbs, Mae	1504
Grubbs, Roy C.	1294
Greenwood, Louisa	1068
Graman, Sophia	1109
Green, Betsey	1463
Griggs, Dora Elizabeth	395
Gravitt, Thomas	1405
Guthrie, Gertie B.	426
Guess, Minnie	762
Guess, Dicy	1185
Harris, Robert C.	55
Harris, Josiephine Beatres	56
Harris, Paul C., Jr.	62
Harris, Charles James	160
Harris, Mamie	476
Harris, Gertrude	477
Harris, Nora	503
Harris, J. H. Rayburn	807
Harris, Jack L.	808
Harris, Sadie. Aline	1103
Harris, Edward A.	1240
Harris, Tarie E.	1407
Harris, Nellie M.	1471
Harris, Clifford	1564
Hazel, J. Crosby	165
Hazel, Lottie	330
Hartshorne, George Ewing	194
Hall, Theodore Byron	201
Hall, William S., Jr.	202
Hall, Sidney	1416
Hall, Frank	1565
Hampton, Henry G.	214
Hampton, Noel	215
Hampton, Burniss Irene	232
Hampton, Mitchell	263
Hampton, Annie Frances	640

Name.	Roll No.
Hampton, Sarah	1018
Hampton, Ollie	1135
Harkins, Claud Hassel	258
Harkins, Mable	259
Harkins, George Lafayette	643
Harkins, Richard	1183
Harkins, Levicey	1451
Hamilton, William Fenton	287
Harkreader, Zula May	328
Hailey, May	363
Hailey, Sue	364
Harlan, David Franklin	374
Harlan, Chilliney	1304
Hallmark, Edna Irene	404
Hallmark, Elick	482
Hamlin, William	540
Harrison, Nellie	670
Harrison, Anna Ardelia	1070
Harrison, Birdie	1331
Harrison, Rhoda	1332
Harrison, Ruth Juanita	1538
Haiakanubbi, Amanda	867
Hardy, Josephine	1239
Hammers, Everett Loyde	925
Hays, Dora Frances	1008
Hayes, Perlie Luella Gertrude	1323
Harley, Willie	1020
Hancock, Kemble	1227
Hancock, Josephine	1322
Hammons, Cleo Inez	1492
Hawkins, Allie May	474
Heskett, Eliza Ann	32
Heskett, Agnes Marie	1264
Henderson, Carmen	94
Henderson, Sam Randolph	335
Henderson, Lilly B.	431
Henderson, Lee O.	620
Henderson, Benjamin F.	719
Herndon, Calvin H.	108
Herndon, Maude	511
Herndon, Leo	818
Henley, Thelma	457
Hendrix, Edgar	546
Henry, Arthur Lafate	742
Henry, Frances	801
Henson, Roxy	1242
Hembree, Rebecca Jincy	1279
Hensley, Pearl	1374
Hekia, John E.	1560
Hickman, Amanda	21
Hickman, Houston Eugene	387
Hickman, Katherine R.	388
Hickman, Edith	471
Hickman, Patsey	1574
Hibdon, Annie Avery	31
Hiarker, Estes	178
Hicker, Daisy	204
Hill, Esther Julia	433
Hill, Clyde	492
Hill, Wynema	1298
Hill, Floy May	1530
Hines, Della May	689
Hiberd, Roy	894
Hibben, Mary Gertrude	982
Hicks, Adam	1383
Hicks, Mary	1384
Hitcher, Adeline	1491
Holloway, Minnie	1466
Holloway, Ruby	327
Holleman, Clittie Elizabeth	341
Hooe, Edna May	421
Hooe, Robert Isreal	422
Homer, Saler	525
Homer, Johnson	754
Homer, Solomon	969
Homer, Sophia	1477
Homer, Willie	1561
Holman, Thelma	501

Name.	Roll No.
Holman, Moses	1354
Hopkins, Elizabeth M.	922
Howze, William Lee	1061
Howze, Jesse Myrtle	1062
Holder, Wilmot Elnora	1275
Holder, Edris Imogen	1276
Hoparkentubbi, Maggie	1284
Hoyt, Olian Vernon	1440
Hotubbee, Allen	1511
Hodges, Dave	697
Human, Eugenia Basil	107
Human, Allen Terrell	243
Hulsey, Earnest T.	205
Huggins, Olla	671
Hunt, Wilburn	693
Huddleston, Nora	402
Huddleston, Frank Jr.	1424
Hudson, Peter Jay Jr.	928
Hudson, Marie	935
Hudson, Calvin	965
Hudson, Cleo	966
Hudson, Roosevelt Easton	1393
Hull, Clem Y.	936
Hutchinson, Willie Alexander	1203
Hutchinson, Jim	1204
Hutchinson, Albert Jerry	1205
Hulsey, Eulah Cordelia	1578
Impson, Troy Silvester	1337
Impson, Laura	1296
Impson, Theodore Roosevelt	1516
Intolabbee, Cepha	236
Ingram, Milburn Cisney	1257
Ingram, Nancy Jane	1258
Ireton, Rufus Claude	1037
Ireton, Frederick Henry	1038
Ireton, Jackson	49
Ireton, Ollie Virgie	1489
Izard, Lora D.	244
Izard, Valley Esther	1281
Jacob, Jonas	857
Jacob, Reason	279
Jacob, Folsom	923
Jacob, Ben	1566
Jacobs, Nita	1321
James, Arabel	18
James, Iles	22
James, Norah	117
James, John Jay	118
James, Bettie P.	495
James, Etta M.	496
James, Abner	547
James, Henry	548
James, Wesley	597
James, Dolly Elizabeth	630
James, Jincy	772
James, Sallie	838
James, Davis	873
James, Lekoda	926
James, Ada Ann	979
James, Rose	1004
James, Gibson	1328
James, Vera C.	1336
James, Ester	1446
James, Bicey	1450
James, Charley	1515
James, Betsy	1533
James, Martin A.	1549
Jackson, Rowan	499
Jackson, Bessie	993
Jackson, Green	1189
Jackson, Simon C.	1197
Jackson, Rosie	1401
Jackson, Luke	1434
Jack, Allen	1509
Jefferson, Joseph	691
Jefferson, Cephus	760
Jefferson, Cain	823
Jefferson, Eliza	824
Jefferson, Ella	855
Jefferson, Helen	860
Jefferson, Foster	861

Name.	Roll No.
Jefferson, Spencer	1409
Jefferson, Ida	1433
Jefferson, Perry	1541
Jennings, Lota	947
Jennings, Adie	948
Johnson, Edith	175
Johnson, Lena	176
Johnson, Caroline	412
Johnson, Simon	596
Johnson, Abel H.	658
Johnson, Ivey May	757
Johnson, Norman Joseph	864
Johnson, Myrtle Zula	876
Johnson, Annie	939
Johnson, Zelpha	1100
Johnson, Ellis	1406
Johnson, Frank	1523
Johnson, Bettie	1525
Johnson, Annie	1537
Jones, Henry	336
Jones, Lewie Haral	427
Jones, Ollie May	459
Jones, Lena	542
Jones, Gladys	544
Jones, Meda	598
Jones, Russell Ray	764
Jones, Acy Louis	765
Jones, Amelia May	785
Jones, Carl	819
Jones, Ida	859
Jones, Ester May	950
Jones, Lula	1167
Jones, Luella	1168
Jones, Rosie Ann	1174
Jones, Bennie	1289
Jones, Willie	1335
Jones, Selton	1342
Jones, Maude Marine	1349
Jones, Edney May	1355
Jones, Gracie Sybil	1356
Jones, Clyde	1377
Jones, Freddierica	1453
Jones, Ella	1470
Jones, Ella	1512
Jones, Albert	1562
John, Harry	795
John, Semiah	822
John, Charley	1265
John, Agnes	1266
John, Sweeney	1502
Joel, Jim	1147
Johnico, Ole	1476
Julius, Mollie	479
Julius, Florence	799
Juzan, Hattie	1382
Karl, Esta V.	339
Kaniatobe, Rhoda	851
Kaniatobe, Johnson	1376
Kaniatobe, Susan	1381
Kaneubbe, Lizzie	1055
Keltner, William H. H. Jr.	25
Kelly, Pearl A.	96
Kelly, Grocie	768
Kelly, Jewel	769
Kemp, Joseph	219
Kemp, Israel	1053
Kemp, Benjamin	1177
Kemp, Guertie	1444
Key, James Leroy	669
Kendrick, Sylma	1439
King, Iler May	1002
King, Betsey	150
King, Zona	299
King, Ella	494
King, Smallwood	820
King, Jack Evelyn	1118
Kirkpatrick, LeRoy F.	46
Kirksey, John Clifton	441
Kirksey, Pearl	442
Kirby, Minnie May	1027
Kinney, Lillie R.	493
Krebbs, May Etta Emaline	275

Name.	Roll No.
Krebbs, Edmond	1031
Krieger, Oscar M.	739
Langley, Essie Viola	78
Langley, Clyde Edward	79
Latimer, Byron H.	104
Latimer, Marie Kathleen	212
Lankford, Douglas Newton	137
Lauchner, Daisy Ruby	242
Lawrence, Ruth	257
Lawrence, Raymond Arthur	1234
Lamb, Lillie M.	322
LaFlore, Charley	1219
Lawechobe, Annie	1225
Lane, Dawie Ophelie	1274
Labor, Earl Lee	1417
Laughlin, Dora Maud	1448
Leslie, William Joseph	84
LeFlore, Mable	186
LeFlore, John Wesley, Jr.	188
LeFlore, Houston	223
LeFlore, Sam	262
LeFlore, Jennie Bryan	466
LeFlore, Anna Ruth	467
LeFlore, Louie Fudge	534
LeFlore, Jeff	813
LeFlore, Tandy	1033
LeFlore, Clara Lee	1277
LeFlore, Ruthie	1318
LeFlore, Lou	1360
LeFlore, Florence	1408
LeFlore, Lorena	1475
Lewis, Brewster	238
Lewis, Charley Allen	559
Lewis, Noa	629
Lewis, Cassie	644
Lewis, Harmon	802
Lewis, Thurman	803
Lewis, Annie Belle	828
Lewis, Mabel	829
Lewis, Wilson	875
Lewis, Porter J.	960
Lewis, Emoline	1162
Lewis, Leona Moria	1362
Lewis, Eliza	1488
Lewis, Ethel Eugenia	1531
Lewis, William Joseph	1278
Lester, Julia Ann	320
Lester, Ralph	321
Lester, Dudley Pitchlynn	934
Lindsey, Waldo	531
Lindsey, Lewis Murray	551
Lloyd, Burnnie Lee	1094
Long, Bertha	131
Long, Jewell V.	183
Loving, Carl Logan	545
Loring, Elbert Homer	970
Locke, Crystal	1230
Lowe, Alvin H.	506
Luce, Herbert	151
Luce, Lester	152
Luper, Roy Ruth	343
Luttrel, Eddie	1153
Lynn, Leola	464
Lynn, Adley V.	566
Lyle, Grady Edwin	639
Lyles, John W.	1025
Mauldin, Edna Grace	110
Mauldin, Roy Jackson	1358
Mason, Clarence	177
Matthews, Losera	192
Manning, Lloyd O.	260
Manning, Speairs A.	741
Marlow, Claud Crofford	303
Massey, Tams Bixby	311
Massey, Sillin Walker	312
Massey, William B.	610
Martin, Madora Jane	382
Martin, Clarence	666
Martin, Bertsworth	1241
Mackey, Beulah Lois	385
Mackey, Sarah Margaret	778
Marcum, Edward C.	416

Name.	Roll No.
Mayo, George	470
Mann, John Lee	541
Maytobe, Lina	830
Maytobe, Casey	831
Marshall, Pearl	1115
Marston, Theodore Mc-Kinley	1312
Marston, Addie	1313
Mays, Rosa Anna	1480
Merryman, Marion Francis	140
Merryman, Johnny Frances	185
Merryman, Carl Ocey	532
Merryman, Groce Ella	1119
Merryman, Sherman	1436
Meryman, Benjamin C.	187
Meadows, Burnett	348
Medell, Everet Lee	680
Meashintubby, Abe	729
Meashintubby, Andrew	1343
Minehart, Rebecca	172
Miller, John B.	350
Miller, Clarence L.	351
Miller, Myrtle Gladys	1228
Miller, James Gordon	1229
Mitchell, H. Gains	136
Mitchell, William Bryant Marion	413
Mitchell, Alice	744
Mitts, Delie Estle	447
Mitts, James Isaac	448
Milton, Sidney	986
Milton, Amaziah	1556
Middleton, May	1137
Morris, Lillian Inez	26
Morris, Clay Franklin	27
Morris, Thelma	709
Morris, Lenora	957
Morris, Fisher Washington	1032
Moore, Louisa	54
Moore, Willis Edgar	81
Moore, Thomas B.	86
Moore, Emeline	88
Moore, Thomas Ellena	129
Moore, Lyman Southard	130
Moore, Jas. William A.	155
Moore, Corinne	222
Moore, Ethan Allen	535
Moore, Lena Cecile	611
Moore, Clifford Wesley	622
Moore, Mary Kathleen	623
Moore, Mary Eunice	707
Moore, Sylvan G.	1007
Moore, James Lillian Thresa	1195
Moore, Robbie A.	1333
Moore, Silena	1392
Moore, Lucie	1449
Moore, Emma	1454
Mouser, John Robert	87
Morgan, Theone	283
Morgan, Louisa Alice	379
Morgan, Juston H.	528
Morgan, Raymond W.	1302
Morgan, Sallie Puryear	1040
Monds, Oda	450
Mowdy, Ruby	460
Motes, Mary Elizabeth	575
Moran, Alton Oline	582
Moran, Author C.	1099
Moran, Elvin	1213
Mozley, Laura Lucille	334
Murray, Helen Verna	40
Muldrow, Mattie Annie	80
Mullens, Alvin Floid	393
Mullin, Amison	1557
Munkus, Ollie Lee	696
Murphy, Ed G. W.	1005
Muncrief, Clinton	1200
McAdoo, Tulous L.	6
McAfee, Elsie	816
McAlester, Nelson	1261

Name.	Roll No.
McBride, Willis Owen	728
McCullough, Vivian Mae	355
McCann, Sampson Francis	398
McCann, Marie	958
McCurtain, Greenwood Mitchell	139
McCurtain, William	148
McClain, Edward George	162
McClain, Notre Dame	436
McCarley, Lola	181
McClendon, Morris Stanley	239
McCarty, Vernon Clay	300
McCarty, Willie May	891
McClure, Dora May	420
McClure, Horace Clay	500
McClure, Racy	856
McCartney, Ruth	550
McClish, Durie	556
McClish, Zelma	558
McCoy, Willie Henry	885
McCarter, Elberta G.	276
McDaniel, Lelia L.	386
McDaniel, Amy	539
McDaniel, Clarence C.	791
McDaniel, Alma Mae	1130
McDonald, Verna Austin	1166
McDonald, Pearly	1543
McFerran, Bennie	705
McFarland, Flarnce Glenn	1000
McGahey, Opal	491
McGahey, Johnnie F.	766
McGee, Solomon	1506
McGee, Emily	701
McGuire, Joel Burrell	453
McIntosh, Sarrah	1044
McKinzie, Benson	111
McKinnon, Edith Irene	247
McKinnon, Mary Virgil	248
McKinney, Jacob	904
McKinney, Thompson	1244
McKinney, Sinsie	1427
McKinney, Elliott	1495
McKee, Willie D.	1429
McLellan, Clara D.	271
McLellan, Stelma	552
McLellan, Velma	553
McLellan, Ora M.	554
McLellan, Samuel J.	1532
McLaughlin, Claude	478
McMurtry, Wallace H.	1078
McMurtrey, Guy	1173
McMurtrey, Thomas Walter	1187
McMurry, Ervin	1131
Nail, Robert	217
Nail, Lillie	218
Nail, Junetta	241
Nail, David Oscar, Jr.	411
Nail, Dellie M.	1009
Nail, Joel	1193
Nail, Alice Eva	1442
Nail, Dock	1569
Naylor, Lestor	1085
Narlett, Grincy	1497
Nelson, Simon	430
Nelson, Bertha Elizabeth	1134
Nelson, Benjamin	1237
Nelson, James	1414
Neal, July	617
Needham, Helen	786
Needham, Herbert Enoch	787
Nero, Jimmy	1571
Nessmith, Susan Myrtle	197
Nix, Grace	24
Nicholson, Lawrence W.	526
Nicar, Amanda E.	753
Nichols, Escar	1108
Norman, Benjamin Hibbert	432
Norman, Irene	1022
Nolen, Rena	1143

Name.	Roll No.
Noel, Agnes	1164
Noah, Sampson	1247
Noah, Annie	1366
Noah, Martin Van	1368
Noah, John	1510
Nowabbi, David	316
Oakes, Mary Margarite	555
Oakes, Martha Ellen	974
Oakes, Myrtle Grace	1013
Oakes, Donald	1029
Oklahambi, Reason	1496
Oliver, Lena	34
Onubby, Stella Frances	463
Ontaiyabi, Louis Stephen	868
Orr, Walter	738
Ott, Green	626
Ott, Martha Jane	1435
Ott, Roy	755
Overstreet, Mamie	635
Overstreet, Daisy Lillie	1430
Owens, Estella	423
Owens, Clarence	543
Owens, Amanda	1129
Paxton, Swinney	60
Paddock, John Clinton	268
Patterson, Albert Roy	346
Patterson, John Walton	675
Patterson, Nancy S.	1462
Payton, Allen	584
Payton, Walter	585
Pate, Vernon	652
Parker, Gabe George	672
Parrish, James Otto	679
Parrish, Lois Aletha	918
Parish, Lizzie	1073
Payte, Roy K.	1320
Penny, Willie Grace	377
Perteet, Earlie	380
Perkins, Archie Lee	581
Perkins, George Johnson	946
Perkins, Lena Bell	1456
Perkins, Simeon D.	1527
Perkins, Fannie	1528
Pearson, Bernard Preston	612
Perry, Houston	613
Perry, Lula	641
Perry, Bertha	1412
Perry, Izora Alice	1413
Perry, Ola Edith	1375
Pebworth, Henry Lee	1163
Peter, Harriet	1206
Peter, Leviney	1273
Phillips, Minnie Lee	909
Pike, Mary P.	269
Pitchlynn, Andy A.	357
Pierce, Douglas J.	1132
Pierce, Leroy	1180
Pickens, Levi	1572
Plummer, Mike Mayers	284
Plummer, Mary A.	839
Platt, Beulah Viola	1210
Powell, Kenney Muse	141
Powell, Vera	636
Potts, Martha Ann	145
Potts, Margaret Jane	146
Pope, Mutien	224
Potter, Arbon Blackburn	806
Pruner, Walter Leonard	687
Pritchard, Jesse R.	1050
Pritchard, Beulah	1082
Pusley, Willie Lee	220
Pusley, Frank William	455
Pusley, Agnes	592
Pusley, Julian	593
Pusley, Vivian Eloise	594
Pugh, Robert Lee	886
Puckett, Mabel	897
Putnam, Fannie	1095
Quincy, Lela Lou	125
Quincy, James Dewit	1142
Quinton, Narciss	1049
Quinton, Annie	1226

Name.	Roll No.
Rabon, Thurman Moore	234
Rabon, Ruby Hellen	468
Rabon, Ottowa Thomas	469
Rabon, Lynn	1003
Rabon, Dovey	1271
Rabon, Boyd	1324
Randell, Eddie	1128
Rail, Hester May	1165
Ratterree, John Henry	1034
Rexroat, Opal Delana	168
Reese, Margie C.	895
Reese, Orville	1501
Reed, Catherine	1192
Reid, Gladess Lee	1233
Reynolds, Elizabeth Eunice	1260
Renick, Nora A.	1305
Riddle, Lee Ray	213
Riddle, Clem	253
Riddle, William H.	580
Riddle, Louisa	1212
Riddle, Lena	1202
Riddle, Joseph	1580
Richards, Samuel Allen	272
Richards, Irene Inez	345
Risener, Charlie	586
Richardson, Samuel Oliver	779
Richardson, Mattie C.	780
Richerson, Maggie Ether	1263
Ripley, John	1403
Ridgeway, Nellie McCurtain	789
Roberts, Clyde	89
Roberts, Henry McKinley	1576
Roberts, Perry	734
Roberts, Irene Exodus	735
Robert, Sudie	862
Robert, Bassie	962
Robinson, Denver Madison	520
Robinson, Theodore R.	949
Robinson, Morley	1286
Robinson, Aldon Freddie	1309
Roberson, Sarah L.	1326
Robertson, Fredie	1520
Rogers, Dwight C.	524
Rockman, Montie J.	720
Roebuck, Minnie Lee	1014
Roebuck, Abbie	1089
Roebuck, Georgia May	1048
Rose, Horace C.	1024
Rose, Preston Harral	1290
Roff, Joseph David	1190
Roden, William Harrison	1481
Roach, Lorena Pearl	1343
Ryan, Clide Bushnell	342
Rushing, Mary Elizabeth	759
Russell, Perry, Jr.	75
Russell, John Jr.	76
Russell, Stella	533
Runton, James C.	713
Rutherford, Lavinia Albertine	1291
Sanguin, Marie	28
Sanguin, Charmian Vaughan	1019
Sauls, Lizzie Elnora	44
Sauls, Clarence	45
Sanner, William Thomas	92
Sanner, Frank	93
Sanner, Charlie	521
Sanner, William Ira	522
Sampson, Etna	938
Sanders, William B.	951
Sanders, George	975
Sage, Clyde	1352
Sage, Claud	1353
Sample, Gussie Lee	1015
Schrock, Lannes William	376
Scantlen, James Russell	435
Scott, Benjamin Thomas	1006

Name.	Roll No.
Scott, Elizabeth	1039
Scott, Norman	1410
Scroggins, Georgie Lee	1457
See, Charles Clifford	74
Sexton, Juanita Ruth	122
Sexton, Ruel Finton	154
Sexton, Richard B.	368
Sexton, Myrtle	901
Sexton, Pearl	902
Sexton, Pleas Porter	1218
Seeley, May Sophina	249
Seeley, Ralph Whitfield	250
Selsor, Thelma Thyra	290
Self, Eloise	437
Self, Guy	1001
Secor, Bessie May	656
Semple, Maude Kathryn	1043
Seago, LaClara A.	1307
Shannon, William Landles	295
Shoemake, Lowell C.	571
Shuler, Roy Hill	573
Shillings, Virgie Lou	1112
Shield, Rosie Lee	1551
Shotube, Charles	1010
Shaw, Rena	1207
Simpson, Henry	1092
Simpson, Lena	42
Singer, Mitchell	138
Sims, Edith	159
Silmon, Turner	366
Silmon, Adam	367
Sittel, Jennette	394
Simmons, John	409
Simmons, Jewel	1253
Sirmans, Daniel Willis	912
Sirmans, Etanee	913
Slinker, William R.	304
Smith, Irene Nellie	3
Smith, Joe Wesley	16
Smith, Marjorie	17
Smith, Ella Gertrude	156
Smith, Clorie	267
Smith, Noland Freeman	373
Smith, Mary Elizabeth	465
Smith, Georgie Lee	649
Smith, Pauline	650
Smith, Jimmie	1198
Smart, Ruth	371
Snow, Annie Marie	390
Sorrells, Charles LeRoy	233
Sorrells, Annie Frances	1255
Sorrells, Nancy Elizabeth	1256
Sorrels, James Edward	356
Sockey, Homer	1083
Sockey, Rosey	1141
Sockey, Lester	1422
Spain, David H.	9
Spain, Thelma Lee	82
Spain, Minnie May	588
Spain, Jimmie B.	489
Spain, Mary Magdaline	737
Sperling, Daisy E.	41
Spann, Martha L.	132
Spring, Elma Edith	134
Spring, Cicero	968
Spring, Julia Lee	972
Spring, Earl	1064
Sparks, Capitolia	216
Spradlin, Orilla	523
Steward, Mattie J.	30
Stewart, Commodore	179
Stewart, Florence	1563
Stathan, Everett F.	142
Stephenson, Wanona Estelle	231
Starks, Bessie Leola	245
Standley, Norma Jane	439
Stanley, Charles S.	483
Stowers, Laura Winnie	519
Stigler, Rupert Bernard	618
Staples, Cecil A.	740
Stanford, Maudie	817

Name.	Roll No.
Strickland, Sarah N. C.	843
Stephen, Sampson	899
Stephen, Lena	1052
Stidham, William Harvey	929
Stidham, Willie	961
Stidham, Pearley Ann	996
Stidham, Harold	1581
Stiles, Bertie May	971
Stiles, Lilia	1208
Stallaby, Mary Ann	1259
Stallings, Oweta	1458
Suddath, Noel Aubry	4
Sumter, Lena Marie	23
Sumter, Milton Leon	324
Sumter, Robert O., Jr.	1285
Sullivan, Samuel Edmond	1310
Summer, Eller	1573
Swink, Randell Henry	415
Swink, William L.	1223
Swarm, Archie Mason	919
Swarm, Amanda Elizabeth	920
Taylor, Mirtie Lee	85
Taylor, Lee Rebecca	98
Taylor, Benjamin Lawson	319
Taylor, Hugh Sylvester	331
Taylor, Myrtle Lela	462
Taylor, Agnes	609
Taylor, Milton Nelson	685
Taylor, Absalom James	686
Taylor, Jesse	858
Taylor, Agnes	1116
Taylor, Eulafay	1357
Taylor, Virla Etna	1459
Taylor, Newcomb Davenport	1579
Tanehill, Theodore	326
Taliaferro, Nannie Lucile	660
Taliaferro, James Vernon	1214
Terry, Agnes Livena	103
Terry, Glenn M.	246
Terry, Thomas Vernon	296
Tecumseh, Julia	702
Terrell, Jesse James	1113
Thompson, Claud V.	59
Thompson, Beula	203
Thompson, Listy	314
Thompson, Daisy M.	706
Thompson, Joseph W.	1231
Thompson, Calvin	1325
Thompson, Silman	1400
Thomas, Willie	115
Thomas, Maggie	285
Thomas, George	286
Thomas, Loise	565
Thomas, Dorthula	914
Thomas, Josephine	983
Thomas, Emma	1568
Tiner, Leroy	337
Tims, Vincenta W.	1045
Tilly, Cornelius	1056
Tigert, Samuel C.	1151
Tigert, Bertha M.	1152
Tobler, Emmet	564
Tohkubbi, Laura	659
Tonihka, Ray	853
Trueblood, William Downard	425
Trammell, John Edgar	633
Trammell, Stella May	634
Truitt, William L.	758
Trohbe, Mary	999
Triplett, Thomas, Jr.	1081
Traut, Annie	1485
Tucker, Carrell	293
Tucker, Grady	294
Tucker, Ronald	301
Tucker, John Hampton Jr.	302
Tucker, Atha E.	529

Name.	Roll No.
Tucker, Clarence J.	530
Tucker, John E., Jr.	700
Tucker, Ozious James W.	892
Turnbull, Minnie	399
Turner, Eunice Melvina	619
Turner, Harrol Van	665
Tubby, John William	661
Tushka, Joseph	850
Tushka, Fostan	1028
Tullihela, Ben F.	1269
Turley, Nalio	1513
Tyler, William W.	763
Underwood, Vermelle	135
Underwood, Clarence Jefferson	579
Underwood, Abbin	1181
Upton, Floyd Manuel	1074
Vail, Gilbert	340
Vawter, Florence Maud	1021
Verner, Pearl	673
Vincent, Garlie	743
Victor, Frank	833
Vice, Lottie May	1545
Watkins, Benjamin Frederick	8
Watkins, Aaron	980
Watkins, Agnes	1503
Ward, Cassie V.	12
Ward, Freida I.	149
Ward, Lena Ola	184
Ward, Elias Jackson	288
Ward, Maggie Lorine	289
Ward, Ambrose Henry	291
Ward, Isom	815
Ward, Nova Cleo	987
Ward, Cleo Irene	1493
Watson, Charley	61
Watson, Washington	835
Watson, Johnnie	1478
Watson, Samuel James	1479
Watson, Mary	1487
Wade, Mary E.	63
Wade, Simon	472
Wade, Willie	931
Wade, Lilly	1154
Wade, Eli	1155
Wade, Clayton	1385
Wade, Willie	1460
Wade, Belinda	1575
Wade, Ethel	211
Walters, Edward	109
Wall, Napoleon B.	112
Wall, Bertha N.	113
Wall, Gilbert	121
Wall, Martha Eloise	147
Wall, Elma May	774
Wall, Gilbert	1030
Wall, Mulcy	1363
Walls, Bennie	1550
Walls, Green M.	313
Wallace, Leona	277
Wallace, Ione	1114
Wallace, Carlo	1398
Washington, Zona	461
Washington, Laura	869
Washington, Sissy	874
Wallen, Absolum	487
Wallen, Isom	648
Walker, Dellar	516
Walker, Hortey	517
Wadley, Dean McKinnon	733
Walcott, Daniel Hailey	1088
West, John Thomas	35
West, Clarence Earl	119
Welch, David Reagan	143
Welch, Pauline	144
Wesley, Mary	880
Wesley, Davis	977
Wesley, Houston	1133
Wesley, Agbert	1217
Wesley, Rhoda	1508
Webster, Samuel	1077
Webster, Nancy · Iva	921
Westbrook, Edker	1428
Weston, Mary	1482

Name.	Roll No.
Whistler, Lena	651
Whistler, Arena	997
Whitner, Harland H.	642
Whiteman, Henry A.	798
Whale, Lindsy	865
Wheeler, Lovina	1138
White, Lillian Aline	1380
Whitson, David Cornelius	128
Williams, Susan	43
Williams, Dessie	434
Williams, Ola May	349
Williams, Martha	514
Williams, Lula Pearl	695
Williams, Sarah	712
Williams, Elizabeth	723
Williams, Wilsie	834
Williams, Mattie	1098
Williams, Della	1232
Williams, Beulah F.	1292
Williams, Leola	1330
Williams, Charlie R.	1338
Williams, Benjamin	1554
William, Mary Ida	924
Winters, Emma	47
Willis, Vira	69
Willis, Susie	126
Willis, Frances	292
Willis, Sam	440
Willis, Lottie	854
Willis, Louisa	981
Willis, Rebecca	990
Willis, Fannie May	1075
Willis, Levi	1319
Willis, Hickman	1524
Wilkins, Alice	57
Wilson, Reader Melvin	353
Wilson, Roberth R.	419
Wilson, Ellenor Jane	674
Wilson, Zel Ora	767
Wilson, Eda	821
Wilson, Allie	845
Wilson, Bryant	846
Wilson, Jordan	900
Wilson, Ida May	905
Wilson, Annie Dovie	906
Wilson, Edward	1026
Wilson, Arther	1046
Wilson, McVay	1150
Wilson, Birdie	1267
Wilson, Susie	1268
Wilson, Clarence	1270
Wilson, Lida Bessie	1283
Wilson, Green	1390
Wilson, Noel J.	1421
Wilson, Judy	1473
Wilson, Anna	1555
Wilkin, Margret	749
Wise, John E. Jr.	489
Wise, Lela	490
Wiltsey, James Ellis	663
Winship, Lincoln	847
Winship, Anderson	848
Winship, John	1091
Wilmoth, Ivy	908
Witt, Jesse Thomas	1104
Wood, Annie	318
Wood, Julius Arthur	984
Woods, Ruby Grace	1096
Woods, Bulah Grace	1514
Worley, Mattie Fay	424
Wooldridge, Boyd Turner	1196
Wooley, Joseph M.	1329
Wright, Reno Cecil	1093
Wright, Mary Ann	1359
Wyatt, Pearl Dude	1251
Wyatt, Bonnie Pearl	1252
Wyers, Wyneter	1097
Yandell, Nettie	756
Yarbrough, Nowita	1314
Yota, Zira	1547
Young, Marion	627
Yoder, Troy	488
Zion, Cleo	266
Zion, Roy	1209
Zion, Floyd	1519

Name.	Roll No.
Burkes, Lelah Morine	453
Burks, Jessie	904
Burney, Delora Estelle	505
Burney, Frank	913
Burris, Buster	683
Burris, Lefes	684
Byington, David	98
Byington, Willie	236
Byington, Lillie	237
Byington, Albert	548
Byrd, Pauline	164
Cash, Henry G.	78
Carey, Josephine F.	115
Carr, Clayton	227
Carr, Ida	702
Carnes, Lorinda	260
Carnes, Ruthie Eugenia	292
Carns, Simpson	672
Cantwell, David Henry	312
Campbell, Farris Monroe	341
Carney, Erlington	350
Carney, Annie Eva	476
Carney, Minnie	792
Case, Fayette Blaine	364
Carter, Nancy Leah	428
Carter, Dana Kelsey	604
Cass, Donald	430
Cassell, Norris	605
Campala, Hampton	670
Caudill, Joseph Jacob	717
Casey, Lula Myrtle	807
Carn, Fannie	885
Choate, Phelix N.	43
Chandler, Nettie Marea	145
Christy, Amos W.	338
Christie, Minnie	888
Channell, Joseph L.	448
Chapman, Velma	468
Chivers, Stella LaFlore	512
Charley, Nellie	675
Charley, Noel	886
Clark, Lee Vester	217
Clark, Mamie	606
Coats, James	5
Cole, Bessie	113
Cole, Lizzie	189
Cole, Martha	681
Cole, Edwin	798
Coleman, Sallie	127
Coleman, Grady D.	204
Colbert, Blanche	238
Colbert, Nathanael	465
Cowling, Loreta Beechwood	304
Cooper, Tony A.	386
Cooper, John M.	427
Cooper, Vivian	499
Cooper, Rebecca E.	635
Cooper, Lena May	834
Cochnauer, Erma Marie	402
Cowen, Nora May	407
Coffman, Luna May	426
Columbus, Annie May	500
Cox, Caleb	637
Conn, Edward	658
Coon, Florence Naomi	689
Cook, Vivian	747
Compelube, Thad	753
Crowder, Willie May	50
Crowder, Francis Ann	64
Crowder, Simon	196
Crowder, Carl A.	673
Crowder, George Stanley	938
Crisp, William Henry Eugene	109
Crosby, Mike	197
Crow, Neveda Belle	221
Crutchfield, Mary	225
Crawford, Lena	241
Crawford, Mattie	740
Crossett, Guy Granville	256
Cranford, Bertie Oral	429
Crittenden, Edgar	549

Name.	Roll No.
Cross, Bonnie Marie	550
Cross, Walter R.	659
Creecy, Winnie Waneta	687
Culberson, Jennie E.	251
Davenport, Eunice Dorris	26
Daniels, Robert E. Lee	303
Davis, Birdie	365
Davis, Julia Josephine	410
Davis, John Edward	493
Davis, Joe T.	607
Davis, Minnie V.	636
Davis, James	889
Daggs, James W.	518
Darneal, Alma	575
Daffern, Wade	519
Devenport, Willie Edward	110
Denby, Yula Byrl	322
Denson, Opal	363
Dills, Gertrude	56
Dillard, Clemency H.	653
Dillard, Ettie Victoria	943
Dowland, Benjamin Franklin	285
Dorset, Anna	746
Dunagan, David Newton	156
Dukes, Theodore F.	213
Dukes, Jewel	242
Dukes, George Gilbert	711
Duer, Eddie	318
Duer, Janey Catharine	823
Durant, Columbus Robbs	406
Durant, Clarence C.	608
Durant, Luie Daniel	710
Durant, Lela May	930
Dwight, James Edgar	172
Dyer, Rincey	463
Dyer, Evalina	833
Dyer, Irene	880
Edgar, Percy Paul	258
Elliott, Earl D.	75
Ellis, Herbert	551
Ellis, Jessie	805
Emeyabbi, Cellin	799
English, Willie Cecil	229
Ervin, Malonea	48
Everidge, Jackson	49
Everidge, Mintie	71
Evans, Irene	949
Farrill, Emry Hendrix	23
Fargo, Charles Hugh	837
Featherston, Frances	431
Ferrante, Rosie Velentie	712
Fitzer, Tobias	16
Fisher, Harvey	496
Fisher, Wilson	517
Finley, Rosie	794
Fowler, Sims	39
Fowler, Oscar S.	159
Fobb, Philiston	66
Fobb, Franklin	577
Fox, Ethel Merree	140
Fout, Nelson	154
Folsom, Robert E.	205
Folsom, Lila May	331
Folsom, Earl	374
Folsom, Albert Pike	474
Folsom, May	661
Folsom, George	739
Folsom, Selina	755
Frazier, John	96
Frazier, Eliza	306
Frazier, Lena	308
Frazier, William	324
Frazier, Francise	944
Fry, Cleveland	194
Freeman, Maudie Bell	408
Freeman, Elizabeth	482
Freeney, Lillian C.	473
Freeny, Mary Elizabeth	537
Franklin, William P.	609
Franklin, Edny	682
Franklin, Kilburt	727

Name.	Roll No.
Fulton, James David, Jr.	91
Fulton, Jim	250
Garland, McCurton Stanford	123
Garland, William Marton	232
Garland, Edna	239
Garland, Willie	578
Garland, Raybon	883
Gardner, Lillie	161
Gardner, Sawyer	300
Gardner, Clemmie Arlie	495
Garlin, Raleigh Lee	353
Gamm, Ivy Deaner	627
Gazaway, Geneva May	806
Gibson, Pipkin P.	69
Gibson, Cyril	768
Gibbs, Virgie Ellen	209
Glenn, Jack M.	45
Gorman, Vermell	27
Goldston, Lora C.	32
Gooding, Oscar B.	132
Gordon, Laura Margaret	257
Going, Fannie	343
Going, McCleyborn	503
Going, George Gibson	723
Going, Jimmie	750
Goins, Mary Elizabeth	950
Goodman, William Aron	479
Gotcher, Herman Everett Ross	610
Goodard, Ray	703
Goold, Ruth	796
Griffith, Anna Wainta	203
Grubbs, Samuel Ross	385
Graham, Ida	467
Graham, Mattie	769
Gray, Luther Emery	693
Guess, May	86
Guess, Eldridge Buen	314
Guess, Zona	611
Harris, Elmer A.	70
Harris, Beatrice	941
Harrison, Vivian Blanche	130
Harrison, Ethel	235
Hawkins, Willie	219
Hawkins, Ruby May	447
Hawkins, Johnie M.	443
Harley, Laura	277
Harley, Leo	873
Hays, Isaac W.	293
Hayes, Bertha Ellis	411
Hayes, Milton Madlynn	612
Harkreader, Willis Franklin	323
Hatchett, Meta Ruth	340
Hancock, Albert	397
Hancock, William W.	654
Hancock, Sophia Margarett	715
Hattox, Ruby	412
Halcomb, Rebecca E.	639
Hallmark, Sarah May	737
Harlan, Joseph Buchanan	742
Hall, Minnie	875
Hampton, Bud	552
Henson, Jake J.	92
Heath, Ollive A.	136
Henderson, James Lamar	202
Henderson, Buster P.	440
Heck, Odie	230
Hensley, Dave	327
Hendrix, Lem Mitchell	389
Hendrix, Flora	940
Henbree, Ay	520
Herndon, Clara Estel	521
Herndon, Beulah	597
Herndon, Ruby	730
Hines, Martin Hulen	155
Hines, Thomas	325
Hibdon, Hobert V.	320
Hill, John Folsom	351
Hill, Carl F.	470

Name.	Roll No.
Hill, Claud	522
Hill, Eunice	726
Hicks, Comby	829
Hight, Mary Yetive	185
Hopkins, Frank Lee	11
Holman, Fannie	28
Holman, Vivion	508
Hooe, Bulah J.	59
Hodge, James Otis	82
Hoyt, Olline	329
Holmes, Mary	523
Holder, Hubert	803
Homma, Aaron	884
Hunt, Flowella Mattie	118
Hutchinson, Milton Parnell	311
Hunter, Ethel	359
Hudson, Goldie W.	579
Husbands, Nancy Ellen	952
Husbands, Francis E.	953
Huggins, Ora	281
Hyden, Henry Wilson	119
Hyde, Isabell	244
Impson, Junior	356
Impson, Viola	830
Impson, Joshua	914
Impson, Lillie	915
Impson, Frank	916
Impson, Roy Vester	939
Intolabbee, Earl Colbert	63
Irons, Aubery R.	40
Ireton, Johnnie Green	174
Isherwood, Frank R.	121
Ischcomer, Emley	398
Izard, John O.	694
Izard, William R.	695
James, Jincy	17
James, Roosevelt	432
James, Melinda	511
James, Incey	580
James, Jacob	581
James, Charles	720
James, Narcissa	826
James, Joetta	827
James, Ada Casteline	840
James, Henry	878
James, Liza	879
Jackson, Grace	33
Jackson, Lemar F.	55
Jackson, Eliza	149
Jackson, Jimson	514
Jamison, Walter	671
Jacob, Peter	752
Jefferson, Laura	83
Jefferson, Susan	147
Jefferson, Preston	525
Jefferson, Carolinsy	820
Jennings, Eliza Jane	524
Jennings, Arthur	719
Jeflow, Ben	906
Jones, Nova M.	7
Jones, Perry B.	53
Jones, Floyd J.	190
Jones, Locial C.	211
Jones, Viola G.	220
Jones, Laura Belle	234
Jones, Everett Vaunto	276
Jones, Eastman	360
Jones, Esta Elma	392
Jones, Noba	401
Jones, Levison	488
Jones, Fely	489
Jones, Charles Alexander	509
Jones, Gibson	553
Jones, Cleo	613
Jones, Hiram F.	651
Jones, Harry Douglas	655
Jones, Jacob, Jr.	716
Jones, Kizzie	814
Jones, Wilson	824
Jones, Tobias	825
Johnson, Alice	124
Johnson, Cleo	409
Johnson, James	946

Name.	Roll No.
John, Mary	490
John, Thomas Aline	582
John, Newton	583
John, Elias	614
John, Siala	652
Johnico, Isable	756
Julius, Solomon	188
Kaniatobe, Raymond	378
Kaniatobe, Watson	380
Keltner, Wallace Leflore	102
Kelly, Gertie Ruth	400
Kellogg, Frances Mariee	526
Kirkpatrick, Alexander	47
Kirby, Walter Taylor	65
Kirby, Horace Turner	584
Killingsworth, Louis M.	287
King, Opal Louise	332
King, Cornelius A.	376
King, Junia Elizabeth	403
Knight, Mary Violetta	477
Krebbs, Tandy Walker	60
Krebbs, Mandy	339
Lauchner, Harry Clay	12
Larecy, Eldon H.	106
Labor, Isaiah	193
Labor, Thornton	758
Ladd, Cecil Pearl	223
LaFlore, John	438
Lance, Novena	507
Lane, Callie	617
Lane, Allie (No. 2.)	618
Lee, Manford	19
Lee, Jeoraldean	783
LeFlore, Emily	37
LeFlore, Silma Cecil	177
LeFlore, Edith O.	222
LeFlore, Henry Clay	243
LeFlore, Byrd L.	275
LeFlore, Ishmon	333
LeFlore, Alice	662
LeFlore, Frank	676
LeFlore, Forbes	744
LeFlore, Allice	757
Lewis, Daisy, Ivanella	224
Lewis, L. Vinsey	585
Lewis, Jesse	650
Lewis, Dorothy	770
Lewis, Mattie Hellen	819
Lewis, Julia B.	948
Lemon, Martha May	808
Lingo, Joe W.	54
Littlefield, Thomas Harold	81
Lively, Albert Eugene	349
Lindsey, Jaunita Albena	528
Little, Flossie	817
Lowe, Elmer	38
Lowry, Agnes Austin	249
Logan, Arnode	264
Lowman, Johnnie	527
Lowery, Ora Lee Bell	909
Loring, Sophia	679
Ludlow, Dixon	741
Ludlow, Corianthan Samuel	839
Ludlow, Nellie Samuel	893
Ludlow, Magdaline	942
Luper, Neva May	57
Manning, Vera	30
Maxwell, Ulia Elsie	34
Martin, Marie	58
Massey, Ray	141
Mathews, Willie Irma	181
Mathews, Thelma Ma	890
Mathiews, Alvin Clayton	437
Mathis, Ether	759
Mambi, Elistin	255
Mays, Phely Bell	282
Mackey, Calvin Perry	321
Mackey, Willis W.	494
Mason, Geo. Isreal	690
Medell, Ophelia F.	195
Mitchell, Lola May	103
Mitchell, Helen E.	133
Mitchell, Louis Tarber	206
Middleton, Welsin	414

Name.	Roll No.
Miyabe, Elsie	433
Miller, Sam	529
Miller, Thomas Young	530
Miller, Sam	917
Mills, Irene	800
Monds, Julia Frances	9
Moore, Beaula Josie	160
Moore, Jessie. Irene	274
Moore, Johnson Douglass	316
Moore, Lolency	413
Moore, Henry F.	638
Moore, Carl	307
Morris, Edna May	441
Morris, Mattie Lorma Vernell	590
Morris, Ibra Cleveland	738
Morrell, Cooper	513
Morgan, Joseph H.	615
Morrison, Cearil	642
Morrison, John Trinnier	713
Muldrow, Henry Lowndes	3
Mullen, Harrold Marion	31
Myer, Kennedy	554
McAlvain, Zella	15
McAlvain, Robbie Marie	270
McAlvain, Neva Leon	691
McAdoo, Gladys Ivy	778
McAlester, Daniel	749
McBride, Dorothy	586
McCalla, Joseph Bailey	14
McClain, Theodore Roosevelt	163
McClain, James Thomas Jr.	170
McClure, Artemissa	167
McClure, Ida May	454
McClure, Chas. Wesley	480
McClure, Bessie	484
McClure, George Eugene	555
McClure, Anna May	704
McCann, Irene	587
McCann, Dixson	663
McCarty, Myrtle Lee	619
McCurtain, Frank Allen	705
McCary, Lessie Arena	810
McDaniel, Eunice	125
McFarland, Samuel	278
McFarland, Maggie Lou	771
McFerran, Harry Deseveridge	279
McGee, Baston	588
McGee, Annice	620
McKinney, Loter Lee	215
McKinney, William Cecil	449
McKinney, Benno S.	589
McLellan, William E.	116
McLellan, Lee	134
McMurtry, Sterling	466
McMurtry, Cora B.	831
Nail, Rufus M.	87
Nail, Malsey	158
Nale, Morris	146
Nale, James Fredric	200
Nakishi, Nattie	714
Nelson, Josephine Elizabeth	13
Nelson, Henry	760
Nelson, Henry	908
Neill, Samuel Leonard	326
Neal, Luther Leonidas	813
Nehka, Phillip	891
Nicholas, Frank Adam	345
Ninas, Mary	745
Norman, Aaron	144
Noah, Leaonias	556
Noah, Silina	809
Noley, Grayson	892
Null, John Edwards	688
Oakes, Harriet E.	77
Odelle, James Gordon	506
Oliver, Agnes Blanch	68
Orndorff, Bertha M.	882
Ott, Sam	344
Overstreet, Mary Margaret	647
Payne, Irene M.	73

Name.	Roll No.
Parrish, William	152
Patterson, Martha Letrice	301
Paddock, Wiley	405
Parker, Wilsie	531
Pebworth, Elva Augustus	245
Pebsworth, Dorothy	366
Perkins, William Hardin	415
Perkins, Laura	725
Pernell, Annie	591
Peter, George	664
Perry, Eva	686
Penny, Samuel W.	216
Phillips, Leola	375
Pitchlynn, Rhoda Beulah	640
Pierce, John Thomas	729
Pierce, Sophia	838
Pickens, Arthur	785
Pickens, Mary	815
Platt, Frank Clifford	186
Plummer, Edwin Wright	187
Plummer, Arbie Ella	207
Potts, Ramsey	169
Pope, Millie	416
Pope, Laman	592
Prince, Neoma Clee	515
Pugh, Tilman S.	761
Puckett, Annie J.	832
Quincy, Jackson	532
Quinton, Mary Ellen	557
Quinton, William	558
Quinton, Ruben	665
Rabon, Vera Gertrude	25
Rabon, Clifford	148
Ralls, Clara A.	20
Randolph, Hiram	151
Ratliff, Jane Lloyd	381
Riddle, Bonnie Bess	199
Riddle, Eitle Florence	622
Richardson, Mattie May	377
Roberts, Henry Mayo	6
Roberts, Joshua	52
Roberts, Albert Dillard	393
Roberts, Benjamin	933
Roebuck, Nancy	129
Roebuck, Clarecy	150
Roebuck, Theodore E.	272
Roebuck, Walter Glenn	731
Robinson, Sylvester	233
Robinson, Joshua	382
Robinson, Nattie	841
Robinson, John	842
Robinson, Zachry T.	728
Roberson, Luke	623
Roberson, Pawline	352
Rosenthal, Willie Willis	309
Roff, Della May	383
Roff, Stanley Ray	736
Rogers, Ethyl Aline	469
Rose, Rockey Ella	533
Ross, Gladys	648
Rockman, Lottie M.	754
Rushing, Jesse Joseph	35
Russell, Escopia	120
Russell, Floyd Bruce	166
Ryan, James Andrews	624
Sanguin, Joseph B.	46
Sam, Stephen	84
Sam, Snoda	248
Sanner, Maggie Oma	99
Sanford, Callie Ester	286
Sauls, Leo	472
Samis, Henry	593
Sanders, Daniel	634
Samuel, Emerson	779
Samuel, Lawrence	780
Schrock, Homer Amos	165
Scantlen, Shairlie Lefile	498
Scott, Simon Lester	571
Scott, George Fulton	621
Scott, Catherine Folsom	643
Sexton, Thompson G.	171
Sexton, James J.	733
Sexton, James	793
Sexton, Joseph, Jr.	881
Self, Auddie Lee	357

Name.	Roll No.
Self, Lillian	765
Shannon, Oberan	346
Shoemake, Elijah	353
Shillings, Zelma Estell	434
Sheegog, Charley, Jr.	534
Sharkey, Lula Belle	772
Sharkey, Fleny	936
Sharkey, Lamos	937
Sims, Ramon	208
Singer, Eva	296
Simmons, Cleo	492
Silmon, Susan	625
Slover, Toy Lee	95
Slinker, James Andrew	626
Smith, Anna Zo	101
Smith, Elgen	355
Smith, Lottie Louisa	369
Smith, Ollie E.	497
Smith, Opal May	536
Smith, Lucy Loretta	559
Smith, Hampton	677
Smart, Ada Mable	471
Southard, Eva	450
Sorrells, Claudie Edward	535
Sorrells, Ruby May	641
Sockey, James Alvin	763
Sockey, William L.	764
Sockey, Josephine	912
Spring, Susan D.	79
Spring, Winter Kelly	478
Spring, James Roby	734
Spring, Veno	786
Spradlin, Bud	218
Spain, Joseph A.	361
Steward, Edna	67
Stewart, Ed	94
Stewart, Lem	762
Stewart, Purcell	773
Stewart, Susie	787
Statham, Artie	85
Sterrett, Margaret Virginia	108
Strickland, Tams Bixby	184
Starks, Almena	191
Stowers, Cecil Calbert	228
Stephen, Louisa	486
Stiles, Lottie Lee	560
Strong, Aloysius Gleason	561
Summer, John Henry	680
Swink, Irene K.	628
Taaffe, Alyce Clair	21
Taylor, Jencey	105
Taylor, Frank Jeffress	138
Taylor, Ida M.	475
Taylor, Martha	570
Taylor, Freymon	894
Taylor, McKinley	954
Taylor, Dona Victoria	822
Taliaferro, Gladice	259
Tashka, Rena	562
Takkubbee, Lavenia	700
Terry, Jessie Francis	143
Terry, Melvin M.	173
Terrell, Mary Elizabeth	929
Thomas, Innez	10
Thomas, Agnes	24
Thomas, Mattie	481
Thomas, Hampton	748
Thomas, Della May	801
Thomas, Lotta	947
Thrasher, Ruth	90
Thompson, Eva Alton	137
Thompson, Rosa Belle	182
Thompson, Harris James	334
Thompson, Paul	678
Thompson, Alice	699
Thompson, Thelma Lee	795
Thompson, Jessie Eli	818
Thompson, John Henry	905
Thompson, Esias	126
Tims, Nora E.	72
Tims, Etline	214
Tillman, John B.	88
Tigert, Lee Roy	305

Name.	Roll No.	Name.	Roll No.
Tiner, Bonnie	743	Whistler, Thompson W.	252
Toole, John	89	White, Nancy	254
Tohkubbi, Alex	379	White, Ora Ida	595
Tonler, Susan	788	Whittle, Walter. Clyde	271
Town, Jesse Johnson	918	Williams, Alvarah Viola	62
Traylor, Walter Lee	76	Williams, Cinsy	368
Trammell, Ruby Lee	226	Williams, Josie Pearl	384
Tushka, Toney	485	Williams, William T.	387
Tubby, Mattie May	629	Williams, Henry	390
Turnbull, Goldia	630	Williams, May	394
Turnbull, Edith	816	Williams, Ike	540
Turnbull, Ozi Dulaney	895	Williams, Ella	789
Turner, James McClure	594	Williams, John F.	835
Tyler, Anna Reva	631	Williams, Rephey	887
Vawter, Alice Roxie	111	Williams, Wincy	893
Vawter, Beatrice Lee	112	Williams, Zegar	899
Vincent, Edgar Morris	162	Williams, Isham	900
Wallace, Essie Lee	8	Williams, Annie	901
Wallace, Lincey	667	Wilson, Candace	104
Wade, James	93	Wilson, Johnnie Lee	131
Wade, Alexander	97	Wilson, James Ethel	157
Wade, Ola Marie	464	Wilson, Islam	210
Walker, Tommie W.	135	Wilson, Vivian Lynn	240
Walker, Louisa	666	Wilson, Theodore Roose-	
Watts, Columbus David	246	velt	315
Waide, John Emory	261	Wilson, Susie Marie	373
Washington, Lawrence	342	Wilson, Preman M.	444
Washington, Timothy	565	Wilson, Alice	541
Washington, Allen	566	Wilson, Record Prather	692
Ward, Orville Leonard	395	Wilson, Mona	774
Ward, Lillie Irene	396	Wilson, Lucie	811
Ward, Sela	399	Wilson, Listie	902
Ward, Homer Baxter	563	Wilson, Beccy	955
Ward, Thelma Dorean	632	Wilkinson, Ollis Quinton	117
Ward, Herbert Zacariah	828	Willis, Green	168
Ward, Julia	874	Willis, Roy	348
Ward, Elisha	446	Willis, Elsie	766
Walls, Lou Evalena	417	Winter, Abe F.	313
Walton, John P.	418	Winters, Hazel V.	510
Wallen, Allen	538	Winters, Charles Thomas	567
Wallen, James	539	Winship, Ina	504
Wallen, Rose Anna	569	Wilkin, Sillian	596
Watkins, Henry	544	Wilkin, Jefferson Davis	812
Watkins, Selley	896	Woodward, Christina V.	100
Watkins, Elton	897	Wood, Fannie	542
Watson, Mamie L.	564	Wood, Trannie	543
Webster, Ethel D.	391	Wood, Ben	767
Weston, Nora	404	Woods, Cleo G.	568
Wesley, Alma	462	Woods, Ruther May	668
Wesley, Jackson	491	Woolery, James H.	932
Wesley, Mary	802	Wright, Rosie Pearl	660
Wesley, Mary	945	Wright, Simon	696
West, Pearlie May	616	Wright, Cellina	903
West, Tommie	708	Yandell, Sim David	299
West, Johnnie	709	Young, Ethel M.	42
Welsh, Nancy	804	Zion, Ethel	649

INDEX TO
CHOCTAWS BY MARRIAGE

Name.	Roll No.	Name.	Roll No.
Birlew, Rebecca	1094	Buckholts, Tommy	1334
Bingham, James B.	1450	Burditt, Mattie	1001
Bishop, Hugh A.	1459	Burnes, Ollie	1208
Blakely, F. C.	199	Burnes, Laura	1209
Blakely, Annie	1285	Burns, Alice	1404
Blalack, Joseph W.	298	Burns, Buckner	1542
Blake, L. L.	957	Burnett, John L.	1243
Blundell, James H.	1283	Burnitt, Alice	1553
Blue, Rhoda	1318	Burkes, Alice V. R.	1272
Blevins, George W.	1465	Burkes, Sarah P.	1572
Boatwright, Alice M.	445	Burkes, Maud Ella	1600
Boatright, Lou E.	50	Burrows, Alabama	1326
Boatwright, Zena	444	Buckhanon, Nanie	1563
Bowles, John	54	Byram, Miles	510
Bohanan, Rosie D.	85	Byford, H. M.	858
Bohanan, Abie	86	Carr, Daniel H.	1
Bohanan, Mary	267	Carr, Frederick H.	566
Bohanan, Lula	814	Carr, Alice C.	859
Bohanan, Ada	1293	Carr, William Madison	1383
Bohanan, Annie	1309	Campbell, Lucy	143
Bond, Edna	116	Campbell, Hugh	490
Bond, Ridgely	462	Campbell, W. H. L.	550
Bond, June H.	681	Campbell, Susan Frances	943
Bond, George M.	1037	Campbell, Katie	944
Bogle, Henry C.	216	Campbell, John	1441
Bogle, Ada B.	1325	Campbell, Susan Jose-	
Boland, Kizzie	362	phine	1561
Bolin, John	1444	Campbell, Sarah A.	1562
Bohreer, John	998	Campbell, Idonia	1607
Bounds, James H.	1035	Campbell, Clara	1613
Boggess, Eliza Barbara	1088	Carroll, James	214
Booker, William P.	1124	Carroll, Laura L.	1361
Boydstun, George A.	1125	Carnes, Myrtle	353
Boydstun, Mary Jane	1442	Cartlidge, Edward	479
Boydston, Hattie	1622	Carrier, Joe G.	542
Bolling, George F.	1130	Carn, Caldonia	563
Bolling, Hazel Belle	1337	Camp, Allie	696
Bolinger, Ella	1156	Camp, Joseph B.	1069
Boykin, James	1167	Camp, Mary	1402
Boswell, Mary	1589	Case, Lee	826
Brown, Charles E.	98	Catlin, James D.	837
Brown, Absalom B.	320	Carson, Jerry	857
Brown, Henry	530	Casey, Wiley P.	960
Brown, John I.	636	Cattuton, Sarah E.	1025
Brown, John T.	725	Carpenter, Walter D.	1152
Brown, Mat	818	Carpenter, Thomas L.	1493
Brown, Lou	920	Camden, A. B.	1386
Brown, George	1036	Childs, F. H.	9
Brown, Armatha	1304	Chandler, James R.	207
Brashears, Myrtle	113	Choate, Belle D.	308
Brashears, Minnie	281	Choate, Mary E.	581
Brashears, Lida B.	295	Choate, Ida	589
Brashears, Martha H.	1234	Choate, Annie M.	1028
Brashears, Bessie	1528	Chunn, Lucy	458
Brewer, Lake	195	Chunn, Allie	464
Brackett, Thomas	368	Chastain, Jefferson D.	738
Brimage, John W.	472	Chivers, Edgar E.	1046
Brimage, George	645	Chapman, James M.	1095
Brennon, Thomas	789	Chaffin, Dorellar	1569
Brennon, Nancy	1252	Cloud, H. D.	55
Brandy, Nettie	905	Clower, Walter F.	424
Brooks, G. W.	958	Clay, Mattie	699
Brooks, William	1038	Cline, Arthur J.	835
Brinkley, Sarah E.	1051	Clark, James B.	969
Brinkley, Carrie	1608	Clark, Ina Katherine	1350
Brady, Robert G.	1058	Clover, Mary F.	1522
Breedlove, Thomas	1265	Cobb, Ben	2
Broughton, Lee	1394	Cobb, Agnes	1635
Bruton, Thomas	1571	Conner, F. L.	4
Burris, Frank	334	Conners, John P.	587
Burris, Rebecca	856	Cowen, John R.	96
Burris, Florence	1611	Cowan, George S.	118
Bugg, John H.	364	Coleman, James M.	197
Buck, Francis E.	446	Coleman, W. A.	596
Buck, Mattie	1547	Coleman, Annie E.	1587
Busby, Smith Jefferson	526	Costen, Thomas J.	200
Eurch, James E.	546	Cochran, W. L.	202
Bullard, Andrew C.	653	Cornelius, Benjamin F.	241
Bullard, Elijah G.	1089	Collins, Gracie	274
Butterly, Nicholas	860	Collins, Henry A.	300
Buckholts, Martha	868	Collins, Daisy	731
Buckholts, Frances E.	874	Collins, Claudie I.	965
Buckholts, Annie J.	878	Collins, Miles S.	1182
Buckholts, Fannie	1084	Cooper, Mary	276
Buckholts, Carrie L.	1284	Cooper, Eliza A.	278

Name.	Roll No.	Name.	Roll No.
Folsom, Vina	474	Goddard, James M.	832
Folsom, Elizabeth G.	524	Goddard, Mary	1427
Folsom, Sallie	553	Goodson, Nettie	1078
Folsom, Maud A.	558	Goodson, Rebecca	1171
Folsom, Annie	770	Goforth, Hanora	1106
Folsom, Sarah	820	Goforth, Mary A.	1381
Folsom, Mary Elizabeth	904	Goldston, James William	1656
Folsom, Tabitha	929	Gowen, Cora	1667
Folsom, Leora	1043	Grant, Alice	5
Folsom, Etta J.	1050	Grant, Mardie	1275
Folsom, Delena	1144	Gregory, Alzia R.	250
Folsom, Lizzie	1222	Gregory, Abraham	520
Folsom, Laura	1390	Gregory, Corda J.	821
Folsom, Mary G.	1551	Grubbs, Eliza C.	447
Folsom, Lee	1618	Grubbs, Carrie	523
Folsome, Lula Belle	219	Grubbs, Ity A.	600
Fortner, Samuel H.	245	Gray, George	1063
Fortson, Josiah R.	484	Griffith, Sarah C.	1168
Forbis, Jane	505	Grady, John M.	1472
Fowler, David A.	509	Guthrie, W. M.	6
Fowler, Hasea L.	949	Gulley, Eugene A.	311
Foster, John E.	908	Guess, Emanuel P.	332
Foster, Minnie B.	938	Guess, Maud	369
Foster, Ida Adella	942	Hartshorne, George E.	51
Foster, Mattie Bell	1226	Harris, Amanda A.	66
Foster, Thomas	1250	Harris, Maggie E.	222
Foster, Eliza Jane	1560	Harris, Susan G.	243
Foucar, Ida L.	1438	Harris, Jack L.	365
Frost, Severe W.	218	Harris, Mary F.	504
Freeney, Fannie	293	Harris, Jonas R.	620
Freeny, Josephine	359	Harris, Maggie E.	631
Freeny, Era	543	Harris, James F.	693
Freeny, Grace	672	Harris, Sarah E.	890
Fry, Thomas W.	919	Harris, Cyrus L.	1291
Freeman, Jasper N.	1139	Harris, Mary E.	1499
Freeman, Joanna	1513	Harris, Frances	1541
Freeman, Zona	1515	Harkins, Viney	74
Fronterhouse, John	1188	Harkins, Hattie	342
Fronterhouse, William	1356	Harkins, Lillie	420
Fronterhouse, Nellie	1357	Harkins, Alice	559
French, Mary B.	1249	Harkins, Mollie	571
Franklin, John Anderson	1654	Harrison, Addell	125
Fulton, James D.	687	Harrison, Bessie	418
Fulton, Jack	983	Harrison, Robert S.	436
Garland, Ellen	17	Harrison, Edgar Lee	557
Garland, Mabel	248	Harrison, Serilda J.	792
Garland, Mary L.	253	Harrison, Lorena	899
Garland, Daniel N.	500	Harrison, Rosa	1009
Garland, Mandy C.	515	Hart, Mattie	178
Garland, Ida	518	Hallmark, John J.	309
Garland, Quay	628	Hardage, Andrew C.	321
Garland, Arizona	906	Hampton, Willie	330
Garland, Jessie Lee	1040	Hampton, Mattie	836
Gardner, Mattie	68	Hampton, Fannie	884
Gardner, Zora	163	Halpin, Michael	347
Gardner, Florence	348	Harrell, Pious D.	374
Gardner, Laura B.	511	Hazel, Nora	456
Gardner, Emily	619	Hazel, Eveline	491
Gardner, Rosetta	1006	Hailey, Daniel M.	466
Gardner, Minnie	1087	Hailey, Grace C.	766
Gardner, Minnie	1558	Hailey, Stella Doyle	767
Gardner, Maud T.	1653	Hailey, Minnie L.	1138
Garner, Alexander T.	841	Haley, Nancy	1435
Gaither, Beal	285	Hardaway, Margaret	651
Garvin, Mattie M.	305	Hankins, Levi	705
Garvin, S. J.	784	Hall, Robert H.	733
Garrison, LaFayette O.	990	Hall, William S.	1306
Garrison, Sarah E.	1142	Hatchett, Jesse M.	744
Gallamore, Elonzo W.	1054	Harper, Isham W.	761
Gentry, Sarah A.	827	Hays, Rose	755
Gills, Emmet K.	409	Hamilton, William H.	782
Gill, Charles J.	440	Hamilton, Hugh H.	1026
Gilstrap, J. F.	536	Hamilton, Alexander B.	1136
Gillum, Harris T.	1119	Hamilton, Lillie	1213
Gibson, Laura	1224	Hamilton, Laura	1267
Gibson, Sallie	1352	Harkreader, Samuel B.	845
Gleason, Michael H.	201	Hamm, Thomas I.	867
Glenn, William I.	675	Hawkins, Margaret	926
Goodnight, John H.	115	Hattox, John W.	1129
Gordon, Reverdy J.	185	Hale, Mary	1174
Gordon, Haywood P.	1446	Hageman, Charles	1186
Goings, Lena	337	Hancock, Henry	1236
Gooding, Minnie Lee	704	Hancock, Viola	1322
Gooding, Georgia A.	708	Harlan, Etta	1264
Gooding, Henry L.	994		

Name.	Roll No.	Name.	Roll No.
Hagewood, Mary J.	1509	Impson, Flora	973
Hardin, Bettie	1570	Impson, Mary J.	1083
Hermon, Joseph G.	13	Ingram, Benjamin .S.	193
Henderson, Wilson L.	106	Ireton, John	499
Henderson, Sarah	1011	Ireton, Minnie Ann	1159
Henderson, Lula	1132	Ireton, Laura	1277
Henderson, Lula	1183	Intolabbee, Ada	829
Henderson, Samuel N.	1294	Ish, William W.	953
Henderson, George W.	1371	Isaac, Margaret	1379
Hembree, William	310	James, Clara	34
Hendrix, Jasper	401	James, Mary	554
Hendrix, Nancy	461	James, Orlener	806
Hendrix, Evelina	1137	James, Edith	817
Hendrix, Myra	1373	James, William A.	921
Hendricks, Martha M.	1195	James, Lela	972
Hendrickson, Mary E.	656	James, Florence	1014
Herndon, Sidney J.	507	James, Gertha	1286
Herndon, Edgar B.	508	James, Winnie	1295
Herndon, Quintus	785	James, Elizabeth M.	1354
Herndon, Ezekiel K.	812	James, Henrietta	1420
Herndon, John C.	1289	Jackson, Belle Z.	425
Hensley, Robert L.	539	Jackson, Jim Thompson	1335
Heskett, Nettie	688	Jackson, Maria	1340
Heskett, Emery E.	984	Jackson, Lucretia	1471
Heath, Chester R.	713	Jefferson, Sarah	32
Hewitt, Joseph C.	752	Jefferson, Annie	1298
Hewitt, George W.	886	Jenkins, John L.	60
Hewett, William J.	1153	Jeter, Joshua B.	240
Heavener, Joseph	901	Jelks, Fred	622
Henson, Virginia	1056	Jennings, Henry C.	1389
Herron, John L.	1178	Jennings, Ida Leona	1466
Heflin, William H.	1449	Jennings, Orotia A.	1482
Hickman, Lawrence Q.	266	Jones, Dovie	137
Hickman, James H.	131	Jones, Charles P.	172
Hickman, Eugene A.	605	Jones, Frances A.	232
Hickman, Samuel	1514	Jones, Frank	489
Hill, Cornelius D.	101	Jones, Mattie	535
Hill, Charles	356	Jones, Malinda	570
Hill, David	575	Jones, Charles W.	598
Hill, Jefferson W.	907	Jones, James A.	686
Hill, Granville G.	1328	Jones, George W.	701
Hiberd, Laura	134	Jones, Eliza B.	833
Hibben, Thomas D.	231	Jones, Martha Ann	863
Hiarker, Sarah	257	Jones, Amanda	922
Hightower, Benjamin F.	583	Jones, Martha E.	923
Hilseweck, Wm. E.	756	Jones, Ida M.	947
Hibdon, Emma Lively	1239	Jones, Daniel	954
Holman, Tuck D.	149	Jones, Ella	988
Holman, Charles R.	228	Jones, William J.	1032
Hoover, D. H.	209	Jones, Martha E.	1080
Howard, William H.	236	Jones, Mary	1227
Hodges, Laura B.	406	Jones, Laura A.	1271
Hodges, Nancy A.	1221	Jones, Rodham T.	1333
Howell, Sallie	498	Jones, John W.	1549
Howell, Henrietta	955	Jones, Ruthie	1632
Homer, Blanche E.	666	Johnson, Van B.	252
Hooe, Archie F.	737	Johnson, James C.	486
Hopkins, Thomas W.	759	Johnson, William	630
Holleman, William G.	842	Johnson, Ben F.	659
Hoyt, Lizzie	917	Johnson, Lydia M.	956
Holson, Texanna	918	Johnson, G. W.	959
Houghton, Charles L.	982	Johnson, Dicie E.	1496
Hoff, Lizzie	1018	Johnson, Roselia	1500
Holloway, Alice	1022	Johns, Margaret	1261
Holly, James	1483	Karl, Frank A.	443
Hotubbee, Nancy	1657	Kayser, Elizabeth H.	728
Hull, Joseph L.	354	Kennady, James F.	25
Hudson, Myrtle	711	Kennedy, Michael	428
Human, Mary J.	799	Kendrick, William D.	229
Human, Mattie E.	1004	Kelly, James J.	230
Hunt, John	976	Kelly, Mollie	423
Hutchings, James W.	1400	Kelly, William R.	1097
Hutchinson, Lillie	1214	Kendle, Charles J.	840
Hutchinson, Matilda	1582	Keltner, William H. H.	888
Hurt, William	1117	Kemp, Rosa E.	1070
Huddleston, May	1610	King, Joanna	23
Husbands, Catherine J.	1670	King, Jackson W.	264
Hybarger, James C.	1101	King, John A.	319
Hynson, Noland	1161	King, Emma	615
Isherwood, William H.	99	King, Sarah J.	769
Izard, Mary L.	156	King, Mary Y.	930
Izard, Tommie	1474	Kirby, Emma	67
Impson, Angeline	157	Kirby, Lizzie	809
Impson, Eveline	964	Kirby, Wyatte T.	1288

Name.	Roll No.	Name.	Roll No.
Kirkpatrick, James C.	71	Love, Kate D.	613
Kirkendall, Joseph	946	Lockley, L. Cornelius	720
Kinghorn, Jennie	1372	Low, Hugh D.	1029
Kinghorn, Thomas A.	1663	Loyd, John J.	1229
Klugh, August	290	Loring, Lulie	1616
Koozer, Charles	891	Lucas, Thomas L.	56
Krieger, Frederick C.	476	Lucas, Spencer	700
Krieger, William	574	Ludlow, Edwin	291
Krebbs, Hattie	911	Lynn, George E.	171
Krebbs, Provie Lee	1477	Lynn, J. Y.	173
Krebbs, Susie Bell	1573	Lyles, Mary L.	646
Latimer, Byron H.	147	Lyle, Robert Thomas	963
Latimer, Osborne S.	234	Matthews, John W.	21
Latimer, James S.	657	Mathews, Andrew J.	748
Labor, Houston	223	Mathews, James S.	1664
Labor, William	363	Maxwell, William	107
Lankford, Thomas N.	307	Mathies, Christopher C.	242
Lawrence, Sarah J.	341	Manning, Laura	346
Lawrence, Ida V.	669	Mayo, John B.	372
Lawrence, Sudie	670	Mayo, James D.	1282
Lawrence, Dollie	865	Massey, Alice Victoria	433
Lawrence, Georgia Ann	1120	Massey, Arizona C.	951
Lanz, Henry	453	Martin, Howard	592
Lane, Bartholomew	746	Martin, Maggie	912
Lane, Mary	1123	Manners, Thomas Edgar	774
Lauderdale, Thomas J.	1033	Mackey, Belle	848
Lauchner, Grant	1413	Mackey, Wayne Lee	1396
Latta, Mary Etta	1557	Marcum, John W.	1000
Langley, Samuel Lee	1596	Marcum, Joshua	1099
Leslie, Mary	10	Marcum, Henry W.	1197
LeFlore, Lama	255	Magner, Eula H.	1061
LeFlore, Bertha	279	Mauldin, Edwin A.	1104
LeFlore, Phoebe E.	350	Marlow, Etta J.	1196
LeFlore, Marion	384	Marshall, Annie Palmer	1240
LeFlore, Anne Mary	385	Marshall, Nancy	1424
LeFlore, Louisa F.	389	Matoy, William M.	1419
LeFlore, Arley M.	480	Maddox, Elliah C.	1505
LeFlore, Keturah	791	Meroney, Harriet C	256
LeFlore, Lizzie	813	Merryman, Ruth	269
LeFlore, Carrie	815	Merryman, Florence A.	270
LeFlore, Daisy	851	Merryman, Ellen	275
LeFlore, Florence H.	986	Merryman, Pairlee	734
LeFlore, Ella	1039	Merryman, Mary	824
LeFlore, Russ	1092	Merryman, Cordelia E.	915
LeFlore, Mamie B.	1194	Merryman, Ora	1314
LeFlore, Josephine	1220	Meggs, William	599
LeFlore, Gertrude	1311	Medell, Albert	757
LeFlore, Mason	1508	Medell, William	1008
LeFlore, Amanda	1529	Messick, Arthur C.	1187
Lewis, Myrtle	283	Messick, Mary F.	1348
Lewis, Cynthia	296	Merry, Louis	1363
Lewis, Martha J.	478	Meek, Ada	1434
Lewis, Thomas B.	740	Mitchell, Bessie	1245
Lewis, Cynthia Eudora	743	Mitchell, Sallie E.	43
Lewis, Rosa	771	Mitchell, Robert B.	194
Lewis, Rosa	1003	Miller, John C.	90
Lewis, John M.	1440	Miller, Maggie M.	755
Lee, Leila C.	534	Miller, James H.	783
Lee, C. W. D.	1672	Miller, Virginia P.	1454
Leewright, Minor	540	Middleton, Charles P.	142
Ledou, Jacob	661	Miashintubi, Mary	1504
Lester, Preston S.	796	Moore, William M.	12
Lemasters, Belle	1375	Moore, Dora M.	120
Leard, James T.	1626	Moore, Robert M.	434
Little, William A.	167	Moore, Joseph J.	652
Link, Robert E.	572	Moore, William C.	758
Lindsey, Lewis	861	Moore, Nannie	846
Littlepage, Patrick H.	1013	Moore, Jasper N.	1072
Livingston, Mollie	1633	Moore, Hattie	1079
Lloyd, John M.	608	Moore, Nancy M.	1085
Lofton, Sarah E.	36	Moore, Dora	1210
Lowery, Crecy A.	159	Moore, Frances Emma	1281
Lowery, Rhoda A.	215	Moore, Elizabeth	1431
Lowery, Isaac S.	719	Moore, Idummea	1512
Lowery, Florence	1418	Moyer, John F.	16
Locke, Mattie B.	180	Morris, Corinne S. M.	103
Locke, Victor M.	778	Morris, Arreathy	65
Locke, Elisha S.	936	Morris, Lawson A.	496
Loman, Susan	227	Morris, John	1552
Loman, Nellie E.	632	Monks, Francis M.	104
Loving, Amanda	514	Monks, John W.	1185
Long, LeRoy	611	Morgan, Dick	152
Long, Charley C.	952	Morgan, Robert A.	1044
Long, Julia	1313	Mote, James R.	246
		Motes, John A.	1255

Name.	Roll No.	Name.	Roll No.
Moran, Willie Agnes	343	McLellan, Ada	1593
Moran, Emma	378	McLellan, Belle	1617
Moran, Fannie	1015	McLaughlin, Ezekiel C.	1052
Moran, Fannie	1588	McLaughlin, Lillie	1662
Monds, Mollie	398	McLain, Susan A.	1455
Moncrief, Annie	450	McMenamin, Laura Lee	62
Moncrief, Lina	882	McMenamin, Michael	208
Mowdy, James M.	512	McMurtry, Della	516
Mouser, Lizzie	808	McMurtry, Mollie T.	819
Mozley, Benjamin F.	1016	McMurtrey, John	1223
Moseley, Daisy	1606	McNeely, James C.	1041
Morse, James M.	1162	Napier, Thomas B.	95
Moss, Homer	1398	Nail, Beulah M.	139
Mugler, Francisco C.	144	Nail, Lou	531
Muldrow, Henry L., Jr.	220	Nail, Millie	568
Muncrief, Virginia	544	Nail, Pearl E.	618
Muncrief, Olivia	1064	Nail, Mary Ann	665
Munkees, Beverly C.	689	Nail, Paralee	706
Murphy, James C.	875	Nale, Mary Isabelle	583
Murphy, Annie	1422	Nale, Luann	879
Murphy, Edna	1525	Nelson, Bithel A.	72
Murphy, Pat	1580	Nelson, Della	742
Murray, Frank	968	Nelson, Ella	1244
Mullen, Joseph S.	1128	Nelson, Lula	1365
McAlvain, Louisa	100	Nelson, Mary Agnes	1426
McAlvain, Mollie Belle	780	Nessmith, David	272
McAlvain, Bell	1540	Neil, Samuel E.	465
McBrayer, John E.	254	Neal, John W.	1042
McBride, Thomas L.	637	Newsom, James	714
McBride, William P.	1218	Needham, Enoch	715
McBride, Emmette C.	1636	Nevins, Vivian Scott	854
McCurtain, Rosie	33	Neukirchner, Clara	1160
McCurtain, Clara E.	855	Newkirk, Sarah M.	1506
McClain, Rufus L.	44	Newman, Julia A.	1621
McClain, Laura B.	111	Nichols, Levi	224
McCoy, Alvah B.	141	Nichols, James H.	1177
McCoy, Sarah E.	1231	Nichols, Maggie B.	1452
McClure, John H.	244	Nicholson, Omer R.	1385
McClure, Poker J.	716	Ninas, William	370
McClure, Mary F.	903	Nix, Gus	722
McClure, Carrie L.	966	Norman, Isaac M.	150
McCarty, Frances	260	Norman, Emma	1447
McCarty, Lizzie Y.	727	Norton, Josiah R.	484
McCarter, Andrew L.	379	Noel, Ida	610
McCaull, James M.	473	Noel, Mary	852
McClendon, James W.	477	Noel, Chaney	1267
McCann, Alice	617	Nolen, Rhoda	902
McCann, Leonia	654	Norris, Sallie	1230
McClung, Willie	1059	Null, Elizabeth	873
McCaughey, Annie M.	1060	Oakes, Josephine E.	80
McCurry, Eliza	1198	Oakes, Margaret A.	82
McCollum, James R.	1324	Oakes, Annie	83
McClard, William C.	1534	Oakes, Lucy E.	238
McDaniel, William	59	Oakes, Cleora	638
McDaniel, Kate	271	Oakes, Rosa E.	993
McDaniel, Mollie	1068	Oakes, Elsie J.	1603
McDaniel, Ida	1126	Oakes, John T.	1666
McDaniel, Commie	1453	Obannon, Jack	562
McDaniel, Mollie	1655	Odell, W. B.	1417
McDaniels, Mary Jane	217	Oliver, Samuel R.	73
McEvers, Newton	1351	Oliver, James R.	698
McFarland, J. B.	69	Oliver, Leonard C.	805
McFerrin, Margaret	183	Olson, Benjamin	979
McFerran, Walter	650	Ollar, Sarah E.	1116
McFadden, Mary E.	1154	Oldham, Minnie	1479
McGilberry, Nora	302	Orr, William E.	430
McGilberry, Mamie	773	Ormsby, James C.	624
McGee, John E.	564	Overstreet, Thomas G.	265
McGee, Nannie	1273	Overstreet, Lillian P.	694
McGuire, Emery O.	1193	Overstreet, Alice E.	776
McGahey, Minnie	1392	Owens, Beacham B.	400
McGahey, Annie	1619	Owens, Katie	664
McIntosh, John G.	1498	Owens, Emma	1305
McKinney, Richard T.	192	O'Neil, Cassandra Frances	695
McKinney, Cleo	552		
McKinney, Leona	591	O'Riley, John	329
McKinney, Bertha W.	1307	Parnell, Roxie	19
McKee, John D.	641	Page, Montie S.	27
McKasson, Thadeus S.	844	Page, Jane	30
McKenzie, Sam	876	Page, Lulu	721
McLellan, Kittie	800	Paddock, Venia	145
McLellan, Mary A. E.	801	Paddock, Mollie	345
McLellan, Sarah	802	Paddock, Reuben	1475
McLellan, Susan E.	803	Parker, Louise E.	639

Name.	Roll No.	Name.	Roll No.
Patterson, Louise E.	639	Reynolds, E. D.	97
Patterson, Martha J.	732	Reynolds, James E.	565
Patterson, Sophronia	1429	Reynolds, Hiram C.	682
Parsons, John M.	897	Reynolds, Dora	1545
Park, Robert Lee	941	Reagan, Robert L.	787
Parke, Nannie H.	1251	Reel, William E.	1031
Paul, William Albert	1148	Rector, James H.	1163
Payton, Amanda Eliza-		Rector, Eliza Ellen	1204
beth	1415	Reed, Major Franklin	1327
Payton, Nancy C.	1439	Reed, James H.	1347
Perkins, Finis L.	186	Rhea, James	937
Perkins, Lena E.	344	Riddle, Elvarine A.	160
Perkins, Ormae H.	1358	Riddle, Florence	288
Perkins, Elizabeth	1501	Riddle, Ella	355
Pebsworth, Willie A.	360	Riddle, Henrietta	807
Pebworth, Octavia	1355	Riddle, Fannie	1110
Perry, Adolphus E.	387	Ritchey, W. H.	169
Perry, Nancy	718	Riggon, S. C.	210
Perry, Dixie	981	Risener, Atwood C.	333
Perry, Mildred A.	999	Risener, William	1629
Perry, Nancy	718	Richards, William W.	376
Peters, Delia	831	Richards, Edwin T.	843
Peter, Minnie	1602	Ridgeway, George W.	399
Pearson, Amelia E.	576	Richerson, John S.	556
Pearce, Thornton D.	975	Richardson, S. O.	862
Pettijohn, Nannie	1157	Riley, Dora	1669
Perse, George R.	1382	Rogers, Benjamin F.	91
Penny, Oren S.	1481	Rogers, Kitie D.	94
Phillips, Charley	176	Rogers, Lizzie	1237
Phillips, Tobe	226	Rogers, Lavega	1510
Phillips, George	1585	Rogers, Emma	1620
Phebus, Margaret	1268	Ross, Lizzie	119
Pickens, Jane	35	Ross, Emma J.	1122
Pigott, Edward	441	Robinson, Allie May	351
Piepgrass, John H.	683	Robinson, Sarah	532
Pitchlynn, Grace M.	691	Robinson, John W.	660
Pierce, Mandie May	850	Robinson, Mary E.	885
Pitts, Alice	1189	Robinson, Sam P.	1067
Pitman, Nora	1660	Robinson, Rosa	1155
Plummer, Sallie L.	377	Robinson, J. W.	1461
Plummer, Laura .B.	381	Robertson, David	729
Plummer, Mary S.	383	Robertson, Albert M.	853
Plummer, Ella Pearl	673	Roberson, James W.	680
Plummer, Minnie	1448	Robb, David N.	373
Plank, Jasper E.	633	Roark, William	411
Plato, Frank W.	883	Rose, Christopher C.	413
Plato, Alton Aladin	1020	Rose, Nancy J.	1296
Powell, Lizzie M.	48	Roach, Robert W.	433
Powell, Mary Etta	1665	Roebuck, Nancy A.	707
Porch, Robert	117	Roebuck, Minnie	811
Pool, Ike K.	182	Rowley, H. B.	793
Poland, Emma L.	213	Rockett, Louis	794
Poland, Emer M. G.	1378	Roberts, John W.	992
Potts, Ada	717	Roberts, Joseph J.	1460
Polloch, Andrew D.	967	Roff, Joe	1057
Polloch, Eliza J.	980	Roff, Pearl	1517
Powers, William J.	1256	Roff, Dottie	1594
Pritchard, William E.	177	Rosenthal, Birdie	1581
Price, William E.	306	Runton, Tabitha	40
Presley, Hattie	1005	Russell, Campbell	124
Prola, John	1199	Russell, William	895
Pusley, Nannie B.	314	Russell, Perry	989
Pusley, Lelan	849	Russell, Dora	1111
Puckett, Liddy	1007	Russell, Calistia	1579
Puckett, Mary E.	1331	Russell, George	1597
Purtle, Thomas	1290	Rushing, Annie	390
Quinn, John	47	Rushing, Joe	1143
Quincy, Allie	102	Sanguin, Alice J.	70
Quincy, Daisy	455	Sanguin, Zula C.	991
Quinton, Katie	1317	Savage, John B.	132
Quinton, Sallie	1516	Sample, Charles ·A.	153
Raulston, Robert M.	14	Samples, James L.	685
Rabon, Rufus	130	Sanders, Ada	336
Rabon, James W.	289	Sanders, John A.	1211
Rabon, William T.	649	Sacra, R. C.	502
Ratliff, Lee W.	237	Sadler, John F.	684
Ralls, Joseph G.	419	Sage, James W.	995
Rainey, David F.	431	Sage, Carrie	1527
Rainey, Jackline	1520	Salter, Henry J.	1098
Ramseyer, Gotleib	1048	Sanner, Lou	1574
Rayel, Robert W.	1049	Scott, John C.	408
Randolph, Wirt	1200	Scott, James	439
Randolph, Ed	1362	Scott, Chopling	1151
	469	Scantlen, James M.	517

Name.	Roll No.	Name.	Roll No.
Sexton, Fannie M.	29	Stidham, Laura	1278
Sexton, Lou	108	Staton, Phoebe C.	1147
Sexton, Maggie	405	Strickland, Phoebe	1253
Sexton, Jessie L.	768	Stealey, Charles L.	1262
Self, John L.	38	Sterling, Mary E.	1301
Self, Thomas	75	Sterrett, Frank M., Jr.	1319
Self, William D.	239	Stephens, Charlotte	1367
Self, John H.	410	Sumter, Robert O.	391
Self, Joseph M.	838	Suddath, Thomas M.	487
See, Charles W.	168	Suttle, Merriman W.	1062
Semple, Charles A.	153	Sutton, Rachel A.	1332
Semple, Helen Mae	595	Swink, David R.	92
Secor, Lucy	317	Swink, William	1456
Seldner, Paul	328	Swinney, Louis A.	494
Selsor, John	395	Taylor, Green	52
Seago, Charles W.	533	Taylor, Martha J.	110
Seeley, George W.	779	Taylor, Allie V.	282
Seybold, Lola	1503	Taylor, Joe N.	495
Sheegog, Charley	174	Taylor, Newcomb B.	1074
Shirey, Edmond M.	567	Taylor, Epps	1082
Shannon, Ober L.	750	Taylor, Robert H.	1086
Shropshire, Joseph J.	823	Taylor, Amanda H.	1397
Shaw, Ola M.	1212	Taylor, Lula	1521
Sittel, Fritz	525	Taylor, Cora	1599
Simmons, Mamie	739	Tanehill, Joseph D.	449
Simmons, Nathaniel H.	948	Taliaferro, James R.	866
Simmons, Ellen	1592	Taliaferro, William N.	962
Simpson, Edward	781	Taliaferro, John D.	1235
Sisney, Emmer	1584	Telle, Emma	432
Skaggs, John	795	Tennant, Lewis C.	451
Slaton, James A.	881	Terry, Noah M.	751
Smith, James A.	20	Terry, Jefferson J.	892
Smith, Nathaniel W.	161	Terrell, Elmer	1658
Smith, William T.	162	Thornton, Joseph E.	175
Smith, Mary E.	263	Thompson, Leona	287
Smith, Joseph P.	492	Thompson, Clemmie	606
Smith, Elizabeth J.	580	Thompson, Benjamin F.	798
Smith, Bird Q.	614	Thompson, Mary Jane	1184
Smith, Anna E.	777	Thompson, Clara May	1279
Smith, Essie	933	Thompson, Mary Ann	1365
Smith, Myrtle	1135	Thompson, Mary	1370
Smith, Charles	1140	Thurlow, Herman C.	690
Smith, Albert	1544	Thomas, Minnie	712
Smiser, Butler S.	393	Thomas, Andrew Jackson	877
Snider, Samuel T.	297	Thomas, John F.	940
Sorrells, George W.	313	Thomas, Marcus D. L.	1105
Southerland, Clara L.	1302	Tiner, Nancy C.	318
Spain, Elizabeth	3	Tiner, Dora	442
Spain, Emma E.	7	Tims, Willie J.	635
Spain, Allie	323	Tindell, Andrew J.	671
Spain, Louisa	371	Tomlinson, Benjamin F.	415
Spain, Hattie E.	493	Toole, Etta E.	584
Spain, Lula M.	555	Toole, Nettie M.	585
Spain, Maggie	1192	Towry, James W.	764
Spain, Cora M.	1276	Traylor, John E.	77
Spain, Martha Elizabeth	1380	Trahern, Virginia P.	122
Spain, Minnie Lee	1387	Trahern, Lula E.	788
Spring, Hattie	76	Travis, Robert A.	340
Spring, Maud M.	640	Trueblood, A. H.	545
Sperling, Henry H.	211	Trout, S. G.	786
Speegle, David L. H.	710	Traut, Henry	931
Spears, David Freeman	1045	Truitt, William M.	1173
Spann, Katie A.	1316	Treep, Josephene	1391
Standley, Lizzie C.	114	Tucker, Edward T.	31
Standley, Bertha M.	392	Tucker, Joseph S.	41
Standley, Etna	1342	Tucker, Ella May	927
Stanley, William M.	627	Tucker, Nancy	1228
Stanley, Ella	1612	Tucker, Janie	1280
Starritt, George A.	170	Turner, James M.	471
Stalcup, Thomas	205	Turner, Lena	579
Sturdivant, Chame	206	Turner, George A.	1175
Stallings, Jared A.	303	Turner, Sarah E.	1180
Strong, John B.	463	Turner, Artie M.	1266
Stanford, Henry C.	597	Turner, Hattie	1590
Stigler, Joseph S.	604	Turner, Katie	1671
Stanton, Inez J.	678	Turnbull, Harriet E.	634
Stewart, Bettie	790	Turnbull, Ettie	1432
Stewart, James W.	1254	Tutt, Richard T.	674
Stewart, John	1443	Tubby, Cora	822
Stewart, Sarah I.	1539	Underwood, May	834
Steward, Samuel P.	887	Underwood, John W.	1300
Starks, Josephine	830	Usray, James	1292
Stidham, Nannie	872	Van Zant, Hannibal G.	135

Name.	Roll No.
Vance, Rus	280
Vail, James W.	427
Vail, John F.	1345
Vawter, James W.	741
Veach, Horatio	138
Victor, Trudy May	273
Victor, Mary J.	1323
Wade, Martha F.	18
Wade, Eliza J.	28
Wade, Margaret	1270
Ward, Lula M.	42
Ward, Mary D.	394
Ward, Lucy D.	396
Ward, Letty	404
Ward, Eliza	485
Ward, Minnie	537
Ward, Helen I.	643
Ward, Mary	839
Ward, Ida L.	910
Ward, Sallie P.	1010
Ward, Lockey	1131
Ward, Rachel C.	1336
Wallen, Sarah	45
Walters, Charles W.	87
Walker, Mattie	126
Walker, Sallie	577
Walker, Martha	1206
Walker, Sambray	1207
Walker, Sam	1303
Walker, Robert L.	1315
Walker, Naomi	1467
Walker, Mary	1627
Wadley, George L.	251
Watkins, Ophelia	261
Wall, Octavia	277
Wall, Chris	529
Walls, Catherine	437
Walls, Nellie Alice	677
Walls, Pink	1133
Wallace, Robert	304
Wallace, John	380
Walden, James C.	327
Watson, Amasa	475
Walcott, Arthur	870
Waide, Whit M.	1488
Weich, Lula M.	109
Welch, Leamon	1368
Westbrook, Andrew J.	454
Webster, Nannie W.	561
West, Thomas J.	1055
West, Liddy	1377
Whiteman, W. J.	64
White, John R.	506
White, Dora	299
White, James Edward	945
Whittenburg, Lorenzo H.	357
Wheeler, Walter R.	397
Wheeler, Robert J.	753
Wheeler, James S.	1165
Wheeler, Lucretia N.	1166

Name.	Roll No.
Whittle, LilHan Delorries	1169
Whiteside, Levicia	1201
Whitlock, William P.	1631
Williams, Isaac W.	63
Williams, Jasper	655
Williams, Thomas H.	847
Williams, Sarah E.	913
Williams, William Franklin	939
Williams, Mary	977
Williams, John R.	1107
Williams, Abbie	1242
Williams, Rocey Lee	1274
Williams, William F.	1343
Williams, Clemmie	1349
Williams, Etta	1436
Williams, Annie	1437
Wilson, Ollie M.	225
Wilson, Maggie	702
Wilson, Alice	1247
Wilson, Samuel R.	1248
Wilson, Matilda	1287
Wilson, William W.	1369
Wilson, Mary	1445
Wilmoth, William M.	358
Wilmoth, John W.	629
Witt, Marion	528
Willis, Samie	560
Willis, Gracie	1205
Willis, Francis M.	1497
Wiltsey, John M.	896
Wood, John W.	179
Wood, Thomas L.	468
Woods, Robert A.	607
Woods, Lyons	1312
Woolery, John	513
Woolery, Dona	950
Wolf, Matt	584
Wooley, William L.	1121
Worley, Jesse A.	1172
Woosley, Mattie	1179
Workman, Dora	1563
Wright, Belle	8
Wright, Mary F.	15
Wright, Helen S. Kiles	196
Wright, Ida B.	375
Wright, Addie L.	658
Wright, James E.	871
Wright, Ida	1146
Wren, Etha	1170
Wyars, John W.	121
Wyatt, Vancie	1202
Yarborough, John C.	190
Yarbrough, James	191
Yandell, John M.	338
York, Wallace	582
Young, Madison C.	586
Young, Catherine	997
Young, Mary A.	1190
Young, Elizabeth A.	1526
Zanola, John	414

INDEX TO
CHOCTAW FREEDMEN

Name.	Roll No.	Name.	Roll No.
Banks, Minnie	1122	Beaver, Thomas	1025
Banks, James S.	2596	Beavers, Charlotte	3413
Banks, R. Calhoun	2597	Beavers, Mary	3414
Banks, Lucy	2598	Beavers, Johnnie	3415
Banks, Luvinia	2599	Beavers, Anna	3416
Banks, Frances	4678	Beavers, Robert	3417
Bailey, Ida	622	Bearden, Virginia	1272
Bailey, Mary Maggie	623	Beltón, Jesse	1294
Bailey, Mary	677	Benson, Frances	1116
Bailey, Needdom M.	678	Benson, Thomas	1117
Bailey, Aron Emitt	679	Benson, Columbus	1118
Bailey, Ivery James	680	Benson, Pearly Beat-	
Bailey, William Presker	681	trice	1119
Bailey, Leona	670	Benson, Susan	3079
Bailey, Leanders	675	Benson, Victoria	3080
Bailey, Stella	1273	Benson, Jodie	3726
Bailey, Dan	2854	Beckwith, Frances	1844
Bailey, Sallie	3689	Belvin, Neata	1951
Bailey, Mattie	3690	Belvin, Barbara	1952
Bailey, Ethard	3691	Beeson, Cora	3754
Bailey, Richard	3692	Beeson, America	3755
Baker, Taylor	894	Belcher, Mary	5391
Baker, Bonnie	895	Bibbs, Martha	578
Baker, Fredonia	896	Bibbs, Pearley	579
Bagley, Nellie	2590	Bibbs, Sam	580
Battiest, Lila	1939	Bibbs, Sarah	581
Battiest, Henry	5368	Bibbs, Fanny	582
Battiest, Mary	5369	Bibbs, Emily	583
Battiest, Davis	5370	Bibbs, Levi V.	869
Battiest, Mattie	5371	Bibbs, Charlie	954
Battiest, Juanita	5372	Bibbs, Nube	3070
Battiece, Joe	2968	Bibbs, Mary	3712
Bassett, Eddie	3187	Bird, Martha	888
Battie, Bettie	3578	Bird, Martin	889
Battie, Frank	3579	Bird, Gertrude	890
Battie, Robert	3580	Bird, Albert	2919
Battie, Charlie	3581	Birdsong, Martha	1094
Battie, Abbie	3582	Birdsong, Austin	1095
Battie, Albert	3588	Birdsong, Allie	2972
Battie, Martin	3589	Birdsong, Douglas	2973
Battie, Sam	3590	Birdsong, John	4490
Battie, Maudie	3591	Birdsong, Tyler	4491
Battie, Claudie	3592	Birdsong, Lucy Ann	4502
Battie, Cora Lee	3593	Birdsong, Violet	4504
Battie, Birdie	5358	Birdsong, Frank	4505
Barrows, Joseph	3906	Birdsong, Willie	4506
Barrows, Edward	3907	Birdsong, Arthur	4507
Barrows, William	3908	Birdsong, Ella	4538
Barrows, Daisy	4315	Binks, William	2667
Barrows, Annie	4316	Binks, Willie	5185
Barr, Katsy	4069	Binks, Robbie	5186
Barr, Emigh	4070	Bidden, Rachael	3384
Barr, Marshall	4071	Biggs, Joe Henry	5162
Barr, Nora	4072	Blair, Henry	113
Barr, Eliza	4113	Blair, Georgia	4640
Barber, Quennie	4427	Blackwater, Annie	1554
Barber, Hestella	4431	Blackwater, Cornelius	
Bartlett, Charley	4645	W.	2373
Barrett, Ellis B.	5197	Blackwater, Lucy Ann	2374
Battle, Dan	5342	Blackwater, Jessie	2375
Battle, Florida	5343	Blackwater, Thomas	5065
Battle, Mary	5344	Blue, Rachel	2388
Battle, Sarah	5345	Blue, Lem	2395
Battle, Jim	5346	Blue, Hardy	2400
Battle, Jodie	5347	Blue, Louis	2401
Battle, Eula	5348	Blue, Delia	2402
Barnhill, Bert	5050	Blue, Angeline	2545
Barnhill, Memory	5361	Blue, Lonnie	4233
Barnhill, John Ceissel	5362	Blue, Tony	4879
Bell, Alice	366	Blunt, Minerva	4391
Bell, Nick	1141	Blunt, Henry	4392
Berry, Lela	794	Blunt, Ella	4393
Berry, Nina	795	Blunt, Mattie	4394
Berry, Malinda	796	Blunt, Minnie	4395
Berry, Nanny	797	Blunt, Myrtie	4396
Berry, Aleck	5130	Blunt, Harvey	4397
Beams, Nellie	853	Blunt, Gurty	4398
Beams, Violet	854	Blunt, Carl	4399
Beams, Emma	855	Blunt, William	4829
Beams, Johnnie	956	Blunt, Joanna	5359
Beams, Simon	3682	Bledsoe, Sarah	4948
Beams, Ella	4290	Blaine, Guy	5124
Beams, Magnolia	4782	Blaine, Eddie	5125
Beaver, Arella	1024		

Name.	Roll No.
Blaine, Sam	5126
Blocker, Rena	5134
Blocker, Leoda	5135
Blocker, Eddie	5136
Blocker, Emsie	5149
Blocker, Andrew	5154
Bolding, Lucy	5056
Bolding, Louisa	5055
Bolding, Mattie	5054
Bolding, Josephine	5053
Bolding, John	1032
Bolding, Louie	1033
Boldin, Philies Ann	5440
Boatwright, Frances	1310
Boatwright, Oliver	1311
Boatwright, Tommy	1312
Boatwright, James	1313
Boatwright, Powhattan	1314
Boatwright, Clayton	1315
Boatwright, George Washington	5252
Bowers, Johnny	1545
Boyd, Horace	1890
Boyd, Isaac	1891
Boyd, Annie	1892
Boyd, Creasie	2156
Boyd, Robert	2157
Boyd, Jimmie	2158
Boyd, Christopher C.	2159
Boyd, Nancy	2259
Boyd, Walter	2260
Boyd, Tommie	2261
Boyd, Lonzo	2262
Boyd, Melinda	2263
Boyd, Lena	3463
Boyd, Mattie	3464
Boyd, James	3517
Boyd, Sam	3654
Boyd, McKinley	3655
Boyd, Isom	3822
Boyd, Silas	3823
Boyd, Emma	3824
Boyd, Nancy	3825
Boyd, Siny	3826
Boyd, Penny	3827
Boyd, Agnes	3828
Boyd, Lila	3829
Boyd, Peter	3830
Boyd, Emanuel	3831
Boyd, Moblie	3832
Boyd, Isham	3833
Boyd, Hattie	3835
Boyd, Seborn	3836
Boyd, Frances	3837
Boyd, Richard	3838
Boyd, Nancy	3839
Boyd, James	3840
Boyd, Emma	4296
Boyd, Daniel	5241
Boyd, Daniel	5304
Boyd, Carry	5305
Boyd, Leo	5387
Bonham. Joe Arthur	4282
Boyles, Ellen	5416
Boyles, Rachel	5417
Brown, Johnie Lee	92
Brown, Tony	201
Brown, Jennie	202
Brown, Rufus	203
Brown, Louis	206
Brown, Holman	214
Brown, Nellie	215
Brown, John	216
Brown, Pearly	217
Brown, Maria	241
Brown, Jim	242
Brown, Houston	243
Brown, Tom	245
Brown, Lebadee	246
Brown, Malissa	247
Brown, Frank	319
Brown, Eliza	320

Name.	Roll No.
Brown, Sweet Magnolia	321
Brown, Will	441
Brown, Otha	442
Brown, Onnie	443
Brown, Crochett	444
Brown, Arabella	445
Brown, Polly	446
Brown, Luther	447
Brown, Alvin	448
Brown, Conley	449
Brown, Clay	450
Brown, Lovely	451
Brown, Judy	452
Brown, Beula	453
Brown, Harris	525
Brown, Frances	526
Brown, Jeffie	527
Brown, Davis	528
Brown, Catharine	529
Brown, Rettie	552
Brown, Roy	558
Brown, Lee	597
Brown, Neptune	761
Brown, Jenny	762
Brown, Katie	763
Brown, Richard	764
Brown, Simon	830
Brown, Matt	951
Brown, Alice	952
Brown, Fannie	1138
Brown, Robin	1197
Brown, Olivia	1233
Brown, Hickman	1234
Brown, William	1235
Brown, Della	1236
Brown, George	1237
Brown, Ada	1437
Brown, Pearly	1438
Brown, Rachael	1492
Brown, Rufus	1493
Brown, Wm.	1494
Brown, Alonzo	1495
Brown, Louis	1496
Brown, Clondell	1497
Brown, Phoebe	1502
Brown, Eliza	1547
Brown, Sallie	1548
Brown, Johnny	1549
Brown, Smith, Jr.	1550
Brown, Rachael	1551
Brown, Mattie	1552
Brown, Malindy	1558
Brown, Chester	1570
Brown, Annie	1571
Brown, Clemmy	1572
Brown, Manuel	1573
Brown, Thomas T.	1574
Brown, Georgianna	1575
Brown, Nettie A.	1576
Brown, Julia F.	1612
Brown, Peter	1613
Brown, Mary	1665
Brown, Sallie Ann	1666
Brown, Jerry	1667
Brown, Smith	1668
Brown, Oscar	1669
Brown, Thomas	1670
Brown, Eva	1671
Brown, Etta	1672
Brown, Jennie	1703
Brown, Rhoda	1704
Brown, Anna	1705
Brown, Simon	1706
Brown, Eastman	1707
Brown, Lucy Ann	1708
Brown, Lewis	1709
Brown, Bertha	1710
Brown, Wilson	1711
Brown, Charlotte	1769
Brown, Rosetta	1872
Brown, Creasie	2012
Brown, Robert	2036
Brown, Thomas	2129

Name.	Roll No.	Name.	Roll No.
Brown, Ruffin	2130	Brown, Davis	4073
Brown, Charity	2131	Brown, Virginia	4102
Brown, Joe	2132	Brown, Isom	4103
Brown, Rachael	2179	Brown, Calvin	4104
Brown, Lou T.	2180	Brown, Cora	4105
Brown, Frankie	2181	Brown, Nora	4106
Brown, Colbert	2182	Brown, Caesar	4270
Brown, Addie M.	2183	Brown, Flora	4284
Brown, Cleo	2184	Brown, Elias	4310
Brown, Anna	2185	Brown, Calonia Easter	4311
Brown, Allie	2219	Brown, John	4312
Brown, Martin Roosevelt	2225	Brown, Edmund	4314
		Brown, Ada	4470
Brown, Tibbett	2342	Brown, Shub	4471
Brown, Richard	2379	Brown, Calvin	4472
Brown, Jonas	2380	Brown, Timothy	4473
Brown, Mahaley	1733	Brown, Arian	4621
Brown, Becky	2389	Brown, Nicholas	4632
Brown, Philip	2391	Brown, Sallie	4669
Brown, Mandy	2393	Brown, Gracie	4670
Brown, Thomas	2397	Brown, Ophelia	4671
Brown, Neptune Jr.	2887	Brown, Cora	4672
Brown, Nancy	2910	Brown, Reuben	4673
Brown, Ruthy	2943	Brown, Barbery	4674
Brown, Josephine	2997	Brown, Phoebe	4736
Brown, Eliza	2998	Brown, Carrie	4952
Brown, Susan	3009	Brown, Myrtle	4960
Brown, Tom	3048	Brown, Ben	5494
Brown, Wiley	3089	Brown, Calvin	5495
Brown, Mary	3090	Brown, Lonnie	4762
Brown, George	3091	Brown, Ples	5048
Brown, Willie	3093	Brown, Mattie	5144
Brown, Netha	3094	Brown, Jim	5166
Brown, Clinton	3095	Brown, Ben	5218
Brown, Arthur	3096	Brown, Henry	5255
Brown, Lulu	3092	Brown, Lillie	5256
Brown, Solomon	3108	Brown, Effie	5257
Brown, Moses	3109	Brown, Silas	5295
Brown, Susan	3110	Brown, Susie	5296
Brown, Mary Lilly	3111	Brown, Alfred	5297
Brown, Amandy	3154	Brown, Lulu May	5298
Brown, Willie	3155	Brown, Emmet	5299
Brown, Pinkie	3156	Brown, Mary	5300
Brown, Mattie	3157	Brown, Cornelia	5301
Brown, Wyatt	3181	Brown, Mat	5302
Brown, David	3249	Brown, Rebecca	5378
Brown, Sylvania	3250	Brown, Davit	5398
Brown, Martin	3252	Brashears, Bill	322
Brown, Verdia	3305	Brashears, Battiest	892
Brown, Mariah	3320	Brashears, Nancy	893
Brown, Robert	3323	Brashears, Polly	1915
Brown, Virgie	3383	Brashears, Richard	1916
Brown, Smith	3742	Brashears, Willie	1917
Brown, Moses	3745	Brashears, Charley	1918
Brown, Ida	3770	Brashears, Henrietta	1919
Brown, Charley	3848	Brashears, Henry C.	1920
Brown, Minny	3872	Brashears, Augustus	1921
Brown, Elisha	3873	Brashears, Flossie	1922
Brown, Benjamin	3874	Brashears, Eugene	1923
Brown, Melina	5431	Brashears, Bat	2577
Brown, Allen	5432	Brashears, Mary Prince	2928
Brown, Sophia	5433	Brashears, Ida	2929
Brown, Minnie	5434	Brashears, Amelia	3144
Brown, Therena	5435	Brashears, Richard	3821
Brown, Charles	5436	Brashears, Ed	4267
Brown, Arbella	5437	Brashears, Carrie.	4319
Brown, Elias S.	5438	Brashears, Charley	5239
Brown, Freedona Idetter	3875	Brashears, Albert	5250
		Brashears, Susie	5351
Brown, Collins	3876	Brackeen, Eva	608
Brown, Melvina	3877	Brackeen, Dora	609
Brown, Moline	3878	Bryant, Walter	1419
Brown, Becky	3879	Bradley, Katie	1591
Brown, Edmund	3880	Bradley, Mabel	1592
Brown, Watson	3910	Brady, Sophie	2085
Brown, John	3911	Brock, Livinia	3215
Brown, Aaron	3912	Briley, John	2346
Brown, George	3913	Bruner, George	2634
Brown, Aggie	3914	Brumley, Mollie	2641
Brown, Green	3915	Brumley, Audrie	2642
Brown, Cornelia	3929	Brewer, Eliza	2989
Brown, Josie	3948	Brewer, Alonzo	2990
Brown, Emma	3954	Brack, Gracie	3196

Name.	Roll No.	Name.	Roll No.
Brack, Margaret	3197	Butler, Frank	459
Brack, Willis	3198	Butler, Mary	460
Brack, Jesse	3199	Butler, Alfred	461
Bruce, William	3318	Butler, Josephine	462
Briggs, Lizzie	3752	Butler, Isaiah	463
Brunner, Rosy	3996	Butler, Marshall	566
Brasco, Matilda	4411	Butler, Rhoda	567
Brasco, Abagail	4412	Butler, Sallie	568
Brasco, Scott	4413	Butler, Isaac	569
Brasco, Livingston	5254	Butler, Aaron	570
Butler, Lemon	49	Butler, Izaer	571
Butler, Ruthie	50	Butler, Violet	595
Butler, Kizzie	60	Butler, Randall	626
Butler, Mason	88	Butler, Luvinia	627
Butler, Newton	89	Butler, Johnny	628
Butler, Betsey	144	Butler, Earle	629
Butler, William	168	Butler, Ollie	630
Butler, Mirah	169	Butler, Henry	5514
Butler, Holman	170	Butler, Francis	631
Butler, Billy	184	Butler, Anderson	658
Butler, Jane	185	Butler, Lilly	659
Butler, Charlie	186	Butler, Sammy	660
Butler, Millie	187	Butler, Morgan	661
Butler, Coleman	188	Butler, Emma	662
Butler, Luvinia	189	Butler, Zebadee	663
Butler, Pearly	190	Butler, Creasie	664
Butler, Ruverdia	191	Butler, McDownie	666
Butler, McCurtain	192	Butler, Lillie Berta	667
Butler, Sarah	220	Butler, William	700
Butler, Lena	221	Butler, Simmy	704
Butler, Liza	222	Butler, Fredonia	705
Butler, Adeline	224	Butler, Clemmie	706
Butler, Lon	225	Butler, James	707
Butler, Paul	226	Butler, John Henry	708
Butler, Betsy	227	Butler, Ella	727
Butler, Thomas E.	260	Butler, Lemon	728
Butler, Florence	261	Butler, Eli	729
Butler, Hannibal	267	Butler, Robert	754
Butler, Matilda	268	Butler, Anderson	756
Butler, Millie	269	Butler, Adolphus	772
Butler, Robert	270	Butler, Janie	773
Butler, Jordon	272	Butler, Adolphus, Jr.	776
Butler, Sam	273	Butler, Isaac	777
Butler, Adelot	274	Butler, Ida May	778
Butler, Anna	300	Butler, Ed	805
Butler, Virgie	303	Butler, Amelia	806
Butler, Israel	304	Butler, Julius	807
Butler, Etha	305	Butler, Oza	808
Butler, Solon	306	Butler, Alfus	809
Butler, Clara	307	Butler, Amand	810
Butler, Annie	323	Butler, Oliver	811
Butler, Isabel	324	Butler, Lizzie	812
Butler, Joe	325	Butler, Elmire	813
Butler, Wheeler	326	Butler, Emly	814
Butler, Luvinia	327	Butler, Henry	849
Butler, Lucy	328	Butler, Christina	850
Butler, Bertha	329	Butler, Lemon	870
Butler, Susan	337	Butler, Sallie	922
Butler, Grant	362	Butler, Ellis	925
Butler, Riley	367	Butler, Prince	974
Butler, Milly	368	Butler, Kitty	1017
Butler, Afun	369	Butler, Wesley	1018
Butler, Robert	370	Butler, Viola	1019
Butler, Callie	371	Butler, Benjamin	1100
Butler, Easter	379	Butler, Kitty	1101
Butler, Fannie	383	Butler, Pilot	1102
Butler, Mattie	384	Butler, Patsy	1103
Butler, Florence	385	Butler, Aaron	1104
Butler, Jacob	386	Butler, Levi	1105
Butler, Mollie	387	Butler, David	1106
Butler, Lee	388	Butler, Roseanna	1107
Butler, Emily	389	Butler, Nancy	1108
Butler, Ader	390	Butler, Joshua	1382
Butler, Albert	391	Butler, Milly F.	1487
Butler, Amanda	392	Butler, Becky	1488
Butler, Adeline	393	Butler, Nettie	1489
Butler, Vester	394	Butler, Lem	1802
Butler, Alvin	395	Butler, Roland H.	1906
Butler, McCoy	396	Butler, Noah	1907
Butler, Elizha	397	Butler, Ida	1908
Butler, General	440	Butler, Emmet	1909
Butler, Winnie	457	Butler, Lucilla	1933
Butler, Lizzie	458	Butler, Pearl	1934

Name.	Roll No.	Name.	Roll No.
Butler, Oscar	1935	Burris, Sylvania	234
Butler, Andrew	1982	Burris, Adeline	235
Butler, Emmie	1983	Burris, Bertha	236
Butler, Ed	2195	Burris, Lenard Nathan-	
Butler, Wm. H.	2266	iel	237
Butler, Orange	2385	Burris, Edward	351
Butler, Dove	2425	Burris, Thomas	377
Butler, Charley	2426	Burris, Lucy A.	378
Butler, Joshua	2692	Burris, Sam	401
Butler, Henrietta	2693	Burris, Frances	402
Butler, George	2694	Burris, Miles	403
Butler, Tennessee	2774	Burris, Ben	405
Butler, Conda Lee	2775	Burris, Jodie	406
Butler, Percy	2776	Burris, Silas	407
Butler, Redelar May	2777	Burris, Ellen	409
Butler, Mason	2787	Burris, Calvin	468
Butler, Lula	2807	Burris, Martha	469
Butler, Vina	2808	Burris, Nathan	483
Butler, Elizabeth	2876	Burris, Emma	484
Butler, Martha	2880	Burris, Samuel	485
Butler, Sarah	2882	Burris, Alexander	486
Butler, David	2892	Burris, Jimmie	500
Butler, Lettie	2897	Burris, Henry	501
Butler, William	2904	Burris, Solomon	502
Butler, Anderson	2905	Burris, James	503
Butler, George	2906	Burris, Lucy	504
Butler, Mack	2907	Burris, Calvin	505
Butler, Lela	2949	Burris, Dave	668
Butler, Amy	2950	Burris, Hattie	669
Butler, Indiana	2983	Burris, Leona	670
Butler, Jay Gould	3306	Burris, Arey	671
Butler, Charlotte	3476	Burris, Gertrude	672
Butler, Roland M.	3487	Burris, Jordan	673
Butler, Willie May	3488	Burris, Mitchell	674
Butler, Wheeler	3506	Burris, Betsie	676
Butler, Emeline	3507	Burris, Jerry	682
Butler, Thompson	3508	Burris, Nancy	683
Butler, Jacob	3509	Burris, Jesse	684
Butler, Henrietta	3510	Burris, Robert	685
Butler, Sarah	3511	Burris, George	686
Butler, Edna	3512	Burris, Abraham	687
Butler, Salome	3513	Burris, Rachel	688
Butler, Jacob, Jr.	3514	Burris, Coleman	689
Butler, Jasper	3516	Burris, Estroy	690
Butler, Laura	3617	Burris, Ruth Ann	743
Butler, Alfred	3618	Burris, Morgan	744
Butler, Ida	3619	Burris, Jefferson	745
Butler, Willie	3620	Burris, Cora	746
Butler, Douglas	3628	Burris, Anderson	747
Butler, Alice	3629	Burris, Dennis	748
Butler, Melissa	3707	Burris, Lewis	936
Butler, Winnie	3708	Burris, Lilly Parker	1536
Butler, Virginia	4100	Burris, Pearl	1537
Butler, John Ross	4101	Burris, Christopher	1538
Butler, Caroline	4326	Burris, Fredreka	1540
Butler, Mabel	4349	Burris, Valentine	2016
Butler, Mary	4367	Burris, Georgia	1539
Butler, George	4370	Burris, Sarah	2782
Butler, Lemon	4371	Burris, Willie	2801
Butler, Molsie	4801	Burris, Albert	2803
Butler, Bessie	4802	Burris, Jacob	2804
Butler, Reggie	4803	Burris, Sanders	2805
Butler, Vivial	4804	Burris, Pricilla	2806
Butler, Wadie	4805	Burris, Simon	2829
Butler, Effie	4972	Burris, Simon	2841
Butler, Charlie	5441	Burris, Lewis	2855
Butler, Ophelia	5175	Burris, John	2859
Butler, Edith	5310	Burris, Delia	2860
Butler, James	5411	Burris, Nathan	2861
Butler, Blandina	5412	Burris, Will	2862
Butler, Harrison	5413	Burris, Thomas	2863
Butler, Maxey	5471	Burris, Mack	2864
Butler, Willie	5474	Burris, Duke	2865
Burris, Arah	59	Burris, Rufus	2866
Burris, Ned	97	Burris, Eddy	2881
Burris, Davis	98	Burris, Annie	3319
Burris, Lee	99	Burris, Jether	3715
Burris, Charley	120	Burris, Irma	4234
Burris, Annie	121	Burris, Salomon	4241
Burris, Enex	122	Burris, Mose	4280
Burris, Hickman	123	Burris, Turner	4870
Burris, Matilda	124	Burris, Martha	4992
Burris, George	174	Burris, Louis	5245

Name.	Roll No.	Name.	Roll No.
Burris, Annie	5490	Cass, Lucy	3868
Burton, Mary Jane	523	Cass, Pearl	3869
Burton, Bettie Allean	524	Cass, Alfred	3870
Burton, Mack	3214	Cass, Walter	3871
Burton, Houston	4026	Cass, Simpson	4309
Burton, Victoria	4027	Carney, Levi	1713
Burton, Sam	4028	Carney, Eliza	1714
Burton, Haywood	4029	Carney, Milly	1740
Burton, Joseph	4030	Carney, Lilly	3378
Burton, Henry	4031	Carney, Joe	3379
Burton, Alonzo	4032	Carney, Eddie	3668
Burton, Hodges	4818	Carney, Aaron	3669
Burton, Gilbert	5293	Carney, Lula	3679
Buckner, Nathan	1027	Carney, Leola	3680
Buckner, Henry	1053	Carney, Nora Belle	4650
Buckner, Margaret	4214	Carson, Emily	1820
Puckner, Cal	4216	Carson, Missouri	1821
Buckner, S. A.	5253	Carson, Henry	1822
Buffington, Willie	1238	Carson, Charlie	1823
Buffington, Jennie	1239	Carson, Jerry	1824
Buffington, Noah	3122	Carson, Frankie	2103
Busby, Raymond	2237	Carson, Polly	2277
Busby, Janie	5016	Carson, Emanuel	2278
Burley, Rosa	3678	Carson, Arthur	2279
Burks, Easter	4571	Carson, Mary	2280
Burks, Louisa	4572	Carson, Eddie	2281
Buckman, Onelia	4619	Carson, Kittie	2290
Buckman, Bertha	5041	Carson, Lasena	2557
Buckman, Joe	5042	Carson, Fleet wood	2558
Buckman, Manuel	5043	Carson, Bessie	2559
Bulger, Emma	5456	Carson, Allie	2560
Bulger, Sissy	5458	Carson, Levvie	3436
Bulger, Geneva	5459	Carson, Thos.	4294
Byrd, Lucy	1256	Carson, Oliver	4295
Byrd, Ida	1265	Carter, Alex	2247
Byrd, Jiles G.	1266	Carter, Silvia	2601
Byrd, Eugene	1267	Carter, Annie	2602
Byrd, Jessie	1491	Carter, Allen	4175
Byrd, Jimmie Vaughan	3271	Carter, Middleton	4177
Byrd, Emma	3986	Carter, Nancy	4178
Byrdsorg, Nicey	5063	Carter, Colonel	4180
Carr, Eva	77	Carter, Jacob	4181
Carr, Dewey McKinley	78	Carter, Amos	4182
Carr, Alberta	79	Carter, Julia	4618
Carr, Maria	2080	Carter, Matilda	4704
Carr, Willie	2081	Carter, Shed A.	4707
Carr, Viney	2082	Carter, Georgia	4708
Campbell, Andrew	1006	Carter, Vinie	4709
Campbell, Rebecca	1526	Carter, Elsie	4710
Campbell, Jessie	1534	Carter, Mahala	4886
Campbell, Mady Estell	1535	Caruthers, Lorena	3317
Campbell, Willie	1544	Cary, Nathan	3622
Campbell, Solomon	1712	Cahill, Lacey	3905
Campbell, Lillie	1718	Cahill, Lue Ella	3909
Campbell, R. Lee	2208	Cahill, Fannie	4866
Campbell, Mary Gennelia	2209	Cahill, Isaac	4867
Campbell, Richmond	2362	Cain, Anarky	4620
Campbell, Eli	2427	Carroll, Howard	4941
Campbell, Texanna	2428	Carroll, Fred	4942
Campbell, Walter	2429	Carroll, Clarence	4943
Campbell, J. D.	2430	Carroll, Ida	5496
Campbell, Bessie	2431	Carroll, Nettie	4944
Campbell, Jess	2432	Carroll, Hazel	4945
Campbell, Edward	2433	Ceaphus, Tincy	3519
Campbell, Willie	2940	Child, Austin	835
Campbell, Jack	3857	Chester, Hester	872
Campbell, Lillie	3858	Chester, Johnson,	873
Campbell, Henry	3859	Chester, Josephine	874
Campbell, Emma	3860	Chester, Benjamin	875
Campbell, Bertha	3861	Chester, Jeff	876
Campbell, Ophelia	3862	Chester, Melvina	877
Campbell, Frances	3863	Cheatham, Sarah	907
Campbell, Jesse	4649	Cheatham, Lem	908
Campbell, McKinley	4715	Cheatham, George	909
Campbell, Erdie	4716	Cheatham, Frank	910
Campbell, Peter	5229	Choat, Henry	1542
Campbell, Jeff	5230	Choat, Edna	1716
Campbell, Joe	5231	Choat, George	2199
Campbell, Ervin	5232	Choat, Amos	2284
Campbell, Florence	5233	Choat, Mandy	2285
Campbell, Pearlie	5234	Choat, William	2286
Campbell, Darthuley	5235	Choat, Levi	2287
Campbell, David	5236	Choat, Allen	2288
Cass, Peter	1699	Choat, Willie	2289
Cass, Silvia	3867	Choat, Dennis	2305
		Choat, Manuel	3664
		Choat, Charley	3665

Name.	Roll No.	Name.	Roll No.
Choat, Mariah	4153	Clark, Farris	3228
Chambers, Alice	1746	Clark, William	3229
Chambers, Vera	5425	Clark, Garret A. H.	3230
Chapman, Charley	1754	Clark, Elliard	3322
Chapman, Nancy	1755	Clark, Jennie	3702
Chapman, Benj.	1756	Clark, Ida	3721
Chapman, Parker	1757	Clark, Idella	5477
Chapman, Jeff	1758	Clark, Bessie	5481
Chatman, Celia	1766	Clark, Suky	5281
Chatman, Della	1961	Clark, Ada	5282
Chatman, Willie	2398	Clark, Pearlie	5283
Chatman, Belle	3020	Clark, Sallie	5284
Chatman, Ruffin	3392	Clark, Lela	5285
Chalk, Ben	1812	Clark, Frank	5286
Chalk, James G.	1813	Clark, Jinnie	5287
Chalk, Arrilla	1814	Clark, Minerva	5414
Chalk, Arthur	2291	Clark, Annie	4933
Chalk, Clyde	2292	Clayton, Piner	1654
Chalk, Willie	2295	Clayton, Willie	1655
Chalk, Lula	2296	Clayton, James	1656
Chalk, Chris	3407	Clayton, Diamond	1657
Chalk, Jesse	3408	Clayton, Anna	1658
Chalk, Rebecca	3409	Clayton, Josephine	2105
Chalk, Earlie	3410	Clayton, Etheline	2106
Chalk, Henry	3661	Clayton, Mittie	2145
Chalk, Harvey	3762	Clayton, Theodore L.	2146
Chalk, Emma	3763	Clayton, Argutha	3355
Chalk, Artelia Carson	3772	Cleveland, Andrew	4434
Chalk, Isaac	5183	Colbert, Andrew	6
Chalk, Tom	5444	Colbert, Hettie	7
Chalk, Emry	5446	Colbert, Josiah	8
Christian, Martha	2613	Colbert, Lewis	10
Christian, Henrietta	2614	Colbert, Eliza	11
Christian, Elizabeth	2615	Colbert, Emanuel	12
Christian, Arthur	2616	Colbert, Robert	22
Christian, John	2617	Colbert, Link	24
Cheadle, Susie	2727	Colbert, Hamp	25
Cheadle, Nicholas	2730	Colbert, Rosa	26
Cheadle, Mary	2731	Colbert, Henry	33
Cheadle, Douglas	2732	Colbert, Georgia	34
Cheadle, Dola	2733	Colbert, Freeman	35
Cheadle, Chloe	3360	Colbert, Rose Anna	36
Chilton, Susan	3377	Colbert, Sukie	404
Chandler, Myra	4509	Colbert, Etta	408
Chandler, Clayton	4510	Colbert, Mary	831
Chandler, Dovie	4511	Colbert, Jim	846
Chandler, Early	4512	Colbert, Mary	847
Chandler, Dock	4513	Colbert, Jeppie	848
Chandler, Warran	4514	Colbert, Angeline	1190
Chism, Jim	4723	Colbert, Howell	1264
Chism, Josephine	4724	Colbert, William	1274
Cherry, James	4904	Colbert, Henrietta	1275
Cherry, Nelson	4905	Colbert, Frances	1276
Cherry, Viocrus	4906	Colbert, Amy	1277
Cherry, Scott	4909	Colbert, William Jr.	1278
Clay, Mary	51	Colbert, Charley	1279
Clay, Vinnie	2618	Colbert, Della	1280
Clay, Rena	2619	Colbert, Annie	1281
Clark, Edmond	535	Colbert, Israel	1302
Clark, Susan	716	Colbert, Susan	1303
Clark, Wilson	717	Colbert, Nicholas	1307
Clark, Isaac	718	Colbert, Eddie	1308
Clark, Garfield	719	Colbert, Hamp	1309
Clark, John	720	Colbert, Nathan	1407
Clark, Paralee	721	Colbert, Florence	5488
Clark, Gilford	722	Colbert, Lanie	5489
Clark, Mary Jane	723	Colbert, Thomas	1634
Clark, Frank	724	Colbert, Creasy	1635
Clark, Ben	1354	Colbert, Elizabeth	1636
Clark, Mary	2410	Colbert, Douglas	1637
Clark, Fred D.	2411	Colbert, Frances	1638
Clark, Agnes	2412	Colbert, Frankie	1639
Clark, Lettie D.	2413	Colbert, Emma	1640
Clark, Cyntha	2414	Colbert, Annie	1641
Clark, Margaret	2984	Colbert, Nellie	1760
Clark, Liffey	2985	Colbert, Madison	1761
Clark, Aaron	2986	Colbert, Leoda	1762
Clark, Simon	2987	Colbert, Rufus	1926
Clark, Morris	3021	Colbert, Clorie F.	1927
Clark, Raindeer	3200	Colbert, Rozie Emma	1928
Clark, Robert	3201	Colbert, Charlie	2014
Clark, Allie B.	3202	Colbert, Lewis	2107
Clark, Florence	3207	Colbert, William G.	2108
Clark, Emily	3225	Colbert, Serena	2109
Clark, Oliver	3226	Colbert, George P.	2110
Clark, Deva	3227	Colbert, Joseph R.	2111

CHOCTAW FREEDMEN

125

Name.	Roll No.	Name.	Roll No.
Colbert, Shelby	2193	Colbert, Nellie	5319
Colbert, Primer	2194	Colbert, Leo	5320
Colbert, Nicodemus	2196	Colbert, Jim	5321
Colbert, Ozi	2197	Colbert, William Mc-	
Colbert, Edwin N.	2198	Kinley	5360
Colbert, Edmund	2217	Cotton, Lillie	112
Colbert, Douglas	2447	Cotton, Andy	651
Colbert, Winchester	2496	Cotton, Essie	652
Colbert, Willie	2499	Cotton, Minnie	653
Colbert, Hardy	2574	Cotton, Caroline	654
Colbert, Ether	2575	Cotton, Lola	655
Colbert, Elizabeth	2576	Cotton, Lilia	656
Colbert, Henry	2664	Cotton, Andy, Jr.	657
Colbert, Mary Ann	3012	Cotton, Willie	1555
Colbert, Manuel	3015	Cotton, Simon	1556
Colbert, Henry Lee	3124	Cotton, Thaddeus	2868
Colbert, Jimmie	3125	Coleman, Ary	125
Colbert, Jane	3126	Coleman, Augustus	147
Colbert, Angeline	3127	Coleman, Settie	148
Colbert, Fannie	3128	Coleman, Starkwell	1115
Colbert, Walter	3129	Coleman, Cloria	1427
Colbert, Gracie	3130	Coleman, Nelson	5121
Colbert, Emma	3131	Cole, Ed	131
Colbert, Albert	3132	Cole, Albert	193
Colbert, Gertrude	3468	Cole, Vina	194
Colbert, Verdie	3469	Cole, Virgie	195
Colbert, Rastus	3470	Cole, Hodges	196
Colbert, Creasie	3485	Cole, Ellen	208
Colbert, Nookie	3568	Cole, Wm. Logan	209
Colbert, Tommie	3569	Cole, Isaac	249
Colbert, Rhoda	3572	Cole, Ruthy	250
Colbert, Hull	3621	Cole, Lillian	301
Colbert, Johnnie	3623	Cole, Ed	624
Colbert, Oliver	3760	Cole, Aline	625
Colbert, Juanita	3761	Cole, William	691
Colbert, Laura	3778	Cole, Lovie	692
Colbert, Andrew	3779	Cole, Webster	693
Colbert, Beulah	3780	Cole, Elizabeth	694
Colbert, Brady	3781	Cole, Lucy	695
Colbert, Sarah	3782	Cole, Lemon	697
Colbert, Oliver	3896	Cole, Thomas	713
Colbert, Robert	3897	Cole, Hattie	714
Colbert, Monroe	4116	Cole, Minnie	715
Colbert, Prentice	4117	Cole, Willie	789
Colbert, Pun	4155	Cole, Hettie	790
Colbert, Cora	4249	Cole, Lottie	851
Colbert, Mile	4355	Cole, Elizabeth	859
Colbert, Lin	4360	Cole, Emma	862
Colbert, Elizah	4363	Cole, Dora	1058
Colbert, Odie	4364	Cole, Sweetann	1064
Colbert, Fannie	4415	Cole, Matthew	2784
Colbert, Frances	4416	Cole, Perry	2785
Colbert, Sarah	4417	Cole, Celia	2795
Colbert, Mary	4418	Cole, Jesse	2867
Colbert, Laura	4419	Cole, Willie	2879
Colbert, Anna	4426	Cole, William	2895
Colbert, Julius	4463	Cole, Daniel	2951
Colbert, R. D.	4485	Cole, Sam	3068
Colbert, Anna L.	4486	Cole, J. L.	3677
Colbert, Estella	4487	Cole, Mary Eliza	3717
Colbert, Julia	4489	Cole, Eugene Lee	3718
Colbert, Susan	4537	Cole, Bessie May	5274
Colbert, Stephen	4575	Cole, John	5421
Colbert, Columbus	4578	Coal, Walter	172
Colbert, Eva	4579	Cobb, Amy	181
Colbert, Nellie	4580	Cobb, Impson	182
Colbert, Levy	4581	Cobb, James	183
Colbert, Leavie	4582	Cooper, Etna	487
Colbert, Gussie	4735	Cook, Emma	1295
Colbert, Lillie	4830	Cook, Isaac	1296
Colbert, Eva	4838	Cook, Lilly	1297
Colbert, Lucretia	4951	Cook, Nellie	1298
Colbert, Bertha	4953	Cook, Eva	1299
Colbert, Willie	4954	Cook, Willie N.	3209
Colbert, Lee	4955	Cox, Lula	2060
Colbert, Dicey	4956	Cox, Lonzo	2061
Colbert, Clyde	4957	Cox, Abraham	2062
Colbert, Edmond	4959	Cox, David	3630
Colbert, Ellen	4961	Cohee, Hattie	2416
Colbert, Frank	5003	Cohee, Amanda	3005
Colbert, Neet	5036	Cohee, Buell	2417
Colbert, Maggie	5037	Cohee, Ivory Ollie	3030
Colbert, Bynum	5066	Colly, Oliver	2505

Name.	Roll No.	Name.	Roll No.
Colly, Maudie	2506	Cubit, Eliza	57
Colly, Mary	2507	Cubit, Jake, Jr.	58
Cochran, Richard	2995	Cubit, Mark	132
Cochran, Henry	2996	Cubit, Melvina	133
Cochran, Mary	3000	Cubit, Alice	134
Cochran, Siny	3001	Cubit, William	135
Cochran, President	3002	Cubit, Minnie	136
Cochran, Frank	3003	Cubit, Aurilla	137
Cochran, Ella	3004	Cubit, Sim	138
Cochran, Nathan	3010	Cubit, Mandy	139
Cochran, Charley	3011	Cubit, Cleveland	140
Cochran, Effie	5195	Cubit, Cassie	141
Cochran, Alex	5196	Cubit, Rathy	142
Collins, Malinda	4516	Cubit, Zelphia	143
Conard, Lewis	5187	Cubit, Mathew	266
Conard, Rennie	5188	Cubit, Emma	380
Conard, Walter	5189	Cubit, Frank	381
Conard, Needy	5190	Cubit, Randolph	478
Conard, Ella May	5191	Cubit, Mary	489
Conard, Lee	5192	Cubit, Phil	537
Conard, Joe Bennett	5193	Cubit, Harriet	538
Conard, Andy	5194	Cubit, John	539
Craig, Anna	1457	Cubit, Randall	540
Craig, Nettie	1458	Cubit, Harrison	541
Craig, Zack	1459	Cubit, Sam	632
Craig, Lula	1460	Cubit, Amy	633
Craig, Mecca	1461	Cubit, Rosy	634
Craig, Dan	1462	Cubit, Henry	635
Craig, Edward	3301	Cubit, Justice	637
Craig, Ada	3302	Cubit, Lee	638
Croons, Elizabeth	2021	Cubit, Johnny	639
Croons, Mary	2022	Cubit, Malvina	815
Croons, Bennie	2023	Cubit, Jack	816
Croons, Hubbard	2024	Cubit, Goodin	817
Croons, Lucy	2025	Cubit, Catherine	818
Crooms, Liddie	3544	Cubit, Mary Belle	9
Crooms, Doretha	3545	Cubit, Birdie	13
Crooms, Abram	3546	Cubit, Harry	2898
Crooms, Tommie	3547	Cubit, Wheeler	2925
Crooms, Evie	3548	Cubit, Asa	4037
Crooms, James	3549	Cubit, Emma	4038
Crooms, Liddie, Jr.	3550	Cubit, Mattie	4339
Crooms, Lenard Grant	3551	Culver, Marion	1989
Crooms, Annie	4679	Cutchlo, Matilda	3881
Crooms, Lavine	4680	Cutchlo, Henry	3882
Crooms, Evalina	4682	Cunish, Louisa	3607
Crooms, Pearl	4683	Cunish, Lenora	2165
Crooms, Ida	4684	Cunish, Joseph L.	2166
Crooms, Cleveland	4685	Cunish, Edna	2167
Crooms, Georgia	4686	Daniels, Lola	313
Crooms, Simon	4687	Daniels, Charlie	314
Crooms, Lonlo	4688	Daniels, John H. G.	315
Crooms, Leona	5049	Daniels, Arthur	316
Crittenden, Jack	3123	Daniels, Willis	317
Crawford, Rosanna	3584	Daniels, Green E.	318
Crawford, Albert	3585	Daniels, Jimmie	838
Crawford, Alonzo	3586	Daniels, Tommy	3049
Crawford, Aisy	3587	Daniels, Green	4402
Crawford, Lula	4681	Daniels, John	4403
Crawford, Grace	4689	Daniels, Eliza	4404
Crawford, Angie	4781	Daniels, Katie	4405
Cris, Vinie	3947	Davis, Helen	1054
Cris, Sam Benjamin	4816	Davis, Matilda	1055
Crutchfield, David	4330	Davis, Sidney	1056
Crutchfield, Curtis	4331	Davis, Jesse	1057
Crutchfield, Edna	4332	Davis, Calvin	1081
Crutchfield, Emma	4333	Davis, Ham	1522
Cravens, Frances	4793	Davis, Dave	2017
Cravens, Evline	4794	Davis, George	2018
Cubit, Ben	37	Davis, Sam	2019
Cubit, Jane	38	Davis, Gertie	2020
Cubit, Douglas	39	Davis, Belton	2620
Cubit, Phillis	41	Davis, Willie	3075
Cubit, Willis	42	Davis, Elizabeth	3077
Cubit, Mary	43	Davis, Minnie	3767
Cubit, Rindy	44	Davis, Nathan	4293
Cubit, Bob	45	Davis, David	5164
Cubit, Mitchell	46	Davis, Anderson	5483
Cubit, Clayborn	47	Dana, James	1801
Cubit, Jake	53	Dana, Luzena	1964
Cubit, Ida	54	Dana, Wm.	1977
Cubit, Callie	55	Dana, Emma	1978
Cubit, Della	56	Dana, Austin	3440
		Dana, Scott	3441

Name.	Roll No.	Name.	Roll No.
Dana, Jimmie	3443	Edd, Johnson	2821
Dana, Theodore	1965	Edd, Ludeller	3710
Dangerfield, Rhoda	4229	Eights, Lillie	2445
Dangerfield, Clemma	4230	Eights, Earnest	2446
Dangerfield, Olly	4231	Ellis, Maria	1361
Dangerfield, Lila	4232	Ellis, Cash	3674
Dangerfield, Cleveland	5030	Elridge, Jake	2392
Daugherty, William E.	4908	Ellison, Willie	2573
Dennis, Frank	863	Epps, Kittie	2763
Dennis, Anna F.	1463	Epps, Winnie	4384
Dennis, Alberta L.	1464	Epps, Pastoria	4387
Dennis, Tom Alphonso	1465	Epps, Carrie	4388
Dennis, Rosa	2992	Epps, Ira	4389
Dennis, James Rosco	33C3	Epps, Leonard	4390
Demus, Albertie	3724	Ervin, Eddie	4557
Demps, Mitchell	4158	Ervin, Pearlie	4559
Demps, Haywood	4159	Ervin, Allie	4560
Demps, Richmond	4160	Errett, Amanda	5242
Dizer, Maria	1213	Eubanks, Eddie	1467
Dizer, Cora	3168	Eubanks, Henry	1480
Douglas, Moses	842	Eubanks, Aaron	1484
Douglas, Gabrella	843	Eubanks, Jesse	1485
Douglas, Mabel	2605	Eubanks, John E.	1486
Douglas, Sopha Myrtle	2612	Eubanks, Minnie	1514
Douglas, Nancy	4863	Eubanks, James	1517
Douglas, Fred	4865	Eubanks, Moses	1523
Douglas, Alice	5174	Eubanks, Richard	1524
Douglas, Raynard	5443	Eubanks, Moses Jr.	1528
Douglas, Emaly	5546	Eubanks, Al	1529
Dockins, Sam	1805	Eubanks, Columbus	1530
Dockins, Minerva	1806	Eubanks, Collie L.	1531
Dodd, Sarah	1976	Eubanks, Cora	1533
Donegay, Cornelius	4281	Eubanks, Thaddeus	1659
Dodson, Marilda	5094	Eubanks, Andrew	1661
Dodson, Thomas	5095	Eubanks, Maria	2354
Dodson, S. W.	5097	Eubanks, Joseph	2355
Dodson, Robt.	5099	Eubanks, Henry	2356
Dotson, Claudie	5399	Eubanks, Willie	2357
Draper, Martha	1490	Eubanks, Alfred	2358
Durant, Walter	382	Eubanks, Frances	3842
Durant, Aleck	3768	Eubanks, Mary	3843
Durant, Millie	5384	Eubanks, Caesar	3844
Duckett, Peggy	636	Eubanks, Susan	3845
Duckett, Lela	2856	Eubanks, Ella	3846
Duckett, Anna	5290	Eubanks, James	3883
Duckett, Northly	5294	Eubanks, Charley	3964
Dunford, Tena	1759	Everidge, Mack	1120
Dunford, Dock	1774	Everidge, Rebecka	1121
Dunford, Charity	1775	Everidge, Cora	1200
Dunford, Zach	1959	Everidge, Charlie	1209
Dunford, Reuben	3395	Everidge, William I.	1342
Dunford, Willie	3396	Everidge, Katie	1343
Dunford, Ephraim	3397	Everidge, Alonzo	1344
Dunford, Aleck	3398	Everidge, Myrtle	1345
Dunford, Daisy	3399	Everidge, Leonard	1350
Dunford, Terry	3405	Everidge, Violet	1351
Dunford, Oscar	3406	Everidge, Bryant	1352
Dunford, Rena	4286	Everidge, Emma	3097
Dunford, Vicey	4287	Everidge, Henry	3098
Dunford, Elsie	4288	Everidge, Impson	3737
Dunford, Lucy	4751	Everidge, Emanuel	3917
Dunford, Phillip	4752	Everidge, Emerson	3918
Duncan, Laura	3296	Everidge, Burton	3919
Duncan, Gertie	3297	Evans, Ben	1518
Duncan, Grover	3298	Ewing, Lula	4235
Duncan, Aleck	3299	Ewing, Cora	4236
Duncan, Shadrack	3300	Ewing, Dick	4237
Dumas, Joanna	5392	Ewing, Candy Cocenia	4238
Eastman, Norvel	1984	Ewings, Rosie	4949
Eastman, Albert	1985	Eyrett, Washington	4826
Eastman, Mary Ann	2368	Farris, Joe	2481
Eastman, Nelson	4919	Farris, Robert	2512
Eastman, Frank	4926	Farris, Jennie	2513
Eastman, Ida	4927	Farris, Henry	2515
Eastman, Aggie	4928	Farris, William	2516
Easton, Thurlow	5506	Farris, O'Niel	2517
Edwards. Sallie	2086	Farris, Manuel	2518
Edwards, Dora	2742	Farris, Verginia	2519
Edwards, Libby	2743	Farris, Bela	2520
Edwards, Louisa	4318	Farris, Mary	2521
Edd, Julia	2815	Factory, Nelly	3811
Edd, Henry	2816	Factory, Eva	3812
Edd, George	2817	Factory, Oscar	3813
Edd, Eli	2818	Factory, Everett	3814
Edd, Mitchell	2819	Factory, Forest	3815
Edd, Millie	2820		

Name.	Roll No.	Name.	Roll No.
Factory, Sylverter	3816	Finley, Myra	2737
Factory, Effy	3817	Finley, Robert	2738
Featherston, Sallie	5450	Finley, Mamie	2739
Featherston, John	5454	Finley, John	3390
Featherston, Clement	5455	Finley, Charlotte	4279
Featherston, Mathew	5465	Fleeks, Cordelia	21
Featherston, Norene	5466	Fleeks, Sampson	3736
Featherston, Roma	5467	Fleeks, Blanche	4967
Featherston, Mathew B.	5468	Fleeks, Minnie	4968
Ferguson, Catherine	1140	Fleeks, Emma	4969
Fields, Fannie	101	Flemins, Jim	562
Fields, Sammy	102	Flemins, Curly	563
Fields, Everett	103	Flemins, Willis	564
Fields, Dan	104	Flemins, Virginia	565
Fields, Clara	105	Flack, Rosetta	2160
Fields, Hewitt	106	Flack, Erdie	2161
Fields, Peggy	107	Flack, Letie	2162
Fields, Lula	108	Flack, Annie	2239
Fields, Arthur	109	Flack, Ollie	2240
Fields, John	110	Flack, Enoch	2339
Fields, Hampton	618	Flack, Sallie	2340
Fields, Eliza	619	Flack, Wade	3535
Fields, Roy	620	Flack, Lucy	3536
Fields, Luler	621	Flack, Eliza	3636
Fields, Elmira	2653	Flack, Earl	3640
Fields, Chaney	2655	Flint, Edmund	2229
Fields, Angeline	2656	Flint, Isom	2382
Fields, Andrew	2657	Floyd, Katie	2869
Fields, Mary	2658	Floyd, Ara	2871
Fields, Louis	2659	Floyd, Frank	2872
Fields, Alex	2660	Floyd, Della	2873
Fields, Ether	2661	Floyd, Emma	2874
Fields, Calvin	3041	Floyd, Pearley	2875
Fields, Adeline	4583	Floyd, Roxey Anna	4973
Fields, Creasie	4988	Folsom, Amelia	1
Fields, Paralee	5047	Folsom, George	70
Fields, William	4663	Folsom, John	71
Fisher, Easter	1191	Folsom, Feina	72
Fisher, Victor	1192	Folsom, Louie	73
Fisher, Albert	1498	Folsom, Jordon	218
Fisher, Minerva	1499	Folsom, Harrison	911
Fisher, Villa	1808	Folsom, Johnson	981
Fisher, Alexander	1855	Folsom, Eliza	982
Fisher, Ella	1856	Folsom, Ephriam	983
Fisher, Martin	1857	Folsom, Dixie	984
Fisher, Tillie	1858	Folsom, Parmelia	985
Fisher, Osborn	1859	Folsom, Georgia	986
Fisher, Reason	1860	Folsom, Willie	1146
Fisher, Charlie	1861	Folsom, Mose	1157
Fisher, Harrison	1862	Folsom, Martha	1158
Fisher, Ellen	1863	Folsom, Frances	1159
Fisher, Moonie	1864	Folsom, Arthur	1160
Fisher, Abiza	1865	Folsom, Henry	1161
Fisher, Emma	1866	Folsom, Isiriney	1162
Fisher, Aleck	2749	Folsom, Dora	1163
Fisher, Nettie	2750	Folsom, Emma	1164
Fisher, Ottie	2751	Folsom, Edgar L.	1165
Fisher, Levi	2752	Folsom, Violet	1166
Fisher, Carl	3033	Folsom, Lizzie	1360
Fisher, Burt	3034	Folsom, Sinie	1405
Fisher, Claude	3035	Folsom, Minnie	1560
Fisher, Mary Lee	3307	Folsom, Robert	1561
Fisher, Owens	3308	Folsom, William	1602
Fisher, Hale	3309	Folsom, Walter	1603
Fisher, Eli	3557	Folsom, William, Jr.	1604
Fisher, Julia	3558	Folsom, Josie	1605
Fisher, Mary	3559	Folsom, Albert	1606
Fisher, Charlie	3560	Folsom, Opal	1607
Fisher, Tom	3561	Folsom, Phoebe	1608
Fisher, Patsy	3562	Folsom, Griffin W.	1609
Fisher, Henry	3563	Folsom, Mary W.	1610
Fisher, Gussie	3564	Folsom, Annie	1611
Fisher, Tony	3565	Folsom, Catherine	1897
Fisher, Lem	3566	Folsom, Jerry	1898
Fisher, Felix	3567	Folsom, Martin	1899
Fisher, Sylverter	3645	Folsom, Susan	1900
Fisher, Rena	3646	Folsom, Sampson	1901
Fisher, Mary Alice	4526	Folsom, Andrew	1902
Fisher, Felix	4528	Folsom, Alice	1903
Fisher, Henry Richard	4732	Folsom, Mandy	1904
Fisher, Frank	5373	Folsom, Florence	1905
Finley, Melissa	2735	Folsom, Henry	2228
Finley, Simon	2736	Folsom, Fredonia	2920

Name.	Roll No.	Name.	Roll No.
Folsom, Lucinda	3059	Frazier, Annie	3729
Folsom, Samuel	3060	Frazier, Alza	3730
Folsom, Elijah	3061	Frazier, Will	3731
Folsom, Dave	3062	Frazier, Phoebe	3732
Folsom, Susan	3063	Frazier, Collin	4115
Folsom, Johnnie	3064	Frazier, Edward	4137
Folsom, Mary Jane	3065	Frazier, Sim	4138
Folsom, Lu Emma	3069	Frazier, Jerry	4350
Folsom, Osborne	3203	Frazier, Johnnie	4351
Folsom, Osborne Jr.	3204	Frazier, Willie	4352
Folsom, Robert	3205	Frazier, Malvina	4589
Folsom, Mattie	3279	Frazier, Jacob	4590
Folsom, Claudie	3331	Frazier, Parthenia	5339
Folsom, Cora Lena	3334	French, Susan	542
Folsom, Willie	3335	French, Green	543
Folsom, Arthur	3336	French, John	544
Folsom, Leanna	3337	French, Gilly	545
Folsom, Frederick	3338	French, Beulah	546
Folsom, Gibson	3670	French, Lucy	547
Folsom, Josephine	3705	French, Mary Ellen	3054
Folsom, Bessie	3706	French, David	3055
Folsom, Louis	3725	French, Dan Jr.	3056
Folsom, Jordan	3926	French, Willie	3711
Folsom, Andrew	3965	Franklin, Charley	975
Folsom, Francis	4484	Franklin, Polly	976
Folsom, Ben	4596	Franklin, Matilda	977
Folsom, Louis	4597	Franklin, Mary A.	978
Folsom, Henry	4598	Franklin, Elzira	979
Folsom, Bennie	4600	Franklin, William	980
Folsom, Isabella	4601	Franklin, Walter	2415
Folsom, Emma	4602	Franklin, Andrew	2418
Folsom, Luther	4603	Franklin, Thomas	2419
Folsom, Isah	4604	Franklin, Matthew	2420
Folsom, Robert	4844	Franklin, Buck	2421
Folsom, Simon	5249	Franklin, David	2422
Foreman, Malinda	2396	Franklin, Fisher	2423
Frazier, Tennessee	23	Franklin, Lydia	2424
Frazier, Fannie	604	Franklin, Palesa	2456
Frazier, McKinney	605	Franklin, Ephram	2461
Frazier, Freeman	606	Franklin, Effie	2462
Frazier, Mary	607	Franklin, Cary	2470
Frazier, Hickman	610	Franklin, Lila	2532
Frazier, Minerva	774	Franklin, Fred	2533
Frazier, Vina	775	Franklin, Aurthur	2534
Frazier, Sarah	861	Franklin, Osborn	2934
Frazier, Emmett	1181	Franklin, Garfield	3013
Frazier, Sylvanie	1182	Franklin, Helen	3024
Frazier, Paralee	1185	Franklin, Eddie	3025
Frazier, Mary	1353	Franklin, Russell	3026
Frazier, Wiley	1413	Franklin, Joe	3029
Frazier, Eddy	1414	Franklin, Minerva	3370
Frazier, Orman	1415	Franklin, Luvinia	3371
Frazier, Eastman	1416	Franklin, George	3372
Frazier, Kansas	1417	Franklin, Toledo	3373
Frazier, Lena	1424	Franklin, Gus	3374
Frazier, Ophelia	2771	Franklin, Odelot	3375
Frazier, Letha	3022	Franklin, Angeline	3376
Frazier, George	3136	Franklin, Julia	3855
Frazier, Joanna	3137	Franklin, Alonzo	3856
Frazier, Clem	3138	Franklin, Richard B.	4273
Frazier, Thos.	3139	Franklin, Lemuel	4274
Frazier, John	3145	Freeman, Georgia Ann	1039
Frazier, Joshua	3146	Freeman, Sylverter	1618
Frazier, Thomas	3148	Freeman, Lula	1619
Frazier, Aurella	3151	Freeman, Mary C.	1620
Frazier, Callie	3152	Freeman, Emma	1621
Frazier, Dave	3153	Freeman, Arthur C.	1622
Frazitr, Noah	3216	Freeman, Viola M.	1623
Frazier, Alfred	3217	Freeman, Patsey	2325
Frazier, Havana	3218	Freeman, Jonas	2326
Frazier, Willie	3281	Freeman, Walton	2327
Frazier, Frances	3282	Freeman, Joe	2328
Frazier, Manuel	3283	Freeman, Lizzie	2330
Frazier, Jack	3284	Freeman, Charley	2331
Frazier, Johnny	3285	Freeman, Dick	2332
Frazier, Davis	3292	Freeman, Ed	2953
Frazier, Matilda	3388	Freeman, George	2955
Frazier, Andy	3389	Freeman, David	2965
Frazier, Charley	3391	Freeman, Jim	2974
Frazier, Hubbard	3481	Freeman, Jim, Jr.	2975
Frazier, Rena	3482	Freeman, Pearly	2976
Frazier, Albert	3727	Freeman, Will	3076
Frazier, Henry	3728	Freeman, Carrie Belle	3333

Name.	Roll No.	Name.	Roll No.
Freeman, Matt	4042	Gary, Nathan	3622
Freeman, Ella	4043	Gary, Jesse	4783
Freeman, Myrtle	4044	Gary, Chester	4784
Freeman, Phoebe	4045	Gary, Molcey	4810
Freeman, Joe	4046	Gary, Ephriam	4947
Freeman, Lurinda	4243	Gardner, Horace	1586
Freeman, Lorenda	4244	Gardner, Isaac	1793
Freeman, Arabella	4340	Gardner, Hettie	1794
Freeman, Rosie	4444	Gardner, Lizzie	1795
Freeman, Mary Lena	4448	Gardner, Charlie	1796
Freeman, Minnie	4499	Gardner, Magnolia	1797
Freeman, Louis	4500	Gardner, Albert	1840
Freeman, John	4531	Gardner, Rutha	1841
Freeman, Joe	4703	Gardner, Emma	1842
Froeman, Elnora	4731	Gardner, Randall	1962
Freeney, Ellen	1249	Gardner, Joe	1966
Freeney, George	4561	Gardner, Sinie	1967
Freeney, Sam	4562	Gardner, Elijah	1968
Freeney, Margaret	4563	Gardner, Tennessee	1969
Freeney, Delphia	4564	Gardner, Dora Lee	1970
Freeney, William	4565	Gardner, LeRoy	1971
Freeney, Jane	4567	Gardner, Ruffin	2000
Freeney, Andrew	4568	Gardner, Ruffin, Jr.	2001
Freeney, Eli	4569	Gardner, Edmund	2006
Freeney, John	4573	Gardner, Bird	2171
Freeney, Ruthie	4574	Gardner, Angeline	2706
Freeney, Louis	4841	Gardner, Myrtle	2707
Freeney, Emma	4842	Gardner, David	3418
Freeney, Henry	5039	Gardner, Elsie	3419
Freeney, Christina	5040	Gardner, Nellie	3420
Fullbright, Wiley	731	Gardner, Evalena	3421
Fullbright, Simpson	732	Gardner, Drucilla	3422
Fullbright, Peter	3890	Gardner, Mary	3423
Fullbright, Sam	3891	Gardner, Pamelia	3424
Fullbright, Estelle	3894	Gardner, William	3425
Fullbright, Julia	5238	Gardner, Abner	3426
Fulsom, Cooper	1815	Gardner, Joe	3427
Fulsom, Janie	1816	Gardner, Israel Lee	3428
Fulsom, Junior	1818	Gardner, Wallace	3429
Fulsom, Vivia May	1819	Gardner, Noah	3431
Fulsom, Nettie	4769	Gardner, Julia	3432
Fulsom; Ida	1817	Gardner, Lula	3433
Fulsom, Maryland	5520	Gardner, Isabelle	3434
Fulsom, Charley	5519	Gardner, Jessie	3435
Fulsom, Ida	5521	Gardner, Julius	4695
Fulsom, Nancy	5529	Gardner, Hubbard	4696
Fulsom, Lula	5531	Gardner, Clay	4789
Fulsom, Ada	5532	Gardner, Tom	4888
Garner, Andrew	146	Gardner, David	5243
Garland, Julius	891	Gardner, Jerome	5270
Garland, Carrie	902	Gardner, Ovy	5271
Garland, Morris	940	Gardner, Odeal	5272
Garland, Mary	941	Gardner, Vicey	5352
Garland, William	942	Gardner, Tennie	5353
Garland, Isaac	943	Gardner, Penny	5354
Garland, Nancy	3066	Gables, Martin	3529
Garland, Clayborn	5374	Gables, Hammond	3530
Gable, Irvin	924	Gables, Arrie	3531
Gable, Albert	931	Gables, John	3532
Gable, Virginia	932	Galloway, Isabel	4179
Gable, Robert	933	Galloway, Lula	5102
Gant, Gus	1129	Galloway, Carrie	5106
Gant, Daries	2386	Gay, William L.	4668
Gant, John	2979	Gaffney, Kizzie	5074
Gant, Eliza	3105	Gaffney, Eddie	5075
Gant, Phoebe	3106	Gaffney, Florida	5076
Gant, Irena	5355	Gaffney, Georgia Ann	5077
Gant, Ollie	5356	Gaffney, Brown	5078
Gant, Ivy	5357	Gaffney, Aleck	5079
Garrett, Hattie	1428	Gaffney, Lilly	5080
Garrett, Mattie	1429	Galbert, Mary	5400
Garrett, David	1430	Galbert, Henry	5401
Garrett, Alexander	1660	Galbert, Cornelia	5402
Garrett, Eliza	1776	Galbert, Dora	5403
Garrett, Reuben	1960	Galbert, Raize	5404
Gary, Albert	1447	Galbert, Elowise	5405
Gary, Israel	1448	Galbert, Augustus	5406
Gary, Ruthy	1449	Galbert, Ethel	5407
Gary, Zekiel	1450	Giddens, Rodella	61
Gary, Henrietta	1451	Giddens, Alberta	62
Gary, Elizabeth	1452	Giddens, Prentiss	63
Gary, Mattie	4291	Giddens, Lola Belle	64
Gary, Lindsey	4292	Giddens, Fancy Nora	65

Name.	Roll No.	Name.	Roll No.
Giddens, James A.	66	Green, Charlie	356
Giddens, Tilman	67	Green, Isaac	357
Giddens, Millie	507	Green, Sarah	1026
Giddens, Willie	508	Green, Anna	1147
Giddens, Curly Oco	2778	Green, Celeste	1148
Giddens, Sarah	3722	Green, Susan	1149
Gilmore, Ada	600	Green, Gertrue	1150
Gibson, Vina	880	Green, Sammy	1151
Gibson, Mary	963	Green, Dinah	1250
Gibson, Joseph	964	Green, Charley	1251
Gibson, Press	2268	Green, Tommy	1252
Gibson, Mary F.	2269	Green, William	1253
Gibson, Jesse	2270	Green, Hattie	1254
Gibson, Leonetta	2271	Green, Benjamin	1255
Gibson, Mary	2272	Green, Delbert	1321
Gibson, Annie	2930	Green, Nellie	1771
Gibson, Louisa	4074	Green, Lillie	1772
Gibson, Australia	4078	Green, Cora	1773
Gibson, Susan	4183	Green, Cora	2046
Gibson, Pearlie	4184	Green, Lee	2058
Gibson, Nettie	4185	Green, Louis	2372
Gibson, Levi	4186	Green, Jerry	3113
Gibson, Australia	4187	Green, Aleck	3213
Gibson, Nona	4188	Green, Jerry	3245
Gibson, Pheona	4189	Green, Rose	3246
Gibson, 'Nathan	4361	Green, Jacob	3403
Gibson, Oliver	4372	Green, Patsy	3404
Gibson, Ellen	4436	Green, Ambrose	4055
Gibson, Kissa	4440	Green, Minerva	4056
Gibson, Hurly	4833	Green, Leanna	4111
Gilbert, Monroe	885	Green, Mollie	4112
Gilbert, Violet	886	Green, Aaron	4488
Givens, Ella	1202	Green, Daniel	4733
Glover, James	1211	Green, Frank	4748
Glover, Mary	1212	Green, Charley	4749
Goings, Lizzie	416	Green, James	4750
Gordon, Emmaline	1867	Green, Mabel	4808
Gordon, Elmer	1868	Green, Clarence	4809
Gordon, Lelia	1869	Green, Dave	5205
Gordon, Carrie Bell	1870	Green, Lizzie	5206
Gordon, Temple	1876	Green, Lawrence W.	5207
Gordon, Albert	1877	Green, Spencer	5208
Gordon, Mattie	1878	Green, Ada Virginia	5209
Gordon, Isaac	1879	Green, Birtha	5210
Gordon, Marion A.	3462	Green, Emma	5497
Gordon, Edna	4902	Green, Evaline	5498
Goodlow, Henry	4020	Greenwood, Frances	1183
Goodlow, Willie	4021	Greenwood, Tishie	2719
Goodlow, Pearley	4022	Greenwood, Lucy	2722
Goodlow, Lucy	4023	Greenwood, George	2723
Goodlow, Lithy	4921	Greenwood, Annie	2724
Goodlow, Roosevelt	4925	Greenwood, Phoebe	3269
Gooding, Minnie	4771	Greenwood, Calvin	3270
Graham, Mary Jane	100	Gray, Hattie	5484
Graham, Mattie	173	Gray, Elbert	5485
Graham, Robert	771	Grundy, Richmond	2064
Graham, Saul	884	Grundy, Rindy	3809
Graham, Malinda	1208	Greer, Eddie	3442
Graham, Abraham	1422	Greer, James	5201
Graham, Rose	1423	Greer, Willie	5203
Graham, Lila	2913	Graves, Sylverter	3633
Graham, Hattie	3987	Graves, Martha	3634
Graham, Isom	3989	Graves, Joe	3672
Graham, Joshua	4057	Graves, Cornelia	3773
Graham, Willie	4058	Graves, Roy	3774
Graham, Mariah	4202	Graves, Tommy	3775
Graham, Dewood	4203	Graves, Ivary	3776
Graham, Jerry	4204	Graves, Henry	3777
Graham, Abraham	4205	Graves, Cora	5530
Graham, Zacnariah	4206	Gross, Mary	3928
Graham, Louisa	4207	Gross, Ida	4320
Graham, Louis	4375	Grayson, Annie	4903
Graham, March	4543	Grice, Florence	5393
Graham, Matilda	5088	Guess, Bell	239
Graham, Alonzo	5089	Guess, Harry	240
Graham, Walter	5090	Guess, John Jr.	1300
Graham, Matt	5091	Guess, Anna	1301
Graham, John	5092	Guess, John	1330
Graham, Mattie	5096	Guess, Isabella	1331
Graham, Willie	5098	Guess, Martin	1332
Graham, Robert	4325	Guess, Billy	1333
Green, Lizzie	352	Guess, Wilson	1334
Green, Irrella	355	Guess, Thomas	1335

Name.	Roll No.	Name.	Roll No.
Guess, Martha	1336	Harris, Jesse	2789
Guess, Columbus	1337	Harris, Margie Ann	2852
Guess, Elba	1338	Harris, Jim	3017
Guess, Jesse	1339	Harris, Rosanna	3244
Guess, Bessie	1340	Harris, Lettie	3524
Guess, Vernetta	1341	Harris, Richard	3612
Guess, Pearlie	3210	Harris, Henry	3648
Guess, Jimmie	3211	Harris, Lou	3649
Guess, Wash	4012	Harris, Lucinda	3675
Guess, Ella	4013	Harris, Jeff	4428
Guess, Johnnie	4014	Harris, Eliza	4584
Guess, Andy, Jr.	4015	Harris, Luvica	4587
Guess, Andrew	4025	Harris, Paralee	4779
Guest, Arabella	1974	Harris, Alexander	4795
Guest, Epluribus	1975	Harris, Lucindy	4796
Guest, Jackie	3765	Harris, Nicey	4797
Guesst, Charley	2383	Harris, Annie	4843
Guesst, Ike	2384	Harris, Sweetie	5093
Gully, Robt.	4283	Harris, John Tom	5349
Hawkins, Hettie	82	Harris, Lillie	5382
Hawkins, Myrtie	83	Harris, Frances	5508
Hawkins, Willis	1500	Harris, Mary	5509
Hawkins, Rebecca J.	1501	Harris, Thomas	5511
Hawkins, Zara	2135	Harris, Josephine	5512
Hawkins, Alfred	2404	Harris, Rosetta	2009
Hawkins, Velma	3489	Harris, Eddie	2010
Hawkins, Annie	4275	Harris, Sam	2011
Hawkins, Frances	4276	Hall, Martin Lee	823
Hawkins, Grant	4277	Hall, Louis	832
Hawkins, Albirda	4278	Hall, Nellie	833
Hawkins, Dan	5340	Hall, Sophina	834
Hawkins, Lewis	5350	Hall, Mary	176
Harris, Rose	114	Hall, Aleck	177
Harris, Billy	118	Hall, Malinda	178
Harris, Washington	265	Hall, Dora	179
Harris, Reuben	330	Hall, Sam	180
Harris, Scott	331	Hall, Ramsey	926
Harris, Ellen	332	Hall, Cynthia	927
Harris, Jacob	333	Hall, William	928
Harris, Viola	334	Hall, Julius	929
Harris, Jency	335	Hall, Johnie	930
Harris, Lewis	336	Hall, Thomas	948
Harris, Sam	572	Hall, Rachel	949
Harris, Catherine	573	Hall, Charity	950
Harris, Daniel	574	Hall, Hattie	966
Harris, Roland	575	Hall, Johnnie or Clem-	
Harris, Rufus	576	mie	5487
Harris, Johnny	577	Hall, Squire	1541
Harris, Ellin	584	Hall, Melissa	1963
Harris, Charles	586	Hall, Fanny	2922
Harris, Henry	587	Hall, Patsy	3703
Harris, Edward	588	Hall, Mamie	3719
Harris, John	589	Hall, Jimmie	4264
Harris, James	590	Hall, Mary	4476
Harris, Celeste	591	Hall, George	4477
Harris, David	592	Hall, Eastman	4478
Harris, Bennie	593	Hall, Sophy F.	4606
Harris, Arthur	734	Hall, Jake	4607
Harris, Julia	901	Hall, Ordell	4608
Harris, Oliver	903	Hall, Robert	4609
Harris, Florence	1004	Hall, Lucinda	4634
Harris, Nancy	1210	Hall, Roosevelt	4635
Harris, Robert	1223	Hall, Ruby	4636
Harris, Rosella	1224	Hall, Alberta	4964
Harris, Vineta	1227	Hall, Josephine	5267
Harris, James	1442	Hall, Minerva	5268
Harris, Ella	1443	Hall, Thomas	5380
Harris, Zeke	1444	Harkins, Nellie	938
Harris, William Gentry	1445	Harkins, Dave	2851
Harris, Della	1446	Harkins, Jackson	2908
Harris, Ruth	1675	Harkins, Mitchell	4717
Harris, Isaac	1676	Harkins, Elvira	4718
Harris, Battice	1722	Harkins, Alfred	4719
Harris, Tennessee	1777	Harkins, Henry	4720
Harris, Delilah	1807	Harkins, Ezekiel	4721
Harris, Nelson	1986	Harkins, Melvin	4722
Harris, Claria A.	2186	Harkins, Mollie	4820
Harris, Lettie	2187	Harkins, Tina	4821
Harris, Walter	2188	Halford, Hattie	1031
Harris, Crittenton	2189	Haywood, Georgia	1059
Harris, Martin	2306	Haywood, Ada	1060
Harris, Hollie	2307	Haywood, Johnnie	1061
Harris, Isaac	2364	Haywood, Nathan	1062
Harris, Martin	2788	Haywood, Mattie	1063
		Haywood, Indiana	2753
		Hampton, Mack	1082

Name.	Roll No.	Name.	Roll No.
Hampton, Ella	1083	Henderson, Louis	1742
Hampton, Veretta	1084	Henderson, Amanda	1743
Hampton, Rosa	1228	Henderson, Mack	1744
Hampton, Wilburn	1229	Henderson, Florence	1745
Hampton, Jesse	1230	Henderson, Isom	1747
Hampton, James	1231	Henderson, Rachel	2047
Hampton, Mary	1232	Henderson, Philip	2049
Hampton, Jerry	1271	Henderson, Oscar	2050
Hampton, Wade	3520	Henderson, Elizabeth	2051
Hampton, Catharine	3521	Henderson, Cora	2052
Hampton, Benson	3522	Henderson, Henry	2053
Hampton, Emma	3980	Henderson, Harvey	2054
Hampton, Lyinz	3985	Henderson, Sally	1646
Hampton, Nancy	5118	Henderson, Henry	1647
Hampton, Robert	5277	Henderson, Nelson	3120
Harrison, William	1088	Henderson, Emma	3121
Harrison, Thomas	1366	Henderson, Gertrude	3345
Harrison, Kizziah	1367	Henderson, Dolly	3757
Harrison, James	1368	Henderson, Jeff	4252
Harrison, Cora M.	1369	Henderson, Cub	4253
Harrison, Catherine	1370	Henderson, Ida	4254
Harrison, Thomas Jr.	1371	Henderson, Caroline	4255
Harrison, Louisa	1372	Henderson, Idella	4256
Harrison, Hattie	1373	Henderson, Harriet	4532
Harrison, Brigham Y.	1953	Henderson, Hannah	4533
Harrison, Paul	1954	Henderson, Joseph	4534
Harrison, Floyd	1955	Henderson, Susie	4535
Harrison, Clyde	1956	Henderson, David	4536
Harrison, Monte Mable	1957	Henderson, Carrie Ethle	5424
Harrison, Ida	2148	Hester, Lee	709
Harrison, Mat	2149	Hester, Edna	2877
Harrison, Minerva	2562	Hendricks, Cynthia	2954
Harrison, Ella	2563	Henry, Laura	4081
Harrison, Sim	2564	Henry, Randall	4082
Harrison, Mattie	2565	Henry, James	4083
Harrison, Hattie	2566	Henry, Robin	4084
Harrison, Mary	3489	Henry, Carrie	4085
Harrison, Myree	4975	Henry, Hirma	4086
Harrison, Ervin	4980	Henry, Levi	4087
Hamilton, Emma	1988	Henry, Ezekiel	4088
Hamilton, Nancy	2409	Henry, Eugene	4089
Hamilton, Peter	2434	Henry, Magnolia	4090
Hamilton, Ruth	2435	Henry, Elmira	4091
Hamilton, Willie	2436	Henry, Randall Lenard	4092
Hamilton, Maxy	2437	Hill, Mary	20
Hamilton, Annie	2438	Hill, Ben	158
Hamilton, Sallie	2439	Hill, John	159
Hamilton, Persia	2440	Hill, Louisa	398
Hamilton, Easter	2478	Hill, Rosa	399
Hamilton, Mahala	4974	Hill, Sam	400
Harlan, Aleck	2399	Hill, Oscar	2822
Harlan, Isabinda	3006	Hill, Hannibal	2870
Harlan, Margaret	3007	Hill, Caroline	3273
Harlan, Mandy	3008	Hill, James	3274
Harlan, Addie	3019	Hill, North	3275
Harvey, Adelaide	2744	Hill, Richard	3276
Harvey, Vinessa	2745	Hill, Bertie	3277
Harvey, Madison	2746	Hill, Cora	3278
Harvey, Osceola	2747	Hill, North	3927
Harvey, Minnitte	2748	Hill, Abagail	4161
Hatley, Virginia	3625	Hill, Celestina	4162
Hatley, Ben	3626	Hill, Roger	4163
Hatley, Laura	3627	Hills, Amelia	1014
Haley, Willis	4107	Hills, Bessie	1015
Haley, James	4108	Hills, Rosey Lee	1016
Haley, Malinda	4109	Hills, Anna	2791
Haley, Lucinda	4420	Hills, Adaline	2792
Haley, Esther	4421	Hilliard, Becky	1958
Haley, Joseph	4422	Hilliard, Lucy	2098
Haley, Clarissa	4832	Hilliard, Janie B.	2099
Harnage, Rhoda	3673	Hilliard, McKinley	2100
Henderson, Olivia	594	Hilliard, Lonzo	2101
Henderson, Ellen	897	Hilliard, Ephram	2102
Henderson, Virgil	898	Hilliard, Annie	3490
Henderson, Clayton	899	Hilliard, Julia	4953
Henderson, Wilson	900	Hines, Henry	2969
Henderson, Dinah	946	Hines, Violet Mary Bell	3078
Henderson, Calafornia	1186	Hines, Sarah	4725
Henderson, Jackson	1187	Hines, Henry	4727
Henderson, Georgia Ann	1188	Hines, John	4728
Henderson, Columbus	1189	Hicks, Tommie	4772
Henderson, Martha B.	1625	Horton, Frank	857
Henderson, Mary	1626	Horton, Kizzie	4156
Henderson, Elijah	1627	Horton, Joe	5289
Henderson, Josephene	1628	Homer, Wiley	1075
Henderson, Sallie	1741	Homer, Rhoda	4406

Name.	Roll No.
Homer, Sarah	4408
Homer, Lincoln	4409
Holford, Josephine	1114
Holford, Amelia	5429
Hotchkins, Henry	1763
Hotchkins, Easter	1764
Hotchkins, Willis	1798
Hotchkins, Mace	4497
Hollin, Minnie	1925
Hollin, Minerva	3467
Holt, Littleton	2343
Hogan, Lorena	2347
Hogan, Ezella	2348
Hogan, Lethia	2349
Hogan, Lebanginus	2350
Hogan, Harvey	2351
Hogan, Madona	2352
Hogan, Bertha May	2353
Hoppy, Maggie	2471
Hollaway, Lou Vesta	2842
Hodges, Charlotte	2958
Hodges, Hannibal	5470
Horn, Ann	3525
Horn, Laura	4788
Horn, Ida	5502
Howell, John	3865
Howell, Lewis	3866
Howell, Jane	4807
Hornback, Sallie	4610
Hornback, Mary	4611
Hornback, Katie	4612
Hornback, Martha E.	4613
Hornback, Della	4614
Hornback, Lucas	5323
Hornback, Della	5324
Hornback, Maria	5325
Hornback, Benjamin	5326
Hopkins, Mose	4929
Hunter, Mary Eliza	987
Hunter, Albert H.	988
Hunter, Elizabeth	989
Hunter, Lucinda	1002
Hunter, Dicey	1283
Hunter, Cornelia	1284
Hunter, George	1285
Hunter, Ellen	1286
Hunter, Cindy	1287
Hunter, Julius	1288
Hunter, Emma	1289
Hunter, Cleveland	1290
Hunter, Melvin	1291
Hunter, Brazel	1292
Hunter, Ward	1362
Hunter, Viola	1363
Hunter, Lavissa M.	1364
Hunter, Charles	1365
Hunter, Joe	3208
Hunter, John	4730
Hunter, Elijah	4996
Hunter, Serena	5303
Hunter, Emanuel	5381
Hunter, Isah	5505
Hutchins, Jennie	1408
Hutchins, Ada	1409
Hughes, Phoebe	2002
Hughes, Willie	2003
Hughes, Anna May	2004
Hughes, Bernice	2048
Hughes, Ernestine	2055
Hughes, Odessa	3523
Humdy, Tillie	2551
Humdy, Edward	2552
Humdy, Rosa J.	3037
Humes, Dennis	3970
Humes, Martha E.	3971
Humes, James	3972
Humes, Monroe	3973
Humphrey, Hattie	4221
Humphrey, Daisy	4226
Humphrey, Ethel	4228
Humphrey, Roy Lee	5029
Hutchison, Matilda	4432
Hyatt, Celestris	5385
Hyatt, Dixie Ivory	5386
Irving, Jimmy	1123
Irving, Bennie	1124

Name.	Roll No.
Irving, Sammy	1125
Irving, Leslie	3102
Irving, Amaretta	4976
Irving, Albert	4977
Irving, Lillian	4978
Irvin, Liza	4979
Ingram, Louisa	3751
Jackson, Willie	223
Jackson, Edmond	206
Jackson, Joe	297
Jackson, Jesse	298
Jackson, Alfred	735
Jackson, Willie	736
Jackson, Annie	737
Jackson, Janie	738
Jackson, Mattie	739
Jackson, Alfred, Jr.	740
Jackson, Abbie	741
Jackson, Harriet	742
Jackson, Caroline	1097
Jackson, Willie	1098
Jackson, Walter	1099
Jackson, Malinda	1222
Jackson, Lula	1357
Jackson, Annie Lee	1358
Jackson, Tenna	1359
Jackson, Elsie	1509
Jackson, Frank	1510
Jackson, Ralph	1511
Jackson, Florida	1778
Jackson, Eliza	1779
Jackson, George	1780
Jackson, Terry	1781
Jackson, Henry	1782
Jackson, Erin	1783
Jackson, Palina	1811
Jackson, Andrew	2336
Jackson, Edward	2797
Jackson, Liversa	2853
Jackson, Sarah	2978
Jackson, Primer	2980
Jackson, Ed	2981
Jackson, Aleck	2982
Jackson, Jesse	3133
Jackson, Molly Ann	3251
Jackson, Aleck	3260
Jackson, Garnett	3261
Jackson, Bertha	3311
Jackson, Carry	3400
Jackson, Laura	3402
Jackson, Laura	3656
Jackson, Eddie	3657
Jackson, Stella	3658
Jackson, Pet	3659
Jackson, Henry	3660
Jackson, Catherine	3685
Jackson, Tela	3714
Jackson, Malinda	3759
Jackson, Isom	3934
Jackson, Julia Ann	3935
Jackson, Willie	3936
Jackson, Ben	3937
Jackson, Anderson	3938
Jackson, Mitchell	3939
Jackson, Josephine	3940
Jackson, Emma	3941
Jackson, Martha	3974
Jackson, Robert	3977
Jackson, Robert	3990
Jackson, Serena	3991
Jackson, Etta	3993
Jackson, Emit	3994
Jackson, Milly	4048
Jackson, William	4080
Jackson, Mary	4134
Jackson, Eldridge	4135
Jackson, Horris Elwood	4136
Jackson, Roxy	4154
Jackson, Eliza	5522
Jackson, Jim	4300
Jackson, Earnest	4759
Jackson, Taylor	5081
Jackson, Legusta	5082

Name.	Roll No.	Name.	Roll No.
Jackson, Janie	5204	James, Lonzo	4960
Jackson, Phyllis	5246	James, Bessie	4774
Jackson, Louis	5247	James, Lida	4775
Jackson, Charles	5248	James, Elsie	4776
Jackson, Harriet	5322	James, Viney	4777
Jackson, Vina	5379	James, Callie	4778
Jackson, Geraldine	5396	James, Lewis	4990
Jackson, Nathan	5397	James, Joseph	4991
James, Everett	640	James, Georgia	4997
James, Solomon	765	James, Reuben	5269
James, Malvina	766	Jacob, Aaron	2442
James, Pearlie	767	Jamerson, Isabinda	2540
James, Anonia	768	Jeffers, Georgia	992
James, Jesse	769	Jeffers, John Henry	999
James, Sylvester	770	Jeffers, Frankie	4319
James, David	1374	Jeffers, Early	4227
James, Isaac	1375	Jeffers, Lonzo	4225
James, Agnes	1376	Jeffers, Ella	4773
James, Stella	1377	Jeater, Armstrong	1137
James, Lucius	1378	Jeter, Alonzo	1269
James, Mary	1379	Jefferson, Minnie	1942
James, Sarah	1649	Jefferson, Josephine	3480
James, John	1848	Jefferson, Shelby	5062
James, Jackson	2088	Jeffries, Johnny	3394
James, Hannah	2089	Jeffries, Lillie	4993
James, Telephus	2090	Jeffries, Herndon	4994
James, Lucinda	2091	Jeffries, Gustava	4995
James, Luanna	2092	Jones, Lettie	75
James, Daniel	2093	Jones, Lydia	488
James, Guy	2094	Jones, Malinda	819
James, Willie	2095	Jones, Lilly	821
James, Jimmie	2096	Jones, Levi	822
James, Sylva	2097	Jones, Maria	1040
James, Lenora	2104	Jones, Henry	1041
James, Hardy	2191	Jones, Ed	1042
James, Willis	2283	Jones, William	1044
James, Calvin	2465	Jones, Vinie	1045
James, Amanda	2466	Jones, Bessie	1046
James, Thomas	2467	Jones, Anna	1047
James, Florry	2468	Jones, Nero	1048
James, Ephriam	2671	Jones, Leola	1854
James, Dina	2672	Jones, John	2136
James, Caesar	2673	Jones, John Britton	2137
James, Almon	2675	Jones, Dave	2138
James, Ephriam, Jr.	2676	Jones, Martha	2267
James, Emma	2677	Jones, Lucinda	2363
James, Voyage	2678	Jones, Zilphia	2586
James, Grant	2679	Jones, Eliza	2624
James, Ether	2681	Jones, Nellie	3067
James, William	2682	Jones, George	3074
James, Leeones	2683	Jones, Isom	3498
James, Mapell	2684	Jones, Edmund	3602
James, Carrie	2685	Jones, Sarah	4785
James, Israel	2686	Johnson, S. D.	90
James, Hattie	2687	Johnson, Robert	364
James, Rodessa	2688	Johnson, Neat	365
James, Ether	3263	Johnson, Albert	599
James, Jim	3444	Johnson, Eliza A.	602
James, Jesse	3445	Johnson, Katie	603
James, Minerva	3446	Johnson, Perry	725
James, Eva	3447	Johnson, Arthur	726
James, Joseph	3448	Johnson, Martin	784
James, Clarissa	3449	Johnson, Mandy	785
James, Martin	3450	Johnson, Kate	786
James, Molly	3451	Johnson, Edner	787
James, Mary	3452	Johnson, H. C.	91
James, Hickman	3453	Johnson, Ellis	788
James, Jacob	3454	Johnson, Winnie	867
James, Martha Ann	3455	Johnson, Aelberta	868
James, Frank	3456	Johnson, Violet	953
James, Emma	3457	Johnson, Georgie	1000
James, Bessie B.	3458	Johnson, James	1001
James, Charlie M.	3459	Johnson, Ella	779
James, Willie	3460	Johnson, Joe	780
James, Lilly	3461	Johnson, Cherry	1043
James, Ellis	3573	Johnson, Anna	1049
James, Effie	3574	Johnson, Nana	1050
James, Clarence	3575	Johnson, James	1089
James, Minny	3576	Johnson, Jenny	1152
James, Bernie Beatrice	3577	Johnson, Ella N.	1153
James, Davis	3975	Johnson, Leona	1154
James, Daisy	3976	Johnson, Ida	1155
James, Thomas	4755	Johnson, Lewis	1156

Name.	Roll No.	Name.	Roll No.
Johnson, Lucinda	1678	Johnson, Aleck	5237
Johnson, Isaiah	1679	Johnson, Minerva	5259
Johnson, Jesse	1680	Johnston, Birdie	5334
Johnson, Rebecca	1681	Jolly, Lemon	2528
Johnson, Dora	1682	Jolly, Lewis	2529
Johnson, Frank	1683	Jolly, Lemon, Jr.	2530
Johnson, Rachael	1684	John, Rebecca	2556
Johnson, Alma	1685	John, Edward William S.	2561
Johnson, Andrew	1686	Joseph, July	2603
Johnson, Robert	1687	Jordon, Pink	2622
Johnson, Duglas	1683	Justice, Minerva	1385
Johnson, Susan	1849	Justice, Hazel	1386
Johnson, George	1850	Judy, Sampson	2570
Johnson, Penny	1851	Kendricks, Eliza	1453
Johnson, Pet	1852	Kendricks, Modessa	1454
Johnson, Hannah	1853	Kendrick, Mary	2497
Johnson, Willie	1880	Kendrick, Tennie	2498
Johnson, Nettie	1980	Keith, Pleas Jonathan	1810
Johnson, John	1981	Keith, Harriet	4887
Johnson, Andrew	2337	Keel, Eddie	2273
Johnson, Rachel	2493	Keel, Mary	2274
Johnson, Aravilla	2494	Keel, Minnie	2275
Johnson, Matilda	2495	Keel, Henry	2276
Johnson, Rosa	2553	Keel, Willie	2728
Johnson, Mannie	2554	Kemp, Josie	2654
Johnson, Marietter	2555	Kirk, Annie	955
Johnson, Albert	2579	Kirk, Robert	957
Johnson, Rachel	2580	Kirk, Henry	958
Johnson, Mina	2581	Kirk, Obediah	959
Johnson, Laura	2582	Kirk, Ludie	960
Johnson, Anna	2583	Kirk, Sadie	961
Johnson, Janie	2584	Kirk, Susan	3723
Johnson, Carrie	2585	Kiel, Lindy	2039
Johnson, Payton	2894	Kiel, Willie	2040
Johnson, Roy	2971	Kiel, Sammie	2041
Johnson, Liversa	2853	Kiel, Ester	2042
Johnson, Levi	3023	Kiel, Osceola	2043
Johnson, Eli	3036	Kiel, Evil	2044
Johnson, Annie	3081	Kiel, Henrietta	2254
Johnson, Jack	3082	Kiel, Laura	2255
Johnson, Virginia	3083	Kiel, Clifton	2256
Johnson, Willie	3084	Kiel, William	2257
Johnson, Joe	3085	Kiel, Gracie	2258
Johnson, Eddie	3086	Kincade, Willis	2308
Johnson, Green	3087	Kincade, Mandy	2309
Johnson, Celia	3604	Kincade, Alice	2310
Johnson, Bertha	3605	Kincade, Horace	2311
Johnson, Silas	3743	Kincade, St. Elmo	2312
Johnson, Harlan	3955	Kincade, Nellie	2313
Johnson, Roland	4079	Kincade, Celia	2314
Johnson, Lena	4145	Kincade, Leola	2315
Johnson, James	4146	Kincade, Laura	2316
Johnson, Isabella	4147	Kincade, Stella	2317
Johnson, Annie	4148	Kingsbury, Jordan	3339
Johnson, Martin	4149	Kingsbury, Lige	3340
Johnson, Sissie	4150	Kingsbury, Ben W.	5523
Johnson, Lucelia	4151	Kingsbury, Ben	3385
Johnson, Rossnna	4152	Kingsbury, Andrew Alfonso	3386
Johnson, Jane	4211		
Johnson, Amos	4212	Kingsbury, Beatrice Legree	3387
Johnson, Savannah	4247		
Johnson, Carter	4345	King, Annie	5377
Johnson, Louis	4346	King, Tommie	5469
Johnson, George	4347	Lake, Lucy	965
Johnson, Sefronia	4348	Last, Fannie	1768
Johnson, Porter	4358	Lawson, Easter	1828
Johnson, Matthew	4381	Lawson, Vester	1829
Johnson, Maria	4382	Lawson, Barbara Ellen	1830
Johnson, Zelphy	4423	Lawson, Alwin	1831
Johnson, Aleck	4441	Lawson, Zora Ida	1832
Johnson, Ann Eliza	4517	Lawson, Pearlie	1833
Johnson, Ella Wynnifred	4518	Lawson, Turner	1834
Johnson, Philip	4519	Lawson, Adlisa	1835
Johnson, Lilly	4539	Lawson, Matilda	4114
Johnson, Eliza	1779	Lawson, Rebecca	4354
Johnson, Clara	4864	Lawrence, Joe	1992
Johnson, Charlotte	5035	Lawrence, Frances	1993
Johnson, Dollie	5038	Lawrence, Lavota	1994
Johnson, Willy	5064	Lawrence, Zachariah	1995
Johnson, Ann	5123	Lawrence, Edna	1996
Johnson, Leoda	5127	Lawrence, Emily	1997
Johnson, Rosanna	5128	Lawrence, Douglass	1998
Johnson, Andrew	5129	Lawrence, Grant	3766

Name.	Roll No.	Name.	Roll No.
Lawrence, Lizzie	3804	Lewis, Lenora	2165
Lawrence, Dewey Ru-		Lewis, Joseph L.	2166
dolph	3805	Lewis, Edna	2167
Lawrence, Merle Goldie	3806	Lewis, Pearl Gardner	2169
Lawrence, Melvin, Jr.	4811	Lewis, Lycurgus	2800
Lathers, Mandy	2200	Lewis, Alfred	2826
Lathers, Willy	2206	Lewis, Fredonia	2827
Lathers, Irene	3624	Lewis, Shepard	2828
Larkin, Millie	2754	Lewis, Abelina	2830
Larkin, Mathew	2755	Lewis, Georga	2831
Larkin, Jim	2756	Lewis, George	2832
Larkin, Tooker	2757	Lewis, Grover	2956
Larkin, Berden	2758	Lewis, Elizabeth	3286
Larkin, Bruce	2759	Lewis, Bert	3287
Larkin, Frank	2760	Lewis, Bryant	3288
Larkin, Rhoda	3088	Lewis, Joe	3380
LaFlore, Lucinda	4317	Lewis, Solomon	3606
LeFlore, Isaac	52	Lewis, Louisa	3607
LeFlore, Victoria	887	Lewis, Jennie	3818
LeFlore, Margaret	947	Lewis, Elizabeth	3819
LeFlore, Austin	2381	Lewis, Isom	3820
LeFlore, Sam	2918	Lewis, Adam	4306
LeFlore, Jack	3361	Lewis, Hettie	4407
Leflore, Michael	596	Lewis, Iole	4410
Leflore, David	2911	Lewis, Alice	4494
Lewis, Emanuel	149	Lewis, Harry	4496
Lewis, Jordon	151	Lewis, Frank	4495
Lewis, Ozella	152	Lewis, Willie	4622
Lewis, Gustave	155	Lewis, Tony	4623
Lewis, Joel	156	Lewis, Bennie	4624
Lewis, Lillie	150	Lewis, Emeline	4633
Lewis, Pearl	160	Lewis, Susan	4647
Lewis, Amy	205	Lewis, George	4648
Lewis, Eldridge	207	Lewis, Joshua	4655
Lewis, Minerva	338	Lewis, Benjamin	4656
Lewis, Charley	339	Lewis, Ida	4657
Lewis, Aleck	340	Lewis, Willie	4658
Lewis, Susan	341	Lewis, Silas	4659
Lewis, Irvin	342	Lewis, Birdie	4660
Lewis, Charity	343	Lewis, Silas	4746
Lewis, Alonzo	344	Lewis, Paralee	4871
Lewis, Mary	345	Lewis, William	4875
Lewis, Zetta	346	Lewis, Eliza	4970
Lewis, Cora	347	Lewis, Cynthia	5033
Lewis, Agnes	348	Lewis, Leroy	5034
Lewis, Roverta	349	Lewis, Elsie	5107
Lewis, Robert	350	Lewis, Willie	5108
Lewis, Judy	470	Lewis, Johnnie	5109
Lewis, Adam	471	Lewis, Susan	5110
Lewis, Frank	472	Lewis, Jackson	5181
Lewis, Winnie	473	Lewis, Joe	5182
Lewis, Della	474	Lewis, William	5408
Lewis, Emmet	475	Lewis, Leaner	5409
Lewis, Teele	476	Lewis, Emma	5541
Lewis, Nettie	477	Lewis, Homer	5410
Lewis, Monroe	749	Leftridge, Amy	210
Lewis, Sim	750	Leftridge, Eliza	211
Lewis, Lon	751	Leftridge, Willie	212
Lewis, Ebenezer	752	Leftridge, Sarah	213
Lewis, Wesley	753	Leftridge, Isabelle	3704
Lewis, James	1052	Lenox, Sophie	1022
Lewis, Nip	1396	Lenox, Lela	1023
Lewis, Jinsey	1397	Lee, Lizzie	3221
Lewis, Sallie	1398	Lee, Charlie	3224
Lewis, Chaney	1399	Lee, Henry	3988
Lewis, Phoebe	1400	Lee, Sam	5024
Lewis, Hattie	1401	Leppord, Virginia	4932
Lewis, Louie	1402	Leppord, Henderson	4934
Lewis, Turner	1403	Leppord, Zelmore	4935
Lewis, Robert	1404	Leppord, Birtie	4936
Lewis, Rosa	1418	Leppord, Isaah	4937
Lewis, Henry	1420	Leppord, Carrie Nellie	4938
Lewis, Somey	1421	Leppord, Paul Omer	4939
Lewis, Rachael	1717	Littlejohn, Anna	275
Lewis, Robert	1738	Littlejohn, Carrie	276
Lewis, Benjamin	1767	Littlejohn, Henry	277
Lewis, Myrtie	1873	Littlejohn, Tommy	278
Lewis, Curtis	1874	Littlejohn, Arthur	279
Lewis, Cordelia	1875	Littlejohn, Emma	280
Lewis, Jane	1936	Littlejohn, Ola	281
Lewis, Jay Gould	1937	Littlejohn, August	282
Lewis, Eli	1938	Littlejohn, Garfield	285
Lewis, Elizabeth	2163	Littlejohn, Emma	2298

Name.	Roll No.	Name.	Roll No.
Littlejohn, Blanche	2294	Maytuby, Martha	2977
Littlejohn, Sophronia	3492	Maytubbee, Isom	4667
Littlejohn, Jesse	3493	Maytubbee, Ida	4853
Littlejohn, Annie	3494	Maytubbee, Mathew	4854
Littlejohn, Willie	3495	Maytubbee, Aurelius	4855
Littlejohn, Laurie	3496	Maytubbee, Leffie	4856
Littlejohn, Hiram	3497	Maytubbee, Leroy	4857
Littlejohn, Mattie	5517	Maytubbee, Mattie	4858
Liggins, Ozella	696	Maytubbee, Alice	4890
Liggins, Ned	698	Maytubbee, Mag	4892
Liggins, Lizetta	699	Maytubbee, Wm.	4893
Liggins, Rosa	2868	Mahardy, Salina	3570
Livingston, Minnie R.	1439	Mahardy, George	4132
Livingston, Frances	1440	Mahardy, Thelmer L.	4133
Ligon, Betty	2604	Mahardy, Sarah	4335
Ligon, Nathaniel	2606	Manning, Mandy	3608
Ligon, Clarence	2607	Manning, Rufus	3609
Ligon, Mitchell	2608	Manning, Lee	3610
Ligon, Gladys	2609	Manning, Leona	3611
Ligon, Leader	2610	Martin, Fannie	3667
Ligon, Shadrack	2611	Martin, Mary	4895
Lovelace, M. Florence	1719	Martin, Lizzie	5156
Lovelace, Charles	1721	Mackey, Mary	3693
Lovelace, Irene	4599	Mackey, Joshua	3700
Lovelace, Thomas	4605	Mackey, Minnie	3701
Lowery, Malvina	1990	Mackey, Minervy	5447
Lowery, John Isaac	1991	Mackey, Johnny	5448
Lowery, Ricy Gee	3518	Mackey, Bessie	5449
Low, Sophie	2300	Maxwell, Hattie	3753
Low, Pearl	2301	Maxwell, Robert	3756
Low, James	2302	Maxwell, Mamie	5278
Low, Walter	2303	Maxwell, Christina	5279
Low, Clara	2304	Maxwell, Porter	5341
Low, Samuel	4299	Maupin, Oddie	5453
London, Steve	3483	Maturby, Jesse	5482
Love, Sookey	2709	Meadows, Enoch	1259
Love, Sibbey	5198	Meadows, Eliza	1260
Lowman, Frank	3950	Meadows, Carrie	1261
Looney, Catherine	4047	Meadows, Frances	1262
Logan, Pinky	4464	Meadows, Estella	1263
Lynch, Sallie	2360	Meadows, Buddie	1791
Lynch, Lawrence	2361	Meadows, Andrew	2377
Lynch, Nicholas	4761	Meadows, Emma	3259
Lynch, Adaline	4762	Merritts, Susan	4469
Lynch, Walton	4763	Meggs, Netta	4965
Lynch, Arthur	4764	Mills, Lum	5461
Lynch, Mattie	4765	Mills, Jimmie	5462
Lynch, Ella	4766	Mills, Lucinda	5534
Lynch, Mandy	4767	Mills, Alice	1091
Lynch, Alice	4768	Mills, Victoria	1092
Lynch, Fanny	5251	Mills, Alice, Jr.	1093
Lynn, George	5184	Mills, Cleveland	1173
Mays, William	1109	Mills, Napoleon	1174
Mays, William Jr.	1110	Mills, Rosy	1175
Mays, Grant	1214	Mills, Arilla	1180
Mays, James	1215	Mills, Elias	1198
Mays, Joe	4245	Mills, Willie	1199
Mays, Amelia	5422	Mills, Margaret	2369
May, York	3356	Mills, Jessie	2370
May, Mason	5503	Mills, Clayton	2371
May, Jesse	5504	Mills, Solomon	2944
Mayes, Mary	4298	Mills, Henry	2945
Mansfield, Lettie	1196	Mills, Lula	2946
Mansfield, Sallie	3134	Mills, George	2947
Mansfield, Houston	3142	Mills, Mack	3182
Mansfield, Avery	3733	Mills, Jimmy	3676
Mat-ub-hee, Della	1257	Mills, Leany	4250
Mat-ub-hee, Jesse	1258	Mills, Erna	4521
Mann, Elsie	1425	Mills, James	4522
Mann, Peter	1426	Mills, Mary Bell	4523
Mann, Israel	2523	Mills, Essie V.	4524
Mann, Henderson	3289	Mills, Christina	4839
Mann, Hydra	3290	Mills, Mitchell	4840
Mabry, Mary	1577	Miller, Eliza	1809
Mabry, Louis	1578	Miller, Polly Ann Eliza	3291
Mabry, Lula	1579	Miller, Siney	3916
Mabry, Willie	1580	Miller, Sina	5428
Mabry, Carrie	1581	Miller, Aleck	4530
Mabry, Walker	1582	Mitchell, Tempie	1871
Mabry, Aaron	1593	Mitchell, Jake	4931
Mabry, Laurence	1594	Mitchell, Annie	5261
Mabry, Lidie	1601	Mitchell, Wayman	
Mabry, Herman	3327	Adolphus	5265
Mabry, Hubbard	5423	Miles, Leander	2474
		Miles, Willie	2480
		Miles, Robert	2531

Name.	Roll No.	Name.	Roll No.
Miles, Virginia	3438	McCoy, John	1564
Miles, Serena	3437	McCoy, Lily	1565
Milton, Sarah	4123	McCoy, Wesley	1566
Milton, Frank	4124	McCoy, William	1567
Milton, Dosy	4125	McCoy, Morris	1727
Milton, Hattie	5101	McCoy, Calvin	2113
Milton, Nobin	5104	McCoy, Turner	2114
Milton, Alice	5105	McCoy, Dora	2115
Minner, Tena	4466	McCoy, Walter	2116
Minner, Ineas	4467	McCoy, King	2117
Minner, Lutitia	4468	McCoy, Dinah	2118
Minner, James	4835	McCoy, Harrison	2119
Minner, Ada	4836	McCoy, Willis	2191
Minner, Garfield	4837	McCoy, Solomon	2173
Moss, Mollie	111	McCoy, William	2207
Moss, Amos	2621	McCoy, Wesley	3378
Moore, Louisa	1074	McCoy, Sam	3671
Moore, William	1728	McCoy, Mary	3681
Moore, Ailsey	1729	McCoy, Noah	3807
Moore, Georgia	1730	McCoy, Dave	3808
Moore, Walton	1731	McCoy, Cordie	3810
Moore, Simon	1732	McCoy, Willie	3953
Moore, Elzina	1734	McCoy, Minerva	4694
Moore, Susie	1735	McCoy, Henry	4697
Moore, Crawford	1736	McCoy, William	4698
Moore, Louisa	1737	McCoy, Charlotte	4699
Moore, Georgie	3539	McCoy, Frances	4700
Moore, David	3540	McCoy, Rosie	4701
Moore, Clarence	3541	McCoy, Lizzie B.	4702
Moore, Leola	3542	McCoy, Preston	4739
Moore, Mark	3543	McCoy, Earnestine	4861
Moore, Charley	3884	McCloud, Charley	1412
Moore, Sampson	4872	McCleary, James	2909
Moore, Clarissa	5460	McCarty, Peter	3357
Moore, Sallie Nolia	5463	McCarty, Alfred	4429
Moore, Geneva	5464	McCarty, Celia	4475
Morris, Creasie	2204	McCarty, Gib	4482
Morris, Mary	3018	McCarty, Mary	5032
Morris, Polly	3666	McCurtain, David	3738
Moses, Vinetta	2226	McCurtain, Elizabeth	3739
Moses, Katie Levicey	2227	McCurtain, Benjamin	3740
Morgan, Lizzie	2798	McCurtain, Johnnie	3741
Mosely, Mattie	3231	McCurtain, Cecil	4262
Mosely, Ladonia	3232	McCurtain, Albert Car-	
Mosely, John Wesley	3233	penter	4263
Mosely, Frank	1589	McChristain, Minerva	3995
Mosely, Leona	1590	McChristain, Mary	3997
Morton, Eva	5452	McChristain, Henry	3998
Murphy, Cella	2147	McChristain, Lillie	3999
Murphy, Carrie	2150	McChristain, Tena	4000
Murphy, Lucy	2151	McChristain, Elmore	4001
Murphy, Lennabelle	2152	McDaniel, Curtis	5472
Murphy, Reuben	2889	McDaniel, Samantha	5473
Murphy, Elias	2890	McDaniel, Jesse	2
Murphy, Clarissa	2891	McDaniel, Vinia	3
Murphy, Sealy	4566	McDaniel, Jimmie	4
Murphy, Mary	4570	McDaniel, Henry	5
Murray, Louisa	2637	McDaniel, Henry	162
Murray, Mary J.	2638	McDaniel, Martha	163
Murray, Claude W.	2639	McDaniel, Sarilda	164
Murray, Sampson	2640	McDaniel, Peggy	165
Murray, Lizzie	2668	McDaniel, Rena	166
Murray, Letha	2670	McDonald, Eda	1145
Murray, Emmet	4004	McDonald, Angeline	2210
Murray, Mollie	4005	McDonald, Henry	2212
Murray, Julia	4006	McDonald, Annie	2213
Murray, Isaac	4007	McDonald, Janie	2214
Murray, Gaines	4008	McDonald, Emmet	2215
Murray, Katie	4239	McDonald, Ed	2244
Murray, Joe	4357	McDonald, Mildred	2245
Munn, Israel	2523	McDonald, Florence	2246
Murchison, Pherdelia	3071	McDonald, Hubert	3771
Murchison, Harry H.	3072	McDonald, Woodie	4297
Musgrove, Susan	5226	McDonald, Ida	4503
Musgrove, Henry	5227	McDonald, Eddie	4508
Musgrove, Henrietta	5228	McFarland, D.	4215
McAfee, Andrew	4191	McGuire, Geo.	422
McAfee, Louvetia	4192	McGuire, Sam	423
McAfee, McKinley	4193	McGuire, Sarah	424
McAfee, Terry	4373	McGuire, Amelia	425
McCoy, Susan	1346	McGuire, Jack	426
McCoy, Michael	1347	McGuire, James	427
McCoy, Lizzie	1348	McGuire, Rovilla	428
McCoy, Mary	1349		
McCoy, Henry	1562		
McCoy, Mollie	1563		

Name.	Roll No.	Name.	Roll No.
McGuire, Kitty	429	Nail, Calvin	2063
McGuire, Love	430	Nail, Susan	2124
McGuire, Lemon	479	Nail, Annie	2125
McGuire, Membra	480	Nail, Eck	2126
McGuire, Estella	481	Nail, Simuel	2127
McGuire, Levella	482	Nail, Herbert	3465
McGuire, Annie	2839	Nail, John	3613
McGuire, Sarah	2840	Nail, Birdie	3847
McGee, James	1587	Nail, Ben	3898
McGee, Richmond	2341	Nail, Sam	3899
McGee, Manuel	4019	Nail, Lewis	3900
McGee, Josephine	4327	Nail, Jack	3901
McGee, Rachel	4328	Nail, Ben, Jr.	3902
McGee, Julia	4329	Nail, Sonny	3903
McGee, Jimmie Henry	4812	Nail, Carrie	3904
McGill, Myrtle	4910	Nelson, Rebecca	197
McGilbry, Susan	5545	Nelson, Floyd	198
McKinney, Sam	1282	Nelson, Aaron	199
McKinney, Robert	1387	Nelson, July Ann	200
McKinney, Lila	1388	Nelson, Winnie	1111
McKinney, Zach	1389	Nelson, William	1205
McKinney, Park	1390	Nelson, Evalina	2783
McKinney, Gibson	1391	Nelson, Nancy	5120
McKinney, Oscar	1392	Neighbors, Emma	1585
McKinney, Henry	1393	Neal, Malinda	1943
McKinney, Joshua	1394	Neal, Maud	1944
McKinney, Nancy	1395	Neal, Pearl	1945
McKinney, Breedlove	1410	Neal, Ed	1948
McKinney, Jake	1466	Neal, Columbus	1949
McKinney, Louis	1673	Neill, Ella	3411
McKinney, Bertie	1674	Newton, Lizzie	5332
McKinney, Wesley	2344	Newton, Amandy	5335
McKinney, John	2376	Newton, Rosie	5336
McKinney, Celestine	3206	Newton, Jesse	5528
McKinney, Garfield	3272	Newberry, Aaron	5419
McKinney, Frenchy	3358	Noland, Mariah	511
McKinney, Buster	3966	Noland, Lucy	512
McKinney, Jerry	4401	Noland, Cleveland	513
McKinney, Veny	5308	Noland, Minervia	514
McKinney, Boling	5536	Noland, Inez	515
McKinney, Maudie Lee	5537	Noland, Dixie	755
McKinney, Lillie Bell	5538	Noland, Lottie	509
McKinney, Chloe	5539	Noland, Laney	510
McKinney, Cleo	5540	Noland, Willard	2848
McKinley, Burrell	2942	Noland, Fred Melvin	2849
McKee, Mimy	4093	Noland, Willie	4930
McLendon, Maggie	3601	Nolen, Parthenia	1167
McNeill, Stella	2154	Nolen, Lewis	1168
McNeill, Franceil	2155	Nolen, Gertrude R.	1169
McQuilla, Lizzie	5302	Nolen, Willie	1170
Napoleon, Isham	454	Nolan, Gertie	2482
Napoleon, Anna	455	Norman, Ida	1629
Napoleon, Link	456	Norman, Myrtle	1630
Napoleon, Eli	858	Norman, Ona	1631
Nash, Collins	530	Norman, Jim	1632
Nash, Maude	531	Norman, Charles	1633
Nash, Catherine	532	Norman, Oda	3744
Nash, Fannie	533	Norris, Charlotte	3477
Nash, William	534	Nourole, Elzie	5389
Nash, Otto	535	Nourole, Gertrude	5390
Nash, Georgia	3892	Nunley, Martha	3163
Nash, Frank	3893	Nunley, Katie	3164
Nash, Florence	3895	Nunley, Mary	3165
Nash, Vina	4525	Nunley, Eddie	3166
Nash, Ellen	4527	Nunley, Carie	3167
Nail, Joe	1383	Nunnely, Ada	3886
Nail, Lucy	1384	Nunnely, Melvina	3887
Nail, Joe	1893	Nunnally, Tom	5131
Nail, Clinton	1894	Nunnally, Willie	5132
Nail, Mamie	1895	Nunnally, Sula	5133
Nail, Lennie	1896	Nunnally, Patsy	5328
Nail, Edmond	2008	Nunnally, Clora	5329
Nail, Alex	2027	Nunnally, Jennie	5330
Nail, Rose	2028	Nunnally, Riley	5331
Nail, Lorenzo	2029	Oats, Emma	4806
Nail, Clarence	2030	Oats, Willie	5022
Nail, Claude	2031	Oats, Hattie	5023
Nail, Aurilla	2032	Oliver, Bertha	2443
Nail, Luzena	2033	Olivtr, Rennie	2464
Nail, Irena	2034	Oliver, Vallie Sue	5244
Nail, Mandy	2035	Osborn, Cornelius	2015
Nail, Wilson	2037	Osborn, James	2190
Nail, Asa	2038	Oscar, Howard	3647

Name.	Roll No.	Name.	Roll No.
Owles, Patsy	1316	Perry, Richmond	5200
Owles, Ebby	1317	Perry, Jincy Jane	5280
Owles, Anna	1318	Peyton, Harrison	1946
Owles, Emma	1319	Peyton, Jerome	1947
Owles, Ed	3212	Pearson, Dave	2318
Owles, Abner	4984	Pearson, Gertie	2319
Owens, Sam	1381	Pearson, Mabel	2320
Owens, Tom	2779	Pearson, Gerlena	2321
Owens, Charlotte	2780	Pearson, Herman	2322
Owens, Mollie	2781	Pearson, Ora	2323
Owens, Ida	4208	Pearson, Hazle	2324
Owens, Douglas	4210	Pendleton, Catherine	2696
Owens, Georgia	4378	Pendleton, Maran	2704
Paris, Jane	905	Pendleton, Burtrum	2705
Paris, Maud	906	Pendleton, Bennie	4894
Paris, Lilla	2567	Phelps, Alice	1999
Paris, Willis	2592	Phillips, Wesley	3028
Paris, Nat	2593	Pitchlynn, Millie	171
Patterson, Emma	1527	Pitchlynn, Allen	358
Patterson, Willie	4966	Pitchlynn, Laveda	359
Patterson, Oma	5418	Pitchlynn, Scroggins	360
Parker, Mose	1653	Pitchlynn, Estella	361
Parker, Margaret	3170	Pitchlynn, Ben	410
Parker, Willie	3171	Pitchlynn, Lucy	411
Parker, Andrew	3172	Pitchlynn, Eda	412
Parker, Rosebun	3173	Pitchlynn, Alvin	413
Parker, Mahaly	3834	Pitchlynn, Roselia	414
Parker, Amanda Ethel	3841	Pitchlynn, Allen	415
Parnell, Julia A.	1784	Pitchlynn, Dallas	612
Parnell, Calvin	1785	Pitchlynn, Victoria	613
Parnell, Nathan	1786	Pitchlynn, Garfield	614
Parnell, Gilbert	1787	Pitchlynn, Louis	615
Parnell, Wyatt	1788	Pitchlynn, Fannie	616
Parnell, Herbert	1789	Pitchlynn, Tommy	617
Parnell, Rayford	1790	Pitchlynn, Horace	914
Parnell, Texana	1792	Pitchlynn, Amanda	915
Patton, Frances	2076	Pitchlynn, Ellen	916
Patton, Charles	2077	Pitchlynn, Purdie	917
Patton, Lena	2078	Pitchlynn, Holsey	918
Payton, Millie	2338	Pitchlynn, Alfus	919
Payton, Queenie	5157	Pitchlynn, Anna	920
Partilla, Rebecca	3716	Pitchlynn, Lela	921
Perkins, James	228	Pitchlynn, Winnie	934
Perkins, Louis	262	Pitchlynn, Prince	1455
Perkins, Cleveland	263	Pitchlynn, Mary	1456
Perkins, Ella	264	Pickens, Henry	1003
Perkins, Louis	710	Pickens, Melvina	1005
Perkins, Louis	711	Pickens, Walton	1322
Perkins, Charlie	712	Pickens, Ephriam	1323
Perkins, Charlie	883	Pickens, John	1324
Perkins, Arnold	2878	Pickens, Terry	1325
Perkins, William	2914	Pickens, Aaron	1326
Perkins, Lucinda	2915	Pickens, Green	3967
Perkins, Richard	2916	Pickens, Sarah	3968
Perry, John	1171	Pickens, Inez	3969
Perry, Arthur	1172	Pickens, Perry	4817
Perry, Annie	2153	Pierce, Louis	4529
Perry, Isaac	2241	Pitner, Eliza Ann	5311
Perry, Gerlethy	2242	Pitner, Pres	5312
Perry, James	2243	Pitner, Benjamin H.	5313
Perry, Lester	2248	Pitner, Rena	5314
Perry, Henry	2710	Powell, Minerva	820
Perry, Jesse	2711	Powell, Harrison	2128
Perry, Frank	2712	Powell, George	2939
Perry, Mary Alice	2713	Powell, Nero	4054
Perry, Ruverta	2714	Powell, Wyatt	4167
Perry, Joe	3294	Powell, Dolly Ann	4168
Perry, Levi	3643	Powell, Plez	4169
Perry, Nettie	3644	Powell, Harvey	4170
Perry, Oliver	3650	Powell, Hettie	4171
Perry, James	3651	Powell, Mahaly	4172
Perry, Eugene	3652	Powell, Easter	4176
Perry, Ora	3653	Powell, Delia Jane	4209
Perry, Sarah	4301	Powell, Myrtle	4271
Perry, Malvina	4302	Powell, Henry	4343
Perry, Nettie	4847	Powell, Florida	4365
Perry, Allen	4876	Powell, Josie	4380
Perry, Bessie	4877	Powell, Cornelius	4637
Perry, Ellen	4878	Powell, Celia	4638
Perry, Celie	5010	Powell, Calvin	4639
Perry, Beatrice	5011	Powell, Martha	4786
Perry, Wesley	5012	Powell, Timothy	4787
Perry, Luther	5013	Powell, Mabel	5004

Name.	Roll No.	Name.	Roll No.
Powell, Ericks	5150	Reynolds, Georgia	2741
Powell, Cherry	5151	Reynolds, Lillian	2935
Powell, Billy	5152	Reed, Abram	1910
Powell, Morris	5153	Reed, Emma	1911
Poleon, Frank	2636	Reed, Andrew	1912
Prince, Hickman	1007	Reed, Premium	1913
Prince, Cinda	1008	Reed, Charlie Demas	1914
Prince, Emma	1009	Reed, Caroline	2139
Prince, Leona	1011	Reed, William	2140
Prince, Henrietta	1012	Reed, Charlie	2141
Prince, Josephine	1013	Reed, David	2142
Prince, Sim	1203	Reed, William Owen	2144
Prince, Bettie	3478	Reed, James	2345
Prince, Malinda	3483	Reed, Seresa	3466
Prince, Caroline	4651	Reed, Minerva	4003
Prince, John	4653	Reed, Catherine	4912
Prince, Henry	4654	Reed, Marion	4914
Prince, Henry	4770	Reed, Arthur	4915
Prince, Warrick	5100	Reed, Emmett	4916
Prince, Cordie	5103	Reed, Tommy	4917
Prince, John	5415	Reed, Gertrude	4918
Pratt, Sarah	1176	Reed, Amanda	5145
Pratt, Garfield	1177	Reed, General	5146
Pratt, Lem	1178	Reed, Ella	5147
Pratt, Willie	3169	Reed, Mobile	5148
Pratt, Monroe	3253	Read, Aaron	1929
Pratt, Eliza	3254	Read, Jimmie	1931
Pratt, Dora	3255	Read, Charlie	1940
Pratt, Josephine	3256	Read, Mammie	1941
Pratt, Pearl	3257	Read, Sylva	3475
Pratt, Minnie May	3258	Rector, Clayton	1987
Pratt, James	4868	Reddick, George	2143
Price, Susan	1662	Reddick, Archie	3603
Price, Verney	1663	Record, Laura	3150
Price, Rebecca	3116	Record, Linnie	3734
Price, George	3117	Record, Joanna	5375
Price, Henry	3118	Record, Newton	5376
Price, Raymond L.	3119	Rentie, Arilla	4577
Pryor, Elsie	3186	Reeder, Sophia	4920
Pryor, Leanna	3188	Richards, Thomas	464
Pryor, Georgia	3189	Richards, Catherine	465
Pryor, Ella	3190	Richards, Nora	466
Pryor, Johnny	3191	Richards, Marahle	467
Pryor, Louis	3192	Richards, Mathew	498
Pryor, Herman Garfield	3193	Richards, Earnest	499
Purdy, Raymond	852	Richards, Girtrude	506
Purdy, Siney	2932	Richards, Primis	548
Purdy, George	2933	Richards, Winnie	549
Purdy, Alex	4971	Richards, Cyrus	550
Pursley, Stephen	1664	Richards, John	551
Pulcher, Andrew	1690	Richards, William	553
Pulcher, Tena	1691	Richards, Annie	554
Pulcher, Lutitia	1692	Richards, James	555
Pulcher, Joshua	1693	Richards, Mayhall	556
Pulcher, Simon.	1694	Richards, George	557
Pulcher, Green	1695	Richards, Jordan	2833
Pulcher, Ned	1696	Richards, Laura	2834
Pulcher, Angeline	4737	Richards, Everidge	2835
Pulcher, Clarence	4740	Richards, Serena	2836
Pulcher, William	4741	Richards, Albertie	2837
Pulcher, Sylvia	4742	Richards, Mary	2838
Pulcher, Harriet	4744	Richards, Lycurgus	2846
Pulcher, Georgie	4745	Richards, Wellington	4385
Radford, Elias	363	Richards, Robert	4386
Radford, Dollie	536	Riley, Shepard	824
Radford, Aaron	2843	Riley, Catherine	825
Radford, Margaret	4049	Riley, Virginia	826
Radford, Julia	4050	Riley, Fannie	827
Radford, Oda Ann	4341	Riley, Kizzie	828
Radford, Umpson	4342	Riley, Jenkins	829
Radford, Edward	4652	Riley, Johnson	1206
Railback, Virginia	4664	Riley, Peter	1207
Railback, Rodric	4665	Riley, Richard	1240
Railback, Hattie	4666	Riley, Margaret	1411
Railback, Ophelia	4851	Riley, Garfield	3158
Railback, Gertrude	4852	Riley, Wm. M.	3159
Reeves, Harriett	238	Riley, Annie	3160
Reeves, Tucker	2793	Riley, Isaac	3161
Reeves, Rennie	2794	Riley, Hannah	3162
Reid, Nancy	860	Riley, Jenkin	4059
Reynolds, Isabelle	1268	Riley, Austin	4060
Reynolds, Lou	1525	Riley, Pearlie	4061
Reynolds, Johnnie	1532	Riley, Archie	4062
Reynolds, James	2740	Riley, Eldonia	4063
		Riley, Chancy	4064
		Riley, Luella	4065

Name.	Roll No.
Riley, Phoebe	4066
Riley, Willie Belle	4067
Riley, Jenkin Jr.	4344
Riley, Joanna	4547
Riley, Marcus	4548
Riley, Tony	4549
Riley, Garvin	4550
Riley, Isaac	4551
Riley, Isabelle	4552
Riddle, Pearlie	1441
Riddle, John	2717
Riddle, Stewart	3683
Riddle, Jackson	4303
Riddle, Liza	4631
Riddle, Willie	4846
Riddle, Peter	4848
Riddle, Mun	4849
Richardson, Lucy	2569
Richardson, Richmond	2571
Richardson, Stephen	2572
Richardson, Jennie	5258
Ridge, Estella	2595
Ridge, Willis	2600
Riston, Henry	2691
Rice, America	3888
Rice, Mattie	3889
Rice, Tobitha	4400
Rice, Jesse Davis	4813
Rose, Simmier	665
Rose, Rena	2931
Rose, Jeffie	4213
Rose, Louisa	4217
Rose, Abram	4218
Rose, Joe	4220
Rose, Nina	4222
Rose, Daniel	4223
Rose, Ada	4224
Rose, Jeff	4376
Rose, Willie	4377
Rose, McKinley	5027
Rose, Pearly	5028
Rose, Green	5317
Robinson, Fannie	841
Robinson, Coe	3295
Roebuck, Richard	1065
Roebuck, Virginia	1067
Roebuck, Adeline	1068
Roebuck, Ben	1069
Roebuck, William	1070
Roebuck, Ella	1071
Roebuck, Isaiah	1072
Roebuck, Frances	1073
Roebuck, Bennie	2957
Roebuck, Henry	3112
Roebuck, Louisa	3920
Roebuck, Mattie	3921
Roebuck, James	3922
Roebuck, Garnett	3923
Roebuck, Samuel	3924
Roebuck, Rosa	3925
Rogers, Rice	1521
Rogers, Susie	1546
Rogers, Martha	1595
Rogers, Eliza	3326
Rogers, Nancy	3328
Rogers, Birdie E.	3329
Rogers, Louis	3330
Rogers, Aleck	5439
Rogers, Lizzie	5122
Rogers, John	5137
Rogers, Clarence	5138
Rogers, Clayborne	5139
Rogers, Marian Odessa	5140
Rogers, Maria	5141
Rogers, Andrew	5142
Rogers, Stephen	5143
Rodgers, Rachael	5165
Ross, Frances	1715
Roberts, Ned	2594
Roberts, Mary	2627
Roberts, James	2628
Roberts, Dina	2629
Roberts, Sam P.	2630
Roberts, Allelia	2631
Roberts, Eva	2632
Roberts, Mazie	2633

Name.	Roll No.
Roberts, Ella	3040
Roberts, Eli	3783
Roberts, Mary	3784
Roberts, Cora	3785
Roberts, Ida	3786
Roberts, Simon	3787
Roberts, Saincy	3788
Roberts, Harvey	3789
Roberts, Noraola	3790
Roberts, Jack	3791
Roberts, George	3792
Roberts, Willie	3793
Roberts, Lyman	3794
Roberts, Vester	3795
Roberts, Maud	3796
Roberts, Ben Carter	4304
Roberts, Lumuel	4305
Roberts, Robert	4368
Roberts, Willie	4369
Roberts, Rena	4950
Roberts, Susie	5275
Roby, Hannah	2718
Roberson, Georgia	4558
Roberson, Birdie	4641
Roberson, Jonathan	4642
Roberson, Caddie	4643
Roberson, Annie	4644
Russell, Jensy	1559
Russell, Frank	2448
Russell, Gat	2453
Russell, William	2454
Russell, Malinda	2455
Russell, Voyage	2457
Russell, Carrie	2458
Russell, William Jr.	2459
Russell, Lewins	2460
Russell, Velma	2463
Russell, Elizabeth	2994
Russell, Zilphia	2999
Russell, Edith	3143
Russell, Matilda	3885
Russell, Julia	4540
Russell, Lorenzo	4541
Russell, Mattie	4542
Sakki, Hannah	1481
Sakki, Lina	1482
Sakki, Eliza Ann	1483
Sandridge, Sallie	2535
Sandridge, Dave	2536
Sandridge, Corina	2537
Sandridge, John	2538
Sandridge, Willie	2539
Sams, Aggie	2663
Samuels, Nathaniel	4873
Samuels, Mabel	4874
Scott, Joanna	879
Scott, Rhoda	1076
Scott, Jim	1077
Scott, Pearl	1078
Scott, Violet	1079
Scott, Henry	1080
Scott, Jake	1139
Scott, Minerva	3735
Scott, Jesse	4822
Self, Tandy	1090
Sexton, Patsy	1596
Sexton, Solomon R.	1597
Sexton, Edmund	1598
Sexton, Benjamin	1599
Sexton, Henry	1600
Sexton, Sam	4625
Sexton, Israel	4626
Sexton, Edward	4627
Sexton, Laura	4628
Sexton, Minnie	4629
Sexton, Johnny	4630
Sexton, Willie	4850
Seely, Henry	3641
Seely, Nora	3642
Severe, Nolia	5451
Shoals, Marthella	353
Shoals, Ned	354
Shoals, Mary	438

Name.	Roll No.	Name.	Roll No.
Shoals, Bennie	439	Shoals, Nelson	5057
Shoals, Luther V.	598	Shoals, Dona	5058
Shoals, Cora	757	Shoals, Mattie	5059
Shoals, Mitchell	758	Shoals, Cora	5060
Shoals, Carrie Viola	759	Shoals, Patsy	5061
Shoals, Nova	760	Shoals, Lucretia	5276
Shoals, Pink	836	Shoals, Clinton	5318
Shoals, Josephine	837	Sholes, Margaret	1825
Shoals, Darilla	839	Sholes, Marina	1826
Shoals, Membry	840	Sholes, Cravens	1827
Shoals, Arthur	881	Sholes, Gracie	1837
Shoals, Matthew	882	Sholes, William	1838
Shoals, Susan	939	Sholes, Hannibal	4661
Shoals, Tony	945	Sholes, Victoria	5044
Shoals, Rosa	1765	Sholes, Jordan	5045
Shoals, Dennis	1770	Shelton, Mary A.	864
Shoals, Elnora	2802	Shelton, Martha J.	865
Shoals, Richmond	2825	Shelton, Charley	866
Shoals, Pleas L.	3039	Shelton, Clara	2912
Shoals, Sump	3099	Shields, Green	1086
Shoals, Foster	3100	Shields, Amy	1293
Shoals, John Parker	3101	Shields, Mary Jane	2960
Shoals, Edith	3401	Shields, Arthur	2961
Shoals, Ophelia	3491	Shields, Willie	2962
Shoals, Louis	3499	Shields, Henrietta	2963
Shoals, Edward	3500	Shields, Rose	4414
Shoals, Paralee	3501	Shields, Florence	4831
Shoals, Rosa	3502	Shields, James	5420
Shoals, Lennie	3503	Shield, Jack	5542
Shoals, Sophie	3504	Shephard, Corellas	1553
Shoals, Anderson	3758	Shoat, Annie	2359
Shoals, Philip	3930	Shirley, Callis	2509
Shoals, Wesley	3931	Shirley, Ginsey	2524
Shoals, Josiah	3932	Shirley, Mack	2526
Shoals, Robert	3933	Shaw, Johnnie	3304
Shoals, Joe	4034	Shaw, Geneva	4075
Shoals, Hattie	4094	Shaw, Luanna	4076
Shoals, Johnson	4095	Shaw, Perry	4077
Shoals, H. C.	4096	Shaw, Enos O.	4825
Shoals, Elsie Ann	4097	Shelby, Angeline	5155
Shoals, Jimmie	4098	Shelby, Charley	5158
Shoals, George	4099	Shelby, Joe	5159
Shoals, Louis	4142	Shelby, George	5160
Shoals, Elvira	4157	Shelby, Jim	5161
Shoals, Rose	4174	Simpson, Buck	5491
Shoals, Creassie	4173	Simpson, Berta	5492
Shoals, Alfred	4194	Simpson, Emily	5493
Shoals, Isadore	4195	Simpson, Penny	519
Shoals, Lola	4196	Simpson, Lawyer	520
Shoals, Porter	4197	Simpson, Maud	521
Shoals, Addie	4198	Simpson, Minimon	2587
Shoals, Sarah	4200	Simpson, Lovard	2588
Shoals, Aaron	4366	Simpson, Earley	2589
Shoals, Clarence	4374	Simpson, Lewis	2847
Shoals, Sarah J.	4430	Simpson, Dan	3050
Shoals, Patsy	4433	Simpson, Mazie	3051
Shoals, Martin	4453	Simpson, Wellington	4024
Shoals, Mary	4454	Singleton, Charlotte Ann	781
Shoals, Foster	4455	Singleton, Georgia Ann	782
Shoals, Eliza	4456	Singleton, Tennessee	783
Shoals, Nubbie F.	4457	Simmons, Henrietta	1201
Shoals, Joseph	4458	Simmons, Manuel	1204
Shoals, Robert	4459	Silos, Wesley	2026
Shoals, Mary	4460	Sims, Malinda	3472
Shoals, Elmira	4461	Sims, Gertrude	3473
Shoals, Wilson	4462	Sims, Sarah Bell	3474
Shoals, Alfred	4515	Sifax, Lovey	5430
Shoals, William	4588	Smith, Alonzo	76
Shoals, S. D.	4591	Smith, David	800
Shoals, Elbert D.	4592	Smith, Webster	801
Shoals, Stephen	5426	Smith, Arthur	802
Shoals, James Carter	5427	Smith, Ida	803
Shoals, Gertrude	5526	Smith, Lilly	804
Shoals, William	5527	Smith, Carrie	944
Shoals, Aleck	4593	Smith, George	1112
Shoals, Moses	4594	Smith, Caroline	1130
Shoals, Ada B.	4595	Smith, Elzira	1179
Shoals, James	4753	Smith, Ludie	1184
Shoals, John	4754	Smith, Della	1304
Shoals, Henry	4814	Smith, Oliver	1305
Shoals, Garfield	4889	Smith, Etta	1306
Shoals, Silas	4891	Smith, Mary	1843
Shoals, Lizzie	5031	Smith, Isabella	1845

Name.	Roll No.	Name.	Roll No.
Smith, Eliza Ann	1846	Stewart, William	3114
Smith, Warsaw	1847	Stewart, Sinie	3115
Smith William	1979	Stewart, Jane	3956
Smith, Dixie	2510	Stewart, Mitchell	3957
Smith, Dave	2809	Stewart, David	3958
Smith, Mose	2810	Stewart, Willie	3959
Smith, Aaron	2811	Stewart, Jimmie	3960
Smith, Eli	2812	Stewart, George	3961
Smith, Albert	2813	Stewart, Ella	3962
Smith, Nellie	2814	Stewart, Liza Ann	3963
Smith, Annie	2896	Stewart, Willie	4321
Smith, Warrick	2941	Stewart, Lucinda	904
Smith, Tennessee	2959	Stanley, Joe	1216
Smith, Mary	2786	Stanley, Arthur	1217
Smith, Silvia	3014	Stanley, Phidelia	1218
Smith, Rosa	3140	Stanley, John	1219
Smith, Robert E.	3141	Stanley, Oliver	1220
Smith, Frances	3174	Stanley, Sam	1221
Smith, Lillie	3175	Stanley, Gabriel	3177
Smith, Ollie	3176	Stanley, Sam	3178
Smith, Ada	3709	Stanley, Pearlie	3179
Smith, George	3764	Stanley, George	3180
Smith, Martha	4199	Stanley, Zachariah	4201
Smith, Hettie	4322	Stanley, Hannah	4544
Smith, Porter	4323	Stanley, Tandy	4545
Smith, Lottie	4324	Stanley, Eva	4546
Smith, May Belle	4439	Stanly, Garland	2984
Smith, Phoebe	4585	Stevenson, Silas	1924
Smith, Harry	4705	Stevenson, Abraham	2444
Smith, Ben	4706	Stevenson, Bertha	2472
Smith, Henry	4711	Stevenson, Dave	2484
Smith, Lillie	4712	Stevenson, Joe	2485
Smith, Ernest	4713	Stevenson, Ellis	2487
Smith, Henry	5515	Stevenson, Nelson	2488
Smith, Earl	4714	Stevenson, Santa Anna	2489
Smith, Charles	4862	Stevenson, Lucy	2491
Smith, Liza	5219	Stevenson, Rena	2492
Smith, Lizzie	5220	Stevenson, Billy	2500
Smith, Joseph	5221	Stevenson, Bankston	2501
Smith, Myrtle	5222	Stevenson, Eliza	2502
Smith, Pearline	5223	Stevenson, Lucy	2503
Smith, Ida	5224	Stevenson, Robert	2504
Smith, Ellis	5225	Stevenson, Standwatie	2511
Smith, Eliza Ann	5363	Stevenson, Cora	2514
Smith, Gardner	5364	Stevenson, Henderson	2522
Smith, Ira	5365	Stevenson, Polly	2525
Smith, Cornell	5366	Stevenson, Cornelius	2527
Smith, Robert	5367	Stevenson, Johnson	2708
Smith, Claudius	5394	Stevenson, Ben	2764
Smith, Maud	5395	Stevenson, Orilla	2991
Smallwood, Filmore	4881	Stevenson, Willie	2993
Smallwood, Jasper	4882	Stevenson, Carser	3027
Smallwood, Clara	4883	Stephenson, Alice	1930
Smallwood, Emma	4884	Stephenson, Cashey	1932
Smallwood, Evalina	4885	Stephenson, George	4447
Spring, Levi	1406	Stakohaka, Willie	1950
Spring, James N.	1512	Star, Anna	2365
Spring, Leo Bennett	1513	Starr, Willie	3321
Spring, Lilly	1515	Striblin, Ellen	3484
Spring, Frederick	1516	Striblin, Lena	3486
Spring, Rebecca	3312	Stribling, Annie	4675
Spring, Beatrice	4257	Stribling, Edna	4676
Spring, Oliver W.	4258	Stribling, Mary A.	4677
Spring, Nettie	4259	Stribling, Josiah	4859
Spring, William Dewey	4260	Stribling, Lorella	4860
Spencer, Mat	2238	Stubblefield, Callie	3537
Stephens, Bettie	251	Stubblefield, Virginia	3538
Stephens, Emeline	253	Suton, Minerva	2333
Stephens, James	254	Suton, Edmond	2334
Stephens, Katie	255	Suton, Edward	2335
Stephens, Effie	256	Sutton, Clarence	4896
Stephens, Roxy	257	Sutton, Henry	4897
Stephens, Winnie T.	258	Sutton, Ellsworth	4898
Stephens, Ollie	490	Sutton, Mamie	4899
Strong, Alice	791	Sutton, Percy	4900
Stewart, Van	871	Sutton, Scottie	4901
Stewart, Malvina	1327	Taylor, Winnie	2007
Stewart, Amanda	1328	Taylor, Sarah	2546
Stewart, Hubbard	1329	Taylor, Lonnie	2547
Stewart, Chaney	1508	Taylor, Robart	2548
Stewart, Willie	1568	Taylor, Birtie	2549
Stewart, William	1583	Taylor, Lizzie	2716
Stewart, Emma	1584	Taylor, John	3016
Stewart, Willie	1677	Taylor, Andrew	3694
Stewart, George	1697	Taylor, Henry	3695
Stewart, Frank	1698	Taylor, James	3696

Name.	Roll No.	Name.	Roll No.
Taylor, Morris	3697	Thomas, Josie	2005
Taylor, Beatrice	3698	Thomas, Sarah	2541
Taylor, Harriet	3699	Thomas, George	2542
Taylor, Salina	4913	Thomas, Ivory	2543
Teel, Carter	4164	Thomas, Nancy	3631
Thompson, Jennie	68	Thomas, Bessie	3662
Thompson, Willie	69	Thomas, Elie	5333
Thompson, May Belle	74	Thurman, Ellen	4432
Thompson, Mary	129	Tims, James	3219
Thompson, Lela	130	Tims, Israel	3220
Thompson, Sylvana	219	Tins, Rosy	3222
Thompson, Robert	433	Tims, Juanita	3223
Thompson, Joe	1468	Tinkshell, Frances	3864
Thompson, Josephine	1469	Tinkshell, Monroe	4307
Thompson, Lee	1470	Tinkshell, Seabell R	4308
Thompson, Ben	1471	Tinkshell, Mollie	4313
Thompson, Cornelius	1472	Titus, Tiny	5457
Thompson, Susan	1473	Timpson, Osborn	5533
Thompson, Mary Jane	1474	Triplett, Felix	1569
Thompson, Caeser	1475	Triplett, Arthur	3280
Thompson, Phoebe	1476	Tuggle, Cora	733
Thompson, Sarah	1477	Turner, Milton	1617
Thompson, Squire	1478	Turner, Emma	3363
Thompson, Armer	1479	Turner, Frank	3364
Thompson, Ben	1503	Turner, Spencer	3365
Thompson, Caroline	1504	Turner, Gatha	3366
Thompson, Hence	1505	Turner, Andrew	3367
Thompson, Belle	1506	Turner, John	3368
Thompson, Levi	1507	Turner, Mary	3382
Thompson, Spence	1614	Tucker, Nip	4018
Thompson, Louisa	1615	Tyson, Ruffin	792
Thompson, Joseph Jr.	1616	Tyson, Jasper	793
Thompson, Jim	2056	Tyson, Watson	798
Thompson, Rachael	2057	Tyson, Pricilla	799
Thompson, Joe	2066	Tyson, Jasper	878
Thompson, Dave	2067	Tyson, George	2544
Thompson, Martin	2068	Tyson, William	3262
Thompson, Richard	2069	Tyner, Henry	2486
Thompson, Henry	2070	Tyler, Dora	2720
Thompson, Alice	2071	Tyler, James William	2725
Thompson, Willie	2072	Tyler, Floyd	2726
Thompson, Nancy	2073	Valliant, Willie	4520
Thompson, Nora	2074	Vaughn, Anna	4907
Thompson, Lena	2075	Vina, Winnie	113
Thompson, Ella	2079	Vina, John	115
Thompson, Mandy	2133	Vina, Paul	116
Thompson, Henry	2249	Vina, Lizzie	117
Thompson, Harrison	2250	Vinson, Alfred	1355
Thompson, Wm.	2251	Vinson, Violet	1803
Thompson, Maria	2252	Vinson, Johnson	1804
Thompson, Robt.	2253	Vinson, Robert	3234
Thompson, Ida	3194	Vinson, Evangelist	3235
Thompson, Joseph	332	Vinson, Eli	3236
Thompson, Aleck	3359	Vinson, Monroe	3237
Thompson, Pink	3978	Vinson, Martin	3238
Thompson, Lucy	3979	Vinson, Harry	3239
Thompson, Eddy	3981	Vinson, Pauline	3240
Thompson, Walter	3982	Vinson, Maggie	3241
Thompson, Jimmie	3983	Vinson, Rosaline	3242
Thompson, Freeman	3984	Vinson, Vinson	3243
Thompson, Richmond	4009	Vinson, Charles	3369
Thompson, Harrison	4010	Vinson, Mollie	3552
Thompson, Hayes	4011	Vinson, Sammie	3553
Thompson, Celia	4033	Vinson, Claudie	3554
Thompson, Jack	4039	Vinson, James	3555
Thompson, Josiah	4040	Vinson, Linard Cliford.	3556
Thompson, Lucinda	4041	Vinson, Henry	4272
Thompson, Walter	4110	Vinson, Bennie	5315
Thompson, Lorena	4261	Vinson, Willie	5316
Thompson, Joe	4269	Vinson, Eddie	5383
Thompson, Anderson	4747	Virgil, Nancy	4248
Thompson, Betsy	4780	Voyd, William	1380
Thompson, Sid	4798	Voyd, Mary Inez	3264
Thompson, Albert	4799	Voyd, Bernice	3265
Thompson, Henry	4800	Voyd, Will Lee	3266
Thompson, Mose	4869	Voyd, Junia V.	3267
Thompson, Dan	5005	Voyd, Ezkiel	3268
Thompson, Nettie	5006	Walker, Ida Bell	2937
Thompson, Pomp	5442	Walker, Rosy	145
Thompson, Willie	5486	Walker, Willis	153
Thompson, Burt	5007	Walker, Sallie	154
Thompson, Florence	5008	Walker, Liddy	372
Thompson, Elmer	5009	Walker, Houston	373
Thompson, Elnora	5388	Walker, Andrew	374
Thomas, Willie	1020	Walker, Jimmie	375
Thomas, I. C.	1021	Walker, Arthur	376

Name.	Roll No.	Name.	Roll No.
Walker, Mary	601	Ward, Lilly	5179
Walker, Rutha	935	Ward, Henry	5180
Walker, Jesse	967	Walls, Emily	990
Walker, Maria	968	Walls, Mary	3031
Walker, Mack	969	Walls, Zenolia	3032
Walker, Scott	970	Wand, Frances	302
Walker, Dickson	971	Walton, Beff '	998
Walker, Leroy	972	Walton, Samuel	3747
Walker, Everette	973	Walton, Sallie	3748
Walker, Alonzo	1701	Walton, Houston	3749
Walker, Velt	1702	Walton, Sam Jr.	3750
Walker, Jimmie	5499	Waldron, Celeste	1126
Walker, Oliver	5500	Waldron, Jesse	1127
Walker, Myrtie	2174	Waldron, George	1128
Walker, Dove	2175	Waldron, Henry	1142
Walker, Celie	2176	Waldron, Sophy	1143
Walker, Mabel	2177	Waldron, Jeff	3103
Walker, Ellen	1700	Waldron, George	5501
Walker, Amon	2178	Waldron, Burba	4246
Walker, Charles	2387	Wade, Aleck	1724
Walker, James	2403	Wade, Byington	1725
Walker, Mary	2790	Wade, Clayton	1726
Walker, Victoria	3073	Wade, Joshua	2390
Walker, Willie	3720	Waters, Robert	1748
Walker, Robert	4734	Waters, James	5337
Walker, Elizabeth	4756	Waters, Alfred	5338
Walker, Gertrude	4757	Watson, John	1752
Walker, Emma	4758	Watson, Maria A.	1753
Walker, Roxy Ann	4985	Wagoner, Columbus	1972
Walker, Emily	4986	Wagoner, Isom	1973
Walker, Olive	4987	Wagoner, Annie	4998
Walker, Mary	4999	Walters, Ida	2045
Walker, Joe	5000	Walters, Celia	2441
Walker, Willie	5001	Walter, Louisa	3147
Walker, Lucinda	5002	Walzer, Alemeta	4251
Warren, Jennie	283	Ware, Nancy	4383
Warren, Charlie	284	Ware, George	4827
Warren, Harriet	2329	Ware, Sam	4828
Washington, Bathya	491	Warner, Fred	4729
Washington, Lawyer	516	Walford, Henry	4791
Washington, Ann	517	Walford, Jimmie	4790
Washington, Mose	518	Walford, Albert	4792
Washington, Annie	522	Warrior, Angeline	4911
Washington, Effie G.	1588	Webster, Manuel	29
Washington, Caroline	2366	Webster, Lewis	30
Washington, Susan	2883	Webster, Louisa	31
Washington, Rosy	2884	Webster, Troy	5163
Washington, Lawyer	2885	Wellington, Jerry	611
Washington, Harvey	2886	Wellington, Mariah	730
Washington, Laurinda	3247	Welch, Jimmie P.	4743
Washington, Ada	3325	Webb, Sylvia	5307
Washington, Rebecca	4068	Webb, Chester	5309
Washington, Elizabeth	4118	West, Ella	5445
Washington, Clayburn	4119	White, Edmond	1624
Washington, Sarah	4120	White, Louisa	1799
Washington, Ida	4121	White, Beatrice	1800
Washington, Charley	4122	White, Ether	2164
Washington, Melvina	2367	White, Forbus	2168
Ward, Harman	923	White, Bennie	2201
Ward, Sampson	1881	White, Eddie	2202
Ward, Solomon	1882	White, Curtie	2203
Ward, Monroe	1883	White, Lonnie	2205
Ward, Mattie	1884	White, Clemmie	2231
Ward, Emma	1885	White, Bessie	2236
Ward, Amos	1886	White, Nancy	3341
Ward, Edmund	1887	White, Dewey	3342
Ward, Willie	1888	White, Fannie	5014
Ward, Birdie	1889	White, Mary	5260
Ward, Mary	2059	White, Jim	5262
Ward, Walter	2134	White, Napoleon	5263
Ward, Maggie	2211	White, Naomi	5264
Ward, Lillie	2216	White, Frank	5266
Ward, Henry	2715	White, Bertha	5306
Ward, Susan	2734	White, Irving	5478
Ward, Howard	3614	White, Sam	5479
Ward, Hattie	3615	White, Robert	5480
Ward, Melia	3616	White, Lilly	5524
Ward, Sloan	3632	White, Harry	5525
Ward, Jane	3533	Whitaker, Patsy	2921
Ward, Johnnie	3534	Whitaker, Irene	2923
Ward, Sophia	5176	Whitaker, Elvira	2924
Ward, Jesse	5177	Whitby, Alex	5199
Ward, Tandy	5178	Williams, Ida	14

Name.		Roll No.	Name.		Roll No.
Williams,	Ella	15	Williams,	Lizzie	2765
Williams,	Ivy	16	Williams,	Rosa Lee	2766
Williams,	Fannie	17	Williams,	Angeline	2767
Williams,	Lizzie	18	Williams,	Napoleon	2768
Williams,	Mary	19	Williams,	Thomas	2769
Williams,	Alfred	27	Williams,	Hettie	2770
Williams,	Edith	28	Williams,	John	2844
Williams,	Eda	93	Williams,	Sallie	2850
Williams,	Albert	94	Williams,	Jennie	2903
Williams,	Major	95	Williams,	Virginia	2936
Williams,	Lena	96	Williams,	Matilda	2952
Williams,	Alice	229	Williams,	Paschal	3052
Williams,	Zebadee	230	Williams,	Dora	3053
Williams,	Mollie	231	Williams,	Vinie	3195
Wilialms,	Relle	232	Williams,	Frances	3412
Williams,	Clay	233	Williams,	Odessa May	3430
Williams,	Joseph	271	Williams,	Charlie	3439
Williams,	Malindy	417	Williams,	Dick	3594
Williams,	Ben	418	Williams,	Louisa	3684
Williams,	Sanders	419	Williams,	Mary	3688
Williams,	Levi	420	Williams,	Angeline	3769
Williams,	Aaron	421	Williams,	Lucinda	3799
Williams,	Cora	494	Williams,	Addie	3800
Williams,	George	496	Williams,	Jesse S. R.	3801
Williams,	Clarissa	497	Williams,	Lela	3802
Williams,	Emma	559	Williams,	Wallace	3803
Williams,	Porter	560	Williams,	Laura	3992
Williams,	Farris	561	Williams,	Phoebe	4051
Williams,	Tony	844	Williams,	Julius	4052
Williams,	Bettie	845	Williams,	Ida	4053
Williams,	Hettie	956	Williams,	Pinky	4139
Williams,	George P.	962	Williams,	Hunt	4140
Williams,	Charley	1029	Williams,	Tina	4141
Williams,	Rosa	1030	Williams,	Luther	4240
Williams,	Sarah Jane	1087	Williams,	Frances	4285
Williams,	Simon	1096	Williams,	Mack	4289
Williams,	Lizzie	5475	Williams,	Salina	4353
Williams,	Tommie	5513	Williams,	Elvira	4359
Williams,	Theoda	5516	Williams,	Charley	4442
Williams,	Corine	5544	Williams,	Charles	4443
Williams,	Virginia	1320	Williams,	Garfield	4445
Williams,	Rufus	1356	Williams,	Ida	4446
Williams,	Edna	1519	Williams,	Susan	4465
Williams,	Nathaniel	1520	Williams,	Mary	4492
Williams,	Josephine	1650	Williams,	Isaac	4493
Williams,	Jim	1651	Williams,	Simon	4576
Williams,	Henry	1652	Williams,	Pearlie	4586
Williams,	Essy	1689	Williams,	Luvinia	4646
Williams,	Edmond	1749	Williams,	Dixie	4690
Williams,	Lillie	1750	Williams,	Charity	4691
Williams,	Raymond	1751	Williams,	Charlie	4692
Williams,	Emma	1836	Williams,	Roland	4693
Williams,	Anna L.	1839	Williams,	Patsy	4819
Williams,	Andy	2083	Williams,	Jesse	4823
Williams,	Emma	2084	Williams,	Elzada	4824
Williams,	Thomas	2112	Williams,	Thomas	4834
Williams,	Sampson	2120	Williams,	Orra	4922
Williams,	Eldora	2121	Williams,	Peter	4923
Williams,	Bertha	2122	Williams,	Adge	4924
Williams,	Sallie	2123	Williams,	Lillie	4989
Williams,	Joana	2170	Williams,	Nellie	5046
Williams,	Elizabeth	2172	Williams,	Sam	5067
Williams,	Martha	2230	Williams,	Charley	5068
Williams,	Richard	2232	Williams,	Lee	5069
Williams,	Ida B.	2233	Williams,	Maxey	5070
Williams,	Cloria L.	2234	Williams,	Hugh	5071
Williams,	Rosana	2235	Williams,	Myrtle	5072
Williams,	Mack	2394	Williams,	Addene	5073
Williams,	Francis	2405	Wilson,	Malinda	2643
Williams,	Mattie	2406	Wilson,	Charles	2644
Williams,	Raford	2407	Wilson,	Serena	2645
Williams,	Anna	2408	Wilson,	Jeff	2646
Williams,	Belle	2449	Wilson,	Mary	2647
Williams,	Wade	2450	Wilson,	Banks	2648
Williams,	Mary	2451	Wilson,	Lydia	2649
Williams,	Henrietta	2452	Wilson,	Harvey	2650
Williams,	Claude	2473	Wilson,	Thomas	2651
Williams,	Jesse	2475	Wilson,	Raman	2652
Williams,	Edna	2476	Wilson,	Margaret Ann	2665
Williams,	Saint Paul	2477	Wilson,	John	2666
Williams,	Hepsy	2479	Wilson,	Irving	2796
Williams,	John E.	2508	Wilson,	Blanche	2799
Williams,	Jennie	2550	Wilson,	Joe	3183

Name.	Roll No.	Name.	Roll No.
Wilson, Nettie	3184	Willis, Lila	4144
Wilson, Emma	3185	Willis, Geo. Cleveland	4356
Wilson, Jinsy	3248	Willis, Emma	4449
Wilson, Cora	3343	Willis, Henry	4450
Wilson, Albert	3479	Willis, Robert	4451
Wilson, Laurey	3344	Willis, Henrietta	4452
Wilson, Walter	3381	Willis, Serena	4498
Wilson, Harriett	3635	Willis, Britt	4501
Wilson, Ellen	3637	Wimbley, Rachel	912
Wilson, Elby	3638	Wimbley, Sam	913
Wilson, Bertha	3639	Wimbley, Fred	2926
Wilson, Belle	3713	Windham, Hense	1543
Wilson, Alonzo	3951	Windham, Jennie	4265
Wilson, Ransa	3952	Windham, Mitchell	4266
Wilson, Hattie	4379	Wilkins, Daisy	3104
Wilson, Richmond	4424	Wilkins, Laura	3107
Wilson, Clayton	4425	Wilkins, Bettie	3149
Wilson, Margaret	4474	Wilburn, Lorena	3526
Wilson, Pearlie	4479	Wilburn, Sophia	3527
Wilson, Frances	4480	Wilburn, Arthur	3528
Wilson, Cora	4481	Wire, Mandy	4126
Wilson, Lizzie	4553	Wire, William	4127
Wilson, Eddie	4554	Wire, Isom	4128
Wilson, Harrison	4555	Wire, Peter	4129
Wilson, Shub	4556	Wire, Calvin	4130
Wilson, Eddie	4963	Wire, Hattie	4131
Wilson, Minerva	5111	Workman, Laura	40
Wilson, Eddie	5112	Workman, Firdnan	48
Wilson, Solomon	5113	Woods, Anna	80
Wilson, George	5114	Woods, Lola	81
Wilson, Ida	5115	Woods, Hamp	167
Wilson, Joe	5116	Woods, Dennis	431
Wilson, Frances	5117	Woods, Mindy	432
Wilson, Mary	5119	Woods, Edic	434
Wilson, Willie	286	Woods, Alford	435
Wilson, Lena	287	Woods, Frank	436
Wilson, Zack	288	Woods, Dennis Jr.	437
Wilson, Zophy	289	Woods, Emma	492
Wilson, Louis	290	Woods, Clarissa	641
Wilson, Lilly	291	Woods, Gilly	642
Wilson, Levi	292	Woods, Preston	643
Wilson, Grant	293	Woods, Emanuel	644
Wilson, Joel	294	Woods, Evalena	645
Wilson, Ardelia	295	Woods, Prentiss	646
Wilson, Johnny	308	Woods, Delbut	647
Wilson, Sylvania	309	Woods, Emma	648
Wilson, William Bryan	310	Woods, Carrie	649
Wilson, Cephus	311	Woods, Jennie	650
Wilson, Simeon	312	Woods, Jimmie	2823
Wilson, Aleck	701	Woods, Luvinie	2824
Wilson, John	702	Woods, Lucy	2845
Wilson, Cherry	703	Woods, Bettie	2857
Wilson, George	1028	Woods, Idella	2964
Wilson, Louisa	1034	Woods, Ida	3313
Wilson, Annie	1035	Woods, Henrietta	3314
Wilson, Gertrude	1036	Woods, Jimmie	3315
Wilson, James	1037	Woods, Esther	3316
Wilson, Elon Franklin	1038	Woods, Tena	4165
Wilson, Sarah	1066	Woods, Oliver H.	4166
Wilson, Wheeler	1131	Woods, George	5240
Wilson, Aaron	1132	Woods, Aleck	5476
Wilson, Delia	1133	Wortham, Hattie	157
Wilson, Thomas	1134	Wortham, Ethel	161
Wilson, Daniel	1135	Wortham, Amanda	1193
Wilson, Johnny	1136	Wortham, Mary	1194
Wilson, Jim	1241	Wortham, Annie	1195
Wilson, Bud	1720	Wortham, William	2899
Wilson, Katie	2218	Wortham, Enoch	2900
Wilson, Eddie	2220	Wortham, Margaret	2901
Wilson, Blaine	2221	Wortham, Dick	2902
Wilson, Priscilla	2222	Wortham, Parthenia	5535
Wilson, Blanche	2223	Wortham, Henry C.	4242
Wilson, Wade	2224	Wooten, Sallie	4615
Willis, Mitchell	175	Wooten, Beatrice	4616
Willis, Rose	991	Wooten, Everett R.	4617
Willis, Ruth	993	Wooten, Prentis Bunion	4845
Willis, Frances	994	Wright, Ruthy	1010
Willis, Cora	995	Wright, Robert	1642
Willis, Thomas	996	Wright, Betsy	1643
Willis, Walter	997	Wright, Modessa	1644
Willis, Emma	2938	Wright, Luvinia	1645
Willis, John	3949	Wright, Essie	1648
Willis, Joe	4143	Wright, Mose	2087

Name.	Roll No.	Name.	Roll No.
Wright, Nancy	2282	Wright, Estella	5170
Wright, Abram	2893	Wright, Alex	5171
Wright, Ed	3324	Wright, Sam	5172
Wright, Henry	3362	Wright, Louise	5173
Wright, Cornelius	3571	Wright, Ellen	5211
Wright, Willie	3583	Wright, Peggy	5212
Wright, Lou	3595	Wright, Ed	5213
Wright, Charlie	3596	Wright, Hannah	5214
Wright, Henrietta	3597	Wright, Florence	5215
Wright, Eli	3598	Wright, Moses	5216
Wright, Arthur	3599	Wright, Ezekiel	5217
Wright, Willie	3600	Wright, Laura Belle	5273
Wright, Mollie	3686	Wright, Eliza	5543
Wright, Mary	3687	Young, Dick	1242
Wright, Martin	3797	Young, Maria	1243
Wright, Millard	3798	Young, Amanda	1244
Wright, Sam	4035	Young, William	1245
Wright, Willie	4036	Young, Henry	1246
Wright, Betsy Jr.	4268	Young, Irella	1247
Wright, Levi	4726	Young, Sarah	1248
Wright, Alf	5167	Young, Henrietta	2674
Wright, Jim	5168	Young, Ceasor	2680
Wright, Floyd	5169	Yocubby, Susan	2988

INDEX TO
MINOR CHOCTAW FREEDMEN.

Name.	Roll No.	Name.	Roll No.
Cubit, Lizzie	69	Harris, Robert	250
Cubit, Carrie	264	Harris, Bob	271
Culver, Rodric	15	Harris, Dasy	272
Culver, Addie May	177	Harris, Lizzie	301
Cutchlo, Henry Jr.	241	Harris, Lulla	326
Cutchlo, Edward	242	Harris, Willie	414
Cutchlo, Roy	243	Harris, Velmore	441
Dana, Alburta	26	Harrison, Leo	269
Dana, Bessie	27	Hampton, Mary	270
Daney, Massey	445	Hampton, Lizzie Leona	444
Dick, Bentley	313	Hawkins, Lucinda	325
Douglass, Pearlie Lee	192	Henderson, Panther	254
Douglass, Hadley	193	Henderson, Celestine	327
Douglas, Purline	381	Henry, Clara	336
Ducket, Wallace	145	Hilliard, Lurrena	373
Ducket, Evereline	151	Hills, Pearley	389
Eights, George	437	Hogan, Weetor	268
Eubanks, Beulah	93	Horton, Burnett T.	314
Eubanks, Brunett	94	Hundy, Edna	44
Everidge, Parker	352	Hundy, Alfred	45
Everidge, Josie May	420	Hutchins, Myrtle	101
Everidge, Lillie	421	Hutchins, Bertha	102
Farris, Howdy	297	Hughes, Essie	165
Farris, Willie	323	Hyatt, Glenn	328
Farris, Burney	324	Jackson, Daisy U.	36
Factory, Leander	248	Jackson, Henry	77
Fields, William	16	Jackson, Edward Earl	79
Fields, Lilly Beil	96	Jackson, Julius Joshua	80
Fields, May Bell	217	Jackson, Bertha	105
Fields, Vestie	218	Jackson, Jesse	353
Fields, Benjamin Frank-		Jackson, Carry	374
lin	386	Jackson, James Henry	401
Finley, Cally	294	James, Earl Lee	103
Finley, Annie	295	James, Maria Bell	104
Fisher, Henry	424	James, Edward	187
Flack, John Henry	361	James, Mary Etta	188
Flack, Eugene	246	James, Isabell	199
Flack, Wesley	360	James, Gurletha	359
Fortune, Hastings An-		James, Dora	416
drew	159	Jacobs, Susie Ann	400
Fortune, Evans Easton	160	Jeffres, Sammy	262
Folsom, Griff	215	Jeffres, Ida Lee	267
Folsom, Fred	216	Jones, Walter	46
Folsom, Hattie	363	Jones, Elzora	164
Folsom, McKinley	409	Jones, Rosa Lee	244
Freeman, John	8	Jones, Lillie Lee	351
Freeman, Rosie Lee	442	Jones, Crenner	256
Franklin, Rossetta	33	Johnson, Viola	78
Franklin, Evilene	34	Johnson, Lola Ann	106
Franklin, Ethel	95	Johnson, Maud	107
Franklin, Effie	219	Johnson, Guss	108
Franklin, Edgar	220	Johnson, Viola	163
Franklin, Adlissie	253	Johnson, Smitha	195
Franklin, Ora	425	Johnson, Inizza	196
Franklin, William	426	Johnson, Lona B.	197
Franklin, Wirt	427	Johnson, Parlie	198
Franklin, Frederick	430	Johnson, Annie	273
Franklin, Videl	446	Johnson, Langres	364
Franklin, Adella	447	Johnson, Gussie	404
Franklin, Ether Mary	453	Justice, Lubirda	111
Frazier, Harry	260	Keel, Rosetta	81
Frazier, Curley	261	Kemp, Lou Venia	178
Fulsom, Ora	391	Kemp, Viola	179
Gables, Birdie	58	Kirk, George, Jr.	208
Gardner, Donie Ester	99	Knowles, Margaretta	184
Gardner, Green	74	Knowles, Hettie May	185
Galbert, Florena	200	Knowles, King	186
Gary, Wilson	251	Larkin, Pelinie	82
Gary, Golatha	252	Lawson, Jimmie	322
Gibson, Robert Estella	75	Lee, Addie May	57
Gibson, Silvester Jr.	97	Lewis, Laurel	83
Gibson, Ward	98	Lewis, Sallie	366
Gibson, Mirvan	415	Lewis, Dennis	367
Gordon, Frances	100	Lewis, Eliza	368
Green, Hattie	255	Lewis, Eva	369
Green, Oscar	265	Lewis, Jennie May	394
Green, Jacob	355	Ligon, Eliza Ann	191
Green, E. M.	423	Littlejohn, Ose	194
Grundy, Osceola	371	Littlejohn, Pink	209
Grundy, Johnie O.	372	Littlejohn, William C.	330
Hall, Ofelia	35	Lowery, Tishey Lee	112
Hall, Floyed Ellwood	149	Lowery, Allen	113
Harris, Arthur	249	Low, Katy	114

Name.	Roll No.
Lovelace, Leuranda	329
Lovelace, Susana	331
Luttrell, Angeline	382
Luttrell, Zora May	383
Maxwell, Rosa	84
Maxwell, Mellnee Artiemisy	210
Mathis, Roy	85
Manning, Butler	274
Mansfield, Henry	282
Minner, Zela	28
Minner, Cornelia	245
Milton, Charlie Walker	115
Miller, Emily	290
Miller, Jessie	465
Mosely, Herman	56
Moore, Orebel	153
Moore, Bessie	283
Moore, Ruby	332
Moore, Hazel	333
Munn, Willie Joseph	334
Murray, Adie	464
McCoy, Charlotte	286
McCoy, Booker T.	443
McDaniel, Burton	18
McDaniel, Nona	213
McGuire, Lottie	211
McGuire, Elmira	212
McGuire, McGaina	408
Nash, Myra Ann	257
Neals, Harry Sullivan	190
Neighbors, Hazel	348
Neighbors, Curtis	349
Neighbors, Ernar	350
Noland, Moses, Jr.	221
Nolen, Pearlie	418
Norwood, Kittie	317
Owles, George Dewey	276
Parker, David	222
Parker, Fannie	335
Pearson, Ethel	1
Pearson, Willie May	2
Pendleton, Exie	42
Pendleton, Rozel	183
Perry, Artvee R.	154
Perry, Clara	291
Perry, Leah	292
Petty, Frank Lee	189
Powell, Ester	410
Powell, Panzy	411
Price, Sarah	116
Pratt, Bessie	318
Pratt, Arabella	319
Pulcher, Ezekial	223
Pulcher, Elsworth	224
Railback, Mamie	23
Railback, Leona	24
Radford, Florida	120
Reed, Hassan	14
Reeves, Della	277
Richards, Eller	117
Richards, Roman	118
Riddle, Joseph	119
Riddle, Edgar	417
Riley, Sallie	225
Riley, James	226
Ridge, Leaford	299
Roberts, Talmage	40
Roberts, Hattie	41
Roberts, Charley	55
Roberts, DeLora Belle	181
Roberts, Etha	182
Roberts, Elree	227
Roberts, Theodore Roosevelt	365
Rogers, Lizzie	86
Rogers, Frank	89
Rogers, Johnie	337
Rogers, Dora	338
Rogers, Nettie	339
Rosemond, Gurither	88
Russell, Henry	370
Russell, Gracie	388

Name.	Roll No.
Russell, Pallecy	405
Samuels, Winetha	121
Samuels, George H.	228
Sanders, Cristena	147
Sanders, Jack Herman	148
Scott, Elizabeth	9
Scott, Lena	390
Shields, Henry	11
Shields, Ida	470
Shields, William	471
Shoals, Eardest	19
Shoals, Gertice	20
Shoals, Jessie James	21
Shoals, Luiretta	22
Shoals, Lula	170
Shoals, Lewis, Jr.	303
Shoals, Clara	321
Shoals, Fred	429
Shelby, Cornelius	150
Shirley, Jensie	461
Sherley, Cathil	462
Sinclair, Ertha M.	152
Sinclair, Alvin	354
Simpson, Ingle	463
Smith, Frederick Douglas	362
Smith, Mary Elizabeth	392
Smith, Anna M.	412
Spring, Grady Porter	166
Stevenson, Jincie	173
Stevenson, Leford	287
Stevenson, Banks	436
Stevenson, Lela	458
Stevenson, Fannie	459
Stahaka, Queenie	438
Taylor, Eveline	51
Taylor, Calvin	50
Taylor, Helen	52
Thomas, Robert Walker	275
Thompson, Charley Leroy	37
Thompson, Duey	298
Thurman, Ada	122
Thurman, Samuel L.	375
Tinkshell, Lula	49
Tilford, Andrew	53
Tilford, Alfonzo	54
Turner, Robert	39
Vinson, Willie May	406
Vinson, George	387
Voyd, Rosa Lee	48
Ward, Fred	31
Ward, Sammie	398
Washington, George	37
Walker, Rena	123
Walker, Wilmer	124
Walker, Ivey May	125
Walker, Turner	126
Walker, Emles Hosey	127
Warren, Dalia	239
Warren, Ora	347
Waters, Jimmie	384
Waters, Flora	385
Webster, Henry	169
White, Ester	38
White, Willa L. D.	128
White, Surrender W.	165
Williams, Henry	10
Williams, Gracie	90
Williams, Merrel L.	167
Williams, Lefert	174
Williams, Alberter	175
Williams, Sam	229
Williams, Minnie Maola	279
Williams, Theodore	285
Williams, Rosbell	289
Williams, Elnorah	376
Williams, Ed	377
Williams, Georgie	393
Williams, Nellie	432
Willis, Carrie	91
Willis, Elias	144
Win, Luverna	132

Name.	Roll No.	Name.	Roll No.
Wilson, Cornelia	320	Workman, Virgal	130
Wilson, Henry	402	Workman, Booker T.	131
Wilson, George	403	Woford, Lee	413
Wilson, Ella	451	Wright, David	129
Wilson, Elmus	452	Wright, Leroy	143
Wooten, Archristful	17	Young, Izora	29
Woods, Claude	278	Young, Thomas	30
Woods, Odessa	284	Younger, Willie L.	172
Woods, George C.	92		

Name.	Roll No.	Name.	Roll No.
Bob, Morris	250	Cooper, Janie	59
Bob, Sallie	336	Cooper, Susie	60
Bob, Willis	509	Cooper, Georgie	61
Bob, Betsie	510	Cooper, James	587
Bob, Johnnis	512	Cooper, Annie	588
Bob, Johnnie	665	Cooper, Lonnie	589
Bob, Martha	666	Cooper, Nancy	590
Bob, Mollie	704	Cooper, Mary	591
Bob, Nancy Jane	866	Cooper, Spencer	1163
Bob, Woodward	868	Cotton, Willie	756
Bob, Lena	869	Cunnatomby, Thompson	491
Bob, Boyd	886	Cunnatomby, Sealy	492
Bob, Lisdy	887	Cuttie, Annie	24
Bob, Preston	888	Dansby, Jacob	19
Bob, Rainey	889	Dansby, Lewis	607
Bob,Lexis	890	Dansby, Isom	625
Bob, Sallie	995	Davis, Tom	31
Bob, Emma	996	Davis, Rena	32
Bob, Alex	1367	Davis, Walton	33
Bob, Edna	1368	Davis, Alice	34
Boston, Lizzie	279	Davis, Emma	35
Boston, Bennie	280	Davis, Oscar	36
Boston, Dora	281	Davis, John	37
Boston, Jim T.	1142	Davis, Alex	62
Bonaham, Ed	1439	Davis, Jeff	258
Brokeshoulder, Morris	343	Davis, Frank	333
Brokeshoulder, Martha	344	Davis, Edna	737
Brokeshoulder, Obediah		Davis, Linnie	738
W.	345	Davis, Louella	739
Brokeshoulder, Severa M.	346	Davis, Julia	862
Brokeshoulder, Adam		Davis, Mary	863
(Ok-lah-nah-nubbee)	933	Davis, Bissie	1280
Brokeshoulder, Minnie	1144	Davis, Fronie	1281
Brokeshoulder, James	1382	Dees, Mary E.	1399
Brokeshoulder, John	1383	Dees, Henry H.	1400
Brokeshoulder, Adam, Jr.	1384	Dees, George A.	1402
Brokeshoulder, Cam-		Dees, Edgar R.	1403
mack	1385	Dees, Oscar E.	1404
Brokeshoulder, Lee	1441	Dees, Fannie E.	1405
Brewer, Frank	1443	Dees, Katiebelle	1406
Bull, John (On-ta-tub-		Dees, Walter T.	1445
bee)	189	Dixon, John	145
Bull, Robert E.	504	Dixon, Feely	146
Bull, Pink	580	Dixon, Julia	615
Bull, Emma	581	Dixon, Columbus	616
Bull, Houston	639	Dixon, Sallie	617
Bull, Asa Elmon	1228	Dixon, John	626
Bull, Susan	1303	Dixon, Mary	627
Burton, Susan S.	1123	Dixon, Leanna	628
Burton, Henry D.	1124	Dixon, Sarah Jane	629
Burton, Austin G.	1125	Dixon, Lena	630
Burton, Susan O.	1126	Dixon, Beauty	631
Burton, Florence A.	1127	Dixon, Doctor	658
Burton, Jewel A.	1128	Dixon, Nancy	659
Byars, Luisa	1244	Dixon, John	1138
Byrnes, Cricket	86	Dixon, Manie	1139
Carter, Nettie Frances	556	Dixon, Ennie	1140
Chubbee, Cully	41	Dixey, Jim	1042
Chubbee, Leanna	213	Draper, Rosie	1182
Chubbee, Susie	527	Draper, Maggie	1183
Chubbee, Rosanna	528	Elix, Davis	260
Chubbee, Julia	529	Ellis, Habett	38
Chubbee, Lucy	530	Ellis, Jim	654
Chubbee, Agnes	531	Ellis, Nancy	655
Chubbee, Anna	532	Ellis, Mary	656
Chubee, Janie	533	Ellis, Leroy	657
Chubbee, Willie	534	Emi-yah-tubbe, Wallace	1015
Chubbee, Pink	535	Emi-yah-tubbe, Nancy	1016
Chubbee, John	1363	Emi-yah-tubbe, Martha	1017
Chubbee, Sallie	1369	Emi-yah-tubbe, Minnie	1018
Charley, Emil	211	Emi-yah-tubbe, Flem-	
Clover, Matilda	1167	mon	1019
Clover, Josiah M.	1168	Emi-yah-tubbe, Johnnie	1020
Clover, Nettie Lee	1169	Farmer, Solomon	842
Clover, Robert Arthur	1170	Farmer, Louisa	843
Clover, Leander Louis	1171	Farmer, Wilson	1326
Clover, Earnest Q.	1198	Farve, Amelia	1161
Clover, Thomas L.	1199	Faure, Marie	1134
Clover, Euguia B.	1200	Fillihemah, Nancy	844
Clover, Mary	1204	Folsom, Andy	1253
Clover, William Marshall	1205	Foley, Davie	130
Clover, Henry H.	1246	Foley, Betsie	524
Clover, Josie	1247	Foley, Oscar	525
Cooper, Jacob	56	Foley, Stella	526
Cooper, Julia	57	Fountain, Lillie M.	1407
Cooper, Foster	58	Franklin, Lou	1178

Name.	Roll No.	Name.	Roll No.
Franklin, Alfus R.	1179	Henry, Lillie	1073
Franklin, Homer Lee	1180	Henry, Josie	1074
Franklin, Quinon Hu-		Henry, John	1087
bert	1181	Henry, George	1101
Frazer, Jacoway	439	Hickman, John	390
Frazer, Frank	440	Hickman, Dennis	391
Frazer, John	441	Hickman, Ben	392
Frazer, Sudie	442	Himonubbe, Shock	915
Frazer, Henry	443	Himonubbe, Bobbie	916
Frenchman, Lotie	1050	Himonubbe, Laben	917
Frenchman, Mollie	1051	Him-o-nubbe, Davis	949
Frenchman, Sally	1226	Him-o-nubbe, Emmon	950
Gibson, Alex	6	Him-o-nubbe, Ella	951
Gibson, Walter	39	Him-o-nubbe, Carson	952
Gibson, Ona	237	Him-o-nubbe. Larbin	953
Gibson, Ben	762	Hochmeah, Mary	947
Gibson, Sallie	763	Horton, Bob	448
Gibson, Mullen	764	Houston, Willie	867
Gibson, Lena	765	Huff, Zeno	1376
Gibson, Lulu	766	Hunter, Joewillie	1201
Gibson, Sammon	767	Hunter, Mary	1202
Gibson, Leona	803	Hunter, Pearl	1203
Gibson, Billie	804	Hussey, William Han-	
Gibson, Christina	805	cock	1
Gibson, Ethan S.	806	Hussey, Alvin McDowell	2
Gibson, Mattie	807	In-pun-nubbee, Mingo	40
Gibson, Emmie	808	Isaac, Lucy	122
Gibson, Sallie	809	Isaac, Clinton	123
Gibson, Willie	810	Isaac, Tennis	124
Gibson, Mollie	811	Isaac, Halmond	125
Gibson, Mike	812	Isaac, Hollis	126
Gibson, Ben	845	Isaac, Nabore	127
Gibson, Sealy	846	Isaac, Tommie	128
Gibson, Jeff	856	Isaac, Mandy	129
Gibson, Lucy	857	Isaac, King	753
Gibson, William	858	Isaac, Eliza	754
Gibson, Ellis	859	Isaac, Siss	755
Gibson, Snowdon	860	Isaac, George	768
Gibson, Amy	861	Isaac, Mary	769
Gibson, Sarah	1047	Isaac, Wilson	775
Gibson, Robison	1048	Isaac, Siney	776
Gibson, Mary Jane	1049	Isaac, Gift	777
Gift, Jim	1327	Isaac, Ellen	778
Gift, Mobella	1328	Isaac, Jim	779
Gift, Sarah	1329	Isaac, Lela	780
Gift, Johnson	1330	Isaac, Rogers	1426
Gift, Effie	1331	Isom, John	26
Gift, Donnie	1332	Isom, Mary	27
Gilmore, Nettie Bessie	799	Isom, Rosie	28
Gilmore, Ramond	800	Isom, John, Jr.	29
Gilmore, Emma	801	Jackson, Melvina	65
Gilmore Mabell	802	Jackson, Marcelene	66
Gilmore, Allen	841	Jackson, Henry	68
Gilmore, Tom	899	Jackson, Sealy	69
Gilmore, Martha	900	Jackson, Becky	292
Gilmore, Johnnie	901	Jackson, Jim	362
Gilmore, Mamie	902	Jackson, Elder	429
Gilmore, Ludie	903	Jackson, Cornelia	660
Gilmore, Benjamin	904	Jackson, Annie	774
Gilmore, Jane	905	Jackson, Billie	847
Golden, Abe	83	Jackson, Jennie	848
Golden, Louisa	84	Jackson, Leroy	849
Golden, Mollie	85	Jackson, Mary	850
Golden, Margaret Ann	1364	Jackson, Charlie	934
Guice, Benjamin J.	1207	Jackson, Frances	935
Guss, Nancy	147	Jackson, Ben	936
Guss, Sina	148	Jackson, Stephen	937
Guss, Rafe	149	Jackson, Tecumseh	961
Guss, Allice	150	Jackson, Sophia	962
Guss, Leanna	1357	Jackson, Walter	963
Ha-cubbee, Mollie	697	Jackson, McElroy	964
Ha-cubbee, Amie (Il-le-		Jackson, Salina	965
mah-ho-ki)	906	Jackson, Winnie	966
Hancock, Jubal A.	5	Jackson, Willis	999
Hawkins, Billy	102	Jackson, Jameson	1000
Hawkins, Jerden	103	Jackson, Ida	1001
Hawkins, Rollis	1137	Jackson, Albert	1002
Hawkins, William	1371	Jackson, Nixie	1003
Hawkins, Jane	1372	Jackson, Nancy	1034
Hawkins, Sillie	1039	Jackson, Bessie	1035
Henderson, Ben	1064	Jackson, Patsey	1036
Henry, John	909	Jackson, Tom	1031
Henry, Sarah	910	Jackson, Joe	1162
Henry, Dennis	911	Jackson, Bob	1354
Henry, Frank	1065	Jackson, Birdie	1355
Henry, Wallace	1072	Jackson, Maseline	1356

Name.	Roll No.	Name.	Roll No.
Jackson, Lizzie	1435	Johnson, Allen	8
Jackoway, Cora	219	Johnson, Lela	9
Jacoway, Charlie	833	Johnson, Louis	197
Jacoway, Mandy	834	Johnson, Mettie	198
Jacoway, Martin	835	Johnson, Henry	220
Jacoway, Oma	836	Johnson, Reecy	221
Jacoway, Elsie	837	Johnson, Amos	222
Jacoway, Onus	838	Johnson, Thomas	223
Jacoway, Davis	938	Johnson, Will	224
Jacoway, Sealy	939	Johnson, Frank	225
Jacoway, Rose	940	Johnson, John	226
Jack, Jim	606	Johnson, Margaret	227
Jack, Billy	608	Johnson, Fayette	228
Jack, Leanna	609	Johnson, Isby	229
Jack, Minnie	610	Johnson, Ostar	230
Jack, Nettie	611	Johnson, Jimmie	231
Jack, Camille	612	Johnson, Lona	232
Jack, Allen	681	Johnson, Andy	251
Jack, Tom	757	Johnson, John	324
Jack, Eliza	758	Johnson, Nancy	325
Jack, Ethel	759	Johnson, Hickman	326
Jack, Silman	760	Johnson, Albert	327
Jack, Evaline	761	Johnson, Wallace	355
Jack, Martha	948	Johnson, Mary	356
Jack, Lena	954	Johnson, Effie	357
Jack, Sarah Jane	955	Johnson, Jim	374
Jack, Willie	956	Johnson, Amie	375
Jack, Nancy	957	Johnson, Lottie	376
Jack, Ellen	958	Johnson, Willie	428
Jack, Lillie	959	Johnson, Isaac	474
Jack, Robert	960	Johnson, Susie (Ah-be-	
Jack, Marsaline	1068	ho ka)	475
Jack, Joe	1069	Johnson, Sallie	476
Jack, Tom	1070	Johnson, Painey	477
Jack, Jane	1071	Johnson, Mattie	478
Jack, Bicey	1279	Johnson, Taylor	585
James, Mollie	353	Johnson, Jennie	586
James, Jeff	354	Johnson, John P.	614
James, Wash	651	Johnson, Cook	745
James, Easter	652	Johnson, Eliza	746
James, Harbar	653	Johnson, Big Wiley	839
James, Ore	709	Johnson, Patsie	840
Jamison, Hattie	398	Johnson, Jesse Porter	983
Jamison, Lula	1155	Johnson, Wiley	997
Jamison, Finis	1156	Johnson, Stela	998
Jamison, Mike	1157	Johnson, Sealy	1077
Jamison, Reuben	1158	Johnson, Maggie	1078
Jamison, Arden	1362	Johnson, Sam	1079
Jamus, Lulu	941	Johnson, Tatum	1080
Jacob, Charley	706	Johnson, Jimmie	1235
Jacob, Louisa	707	Johnson, Amy	1236
Jacob, Ebbie	708	Johnson, Freeman	1237
Jasper, John	121	Johnson, Mamie	1377
Jefferson, Thomas	1147	Johnson, Nochee	1378
Jefferson, Mary Jane	1419	Johnnie, Lucy	422
Jefferson, Ike	1420	Johnnie, Hickman	423
Jefferson, Velma	1421	Johnnie, Sutt	424
Jefferson, Susie	1422	Johnnie, Criset	425
Jefferson, Abney	1423	Johnnie, George G.	426
Jeff, Eliza	431	Johnnie, Freeney	427
Jeff, Alice	932	Johnston, Isham	922
Jeff, George	1061	Johnston, Lenna	923
Jeff, Lula	1062	Johnston, Jesse	924
Jimmerson, Joe	1066	Johnston, Lena	925
Jimmerson, Martha	1067	Johnston, Malissie	926
Jimmerson, Lucy	1095	John, Sidney	215
Jim, Lucy (Lo-mah)	131	John, Bettie	216
Jim, Ellen	244	John, Eva	217
Jim, Stephen	347	John, Ella	218
Jim, Betsy	348	John, Lewis	409
Jim, Austin	459	John, Simpson	410
Jim, Ola	460	John, Sam	553
Jim, Martha	461	John, Nancy	554
Jim, Bessie	462	John, Big (Ondochatub-	
Jim, Filleah	684	bee)	601
Jim, Rosie	685	John, Sally	602
Jim, Thomas	686	John, Charley	603
Jim, Salena	687	John, Lena	604
Jim, Simpson	710	John, Julia	605
Jim, Eliza	711	John, Simon	676
Jim, Robert	712	John, Georgia	677
Jim, Egburt	713	John, Johnnie	678
Jim, Tessie	714	John, Minnie	679
Jim, Clemmon	715	John, Alex	680
Jim, Evan	716	John, Jack	702
Johnson, Frank	7	John, Olevia	703

Name.	Roll No.	Name.	Roll No.
John, Enil	1153	Lick, John (Hintubbee)	942
Jones, Annie C.	1340	Lise, Lissie	661
Jones, Maud	1341	Martin, Sallie	751
Jones, May	1342	Martin, Bettie	613
Jones. Leonard H.	1343	Martin, Jacob	752
Jordan, William G.	1213	Martin, Sam B.	770
Joshua, Levisa	63	Martin, Winnie	771
Karr, Nancy F.	1176	Marris, Elizabeth	943
Karr, Lon	1177	Marris, Forgy	1160
Kelly, Joe	42	Marris, Minerva	1241
Kelly, Lizzie	43	Marris, Jim	1258
Kelly, Fannie	1088	Marris, Arch	1259
Kelley, Sealy	1295	Marris, Annie	1260
Kelley, Presley	1296	Marris, Dibbin	1261
Kelley, Lloyd	1297	Marris, Wench	1262
Kelley, Eula	1298	Marris, Steve	1263
Lafontain, Victoria	1132	Marris, Nancy	1264
Lehuw, Willie Ann	1208	Marris, Missy	1265
Lehuw, Floyd	1209	Marris, Mat	1266
Lehuw, Ophelia	1210	Marris, Liss	1267
Lenochan, Campbell	1345	Marris, Tom H.	1287
Lewis, Smith	208	Marris, Christian	1288
Lewis, Chuly	209	Marris, Winner	1289
Lewis, Jacob	210	Marris, Coleman	1290
Lewis, Young	243	Marris, Nannie	1291
Lewis, David	307	Marris, Jane	1292
Lewis, Emely	308	Marris, Lillie	1293
Lewis, Sina	335	Marris, Tennis	1294
Lewis Jim	400	Marris, Bobo	1299
Lewis, Moseley	401	Marris, Otis	1300
Lewis, Mary	402	Marris, Sanderson	1301
Lewis, Sarah	403	Marris, Lula	1302
Lewis, John	514	Marris, Marris	1304
Lewis, Jim	557	Marris, Sam	1309
Lewis, Leanna	690	Marris, George	1310
Lewis, William	691	Marris, Sealy	1379
Lewis, Thomas	692	Marshall, Susan Cor-	
Lewis, Nelson	693	nelia	1129
Lewis, Mary	694	Marshall, Valentine	1130
Lewis, Annie	695	Marshall, John H.	1131
Lewis, Easter	696	Marshall, Charles Har-	
Lewis, Mollie	727	old	1141
Lewis, Martha	728	Marx, Sallie V.	1409
Lewis, Caroline	732	Marx, Moses	1410
Lewis, Ollie	733	Marx, Miriam	1411
Lewis, Martha	734	Marx, Philip Aaron	1412
Lewis, Charles (Kon-ni-ah-tubbee)	735	Meely, Leanna	314
Lewis, Lila	736	Meely, Kelley	315
Lewis, Sim	740	Meely, Botman	316
Lewis, Minnie	741	Meely, Eunice	317
Lewis, Lonie	742	Meely, Sallie	318
Lewis, Jesse	743	Meely, Jim	747
Lewis, John	744	Meely, Lula	748
Lewis, Noble	789	Meely, Amos	749
Lewis, Webb	790	Meely, Fannie	750
Lewis, Mary	912	Meely, Clark	772
Lewis, Jim	913	Meely, Mary	773
Lewis, Jeffie	914	Meely, John G.	1224
Lewis, Sam	967	Mingo, Samuel Alexan-	
Lewis, Pollie	968	der	1154
Lewis, Jim	969	Moncrief, Joseph	1414
Lewis, Dorano	970	Moore, Ellen	1316
Lewis, Ump	971	Moore, John M.	1317
Lewis, Claire	972	Moore, Lizzie B.	1318
Lewis, Charlie	973	Moore, Callie H.	1319
Lewis, Sallie	974	Moore, Elisha N.	1320
Lewis, Larnie	975	Moore, Mattie J.	1321
Lewis, Minnie	976	Moore, Maggie N.	1322
Lewis, Bud	977	Moore, Rutha E.	1323
Lewis, Rody	978	Moore, Willie N.	1324
Lewis, Betty	982	Moore, Lillie A.	1325
Lewis, John	1102	Morrison, George W.	1386
Lewis, Lucy	1103	Morrison, Emma Z.	1387
Lewis, Dan	1104	Morrison, Amma May	1388
Lewis, Jim	1105	Morrison, Henry B.	1389
Lewis, Lewis	1146	Morris, Clemmans	255
Lewis, Dan	1148	Morris, Frank	256
Lewis, Little Tom	1229	Morris, Tracy	257
Lewis, Lonie	1230	Morris, Watkins	291
Lewis, William	1231	Morris, J. P.	563
Lewis, Rufus	1232	Morris, Bessie	564
Lewis, Jennie	1358	Mosely, Maggie	1333
Lewis, Mary	1428	Mose, John	595
Lewis, Lonie	1431		
Lewis, Frank	1360		

Name.	Roll No.	Name.	Roll No.
Mose, Lula	596	Pebworth, Josie Viola	1197
Mose, Steen	597	Pebsworth, Roscoe W.	1219
Mose, Frank	598	Pebsworth, Jepthar A.	1220
Mose, William Davis	599	Pebsworth, Marshal H.	1221
Mose, Lark Davis	600	Pebsworth, Vassie V.	1217
Mose, Ike Moses	717	Pebsworth, Void Preston	1218
Moses, Ann	718	Peter, Sooky	1429
Moses, Nicey	719	Peter, Emely	479
Moses, Lottie	720	Peter, Nathan	480
Moses, Edna	721	Peter, Thompson	1093
Moses, Elsie	722	Peter, Richardson	1094
McCormick, Sara Jane	1145	Phillip, Wesley	132
McClosky, Charlie	1172	Phillip, Maggie	133
McDonald, Susanna	1149	Phillip, Sock	158
McDonald, Lucy	1150	Phillip, Ples Tinsley	159
McDonald, Indian	1268	Phillip, Bettie	160
McDonald, Lee	1269	Phillip, Lewis	161
McDonald, Lee Poe	1270	Phillip, Celia Ann	162
McDonald, William	1271	Phillip, Mack	619
McDorald, Mack	1272	Phillip, Sallie	620
McDonald, Viney	1273	Phillip, Arlena	621
McDonald, Hugh	1274	Phillip, Mary	622
McDonald, Sealy	1275	Phillip, Williamson	1004
McDonald, John Patty	1276	Phillip, Jinnie	1005
McDonald, Mollie	1277	Phillip, Leanna	1006
McDonald, Jane	1278	Phillip, Sina	1007
McMillan, Lonie	1250	Phillip, Albert	1008
McPhail, Laura K.	1390	Phillip, Dibin	1009
McPhail, Frank	1391	Phillip, Bob	1010
McPhail, Myra	1392	Phillip, Lucie	1081
McPhail, Fannie	1393	Phillip, Lesa	1082
McPhail, Grace	1394	Phillip, Sis	1370
McPhail, Gates	1395	Phillips, Meeks	247
McPhail, Preston	1396	Phillips, Caroline	821
McPhail, Virgil	1397	Phillips, Lena	822
McPhail, Homer	1398	Phillips, Sealia	823
Neal, Jeff D.	303	Phillips, Germain	824
Neal, Dora	304	Phillips, Custer	825
Neal, Cora	305	Philip, Masey	30
Neal, Earnest	306	Philip, Nancy	456
Neal, Nancy	407	Philip, Thomas	470
Neal, John (Me-ah-ta-kubbee)	334	Philip, Louisa	471
		Philip, John Lumpkin	472
Ned, Annie (Mehiotimah)	261	Philip, Winston	623
Ned, John	262	Philip, Tom	624
Ned, Francis	263	Philip, Sallie	826
Ned, Frank	264	Philip, George	944
Ned, Ernest	265	Philip, Bettie	945
Ned, Reuben	266	Philip, Sissy	946
Ned, Willie	877	Philip, Elijah	1248
Ned, Lona	878	Philip, Edmond (or Farbus)	1249
Ned, Maryin	879	Pistemah, Nancy	236
Ned, Russell	880	Pistubbee, Tinsley	907
Ok-chi-tubbee, Josephene	683	Pistubbee, Archie	908
Old, Hannah	295	Pis-tubbee, Horace	451
Onah-fal-a-ma-tubbee	705	Pis-tubbee, Lena	452
Parker, Logan	648	Pis-tubbee, Mattie	453
Parker, Sidney	649	Pis-tubbee, Seleah	454
Parker, Jim	650	Pis-tubbee, Maggie	455
Parker, John	1055	Plummer, Frank E.	1254
Parker, Mary	1056	Plummer, Frank S.	1255
Parker, Joseph	1057	Plummer, Raymond S.	1256
Parker, Frances	1058	Plummer, Joseph R.	1257
Parker, Ninnie	1059	Polk, Jim	253
Parker, Sasteline	1060	Polk, Melissie	254
Patterson, Emma	1442	Post-Oak, Malissa	516
Patterson, Doroth A.	1214	Post-oak, Johnson	1117
Patterson, Shelby A.	1215	Post-oak, Susie	1118
Patterson, Howell M.	1216	Post-oak, Eli	1119
Pebworth, William	1184	Post-oak, Sweeney	1120
Pebworth, William H.	1185	Post-oak, Jim	1164
Pebworth, Lillie May	1186	Post-oak, Mary	1165
Pebworth, Pearl	1187	Post-oak, Jim Brown	1166
Pebworth, Zelma	1188	Postoak, Jack	141
Pebworth, Maggie	1189	Postoak, Fee Kelly	142
Pebworth, Josie	1190	Postoak, Sam	143
Pebworth, David	1191	Postoak, William	332
Pebworth, Artie	1192	Postoak, Bessie	1424
Pebworth, Charley	1193	Postoak, Sarah	212
Pebworth, Lee	1194	Porter, Jesse	723
Pebworth, Clarence	1195	Porter, Betsey	724
Pebworth, Joe	1196	Porter, Jenkins	725

Name.	Roll No.	Name.	Roll No.
Porter, Thornton	726	onah)	814
Primus, Ben	259	Shoemaker, Sister	815
Primus, Seaby	432	Shoemaker, Coleman	816
Rasha, Mary	414	Shoemaker, Henry	817
Rasha, Jim	415	Shoemaker, Selest	818
Rasha, John	416	Shoemaker, Will	819
Reed, Kit	1037	Shoemaker, Sally	820
Reed, Victoria	1038	Shoemaker, Wiggin	979
Reed, Linnie	1366	Shoemaker, Margaret	
Reese, Salina	322	(Ish-te-mah)	980
Reese, Manuel	323	Shoemaker, Emerson	981
Reese, Fannie	363	Shoemaker, Jim	1359
Reese, Lelia	984	Shoemaker, Susie	1238
Reese, John	1361	Shoemake, Jackson	
Ricketts, Freddie C.	1211	(La-we-tubbee)	151
Ricketts, Dossie	1212	Shoemake, Jennie	152
Robinson, Dilese	493	Shoemake, Watson	153
Robinson, Annie	494	Shoemake, Ernest	154
Robison, Mary Jane	729	Shoemake, Manat	155
Robison, Alice	730	Shoemake, Ada	156
Robison, Eula	731	Shoemake, Rhoda	157
Roe, J. Folsom	3	Shook, Bettie	885
Roe, Jeannette C.	4	Simpson, Jefferson	267
Roe, Harry F.	1222	Simpson, Sallie	268
Roe, Tannie T.	1223	Simpson, Marcelline	269
Sampson, Johnson	73	Simpson, Backus	270
Sampson, Sallie	74	Simpson, Barnett	271
Sampson, Senie	75	Simpson, Mary Corria	272
Sampson, Jim	76	Simpson, Beeley	309
Sampson, George	77	Simpson, Leslie	310
Sampson, Sealy Ann	78	Simpson, Jennie	495
Sampson, Pauline	79	Simpson, Lewis	496
Sampson, Gus	80	Simpson, Adaline	497
Sampson, Bennie	81	Simpson, George	498
Sampson, Mary Ann	82	Simpson, Sims	499
Sampson, John	179	Simpson, Johnnie	500
Sampson, Louisiana	180	Simpson, Celia	501
Sampson, Emeline	181	Simpson, Leta	502
Sampson, Steve	182	Simpson, Cinda	503
Sampson, Oscar	183	Simpson, Gill	545
Sampson, Arlone	184	Simpson, Mertine	546
Sampson, Spence	185	Simpson, Sockie	682
Sampson, Artis	186	Simpson, Sam	781
Sampson, Cenie	187	Simpson, William	986
Sampson, Lillie	543	Simpson, Caroline	987
Sampson, Salonie	544	Simpson, Ben	988
Sampson, Selia	1438	Simpson, Fannie	989
Sam, Huddleston	94	Simpson, Ira	990
Sam, Tilwa	511	Simpson, Mabel	991
Sam, Dennis	637	Simmons, Leona	191
Sam, Acy	638	Simmons, Robert	192
Sam, Thomas	640	Simmons, Maggie	193
Sam, Minnie	641	Simmons, King	194
Sam, Amos	642	Simmons, Pigfoot	195
Sam, Joe	643	Simmons, Mamie	196
Sam, George	644	Simon, Albert	592
Sam, Delia	645	Simon, Mary Jane	593
Sam, Nancy	646	Simon, Amos	594
Sam, Sis	647	Smith, Sehorn	91
Sam, Wallace	1022	Smith, Emma	92
Sam, Jim	1089	Smith, Mollie	328
Scott, Emil	406	Smith, Amon	329
Scott, Chubby	865	Smith, Sibbie	330
Scott, Liza	1239	Smith, Martin	331
Scott, Aline	1240	Smith, Jeff	377
Seals, Annie	1252	Smith, Mary Jane	378
Seals, Emma	1334	Smith, Williamson	379
Seals, James	1335	Smith, Emma	380
Seals, Ora	1336	Smith, Isabel	381
Seals, Kernell	1337	Smith, Richardson	382
Seals, Ada	1338	Smith, Bettie	383
Seals, Talmadge	1339	Smith, Doyle	384
Shoemaker, Billy	404	Smith, Louiana	385
Shoemaker, Eliza	405	Smith, Mack	992
Shoemaker, Willie	463	Smith, Victoria	1349
Shoemaker, Lucy	464	Snider, Ester D.	1352
Shoemaker, Joe	465	Snider, Sarah Pearl	1351
Shoemaker, Amie	466	Snider, Beulah Lee	1353
Shoemaker, Dock	467	Sockey, Will	163
Shoemaker, Fannie	468	Sockey, Solomon	673
Shoemaker, Dan	469	Sockey, Phoebe	674
Shoemaker, Ben	813	Sockey, Mary	675
Shoemaker, Mary (Sti-		Sockey, Rafe	1108

Name.	Roll No.	Name.	Roll No.
Sockey, John	1225	Thompson, Allison	852
Sockey, Bettie	1305	Thompson, Martha	853
Sockey, Maggie	1306	Thompson, Lena	855
Sockey Rafe	1307	Thompson, Lem	1023
Sockey, Ned	1308	Thompson, Suala	1024
Solomon, Winnie	67	Thompson, Lonie	1025
Solomon, Fannie	1041	Thompson, Sydney	1026
Stallaby, Anderson	864	Thompson, Leona	1027
Stafford, Tinnie	1350	Thompson, Marsaline	1028
Stemona, Eliza	523	Thompson, Austin	1314
Stephen, Jim Polk	412	Thompson, Arba Lou-	
Stephen, Agnes	413	venia	1380
Stephen, Frank	669	Tomby, Frankson	287
Stephen, Lissie	670	Tomby, Fannie	288
Stephen, Allie	671	Tomby, Sibena	289
Stephen, Eliza	672	Tomby, Limmer	290
Stoliby, Folsom	851	Tom, Lina	16
Stout, Sis	1151	Tom, Amos	17
Stout, Terese Annie	1152	Tom, Leona	18
Stout, Usan	1432	Tom, Ahleen	70
Stribbling, Frank	1135	Tom, John	71
Sturdevant, Charley	613	Tom, Sallie	72
Sweeney, Robert	87	Tom, Thomas	473
Sweeney, Ara Ann	88	Tom, Nicholas	918
Sweeney, Joseph	89	Tom, Watson	919
Sweeney, Frank	90	Tom, Moses	920
Taylor, Battiste	11	Tom, Sicily	921
Taylor, Elizabeth	12	Tom, Willie	927
Taylor, Lem	13	Tom, Willie	1014
Taylor, Stanley	14	Tom, Sealy Ann	1040
Taylor, Louisa	15	Toby, William	64
Taylor, Lawrence	515	Toby, Lewis	114
Taylor, Willie	928	Toby, Ellen	115
Taylor, Jennie	929	Toby, John	178
Taylor, Elizabeth	930	Tonubbee, Jackson	1136
Taylor, Johnson	931	Tonubbee, Sissie	1282
Taylor, Frank	1075	Tonubbee, Lewis	1283
Taylor, Lulie	1076	Tonubbee, Robert	1284
Taylor, Madeline	1090	Tonubbee, Murphy	1285
Taylor, Nettie	1091	Tonubbee, Lottie	1286
Taylor, Mary	1092	Tooklo, Sealy	296
Taylor, Henry	1133	Tooklo, Leo Jim	297
Taylor, Mollie	1440	Tookolo, William O.	507
Temona, Sallie	408	Tookolo, Lillie	508
Thomas, Bob	49	Tookolo, John Henry	1365
Thomas, Daley	50	Toonubbee, Allen	796
Thomas, Ramsom	51	Toonubbee, Siss	797
Thomas, Berry	52	Toonubbee, Bissie	798
Thomas, Emeline	53	Tubbee, Columbus	486
Thomas, Sam	54	Tubbee, Willis	487
Thomas, Samawail	55	Tubbee, Martha	488
Thomas, Smith	293	Tubbee, Lucy	489
Thomas, Elijah	668	Tubbee, Ada	490
Thomas, John B.	698	Tubbee, Robert	1433
Thomas, Emma	699	Tucker, George	1173
Thomas, Ada	700	Tucker, Henry	1245
Thomas, Henry	701	Tuffamah, Ishman	358
Thomas, Charlie	870	Tuffamah, Suella	359
Thomas, Mary	871	Tuffamah, Moses	360
Thomas, Peter Foster	872	Tuffamah, Emma	361
Thomas, Esau	873	Umber, Ida	445
Thomas, Risher	874	Umber, Joe	446
Thomas, Enoch	875	Umber, Minnie	447
Thomas, Nicholas	876	Waiter, Martha	541
Thomas, Anison	1106	Waiter, Robert	542
Thomas, Silman	1121	Wallace, Tom	25
Thomas, Beckey	1122	Wallace, Jim	112
Thomas, Sincum	1233	Wallace, Mary	113
Thomas, Martha	1234	Wallace, Jim	116
Thompson, Ben	558	Wallace, Lizzie	117
Thompson, Martha	559	Wallace, Walter	118
Thompson, Leona	560	Wallace, David	119
Thompson, Thomas	561	Wallace, Mary	120
Thompson, Maggie	562	Wallace, John	199
Thompson, Chapman	1227	Wallace, Leona	200
Thompson, Isaac	368	Wallace, William	201
Thompson, Betsy	369	Wallace, Comby	214
Thompson, Jimmie	370	Wallace, Wesley	1029
Thompson, Sarah	371	Wallace, Letitia	1030
Thompson, Arthur	372	Wallace, Lemmie	1032
Thompson, Leonie	373	Wallace, Earley	1033
Thompson, Simmons	481	Wallace, John B.	1043
Thompson, Callie	482	Wallace, Lillie	1044

Name.	Roll No.
Wallace, Arna	1045
Wallace, Ora	1046
Wallace, Aben	1373
Wallace, Sota	1374
Wallace, Bill	1418
Wampler, Amanda L.	1344
Wampler, George W.	1346
Wampler, John	1347
Wampler, Daniel Edgar	1348
Washington, Sallie	1427
Washington, Billy	536
Washington, Liza	537
Washington, Hannah	538
Washington, Martha	539
West, John	555
Wickson, Sim	248
Wickson, David	249
Wickson, Mike	517
Wickson, Amie	518
Wickson, Cleo	519
Wickson, Leotie	520
Wickson, Nancy	521
Wickson, Holliston	522
Wickson, John (Con- ne-ma-tubbee)	579
Wilkerson, Sam (or John)	134
Wilkerson, Annie	135
Wilkerson, Mollie	136
Wilkerson, Lemie	137
Wilkerson, Isetralen	138
Wilkerson, Mary	139
Wilkerson, Cora	140
Wilkinson, Harrison	898
Williamson, Ben (Ni- noc-e-lubbee)	298
Williamson, Amie	299
Williamson, Joe	300
Williamson, Pres	301
Williamson, Rosie	302
Williamson, Joe	386
Williamson, Deanna	387
Williamson, Steve Smith	388
Williamson, Malissa	389
Williamson, Flamus	457
Williamson, Tom	1011
Williamson, Mary	1012
Williamson, Davie	1013
Williamson, Edmund	1107
Williams, Rainy	393
Williams, Bettie	394
Williams, Maggie	395
Williams, Cathlena	396
Williams, Micheal	397
Williams, Jack	417
Williams, Emaline	418
Williams, Mamie	419
Williams, Smith	420
Williams, Smith	458
Williams, Tom	573
Williams, Mary	574
Williams, Chlorie	575
Williams, Sam	576
Williams, Harvey	577
Williams, Susan	578
Williams, Telan	985
Willie, Billy	190
Willis, Mary	44
Willis, Silli	45
Willis, Mandy	46
Willis, Anna	47
Willis, Abel	48
Willis, John (Tom-ola- tubbee)	95
Willis, Susie Ami (or Susie Ann	96
Willis, Lee	97
Willis, Adolphus	98
Willis, Will	99
Willis, Walter	100

Name.	Roll No.
Willis, Mary	101
Willis, Mack	144
Willis, John	164
Willis, Hickman	165
Willis, Margaret	166
Willis, Lillie	167
Willis, Fannie	168
Willis, Elma	169
Willis, Sam Houston	170
Willis, Riley	319
Willis, Lona	320
Willis, Robison	364
Willis, Lizzie	365
Willis, Davie	366
Willis, Ballison	367
Willis, Jim	430
Willis, Wallace	433
Willis, Nancy	434
Willis, Fannie	435
Willis, Charlie	436
Willis, Eddie	437
Willis, Moses	438
Willis, John (Il-le-ah- Tubbee)	572
Willis, Charley	582
Willis, Tishomingo	1063
Willis, Solomon	1143
Willis, Hugh	1251
Willis, William	1413
Willis, Nannie	1437
Wilmond, Raymond	1444
Wilson, Billy	171
Wilson, Maggie	172
Wilson, Sampson	173
Wilson, Sammie	174
Wilson, Jimmie	175
Wilson, Freeman	176
Wilson, Dick Russell	177
Wilson, Sam	411
Wilson, Willie	881
Wilson, Janie	882
Wilson, John	883
Wilson, Donald	884
Wilson, Katie	1174
Wilson, William C.	1175
Wiltshire, Fannie E.	1408
Womack, Maggie	1086
Wood, Mary E.	1401
Yearby, Thomas	1242
Yearby, Christie	1243
Yearby, Jesse	1375
Yearby, Nancy	1425
Yearby, Joseph	1434
York, Dixon	104
York, Josephine	105
York, Sydney	106
York, Bettie	107
York, Sallie	108
York, Lee	109
York, Alice	110
York, Lula	111
York, Scott	238
York, John	239
York, Taylor	240
York, Evan	241
York, Pauline	449
York, William	450
York, Pickens	505
York, Nannie	506
York, Solomon (Tuck- a-lum-bee)	540
York, Rufus	547
York, Malissa	548
York, Ida	549
York, Jamison	550
York, Jesse	551
York, Annie	552
York, Amos	993
York, Bettie Lee	994

INDEX TO
NEW BORN MISSISSIPPI CHOCTAWS

INDEX TO
MINOR MISSISSIPPI CHOCTAWS.

Name.	Roll No.	Name.	Roll No.
Phillip, Minnie	97	Thompson, Will	51
Philip, Asie	12	Thompson, Sallie	96
Philip, Sid	23	Thompson, Jim	119
Philip, Eli	46	Tonubbee, Lizzie	28
Philip, Adam	99	Tookolo, Ida Rena	125
Pis-tubbee, Sinnes	153	Tubbee, Lena	161
Plummer, Charles W.,		Tubbee, Effie	182
Jr.	151	Tubbee, Rachel	183
Post-oak, May Jane	848	Tubbee, Annie	184
Post-oak, Sam	127	Tubbee, Maisie (or	
Post-oak, Lena	162	Bessie)	185
Post-oak, Oscar	163	Tubbee, Betsey	186
Postoak, James	82	Tucker, Docia May	130
Risher, None	43	Wallace, Ida	26
Sám, Abel	6	Wallace, Meeley	73
Sam, Rhody	98	Wallace, Annie	74
Scott, Luciel	14	Wallace, Newt	155
Seals, Willie	87	Wallace, Lee	156
Seals, Anna	94	Wallace, Jennie	176
Shoemaker, Arlie	4	Wickson, Winnie	24
Shoemake, Labon	112	Wickson, James	25
Simpson, Easton	57	Wilkerson, Lonnie	72
Simpson, Jennie	179	Williamson, Tom	
Simpson, Barnard	85	Frank	107
Smith, Martha Jane	67	Williams, Jamen	47
Smith, William B.	68	Willis, Willis	52
Sockey, Robert	141	Willis, Mary	56
Stephen, Wade	90	Willis, Neffie	160
Stribling, Jimmie Jef-		Willis, Willie	164
ferson	159	Willis, Sarah Jane	165
Sweeney, Minna	54	Willis, Henney Lee	166
Taylor, Mamie Annie	40	Wilson, Lelia	13
Taylor, Ritchard	145	Wilson, Marvin Alma	81
Taylor, Emily F.	144	Wood, Sammie D.	173
Taylor, Dewey W.	146	York, Annice	70
Taylor, Celestine	180	York, Wm. Baston	136
Thompson, Ida Jewell	21		

Name.	Roll No.	Name.	Roll No.
Anderson, Elsey	3217	Atkinson, Mattie	3663
Anderson, Dickson	3590	Atkinson, Susan B.	3664
Anderson, Joe	3631	Atkinson, Thos. James	3665
Anderson, Hagen	3633	Austin, Mattie	2812
Anderson, Frank	3634	Ayakatubby, Thompson	21
Anderson, Edward	3635	Ayakatubby, Mina	22
Anderson, Ralph	3636	Ayakatubby, Agnes	23
Anderson, John	3637	Ayakatubby, Mary	24
Anderson, Edith	3638	Ayakatubby, Dixson	25
Anolitubby, Shosha	1103	Ayakatubby, Dorena	26
Anglin, Albert Thomas	1824	Ayakatubby, Minnie	27
Anglin, Lucy Obedient	4590	Ayakatubby, Ida	454
Anglin, Annie May	4591	Ayahakatubby, Amy	1097
Anglin, Lillie Rhode	4592	Ayahakatubby, Alice	2208
Anglin, Sydney C.	4593	Barr, Alta	1161
Anoletubby, Ellis	2399	Barr, Addie	1162
Anoletubby, Annie	2400	Barr, Ema	1163
Anoatubby, Lankford	2846	Barr, Maddie May	1164
Anoatubby, Jane	2847	Barr, Sam T.	1165
Anoatubby, Ida	2848	Baker, Mary H.	1327
Anoatubby, Atchison	2930	Baker, Mary V.	4529
Anoatubby, Minnie	2931	Baker, Charles Wesley	4530
Anoatubby, Lee	2932	Baker, Ada Gertrude	4531
Anoatubby, McKinzie	2933	Baker, John Garland	4532
Anoatubby, Zola	2934	Baker, William Lee	4533
Anoatubby, Richman	2935	Baker, Flora Bell	4534
Anoatubby, Elsie	4170	Baker, Franklin Bryan	4600
Apala, Kizzie	37	Baker, Fannie	4823
Apala, Henrietta	38	Baker, Louise C.	4824
Apala, Ophelia	39	Baker, Colbert Latimer	4825
Apala, Lemuel	40	Bass, Margaret	1722
Apala, Mulbert	41	Ball, Myrtle Virginia	1825
Apala, Nicholas	3135	Ball, Ada Clifford	1826
Apala, Martha	3136	Bates, Emma	3462
Apala, Sophia	3138	Bates, William A.	3463
Apala, Leticia	3858	Bates, Thomas B.	3464
Apala, Joseph	3160	Bates, Nora E.	3465
Apala, Myrtle Paul	4004	Bates, Ned	3466
Arpealer, Aaron	180	Bates, Charles M.	3467
Arpealer, Silbey	181	Bates, Emma M.	3468
Arpealer, Gilbert H.	182	Barnes, Mary Eliza	3691
Arpealer, Juliann	185	Barnes, Samuel Paul	3692
Arpealer, William	254	Bailey, Annie L.	4584
Arpealer, Sippy	255	Bailey, Richard Furman	4585
Arpealer, Sophia	256	Bailey, Pontotoc P.	4586
Arpealer, Lyntch	257	Bailey, Jewel	4587
Arpealer, Nellie	258	Baldwin, Lee P.	4632
Arpealer, Katie	259	Barker, Eula	4793
Arpealer, Semaney	4010	Barker, Minnie	4794
Arpealer, Noley	4930	Barker, Thomas M.	4795
Arpealer, Melvina	4958	Barker, Charles C.	4798
Arnold, Luther W.	3801	Barker, Stella A.	4799
Archerd, Henry Adolphus	4502	Bacon, Sam J.	4869
Archerd, Martha	4501	Bacon, Bailey	4870
Archerd, James Edward	4503	Bacon, Nellie	4871
Archerd, Charles Vernon	4504	Bacon, Sammie	4872
Archerd, Effie Jane	4505	Bacon, William Henderson	4873
Archerd, Cora Maude	4506	Bacon, Will Hubbard	4874
Archerd, Max	4507	Bacon, Anna	4875
Archerd, Nancy Jane	4508	Bacon, Gertrude	4876
Archerd, J. William	4510	Bacon, William J.	4879
Archerd, Sydney E.	4511	Bacon, Frances Belle	4880
Archerd, John William	4513	Bacon, Robert	4881
Archerd, Pineo	4514	Bacon, Henry Clinton	4882
Ard, Emet	4555	Bacon, Epsey	4951
Ard, Maud Lena	4556	Benton, Wesley	289
Ard, Albert Devro	4547	Benton, Peter	30
Ashton, Julia V.	321	Benton, Ellen	31
Ashton, Annie Lucy	324	Benton, Louis	694
Ashton, Alfrod Jackson	325	Benton, Ellen	695
Asbury, Alice	1301	Benton, Nora	697
Asbury, Myrtle	1302	Benton, James L.	698
Asbury, Wm. Douglas	1303	Benton, Adaline	700
Asbury, Nellie	1304	Benton, Earnest	1020
Asbury, Edgar Allen	1305	Benton, Hattie Adeline	1021
Asbury, Eula	1306	Benton, Thomas	2649
Asbury, Rual O.	1307	Benton, Davis	4052
Atkins, John	211	Benton, Elizabeth	4619
Atkins, Hattie	212	Benton, Isaac B.	4620
Atkins, Abner	213	Benton, Eliza M.	4621
Atkins, Susie	214	Benton, Verna	4623
Atkins, Abel	215	Beans, Rosa	48

Name.	Roll No.
Beans, Tienie	4765
Berkett, Jennie	710
Berkett, George	711
Berkett, Eddie	712
Bean, Felin	728
Bean, Mary	2296
Bean, John	2297
Bean, Ben	2298
Bean, William P.	2299
Beam, Andrew	2085
Beam, Sinie	4679
Bee, Ebin	2787
Bee, Dollie	4128
Beaver, Harriett	3155
Beaver, Rachel	3156
Beshirs, Aaron	3474
Beshirs, Laura Belle	3475
Beshirs, William	3476
Beshirs, James Alexander	3477
Beshirs, Joel Everidge	3478
Beshirs, Aaron, Jr.	3479
Beshirs, Ada	3481
Beshirs, Francis	4193
Beeler, Georgia A.	3762
Beeler, Fred Grant	3764
Beeler, Melton	3765
Beeler, Julia	3766
Beeler, George R. Jr.	3767
Beeler, Sarah Louisa	3769
Bell, Alta Pearl	4460
Bell, Joe Edgar	4461
Bell, James Smith	4462
Belvin, Josephine	4624
Belvin, Elizabeth	4625
Belvin, Arabella	4626
Belvin, Rosa Ellen	4627
Belvin, James Charley	4628
Belvin, William Guy	4629
Belvins, Lemuel	1369
Belvins, Susie	1370
Belvins, Wirtie Clyde	1371
Belvins, Robert Earl	1372
Belvins, Susie P.	1373
Billis, Melissa	2315
Billis, Minnie Bell	4145
Blue, Rosa	373
Blunt, Galloway	738
Black, Kissie	1492
Black, Mamie Wilbert	1493
Black, Ida	1842
Black, Overton	1843
Black, John Dechard	1844
Black, Sophia Ellen	1845
Black, Camelia	1847
Black, Henretta	1848
Black, Willie	5057
Black, May	5058
Black, Effie	5059
Blake, Callie	1784
Blocker, Ada	3944
Blocker, Hallie J.	3945
Blocker, Abner	3946
Blackwood, Amelia C.	4671
Blackwood, Georgia M.	4672
Blackwood, Robert G.	4673
Blackwood, Nora I.	4674
Blackwood, Jemima C.	4675
Blackwood, Andrew C. Jr.	4676
Bolen, Wicey	163
Bolen, Morgan	164
Bolen, James E.	165
Bolen, Joseph	166
Bourland, Frances	512
Bourland, Norman Dale	514
Bourland, Estelle Valeria	515
Bourland, Henry	1423
Bourland, Clemmie	1424
Bourland, Ben	1425
Bourland, Bessie	1426
Bourland, William	1427

Name.	Roll No.
Bourland, Charles Howard	1428
Bourland, Elsie	2173
Bourland, William Howard	3708
Bourland, William Franklin	4379
Bourland, James Patrick	4380
Bourland, Lulu Catherine	4381
Bourland, Lorinda Melvina	4382
Bourland, Robert Love	4383
Bourland, Michael Frazier	4384
Bonie, Eva	968
Bonie, William N.	969
Bonie, Lois	970
Bonner, Iszoda	1830
Bonner, Flora	1831
Bonner, Whitmel Francis	1832
Bonner, Margaret	3040
Bond, Adelide	1988
Bond, Reford	1989
Bond, Edward	1990
Bond, Lizzie	2672
Bond, Galloway	4277
Bond, Jesse	4278
Boyd, Thomas	2206
Boyd, Robert Lewis	2310
Bowlin, Maggie	2486
Bowlin, Tressa	2491
Bowlin, Sudie	2492
Boles, Mary E.	3322
Boles, Maude E.	3323
Boles, Sylvia	3324
Boles, William Walter	3325
Bouie, Henry	4048
Brown, Levi	46
Brown, Elizabeth	47
Brown, Scott	49
Brown, Andy	50
Brown, Margaret	100
Brown, Harley	138
Brown, Abel	139
Brown, Edmundson	140
Brown, John	141
Brown, Linton	158
Brown, Lowina	161
Brown, Lillie	167
Brown, Aaron	168
Brown, Wilken	198
Brown, Louisa	209
Brown, Melisia	236
Brown, Robert	263
Brown, Houston	326
Brown, Lizzie	376
Brown, Clarence	377
Brown, Joseph	378
Brown, Harris	437
Brown, Daniel	439
Brown, Epsie	440
Brown, Willis	441
Brown, Eddie	442
Brown, Luffie	459
Brown, Sallie	460
Brown, Julia	461
Brown, Lonie	462
Brown, Lucy	561
Brown, Mason	563
Brown, Willie	564
Brown, James	565
Brown, Gabrel	568
Brown, Lucy	569
Brown, Alley	625
Brown, Allen	642
Brown, Betsey	643
Brown, Halison	666
Brown, Tecumseh	805
Brown, Henderson	1011
Brown, Susan	1013
Brown, Sarah	1166

Name.	Roll No.	Name.	Roll No.
Brown, Loman	1168	Brown, Nealie	3192
Brown, Sisy	1169	Brown, Willis	3198
Brown, Benson	1362	Brown, Edmonson	3210
Brown, William	1412	Brown, Malinda	3211
Brown, Annie	1413	Brown, Julia	3212
Brown, Nancy	1414	Brown, Lulu	3213
Brown, Lucy	1415	Brown, Nannie	3214
Brown, Frances	1416	Brown, Bettie	3215
Brown, Roberson	1542	Brown, Sampson	3447
Brown, Hattie	1543	Brown, Stella M.	3721
Brown, Leonard	1544	Brown, Jerome	3974
Brown, Jesse	1545	Brown, Benjamin F.	3975
Brown, Myrtle	1546	Brown, Ellen	4031
Brown, Lou	1609	Brown, Minerva Lee	4096
Brown, Hattie	1647	Brown, Otto	4110
Brown, Henry	1650	Brown, Virginia Cath-	
Brown, Joe	1728	erine	4123
Brown, Mary	1729	Brown, George	4124
Brown, Joe	1730	Brown, Florence	4132
Brown, Guy	1734	Brown, Gipson Albert	4183
Brown, Douglas Cooper	1891	Brown, Victoria May	4425
Brown, Susan	1900	Brown, Charles A.	4774
Brown, Josiah	1926	Brown, Nathaniel	4775
Brown, Cyrus Harris	1927	Brown, Martin E.	4778
Brown, William Josiah	1928	Brown, Martha J.	4779
Brown, James Lewis	1929	Brown, Joe E.	4780
Brown, Guy	1930	Brown, Bessie A.	4782
Brown, Ethel	1931	Brown, Susan Frances	4884
Brown, Cyrus Harris	1932	Brown, Eben Foster	4885
Brown, Martha	2098	Brown, Natha	4886
Brown, Elsie	2155	Brown, Amos	4887
Brown, John	2156	Brown, Kelo	4972
Brown, Edna	2157	Brown, Sippy	4974
Brown, Lucy	2158	Browne, Alice	470
Brown, Willie	2159	Branum, Mattie	1245
Brown, Ethel	2160	Brittain, Frank	1255
Brown, Lena	2191	Brittain, Eveline	1256
Brown, Loman	2240	Brady, Caroline	1294
Brown, Wesley	2244	Brittenburg, James N.	1382
Brown, Julia	2412	Brittenburg, Mary Ann	1383
Brown, Mamie	2413	Brittenburg, Norma S.	1384
Brown, Rachel	2414	Browning, Josiah	1933
Brown, John	2424	Browning, Albert	1934
Brown, Mollie	2425	Browning, Lovie Ann	1935
Brown, Milton	2427	Browning, Bula	1937
Brown, Frances	2429	Bridges, Nettie	2139
Brown, Overton	2542	Bridges, Marion F.	2140
Brown, Chicklin	2582	Bridges, Juanita Zelma	2141
Brown, Linda	2583	Bradley, Edwin	2782
Brown, Levi	2584	Bradley, Bruce	4290
Brown, Holmes	2586	Bradley, Frank Colbert	4829
Brown, Laura	2587	Bradley, Clara Hicks	4830
Brown, Lucy	2588	Bradley, Earnest	4831
Brown, Frances	2601	Bradley, Nellie	4832
Brown, Emely	2619	Bradley, Holmes	4833
Brown, Marial	2620	Brooks, Elizabeth	3011
Brown, Willis P.	2657	Brooks, Alexander	3013
Brown, Gincy	2658	Brooks, Steve	3014
Brown, Betsey	2659	Brailey, Nettie	4118
Brown, Agnes	2660	Brawdy, Johnson	4306
Brown, Esias	2661	Brawdy, Dave	4307
Brown, Susan	2662	Burris, Colbert A.	143
Brown, Hobert	2691	Burris, Marvin J.	144
Brown, Andrew L.	2714	Burris, Daisy	146
Brown, Susan	2828	Burris, Cecilia	147
Brown, Joe	2832	Burris, Lillie B.	148
Brown, Slack	2849	Burris, Elsie	342
Brown, Lucy	2850	Burris, Elias	357
Brown, Carrie	2851	Burris, Isaac A.	490
Brown, Lela	2852	Burris, Celia J.	491
Brown, Elta	2853	Burris, Mary C.	492
Brown, Calvin	2914	Burris, Maude C.	493
Brown, Neta	2917	Burris, Colbert A., Jr.	494
Brown, Sampson	2959	Burris, Noah	654
Brown, Patsey	2960	Burris, Amy	739
Brown, Flora Belle	2961	Burris, Mack	740
Brown, Lily	2968	Burris, Ada	792
Brown, Ben	2969	Burris, George	1102
Brown, Martin	2976	Burris, Melton	1497
Brown, Melton Perry	3020	Burris, Lillie	1498
Brown, Sibby	3173	Burris, Bessie	1499
Brown, Gipson	3190	Burris, Robert Lee	1500
Brown, Lolah Rachel	3191	Burris, George Wash-	

Name.	Roll No.	Name.	Roll No.
ingtin	1948	Byrd, Susan F.	4613
Burris, Lemuel Colbert	1949	Byars, Catherine	1674
Burris, Emily	1950	Byars, Thomas N.	1675
Burris, Hindman H.	2636	Byars, William C.	1676
Burris, Viola J.	2637	Byars, Charlie T.	1677
Burris, Hinmon Harrison	2638	Byars, Samuel T.	1678
		Byars, Nancy E.	1680
Burris, Ben	2793	Byars, Roy N.	1681
Burris, Sim	2835	Byars, Alice Ophelia	1682
Burris, Bettie	2836	Byars, Jim Jones	1683
Burris, Isaac	2837	Byfield, Elsie	2681
Burris, Eastman	2838	Bynum, Joseph	2727
Burris, James	2839	Bynum, Lulu	2728
Burris, Sarah	2840	Bynum, Remonia	2729
Burris, Nancy	2841	Bynum, Lucy	2730
Burris, Joe H.	2871	Bynum, Charley	2731
Burris, Vina	2872	Bynum, Netterville R.	2732
Burris, Walsie	2873	Bynum, Julius Colbert	2733
Burris, William	3977	Bynum, Joseph Jr.	4163
Burris, Eben	3978	Bynum, Effie	4482
Burnett, Harriet I.	796	Bynum, Willis	4483
Burnett, Charles M.	797	Cass, Lewis	169
Burnett, Benjamin Franklin	798	Cass, Rhoda Nail	170
Bunch, Emma	1115	Cass, William M.	171
Bunch, Thomas P.	1116	Cass, Levi	675
Bunch, Maudie M.	1117	Cass, Lizzie	1085
Bunch, Albert C.	1118	Cass, Benjamin	1086
Burks, Royden	1334	Cass, Sam	2465
Burks, William	1335	Carney, Martin	417
Burks, Vera	1336	Carney, Lottie	418
Burks, Rowena	1337	Carney, Bina	419
Burks, Johnie Wenona	1338	Carney, Jimpson	420
Burney, W. B.	1742	Carney, Lee	421
Burney, Julian	1743	Carney, Morris	422
Burney, Una	1744	Carney, Lucy	423
Burney, Valey	1745	Carney, Sampson	781
Burney, Blanch	1746	Carney, Thomas	783
Burney, Wessie	1747	Carney, Harriet	784
Burney, Clay P.	1748	Carney, Burney	882
Burney, Douglas Johnson	1749	Carney, Joseph	883
		Carney, Martha	884
Burney, Louisa	2478	Carney, Mary	885
Burney, Bennie Bennett	2479	Carney, Reubin	886
Burney, Paul Earnest	2480	Carney, Andrew	888
Burney, Arvilla	2481	Carney, Annie	889
Burney, Albert Sydney	3022	Carney, Gilbert	2087
Burney, Sydney Guy	3023	Carney, William	2125
Burney, Joseph	3024	Carney, Katie	2444
Burney, Tams Bixby	3025	Carney, Johnson	2571
Burney, Geraldine	3026	Carney, Cicen	3172
Burney, Edward Sehon	3722	Carney, Philip	4288
Burney, Wessie Ella	3723	Carney, Maltsie	4763
Burney, Joseph Calhoun	3724	Carter, Watson	1090
Burney, Edward Everett	3725	Carter, Serena	1523
Burney, Overton Love	3726	Carter, C. D.	1527
Burney, Ada Bessie	3727	Carter, Stella Laflore	1528
Bussell, Luey	2200	Carter, Italy Cecil	1529
Bussell, Stephen	3012	Carter, Benjamin W.	1530
Burch, Charles E.	2602	Carter, John E.	1639
Burns, Mollie	4497	Carter, Ida	2053
Burns, Annie	4498	Carter, Williston	2054
Burns, Charley Francis	4499	Carter, Colbert	3488
Burns, Eli Pickens	4500	Carter, Henry E.	3489
Byrd, Ida	4	Carter, Alberta	3490
Byrd, Eugean	7	Carter, Julia Josephine	4101
Byrd, Chester Temple	8	Carter, Stella E.	4194
Byrd, J. W.	199	Carter, Florence	4911
Byrd, Emma M.	200	Cash, Alice	1148
Byrd, Johnson	201	Cash, Patterson Shi	1149
Byrd, Stella V.	202	Cash, Tyree	1150
Byrd, Louisa	624	Cash, Elpha	1151
Byrd, William L.	1024	Carlton, Frances	1717
Byrd, B. F.	1455	Carlton, Josie	1718
Byrd, Mamie	1456	Carlton, Guy	1719
Byrd, Lonnie E.	1457	Carlton, Pearlie	1720
Byrd, Roy Neal	1458	Carlton, George R.	1721
Byrd, Lula May	1459	Camp, Calvin	2055
Byrd, George Franklin	1461	Camp, Sissy	2056
Byrd, William L., Jr.	1462	Camp, Nancy	2057
Byrd, Benjamin F.	1464	Camp, Lyman	2058
Byrd, Palmer W.	4011	Carroll, Joel Henry	2145
Byrd, Timmie	4029	Carroll, James Calvin	2146
		Carrell, Mary	3554

Name.	Roll No.	Name.	Roll No.
Carrell, Richard	3559	Christian, Ed	4549
Carrell, Alice	3560	Chisholm, William F.	3707
Carrell, Stella	4201	-Chitwood, Mary	3754
Carrell, Joe	4202	Chitwood, Emil	3755
Cain, Lottie	2485	Chitwood, Silas	3756
Carhee, Julia	2603	Chitwood, Lena	3757
Carhee, Florence	2604	Chitwood, William Col-	
Carhee, Alice	2605	bert	3758
Capey, Wallace	2822	Chitwood, Walter Belvin	3759
Calhoune, Charles	2863	Chitwood, David P.	3760
Calhoune, Emily	3203	Chitwood, Lee	3761
Caraway, Mary	3551	Chuffatubby	3898
Caraway, Lonzo E.	3553	Chief, Louena	3979
Campbell, Lewis	3658	Choate, Willie	4961
Campbell, Charles B.	3792	Cicin	3966
Campbell, Annie Belle	3793	Clopton, Susie	707
Campbell, Charles W. W.	3794	Clopton, Fannie	708
Campbell, Mary Ellen	3795	Clopton, Maggie	709
Campbell, Milton Bryant	3796	Clopton, Thomas W.	713
Campbell, Stella Ber-		Clopton, Sophia Easter	714
nard	3797	Clopton, Luella	4032
Campbell, Frances B.	3798	Clayton, Tansey A.	1364
Campbell, Effie May	3799	Clayton, Indianola D.	1365
Campbell, Montford T.	3821	Clayton, Lockie S.	1366
Campbell, Holmes Col-		Clayton, William Her-	
bert	3822	bert	1367
Campbell, Lawrence	3823	Clayton, Paul Sharpe	1368
Campbell, John	3824	Clayboun, Celia	2954
Campbell, Rex	3825	Colbert, Humphrey	13
Campbell, Charles T.	3827	Colbert, Salina	14
Campbell, Ada Pearl	4386	Colbert, Jackson R.	15
Campbell, William G.	4389	Colbert, Mary Wolfe	16
Cartlidge, Benj. F.	4148	Colbert, Lucy	18
Cartlidge, Nadean	4149	Colbert, Amanda	19
Cawdell, Jay	4528	Colbert, Walton	66
Casey, Lula	4583	Colbert, Louisa	67
Carr, Celin	5003	Colbert, Amanda	68
Chapman, Harriet E. G.	53	Colbert, Minnie	69
Chapman, Charles L.	54	Colbert, Frank	70
Chapman, James W.	55	Colbert, Serena	71
Chapman, Virginia C.	56	Colbert, Nora	72
Chapman, Claud C.	57	Colbert, Mack	73
Chapman, Richard F.	58	Colbert, Wilburn	265
Chapman, Susan	4309	Colbert, Gipson	297
Chapman, Edward	4310	Colbert, Dougherty C.	524
Chapman, Ellen	4311	Colbert, Harley Hum-	
Chapman, James Thomas	4312	phrey	525
Chapman, John Napo-		Colbert, Denovo A.	526
leon	4313	Colbert, Zeno Penner	527
Chase, Grove E.	1723	Colbert, Jessie	619
Chase, Gussie	1724	Colbert, James E.	892
Chase, Emmet	1725	Colbert, James	893
Chase, Abel D., Jr.	1726	Colbert, Leila	894
Chase, Lennie Mabel	1727	Colbert, Holmes	895
Chase, Nancy	1783	Colbert, Ben	896
Chummuttie, Tennessee	1906	Colbert, Theodore	897
Chastain, Mary	2044	Colbert, Edmon	903
Chastain, Alec	2045	Colbert, Joshua	904
Chastain, Jessie	2046	Colbert, George	956
Chigley, Nelson	2257	Colbert, Sukey	957
Chigley, Julia	2258	Colbert, Dougherty	959
Chigley, Mose	2259	Colbert, Richard Floyd	960
Chigley, Wyatt	2260	Colbert, Abijah	961
Cheadle, Martin Van		Colbert, Laura D.	962
Buren	2698	Colbert, Benis	1053
Cheadle, Mary V.	2699	Colbert, Lucy	1055
Cheadle, Tommie	2700	Colbert, Cubby	1057
Cheadle, Overton	2701	Colbert, Jim	1058
Cheadle, Lurena	2702	Colbert, Ed F.	1782
Cheadle, Ellis	2703	Colbert, Lydia	1969
Cheadle, Lillian Hor-		Colbert, Martha	1970
tense	3516	Colbert, Icy	1972
Chester, Jinsie	2877	Colbert, Alice	1973
Chester, Joel	2895	Colbert, Humphreys	1974
Chosholm, Sallie	2962	Colbert, Mary	2106
Christian, Tom	3021	Colbert, Margaret	2137
Christian, Lee	3030	Colbert, Frank	2161
Christian, John	3031	Colbert, Jeff	2175
Christian, Lottie	3032	Colbert, Lyman	2432
Christian, Walter	3036	Colbert, Burney	2483
Christian, Holmes	3038	Colbert, Mary	2599
Christian, Maude	3039	Colbert, Ida O.	2644
Christian, Mattie E.	4515	Colbert, Dixie H.	2721

Name.	Roll No.
Colbert, Bulah	2722
Colbert, Mamie	2723
Colbert, Holmes	2724
Colbert, Effie	2725
Colbert, Elmer	2726
Colbert, Willie	2880
Colbert, Thanet	2882
Colbert, Louis V.	2896
Colbert, Eva Lou	2897
Colbert, Elizabeth Honor	2898
Colbert, Eula Emily	2899
Colbert, Amy	2900
Colbert, Julia May	2901
Colbert, Sim	3242
Colbert, Jim	3243
Colbert, Ben	3244
Colbert, Aden	3245
Colbert, Allie Lee	3246
Colbert, Billie	3592
Colbert, Lamon	3619
Colbert, Harley Eugene	3639
Colbert, Richard G.	3640
Colbert, Holmes	3666
Colbert, Frank Overton	3667
Colbert, Nora	958
Colbert, Nancy	1056
Colbert, Sam Tilden	3689
Colbert, Thomas Rutherford	3690
Colbert, James Beldon	3693
Colbert, Albert D.	3699
Colbert, William	3896
Colbert, Guy	4006
Colbert, Liza Lessie	4020
Colbert, Zona	4038
Colbert, Elizabeth	4081
Colbert, Martin Jr.	4084
Colbert, Benj. Franklin	4085
Colbert, Cecil Calvin	4086
Colbert, Tolbert Ray	4087
Colbert, Mamie Marie	4088
Colbert, Luther Earl	4089
Colbert, Judie	4147
Colbert, Marion Estelle	4206
Colbert, Walter	4279
Colbert, Czarina M.	4280
Colbert, Walter Cevera	4281
Colbert, Charley	4374
Colbert, Cornie	4376
Colbert, Lela	4377
Colbert, Joe E.	4427
Colbert, Annie R.	4428
Colbert, Nancy Louisa	4429
Colbert, Henry Tuttle	4430
Colbert, Lettie M.	4431
Colbert, Joseph E.	4432
Colbert, Salina	4564
Colbert, Martha	4569
Colbert, Ben	4570
Colbert, Deen	4599
Colbert, Isabel	4660
Colbert, Emil Franklin	4667
Colbert, Oscar	4668
Colbert, Eula	4669
Colbert, Henry C.	4693
Colbert, Rufus	4694
Colbert, Ruth	4695
Colbert, Benjamin H.	4733
Colbert, Gladdes	4757
Colbert, Annie	4790
Colbert, James	4941
Colbert, Holmes B.	4993
Collins, Odus Lynn	101
Collins, Wm. B.	102
Collins, S. C.	103
Collins, George R., Jr.	104
Collins, Norah	304
Collins, Edmund	333
Collins, Lema	915
Collins, Oscie	916
Collins, Alphus	937
Collins, Lee	938
Collins, George	1522

Name.	Roll No.
Collins, Hettie	1687
Collins, James P.	1688
Collins, George H.	1689
Collins, Andrey B.	1690
Collins, Theodore	1692
Collins, John	1691
Collins, Ben Carter	2107
Collins, Hettie	2108
Collins, Lousianna	2321
Collins, Thomas	2322
Collins, Edward	2323
Collins, Tennie	2333
Collins, Maggie	2334
Collins, Allie	2335
Collins, John	2336
Collins, Berry E.	2337
Collins, Virgie	2338
Collins, Albert, Jr.	2340
Collins, Roy	2341
Collins, Mary Etta	2342
Collins, Ben, F.	2355
Collins, Mary Annetta	2356
Collins, Benjamin F.	2357
Collins, Serena	2484
Collins, Sarah A.	3328
Collins, Maude	3329
Collins, Dannie	3330
Collins, Charley	3331
Collins, Cecil Cline	4007
Collins, Nancy	4378
Colley, Ella	351
Colley, Lillie	352
Colley, Lydia	353
Colley, John R.	354
Coleman, Louisa	583
Conohotubby, Susanna	729
Columbus, Etta	1069
Columbus, Byars	2419
Columbus, Ephus	2420
Columbus, Dawes Tandy	2421
Columbus, Lizzie	2422
Cook, Mary	1308
Cook, Charles	1309
Cook, Stella	1310
Cook, Levera	1311
Cook, William Nye	1313
Cook, Cleo	1314
Coffey, Charley	1537
Coffey, Amanda Virginia	1592
Coffey, William Lee	1593
Coffey, Taylor Overton	1594
Coffey, Merritt Price	1595
Coffey, Earnest	1596
Coffey, Mary Alvirta	1597
Coffey, Anderson Wolford	1598
Coffey, Sale	1599
Coffey, Walter	1600
Coffey, Ivy	1615
Coffee, Luella	3046
Coffee, John Lewis	3047
Coffee, Cora	3048
Coffee, Mamie	3049
Coyle, James Thomas	1652
Coyle, Albert Pike	1653
Coyle, Benjamin Harrison	1654
Coyle, Earnest Earl	1655
Coyle, Mabel Pearl	1656
Coyle, Lillie Audry	4111
Coyle, Violet Teresa	4112
Cox, Ada E.	1776
Courtney, Ziley	2081
Courtney, Peter	2082
Courtney, Ben	2569
Courtney, Ellen	2570
Courtney, Ben Jr.	2572
Courtney, Willie	2573
Courtney, Adelaide	2574
Courtney, Sally	2575
Courtney, Tyson	2576
Courtney, Sophia	2577
Courtney, Sammie	2578

Name.	Roll No.
Courtney, Betsie	2579
Courtney, Elsie Sena	2580
Courtney, Adeline	2581
Cole, Ellen	2245
Cobb, Jim	2262
Cobb, Virginia	2263
Cobb, Calvin	2264
Condon, Lucy	2415
Condon, Michael Jefferson	2472
Cooney, Alpha	2627
Cooney, Neita Carine	2628
Cooney, Wallace Franklin	2629
Cooney, Myrtle Lee	4189
Cohee, Johnson	2712
Cohee, Emeline	2713
Coss, Jimmie	2715
Coss, Emma	2716
Conway, Joel	3129
Conway, Nancy	3130
Conway, Lizzie	3131
Conway, Bessie	3132
Corley, Charley	3511
Corley, Sallie	3512
Cooper, Demis Mattie	3852
Cooper, Lydal F.	3853
Cooper, Charles Christopher	3854
Cooper, Frances M.	3855
Cooper, Pattie Ross	3856
Cooper, Happy	3857
Conner, Ada B.	4253
Conner, Edna	4606
Cochran, William Hunter	4323
Cochran, Willie	4324
Cochran, Vertis	4325
Cochran, Samuel T.	4326
Cochran, Arnaca	4696
Cochran, Martin	4697
Cochran, Turner	4699
Cochran, Nellie	4700
Cochran, Ruth	4701
Cochran, Lettie	4702
Connelly, John William	4348
Connelly, Elizabeth	4349
Connelly, Alfred	4350
Connelly, William	4351
Connelly, Henry N.	4352
Connelly, Jennie	4353
Connelly, Emma May	4354
Connelly, John W.	4355
Connelly, Irene	4356
Cofer, Bettie	4240
Cofer, Andrew Jackson	4241
Cofer, Emma Lena	4242
Cofer, Geo. Edward	4243
Cofer, Jesse Freeman	4244
Cofer, Virgil Lee	4245
Costello, Charles Leavitt	4603
Cowoy, Asaw	4976
Compton, Sallie	4997
Compton, Pearl	5001
Cravatt, Katie	426
Cravatt, Angeline	427
Cravatt, Maggie	428
Cravatt, Lila	429
Cravatt, Ina	430
Cravatt, Clarence	431
Cravatt, Randers H.	996
Cravatt, Mary	997
Cravatt, Irvin	998
Cravatt, Elvina	999
Cravatt, Forbus D.	1046
Cravatt, Lena	1047
Cravatt, Amanda	1048
Cravatt, Stella	1049
Cravatt, Overton	1052
Cravatt, Tom	2473
Cravatt, Ben	2474
Cravatt, Lubocea D.	2477
Cravatt, Imogene	2633

Name.	Roll No.
Cravatt, Albert	2633
Cravatt, Allen W.	4239
Creecy, Gracie	2345
Creecy, Juel	2347
Creecy, Clara Susie	4596
Criner, Eunice	1235
Criner, Joe W.	1330
Criner, George	1785
Criner, Norma	1786
Criner, John	1788
Criner, Robert Franklin	1789
Criner, John Adolphus	1790
Criner, Joe William	1791
Criner, Frank	1792
Criner, Alva	1793
Criner, Buck	1794
Criner, Charles Cook	1795
Criner, Frank	3729
Crosby, Annie	123
Crockett, Hayes	2348
Crockett, Joseph McKinley	2349
Crockett, Majar	2372
Crockett, Mack	2373
Crockett, Elizabeth	2374
Cravens, Mary	3308
Cravens, Charles Thomas	3309
Cravens, John James, Jr.	3311
Cravens, Tullas Russell	4190
Cruce, Chickie	4495
Cruce, Lorena Jane	4496
Crummey, Tennie	4156
Crummey, Clarence	4157
Cuberry, Davis	17
Cutchontubbee, Shimoheche	2351
Cumley, Irvan	2669
Cummeutubby, Palmer	2807
Culberson, James	3912
Davis, Martha	28
Davis, Maggie P.	29
Davis, Julius	262
Davis, Henry	508
Davis, Samuel C.	686
Davis, Matilda F.	687
Davis, Arvilla	688
Davis, Julia	1833
Davis, Dora Stella	1834
Davis, James Russell	1835
Davis, Nora Belle	1836
Davis, Benjamin	1837
Davis, John Henry	1838
Davis, Daniel	2354
Davis, John Lowery	2818
Davis, Mattie	4877
Davis, Marian Jessie	4878
Dana, Peter	230
Dana, Agnes	231
Darin, Markham	266
Dawkins, Minnie	595
Dawkins, Wallace	601
Dawkins, Lonnie E.	602
Davenport, Julia A.	2626
Daily, Henry	4952
Daily, Jimmie	4953
Daily, Elizabeth	4954
Daily, Emma	4955
Dearring, Richard	383
Dearring, Kilsie Collins	4664
Decherd, Eugenia	1435
Deel, Hattie Johnson	3838
Deel, Bonnie Owenby	3839
Deel, Homer	3840
Deshan, Albert	3915
Deshan, Dovie	3916
Dennis, Jessie	4554
DeArmon, Laura	4580
DeArmon, Ester Lee	4581
DeArmon, Oramay	4582
Dickerson, Lillie	464
Dickerson, Leo Earl	465
Dickerson, Robert R.	466
Dickerson, Amanda	2992

Name.	Roll No.
Dickerson, Cecil R.	4019
Dillard, Lizzie	2132
Dillard, Dick	2133
Dillingham, Amanda	3605
Dilbeck, Luella	4578
Dilbeck, Floyd Edwin	4579
Dick, Martin	4865
Douglas, Nancy L.	1374
Doak, Lovie Lee	4827
Doak, Henry Love	4828
Doak, Lula E.	4861
Downing, Mose	4893
Downing, Mary Mozelle	4894
Drew, Mary V.	4925
Durant, Ashome	187
Durant, Jacob	188
Durant, Burney	189
Durant, Julius	190
Durant, Preman J.	191
Durant, Mollie	293
Duke, Billy	414
Duke, Lankford	415
Duke, Tip Graham	416
Duke, Dora	1070
Duke, Lucy	2388
Duke, Sam	3425
Duffy, Edith Ethel	993
Duffy, Ethel Cecelia	994
Duffy, Esther Clementine	995
Durin, Wesley	1067
Dulin, Simpson	1285
Dulin, Ola Lee	1286
Duroderigo, Albert Franklin	1658
Durederigo, Eliza	1659
Duroderigo, Columbus	3808
Duncan, Eliza	2202
Duncan, Lewis	3204
Duncan, James	3274
Duncum, William Henry	2293
Duncum, Thomas Brown	2294
Duncum, Charles Lewis	2295
Duncum, John Lawton	2300
Duncum, Roy E.	4141
Duncum, Silas Floyd	4142
Duncan, John W.	4759
Duncan, Frona	4965
Durham, John	2487
Durham, Arthur	2488
Durham, Sudie	2489
Durham, Berry	2490
Durham, Stella	4153
Dunigan, Lela	2680
Dunigan, Ethel Jennie Bell	2683
Duckworth, Lou	3563
Duckworth, Benjamin Allen	3564
Duckworth, Maude	3566
Duckworth, Claud Gay	3567
Duckworth, Sallie	3568
Duckworth, Berry A., Jr.	3569
Duckworth, Wiley J.	3570
Duckworth, Perry Polaski	3571
Duckworth, Thomas	3653
Duckworth, Lausson	3654
Duckworth, Raymond	3655
Dyar, Calvin	544
Dyar, Sallie	545
Dyar, Fannie	546
Dyar, Joe	547
Dyar, Annie	750
Dyar, Katesy	752
Dyar, Susan	4023
Dyer, Dawes	126
Dyer, Adeline	179
Dyer, Tecumseh	1104
Easter	264
Eastwood, Emma Luella	2142
Eastwood, Arthur Franklin	2143

Name.	Roll No.
Easky, Ruth	3403
Easky, Tandy	3404
Eastman, Lorena	3518
Earl, William	3718
Earl, Katie Ethel	3719
Earl, Edith May	3720
East, Frances	4315
Easton, Henry	4595
Ebisch, Mattie	1759
Ebisch, Wagoner	1760
Ebisch, C. A. Frederick	1761
Ebisch, May	1762
Ebisch, Lidda	1763
Ebisch, W. T. Ernest	1764
Edwards, Esias	403
Edwards, Binum	616
Edwards, Daniel	1139
Edwards, Nellie	1140
Edwards, Sam I.	1141
Edwards, Pocahontas	4527
Elmy	497
Elementoner	504
Elliott, Hannah	1333
Elliott, Olivia	1339
Eldridge, Jim Jr.	2012
Eldridge, Emily	2013
Elmore, Lorena	4777
Elmore, Floyd Lee	4781
Ensharkey, Carrie	2642
Ensharkey, C. A.	2684
Ensharkey, Serena	2685
Ensharkey, Ada	2686
Ensharkey, Sampson	2687
Escue, Walter	3818
Escue, Ida	3819
Eyatubby, Ben	3817
Factor, Isteph Ifyaka	749
Factor, McCurtain	844
Factor, Henry	2520
Falata, Kuneatcha	2819
Falata, Linho	2820
Fallin, Jesse	3956
Feland, John R.	3380
Feland, James C.	3381
Feland, Maggie	4522
Feland, Hattie	4523
Feland, Lucretia Graham	4524
Feland, Columbus Scott	4525
Feland, William Thomas	4526
Filmore, William	159
Filmore, Henry	786
Fillmore, Selan	2446
Fillmore, Mollie	2447
Fillmore, Robert	2448
Fillmore, Maria	2449
Fillmore, Nellie	2450
Fillmore, Marcum	2451
Fillmore, Mary Ann	2640
Fillmore, Epsie	2648
Fillmore, Jennette	2650
Fillmore, Hannah	2651
Fillmore, Isaac	2810
Fillmore, Charles Wilson	2811
Fillmore, Benjamin Franklin	3784
Fillmore, Robert	3785
Fillmore, Frank	3786
Fillmore, Emly Lebell	3787
Fillmore, Benjamin	3834
Fillmore, Frances	4152
Fillmore, Jacob	4302
Fillmore, Silas	4304
Fillmore, Elias	4305
Fillmore, Julia	4708
Fitch, Mary Ellen	1736
Fitch, Joe	1737
Fitch, Maude	1738
Fitch, Eliza Easter	1739
Fisher, Amanda	2279
Fisher, Lewis Keel	2286
Finley, Mary C.	4405
Finley, Rosa Lorina	4409
Finley, Emma Elzada	4410

Name.	Roll No.
Fletcher, Maude	2029
Fletcher, Claudie	2030
Fletcher, Joe	2094
Fletcher, Thomas B.	2776
Fletcher, John Henry	2777
Fletcher, Katie May	2778
Fletcher, Virgie	2779
Fletcher, Abner Brown	2780
Fleming, Willie Hampton	4276
Flemmings, Joe	4300
Folsom, Phoebie	250
Folsom, Eli	479
Folsom, Frank	480
Folsom, Lyman	500
Folsom, Jane	501
Folsom, Mulbert	502
Folsom, Clicy	503
Folsom, Sampson	793
Folsom, Margany	3428
Folsom, Joseph P.	3429
Folsom, Tandy	3431
Folsom, Alice Julia	3432
Folsom, Mollie	3596
Folsom, Basey	3597
Folsom, Daisy	3598
Folsom, Minnie	3599
Folsom, Alice	3600
Folsom, Israel R.	3601
Folsom, David	3750
Folsom, Myrtle	3751
Folsom, Nora	3752
Folsom, Minerva	4028
Folsom, Jefferson	4030
Folsom, Agnes	4209
Folsom, Virgil	4210
Folsome, Catherine	2389
Folsome, Isaac	3119
Folsome, Minnie	3120
Folsome, Willie	3121
Folsome, John	4303
Ford, Sallie	481
Ford, Willie	482
Ford, Nannie	483
Ford, Mary	484
Ford, Mollie Willis	4412
Ford, Mollie Willis, Jr.	4413
Ford, Hugh W.	4414
Ford, John J.	4415
Foster, Henry C.	1574
Foster, George	1575
Foster, William	1576
Foster, Lizzie	1577
Foster, Florence	1578
Fox, Frank F.	4546
Fox, Jay J.	4547
Fox, Wallace W.	4548
Frazer, Maulsie	356
Frazier, Eastman	550
Frazier, Mollie	551
Frazier, Colsen	552
Frazier, Elizabeth	553
Frazier, Sylvia	789
Frazier, Agnes	790
Frazier, Mary	791
Frazier, Jim	1100
Frazier, Lottie	1101
FrazierThompson	2509
Frazier, Elsie*	2510
Frazier, Victoria	2545
Frazier, Minnie	2546
Frazier, Fletcher	2547
Frazier, Rhoda	5012
Friend, Retta	1225
Friend, Alice	1226
Friend, Dorset Carter	1227
Fryrear, Rosa	1287
Fryrear, Ema	1288
Fryrear, Annie May	1289
Fryrear, Emet	1290
Fryrear, Robert O.	1293
Fry, Sammie J.	1524
Fry, Sophia	1525

Name.	Roll No.
Froman, Levina	2128
Froman, Celescaby	2129
Franklin, Martha A.	3250
Franklin, Jesse James	3383
Franklin, Johnson	3384
Franklin, Joe	3385
Franklin, Edna Lou Sophia	3386
Franklin, Samuel Wesley	3387
Franklin, Dollie Ulis	3388
Francis, Katie	4219
Francis, Percy	4220
Francis, Bertram	4221
Fulsom, Charlie	44
Fulsom, Tennessee	1022
Fulsom, Lela	2038
Fulsome, Liza Ann	195
Fulsome, Sina	457
Fulsome, Pharo	458
Fulsome, Isaac	1120
Fulsome, Edmon	2502
Futishcha, Johnnie	153
Futischa, Wincy	402
Futischa, Joe	404
Fussell, Alice	172
Fussell, Charley	173
Fussell, Monie	174
Fussell, Lola Francis	175
Gallatin, Minnie	1419
Garland, Jake	1705
Gaddis, William Manuel	1799
Gaddis, William B.	1801
Gaddis, Sallie	2433
Gaddis, Claude	2435
Gaddis, Lizzie	2436
Gaddis, George L.	3875
Gaddis, Lee Jefferson	3876
Gaddis, George	4172
Gaddis, Will	4932
Gates, Bennington	2405
Garrett, Lula	2752
Garrett, Jessie Lynn	2757
Gardner, Annie	3086
Gardner, John	3087
Gardner, Cleveland	3088
Gardner, Sam	3089
Gardner, Maggie	3090
Gardner, Albert	3091
Gardner, Susie	3407
Gardner, Sudie	3408
Gardner, Dollie	3409
Gardner, Fitzhugh L.	3410
Garsides, Fannie	4652
Garsides, Ben	4653
Garsides, Alex	4654
Garsides, Jim	4655
Garsides, Nellie	4656
Garsides, Mattie	4657
Garsides, Joe Jr.	4658
Gipson, William	473
Gipson, Liza	696
Gipson, Martha	699
Gipson, Ethel May	701
Gipson, Murtle	702
Gipson, Abner	829
Gipson, Eddie	830
Gipson, Wilburn	841
Gibson, Minnie	1171
Gibson, Mitchell	1172
Gibson, Jane	1173
Gibson, Lucy	1174
Gibson, Mississippi	1175
Gibson, Josiah	1176
Gibson, Emily	3788
Gibson, Nancy	3789
Gibson, Hickman	3790
Gibson, Millenda	3791
Gibbons, Amelia J.	4478
Gibbons, Murray	4479
Gibbons, Margaret C.	4480
Gibbons, Migs E.	4481
Gilliam, Mary Elizabeth	1981
Gilliam, Olivette Herndon	1982

Name.	Roll No.	Name.	Roll No.
Gilliam, James Sanders	1983	Grayson, Rena	3963
Gilliam, John Overstreet	1984	Gray, Ada B.	4509
Gilliam, Sallie Louisa	1985	Gray, Lon	3776
Gilliam, Lula Maude	1986	Gray, Robert	3777
Gilliam, Howard Preston	1987	Gray, Vidi	3778
Gilliam, Ona	5008	Gray, Elsie	3779
Gilliam, Clemmie	5009	Greenwood, Sarah	233
Gilbert, Lucy	2101	Greenwood, Thos. W.	234
Gilbert, Ida	2102	Greenwood, Mattie	235
Gilbert, Elvie	2103	Greenwood, Bessie	322
Gilbert, Lela	4130	Greenwood, Julius T.	323
Gilbert, Jennie	4131	Greenwood, Tom	507
Gilmore, Sarah A.	4721	Greenwood, Hogen	762
Gilmore, Monteray	4722	Greenwood, Mahall	763
Gilmore, Roscoe C.	4723	Greenwood, Linsey	764
Gilmore, Louina B.	4724	Greenwood, Jesse	765
Gilmore, Flavions J.	4725	Greenwood, Bessie	767
Gilmore, Lena A.:	4726	Greenwood, Gincy	946
Gilmore, John N.	4727	Greenwood, Bert	947
Gilmore, Edwin F.	4728	Greenwood, Lee	948
Gordon, Emily	1536	Greenwood, Catherine	949
Godfrey, Louisa	1943	Greenwood, Myrtle	1547
Godfrey, Annie	3230	Greenwood, Betsey	1610
Godfrey, Wilbur Elmer	3232	Greenwood, Pearl	1611
Godfrey, Mary Pearl	3461	Greenwood, Susie	1907
Godfrey, Mary C.	3482	Greenwood, Jackson	2105
Godfrey, Frank E.	3484	Greenwood, Eula	2127
Godfrey, Charles B.	3485	Greenwood, Simeon	2280
Godfrey, Harriet Edna	3486	Greenwood, Emaziah	2281
Godfrey, Earl Jay	3487	Greenwood, Lem	2282
Gooding, John Franklin	3146	Greenwood, Edmon	2283
Gooding, Charles Lemuel	3299	Greenwood, Lizzie	2498
Gooding, Charles Holmes	3300	Greenwood, Frank	2544
Goforth, Solomon	3185	Greenwood, Jeff	2548
Goforth, Sarah	3256	Greenwood, Barney	2549
Goforth, Fred W.	3257	Greenwood, Isaac	2770
Goforth, Nora	3258	Greenwood, Nellie	2771
Goforth, Eli P.	4222	Greenwood, Hicks	2772
Goforth, Sophina	4223	Greenwood, Emma	2773
Goforth, Charlotte	4224	Greenwood, Jimmy	2774
Goforth, Bessie	4225	Greenwood, Josie Ann	2775
Goforth, Odelia	4226	Greenwood, Henry	2806
Goforth, Solomon	4227	Greenwood, Stephen	3980
Goforth, William	4228	Greenwood, Jensie	3981
Goforth, Grover C.	4229	Greenwood, Lela	3982
Goforth, E. P., Jr.	4230	Greenwood, Lottie	4035
Goforth, Ruth	4231	Greenwood, George	4120
Goforth, William H.	4339	Greenwood, Myrtle	4164
Goforth, Mary	4340	Greenwood, Robert	4747
Goforth, Lena May	4341	Greenwood, Alphens	4767
Goforth, Joe H.	4390	Grant, C. J.	1246
Goforth, Jessie	4391	Grant, Calvin F.	1247
Goforth, Louisa	4910	Grant, Tom P.	1248
Good, Minnie E.	3326	Grant, Mattie C.	1249
Good, Ruth E.	3327	Grant, Nora J.	1250
Goode, Ada	4436	Graham, Menerva	3377
Goode, Lily	4437	Graham, Fred J.	3378
Goins, Susan	3730	Grinslade, Sallie	3390
Goins, Charles Calvin	3731	Grinslade, Benjamin	
Goins, Melinda Alzina	3732	Jackson	3391
Goins, Vaney Dixon	3733	Grinslade, William Ed-	
Goins, Ludie Napoleon	3734	ward	3392
Goins, Susie Alice	3735	Grinslade, Martha Eliza-	
Goldsby, Dettie	3906	beth	3393
Goldsby, Frank Walter	3907	Grinslade, John Wilson	3394
Goldsby, Frank Walter		Grinslade, Albert Milton	3395
Jr.	3908	Grinslade, Henry Martin	3396
Goldsby, Bryan	3909	Grinslade, Walter Lee	3397
Goldsby, Nellie	3910	Grinslade, Hattie May	3398
Goldsby, Clay	3911	Griggs, Dora	3802
Goldsby, Richard O.	4214	Green, Minnie	3836
Gooch, Cora Eugenea	4083	Green, Roy C.	3837
Grayson, Gibson T.	132	Green, Redie Jackson	4062
Grayson, Ema	133	Green, William Elvie	4063
Grayson, Felix	134	Green, Myrtle Emma	4064
Grayson, James J.	135	Green, Daniel	4316
Grayson, Annie	136	Graves, Ellen	4659
Grayson, Acey	628	Gully, Jim	124
Grayson, John	913	Guynes, Margarett	742
Grayson, Louisa	914	Guynes, Charles Monson	744
Grayson, Tennie	917	Guynes, David J.	745
Grayson, Lizzie	2215	Guy, Douglas D.	1463
Grayson, Maggie	2219	Guy, William Malcolm	1944

Name.	Roll No.
Guy, Cerena Josephine	1945
Guy, Angeline Elizabeth	1946
Guess, Joe	3416
Guess, Robert	3417
Guess, Edward	3418
Guess, Robert, Jr.	3419
Guess, Emmet	3420
Guess, Jeff	3421
Guess, Elizabeth	3422
Guess, Joe, Jr.	3593
Guess, Jimmie	4204
Harris, Walton	45
Harris, Joe	1025
Harris, Ema	1026
Harris, Halis	1027
Harris, Serena	1616
Harris, Daisy	1617
Harris, Bennie	1618
Harris, Mary	1871
Harris, Tommie	1872
Harris, Lucy	1873
Harris, William	1886
Harris, Lucretia	1887
Harris, Bertie	1888
Harris, John	1889
Harris, Hettie	1890
Harris, Tipton Shirley	2000
Harris, Delos	2001
Harris, Fred	2002
Harris, Irene	2003
Harris, Jennie	2004
Harris, Hettie	2041
Harris, Benjamin Franklin	2652
Harris, Hindmon H.	2653
Harris, Loren Thomas	2654
Harris, Martha	2749
Harris, Lila	3448
Harris, Wes	3449
Harris, Emma	3450
Harris, Louisa	3884
Harris, Amanda	4065
Harris, Henderson	4121
Harris, Mamie	4192
Harris, R. M.	4282
Harris, Jennie	4283
Harris, Dixie	4284
Harris, Halley	4285
Harris, Robert Maxwell	4286
Harris, Frank	4686
Hawkins, Morris H.	89
Hawkins, Charlie	90
Hawkins, Lena	400
Hawkins, Nelson	505
Hawkins, Mille	508
Hawkins, Lewis	510
Hawkins, Patsey	511
Hawkins, Minnie	1538
Hawkins, Scott	1995
Hawkins, Ruby	1996
Hawkins, Jessie	1997
Hawkins, Fannie Doria	1998
Hawkins, Abbie Dee	1999
Hawkins Ledicy	2242
Hawkins, Sam	2365
Hawkins, William Lloyd	2366
Hawkins, Eliza	2408
Hawkins, Lila	2551
Hawkins, Betsey	2552
Hawkins, Sarah	2553
Hawkins, George	2758
Hawkins, Josie	2767
Hawkins, Molsie	2768
Hawkins, William	3728
Hawkins, Winnie	4015
Hawkins, Kingsberry	4289
Hawkins, May	4711
Hawkins, Frances Terry	4712
Hayes, Agnes	218
Hayes, Clara	219
Hayes, Nora	220
Hayes, Joseph William	4012
Hayes, Daniel	4988

Name.	Roll No.
Hayes, Minnie	4989
Hayes, Maggie	4990
Hayes, Edward	4991
Hays, Amos H.	336
Hays, Bettie	337
Hays, Amanda	338
Hays, Ida	339
Hays, Daniel	340
Hays, Sarah	341
Hays, Emma E.	1421
Hays, Thomas Wesley	1422
Hays, Louisa	2329
Hays, Amelia	3055
Hays, Willie	3056
Hays, James Osa	3057
Hays, Viola	3058
Hays, Eula	3059
Hays, John Benjamin	3936
Hays, Buna	3937
Hays, Alice	3938
Hays, Samuel	4959
Hatcher, Lillie May	513
Hatcher, Lula May	516
Hatcher, Robert Norman	518
Harjo, Lucy	571
Harjo, Alice	572
Harjo, Lem	573
Harjo, Lewis	574
Harjo, Mattie	575
Harjo, Mary	800
Harjo, Oscar	4766
Harjo, Salina	4992
Harrison, Daniel P.	816
Harrison, William F.	817
Harrison, Laura	818
Harrison, Tena	819
Harrison, Cecilia	820
Harrison, Mamie	821
Harrison, Pearl	822
Harrison, Ella	823
Harrison, Frances V.	824
Harrison, Arthur D.	825
Harrison, Maud	3092
Harrison, Emma Eveline	3094
Harrison, Pollie	3862
Harrison, Laura J.	3863
Harrison, John Thomas	3864
Harrison, Mary	4566
Harlin, George	1539
Harlin, Belton	1540
Harlin, Ruth G.	1541
Hassell, Willie	1001
Hassell, Bernice	1003
Harney, Sison	1488
Hardy, Janetta	1516
Hardy, Vinnie	1517
Hardy, Charles R.	1519
Hall, Henrietta	1520
Hall, George J.	1521
Hare, Samuel J.	1861
Hare, Sarah	2815
Hare, Walter	2816
Hare, Charles	2817
Hamilton, Sallie	1959
Hamilton, Matilda	2120
Hamilton, Aaron	2499
Hamilton, Simeon	2500
Hamilton, Jency	2663
Hamilton, Henderson	3050
Hamilton, Tommie	3815
Harrell, Tandy Lee	2114
Harrell, Almarine	2115
Harrell, Mary Lee	2116
Harkins, Mary	2288
Harkins, Charley	2289
Harkins, Lula	2290
Harkins, Robert	2291
Harkins, Nettie Inza	2292
Harkin, Sikey	4973
Hart, Sallie	2464
Hart, Johnslin	2467
Hart, Jackson	2707
Hardwick, Joe B.	3041

Name.	Roll No.
Hardwick, Lilburn	3060
Hardwick, Birt	3062
Hardwick, Eastman	3063
Hardwick, Janie	3064
Hardwick, Maryetta	3065
Hardwick, David	3269
Hardwick, Mattie	8110
Hardwick, Frank H.	8111
Hancock, Robert M.	8122
Hancock, Flora Viola	8123
Harper, Joseph Lea	8438
Harper, Helen Josephine	8439
Harper, Joshua Robert	8440
Harper, Bettie Leona	8441
Hayward, Mona E.	8443
Hampton, Bessie	3507
Hampton, Lela	3508
Hampton, Hollis	3509
Hampton, Mary	3513
Hampton, Alice I.	3514
Hampton, Lethe T.	3515
Hampton, Herbert R.	4195
Hawley, Lizzie	3953
Hawley, Alice	3954
Hawley, Lydia	3955
Hamblin, Charley M.	4263
Hamblin, Albert H.	4361
Hamm, Mattie L.	4472
Hamm, Charles Wesley	4473
Haynes, Julia	4665
Halsell, Susan	4792
Halsell, Annie Laurie	4792
Harden, Elizabeth	4897
Harden, Sarah E.	4898
Harden, Andrew J., Jr.	4899
Harden, Frank Byrd	4900
Harden, Maude	4901
Harden, Josiah	4902
Harden, Wood M.	4903
Harden, Bland V.	4904
Harden, Dewey	4905
Harden, Daws	4906
Henderson, Tom	838
Henderson, Nancy	839
Henderson, Frances	840
Henderson, John	1059
Henderson, Mollie	1061
Henderson, John	1508
Henderson, Loisa	1554
Henderson, Charles Colbert	1555
Henderson, Luella	1556
Henderson, John Thomas	1557
Henderson, Phelma	1558
Henderson, Addie Ruth	1559
Henderson, Ceza	2247
Henderson, Serena	2248
Henderson, Sessum	2562
Henderson, Campbell	2798
Henderson, Frances	2801
Henderson, Norah	2802
Herndon, Myrtle Gale	1626
Herndon, John Milton	1627
Herndon, Otto A.	1628
Herndon, Clyde Elwood	1629
Hewitt, Thomas	1340
Hewitt, Stella	1341
Hewitt, Julius	1342
Hewitt, Sam	1344
Heald, William	1661
Heald, Benjamin	1662
Heald, Charles H.	1663
Herman, Vicy	1994
Hearrell, Jesse B.	2047
Hendrickson, Susan	2172
Hillhouse, Louisa	776
Hillhouse, Walter	3928
Hillhouse, Jefferson	4037
Hill, John Edgar	1403
Hill, Wm. Riley	1404
Hill, Ude	1405
Hill, Harry Vernon	1406
Hill, Susie	1407

Name.	Roll No.
Hill, Thomas J.	1408
Hill, Mamie	2961
Higgins, Frances	1144
Higgins, Nebby C.	4077
Higgins, Patsey Ann	4078
Hickentubby, Mina	2600
Hickentubby, Lucy	2718
Hicks, Tom	3032
Hicks, Daniel L.	3055
Hihcha, Lottie	2911
Hilton, Minnie	4295
Hilton, Loma Ruth	4301
Holloway, Kitsie	51
Hopping, Rosa Ella	521
Hopping, Augustus M.	522
Hopping, Gordon	523
Hotubby, Julia	941
Hotubby, Semie	942
Hotubby, Robert	943
Hotombby, Chehota	2394
Howell, Calvin H.	1207
Howell, Brunetta	1385
Howard, Mary I.	1212
Howard, Harriet May	1213
Howard, William Bryan	1214
Howard, Allie Viola	1215
Howard, Robert Lee	1216
Howard, Kitty	1328
Howard, Charlie	2205
Hogue, Henry	1329
Holden, Annie	2641
Holden, John	3982
Holden, McKenzie	3983
Holden, Amos	1963
Holden, Sukey	1964
Holden, James	1965
Holden, Annie	1966
Holden, Armon	1967
Holden, Emily	1971
Holden, Alemon	2437
Holden, Lucy	2438
Holden, Johnie	2439
Holden, Siney	2440
Holden, Emma	2441
Holden, Elsie	2442
Holden, Walter	2443
Holcomb, Fannie E.	2060
Holcomb, Millard Fillmore	2061
Holcomb, Pleassent	2062
Holcomb, Martha Easter	2063
Holder, Lottie	3051
Holder, Eula	3052
Holder, Ardie	3053
Holder, Daisy	3054
Holoata	2454
Holoata, Sier	2455
Houston, Frank	3527
Hoffman, Fannie	3388
Hoffman, George L.	3389
Hoffman, Willie Thomas	3390
Hucklochubby, Robert son	629
Hughes, Mamie	768
Hughes, Fannie C.	769
Hughes, Eula A.	770
Hughes, Mamie M.	771
Hughes, Missouri V.	4036
Hull, Sippia	1260
Hull, Theodore	1261
Hull, Lucius Irvin	1262
Hull, Flora	1263
Hull, Bessie	1264
Hull, Jesse	1265
Hull, Joseph K.	1266
Hull, William Jesse	1267
Hunnatubby, Easter	2201
Hunnatubby, Isum	2430
Hunnatubby, Eddie	2431
Hunnatubby, Delphia	2963
Hutchins, Lizzie	2235
Hutchins, Lillian May	2236
Hutchins, Alvia Ross	2237

Name.	Roll No.	Name.	Roll No.
Hutchins, Mamie	2350	James, Wesley	3583
Hutchins, Lola Melissa	2353	James, Eloise	3947
Hutchins, Hattie O.	4067	James, Rufus	3948
Hutchins, Daisy May	4068	James, Perline	4005
Hume, Olena	2402	James, McKee	4246
Hume, Benjamin Alfred	2403	James, Rhoena	4247
Hume, Paul Earnest	2404	James, Benj. D.	4248
Humes, Jesse	2383	James, Frank	4249
Humes, Melton	2384	James, Jesse	4250
Humes, Emma	2385	James, Elsie	4411
Humes, Loomis	2386	James, Elsie A.	4709
Hunnicutt, Daisy	3942	James, Simeon	4751
Hunnicutt, Calvin H.	3943	James, Wilson H.	4834
Hurley, Bertha	4756	James, Jacob	4835
Hybarger, Laura T.	3917	James, Gilbert	4836
Immotichey, Robert	449	James, Moses	4837
Immotichey, Molliean	450	James, Joseph	4838
Immotichey, Holmes	451	James, Cephus	4839
Immotichey, Harriet	453	James, Ruthielane	4840
Immotichey, Sam	1012	James, Miriem	4841
Immotichey, Melvina	4571	James, Annie	4858
Immoticha, Clarisa	471	James, George Newton	4889
Immohotichey, Jesse	641	James, Sallie Ann	4890
Imatobby, Calvin	4687	James, Malsy	4891
Imatobby, Susie	4688	Jack, Mary	3844
Imatobby, Hannah	4689	Jack, Walter	3845
Imatobby, Lonnie	4690	Jack, Hazel Gladus	4212
Isaac, William	570	Jackson, Annie D.	655
Ishtincheyou, Fomister	901	Jackson, Lizzie	657
Ishtincheyou, Annie	902	Jackson, Crudip	658
Illetewahke, Charles	963	Jackson, Zenobia	659
Illetewahke, Betsey	964	Jackson, Thomas P.	660
Illetewahke, Caroline	965	Jackson, Wm. Byrd	661
Illetewahke, Malvina	966	Jackson, Juanita	662
Illetewahke, Peggy	967	Jackson, Wynona	663
Illetewahke, Noah	4045	Jackson, Othelo	664
Illetewahke, Sam	4046	Jackson, Jerole W.	665
Illetewahke, Cathy	4047	Jacobs, John B.	3800
Isheatubby,	1072	Jemison, Hula E.	845
Ingram, Mollie	1633	Jemison, Joe	846
Ingram, Lydia	1634	Jemison, Gertrude	847
Ingram, Gertie	1635	Jemison, Jennie	848
Ingram, Hettie	1636	Jemison, Vera	849
Ingram, Clytie	1637	Jenkins, Jennie	1588
Ingram, William Hobart	1638	Jenkins, Minnie	1589
Ingram, Ruby	1640	Jenkins, James	1590
Irvin, Emmie Elizabeth	4512	Jenkins, Boyd	4109
James, Emmet	472	Jefferson, Morris	1991
James, Gipson	578	Jefferson, Hilda E.	1992
James, Alba	580	Jefferson, Tecumseh	2059
James, Sylva	581	Jefferson, Martin	2083
James, Lavin	582	Jefferson, Alec	2113
James, William	590	Jefferson, Edmon	2916
James, Annie	591	Jefferson, Simeon	4868
James, Daniel	592	Jeflow, Joe	3576
James, Joe	593	Jeflow, Sallie	3577
James, Mary	667	Jennings, Henrietta L.	4269
JJames, Walter	668	Jennings, Daisy	4270
James, Arthur	669	Jennings, Thenia	4271
James, Johnson	670	Jennings, Louisa	4272
James, Jennie	850	Jennings, Alvers	4273
James, Osceola W.	851	Jennings, James	4274
James, Dixson	856	Jennings, John	4275
James, June	857	Jennings, Mary J.	4630
James, Culberson	858	Jennings, James A.	4631
James, George	1363	Jennings, Charles T.	4635
James, Lucy	1909	Jennings, Lizzie	4927
James, Fulsom	2049	Jennings, Robert J.	4928
James, Nelson	2051	Jennings, Mary Jane	4929
James, Henry	2183	Jimmy, William	2634
James, Walton	2192	Jimmy, Loman	2635
James, Minnie	2193	Jimmy, Rena	2964
James, Turner	2194	Jimmy, Johnson	4597
James, Felix	2195	Johnson, Napoleon B.	109
James, Moses	2196	Johnson, Leewellyn	110
James, Zelia	2197	Johnson, Gertrude	111
James, Joseph	2198	Johnson, Chisolm	335
James, Thomas	2630	Johnson, Mason	385
James, Lawrence	2781	Johnson, Hunos	386
James, Alex	3561	Johnson, Henry	387
James, Emerson	3573	Johnson, Willie	388
James, Frank	3574	Johnson, Arthur	389
James, Albert Levi	3575	Johnson, Scott	390

Name.	Roll No.	Name.	Roll No.
Johnson, Newton	396	Johnston, Jesse	976
Johnson, Adaline	397	Johnston, Robert E.	977
Johnson, Markey	398	Johnston, Edwin Bates	978
Johnson, Elum	399	Johnston, Isaac	1178
Johnson, Mary	405	Johnston, Lem	1179
Johnson, Sampson	455	Johnston, Orin A.	1180
Johnson, Jane	456	Johnston, Cora E.	1181
Johnson, Millie	463	Johnston, Clarence F.	1182
Johnson, Louisa	477	Johnston, Elsie May	1183
Johnson, Gipson	478	Johnston, Eva Pearl	1184
Johnson, Nancy	610	Johnston, Albert S.	1202
Johnson, Thompson	611	Johnston, Lawrence	
Johnson, Lucy	612	Lister	1953
Johnson, Frances	613	Johnston, Willie	1954
Johnson, Solomon	614	Johnston, Dellena	1955
Johnson, George	615	Johnston, Maggie May	1956
Johnson, Isaac	620	Johnston, Annie	1957
Johnson, Jincy	626	Johnston, Douglas	
Johnson, Slone	891	Henry	2621
Johnson, Ema	905	Johnston, Bettie L.	2622
Johnson, Rena	906	Johnston, Llewellyn	2623
Johnson, E. B.	979	Johnston, Juanita	2624
Johnson, Veta	980	Johnston, Douglas	
Johnson, Ina	981	Harper	2625
Johnson, Neal R.	982	Johnston, Malissa	2656
Johnson, Montford T.	983	Johnston, Carrie	4049
Johnson, Froma Adelaide	984	Jones, D. H.	210
Johnson, Benj. F.	985	Jones, Susan	274
Johnson, Arline	986	Jones, Nancy	746
Johnson, Adelaide B.	987	Jones, Ellen	903
Johnson, Gertrude	988	Jones, James	912
Johnson, Ira Montford	989	Jones, Burney	1155
Johnson, James Wolf	990	Jones, Jane	1156
Johnson, Charles Boggy	991	Jones, Joseph	1157
Johnson, Vivian	992	Jones, Mary	1158
Johnson, Emely	1619	Jones, Mary Ella	1236
Johnson, Maybell	1620	Jones, Eaman Mays	1237
Johnson, Willie M.	1621	Jones, Erin Murray	1238
Johnson, Lola Maude	1622	Jones, Wesley	3526
Johnson, Wesley R.	1623	Jones, Amelia	3672
Johnson, Zella Marigold	1624	Jones, Carrie	3701
Johnson, Elba	1625	Jones, Frankie Velma	3702
Johnson, Laura L.	1796	Jones, Mattie	3703
Johnson, Ben	1797	Jones, Neoma	3704
Johnson, William A.	1798	Jones, Ruth	3705
Johnson, William	2406	Jones, Vera Nelson	3706
Johnson, George A.	3528	Jones, Sallie	3958
Johnson, Sallie Eliza-		Jones, William Sammie	
beth	3529	E.	3959
Johnson, Iney	3530	Jones, Moses	4040
Johnson, Louisa	3531	Jones, Hettie L.	4207
Johnson, Henry Belton	3771	Jones, Johnnie	4864
Johnson, Robert Miller	3772	John, McKinney	1080
Johnson, Virgie	3773	John, Seliom	2203
Johnson, William Mont-		John, Nellie	2204
ford	3774	John, Sanders	3174
Johnson, Tilford Thomas	3775	John, Stephen	3985
Johnson, Claudie	3835	John, Hannah	3986
Johnson, James T.	3846	John, Nancy	3987
Johnson, Thomas Wreen	3847	John, Amanda	3988
Johnson, Dewey Reeves	3848	John, Tecumseh	3989
Johnson, Willie	3861	John, Mary	3990
Johnson, James M.	3868	John, Edward	3991
Johnson, Lenorah	3869	John, Grover	4180
Johnson, Eliza	4039	Jordan, Mollie	1839
Johnson, Graham Belton	4050	Jordan, Martha	1840
Johnson, Lucretia	4097	Jordan, Anneta	1841
Johnson, Mulford	4748	Jordon, Ethel	4543
Johnson, Emma	4797	Jordon, James Earl	4544
Johnson, Samuel	2407	Jordon, Earnest Cecil	4545
Johnson, Eastman	2541	Jordon, Benj. Gaston	4601
Johnson, Holmes	4919	Jordon, Ola May	4602
Johnson, Carrie	4920	Juzan, Eliza	217
Johnson, Ebatamby	4921	Juzan, Thomas	3006
Johnson, Rosa Lee	4979	Kaney, Mary	1489
Johnson, Elcie	4981	Kaney, Robert Harmon	1491
Johnston, B. F.	310	Kaney, Margaret	1548
Johnston, William	827	Kaney, Lafayette	1952
Johnston, Joseph E.	971	Kaney, Gilbert	2238
Johnston, Viola	972	Kaney, Frances	2239
Johnston, Neoma	973	Kaney, Willie	2825
Johnston, Henry	974	Kaney, Harmon	3081
Johnston, Sydney	975	Kaney, Ida Belle	3082

Name.	Roll No.	Name.	Roll No.
Kaney, Lottie	4102	Kemp, Elzira	3189
Kaney, Billie	4103	Kemp, Julia	3195
Kaney, Eastman	4104	Kemp, Joe	3433
Kaney, Lucy	4105	Kemp, Henry	3434
Kaney, Alice	4106	Kemp, Lenora	3435
Kaney, Joanna	4107	Kemp, Robert Lemuel	3436
Kay, Fred	4287	Kemp, Joseph Franklin	3437
Kay, Minnie	4327	Kemp, Alexander Com-	
Kay, Charley	4328	modore	3442
Kanawa, Louana	4403	Kemp, David	3443
Kanawa, Albert	4404	Kemp, Charley	3444
Kennedy, Mary C. I.	316	Kemp, Martha Myrtle	3445
Kennedy, Tandy Alfred	317	Kemp, Rhoda	3491
Kennedy, Daisy Ellen	318	Kemp, Mary Eliza	3595
Kennedy, Julia Elizabeth	319	Kemp, Jackson	3641
Kennedy, William D.	320	Kemp, Martha N.	3642
Kennedy, Maulsie	2971	Kemp, Frank	3643
Kennedy, W: J. Bryan	2974	Kemp, Annie	3644
Kennedy, George W.	2975	Kemp, Estella	3645
Keel, Hogan	735	Kemp, Lillie	3646
Keel, Emely	736	Kemp, Walton C.	3647
Keel, Billie	864	Kemp, Frankie	3648
Keel, Lizzie	865	Kemp, Elizabeth Min-	
Keel, Ella	866	erva	4054
Keel, Ida	867	Kemp, Theodocia Aba-	
Keel, Ada	868	gail	4055
Keel, William	869	Kemp, Eli Clem	4056
Keel, Lewellen	870	Kemp, James Earl	4057
Keel, Leo	871	Kemp, Frances Eliza-	
Keel, Ida	1409	beth	4058
Keel, Guy	1866	Kemp, Mary Montressa	4059
Keel, Lula	1867	Kemp, Raymond Herrel	4060
Keel, William Simon	1868	Kemp, Joel L.	4061
Keel, Lewis Colbert	1869	Kemp, Lela	4181
Keel, Johnson	2324	Kemp, Eva	4182
Keel, Alice	2325	Kemp, Roberson	4333
Keel, Eula	2326	Keberry, Jimmie	2314
Keel, May	2327	Keffer, Alvira	3229
Keel, Dora	2328	Keffer, Willie	3231
Keel, Madelaine	2330	Keirsey, Mittie Jose-	
Keel, Lewis, Jr.	2331	phine	3283
Keel, Simon	2332	Keirsey, James D.	3284
Keel, Gipson	2535	Keirsey, Clifford C.	3285
Keel, Pearilee	2536	Keirsey, Agnes Maude	3286
Keel, Lizzie	2537	Keirsey, William Con-	
Keel, Hattie	2538	way	3287
Keel, Archison	2539	Keirsey, Vivian	3288
Keel, Thomas	2540	Keirsey, Benjamin C.	3289
Keel, Mollie	2557	Keirsey, Milton.	4187
Keel, Noah	2561	Kepo, Cephus	3630
Keel, Sanders	2937	Keno, Emily	3809
Keel, Simon, Jr.	2938	Keno, Houston	3810
Keel, Colbert	2981	Keno, Martha	3811
Keel, Caroline	2982	Keno, Mattie	3812
Keel, Minnie	2983	Keno, Lizzie	3813
Keel, Belton	2984	Keno, Fannie	3814
Keel, Bennie	2985	Keno, Frank	3815
Keel, Willie	3992	Keno, Carrie	3816
Keel, Freeman	3993	Keener, Maulsey	3894
Keel, Maulsie	4069	Keener, Thomas Butler	3895
Keel, Overton	4117	Keys, Thomas	4819
Keel, Bertha	4154	Keys, Willie	4820
Keel, Phoebe	4155	Keys, Charlie	4821
Keel, Cabon	4680	King, Wall	129
Keel, Eastman	4681	King, Celian	130
Keel, Dan	4769	King, Callie Boyd	1485
Kerr, Irene	1396	King, Marie Boyd	1486
Kerr, Lockhart B.	1397	King, Clemmie Lelia	1487
Kerr, Rita	1398	King, Patsey	131
Kerr, Waite Tecumseh	1399	King, Cornelia	2900
Kernel, George	1494	King, Allie	3901
Kernel, Charley	1496	King, Andrew	4008
Kemp, Joel Carr	1913	King, Anderson	4009
Kemp, George	2518	King, Billy	4773
Kemp, Jemima	2519	King, Robert O.	4859
Kemp, Benjamin Frank-		King, Lou M.	4860
lin	2709	King, Arthur	4982
Kemp, Elsie	2710	Killcrease, Isum	303
Kemp, Levi	3183	Killcrease, Thompson	444
Kemp, Lulu	3184	Killcrease, Tohkey	445
Kemp, Wellington Mar-		Killcrease, Eastman	541
tin	3187	Killcrease, Robin	542
Kemp, Levi Pitman	3188	Killcrease, Agnes	543

Name.	Roll No.	Name.	Roll No.
Levi, Edmon	812	Love, Edward Davis, Jr.	3614
Levi, Milsey	813	Love, Felix Theodore	3615
Levi, Jackson	814	Love, Ula	3616
Levi, Mattie	815	Love, Francis Marion	3618
Lee, Margaret	384	Love, Lottie Lillian	4113
Lee, Katie	1325	Love, Arthur	4186
Lee, Sam	1326	Love, Joe N.	4857
Lester, Moran S.	1470	Loman, Eli	272
Lester, Wesley	1471	Lowrance, Mary Easter	1874
Letty, Mary	2016	Lowrance, Oscar K.	1375
Letty, Carry	2019	Lowrance, Charles Or-	
Lemon, Maria	3353	rick	1876
Lemon, Bennie	3354	Lowrance, Robert H.	3879
Lemon, Fannie	3355	Lowrance, Dora Isabella	3880
Lemon, Willie	3356	Lowrance, Bernice Sloan	3881
Lemon, Maggie	3357	Lowmer, Emely	2671
Lemon, Robert Emory	3358	Lowmer, Mulsie	2674
Lemon, Mary K.	3359	Lomer, Adam	2885
Leftwich, Minnie C.	4805	Lomer, Malinda	2886
Leftwich, Velma	4806	Lomer, Wesley	2887
Leftwich, George C.	4807	Lomer, Amanda	2889
Leftwich, Dewey	4808	Lomer, Susan	2890
Leftwich, James Brooks	4809	Lone, Elie	2416
Leecraft, Lelah M.	3411	Lomer, Sophia	2891
Leecraft, Bertram M.	3412	Lomer, Lillie	2892
Leecraft, Mildred	3413	Long, Wydia Caroline	4175
Leecraft, Frances	3415	Long, Harry Jerome	4176
Lilliard, Mary Louise	344	Long, Paul Edward	4177
Lilliard, Rossie O.	345	Lynch, Georgie Vann	4646
Liley, Dotson	529	Mayer, Cornelia	11
Lindsey, Ethel	4776	Mayer, Myrtle J.	12
Lindsey, Gracie	4782	Mayer, Betsie	1436
Loving, Isabelle	20	Mayer, Cecil Joseph	4002
Love, Slone	594	Maryacher	1028
Love, Edmon P.	596	Maytubby, Eastman	1064
Love, Grace	597	Maytubby, Minnie	1065
Love, Claude	598	Maytubby, Franklin	1066
Love, Eunice	599	Maytubby, Joe S.	2273
Love, Addie	600	Maytubby, Hagan	2558
Love, Sallie G.	1315	Maytubby, Ben	2559
Love, Buck	1316	Maytubby, Sam	2676
Love, Frank C.	1317	Maytubby, Sena	2717
Love, Robert B.	1318	Maytubby, Peter	3620
Love, Grace E.	1319	Maytubby, Jesse D. Y.	3622
Love, Pearl G.	1320	Maytubby, Bessie	3623
Love, George C.	1321	Maytubby, Elihu Ben-	
Love, Joe	1322	nett	3624
Love, R. J., Jr.	1324	Maytubby, Lillie	3625
Love, Sam	1350	Maytubby, Samuel W.	4332
Love, Ruby Jewel	1352	Maytubby, Samuel W.	
Love, Lizzie Melvina	1353	Jr.	4335
Love, Lauta Overton	1355	Maytubby, Floyd E.	4336
Love, Annie	1356	Maytubby, Dudley	4337
Love, George	1357	Maytubby, Kalitoe	4338
Love, Will E.	1684	Maytubby, Peter, Jr.	4375
Love, Alvia	1685	Maytubby, Mary	4682
Love, Frank	1686	Maytubby, Polly	4683
Love, Thomas B.	1751	Maytubby, Simeon	4684
Love, Lena Belle	1752	Maytubby, Peter P.	4685
Love, Robert Howard	1753	Maytubby, Lymon	4771
Love, Clara Maude	1754	Maytubby, Silas	4772
Love, Mary Hazel	1755	Martin, Ida K.	1386
Love, Clifton Nathaniel	2842	Martin, Tom G.	1387
Love, Mary Olena	2843	Martin, Ida M.	1388
Love, Ruby	2845	Martin, Verbeth McIver	1389
Love, Overton	3101	Martin, Martha	2928
Love, Harriet	3102	Martin, Stonewall Jack-	
Love, Ruby Belle	3103	son	2929
Love, Hattie Byrd	3104	Martin, Dick	4865
Love, Jodie Jessie Me-		Maxwell, Wisdom	1429
hota	3105	Maxwell, Malinda	1430
Love, Henry O.	3106	Maxwell, Birtha	1433
Love, Benjamin	3247	Maxwil, Tommie	3194
Love, Joseph Henry	3248	Massey, Juel	2493
Love, Mary Adline	3249	Massey, Bennie W.	2494
Love, Isaac Newton	3346	Massey, Marietta	3070
Love, Mart	3367	Massey, Nancy Elizabeth	3565
Love, Pierre Sparlin	3368	Massey, Berry Esther	3572
Love, Edward Davis	3609	Mattahoya	2769
Love, Hercules Martin	3610	Mashburn, Laura A.	3402
Love, Caryann Edna	3611	Maupin, Helen E.	3414
Love, Dolceny	3612	Maupin, Laurina P.	4484
Love, Samuel	3613	Marshall, Lillie	4362

Name.	Roll No.	Name.	Roll No.
Marshall, Hazel	4363	Morris, Lena	4966
Marshall, Colbert	4364	Morris, Lilla	4399
Mays, Susan E.	4439	Moore, Gracie	1259
Mays, Willie	4440	Moore, J. B.	1392
Mays, T. G.	4441	Moore, Helen Foster	1257
Mays, Clarence	4442	Moore, Nancy	2126
Melville, Jane Perry	154	Moore, Thomas	2517
Melville, Samuel C.	155	Moore, Charles	2696
Melville, Frances	447	Moore, Ellen	3037
Melville, Leon	448	Moore, Thomas W.	3259
Merchant, Melvina	1583	Moore, Monroe	3260
Merchant, Victoria	1584	Moore, Thomas Nowel	3290
Merchant, Harry	1585	Moore, Samuel Riley	3291
Merchant, Irene	1586	Moore, Lillie Armildia	3292
Merchant, Ellen	1587	Moore, Cordelia	3293
Melton, Mary Jane	2190	Moore, Roxie Mildred	3294
Melton, Ed	4998	Moore, Nancy M.	3295
Melton, Jesse	4999	Moore, Luke Prior	3379
Melton, Rosa	5000	Moore, Lemuel Capel	3492
Merriman, Crecy	3061	Moore, Charles Edward	3493
Meeks, Betsey	3199	Moore, Ella Minerva	3494
Meeks, Reubin	3200	Moore, Nettie May	3495
Meeks, Dosia	3201	Moore, Ludie Grace	3496
Mead, Frances Eliza-		Moore, Daisy	3497
beth	3347	Moore, Ruby	3498
Mead, Walter Bradford	3348	Moore, Lemuel Paul	3499
Mead, Martha Frances	3349	Moore, Eugene Capell	3500
Mead, Levi Landers	3350	Moore, Walter	3501
Mead, Simon Minor	3351	Moore, Wesley	4133
Mead, Abigale	3352	Moore, Estella	4134
Miller, William	176	Moore, Ethel	4135
Miller, Colbert	177	Moore, William Jennings	4161
Miller, Eli	2088	Moore, Viola Myrtle	4162
Miller, Sarah	2089	Moore, Mary Ellen	4357
Miller, Annie	2090	Moore, Harold	4358
Miller, Mulbert	2091	Moore, Claude M.	4350
Miller, Stella	2092	Moore, Floy	4360
Miller, Julia	3196	Moore, Jessie E.	4449
Miller, Robert Johnston	3198	Moore, Carrie Imogene	4450
Miller, John M.	3683	Moore, Lillie	4677
Miller, James	3684	Mobley, Tennie	1808
Miller, Willie G.	3685	Mobley, Helen Louise	1809
Miller, Sophia	3994	Mobley, Gerald Farley	1810
Miller, Stephen Sheuno	3995	Mosely, Palmer Simeon	2020
Miller, Dora	4535	Mosely, Amanda J.	2021
Miller, Laura	4536	Mosely, Flora	2022
Mitchell, Agnes	498	Mosely, Nannie P.	2023
Mitchell, Rilla	1191	Mosely, Wilson H.	2024
Mitchell, Jessie Pauline	1192	Mosely, Palmer S., Jr.	2025
Mitchell, George	1193	Mosely, Bessie	2026
Mitchell, Mantie	1194	Mosely, Garnett F.	2028
Mishontombby,	1093	Mosely, Sarah	3949
Mishontombby, Liza	1094	Mosely, Ava	3950
Mishontombby, Aaron	1106	Mosely, Annie	3951
Mishontaumbby, Jincy	4066	Mosely, Varnia Susie	4125
Mishontaumbby, Jackson	4788	Mosley, Forbus	2220
Mishontaumbby, Iba	4962	Mosley, Maria	2221
Milligan, Ida	2121	Mosley, Riley	3154
Milligan, Clell Franklin	2122	Monday, Mary	3043
Milligan, Simon James	2123	Monday, Jim	3044
Milligan, Lenora Dell	2124	Monday, Everet	3045
Mike, Morina	2507	Morrison, Ella Gertrude	3340
Middleton, Bessie	3557	Morrison, Elva	3344
Middleton, Nora	3558	Moit, Emily A.	4416
Minter, Sallie L.	3820	Moreland, Fannie	4818
Minter, Sinie L.	3826	Moutray, Perry	4945
Minter, Agnes	3830	Murray, J. A.	1195
Minor, Thos. J., Jr.	4940	Murray, Frankie Lee	1196
Minor, Sarah Lucinda	4983	Murray, Henry C.	1197
Monroe, William	474	Murray, Laura	1507
Monroe, Sarah	475	Murray, Robert Lovard	3276
Monroe, Lizzie	476	Murray, Louie	3277
Monroe, Josephine	804	Murray, Mildred P.	3278
Morris, Annie	1112	Murray, Robert L., Jr.	3279
Morris, Caline	1239	Murray, Lucile	3280
Morris, Mary	1240	Murray, Minnie Agnes	3281
Morris, Tecumseh	1241	Murray, Cecil Collins	3282
Morris, Susie	1242	Murray, Meigs Colbert	3296
Morris, Nellie	1243	Murray, Madge	3297
Morris, Elizabeth	4396	Murray, Meigs Colbert	
Morris, Joseph Daniel	4397	Jr.	3298
Morris, Catherine	4398	Murray, Hinton	3301
Morris, Lena	4400	Murray, Mattie	3302

Name.	Roll No.
Murray, George G.	3316
Murray, Helen	3317
Murray, Alice H.	3940
Murray, Massena Bancroft	3941
Murray, Leo Edward	4188
Murray, George Gordon	4191
Murray, Johnston	4217
Mulkey, Elsie	1698
Mulkey, Charlie S.	1699
Mule, Joe	2789
Mule, Joanna	2790
Mule, Amanda	4166
Mutz, Ida	3066
Mutz, Ada	3067
Mutz, Fred	3068
Mutz, Henry Overton	3069
Mutz, Lizzie	3076
Mutz, Mamie Frances	3077
Mutz, James Henry	3078
Mutz, Edwin Willis	3079
Mutz, Jesse Lee	3080
Mutz, Joe Franklin	4598
Muckintubby, Katie	3603
Muckintubby, Ada	4866
Myers, Patsey	1502
Myers, Malinda	1503
Myers, George	1504
Myers, Maude	1505
Myers, Thomas David	1506
Myers, Alice M.	3886
Myers, Gretchen	3887
Myers, Eula	4438
McAlester, Rebecca	3333
McAlester, Sudie	3334
McAlester, James Burney	3335
McAlester, William Berry	3336
McAlester, Rebecca Leo	3337
McAlester, James J., Jr.	3338
McBride, Lovica Colbert	4737
McBride, Hettie A.	4738
McBride, Coorinne	4739
McBride, Hiram Hadyn	4740
McBride, Lovica Czarina	4741
McBride, Colbert Marrow	4742
McBride, Walter C. Ben	4743
McBride, Mildred Mahota	4744
McBee, Millie	4770
McCarty, Katsey	787
McCarty, Sonie	788
McCarty, Tom	794
McCarty, Nancy	795
McCarty, William	1916
McCarty, Mary Elizabeth	1917
McCarty, Nettie	1918
McCarty, James William	1919
McCarty, Claudie Eugene	1920
McCarty, Jennie Lou Mittie	1921
McCarty, Jefferson Odie L.	4122
McCurtain, Edmon	1050
McCurtain, Humphrey	1051
McCurtain, Zeno	1083
McCurtain, Madeline	1084
McCurtain, James Cotton	2417
McCurtain, Fykie	2418
McCurtin, Buster	4034
McClure, Imon	1228
McClure, Lillie	1229
McClure, Imon O.	1231
McClure, John W.	1232
McClure, Ed	1107
McClure, Tecumseh Jr.	1109
McClure, Amanda	1110
McClure, Tamsey	1111
McClure, Jemison Gordon	4833

Name.	Roll No.
McCrummen, Susie	1234
McCauley, Elmer	1706
McCauley, Peachie	1850
McCauley, Susie	1851
McCauley, Junie	1852
McCauley, Wm. Watkins	1853
McCurley, Carrie	2131
McCann, Mary	2521
McCoy, Joe	2743
McCoy, Jake	2745
McCoy, Bettie	2746
McCoy, Zena	2747
McCoy, Tommie	2748
McCoy, Parthenia	3657
McCoy, Athen Elonzo	3659
McCoy, Sallie Goldsby	3905
McCall, Mamie	4729
McCall, William Aubry	4730
McCall, Cora Bell	4731
McCall, Etta A.	4732
McClish, Ruben	4907
McDonell, Susan	1811
McDonell, Norval	1813
McDonell, Cleveland	1814
McDonell, Isaac	1815
McDonell, Eliza Jane	1816
McDonell, Nona	1817
McDonell, Nocodemus	1818
McDonell, Josephus	1819
McDuffie, Rebecca	3015
McDuffie, Myrtle May	3016
McDuffie, Morey Emily	3017
McDuffie, Juzan Ben	3018
McDuffie, Indiola	3019
McDonald, Albert S.	3562
McDaniel, Jennie	4698
McDaniel, Annie L.	4703
McGee, Billie Perry	343
McGee, Lucy	945
McGee, Harriet	950
McGee, Jesse	1646
McGee, Minnie	2177
McGee, Isaac	2178
McGee, Hiram	2390
McGee, Cornelius	2391
McGee, Nettie	2392
McGee, Hattie	2393
McGee, Reubin	2695
McGee, Alex	3112
McGee, Eula	3113
McGee, Willie	3114
McGee, Imon	3116
McGee, Annie	3117
McGee, Frank	3118
McGee, Susan	3345
McGee, Fulsome	3629
McGee, George	3913
McGee, Florence	5049
McGee, Mattie	5050
McGee, John	5051
McGee, Allison	5052
McGee, Wade	5053
McGee, Ruby	5054
McGee, Oliver	5055
McGee, Elsie	5056
McGlasson, Emma	1735
McGlasson, Jesse	1740
McGlasson, Lula	1741
McGuire, Elsie	2251
McGuire, Louisa	2255
McGuire, Sam	2879
McGill, Hoah	2724
McGill, Eliza	2735
McGill, Henry	2736
McGill, Rose	2737
McGill, Ella	2738
McGill, Sallie	2739
McGill, Mack	2740
McGill, Ida May	2742
McGeehee, William	2753
McGeehee, Josie	2754
McGeehee, Bessie	2755
McHardy, Wyatt	2794

Name.	Roll No.
McKinney, Albert Thomas	2316
McKinney, Granville	2317
McKinney, Tommie	2318
McKinney, Pontie	2319
McKinney, Tishie	2320
McKinney, Labon	2694
McKinney, Lauretta	3270
McKinney, Turner	4151
McKinney, Allen	4605
McKinney, Oyd	4647
McKinney, Harris	4648
McKinney, Laura Etta	4649
McKinney, Cecial Berthal	4650
McKinney, Maude Lee	4651
McKinney, Bertha	4752
McKinney, Georgie	4980
McKeel, Cora Chrisolm	3872
McKeel, John C.	3873
McKeel, William Bynum	3874
McKellop, William	3996
McKellop, William L.	3997
McLish, Leondus	192
McLish, Sallie	193
McLish, Lee	1015
McLish, Richard H.	1641
McLish, Jerry J.	1642
McLish, Richard R.	1643
McLish, Otwell	1644
McLish, Wm. Bourland	2040
McLish, Turner Bynum	2287
McLish, Lottie	2554
McLish, Esaw	2874
McLish, Annie	2965
McLish, Millie	3071
McLish, Alice	3073
McLish, Allie	3074
McLish, Rosie	3075
McLish, Henry F.	3780
McLish, Nina	3781
McLish, Lena	3782
McLish, Clara	3783
McLish, Frazier	3805
McLish, Ollie	3957
McLish, Glenn	4211
McLish, Holmes	4950
McLeod, Julia	556
McLean, Liesiny	777
McLane, John	832
McLane, Margaret	833
McLane, Clinton	834
McLane, Lenus	835
McLane, Ainusiah	837
McLane, Willie B.	1515
McLaughlin, John Duke	3235
McLaughlin, Amanda Louisa	3236
McLaughlin, John Bunyan	3237
McLaughlin, Benjamin	3238
McLaughlin, Tunkie	3239
McLaughlin, Cravens	3240
McLaughlin, James R.	3446
McLaughlin, Duke	4185
McMillan, Nancy	1476
McMillan, Minnie	1477
McMillan, Rosie Rena	1478
McMillan, Joseph T.	1479
McMillan, Bertha Frances	1480
McMillan, Alva Linzie	1481
McMillan, Lillian Ethel	1482
McMillan, Mary	1657
McMillan, Lillie Myrtle	1616
McMorries, Alice	3452
McMorries, Lee, Jr.	3460
McNally, John R.	3902
McNally, Lena	3903
McNally, William Otie	3904
McSwain, Laura	3095
McSwain, Harry	4844
McSwain, Minnie	4845

Name.	Roll No.
McSwain, Bessie	4846
McSwain, Romey	4847
McSwain, Belle	4848
McSwain, Maud	4849
McSwain, Willie	4850
McSwain, Charles H.	4851
McSwain, Joel D.	4852
McSwain, Luella	4853
Nail, George	251
Nail, Harrison	760
Nail, Silas W.	2052
Nail, Jessie	2189
Nail, Webster	2664
Nail, Selina	2665
Nail, Alfred	2666
Nail, Mallsey	2667
Nail, Dilsie	2668
Nail, Suckie	2675
Nail, Alfred	3897
Nash, Lizzie	4704
Nash, Esther	4705
Nash, Ruth	4706
Nash, Mary	4707
Naponahoyah	2050
Nelson, Ward	106
Nelson, Jaynson	365
Nelson, Silas	366
Nelson, Albert	367
Nelson, Maggie	368
Nelson, Adeline	369
Nelson, Cena	370
Nelson, Cornelius	576
Nelson, Linty	577
Nelson, Columbus	806
Nelson, John	807
Nelson, Malissa	808
Nelson, Fate	809
Nelson, Lulu	810
Nelson, Sim	811
Nelson, Phillip	4791
Nelson, Chilley	4826
Nelson, Minnie	4888
Ned, John	907
Ned, Osborn	909
Ned, Ida	910
Ned, Abe	911
Ned, Ellis	2039
Ned, Watson	3939
Ned, Solomon	4168
Neal, Oliver	1105
Neal, Isabella	4622
Newton, Ruthie V.	1713
Newton, Ed	1714
Newton, Willie Ida	1715
Newton, Calvin	1716
Newberry, Levi	2468
Newberry, Katie	2469
Newberry, Jane	2470
Newberry, Martha	2967
Newberry, Martin	3147
Newberry, Joe	3148
Newberry, Franklin	3149
Newberry, Calvin	3150
Newberry, Burney	3151
Newberry, Mattie Ava	3152
Newberry, Wilson	3153
Newberry, Lucy	3219
Nesbit, Arthur H.	4758
Neighbors, William	4636
Neighbors, Bulah G.	4637
Neighbors, Winnie L.	4638
Nichols, Sarah Lottie	1451
Nichols, Winnie Elsie	1452
Nichols, Lee	1453
Nichols, Susan M.	1531
Nichols, Robert H.	1532
Nichols, Walter	1533
Nichols, Daisy	1534
Nichols, Clyde Cleveland	1535
Nichols, Hannah	3891
Nichols, Earnest Lee	3892
Nichols, Bessie May	3893

Name.	Roll No.
Nichols, Velary Etta	4082
Nichols, Joe B.	4099
Nichols, Stanwaite	4422
Nichols, Lena	4423
Nichols, Jewel	4424
Nolatubbee, Ella	584
Nolatubbee, James	585
Norton, Henry	1613
Norton, Sealy	4607
Norton, Thomas Owen	4608
Norton, Henry Taylor	4609
Norton, Lewis Bird	4016
Norton, Jesse Melton	4611
Norman, Catherine	1614
Norman, William J.	4735
Norman, Virginia Elizabeth	4736
Norris, Josephine	1777
Norris, Minnie	1778
Norris, Maude	1779
Norris, T.	1781
Noletubby, John Anderson	3161
Noletubby, Jessie	3162
Noletubby, Jackson	3163
Noletubby, Tandy	3164
O'Brien, Katie	3405
Okayambby, Sylvia	2827
Okayambby, Albert	2830
Okayambby, Liza	2831
Okchantubby, Winey	2936
Oliphant, Jennie	1276
Oliphant, Willie	1277
Oliphant, Lucile M.	1278
Oliphant, Oscar Paul	1279
Oliphant, Ruth O.	1280
Oliphant, Claude Waite	4091
Onahintubby, Malissa	2824
Opeasubby	2614
Orphan, Levi	311
Orphan, Rena	312
Orphan, Suckey	313
Orphan, Elmer S.	314
Orphan, Eugene F.	315
Orphan, Myrtle	4662
Orphan, Sina	4663
Orndorff, Calvin P.	3406
Orr, Harriet	3935
Osavior, Frank	4116
Ott, Eliza Wade	1033
Ott, Joel	1035
Overton, Frankie	2946
Overton, Ruel Joseph	2994
Overton, Viola	2995
Overton, Jewel	2996
Overton, Stella M.	2997
Overton, Frank	4174
Owens, David	150
Owens, Seely	151
Owens, Frank	152
Owens, Solomon	2223
Owens, Bendie	2228
Owens, Minnie	3925
Owens, Vera V.	3926
Owens, Ider Elvira	3927
Owens, Abe	4768
Owens, Laura Vaginia	4964
Parnacher, Titas	528
Parnacher, Devet	779
Parnacher, Nolens	780
Parnacher, Calvin	951
Parnacher, Nannie	952
Parnacher, Roberson	953
Parnacher, Lizzie	954
Patterson, James E.	4538
Patterson, Docia M.	4539
Patterson, Charles Olander	4540
Patterson, Leona	4541
Patterson, James Earl	4542
Paul, Abby	1108
Paul, Joe M.	2972
Paul, William Ikard	2973

Name.	Roll No.
Paul, William H.	3920
Paul, William George	3923
Paul, Victoria	3923
Paul, Nettie May	4024
Paul, Smith W.	4090
Paul, Samuel Jackson	4095
Paul, Sammie	4862
Parker, Wilson	1603
Parker, John T.	1604
Parker, Victoria Sophronia	1605
Parker, Charles Benjamin	1606
Parker, William Guy	1607
Parker, Laura Belle	1608
Parker, Simon	2864
Parker, Bert	2865
Parker, Ed	2866
Parker, Aley	2867
Parker, Dovie	2868
Parker, Kaloolah	2869
Parker, Claud	2870
Parker, Louis	2876
Parker, John Wesley	3001
Parker, Ella Rennie	3002
Parker, Douglas H. J.	3004
Parker, Wesley	3186
Parker, Emily Frazier	4755
Parker, Wesley Lee	5005
Parker, Homer J.	5006
Palmer, Rhoda	1922
Palmer, Joseph	1923
Palmer, Lafayette	1924
Palmer, Elizabeth M.	1925
Palmer, Amanda	2800
Payne, Thomas H.	3686
Perry, Albert	75
Perry, Charles Guy	76
Perry, Ella	77
Perry, Billie	78
Perry, Eliza	79
Perry, James	80
Perry, Lee	81
Perry, Tena	82
Perry, Wilson	83
Perry, Stephen	300
Perry, Charles J.	327
Perry, Eli	328
Perry, Geo. H.	380
Perry, Theodore	467
Perry, Annie	468
Perry, Mary	469
Perry, Thomas J.	717
Perry, Zelda Marie	718
Perry, Benjamin Franklin	719
Perry, Simon	720
Perry, Cicen	721
Perry, Lucy	722
Perry, Edward	723
Perry, Clifton	939
Perry, Jeff	1009
Perry, Benny	1010
Perry, Houston	1081
Perry, J. M.	1096
Perry, Henry Kilpatric	3176
Perry, Lucian Rains	3177
Perry, Amy	3660
Perry, Coleman	3662
Perry, Bettie	4051
Perry, Annie	4232
Perry, Tandy F.	4233
Perry, Juanita	4234
Perry, Minnie	4235
Perry, Lillie M.	4236
Perry, Roxy	4237
Perry, Theodore Mosly	4238
Perry, Joseph	4255
Perry, Matilda	4256
Perry, Charles E.	4257
Perry, Joel F.	4258
Perry, Lela A.	4259
Perry, James W.	4260

Name.	Roll No.	Name.	Roll No.
Perry, Clemmie May	4261	Phelps, Emma	3208
Perry, Mildrid Catherine	4262	Phelps, Bessie	3209
Perry, Charley	4308	Phelps, Willie	4184
Perry, Eli	4329	Pikey, Katie	1145
Perry, Lillie Marie	4330	Pikey, Mollie	4073
Perry, Hattie Lee	4331	Pikey, Minerva	4074
Perry, Carlos Troy	4332	Pikey, Sophia	4075
Perry, Willie Clay	4334	Pikey, Montford J.	4076
Perry, Minnie May	4345	Pikey, Thos. Benson	4077
Perry, Frank Calvin	4346	Pikey, Catherine	4078
Perry, John Henry	4347	Pikey, Delila	4962
Perry, Conce D.	4572	Pickens, Edmon	1914
Perry, Ida Fay	4573	Pickens, Edmond Hiram	2233
Perry, Maude	4574	Pickens, George W.	2234
Perry, Allen Wesley	4575	Pickens, Ziley	2275
Perry, Emma J.	4670	Pickens, Johnie	2276
Perry, Jacob	4746	Pickens, Tommie	2277
Perry, Martha	4908	Pickens, Dave	2278
Perry, Albert	4909	Pickens, Hiram	2638
Peter, Jack	395	Pickens, Clayburn	2854
Peter, Pitman	2445	Pickens, Anna	2855
Peter, Martha	2977	Pickens, Nora	2856
Peter, Ella	2978	Pickens, Ihunter	2902
Peter, Noel	2979	Pickens, Annie	2903
Peter, Enos	2980	Pickens, Leona	2905
Peter, Harvey	3178	Pickens, Eli	2906
Peter, Jane	3179	Pickens, Joseph	2907
Peter, Simon	3180	Pickens, Apsie	2908
Peter, Rosa Anna	3181	Pickens, Hattie	2909
Peter, Jesse	4173	Pickens, Jane	2910
Pettigrew, Mose	554	Pickens, Gincy	3532
Pettigrew, Louvinia	555	Pickens, Sampson	3533
Pettigrew, Amon	715	Pickens, Frances	3534
Pettigrew, Lena	716	Pickens, Isaiah	3535
Pettigrew, Frances	2670	Pickens, William	4129
Pettigrew, Elizavene	4033	Pickens, Aaron	4150
Pettigrew, Bynum	4960	Pickens, Mina	4169
Petigrew, Oscar	2216	Pickens, Eunice	4426
Petigrew, Viola	2217	Pickens, Lizzie	4754
Petigrew, Arch McCannon	2218	Pierce, Eliza	2261
Petigrew, Joe	2708	Pitts, Rebecca	4995
Perkins, Jane	1082	Pitchlyn, Eli	2719
Perkins, Mary	2382	Pitchlynn, Sudie	3621
Perkins, Edward	2387	Pitchlynn, Sophia M.	3626
Perkins, Laura B.	3399	Porter, Joe	224
Perkins, Hearl M.	3400	Porter, Elsie	225
Perkins, Julia Frances	3401	Porter, Mary	226
Perkins, Joe	4745	Porter, Herbert	227
Perriman, Lizzie	880	Porter, Hamp	228
Perriman, George	881	Porter, Mollie	229
Pettenridge, Charley	1292	Porter, Franklin	271
Penner, Amanda	1862	Porter, Oshway	650
Penner, Charley	1863	Porter, Betsey	651
Penner, Cyrus	1864	Porter, Chetona	652
Pershica, Millie	2533	Porter, Johnson	785
Pershica, Ben	2955	Porter, Harrison	854
Pershica, McLane	2956	Porter, Icey	855
Pershica, Fred	2957	Porter, Edmon	2523
Percival, Kate	3673	Porter, Robert	2524
Percival, Edward H.	3674	Porter, Jody	2525
Percival, Lela	3676	Porter, Sebena	2688
Percival, Fred	3677	Porter, Susie	2689
Percival, Claude	3678	Porter, Elmina	2690
Percival, Brit	3679	Porter, Jackson	751
Percival, Ottis	3680	Porter, Ben	4022
Phillips, Sallie Walker	91	Porter, Mamie	4565
Phillips, Ada	92	Porter, Angeline	4933
Phillips, Louisa	93	Porter, Carl Richard	4937
Phillips, Lucy	94	Porter, Andrew	4938
Phillips, Hill, Jr.	95	Porter, Lilie	4939
Phillips, Elmer	96	Pound, Tom	898
Phillips, Robert B.	97	Pound, Cornelia Eldora	1004
Phillips, Winona	98	Pound, Lillie	1005
Phillips, William Thomas	2073	Pound, Lela S.	1006
Phillips, Charles Rooks	2074	Pound, Helena	1007
Phillips, Rolla H.	2075	Pound, Mabel A.	1008
Phillips, John E.	2076	Pound, Carrie	3451
Phillips, Annie Louisa	2077	Pound, Nina	3454
Phillips, George E.	2078	Pound, Willie	3455
Phillips, William Ross	2079	Pound, Florence	3456
Phillips, Joseph R.	3144	Pound, Lizzie	3457
Phillips, Harry H.	3145	Pound, Madge	3458
		Poff, Maggie May	1135

Name.	Roll No.
Polk, Nannie	2031
Polk, Jodie Ellify	2032
Polk, Oscar Alinton	4119
Polomishtubby, Onahhy-yah	2921
Polomishtubby, Wesley	2920
Potts, Joseph B.	3360
Potts, Pearl	3361
Potts, Jewel	3362
Potts, Frank	3363
Potts, Joseph B., Jr.	3364
Potts, Ruby	3365
Potts, Douglas Howard	3366
Potts, John Taylor	3539
Potts, Goldey Abner	3540
Potts, John Taylor Jr.	3541
Potts, Allie May	3542
Potts, Mary Myrtle	3543
Potts, Annie Eliza	3544
Potts, Benjamin Alexander	4198
Potts, Robert	4863
Potts, Fannie E.	4912
Potts, Nina June	4913
Potts, Maud	4914
Potts, Lela	4915
Potts, Joel Cecil	4916
Powell, Ellen Jane	4366
Powell, Annie Viola	4367
Powell, Charles Ambrose	4368
Powell, Roy	4369
Powell, Rutha	4370
Powell, Preston	4371
Powell, Mary	4372
Powell, Thomas Clifford	4373
Powell, Samuel	4633
Pollock, Georgia	3453
Pope, Frank	3525
Price, Louvira	588
Price, Katie	589
Price, Mollie	1630
Price, Thomas Guy	1631
Price, Therian Bogart	1632
Price, Bisey	1693
Price, Benjamin Franklin	1694
Price, Jennie Belle	1695
Price, Ellis	1696
Price, Beula	1697
Pratt, Thomas	2912
Pratt, Robert	2913
Pratt, Robert	3072
Pruitt, Alice	3536
Pruitt, James Thomas	3537
Pruitt, Cecil Ray	3538
Priddy, Melvin	3882
Priddy, Cecil Lewis	3883
Pusley, Irene	261
Pusley, James	3627
Pusley, Mattie Jewell	3628
Pusley, Harriet	4661
Puller, Charles	485
Puller, Peter	486
Puller, Thomas	487
Puller, Mike	488
Puller, Nieby	489
Purtle, Kitty	692
Purtle, John Allen	693
Pytchlyn, George	3687
Pytchlyn, Jeff	4934
Pytchlyn, Isabella	4935
Pytchlyn, Mawlsey	4936
Pybas, Dora	4443
Pybas, Fannie Belle	4444
Pybas, Pat	4445
Pybas, Daisy	4446
Pybas, Lee Winston	4447
Pybas, Nellie H.	4448
Quincy, Thomas	2048
Quincy, Herbert M.	2401
Randolph, Elizabeth	1208
Randolph, Joe M.	1209
Randolph, Olive E.	1210

Name.	Roll No.
Randolph, Paul William	1211
Randolph, Nellie P.	3960
Randolph, Sobe	3962
Randolph, Fay	4080
Ravia, Mollie	3266
Ramsey, Mabel	3332
Ray, Mollie	3521
Ray, Vivian	3522
Ray, Opal	3523
Ray, Robert L.	3524
Raines, Nancy	3578
Raines, John	3580
Raines, Lillie	3581
Raines, Rosa	3582
Rains, Catherine	4342
Rains, Bessie	4343
Ragland, Wm. Nathan	4406
Ragland, Walter D.	4407
Ragland, Roy Nelson	4408
Rennie, Lula D.	145
Rennie, Louise Ella	149
Rennie, Catherine Rooks	1331
Rennie, George Burney	1332
Rennie, William	1892
Rennie, Mary Ellen	1893
Rennie, Mary Adeline	1894
Rennie, Jessie D.	1895
Rennie, Nora	1896
Rennie, Cecil C.	1897
Rennie, Claude C.	1898
Rennie, Mary M.	3828
Rennie, Alexander, Jr.	3829
Rennie, John F.	3924
Reed, Frank	245
Reed, Icy	246
Reed, Jincy	247
Reed, Diana	248
Reed, Edmon	249
Reed, Kissen	3585
Reed, Rhoda	3586
Reed, Jimmy	3587
Reed, Hagen	3588
Reed, Ed	3589
Reed, Simon	3591
Reed, Ivan	4014
Reed, Robinson	4203
Reynolds, Zack	1170
Reynolds, Sarah Ann	3272
Reynolds, Darius	3369
Reynolds, Elizabeth	3370
Reynolds, Elsie D.	3371
Reynolds, James	3372
Reynolds, Mamie	3373
Reynolds, Manilla	3374
Reynolds, Colbert U. H.	3376
Reynolds, Frank	3426
Reynolds, James Allen	3427
Reynolds, Ben F.	3688
Reynolds, Willie	4550
Reynolds, Frank	4551
Reynolds, Seldan	4552
Reynolds, Ethel	4553
Reynolds, Ida	4867
Reirdon, Claudie Ella	2065
Reirdon, Thelma O.	2072
Ream, James Boudinot	2564
Ream, Mary	2565
Ream, Robert Lee	2566
Ream, Leona	2567
Ream, Robert Lee, Jr.	2568
Reagan, Stella	4944
Rhoda,	4943
Richardson, Walton	557
Richardson, Stephen	558
Richardson, Dora	559
Richardson, Frank	560
Rice, Serena M.	703
Rice, Kittie Jane	704
Rice, Susie Meanda	705
Rice, Lizzie Evaline	706
Rider, Thomas Lewis	4713
Rider, Ollie Austin	4714
Rider, Freddie Fay	4715

Name.	Roll No.	Name.	Roll No.
Rodke, Lizzie	278	Scoby, Lela	2751
Rodke, Leo	279	Scoby, William Arthur	2756
Rodke, Loreno	280	Scarlett, Louisa	3124
Rodke, David L.	281	Scarlett, Edward J.	3135
Roberts, Wilson	638	Scarlett, Richard J., Jr.	3126
Roberts, Elsie	639	Scales, Mattie	3139
Roberts, Josephine	640	Scales, Claude	3140
Robeson, Jane	1054	Scales, Mamie	3141
Robeson, Eliza	1060	Scales, Winnie	3142
Robison, Hattie Adeline	1820	Scales, Grace	3143
Robison, Addie L.	1821	Sealy, Eli	84
Robison, Altai E.	1822	Sealy, Annie	85
Robison, Luther F.	1823	Sealy, Josephine	86
Robinson, Eliza	2138	Sealy, Sampson	88
Robinson, Susan	2174	Sealy, Sallie	125
Robinson, Eliza	3216	Sealy, Watson	646
Roberson, Simon	2589	Sealy, Grayson	648
Roberson, Martha	2590	Sealy, Susan	801
Roberson, Lila	2591	Sealy, Culberson	802
Roberson, Benjamin	2592	Sealy, Malinda	944
Roberson, Easter	2593	Sealy, Henry	1014
Roberson, Tilman	2594	Sealy, Ben	1044
Roberson, Logan	2595	Sealy, Viney	1045
Roberson, Caroline	2596	Sealy, Eli	1393
Roberson, Davison	2597	Sealy, Esau	1394
Roberson, Hattie Mary	2598	Sealy, Maggie	1395
Roberson, Emeline	2616	Sealy, Clarence	1731
Rodgers, Nora	1167	Sealy, Holmes	1732
Ross, Ada	2163	Sealy, Alice	1733
Ross, Homer Wilson	2164	Sealy, Josephine	1812
Ross, Bessie	2165	Sealy, Dave	1938
Ross, Bettie	2166	Sealy, Annie	1939
Ross, Thomas Cecil	2167	Sealy, Limond	1941
Ross, Joseph F.	4178	Sealy, Ely	1942
Roark, Alphonso Bailey	3469	Sealy, Rosa	2209
Roark, Annie L.	3470	Sealy, Henry	2210
Roark, William Edgar	3471	Sealy, Esther	2253
Roark, Ruthie Pearl	3472	Sealy, Ethel	2254
Roark, Charlie Yelser	3473	Sealy, Joe	2364
Rowe, Letitia	4393	Sealy, Annie	2466
Rowe, Rena	4394	Sealy, Charley	2511
Rowe, Alaric	4395	Sealy, Thompson	2513
Russell, Sissy	346	Sealy, Gilbert	2514
Russell, Silas	2529	Sealy, Lela	2515
Russell, Margerette	2530	Sealy, Susan	2516
Russell, Richard	2532	Sealy, Willie	3085
Russell, Ellis	2857	Sealy, Permelia	4931
Russell, Hattie	2858	Sealey, Adam	186
Russell, Edmond	2859	Sealey, Sina	2118
Russell, Eula	2860	Sealey, Louisa	3918
Russell, Richard	2861	Sealey, Julius	4977
Russell, Lula Myrtle	2862	Seeley, Joe	205
Russell, Arthur	2875	Seeley, Parley	206
Russell, Kate	4594	Seeley, Walter	207
Rucker, Rutha	4576	Seeley, Alonzo	208
Rucker, Mamie Arenia	4577	Seely, Lewis	2460
Ryle, Mattie	1549	Seely, Ellen	2461
Ryle, Emma	1550	Seely, George	3182
Ryle, Nannie May	1551	Seely, Isham	3885
Ryle, Jessie Lee	1552	Seely, Odus	4978
Ryle, W. H.	1553	Seeney, Nellie	2617
Ryan, Thomas Walker	4385	Seawright, Jack	2162
Ryan, Gussie Van Buren	4387	Seawright, Lula	2168
Ryan, Elbert Lewellyn	4388	Seawright, Stella Adeline	2169
Sadler, Ginsey	1379		
Sadler, Lavina	1380	Seawright, Ula	2170
Sadler, James	3669	Seawright, Leala	2171
Sadler, William	3670	Seifried, Charley	4392
Sadler, Joseph	3671	Seifried, William T.	4558
Saffron, Lizzie E.	1993	Seifried, Minnie	4559
Sanders, Sarah Jane	2093	Seifried, Henry	4560
Sacra, Mattie	2939	Seifried, Mattie	4561
Sacra, Lillie	2940	Seifried, Mary	4562
Sacra, Estelle	2941	Seifried, Lucy	4563
Sacra, Edward	2942	Seifried, Eula Beatrice	4710
Sacra, Marie	2943	Shield, Mandy	252
Sacra, Leston	2944	Shield, Jacob	253
Sacra, Nettie Loyce	2947	Shield, Watson	617
Sacra, Malachia	4171	Shield, Mary Jane	618
Scott, Mary	1062	Shield, Simon	637
Scott, Wilburn	1063	Shield, Esau	4957
Scott, Louisa	1901	Shields, Henry	2343
Schoeppe, Elizabeth	1526	Shields, Ennet	4967

Name.	Roll No.	Name.	Roll No.
Shico, Elonzo	831	Souse, Dory	1513
Shico, Frank	3165	Spain, Mary E.	1297
Shico, Louisa	3166	Spain, Jessie	1298
Shico, Mamie	3167	Spain, McKnightle	1299
Shico, Douglas	3169	Spain, Georgia	1300
Shico, Martin	4365	Spain, Sallie P.	4094
Shannon, Daisy	1206	Sparks, Dollie	4433
Shannon, Laura G.	4451	Sparks, Richard L.	4434
Shannon, Thressa May	4452	Sparks, Ethel	4435
Shannon, Joseph Scott	4453	Sparks, Nellie Gaines	4842
Shannon, Robert Lee	4454	Speed, Willie Grant	1252
Shannon, Charlie Foster	4455	Speed, Charles J.	1253
Shannon, Annie Laura	4456	Speed, Samuel J.	1254
Shannon, Murphy Lena	4457	Spencer, Margaret E.	4854
Shannon, Ida Estella	4458	Stephen, Gano	267
Shannon, Willie Inez	4459	Stephen, Lincey	268
Shannon, Nora	4463	Stout, Jeff	282
Sharp, Sallie	1908	Stout, Tena Thomas	283
Sharp, Mary Gladys	1910	Stout, Liza	285
Sharp, Lillie	2744	Stout, Lonzo	286
Sharp, Ruby	2750	Stick, Albert	372
Shuckey, Patsey	2456	Stick, Henry	499
Shelton, Clemmie	2945	Stick, Rogers	530
Shelton, Myrtle C.	4254	Stick, Minnie	531
Short, Lizzie	3107	Stick, Amosin	532
Short, Morris L.	3108	Stick, Mary	533
Short, Thomas W.	3273	Stick, Lottie	534
Short, Ethel	3275	Stick, Charles	535
Short, Effie Jane	3675	Stick, Nora	536
Short, Ode	3681	Stick, Linton	537
Short, Holmes	3682	Stick, Billie	872
Short, William Walter	3841	Stick, Nellie	873
Short, Robert P., Jr.	3842	Stick, Katie	874
Short, Thomas Clyde	3843	Stick, Mattie	975
Short, Maury	4179	Stick, Lillie	876
Shirley, Willie	3930	Stick, Eddie	877
Shwinogee, Sam	4761	Stick, Emily	879
Ship, Susan	3251	Stick, Kinney	923
Ship, Mary	3252	Stick, Malissa	924
Simpson, Mattie	2027	Stick, Fannie	925
Skeen, Matilda	772	Stick, Silsey	926
Skeen, James Walter	773	Stick, Morris	4975
Skeen, Emily Frances	774	Story, James C.	678
Skeen, Cora Tamsie	775	Story, Corbett	679
Skinner, Permelia	3606	Story, Etter	680
Skinner, Russell F.	3607	Story, Jake	681
Skinner, Mollie Vernon	3608	Story, Sam	1495
Smith, Martha C.	348	Story, Lotta Estella	4208
Smith, Mable M.	349	Statler, Dacie	852
Smith, Morris B.	350	Statler, Lilia	853
Smith, Malisie	747	Strickland, Charles Guy	1133
Smith, Mary A.	1672	Strickland, Wm. Doug-	
Smith, Lillian Estelle	1673	lass	1134
Smith, John	2033	Strickland, Tom	1152
Smith, Ticy	2034	Strickland, Glassey	1153
Smith, Loman	2035	Strickland, C. W.	1154
Smith, Ella	2036	Strickland, Walter	2358
Smith, Melton	2037	Strickland, John	2359
Smith, Minnie O.	2471	Strickland, Granville	2360
Smith, Mollie	2998	Strickland, Joseph Bry-	
Smith, Nancy	3127	an	2361
Smith, Jordan Cutchin-		Strickland, Meda Ann	2362
tubby	3128	Strickland, Ada May	2363
Smith, Zona	3555	Strickland, Homer	4146
Smith, Myrtle	3556	Stewart, Josephine	1185
Smith, Lelia	4126	Stewart, Wiley	1186
Smith, Lindsey	4127	Stewart, Frank	1187
Smith, Frank	4291	Stewart, John	1188
Smith, Mollie	4292	Stewart, Earl	1189
Smith, Birdie	4293	Stewart, Addie	1190
Smith, Richard	4294	Stewart, Mary Frances	1473
Smith, Rector	4295	Stewart, Eugene	1474
Smith, Cheadle	4296	Stewart, Gertrude M.	1475
Smith, Dewey	4297	Stewart, Minnie	2611
Smith, Katie	4298	Stewart, Georgia	2612
Smith, Kittie	4917	Stewart, Lettie Bell	2613
Smith, Winnie	4918	Stewart, Calvin	2999
Smith, Hobart	4922	Stewart, Ben	3000
Smith, Martha	4923	Stewart, William	4158
Smith, Esaw	4924	Staton, Laura	1375
Souse, Georgia	1510	Staton, Will	1376
Souse, Lula	1511	Staton, Ludie David	1377
Souse, Rix	1512	Staton, Nita May	1378

Name.	Roll No.	Name.	Roll No.
Statons, Marina B.	3253	Thomas, Tom	4143
Statons, William Alma	3254	Thomas, Fannie	4892
Statons, Arthur Edward	3255	Thurston, David Jeff	587
Stevenson, Malinda	1390	Thornton, Carrie Mur-	
Stevenson, Mary	1391	ray	1580
Stephenson, Victoria	1648	Thornton, Robert	1581
Stephenson, Wayne	1649	Thornton, Anita	1582
Stephenson, Ivry	1651	Thompson, Martha	1976
Stone, Josephine	1664	Thompson, Robert	1977
Stone, James B.	1665	Thompson, Alexander	1978
Stone, Mary	1666	Thompson, Wilson	1979
Stone, Lacy	1667	Thompson, Angeline	1980
Stone, William C.	1668	Thompson, Mattie	2704
Stephens, Agnes	2462	Thompson, Inez	2705
Steele, Amelia	3007	Thompson, Thomas Benj.	2783
Steele, Willie	3008	Thompson, Eugene Ross	2784
Steele, Thomas	3009	Thompson, Mary Fran-	
Steele, Overton	3010	ces	2785
Sturdivant, Luke Love	3717	Thompson, Iona	2786
Sturdivant, Isabella	3753	Thompson, Flora Mary	2987
Stumbaugh, Lula	3983	Thompson, James Willis	2988
Stumbaugh, Helen Maud	3984	Thompson, Eula	2989
Sturges, Louise	4537	Thompson, Lillian	2990
Stowers, Mary Elizabeth	4800	Thompson, Stella	2993
Stowers, Mamie E.	4801	Thompson, Siney	3218
Stowers, Thomas Cecil	4802	Thompson, Minnie	3233
Stowers, Mattie Lucile	4803	Thompson, Rubie	3234
Stowers, Lottie Esther	4804	Thompson, Culberson	3424
Sullivan, Michael Jos.	1038	Thompson, Green Wood	3480
Sullivan, Edward A.	1039	Thompson, Henry	3594
Sullivan, Ellen	1040	Thompson, Gladys Try-	
Sullivan, Anna L.	1041	phenia	4165
Sullivan, Robert E.	1042	Thompson, Minnie Lee	4318
Sullivan, Florence	1043	Thompson, Mamie Fran-	
Surber, Maudie	4634	ces	4319
Taylor, Nancy	2130	Thompson, Robert Lee	4320
Taylor, Johnie	2134	Thompson, Emma Au-	
Taylor, Robert	2135	gusta	4321
Taylor, John W. P.	2136	Thompson, Jessie May	4322
Taylor, Vernie Dillard	2147	Thompson, Selena Isa-	
Taylor, Sarah Lucinda	2148	bella	4314
Taylor, Leo	2149	Thompson, Jacob Loren	4612
Taylor, Annie	2555	Thompson, Charles Wil-	
Taylor, Daniel Alexan-		liam	4968
der	4136	Thompson, Thaxton	
Taylor, Mary Ann	4421	Rosa	3310
Taylor, Lula	4588	Thompson, Lais Ethel	3313
Talley, Willie N.	1400	Thomson, Della May	3763
Talley, Thomas P.	1401	Thomson, William Paul	3768
Talley, Sudie B.	1402	Tohm, Wilson	918
Tabor, Rhoda	3649	Tohm, Nedo	919
Tabor, Frances	3650	Tohm, Maggie	920
Tabor, Juanita	3651	Tohm, Mamie	921
Tabor, Electer	3652	Tohm, Acey	922
Tabor, Agnes Retta	4205	Townsley, Pheby	1960
Thomas, Isaac	204	Townsley, Rosie	1961
Thomas, Minnie	284	Townsley, Maggie	1962
Thomas, Bob	436	Trentham, Henderson	63
Thomas, Joe L.	689	Trentham, Lena	64
Thomas, Mamie	690	Trentham, Mary	65
Thomas, Willie	1159	Truax, Mary	112
Thomas, Amanda	1560	Truax, Pearl E.	113
Thomas, Minnie	1849	Truax, Ruby G.	114
Thomas, Russell Gard-		Truax, William B.	115
ner	1854	Truax, Jewel	116
Thomas, Charles Cruce	1855	Troop, Cecil Gordon	4114
Thomas, John	2005	Turnbull, C. W.	1203
Thomas, Martha Belle	2006	Turnbull, Loyd Mertin	1204
Thomas, Rosabelle	2007	Turnbull, Clarence Rex	1205
Thomas, Alta	2008	Turnbull, Ryan	1669
Thomas, John	2009	Turnbull, Roy	1670
Thomas, Gracie	2010	Turnbull, Virgil Lester	1671
Thomas, Heck	2883	Turnbull, Estella	2395
Thomas, Charley	3736	Turnbull, Delburt	3547
Thomas, Wm. Montgom-		Turnbull, Albert	3548
ery	3737	Turnbull, Ora May	3549
Thomas, Lillie Asley	3738	Turnbull, Cecil Ryan	3950
Thomas, Jefferson	3739	Turnbull, Dollie	3952
Thomas, Jessie May	3740	Turnbull, Dick	4474
Thomas, Callie Ray	3741	Turnbull, Claude	4475
Thomas, Donnie Eveline	3742	Turnbull, Fannie	4476
Thomas, Charles N. D.	3743	Turnbull, Adel	4477
Thomas, Isaac Alva	4115	Turman, Vinnie Ream	1827

Name.	Roll No.	Name.	Roll No.
Turman, Annie Ream	1828	Vaughn, Jesse	1490
Turman, Louis Boudinot	1829	Vail, Willie	1870
Tushkatomby, Mamie	2434	Vail, Vergie	4678
Tushkatomby, James	4946	Van Zandt, Eva May	2720
Tushkatomby, Hattie	4947	Vann, Lottie	4639
Tushkatomby, Willie	4948	Vann, Jim	4640
Tushkatomby, Clara	4949	Vann, Lolo	4641
Tussy, Jane	2821	Vann, William	4642
Tussy, Lila	3709	Vann, David	4643
Tussy, Mary Elizabeth	3710	Vann, Arthur	4644
Tussy, Martha Jane	3711	Vann, Jennie	4645
Tussy, Lucy Lee	3712	Venable, Dollie	3267
Tussy, Lola May	3713	Venable, Beulah	3268
Tussy, Alex Hugh	3714	Venable, Laura	3269
Tussy, Lilla F.	3715	Victor, Emmet L.	2677
Tussy, Minnie Edna	3716	Victor, Wilson L.	2678
Tuttle, Carrie M.	3744	Victor, Julious Thomas	2679
Tuttle, Virginia Molette	3745	Walker, Tandy C.	1
Tuttle, Nora Alma	3746	Walker, J. T.	2
Tuttle, James Bond	3747	Walker, J. C.	3
Tuttle, Charles Campbell	3748	Walker, G. C.	5
Tuttle, Barbara Ann	3749	Walker, Minnie	6
Tushawaha, Willie	3770	Walker, Mary Cornelia	9
Turner, Edward B.	3865	Walker, Robert T.	10
Turner, Clifford	3866	Walker, David	99
Turner, Ethel	3867	Walker, James W.	391
Turner, Laura E.	4213	Walker, Noah	392
Turner, Daisy	4815	Walker, David	393
Turner, Ludie May	4816	Walker, Lizzie	394
Turner, Mary	4817	Walker, Amy	548
Tyson, Joe	677	Walker, Amon	549
Tyson, Ed	1073	Walker, Delia	1410
Tyson, Susan	2119	Walker, Thomas H.	1411
Tyson, Elonzo	2543	Walker, Alice	3998
Tyson, Willie	3807	Walker, William D.	3999
Tyubby, Sam	2249	Walker, Robertha	4000
Tyubby, Nancy	2250	Walker, Daisy O'Dean	4001
Tyubby, Noel	2252	Walker, Vicy	4417
Tyubby, Richmond	2256	Walker, Theodore D.	4734
Tyubby, Leah	2904	Walton, Salina	160
Tyubby, Nicey	2911	Walton, Tecumseh	519
Underwood, George	42	Walton, Holmes	520
Underwood, Gabriel	117	Walton, Simon	539
Underwood, Nancy	118	Walton, Josiah S.	621
Underwood, Wesley	119	Walton, Emely	622
Underwood, Alice	120	Walton, Maggie	623
Underwood, Bina	121	Walton, Carney	627
Underwood, Hagen	122	Walton, Powell	3584
Underwood, Louis	123	Walton, Davis	3952
Underwood, Phoebe	127	Walton, Virgie	4021
Underwood, Rena	203	Watters, Joe	360
Underwood, Johnie	273	Watters, Even	362
Underwood, Burney	355	Watters, Hamilton	363
Underwood, Intolubby	1018	Watters, Polly	364
Underwood, William	1071	Wall, Billie	496
Underwood, Daisy	2284	Wade, George	644
Underwood, Rosa	2285	Wade, Eliza	645
Underwood, Ben	2428	Wade, Lizzie	1023
Underwood, Joe	2556	Wade, Nancy	4025
Underwood, Jimpson	2606	Wade, Missie	4026
Underwood, Sarah	2607	Wade, Mamie	4027
Underwood, Lena	2608	Wade, Maggie	4996
Underwood, Daniel	2609	Walner, John H.	1177
Underwood, Thomas	2646	Walner, Robert	1345
Underwood, Phoebe	2647	Walner, John	1346
Underwood, Elonzo	2697	Walner, Jim	1347
Underwood, Salina	2813	Walner, Ebb	1348
Underwood, Matlain	2814	Walner, Frank	1349
Underwood, Edgar	3205	Walner, Lula	4264
Underwood, Allen	3206	Walner, Susan V.	4265
Underwood, Lewis	3207	Walner, Acca	4266
Underwood, Mollie	3967	Walner, Julia	4267
Underwood, Silena	4041	Walner, Hugh	4268
Underwood, Martha Hoey	4042	Waldon, Albert	1198
Underwood, Isaac	4140	Waldon, Verona H.	1199
Underwood, Willie Bond	4749	Waldon, Thomas Wm.	1200
Underwood, Lewis	4760	Waldon, Clara May	1201
Vance, Jefferson	940	Waldon, Hosey	1217
Vanderslice, Walter	1137	Waldon, Susie	1218
Vanderslice, Jacob	1138	Waldon, Sina	1219
Vanderslice, Eliza	1142	Waldon, Evelene	1220
Vanderslice, Maulsie Bula	4070	Waldon, Sadie	1221
		Waldon, Hosea Thomas	1222

Name.	Roll No.	Name.	Roll No.
Waldon, Burney Duglas	1224	Wells, Norman	243
Waldon, Sophia	1358	Wells, Robert L.	244
Waldon, Jimmie	1359	Wells, John Franklin	3858
Waldon, Bill Byrd	1361	Wells, Charles M.	4013
Waldon, Bert	4079	Welch, Bessie	3520
Waite, A. R.	1268	Welch, Robert C.	4614
Waite, Verdi V.	1269	Welch, Mildred B.	4615
Waite, Grace C.	1270	Welch, Charles A.	4616
Waite, Winifred	1271	Welch, Fitzhugh Lee	4617
Waite, Leo E.	1272	Welch, Lucile Matilda	4618
Waite, Emely	1273	Welch, Alice	4784
Waite, Mary	1281	Welch, Joe	4785
Waite, Katie	4789	Welch, Makey	4786
Watkins, Eugean	1420	Welch, Earl	4787
Watkins, James	1444	Welch, Frank	4813
Watkins, James Artie	1445	Welch, John H.	4814
Watkins, William Eugenus	1446	Webb, Stella LaFlore	1756
		Webb, Guy LaFlore	1757
Watkins, W. R., Jr.	1591	Webb, Daisy Maude	1758
Watkins, Henry Patton	4098	Webb, Isabella Abigale	3261
Watkins, Calvin D.	4493	Webb, Joel F.	3662
Watkins, Oscar Oliver	4494	Webb, George W.	3263
Watkins, Albert Elverson	4589	Webb, William H.	3264
		Webb, John M., Jr.	3265
Wasson, Nannie E.	1465	White, Leona	861
Wasson, Emma Janette Chloe	1466	White, Alice	862
		White, Willie	1113
Wasson, Joseph J.	1467	White, James	1114
Wasson, Victor B.	4100	White, Harry Harvel	2179
Washington, May Ellen	1601	White, Malissa A.	2301
Washington, John Richard	1602	White, Lula M.	2302
		White, Ethel D.	2303
Washington, George	2211	White, Oscar D.	2304
Washington, Johnie Lou	2212	White, Walter S.	2305
Washington, Clela May	2213	White, Illynoyah	2306
Washington, Osler Flint	2214	White, Harvel E.	2130
Washington, Hugh	2375	White, Lucy V.	2307
Washington, Isaac Monroe	2376	White, Samuel Benj.	2308
		White, Thomas W.	2309
Washington, George Edwin	2377	White, Cora Malissia	4137
		White, Ethel S.	4138
Washington, Jeremiah C., Jr.	4855	Wheatley, Louisa	1434
Washington, Russell L.	4856	Whitesel, Mary Elizabeth	3096
Warren, Reuben H.	1708	Whitesel, Katie May	3097
Warren, Mabel	1709	Whitesel, Freddie Jerome	3098
Warren, Mary Catherine	1710		
Warren, Ruth Bixby	1711	Whitesel, Willis Love	3099
Warren, Nannie C.	1707	Whitesel, Zula	3100
Warren, William Byrd	1712	Whitthorne, Angie	3304
Watts, Will	2243	Whitthorne, Martin	3305
Ward, William Thomas	2378	Whitthorne, Matthew Thomas	3307
Ward, Estelle	2379		
Ward, Estwill	2380	Whitthorne, Hardin Coleman	4189
Ward, Beatrix Theodosia	2381		
Ward, Houston	2922	Wilson, Salan	401
Watson, Noah	4417	Wilson, George T.	434
Watson, Hugh L.	4418	Wilson, Ruth	435
Wallace, Nannie	4485	Wilson, Elsie	566
Wallace, Esther B.	4486	Wilson, Kate	1017
Wallace, Elizabeth Vashti	4487	Wilson, Joseph B.	1295
		Wilson, Stephen	2643
Wallace, Albert Ned	4488	Wilson, Newton G.	2692
Wallace, Samuel Lee	4489	Wilson, Willie	2693
Wallace, Leo Edmond B.	4490	Wilson, Icy	2966
Wallace, George Blanchee	4491	Wilson, Sue Ellen	4092
		Wilson, Claude Allen	4093
Wallace, Harold M.	4926	Wilson, John D.	4516
Waatkins Emma A.	4492	Wilson, Augusta Jessie	4517
Watehall, Nicholas Mondavis	4810	Wilson, Gracie Ethel	4518
Watehall, Samuel Dixon	4811	Wilson, Laura Lee	4519
Watehall, Bruce Love	4812	Wilson, Clara May	4520
Waitman, Ludia	4895	Wilson, Frankie Florence	4521
Waitman, Henry T.	4896		
Wesley, Stone	156	Wilson, Eva	5007
Wesley, Selina	157	Wilson, Roy G.	5010
Wesley, Lizzie	766	Wilson, Joseph P.	5011
Wells, Willard W.	238	Williams, Sukey	540
Wells, W. W., Jr.	239	Williams, Sophia	671
Wells, James F.	240	Williams, Sylvia	672
Wells, Claude W.	241	Williams, Silas	673
Wells, Ida L.	242	Williams, Boyle	674
		Williams, Ella	1469

Name.	Roll No.	Name.	Roll No.
Williams, Orin	1472	Wolf, Esau	5004
Williams, Emely	3877	Worcester, Lyman D.	294
Williams, Katie M.	3878	Worcester, Overton	295
Williams, Jennie L.	4464	Worcester, Mattie	296
Williams, Lella	4465	Worcester, Simeon	298
Williams, Wade	4466	Worcester, Laban	299
Williams, Alonzo	4467	Worcester, Arlington	
Williams, Allie	4468	Telle	1915
Williams, Sam, Jr.	4469	Wolfenbarger, Rella	1437
Williams, Susan Eliza-		Wolfenbarger, Joseph	1438
beth	4470	Wolfenbarger, Lula	1439
Williams, David S.	4471	Wolfenbarger, Birdie	1440
Williams, Isum	4466	Wolfenbarger, James	
Williams, Johnnie	5002	Hanson	1441
Wisdom, George	603	Wolfenbarger, Launa	1442
Wisdom, Carolins	604	Wolfenbarger, Garnett	1443
Wisdom, Linhey	605	Worsham, Lucretia	1802
Wisdom, Lem	606	Worsham, Richard	1803
Wisdom, Frances	607	Worsham, Samuel	1804
Wisdom, Cleveland	608	Worsham, Mattie	1805
Wisdom, George	609	Worsham, Jewel	1806
Wisdom, Felix	761	Worsham, Birdie Guy	1807
Willis, Johnson	1098	Wooten, Lillie	2394
Willis, Frances	1765	Woody, Ada	2915
Willis, Floradel	1766	Woody, Guy	2918
Willis, Archie Leonard	1767	Woody, Brice	2919
Willis, Holmes	2923	Wright, Martha	194
Willis, William	2924	Wright, Frank	269
Willis, Sydney	2925	Wright, William	276
Willis, Hortense	2926	Wright, Serena Fulsom	277
Willis, Overton Love	2927	Wright, Jimpson	359
Willis, J. Hamp	2951	Wright, Sophia	371
Willis, Emma	2952	Wright, Dillard	374
Willis, Helen Robenia	2953	Wright, Delilah	1000
Willis, Raleigh Britton	3027	Wright, Willie Mazeppa	3850
Willis, Holmes Ulysses	3028	Wright, Pearl	3851
Willis, Hamilton	3502	Wright, Wilson	3919
Willis, Lemmie	3503	Wright, Oran R.	4196
Willis, Agnes	3504	Wright, Monge P.	4197
Willis, Robert B.	3505	Wright, Thomas	4215
Williford, Richard	1514	Wright, Davis	4216
Winchester, Luther E.	3963	Wright, Sam B.	4691
Winter, Anna Louise	4822	Wright, Gertrude	4692
Wolfe, Charlotte	196	Wray, Daisy	1468
Wolfe, Sale	197	Wray, Serena Belle	3694
Wolfe, Mary	230	Wray, Lester W.	3695
Wolfe, Agnes	347	Wray, David Walker	3696
Wolfe, Mose	1037	Wray, Carrie E.	3697
Wolfe, Mattie	1911	Wray, William Thomas	3698
Wolfe, Frances	1912	Yarborough, William	
Wolfe, Lizzie	2042	Henry	3339
Wolfe, Solbun	2043	Yarborough, Minnie May	3341
Wolfe, Robinson	2795	Yarborough, George Au-	
Wolfe, Ida	2796	gustus	3342
Wolfe, Johnnie	2797	Yarborough, James Mar-	
Wolfe, Welburn	2805	tin	3343
Wolfe, Nelson	3804	Yates, Rachel	3870
Wolfe, Alum	4251	Yancey, Minnie	32
Wolfe, Chiminayne	4252	Yancey, Lillian	33
Wolf, Monroe	1484	Yancey, Clara	34
Wolf, Susan	1570	Yancey, Ermi Ancher	36
Wolf, Frank	1571	Yancey, Mattie Ella	4033
Wolf, May	1579	Yoakum, George H.	1121
Wolf, Bella	1612	Yoakum, Leonard	1122
Wolf, Delphia	2086	Yoakum, Mary B.	1123
Wolf, Malinda	2095	Yoakum, John T.	1124
Wolf, Sallie	2096	Yoakum, Beulah Pearl	1125
Wolf, Jim	2097	Yoakum, Una Lee	1126
Wolf, Key	2265	Young, Adaline	1561
Wolf, Davison	2266	Young, Lizzie Bell	1562
Wolf, Wicy	2267	Young, Lucy Branferd	1563
Wolf, John	2268	Young, Carrie Lee	1564
Wolf, Abel	2269	Young, Mattie Lou	1565
Wolf, Elias	2270	Young, James Granville	1566
Wolf, Loman	2272	Young, Nancy Colbert	1567
Wolf, Josephine	4018	Young, Patsey	1568
Wolf, Jessie	4108	Young, Bettie May	1569

INDEX TO
NEW BORN CHICKASAWS BY BLOOD

Name.	Roll No.	Name.	Roll No.
Coffee, Willie Lucile	481	Godfrey, Bessie Annie	274
Cotner, Holmes Russell	75	Grayson, Leo Mayfield	8
Condon, Clarence Douglas	113	Grayson, Miller Woodson	398
		Greenwood, Cecil	73
Cochran, Vaughon	203	Greenwood, Alice	305
Connelly, Leslie	204	Greenwood, Cora	381
Coyle, Cecil Earl	234	Greenwood, Ella	519
Collins, Louise Maud	245	Greenwood, Nora	548
Collins, Garland Wardlow	299	Grinslade, Henryetta	162
Collins, Vernon	383	Green, Roman	220
Cotner, Lawana C.	445	Gray, Ruel Archey	341
Courtney, Emma	569	Hayes, Carrie	10
Criner, Sallie Joe	62	Hays, Vivian	190
Criner, Luther Herbert	63	Hatcher, Mary Ellen	18
Creecy, Pearl	103	Harrison, Earle Eugene	20
Crockett, George	106	Harrison, Lillie	21
Cravatt, Ramona	112	Harrison, Vivian	136
Cravatt, Darias A.	380	Harrison, Jas. Anderson	146
Cravatt, Fred	409	Hawkins, Betty Wade	78
Cravatt, Rena	410	Hawkins, Margaret	125
Cravens, Thyra Fay	500	Hawkins, Nicy	270
Culbarson, Rachel	446	Hawkins, May	423
Culbarson, Gilbert	524	Harrell, James L.	87
Davis, Samuel C., Jr.	19	Hardwick, Herman	141
Davis, Herschell W.	77	Hardwick, Waneta	142
Davis, George Lowery	126	Hardwick, Dave	291
Deshan, Darcey	188	Harper, Joseph E. Johnston	167
Denny, Almina	575	Hayward, Edna May	169
Dilbeck, Montelee	29	Hawley, Daisy	191
Dickerson, Fleda	424	Hawley, Nellie	192
Dick, LeRoy	528	Hamblin, Mary Ruth	195
Dobbs, Martha Ann	32	Hamblin, Lela Mildred	
Doak, Vivian Nail	56	Beatrice	196
Dowdy, Oma	140	Harkins, Lucy May	272
Downing, Roy Thomas	295	Harden, Viola Iona	277
Draughon, Byrd Love	142	Harris, Battiest	283
Durant, Eathem Lee	9	Harris, Claud Laten	418
Duncan, Johny Odus	155	Halsell, Thomas E. C.	309
Duckworth, Mattie Thomas	174	Harwood, Omal Earl	325
Dunigan, Roxie	333	Hassell, William Henry	342
Duffy, Burris Donaven	394	Hampton, Edward	345
Dulin, James P.	436	Hampton, Burnie C.	390
Duroderigo, Peachie Viola	496	Hancock, Clarence R.	384
Durin, May Pearl	537	Hamm, Thomas Colville	389
Eddleman, Dale	230	Hamilton, Zora	427
Elmore, Claud Franklin	211	Harlin, Delter	440
		Hale, Hanley Harvey	508
Elliott, John Cyrus, Jr.	472	Harrell, Jeff	478
Finley, Johnie L.	322	Higgins, Thomas H.	31
Fillmore, Mandy	382	Hilton, Edith	357
Filmore, Allice Victoria	520	Horton, Burruss Andrew	13
Fletcher, Burney Johnson	259	Horton, Thelma	475
		Howard, Ulalia Ruth	36
Flemmons, Frank	515	Hogue, John L. W.	44
Folsom, James	347	Hutchins, Ira William	261
Ford, Fannie	488	Hutchins, John Ellis	324
Ford, Jewell	489	Hughes, Thomas Jefferson	289
Friend, Estella M.	38	Hudgeons, Roy	490
Friend, Douglas H.	435	Immohotichey, Jonas	235
Francis, R. Miller	193	Jack, Roland	185
Fry, Florence Marzett	271	James, Ruble Rhoener	194
Fryrear, Eddie Lee	437	James, Lela	240
Furgerson, Leon May	370	James, Lavader Jewel	304
Fussell, Paul	417	James, Almeda	470
Gaddis, Arthur O. Love	64	Jackson, Heawatha May	326
Gaddis, Eva	400	Jemison, May	22
Gaddis, Pearl	401	Jefferson, Tommy	127
Gaddis, Clifton	513	Jefferson, Salina	577
Gardner, Zella Bernice	145	Jennings, Vernon H.	221
Gardner, Winona	454	Jeflow, Joseph	506
Garrett, Uldean	412	Johnson, Cecil Elihu	47
Gibson, Rodie	34	Johnson, Ula	48
Gibson, Sylvia	533	Johnson, Elizabeth	184
Gilmore, Conchoella B.	406	Johnson, Edward B., Jr.	337
Gooch, Gladys Morine	41	Johnson, Josephine Olive	433
Gooding, Sadie Bell	158	Johnson, Elihu Bennett	441
Goins, Josephine Lucy	222	Johnson, Susan	566
Goins, Charles Reuben	223	Jordan, William T.	282
Goforth, Irene Stella	252	Jordan, Edgar Ray	456
Goforth, Clifton Leeper	263	Jones, Ernest Leon	374
Godfrey, Addie Mary	273	Jones, Charles Marvin	375

Name.	Roll No.
Randolph, Norma Lucille	366
Randolph, Maude Elizabeth	535
Reirdon, Rebecca Louise	84
Reynolds, Eddie Leroy	178
Ream, Allinton Guy	288
Ream, Vinnie	287
Rennie, Hortense Hiahwah-nah	308
Rennie, Helen	393
Reed, Rosevelt	340
Reed, Lillie May	556
Rider, Gussie Agnes	216
Rice, Odneal	428
Richardson, Liza	543
Ross, Amos	90
Ross, Icy Myrtle	98
Roberson, Amon	114
Roller, George Martin	152
Rowe, Vera	209
Rodke, Benjiman P.	307
Robison, Bluford	323
Roberts, Nancy	498
Robeson, Charley	550
Rucker, William Clayton	364
Russell, Eliza	504
Russell, Evison	505
Seawright, Lucy	91
Seawright, Bessie	92
Sealy, Either	144
Sealey, Gouldey	492
Seely, Vinnie May	557
Seifried, Jessie A.	208
Self, Sarah Arinda	552
Self, Joseph W.	553
Shelton, Van Noy	133
Shannon, Winnie Elizabeth	246
Short, Thomas Thedore	339
Shico, Mary	359
Shield, Wisie	420
Sharkey, Mattie	458
Spencer, Wesley	217
Spencer, Irene	218
Spence, William Wellington	425
Stewart, Charlie Claud	12
Stewart, Edna Lucile	137
Stewart, Charley Elmer	231
Stanton, Missouria D.	33
Stanton, Marrley M.	517
Straughn, Sidney Ceicel	61
Stanfield, Isaac Edward	79
Stick, Reller	95
Strickland, Thomas Edmond	104
Strickland, Vineta	105
Strickland, Malita Fay	402
Stephenson, Annie	249
Stout, Mica	278
Statons, Sam Potts	303
Story, Olla	349
Stowers, Minnie Beatrice	371
Stowers, James Royce	372
Statler, James J.	431
Surrell, Matilda Pocahontas	236
Taylor, Jewel	89
Taylor, Frank R.	247
Taylor, George Porter	368
Thomas, Douglass H. G.	68
Thomas, Lavera	80
Thomas, Alpha	181
Thomas, Alma	182

Name.	Roll No.
Thompson, Bettie Lou	119
Thompson, Martin Epps	120
Thompson, Avise Minnitte	311
Thompson, Minerva B.	516
Thompson, Jesse	563
Thonson, VirginiaMay	269
Thaxton, Earnest Leon ard	297
Thornton, Golda	329
Thurston, Cordie Marie	578
Tinsley, Edith Audrey	226
Townsley, Monroe James	74
Trentham, Bessie	3
Truax, Opal	6
True, Lena May	224
True, Lottie Belle	225
Troute, Roland	267
Turnbull, John B.	51
Tussy, LottieKate	265
Tucker, George Wilson	352
Turner, Evert Allen	421
Turner, Roscoe Hampton	459
Tyson, Mable	94
Underwood, Jessie	7
Underwood, Amanda	544
Underwood, Ada	554
Underwood, Joe	561
Underwood, Vinie	568
Vail, Minnie	72
Vann, Cloy	477
Venable, Ruth	248
Victor, Hazel	257
Walker, Tandy C., Jr.	1
Walker, Maimie	422
Watkins, Bessie May	49
Watkins, Rosalee Levina	268
Watkins, Ruby Isabelle	493
Watkins, Henry Furmon	494
Ward, Elizabeth Corine	107
Ward, Morine	464
Walthall, Gracie	180
Waldon, Roy Oscar	243
Waldon, Turner Clyde	244
Waldon, Floyd	376
Warren, Marguerite N.	294
Walton, Kutman	298
Wagner, Leroy E.	358
Wade, George, Jr.	487
Walner, Florence M.	540
Webb, John Wesley	153
Webb, Abrigale	154
Welch, Edgar Warren	212
Welch, Clayton	460
Welch, Paul B.	461
Wells, Florence E.	405
White, Wilber S.	93
Williams, Ruth	52
Wilson, Pearl Caroline	134
Wilson, Anna Aleen	260
Willis, Margaret Evelyne	139
Willis, Juanita	264
Willis, Janise Hortense	334
Willis, William Wiley	353
Williamson, Shirley	229
Wolf, Ruben	86
Worsham, Gertrude	442
Worcestor, Edmond	447
Wright, Samuel Pickens	507
Young, Charles Ruben	55
Yoakum, George W.	165
Yoakum, John M.	521
Yancey, Agnes Lorena	351
Youngblood, Juneta	385

Name.	Roll No.
Harjo, Fannie	250
Harjo, Susan	251
Hayes, Rosie	270
Hayes, Henry Charles Preston	317
Hays, Hazel M.	292
Harrell, Tandy Edwin	287
Heald, Cecil Chester	313
Heald, Vinnie Lucile	314
Holt, Emily	7
Horton, Nannie Fay	19
Horton, Arnoid Liffie	285
Holden, Clamy	72
Hornbeck, William Stevens	171
House, Lester E.	234
Hughes, Flora Lucile	147
Immohotichey, Jackson	117
James, Rossie Jewel	102
James, Leona	240
James, Lizzie	263
Jackson, William H., Jr.	265
Jennings, Ruby M.	262
Johnson, Henry Belton Jr.	5
Johnson, Edna	18
Johnson, Mary Lee	75
Johnson, Tilford Thomas, Jr.	76
Johnson, Earl O.	100
Johnson, Crawford	126
Johnson, Kizzie Ann	145
Johnson, Ella	229
Johnson, Calvin	252
Johnson, Charles	253
Johnston, Clay Tyree	150
Jones, Wesley	190
Jones, Geneva Lorene	212
Kaney, Willie Pearl	180
Keel, Sadie	3
Keel, Ellis	291
Kingsberry, Willie May	106
Killcrease, Doler	163
Killcrease, Billie	269
Killcrease, Josie	312
Landers, Birie Nuton	58
Lasater, Carrol	271
Lawrence, Annie	277
Lowrance, Kenneth	202
Love, Lindsey Spencer	204
Lucus, Holmes Ruthwin	146
Lynch, Raymond	289
Massey, Gladys Eulah	69
Mays, Clarence Elmo	86
Maytubby, Alice India	203
Melville, Codelia D.	162
Mead, William Minor	213
Miller, Mary	276
Milligan, Lida Lois	301
Mobley, Aurelia Guy	44
Morrison, Eugene Ward	93
Morris, Pike	214
Moore, Charles M.	259
Mulkey, Jerome C.	35
Mutz, Lela	71
Mutz, Lem	107
Murray, William Henry	231
Myers, Tommie Ima	87
Myers, Joseph L.	113
McCoy, Charley	165
McCoy, Mary	166
McCauley, James Thomas	182
McDonald, Myrtle Pink	66
McGee, Ernsby	215
McGee, Joseph	216
McGill, Douglas	241
McKinney, Lafayette King	61
McKinney, Williams	299
McLish, Sherman	247
McMorries, Ina	2
McSwain, Clarence Thomas	302
Nesbit, George Rennie	32

Name.	Roll No.
Nelson, Swill	95
Ned, Nora	226
Nichols, Charley Daniel	169
Nolatubbee, J. Z.	141
Nolen, Floyd	297
Oliver, Bessie Wade	294
Osborn, Alma Bertha	217
Ott, McKinley	307
Owens, Ola	14
Owens, Virgil	290
Paul, Opael Beatrice	88
Parnacher, Fannie	132
Parker, Tena Nell	77
Perry, Waunona Laurice	10
Perry, Rula Elen	16
Perry, Frances	131
Perry, Bygimie	133
Perry, Lelia Sarah	284
Perry, Jefferson Dale	68
Perkins, George Wesley	218
Pettigrew, Foster	315
Pettigrew, Hinabe	316
Pitchlynn, Everett Lee	34
Pickens, Nicholus	200
Pickens, Lewis	296
Pitts, Maggie May	288
Porter, May Belle	8
Porter, Nellie Lula	161
Potts, Clarence James	13
Potts, Ovis	85
Pound, Willie V.	49
Polk, Lucile	193
Polk, Velma	242
Price, Leo Quitman	12
Presley, Waneta	149
Pratt, Henry	196
Pusley, Myrtle May	155
Pybas, Lula Agnes	99
Pytchlyn, William	114
Ray, Howard Burney	27
Ray, Thomas C.	104
Ray, Louise Tyler	305
Reirdon, Ethel Lorine	11
Reagan, Wauneta	55
Reagan, Wenona	56
Ream, Boudinot	98
Ream, Annie Louise	51
Reed, Wilkinson	219
Reed, Julia	327
Reynolds, Ruby	293
Rice, Marshall Elmer	21
Ross, James Lee	41
Rowe, Lero	65
Rotenberry, Mattie Marie	83
Roark, Ruby Lourinda	89
Russell, Henry	160
Ruddell, Joseph Linn	197
Scarlett, John Slain	70
Sealy, William Hearst	121
Sealy, Simon	134
Sealy, Richmond	135
Sealy, Clarie	175
Sealy, Lillie Myrtle	243
Sealy, Simon	272
Sealy, Rosa	275
Self, Cecil Newton	183
Short, Jesse Factor	73
Sittel, Earstine Virginia	101
Skinner, William L.	220
Smith, Helen Scales	9
Smith, Johnnie	225
Smith, Luther Bell Jr.	254
Strickland, Augustus	42
Strickland, Paul Jones	249
Staton, Ruble S.	48
Stanfield, Jewell	84
Stewart, Wiley Scott	90
Stewart, Earl Clifton	198
Story, Burl	94
Stanton, Sarah Hall	137
Straughn, Lyndel Ella May	191
Sumpter, Lillie	139

Name.	Roll No.
Thaxton, Tullas Ottis	25
Thomas, Felcie Marie	40
Tinsley, Ruby	125
Tindall, Howard Amon	164
Townsend, Willie May	181
Townsley, William	222
Tracy, Calvin Bradley	173
Tuttle, Holmes Paul	81
Tucker, Cassie Ellen	122
Turner, Grace	186
Tyubby, Sofa	230
Underwood, Lara	306
Underwood, Viola	311
Vann, Juanita	227
Walner, William Robert	36
Walker, George H.	47
Walker, Emmer	109
Ward, Ellen	74
Ward, Julia McLish	221
Wasson, Don Raphael	112
Watkins, Overton Love	194
Weightman, Bouden	167
Welch, Daniel M.	281

Name.	Roll No.
Wells, Bert M.	331
White, Cyrus D.	26
White, Marvin	364
Wheatley, Albert	118
Wilson, Mary Opal	1
Wilson, Gladys	159
Wilson, Cyrus Mose	199
Willis, Hazel	29
Willis, Ozro	142
Willis, Aubrey	235
Williams, George Kelton	46
Williams, Earnest Howard	172
Williams, Charlie	261
Williams, Martha	279
Worley, McMay	110
Worcester, Mamie	303
Wolfe, John Irvin	308
Wray, Samuel Noble	119
Wynn, Daisy Bell	67
Youngblood, Johnson Colbert	187
Yokum, Rebecca	267

INDEX TO
CHICKASAWS BY MARRIAGE

Name.	Roll No.	Name.	Roll No.
Colbert, Ida	518	Gardner, Edna O.	461
Colbert, Abbie	533	Gaddis, Georgia	468
Colbert, Nancy	551	Garsides, Joseph	535
Colbert, Rebecca	578	Gibbons, James E.	279
Cooper, William W.	63	Gilliam, John O.	430
Conrady, Henry	100	Godfrey, Joseph H.	56
Cook, William V.	106	Godfrey, Peter	439
Collins, Dan	152	Gooding, Sarah W.	150
Collins, Ed	324	Goode, C. A.	257
Collins, James P.	313	Good, Albert	157
Collins, George R.	245	Goodall, Mary	571
Collins, Charles	391	Goldsby, Minnie	231
Collins, Thomas W.	497	Goforth, Alba	530
Cooney, Frank	192	Gordon, Richard J. D.	600
Coffee, Thomas Jefferson	224	Graham, Edward	161
Colley, William E.	248	Graham, Thomas M.	580
Cornish, John H.	377	Grant, Carrie L.	205
Condon, Michael Charles	392	Grant, Thomas	256
Costella, Charles E.	442	Grinslade, Henry	340
Conway, Elizabeth J.	470	Green, Etta	345
Connaway, Philip K.	483	Green, Fred C.	486
Coleman, Maggie A.	503	Greenwood, Samuel A.	625
Cox, William R.	511	Grunden, Martha A.	449
Conner, James O.	525	Gray, Amanda	520
Cochran, Carrie	529	Guy, Maggie J.	186
Cochran, Lynch Bailey	552	Hatcher, Andrew J.	3
Cole, John	601	Hardy, Walter	15
Criner, Lizzie	11	Hawkins, Lucy Belle	40
Criner, Minnie	24	Hawkins, Joseph Walter	211
Criner, Etta	185	Hawkins, Wyatt S.	241
Cruce, Lee	238	Hawkins, Eliza Jane	639
Creecy, Frank	325	Hare, Minnie F.	43
Cravens, John James	338	Hare, Laura J.	123
Craig, Amanda J.	369	Hare, Francis M.	298
Crow, P. C.	424	Hancock, Katie	50
Crummey, George	616	Harrell, Sudie	126
Davis, John	26	Hawley, Arthur E.	178
Davis, Linnie K.	84	Harrison, George William	194
Davis, Gabrel Marion	453	Harrison, Mary	301
Davenport, Albert E.	41	Hays, Jesse S.	333
Daniel, James	613	Hays, John S.	464
Deshan, Iva A.	65	Hayes, Charley	619
Deckerd, N. G.	273	Harris, Irene	282
Deel, Bennett B.	293	Harper, Viola	406
Dennis, A. B.	527	Harden, Andrew J.	419
Dickerson, L. D.	249	Hamblin, Henry C.	437
Dillingham, Nathan Thomas	476	Hamblin, Jessie I.	438
Doak, James	358	Hall, John W.	467
Doak, Dudley Nail	573	Halsell, Samuel D.	473
Dorchester, John M.	371	Herndon, Ellwood	216
Downing, Mattie	418	Henderson, C. W.	212
Drew, Byron	603	Heald, Charles Hobart	496
Durant, Mary	70	Higgins, Thos. H.	95
Duffy, Patrick	90	Hill, John T.	109
Duncum, Ella	189	Hilton, Charles N.	443
Duncum, Lottie M.	615	Hiser, Mincy	448
Duncan, Sallie	374	Howard, William B.	8
Duncan, Martha E.	399	Howard, Ella	433
Eastwood, Lewis James	512	Howard, Frank	589
East, Theophilus H.	648	Hopping, Augustus	82
Ebisch, Christian Frederick	118	Hoffman, Jesse	174
Elliott, John Cyrus	107	Hogue, Beulah	182
Evans, Elizabeth Ann	566	Holcomb, Sparrell Harvey	187
Filmore, Linna	1	Holford, George M. D.	375
Fillmore, Sallie	61	Holford, Boon	586
Fitzhugh, John M.	349	Hogard, Minnie	495
Fitch, D. H.	502	Holder, George Washington	608
Fletcher, Sally V.	138	Hutchins, John	39
Ford, Robert P.	81	Hutchins, William Andrew	188
Fox, Franklin Marion	487	Hughes, A. B.	200
Folsom, Rosa	519	Hull, Belle Langdon	206
Froman, Perry	127	Hull, William	264
Friend, Thomas L.	181	Hunnicutt, Thomas M.	232
Fryrear, S. Burl	208	Hume, William Robert	432
Franklin, Edward Q.	403	Hybarger, David C.	176
Franklin, Joseph M.	454	Ingram, W. R.	20
Francis, B. L.	491	Irvin, Walter	288
Fussell, James E.	76	Irwin, Jennie	569
Gardner, Benjamin Shannon	147	Jackson, William H.	199
Gardner, Janie May	445	James, Mary J.	351
		James, Liddy Ann	417

Name.	Roll No.	Name.	Roll No.
Jennings, R.W.	236	Mashburn, John Horton	404
Jennings, Mary E.	540	Marshall, J. Horace	532
Jenkins, Peter	215	Melton, George Arnold	36
Jemison, William P.	508	Merchant, E. E.	214
Johnson, John	19	Merriman, Tate	239
Johnson, Drucilla	74	Melville, Martin C.	300
Johnson, Effie M.	169	Mead, Santford Minor	402
Johnson, Minnie	198	Mitchell, Gaines A.	7
Johnson, Mollie E.	203	Miller, Norman	235
Johnston, Georgianna	32	Minter, Willis H.	485
Johnston, Mary Catherine	303	Minter, William H.	553
Jones, Osceola	33	Morris, William Franklin	9
Jones, Winfield Scott	102	Morris, Joseph E.	304
Jones, James Milton	233	Morris, Wharton H.	556
Jones, Charles L.	368	Morris, John W.	558
Jones, Frank W.	411	Morris, Olive J.	587
Jones, James Pate	440	Monday, Alexander Elson	145
Jordan, Jesse L.	121	Moore, E. M.	262
Jordan, William Gaston	344	Moutray, Mathew G.	636
Joins, U. S.	635	Mutz, George	49
Juzan, Eliza	330	Mutz, Jake	146
Kemp, Mary	51	Mulkey, John C.	117
Kemp, Marilous E.	54	Murray, Henry F.	153
Kemp, Susan A.	151	Murray, Laura	156
Kemp, Penelope Catherine	328	Murray, William H.	177
Kennedy, John W.	77	Murray, Cora	254
Keel, Pearl	110	Murray, Annie	364
Keirsey, William D.	154	Murray, Maye	617
Kerr, Perry N.	309	Myers, Winfield Scott	173
Keffer, Nick	400	Myers, Joseph F.	258
Kingsbery, Sallie	132	McAlester, Asa	53
King, Felix J.	210	McAlester, James Jackson	401
Kinney, John H.	318	McBride, Hiram Young	243
Kimberlin, William G.	463	McCrummen, E. L.	101
Krouse, Christian	337	McCarty, Sampie	218
LaConte, Benjamin C.	38	McClure, Jennie	459
Lanham, Perry G.	91	McDuffee, Edward Harvey	331
Lanham, Scott W.	286	McDonald, William	585
Land, C. M. C.	94	McGee, Maggie	335
Lael, Noah	96	McKeel, John Francis	522
Latta, Rebecca	130	McLish, Rosa	113
Latta, Allen	471	McLish, Cora	484
Lasater, Milas	265	McLish, Esther	501
Law, A. H.	356	McLaughlin, Corrilla	226
Lannom, William R.	509	McMorries, Lee W.	55
Lane, Joseph C.	524	McMillan, George W.	277
Lee, Fred O.	80	McNally, Lula	488
Lee, Samuel S.	446	McSwain, Charles	565
Lemon, Robert Breckenridge	159	Nash, Henry C.	294
Lewis, Mary L.	297	Newton, William Calvin	22
Leedy, James T., Sr.	380	Neighbors, Lillian Ethel	68
Leecraft, Arthur N.	405	Neighbors, Conrad	640
Leftwich, James	410	Newberry, Mattie	397
Lester, E. W.	428	Neal, W. R.	582
Leming, Tom	595	Nichols, R. L.	14
Lillard, Benjamin F.	247	Nichols, Alexander	112
Lishtubby, Lizzie	633	Nichols, Louis	175
Love, Nellie	44	Norman, Sallie	242
Love, Mary M.	116	Norman, Daniel S.	574
Love, Minnie	160	Norman, Nelson H.	579
Love, Melvina	269	Norris, Tom	388
Love, Mary Caroline	407	Noletubby, Land	398
Love, Phoebe H.	489	Norton, Yancey W.	534
Love, Hattie Simpson	638	Nolatubbee, Bessie	591
Loving, Wesley D.	72	Nutt, William E.	523
Long, Samuel D.	144	Oliphant, Sam R.	207
Lowrance, Sophia Elizabeth	172	Owens, Neely A.	347
Lowrance, Willis B.	429	Owens, Samuel	543
Lucas, Edward B.	223	Owens, Alfred	560
Lynn, George Riley	583	Orr, James A.	414
Martin, Tom H.	13	Osacior, Dollie	469
Martin, Charles Benjamin	143	O'Donnell, John	610
Maytubby, Tobitha	58	O'Brien, Joe Frank	515
Maytubby, Lulu A.	295	Palmer, Thomas L.	29
Massey, John W.	135	Parker, Laura	46
Mays, David	260	Parker, Alice I.	48
Mays, George W.	493	Patterson, Mollie J.	343
Maupin, Charles Stuart	280	Paul, Sarah J.	460
Mayer, Bruno	381	Paul, Jennie	462
Mayer, George	572	Paul, Victoria May	554
		Paul, John	568
		Payne, Thomas B.	478

Name.	Roll No.	Name.	Roll No.
Passmore, C. C.	507	Sparks, J. B.	352
Penner, Felix	28	Spivey, Cora M.	563
Perry, Kittie Peddycoart	88	Statler, Gale	4
Perry, Annie M.	252	Stevenson, John H.	71
Perry, Emma Frank	531	Story, Eliza	82
Perkins, Walter William	162	Story, Zula J.	362
Percival, Taylor	517	Strickland, Jettie	98
Phillips, Hill	73	Strickland, Carrie	190
Phillips, Mary M.	149	Staton, Elijah	108
Phillips, Nettie A.	220	Stewart, Ben M.	312
Phillips, Thomas Jefferson	322	Standifer, Frank	365
Phillips, Dora	372	Sturdivant, Minnie	441
Pierce, George	222	Strite, Arminta	474
Pitman, N. R.	354	Sullivan, Daniel	458
Pound, William T.	6	Summers, Bettie	559
Pound, Mattie	237	Taylor, Daniel	129
Pound, George W.	341	Taylor, Lena	427
Polk, Lon	34	Taylor, Stephen Lee	492
Powell, Thomas Porter	179	Taylor, Lillie M.	584
Powell, J. H.	607	Taylor, William V.	588
Potts, Nannie V.	225	Talley, William	420
Potts, Edward Forest	618	Thomas, Mattie	85
Pollock, Lee	227	Thomas, Charles W.	122
Poe, George M.	373	Thomas, Jane	321
Poyner, Louisa J.	451	Thomas, Laura	284
Priddy, Siddie	64	Thompson, Bertie	139
Pratt, Alice	141	Thompson, James P.	339
Price, C. C.	387	Thompson, J. W.	655
Pruitt, Willis	577	Thompson, William Ashley	513
Pusley, Mary J.	165	Thaxton, Tullas	197
Pybas, Boy	261	Thornton, William D.	213
Randolph, James	180	Thomson, William H.	229
Randolph, Thomas H.	234	Thacker, Zachary T.	541
Randolph, W. C.	308	Thurston, D. J.	524
Ravia, Joseph	548	Tomlinson, Mary Y.	498
Raines, Stephen M.	550	Truax, Geo. Henry	75
Ray, Henry Lorin	602	Trentham, Belle Smith	299
Reidon, Joseph P.	35	Trentham, Joseph	581
Ream, Mattie	327	Troop, Jesse L.	634
Ream, Ona O'Neal	285	Turnbull, Ida May	57
Reynolds, Sarah Jane	359	Turnbull, Lottie	114
Reynolds, Charles A.	526	Turnbull, Maude	275
Rennie, Minnie A.	490	Turnbull, Jettie Lemons	599
Rice, O. E.	86	Turman, Louis N.	420
Rodke, Lawrence	2	Tuttle, James H.	168
Ross, James F.	435	Tussy, Henry B.	481
Ross, Martha A.	597	Turner, Hiram G.	536
Roark, Dora	549	Turner, Mazeppa T.	609
Robinson, O. P.	632	Tucker, George R.	562
Ralston, Sarah E.	646	Tuskatomby, Orlena	593
Russell, Clesteen	45	Underwood, Mary	355
Ryle, Whitmill A.	16	Vanderslice, Robert J.	383
Ryan, Stephen Walker	637	Van Zandt, Isaac N.	434
Sadler, Joseph	12	Venable, Robert L.	196
Sadler, Jane	477	Victor, Lee	393
Sacra, Ed	287	Washington, William Edward	18
Scales, George W.	336	Washington, Kate	37
Scoby, Arthur E.	370	Washington, Mollie	133
Scott, John P.	382	Washington, Jeremiah C.	357
Scarlett, Richard James	396	Warren, William F.	21
Schoeppe, Fred L.	421	Waite, Mary E.	104
Sealy, Julie	30	Waldon, Tom	306
Sealy, Daily	271	Waldon, Eddie	624
Self, James	346	Walker, Thomas	311
Seay, O. W.	367	Walker, Mary I.	570
Shannon, Jesse R.	204	Wallace, William G.	319
Shannon, William T.	263	Watkins, George W.	323
Shannon, J. R.	268	Watkins, Nora	274
Short, John C.	228	Wasson, Clark B.	465
Short, Robert P.	500	Walthall, George O.	482
Shelton, William J.	348	Waitman, General J.	645
Skeen, Cicero A.	89	Webb, George H.	23
Smith, Tom	47	Webb, John M.	152
Smith, Charles S.	79	Welch, William A.	240
Smith, Robert E.	134	Welch, Adelia	296
Smith, Alfred M.	423	Welch, Nellie A.	623
Smith, Jourdan Anderson	472	Weaver, James Wilson	456
Smith, Wood	528	Whitesel, Jerome	148
Snowden, William H.	546	Whitthorne, Thomas K.	155
Souse, John	466	White, Annie	389
Speed, James L.	10	White, Samuel McKinley	390
Sparks, George W.	255		

Name.	Roll No.	Name.	Roll No.
Williams, Nelson C.	59	Woody, Charles H.	69
Williams, Charles L.	171	Woody, John L.	366
Williams, Samuel L.	270	Wooten, James Henry	326
Williams, Clara J.	422	Woolsey, N. B.	376
Williams, John F.	450	Worsham, John Farley	317
Willis, Viola	142	Wolfe, Iva P.	627
Willis, Anna	164	Wright, Isaac S.	62
Willis, Margaret	332	Wright, Nettie	475
Wilson, Emma B.	266	Wray, Samuel L.	167
Wilson, Lillie Luella	479	Wray, William B.	276
Wiggs, Richard C.	360	Young, Granville W.	17
Williford, Joe	504	Yoakum, Minnie A.	93
Williford, Nannie	505	Yancey, James I.	244
Winter, George Alexander	557	Yarborough, George	620
		Yates, Alonzo Pleasant	628

INDEX TO
CHICKASAW FREEDMEN

Name.	Roll No.	Name.	Roll No.
Allen, Minnie	319	Anderson, Buck	2533
Allen, Ollie	320	Anderson, Margaret	2534
Allen, Mary	321	Anderson, Lidy	2535
Allen, Calvin	502	Anderson, Donie	2536
Allen, Martha	844	Anderson, Silvia	2537
Allen, Gloster	847	Anderson, George	3028
Allen, Rhoda	848	Anderson, Minerva	4048
Allen, Zach	849	Anderson, Arbella	4075
Allen, Lena	850	Anderson, Katie	4109
Allen, Clarietta	851	Anderson, Elvira	4110
Allen, Martha	852	Anderson, Lee Etta	4235
Allen, Monie	853	Anderson, Creasy	4521
Allen, Dona McKinley		Anthony, Odele	3434
Hubbard M.	854	Andrews, Kissiah	3779
Allen, Lillie E.	855	Armstrong, Lucy	611
Allen, Stephen	856	Armstrong, Tom	3969
Allen, Albert	866	Augustus, Bettie	299
Allen, Manuel	867	Austin, Henrietta	3315
Allen, John	868	Austin, Charley	3316
Allen, Pleasant	1061	Austin, Lula	3822
Allen, Alter	1063	Austin, Ethel	3823
Allen, Arden	1064	Bachelor, Maria	2257
Allen, Ella Wilmer	4817	Bachelor, Comadore	
Allen, Ina	1065	Dewey	2258
Allen, Aramenta	1066	Barr, Ellen	3232
Allen, Verna M.	1067	Barr, Anderson	3238
Allen, Secil M.	1069	Barlow, Fannie	3273
Allen, Ona	1071	Barlow, Clifford	3278
Allen, Nellie	1072	Bailey, Jackson	3733
Allen, Lena	1073	Baily, Martha	4017
Allen, Winnie	1074	Baily, Marilda	4018
Allen, Ellen	1075	Baily, Alonzo	4019
Allen, General	1076	Baily, Elzira	4021
Allen, Maud	1077	Bayles, Mary	3841
Allen, Adel	1078	Barber, Eugene J.	4276
Allen, Beulah	1079	Barker, Bennie	4386
Allen, George	1080	Barker, Johnnie	4387
Allen, Sam	1546	Bacon, Cornelius	4571
Allen, Mary	1547	Bennett, Bud	290
Allen, Allie	1549	Bennett, Roberta	2167
Allen, Lula	1550	Bennett, Alberta	2168
Allen, Zuruleka	1551	Bennett, Isadora	2420
Allen, Prince	1552	Bennett, Rosevelt	2423
Allen, Adel	1553	Bennett, William	2460
Allen, Ella	1554	Bennett, Ella	2461
Allen, Martha	1555	Bennett, Nora	2462
Allen, Lovey Anna	1556	Bennett, Gilbert	2463
Allen, Rosa	2754	Bennett, James	2464
Allen, Squire	3395	Bennett, Louis	2827
Allen, Columbus	3397	Bennett, Gertrude	2828
Allen, Charley	3989	Bennett, Louis, Jr.	2829
Allen, Victoria	4196	Bennett, Hazel	2830
Allen, Edna E.	4197	Bennett, Sydney	2831
Allen, Thomas Clarance	4198	Bennett, Lena	2832
Allen, Glenn	4266	Bennett, Edward P.	2833
Allen, Jemima	4267	Bennett, Adolphus	4616
Albert, Ella	1458	Bend, Minerva	1336
Albert, David	1462	Bend, Leander	1338
Albert, Bertha	1463	Bend, Lucinda	1339
Albert, Helen	1464	Bend, Cleveland	1340
Albert, John	1465	Bend, Henry E.	1342
Albert, Susan	1466	Bend, Orilla	1344
Albert, Letha	1467	Beasley, Nellie	3260
Albert, Rafard	4309	Beasley, T. Rosenfelt	3268
Alberson, Viola	2518	Belford, Jeff	3851
Alberson, Tom	4568	Beatty, Mary Jane	4117
Alop, Martha	3131	Beatty, Lila Ann	4118
Alop, George	3132	Beatty, Ida May	4119
Alop, Ora	3133	Bishop, Sallie	272
Anderson, Caldonia	1188	Bice, Lee	2185
Anderson, Wister	1189	Bice, Becky	2186
Anderson, Roxanna	1211	Bice, William	2187
Anderson, Bob	2104	Bice, Aleck	2189
Anderson, Sallie	2105	Bice, Venia	2190
Anderson, Paris	2106	Bice, Raford	2191
Anderson, Alva	2107	Bice, Jim	2192
Anderson, George	2108	Bice, Eliza	2193
Anderson, Simon	2109	Bice, Rosa	2194
Anderson, Loratia	2110	Birt, Sallie	2564
Anderson, Betsy	2236	Birt, Levy	2574
Anderson, Kittie	2359	Birdsong, Caroline	4113
Anderson, Loss	2362	Birdsong, Melvina	4114
Anderson, Floyd	2363	Blue, Margaret	60

Name.	Roll No.	Name.	Roll No.
Blue, Isaiah	65	Boyd, Aleck	3255
Blue, Daniel	92	Boyd, Isom	3866
Blue, Kisse	93	Boyd, Claude F.	4261
Blue, Rhoda	94	Bowen, Rosa	2893
Blue, Dilsie	98	Bruner, Leo	5
Blue, Sam	108	Bruner, Mary	61
Blue, Carolina	225	Bruner, Isabella	62
Blue, Carrie Bell	241	Bruner, Amelia	63
Blue, Israel	301	Bruner, Willie	64
Blue, Mary	325	Bruner, Annie	160
Blue, Joe	341	Bruner, Charley	161
Blue, Amy	342	Bruner, Alfred	162
Blue, Jencie	344	Bruner, Gertrude	269
Blue, Willie	345	Bruner, Susan	513
Blue, Alice	346	Bruner, Jesse James	515
Blue, Laura	347	Bruner, Angie	556
Blue, Adeline	348	Bruner, Ellen	557
Blue, Henry	349	Bruner, Manuel	558
Blue, Albert	350	Bruner, Davis	559
Blue, Sallie	351	Bruner, Sarah	1212
Blue, Agnes	352	Bruner, Bud	1213
Blue, Peter	372	Bruner, August	1214
Blue, Aaron	396	Bruner, Soloman	1215
Blue, Bessie	397	Bruner, Charley	1216
Blue, Jessie	398	Bruner, Palesa	1217
Blue, Ellen	403	Bruner, James	1218
Blue, Pompey	463	Bruner, Lulu	1219
Blue, Mimey	464	Bruner, Caroline	1277
Blue, Tom	465	Bruner, Angeline	1406
Blue, Isabella	466	Bruner, Rubessa	1407
Blue, Willie	468	Bruner, Harvey	1408
Blue, Charley	469	Bruner, Ernest	1409
Blue, Claraisse	470	Bruner, Olive	1410
Blue, Israel	472	Bruner, Edward	1411
Blue, King	494	Bruner, Eliza	1683
Blue, Ellen	1577	Bruner, Reuben	1690
Blue, Ida E.	1579	Bruner, Yucum	1691
Blue, Joe	1580	Bruner, Sena	1692
Blue, Gertie	1581	Bruner, Elmira	1755
Blue, Craven	1584	Bruner, Rose	1757
Blue, John	1585	Bruner, Legus	1758
Blue, Napoleon B.	1586	Bruner, Rachel	1759
Blue, Noah	1587	Bruner, Columbus	1760
Blue, Smith	1590	Bruner, Cephus	1761
Blue, Virginia	1591	Bruner, Joe	1762
Blue, Torrence	1592	Bruner, Maria	2818
Blue, Letha	1593	Bruner, Samantha	2821
Blue, James	1594	Bruner, Bettie	2822
Blue, Princella	1595	Bruner, Arthur	2823
Blue, Hattie	1596	Bruner, Izora	2824
Blue, Nero	1880	Bruner, Marcena	2825
Blue, Wesley	1899	Bruner, Samuel	2826
Blue, Andrew	4220	Bruner, Dollie	4217
Blue, Alfred	4226	Bruner, Jeanette	4221
Blue, Mattie	4230	Bruner, Lulu	4222
Blue, Cornelius	4238	Bruner, Grant	4223
Blue, Sam	4623	Bruner, Ethel	4304
Blue, William	4680	Bruner, Joanna	4346
Black, Nephi	415	Bruner, Polly	4347
Black, Josie	416	Bruner, Edgar	4348
Black, Jackson	513	Bruner, Lizzie	4349
Black, Harriett	514	Bruner, Richard	4350
Black, Alice	515	Bruner, Victoria	4351
Black, Andy	521	Bruner, Joseph	4398
Black, Lifley	523	Brown, Almos	55
Black, Willie	524	Brown, Tom	56
Black, Cleveland	525	Brown, Silvia	57
Black, Prince	526	Brown, Ben	87
Black, Mary	527	Brown, Alberta	99
Black, Calvin	528	Brown, Albert	101
Black, Andy	529	Brown, Annie	102
Bly, Mary	883	Brown, Mamie	105
Bly, Elliott	884	Brown, Craven	123
Bly, Ethel	885	Brown, George	124
Block, Blanch	1170	Brown, Julia	173
Block, Ahart	1171	Brown, Lou	310
Block, Rachel	1172	Brown, Jonas	362
Block, Genevie	1173	Brown, Mitchell	379
Block, Viola Jane	1174	Brown, Betsie	388
Blackwater, Celia	3669	Brown, Lemuel	395
Boyd, Mary	828	Brown, Agnes	417
Boyd, Eli	1736	Brown, Tony	429
Boyd, Emma	3026	Brown, Belzora	504

Name.	Roll No.	Name.	Roll No.
Brown, Watt	530	Brown, Johnson	4008
Brown, Melvina	531	Brown, Winnie	4027
Brown, Bertha	532	Brown, Thomas	4104
Brown, John	578	Brown, Harry	4105
Brown, Liza	579	Brown, Reenie	4180
Brown, Pink	580	Brown, Ogous	4213
Brown, Douglass	581	Brown, Viola	4219
Brown, Cephas	582	Brown, Julius	4224
Brown, Jimmie	583	Brown, Lizzie	4239
Brown, Wesley	584	Brown, Susie	4244
Brown, Harrison	586	Brown, Benjamin	4245
Brown, Margaret	587	Brown, Myrtle Lee	4305
Brown, Tom	4790	Brown, Cleveland H.	4340
Brown, Janey	588	Brown, Hannah	4354
Brown, Walter	589	Brown, Eugene	4392
Brown, Sallie	590	Brown, Geneva	4393
Brown, Vinnie	591	Brown, Arthur	4474
Brown, Peter	616	Brown, Mary	4522
Brown, Bennie	617	Brown, Silas	4523
Brown, Delia	941	Brown, Alice	4524
Brown, Catherine	942	Brown, Otis	4525
Brown, Walter	943	Brown, Eliza	4712
Brown, Foster	944	Brooks, Betsy	649
Brown, Lydia	1264	Brooks, Mary	4740
Brown, George	1265	Brewer, Emily	1657
Brown, Jacob	1266	Bright, Charley	1703
Brown, Hardy	1393	Bright, Margaret A.	3179
Brown, Susan	1400	Bright, Daisy	3180
Brown, Eddie	1658	Bright, William	3181
Brown, Charley	1733	Bright, Redella	3182
Brown, George	1734	Bright, Bennie	3183
Brown, Fannie Mary	1735	Bright, Alonzo	3184
Brown, Charles	1891	Bright, Eveline	3185
Brown, Robert	1894	Bradley, Sallie	4829
Brown, Alonzo	1961	Brashears, Mary W.	2183
Brown, Emma	1962	Brashears, Bessie	2184
Brown, McKinley	1966	Bryant, Melvina	4006
Brown, Samantha	1967	Brock, Joe	4771
Brown, Delia	1005	Burk, Lizzie	1192
Brown, Margaret	1012	Butler, Carrie	1716
Brown, Lillie	2171	Butler, Maulsy	1719
Brown, Tilford	2172	Butler, Edmund	2019
Brown, Ollie	2200	Butler, Minnie O.	2020
Brown, James	2201	Butler, Andrew	2021
Brown, Ozie	2202	Butler, Celia	3595
Brown, Verda	2203	Butler, Jimmie Gooden	4072
Brown, Thomas	2716	Butler, Daniel	4143
Brown, Mary	2717	Butler, Davodie	4144
Brown, Jennie	2718	Butler, Andrew	4145
Brown, Willie	2914	Butler, Emma	4190
Brown, Charley	2953	Butler, Andrew	2131
Brown, Lizzie	3154	Butler, Maryland	4343
Brown, May	3157	Burney, Newton	1886
Brown, Ozie	3158	Burney, Chris	1887
Brown, Frances	3229	Burney, Narcissa	3304
Brown, Jackson	3230	Burney, Ida	3305
Brown, Alfred	3231	Burney, Rector	3306
Brown, Lucinda	3245	Burney, Nola	3307
Brown, Simon	3246	Burney, Becky	3308
Brown, Willie	3247	Burney, Leonard	3309
Brown, Edmond	3248	Burney, Eddie B.	3310
Brown, Henderson	3249	Burney, William M.	3311
Brown, Alice	3250	Burney, Ben	3312
Brown, Angie	3251	Burney, Rachel	3313
Brown, Mat	3385	Burden, Minervia	3524
Brown, Ben	3386	Burden, Daisy	3915
Brown, Mary	3558	Burden, George	3916
Brown, Aran	3559	Burden, Viola	3917
Brown, Jennie	3560	Burden, Warnie	3918
Brown, Victoria	3561	Burden, Minnie	3921
Brown, Lizzie	3562	Buckler, Ed	3751
Brown, Susan	3563	Buckler, Mary	3752
Brown, Henry	3564	Burton, Arthur	4010
Brown, Primus	3665	Burton, Webster	4427
Brown, William	3666	Burton, Sallie	4428
Brown, Tinny	3668	Burton, Green	4429
Brown, Wash	3741	Burton, George	4430
Brown, Caroline	3789	Bullocks, Robert	4318
Brown, Mary	3790	Burns, Robert	4791
Brown, Lula	3791	Burns, Ben	4792
Brown, McClellan	3855	Burns, Martha	4793
Brown, Amelia	3870	Burns, Jim	4794
Brown, Nancy	3996	Burns, John	4795

Name.	Roll No.	Name.	Roll No.
Burns, Laura	4796	Cheadle, Daisy	3058
Burns, Isaiah	4797	Cheadle, Bill	8059
Burns, Viola	4798	Cheadle, Lurinda	3060
Burns, Edna	4799	Cheadle, Wesley	3061
Byas, Ella	4046	Cheadle, Mary	3062
Cass, William	324	Cheadle, Estella	3063
Cass, Fannie Jane	537	Cheadle, Garfield	3064
Carolina, Maggie	1453	Cheadle, Albert	3068
Carolina, Luvinia	1651	Cheadle, Henderson	3367
Caldwell, Lucy	1532	Cheadle, Amos	3368
Caldwell, Macy	1533	Cheadle, Clarence	3405
Caldwell, Blanche	1534	Cheadle, Addie	3406
Caldwell, George	1535	Cheadle, Ella	3407
Caldwell, Effie	1536	Cheadle, Thomas	3408
Caldwell, Matilda	2874	Cheadle, Elsie	3409
Caldwell, Thomas	2875	Cheadle, Cleveland	3410
Caldwell, Richard	2876	Cheadle, Benjamin	3411
Caldwell, Houston	2877	Cheadle, Jack	3414
Caldwell, Eliza	2878	Cheadle, Angie	3415
Caldwell, Gattie	2879	Cheadle, George	3416
Carson, Sarah	1566	Cheadle, Grant	3417
Carson, Henry	1567	Cheadle, Martin	3418
Carson, Cap	1568	Cheadle, Maud	3419
Carson, Pearl	1569	Cheadle, Rena	3420
Carson, Frances	1570	Cheadle, Rector	3421
Carson, Gertha	1571	Cheadle, Carrie	3577
Carson, Ermer	1572	Cheadle, Turner	3593
Carson, Georgia	1573	Choate, Walter	302
Carson, Richmond	1574	Choate, Emma	303
Carson, Calvin	1575	Choate, Henry	331
Carson, Doc	3290	Choate, George	3375
Campbell, Agnes	2794	Choate, Birdie	3379
Campbell, Charles	2798	Chawanochubby, Samuel	374
Campbell, Frances	2799	Chief, James	451
Campbell, Fred	2800	Childs, Violet	972
Campbell, Etta	2801	Childs, Helen	975
Campbell, Johnson	2802	Childs, Emma	976
Campbell, Patsy	3871	Christian, Wm.	2040
Carroll, Parthena	3210	Christian, Margaret	2041
Carter, Marshall	3372	Christian, Thos.	2309
Carter, Lucy	3373	Christian, Caro	2312
Carter, Harrison	3374	Christian, Sallie	2923
Carter, Lee	3375	Christian, Fleet	2927
Carter, Beulah	3376	Christian, Effie	2928
Carter, Lula	3377	Christian, Floy	2931
Carter, Ludy	3378	Christian, Cliff	2925
Carter, Summer	3379	Cherry, Annie	3164
Carter, Felix	3380	Cherry, Clifton	3165
Carter, Irene	3381	Cherry, Cleveland	3166
Carter, Arthur	3382	Cherry, Myrtle	3167
Carter, Mary J.	3383	Cherry, Bynton	3170
Carter, Tena	4536	Cherry, Louisa	4596
Carter, Maggie Hellenia	4537	Cherry, Jennie	4597
Carney, Joanna	3695	Cherry, Pearlie	4598
Carney, Simpson	3696	Cherry, James	4599
Carney, Aaron	3997	Cherry, Doctor	4600
Calhoun, Isabella	4099	Cherry, Olcie	4601
Carlina, Bertha	4286	Cherry, Melvina	4602
Charles, Nellie	48	Cherry, David	4603
Charles, Nancy	50	Cherry, Jonas	4604
Charles, Manuel	54	Cherry, T. C.	4605
Charles, Amos	73	Chesnut, Ida	3556
Choice, Albert	136	Chesnut, Fannie	3557
Chico, Unity	163	Chapman, Hattie	4009
Chico, Mary	3227	Chandler, Sam	4167
Chico, Sarah	3228	Childers, John	4595
Chico, Wilson	3423	Childers, Arthur	4764
Chico, Betsy	3951	Childers, Dick	4765
Chico, Louisa	3952	Childers, Georgia	4766
Chico, Angie	3956	Childers, Robert	4767
Cheadle, Lugina	179	Childers, Leroy	4768
Cheadle, Patrick H.	180	Childers, Mary	4769
Cheadle, Ida May	181	Childers, Henry	4800
Cheadle, Johnica	182	Childers, Ora	4801
Cheadle, Annie B.	183	Childers, Henry, Jr.	4802
Cheadle, Winnie	184	Clark, Coleman	121
Cheadle, Thomas	185	Clark, Fannie	122
Cheadle, Moses	186	Clark, Silvia	132
Cheadle, Ida M.	196	Clark, Elzira	193
Cheadle, Oweneby	198	Clark, Abner	194
Cheadle, Eugene	200	Clark, Millie	221
Cheadle, Douglas	3051	Clark, Robert	222
Cheadle, Sam	3057	Clark, Nelson	223

Name.	Roll No.	Name.	Roll No.
Clark, Mason	231	Colbert, Mack	489
Clark, Monroe	232	Colbert, Sallie	490
Clark, Abel	233	Colbert, Silas	491
Clark, Aleck	234	Colbert, Nelson	538
Clark, Clifford	262	Colbert, Richard	637
Clark, Richmond	263	Colbert, Ella	638
Clark, Griffith	264	Colbert, Leonard	639
Clark, Carnelius	265	Colbert, Zeno	692
Clark, Joe	391	Colbert, Alva	693
Clark, Willie	392	Colbert, Mary	694
Clark, Cornelia	393	Colbert, Sam	695
Clark, Minnie	394	Colbert, Mary	801
Clark, Fleet	406	Colbert, Carrie	1026
Clark, Paralee	418	Colbert, Ora	1029
Clark, Jesse	419	Colbert, Patsy	1141
Clark, Albert	420	Colbert, Martha	1334
Clark, Lanie	421	Colbert, Miles	1480
Clark, Dallas	422	Colbert, Rose	1629
Clark, Liley	440	Colbert, Manuel	1652
Clark, Israel	441	Colbert, Lillie	1653
Clark, Houston	442	Colbert, Teddie	1654
Clark, Nathan	443	Colbert, Sylvester	1655
Clark, Harrison	444	Colbert, Rayford	1656
Clark, Sookey	503	Colbert, Tobias	1672
Clark, Patsy	1582	Colbert, Boston	1673
Clark, Dixie	1589	Colbert, Robert	1675
Clark, Amelia	3546	Colbert, Allen	1737
Clark, Nicey	3548	Colbert, Nettie	1738
Clark, Joseph	3549	Colbert, Peter	1739
Clark, Delia	3551	Colbert, Paul	1740
Clark, Earnest	3552	Colbert, McKinley	1741
Clark, Perry	4216	Colbert, Robert	2330
Clark, Gertie	4227	Colbert, Rena	2944
Clark, Ephraim	4233	Colbert, Estella	2945
Clark, Luella	4236	Colbert, Lillie Bell	2946
Clark, Victoria	4388	Colbert, Mimy	3015
Clark, Silla	4551	Colbert, Malsy	3017
Clark, Lewis	4552	Colbert, George	3018
Clark, James	4553	Colbert, Rachel	3019
Clark, Walsy	4554	Colbert, Elizabeth	3020
Clark, Minnie	4555	Colbert, Hattie	3021
Clark, Lena	4556	Colbert, Vinetta	3022
Clark, Ernest	4557	Colbert, Soloman	3217
Clark, Alice	4558	Colbert, Becky	3218
Clark, Frank	4689	Colbert, Sam	3219
Clay, Isabella	1975	Colbert, Nellie	3220
Clay, Zeno	1976	Colbert, John	3221
Clay, Samuel	1977	Colbert, Amos	3222
Clay, Hezekiah	1978	Colbert, Tobe	3223
Clay, Tannis	1979	Colbert, Ella	3224
Clay, Delora	1980	Colbert, Lila	3225
Clay, Bohanon	1981	Colbert, Calvin	3292
Clay, Lou Creasy	1982	Colbert, Tobe	3362
Clay, St. Paul	1983	Colbert, Charlotte	3363
Clay, Lovinia	1984	Colbert, Elijah	3526
Clay, Jennie	1985	Colbert, Thomas	3527
Clay, Sim	1991	Colbert, Jody	3528
Clay, Rhoda	1992	Colbert, Peggy	3544
Clay, Cornelius	1993	Colbert, Polly Ann	3597
Clay, Elgy	4342	Colbert, Richard	3599
Clemons, Maudie	2268	Colbert, Tandy	3600
Cochran, Agnes	72	Colbert, John	3601
Cochran, Agnes	322	Colbert, Clarence	3602
Cochran, Jesse James	327	Colbert, Lucy	3628
Cochran, Freeman	329	Colbert, Andrew	3639
Cochran, Lizzie	2665	Colbert, Gottie	3640
Cochran, Mary	4229	Colbert, Wesley	3649
Colbert, Georgia	128	Colbert, Nettie	3650
Colbert, Shadrack	145	Colbert, Lewis	3651
Colbert, Nelson	147	Colbert, Lindy	3652
Colbert, Liddy	148	Colbert, Orilla	3653
Colbert, Lem	150	Colbert, Henry	3743
Colbert, Agnes	326	Colbert, Jacob	3813
Colbert, Simon	332	Colbert, Ader	3814
Colbert, Rosa	333	Colbert, Febby	3842
Colbert, Margaret	334	Colbert, Robert	3844
Colbert, Buck	335	Colbert, Willie	3930
Colbert, Lillie	336	Colbert, Willie Gerta	3931
Colbert, John	337	Colbert, Jim	4000
Colbert, Jim	338	Colbert, Henry	4026
Colbert, George	339	Colbert, Alice	4165
Colbert, Riley	340	Colbert, Evie	4166
Colbert, Benjamine	473	Colbert, Lizzie	4231

Name.	Roll No.	Name.	Roll No.
Colbert, Agnes	4237	Cox, Leonard	3287
Colbert, Myrtle	4246	Cox, Jackson	3289
Colbert, Rex	4316	Cowan, Lizzie	3422
Colbert, Laura	4325	Cotton, Mollie	4061
Colbert, Leford	4328	Cotton, Robert	4065
Colbert, Claudie	4330	Cotton, Beulah	4066
Colbert, Thomas	4329	Cotton, Lee	4067
Colbert, Dave	4576	Cotton, Walter	4068
Colbert, Dave	4609	Cotton, Verdarepunga	4070
Colbert, Ellen	4626	Cobb, Amelia	4379
Colbert, John	4627	Colbut, Jerry	4410
Colbert, Sam	4629	Colbut, Martha	4433
Colbert, Si	4630	Colbut, Landon	4495
Colbert, William	4632	Cravatt, Robert	628
Colbert, Stewart	4633	Cravatt, Caroline	629
Colbert, Rachel	4634	Cravatt, Ben	630
Colbert, Mat	4637	Cravatt, Lelia	631
Colbert, Hulbart	4638	Cravens, George	1831
Colbeat, Mary	4639	Cravens, Georgia	1832
Cooper, Susan	191	Cravens, Jennie	1832
Cooper, Allie	192	Cravens, Ollie	1834
Cobrey, George	209	Crooms, Lula	2748
Covan, Charlotte	283	Crooms, Gavin	2752
Covan, Sam Jones	286	Crooms, Fleetwood	2753
Conley, Lonnie	447	Crathers, Joanna	3078
Conly, Lela	2338	Croomes, Harvey	3159
Conly, Clara	2360	Crockett, Maud	3174
Conly, Richard	2361	Crockett, Carrie	3177
Conly, Reta	3596	Crittenden, Mattie	3554
Cohee, Charles	620	Crittenden, Ada	3555
Cohee, Sallie	621	Crane, Annie	4149
Cohee, Willie W.	622	Crane, Sammie	4151
Cohee, Mattie	623	Crane, Sarah	4152
Cohee, Bertha	624	Crane, Robert	4153
Cohee, Lillian	625	Crane, Henry	4154
Cohee, Serena	1412	Crane, Delilah	4155
Cohee, Eddie	1413	Crane, Rella	4156
Cohee, Washington	1414	Crane, Tena	4157
Cohee, Annie	1415	Crane, Ellison	4158
Cohee, Letha	1441	Curry, Sim	1133
Cohee, Leroy	1446	Curry, Elsie	3898
Cohee, Syrena	1447	Culpepper, Serena	1704
Cohee, Malinda	2845	Culpepper, John	1705
Cohee, Hence	2846	Culpepper, Ella	1706
Cohee, Wayne	2847	Culpepper, Pauline	1707
Cohee, Lafayette	2852	Culpepper, Ida	3604
Cohee, Amanda	2853	Cunish, Joe	3029
Cohee, Calvin	2854	Cummings, Luzina	3843
Cohee, Ernest	2855	Cummings, Young	3845
Cohee, Perry	2856	Cummings, Fannie	3846
Cohee, Henry L.	2857	Cummings, Jasper	3847
Cohee, Charlie	2858	Davis, Richard	765
Cohee, Leora Elizabeth	2859	Davis, Ella	766
Cole, Delilah	1665	Davis, Ida	768
Cole, Jeff	1671	Davis, Josh	769
Cole, Mattie	1830	Davis, Delphia	770
Cole, Josie	2339	Davis, Moses	771
Cole, Mary	4531	Davis, Hall	772
Cole, Frances	4549	Davis, Ivy	773
Cole, Lillie	4550	Davis, Mariah	1004
Cole, Henry	4688	Davis, Luvina	1677
Colly, Lony	1756	Davis, Wesley	2405
Cook, Julia	1957	Davis, Lila	2472
Cook, Ran	1959	Davis, Willard	2473
Cook, Jessee	1960	Davis, Luke	2474
Coker, Zelphia	2175	Davis, Matilda	2480
Coker, Diek	2181	Davis, Hattie	2484
Combs, Fanny	2317	Davis, Manuel	2499
Combs, Beatrice	2318	Davis, Carrie	3648
Combs, Dorsey	2319	Davis, Cassie	4007
Combs, Edna	2320	Davis, William	4489
Colb, Robert	2838	Davis, Alverta	4625
Colb, Samuel	2839	Davis, Matilda	4642
Colb, Fleetwood	2840	Davis, Joe	4644
Colb, Penman	2841	Davis, William	4645
Colb, Wilmore	2842	Davis, Frances	4647
Colb, Robert, Jr.	2843	Davis, Charley	4648
Colb, Lonnie	2844	Davis, Matilda Jr.	4649
Coldwell, Victoria	2916	Davis, George	4650
Cox, Mary	3283	Davis, Ralph L.	4652
Cox, Pierce	3284	Davis, Nimrod Peter	4655
Cox, Virta	3285	Davis, Nimrod	4656
Cox, Melinda	3286	Davis, Priscilla	4657

Name.	Roll No.	Name.	Roll No.
Davis, Martha Athale	4658	Dunford, Monroe	474
Daniel, Ebenezer	1088	Dunford, King	476
Davies, Edward	1271	Dunford, Hattie	477
Davies, Andrew	1272	Dunford, John	501
Davies, Carrie	1273	Dunford, Laura	4389
Davidson, Jennie	1631	Dunford, Leon	4390
Daly, Hattie	2701	Dunford, Andrew	4391
Daly, Bert	2714	Dunford, Rosetta	4614
Daly, Gardy	2715	Dunmas, Lynch	304
Daniels, Rachel	3008	Dunmas, Mattie	305
Daniels, Willis	4082	Duncan, Amanda	2588
Danna, Nancy	3024	Duncan, Mintora	2589
Danna, Frank C.	3027	Duncan, Anna May	2590
Darnell, Ardena	3748	Durant, Myra	4380
Dawson, Hannah	3975	Durant, Etha	4381
Dawson, Hugh	3976	Durant, Maple	4382
Dawson, Lucy	3977	Dyer, Salina	1923
Daugherty, Bessie	2336	Dyer, Lela Bell	1929
Dana, Lizzie	4502	Dyer, Thomas	2413
Dana, Willie	4503	Dyer, Ellen	2414
Dana, Emmett	4504	Dyer, Levy J.	2415
Dana, Lizzie Jr.	4505	Dyer, Myrtle	2416
Dana, Samuel	4506	Dyer, Claude	2417
Dana, Sarah	4507	Dyer, Ona	2418
Dana, Naomi	4508	Dyer, Jim	2860
Dailey, Hannibal	4606	Dyer, Eliza	2861
Dailey, Ananias	4693	Dyer, Frank	2862
Dailey, Obie	4694	Dyer, Jennie	2863
Dailey, Dorcas	4695	Dyer, Columbas	2864
Dailey, Paris	4721	Dyer, Victoria	2865
Dailey, William	4739	Dyer, Mamie	2866
Dailey, Mabell	4824	Dyer, Sugga	2867
Dailey, Dessie	4825	Dyer, Lucy	2868
Danforth, Melvin	4808	Dyer, Ed	2907
Danforth, Eugene	4809	Dyer, Ceasar	2908
Deason, Sarah	4789	Dyer, Robert	2910
Denmark, Rachel	2817	Dyer, Ida	2911
Deer, Molsey	4491	Dyer, Rebecca	2912
Dindy, Celia	1193	Dyer, Nettie	2913
Dindy, Sallie	1194	Eastman, Serena	1134
Dindy, Frazier	1195	Eastman, Tolly	1135
Dindy, Rebecca	1196	Eastman, Frances	1137
Dindy, Edmund	1197	Eastman, Higie	1138
Dindy, Caesar	1198	Eastman, Annie	1139
Dindy, George	1199	Eastman, Patsy	1140
Dindy, Rosa	1200	Eastman, Reube	1142
Dixon, Minnie	2546	Eastman, Carrie	1583
Dixon, Annie	2547	Eastman, Viva Oneta	1588
Dixon, Eula	2548	Eastman, Eli	2954
Dixon, Bulah	2549	Eastman, Edward	2956
Dinwiddie, Cornelia	3004	Eastman, Bertha	2957
Dinwiddie, Malachia	3005	Eastman, Myrtle	2958
Dinwiddie, Almer	3006	Eastman, Malinda	3933
Dinwiddie, Theodo	3007	Eastman, Frank	3944
Dick, Martha	4501	Eastman, Richard	3986
Douglass, Lonnie	791	Eastman, Abram	2955
Douglass, Nellie	792	Eastman, Sallie	4370
Douglass, James	793	Eastman, Carl	4371
Douglass, Alexander	794	Eastman, Rosa Ann	4372
Douglass, Ramond	795	Eastman, Odessa	4373
Douglass, Beulah	796	Eastman, James L.	4374
Douglass, Ernest	797	Edwards, Ben	864
Douglass, Lula	798	Edwards, Rosa	865
Douglass, Vernie	799	Edwards, Dick	870
Douglass, Anna	4258	Edwards, Gertie	871
Douglass, Alma	4259	Edwards, Theodore R.	873
Douglass, Grady	4272	Edwards, Elijah	874
Doser, Nora	1666	Edwards, Hattie	4025
Doser, Alice	1667	Edwards, Ida	4199
Douglas, Zadie	2237	Edwards, Fleetwood	
Douglas, Ludy	2239	Frank	4200
Douglas, Seymore	2240	Edwards, Charley Lee	4201
Douglas, Hercules	2661	Edwards, Violet	4775
Douglas, Ross	2662	Edwards, Walter	4776
Douglas, Willie B.	2663	Edwards, Gussie	4777
Douglas, Cleveland	3608	Edwards, Cleveland	4842
Douglas, Dona	4814	Edwards, William	4843
Douglas, Sarah	4815	Eights, Benj.	1288
Douglas, Dennis	4816	Elliott, Elsie	2990
Doctor, James	3856	Elliott, Samuel B. E.	2991
Drain, Ellis	1027	Elliott, Swift R.	2992
Dunford, Betsie	88	Elliott, Vaucius Cancu-	
Dunford, Lucy	249	lee	2993

Name.	Roll No.	Name.	Roll No.
Ellis, Mary Ann	4548	Flax, Albert	3233
Errett, James	4098	Flax, James	3234
Erwin, Ollie May	4285	Flax, William	3235
Escue, Mahale	2492	Flax, Pleasant	3236
Esters, Nettie	4035	Flax, Mary	3237
Esters, Roosevelt	4039	Flacks, Lizzie	3831
Eubanks, Sampson	3736	Florence, Matilda	4488
Eubanks, Hattie	3738	Foreman, Alice	40
Everhart, Fanny	1701	Foreman, Jackson	51
Even, Kirby	1958	Foreman, Jeff	66
Evans, Lottie	3188	Foreman, Claude	67
Evans, Effie	3189	Foreman, May	68
Evans, Joanna	3190	Foreman, Ned	69
Evans, Louisa	3191	Foreman, Frances	70
Evans, Mimy	3192	Foreman, Susie	4225
Evans, Jesse	3193	Forrester, Zilphia	246
Evans, Amanda	3737	Fort, Cleveland	1048
Evans, Frankie	3740	Fort, Elzerine	1049
Everidge, May	4830	Fort, Coleman	1050
Ewing, Fannie	4073	Foster, Jodie	1132
Ewing, Mary	4081	Ford, Malinda	2816
Falless, Adeline	1018	Frazier, Tony	12
Falless, Zack	1019	Frazier, Zila	13
Falless, Dick	1020	Frazier, Sookey	111
Farrar, Henry	2118	Frazier, Simon	112
Farrow, Hannah	2909	Frazier, Harriet	130
Factor, Bungy	3084	Frazier, Cora	4011
Factor, Rachel	3085	Frazier, Asa	4012
Factor, King	3097	Frazier, Isaac	4013
Factor, Eliza	3098	Frazier, Randies	4131
Factor, Garfield	3099	Frazier, Sylvester	4132
Factor, Roxy	3100	Frazier, Olevia	4133
Factor, Lindy	3101	Frazier, Ella	4177
Factor, Guy	3102	Frazier, Isaac	4178
Factor, Fannie	3103	Frazier, Marietta	4232
Factor, Sarah	3630	Frazier, Rossey	4812
Factor, Arch	4053	Frazier, Nicy	4464
Factor, Edna	4256	Frazier, Chirp	4465
Factor, Aaron	4257	Frazier, Frank	4466
Factor, Joe	4850	Frazier, Julia	4467
Factor, Lillian	4851	Frazier, Hillard	4468
Fagins, Elmore	4284	Frazier, Jesse	4469
Finley, Zilphia	535	Frazier, Luella	4470
Finley, Israel	3065	Frazier, Robert	4471
Finley, Aaron	3066	Franklin, Wash	52
Finley, Minnie	3067	Franklin, Mary	53
Finley, Melvina	3147	Franklin, Sallie	58
Finley, Melissa	3153	Franklin, Jeff	79
Finley, Jack	3671	Franklin, Harriet	80
Finley, Mary	3672	Franklin, Peter	81
Finley, Jim	3673	Franklin, Lee	82
Finley, Scott	3692	Franklin, Henry	83
Findley, Liza	640	Franklin, Dougherty	84
Fisher, Aaron	2803	Franklin, Albert	85
Fisher, Martha	2804	Franklin, Albert	235
Fisher, Thompson	2806	Franklin, Kittie	236
Fisher, Susie	2807	Franklin, Lulu	237
Fisher, Minnie	2808	Franklin, Henrietta	238
Fisher, Riley	2809	Franklin, Alfred	239
Fisher, Elizabeth	2810	Franklin, Josephine	278
Fisher, Joanna	3612	Franklin, William	279
Fisher, Martha	4449	Franklin, Henry	376
Fisher, Ellen	4450	Franklin, Mary	377
Fisher, Patella	4451	Franklin, Jannett	737
Fisher, Burl	4452	Franklin, Liddy	789
Fisher, Roy	4453	Franklin, Solomon	790
Fisher, Bill	4579	Franklin, Sanders	800
Fisher, Sidney	4580	Franklin, Frances	829
Fisher, Mattie Lee	4710	Franklin, Addie	330
Fitchgerl, Caroline	3364	Franklin, Willie	831
Fields, Lena	3990	Franklin, Isaac	832
Fields, Eva	4063	Franklin, Bart	840
Fields, Lona	4069	Franklin, Cassie	841
Fields, Lucy	4185	Franklin, Susanna	897
Finn, Polly	4441	Franklin, Martha	898
Finn, Ella	4442	Franklin, Alexander	900
Finn, Chris	4443	Franklin, Mamie	901
Finn, Lena	4444	Franklin, Nelson	902
Fletcher, Celia	188	Franklin, Delia	903
Flint, Serena	3107	Franklin, Henry	904
Flint, Frank	3108	Franklin, Andrew	921
Flint, Israel	3109	Franklin, Fanny	957
Flint, Luella	3110	Franklin, Minerva	964

Name.	Roll No.	Name.	Roll No.
Franklin, Phebe	969	Franklin, Jonas	4736
Franklin, Russell	1013	Franklin, Nettie	4737
Franklin, Resa	1014	Franklin, James	4738
Franklin, Mark	1015	Freeman, Thomas	4116
Franklin, Catherine	1180	Fulsom, Nancy	3257
Franklin, Grant	1181	Fulsom, Willie	3261
Franklin, Levi	1182	Fulsom, Arthur	3262
Franklin, Isabella	1183	Fulsom, Dicy	3263
Franklin, Gool	1184	Fulsom, Henry	3264
Franklin, Elvira	1185	Fulsom, Martin	3265
Franklin, Mary M.	1186	Furr, Annie	4543
Franklin, Bennie	1187	Furr, Truvine	4544
Franklin, Caesar	1223	Furr, Alpha	4545
Franklin, Sarah	1224	Furr, Evvia Lenerdia	4546
Franklin, Rufus	1225	Furr, John Almer	4547
Franklin, Ada	1226	Gaines, Margaret	30
Franklin, Robert	1227	Gaines, Anderson	31
Franklin, Mattie	1228	Gaines, Dotchie	32
Franklin, Becky	1229	Gaines, Lela	33
Franklin, Lottie	1230	Gaines, Minnie	34
Franklin, Robert	1231	Gaines, Sydney	2205
Franklin, James	1248	Gaines, Theo E.	2206
Franklin, Elnora	1249	Gaines, Ola May	2207
Franklin, Myrtle	1250	Gaines, Josh	2208
Franklin, Perry	1251	Gaines, Eliza	2209
Franklin, Monroe	1296	Gaines, Ada	2210
Franklin, Alice	1360	Gaines, Wilburn	2211
Franklin, Nora	1361	Gaines, Claudie	2212
Franklin, Ellen	1373	Gaines, Mabel	2213
Franklin, Nellie	1374	Gaines, Ora	2214
Franklin, Madgie	1375	Gaines, Adaline	2215
Franklin, Letha	1376	Gaines, Lottie	2216
Franklin, Billy	1377	Gaines, Richmond	2217
Franklin, Eliza	1379	Gaines, Lup	2218
Franklin, Lefannel	1385	Gaines, Billy	2219
Franklin, Otis	1386	Gaines, Jack	2220
Franklin, Palina	1787	Gaines, Annie	2221
Franklin, Ellen	1791	Gaines, Vennie	2222
Franklin, Savanah	1871	Gaines, Ogie	2223
Franklin, Philip	1874	Gaines, Elsie	2224
Franklin, Lillie	1875	Gaines, Effie	2225
Franklin, Frazier	1876	Gaines, Luvinia	2226
Franklin, Allen	1877	Gaines, Lee	2227
Franklin, Frank	1878	Gaines, Sheerwood	2228
Franklin, Annie	1879	Gaines, Phil	2229
Franklin, Isaac	1892	Gaines, Adeline	2230
Franklin, Angie	1963	Gaines, Sallie	2231
Franklin, Viney	1968	Gaines, Lawrence	2232
Franklin, Johnson	1969	Gaines, Emily	2233
Franklin, Andrew	1970	Gaines, Rosa	2238
Franklin, George	1971	Gaines, Eddie	2241
Franklin, Letha	1972	Gaines, Esther	2242
Franklin, Emily	2022	Gaines, Lela	2243
Franklin, Audray	2174	Gaines, Martha	2244
Franklin, Maria	2523	Gaines, Elwood	2245
Franklin, Bart	2525	Gaines, Shoak	2246
Franklin, Ida	2526	Gaines, Cora	2247
Franklin, Ada	2527	Gaines, Addison	2248
Franklin, Frances	2528	Gaines, Jerry	2249
Franklin, Russell	2893	Gaines, Nora	2250
Franklin, Rosella	2894	Gaines, Snowflake	2251
Franklin, George	2895	Gaines, Mattie	2252
Franklin, Houston	2896	Gaines, Jennie	2253
Franklin, Julia	2897	Gaines, Eugene	2261
Franklin, Annie	2898	Gaines, Stafford	2262
Franklin, Gertie	2899	Gaines, Ross	2263
Franklin, Pandy	2900	Gaines, Roy	2264
Franklin, Adella	2901	Gaines, Felix	2265
Franklin, Celia	2932	Gaines, Everet	2266
Franklin, Hester	2933	Gaines, Hence	2267
Franklin, Willie	4062	Geines, Gussie	2269
Franklin, Gussie Viola	4254	Gaines, Sophia	2270
Franklin, Charley	4262	Gaines, Jesse	2271
Franklin, Anna May	4270	Gaines, Floyd	2272
Franklin, Almeda	4271	Gaines, Eddie	2273
Franklin, Maud	4274	Gaines, Willis	2276
Franklin, Ernest	4283	Gaines, Ernest	2277
Franklin, Lelia	4291	Gaines, Fanny	2278
Franklin, Susie	4292	Gaines, Willie	2279
Franklin, Willis	4293	Gaines, Lizzie	2280
Franklin, James	4294	Gaines, Elmo	2281
Franklin, Ora	4336	Gaines, Bertie	2282
Franklin, Minnie	4735	Gaines, Henry	2283

Name.	Roll No.	Name.	Roll No.
Gaines, Myrtle	2284	Gillispie, Rufus C.	167
Gaines, Florence	2285	Gillispie, Benjamin B.	168
Gaines, Irby	2286	Gillispie, Friendly J.	169
Gaines, Lucelle	2287	Gillispie, Frank M. O.	170
Gaines, Ida	2288	Gillispie, Cluna L.	171
Gaines, Orby	2289	Gillispie, Julia A.	172
Gaines, Artie May	2290	Gillispie, Zeddy H.	173
Gaines, Mack	2291	Gillispie, Rado	174
Gaines, Susan	2292	Gillispie, Alberta Savan-	
Gaines, Lonnie	2294	nah	175
Gaines, Tennie	2295	Gillispie, Andrew J.	177
Gaines, Enoch	2296	Gibson, Mary	634
Gaines, Gracie	2297	Gibson, Turner	635
Gaines, Franklin	2299	Gibson, Lulu	636
Gaines, Mitch	2300	Gibson, Charley	3690
Gaines, Mamie	2301	Gibson, Lottie	3693
Gaines, Millard	2302	Giles, Frank	1372
Gaines, Sherwood	2303	Givens, Eliza	1557
Gaines, Huland	2304	Givens, Clarence	1558
Gaines, Pearl	2314	Givens, Bertie	1559
Gaines, Wilburn	2343	Givens, Franklin	1560
Gaines, Bettie	2344	Givens, Ellen	1561
Gaines, Marian	2345	Givens, Ernest	1562
Gaines, Herron	2346	Givens, Lee P.	1563
Gaines, Lulu	2347	Givens, Lucy	4542
Gaines, Richmond	2348	Gibbs, Theodore	1668
Gaines, Rogers	2349	Gibbs, Henrietta	1669
Gaines, May	2350	Gibbs, Mary	1670
Gaines, Willie	2351	Gibbs, John Henry	4317
Gaines, Sam	2355	Gibbs, Emma	4610
Gaines, Macky	2356	Gibbs, Coranie	4853
Gaines, Aleck	2666	Glover, William	478
Gaines, Isabella	2667	Glover, Zilphia	479
Gaines, Louisa	2668	Glover, Isaac H.	480
Gaines, Jimmie	2669	Glover, Emily	481
Gaines, Wesley	2670	Glover, Charity	482
Gaines, Arthur	2671	Glover, Charity	3852
Gaines, Ginsey	2672	Gorden, McCullough	845
Gaines, Edmund	2673	Gorden, Allen	846
Gaines, Caroline	2674	Goldsmith, Addie	1388
Gaines, Maud	2675	Goldsmith, Tecumseh	1389
Gaines, Joanna	2677	Goldsmith, Crissy	1390
Gaines, Sivilla	2678	Goldsmith, Carrie	1391
Gaines, Hudson	2687	Goldsmith, Captain S.	1392
Gaines, Maria	2688	Goldsmith, Henry	1394
Gaines, George	2689	Goldsmith, Mabel	1395
Gaines, Ed	2690	Goldsmith, Lincoln Jef-	
Gaines, Frank	2691	ferson	1396
Gaines, Ollie	2692	Goldsmith, Solomon	1397
Gaines, Boy	2693	Goldsmith, Loyd Levi	1398
Gaines, Philip	2694	Goldsmith, Ross	1399
Gaines, Dave	2948	Goldsmith, Otis	4301
Gaines, Lila	3369	Goldsmith, Orange	4302
Gains, Bertha	4344	Goldsmith, Guy	4303
Gates, Lena	91	Goff, Frank	2156
Gates, Alice	96	Goff, Lou	2157
Gates, Si	97	Gooding, Isom	2642
Gamble, Jack	247	Gooding, Lincoln	2643
Gas, Madrid	1062	Gooding, Billy	2644
Gas, Consie	1068	Gooding, Bob	2645
Garrett, Juanita	3035	Gooding, Stephen	2646
Garrett, Eva	3036	Gooding, Jim	4663
Gasper, Susan	3530	Gooden, Dora	2702
Gasper, Nora	3531	Gooden, John Wesley	2712
Gasper, Palina	3532	Gooden, Allen	2720
Gasper, Leola	3533	Gooden, Albert	2721
Gasper, Frank	3534	Gooden, Thomas	2722
Gasper, Robert	3535	Gooden, William	2723
Garmany, Brady	4002	Gooden, Bettie	2724
Gay, Nancy Abigall	4150	Gooden, Zadie	2725
Gay, Henry C.	4159	Gooden, Walter	2726
Gay, Manervy	4160	Gooden, Gilbert	2727
Gardner, Garfield	4210	Gooden, Perry	2728
Gatewood, Theresa	4478	Gooden, Claude	2729
Gatewood, Alice	4697	Gooden, Allie	2730
Gatewood, Newton	4698	Gooden, Sam	2731
Gatewood, Delphia	4699	Gooden, Rosella	2732
Gatewood, Albert	4700	Gooden, Mirtle Lee	2733
Gatewood, Eliza	4701	Gooden, John	4064
Gentry, Cora	1813	Gooden, Nena	4071
Gillispie, Isabella	164	Gordon, Mary	3241
Gillispie, Christopher C.	165	Gordon, Peter	3244
Gillispie, George M.	166	Gordon, Emma	3631

Name.	Roll No.	Name.	Roll No.
Gordon, John	3632	Gunn, Milly	4084
Gordon, Vivian	3633	Harris, Eliza	41
Gordon, Sam	3634	Harris, Sophia	42
Gordon, Sarah	3635	Harris, Seegle	43
Gordon, Izora	3636	Harris, Margaret	44
Gordon, Lewis	3637	Harris, Claudie	45
Gordon, Frank James	3959	Harris, Cleveland	46
Gordon, Famey	4368	Harris, John	47
Gordon, Abe	4492	Harris, Minnie	2274
Golden, Matilda	3810	Harris, Claude	2275
Goodman, Amanda	3848	Harris, Robert	2340
Goodman, Fred	3849	Harris, William	2695
Goodman, Louisa	3850	Harris, Mollie	2696
Grayson, Serena	10	Harris, Leslie	2697
Grayson, Mary	220	Harris, Annie	3344
Grayson, Eliza	343	Harris, Sarah	3603
Grayson, Athan	353	Harris, Charley	3895
Grayson, Sarah	1468	Harris, Abner	3242
Grayson, Stella	1469	Harris, Dora	4447
Grayson, Della	1470	Harris, Dave	4448
Grayson, Blanche	1471	Harris, Wilson	4662
Grayson, Everett	1472	Harris, Martha	4724
Grayson, Mattie	1473	Hampton, Silvia	146
Grayson, Agnes	1662	Hampton, Sallie	3490
Grayson, James	1663	Hampton, Geneva	3491
Grayson, Nellie	1664	Hampton, Frances	3492
Grayson, Frances	1678	Hampton, Hamp	3493
Grayson, Cubby	1679	Hall, Ella	207
Grayson, Julius	1680	Hall, Theodore	208
Grayson, Zilphia	1681	Hall, Katie	881
Grayson, Edmond	1682	Hall, Gabriel	882
Grayson, Fanny	1683	Hall, Malinda	1087
Grayson, Orilla E.	3280	Hall, Familiar	1608
Grayson, Sallie	3824	Hall, George	1609
Grayson, Fred	3825	Hall, Lula	2742
Grayson, Mittie	3826	Hall, Jamison B.	2743
Grayson, Arnett	3827	Hall, Rosa Arvilla	2744
Grayson, Eva	3828	Hall, Henrietta	2745
Grayson, Lovey May	3829	Hall, Sephronia	2972
Grayson, Dave	4399	Hall, Van	2973
Griffin, Rosa	100	Hall, Ella	2974
Griffin, Pernelia	1659	Hall, Harold	2975
Griffin, James H.	1661	Hall, Georgia	2976
Grey, Julia	201	Hall, Sephronia, Jr.	2977
Grey, Columbus	205	Hall, Etha	2978
Grey, James U.	206	Hall, Araminta	3521
Grayham, Willie	203	Hall, Claude	3934
Grayham, Julius	204	Hall, Carrie	3935
Grimmett, Sophia	354	Hall, Lora	3936
Grimmett, Shelly	356	Hall, Belfry	3937
Grimmett, Amy	357	Hall, Ida	4188
Grimmett, Bessie	358	Hall, Arthur	4189
Grimmett, Lou	359	Hall, David	4729
Grimmett, Tamzey	360	Harlan, Elijah	401
Grimmett, Alter	361	Harlan, Callie	402
Greenwood, Lucy	536	Harlan, Joe	450
Greenwood, Penny	4197	Harlan, Martha	452
Greer, Mary Ann	1270	Hawkins, Soloman	632
Green, Joe	1287	Hawkins, John	633
Green, Julia	3194	Hawkins, Culosh	2000
Green, Nancy	3424	Hawkins, Salina	2001
Green, Lewis	3425	Hawkins, Mary	2002
Green, Lafayette	3426	Hawkins, Ben	2003
Green, Jewell	3427	Hawkins, Joe	2004
Green, Pearl	3428	Hawkins, Fay	2005
Green, Caldonia	3701	Hawkins, Richard	2006
Green, William	4148	Hawkins, Mellette	2007
Green, Claiborne	4296	Hawkins, Charlotte	3714
Green, Lillie	4355	Hawkins, Willie	3715
Gresham, Chaney	1617	Hawkins, Riley	3716
Gresham, Walter	1620	Hawkins, Parthena	3717
Grant, Gus	1724	Hawkins, Julia	3718
Gray, Nathan	3872	Hawkins, Dick	3719
Gray, Sam	3873	Hawkins, Felix	3720
Gunn, Hattie	1482	Hawkins, Granville	3721
Gunn, Simon	1483	Hawkins, Sallie	3722
Gunn, Mary	1484	Hawkins, Neely	3770
Gunn, Bert	1485	Hawkins, Matilda	3771
Gunn, Katie	1486	Hawkins, Joe	3772
Gunn, Dora	1487	Hawkins, Lucy	3773
Gunn, Corine	1488	Hawkins, Henrietta	3774
Gunn, Linda	1489	Hawkins, Lewis	3775
Gunn, Samuel Dovy	1490	Hawkins, Cornealias	3776

Name.	Roll No.	Name.	Roll No.
Hawkins, Lemuel	3777	Homedy, Royal	2632
Hawkins, Veola	4409	Homedy, Simon	2633
Hamilton, Marcus	776	Homedy, Aretta	2634
Hamilton, Laura	778	Homedy, Thomas	2635
Hamilton, Arthur	779	Homedy, Amanda	2636
Hamilton, DeWitt	780	Homedy, Jeanie	2637
Hamilton, Charley	781	Homedy, Mary	2638
Hamilton, Alice	782	Homedy, Frank	2639
Hamilton, Willie	785	Homedy, Clarence	2640
Hamilton, Rhoda	786	Homedy, Lawrence	2641
Hamilton, Cleveland	787	Homedy, Harriet	4288
Hamilton, Tande	788	Hodges, Sephronia	1804
Hamilton, Edy	1286	Horn, Elisa	2332
Hamilton, Jennie	1292	Horn, Charley	2333
Hamilton, Almerine	1298	Horn, Jim H.	2334
Hamilton, George	1792	Horn, Lena M.	2335
Hamilton, Ellen	1793	Hornbeak, Lillie	2352
Harper, Jeff	1106	Hornbeak, Luther J.	2353
Harper, Patys	1107	Hornbeak, Beatrice	2354
Harper, Effie	1108	Houston, Loura	2698
Harper, Robert	1109	Houston, D. McKinley	4821
Harper, Jeff Jr.	1110	Houser, Ed Allen	2757
Harper, William	1111	Houser, Lenora Allen	4839
Harper, Vera	1112	Holman, Willis	4093
Harper, Cap	1113	Holman, Calvin	4094
Harper, Bessie	1114	Holman, Eli	4095
Harper, Felix	1116	Holman, Alberta	4096
Harper, Patsy	1176	Holman, Davis	4097
Harper, Robert B.	1602	Holman, Harry	4169
Harper, Birfet	1603	Holman, Cyrus	4170
Harper, Cora	1604	Holman, Lula	4171
Harper, Amy	1605	Holman, Blaine	4172
Harper, Pernie	1606	Holman, Harrison	4173
Harper, Henry	1607	Holman, Lilly	4832
Harper, Thomas	1616	Howell, Delilah	4163
Harper, Clarence	1618	Hornback, Mary	4559
Harper, Claude	1619	Hornback, Harriet	4560
Harry, Tommy	1686	Hornback, McKinley	4561
Harkins, Mattie	3497	Hornback, Isaac L.	4562
Harkins, Thetas	3504	Hornback, Burnell	4563
Hathaway, Randolph	3987	Hornback, Theodore	4564
Hathaway, Cleo	3988	Hopkins, Maria	4570
Harrison, Frances	4015	Hopkins, Tom	4664
Harrison, Lou	4022	Hogan, Aaron	4703
Harrison, Lucinda	4023	Hogan, Membry	4704
Haynes, Nettie	4195	Hogan, Jim	4705
Harp, Sallie	4400	Hogan, Almerine	4706
Harp, Melton	4401	Hogan, Chap	4707
Harp, Charley	4402	Hogan, Caleb	4708
Harp, Victoria	4403	Hogan, William	4709
Harp, Henry	4404	Humby, Dewey	1404
Harp, Rosa	4405	Huntley, Lillie	1660
Hendersy, Lettie	287	Humdy, Charley	1932
Henderson, Jessee J.	288	Humdy, Isaac	1933
Henderson, John	3750	Humdy, Jack	2080
Henderson, Kittie	4043	Humdy, Maria	2081
Henderson, James	4044	Humdy, Bossy	2082
Henderson, Dwight	4045	Humdy, Caroline	2083
Heard, Margaret	835	Humdy, Calvin	2940
Heard, Mahomedy	837	Humdy, Peter	2941
Heard, Ida	838	Humdy, Arthur	2942
Hennesy, Arminta	1124	Humdy, Hattie	2943
Hennesy, Ernest	1125	Humphreys, Jeff	3700
Hennesy, Smyra	1126	Humphreys, Willie	4268
Hennesy, Moody	1127	Humphrey, Fred	4667
Hennesy, Sudie	1128	Ingram, Amanda	3317
Hervey, Matilda	2293	Ingram, Fred	3318
Harvey, Anna May	2298	Irvins, Agnes	3811
Hines, Theoda	1612	Ireland, Ben	3816
Hicks, Minerva	3894	Impson, Lucy	4517
Hicks, Daniel	4666	Jackson, Kate	135
Hill, Mack	4125	Jackson, Philip	373
Hill, Mary	4187	Jackson, Yoch	496
Hooks, Delia	767	Jackson, Letha	497
Hooks, Jessie	774	Jackson, Frank	498
Hooks, Amy	1506	Jackson, Cassie	618
Hooks, Savana	1512	Jackson, Shoniko	619
Holder, Mollie	1158	Jackson, Oliver	661
Homedy, Isaac	1220	Jackson, Margaret	662
Homedy, Melvina	1221	Jackson, Garfield	663
Homedy, Sam	1222	Jackson, Samuel	664
Homedy, Edmund	2630	Jackson, Henry C.	665
Homedy, Malinda	2631	Jackson, Rhody	666

Name.	Roll No.	Name.	Roll No.
Jackson, Arry B.	667	Jackson, America	3145
Jackson, Robert	1178	Jackson, Aaron	3146
Jackson, Harriett	1179	Jackson, Rufus	3148
Jackson, Wiley	1326	Jackson, Robert	3149
Jackson, Samuel	1329	Jackson, Overton	3150
Jackson, Ella	1330	Jackson, Lucinda	3151
Jackson, Xelia	1331	Jackson, Lizzie	3152
Jackson, Welburn	1333	Jackson, Charley	3430
Jackson, Lula	1334	Jackson, Hannah	3431
Jackson, Ben	1420	Jackson, Miles	3433
Jackson, Arthur	1421	Jackson, Rebecca	3435
Jackson, Ben	1422	Jackson, Robert	3438
Jackson, Hattie	1423	Jackson, Margaret	3439
Jackson, Lydia	1632	Jackson, Stonewall	3853
Jackson, John	1633	Jackson, Riley	2132
Jackson, Dora	4783	Jackson, Lydia O.	2133
Jackson, Charity	4784	Jackson, Dewitt	4314
Jackson, Fred	4785	Jackson, William	4608
Jackson, Elmer	4786	Jackson, Josie	4617
Jackson, Silvia	4813	James, Rhoda	539
Jackson, Rosanna	4819	James, Emma	601
Jackson, Julia	1634	James, Palina	602
Jackson, Arrena	1636	James, Alice	603
Jackson, Frank	1637	James, Zach	604
Jackson, Rachel	1638	James, Gertie	605
Jackson, Flossy	1639	James, Louisa	606
Jackson, Calvin	1640	James, Polly	607
Jackson, Kelton	1641	James, Bertha	608
Jackson, William	1642	James, Gabe	1032
Jackson, Bessie	1643	James, Serena	1247
Jackson, Leford	1825	James, Rosa	1382
Jackson, Tilford	1826	James, Henry	1517
Jackson, Prudence	1827	James, Calvin	1518
Jackson, Susan	1922	James, Willie	1519
Jackson, Raford	1925	James, Rosella	1520
Jackson, Mattie	1926	James, Andy	1521
Jackson, Enzy	1927	James, Mary	2188
Jackson, Dora	1928	James, Cleveland	2519
Jackson, McLean	1924	James, Willis	3025
Jackson, Lee	2074	James, Jennie	3252
Jackson, Estella	2075	James, Simon	3348
Jackson, Sed	2076	James, Lewis	3349
Jackson, Ed	2077	James, Lewis	3578
Jackson, Matthew	2078	James, Cattie	3679
Jackson, Insie	2079	James, Jesse	3580
Jackson, Liny	2170	James, Mitchell	3581
Jackson, Parlee	2173	James, Minnie	3582
Jackson, Joe	2373	James, Etta	3629
Jackson, Rhoda	2374	James, Solomon	4611
Jackson, Ross	2376	James, Willis	4716
Jackson, Ruth	2380	James, Walter	4717
Jackson, Frank	2397	Jacobs, Willie	731
Jackson, Susie	2398	Jacobs, Willis	1278
Jackson, Mollie	2399	Jacobs, Tempy Ann	4251
Jackson, Nervus	2400	Jacobs, Icie	4681
Jackson, Maud	2401	Jacobs, Louis	4682
Jackson, Riva	2402	Jacobs, Pearlie	4683
Jackson, Guy	2403	Jacobs, Jesse	4684
Jackson, Willie	2404	Jacobs, Salina	4685
Jackson, Joe	2409	Jacobs, Idella	4686
Jackson, Cora	2410	Jacobs, Ralph Edward	4687
Jackson, Eva	2411	Jameson, Arthur	1696
Jackson, Herbert	2412	Jameson, Millie	1697
Jackson, Cullin	2587	Jameson, Isaac	1698
Jackson, Andrew	2902	Jameson, Lizzie	1699
Jackson, Minerva	2903	Jefferson, Ella	3867
Jackson, Jersey	2904	Jefferson, Josephine	4085
Jackson, Freeman	2905	Jefferson, Bennie	4086
Jackson, Melton	2906	Jefferson, Daisy	4383
Jackson, Gabe	2961	Jefferson, Pearlie	4384
Jackson, Mary	2962	Jefflo, Willie	3954
Jackson, Margaret A.	2964	Jenkins, Lena	4031
Jackson, Eveline	2965	Jenkins, Hiram	4032
Jackson, Zedick	3088	Jenkins, Lois	4033
Jackson, Minnie	3089	Jenkins, Ermnie	4034
Jackson, Albert	3090	Johnson, Phoebe	86
Jackson, Josie	3091	Johnson, Creasy	89
Jackson, Fred	3092	Johnson, Sarah	137
Jackson, Robert	3093	Johnson, Birdie	138
Jackson, Hattie	3094	Johnson, Willis	139
Jackson, Leford	3095	Johnson, Isaiah	140
Jackson, Viola	3096	Johnson, Alice	141
Jackson, Emily	3144	Johnson, Handy	142

Name.	Roll No.	Name.	Roll No.
Johnson, Mandy	261	Johnson, Eleva	2814
Johnson, Levi	314	Johnson, Lurisse	2815
Johnson, Siney	316	Johnson, Lou	3291
Johnson, Lulu	317	Johnson, Russie	3293
Johnson, Manuel	363	Johnson, James	3294
Johnson, Annie	364	Johnson, Marina Matley	3295
Johnson, Wesley	366	Johnson, Harriet	3404
Johnson, Simon	367	Johnson, Evaline	3412
Johnson, Sina	368	Johnson, Mariah	3413
Johnson, Maud	454	Johnson, Mack	3536
Johnson, Herbert	455	Johnson, Dora	3641
Johnson, Chambers	493	Johnson, Toma	3758
Johnson, Aleck	548	Johnson, Joshua	3869
Johnson, Rachel	668	Johnson, Julia	4047
Johnson, Eliza	669	Johnson, Jim	4115
Johnson, Hettie	670	Johnson, Irene	4141
Johnson, Julie	671	Johnson, Belle	4193
Johnson, Dallas	673	Johnson, Serear	4194
Johnson, Jane	947	Johnson, William	4234
Johnson, Nora	948	Johnson, Malinda	4248
Johnson, Lonnie	1293	Johnson, Mary	4249
Johnson, Mary	1294	Johnson, David McKin-	
Johnson, Byrd	1295	ley	4250
Johnson, Samuel	1460	Johnson, Rayford	4394
Johnson, Ophelia	1461	Johnson, Wellington	4415
Johnson, Bynton	1644	Johnson, Daisy	4416
Johnson, Dora	1645	Johnson, Tiny	4417
Johnson, Effie	1646	Johnson, Effie	4418
Johnson, Selina	1687	Johnson, Maggie	4535
Johnson, Sanders	1913	Johnson, Breedlove	4565
Johnson, Sim	1914	Johnson, John	4566
Johnson, Angy	1915	Johnson, George L.	4567
Johnson, Dora	1916	Johnson, Andrew	4572
Johnson, Lettie	1917	Johnson, Charlie	4575
Johnson, Jesse	1918	Johnson, Edna	4690
Johnson, Benjamin	1919	Johnson, Mary	4696
Johnson, Mat	2023	Johnson, Jimpson	4773
Johnson, Ora Bell	2048	Johnson, Nelson	4774
Johnson, Malinda	2204	Johnson, Myrtle	4822
Johnson, Jack	2563	Jones, Millie	1335
Johnson, Ely	2565	Jones, Ida	2770
Johnson, Bettie	2566	Jones, William McKinley	2771
Johnson, Bennie	2567	Jones, Bessie	2929
Johnson, Mary F.	2568	Jones, Belle	2926
Johnson, Elsie	2569	Jones, Sallie	2930
Johnson, Clifford	2570	Jones, James	3009
Johnson, Claude	2571	Jones, Lillie	3010
Johnson, Carson	2572	Jones, Samuel	3011
Johnson, Elmore	2573	Jones, David	3643
Johnson, Dan	2575	Jones, Agnes	4191
Johnson, Alice	2576	Jones, Willie	4192
Johnson, Manuel	2577	Jones, Mary	4407
Johnson, Dave	2578	Jones, Mary	4454
Johnson, Nathaniel	2579	Jones, Callie	4455
Johnson, William	2580	Jones, Clyde	4456
Johnson, Eastman	2581	Jones, Getta	4457
Johnson, James	2582	Jones, Charley Jr.	4458
Johnson, Ab	2583	Jones, Mary Helena	4538
Johnson, Matilda	2584	Jones, Elijah	4539
Johnson, Texana	2585	Jones, Emma	4540
Johnson, Allie D.	2586	Jones, Silas	4541
Johnson, Ed	2620	Jones, Tener	4730
Johnson, Eliza	2621	Joseph, Joe	1847
Johnson, Julia A.	2622	Joseph, Sam	2169
Johnson, Albert	2623	Joseph, Nancy	2419
Johnson, Izora	2624	Joseph, Martha	2421
Johnson, Linton T.	2625	Joseph, Jewell	2422
Johnson, Clarence	2626	Joseph, Mary Claud	4332
Johnson, Fleetwood	2627	Joseph, Howard	4335
Johnson, Alda	2628	Jordan, Charley	2310
Johnson, Lafate	2629	Jordan, Angeline	2311
Johnson, Lydia	2784	Johns, Ida	3694
Johnson, Joseph	2785	Kemp, Lou Ethel	129
Johnson, Manly	2786	Kemp, Susan	144
Johnson, Melissa	2787	Kemp, Frances	154
Johnson, Ella	2788	Kemp, Ebenezer	1055
Johnson, Henryetta	2789	Kemp, Alice	1056
Johnson, Moses	2790	Kemp, Fred D.	1057
Johnson, Mary	2791	Kemp, Laurel	1058
Johnson, Hattie	2792	Kemp, General T.	1059
Johnson, Sylvester	2793	Kemp, Emily	1060
Johnson, Grant	2812	Kemp, Lorena	1070
Johnson, Elmore	2813	Kemp, Smith	1081

Name.	Roll No.	Name.	Roll No.
Kemp, Nathaniel	1082	Kemp, Charley	3794
Kemp, Malena	1083	Kemp, Henry	3795
Kemp, Missouri	1085	Kemp, Ellen	3796
Kemp, Lottie	1086	Kemp, Orilla	3797
Kemp, John	1089	Kemp, Stella	3798
Kemp, Meline	1090	Kemp, Emma	3799
Kemp, Gabriel	1091	Kemp, Rosa	3925
Kemp, Louis P.	1092	Kemp, Viney	3968
Kemp, Harriett	1130	Kemp, Sanders	3970
Kemp, Althurman	1131	Kemp, Minerva	3971
Kemp, Betsy	1290	Kemp, John H.	3972
Kemp, Peggy	2510	Kemp, Ida	3973
Kemp, Albert	2511	Kemp, Sanders Jr.	3974
Kemp, Dave	2512	Kemp, Joanna	3978
Kemp, Jackson	2514	Kemp, Thelma	4277
Kemp, Manuel	2515	Kemp, Jesse	4326
Kemp, Mollie	2517	Kemp, Lillie O.	4327
Kemp, Jesse	2521	Kemp, Leota	4356
Kemp, Lillia	2522	Kemp, Isaac	4472
Kemp, Albert	2980	Kemp, Zack	4532
Kemp, Julia	2981	Kemp, James	4533
Kemp, Willie	2982	Kemp, Jeff	4534
Kemp, Maud	2983	Kemp, Jesse	4578
Kemp, Nora	2984	Keel, Jacob	382
Kemp, Edna	2985	Keel, Annie	383
Kemp, Viola	2986	Keel, Dan	384
Kemp, Alverson	2987	Keel, Charley	389
Kemp, Rocksey Anna	2988	Keel, Soloman	453
Kemp, Cardy	2989	Keel, Robert	3320
Kemp, Mary	3056	Keel, Elizabeth	3321
Kemp, Henry	3111	Keel, Charley	3322
Kemp, Martha	3112	Keel, Annie	3323
Kemp, George	3113	Keel, Izora	3324
Kemp, Roy	3114	Keel, Mat	3325
Kemp, Louis	3115	Keel, Lula	3326
Kemp, Israel	3116	Keel, Sarah J.	3327
Kemp, Felix	3117	Keel, Rosa B.	3328
Kemp, Cobb	3118	Keel, Silas	3329
Kemp, Edmund	3119	Keel, Lance	3330
Kemp, Mattie	3121	Keel, Simon	3331
Kemp, Adam	3175	Keel, Leonard	3332
Kemp, Viola	3176	Keel, Adeline	3333
Kemp, Alexander	3253	Keel, Levi	3334
Kemp, Martin	3254	Keel, William	3335
Kemp, Malinda	3255	Keel, Den	3538
Kemp, Sam	3350	Kennedy, Belle	1164
Kemp, Annie	3351	Kennedy, Moses	1169
Kemp, Nellie	3352	Kersey, Susan	2406
Kemp, Frances	3353	Kersey, Jackson	2407
Kemp, Etta	3354	Kersey, Letha	2408
Kemp, Nora	3355	Kelly, Letha	3186
Kemp, Turner	3356	Kelly, Julia	3187
Kemp, Claude	3357	Kenrick, Addie	2664
Kemp, Otis	3358	Kingsberry, Ida	387
Kemp, Smith	3442	Kirk, Lena	446
Kemp, Zilphia	3443	Kirk, Lillian	448
Kemp, Lou	3445	Kiah, William	3297
Kemp, Zetta	3446	Kiah, Bob	4490
Kemp, Jesse	3447	Kimbale, William	3724
Kemp, Cleveland	3448	Kimbale, Letha	3725
Kemp, Albert	3449	Kirklin, Sallie	3857
Kemp, Henry	3494	King, Lizzie	3913
Kemp, Louisa	3495	King, Phillip	~~3141~~ 4147
Kemp, Rose	3496	Kinzie, John	4446
Kemp, Wallington	3498	Lamey, William	1347
Kemp, Israel	3499	Lamey, Rose	1348
Kemp, Lula	3500	Lamey, Sampson	1349
Kemp, Levi	3501	Lamey, Eddie	1350
Kemp, Willie	3502	Lamey, Tommie	1351
Kemp, Louis	3503	Lamey, Albert	1352
Kemp, Henry	3584	Lamey, Charley	1353
Kemp, Liffy	3592	Lamey, Daisy	1354
Kemp, Stella	3697	Lamey, Evelina	1355
Kemp, Lee	3706	Lamey, Irene Malena	1363
Kemp, Fannie	3707	Lamey, Elizabeth	1753
Kemp, Cordelia	3708	Lamey, Dewey	1754
Kemp, Parthenia	3709	Lamey, Simmion	3679
Kemp, Hattie	3710	Lamey, Alice	3680
Kemp, Columbus	3767	Lamey, Robertson	3682
Kemp, Lem	3768	Lamey, Noah	3683
Kemp, Joe	3783	Lamey, Bossie	3684
Kemp, Fenton	3792	Lamey, Mary	3685
Kemp, Emily	3793	Lamey, Tippie	3686

Name.	Roll No.	Name.	Roll No.
Lamey, William	3687	Love, Ella	1118
Lamey, Robert	4323	Love, Amos	1119
Lawrence, Pearl	3042	Love, Aaron	1120
Lawrence, Melvin	3336	Love, Richmond	1121
Lawrence, Rob	4360	Love, Lawrence Jr.	1122
Lawrence, Jennie	4361	Love, Lucy Ann	1123
Lawrence, Sam	4362	Love, Leander	1322
Lawrence, Frances	4363	Love, Comela	1323
Lawrence, Willie	4364	Love, Richmond	1324
Lawrence, Leo	4365	Love, Hannah	1325
Lawrence, Florence	4366	Love, Jack	1346
Lawrence, Mabel	4367	Love, Dave	1491
Lane, Susan	4718	Love, Julia	1492
Lane, Johnnie L.	4719	Love, Ben	1493
Lane, Jimmie	4720	Love, Odee	1494
Lewis, Douglass	71	Love, Leora	1495
Lewis, Eli	449	Love, Mange	1496
Lewis, Nettie	950	Love, Lula	1497
Lewis, Gracie	951	Love, Jane	1500
Lewis, Nora	952	Love, Lena	1501
Lewis, Dick	958	Love, Emily	1502
Lewis, Luetta	954	Love, Fred	1895
Lewis, Willie	955	Love, Bettie	1896
Lewis, Osbon Alberta	956	Love, Leslie	1897
Lewis, Newton	1437	Love, Gertrude	1900
Lewis, Serena	1438	Love, Rebecca	2368
Lewis, Ioda	1439	Love, John Jr.	2372
Lewis, Sarah	1448	Love, Abe	2529
Lewis, Raford	1449	Love, Esther	2530
Lewis, Emily	1450	Love, Thomas	2531
Lewis, Caroline	1451	Love, William	2532
Lewis, Richard	1452	Love, Simon	2538
Lewis, Betty	3069	Love, Patsy	2539
Lewis, Hannah	3070	Love, May	2540
Lewis, Robert A.	3071	Love, Frances	2541
Lewis, Edward	3087	Love, Ben	2542
Lewis, Elizabeth	3205	Love, Mimy	2543
Lewis, Edmund	3339	Love, Allie	2544
Lewis, Sallie	3340	Love, Viney	2545
Lewis, Maud E.	3341	Love, Aaron	2550
Lewis, Myrtle	3342	Love, Si	2551
Lewis, Ethel	3343	Love, Excellent	2676
Lewis, John Oliver	3347	Love, Mink	2851
Lewis, Wash	3370	Love, Peter	3082
Lewis, Perry	3371	Love, Mary	3105
Lewis, Rose	3451	Love, Alexander	3106
Lewis, Julius	3453	Love, Viney	3160
Lewis, Walter	3454	Love, Dona	3161
Lewis, Simon W.	3888	Love, John	3162
Lewis, Sallie	3889	Love, Minnie	3163
Lewis, Isaac	3890	Love, Becky	3272
Lewis, Calvin	3891	Love, Lizzie	3274
Lewis, Owens	3892	Love, Simon	3275
Lewis, Bertha	3893	Love, Jesse	3276
Lewis, Caroline	4573	Love, Hattie	3277
Lewis, William	4574	Love, Joe	3387
Lewis, Lee	4691	Love, Liddy	3388
Lewis, Lorenzo	4702	Love, Missie	3389
Lewis, Alice Gracie	4836	Love, Mattie	3390
Leader, Jane	107	Love, Cliff	3391
Lee, Georgia	270	Love, Richard	3392
Lee, Bessie	4677	Love, Tonie	3393
Lee, Witson	4678	Love, James	3458
Lee, Emmet	4679	Love, Hannah	3459
Lin, Daisy	1151	Love, Frank	3460
Lin, Jesse	1154	Love, Joe	3461
Lin, Ada	4281	Love, James Jr.	3462
Lin, Geneva	4282	Love, Edward	3463
Lincoln, Josephine	1442	Love, Oliver	3464
Lincoln, Eveline	1443	Love, Stella	3465
Ligon, Viney	3591	Love, George	3466
Ligon, Nellie	4640	Love, Amanda	3467
Ligon, Frank	4778	Love, Hannah Jr.	3468
Livingston, Lillie	4510	Love, Sam	3480
Love, Bill	430	Love, Frankie	3481
Love, Mary	431	Love, Bessie	3482
Love, Perry	432	Love, Bertie	3594
Love, Jimmie	433	Love, Dave	3622
Love, Sallie	434	Love, Horace	3623
Love, Estella	437	Love, Philip	3624
Love, Albert	439	Love, Irene	3625
Love, Savannah	1028	Love, Elmer	3626
Love, Lawrence	1117	Love, Overton	3627

Name.	Roll No.	Name.	Roll No.
Love, Caleb	3759	Mathews, Suesberry	3887
Love, Albert	3760	Marshall, Estella	3945
Love, Melvina	3761	Mayo, Rena	4807
Love, Della	3762	Merriman, Isabella	250
Love, Aleck	3763	Merriman, Jack	251
Love, Cuny	3764	Merrfman, Susan	253
Love, Gloster	3765	Merriman, Flora	254
Love, Kazelle	3806	Merriman, Claudie	255
Love, Biddy	3807	Merriman, Mandy	256
Love, Dewey	3808	Merriman, Laura	257
Love, Herman	3809	Merriman, Martna	3550
Love, Robert	3835	Merriman, Douglas	3553
Love, Kissiah	3900	Merrican, Oscar	428
Love, Jack	3901	Melton, Janie	1136
Love, Jake	3902	Melton, Francis	1143
Love, Brit	3904	Melton, Leona	4280
Love, Emma	3905	Mimms, Minnie	22
Love, Jeanie	3906	Mimms, Odessa	23
Love, Isom	3907	Mimms, Hortense	24
Love, Amos	3909	Mims, Mathew	26
Love, Morris	3910	Mims, Osisie	28
Love, Ed	3911	Mitchell, Martha	143
Love, Rosa	3912	Mitchell, Silvia	423
Love, Mary	4345	Mitchell, Elnora	424
Love, Charity	4408	Mitchell, Malsy	425
Love, Netty	4476	Mitchell, Minnie	427
Love, Kizzia	4477	Mitchell, Emma	1846
Love, June	4583	Mitchell, Squire	3207
Lofton, Martha	2513	Mitchell, Frona	4810
Lofton, Rosa	2516	Mitchell, Elizabeth	4811
Loftus, William M.	2520	Mitchell, James	4833
Loftus, Callie	2552	Mitchell, Amy	4834
Loftus, Henry	2553	Mitchell, Minnie	4835
Loftus, Melissa	2554	Mike, Aleck	217
Loftus, Elias	2555	Mike, Fheobe	218
Loftus, Jack	2556	Mike, Lora	219
Loftus, Josephine	2557	Mike, Charley	1873
Loftus, Guy	2558	Miller, Jimmie	386
Loftus, Thetis Geo.	2559	Miller, Lou	2150
Loftus, James	2795	Miller, Belle	2151
Loftus, Zach	2796	Miller, Melton	2152
Loman, Henry	3897	Miller, Clara	2153
Lucas, Hettie	3744	Miller, O. D.	2154
Luckly, Ginsey	3896	Mikey, Josiah	543
Luckey, Victoria	4670	Miles, Belton	1044
Luckey, James	4671	Miles, Matthew	1045
Luckey, Cliflus	4672	Miles, Joanna	1046
Luckey, Robert	4673	Miles, Lucy	1047
Luckey, Ada	4674	Miles, Alice	1232
Luckey, Jesse	4675	Miles, Oliver	1233
Luckey, Polk	4676	Miles, Amanda	1234
Lynch, America	4840	Miles, Mary	1236
Lynch, Lelia	4841	Miles, Rosa	1237
Lynch, Venita	2950	Miles, Dora	1238
Lynch, Clemons	2951	Miles, Seney Ann	1239
Lynch, Clarissa	2952	Miles, Cresy	1240
Lynn, Malinda	3745	Miles, Nishey	1241
Mahardy, Hattie	1356	Miles, Eddie	1242
Mahardy, Meanna	1357	Miles, McCannon	1244
Mahardy, Alethia	1358	Miles, Mattie Bee	1245
Mahardy, Mattie	3698	Miles, Minnie Lee	1246
Mahardy, Joanna	3699	Miles, Kittie	1474
Mays, Clifton	1405	Miles, Jesse	1475
Mason, Lizzie	1610	Miles, Cora	1476
Mason, Andy	4128	Miles, Belle	1477
Mason, Geraline	4129	Miles, Sallie	1478
Mason, Walter	4130	Miles, Richard	1479
Martin, Bee	2482	Mintfield, Edmund	2684
Martin, Wilson	2481	Mintfield, Becky	2685
Martin, Frances	2757	Mintfield, Rogers	2686
Martin, Walter	2758	Monroe, Kittie	483
Manning, Alva	3120	Monroe, Isabella	484
Manning, Pearl	3139	Monroe, Johnson	485
Manning, Gertie Obelia	3143	Monroe, Willie	486
Manning, Tenny	4787	Monroe, Billie	488
Manning, Ray	4788	Monroe, Willis	3547
Mathews, Henry	3880	Moses, Aaron	549
Mathews, Caddie	3881	Moses, Turner	550
Mathews, Robert	3882	Moses, Emily	551
Mathews, Arthur	3883	Moses, Jim	552
Mathews, McCoy	3884	Moses, Martha	553
Mathews, Myrtle	3885	Moses, Mary	554
Mathews, Allie	3886	Moses, Lewis	555

Name.	Roll No.	Name.	Roll No.
Moses, Reuben	560	McCarty, Rena	4635
Moses, Elsie	561	McCarty, Hattie	4636
Moses, Oliver	562	McDermott, Lucy Ann	385
Moses, Legus	563	McDonald, Henry	3047
Moses, Vicey	3301	McDonald, Viny	3048
Moses, Ben	3302	McDonald, Jesse	3049
Moses, Louvinia	4475	McDonald, Paul	3050
Montgomery, Ivason	1156	McDonald, Carrie	4837
Molton, Kittie	2805	McDonald, Fred	4838
Molton, Marion	2811	McFarland, Texanna	3903
Morrow, Lucy	3259	McFarland, Jesse	3908
Morrow, Thetus	3266	McGilbarry, Soloman	9
Morrow, Willie	3267	McGee, Dora	2381
Morrow, Emma	3432	McGee, Annie	2382
Mohuntubby, Kissiah	3337	McGilvery, Jinsy	4121
Mohuntubby, Louina	3338	McKinney, Louvisa	880
Moore, Oscar	3346	McKinney, Lucy	1305
Moore, Lizzie	3899	McKinney, William	2088
Moore, Emily	3991	McKinney, Emily	2089
Moore, Dora	3992	McKinney, Angeline	2091
Moore, Cassie	3993	McKinney, Roxanna	2092
Moore, Willie	3994	McKinney, Caroline	2093
Moore, Eliza	3995	McKinney, Ethel	2094
Moore, Martha	4074	McKinney, Lafayette	2095
Moore, Caroline	4641	McKinney, Rena	3086
Moore, Henry	4755	McKinney, Vicey	4581
Moody, Siny	3778	McKinney, Ora	4582
Morris, Frances	4182	McKenzie, Mary	1890
Morris, James W.	4183	McKenzie, Garrett	4338
Morris, Bulla M.	4184	McLish, Sam	4134
Morris, Dock	4241	McLish, Alfred	4135
Morris, Unc	4242	McLish, Frances E.	4136
Murray, Joe	456	McLish, Estelle	4137
Murray, Jodie	458	McLish, Tony	4434
Murray, Willie	459	McLish, Thomas	4435
Murray, Dudley	460	McLish, Matilda	4436
Murray, Hattie	461	McLish, Frederick	4437
Murray, Joe	894	McLish, Rafe	4763
Murray, Lovard	1997	McMillan, Viola	2919
Murray, Laura	1998	McMillan, Clarence	2921
Murray, Elizabeth	2090	McMillan, Sarrah	2922
Murray, Orie Cleo	2096	Napoleon, Jane	1995
Murry, Lennie	716	Nail, Jonas	3083
Munn, Lishia	1710	Nail, Lucy	3211
Munn, Annie	1711	Nail, Winnie	3212
Murphy, Rose	4107	Nail, Viola	3213
Murphy, May	4108	Nail, Celia	3667
Myers, Ida	544	Nail, Etta	3874
Myers, Lulu	545	Nail, Byington	3875
Myers, Aleck	546	Nail, Annie	3876
Myers, Fred	547	Nail, Willie Viola Jus-	
McAfee, Hannah	4103	tice	3877
McCain, Irwin	14	Nail, Amos	3953
McCain, Mary	15	Nail, Byington	4353
McCain, Fannie	16	Nail, Peter	4375
McCain, Zilphia	17	Nail, Lee	4376
McCain, Cornelia	18	Nail, Almeta	4377
McCain, Raswin	19	Nail, Luther	4378
McCain, James	20	Nance, Fanny	3734
McCain, Alva	21	Nance, Freddy	3735
McCain, Claude	25	Nance, Bertha	3739
McCain, Gertrude	27	Nance, Gidion	4358
McCoy, Jackson	2924	Naner, Ion	4359
McCoy, Malinda	4519	Nero, Lucy	126
McCoy, Oliver	4520	Nero, Leonard	564
McCoy, Jane	4526	Nero, Nancy	565
McCoy, Willie	4527	Nero, Scio	566
McCoy, Wesley	4528	Nero, Henry	569
McCoy, Henry	4529	Nero, Silvia	570
McCoy, Sam	4530	Nerb, Orilla	571
McCoy, Rachel	4714	Nero, Charley	572
McCoy, Nettie	4715	Nero, Frances	573
McClendon, Rosella	3195	Nero, Malsy	574
McClendon, Alberta	3196	Nero, Jesse	575
McClendon, Willie	3197	Nero, Abe	576
McClendon, George	3198	Nero, Levey	577
McClish, Tommy	3638	Nero, Henderson	1021
McCorrell, Bell	4589	Nero, Ed	4174
McCorrell, Laura	4590	Nero, Mary Jane	4175
McCorrell, Atwood	4591	Nero, Ceaser	4176
McCorrell, Mattle	4592	Nero, Mattie	4243
McCorrell, Sally	4593	Newberry, Maud	675
McCorrell, Joe	4594	Newberry, Gertie	783

Name.	Roll No.	Name.	Roll No.
Newberry, Caldonia	915	Paris, Ellen	2111
Newberry, Louis	916	Paris, Eddie	2112
Newberry, Calvin	917	Patrick, Walter	3054
Newberry, Moria	918	Patrick, Carrie	3169
Newberry, Lulu	919	Patrick, Amanda	3455
Newberry, Liddy	920	Patrick, Bob	3456
Newberry, Ethel	922	Patterson, Ethel	3079
Newberry, May Bell	923	Payton, Charley	3155
Newberry, Simon	924	Payton, Maud	4486
Newberry, Angeline	925	Payton, Leroy	4487
Newberry, Isom	926	Parks, Fanny	3746
Newberry, Bertha	927	Parks, Monteville	3747
Newberry, Ben	928	Parker, Eddie	4020
Newberry, Lula	4831	Perry, Eliza	266
Newberry, Lillie	929	Perry, Joe	267
Newberry, Willie	930	Perry, Dillard	268
Newberry, Mollie	931	Perry, Jane	414
Newberry, Effie	932	Perry, Russell	540
Newberry, Wiley	933	Perry, Calvin	610
Newberry, Willie Jr.	934	Perry, Washington	627
Newberry, Zadie	935	Perry, William	1033
Newberry, Nettie	1907	Perry, Ellen	1034
Newberry, Essie	1908	Perry, Elmira	1035
Newberry, Ernest	1909	Perry, Elizabeth	1036
Newberry, Ophelia	1910	Perry, Florence	1037
Newberry, Harold	1911	Perry, Nero	2959
Neel, Jane	3124	Perry, Ann	2960
Neel, Mindy	3125	Perry, Bertha	3206
Neel, Simmy	3126	Perry, Susan	3440
Neel, Hattie	3127	Perry, Frank	3441
Neel, Reuben	3128	Perry, Bungy	3654
Neel, Raymond	3129	Perry, Hester	3655
Neel, Julius	3130	Perry, Edmund	3656
Nelson, Sarah	3178	Perry, Dave	3657
Neal, Arlee Jemima	4569	Perry, Joe	3658
Nims, Lillie	127	Perry, Robert	3659
Nowell, Lizzie	49	Perry, William	3660
Noel, Charley	74	Perry, Tommy	3661
Noel, Rachel	75	Perry, Melvin	3662
Noel, Nicy	76	Perry, Cleveland	3663
Noel, Dee	77	Perry, Galaway	3664
Noel, Fanny	78	Perry, Eastman	3675
Noel, Ginnie	4218	Perry, Charlotte	3960
Nolitubby, Si	407	Perry, Foreman	3961
Nolitubby, Sam	408	Perry, Mamie	3962
Nolitubby, Robert	409	Perry, Harrison	3963
Nolitubby, Sarah	410	Perry, Nettie	3964
Nolitubby, Robertson	411	Perry, Elmer	3965
Nolitubby, Dicy	412	Perry, Litsy	3966
Nolitubby, Ella	413	Perry, Wilber	3967
North, Eliza	1202	Perry, Ellen	3999
Owens, Annie	2155	Perry, Catherine	4668
Owens, Arthur	2158	Perry, Douglas	4669
Owens, Maud	4040	Perry, Jeff	4781
Owens, Hattie	4041	Perry, Nathaniel L.	4803
Owens, Willie	4042	Peters, Zilphia	284
Ogles, Winnie	2308	Peters, Sallie	499
Oldhom, Henry	2315	Peters, Robert	511
Oscar, Willie	3044	Peters, Jackson	842
Oscar, Ada	3045	Peters, Brown	962
Oscar, Atwood	3046	Peters, Swain	967
Payne, Wittie	151	Peters, Leora	968
Payne, Ellen	1040	Peters, Willie	973
Payne, Leora	1041	Peters, Malsy	974
Payne, Mary Rose	1042	Peters, Joe	977
Payne, Jerusha	1190	Peters, Brown	978
Payne, Salina K.	4804	Peters, Nettie May	979
Payne, Catherine Virginia	4805	Peters, Samuel J.	980
		Peters, Melissa	993
Payne, Consola	4806	Peters, Roosevelt	999
Paul, Dona	285	Peters, Katie	1381
Paul, Susan	435	Peters, Ruthie	4263
Paul, Willie	869	Peters, Olie	4264
Patton, Eula	982	Peters, Clora	4265
Patton, Georgia Ann	983	Peters, Jack	4613
Patton, Minerva	2591	Peoples, Caldonia	875
Patton, Nancy	2592	Peoples, John W.	876
Patton, Maud	2593	Peoples, Linnie M.	877
Patton, Cornelia	2594	Peoples, Flavius	878
Patton, I. Talerner	2595	Peoples, Beersheba	879
Patton, Edward	2596	Pettus, Becky	886
Patton, Bella	3038	Pettus, Charley	887
Patton, George	3039	Pettus, Allen	888

Name.	Roll No.	Name.	Roll No.
Pettus, Walker	889	Potts, Lucy	3979
Pettus, Virginia	891	Potts, Sylvester	3980
Pettus, Edward	892	Potts, Willie	3981
Pettus, Liddy Ann	893	Potts, Myrtle	3982
Pettus, Mary Eliza	895	Powell, Ed	3243
Pettus, Fanny	1648	Poole, Lizzie	4432
Pettus, Buell	4315	Prince, Aleck	738
Petty, Mary	1038	Prince, Agnes	739
Pearsey, Tony	2647	Prince, Polly	740
Pearsey, Mary	2648	Prince, Ben	741
Pearsey, Lorenzo	2649	Prince, Emery Ann	742
Pearsey, Isaac	2650	Prince, Dora	743
Pearsey, Gibson	2651	Prince, Eva	744
Pearsey, Edward	2652	Prince, Park	745
Pearsey, Isom	2653	Prince, Harrison	746
Pearsey, Alfred	2654	Prince, Virgie	747
Pearsey, Roy	2655	Prince, Rosella	748
Pearsey, Matilda	2656	Prince, Adlissy Alexander	750
Pearsey, Robert	2657	Prince, Calvin	751
Pearsey, Overton	2658	Prince, Charley	752
Pendleton, Geneva	3598	Prince, Eliza	754
Phillips, Mary	125	Prince, Matilda	755
Phillips, Thomas	612	Prince, Jesse	756
Phillips, Lucinda	824	Prince, Mattie	757
Phillips, Sammie	825	Prince, Noble	758
Phillips, Henry	826	Prince, Eddie	759
Phillips, Cornelia	827	Prince, Richmond	905
Pickens, William	1944	Prince, Louvina	906
Pickens, Carrie	1945	Prince, Grant	907
Pickens, John	1947	Prince, Henderson	908
Pickens, Thomas	1948	Prince, Holmes	909
Pickens, Lif	1949	Prince, Florence	910
Pickens, Horace W.	1950	Prince, Nelia	911
Pickens, Eddie	1951	Prince, Mollie	912
Pickens, Eastman	1952	Prince, Charlotte	913
Pickens, Leon	1953	Prince, Sherman	914
Pickens, Rodgers	1954	Prince, Minerva	1621
Pickens, Reece Belt	1955	Prince, Newton	1862
Pickens, Julia	1964	Prince, America	1863
Pickens, Edna	1965	Prince, Wesley	1864
Pickens, Ena	1973	Prince, Elvira	1865
Pickens, Ben	1986	Prince, Rosa	1866
Pickens, Elizabeth	1987	Prince, George	1867
Pickens, Sim	1988	Prince, Ollie	1868
Pickens, Surrena	1989	Prince, Clayton	1869
Pickens, Robeta	1990	Prince, Verna	1870
Pickens, Henry	2024	Prince, Irvin	1872
Pickens, Josie	2025	Prince, Wes	2936
Pickens, Amanda	2026	Prince, Jessie Rosetta	2937
Pickens, Alverson	2027	Prince, Moses	4289
Pickens, Grant	2028	Preuilt, Hattie	764
Pickens, Nannie	2029	Price, Litha	1522
Pickens, Henrietta	2030	Price, Dan	1523
Pickens, Elmon	2031	Price, Gertrude	1524
Pickens, Lyman	2032	Price, William	1525
Pickens, Julia	3957	Price, Nora	1526
Pickens, Henry	4014	Price, Ona	1527
Pickens, Mandy	4445	Price, Charley	1528
Pickett, Jim	3769	Price, Si	1529
Plummer, Santee	641	Price, Scott	1530
Plummer, David	1765	Price, Valley	1531
Plummer, Maggie	3922	Price, Henry	3607
Plummer, Izerio	4335	Pratt, Albert	3543
Poe, Tildy	113	Pratt, Birdie	4481
Poe, Eveline	114	Pratt, George R.	4482
Poe, Annie	115	Pratt, Virgil Summer	4483
Poe, Lucinda	116	Puller, Moses	4240
Poe, Daniel	117	Quinn, Amy	303
Poe, Millard	118	Quinn, Jimmie	306
Poe, Eddie	119	Quinn, Walter	307
Poe, Jimmie	120	Quinn, Cora	308
Porter, Rachel	1253	Randolph, Thomas	2145
Porter, Rubie	1263	Randolph, Clara	2146
Porter, Celia	3784	Randolph, Thomas, Jr.	2147
Pollen, Salina	1647	Randolph, Ida	2148
Powers, Harriet	2597	Randolph, George	4369
Powers, Dovie	2598	Randolph, Jesse	4414
Powers, Thurston	2599	Ranson, Celia	4845
Powers, Odessa	2600	Ranson, Isiah	4846
Powers, Leo	2601	Ranson, Janey	4847
Poleon, Walter	2915	Ranson, Mary	4848
Poleon, Maud	2917	Ranson, Joe	4849
Poleon, Bertha	2918	Reese, Harvie	426
		Reese, Susan	4480

Name.	Roll No.	Name.	Roll No.
Reed, Henry	3014	Roberts, Maree	2039
Reed, Sarah	3868	Roberts, Louis	2051
Reed, Robert	4028	Roberts, Legenia	2052
Reynolds, Sarah	3702	Roberts, John	2053
Reynolds, George	4059	Roberts, Pearl	2054
Reynolds, Rufus	4060	Roberts, Lillie	2055
Reynolds, Georgiana	4168	Roberts, Ada	2056
Reynolds, Alice	4462	Roberts, Collis	2057
Reynolds, Alice	4615	Roberts, Edmund	2321
Reynolds, Frank	4661	Roberts, Sarah	2322
Reynolds, Moses	4725	Roberts, Rachel	2323
Reynolds, Epsie	4726	Roberts, Jamena	2324
Reynolds, Wheeler	4727	Roberts, Charley	2325
Reynolds, Pomp	4741	Roberts, Marcus	2326
Reynolds, Lawrence	4742	Roberts, Jack	2327
Reynolds, Nelson	4743	Roberts, Laura	2328
Reynolds, Alice	4744	Roberts, Rodie	2329
Reynolds, Miles	4745	Roberts, Alice	2331
Reynolds, Florence	4746	Roberts, Richard	2377
Reynolds, Gertie	4747	Roberts, Kate	2378
Reynolds, Cordie	4748	Roberts, Grove	2379
Reynolds, Virgie	4749	Roberts, Mahale	2772
Reynolds, Mandie	4750	Roberts, Aleck	2773
Reynolds, Leggett	4751	Roberts, Guy	2774
Reynolds, Annie	4752	Roberts, William	2775
Reynolds, Nellie	4753	Roberts, Newton	4308
Reynolds, Jessie	4754	Ross, Adeline	863
Reynolds, Thomas	4756	Ross, Dusie	2149
Reynolds, Claude	4757	Ross, Jane	2305
Reynolds, Martha	4758	Ross, Titus	2306
Reynolds, William	4782	Ross, Angeline	2307
Reynolds, Charley	4759	Ross, Charles	4485
Reynolds, Fred	4760	Rollen, Anica	1279
Reynolds, Floyd	4761	Roy, Rosa	1934
Reynolds, Luther	4762	Roy, John Henry	1935
Reeves, Crosetta	3801	Roy, Ada Lee	1936
Reeves, Catherine	3802	Rodville, Susie	3043
Reeves, Linzy	3834	Roby, William	3200
Redfield, Clem	3955	Roby, William H.	3201
Redfield, Jim	3958	Roby, Annie	3202
Read, Malinda	4164	Roby, Katie	3203
Rentie, Isador Elnora	4324	Roby, Mary	3204
Rhone, Mary	4111	Rogers, Fannie	3943
Richardson, Willie	240	Rodgers, Virginia	4161
Richardson, Laura	1773	Rodgers, Rosevelt	4162
Richardson, Amanda	1774	Roff, Abe	4202
Richardson, Robert	1775	Roff, Tom	4203
Richardson, Elmira	1776	Roff, Nannie	4204
Richardson, Adeline	2870	Roff, Mattie	4205
Richardson, Munford	2871	Roff, Will	4206
Richardson, Major C.	2872	Roff, Seely	4207
Richardson, Octavia	2873	Roff, Poncy	4208
Richardson, Lena	2884	Roebeck, Bettie	4518
Richardson, Isabella Amanda	3122	Rody, Malinda	4723
Ridge, Solomon	2819	Russell, Amy	131
Ridge, Edgar	2820	Russell, Elijah	210
Rivers, Coleman	3123	Russell, Mary	211
Richards, Dan	3858	Russell, Ethel	212
Richards, Belle	3859	Russell, Verment	213
Richards, Ed	3860	Russell, Eveline	214
Richards, Albert	3861	Russell, Arline	215
Richards, Anderson	3862	Russell, Francis	216
Richards, Almeda	3863	Russell, Nero	242
Richards, Ada	3864	Russell, Isabella	243
Riley, Henderson	4126	Russell, Andrew	244
Riley, Sukey	4127	Russell, Shadrack	245
Richmond, Rosa	4628	Russell, Henry	289
Richmond, Estella	4631	Russell, Arthur	500
Rose, Nicy	378	Russell, Amanda	646
Rose, Izarah	381	Russell, Jinnie Ann	648
Rose, Jesse	3788	Russell, Agnes	654
Rose, Cornelius	4100	Russell, Henry	655
Rose, Silvey	4101	Russell, Ruthie	656
Rose, Anna Christina	4102	Russell, McClure	657
Roberts, Floyd	380	Russell, Rachel	658
Roberts, Henrietta	1613	Russell, Ada	659
Roberts, Lizzie	1614	Russell, Virgie	660
Roberts, Minnie	1615	Russell, Henrietta	1289
Roberts, Willie	1999	Russell, Janie	2560
Roberts, Tuck	2033	Russell, Ludle	2561
Roberts, Murdie	2038	Russell, Reasie	2562
Roberts, Martha	2034	Russell, Susan	3288
Roberts, Addie	2035	Russell, Mary	4106
Roberts, Luvinia	2036	Russell, Roosevelt	4247
Roberts, Claudie	2037	Russel, Narcissa	541
		Sampson, Amos	613

Name.	Roll No.	Name.	Roll No.
Sampson, Jeff	1901	Smith, Ollie	994
Sampson, Henrietta	1902	Smith, Mary	995
Sampson, Zedick	1903	Smith, Isaah	996
Sampson, Henry	1904	Smith, Eppie	997
Sampson, George	1905	Smith, John	998
Sampson, Isabella	1906	Smith, Lizzie	1001
Sampson, Maybell	4339	Smith, Alfred	1002
Samuels, Rebecca	1155	Smith, Susie	1094
Samuels, Clarence	1159	Smith, Lynton	1095
Samuels, Bertha	1157	Smith, Stephen	1096
Samuels, Charley	1817	Smith, Bill	1097
Samuels, Henry	2997	Smith, Lawrence	1098
Sandridge, Mary	4852	Smith, Frank	1099
Scott, Houston	371	Smith, Clara	1100
Scott, Ann	4112	Smith, Samuel	1101
Sealy, Rosa	248	Smith, Dixie, Jr.	1102
Sealy, Thomas	3541	Smith, Laura	1104
Sealy, Lou	3542	Smith, Ruth	1105
Sears, Malinda	1093	Smith, Joe	1160
Seitz, Lula	4001	Smith, Jane	1161
Seitz, Willie C.	4003	Smith, Ed	1162
Seitz, James	4004	Smith, Burrell	1163
Seitz, Jessie	4005	Smith, Ellen	1165
Shell, Callie	1299	Smith, Patsy	1166
Shell, Sidney	1300	Smith, Zach	1167
Shell, Jackson	1301	Smith, Louis	1168
Shell, Mattie	1302	Smith, Richard	1306
Shell, Gussie	1303	Smith, Elwood	1307
Shell, Arlena	1304	Smith, Melvina	1308
Shell, Leford	4255	Smith, Areta	1309
Shell, Carrie	4494	Smith, Walter	1310
Shell, Levi	3865	Smith, Ada	1311
Shirley, Amy	1794	Smith, Bertha	1312
Shirley, Belle	1795	Smith, Abe	1313
Shirley, Albert	1796	Smith, Cora	1314
Shirley, Vick	1798	Smith, Barney	1315
Shannon, Ann	2042	Smith, Melissa	1803
Shannon, Ed	2043	Smith, Henry	1881
Shannon, Alice	2044	Smith, Elizabeth	3000
Shannon, Isaac	2045	Smith, James G.	3001
Shannon, Jennie	2046	Smith, Mertle	3002
Shannon, Press	2047	Smith, Edeth	3003
Shannon, Albert	2058	Smith, Annie	3470
Shannon, Martha	2059	Smith, Katie	3572
Shannon, Lomy	2060	Smith, Amanda	3573
Shannon, Prudence	2061	Smith, Clarence	3574
Shannon, Kates Anna	2062	Smith, Lula	3575
Shannon, Ella	2063	Smith, Columbus	3576
Shannon, Mary Ann	2064	Smith, Charles	3924
Shannon, Leford	2493	Smith, Luke	4253
Shannon, Mary	2494	Smith, James Henry	4275
Shannon, Turner	2495	Smith, Cleveland	4298
Shannon, Linnie	2496	Smith, Celia	4299
Shannon, Luda	2497	Smith, Nelius	4300
Shannon, Henry	2498	Smith, Charley	4352
Shannon, Henry	4484	Smith, Esau	4473
Shaw, Sallie	2357	Smallwood, Media	2313
Shaw, Minnie O.	2358	Smallwood, Welton	2316
Shoeape, Miley	3319	Sparks, Isom	280
Shatubby, Lila	3345	Sparks, Sina	281
Shelton, Harriett	3938	Sparks, Martha	1597
Shelton, Albert	3939	Sparks, Holmes	1598
Shelton, Ben	3940	Sparks, Nicy	1599
Shelton, Hamilton	3941	Sparks, Altha I.	1601
Shelton, Lela	3942	Sparks, Mack	4311
Shields, Thomas	4016	Sparks, Cleveland	4312
Shepard, Dicy	4411	Sparks, Birthen	4313
Shepard, Albert	4412	Spigener, Sarah	681
Shepard, Henry Nail	4413	Spigener, Darmer	686
Simkins, Quida	4036	Spigner, Elvenia	687
Simkins, Guy	4037	Spencer, Aleck	717
Simkins, Lillie	4038	Spencer, Jennie	718
Sifax, Dicky	4123	Spencer, Laura	719
Simpson, Rosa	2452	Spencer, Spencer	720
Skelton, Minnie	4646	Spencer, Cora	721
Skelton, Ruth	4653	Spencer, Raford	722
Skelton, Theresa	4654	Spencer, Winchester	723
Smith, Nelson	152	Spencer, Manuel	724
Smith, Sallie	189	Spencer, Minnie	725
Smith, Albert	277	Spencer, Andrew	726
Smith, Susanna	315	Spencer, Bill	727
Smith, Wesley	375	Spencer, Gracie	728
Smith, Maggie	438	Spencer, Edna	729
Smith, Hannah	990	Spencer, Beaulah	730
Smith, Joseph	991	Spencer, William	1053
Smith, Daniel	992	Spencer, Minerva	1054

Name.	Roll No.	Name.	Roll No.
Spencer, Henry	1208	Stevenson, Etta	2069
Spencer, Jennie	2195	Stevenson, Docia	2070
Spencer, Dollie	2196	Stevenson, Novata	2071
Spencer, Nancy	2197	Stevenson, Emett Cears	2072
Spencer, Alonzo	2198	Stevenson, Arrene	2073
Spencer, Arrie	2199	Stevenson, Veta	4820
Spears, Maggie	2259	Stevenson, Mimy	2084
Spears, Mittie	2260	Stevenson, Tom	2085
Speer, Harriett	3545	Stevenson, Harriett	2086
Spiers, Perlie May	3712	Stevenson, Felix	2087
Speers, Joanna	3713	Stevenson, Dave	2424
Spigner, Almefine	4269	Stevenson, Mary	2425
Springer, Bessie	4509	Stevenson, Sam	2426
Springer, Jesse	4511	Stevenson, Banks	2427
Springer, Richard	4512	Stevenson, Raford	2428
Stroud, Emma	106	Stevenson, Cleve	2429
Stephenson, Lena	457	Stevenson, Amos	2430
Stephenson, Memory	462	Stevenson, Ernest	2431
Stephenson, Dave	784	Stevenson, Isaac	2439
Stephenson, Jake	4319	Stevenson, Emma	2440
Stevenson, Lizzie	533	Stevenson, Serena	2441
Stevenson, Mack	709	Stevenson, Carrie	2442
Stevenson, Minerva	710	Stevenson, Angie	2443
Stevenson, Hardy	711	Stevenson, Isabella	2444
Stevenson, Robert	712	Stevenson, Sophia	2445
Stevenson, Allen	715	Stevenson, Henry	2450
Stevenson, Lizzie	734	Stevenson, Lou	2451
Stevenson, Susan	760	Stevenson, James A. G.	2453
Stevenson, Rufus	762	Stevenson, Eli	2454
Stevenson, Tilro	823	Stevenson, Dave	2455
Stevenson, Catherine	896	Stevenson, Bettie	2456
Stevenson, Peter	1365	Stevenson, Kizzie	2457
Stevenson, Lizzie	1366	Stevenson, John	2458
Stevenson, Angeline	1367	Stevenson, William	2459
Stevenson, Jay C.	1368	Stevenson, Charley	2465
Stevenson, Albert	1401	Stevenson, Estella	2466
Stevenson, Ida	1402	Stevenson, Leonard	2467
Stevenson, Carrie	1403	Stevenson, Lonnie	2468
Stevenson, Georgia Ann	1712	Stevenson, Mary	2469
Stevenson, Benjimin	1713	Stevenson, Louis	2470
Stevenson, Robin	1714	Stevenson, Elsie	2471
Stevenson, Levy	1715	Stevenson, Louis	2475
Stevenson, Malsy	1717	Stevenson, Elsie	2476
Stevenson, Ida	1718	Stevenson, Garfield	2477
Stevenson, Thomas	1720	Stevenson, Rufus	2478
Stevenson, Alice	1721	Stevenson, Isora Bell	2479
Stevenson, Amy	1722	Stevenson, Allie	2483
Stevenson, Dud	1723	Stevenson, Robert	2485
Stevenson, Henry	1725	Stevenson, Bessie	2486
Stevenson, Houston	1726	Stevenson, Elmore	2487
Stevenson, Robert	1742	Stevenson, L. G. Elnora	2488
Stevenson, Joanna	1743	Stevenson, Isreal	2489
Stevenson, Angeline	1744	Stevenson, George	2490
Stevenson, Brown	1745	Stevenson, Manly	2491
Stevenson, Chaney	1747	Sevenson, George	2500
Stevenson, Alfred	1748	Stevenson, Frances	2501
Stevenson, Annie	1749	Stevenson, Samuel	2502
Stevenson, Dick	1750	Stevenson, Paul	2503
Stevenson, Hannah	1751	Stevenson, Nora M.	2504
Stevenson, Edward	1752	Stevenson, Pearl	2505
Stevenson, Viney	1764	Stevenson, Annie	2506
Stevenson, Flora	1767	Stevenson, Edgar	2507
Stevenson, Lorata	1768	Stevenson, Ollie	2508
Stevenson, Samuel	1769	Stevenson, Buena	2509
Stevenson, Fleetwood	1770	Stevenson, Philip	2524
Stevenson, Simpson	1771	Stevenson, Elwood	2747
Stevenson, Elijah	1778	Stevenson, Joe	2749
Stevenson, Amos	1779	Stevenson, Merriman	2750
Stevenson, Riley	1780	Stevenson, Gertha	2751
Stevenson, Jackson	1781	Stevenson, Mary Ann	2755
Stevenson, Althea	1799	Stevenson, Zeno	2756
Stevenson, Hattie	1800	Stevenson, Philip	2759
Stevenson, Ethel	1801	Stevenson, Harriett	2760
Stevenson, Wavey	1802	Stevenson, Henry	2761
Stevenson, Monroe	1805	Stevenson, Jennie	2762
Stevenson, Josie	1806	Stevenson, Lela	2763
Stevenson, Serena	1807	Stevenson, Charley	2764
Stevenson, Manuel	1808	Stevenson, Carey	2765
Stevenson, Arthur	1888	Stevenson, Joanna	2766
Stevenson, Sallie	1889	Stevenson, Dixie	2767
Stevenson, Amy	2049	Stevenson, Zeno	2768
Stevenson, Adge	2067	Stevenson, Leon	2769
Stevenson, Minerva	2068	Stevenson, Polly	2885

Name.	Roll No.	Name.	Roll No.
Stevenson, Hiram	2891	Taylor, Tom	817
Stevenson, Roxey	2934	Taylor, Bessie	818
Stevenson, Martha	3429	Taylor, Sarah	819
Stevenson, Will	3483	Taylor, Amos	820
Stevenson, Mollie	3484	Taylor, Lafayette	821
Stevenson, Tandy	3485	Taylor, Margaret	965
Stevenson, Elsie	3486	Taylor, Violet Ann	970
Stevenson, Mosey	3487	Taylor, Cadee '	971
Stevenson, Ben	3488	Taylor, Lucy	1177
Stevenson, Levi	3489	Taylor, Burrell	1996
Stevenson, Charley	3539	Taylor, Judge	2065
Stevenson, Ethel	3540	Taylor, Nellie	2066
Stevenson, Margaret	3674	Taylor, Robert	2113
Stevenson, Lewis	3677	Taylor, Mimy	2114
Stevenson, Lula	3678	Taylor, Calvin	2115
Stevenson, Alena	3920	Taylor, Amy	2116
Stevenson, Emma	4211	Taylor, Murdie	2117
Stevenson, Canelia	4252	Taylor, Mary	2129
Stevenson, Alma	4260	Taylor, Mose	2119
Stevenson, Lon	4273	Taylor, Melvin	2120
Stevenson, Malinda	4320	Taylor, Littie	2121
Stevenson, Bebee Ada	4322	Taylor, Willie	2122
Stevenson, Zach	4396	Taylor, Orie	2123
Stevenson, Leford	4397	Taylor, Nonie	2124
Stevenson, Lela	4624	Taylor, Edna	2125
Stewart, Julius	761	Taylor, Linzy	2126
Stewart, Myra	763	Taylor, William M. K.	2127
Stewart, Isaac	3396	Taylor, Nevada	2128
Stewart, Thomas	4024	Taylor, Mose	2134
Stewart, Jesse	4079	Taylor, Emily	2135
Stewart, Earnest	4080	Taylor, Henry	2136
Stewart, Lucy	4513	Taylor, Lila	2137
Stewart, Birdie	4514	Taylor, Benjimen	2138
Stewart, Ruby	4515	Taylor, Amanda	2139
Stewart, Mabel	4516	Taylor, Doeson	2140
Stevison, Alfred	1861	Taylor, Josie Belle	2141
Stanfield, Susie	2159	Taylor, Nancy	2142
Stanfield, Louisa	2160	Taylor, Ernest	2143
Stanfield, Belle	2161	Taylor, Crissie	2144
Stanfield, William	2162	Taylor, Lizzie	2436
Stanefild, Samantha	2163	Taylor, Harvey	2438
Stanfield, Lenora	2164	Taylor, Frank	3609
Stanfield, Zach	2165	Taylor, Wash	3610
Stanfield, Henry	2166	Taylor, Jane	3611
Stone, Viny	3785	Taylor, Mary	2129
Stone, Annie	3786	Tatum, Daisy	1274
Stone, Lovingstone	3787	Tatum, Evelina	1275
Stephen, Abagail	4083	Tecumseh, Sarah	626
Stephens, Jane	4419	Thomas, Nancy	542
Stephens, Ella	4420	Thomas, Julia	1144
Stephens, Bettie	4421	Thomas, Amanda	1145
Stephens, Malsy	4422	Thomas, George	1146
Stephens, Monroe	4423	Thomas, Susie	1147
Stephens, John	4424	Thomas, Juanita	1148
Stephens, Jesse	4425	Thomas, Willie	1149
Stephens, Bessie	4426	Thomas, Isaac	1150
Stahaker, Ella	4498	Thomas, Winnie	1152
Stahaker, Mary	4499	Thomas, Harriett	1564
Summers, Lizzie	802	Thomas, Orilla	3214
Summers, Henry	803	Thomas, Bessie	3215
Summers, James	804	Thomas, Priscilla	3216
Summers, Elizabeth	805	Thompson, Henrietta	1327
Summers, Lucy	806	Thompson, Sellisie	1328
Summers, George	807	Thompson, Lucretia	2963
Summers, Irena	808	Thompson, Riley	2966
Summers, Lufus	809	Thompson, Partheenie	2967
Summers, Parthenia	810	Thompson, Lurina	3134
Summers, Hannah	1426	Thompson, Lilly	3135
Summers, Carrie	1702	Thompson, Caesar	3136
Summers, Bula	4306	Thompson, Angeline	3137
Sutton, Annie	3821	Thompson, Minnie	3138
Swindle, Isadora	691	Thompson, Elzora	3140
Swindle, Georgia	696	Thompson, Robinson	3141
Swindle, Hattie	697	Thompson, Rob	3142
Swindle, Willard	698	Thompson, Albert	3613
Taylor, Harriet	260	Thompson, Alice	3614
Taylor, Jennie	585	Thompson, Link	3615
Taylor, Henry	811	Thompson, Pink	3616
Taylor, Susan	812	Thompson, Ross	3617
Taylor, Willie	813	Thompson, Albert, Jr.	3618
Taylor, Zach	814	Thompson, Jesse	3619
Taylor, James	815	Thompson, Blanche	3620
Taylor, Sam	816	Thompson, Pearley	3621

Name.	Roll No.	Name.	Roll No.
Thompson, Frank	3726	Vaughner, Lucy	4731
Thompson, David	3727	Vaughner, Laura	4732
Thompson, Dora	3728	Vaughner, Joseph	4733
Thompson, Mary	3729	Vee, Chaney	3932
Thompson, Vicy	3730	Vinson, Ellen	4142
Thompson, Eli	3731	Vinson, Lindsey	4146
Thompson, Celia	3732	Vinson, Jenie Pearmy	4463
Thompson, Albert	3780	Vinson, Willie	4734
Thompson, Sam	3781	Vollen, Mary	59
Thompson, Nelson	3782	Walker, Louisa	155
Thompson, Mittie	3946	Walker, Emily	158
Thompson, Clifton	3947	Walker, Joanna	159
Thompson, Cleve	3948	Walker, Julia	609
Thompson, Lesley	3949	Walker, Manuel	614
Thompson, Blake	3950	Walker, Martha	949
Thompson, Willie	4120	Walker, Jennie	1025
Thompson, Simon	4124	Walker, Simon	1051
Thompson, Thaney	4290	Walker, Harriett	1052
Thompson, Jim	4493	Walker, Zilphia	1316
Thompson, Jincy	4772	Walker, Robert	1317
Thurman, Frances	4138	Walker, Lillian	1318
Thurman, Winnie	4139	Walker, Melvina	1319
Tipkins, Louisa	3366	Walker, Dosie	1320
Tillman, Amanda	3927	Walker, Jimmie	1444
Tillman, Nelson	3928	Walker, Johnie	1445
Tillman, Maggie	3929	Walker, Lizzie	1727
Tillman, Phillip	4779	Walker, Nelson	1728
Tillman, Porter	4780	Walker, Josephine	1729
Tillman, Joe	4844	Walker, Rufus	1730
Towser, Polly	134	Walker, Robert	1731
Townsend, Fannie	323	Walker, Martha	1732
Tobler, Rosa	843	Walker, Bailey	1006
Toles, Ellen	2337	Walker, Hattie	1007
Toles, Bart	2341	Walker, Seymour	1008
Toles, Frank	2342	Walker, Bertie	1009
Towns, Edna	2396	Walker, George	1010
Torrence, William	2970	Walker, Mary	1011
Townsley, Sophia	3226	Walker, Laura	3681
Triplett, Eveline	3012	Walker, Essie	3688
Triplett, Cephas	3013	Walker, Henry	4215
Trainell, Clarence	4140	Walker, Cardeil	4307
Trim, Elsie	4385	Walker, Jane	4459
Tutler, Lizzie	1267	Walker, McKennon	4460
Tutler, Oscar	1268	Walker, Devere	
Tutler, Harriett	1269	Garnetta	4461
Turner, Edna	4278	Washington, Mary J.	959
Turner, Calline	4279	Washington, Frank	960
Twyman, Lula	3016	Washington, Wilburn	961
Twyman, Willie	3023	Washington, Allie	3279
Tyson, Stephen	505	Washington, Angeline	3281
Tyson, Paralee	506	Washington, Mary	3282
Tyson, Lynch	507	Washington, Burney	4049
Tyson, Cody	508	Washington, Lucy	4496
Tyson, Sophia	509	Washington, Abner	4497
Tyson, James	510	Washington, Agnes	4665
Tyson, Moses	1565	Ward, Florence	1016
Tyson, Nettie	1809	Ward, Amie	1023
Tyson, Jim	1810	Ward, Willie	1828
Tyson, Fletch	1811	Ward, Fannie	3080
Tyson, Miranda	1812	Ward, Hattie	3081
Tyson, Aleck	3030	Ward, Thomas	3606
Tyson, Marietta	3031	Ward, Israel	3670
Tyson, Thomas	3032	Watts, Rhoda	1252
Tyson, Tom	3033	Watts, Houston	1254
Tyson, Becky	3034	Watts, Simpson	1255
Tyson, Russell	3037	Watts, Josie	1256
Tyson, Jackson	3199	Watts, Dethadue	1257
Tyson, Muck	3676	Watts, Daniel	1258
Tyson, Stephen	3742	Watts, Henison	1259
Tyson, Blanch	4331	Watts, Lawrence B.	1260
Tyner, Nancy	1782	Watson, Serena	1359
Tyner, Alva	1783	Watson, Sarah Mays	1364
Underwood, Edmund	642	Waters, William	3052
Vaughn, Tennessee	512	Waters, Susan	3053
Van, Rachel	592	Waters, Amanda	3055
Van, Mary	594	Wade, Lena	3239
Van, Laura	596	Wade, Nelson	3240
Van, Emily	597	Walton, Emma	3314
Van, Riner	598	Walton, Rena	3836
Van, Dave	599	Walton, Fleater	3837
Van, Irvin	600	Walton, Charlie	3838
Vanley, Louisa	3384	Wesley, Eli	3723
Vanley, Austin	3812	Whitaker, Susan	2018
		Whaley, Millie	2679
		Whaley, Savanna	2680
		Whaley, Sam	2681

Name.	Roll No.	Name.	Roll No.
Whaley, Earl	2682	Williams, Beulah	1543
Whaley, Jake	2683	Williams, Lula	1544
Whitlow, Harriett	2848	Williams, Helen	1545
Whitlow, Lufus	2849	Williams, Sadie	1676
Whitlow, Paul	2850	Williams, Estella	1766
Wheeler, Emeline	3365	Williams, Izora	1772
White, Stella	3436	Williams, Wilton	1784
White, Robert	3437	Williams, Ellen	1785
White, Sallie	3800	Williams, Ebenezer	1786
White, Josie	3803	Williams, Henrietta	1788
White, John	3804	Williams, Mattie	1789
White, Isaiah	3805	Williams, Irene	1790
White, Mamie	3926	Williams, Becky	1814
White, Laura	4722	Williams, Janie	1815
White, Ludie	4826	Williams, Agnes	1816
Whitson, Martha	3469	Williams, Charley	1818
Whitson, Nellie	3471	Williams, Jennie	1819
Whitson, Ben	3472	Williams, Andrew	1820
Whitson, Lizzie	3473	Williams, Allie	1821
Whitson, Bob	3474	Williams, Jesse	1822
Whitson, George	3475	Williams, Rebecca	1823
Whitson, Ed	3476	Williams, Lou	1829
Whitson, Gipson	3477	Williams, Ellis	1835
Whitson, John	3478	Williams, Viney	1836
Whitson, Plummer	3479	Williams, McKinzie	1837
Williams, Rena	615	Williams, Joe	1838
Williams, James	643	Williams, Reuben	1839
Williams, Martha	644	Williams, Lula	1841
Williams, John	645	Williams, Henry	1843
Williams, Salina	647	Williams, Angeline	1845
Williams, Martin	650	Williams, Johnson	1858
Williams, Emily	651	Williams, Jennetta	1859
Williams, George W.	652	Williams, Martin	1860
Williams, Eastman	653	Williams, Butch	1930
Williams, Sam	676	Williams, Mary	1931
Williams, Henry	678	Williams, Bertie Lorena	2008
Williams, Mat	679	Williams, Man	2391
Williams, Joanna	682	Williams, Aaron	2392
Williams, Jackson	683	Williams, Missie	2393
Williams, Cleveland	684	Williams, Frank	2394
Williams, Andy	685	Williams, Allie	2395
Williams, Jim	688	Williams, Berry	2432
Williams, Ida	689	Williams, Patsy	2433
Williams, Ernest	690	Williams, Samuel	2434
Williams, Henderson	699	Williams, Calvin	2435
Williams, Josephus	700	Williams, Jim	2437
Williams, Mary	701	Williams, Buck	2446
Williams, Benj.	702	Williams, Hattie	2447
Williams, Katie	703	Williams, Gertie	2448
Williams, Albert	704	Williams, Drew	2449
Williams, Carrie	705	Williams, Caroline	2659
Williams, Ruthie	706	Williams, John	2660
Williams, Ulcum	707	Williams, Clifford	2705
Williams, Silas	708	Williams, Sam	2706
Williams, Rose	1017	Williams, Maria	2707
Williams, Andrew	1030	Williams, Clem	2708
Williams, Jones	1031	Williams, Ellard	2709
Williams, Tom	1204	Williams, Lomy	2710
Williams, Ada	1205	Williams, Eddy	2711
Williams, Travis	1206	Williams, Nuan	2713
Williams, Lillie	1207	Williams, Jennie	2797
Williams, Harvey	1209	Williams, Owensby	2869
Williams, Ivory Ives	1345	Williams, Mary	2880
Williams, Fannel	1383	Williams, Archie	2881
Williams, America	1435	Williams, William H.	2882
Williams, Ben	1436	Williams, Newton	2883
Williams, Manuel	1503	Williams, Elijah	2886
Williams, Lucy	1504	Williams, Flora	2887
Williams, Ross	1505	Williams, Cephas	2888
Williams, Richard	1507	Williams, Dixie	2889
Williams, Frances	1508	Williams, Arree	2890
Williams, Cub	1509	Williams, Susie	2935
Williams, Mattie	1510	Williams, Ben	2938
Williams, Timisy	1511	Williams, Frances	2979
Williams, Johny	1513	Williams, Frances	3041
Williams, Eliza	1514	Williams, Nellie	3168
Williams, Manuel	1515	Williams, Millie	3171
Williams, Willie	1516	Williams, Doc	3457
Williams, Malsy	1537	Williams, Lizzie	3585
Williams, Fleetwood	1538	Williams, Alphonso	3586
Williams, Charley	1539	Williams, Liffy	3587
Williams, Martha	1540	Williams, Cora	3588
Williams, Jimmie	1541	Williams, Basha	3589
Williams, Tommie	1542		

Name.	Roll No.	Name.	Roll No.
Williams, Cornelia	3590	Wilson, Everlena	989
Williams, Addie	3749	Wilson, Nancy	2097
Williams, Willie	3753	Wilson, Philip	2098
Williams, Isaah	3754	Wilson, Colbert	2099
Williams, Charley	3755	Wilson, Beulah	2100
Williams, Doretha	3756	Wilson, Jimmie	2101
Williams, Polly	3815	Wilson, Mugy	2102
Williams, Glendi	3817	Wilson, Earnest	2103
Williams, Archie	3818	Wilson, Nancy	2746
Williams, Shirley	3819	Wilson, Laman	2920
Williams, Seymour	3820	Wilson, Dick	2939
Williams, Garfield	3854	Wilson, Ellen	3766
Williams, Eliza Ann	3983	Wilson, Pearl	3919
Williams, Lee	3984	Wilson, Viola	3923
Williams, Roberta	3985	Wilson, Caroline	2375
Williams, John	4029	Wilson, Frank	4584
Williams, Took	4030	Wilson, William R.	4585
Williams, Hattie	4051	Wilson, Nellie	4586
Williams, Elmira	4052	Wilson, Weada Bell	4587
Williams, Willie	4087	Wilson, Sindy Riler	4588
Williams, Jim	4088	Williamson, Patsy	2739
Williams, Henry	4089	Williamson, Jimmie	2740
Williams, Georgia	4090	Williamson, Buster	2741
Williams, Bevys	4091	Wilkes, Lutie K.	2719
Williams, Spencer	4092	Windom, Susan	3072
Williams, Alice	4122	Windom, Nora	3074
Williams, Arabella	2130	Windom, Sim	3075
Williams, Geronimo	4287	Windom, Jesse	3076
Williams, Sam	4297	Windom, Willie	3077
Williams, Elnora	4310	Windom, Augustus	3078
Williams, Della May	4321	Wilkerson, Mary	3258
Williams, Susa	4334	Wilkinson, Florida	3269
Williams, Irena	4341	Wilkinson, Ethel	3270
Williams, Robert	4395	Wilkinson, Georgie M.	3271
Williams, Rachel	4431	Wilkins, Serena	3565
Williams, Oliver	4438	Wilkins, Joe	3566
Williams, Joe	4479	Wilkins, James	3567
Williams, Dan	4577	Wilkins, Larry	3568
Williams, Ellen	4607	Wilkins, Frances	3569
Williams, Marcus	4618	Wilkins, Oliver	3570
Williams, Cora	4619	Wilkins, Lucy	3571
Williams, Kimble	4620	Wilder, Callie	3703
Williams, Maise	4621	Wilder, Wesley	3704
Williams, Joe	4622	Wilder, Nora	3705
Williams, Edna	4659	Windon, Eugene	3839
Williams, Leanna	4660	Windon, George	3840
Williams, Madie	4692	Wims, Joyce E.	4643
Williams, Nancy	4728	Wims, Alma Lejester	4651
Williams, Cora Lee	4818	Wolf, Liddy	190
Williams, Roxy	4823	Wolf, Jane	3394
Wiley, Jemima	857	Wolf, Jack	3398
Wiley, Gloster	858	Wolf, Julia	3399
Wiley, Willie	859	Wolf, Hilly	3400
Wiley, Hettie	860	Wolf, Major	3401
Wiley, Mary Ann	862	Wolf, Pamelia	3402
Willis, Dora	936	Wolf, De Etta	3403
Willis, Arthur	937	Worley, Melvina	1848
Willis, Richard	938	Worley, Frank	1849
Willis, Cully	939	Worley, Rufus	1850
Willis, Amiel	940	Worley, Eastman	1851
Willis, Betty	2234	Worley, Anna	1852
Willis, Jennie	2235	Worley, Abb	1853
Willis, Thomas	2699	Worley, Wilson	1854
Willis, Amanda	2700	Worley, James	1855
Willis, Ayers	2703	Worley, John	1856
Willis, Walter	2704	Worley, Albert	1857
Willis, Bal	2834	Worley, Emma	2734
Willis, Mink	2836	Worley, Rosa	2735
Willis, Brit	2837	Worley, Hugh	2736
Willis, Isabella	3208	Worley, Becky	2737
Willis, Daniel	3209	Worley, Sidney	2738
Willis, Napoleon	3296	Woods, Janey	3156
Willis, Josiah	3298	Wright, Martha	2364
Willis, Robert	3299	Wright, Hattie	2365
Willis, Wade	3300	Wright, James	2366
Willis, Mary	3914	Wright, Benjamin	2367
Willis, Norval	3998	Wright, William	2369
Wilson, Callie	981	Wright, Hardy	2370
Wilson, Lugenia	984	Wright, Eddie	2371
Wilson, Fanny	985	Wright, Aaron	2602
Wilson, Anderson	986	Wright, Clemon	2603
Wilson, Arthur	987	Wright, Walter	2604
Wilson, Burtie	988	Wright, Edward	2605
		Wright, Ebbie	2606
		Wright, Calvin	2607
		Wright, Velar	2608

Name.	Roll No.	Name.	Roll No.
Wright, Overton	2609	Yates, Henderson	1921
Wright, Ada	2610	Yates, William	2995
Wright, Dewey	2611	Yates, Willie	2996
Wright, Orange	2612	Yates, Willie May	2998
Wright, Joe	2613	Yates, George	3644
Wright, Rosa	2614	Yates, Matilda	3645
Wright, Birdie	2615	Yates, Pansie	3646
Wright, John	2616	Yates, Lee Ella	4357
Wright, Nora	2617	Yocubby, Louisa	300
Wright, Bertha	2618	Yocubby, Robert	400
Wright, Dink	2619	Young, Mimy	732
Wright, Willie	3452	Young, David	735
Wright, Mary	4054	Young, James	1280
Wright, Eddie	4055	Young, Martha	1281
Wright, Minnie	4056	Young, Ollie	1282
Wright, Birdie	4057	Young, Andy	1283
Wright, Esther.	4711	Young, Mattie	1284
Wright, Walter	4827	Young, Arthur	1285
Wright, Elbert	4828	Young, Escle	2255
Yates, George	1424	Young, Queenie	2254
Yates, Louisa	1425	Young, Laura	2256
Yates, Retta	1427	Young, James Gaddis	4295
Yates, Leah	1428	Younger, Margaret	1369
Yates, Sallie	1429	Younger, Josephus	1370
Yates, Paletha	1430	Younger, Orena	1371
Yates, Andrew	1431	Younger, Lela	3444
Yates, Walter	1432	Younger, Roy	3450
Yates, Mary	1433	Younger, Alberta	3711

INDEX TO
CHEROKEES BY BLOOD

Name.	Roll No.	Name.	Roll No.
Adair, James F., Jr.	5062	Adair, Susan J.	21865
Adair, John M.	5793	Adair, Emma F.	22044
Adair, James W.	6341	Adair, Frank C.	22544
Adair, Frankie M.	6569	Adair, Ezekiel S.	22545
Adair, William P.	6803	Adair, Talitha J.	22546
Adair, Arthur	6804	Adair, Timothy M.	22586
Adair, Edward S.	6865	Adair, Sallie	22609
Adair, Rebecca C.	6866	Adair, Robert E.	23469
Adair, John H.'	6867	Adair, Ida L.	23470
Adair, William T.	6868	Adair, Rollin E.	23471
Adair, Lokie C.	6869	Adair, George	23472
Adair, Clemmie D.	6870	Adair, Fred B.	23473
Adair, Robert P.	6871	Adair, John W. P.	23474
Adair, Annie	6872	Adair, William P.	23532
Adair, Bluele	6895	Adair, Maggie R.	23533
Adair, Virgil H.	7682	Adair, DeWitt J.	23534
Adair, Robert L.	7683	Adair, Walter . T.	23535
Adair, Minnie	7684	Adair, Mary E.	23536
Adair, Peyton	7685	Adair, Fannie	23568
Adair, Clarence L.	7686	Adair, Walter T.	23569
Adair, Peyton A.	7687	Adair, Lola	23570
Adair, Magnolia	7688	Adair, Viola	23829
Adams, Arther T.	7903	Adair, Millard H.	23830
Adair, Ethel L.	8395	Adair, Winnie	23831
Adair, Charles L.	9709	Adair, John W.	25245
Adair, Cora M.	9710	Adair, John W., Jr.	25246
Adams, Carrie F.	10287	Adair, Eugene M.	25247
Adams, Leo D.	10288	Adair, George A.	25248
Adams, William H.	10289	Adair, Edward T.	25249
Adams, James H.	10290	Adair, Sabina	27083
Adams, Fred M.	10291	Adair, Lizzie	27108
Adams, Samuel	10672	Adair, Samuel H.	27124
Adams, Clarence P.	10673	Adair, Sarah S.	27125
Adams, Joseph L.	10674	Adair, Florance W.	27126
Adair, Rollin K.	12475	Adair, Venia F.	27127
Adair, Rachel T.	12476	Adair, Gulah R.	27128
Adair, William D.	12478	Adair, John T.	27129
Adair, Sue T.	12479	Adair, Watie M.	27130
Adair, Sadie K.	12480	Adair, Juanita A.	27131
Adair, Rachel M.	12481	Adair, Carlotta R.	27132
Adair, Thomas J.	13864	Adair, Betsy	27173
Adair, Lena	13865	Adair, Sarah L.	27183
Adair, Emily	13866	Adair, John L.	28279
Adair, Cherokee C.	13989	Adair, Isaac	28574
Adair, Norma B.	14109	Adair, Alice	28601
Adair, Samuel T.	15370	Adair, Etta	28602
Adair, Otha M.	15371	Adair, Olney M.	28603
Adair, Mary E.	15372	Adair, William P. R.	28604
Adair, George W.	15373	Adair, Arthur F.	28848
Adair, Samuel W.	15374	Adair, Mollie E.	28849
Adair, Lula E.	15375	Adair, Arthur L.	28850
Adair, Lillie	15376	Adair, Owen L.	28851
Adair, Lucinda	15382	Adair, Mack	29843
Adair, Luther M.	15383	Adair, Henry G.	30239
Adair, Sarah L.	15384	Adair, Caroline	30240
Adair, William L.	15385	Adair, Mintie	30241
Adair, Mary	15386	Adair, George	30242
Adair, Myrtle L.	15387	Adair, Ute	30243
Adair, Altie	15388	Adair, Katie	30244
Adair, Callie B.	15389	Adair, Levi	30245
Adair, Emmett M.	15390	Adam, Richard	30269
Adair, Nona Bertha	15391	Adams, Bertha M.	31159
Adair, Thomas	15561	Adams, Rosa L.	31160
Adair, Joseph F.	16533	Adams, Carry F.	31161
Adair, John W.	16565	Adams, Abner G.	31555
Adair, Nan L.	16566	Adams, Lottie J.	31556
Adair, John Walter	16567	Adams, Judson H.	31557
Adair, Joseph F. R.	16568	Adams, Josephine R.	31558
Adair, McLeod L.	16569	Adams, Hiram V.	31559
Adair, David D.	16570	Adams, Reuben B.	31560
Adair, Samuel	16892	Adams, Nathan F.	32095
Adair, Mary	16893	Adams, Viola M.	32096
Adair, Jennie M.	16894	Adams, Emmett L.	32097
Adair, Edna B.	16895	Adam, Maudie	32514
Adair, Levi C.	16896	Adair, John	32684
Adair, Susan E.	16897	Addington, William J.	7230
Adams, Edith	17656	Addington, Addison B.	7232
Adams, Luther	17657	Addington, Alice D.	19540
Adams, Charlie	17658	Addington, Belle	2338
Adair, Annie	19190	Addington, Cicero	2335
Adair, Jacob	19191	Addington, Clarance G.	2337
Adair, Sam	19192	Addington, Delora P.	7233
Adair, Albert	19250	Addington, Frederick F.	20205

Name.	Roll No.
Addington, Henry E.	10543
Addington, Henry J.	24559
Addington, Ida B.	10542
Addington, Jesse J.	10541
Addington, Joel C.	7229
Addington, Margaret A.	10538
Addington, Mollie L.	2336
Addington, Oscar P.	7231
Addington, Truman C.	10539
Adkins, Eugene S.	23525
Adkins, Amy	11322
Adkins, Mary	5492
Adkins, Tillie	11318
Adkins, Hattie J.	23524
Adkisson, Callie M.	16648
Adkisson, Clarence M.	16644
Adkisson, Jasper N.	16642
Adkisson, Jennie M.	25260
Adkisson, John W.	25258
Adkisson, Kittie	16646
Adkisson, Milow	25259
Adkisson, Paralee	16647
Adkisson, Samuel	25257
Adkisson, Samuel A.	25255
Adkisson, Susan	25256
Adkisson, Susan J.	15406
Adkisson, Susie	16643
Adkisson, Thomas E.	16645
Agent, Arch	18420
Agent, Dick	18418
Agent, Ella	32339
Agent, Polly	18419
Agent, Wartuck	18421
Agnew, Cephus	5792
Agnew, Ellen	5790
Agnew, Mary E.	5789
Agnew, Robert M.	5784
Agnew, Walter L.	5791
Agnew, Walter S.	5788
Adkins, Eugene S.	23525
Adkins, Hattie J.	23524
Aikins, Anna	2235
Ainsworth, Cornelia	21505
Ainsworth, Emma	21510
Ainsworth, Mamie	21512
Ainsworth, Margarett	21504
Ainsworth, Myrtle	21511
Ainsworth, Spencer	21509
Ainsworth, Thomas	21507
Ainsworth, Willie	21508
Akin, Effie	32714
Akin, Velva May	32715
Akin, Andy T.	771
Akin, Jennie	772
Akin, Ellis A.	773
Akin, Modie	774
Akin, Watie T.	775
Akin, William O.	776
Akin, Thomas F.	777
Akin, Mabel T.	778
Akin, Jennie L.	779
Akins, Frank R.	2205
Akins, Eudorah A.	2206
Akins, Jesse O.	2207
Akins, Robert L.	2208
Akin, Margarette T.	2339
Akin, Mary	3495
Akin, Alfred N.	3496
Akin, Ras C.	5538
Akin, Carrie	5539
Akin, Charles F.	5540
Akin, Arch P.	5541
Akin, Fannie C.	8743
Akin, Strange W.	8744
Akin, Raymond P.	8745
Akin, Don	32677
Alberty, Margaret	209
Alberty, John	669
Alberty, Ellis	829
Alberty, Martha	830
Alberty, Spencer L.	831
Alberty, William H.	832
Alberty, Lula L.	833

Name.	Roll No.
Alberty, Watie M.	834
Alberty, Albert C.	928
Alberty, Ellis C.	1051
Alberty, Willam W.	1052
Alberty, Moses	1053
Alberty, Peter	1054
Alberty, Jack W.	1208
Alberty, Ida L.	1209
Alberty, Minnie	1210
Alberty, Elbridge	1211
Alberty, Delilah	1392
Alberty, Andrew J.	1682
Alberty, Theodocia	1683
Alberty, William L.	1684
Alberty, Bishop M.	1686
Alberty, Samuel J.	1687
Alberty, John	1858
Alberty, Emily C.	1859
Alberty, Oscar L.	1860
Alberty, Mollie	1861
Alberty, Mattie	1997
Alberty, Katie	5166
Alberty, Cornelius	5167
Alberty, Charity	6283
Alberty, Joshua	6881
Alberty, Ellis C.	7004
Alberty, Susan	7005
Alberty, Cecil E.	7006
Alberty, Nanie W.	7007
Alberty, Maggie M.	7008
Alberty, Bernice L.	7009
Alberty, Roxie D.	12622
Alberty, Alfred T.	12624
Alberty, Eli S.	12687
Alberty, Bluford W.	14103
Alberty, Clara C.	14104
Alberty, John A.	14105
Alberty, Annie L.	14106
Alberty, Bluford W., Jr.	14107
Alberty, Martha C.	14108
Alberty, Edward W.	14839
Alberty, Nannie	14840
Alberty, William P.	14979
Alberty, Beulah	14980
Alberty, Minnie Bell	14981
Alberty, Eliza M.	14999
Alberty, Ellis R.	22352
Alberty, Gibson W.	22354
Alberty, Jacob	22363
Alberty, Ella	22365
Alberty, Myrtle	22366
Alberty, Fred	22367
Alberty, George	22368
Alberty, Ellis D.	22369
Alberty, John T.	22370
Alberty, Joseph V.	22382
Alberty, Clara	22383
Alberty, Tota	22384
Alberty, Fannie	22385
Alberty, Joseph V.	22386
Alberty, John G.	22570
Alberty, Grover L.	22572
Alberty, Emmett A.	22573
Alberty, Daily	22574
Alberty, George G.	22575
Alberty, Moses L.	25084
Alberty, Ida L. M.	25085
Alberty, James Q.	25086
Alberty, Rena R.	25087
Alberty, Joseph R.	26332
Alberty, Bertha	26333
Alberty, William A.	26334
Alberty, Jesse	26335
Alberty, Lucy C.	26336
Alberty, John B.	26337
Alberty, Mary	27517
Alberty, Elizabeth	27938
Alberty, Callie	27947
Alberty, Robert	27948
Alberty, Harris	27949
Alberty, Lora M.	27950
Alberty, Jake	27976
Alberty, Anna	27977

Name.	Roll No.	Name.	Roll No.
Alberty, John	27978	Allen, Susan	4399
Alberty, Flora	27979	Allen, Marcellus	4400
Alberty, William	27980	Allen, Isom M.	4401
Alberty, Arther	27981	Allen, China F.	4402
Alberty, David R.	27987	Allen, Thomas P.	7882
Alberty, Beatrice	27988	Allen, Pearl M.	7883
Alberty, George	28159	Allen, Neoma	7884
Alberty, John	28160	Allen, Pluma	7885
Alberty, Thomas B.	28537	Allen, Amariah C. B.	8272
Alberty, Julia	28538	Allen, Rosa E.	8545
Alcorn, Mary E.	5115	Allen, Eva V.	8546
Alcorn, Joseph H.	5126	Allen, Mamie L. N.	8547
Aldridge, Ruth A.	10212	Allen, Sarah E.	8675
Alexander, Joe	3680	Allen, Susie	9505
Alexander, Saphronia	3941	Allen, William R.	9506
Alexander, Lillian	3942	Allen, Clarence V.	9507
Alexander, Maud	3943	Allen, Ethel E.	9508
Alexander, Fay	3944	Allen, Johana	9509
Alexander, Kate	3945	Allison, John R.	11188
Alexander, Paralee	4624	Allison, Willie	11189
Alexander, James F.	4625	Allison, Elmie R.	11190
Alexander, Samuel D.	4626	Allison, Jimmy	11191
Alexander, Elmer H.	7399	Allison, John	11192
Alexander, Effie L.	9946	Allison, Mary E.	11193
Alexander, Una	9947	Allison, Una	11194
Alexander, William H.	11229	Allison, Sabra	11195
Alexander, Lewis	14600	Allison, Edgar H.	11196
Alexander, Nora	16089	Allen, Jennie	11209
Alexander, James	17154	Allen, John	11351
Alexander, Aggie	17155	Allen, Henry F.	12174
Alexander, Andy	17156	Allen, Wilburn O.	12175
Alexander, John	17157	Allen, John W.	12176
Alexander, Job	20099	Alloway, Neely	12311
Alexander, Caroline	20100	Alloway, Mamie	12312
Alexander, Carrie	20101	Allen, Emma	13160
Alexander, Weston	20102	Allen, Ella	13161
Alexander, Jennie	20103	Allen, Joseph C.	13876
Alexander, Thompson	22972	Alloway, Delilah	12305
Alexander, Stephen D.	26838	Alloway, William A.	12307
Alexander, John	28454	Alloway, Salina	12308
Aleck, James	19488	Alloway, Belle	12309
Aleck, Nellie	19489	Alloway, Leroy	12310
Aleck, Nannie	19490	Allen, Nancy A.	15130
Aleck, Coon	19491	Allen, Lewis B.	15230
Aleck, Polly	19492	Allen, Ethel V.	15231
Aleck, Johnson	19493	Allen, Anna M.	15232
Aleck, John	25596	Allen, Olla J.	15233
Aleck, Lydia	25597	Allen, Oscar R.	15234
Aleck, Ailsey	27617	Allen, William B.	17347
Aleck, Aquilla	27618	Allen, Jefferson	18590
Aleck, Celia	27619	Allen, Senie	18591
Alfred, Bob	18764	Allen, Sarah	18592
Alfred, Fannie	18763	Allen, Aaron	18593
Alfred, Maggie	18761	Allen, Michael	20355
Alfred, Nannie	18765	Allen, Oceola	21774
Alfred, Sue	18762	Allen, Theodore	21830
Alfred, Willie	18766	Allen, Lillie B.	21989
Alfrey, Curtis C.	31909	Allen, Annie J.	22078
Alfrey, Genevieve	31908	Allen, Ada D.	22079
Alfrey, Nannie A.	31907	Allen, Ida E.	22080
Allen, Alice	122	Allen, William C.	22081
Allen, Walter A.	1708	Allen, John O.	22082
Allen, Edward	1709	Allen, Sarah	23518
Allen, Hugh M.	1710	Allen, William A.	23519
Allen, Mary L.	1711	Allen, Elmer H.	23520
Allen, Cephas A.	1712	Allen, Arther L.	23521
Allison, John L.	1904	Allen, Thea Brant	23522
Allison, Amos L.	1905	Allen, Ruth A.	27641
Allison, Mildred M.	1906	Allen, Gretchen	27647
Allison, Laura J.	2064	Allen, Georgia	28133
Allison, Mildred T.	2092	Allen, Charles W.	28378
Allison, Edgar G.	2093	Allen, Estella M.	28379
Allison, Narcenie	2094	Allen, Henry	28775
Allison, Ella N.	2238	Allen, Joseph H.	28776
Allison, Laura B.	2247	Allen, Edna C.	28777
Allison, Payton	2248	Allen, Herbert E.	28778
Allison, Clara	2249	Allen, Annie	29133
Allison, Edith	2250	Alleck, William	29055
Allen, Susan	3806	Allison, Edgar R.	22684
Allen, Thomas M.	3958	Allison, Hughey	29266
Allen, William W.	3959	Allen, Mary J.	29908
Alen, Robert B.	3960	Allen, Annie E.	30143
Allen, George W.	4207	Allen, Rosa	30144

Name.	Roll No.	Name.	Roll No.
Allen, Gracie	30145	Anderson, Lizzie	16586
Allen, Robert I.	31330	Anderson, Willie May	16587
Allen, Jesse K.	31352	Anderson, James	18685
Allen, Della M.	31353	Anderson, Saran	18686
Allen, Frank I.	31354	Anderson, Amanda	18687
Allen, Rufus	31355	Anderson, George	18688
Allen, Agnes V.	31356	Anderson, Bettie	18689
Allen, Alta M.	31357	Anderson, Samuel	18690
Allen, William F.	31416	Anderson, Nellie	21627
Allen, Rufus M.	31475	Anderson, Renie	21628
Allen, Jane	32076	Anderson, Jesse	21629
Alltime, William B.	31376	Anderson, Austin	21771
Alston, Williamina	5981	Anderson, Rachel C.	27697
Alston, Susan E.	5982	Anderson, Charles J.	31064
Alston, Elizabeth B.	5983	Anderson, Annie M.	31065
Alston, Sarah C.	28627	Anderson, Lula M.	31066
Alston, William C.	28628	Anderson, Jesse M.	31067
Alston, Rutledge B.	28629	Anderson, Nellie	31169
Alton, Charles J.	11702	Anderson, John	31190
Alton, David C.	11700	Anderson, Samuel	31227
Alton, Percy S.	11701	Anderson, George T.	31228
Alton, Susan E.	11699	Anderson, Anna	31313
Alton, Dorah E.	30254	Andre, Eliza	5437
Alvis, Fannie H.	13970	Andre, Paul	5439
Alvis, Oneita E.	13973	Anddoe, Nancy	12747
Ames, David L.	15293	Andrews, Polly	4841
Ames, George L.	15292	Andrews, Susie	5819
Ames, Hiram L.	15295	Andrews, Sarah C.	9896
Ames, Julia A.	15291	Andrews, Mary A.	9897
Ames, Sallie A.	15294	Andrews, Alvin F.	9898
Ammons, Mary	19088	Andrews, Esther R.	9899
Ammons, Norwood	19089	Andrews, Clyde E.	9900
Amis, Amanda A.	12158	Andrews, Mary	22549
Amis, Edwin R.	12161	Angel, Ida A.	578
Amis, James E.	12160	Angel, Jesse	580
Amis, Margaret E.	12162	Angel, Laura A.	581
Amis, William A.	12159	Angel, Rebecca	577
Amos, Minnie E.	28522	Angel, William Ira	579
Amos, Pansy M.	28523	Anglin, Dessa P.	22498
Anderson, Joanna	2843	Anglin, Georgia A. O.	22496
Anderson, James C.	2847	Anglin, Lona M.	22497
Anderson, Richard	3256	Anglin, Maud V.	22499
Anderson, Edward A.	3257	Anible, Caledonia E.	4083
Anderson, Robert E.	3258	Anspach, Leo	14
Anderson, Pearl	3259	Anspach, Mary E.	6
Anderson, Charles	3260	Anspach, Ruth A.	13
Anderson, Samuel	3261	Antoine, George K.	28213
Anderson, Delilah	3262	Antoine, James W.	28209
Anderson, Lorenzo D.	3263	Antoine, Joseph M.	28210
Anderson, John W.	3264	Antoine, Olive	28175
Anderson, Emma	3265	Antoine, Sarah E.	28174
Anderson, Ella M.	3266	Antoine, William C.	28211
Anderson, Minnie B.	4586	Archer, John R.	273
Anderson, Cynthia C.	4587	Archer, Mary F.	6679
Anderson, Louisa	4605	Archer, Anna B.	8162
Anderson, John D.	4606	Archer, Ina	8163
Anderson, William M.	4607	Archer, Otto	8164
Anderson, Joseph E.	4608	Archer, Fannie B.	8165
Anderson, Mark	4609	Archer, John W.	11581
Anderson, Fannie	4610	Archer, Mattie E.	11582
Anderson, Ida Lee	4611	Archer, John E.	11583
Anderson, Nancy M.	4897	Archer, Robert V.	11584
Anderson, Ora J.	4898	Archer, Leroy	11585
Anderson, John F.	4899	Archer, Thomas J.	11586
Anderson, Maude A.	4900	Archer, Mabel G.	11904
Anderson, Susan	4901	Archer, James V.	11905
Anderson, Mary P.	4902	Archer, Georgia J.	11906
Anderson, Theodora	4903	Archer, Annie	18813
Anderson, Henry M.	4904	Archer, Florence	24703
Anderson, Jesse M.	4905	Archer, Carlotta	26423
Anderson, William C.	4006	Arch, Steve	21131
Anderson, Jessie A.	8063	Arch, Elgin	21132
Anderson, Ray Charles	8064	Arch, Ella	27508
Anderson, Mabel W.	8191	Arch, Minnie	27509
Anderson, Gladys M.	8192	Arch, Eyahni	32644
Anderson, Helen R.	8193	Archilla, Jennie	27596
Anderson, Preston R.	8194	Arch, Polly	32645
Anderson, Amanda	10421	Arch, Sallie	32646
Anderson, Neven T.	10422	Arch, Sam	32647
Anderson, Lillian E.	15867	Arch, Sahhoya	32751
Anderson, Julia E.	15868	Arledge, John	6780
Anderson, Ada D.	15869	Arledge, Maude	28098
Anderson, William B.	16585	Armor, Cynthia A.	7283

Name.	Roll No.
Armor, Daisy L.	7284
Armor, James O.	7287
Armor, Myrtle P.	7286
Armor, Norma O.	7285
Armstrong, Richard A.	7530
Armstrong, Thomas F.	16782
Armstrong, Mary E.	21635
Armstrong, Harold S.	21636
Armstrong, Carrie P.	24349
Armstrong, Albert H.	25039
Armstrong, John	28718
Armstrong, Flora D.	30913
Armstrong, Carroll McT.	30914
Armstrong, William L.	30915
Armstrong, Henry	31088
Armstrong, Minnie B.	31089
Armstrong, Nettie M.	31090
Armstrong, Lucinda	31091
Armstrong, Rosalie	31152
Armstrong, Myrtle R.	31460
Armstrong, Ruby D.	31461
Armstrong, Henry F.	31476
Armstrong, John L.	31477
Armstrong, Mary V.	31478
Armstrong, Charles F.	31498
Armstrong, Violet	31542
Arnold, Victoria	13188
Arnold, Myrtle	13189
Arnold, Isaac C.	13190
Arnold, George W.	13191
Arnold, Mary	13192
Arnold, Herbert	13193
Arnold, Halbert	13194
Arnold, Joseph	13195
Arnold, Sallie L.	13196
Arnold, William	16101
Arnold, Lucy	16186
Arnold, Nancy	16187
Arnhart, Mariah J.	22259
Arnhart, Oowala C.	22260
Ar-nee-cher, John	25622
Ar-nee-cher, Elsie	25623
Ar-nee-cher, Levi	25624
Ar-nee-cher, Fannie	25625
Ar-nee-cher, Jacob	30519
Ar-nee-cher, Bud	30520
Arrowood, Goldie B.	6457
Arrowood, Mertie P.	6453
Arrington, Myrtle M.	8196
Arrow, Cheledia	19822
Arrow, William	19821
Arterberry, Mary A.	29454
Arterberry, Porter W.	29455
Arwood, Cornelia C.	12969
Arwood, John A.	12971
Ashley, Amy M.	5017
Ashley, Ora B.	5016
Ashley, Texas R.	5011
Ashes, Buck	25441
Ashes, John	25437
Ashes, Joseph	25440
Ashes, Martha	25439
Ashes, Sarah	25438
Atchison, Sarah A. I.	7499
Athey, Lizzie K.	7666
Atkins, Arthur	31744
Atkins, Edna E.	31745
Atkins, Edward C.	31746
Atkins, George J. F.	31747
Atkins, Lizzie	31743
Atkisson, Bertha B.	31431
Audrain, Anna C.	9985
Audrain, Charles L.	570
Audrain, Clyde W.	567
Audrain, Eliza J.	564
Audrain, Francis C.	566
Audrain, Frank G.	9982
Audrain, Frank G.	9987
Audrain, James R.	9988
Audrain, John P.	9990
Audrain, Maggie D.	9989
Audrain, Maggie F.	555

Name.	Roll No.
Audrain, Mamie I.	9986
Audrain, Melissa	9983
Audrain, Ralph R.	9984
Audrain, Richard O.	568
Audrain, Winfield S.	563
Audrain, Scott R.	569
Augerhole, Betsy	18922
Augerhole, Eli	32304
Augerhole, Hattie B.	4657
Augerhole, Lydia	4659
Augerhole, William W.	4658
Austin, Charles	21977
Austin, Josie	3858
Austin, Lizzie	3856
Austin, Malinda	3855
Austin, Minnie	3857
Austin, Sevolia	21979
Austin, Walter	21978
Austin, William	3860
Austin, Zerilda	21980
Austin, Zula	21976
Autry, Mary C.	30078
Avant, Artie May	30733
Avant, George W. T.	30731
Avant, Mary M.	30732
Avant, Troy M.	30734
Ayers, Alice	4493
Ayers, Nannie	28608
Ayers, Virginia	4492
Backbone, Calvin	5527
Backbone, Daniel	6165
Backbone, Lydia	21159
Backbone, Polly	6286
Backman, William	17071
Backward, Daniel	18161
Backward, Nellie	18162
Backward, Evans	18163
Backward, Sampson	18164
Backward, Ada	18165
Backward, Eli	32866
Backwater, John	19786
Backwater, Lizzie	19787
Backwater, Susie	19788
Backwater, William	19789
Backwater, Nannie	19790
Backwater, Katie	19791
Backwater, Betsy	25205
Backwater, Sarah	29035
Backwater, Joe	29892
Backwater, Lizzie	29893
Backwater, Nancy	29894
Backwater, Ball	29895
Backwater, Oo-ya-hu-shy	29896
Backwater, Susan	29898
Backwater, Laura	30457
Backwater, Katie	30458
Backwater, Nooyah	30580
Bachtel, Mary J.	7357
Bachtel, Daniel L.	7358
Bachtel, Otis	7359
Bachtel, Elzy	7360
Bacon, Thomas S.	8987
Bacon, Bernice M.	11679
Bacon, William D.	12144
Bacon, John L.	12145
Bacon, Charley B.	12146
Bacon, John H.	13646
Bacon, Treesy P.	13647
Badger, Lillie	14738
Badger, Emiline	14739
Badgett, George M.	24165
Badgett, Mary	24164
Badgett, William R.	24163
Baggett, Pearl	28545
Baggett, Julia	28546
Baggett, Pearl E.	28547
Baggett, Gracie	28548
Baggett, Daisy	28549
Bailey, John H.	8853
Bailey, Lula A.	8854
Bailey, Matilda A.	8855
Bailey, Sarah A.	8856

Name.	Roll No.	Name.	Roll No.
Bailey, Franklin E.	8857	Baldridge, Inis M.	6278
Bailey, Hazel J.	8858	Baldridge, Mike	6301
Bailey, Benjamin L.	12896	Baldridge, Lucy	6302
Bailey, Hiram	12897	Baldridge, Blue	17480
Bailey, George F.	17514	Baldridge, Betsy	17481
Bailey, Sarah E.	17515	Buldridge, George	18985
Bailey, Elizabeth D.	17516	Baldridge, Alice	18986
Bailey, George A.	17517	Baldridge, Albert	18987
Bailey, Jennie L.	17518	Baldridge, Jim	18988
Bailey, Samuel M.	17519	Baldridge, Dick	20552
Bailey, Josephine E.	17520	Baldridge, Naki	20553
Bailey, Sallie E.	17521	Baldridge, Jack	20554
Bailey, Charley	17977	Baldridge, William	20555
Bailey, Jennie	17978	Baldridge, Anleach	20556
Bailey, George	19637	Baldridge, Sequoyah	20557
Bailey, Nannie	19638	Baldridge, Susie	21141
Bailey, Polly	20112	Baldridge, Coleston	21604
Bailey, Steve	20113	Baldridge, Lelia	21605
Bailey, Malinda A.	27416	Baldridge, Richard	25696
Bailey, Amanda W.	27417	Baldridge, Jennie	25697
Bailey, John C.	27418	Baldridge, James B.	29312
Bailey, Frances A.	27419	Baldridge, Will	29313
Baird, Susie	9961	Baldridge, Charley	29314
Baird, Neva L.	9962	Baldridge, Charles	30117
Baird, Jettie I.	9963	Baldridge, Johnson	30118
Baker, Bertha E.	444	Balew, Susan	6272
Baker, Thomas Porter	445	Balew, Callie	6273
Baker, Gladdes	447	Balew, Jennie	6274
Baker, Luella	4872	Balew, Jack	17611
Baker, Maggie M.	6772	Balch, Charlotte	10430
Baker, Ollie J.	6773	Ballard, William	468
Baker, John O.	6774	Ballard, Charlotte	469
Baker, Odessa M.	6775	Ballard, Jane Anna	470
Baker, Eliza	7288	Ballard, Lucinda	472
Baker, Freddie E.	7289	Ballard, William H.	473
Baker, Etta M.	7290	Ballard, Ruth	474
Baker, Sallie E.	7769	Ballard, Ethel	475
Baker, Millie L.	7770	Ballard, Zo	476
Baker, Mabel	7771	Ballard, Sarah	477
Baker, Eva P.	7772	Ballard, Arch	2910
Baker, Effie M.	7773	Ballard, William R.	2911
Baker, Mary A.	8204	Ballard, Thomas	2912
Baker, Melissa E.	8205	Ballard, Ruth	4283
Baker, Myrtle E.	8206	Ballard, Mary M.	4287
Baker, Pauline	8207	Ballard, Brice	5466
Baker, Josephine	9056	Ballard, Jessie	5758
Baker, Lee M.	9057	Ballard, Sarah	7303
Baker, William L.	9058	Ballard, Barney F.	7335
Baker, Calvin	9059	Ballard, Edna P.	7336
Baker, Bertha H.	9064	Ballard, Nellie G.	7337
Baker, Hattie L.	9065	Ballard, Eva M.	7338
Baker, Susie J.	17224	Ballard, Henry C.	7588
Baker, Elizabeth	24919	Ballard, Nancy A.	7589
Baker, Webster C.	24921	Ballard, Evelyn J.	7590
Baker, Maud	26801	Ballard, Mabel L.	7591
Baker, Goldie M.	26802	Ballard, James Q.	7592
Baker, Mary	31012	Ballard, Thomas H.	7593
Baker, Sarah Ellen	31018	Ballard, Randolph	8575
Baldridge, George W.	3527	Ballard, Miriam	8576
Baldridge, Nannie	3528	Ballard, Robert A.	8577
Baldridge, Lucy J.	3529	Ballard, James R.	8578
Baldridge, Rosie Ann	3530	Ballard, John W.	8579
Baldridge, Ada	3531	Ballard, Claude R.	8580
Baldridge, William	3532	Ballard, George B.	8581
Baldridge, Floyd E.	3533	Ballard, Joseph M.	8582
Baldridge, Mary	3534	Ballard, Thomas	8792
Baldridge, Blueford	3535	Ballard, Jesse L.	8793
Baldridge, George	3536	Ballard, Willie A.	8794
Baldridge, Eliza Jane	3537	Ballard, Lula A.	8795
Baldridge, Della E.	3538	Ballard, Archable L.	8989
Baldridge, Mike Jr.	26409	Ballard, Tuxy	15131
Baldridge, Columbus	4764	Ballard, Mary	15132
Baldridge, Nancy	4765	Ballard, Alexander	15133
Baldridge, Cora	4766	Ballard, Elias	15134
Baldridge, Joseph	4767	Ballard, DeWitt	15135
Baldridge, Belle	4768	Ballard, Maybelle	15136
Baldridge, Nelson	4769	Ballard, George	15137
Baldridge, Takie	4770	Ballard, Jack	15138
Baldridge, Maggie	5303	Ballard, Percy P.	18314
Baldridge, Johnson	5341	Ballard, Adoh B.	15834
Baldridge, James	5719	Ballard, Harlin E.	15835
Baldridge, Archilla	6276	Ballard, Forest Abrain	15836
Baldridge, Swimmer	6277	Ballard, Cynthia E.	16375

Name.	Roll No.	Name.	Roll No.
Ballard, Ella Mae	16376	Bankhead, Eddie J.	10922
Ballard, William	16774	Bannon, Delilah	16890
Ballard, Sallie	16775	Banty, Cornelius	18738
Ballard, Thomas H.	16776	Banty, Fannie	30467
Ballard, John J.	16777	Banty, Looney	30468
Ballard, Carrie M.	16778	Banty, Lila	30469
Ballard, Donald L.	16779	Barker, George H.	31050
Ballard, Sarah J.	16950	Barker, Henry J.	31051
Ballard, Mary I.	16951	Barker, Fred A.	31052
Ballard, Malinda A. E.	22931	Barker, Effie	31053
Ballard, James F.	23488	Barker, Elmer	31054
Ballard, Henry T.	23489	Barker, Arthur	31055
Ballard, John C.	23490	Barker, Curtis	31056
Ballard, William H.	27802	Barker, Herbert	31057
Ballard, Wenona L.	27803	Barker, Ona	31058
Ballard, George W.	28697	Barker, William H.	4534
Ballard, William M.	28884	Barker, Mary A.	10061
Ballard, Daisy B.	28885	Barker, Josephine G.	10062
Ballard, Johnnie A.	30139	Barker, Ethel Goldie	10063
Ballard, Stella L.	30140	Barker, Eva	10064
Ballard, Goldie	30880	Barker, Sequoyah	10065
Ballard, DeAuburn	30881	Barker, Artemus B.	10066
Ballard, Guy R.	30882	Barker, Dennis A.	10067
Ball, James T.	10991	Barker, Anna E.	10068
Ball, Lydia J.	10992	Barker, Emaline	10111
Ball, William E.	10993	Barker, Mary A.	10112
Ball, Lucy	10994	Barker, Ollie T.	10997
Balentine, William H.	5681	Barker, William E.	10998
Balentine, Mary D.	5682	Barker, Goldie M.	13870
Balentine, William H.		Barker, Charles	17213
Jr.	5684	Barker, Susie	17214
Balentine, Annie M.	5685	Barker, Joseph	17215
Balentine, Mary E.	7330	Barker, Emma	17216
Balentine, Mary E.	7331	Barker, Rosa B.	29610
Balentine, Ellen S.	7332	Barnett, Frank M.	448
Balentine, Perry P.	14124	Barker, Jennie	29151
Balentine, Johnanna	14125	Barnett, Jessie Lee	449
Ballenger, Ida L.	7678	Barnett, Kinnie L.	450
Ballenger, Alma L.	7679	Barnett, Georgia Ellen	451
Ballinger, Julia A.	8640	Barnett, Edward	640
Ballinger, Mary E.	8641	Barnett, Ida S.	641
Ballinger, Achillis W.	8642	Barnett, Lula A.	642
Ballinger, Dewey H.	8643	Barnett, Frank Edward	643
Ballinger, Opal	8644	Barnett, Charles G., Jr.	4015
Ballou, Jefferson	8765	Barnett, Alman	4582
Ballou, George	15744	Barnett, Robert P.	4583
Ballou, Tom	20716	Barnett, Mabel	8060
Ballou, Sallie	20717	Barnett, Henry	13559
Ballou, Sam	20719	Barnett, George W.	14329
Ballou, Lizzie	20720	Barnett, Julia A.	15792
Ballou, Bird	20721	Barnett, Robert E.	15793
Ballou, Tom	20722	Barnett, James W.	16126
Ballou, Nelson	25901	Barnett, Iva May	16127
Ballou, Peter	25902	Barnett, Ida R.	16128
Ballou, Annie	30631	Barnett, Cora	16129
Ballew, Josie	30365	Barnett, George	16900
Ballew, Thomas J.	30366	Barnett, Benjamin	16901
Ballew, Ada B.	30367	Barnett, John	16902
Ballew, William Freder-		Barnett, Jesse	16903
ick	30368	Barnett, Joel	28136
Balloue, John	21326	Barnett, Laura B.	31485
Balloue, Vinnie	21327	Barnett, Cornelious O.	31486
Balloue, Charlie	21328	Barnett, Robert T.	31487
Balloue, James	25986	Barnet, Nora Mabel	4584
Balloue, Alice	25987	Barnet, Mary	31232
Balloue, Joe	25988	Barnes, Charlie	3064
Balridge, Rachel	4020	Barnes, Bonnie	3065
Balridge, Emma	4021	Barrick, David A.	3142
Bandy, Martha E.	304	Barrick, Emma J.	3143
Bandy, Jasper R.	305	Barrick, Emaline	2637
Bandy, George H.	306	Barrick, Marion F.	18053
Bankhead, John T.	13404	Barrow, Jennie	3483
Bankhead, Eunice A.	13405	Barrow, Lillie A.	3484
Bankhead, Joel T.	13406	Barrow, Ida H.	3485
Bankhead, John H.	13407	Barrow, James H.	3486
Bankhead, Clara M.	13408	Barrow, Mary E.	3487
Bankhead, Frank G.	13449	Barrow, Cicero	3488
Bankhead, George W.	10916	Barr, Tottie	252
Bankhead, Trader	10917	Barr, Susan L.	10750
Bankhead, John	10918	Barr, Ada F.	29219
Bankhead, Charles	10919	Barr, James William	29220
Bankhead, Susan	10920	Barry, Lizzie A.	2542
Bankhead, Late	10921	Barry, Clyde	2543

Name.	Roll No.	Name.	Roll No.
Barry, Clarina	2544	Barnes, Vivian N.	22752
Barry, Billie B.	2545	Barnes, Curtis	22753
Barry, Stella M.	2546	Barnes, Katie	22754
Barry, Ralph L.	21583	Barnes, Agnes	26938
Barrett, Lee	8221	Barnes, Servetus B.	26939
Barrett, Lizzie	8222	Barnes, George D.	26940
Barrett, Mary	8223	Barnes, Oscar E.	26941
Barrett, Alice B.	8224	Barnes, Hiram	27388
Barrett, Ella W.	8685	Barnes, Wenona	27389
Barrett, Edgar P.	8686	Barnes, Charles	27390
Barrett, Vida	8687	Barnes, Jane	27391
Barrett, George	8688	Barnes, Cornelius	27392
Barrett, Carl	8689	Barnes, Oscar	27393
Barrett, Earl	8690	Barnes, Clinton	27394
Barrett, Robert Byron	8691	Barnes, Beulah	27395
Barrett, Saphronia W.	11501	Barnes, Mary M.	29318
Barrett, John C.	11178	Barnes, Lucy W.	29319
Barrett, Victoria S.	11179	Barnes, Sadie E.	29320
Barrett, Flavius L.	11180	Barke, Martha A.	3380
Barrett, Bessie	27585	Barke, Louella	26344
Barthel, Annie	5335	Barke, William D.	30056
Barthel, Frank Jr.	5336	Barlow, Julius	12206
Barthel, Mamie	5337	Barlow, Maggie	12207
Barthel, William W.	5338	Barlow, Clarance	12208
Barks, Victoria	7867	Barlow, John M.	22146
Barks, Willie H.	7868	Barritt, Susie H.	12680
Barks, Grace E.	7869	Barritt, Emery L.	12681
Barton, Cynthia	8495	Barritt, Archie E.	12682
Barton, Mary V.	10038	Barney, Minnie	12970
Barton, Edwin H.	10039	Barney, Jessie I.	12972
Bard, Laura M.	11877	Barney, Felix	13315
Bard, Emily L.	11878	Barger, Agnes	13453
Bard, Robert B.	11879	Barger, Bessie	13454
Bard, Elizabeth H.	12154	Barger, Carl	13455
Bard, Sarah B.	12155	Barger, William E.	21652
Bard, Laura M.	12156	Barger, John W.	21660
Bard, Thomas D., Jr.	12157	Barger, Elizabeth	21661
Barnard, Emma W.	8929	Barger, Myrtle C.	21662
Barnard, James W.	8930	Barger, Joseph F.	21892
Barbee, John	9094	Barger, Maggie C.	21893
Barbee, Othie	9095	Barger, Emma Minnie	21894
Barbee, Claud	9096	Barger, Charley W.	26015
Barbee, Wiliam	9097	Barger, Annie C.	26016
Barbee, Fleetie	9098	Barger, Samuel R.	26017
Barnes, Turner	3146	Barger, Lillie F.	26018
Barnes, Samuel	3147	Barger, Samuel F.	32236
Barnes, Dora L.	3822	Barger, Esta May	32237
Barnes, Etta M.	3823	Barger, Bessie Irene	32238
Barnes, William L.	3824	Barger, Gilbert Elton	32239
Barnes, Joseph D.	3825	Barger, Roy Franklin	32240
Barnes, Ethel M.	3826	Barger, Lula A.	32241
Barnes, Pearl	3828	Barber, David	16955
Barnes, James	5453	Barber, Maud	16956
Barnes, Mattie M.	5454	Barber, Johnson	17158
Barnes, Myrtle L.	5455	Barber, Jennie	17159
Barnes, Jennie E.	5456	Barber, Cherokee M.	26107
Barnes, Argonia	5457	Barber, Josephine	28498
Barnes, Thomas F.	5458	Bark, Andrew	18199
Barnes, Emma	5459	Bark, Nannie	18200
Barnes, Vertie	5460	Bark, Webster	18201
Barnes, William A.	5461	Bark, Looney	18202
Barnes, Alexander	5605	Bark, Lizzie	18203
Barnes, Martha	5606	Bark, Robert	18225
Barnes, Nancy B.	5607	Bark, George W.	18565
Barnes, Antonia	5608	Bark, David	19662
Barnes, Mary L.	5609	Bark, John	21169
Barnes, Malinda	5610	Bark, Lizzie	21170
Barnes, John T.	12887	Bark, Richard	21171
Barnes, Ellis	12888	Bark, Joseph Lee	21172
Barnes, Elby E.	12889	Bark, Nancy Jane	21173
Barnes, Alexander	12890	Bark, Daisy	21174
Barnes, Basheba	12891	Bark, Scrub	27495
Barnes, Mary E.	12892	Bark, Samuel	27496
Barnes, Clem	12893	Bark, Eliza	29039
Barnes, Maud L.	508	Bark, Mary	30493
Barnes, John T., Jr.	12894	Bark, Willie	30687
Barnes, Rachel C.	13863	Bark, Eliza	32074
Barnes, Henry C.	14011	Bark, Suday	32269
Barnes, Henry N.	14012	Bark, Celia	32270
Barnes, Robert O.	14013	Barehead, Peter	19797
Barnes, Jennie	15326	Barehead, Sarah	19798
Barnes, Eliza	22750	Barnoskie, Cat	21062
Barnes, Alfred F.	22751	Barnoskie, Sutteer	21063

Name.	Roll No.	Name.	Roll No.
Barnoskie, Simerheetly	21064	Baugh, Roscoe R.	9176
Barnoskie, Conseen	21065	Baugh, Edgar	9177
Barnoskie, Jennie	21067	Baugh, Robert L.	23396
Barnoskie, Linda	21068	Baugh, Robert L., Jr.	23398
Barnoskie, Clawyasta	25921	Baugh, Rebecca E.	23399
Barnwell, Elizabeth	21524	Bazzell, Mittie A.	7749
Barnwell, Stephen E.	21525	Bazzell, Clarence	7750
Barnwell, Middleton S.	21526	Bazzell, Jessie	7751
Barnwell, Carleton	21527	Bean, Nancy J.	1352
Bartles, Joseph A.	32224	Bean, Charles	1674
Bartles, Nannie M.	32531	Bean, Sam	1675
Barndollar, Nonie	32733	Bean, Pearl	1676
Barndollar, Pratt	32226	Bean, Mack	1677
Baskins, Rachel	25883	Bean, Kate	1678
Baskins, Annie Augusta	25884	Bean, Lee	1679
Bass, Josie G.	30256	Bean, George P.	1680
Bass, Robert M.	30257	Bean, John M.	1756
Batt, Jack	1793	Bean, Nannie E.	1757
Batt, Lucy	1794	Bean, Sarah Z.	1758
Batt, Moses	1795	Bean, Ruth A.	1759
Batt, Charles	1796	Bean, Mary L.	1760
Batt, John	1801	Bean, Jennie A.	1761
Batt, Mary	1802	Bean, Thomas H.	1762
Batt, Joe	2010	Bean, Jessie B.	1763
Batt, Charley	2572	Bean, John A.	1764
Batt, Jane A.	2573	Bean, Mark	1850
Batt, Eliza	15216	Bean, Rachel A.	2224
Batt, Daniel	15217	Bean, Edgar	2517
Batt, Ned	17724	Bean, Mark	2518
Batt, Flora	17725	Bean, Susan	5591
Batt, Emma	17726	Bean, Ellen	5600
Batt, Benjamin	17727	Bean, Walter	6882
Batt, Adam	17728	Bean, Joseph	6883
Batt, Ruth	17729	Beasly, Ida Q.	3124
Batt, Akie	18912	Beasly, Quesenbury	3125
Batt, Nannie	19097	Bearpaw, Samuel	3968
Batt, Isaac	27111	Bean, Carl	6884
Batt, Mary E.	27112	Bean, Alice	6885
Batt, Eva C.	27113	Beatty, Charles L.	8479
Batt, Annie	27958	Beatty, Ida	8746
Bateman, Jasper N., Jr.	2802	Beaver, Runaway	8900
Bateman, Liddy	2803	Beaver, Emma	8901
Bateman, John	2804	Beaver, Isaac	8902
Batie, Emaline	5041	Beaver, Mary	9864
Battenfield, Lillie	5384	Bear, Frank	9865
Battenfield, LaVanch	5385	Bear, Cleveland	9866
Bates, Paulinia	644	Beavers, Sarah M.	11297
Bates, Charles A.	645	Bean, Edward R.	11491
Bates, Josephine	647	Bean, Tooyah	11653
Bates, Herbert G.	648	Bean, Bryant W.	11754
Bates, Mollie	26850	Bean, Henrietta	11755
Bates, Fannie	26853	Bean, Lucy J.	11756
Bates, Beulah	26854	Bean, Nannie	11757
Batey, Robert S.	12963	Beard, Beulah M.	12424
Bat, Eli	15014	Beattie, Samuel	13836
Bat, Emily	15015	Bean, Fannie R.	14145
Bat, Susan	15016	Beavert, Thomas E.	14792
Bat, Ellis	15604	Beavert, Mary L.	14793
Bat, Susie	15605	Beavert, Lillie	14794
Bat, Jack	15606	Beavert, Alice	14795
Bat, Sarah	15607	Beavert, Jennie	14796
Bat, James	15608	Beavert, Jefferson	14797
Bat, Jennie	15609	Beavert, Charlotte	14798
Bat, Josiah	19738	Beavert, Eloise	14799
Bat, Betsy	29046	Beavert, Henrietta	14800
Battie, Robert	15029	Bean, Robert B.	14806
Battie, William	29941	Bean, Phenia	14807
Battie, Wilborn	29942	Bean, William M.	14809
Battie, Elias	29943	Bean, Robert B., Jr.	14810
Battie, Willie	29944	Bean, Hulbert	14852
Battie, Jennie E.	29946	Bean, Elizabeth	14853
Batson, Beulah L.	21949	Bean, Mary D.	14854
Battles, Emily J.	30743	Bean, John W.	15428
Battles, Laura	32793	Bean, Richard D.	15429
Battles, Lax	32794	Beavers, Wyly	15646
Battles, Addie	32795	Bean, Mary	16428
Battles, Zeb	32796	Bean, Sallie	16429
Battles, Willie	32797	Bean, Walter	16430
Baughman, Temperance	1647	Bean, Jeff	16431
Baugh, Nannie S.	5390	Bean, John	16432
Baugh, Joel L.	9173	Bean, Mary E.	16433
Baugh, Charlotte	9174	Bean, Russell A.	17121
Baugh, Joel L., Jr.	9175	Bean, Mary E.	18027

Name.	Roll No.	Name.	Roll No.
Beargrease, Ellen	18047	Beavers, Ella I.	21531
Beamer, John W.	18095	Bean, Sarah A.	21566
Beamer, Alice	18096	Beane, Mark A.	23184
Beavers, Tom	18227	Bean, Nannie	23259
Beavers, Lucy	18228	Beatty, Bessie	24772
Beavers, Rabbit	18229	Beatty, Maud	24773
Beavers, Cherry	18230	Beamer, Lydia	25119
Beavers, Mary	18231	Beamer, Ora	25120
Beamer, Lucy	18239	Beamer, William	25121
Beamer, James	18242	Beamer, Rosa	25122
Beamer, Lewis	18393	Beaver, Daniel	25334
Beamer, Alice	18394	Beaver, Susan	25335
Beamer, Louanna	18395	Bearpaw, Nellie	25767
Beamer, Emiline	18396	Bearpaw, Salcy	25784
Beamer, Ada	18397	Bearpaw, Charles	25845
Beamer, George	18398	Bearpaw, Jennie	25846
Beamer, Nancy	18409	Bean, Joseph S.	26141
Beamer, Sam	18962	Bean, Albert	26142
Beanstick, Charley	19236	Bean, Mark	26143
Beanstick, Susie	19237	Bean, Ruby	26144
Bean, Edna E.	19289	Bean, Dennis B.	26145
Bean, Everette A.	19290	Beaver, Lucy	26154
Bearpaw, Culstiah	19548	Beaver, Grant	26180
Beaver, Washington	19572	Beaver, Katie	26181
Beaver, James	19585	Beaver, William	26182
Beaver, George	19586	Beaver, James	26183
Beaver, Otto	19587	Beaver, Cah-la-te	26184
Beaver, Charlotte	19588	Beaver, Jennie	26185
Beaver, Lilly	19589	Beaver, Cloud	26186
Bear, Lewis	19624	Bean, Etta L.	26668
Bear, Nancy	19625	Bean, Eliza E.	26669
Bear, Simon	19626	Bean, Lorena	26670
Bear, Oscar	19627	Bean, Tot	26671
Bear, Polly	19628	Bean, Dot	26672
Bear, Johnson	19629	Bean, William P.	26673
Bear, Conseen	19630	Bean, Jesse E.	26674
Bearpaw, Daniel	19632	Bearpaw, Dave	27501
Beaver, William	19792	Bean, Adam	28469
Beaver, Josie	19793	Beanstick, Sut	29095
Bearpaw, Charles	19850	Beanstick, Dicie	29096
Bearpaw, Addie	19851	Beanstick, Sarah	29097
Bearpaw, Lugie	19852	Beanstick, Huston	29098
Bearpaw, James	19877	Bean, Jack	29708
Bearpaw, Annie	19878	Bean, Susie	29709
Beaver, Clem	19951	Beane, Thomas A.	29905
Beaver, Sallie	19952	Beamer, John	30025
Beaver, Steve	19953	Beamer, Sarah J.	30026
Beaver, Cindy	19954	Beamer, Pearlie B.	30027
Bean, Raven	20106	Beamer, Oliver C.	30028
Bean, Nannie	20114	Beamer, Lou	30029
Bearpaw, Sargiyah	20133	Beamer, Nancy	30030
Bearpaw, Polly	20207	Beamer, Lee F.	30031
Bearpaw, Johnson	20208	Beavers, Alsie	30465
Bearpaw, Sally	20209	Beavers, Jim	30466
Beaver, Mohawk	20220	Bean, Joe	30478
Beaver, Martha	20221	Bean, Susannah	30479
Beaver, Lesley	20222	Bean, Nancy	30480
Beaver, Tarnie	20223	Bean, John	30481
Beaver, Annie	20224	Bean, Will	30482
Beaver, Arleacher	20225	Bean, Ollie	30483
Beanstick, John	20237	Bean, Sallie	30484
Bean, Thompson	20259	Bean, Coh-tah-ne	30708
Bearpaw, Celia	20289	Beaver, Ollie	31170
Bearpaw, Cul	20280	Beaver, Dalton	31171
Bean, Hail	20316	Beaubien, Susie A.	31366
Bean, Betsy	20317	Beaubien, Laura M.	31367
Bear, George	20331	Beaubien, Arthur W.	31368
Beamer, William	20346	Beaubien, Robert E.	31369
Beanstick, Peggie	20420	Beaubien, Lula M.	31370
Bearpaw, Nancy	20496	Beaubien, James W.	31371
Beanstick, Wuttie	20502	Beaver, Donnie	31411
Beanstick, Becky	20505	Beaver, Frank	31312
Beaver, Susie	20512	Beaver, Alonzo	31413
Beaver, Creek	20544	Beaver, Betsie	32516
Beaver, Jennie	20545	Beatty, William T.	31953
Beaver, Annie	20547	Beavers, Willie	31963
Beaver, Eliza	20548	Beartoater, Davis	32045
Beaver, Dora	20549	Beck, Sabra	1253
Beaver, Samuel	20550	Beck, Weatherford	1254
Beaver, Maggie	20551	Beck, Eula	1255
Beaver, William	20700	Beck, Guy	1256
Bearpaw, Isaac	20702	Beck, Tony A.	1274
Beaver, Charlie	20743	Beck, Sarah A.	1275
Bean, Jim	21257	Beck, Aaron H.	1276
Bean, Elsie	21407		
Beavers, Susan L.	21530		

Name.	Roll No.	Name.	Roll No.
Beck, Josephine	1277	Beck, Joe	25144
Beck, Richard	1310	Beck, Jessie	25145
Beck, Ida A.	1311	Beck, Ada P.	25146
Beck, Roy L.	1312	Beck, Harvey M.	27844
Beck, Maggie M.	1313	Beck, Gertrude B.	27845
Beck, Eddie A.	1315	Beck, Walter R.	27846
Beck, William	5715	Beck, William A.	27847
Beck, Dora	5716	Beck, Stella M.	27848
Beck, Amy	5717	Beck, Joseph	28551
Beck, Ezekiel	6421	Beck, Jeffrey	25552
Beck, Jesse	6422	Beck, Harling	28553
Beck, Thomas J.	6424	Beck, Samuel	28554
Beck, Irena	6425	Beck, John	28555
Beck, James	6426	Beck, John	28886
Beck, Cogin	6427	Beck, Ida	28887
Beck, Samuel	6428	Beck, Ezekiel	28888
Beck, Sallie	6423	Beck, George	28889
Beck, Vivia	6430	Beck, Sabra E.	28890
Beck, Maud	6429	Beck, Cherry M.	28891
Beck, Lucian	6431	Beck, Klon L.	30438
Beck, Macy	6432	Beck, Frederick	32687
Beck, Oren	6499	Beets, Augusta	8871
Beck, Letha	6500	Beets, Bertha	8872
Beck, William A.	7465	Beets, Everett R.	8873
Beck, Robert	7716	Beets, Wesley E.	8874
Beck, Henry	7745	Beeson, Edward B.	26220
Beck, Robert	7746	Beeson, John E.	30932
Beck, Sarah	7851	Bee, Julia A.	30405
Beck, Louisa	8096	Bee, Mary	30409
Beck, Thomas	8099	Beeson, Mary F.	30931
Beck, Tecumseh	8100	Beeson, Perry H.	21682
Beck, Lillie B.	9161	Bee, Willora C. J.	30408
Beck, Susan E.	10032	Beffa, Sarah A.	10277
Beck, Lula B.	10033	Bell, Lizzie	891
Beck, Daniel S.	10034	Bell, Hooley	892
Beck, Rufus S.	10035	Bell, Minerva	3490
Beck, Grace P.	10036	Bell, Margaret O.	3491
Beck, John W.	12101	Bell, Triphenia	5481
Beck, Cynthia	12102	Bell, George W.	6690
Beck, Jessie B.	12103	Bell, Lucian B.	8673
Beck, John B.	12104	Bell, Mary F.	8674
Beck, David M.	13078	Bell, MattieM.	10976
Beck, Osborn A.	13079	Bell, Daniel H.	10977
Beck, Wesley C.	13080	Bell, James E., Jr.	10978
Beck, David M., Jr.	13081	Bell, Pearl	10979
Beck, Martha A.	13082	Bell, Mark R.	10980
Beck, Walter F.	13083	Bell, Robert H.	12643
Beck, George L.	13084	Bell, Mattie J.	12874
Beck, Ellis	13085	Bell, Toka J.	12876
Beck, Maud M.	13086	Bell, Martin	12994
Beck, Susie	13087	Bell, Minnie C.	12995
Beck, Lucy	13088	Bell, Emma W.	12996
Beck, Charles M.	13280	Bell, Ida L.	12997
Beck, Carrie	13281	Bell, Andrew L.	12998
Beck, Belle D.	13282	Bell, Ella	12999
Beck, William F.	13593	Bell, Martin W.	13000
Beck, William P.	14095	Bell, Fortner D.	13001
Beck, Joseph	14096	Bell, George M.	13002
Beck, Susie	14097	Bell, Tilden	16149
Beck, John	16333	Bell, Elizabeth	16150
Beck, Malinda J.	17315	Bell, Pearl	16152
Beck, Isaac C.	17316	Bell, James M.	16814
Beck, James T.	17329	Bell, Sherman	17949
Beck, Eliza	17330	Bell, Samuel	18460
Beck, Claude	17331	Bell, Lizzie	18461
Beck, Malinda	17332	Belt, Stan	18492
Beck, Nannie	17333	Belt, Thomas	18629
Beck. Homer	17334	Belt, Mary	18630
Beck, Chessie	18137	Belt, Lydia	18631
Beck, John H.	22477	Belt, Cooweescoowee	18632
Beck, Lora	23842	Bell, Stephen C.	20029
Beck, Cornelius	23843	Bell, Jennie	20030
Beck, Albert	23844	Bell, Charlotte	20043
Beck, Sina	23845	Belt, Col-lee-sowee	25594
Beck, Ida	23846	Belt, Lee	25595
Beck, Mary E.	23847	Bell, Iola M.	28127
Beck, William H.	23848	Bell, Raymond B.	28128
Beck, Dewey	23849	Bell, Henry C.	28129
Beck, Oscar	23850	Bell, Nellie	28130
Beck, Rutherford	25140	Bell, Willard	28131
Beck, Homer	25141	Bell, Minnie R.	28766
Beck, Stella	25142	Bell, Alfred E.	28767
Beck, Ary	25143	Bell, Laura P.	28768

Name.	Roll No.	Name.	Roll No.
Bell, Lorena	28769	Bennett, Annie L.	12829
Bell, William	30318	Bennett, Winston G.	12830
Bell, Frances	30320	Bennett, Mary	12662
Bell, Percy	30321	Benge, Jessie L.	13999
Bell, John	30322	Benge, Annie L.	14160
Bell, Frank	30323	Bendabout, Lydia	18177
Belt, Martha	32385	Benge, Ross L.	14575
Benge, Pickens	2564	Benge, Lucy	14576
Benge, Pearl	2565	Bennett, Emily	16824
Benge, Houston	2566	Bennett, Anna C.	17250
Benge, John	3481	Bennett, Anna L.	17251
Benge, Sallie	3482	Bennett, Martha McK	17252
Benge, Obediah	3549	Benge, John H.	18133
Benge, Ridge Otto	3551	Bennett, Phillip	18258
Benge, David W.	3744	Bennett, Arley	18259
Benge, Lizzie J.	3745	Bendabout, James	18937
Benge, James M.	3746	Bendabout, Lizzie	18938
Benge, Dooley	3747	Bendabout, Rufus	18939
Benge, Thomas	3801	Bendabout, Jensie	20198
Benge, Rhoda	3808	Bendabout, Judge	20199
Benge, Mary	3809	Bendabout, Bob Taylor	20200
Benge, Columbus	3810	Bendabout, Blunt	20203
Benge, Louella	3811	Bendabout, Charlie	20594
Benge, Richard	3812	Bendabout, Diana	20595
Benge, Sarah	3813	Bendabout, Martha	20596
Benge, Hooley	3837	Benge, Richard	21059
Benge, May	3838	Benge, Nancy	22068
Benge, Emmet	3839	Benge, George	22875
Benge, Samson	3840	Benge, Obediah, Jr.	22876
Benge, Tug Lee	3842	Benge, Louie	23086
Benge, Henry	4131	Benge, Arlie	23087
Benge, Mack	4132	Benge, Elnora	23088
Bennett, Mary	4321	Bendure, Ella M.	24837
Benge, Samuel H.	4499	Bendure, Etta A.	24838
Benge, Nancy	4500	Bendure, Nettie M.	24839
Benge, Jennie	4501	Bendure, Lillie A.	24840
Benge, Samuel H., Jr.	4698	Bendabout, Mary	25762
Benge, Sallie	4699	Bendabout, Mose	25839
Benge, Carrie	4700	Bendabout, Lucy	25840
Benge, Samuel	4701	Bendabout, Lydia	25841
Benge, Jack R.	4702	Benge, Calvin	25702
Benge, Martin V.	4785	Benge, Riddle	27336
Benge, Adna S.	4786	Benge, Takey	27337
Benge, Amy	4788	Benge, Jack	27338
Benge, Martin V., Jr.	4789	Benge, Pickens	27339
Benge, John	4790	Benge, Nelson	28081
Benge, Emma	4791	Benge, Emma	28082
Benge, Ruth	4792	Benge, Jimmie	30163
Benge, Leo	4793	Benge, John	30164
Benge, Charley S.	4794	Bendabout, Quatie	32032
Benge, Louie R.	4801	Bendabout, George	30460
Benge, Floyd	4802	Benbo, Sadie	31243
Benge, Robert	4842	Berry, Amos E.	192
Benge, Theodore	4848	Berry, Etta M.	193
Benge, Richard	4849	Berry, Elisha C.	194
Benge, John	5411	Berry, Elizabeth	3777
Benge, Jennie	5414	Berry, Florence L.	4686
Benge, Mad	5415	Berry, George E.	4692
Benge, James	5416	Berry, Ibbie	7134
Benge, George W.	6037	Berry, Otie A.	7135
Benge, Fannie F.	6038	Berry, Silvey G.	7136
Benge, Samuel A.	6039	Berry, Jay C.	7149
Benge, Minnie	6040	Berry, Charles M.	7559
Benge, George F.	6041	Berry, John W.	8804
Benge, Albert	6042	Berry, Frances L.	10395
Benge, Houston	6043	Berry, Wesley B.	10396
Benge, Eliza	6044	Berry, Lee B.	10397
Benge, Cora	6045	Berry, Maud E.	10398
Benge, Oce P.	6856	Berry, Ida	10925
Benge, Mattie A.	6857	Berry, Tacy E.	10928
Benge, Georgia	6858	Bertholf, Thomas E.	11135
Benge, Elinor	6859	Bertholf, Percy E.	11136
Benge, Lella	6860	Berryhill, Elnora	12688
Benge, Dora	6861	Berryhill, Crystle May	12689
Benge, Lenora L.	6862	Berry, Almedia	12880
Benge, James F.	9044	Berry, Homer	12881
Bennett, Mary E.	10270	Bertholf, Richard R.	16996
Bennett, Clem	10271	Bertholf, Octavia M.	16997
Bennett, Marion	10272	Bertholf, William T.	16998
Benge, Cornelia C.	11062	Bertholf, Bettie	16999
Bendure, John B.	12274	Bertholf, Mannie B.	17000
Bendure, Charles	12277	Bertholf, Grover C.	17001
Bendure, Edward	12283	Bertholf, Claude M.	17002
Benge, Joseph	12394	Bertholf, Richard	17003
		Bertholf, John R.	17395

Name.	Roll No.	Name.	Roll No.
Bertholf, Thomas	21612	Bigknife, Susan	9641
Bertholf, Electra	28335	Bigknife, Mariah	9642
Bertholf, William H.	28343	Bigham, Eva M.	10230
Berry, Emma D.	21961	Bigham, Addie M.	10231
Berry, Mary E.	21962	Bigelow, Emma	10966
Berry, Louella	22300	Bigelow, William	10965
Berry, Ivan	22301	Bigby, Charles T.	15408
Berry, Lemuel	22303	Bigby, Narcissa	15409
Berry, Eva	22302	Bigby, Charles T.	15410
Berry, Lucinda	22304	Bigby, Margaret A.	15457
Berry, Emma	28150	Bigby, Walter D.	15452
Berry, Woda	28151	Bigby, Sabina E.	15453
Berd, Nancy E.	29760	Bigby, Maudie M.	15454
Berd, Beatrice J.	29761	Bigby, Mamie S.	15455
Berd, Harold B.	29762	Bigby, William J. B.	15456
Betterton, William Catherine	189	Bigbey, Samuel A.	15801
Bethel, Clarance	3885	Bigbey, Louvinia	15802
Bethel, Claud G.	3749	Bigbey, Walter	16604
Bethel, Dona B.	4127	Bigbey, Fannie	16605
Bethel, Dora E.	4126	Bigbey, Samuel	16606
Bethel, George	3748	Bigbey, Susan E.	16607
Bethel, Lillian	4124	Bigfeather, Ben	17383
Bethel, Louie L.	4130	Bigfeather, Lucy	17384
Bethel, Madgie L.	4129	Bigfeather, Polly	17385
Bethel, Tilitha M.	4125	Bigfeather, Benjamin	17386
Bethel, William	4123	Bigfeather, Lydia	17387
Bethel, William E.	4128	Bigfeather, George	17388
Bever, George	12692	Bighead, Quarleyukah	18254
Bezonia, Delitha May	4379	Bighead, George	18255
Bible, Lewis	10521	Bigfeather, John	18260
Bible, James P.	10522	Bigfeather, Polly	18261
Bible, Chris R.	10524	Bigfeather, Susie	18262
Bible, Vera M.	10525	Bigfeather, Sallie	18263
Bible, Ary	10526	Bigfeather, George	18264
Bible, Evert	10527	Bigfeather, Mary A.	18265
Bible, William H.	10548	Big Acorn, Nancy	18576
Bible, Eliza J.	10549	Big Acorn, Jesse	18577
Bible, George	10552	Big Acorn, Elsie	18578
Bible, William T.	10553	Big Acorn, Ollie	18579
Bible, John A.	10554	Big Acorn, Takie	18580
Bible, Katie	10555	Big Acorn, Ezekiel	18581
Bible, Maud	10556	Big Acorn, Pollie	18582
Bible, Rebecca	11428	Bigfeather, Wash	19177
Bible, Willis	11429	Bigfeather, Charlotte	19178
Bible, James T.	11819	Bigfeather, Pearl	19247
Bible, Mary L.	11820	Bigfeather, Rider	19859
Bible, Eva M.	11821	Bigfeather, Buck	20145
Bible, George P.	11822	Bigfeather, Sallie	20146
Bible, Josephine A.	11823	Bigfeather, Lucinda	20701
Bible, Sarah A.	11824	Bigbey, Thomas	22623
Bible, Addie L.	11825	Bigbey, Edith	22625
Bible, William	12237	Bigbey, Clarence G.	22626
Bible, Willie A.	12238	Bigbey, Corda M.	22627
Bible, Clem P.	12239	Bigbey, David T.	27116
Bible, Bessie A.	12240	Bigbey, Nannie J.	27117
Bible, Bertha E.	12241	Bigbey, Arthur E.	27118
Bible, Eulalie	12242	Bigbey, Henry C.	27119
Bible, Pearl	12243	Bigbey, Abe	27120
Bibles, Margaret	13263	Bigbey, Martha I.	27121
Bibles, Henry	13264	Bigbey, Walter A.	27122
Bibles, Louis	13268	Bigbey, David L.	27123
Bibles, Jessie	13269	Bigfeather, Jennie	29142
Bible, Arthur	26633	Bigfeather, Mitchell	29827
Bible, George L.	26634	Bigfeather, Lucy	29828
Bice, Benjamin F.	13298	Bigfeather, Gussie	29829
Bice, Lela	13299	Bigfeather, Mary	29830
Bickford, Maggie B.	30127	Bigfeather, Arley	30475
Bigbey, James L.	1862	Bigfeaher, Katie	30476
Bigbey, Nancy C.	1863	Bigfeather, Wuttie	30477
Bigbey, Malinda J.	1864	Bigmule, James	31249
Bigbey, Thomas W.	1865	Bigjohn, Nannie	31308
Bigbey, David E.	1866	Bigjohn, Perry	31310
Bigbey, Edward C.	1867	Bigheart, Alice	31712
Bigbey, Samuel A.	1868	Bigknife, Nancy	32825
Bigbey, Sarah C.	1869	Bill, Charley	31646
Bigbey, Minnie C.	1870	Billingslea, Dollie W.	9761
Bigbey, Thomas B.	1911	Billingslea, Frank D.	21815
Bigby, John	6103	Billingslea, Homer	29176
Bigby, Betsy	6104	Billingslea, Jenette	9760
Biggers, Lillian C.	7061	Billingslea, Joe	9762
Bigknife, Sam	8365	Billingslea, McLeod	29175
Bigknife, James	9640	Billingslea, Robert	29177
		Bingham, Carrie L.	21684

Name.	Roll No.	Name.	Roll No.
Bingham, Mamie	24048	Bird, William	30637
Bingham, Tom Farrar	24049	Bird, Susan	30638
Birchfield, Annie	1421	Bishop, Ida	21506
Birchfield, John A.	1420	Bitting, Emma	29920
Bird, Scott	2034	Bitting, John	13929
Bird, Nancy	3619	Bitting, Kellie	29919
Bird, Emily	4829	Bitting, Leppoe	29918
Bird, Elizabeth	4830	Bitting, Mary J.	13926
Bird, Tresse	4831	Bitting, Nicholas Jr.	13927
Bird, Cindia	4833	Bitting, William	13928
Bird, Rachel	6350	Bivin, David T.	10147
Bird, Joseph	6351	Bivin, Saphronia	8153
Bird, Digonatsali	15567	Bivin, Walter M.	10234
Bird, John A.	16316	Bivins, Emma	10457
Bird, Delilah	16558	Bivins, Joseph	10459
Bird, Charles	16559	Bivins, May D.	10458
Bird, Cornelius	17852	Bixler, Nancy	31189
Bird, James	17884	Blaylock, Sarah Ann	417
Bird, Daniel	17989	Blaylock, Artilla C.	419
Bird, Nancy	17990	Blaylock, Lottie Ann	420
Bird, Nathaniel A.	17991	Blaylock, Julius T.	421
Bird, Sarah	17997	Blaylock, Alice Evaline	422
Bird, Jennie	17998	Blaylock, Lillie May	423
Bird, Nellie	17999	Blaylock, James J.	424
Bird, Nannie	18000	Blackwood, Nellie	2053
Bird, Will	18256	Blair, John	2438
Bird, William	18257	Blair, Jennie	2439
Bird, Charlotte	18266	Blair, Eliza	2440
Bird, Mack	19390	Blair, Louie	2441
Bird, Rachel	19391	Blair, Elizabeth	2950
Bird, Jess	19392	Blair, George	3239
Birdchopper	19693	Blair, Ada	3240
Birdchopper, Jennie	19694	Blair, Zella L.	3241
Birdchopper, Mike	19695	Blair, Tomma Retta	3242
Birdchopper, Lewis	19696	Blackmon, Lou	3428
Bird, Charley	19703	Blackmon, Jesse L.	3429
Bird, Hester	19704	Blackard, Clara	3592
Bird, William	19750	Blackard, Irene	3593
Bird, Jennie	19751	Blackard, Joe	3594
Bird, Susie	19752	Blackstone, Mollie L.	4254
Bird, Maggie	19753	Blackstone, Gipsy	4255
Bird, Sarah	19754	Blackstone, Frank F.	4256
Bird, Susan	20305	Blackstone, Edward F.	4504
Bird, Samuel	20306	Blackstone, George	5474
Bird, James	20307	Blackstone, Gracie	5475
Bird, Thomas	20671	Blackstone, Pearl M.	5476
Bird, Lewis	20781	Blackfox, Enola	6293
Bird, Betsy	20782	Blackfox, Elsie	6294
Bird, Jesse	20783	Blackfox, James	6295
Bird, Lucy	20784	Blackfox, Arlie	6296
Bird, Annie	20785	Blackfox, Lizzie	6297
Birdtail, James	21024	Blackfox, Charlotte	6298
Birdtail, Annie	21025	Blackfish, George T.	7568
Birdtail, John	21027	Blackfish, Allie A.	7569
Birdtail, Dave	21028	Blackfish, Charles A.	7570
Birdtail, Sam	21029	Blair, Lizzie	7613
Bird, Lizzie	21193	Blair, Harrison	7614
Bird, John	21269	Blair, Jimmie M.	7615
Birdtail, Eliza	21423	Blair, John	7616
Bird, Nellie	21847	Blair, George	7620
Bird, Thomas	25578	Blackfeather, Johnson	7953
Bird, Charley	25579	Blackfeather, Nancy	7954
Birdchopper, Benjamin	25586	Blakemore, Retta M.	8301
Birdchopper, Caleb	28380	Blakemore, Gracie D.	8302
Birdchopper, Huckle-		Blakemore, Oce	8303
berry	28241	Blakeman, Lydia J.	10241
Birdchopper, Lucy	28381	Blair, Katie	10722
Bird, Dave	25722	Blair, Annie	10723
Bird, Cynthia	25723	Blair, Emma	12552
Bird, Andrew	25724	Blair, Frank	12553
Bird, Winnie	25725	Blake, Georgia A.	12813
Bird, Ninnie	28072	Blake, Jennie A.	12814
Bird, Peter	28576	Blake, Nita E.	12815
Bird, Mollie	28577	Blake, John F.	12816
Bird, Sarah J.	28979	Blake, Albert W.	12817
Bird, Charley M. C.	28980	Blake, Georgia K.	12818
Bird, Christie	29044	Blackwood, Cora A.	13692
Bird, Bettie	29802	Blackwood, Henry F.	13693
Bird, Francis M.	30410	Blackwood, Minnie M.	13694
Bird, Pearly	30411	Blackwood, James A.	13695
Birdchopper, Wawdi-		Blackwood, Ida C.	13696
yawhi	30563	Blair, William	13727
Bird, Rome	30573	Blackbird, Rebecca	15252

Name.	Roll No.
Blackstone, Robert W.	16054
Blackstone, Annie M.	16055
Blackstone, John	16056
Blackhaw, Annie	16377
Blackhaw, Lydia	16378
Blackhaw, Emma	16380
Blackstone, Pleasant N.	16745
Blackstone, Nannie	16746
Blackstone, Josephine	16747
Blackstone, Napoleon D.	16748
Blackstone, Peachie R.	16749
Blackstone, George E.	16750
Blackstone, Kate	16751
Blackstone, DeWitt	16786
Blackstone, Robert D.	16799
Blake, Effie M.	17609
Blake, James H.	17610
Black, Alsey	17708
Black, Calvin	17710
Black, Lucian	17711
Black, Benjamin	17712
Blackbird, Dave	18156
Blanket, Peter	18240
Blackbear	18537
Blackbear, Sallie	18538
Blackbear, Leestie	18539
Blackbear, Alkinny	18540
Blackbear, Coowee-scoowee	18541
Blackbear, Locust	18542
Blackbear, Oo-ta-li-ta	18543
Blackbear, Teacher	18544
Blackbear, Ca-na-he-ya-du	18545
Blackbear, Uh-ska-jah-wee	.18546.
Blackbear, Scales	18594
Blackwood, Isaac	19079
Blackwood, Annie	19080
Blackwood, Jennie	19081
Blackwood, Wahleah	19082
Blackwood, Henry	19083
Blackbird, Wilson	19133
Blackbird, Nellie	19134
Blackbird, William	19135
Blackbird, James	19136
Blackbird, Susie	19137
Blackwood, Lucy	19186
Blackwood, Sallie	19187
Blackbird, James	19458
Blackbird, Lucy	19459
Blackbird, Handup	19460
Blackbird, Toolate	19461
Blackfox, Nancy	19820
Blackfox, John	20058
Blackwood, Hoolie	20082
Blackwood, Julia	20083
Blackwood, Leona	20084
Blackwood, Jim	20085
Blackwood, Lizzie	20086
Blackwood, Jennie	20096
Blackwood, Martin	20097
Blackwood, Lydia	20098
Blackwood, Dave	20120
Blair, John	20206
Blackfox, Eli	20261
Blackfox, Nelly	20283
Blackfox, Ned	20284
Blackfox, Annie	20285
Blackfox, Jennie	20286
Blackbird, Joseph	20287
Blackfox, Darkey	20295
Blackfox, Benjamin	20296
Blackfox, David	20297
Blackfox, Wilson	20298
Blackfox, Sam	20574
Blackfox, Lucy	20575
Blackfox, Joe	20576
Blackfox, Susan	20577
Blackfox, Sallie	20578
Blackfox, Jonathan	20579
Blackfox, Charlotte	20580
Blackbird, Susie	21280
Blackbird, John	21281
Blackfox, Ellis	21345
Blackfox, Susie	21346

Name.	Roll No.
Blackwood, Martha J.	21489
Blackwood, Dora M.	21490
Blackwood, Joseph L.	21491
Blakemore, Janie R.	21613
Blackwood, Emma E.	22629
Blackwood, Lida A.	22630
Blackwood, William I.	22631
Blackwood, Cora	22632
Blackwood, Leander	22633
Blackwood, Burr	22634
Blackwood, John H.	22635
Blackhawk, Cooey	22951
Blakeny, Robert I.	23767
Blakeny, George R.	23769
Blakeny, Donald F.	23770
Blackwood, James	26086
Blair, Arthur	26155
Blair, William E.	26156
Blair, Bulah M.	26158
Blair, Edna	26157
Blair, Eliza	27250
Blair, Lee	27251
Blair, Douglas	27252
Blair, Callie	27253
Blair, Dewey	27254
Blackbird, Joe	27266
Blackbird, Nancy	27267
Blackbird, Josie	27268
Blackbird, Jennie	27270
Blackbird, John	27271
Blackbird, William	27272
Blackbird, Belle	27273
Blackbird, Annie	27274
Bladon, Lenora N.	27307
Bladon, Marion	27309
Bladon, Aggie E.	27310
Blair, Thomas	27311
Blair, Margarett	27312
Blair, Maud	27313
Blair, Jesse T.	27314
Blair, Maggie	27315
Blair, Pearl	27316
Blackfish, Mary A.	28705
Blackfish, Hiram	29254
Blakeney, Kate	29281
Blackwell, King D.	29490
Blackwell, Solomon	29491
Blackwell, Hazel	29492
Blackwell, Rosa	29493
Blackbird, David	29539
Blair, Lila	29736
Blackbear, Cynthia	30511
Blackbear, Ga-la-nu-du	30512
Blackfox, Tagahtluga .	30620
Blackfox, Jesse	30697
Blackfox, Sunday	30698
Blackfox, Emma	30699
Black, Albert	31166
Black, Daniel E.	31167
Black, Henry Clyde	31168
Blair, Amelia	31654
Blair, James L.	31655
Blasingame, Vinnie C.	31883
Blasingame, Elbert L.	31884
Blasingame, Ellis W.	31885
Blasingame, Earl D.	31886
Blasingame, Alexander, Jr.	31887
Blasingame, Elmer H.	31888
Blasingame, James R.	31889
Blasingame, William A.	31890
Blasingame, George L.	31891
Blasingame, Grace D.	31892
Blackbird, George	32292
Blackbird, Alie	32293
Blalock, Charley	32593
Blalock, Rosa	32594
Blalock, William Henry	32595
Blakeney, John T.	32760
Blakeney, John S.	32761
Bledsoe, Belle	7400
Bledsoe, Edna	7405
Bledsoe, Henry W.	7401
Bledsoe, Joel C.	7403
Bledsoe, Sallie M.	7402
Bledsoe, Susie	17973

Name.	Roll No.	Name.	Roll No.
Bledsoe, William A. G.	7404	Bluejacket, Eunice	30013
Blevins, Nancy	7494	Bluejacket, Robert O.	30014
Blevins, Jackson	7495	Bluejacket, David	30186
Blevins, Joe	9043	Bluejacket, Eliza	30187
Blevins, Ross	9092	Bluejacket, Eddie M.	30188
Blevins, Jeff	9305	Bluejacket, Lizzie	30189
Blevins, Augusta	15516	Bluejacket, Charles D.	30190
Blevins, Ollie	15517	Bluebird, Samuel	30715
Blevins, Joseph	15677	Bluebird, Nellie	30716
Blevins, William V.	15678	Bluebird, Rachel	30717
Blevins, John C.	15679	Blue, Martha	32306
Blevins, George	15683	Bluebird, Checowee	32355
Blevins, Pleasant	15684	Bluebird, Gallitsa	32356
Blevins, Burrell	15685	Bluebird, Oolutsa	32357
Blevins, Laura Elen	25385	Bluejacket, Josephine	32471
Blevins, Sally Belle	25386	Blythe, Aubrey A.	30905
Blevins, Pleasant	25546	Blythe, Burton N.	26211
Blevins, Joseph	25547	Blythe, Charles F.	30908
Blevins, Elizabeth	25548	Blythe, Elijah	10300
Blevins, James	25549	Blythe, Eliza	17201
Blevins, Leroy C.	28698	Blythe, Ermer L.	30906
Blevins, John T.	28699	Blythe, Farry A.	30904
Blevins, Walter L.	28700	Blythe, Jack	4622
Blevins, William	30842	Blythe, Jackson	17200
Blevins, Apsia	30843	Blythe, James C.	10143
Blevins, Edna	30844	Blythe, Jemima S.	7488
Blevins, Minnie Lee	32397	Blythe, Jesse L.	30907
Blevins, Nellie May	32398	Blythe, John E.	30902
Blossom, Betsy	18197	Blythe, Mary J.	30903
Blossom, Jack	29667	Blythe, Napoleon B.	30900
Blossom, Jennie	18556	Blythe, William H.	30901
Blossom, Joe	18196	Boatman, Edgar	12621
Blossom, John	18555	Boatman, Sarah L.	12619
Blossom, Lila	29666	Boatright, Roy E.	29447
Blossom, Muggy	18198	Bob, Emeline Lemblese	31267
Blossom, Thomas	29669	Bobb, Frank	8257
Blosser, Joseph D.	10349	Bobb, George	8255
Blossom, Betsie	30471	Bob, Samuel	31667
Blossom, Joe	30503	Bobb, Susan	8256
Blossom, Maggie	30473	Boggs, Blue	25838
Blossom, Ned	30472	Boggs, Polly	4887
Blossom, Osie	30504	Bogle, Claud	31905
Blossom, Will	30505	Bogle, Edna N.	31902
Blossom, William	30474	Bogle, James E.	31901
Bluejacket, Thomas	8505	Bogle, John H.	31903
Bluejacket, May B.	8506	Bogle, Marvin R.	31904
Bluejacket, Henry C.	9027	Bogle, Nancy J.	31900
Bluejacket, Helene M.	9028	Bogle, Nancy Edith	31906
Bluejacket, William C.	9029	Bolyn, Elizabeth	5828
Bluejacket, Eliza	9565	Bolyn, Worcester	5841
Bluejacket, Alexander C.	9566	Boling, Julia M.	11211
Bluejacket, Gertrude	9568	Bolyn, Charles	15346
Bluejacket, Lillie E.	9567	Boland, Ross	17015
Bluejacket, Willis J.	9569	Boland, Katie	17016
Bluejacket, Mollie	13440	Boland, John	17017
Bluebird, Elias	15215	Boland, Annie	17018
Blue, Jane	16366	Boland, Elizabeth	17019
Bluejacket, Simon	17586	Boland, Moses	17020
Bluebird, William	18440	Boland, Eve	17021
Bluebird, Jack	20902	Boland, Jeremiah	17022
Bluebird, Peggy	20903	Boland, Robert	17023
Blue, Lizzie	21419	Boland, Nellie	17024
Bluejacket, Silas D.	21909	Bolin, Leonard	17774
Bluejacket, Burtie	21910	Bolin, Jennie	17775
Bluejacket, Bonnie	21911	Bolin, Lucile	17776
Bluejacket, Elsie M.	21912	Bolin, Lucien W.	17777
Bluejacket, Oscar	21913	Bolyn, Lucy	17914
Bluejacket, Henry	21914	Bolyn, Charlie	18975
Bluejacket, Mike	21915	Bolyn, Redbird	18976
Bluejacket, Pearl T.	24047	Bolyn, William	19317
Bluejacket, Ed	25062	Bolyn, Nannie	19318
Bluejacket, Karl M.	25063	Bolin, Alice	19535
Bluejacket, Sylvia	25064	Bolyn, Betsy	19893
Bluejacket, Laura E.	25065	Bolyn, Wolfe	19894
Bluebird, Luke	25591	Bolyn, Peggie	19895
Bluebird, Charlie	25936	Bolyn, Ratler	19896
Bluejacket, Louisa	27636	Bolyn, Jennie	19897
Bluejacket, Louis	27638	Bolyn, Tiana	19898
Bluejacket, Lucinda	27639	Bolyn, Charles	20171
Bluejacket, Amanda	27640	Bolyn, Sarah	20172
Bluejacket, Everett J.	28723	Bolyn, Sallie	20173
Bluejacket, William F.	30010	Bolyn, John	20174
Bluejacket, Nellie	30011	Bolyn, Lydia	20175
Bluejacket, Russell P.	30012		

Name.	Roll No.	Name.	Roll No.
Bolyn, Martha	20176	Boudinot, Mary C.	5579
Bolin, William	20515	Boudinot, Mary C.	5580
Bolin, Martin	25755	Boudinot, Richard F.	5578
Bolin, Annie	25756	Boudinot, Sallie	30261
Bolin, William	25757	Boudinot, William P.	5583
Bolin, Sam	25758	Bowden, Emiline	12640
Bolin, Richard	25759	Bowden, Eva I.	12642
Bolin, John	25760	Bowden, Florence	21026
Bolin, Lillie	25771	Bowden, Lola M.	12641
Bolyn, Jackson	25842	Bowden, Louisa J.	5181
Bolyn, Josh	25843	Bowen, Clara A.	10077
Boles, Leo	27420	Bowen, Sanford M.	10078
Boles, Richard	27421	Bowen, Thelma E.	10079
Bolyn, Jennie	28420	Bowers, Ida	12547
Boles, Nannie	30105	Bowers, Paul W.	12548
Boles, Thomas	30425	Bowles, Betsy	1502
Bolen, Harry O.	30984	Bowles, Jennet	19956
Bolen, Adnia	30985	Bowlin, Tooka	20132
Bolen, Minnie	21334	Bowlin, Tuckie	22025
Bond, Albert Harlin	23731	Bowman, Clara	30122
Bond, Eddie S.	23729	Bowman, Delilah Dorsey	32449
Bond, Ida May	363	sey	32449
Bond, Lillian	366	Boyd, Henry A.	11315
Bond, Mabel O.	365	Boyd, Jane F.	12379
Bond, Tottie	364	Boyd, Joseph M.	29808
Bond, William Penn	23730	Boyd, Ruby A.	11314
Bone, Frank E.	10927	Boyd, Sallie C.	11313
Bone, Ruth J.	10926	Boydstun, Beulah	3229
Boney, Betsy	19819	Boydstun, Domah R.	3228
Boney, Esiah	30513	Boydstun, Manuel P.	3230
Boney, Nancy	18567	Boydstun, Minnie D.	3226
Boney, Ollie	30547	Boydstun, Viva	3227
Boney, Peggy	19374	Boydstun, Willie E.	3231
Boney, Rabbit	18521	Boyer, Edna E.	13170
Boney, Sakie	19412	Boyer, Lydia	13169
Boney, Sam	19411	Boyle, Ambrose	22307
Boney, Sarah	18600	Boyle, Hugh	21975
Boney, Steve	18566	Boyles, Alie	28834
Boney, Swimmer	18599	Boyles, Charlie	17915
Bonham, Addie	4390	Boyles, George W.	15286
Bonham, Bertha L.	4393	Boyles, Margaret	15884
Bonham, Gertrude I.	4394	Boyles, Martha	14993
Bonham, Howard B.	4395	Boyles, Oliver O.	14994
Bonham, Nannie A.	4392	Boyles, Peggy	17913
Bonham, Vaughn E.	4391	Boyles, William H. H.	14995
Boot, William	7919	Boyls, Mamie	29042
Boot, Nellie	7920	Branson, Emma	658
Boot, Cornelius	7921	Branson, Eliza	659
Boots, Eliza	7931	Branson, Lucy	660
Boone, Ora C.	10294	Branson, William Francis	661
Boone, Cecil W.	10295	cis	661
Boone, Raymond A.	10296	Bramwell, Renda P.	682
Boone, Maude	11168	Bramwell, Lillie May	686
Boone, George H.	11169	Bradford, Elizabeth J.	1161
Boone, Walter	11170	Bradford, John C.	1162
Boone, Ethel M.	11171	Bradford, Jennie L.	1163
Boothe, Rebecca A.	12059	Bradford, Timothy E.	1164
Boothe, Frances L.	12060	Brackett, Benjamin	2331
Boothe, Grover G.	12061	Brackett, William T.	2332
Boothe, Francis M., Jr.	12062	Brackett, Amelia E.	2334
Booth, Frank H.	17294	Brackett, Daniel R.	2341
Booth, William F.	17295	Brackett, Callie M.	2342
Booth, Minnie M.	17296	Brackett, Clara E.	2343
Booth, Florence M.	17297	Brackett, Susie	2462
Booth, Edwin J.	17298	Brackett, Elizabeth J.	2463
Booth, Edna M.	17299	Brackett, Annie M.	2464
Booth, Dollie M.	17300	Bradley, Benjamin	2597
Boone, Mary	31580	Bradley, Bertha	2595
Boone, Luther	31581	Bradley, Cyntha A.	2592
Boswell, Linda	13368	Bradley, David	3611
Boswell, Richard E.	13369	Bradley, Frederick G.	2598
Boswell, Iva	13370	Bradley, George	2600
Boswell, Manerva	22879	Bradley, Henrietta	21788
Boswell, Charles S.	22880	Bradley, Jesse	3610
Boswell, Frank	22881	Bradley, John Q.	2593
Bosworth, Anna	31509	Bradley, Nora	2594
Boudinot, Annie S. M.	17959	Bradley, Robert	2596
Boudinot, Caroline F.	27820	Bradley, Walter	2599
Boudinot, Eleana M.	5581	Brandwiede, Frank	3929
Boudinot, Franklin J.	17953	Brandwiede, Sallie	3928
Boudinot, Franklin J., Jr.	17960	Bragg, Elizabeth	4490
		Bray, William H.	4861
Boudinot, Harriett G.	5582	Bray, Elita	5056

Name.	Roll No.
Bray, George R.	5298
Bredshaw, James L.	5536
Brandon, Fred I.	8359
Brackett, Margaret	8684
Branham, Maggie J.	10091
Branham, Bertrand D.	10092
Brady, Martha A.	10655
Brady, Otto M.	10656
Bray, Richard R.	11606
Bray, John	11637
Bradshaw, Nora	12163
Bradshaw, Rosa E.	12164
Bradshaw, Auda L.	12165
Bradshaw, Jehu E.	12166
Bradshaw, Dennis C.	12167
Bradshaw, Thomas McK.	12168
Bradshaw, Emma T.	12255
Brady, Etheral	12291
Brady, Edgar	12292
Brady, Zeb V.	12314
Brady, Addie E.	12315
Brady, Zeb A.	12316
Brady, Phoebe B.	12317
Brady, Calvin L.	12318
Branson, Laura E.	12716
Branson, Charles R.	12717
Brantley, Mary A. E.	14259
Bradford, Susie	14447
Bradford, Mamie	14448
Bradford, Buff	14449
Bradford, Riley	14450
Brackett, Alice	15226
Brackett, Jeff	15227
Brackett, Dovie	15228
Brackett, Josie	15229
Brassfield, John	15360
Brannon, Elizabeth	16306
Bracken, Cornelia	16729
Bracken, Harry W.	16730
Bracken, Alton E.	16731
Bracken, Gracie P.	16732
Bracken, Donald R.	16733
Bracken, Herbert S.	16761
Branan, Emma H.	17539
Branan, Clifford B.	17540
Branan, Edward H.	17541
Branan, William C.	17542
Brady, Rachel C.	17545
Brady, Ruth T.	17546
Brady, Bessie	17547
Brady, Henry T.	17548
Brackett, Mige L.	21553
Brackett, Augustus	21595
Brackett, Robert L.	21796
Brackett, Sarah	21866
Brackett, John W.	22065
Brackett, Jefferson	22066
Brackett, Thomas B.	22067
Bray, Lucy	23098
Brandon, Lola L.	23762
Brandon, Frank E.	24185
Bradshaw, Louisa	24647
Bradshaw, Delpha	24648
Bradshaw, Stella	24649
Bradshaw, Eddith	24650
Bradshaw, J. D.	24651
Bradshaw, Jesse P.	24824
Bradshaw, Albert H.	24825
Bradshaw, Ellen	25175
Bradshaw, Charles T.	25176
Bradshaw, Sopha	25177
Bradshaw, May	25178
Bradshaw, Jahu	25179
Bradshaw, Spurgen	25180
Bradshaw, Stella E.	25181
Brassfield, Jay	25235
Brassfield, Abner	25236
Brackett, William L.	26202
Brackett, Lucinda	26203
Brackett, Bayless	26204
Brackett, Jesse	26205
Brady, Lucinda	26387

Name.	Roll No.
Brackett, William H.	26867
Brackett, Addie	26868
Brackett, Ed	26869
Brackett, Fanie	26870
Bradshaw, Mary	27240
Bradshaw, Willie R.	27241
Bradshaw, Dixie A.	27242
Brady, George W.	28123
Brady, Florence E.	28126
Brady, William F.	28125
Bradshaw, Ethel F.	28795
Brackett, Daniel	29317
Brackett, Agnes	29412
Brackett, Charles A.	29528
Brackett, Adam	30776
Brackett, Benjamin	30777
Brackett, Lizzie M.	30778
Brackett, Annie	30779
Bratcher, James T.	31548
Bratcher, Charles E.	31549
Bratcher, Mamie	31550
Bratcher, William P.	31551
Bratcher, Myrtle M.	31552
Bratcher, Nettie	31553
Bratcher, Olena	31554
Bradshaw, Florence P.	31817
Bradshaw, Myrtle	31818
Bradshaw, Claude	31819
Brauer, Etta	31854
Branum, Rhoda M.	32186
Brackett, William	32762
Breedlove, Emily W.	526
Breedlove, Waller W.	619
Breedlove, Priscilla	620
Breazeale, Eliza	2896
Breedlove, Carrie W.	4006
Breedlove, William O.	4007
Breedlove, John C.	4008
Breedlove, Cassie	4009
Breedlove, Wharton	4010
Breedlove, Walton D.	4011
Breedlove, Charles W.	4012
Brewer, Delia A.	4324
Brewer, Thomas F.	4540
Brewer, Choowee	4541
Brewer, William S.	4542
Brewer, Eva	4543
Brewer, Thomas F.	4544
Brewer, William L.	4612
Brewer, Nancy	4613
Brewer, David B.	4614
Brewer, Richard T.	4615
Brewer, Jack W.	4918
Brewer, Fannie	4919
Brewer, Charley E.	4920
Brewer, Jack W.	4921
Breedlove, Mary B.	5998
Breedlove, Willoughby W.	6001
Bread, William	6198
Brewer, Cherokee	6734
Brewer, Mary D.	6735
Brewer, William M.	6736
Brewer, John G.	6737
Brewer, Carrie	6738
Brewer, Mary G.	6739
Bread, Samuel	8637
Bread, Mary	8638
Breker, Annie E.	9343
Breker, Louis H.	9344
Breker, Flossie B.	9345
Breeden, Rebecca	11203
Breeden, Bessie M.	11204
Breeden, John L.	11205
Breeden, Raymond E.	11206
Breeden, Susie	11207
Breeden, Gertie	11208
Breeden, Martha J.	11614
Breeden, Sarah	11615
Breeden, John W.	11616
Breeden, Maggie D.	11617
Brewer, George W.	14971
Brewer, Anna	14972
Brewer, Richard R.	14973

Name.	Roll No.	Name.	Roll No.
Brewer, Cherokee	14975	Brown, Jack	1852
Brewer, Lucile G.	14977	Brown, Narcissa	1853
Brewer, John W.	16139	Brown, John Jr.	1854
Brewer, Thurza	16140	Brown, Kellah	1855
Brewer, Floyd W.	16141	Brown, Martha W.	2211
Brewer, Sallie L.	16142	Brown, William D.	2212
Brewer, Jewel	16143	Brown, Lula J.	2213
Brewer, William D.	16988	Brown, Martha	2214
Brewer, Pearl S.	16989	Brown, Myrtle	2215
Brewer, Alfred	16990	Brown, Lottie	2216
Brewer, Nellie	16991	Brown, Robert B.	2217
Brewer, Edith	16992	Brown, Grover F.	2218
Brewer, Earl	16993	Brown, Ray McK.	2219
Brewer, Oliver P.	17588	Brown, Marvin	3292
Bread, Cherokee	18289	Brockman, Emma J.	3471
Bread, Celia	18290	Brown, Bell	4815
Bread, Jennie	18291	Brown, Ada	4816
Bread, Gilouneske	18292	Brown, Mary	4817
Bread, Nancy	18293	Brown, Charles	4818
Bread, Wilson	20778	Brown, Louis	4819
Bread, Nannie	20779	Brown, John	4820
Brewer, William P.	22115	Brown, Finis	4821
Brewer, George	25732	Brown, Quinn	4862
Breedlove, James W.	28180	Brown, William J.	4863
Brewer, Mack	28367	Brown, Benjamin	4864
Brewer, Susie	28368	Brown, Gertie	4865
Brewer, Benny F.	29992	Brown, Amanda D.	4866
Brewer, William I.	30212	Brown, Manchie	4867
Brewer, Hattie E.	30213	Brown, Thomas J.	4868
Brewer, Jessie	30214	Brown, Robert L.	4869
Bread, Oct-te-yah	30485	Brown, Eugene	4870
Bright, Noah	758	Brown, Ann E.	4926
Bright, John H.	791	Brown, James	5042
Bright, Ella	879	Brown, Watie	5043
Bright, William	1153	Brown, James Jr.	5044
Bright, Sallie	1154	Brown, Mary J.	5630
Briley, Tennessee V.	3763	Brown, Viola	5631
Briley, William E.	3764	Brown, Sam H.	5632
Briley, Nettie M.	3765	Brown, Delora	6261
Brimage, Susan	4413	Brown, Delores E.	6268
Britton, William	7989	Brown, Palmira	6600
Britton, Jeff	7990	Brown, Myrtle	6601
Britton, Mary	8967	Brown, James B.	6602
Brink, Lydia	11560	Brown, William M.	6603
Brink, George F.	11561	Brown, Lillie M.	6604
Brink, Mary A.	11562	Broaddus, Corintha	7169
Brink, Charles N.	11563	Broaddus, Dora May	7170
Brink, Albert L.	11564	Brown, Mary	7224
Brink, William T.	11565	Brown, Henry F.	7225
Brink, Hooley	11566	Brown, Rhoda	8097
Brink, James	11567	Brown, Henry	8098
Bridges, Fannie	12223	Brown, Olive G.	8181
Bridges, Guss	12224	Brown, Fannie M.	8182
Bridges, Thomas H.	12225	Brown, Bertha L.	8183
Brimage, Alexander	15738	Brown, Sadie M.	8184
Brimage, Fred	15832	Brown, Celia	8199
Brimage, Cora F.	15833	Brown, Thompson	8200
Bridge, Runaway	18531	Brown, Richard	8201
Bridge, Nellie	18532	Brown, William	8226
Brimage, Ethel May	21842	Brown, Eddie	8227
Bright, Marion	22355	Brown, Herman	8228
Bright, Henry	22357	Brown, Emily	8229
Bright, Samuel	22387	Browning, Mary J.	8814
Bright, Barshey	22388	Browning, Fannie M.	8815
Bright, Charly	22389	Browning, Robbie .E.	8816
Brimage, Thomas	22847	Brown, Margaret	8911
Brickey, Gertrude	25088	Brown, Sarah A.	9551
Brickey, Mamie R.	25089	Brown, Addie J.	9552
Brickey, Mary M.	25090	Brown, Elizabeth	9553
Brickey, James S.	25091	Brown, Jesse C.	9554
Bright, Letha	28539	Brown, Garland A.	9555
Bridge, Nancy	30502	Brown, Maud S.	9556
Brown, John W.	978	Brown, Effie E.	9557
Brown, Ida B.	979	Broaddus, Rebecca J.	9916
Brown, Mary J.	980	Brock, Charles R.	9918
Brown, Myra	981	Brock, Robert E. L.	9919
Brown, Richard	982	Brown, Larkin	9964
Brown, Florence	983	Brown, Martha A.	9965
Brown, Robert A.	984	Brown, Elmer E.	9966
Brown, Demaris	985	Brown, Fannie S.	9967
Brown, James	1294	Brown, Bertha M.	9968
Brown, Josephine	1770	Brown, William H.	9969
Brown, John L.	1851	Brown, Rebecca	10544

Name.	Roll No.	Name.	Roll No.
Brown, Mabel A.	10545	Brown, James E.	16242
Brown, Eliza	10618	Brown, Ella M.	16243
Brown, Henry L.	10619	Brown, Ida A.	16244
Brown, Louis L.	10748	Brown, Lelia F.	16245
Brown, Minnie	11319	Brown, Ruth E.	16246
Brown, Josephine	11320	Brown, Samuel Fill-	
Brown, Emma	11321	more	16247
Brown, Sarah E.	11364	Brown, Lillie	16503
Brown, Mollie V.	11365	Brock, Walter J.	16910
Brown, James M. Jr.	11366	Brock, Susie E.	16911
Brown, Edna M.	11367	Brock, George	16912
Brown, Hiram C.	11368	Brock, Gleason K.	16913
Brown, Manley E.	11369	Brown, Rachel	16925
Brown, Frances E.	11454	Brown, Samuel T.	16926
Brown, Mary E.	11455	Brown, Josiah	16927
Brown, Beatrice	11456	Brown, Jennettie	16928
Brown, Eva J.	11983	Brown, Maggie	17865
Brown, Johnnie A.	12199	Brown, Nannie E.	17866
Brown, Sereni E.	12200	Brown, Frank G.	17902
Brown, Laura E.	12201	Brown, Jim	18048
Brown, John L.	12202	Brown, Cassie	18054
Brown, Addie M.	12203	Broner, Lydia	20546
Brown, Martha E.	12204	Brown, Rufus	20939
Brown, Marion E.	12205	Brown, John B.	21685
Brown, Rufus H.	12226	Brown, John	21787
Brown, Nellie C.	12227	Brown, James	21806
Brown, Bessie M.	12228	Brown, Martha	22482
Brown, Letha F.	12229	Brown, Artie	22483
Brown, Florence B.	12230	Brown, Henry M.	22488
Brown, Nora L.	12231	Brown, Mary	22489
Brown, Jesse	12557	Brown, Baskum	22490
Brock, Mary M.	12588	Brown, Eliza	22491
Brock, Joseph C.	12589	Brown, Martha	22492
Brock, Lula G.	12590	Brown, William	22493
Brock, Mary M.	12591	Brown, Sarah M.	22494
Brown, Nancy L.	12721	Brown, Luduskey A.	22592
Brown, Albert B.	12722	Brown, John	22593
Brown, Effie M.	12723	Brown, Cornelius	22594
Brown, Nora A.	12724	Brown, Benjamin	22595
Brown, Roy T.	12725	Brown, Eliza	22861
Brown, William O.	12726	Brown, Morris	24441
Brown, Annie B.	12954	Brown, Helen	24443
Brown, William A.	12955	Brown, Eva M.	24444
Brown, Laura J.	12956	Brown, Mabel O.	24445
Brown, Florence L.	12957	Brown, Floyd F.	24446
Brown, Beulah B.	12958	Brown, Frank	24459
Brown, Eugenia D.	12959	Brown, Mary	24460
Brown, Annie B.	12964	Brown, Nannie	24461
Brown, Maude E.	13117	Brown, George C.	25564
Brown, Foster G.	13118	Brown, Mary M.	25565
Brown, Carl J.	13119	Brown, Tennessee B.	25566
Brown, Ulla M.	13120	Brown, Fannie A.	25567
Brock, Louis C.	13555	Brown, Frederick F.	25568
Brock, Nona P.	13556	Brown, Nancy I.	25569
Brock, Della	13557	Brown, Robert E. L.	25570
Brock, Jesse R.	13558	Brown, Lula	25928
Brown, Martin R.	13842	Brown, George	25929
Brown, Nannie E.	13843	Brown, Ruth	26664
Brown, Anna E.	13844	Brown, Earnest E.	26665
Brown, Catherine	13845	Brown, Rebecca A.	26666
Brown, Ida B.	14530	Brown, William M.	26667
Brown, Roscoe A.	14532	Brown, Annie	27478
Brown, Geneva B.	14533	Brown, Polly	27628
Brown, Charles F.	14534	Brown, George T.	27629
Brown, Charles G.	15624	Brown, Josie	28504
Brown, Rachel E.	15625	Brown, Nancy	28507
Brown, Etta B.	15626	Brown, Alsie	28508
Brown, Nannie L.	15627	Brown, Elizabeth J.	28660
Brown, Eliza	15783	Brown, Lottie M.	28665
Brown, Polly A.	15784	Brown, James H.	28743
Brown, Florence	15785	Brown, Bertha A.	28744
Brown, George H.	15967	Brown, Emmit Cecil	28745
Brown, Maude F.	16033	Brooks, Lafayette E.	29267
Brown, Addie V.	16034	Brooks, Fay T.	29268
Brown, Bertha E.	16035	Brown, Susan L.	29269
Brown, Mary E.	16036	Brown, Margaret C.	29270
Brown, Charles	16103	Brown, Florence R.	29271
Brown, Frank J.	16104	Brown, James M.	29272
Brown, Pearl J.	16105	Brown, William J.	29273
Brown, Charles A.	16106	Brown, Amanda	30959
Brown, George R.	16107	Brown, George W.	31005
Brown, Eula V.	16108	Bronson, Maggie E.	31096
Brown, Flora	16237	Bronson, Luella	31097

Name.	Roll No.	Name.	Roll No.
Bronson, James	31098	Bryan, Joel M., Jr.	6960
Bronson, William	31099	Bryan, Charles V.	6961
Brown, Charles	31301	Bryan, Ett	6962
Brown, Matilda	31345	Bryan, Jessie M.	6964
Brown, Eben W.	31346	Bryan, Rachel B.	11791
Brown, Ida May	31347	Bryan, Eula P.	15750
Brown, Katie	31675	Bryan, Roy V.	15751
Brown, Lucinda	31676	Bryan, Clifford	15752
Brown, Annie	31677	Bryan, Cleo C.	15753
Brown, Mary	32003	Bryan, Guy G.	15754
Brown, Frances O.	32212	Bryan, Eula E.	15755
Brown, Daniel R.	32213	Bryan, Mastie Chancey	15756
Brown, John J.	32214	Bryce, Georgia C.	11921
Brown, Cora B.	32215	Bryce, Charles M.	11922
Brown, Effie L.	32216	Bryce, Anna L.	11923
Brown, Robert	32752	Bryce, Walter J.	11924
Brown, Nellie	32753	Buchanan, James	5124
Brown, Irene	32754	Buck, Jumper	6185
Brown, Elmer	32755	Buckskin, James	6319
Brown, Viola	32756	Buckskin, Jennie	6320
Bruner, Mary	2068	Buck, Steve	7520
Bruner, Isaac N.	2261	Buck, Bettie	7521
Bruner, Clarence M.	2262	Buck, Noah	7522
Bruner, Jalina C.	2263	Buckmaster, Cenia	13714
Bruner, George S.	2271	Buckmaster, Mary	13715
Bruner, Mary E.	2272	Buckmaster, Birdie E.	13716
Bruner, Ivory I.	2273	Buckner, Mary	14325
Bruner, Rice A.	2274	Bucket, David	17678
Bruner, Theodore S.	2567	Bucket, Aggie	17679
Bruner, Mary M.	2568	Bucket, Bettie	17680
Bruner, Florence E.	2569	Bucket, Jack	17681
Bruner, Josie H.	2570	Bucket, Daws	17682
Bruner, Letha A.	2580	Bucket, Samuel	17683
Bruner, John R.	2581	Bucket, Lou	17684
Bruner, Claud	2582	Buckskin, George	17972
Bruner, Amos C.	21809	Buckskin, Frank	18211
Bruton, Calvin	3467	Buckskin, Sam	18212
Bruton, Walter C.	3468	Buckskin, Sic-a-towie	19440
Bruton, Wilson O.	3492	Buckskin, Aggy	19441
Bruton, Caswell B.	3493	Buckskin, Joseph	19453
Bruton, Robert O.	3494	Buckskin, Wahley	19454
Bruere, Lydia	12729	Buck, John	19968
Bruere, Louisa S.	12730	Buck, Jennie	19969
Bruere, Charles A.	12731	Buck, Jack	19970
Bruere, Susie J.	12732	Buckhorn, Jack	20708
Bruere, Louis	12733	Buckhorn, Lizzie	20709
Bruere, Clarinda	12734	Buckhalter, Frances Louise	21576
Bryson, Jennie M.	1927	Buckner, Minnie	21745
Bryson, Mary J.	1928	Buck, Taylor	23336
Bryson, William Etta	1929	Buck, William	23337
Bryant, James A.	6778	Buckner, Mary C.	25123
Bryant, Margaret J.	8560	Buckner, Joel M.	25124
Bryant, Martha A.	8562	Buckner, Sarah L.	25125
Bryant, Lou L.	8563	Buckner, Leland D.	25126
Bryant, Lottie S.	8564	Buckner, James	25127
Bryant, Bertha M.	8565	Buckner, Neoma V.	25128
Bryant, Lucinda	8566	Buckner, Martha A.	25513
Bryant, William C.	8567	Buckner, Ivory C.	25514
Bryant, Inola	8568	Buckner, Parthenia L.	25515
Bryant, Jessie V.	8569	Buckner, Lola L.	25516
Bryant, Myrtle B.	10046	Buckner, Strauther R.	25517
Bryant, Luther R.	10047	Buckner, Tams E.	25518
Bryant, Calvin A.	10048	Buckskin, Joe M.	25576
Bryant, Theodore Orvil	10049	Buck, Lydia	26454
Bryant, Jennie	12438	Buck, Jennie	26397
Bryant, Joseph V.	21618	Buchanan, Josephine	26426
Bryant, Vinnie	21619	Buchanan, Walter	26427
Bryant, Leonidas	21620	Buchanan, Myrtle	26428
Bryant, Jesse	21621	Buchanan, Edgar	26429
Bryant, Cullen	21622	Buchanan, Ann	26430
Bryant, Bertha	21623	Buchanan, Clyde	26431
Bryant, Hattie E.	21624	Buckskin, Littlebird	29672
Bryant, Benjamin F.	22437	Buckskin, Katie	29673
Bryant, Alice	22439	Buchanan, Bertha L.	30067
Bryant, Leona	22440	Buckskin, Delegates	30516
Bryant, Rhoda	22441	Budder, Lewis	8332
Bryant, Florance	22442	Budder, Jesse	8484
Bryant, John	22443	Budder, Nellie	8485
Bryant, Susan	22444	Budder, Henry	8486
Bryant, Clarence R.	23444	Budder, Jennie	8487
Bryant, Benjamin F.	26525	Budder, Canuka	8488
Bryant, Minnie	29786	Budder, Watt	8489
Bryan, Joel M.	6957	Budder, Oochalatah	8490
Bryan, Maggie J.	6958	Budder, Jack	18503
		Budder, Dave	29676

Name.	Roll No.	Name.	Roll No.
Budder, Cewee	29677	Bumgarner, John W.	18760
Budder, Ned	26678	Bumgarner, Samuel H.	8263
Buffington, Alexander		Bump, Cordie S.	11450
C.	3702	Bump, Hurshell P.	11451
Buffington, Stella M.	3703	Bunch, Eli	17825
Buffington, Annie L.	3704	Bunch, Alex	18011
Buffington, William E.	3705	Bunch, Eliza	18012
Buffington, Georgia L.	3706	Bunch, Mary	18013
Buffington, John R.	7032	Bunch, Ollie	18014
Buffington, Nannie J.	7033	Bunch, Lizzie	18015
Buffington, Carrie R.	7034	Bunch, Jesse	18016
Buffington, Charles R.	7035	Bunch, Jack	18018
Buffington, Hallie H.	7036	Bunch, Samuel	18019
Buffington, Joel W.	7037	Bunch, Nancy	18017
Buffington, Mary J.	7038	Bunch, Noah	18373
Buffington, Cherry G.	7039	Bunch, Ollie	18374
Buffington, James	8407	Bunch, Rebecca	18923
Buffington, Hazel Marie	8408	Bunch, Charles	19014
Buffington, Charles	8423	Bunch, Nannie	19015
Buffington, Lucian W.	8614	Bunch, James	19016
Buffington, Nannie	8615	Bunch, Jack	19017
Buffington, Daniel W.	8636	Bunch, Mary	19018
Buffington, Thomas M.	9823	Bunch, Adaline	19019
Buffington, John E.	15877	Bunch, Lee	19020
Buffington, Ellis W.	16461	Bunch, Tom	19117
Buffalofish, Hunter	20538	Bunch, Ollie	19118
Buffalofish, Aggie	20539	Bunch, Levi	19119
Buffington, Dave	21216	Bunch, Dicie	19120
Buffington, Charlotte	21217	Bunch, Tunie	19121
Buffington, Susie	21221	Bunch, Jennie	19122
Buffington, Fannie E.	22341	Bunch, Jennie	20155
Buffington, Mary Etta	22342	Bunch, Lizzie	20156
Buffington, Grover	22343	Bunch, Richard	20157
Buffington, John D.	22344	Bunch, Peggie	20158
Buffington, Lucille	24402	Bunch, John	20159
Buffington, Sue Nell	24403	Bunch, Jug	20160
Buffington, Lillian M.	24404	Bunch, Annie	20161
Buffington, Thomas C.	28947	Bunch, John	20162
Buffington, Mollie C.	28948	Bunch, Betsy	20163
Buffington, Colbert W.	28949	Bunch, Etta	20164
Buffington, Stella K.	28950	Bunch, Jack	20165
Buffington, Thomas C.		Bunch, Susie	20166
Jr.	28951	Bunch, Nancy	20167
Buffington, Webster	30003	Bunch, Henry	25733
Buffington, Lucian	30741	Bunch, Missouri	25734
Buffington, Alex	30742	Bunch, Jennie	25735
Buffalo, Lula	31180	Bunch, Sarah	25736
Buffalo, James	31217	Bunch, Bird	25737
Buffalo, Josie	31181	Burgess, Jessie M.	2233
Buford, Jesse	31137	Burgess, Louena V.	12536
Bugher, Florence	8391	Burgess, Flora E.	12537
Bugher, Charles	8392	Burgess, Laura M.	12538
Bugher, Oma	8393	Burgess, Sidney E.	12539
Bug, Return	29674	Burgess, Ben	12540
Bug, Ca-ho-ker	29675	Burgess, John	12558
Bullock, Fannie	5749	Burgess, Cooie	12559
Bullock, Floyd	5752	Burgess, Mary J.	12560
Bullard, Lucy I.	17308	Burgess, William A.	12561
Bull, Thomas	18401	Burgess, James O.	12562
Bullfrog, Nancy	18902	Burgess, John S.	12563
Bullette, George	31195	Burgess, Carrie	12564
Bullette, Rosie	31196	Burgess, Alma	12565
Bullett, Josie	31212	Burgess, Daniel	12566
Bullette, Mabel Z.	31587	Burgess, William	24882
Bullette, George C.	31588	Burgess, Jesse B.	28046
Bullette, Mary A.	31589	Burrow, Sarah A.	2618
Bullette, Floyd C.	31590	Burrow, Charles H.	2619
Bullett, Nellie F.	31598	Burrow, William D.	2620
Bullett, John E.	31597	Burrow, Bertha L.	2622
Bullett, Jessie E.	31599	Burrow, Joseph W.	2623
Bullett, Georgia P.	31600	Burrow, Franklin E.	2625
Bullette, Frank S.	31611	Burrows, James	5192
Bullette, Sonoma	31612	Burrows, Walter R.	5193
Bulawsky, Josephine	31755	Burrows, Whit	5194
Bulawsky, Dora	31756	Burrows, William A.	5195
Bulawsky, Ida	31757	Burrows, Alta M.	5196
Bulawsky, Annie	31758	Burrows, Tobe	5197
Bulawsky, Blanche	31759	Burrows, Samantha L.	5198
Bulawsky, May	31760	Burrows, Charles C.	11198
Bulawsky, Oscar	31761	Burrows, Thomas C.	11199
Bullett, Levi	32806	Burrows, John H.	11200
Bumgarner, Charlotte E.	8260	Burrows, Edward M.	11201
Bumgarner, James L.	8259	Burrows, Christopher B.	11202
Bumgarner, Jessie L. B.	8261		
Bumgarner, John B.	8262		

Name.	Roll No.
Burton, Emily B.	4105
Burton, Maud M.	4106
Burton, Alice L.	4107
Burton, Maude F.	12046
Burr, Benjamin F.	4302
Burton, Gladys	12047
Burr, Frank	4303
Burr, Joseph	4304
Burr, Sylvia	4305
Burr, Andy	5125
Burr, James W.	17904
Burr, Frank R.	21848
Burr, Aaron	22140
Burr, Eddie B.	22141
Burr, Eliza	22981
Burr, Charles	22982
Burr, Josie.	22983
Burr, Maggie B.	23576
Burr, John W.	23577
Burr, Jesse E.	25378
Burr, Maggie E.	25379
Burr, Nina A.	25380
Burr, Harris E.	25381
Burr, Robert	25382
Burr, George W.	28375
Burr, Calvin	28376
Burr, Alexander	28377
Burk, Emma	4317
Burk, Fannie M.	4685
Burk, Otto P.	4691
Burk, Amy	4687
Burk, Helen E.	4688
Burk, Eva	4689
Burk, Fanny R.	4690
Burke, Martha	7512
Burke, Thomas W.	7513
Burke, William R.	7514
Burke, John S.	7515
Burke, Walter L.	7516
Burks. Elmer H.	7902
Burckhalter, Tom C.	7455
Burckhalter, Opal L.	7456
Burns, Bernard D.	7525
Burns, Etta H.	8517
Burns, Lily D.	8518
Burnett, Ethel P.	8386
Burnett, Alta C.	8387
Burnett, Annie F.	13627
Burnett, Mary B.	13626
Burnett, Tommie R.	13628
Burt, Alice	25395
Burton, Laura O.	31415
Bushyhead, Dennis W. Jr.	748
Bushyhead, Sarah C.	1337
Bushyhead, Louis	1338
Bushyhead, George	6187
Bushyhead, Jacob	6229
Bushyhead, Robert	6777
Bushyhead, Smith	11466
Bushyhead, Mamie E.	11467
Bushyhead, Augustus	11468
Bushyhead, Delilah	11594
Bushyhead, George W.	11984
Bushyhead, Eloise P. B.	13829
Bushyhead, James B.	13831
Bushyhead, Frances T.	13832
Bushyhead, Jesse	17667
Bushyhead, Jane	17668
Bushyhead, William	17669
Bushyhead, John	17671
Bushyhead, Maggie	17672
Bushyhead, Cornelius	17673
Bushyhead, Eddie	17674
Bushyhead, Lucinda	17675
Bushyhead, Rurus	17676
Bushyhead, Jesse	17957
Bushyhead, Kahawker	20370
Bushyhead, George	20830
Bushyhead, Jennie	20831
Bushyhead, Ada	25587
Bushyhead, Charlie	28516
Bushyhead, Maggie	29157

Name.	Roll No.
Bushyhead, Henry	32901
Bush, Eliza	5359
Bush, Edna	5364
Bush, Mary	18964
Bush, Nannie	19304
Bush, Dave	25704
Bush, Bettie	25705
Bush, Sam	25706
Bush, Ben	25707
Buster, William	11731
Buster,. Rosa Ellen	11732
Buster, Charles W.	11733
Buster, Thomas V.	11734
Buster, John W., Jr.	11882
Buster, William T.	11883
Buster, Hunter	19909
Buster, Betsy	19910
Buster, Gegoowie	19911
Buster, Polly	19912
Buster, Dargie	19913
Buster, Celia	19914
Buster, Lipsie	19915
Buster, Tiger	19916
Buster, Nellie	20842
Buster, Tom	20843
Buster, Dorster	20844
Buster, Club	20845
Buster, Ijarker	20846
Buster, Rachel	21121
Buster, Wallese	21222
Buster, Aggie	21223
Buster, Isaac	21224
Buster, Robert	21225
Buster, Aggie	28518
Buster, Susie	32073
Bussey, Dottie	11759
Bussey, Dora	11760
Bussey, Francis M. Jr.	11761
Bussey, Freddie M.	11762
Bussey, Milliard F.	11763
Bussey, Johnnie H.	11764
Bussey, George W.	11765
Bussey, Martha	12007
Bussey, Heck	12008
Bussey, Nicholas	12009
Bussey, John	12260
Bussey, Emma	12556
Busheyhead, Jesse C.	11874
Busheyhead, Oowala E.	11875
Busheyhead, Edward R.	11876
Busheyhead, Martha	11985
Busheyhead, William T.	11986
Busheyhead, Charlotte	11987
Busheyhead, James W.	11988
Buse, Nancy R.	14765
Buse, Onie M.	14766
Buse, Charles F.	14767
Buse, Ada E.	14768
Buse, Samuel T.	14769
Butler, James P.	502
Butler, James	503
Butler, Aaron	4758
Butler, Nora	4759
Butler, Leona L.	4760
Butler, Emmett	4761
Butler, Charles C.	4762
Butler, William	5223
Butler, Carrie L.	5737
Butler, Willie E.	5738
Butler, Richard V.	5887
Butler, Samuel H.	5888
Butler, Helen	7862
Butler, Grace	7863
Butler, Elizabeth	7864
Butler, Helen	7865
Butler, John O.	13687
Butler, Sallie	13688
Butler, Lucien B.	13690
Butler, Frances H.	13830
Butler, James H.	15005
Butler, Emeline	15006
Butler, Bear	17083
Butler, Lydia	17084

Name.	Roll No.	Name.	Roll No.
Butler, Josie	17085	Byers, Offie	3005
Butler, Susie	17423	Byers, William E.	3006
Butler, Nancy	22277	Byers, John	3007
Butler, John W.	25056	Byers, James	3047
Butler, Robert R.	25058	Byers, Wilson	3203
Butler, Mary U. E.	25059	Byers, Thirsty Lee	3204
Butler, Joseph B.	25060	Byers, Emma A.	10297
Butler, Robert E.	26111	Byers, Wilma A.	10298
Butler, George O.	27780	Byers, Jessie May	10299
Butler, Kittie E.	27781	Byers, Dave	19521
Butler, Kathleen P.	27782	Byers, Annie	19522
Butler, Daniel R.	27783	Byers, Sallie	19523
Butler, James L.	27784	Byers, Eliza	19524
Butler, Pierce P.	27785	Byers, Betsy	20527
Butler, George	28927	Byrd, Annie D.	9311
Butler, Charlotte	28928	Byrd, Eva R.	9312
Butler, Robert	28929	Byrd, Fitzhugh L.	9313
Butler, Susan	28930	Byrd, Susan P.	9314
Butler, Samuel	28931	Byrd, Bettie	9342
Butler, Gee Dick	28932	Byrd, Decator F.	9871
Butler, Curtis	28933	Byrd, Dimmie F.	10019
Butler, Katie	28997	Byrd, Nina	10123
Butler, Mattie L.	32663	Byrd, Alfred	10124
Butler, Frank L.	32664	Byrd, Maud M.	10125
Butler, Myrtle	32665	Byrd, Minnie L.	10126
Butler, William J.	32676	Byrd, Louisa J.	10127
Butts, Cordelia	15186	Byrd, Henry H.	13115
Butts, Naeta M.	15187	Byrd, Daisy E. L.	13116
Butts, Cherokee	15588	Byrd, Cynthia	14355
Butts, Edna M.	26250	Byrd, Jane	24962
Butts, Gertie	26251	Byrd, Daisy D.	24963
Butts, Ella S.	30301	Byrd, Elizabeth	24985
Butts, Harvey W.	30302	Byrd, Henry A.	24986
Butts, Silvia E.	30303	Byrd, Randolph S.	24987
Butz, Helen	31984	Byrd, Mary E.	24988
Buzzard, James	2550	Byrd, Leroy A.	24989
Buzzard, Berry	2551	Byrd, Lillie M.	24990
Buzzard, Hardy	2552	Byrd, Robert	24991
Buzzard, George	2553	Byrd, Minervia J.	24992
Buzzard, Tom	2554	Byrd, Theodore	24993
Buzzard, Eliza	7918	Byrd, Maggie E.	26373
Buzzard, Jessie	17450	Byrd, Richard C.	32705
Buzzard, William	18639	Byrd, Josie P.	32706
Buzzard, Lucy	18640	Byrd, Ethel M.	32707
Buzzard, Jackson	18646	Byrd, Maggie A.	32708
Buzzard, Sam	19359	Byrd, Ella M.	32709
Buzzard, Annie	19361	Byrd, Richard A.	32710
Buzzard, Elizabeth	19360	Byrd, Laura J.	32711
Buzzard, Adam	19362	Byrd, Miles L.	32712
Buzzard, Nellie	19363	Byrd, Ruby M.	32713
Buzzard, Cornelius B.	19367	Byron, Cora M.	31511
Buzzard, Lucy	19368	Cabe, Katie	12518
Buzzard, Jackson	19464	Cabe, Marven	12520
Buzzard, Betty	19739	Cabbagehead, Pay-	
Buzzard, Jackson	19794	master	32406
Buzzard, Sallie	19795	Cabbagehead, Sarah	32407
Buzzard, Nellie	19853	Cabbagehead, Lizzie	32408
Buzzard, Lydia	20135	Cabbagehead, Jennie	32787
Buzzard, John	30536	Caesar, James	10243
Buzzard, Celia	30581	Cah-no-hyat, George	20343
Buzzard, Nancy	32034	Callahan, Drury Q.	1703
Buzzard, Daniel	32035	Callahan, Benjamin P.	1704
Buzzard, Joe	32036	Callahan, William R.	1705
Buzzard, John	32037	Callahan, James A.	1706
Buxton, Susie	9082	Callahan, Georgia C.	1707
Buxton, William C.	9083	Callahan, Alice	22180
Byers, Nick	2065	Callison, Emily M.	4999
Byers, Ellen	2066	Callison, Bertha E.	5000
Byers, Alfred	2067	Callison, Jesse L.	5001
Byers, Joe	2280	Calvert, Sarah A.	9675
Byers, Ann	2773	Calvert, Amanda A.	9676
Byers, Fannie	2774	Calvert, Charley E.	9677
Byers, Ezekiel	2775	Calvert, Lela D.	9678
Byers, Lizzie	2776	Calvert, Cynthia J.	24705
Byers, Cornelia	2777	Calvert, Robert	24706
Byers, Nickademus	2778	Calbert, Samuel A.	14862
Byers, William H.	2997	Calbert, Roberta	14863
Byers, Ellen E.	2998	Calbert, Willie M.	14864
Byers, Henry C.	2999	Caldwell, John L.	24418
Byers, Charles W.	3001	Caldwell, Mariah F.	24419
Byers, Sarah A.	3002	Caldwell, Benjamin M.	24420
Byers, Leona M.	3003	Caldwell, Joella M.	24421
Byers, Mary	3004	Caldwell, Annie	30794
		Caldwell, Isaac B.	30795

Name.	Roll No.	Name.	Roll No.
Caldwell, Elsie F.	30796	Candy, George	21811
Caldwell, Francis A.	30797	Candy, Allen	29938
Caldwell, Tule	30798	Candy, Mabel	29939
Caldwell, Lula	32624	Candy, Rachel	15864
Campbell, Alex	4467	Candy, Lewis J.	15865
Campbell, May	4468	Candy, Josephine	15866
Campbell, Minnie	4469	Candy, Deertrack	20996
Campbell, James A.	4470	Candy, John	20997
Campbell, William L.	4681	Candy, Mary Augusta	20998
Campbell, Herbert	4682	Candy, George	25952
Campbell, Hugh W.	4683	Candy, Nancy	25953
Campbell, Flora	6753	Canoe, Lydia	15892
Campbell, Zelma	7672	Canoe, Samuel	15893
Campbell, Noma W.	7676	Canoe, Jennie	15894
Campbell, George L.	12684	Canoe, Katie	15895
Campbell, Gaylena	12685	Canoe, Benjamin	15896
Campbell, Charles H.	12686	Canoe, Louisa	15898
Campbell, John	13327	Canoe, Arch	15906
Campbell, Glenn	13328	Canoe, Ailsy	15907
Campbell, Mathew	13329	Canoe, Martin	15908
Campbell, William W.	15500	Canoe, Ellis	18968
Campbell, Wilson	16304	Canoe, Bettie	20197
Campbell, Nancy	16305	Canoe, George	25645
Campbell, John	16841	Canoe, Jennie	25646
Campbell, Miles	16842	Canoe, Chickoowa	25647
Campbell, James P.	16859	Canoe, Beaver	25648
Campbell, William R.	17809	Canoe, Mary	2509
Campbell, Abraham	18223	Canoe, Ida	18010
Campbell, Bean	20381	Cantrell, Clara	21585
Campbell, John	20870	Cantrell, Charles	21586
Campbell, Olce	20871	Cantrell, Maud M.	27664
Campbell, Oolskuntny	20875	Cantrell, Ruthie M.	27665
Campbell, Susan	20876	Cantrell, Walter J.	27666
Campbell, Joseph	26729	Cantrell, Ida B.	9901
Campbell, Mary A.	26902	Cantrell, Mabel L.	9902
Campbell, Lucy A.	27747	Cantrell, Louie E.	9903
Campbell, Charlotte	28505	Canary, Anola J.	26240
Camel, Rope	28926	Canary, Emma P.	26241
Campbell, Delora	29489	Canary, Simeon C.	26242
Campbell, Mary E.	30266	Canary, James H.	26243
Campbell, Herbert L.	31609	Canary, Elmira L.	26244
Camp, Mary A.	23608	Canup, Viola G.	29989
Camp, Claud F.	23609	Canup, Harry T.	29990
Camp, Jennie M.	23610	Capps, Charlotte	1364
Cannon, John C.	869	Capps, Lillie M.	1367
Cannon, Mary R.	870	Capps, Mary	5755
Cannon, Walter	871	Capps, Henry	19596
Cannon, Bular	872	Capps, Amanda E.	29441
Cannon, Cora	873	Capps, Seaneath L.	29442
Cannon, Anna B.	7454	Captain, George	31582
Cannon, Spencer W.	13022	Carey, Robt. E. L.	210
Cannon, Wilson L.	14065	Carey, Sarah A.	211
Cannon, Alice	14066	Carey, Myrtle	212
Cannon, Grover	14067	Carey, Lillie	213
Cannon, Frank	14068	Carey, Lucy	214
Cannon, Mance	14069	Carey, Winnie	215
Cannon, Adah	14070	Carey, Ray E.	216
Cannon, Oscar	16271	Carey, Edmond D.	217
Cannon, Zoe M.	22033	Carey, Lydia Ann	218
Cannon, Leonard L.	22034	Carey, Susan	219
Cannon, Edwin B.	22371	Carey, Charlotte B.	220
Cannon, Charles L.	22372	Carey, Edmond L.	221
Cannon, Claud	22374	Carey, George B.	222
Cannon, Maud	22375	Carey, Stonewall J.	223
Cannon, Aud	22376	Carey, Bruce	224
Cannon, Caud	22377	Carey, David L.	9971
Cannon, Ruth	22378	Carey, Emma M.	10885
Cannon, Bertha	26026	Carey, Flona V.	10886
Cannon, Wirt	26027	Carey, Sansa V.	10887
Cannon, Maggie M.	26028	Carey, Majora B.	10888
Cannon, Sterling P.	27801	Carey, William V.	10889
Cannon, Al	29755	Carey, Sabra	15001
Cannon, Roxie	30319	Carey, Silas	15432
Cannon, Mattie Edna	30324	Carey, Mike Jr.	16159
Cannon, Ira	724	Carey, Jennie	16160
Cannon, Cora V.	725	Carey, Nora	16162
Cannon, George L.	12931	Carey, Susan	16198
Cannon, Robert L.	12932	Carey, Daniel	16199
Cannon, Ada N.	12933	Carey, Katie	16200
Canada, Henry L.	10460	Carey, Frances	17640
Canada, Fannie E.	10950	Carey, George	17659
Canada, Ida C.	10951	Carey, Walter	17660
Candy, Jess	21096	Carey, Thomas	17661
Candy, Samuel	11536	Carey, Rhoda	17662
Candy, Sallie	21097	Carey, Eliza	18253

Name.	Roll No.	Name.	Roll No.
Carey, Sallie	18273	Carter, Delora B.	12704
Carey, Jesse	18274	Carter, Candis J.	12705
Carey, Madison	18275	Carter, Emery W.	12706
Carey, Sallie	18276	Carter, Jerdie B.	12707
Carey, Lewis	18277	Carter, Margaret C.	12709
Carey, Nancy	18278	Carter, Carrie E.	14361
Carey, Clem	18279	Carter, Sue A.	14362
Carey, Nellie	18280	Carter, James P.	14363
Carey, Nelson	18281	Carter, Nancy C.	15189
Carey, Dick	18552	Carter, James I.	15190
Carey, Jennie	18553	Carter, Lula	15191
Carey, Linnie	18554	Carter, Albert	15192
Carey, Dick	21256	Carter, Sarah M.	15193
Carey, Julie Mary	21841	Carter, Mary	17528
Carey, Annie	22028	Carter, Minnie L.	29438
Carey, Thomas	22029	Carter, Pearl I.	29439
Carey, Harlan	22030	Carter, Ada P.	29440
Carey, Robbin L.	24428	Carlile, Thomas	3279
Carey, Rachel J.	24429	Carlile, Myrtle	3280
Carey, Lucy	29054	Carlile, Arthur	3281
Carey, Aaron	29056	Carlile, Wiliam	3461
Carey, Annie	29057	Carlile, William A.	3462
Carey, James	29058	Carlile, Leo A.	3463
Carey, Jesse J.	29059	Carlile, Maud E.	3464
Carey, Samuel	29060	Carlile, Effie E.	3465
Carey, Dewey	29061	Carlile, Mary N.	3466
Carey, Ayla	29062	Carlile, Mary L.	4296
Carey, Joseph	29063	Carlile, Robert B.	6089
Carey, Steve	29064	Carlile, Thomas J.	14696
Carey, Amanda	29065	Carlile, Viana E.	14697
Carey, Mollie	29066	Carlile, Thomas H.	14698
Carey, Bulah E.	30019	Carlile, John H.	14699
Carey, Ruth	30020	Carlile, Walter E.	14700
Carey, William R.	30021	Carlile, Edward A.	14701
Carey, Joella	30022	Carlile, Levi	14702
Carey, Lelia M.	31430	Carlile, Virgil D.	14703
Carey, Joe	32274	Carlile, Clarence G.	14704
Carey, Lewis	32275	Carlile, Stephen N.	14294
Carnes, Jeff D.	1189	Carlile, John	14705
Carnes, Henry A.	1190	Carlile, Johnan	14706
Carnes, John J.	1191	Carlile, Ada B.	14707
Carnes, Dempsey A. N.	1192	Carlile, Alice B.	14708
Carnes, Oscar	1193	Carlile, Maggie	14899
Carnes, Angie	1194	Carlile, Stephen F.	15120
Carnes, George W.	1195	Carlile, Willie A.	15121
Carnes, Robert H. L.	1196	Carlile, Mattie M.	15122
Carnes, George B.	1197	Carlile, William K.	15501
Carnes, Ida	1198	Carlile, Emma	15502
Carnes, Cora L.	1199	Carlile, Annie M.	15503
Carnes, Lizzie L.	1200	Carlile, Carrie E.	15504
Carnes, Walter R.	1201	Carlile, Henrietta	15505
Carnes, Ada Ann	1202	Carlile, William K., Jr.	15506
Carnes, John W.	1287	Carlile, Bluie J.	15507
Carnes, Susan	1288	Carlile, Henry H.	15745
Carnes, Roscoe	1289	Carlile, Lizzie N.	15746
Carnes, Coney	1290	Carlile, Thomas K.	15747
Carnes, Dianna	1291	Carlile, Charles A.	17119
Carnes, Elizabeth P.	1292	Carlile, Henrietta	27955
Carnes, Anna F.	1293	Carlisle, Mary	29778
Carnes, Andrew J.	1305	Carman, Katie J.	5072
Carnes, Joseph E.	1306	Carman, Hugh	5073
Carnes, Maudie J.	1307	Carman, Daniel	5074
Carnes, George W.	1308	Carman, William A.	5075
Carnes, Earl J.	1309	Card, Carrie E.	6916
Carnes, Gertie	21827	Carr, John G.	7090
Carden, Minnie M.	2359	Carr, Sarah A.	10144
Carden, John	2360	Carr, Josie M.	10145
Carden, Etta	2361	Carr, Beulah M.	10146
Carden, William	2362	Carr, Frank M.	10233
Carden, Rass	2363	Carr, William A.	10429
Carden, Lillie	2364	Carr, Vida	23057
Carden, Ida L.	2365	Carr, Lillian May	23060
Carden, Kate	2366	Carr, Ollie Ponder	23061
Carden, Lola B.	2367	Carr, Edwin E.	24158
Carter, Mary B.	2654	Carr, Minnie	32625
Carter, Albert E.	2655	Carr, Clyde	32626
Carter, Ola M.	9398	Carr, Susan M.	8973
Carter, Florence E.	9399	Carr, Tessie	32627
Carter, Mai M.	9400	Carr, Fannie J.	8974
Carter, William S.	9401	Carr, Edward	32628
Carter, Alma A.	9402	Carpenter, Ben	8586
Carter, Frank	9403	Carpenter, Angeline	8587
Carter, Clifton	9404	Carpenter, Lorenzo	8588

Name.	Roll No.	Name.	Roll No.
Carpenter, Grace	8589	Catcher, John	2011
Carpenter, Zonie	8590	Catcher, Susie	2012
Carpenter, Mary	8639	Catcher, Lettie	2013
Carpenter, Olive	8924	Catcher, Charles	2014
Carpenter, Alma Louis	8925	Catcher, Rachel	2015
Carpenter, Cora	27602	Catcher, Charles	2623
Carpenter, Claude	28910	Catcher, Ann	2924
Carpenter, Mollie R.	30771	Catcher, Betsy	2025
Carselowey, Kate A.	9512	Catcher, George	2026
Carselowey, Florence M.	9513	Catcher, Rosa P.	31990
Carselowey, Pauline R.	9514	Catcher, Cloe	31991
Carselowey, Arthur A.	9515	Catcher, Mary	2027
Carselowey, Stella E.	9516	Catcher, Tom	2028
Carselowey, James R.	13568	Catcher, George	2086
Carselowey, James M.	13569	Catcher, Charlotte	2087
Carselowey, Charles V.	13588	Catcher, Mollie	2088
Carrington, Wylie V.	10547	Catcher, Nannie	2089
Cary, Nellie	12404	Catcher, Georgie A.	2090
Cary, Georgia E.	12405	Catcher, Louis	2392
Cary, William	12406	Catcher, Sarah	2393
Carroll, Lola A.	14260	Catcher, Emma	2394
Carroll, Lula B.	14261	Catcher, Levi	17907
Carroll, Joe B.	14262	Catcher, Charles	18069
Carroll, Nellie	14728	Catcher, Lou	18070
Carroll, Henry L.	15671	Catcher, Frank Edward	18117
Carroll, Mary C.	26172	Catcher, John	18315
Carroll, Myrtie J.	26173	Catcher, Sis	22112
Carroll, Clemmie	26174	Catcher, Cornelius	27215
Carroll, Gilley M.	26175	Catcher, Bettie	27216
Carroll, Jesse L.	26176	Catcher, William	27217
Carroll, Charlie	29613	Catcher, Maud P.	27218
Carcawee, Dick	15148	Catcher, Richard	28251
Carrick, Lydia	15331	Catron, Lafayette	17982
Carrick, Susie	15332	Catron, Jefferson D.	17983
Carrick, Robert	15333	Catron, Josephus	17984
Carrick, Maggie	15334	Catron, Louanna G.	17985
Carrick, Lelia	15335	Catron, Julius	17992
Carrick, Ila I.	15336	Catron, Mary	25924
Carrick, Cornelius	15337	Catron, Frank L.	26029
Carver, Jerry	15831	Catron, Phoebe	26071
Carver, Josie	21487	Catron, Maggie	26072
Carver, Donie	21488	Catron, Lafayette	26073
Carver, Lizzie	27877	Catron, George	26074
Carver, Walter	27878	Catron, Thomas	26075
Carver, Pearl	27879	Catron, Maud B.	26076
Carver, Nannie	27907	Catron, Ola	26077
Carver, Joanna	27908	Catron, Etta	26078
Carver, Frank	27909	Catron, John	27804
Carselowry, Joe	16846	Catron, Toolie	29972
Cartwright, John H.	17125	Caulk, Melton M.	7765
Cartwright, Lelia Etta	17126	Caulk, Arther F.	7766
Cartwright, William T.	17127	Caulk, Rhoda	7767
Carcarwee, Susie	17895	Caulk, Maud	7768
Carcarwee, Ross	17896	Caulk, Pleasant	7774
Carroll, May	32859	Caulk, Millard	7775
Carseluke, Knight	32872	Caulk, Jewel	7776
Carseluke, Ce-kie	32873	Caulk, Gratten	7777
Cash, Nancy E.	4464	Caulk, Audry	7778
Cash, James M.	4465	Caulk, Eleanor	7779
Cash, Samuel A.	21964	Caulk, Edward H.	9335
Cash, John A.	22075	Caulk, Mary A.	32466
Case, Mattie	5903	Caulk, Bessie	32467
Cass, Lewis P.	7550	Caulk, Jesse	32468
Cass, Oreana	7551	Caulk, Laura	32469
Cass, Ruby M.	7552	Caulk, Otis	32470
Cass, Pearl M.	7553	Caudrey, Lewis C.	15059
Cass, Gracie B.	7554	Caudrey, Eliza	15060
Cass, Cornelia C.	7555	Caudrey, Mary	15061
Cass, Iddo G.	8036	Caudrey, Jennette	15062
Cass, Corbet	8037	Caudrey, Emma	15063
Cass, Mary E.	8038	Caudill, Elrilda	32735
Cass, Jessie	8039	Caudrey, Belle	15064
Cass, Bruce A.	26596	Cave, Minora	8073
Cason, Sarah M.	7854	Cave, James L.	8074
Cason, Bertha M.	7855	Cave, Annie	8075
Cason, George B.	7856	Cave, Ona	8076
Casey, Robert	14828	Cave, William C.	8077
Casey, John	27422	Cave, Katie M.	8078
Casey, Arch	28764	Cave, Earl	8079
Casey, William P.	31920	Cave, Leda G.	8080
Cates, Emma C.	1281	Cavalier, John T.	8936
Cates, Leona A.	1282	Cavalier, Eliza E.	8937
Cates, Edmond E.	1283	Cavalier, Cicero	8938
Cates, Syble E.	1284	Cavalier, Theodore	8939
Cates, Newton L.	1285	Cavalier, Markham	8940
		Cavalier, Scott	8941

Name.	Roll No.	Name.	Roll No.
Cavalier, Curtis	8942	Chambers, Minnie L.	11675
Cavalier, John T.	16924	Chambers, Joseph	11676
Caywood, Lillie	6186	Chambers, Evans	11677
Caywood, Mary E.	8443	Chambers, Claud S.	11678
Caywood, William M.	8444	Chambers, Juliette S.	11680
Caywood, Herbert T.	14382	Chambers, Willey E.	11838
Caywood, Moses S.	14384	Chambers, Nannie E.	11839
Caywood, Lizzie	18451	Chambers, Joseph W.	11840
Caywood, Fannie	18452	Chambers, Tuxy	11841
Caywood, Albert W.	18453	Chambers, Teecy	11842
Caywood, Bruce	18454	Chambers, Elizabeth	11898
Caywood, Joseph	18455	Chambers, Maxwell	11976
Caywood, Thomas P.	18456	Chambers, Catherine	11990
Caywood, William F.	26717	Chambers, Teesey	12021
Caywood, Elizabeth	27491	Chambers, Henry	12099
Caywood, Butler	27492	Chambers, Charles P.	12399
Caywood, Christopher	27493	Chambers, William M.	12430
Caywood, Lemuel J.	27494	Chambers, Nancy J.	12439
Cearley, Sion A.	9127	Chambers, David	12600
Cearley, Sarah L.	16391	Chambers, William A.	26684
Cearley, John G.	16392	Chambers, Maud B.	26685
Cearley, Charles S.	16393	Chambers, Mary E.	26686
Cessna, Sallie V.	10621	Chambers, Katie	26687
Chatham, Mary A.	383	Chambers, Robert P.	26688
Chandler, Cornelia C.	398	Chambers, William L.	26689
Chandler, Claud A.	399	Chambers, William W.	27748
Chandler, Felix C.	400	Chambers, Jesse S.	27749
Chandler, Myrtie May	401	Chambers, Leo	27750
Chandler, John DeWitt	402	Chambers, Joseph H.	27751
Chandler, Benjamin H.	403	Chambers, Bessie L.	27757
Chandler, Homer E.	405	Chambers, Floyd B.	27758
Chandler, Fannie W.	404	Chambers, John Q.	28048
Chandler, Robert E.	406	Chambers, Tarchechee	28049
Chandler, Otto C.	407	Chambers, James	28802
Chandler, Lura C.	408	Chambers, John Q.	28803
Chandler, Fannie E.	484	Chambers, Clementine	28804
Chandler, James A.	485	Chambers, Mack	29309
Chandler, Rebecca C.	486	Chambers, Hallie O.	29310
Chandler, Oliver K.	487	Chambers, Lorenzo D.	29728
Chandler, Jeanette B.	488	Chambers, Elsie	29729
Chandler, John W.	489	Chambers, George S.	31685
Chandler, Benjamin E.	490	Charboneau, Emma L.	5374
Chandler, Ethel M.	491	Charboneau, Charles	5375
Chandler, Ida C.	492	Charboneau, Mary M.	5376
Chandler, Richard	4005	Charboneau, John H.	5377
Chandler, Thomas A.	7811	Charboneau, Annie	23213
Chandler, Norma	7812	Chastain, Rhoda	7226
Chandler, Collis	7813	Chastain, Elvin	7227
Chandler, Ann E.	8186	Chastain, Earnest	7228
Chandler, Vann S.	8187	Chastain, Nancy J.	16061
Chandler, Nannie L.	8188	Chastain, Robert	16062
Chandler, David	8189	Chastain, Bertha M.	16063
Chandler, Claud D.	8701	Chastain, Belle	16064
Chandler, Sarah M.	8709	Charlesworth, Mary J.	8607
Chandler, Susan	15434	Charlesworth, Walter M.	8608
Chandler, David	15435	Charlesworth, Frederick W.	8609
Chandler, Ella J.	15436	Charlesworth, Oliver E.	8610
Chandler, Henry	15437	Charlesworth, Adolphus	8611
Chandler, Samuel W.	15592	Charlesworth, Blanche	8612
Chandler, William P.	16294	Chamberlin, Arthur F.	8862
Chandler, John C.	16295	Chamberlin, Dollie E.	8863
Chandler, Eliza	16502	Chamberlin, Catherine B.	8864
Chandler, Louisa L.	30940	Chamberlin, Arthur F. Jr.	8865
Chandler, Annie J.	30941	Chamberlin, Robert L.	8903
Chandler, Robert E.	30942	Chamberlin, Amory P.	8904
Chandler, Mary E.	30943	Chamberlin, Freeda E.	8905
Chandler, James A.	30944	Chamberlin, Laura H.	23926
Chandler, Burges G.	30945	Chamberlin, Edward R.	23927
Chandler, Mary Magdaline	32721	Chamberlin, John R.	23928
Chandler, George	32722	Chamberlin, Ethel L.	23929
Chancellor, Mellie J.	418	Chamberlin, Martha E.	23930
Chancellor, Meda	425	Chamberlin, William C.	9049
Chambers, Mary F.	2731	Chemberlain, Clara E.	9050
Chambers, Robert	4888	Chamberlain, Winfred C.	9051
Chambers, Vann	11298	Chamberlain, Margaret L.	9052
Chambers, Jennie	11299	Chamberlain, Milo R.	9053
Chambers, Louis	11300	Chamberlain, Cline L.	9054
Chambers, Vann, Jr.	11301	Chamberlain, Quatie E.	9055
Chambers, Clarence	11302	Chamberlain, Nelson B.	9213
Chambers, Alsie C.	11303	Chamberlain, Mariah E.	9214
Chambers, Joanna	11304	Chamberlain, William N.	9215
Chambers, Robert E.	11311	Chamberlain, Abbie O.	9216
Chambers, William D.	11312	Chamberlain, Erastus	9217
Chambers, Ezekiel P.	11478	Chamberlain, Mary E.	9218
Chambers, Teesey	11674		

Name.	Roll No.
Chamberlain, Clarence E.	9219
Charley, Frank	10364
Charley, Lemuel	10365
Charley, Samuel	12083
Charley, Frank	31184
Chaney, Julia	10495
Chaney, Eliza	10496
Chaney, Mamie	10497
Chaney, Della	10498
Chaney, Ethel	10499
Chaney, Lou E.	10500
Chaney, George W.	10501
Chaney, Florence E.	10502
Chaney, Susan B.	10551
Chaney, Charles E.	10855
Chaney, James	10856
Chaney, Charles	10857
Chaney, Artie	12359
Chaney, John	12360
Chaney, Thomas J.	12361
Chaney, George S.	12362
Chaney, Edna	12364
Chaney, William	30007
Chaney, Ada	30008
Chaudoin, Janeanna	16439
Chaudoin, Mary J.	16440
Chaudoin, Elva	16441
Chair, Johnson	17925
Chair, Quatie	17926
Chair, Rabbit	17927
Chair, Stout	28398
Chair, Margaret	28399
Chair, Benjamin	28400
Chair, Levi	28401
Chair, James	28402
Chair, Narcie	28403
Chair, Lydia	28404
Chair, Bettie	28426
Chair, Samuel	28427
Chair, Annie	28428
Chair, Phoebe	28429
Chair, Katie	32266
Charles, Lazarus	19651
Charles, Nancy	19652
Charles, Thompson	20021
Charles, John	20022
Charles, Polly	20023
Chanley, Josie B.	21916
Chanley, Maggie	21917
Chanley, Gracie E.	21918
Chance, Maggie	26947
Chance, James	26948
Chance, Myrtle	26949
Chance, Ida	26950
Chance, William	26951
Chapman, Cynthia E.	29247
Chapman, Mary E.	29248
Chapman, Don L.	29249
Chapman, Willis B., Jr.	29250
Chapman, Annie L.	29251
Chapman, Joseph W.	29252
Chapman, Georgie R.	29253
Cheek, Rosa E.	3180
Cheek, Flora I.	3181
Cheek, Murta G.	3182
Cheek, George A.	3183
Cheek, Eli L.	3184
Cheek, Butin D.	3185
Cheek, Nina M.	3186
Cheek, Morjie M.	3187
Cheek, Eva	3188
Cheek, Lula D.	23629
Cheek, Pleasant J.	23630
Cheater, Charles	8796
Cheater, Lacy	19442
Cheater, Katie	19443
Cheater, John	19444
Cheater, Joe	19450
Cheater, John	19455
Cheater, Ike	19456
Cheater, Jennie	19457
Cheater, George	19462
Cheater, Becky	19463
Cheater, Benjamin	19804
Cheater, Annie	19805
Cheater, Chiccowie	19806

Name.	Roll No.
Cheater, Enole	27824
Cheater, Katie	27825
Cheater, John	27826
Cheater, Marie	27827
Cheater, Bessie	30584
Cheater, Stan	32038
Cheater, Awy	32039
Cheater, Sut Beck	32040
Cheater, Ah-kah-te-yuh	32301
Chewie, Willie	21014
Chewie, Annie	32075
Chesnut, Holly	25074
Chewey, William	26060
Chewey, Annie	26061
Chewey, Och-tee-yah	30723
Chewey, Oo-dee-we-ske	30724
Cheney, Thomas C.	29660
Cheney, Florence E.	14531
Childers, Charley C.	2657
Childers, William	2658
Childers, William W.	2659
Childers, Charles A.	2660
Childers, Pearl	2661
Childers, Lemuel J.	2662
Childers, John C.	2663
Childers, Luella	3201
Childers, James A.	3202
Childers, John	3301
Childers, Nancy	3302
Childers, Robert	3595
Childers, William C.	3596
Childers, Eliza C.	3597
Childers, Florence E.	3598
Childers, Robert R.	3599
Childers, John C.	12267
Childers, Thomas J.	12525
Childers, Mary L.	22016
Childers, Lucretia M.	25107
Childers, Thomas B.	25108
Childers, Levi	29167
Childers, Noah	29168
Childers, Dolley E.	29169
Childers, Eliza B.	29170
Childers, William	29580
Childers, William S.	29581
Childers, Tandy S.	29582
Childers, Sophia N.	29583
Childers, Ben F.	29584
Childers, Sarah V.	29585
Childers, Gladdys Augustus	29586
Childers, Viola O.	31432
Childers, Warren F.	31433
Childers, Mary A.	31434
Childers, William W.	31435
Childers, Eudora E.	31436
Childers, Gertrude A.	31437
Childers, Eulalie	31438
Chilson, Rena L.	9017
Chirley, Ross	12094
Chirley, Elie	12095
Chitwood, Lucy A.	9765
Chitwood, Walter	9766
Chitwood, Mamie J.	9767
Chitwood, Homer F.	9768
Chisholm, Eliza	16298
Chisholm, Buster	16300
Chisholm, Nancy	30870
Chisholm, Webster	30871
Chisholm, Lizzie	30872
Chisholm, Ollie	30873
Chisholm, Davis	30874
Chisholm, Lillie	30875
Chisholm, Sallie	30876
Chisholm, John	30877
Chisholm, Lucy	30878
Chisholm, Rosa	30879
Chisholm, Alice	32197
Chisholm, James	32198
Chisholm, Harry	32199
Chisholm, Daniel	32200
Chicken, Betsy	19102
Chicken, Elk	19103
Chicken, Nancy	19639
Chicken, Nancy	20053

Name.	Roll No.
Chicken, Ned	32190
Chicken, Cora	32191
Chicken, Levi	32192
Chickenroost, Lizzie	19305
Chinarche, John	26559
Chinarche, William T.	26560
Chickilly, Nancy	29885
Childress, Lucy M.	31450
Childress, Lucille E.	31451
Chick-a-lee-lee, Nellie	32683
Choate, Richard B.	2373
Choate, Lydia	2374
Choate, Robert M.	2375
Choate, Edward E.	2376
Choate, Mary A.	2429
Choate, Charles S.	2864
Choate, Marion D.	2873
Choate, Lilly	3138
Choate, George W.	3196
Choate, Loretta	3868
Choate, James	3888
Choate, Bettie M.	3889
Choate, William	5254
Choate, Mary	5413
Choate, Charley	5417
Choate, John B.	6928
Choate, Robert M.	6929
Choate, Isabelle	6930
Choate, Rufus M.	6968
Choate, William P.	6969
Choate, Charley	17265
Choate, Samuel	20907
Choate, George	26983
Choate, Elizabeth	26984
Choate, Felix R.	26985
Choate, Rufus	26986
Choate, Jane	26987
Choate, Douglass	26988
Choate, Silas	27246
Choate, Ellen	28620
Choate, John C.	2415
Choate, Fannie	2416
Choate, Joshua	2417
Chouteau, John	8195
Chouteau, Tessie J.	8197
Chouteau, Edmond	8702
Chouteau, Corbett E.	8703
Chouteau, Byron	8704
Chouteau, Benjamin F.	13502
Chouteau, James W.	13503
Chouteau, Frederick L.	13531
Chouteau, Adele A.	13532
Chouteau, Samuel C.	13533
Chouteau, Nancy J.	13534
Chouteau, Frederick L. Jr.	13535
Chouteau, William	23686
Chouteau, Bessie	23688
Chouteau, Jesse	23689
Chouteau, Mable	23690
Chouteau, Alexander L.	30192
Chouteau, Cyrus C.	30193
Chouteau, Morris F.	30194
Chouteau, James C.	30195
Chouteau, Julia W.	30196
Chouteau, Francis E.	30809
Chouteau, Francis E. Jr.	30810
Chouteau, Cyprian W.	30811
Chouteau, Karl F. A.	30812
Choteau, Benjamin C.	8661
Choteau, Mariah H.	8662
Choteau, Benjamin C. Jr.	8663
Choteau, Albert T.	8664
Choteau, Blanche B.	8665
Choteau, Mariah H.	8666
Choteau, Charles	10906
Choteau, Charles P.	10907
Choteau, Mary F.	10908
Choteau, Catherine M.	10909
Choteau, Arthur D.	10910
Choteau, Franklin	11109
Chopper, Daylight	8883
Chopper, Jennie	8884

Name.	Roll No.
Chopper, Seekie	26487
Chopper, Eliza	26488
Chopper, Joseph	26489
Chopper, Emma	26490
Choctaw, Aryahnula	25911
Choctaw, Lizzie	32043
Christie, James	900
Christie, Lula C.	901
Christie, Lucy	902
Christie, Ella M.	903
Christie, Jane	993
Christie, Nancy E.	994
Christie, George W.	1401
Christie, Ada E.	1402
Christie, Mary B.	1403
Christie, Ollie	1404
Christie, Ella	1405
Christie, Janie	1406
Christie, Pheasant	1797
Christie, Lucy	1798
Christie, Jacksôn	2230
Christie, William	2526
Christie, Buffalo	2527
Christie, Akie	2528
Christie, Jennie	2529
Christie, Charles	2530
Christie, Eliza	2531
Christie, Jincy	2532
Christie, Richard	2533
Christie, George	2534
Christie, Nannie	2535
Christie, Mary	2536
Christie, Callie	2571
Christie, Nancy	8056
Christie, Sallie	8057
Christie, John	8058
Christie, Jackson	16511
Christie, Betsy	18194
Christie, Alexander	18895
Christie, Arch	18896
Christie, Nellie	18977
Christie, John	18978
Christie, Lydia	18979
Christie, Jennie	18980
Christie, Richard	18981
Christie, Jennie	19189
Christie, Dick	19582
Christie, Walker	19867
Christie, Sallie	19868
Christie, Zeke	19941
Christie, John	19942
Christie, Rachel	20179
Christie, Mary	20180
Christie, Mollie	20425
Christie, Taylor	20597
Christie, Annie	20598
Christie, Albert	20600
Christie, Fannie	20599
Christie, Annie Jr.	20601
Christie, Jane	20602
Christie, Dick	20649
Christie, Annie	20867
Christie, Watt	20946
Christie, Sunday	21283
Christie, Jennie	21284
Christie, Annie	21285
Christie, Sallie	21286
Christie, Arch	21287
Christie, Daniel	21288
Christie, Maggie	21324
Christie, Nancy	21361
Christie, Cindie	21440
Christie, Alice	21828
Christie, Margaret	21829
Christie, Annie	21835
Christie, Jennie	22839
Christie, Nannie	22840
Christie, Cherokee	22841
Christie, Angie M.	22842
Christie, Charlie	25585
Christie, Annie	26062
Christie, George	26063
Christie, Lucy	26064

Name.	Roll No.	Name.	Roll No.
Christie, Katie	26065	Chuculate, Bush	19148
Christie, Betsey	26066	Chuculate, Katie	19149
Christie, Lacy	26067	Chuculate, Charley	19150
Christie, Ned	26068	Chuculate, John	19174
Christie, Annie	26070	Chuculate, Nakie	19175
Christie, Susie	26069	Chuculate, John	19292
Christie, Richard	27232	Chuculate, Lizzie	19293
Christie, Katie	27233	Chuculate, Ben	19297
Christie, Elizabeth	27234	Chuculate, Berman	19298
Christie, Jesse	27235	Chuculate, Jennie	19837
Christie, Daniel	27236	Chuculate, Walker	19847
Christie, John	27237	Chuculate, Jim	20511
Christie, Nancy	27238	Chuculate, Nellie	21518
Christie, Lacie	28467	Chuculate, Wesley	25636
Christie, Goback	29158	Chuculate, William	25655
Christie, Susan	29159	Chuculate, Lucy	25656
Christie, Annie	29160	Chuculate, Sam	25657
Christie, Watt	29161	Chuculate, John	25658
Christie, Israel	29730	Chuculate, Daniel	25708
Christie, Isaac	29738	Chuculate, Bettie	25709
Christie, Stand	29789	Chuculate, Nellie	25710
Christie, Rachel	29915	Chuculate, George	25711
Christie, William	29977	Chuculate, Ice	25712
Christie, Mary	29978	Chuculate, Katie	25713
Christie, Springfrog	29979	Chuculate, Claud	25714
Christie, William Jr.	29980	Chuculate, Eli	27223
Christie, Jack	29981	Chuculate, Louisa	27224
Christie, Watt	29982	Chuculate, Boon	27225
Christie, Peggie	29983	Chuculate, Nannie	27226
Christie, Joseph	29984	Chuculate, Alexander	27227
Christie, Thomas	29985	Chuculate, Sallie	28361
Christie, George	29986	Chuculate, Tom	28472
Christie, Stephen	32369	Chuculate, Rebecca	28473
Christie, James	32587	Chuculate, Mary	29104
Christie, Nancy	32588	Chuculate, Moses	29796
Christie, Wat	32589	Chuculate, Ollie	29797
Christie, Charlotte	32590	Chuculate, John	29844
Chromister, Mary	3895	Chu-cu-late, Mary	32903
Chromister, Lawrence	3896	Chuwalooky, David	7894
Christy, Jesse S.	12785	Chuwalooky, Leann	7895
Christian, Osgood F.	17509	Chuwalooky, Beaver	7896
Christian, William T.	17944	Chuwalooky, Jennie	7897
Christian, Susan	23886	Chuwalooky, Lydia	7898
Christian, Ethel M.	23887	Chuwalooky, William	7899
Christian, Ora F.	23888	Chuwalooky, Lydia	10094
Christian, Samuel	23889	Chuwalooky, Quatie	10095
Christian, Ray	23890	Chu-wa-looky, Richard	8773
Christian, Mary C.	26218	Chu-wa-looky, Lizzie	8774
Chrismon, Ida	23758	Chu-wa-looky, John	8775
Chrismon, William	23759	Chu-wa-looky, Cora	8776
Chrismon, Allen	23760	Chu-wa-looky, Ella	8777
Chucuerlate, Zeke	2511	Chu-wa-looky, Lucy	8778
Chucuerlate, Lizzie	2512	Chu-wa-looky, Sarah	8779
Chucuerlate, Josie	2513	Chu-wa-looky, Chic-a-	
Chucuerlate, John	2514	lee-lee	8945
Chuculate, Isaac	2587	Chu-wa-looky, Che-	
Chuculate, George W.	2951	wa-nes	8946
Chuculate, Elmira	2952	Chu-wa-looky, Ah-	
Chuculate, Perry L.	2953	leecher	8947
Chuculate, Bulah	2954	Chu-wa-looky, Annie M.	8948
Chuculate, George	2955	Chu-wa-looky, Walsie	8949
Chuculate, Moses B.	2956	Chu-wa-looky, Olcie	8950
Chuculate, Samuel	3364	Chunestudy, John	17752
Chuculate, Vinnie	3365	Chunestudy, Polly	17753
Chuculate, Bonnie	3366	Chunestudy, Josiah	18524
Chuculate, William	3836	Chunestudy, Bettie	18525
Chuculate, Wyly	15991	Chunestudy, Willie	18526
Chuculate, Richard	18140	Chunestudy, William	19385
Chuculate, Ellis	18141	Chunestudy, Lydia	19386
Chuculate, Eliza	18142	Chunestudy, Benjamin	19387
Chuculate, Charley	18143	Chunestudy, Andy	19388
Chuculate, Peggie	18144	Chunestudy, Robert	19389
Chuculate, David	18145	Chunestudy, Jalum	19393
Chuculate, Levi	18146	Chunestudy, Mary	19394
Chuculate, Duval	18147	Chunestudy, Joe	19818
Chuculate, Rachel	18916	Chunestudy, Mollie	20591
Chuculate, Charles	18969	Chunestudy, Katie	30543
Chuculate, Eliza	18970	Chunestudy, Guyuche	30544
Chuculate, Jennie	18983	Chunestudy, Smoke	30645
Chuculate, Conseen	19095	Chunestudy, Cartayah	30624
Chuculate, Sarah	19096	Chunestudy, Wolfe	30625
Chuculate, Wesley	19116	Chuckuluck, Tom	18487
Chuculate, Bettie	19147	Chuckuluck, Nancy	18488

Name.	Roll No.	Name.	Roll No.
Chuckuluck, Tyler	25592	Clark, William	10052
Chuckuluck, Polly	25593	Clark, Mary A.	11006
Chunawah	18675	Clark, George William	11007
Chuwee, Sarah	18901	Clark, William H.	12920
Chuwee, Deliah	19648	Clark, Lilla J.	12921
Chuwee, Frame	19991	Clark, James W.	12922
Chuwee, Sarah	19992	Clark, Mabel C.	12923
Chuwee, Charley	19993	Clark, Raleigh P.	12924
Chuwee, Susie	19994	Clark, Rosa Blanche	12925
Chuwee, John	19995	Clark, Silas D.	14046
Chuwee, Nan	19996	Clark, Elizabeth	14047
Chuwee, Looney	19997	Clark, Levi K.	14048
Chuwee, Takey	20000	Clark, Robert L.	14049
Chuwee, Mary	20009	Clark, Blue D.	14050
Chuwee, Samuel	20361	Clark, Jennie	14051
Chuwee, Samuel	25853	Clark, Joel M.	14052
Chuwee, Nancy	29705	Clark, Evin P.	14053
Chuwee, Sallie	29706	Clark, Martin V.	14054
Chuwee, Jesse	29707	Clark, Jay T.	14604
Chulio, Jack	19107	Clark, Mary A. Jr.	14605
Chulio, John	19576	Clark, Jesse J.	14606
Chulio, Nancy	19577	Clark, Jennie R.	14607
Chulio, Liza	19578	Clark, Maggie C.	14608
Chulio, Ratler	19579	Clark, Frank C.	14609
Chulio, Bear	19580	Clark, Clarence J.	14610
Chulio, Ned	25667	Clark, Taylor	14915
Chulio, Jennie	25668	Clark, Dillie	14916
Chulio, Susie	29025	Clark, Delilah	14917
Chubbuck, Ross	27357	Clark, Silas D.	14918
Chuwie, William	28954	Clark, Jay T.	14919
Church, Mary B.	32601	Clark, Ada	15491
Clay, Henry	2181	Clark, Ethel	15492
Clay, James H.	2188	Clark, Charles	21043
Clay, Susie J.	2189	Clark, William	21801
Clay, Susan	2229	Clark, Joel B.	23751
Clay, Rachel	3179	Clark, Olola	23753
Clay, Columbus	5308	Clark, George W.	23862
Clay, Lovely	5467	Clark, Lydia A.	23863
Clay, Henry	5468	Clark, George W. Jr.	23864
Clay, Riley	14891	Clark, Ross	23865
Clay, James A.	14892	Clark, Emily L.	26845
Clay, William	14893	Clark, Sarah E. R.	26846
Clay, Nancy Ann	26314	Clark, Lucy C.	26847
Clay, Minnie	30098	Clark, Addie C.	26848
Clay, William	30099	Clark, Emily L.	26849
Clay, Annie	30100	Clark, William Jr.	27806
Clay, Lucy	30101	Clark, Myrtle	29145
Clay, Freddie D.	30102	Clark, Lorinda E.	30982
Clay, Jesse A.	30103	Clark, Annis	30983
Clay, Thomas	32730	Clark, Bessie E.	32144
Clay, Jennie	32731	Clark, Susie	32145
Clapp, Alcie	2779	Clasby, Fannie	7459
Clapp, James	2780	Clasby, Annie M.	7460
Clapp, Frances	2781	Clasby, Phillip R.	7461
Clark, Perry	4771	Clasby, Robert L.	7462
Clark, Jennie	4772	Clasby, James R.	7463
Clark, Myrtle	4773	Clasby, Thomas M.	7464
Clark, Bud	5047	Clawson, Vinita I.	9108
Clark, Lucinda	5048	Clawson, Mirah Catherene	9109
Clark, John	5049		
Clark, Albert	5050	Claghorn, Peggy	12756
Clark, Louisa	5051	Clak, Eva M.	23866
Clark, Martha	5052	Clapper, Emma J.	24166
Clark, Austin	5053	Clapper, Zella M.	24167
Clark, Elita	5054	Clapper, Ora Lee	24168
Clark, Ruth	5055	Clarke, Martha C.	29240
Clark, Herman	5522	Clarke, Helen I.	29241
Clark, Peggy	5523	Clarke, Dana C.	29242
Clark, Alice	5547	Cleland, George W.	5974
Clark, Stella O.	5548	Cleland, George W., Jr.	5975
Clark, Charles A.	5550	Cleland, James B.	5976
Clark, William A.	6487	Cleland, Amelia C.	5977
Clark, Joseph J.	6488	Cleland, Emmett S., Sr.	5978
Clark, Lucy J.	6489	Cleland, Emmett S., Jr.	5979
Clark, Mary L.	6490	Cleland, Marion W.	5980
Clark, Clarinda S.	6491	Cleland, James B.	17341
Clark, Elizabeth	8356	Cleland, Thomas T.	17342
Clark, Hiram N.	8357	Clepper, Sallie	7221
Clark, Russell W.	8358	Clepper, Bruce	7222
Clark, Elizabeth	8369	Clepper, Sarah A.	7223
Clark, Lydia M.	8421	Cleghorn, Fannie	12402
Clark, Johnson	8445	Cleghorn, Thomas	12403
Clark, Leona E.	8446	Clevenger, Nellie	26521
Clark, William	10050		
Clark, John F.	10051		

Name.	Roll No.	Name.	Roll No.
Cleveland, Bark F.	26731	Coats, Annie L.	9560
Cleveland, Cornelia C.	26732	Coats, John W.	9756
Cleveland, Byron F.	26733	Coats, Floyd	9757
Clingan, Sherman A.	5096	Coats, Samuel B.	13374
Clingan, William D.	5381	Coats, Willie B.	13375
Clingan, Mary J.	5382	Coats, Myrtle M.	13376
Clingan, Samuel D.	5333	Coats, John M.	13392
Clingan, Cora M.	5387	Coats, John	15673
Clingan, Judge K.	12960	Coats, Clara A.	21632
Clingan, Claude C.	12961	Coats, William	21633
Cline, Ben D.	16553	Coats, Thomas M.	21634
Cline, Dora	16554	Coats, Henry L.	23449
Cline, Johnnie	16555	Coats, Carrie M.	23451
Cline, Raymond	16556	Coats, William M.	23452
Cline, Roy	16557	Coats, Ethel M.	24050
Cline, John T.	17105	Coats, Canzada	27570
Cline, Ezekiel	17437	Coats, Novada	27571
Cline, Eli	17438	Coats, William	28090
Cline, Albert R.	17439	Coats, Bertha E.	28091
Cline, Amanda M.	17440	Coats, John H.	28093
Cline, William P.	17441	Coats, George McK.	28094
Cline, Timothy E.	17442	Coats, Charles J.	28096
Cline, Maud	17443	Coats, William P.	28095
Clinkscales, Louis D.	23967	Coast, Alice M.	21920
Clinkscales, Albert S.	23968	Cobb, Joseph B.	4892
Clinkscales, John W.	23969	Cobb, Evelyn	4893
Clifton, Mattie	26676	Cobb, Florence	4894
Cloud, Charles C.	904	Cobb, Joseph J.	4895
Cloud, Mary J.	905	Cobb, Isabel	4896
Cloud, John M.	906	Cobb, James C.	5709
Cloud, Mattie B.	907	Cobb, James E.	5710
Cloud, Joel B.	908	Cobb, Charles H.	5711
Cloud, Caldonia	909	Cobb, Andrew J.	5712
Cloud, Pearl	910	Cobb, William W.	5713
Cloud, Martha C.	1512	Cobb, Susannah M.	5714
Cloud, William M.	1513	Cobb, Isabel	5938
Cloud, George S.	1765	Cobb, Alexander C.	5942
Cloud, Jesse J.	1766	Cobb, Gilbert B.	5943
Cloud, James L.	1775	Cobb, Mary I.	5944
Cloud, Sarah J.	1776	Cobb, William A.	5945
Cloud, Thomas	1777	Cobb, Irene	5946
Cloud, James S.	1778	Cobb, Mary E.	8282
Cloud, Emma J.	1779	Cobb, Artie	8283
Cloud, John C.	1780	Cobb, Samuel A.	8284
Cloud, John E.	6440	Cobb, Mary E.	8285
Cloud, James H.	11901	Cobb, Clarissa	8286
Cloud, John J.	12105	Cobb, Hutton V.	8287
Cloud, Henry	13611	Cobb, Absalom McD.	10842
Cloud, Lizzie	18157	Cobb, Lillie E.	10843
Cloud, Joshua	21615	Cobb, Charles R.	10844
Cloud, Robert L.	22694	Cobb, William McD.	10845
Cloud, Noah S.	22695	Cobb, John R.	10846
Cloud, Susie	22696	Cobb, Schooler S.	10847
Cloud, Robert	22697	Cobb, Howell	11148
Cloud, William	22698	Cobb, Mary E.	16752
Cloud, Leona	22699	Cobb, Simpson C.	16753
Cloud, Richard H.	26338	Cobb, Susie E.	16754
Cloud, Noah	27503	Cobb, Benjamin	16755
Cloud, Katie	29624	Cobb, Edith M.	16756
Cloud, Arch	29665	Cobb, Grover C.	16757
Cloud, Crickett	29716	Cobb, Ula E.	16758
Clyne, Ed	759	Cobb, Mary E.	16759
Clyne, Jane	760	Cobb, Sam	19468
Clyne, Timothy W.	13316	Cobb, Lizzie	19469
Clyne, Elma	25048	Cobb, Rufus B.	29224
Clyne, Emma B.	26320	Cobb, Samuel S.	29341
Clyne, John	26321	Cobb, Phil H.	29342
Clyne, Sallie	26322	Cobb, Paul P.	29343
Clynes, William	18134	Cobb, Samuel S., Jr.	29344
Clynes, John	18135	Cobb, Evaline	29999
Clynes, Sallie	18136	Cobb, James	30108
Clynes, Bettie	32057	Cobb, Jefferson	30109
Coats, James	6934	Cobstill, Martha J.	5322
Coats, Susie D.	6935	Cobstill, Mark	5324
Coats, Jennie B.	6936	Cobstill, Lucinda	5325
Coats, James M.	6937	Cobstill, Jesse	5326
Coats, Elmer E.	6938	Cobstill, Pearl	5327
Coats, James E.	9521	Cobstill, Jacob	5328
Coats, Annie M.	9522	Coble, Robert	30184
Coats, Claud E.	9523	Coble, Mary K.	31331
Coats, Charles F.	9531	Coble, Mattie M.	31332
Coats, Lilly E.	9532	Coble, Susie E.	21333
Coats, Louisa J.	9559	Cochran, Columbus	2409

Name.	Roll No.	Name.	Roll No.
Cochran, Eve	2410	Cochran, Jack	25652
Cochran, James	2411	Cochran, Curtis	25653
Cochran, Sallie	2412	Cochran, Eliza	26385
Cochran, Narcissus	2413	Cochran, Lewis	26975
Cochran, Price	5221	Cochran, Betsy	26976
Cochran, Malcolm M.	5407	Cochran, Mary	26977
Cochran, Arch	5537	Cochran, Willie	26978
Cochran, Sarah	6192	Cochran, Oscar	26979
Cochran, George W.	11650	Cochran, Annie	26980
Cochran, Julia	11651	Cochran, Jennie	26981
Cochran, Joseph	11652	Cochran, Watt	26982
Cochran, Jesse Jr.	13249	Cochran, Henry	27156
Cochran, Henry C.	13642	Cochran, Eva	27157
Cochran, Nannie V.	13643	Cochran, Lydia	27158
Cochran, Sallie P.	13644	Cochran, James	27159
Cochran, Henry C.	13645	Cochran, Dollie	27423
Cochran, Jesse	13657	Cochran, Hooley	27424
Cochran, Susan	13658	Cochran, Ada	27425
Cochran, Clinton	13659	Cochran, Jesse	27426
Cochran, John	13660	Cochran, Jennie	27484
Cochran, Clarence	13661	Cochran, Annie	27485
Cochran, Katie	14435	Cochran, William	27486
Cochran, Silas	14436	Cochran, Stop	27487
Cochran, Sallie	14437	Cochran, Stacy	27834
Cochran, Sequoyah	14988	Cochran, Felix	28073
Cochran, Trudy	14989	Cochran, Ned	28666
Cochran, Dora B.	15002	Cochran, Lewis	28996
Cochran, Landon	15007	Cochran, Mary	29040
Cochran, Walker	15317	Cochran, Isabelle	29041
Cochran, Nancy	15318	Cochran, Nancy	29897
Cochran, Wind	15319	Cochran, Alexander	30360
Cochran, Judy	15320	Cochran, Joseph	30361
Cochran, James	15347	Cochran, Jesse	30362
Cochran, Annie	15348	Cochran, William	30363
Cochran, Lillie	15349	Cochran, Loam	30642
Cochran, Jennie	15350	Cochran, Cindia	30643
Cochran, Thomas	17372	Cochran, William	30644
Cochran, Maggie	15881	Cochran, Too-late	30645
Cochran, George	15882	Cochran, William	31992
Cochran, Emma	15990	Cochran, George	32007
Cochran, Maggie J.	16349	Cochran, Ah-no-he	32333
Cochran, Lena M.	16350	Cochran, John	32809
Cochran, Lydia B.	16351	Cochrum, John	2419
Cochran, Susan	16521	Cochrum, Naressa	2420
Cochran, Alcie	16522	Cochrum, Annie	2421
Cochran, Jackson	16677	Cockrum, George	2457
Cochran, George	17366	Cockrum, William	14992
Cochran, Arch	17839	Cockrum, Taylor	15000
Cochran, Lizzie	17840	Cockrum, Lizzie	18449
Cochran, Mallie	17841	Cockrum, Ned	18450
Cochran, Carrie	17842	Cockrum, John	19977
Cochran, Joseph L.	17843	Cockrum, Russell	26974
Cochran, Zell	17844	Cockrum, Sallie	27115
Cochran, Edwin L.	17845	Cockrell, Mary	9165
Cochran, Scott	17873	Cockrell, Lillie	9166
Cochran, Isabell J.	18243	Cockrell, Percy	9167
Cochran, DeWitt C.	18347	Cockrell, Pearl	9168
Cochran, Sallie	18378	Cockrell, Stella	9169
Cochran, Charlotte	18522	Cochram, Sanders	19251
Cochran, Cornelia	18936	Coffman, Cornelia Jane	269
Cochran, Jesse	19001	Coffman, Jesse S.	272
Cochran, George	19003	Coffee, George	11556
Cochran, Annie	19004	Coffee, Lila G.	28845
Cochran, Charlie	19005	Coffee, Ruby L.	28846
Cochran, Rufus	19006	Coffee, Violet P.	28847
Cochran, Ollie	19007	Cohee, Martha	348
Cochran, Emma	19008	Coker, Lewis C.	10769
Cochran, Sally	19009	Coker, Calvin F.	10770
Cochran, Josie	19010	Coker, Arthur L.	10771
Cochran, Dora	19011	Coker, Mary L.	10772
Cochran, Henry	19012	Coker, Benjamin F.	10773
Cochran, Cora	19013	Coker, Kittie	10774
Cochran, Sam	20497	Coker, Cynthia E.	10775
Cochran, Mary	20500	Coker, William W.	11066
Cochran, Jennie	20501	Coker, Mary E.	11067
Cochran, Beckey	21810	Coker, Minnie M.	11068
Cochran, Ella	23158	Coker, Calvin	11143
Cochran, Susie	23159	Coker, David N.	11459
Cochran, Annie	23160	Coker, Ora	24671
Cochran, Louis	23161	Coker, May	24672
Cochran, Dollie	23162	Coker, George W.	24673
Cochran, Celia	23163	Coker, Bertha L.	24674
Cochran, George Jr.	25651	Coker, Maud E.	24675

Name.	Roll No.	Name.	Roll No.
Coker, Lizzie	26645	Collins, Rachel	28320
Coker, Samuel C.	26646	Collins, Henry	28731
Coker, Manassee M.	26647	Collins, Addie	28732
Coker, Eliza J.	29164	Collins, Lulu E.	28733
Coker, John R.	26678	Collins, George D.	28734
Coker, Josie J.	26679	Collins, Elmer H.	28735
Coker, James M.	29204	Collins, John W.	29301
Coker, Joseph	29205	Collins, Eliza	30005
Coker, Charles	29206	Collins, Annie	30006
Coker, Ethel	29207	Collins, George O.	31604
Coker, Crate	29208	Collins, Thomas E.	32151
Coker, Luella I.	29209	Collins, William L.	32156
Coker, Floyd	29210	Coleman, Kire	2838
Coker, William P. A.	31583	Coleman, Delilah J.	2839
Coker, Frank R.	31584	Coleman, Henry	3946
Coker, Calvin E.	31585	Coleman, Charles	3948
Coker, Joseph C.	31586	Coleman, Nancy	3947
Coker, John R.	31615	Coleman, Joseph	3949
Coker, Charles	31628	Coleman, Jennie	3950
Coker, Mary E.	31629	Coleman, Susan	3951
Coker, Lillie C.	31630	Coleman, John	3952
Coker, Eliza J.	31631	Coleman, James A.	4403
Coker, Cherokee	31632	Coleman, Nannie	4404
Coker, Varana E.	32005	Coleman, Eva	4405
Collins, Nancy	1050	Coleman, Tommie	4406
Collins, Ruthie M.	2306	Coleman, Ella	4407
Collins, Robert E.	2691	Coleman, Timothy	4408
Collins, David H.	2949	Coleman, Minnie	4925
Collins, Mary M.	4420	Coleman, John	5328
Collins, Wyoming	4421	Coleman, Newton E.	5329
Collins, Sirl	4422	Coleman, Samuel G.	5330
Collins, Lindsey	4423	Coleman, Birtha L.	5331
Collins, Ulyssus G.	4424	Coleman, Lydia	16709
Collins, Robert V.	4705	Coleman, Samuel M.	16708
Collins, Andy	4706	Coleman, John	17604
Collins, Lutitia	4707	Coleman, Nancy	17605
Collins, James D.	4708	Coleman, Peggie	19344
Collins, Margaret	4965	Coleman, Dick	19345
Collins, Thomas K.	4966	Coleman, Emma	19346
Collins, Christianna	4967	Coleman, Kiah	19347
Collins, Coleman C.	4968	Coleman, Esther	19348
Collins, Florence	4969	Coleman, Arch	21115
Collins, Fay J.	4970	Coleman, Beckie	23200
Collins, Sammie M.	4971	Coleman, Joel	23201
Collins, Katie A.	9162	Coleman, Willis	23202
Collins, John T.	9163	Coleman, William	27333
Collins, Arizona	11506	Coleman, Caller	32299
Collins, Jennie	12398	Coleman, Gooweestah	32300
Collins, Annie	12577	Colby, James	3758
Collins, Mary F.	12578	Collier, Joseph S.	3916
Collins, Albert H. Jr.	12579	Collier, Jesse	3917
Collins, Eli. H.	12580	Collier, Hattie M.	3918
Collins, Augusta B.	12581	Collier, Charles A.	12369
Collins, Susan Catherine	12582	Collier, Abraham	21004
		Collier, Mack	26088
Collins, Ida M.	12755	Collier, Bettie	30126
Collins, Clifford H.	15218	Collier, Missouri A.	30128
Collins, Mary E.	15219	Collier, Jasper N.	30129
Collins, John H.	15632	Collier, Alice M.	30130
Collins, Jennie	15633	Collier, William A.	30131
Collins, Mollie	15634	Collins, Clark L.	30783
Collins, Mary E.	15635	Collins, Ira J.	30784
Collins, Thomas	15636	Collier, Richard	4218
Collins, Willie	15637	Collier, Flora	9121
Collins, John P.	15689	Collier, Kate	9122
Collins, Henry, Jr.	21718	Cole, Lorena	6262
Collins, Gracie	21719	Cole, John M.	6263
Collins, Delana A.	22567	Cole, Vian	6264
Collins, Clarence A.	22568	Cole, Clem	6265
Collins, Thomas A.	22901	Cole, Felix	6266
Collins, Samuel	22903	Cole, Drucilla	6267
Collins, Thomas Jr.	22904	Cole, Mary S.	6306
Collins, Irvin	22905	Cole, Mary A.	6307
Collins, Okla	22906	Cole, Jennie E.	6308
Collins, Jeffrey	24203	Cole, Maud L.	6309
Collins, James B.	24204	Cole, Effie O.	6310
Collins, Senie B.	24205	Cole, Paul	6311
Collins, Tennessee	25557	Cole, Daniel B.	6312
Collins, Ada B.	25558	Cole, Lucy	11393
Collins, Benjamin F.	25559	Cole, Birtie	11394
Collins, Nellie	25560	Cole, Mary E.	11395
Collins, Hazel I.	25561	Cole, Jack N.	11396
Collins, Ira J.	28319	Cole, Owen W.	11397
		Cole, Cora L.	23362
		Colvard, Sarah	6729

Name.	Roll No.	Name.	Roll No.
Colvard, Stacy L.	6730	Conklin, Sarah P.	8933
Colvard, Myrtle M.	6731	Conkiln, Henry D.	8934
Colvard, Robert E. Lee	6732	Conklin, Margret E.	8935
Colvard, Oden	28642	Connelley, Sophia	12742
Colvard, Lettie	7001	Conseen, Lillie	15327
Collier, Charlotte	7002	Conseen, Franklin	15330
Collier, William E.	7003	Conseen, Thomas F.	15345
Colston, Cynthia	7928	Conseen, Nannie	17504
Colston, Fannie	7929	Conseen, Dora	26574
Colston, Sam	19427	Connally, Bettie	17047
Colston, Sterling	21699	Connally, James D.	17048
Colston, Clementine	21700	Constitution, Ooliscasti	18628
Colston, Charles	26289	Constitution, Dave	19465
Colston, Mary S.	26290	Constitution, Coowee-	
Colston, Bertha M.	26291	scoowee	19466
Colston, Lewis R. B.	28389	Constiution, Lizzie	19467
Colyer, Sarah	17891	Constitution, Teacher	19713
Colyer, Martin	32277	Constitution, Katie	19714
Colwell, Arthur	27604	Constitution, Jennie	30550
Colvin, Myrtle L.	32919	Constitution, Teekah-	
Colvin, Ella	32926	toonah	30567
Combs, Martha	6095	Condreay, Barbara A.	22415
Combs, Mary E.	6096	Condreay, Edward	22417
Combs, Edith M.	6097	Condreay, Charles	22418
Combs, Annie	8875	Condreay, Hattie	22419
Combs, Minnie A.	29770	Condreay, Mary	22420
Combs, Ray A.	29771	Condreay, Harris	22421
Combs, Vernon R.	29772	Condreay, Minnie	22422
Comfort, Dora	8995	Condry, Rebecca	26236
Comfort, William	8997	Condry, Joseph S.	26237
Comfort, Florence	8998	Condry, Georgia A.	26238
Comer, Mary McC.	11777	Condry, Lola Biddy	26239
Comer, Charles McC.	11778	Condry, Mary A.	28161
Comer, Mary E.	12110	Condry, Sterling H.	28162
Comer, Leona M.	12111	Connor, Albert A.	27854
Comer, Wm. J. B.	12112	Connor, Annie E.	27855
Comingdeer, Nick	18333	Connor, Clara E.	27856
Comingdeer, Eliza	18334	Connor, Ella N.	27857
Comingdeer, Joseph	18984	Connor, Echo M.	27858
Comingdeer, Mary	28470	Connor, Johnnie H.	27859
Comingdeer, Hunter	28837	Connor, Mamie G.	32209
Comingdeer, Bessie R.	28838	Connor, Oliver A.	32210
Coming, Wilson	18359	Connor, Rosanna S.	32526
Coming, Joe	19404	Connell, Belle	28027
Coming, Lizzie	19405	Connell, Jimmie	28028
Coming, Dick	19406	Cooper, Sophronia B.	139
Coming, Diana	19407	Cooper, Claud D.	140
Coming, Dave	19408	Cooper, Joanna	11012
Coming, Darkey	30546	Cooper, Oceola	11013
Coming, John	32041	Cooper, Laura E.	14161
Coming, Lydia	32042	Cooper, Juan G.	14162
Comstock, Nita	32575	Cooper, Alice B.	14163
Conner, Anna	471	Cooper, Samuel N.	26920
Conner, Francis William	478	Cooper, Elizabeth A.	29388
Conner, Rebecca J.	621	Cooper, John W.	29389
Conner, Crawford	622	Cooper, Joseph	29722
Conner, Lula M.	623	Cooper, Saphronia	29723
Conner, Leonard	624	Cooley, Mary	356
Conner, Alonzo	22319	Cooley, Robert	357
Conner, Kate E.	22320	Cooley, Charley	358
Conner, Nevada M.	22321	Cooley, Jennie	359
Conner, Lon Jay	22322	Cooley, Josie	360
Conner, Clifton Sidney	22323	Cooley, Mollie	361
Conner, Lucy J.	23726	Cooley, Richard	362
Connor, Lucinda	31336	Coon, John	1964
Connor, Ida	31337	Coon, Darkie	1965
Conner, Josephine	31407	Coon, Ball	1966
Conner, Frank I.	31408	Coon, Joe	1967
Conner, Viola	31409	Coon, Chowweeyuk	1968
Conley, Carrie A.	2769	Coon, Newt	1969
Conley, Ruth	2771	Coon, Nellie	4019
Conley, Jessie A.	3139	Coon, Bernard L.	4838
Conley, Sarah	3140	Coon, Ella	12355
Conley, Maggie I.	16727	Coon, Alice	12356
Conley, William Brann	25822	Coon, Bertha	12357
Conley, Charles W.	20706	Coon, Annie	12358
Conrad, John H.	6125	Coon, Wolfe	18065
Conrad, George	6126	Coon, Sarah	18060
Conrad, Medly J.	6127	Coon, Rabbit	18067
Conrad, Alice V.	14236	Coon, Mary	18068
Conrad, Myrtle M.	14237	Coon, Linnie	19063
Conrad, George	21158	Coon, Richard	19647
Coney, Eliza J.	8682	Coon, Deekilasky	20835
Coney, George	8683	Coon, Annie	20836
Conklin, Annie L.	8931		
Conklin, Bertha M.	8932		

Name.	Roll No.
Coon, Joe	20837
Coody, Ella	4629
Coody, William S.	4630
Coody, Jesse	4631
Coody, Sarah	4632
Coody, Annie F.	4633
Coody, Callie	4634
Coody, Bessie	4635
Coody, Daniel R.	5740
Coody, Edward	5741
Coody, Mary	5742
Coody, Alice	5743
Coody, Charles	5744
Coody, Lila	5745
Coody, Sallie	5746
Coody, Betty	5747
Coody, Robert	5748
Coody, John H.	8185
Coody, Belinda G.	10875
Coody, Richard H.	11123
Coody, Oscie A.	17472
Coody, David H.	17473
Coody, Lida R.	17474
Coody, Jennie	19875
Coody, Richard	19876
Coody, John H.	30237
Coody, Mary A.	30238
Coodey, Lewis R.	5018
Coodey, Daniel R.	5045
Coodey, Sarah E.	12656
Coodey, Myrtle U.	23110
Coodey, Lewis W.	23111
Coodey, Benjamin L.	23112
Coodey, Daniel	5046
Cook, Nancy	5300
Cook, Andrew J.	5301
Cook, Fannie	5302
Cook, Annie M. W.	9254
Cook, Susan	9455
Cook, Thomas M.	9456
Cook, Lila	9810
Cook, Florence	27569
Cook, Henry A.	29504
Cook, William D.	32562
Cookson, John H.	15266
Cookson, Joseph	15267
Cookson, Eliza	15268
Cookson, Jack	15269
Cookson, Levi	15270
Cookson, Clement	15271
Cookson, Ella	15272
Cookson, Betty	15273
Cookson, Reese	15274
Cookson, Lizzie B.	15617
Cookson, Lucinda E.	15618
Cookson, George H.	15619
Cookson, William K.	15620
Cookson, Levi	20622
Cookson, Aggie	20623
Cookson, Thomas	20624
Cookson, Ogden L.	20625
Cookson, Elinor B.	20626
Cookson, John H.	20627
Cookson, Andrew F.	20628
Cookson, Andrew G.	20659
Cookson, Maggie	20660
Cookson, Levi M.	20661
Cookson, Ada	20662
Cookson, Annie	20663
Cookson, Levi	29996
Cookson, Andrew	29997
Cooweescoowee, George	21383
Cookinghead, Nancy	29817
Cookinghead, Rosie	29818
Cookinghead, Jackson	29825
Cookinghead, Johnson	29826
Copple, Manerva	6014
Copple, Perry	6015
Copeland, Alexander	244
Copple, Minnie	6016
Copeland, Nancy E.	245
Copeland, Rabbit B.	248
Copeland, Bertha M.	249

Name.	Roll No.
Copeland, George W.	250
Copeland, Cordelia	251
Copeland, Verena	2754
Copeland, Charlotte E.	2755
Copeland, James A.	2756
Copeland, Andrew J.	2757
Copeland, Polly E.	2758
Copeland, James R.	10024
Copeland, Cordelia J.	10025
Copeland, Dollie	26282
Copeland, Robert F.	26283
Copeland, William M.	26284
Copeland, Nola E.	26285
Copenger, William	15824
Corntassel, Adam	751
Corntassel, Lutitia	752
Corntassel, Benjamin	753
Corntassel, Mary Ann	754
Corntassel, John	755
Corntassel, Alexander	766
Corntassell, Lewis	1028
Corntassell, Betsy	1029
Corntassel, Maude	17716
Corntassel, Rachel	18222
Corntassel, Nancy	19990
Corntassell, Thomas	22466
Corntassell, Lizzie	22467
Corntassell, John	22468
Corntassell, Jennie	22469
Corntassell, James	22470
Corntassell, Thomas	22471
Corntassel, John	28715
Corntassell, Robert	30121
Corntassel, Jesse	7977
Cordray, Mary E.	1110
Cordray, Henry H.	1111
Cordray, James T.	1112
Cordray, Edward C.	1113
Cordray, Uthie M.	1114
Cordray, Nannie B.	1115
Cordray, Allie B.	1116
Cordray, George W.	1117
Cordray, Leona B.	1118
Cordray, Albert Sidney	1119
Cordray, Wilson	4552
Cordray, James B.	5391
Cordray, Andy	5440
Cordray, Mary B.	23243
Cordray, Annie I.	23244
Cordray, Connell	23245
Cordray, Joseph	27369
Cordray, John W.	27384
Cordray, May	27385
Cordray, Sarah	27386
Cordray, Charlotte	27387
Cordray, Susan	27397
Cordray, David S.	30085
Cordon, Mattie	2641
Cordon, Fannie	2642
Cordon, Mamie M.	2643
Cornelius, Nancy	2748
Cornelius, Iola	2752
Cornelius, Lizzie	18185
Cornelius, Henry	18195
Cornelius, Peter	30461
Correll, Lucy	3232
Correll, Bullet	3233
Correll, Minnie	3234
Correll, Charlotte	3235
Correll, Sadie	3236
Correll, Nola	3237
Correll, Phillip W.	3238
Cordrey, Thomas	4555
Cordrey, Hugh	4556
Cordrey, Bessie	4557
Cordrey, Ada	4558
Cordrey, Clifford	4560
Cordrey, Willie A.	5087
Cordrey, Ellie	5088
Cordrey, Frank B.	5258
Cordrey, Percy L.	17647
Cordrey, Laura	23170
Cordrey, William	29609

Name.	Roll No.	Name.	Roll No.
Cordry, Andy	5787	Couch, Thomas L.	7799
Cordry, Annie	27610	Couch, Nellie	10102
Cornatzer, Cornelia J.	8297	Couch, John F.	12484
Cornatzer, Caroline B.	8341	Couch, Clara C.	12910
Cornatzer, Walter C.	8623	Couch, Cherokee R.	12911
Cornatzer, Winnie D.	8624	Couch, Marion W. Jr.	12912
Cornatzer, Cyrus C.	30191	Couch, James C.	12913
Cornwell, James	10431	Couch, Jesse T.	13666
Corn, Hannah	10445	Couch, Charles E.	12914
Corn, Earl	10446	Couch, Floy E.	13667
Corn, William H.	10447	Couch, Susie I.	17025
Corn, Archie	10468	Couch, Stella I.	26315
Corn, Ethel L.	28185	Couch, Thelma L.	26316
Corn, James A.	28186	Couch, Mitchell M.	27728
Corn, Callie M.	28187	Couch, Cynthia	27729
Corn, Grace E.	28188	Couch, Ida M.	31395
Corn, Emma L.	28189	Couch, Victor C.	31396
Corn, Percy J.	28190	Couch, Elna	31397
Corn, Dora	29922	Coughran, Katie	5848
Corn, Alvina	28823	Coughran, Berdie	5854
Corn, Kruger C.	29924	Coughran, Lydia	17317
Cormicle, Mary	13095	Coughran, Mary	17318
Cormicle, Clarence L.	13096	Coughran, Jesse	17319
Cormicle, Annie J.	13097	Coughran, Lillie	17320
Cormicle, Walter	13098	Coughran, Bessie	17321
Cormicle, Thomas C.	13099	Coughran, Eliza	17322
Cormicle, Mary E.	13100	Coughran, Lewis J.	17323
Cormicle, Levi P.	13101	Coughran, William J.	17324
Cormicle, Milton R.	13102	Coughran, Franzel	17325
Cormicle, Lincoln R.	13103	Coughran, Leonard	17326
Cormicle, William C.	13104	Coughran, Herbert	17327
Cormicle, Allen F.	13489	Coughran, Laura	17328
Cornshucker, Sallie	17908	Countryman, George A.	7380
Cornshucker, Tom	17909	Countryman, Zimerhew	7381
Cornshucker, Sam	17910	Countryman, Andrew	7382
Cornshucker, Watie	17911	Countryman, George W.	8219
Cornshucker, Arch	17912	Countryman, Minerva	8220
Cornshucker, George	19705	Countryman, John M.	8235
Cornshucker, John	20780	Countryman, Hooley	9171
Cornshucker, Lizzie	32047	Countryman, James T.	9904
Cornsilk, Steve	18737	Countryman, Eliza	9905
Cornsilk, Jennie	19279	Countryman, Lafayette	9906
Cornsilk, William	19280	Countryman, Henry	9907
Cornsilk, Jack	19281	Countryman, Sam	9908
Cornsilk, Jennie	19282	Countryman, Saber	24222
Cornsilk, Johnson	19283	Countryman, George	24223
Cornsilk, Lucy	20730	Countryman, Nora	24224
Cornsilk, Charles	32453	Countryman, Annie	24225
Cornsilk, Eliza	32454	Countryman, Edna	24226
Cornsilk, Nora	32456	Countryman, Earl N.	24227
Cornsilk, Leona	32455	Countryman, Walter	24228
Cordreay, Ada B.	21606	Countryman, Andrew J.	27533
Cordreay, Josie M.	21607	Countryman, Zimerhew	27534
Cordrey, Bradley	21686	Countryman, John M.	27535
Cordreay, Thomas J.	23240	Countryman, Arther R.	27536
Corban, Sarah B.	21708	Countryman, Jackson	27537
Cornatzer, Lycurgus L.	24051	Countryman, Clara B.	27538
Cornatzer, Adelia M.	24053	Countryman, John A.	30035
Cornatzer, Tessie	24054	Countryman, Jane A.	30036
Cornatzer, Onas L.	24055	Countryman, W. T.	30037
Cornatzer, Vesta	24056	Countryman, Nora	32347
Coram, Ollie	27182	Courtney, Ann E.	8241
Coram, Verley M.	28419	Courtney, Edward E.	8242
Costen, Mary E.	10315	Courtney, Jessie L.	8244
Costen, Margaret M.	13895	Courtney, Minerva	8243
Costen, Cassie B.	13896	Courtney, Lula B.	8245
Costen, Eda B.	13897	Courtney, Ethel C.	8246
Costen, Robert R.	13898	Courtney, Opal	8247
Costen, Samuel H.	13899	Courts, Sarah E.	10809
Costen, William T.	13900	Courts, John W.	10810
Costen, Meridith C.	13901	Covey, Susan	9320
Costen, Elizabeth L.	13902	Covey, Beulah L.	9321
Costen, Eula W.	13903	Covey, Preston C.	9322
Conseen, Eliza	14000	Covey, Bessie L.	9323
Conseen, Maggie D.	14001	Covey, George R.	9324
Couch, Georgia L.	3685	Covel, John H.	26698
Couch, Louellen	6090	Covel, Lizzie B.	26699
Couch, Ina B.	6091	Covel, Ella M.	26700
Couch, Frankie	6092	Covel, Jesse C.	26701
Couch, Dondine	7795	Covel, Henry O.	26702
Couch, George F.	7796	Cowels, Edmond	246
Couch, Lorenzo M.	7797	Cowels, Cora Bell	247
Couch, Lucy N.	7798	Cowart, William L.	1621

Name.	Roll No.	Name.	Roll No.
Cowart, Laura V.	1622	Coyne, Johnanner	9288
Cowart, James S.	1623	Coyne, Maggie	9472
Cowart, Mary A.	1624	Coyne, Mary E.	9473
Cowart, William L., Jr.	1625	Coyne, Agnes M.	9474
Cowart, Charles M.	1626	Coyne, Patrick W.	9475
Cowart, Norma .E.	1627	Coyne, Peter	9476
Cowart, John E.	1628	Craft, George W.	14673
Cowart, Jesse T.	1629	Craig, Nannie	4852
Cowart, Laura A.	20131	Craig, Addie	4853
Cowart, Slater	21541	Craig, Amon H. Jr.	4854
Cowart, Jennie	21542	Craig, Clifford C.	4855
Cowart, John	21543	Craig, Warren R.	4856
Cowart, Alice	21544	Craig, Carl E.	9263
Cowart, Cynthia	21545	Craig, Granville	9273
Cowart, Mary	21546	Craig, Robert W.	9371
Cowart, Collins	'21547	Craig, William L.	9817
Cowart, Nettie	21548	Craig, Clara R.	9818
Cowan, Alexander C.	6657	Craig, Thursey	14736
Cowan, Stella	6658	Craig, Coleman	14737
Cowan, Cherry	6659	Craig, Annie L.	14820
Cowan, Terry	6660	Craig, Buell	14821
Cowan, Louie	6661	Craig, Leonard	14822
Cowan, Georgia H.	6662	Craig, Anna M.	14823
Cowan, Alex F.	6663	Craig, Amina	15139
Cowan, Andrew Jasper	6664	Craig, Margaret	15140
Cowan, Felix G.	24086	Craig, Arthur	15141
Cowan, Felix G.	27588	Craig, Samuel	15142
Cowles, Martha A.	9032	Craig, George F.	24249
Cowles, Maggie M.	9033	Craig, Anna J.	24250
Cowles, Joseph W. .	9034	Craig, Elgy C.	24259
Cowles, William L. S.	9035	Craig, Laura	24260
Cowles, James C., Jr.	9036	Craig, Ellis	25365
Cowles, Viola J.	9037	Craig, William	25366
Cowles, Lucian B.	9038	Craig, Fredie	25367
Cowles, Goldie P.	9039	Craig, Elor	25368
Cowles, Harry D. B.	9040	Craig, Delilah	29995
Cowles, Martha A.	9041	Crain, Nancy	4998
Cowles, Charley E.	13402	Crain, Nannie	17301
Cowand, Mary	23067	Crain, Doney	17302
Cowand, Thomas W.	23068	Crain, Bessie	17303
Cowand, John N.	26374	Crain, Ellen	28877
Cowells, Caleb W.	23727	Crain, Joseph	32262
Cowden, Myrtle	28641	Crane, Henry O.	5478
Cowden, Annie Mildren	28643	Crane, Sarah C.	5479
Cox, Herbert R.	9073	Crane, Arthur Lee	5480
Cox, Emma J.	9769	Crane, George W.	16858
Cox, Zeno Merritt	9772	Crane, Louisa J.	26825
Cox, Rebecca L.	9935	Crane, Henry B.	26826
Cox, Stephen F.	9936	Crane, Maud M.	26827
Cox, Lettie L. L.	9937	Crane, Frances	28324
Cox, Marcus G.	9938	Crane, Nora	28325
Cox, Florence D.	9939	Crane, Ella	28326
Cox, John S.	9949	Crawford, Florence	10386
Cox, Martha J.	9950	Crawford, Mery Pearl	10388
Cox, Dovie	9951	Crawford, Jack	16514
Cox, Marshal	9952	Crawford, Katie	16515
Cox, Leonard	9953	Crawford, George	21057
Cox, Nannie	10001	Crawford, Katie	21108
Cox, Rosetta A.	10252	Crawford, Ned	27500
Cox, Robert E.	10253	Crafton, Mary C.	13791
Cox, Elsie B.	10254	Crafton, Mary L.	13792
Cox, Cora I.	10389	Crafton, Kathleen A.	13793
Cox, Loyd George	10390	Crafton. Susan E.	13794
Cox, Sallie	11740	Craft, Minerva	14547
Cox, Frank M.	11741	Craft, Dennis	14548
Cox, James D.	11742	Craft. James	14549
Cox, Cora I.	11743	Cramp, Sallie	17592
Cox, George A.	15031	Cramp, Katie	17593
Cox, Sallie	15073	Cramp, Tilden	17607
Cox, Robert A.	16851	Cramp, Johnson	25507
Cox, Ancel L.	16852	Crapo, Jim	18722
Cox, J. D.	24373	Crapo, Collin	18723
Cox, Elvy C.	28696	Crapo, Lewis	21194
Cox, Frederick	28783'	Crapo, Linda	21195
Cox, Mary A.	28784	Crapo, George	21196
Cox, Edna L.	28785	Crapo, Pollie	21197
Cox, Nettie M.	28812	Crapo, Eliza	21204
Cox, Ralph M.	28813	Crapo, Nelson	21205
Cox, Florence E.	30895	Crapo, Albert	21206
Cox, William J.	30896	Crapo. Lela	25967
Cox, Lena L.	30897	Crapo. Lewis Buchanan	25968
Coyne, Isabel J.	9284	Crawler. Joe	18974
Coyne, Patrick W.	9285	Crail, Linie J.	21944
Coyne, Ibbie J.	9286	Crail. Dellie	21945
Coyne, James Jesse	9287	Crail. John H.	21946
		Crail, Myrtle J.	21947

Name.	Roll No.
Crail, Dora B.	21948
Crapo, Charlie	27331
Cravens, Kate	29936
Creeden, Ida L.	4079
Creeden, Nellie L.	4080
Creech, Jeff	5256
Creech, Nettie	5257
Creech, Rebecca E.	12248
Creech, Ruth	12249
Creech, Alice	12250
Creech, Lula	12251
Creech, William	12252
Creekkiller, Mary	19419
Creekkiller, Jay G.	19420
Creekkiller, Rachel	19421
Creekkiller, Lydia	19422
Creekkiller, Jeff	21457
Creekkiller, Cartaye	21458
Creekkiller, Sarah	21459
Creekkiller, Peggie	21460
Creekkiller, Mary	21461
Creekkiller, Ooloochee	21462
Creekkiller, Henry	21463
Creekkiller, Scott	25773
Creek, Mary E.	24679
Creek, Nellie M.	24680
Creek, Annie L.	24681
Creek, John S.	24682
Creek, Lillie	30996
Creek, Sullivan	30997
Creek, John W.	30998
Creek, Arizona	30999
Creek, Florence	31000
Crenshaw, Katie	5633
Crenshaw, Mary	5634
Crittenden, Vinnie R.	655
Crittenden, Joseph	656
Crittenden, Carl	657
Crittenden, Israel	691
Crittenden, George	715
Crittenden, Nancy J.	716
Crittenden, Susan E.	717
Crittenden, John H.	718
Crittenden, Rebecca A.	719
Crittenden, Jessie	720
Crittenden, Georgie A.	721
Crittenden, Dewey	722
Crittenden, Charles D.	723
Crittenden, Henry C.	780
Crittenden, Mary S.	781
Crittenden, Charles L.	782
Crittenden, William H.	783
Crittenden, Cicero	784
Crittenden, Pearl	785
Crittenden, Thomas R.	786
Crittenden, Susan F.	787
Crittenden, Myrtle I.	788
Crittenden, Alice	1241
Crittenden, Martin	1242
Crittenden, Richard H.	1260
Crittenden, Allie F.	1261
Crittenden, Robert L.	1262
Crittenden, James	1326
Crittenden, Bruce	1327
Crittenden, Ada	1328
Crittenden, Lizzie	1329
Crittenden, Edith	1330
Crittenden, Mose	1331
Crittenden, Minnie	1332
Crittenden, Beckey	1333
Crittenden, James	1334
Crittenden, William C.	1335
Crittenden, Benjamin	1356
Crittenden, William P.	1919
Crittenden, James	2157
Crittenden, Riley	2158
Crittenden, Ella	2159
Crittenden, Maudie B.	2160
Crittenden, Cicero	2161
Crittenden, Maggie M.	2162
Crittenden, Sanders	2287
Crittenden, James E.	2288
Crittenden, Mary A.	2289
Crittenden, Ora A.	2290

Name.	Roll No.
Crittenden, Thomas C.	2291
Crittenden, Richard	3844
Crittenden, Isaac M.	4531
Crittenden, Eliza J.	4533
Crittenden, George	5143
Crittenden, Jimmie	5144
Crittenden, Robert	5145
Crittenden, Charles	5146
Crittenden, Freddie	5147
Crittenden, William	6057
Crittenden, Lewis	6058
Crittenden, Christopher C.	6970
Crittenden, Nancy.	6971
Crittenden, Leroy	6972
Crittenden, Sallie	6973
Crittenden, Thomas	6974
Crittenden, Columbus	6975
Crittenden, Samuel	6976
Crittenden, Lecta	7238
Crittenden, Cornelius	7362
Crittenden, Andy	11259
Crittenden, Killie	11537
Crittenden, Barbara A.	11538
Crittenden, Christina B.	11539
Crittenden, Walter	12870
Crittenden, Rachel P.	12871
Crittenden, Albert C.	31978
Crittenden, William C.	14278
Crittenden, Lelia M.	14396
Crittenden, Hedgman	14397
Crittenden, Jennie	14652
Crittenden, Melvina	14653
Crittenden, Martha	15028
Crittenden, Jackson	16277
Crittenden, Ned	16402
Crittenden, Carrie	16403
Crittenden, Blue	16404
Crittenden, Lucinda	16405
Crittenden, Clem	16410
Crittenden, Thomas	16411
Crittenden, John	16629
Crittenden, Arthur D.	16630
Crittenden, John	17104
Crittenden, Mattie A.	18051
Crittenden, Alexander	18897
Crittenden, Peggy	19608
Crittenden, James	19609
Crittenden, Mary	19610
Crittenden, Jesse	19653
Crittenden, Mary	20275
Crittenden, Samuel	20299
Crittenden, Henry	20300
Crittenden, Watt	20301
Crittenden, Charles	20302
Crittenden, Lizzie	20303
Crittenden, James	20771
Crittenden, Nelson	20798
Crittenden, Jennie	20799
Crittenden, Susan	20800
Crittenden, Hummingbird	20801
Crittenden, Jesse	21263
Crittenden, Ellen	21264
Crittenden, Joe	21265
Crittenden, James F	21653
Crittenden, Nancy L.	21863
Crittenden, Nannie E.	22478
Crittenden, James	22500
Crittenden, Isaac	26957
Crittenden, Lydia	26958
Crittenden, Joseph	26959
Crittenden, Taylor	26960
Crittenden, Mitchell	26961
Crittenden, William	27039
Crittenden, Jane	27383
Crittenden, Wilson	29050
Crittenden, Becky	29051
Crittenden, William	29084
Crittenden, Abraham	29479
Crittenden, George R.	29480
Crittenden, Corda	29481
Crittenden, Ira C.	29482

Name.	Roll No.
Crittenden, Charles F.	29483
Crittenden, Mary	29635
Crittenden, Felix	29704
Critenden, Walter J.	29935
Crittenden, Coo-tah-ye	30597
Crittenden, Lydia	30654
Crittenden, Infant	30655
Crittenden, Emily	30819
Crittenden, Lewis	30820
Crittenden, David	30821
Crittenden, Lula	30822
Crittenden, Walter	30823
Crittenden, Melvina	31702
Crittenden, Tom	32071
Crittenden, Andrew F.	32383
Crittenden, Nannie	32394
Crittenden, John	32395
Crittenden, Charley	32504
Crittenden, Katie	32515
Crittenton, George W.	10464
Crittenton, Jessie B.	10465
Crittendon, Joel	15401
Crittendon, Ada M.	25237
Crittendon, Bessie E.	25238
Crittendon, Rosie E.	25239
Crittenden, Jack	25816
Crittenden, Sallie	25817
Crittenden, Luke	25818
Crittenden, Kate	26010
Crittenden, Charles W.	26036
Crittenden, Katie A.	26037
Crittenden, James	26038
Crittenden, Mary J.	26039
Crittenden, Leroy	26040
Cripps, Josie E.	11234
Cricket, Charles	28369
Crockett, Sallie	328
Crockett, Gordon R.	330
Crockett, Mary A.	7667
Crockett, Willia P.	7668
Crockett, Inez B.	7669
Crotzer, Emma Lee	461
Crotzer, Rose A.	462
Crotzer, Stella M.	463
Crotzer, Effie L.	464
Crotzer, Edward F.	465
Crotzer, Carl L.	466
Crotzer, Lucile Girtrude	467
Crotzer, Fannie	534
Crotzer, Annie M.	535
Crotzer, Minnie	536
Crotzer, Henrietta	537
Crotzer, Phoebe	538
Crotzer, Lottie L.	539
Crotzer, Maudie	540
Crotzer, Sybil	541
Crowder, Polly	709
Crowder, William P.	710
Crowder, Nelson	711
Crowder, Polly	712
Crowder, Charles	1157
Crowder, Georgia	26618
Crowder, Ethel L.	26619
Crowder, Iva N.	26620
Crossland, Eliza	3613
Crossland, Bettie	3614
Crossland, Alfred	3615
Crossland, Ada	3616
Crossland, Effie	3617
Crossland, Bennett	3618
Crossland, Lizzie	4332
Crossland, Josephus	4333
Crossland, Katie	4334
Crossland, Lottie	4336
Crossland, Jeter R.	4337
Crossland, William	4835
Crossland, Samuel	4929
Crossland, Ada	26375
Crossland, Richard	26376
Crossland, William	26377
Crossland, Joseph	26378
Crossland, Thomas	26379
Crossland, Frances	26380

Name.	Roll No.
Croslin, Buck	3735
Croslin, Maud	3736
Croslin, Rudie	3737
Croslin, Squirrel	3738
Croslin, Ruth	3739
Croslin, Minnie	3740
Crosslin, Richard	3936
Crosslin, Calvin	3937
Crosslin, Samuel	3938
Crosslin, George	3939
Crow, Claude	5533
Crow, Clarence	5534
Crow, William	5535
Crow, Margaret	16328
Crow, Charles	16329
Crow, John	16330
Crow, Jesse	16331
Crow, Andrew J.	17956
Crow, Thomas	20994
Crow, William	29503
Crow, Laura E.	32717
Crow, Anabel	32718
Cromwell, Zeddie R.	10824
Crowell, Mary E.	17049
Crowell, Erda V.	17050
Crowell, Allie B.	17051
Crowell, Frank M.	17052
Crowell, Hunter K.	17053
Crocker, Ella L.	22588
Crocker, Charles C.	22589
Crocker, Neicey	22590
Crocker, Martha L.	26198
Crocker, John H.	26199
Crocker, Lois B.	26200
Crocker, Blanche G.	26201
Crozier, Doris V.	28742
Crutchfield, Thomas	5772
Crutchfield, Mary	5773
Crutchfield, Eli	5774
Crutchfield, Lewis	5775
Crutchfield, Sarah	5776
Crutchfield, Baby Alice	5777
Crutchfield, David	6654
Crutchfield, Lelia	6655
Crutchfield, John H.	8398
Crutchfield, Vinita C.	11917
Crutchfield, James M.	12482
Crutchfield, Alice	12483
Crutchfield, John K.	13755
Crutchfield, Leroy C.	13756
Crutchfield, Ewing H.	13757
Crutchfield, Willie M.	13758
Crutchfield, Nannie	15909
Crutchfield, Taylor F.	24235
Crutchfield, Edward	27442
Crutchfield, Claude	28099
Crutchfield, Mary	28100
Crutchfield, Ray	28101
Crutchfield, Henry G.	28102
Crutchfield, Ida S.	32483
Crutchfield, Lee Roy	32484
Crutchfield, Maggie	32486
Crutchfield, Cuba	32485
Crutchfield, Charles	32487
Culbertson, Ida H.	50
Culbertson, Edwin E.	51
Culbertson, Frank H.	52
Culver, Bessie	21789
Culver, Maggie	4488
Culver, Maggie	4489
Culwell, Irvin J.	12085
Cumpton, Thomas M.	5611
Cumpton, Chelia	5612
Cumpton, Emmett	5613
Cumpton, Glenn	5614
Cumpton, Charles	5615
Cumpton, John B.	5616
Cumpton, James L.	21609
Cumpton, Clark W.	22073
Cummins, Emily G.	12052
Cummins, David W.	12053
Cummins, Edna I.	12054
Cummins, Ruby E.	12055

Name.	Roll No.	Name.	Roll No.
Cummins, Mary F.	12056	Currey, George B.	19430
Cummings, Kitty A.	15644	Currey, Charles T.	19431
Cummings, Rosan	15645	Currey, Albert W.	19432
Cummings, Evans	17860	Currey, Florence	19433
Cummings, Francis M.	17861	Currey, Benjamin F.	19434
Cummings, Jesse	17862	Currey, Claude P.	19435
Cummings, Rebecca	17863	Currey, May	19436
Cummings, Lewis	17864	Curtsinger, Louisa F.	26206
Cummings, Maggie	20670	Curtsinger, Fred	26207
Cummings, John	20672	Curtsinger, Etta	26208
Cummings, Wilson	30001	Curtsinger, Lena	26209
Cummings, Lizzie	30002	Curtsinger, Clifford	26210
Cumming, Maggie E.	23790	Curleyhead, Lillie	31146
Cumsey, Aggie	28502	Curleyhead, Rosie	31147
Cumsey, Key	28503	Curleyhead, Katie	31148
Cumpston, Mary F.	30223	Cureylhead, Josie	31149
Cumpston, Emily	30224	Curleyhead, Catherine	
Cumiford, Pleasant	31945	A.	31150
Cumiford, Robert S.	31946	Curleyhead, Roy	31151
Cumiford, Henry S.	31947	Czarlinkow, Robert	3622
Cumiford, Julia A.	31948	Czarnakow, Caroline	18299
Cumiford, Benjamin F.	31949	Czarnikow, Charles	30787
Cumiford, Beulah C.	31950	Czarnikow, Joel B.	30788
Cumiford, Watt	31951	Czarnikow, George	30789
Cumiford, Margarett	31952	Czarnikow, Bula A.	30790
Cunningham, Lizzie	4964	Czarnikow, Bertha	30792
Cunningham, Thomas F.	5438	Czarnikow, Maudie	30791
Cunningham, Mabel C.	7240	Czarnikow, Robert Jr.	30793
Cunningham, Neva	7241	Dail, Mary E.	8424
Cunningham, James W.	7242	Dail, Mary T.	8425
Cunningham, Lou O.	7243	Dail, Mark L.	8426
Cunningham, Mary	10103	Dail, William S.	8427
Cunningham, Henry	10104	Daly, Marshall	3854
Cunningham, James M.	10105	Daley, Timothy	4092
Cunningham, Eliza E.	10106	Daley, Rufus L.	4093
Cunningham, Charles F.	10107	Dale, Joseph O.	10638
Cunningham, Levander	10108	Dale, James F.	11011
Cunningham, Maggie	10109	Daley, Homer	17838
Cunningham, Alfred C.	12741	Dallas, Rosa L.	31510
Cunningham, Jeter T.	13745	Dallas, Lena G.	32094
Cunningham, Andrew B.	14029	Dameron, Louella	7972
Cunningham, Sam Ella	14030	Dameron, Samuel D.	7973
Cunningham, William		Dameron, William O.	7974
C.	15464	Dameron, Richard C.	7975
Cunningham, Erna	15465	Dameron, John J.	7976
Cunningham, Foster B.	15466	Dameron, John L.	8428
Cunningham, William		Dameron, Mattie L.	8429
P.	15487	Dameron, Henry A.	8430
Cunningham, Dora	15488	Dameron, Rex E.	8431
Cunningham, Ward A.	15489	Dameron, Eva N.	8432
Cunningham, Lillie M.	15508	Dameron, Birdie A.	8433
Cunningham, Jeter T.	26703	Dameron, Lee L.	8434
Cunningham, Kezia C.	26704	Dameron, John T.	8435
Cunningham, Bell	26705	Dannenberg, John H.	1537
Cunningham, Albert S.		Dannenberg, Johnnie H.	1538
J.	26706	Dannenberg, Louis B.	1539
Cunningham, Rozanna	26707	Dannenberg, Robert C.	1540
Cunnigan, George	17730	Dannenberg, Sarah W.	1541
Cunnigan, Sarah	17731	Dannenberg, Thomas N.	1591
Cunnigan, Cynthia	17732	Dannenberg, Ida E.	1592
Curtis, Vinnie R.	3295	Dannenberg, George R.	1593
Curtis, Joe W.	3296	Dannenberg, Lewis B.	1594
Curtis, Dave	3297	Dannenberg, Jane E.	1595
Curtis, Lula H.	7377	Dannenberg, John F.	1596
Curtis, Mary	7786	Dannenberg, Leonard L.	1597
Curtis, Dulcie I.	7787	Dannenberg, Gladys	1598
Curtis, Amy O.	7788	Dannenberg, William H.	1608
Curry, Laura	5102	Dannenberg, Lewis L.	1644
Curry, Lenora	5103	Dannenberg, William	1734
Curry, Jesse	5104	Dannenberg, Daniel E.	1823
Curry, Mamie	5105	Dannenberg, Richard	30678
Curry, Angie	5106	Dannenberg, Fannie	32128
Curry, Mattie	9021	Dannenberg, Richard M.	
Curry, Ethel M.	9022	Jr.	32129
Curry, Margarett E.	10511	Dannenberg, Esther	32603
Curry, Charles J.	10512	Dannenberg, Richard	
Curry, Susan L.	10513	M.	17102
Curry, Annie M.	10514	Dannenberg, Joseph R.	17103
Curry, Sabrina	10515	Dannenberg, John C.	14156
Curry, Minnie V.	10516	Dannenberg, Okia	14157
Curry, Albert	10517	Dannenberg, Yancey N.	14158
Currey, Frances S.	19428	Daniel, Alice R.	7304
Currey, Clarence E.	19429	Daniel, Lula M.	7305

Name.	Roll No.	Name.	Roll No.
Daniel, Eliza J.	7306	Darnell, Elbert	634
Daniel, Martha E.	7307	Darnell, Robert E.	635
Daniel, Emma E.	7308	Dassler, Henry	4763
Daniel, William A.	7309	Dassler, Dora E.	23077
Daniel, Edgar J.	7310	Dassler, Sudie M.	23078
Daniel, Walter S.	7311	Dassler, Mary	23079
Daniel, John R.	7637	Daugherty, Silk	2153
Daniel, Drucilla M.	7638	Daugherty, Mary	2154
Daniel, Mable E.	7639	Daugherty, Ellen	2155
Daniel, Ralph Clinton	7640	Daugherty, Mary	2156
Daniel, Jessie J.	7712	Daugherty, William	6036
Daniel, Allen W.	15968	Daugherty, Andrew E.	6864
Daniel, Virgil A.	15969	Daugherty, Charles B.	7040
Daniel, Osceola P.	15970	Daugherty, William	7533
Daniel, John C.	15971	Daugherty, David	7680
Daniel, Lella B.	15972	Daugherty, Rose	8108
Daniel, Nannie Chris-		Daugherty, Thomas	8511
tina	15973	Daugherty, William I.	8512
Daniel, Lizzie	18641	Daugherty, Lorena	8513
Daniel, John	18642	Daugherty, Edward	8976
Daniel, Elsie	18643	Daugherty, Elizabeth	10582
Daniel, Adolphus	18644	Daugherty, Emmett	10586
Daniel, Kate	18645	Daugherty, Catherine	10587
Daniel, Marma D.	23649	Daugherty, Amy	10588
Daniel, Freeman A.	23650	Daugherty, Mary E.	10589
Daniel, Edna L.	23651	Daugherty, Belle C.	11691
Daniel, John M.	23658	Daugherty, Lou T.	11692
Daniel, Marmaduke	23807	Daugherty, Ridley	13653
Daniel, Lavonia S.	23809	Daugherty, Annie	17995
Daniel, Louisa	26432	Daugherty, Jennie	17996
Daniel, Catherine B.	27334	Daugherty, Eva	18422
Daniel, Ross I.	16666	Daugherty, Moses	19222
Daniel, Ida C.	16667	Daugherty, Linda	19223
Daniel, Josie B.	16668	Daugherty, Wutie	19224
Daniel, Mary J.	16669	Daugherty, John	19225
Daniel, Osie A.	16670	Daugherty, Polly	19226
Daniel, Eliza B.	16671	Daugherty, George	19227
Daniel, Emma B.	16672	Daugherty, Nellie	19228
Daniels, Robert	8014	Daugherty, Soap	19229
Daniel, James H.	9154	Daugherty, Henry	19329
Daniels, Emma	10164	Daugherty, Nannie	19330
Daniels, Richard	10165	Daugherty, Daniel	19331
Daniels, Lucy	10166	Daugherty, Rachel	19332
Daniels, George Jr.	10167	Daugherty, George	19563
Daniels, Oce	10168	Daugherty, Mary	19564
Daniels, Maggie	10169	Daugherty, Lydia	20251
Daniels, Joseph M.	10679	Daugherty, Frederick	20848
Daniels, Jennie	18935	Daugherty, James	20885
Daniels, Sallie	20541	Daugherty, Betsy	21861
Daniels, George	24486	Daugerty, Money	22944
Daniels, Edna	24488	Daugerty, Jennie	22945
Daniels, Susan	27712	Daugherty, Jane L.	23478
Daniels, Ada	27713	Daugherty, Lillie	23764
Daniels, Arthur	27831	Daugherty, Carrie	23765
Daniels, Ella	27832	Daugherty, Frank	23820
Daniels, Andy	27833	Daugherty, Sam	25633
Daniels, Ludie	32123	Daugherty, Elk	27208
Daniels, George	28085	Daugherty, Scott	27209
Daniels, Sallie	28086	Daugherty, Callie	27210
Daniels, Peter	28087	Daugherty, Florence	27621
Daniels, Sarah	28088	Daugherty, Frank L.	27630
Daniels, Peggy	28089	Daugherty, Joella	27631
Daniels, Tom	28412	Daugherty, Joseph	27632
Daniels, John A.	13589	Daugherty, Robert B.	28600
Daniels, Lula M.	13590	Daugherty, Addie	29537
Daniels, William A.	13591	Daugherty, Esther	29538
Daniels, John F.	13592	Daugherty, Diana	29791
Danneberg, George L.	22560	Daugerty, George	29812
Dannenburg, Nathaniel		Daugerty, Lydia	29813
B.	25041	Daugerty, Helen	29814
Dannenburg, Sarah E.	25042	Daugerty, Toy-nee-che	29815
Dannenburg, Beatrix R.	25043	Daugerty, Jack	29816
Dannenburg, Oby L.	25044	Daugherty, Susan	30347
Dannenburg, Alice N.	25045	Daugherty, James	30348
Dannenburg, Henry G.	25046	Daugherty, Akie	32228
Dannenburg, Waldemar	25047	Daugherty, Susan	32464
Dancer, Myrtle M.	27717	Daugherty, Daisy	32465
Dancer, Beulah G.	27718	Davis, Artelia	391
Dancer, Dora S.	13625	Davis, Katy Rosana	392
Dancer, Jesse E.	13629	Davis, Nellie Jane	393
Danderson, John O.	28138	Davis, Thomas Ezra	394
Darnell, Sanora V.	632	Davis, Joel Albert	395
Darnell, Cora M.	633	Davis, William J.	396

Name.	Roll No.	Name.	Roll No.
Davis, Bertha Perrilla	397	Davis, Sarah	17788
Davis, William H.	1931	Davis, Henry	17789
Davis, Eliza	1932	Davis, George W.	17791
Davis, Andrew	2707	Davis, Dave	18519
Davis, Charley	2712	Davis, Annie	18520
Davis, Barney	2713	Davis, Nancy	18680
Davis, Mary	2714	Davis, Henry	18681
Davis, James	2734	Davis, Jug	18712
Davis, Ora E.	2735	Davis, Betsy	18713
Davis, Annie L.	2736	Davis, Charles	18714
Davis, Marvin	2737	Davis, Leona	18715
Davis, Mary A.	3914	Davis, Mollie	18716
Davis, Elias E.	4298	Davis, Carrie	18718
Davis, Ammon H.	4299	Davis, Jennie	18721
Davis, Jetter	4300	Davis, Ross	18733
Davis, Lenora	4616	Davis, Jennie	18734
Davis, Sarah A.	4617	Davis, Lugie	18735
Davis, Tempy S.	4618	Davis, George	19471
Davis, Dosh B.	4834	Davis, Nannie	19472
Davis, Jennie	4930	Davis, Jack	19473
Davis, Pearl A.	4931	Davis, Davis	19823
Davis, William C.	4932	Davis, Alexander	19825
Davis, Sadie A.	4933	Davis, Nicholas	19826
Davis, Polly	5696	Davis, Nellie	20380
Davis, Minerva T.	5697	Davis, Or-kon-stor-ter	20906
Davis, Amanda	5698	Davis, Thompson	21289
Davis, Mary	5699	Davis, Sarah	21300
Davis, Sallie A.	9445	Davis, Mary	21301
Davis, Edna G.	9446	Davis, Curtis	21302
Davis, Ellis L.	9447	Davis, Napoleon	21786
Davis, Mable Bell	9448	Davis, Watie E.	22064
Davis, John W.	10075	Davis, Cicero	22083
Davis, Violet	10076	Davis, Mary L.	22136
Davis, Susan	10448	Davis, Daniel B.	22155
Davis, Susan E.	11522	Davis, Duell A.	22156
Davis, Jeff	11559	Davis, Jas. Preston	23085
Davis, Hattie B.	11891	Davis, Joseph W.	24066
Davis, John B.	11954	Davis, Barilla A.	24067
Davis, Lizzie	11955	Davis, Amanda	24068
Davis, Jeff	11956	Davis, Florence	24069
Davis, Jesse	11957	Davis, Joseph J.	24070
Davis, Jetar	11958	Davis, Hattie M.	24071
Davis, Ezekel	11959	Davis, James H.	24072
Davis, William	12327	Davis, Mattie B.	24073
Davis, Thomas	12395	Davis, Kim	24907
Davis, Chauncey	12396	Davis, Andrew	25325
Davis, Alice V.	12948	Davis, Eugene	25326
Davis, John B.	12949	Davis, Coh-he-neh	25934
Davis, Lyta	12950	Davis, Mexican	25935
Davis, Arthur C.	12951	Davis, John	26057
Davis, Mabel	12952	Davis, Mary	26058
Davis, Frank	12953	Davis, Burwell M.	26059
Davis, Ellen C.	12962	Davis, Alexander D.	26628
Davis, Edna E.	13238	Davis, John	26860
Davis, Mack O.	13239	Davis, Susan J.	26861
Davis, Leeola	13240	Davis, Joe L.	26862
Davis, Roy	13241	Davis, Samuel T.	26863
Davis, Arizona	13242	Davis, Caroline	26864
Davis, Louis H.	13243	Davis, Jack	26865
Davis, Mary L.	14129	Davis, Ellen	26918
Davis, David	14818	Davis, Alfred	27243
Davis, Linnie F.	14819	Davis, Elizabeth	27244
Davis, James	15194	Davis, Maudie	27245
Davis, Laura	15195	Davis, Julius	27581
Davis, Alley	15196	Davis, Hannah M.	27761
Davis, Kyle	16059	Davis, Lee F.	27762
Davis, Kinney	16388	Davis, Joel M.	27763
Davis, Caroline	16939	Davis, Theodore	27764
Davis, Flora	16940	Davis, Asa	27765
Davis, Thompson	16942	Davis, Isaac	27766
Davis, Samuel T.	17072	Davis, John W.	27767
Davis, Lucinda	17073	Davis, Sidney M.	27768
Davis, Lowrey	17120	Davis, Perry	28318
Davis, Stand W.	17137	Davis, Nellie	28668
Davis, Sidney	17430	Davis, Ella	28669
Davis, Rachel	17431	Davis, John	28670
Davis, Nannie	17432	Davis, Mack	28671
Davis, Christine	17433	Davis, Katie	28975
Davis, Pauline	17434	Davis, George	29139
Davis, Robert L.	17446	Davis, Willie H.	29283
Davis, Mattie	17447	Davis, Nannie	29332
Davis, Fixin	17786	Davis, Sanford L.	29333
Davis, John	17787	Davis, Leo J.	29334

Name.	Roll No.	Name.	Roll No.
Davis, Lorena G.	29335	Dawson, James W.	31766
Davis, Polly	30064	Dawson, Thomas P.	31767
Davis, Samuel	30382	Dawson, Mariee J.	31768
Davis, Annie	30383	Dawson, John	31769
Davis, John	30384	Dawson, Robert B.	31770
Davis, Oo-cha-la-na-he	30501	Dawson, Iola M.	31771
Davis, Sampson	30554	Dawson, Lemuel H.	31772
Davis, Mary	30615	Dawson, Rosa B.	31773
Davis, Bruce	31647	Dawson, Charles B.	31774
Davis, Doode	31649	Dawson, Hattie J.	31775
Davis, Georgia A.	31650	Dawson, Jennings B.	31776
Davis, Virginia	31651	Dawson, James U.	31777
Davis, Cyrus	31656	Dawson, Vergal C.	31778
Davis, John D.	31657	Dawson, Joseph R.	31779
Davis, George	31658	Dawson, Clarence E.	31780
Davis, Maud	32066	Dawson, Council J.	31781
Davis, John P.	32549	Dawson, Elmer A.	31782
Davis, Gertrude	32550	Dawson, Cleo	31783
Davis, Pluma	32551	Dawson, Rufus T.	31784
Davis, Diana	32637	Dawson, Edgar	31785
Davis, Miller	32693	Dawson, Wilborn	31786
Davis, Mary L.	32694	Dawson, James R.	31787
Davis, Sallie S.	32695	Dawson, Vinnie D.	31788
Davis, Earl T.	32696	Dawson, Ermine C.	31789
Davis, John M.	32697	Dawson, Edwin C.	31790
Davis, Lorenzo Newton	32916	Dawson, Ancil F.	31791
Davidson, Ermina J.	8026	Dawson, Florence	32654
Davidson, Annie L.	8027	Dawson, Francis Marion	32704
Davidson, Rutha	8028	Dawes, Mary L.	28167
Davidson, Percy R.	8928	Dawes, Sallie	28168
Davidson, William	10433	Dawes, Ida	28169
Davidson, Mary M.	24539	Dawes, Ada	28170
Davidson, Susan M. P.	24540	Dawes, Opal	28171
Davidson, Gracie L.	24541	Dawes, Loyd R.	13211
Davidson, Bert	32777	Dawes, William D.	13212
Davenport, Millard G.	10002	Dawes, Cora B.	13213
Davenport, Grace	10003	Dawes, Claude	13214
Davenport, Dorothy	10004	Dawes, Essie	13215
David, Stephen	17870	Dawes, Johnathan W.	13422
David, Nellie	17871	Dawes, Samson	14928
David, Betsy	17872	Dawes, Phoebe J.	30317
David, Polly	17874	Day, William A.	8210
David, Sallie	17875	Day, Ruth S.	8211
Dave, Key	32520	Day, Mary E.	8212
Dawson, Dora	6605	Day, William A., Jr.	8213
Dawson, James	6606	Day, Mattie S.	8214
Dawson, Samuel	6607	Day, Clarence	31326
Dawson, Charles	6608	Day, Harrison	31327
Dawson, Laura	6799	Day, Nora	31328
Dawson, Stephen E.	6800	Day, Grace	31653
Dawson, Jeff	6801	Daylight, Sarah	29806
Dawson, Joseph F.	6802	Dazley, Robert	4429
Dawes, Mary A.	7585	Dazzler, Aggie	15174
Dawson, Fannie L.	10480	Dazzler, John W.	15175
Dawson, John Hubert	10482	Dazzler, James L.	15176
Dawson, Rebecca	25243	Dazzler, Oce	15177
Dawson, George H.	25244	Dazzler, Charles	15178
Dawson, Robert L.	31716	Deal, John H.	1771
Dawson, Elbert B.	31717	Deal, Clara O.	1772
Dawson, Ralph E.	31718	Deal, Charlie	2076
Dawson, Richard W.	31719	Deal, William W.	13011
Dawson, Ina E.	31720	Deal, Mack	27774
Dawson, William C.	31731	Deal, Edgar L.	27775
Dawson, John	31733	Deal, Ethel	27776
Dawson, William R.	31734	Deal, Cornelius	27777
Dawson, Francis M., Jr.	31735	Deal, Robert L.	28158
Dawson, Francis M.	31736	Deal, Joseph	32413
Dawson, Lula	31737	Dean, Nancy J.	14480
Dawson, Ray	31738	Dean, Presha M.	14481
Dawson, Jessie J.	31739	Dean, Mary C.	14482
Dawson, Jacob L.	31740	Dean, Samantha J.	14483
Dawson, Hugh A.	31741	Dean, William A.	14484
Dawson, Laura A.	31742	Dean, Jefferson D.	14485
Dawson, Samuel R.	31748	Dean, Eva E.	14486
Dawson, August	31749	Dean, Percy S.	14487
Dawson, Mate	31750	Dean, Mamie E.	14488
Dawson, Robert	31751	Dean, Nannie	23277
Dawson, Albert H.	31752	Dean, Nannie	23277
Dawson, Ralph H.	31753	Dean, Claud	23278
Dawson, Alford	31754	Dean, Bessie M.	23279
Dawson, John W.	31763	Deatherage, Mariah A.	25377
Dawson, Orle H.	31764	Deatherage, Sallie M.	25378
Dawson, Burr R.	31765	Deckman, Tracy	26561

Name.	Roll No.	Name.	Roll No.
Deckman, Laura B.	26562	Dew, Jennie	18188
Deerhead, John	6284	Dew, Aily	18193
Deerhead, Lizzie	6285	Dew, Oce	18476
Deerhead, Oce	20714	Dew, William	18477
Deerhead, Nannie	32862	Dew, James	18478
Deems, Edna	12296	Dew, George	18479
Deems, John	12323	Dew, Jack	27830
Deerinwater, Bessie	16763	Dew, Famous	28500
Deerinwater, Richard	16764	Dew, Jefferson	30499
Deerinwater, George	21116	Devine, Charles W.	21485
Deerinwater, Keener	21142	Devine, James T.	21486
Deerinwater, Katie	21143	Devine, Thomas	21535
Deerinwater, Wakie	21144	Devine, James	21536
Deerinwater, Levi	21424	Devine, Joel M.	21537
Deerinwater, John	27299	Devine, William	21538
Deerinwater, Charles	27300	Devine, Jackson	21539
Deerinwater, Sam	32384	Devaughn, Arthur E.	3451
Deerinwater, Lizzie	32430	Devaughn, Sarah L.	3452
Deer-in-water, Aleck	18353	DeVaughn, George F.	3453
Deer-in-water, Annie	18354	DeVaughn, Daniel R.	4081
Deer-in-water, George	20460	DeVan, Mahala E.	10574
Deer-in-water, Lucinda	20461	DeVan, Addie	10575
Deer-in-water, Charley	20462	DeVan, Carrie	10576
Deer-in-water, Sallie	20463	DeVan, Eva	10577
Deer-in-water, Tom	20464	DeVan, Benjamin F.	10578
Deer-in-water, John	20465	Deupree, Maude E.	30166
Deer-in-water, Lucy	20466	Deupree, Charlotte B.	30167
Deer-in-water, Dick	20467	Dial, Nathaniel H.	6406
Deer-in-water, Susie	20468	Dial, Hugh H.	6407
Deer-in-water, Star	21095	Dial, Nola M.	6408
Dege, Charles F.	21673	Dial, Bettie E.	6409
Dege, Laura A.	23797	Dial, Lela A.	6410
Dege, Mary E.	23798	Dial, Daniel F.	6411
Dege, Phillip S.	23799	Dial, Grace B.	6412
Dege, John J.	23800	Dial, James Hastings	6413
Dellis, George	4037	Dial, Newton	6814
DeLozier, Georgia V.	13519	Dial, Thomas	14695
DeLozier, Fountain G.	13520	Dial, Nancy	29152
DeLozier, Manford E.	13521	Dial, Mattie	30407
DeLozier, John E.	13522	Dick, Thomas E.	7753
DeLozier, Ralph A.	13523	Dick, Jessie	7754
DeLozier, Hazel M.	13524	Dick, Ira M.	7755
DeLozier, Vivian	1352b	Dick, Mary E.	7756
DeLozier, Evaline	14589	Dick, Joanna	7757
DeLozier, Roberta E.	14590	Dick, Isaac J.	7758
DeLozier, Carlyle A.	14591	Dick, Mary	7849
DeLozier, Virginia S.	32662	Dick, Mary	7850
Delano, Charles H.	16909	Dick, Laura C.	8436
Dellis, Boot	18785	Dick, Walter	8437
Delay, Albert I.	26030	Dick, George	8438
Delay, Clara C.	26031	Dick, Myrtle	8439
Dempsey, Sallie M.	5313	Dick, Ellis	8440
Dempsey, James W.	5314	Dick, Mary	8441
Dempsey, Jennie	5315	Dick, Lorenzo	8442
Dempsey, Charles Oscar	5316	Dick, Washington	8650
Denton, Josephine	2588	Dick, Amos	8676
Denton, John T.	8355	Dick, Jacob	10153
Denton, Rufus	11337	Dick, Joseph	10154
Denton, Younce	11338	Dick, Alsie	10155
Denton, Frank	11649	Dick, Cassie	10156
Denton, William C.	21720	Dick, Ellen	10157
Denton, Effie	29542	Dick, Bessie	10158
Denton, Margie	29543	Dickey, Callie E.	10999
Denny, Phoeba	3426	Dickey, Effie E.	11000
Denny, Noble	28760	Dickey, Pearl May	11001
Denny, Lewis J.	28761	Dickey, William	11242
Denny, Emmett A.	28762	Dick, Ellis	11243
Denney, Rachel	3920	Dick, Annie	13441
Denney, Alice J.	11305	Dick, Frank W.	13442
Dennis, Viola	7700	Dick, Mary J.	13443
Dennis, Samuel B.	7702	Dick, John	13444
Denbo, Letitia V.	11688	Dick, Eva	13445
Denbo, Robert L.	11689	Dick, Andrew	16415
Denbo, Oce	11690	Dick, George	16416
Denbo, John L.	11907	Dick, John H.	17572
Denbo, Laura A.	11908	Dick, Oce	17792
Denbo, Robert E.	11909	Dick, Willie	17793
Denbo, John L.	11910	Dick, Coleman	18110
DeShane, Caleb	13048	Dick, Katie	18111
DeShane, Rosetta	13049	Dick, Ollie	18112
DeShane, Alfred	13050	Dick, Watt	18113
DeShane, Ida M.	13051	Dick, Josie	18114
DeShane, Washington	13052	Dick, Gee	18551

Name.	Roll No.	Name.	Roll No.
Dick, John	18863	Dixon, Henrietta	9449
Dick, Nancy	20849	Dixon, Edith	9450
Dick, George	20850	Dixon, Isaac E.	9451
Dick, Wahlesah	20851	Dixon, James W.	9452
Dick, Lilly	20852	Dixon, Mabel L.	9453
Dick, George	20929	Dixon, Jennie	27506
Dick, Betsy	20930	Dixon, William	27507
Dick, William	20975	Dixon, Isaac	28939
Dick, Charles A.	22135	Dixon, Lula B.	31494
Dick, Bertha	24109	Dixon, Annie M.	31495
Dick, Arthur	24110	Dixon, Claude	31496
Dick, Ada	24111	Dixon, Riley	31497
Dick, Bessie M.	24112	Dobkins, Ben	9803
Dick, Effie	24113	Dobkins, Hugh C.	27696
Dick, Annie	25369	Dobson, Sarah	14330
Dick, Jane	25601	Dobson, Wallace	14331
Dick, William	25949	Dobson, Mary J.	14332
Dick, Sallie	25950	Dobson, Harry L.	14333
Dick, Maggie	25951	Dobson, Arthur R.	14334
Dick, Eli	25964	Dobson, Eugenia	14335
Dick, Jennie	25965	Dobson, Bonnie L.	16447
Dick, Sooky	25966	Dobbs, Annie	19600
Dick, George	27593	Dobbs, William R.	19601
Dick, Sallie E.	27926	Dobbins, James	29952
Dick, Jennie	29134	Doctor, John	18876
Dick, Irena	31670	Doctor, Aginni	1887
Dick, Jennie	32072	Doctor, Lizzie	25627
Dick, Malinda	32263	Dodson, Eliza	7480
Dick, Laura B.	32264	Dodson, Alma P.	7481
Dickson, Ollie W.	8291	Dodge, Sarah E.	10858
Dickson, Cynthia	13494	Dodge, Ada M.	10859
Dickson, Claude N.	13495	Dodge, James J.	10860
Dickson, Serena	13496	Dodge, Margaret M.	10861
Dickson, Paul	13497	Dodge, William A.	10862
Dickson, Beulah	13498	Dodge, Alma E.	10866
Dickson, Thomas B., Jr.	13499	Dodge, Fidella	10867
Dickins, Irene	29443	Dodge, Robinson Gaddis	10868
Dickins, Miriam	29444	Dodge, Nancy J.	24694
Di-gah-dee-nah-i, Celia	25774	Dodge, Jessie I.	24695
Dildine, Rachel	14300	Dodge, Watie F.	24696
Dildine, James	14301	Dodge, Dewey L.	24697
Dildine, Leathy	14303	Dodge, Cora A.	31529
Dildine, Hester	14304	Dodge, Iris N.	31530
Dildine, Andrew	14305	Dodge, Susan F.	32086
Dildine, Silas	14306	Dodge, Bertha L.	32087
Dildine, Isaac	14307	Dodge, Clem V.	32088
Dildine, Jacob	14308	Dodge, William N. Jr.	32089
Dildine, Sarah Mariah	14309	Dodge, Kay V.	32090
Dinsmore, May B.	14060	Dodge, Susie I.	32091
Dinsmore, Willie	14061	Dodge, Gertrude J.	32092
Dinnis, Peter	19706	Dodge, Charles W. H.	32093
Dinnis, Mary	19707	Dog, Stephen	20308
Dinnis, Nancy	19708	Dog, Nancy	20309
Dinnis, Rachel	19709	Dog, Tinna	20310
Dinnis, Susan	19710	Doherty, Robert E.	6444
Dinnis, Jennie	19711	Doherty, Walter L.	7211
Dinnis, Jim	30566	Doherty, Mary B.	7212
Dirt, Katie	4016	Doherty, Elizabeth C.	7213
Dirtthrower, George	9048	Doherty, William L.	7214
Dirteater, Robin	18415	Doherty, Ella M.	7215
Dirteater, Ella	18416	Doherty, Letha	7216
Dirteater, Maggie	18417	Doherty, James E.	7217
Dirteater, Charles	18423	Doherty, William H.	8527
Dirteater, Annie	18424	Doherty, Josie L.	8528
Dirteater, Stan	18426	Doherty, Claud H.	8529
Dirteater, Moses	18427	Doherty, William H.	8530
Dirteater, Dick	18428	Doherty, John H.	8531
Dirteater, Henry	18429	Doherty, Percy C.	8532
Dirteater, Bell	18498	Doherty, James R.	21777
Dirteater, Joe	18871	Doherty, Lizzie	21778
Dirteater, Lizzie	18872	Doherty, Edna	21779
Dirteater, Nancy	30515	Doherty, John M.	22000
Dirtseller, Rider	19477	Doherty, Sarah E.	22001
Dirtseller, Oosquinna	19478	Doherty, Leona A.	22002
Dirtseller, Ooyustutah	19479	Dolen, Sarah	6909
Dirtseller, Jesse	19480	Dolen, Josephine	6910
Dirtseller, Achinnie	30555	Dolen, Clarry M.	6911
Dirtseller, Adolphus Washington	32805	Dolen, Ida May	6912
Dirttrack, Charlotte	20368	Dollahite, Edith	7219
Dirtpot, Nellie	26597	Dollahite, Veria	7220
Dishman, Jessie	11339	Dolly, Ah-ta-nah	20397
Diver, Bunch	30533	Dollar, Celia	20422
		Dollar, Sarah	20423

Name.	Roll No.	Name.	Roll No.
Donaldson, Frank M.	7355	Downing, Betsy	1169
Donaldson, Fleety	7356	Downing, Thomas	1170
Donaldson, Rachel S.	7840	Downing, Lucy	1171
Donaldson, William C.	7841	Downing, Clem	1172
Donaldson, Ola M.	7842	Downing, Joshua	1173
Donaldson, Annie	7843	Downing, Rufus	1214
Donaldson, Artie	7844	Downing, Ruthie	1497
Donohoo, Delen R.	7363	Downing, Jackson	3670
Donohoo, Madaline	7364	Downing, Mary	3671
Donohoo, Paul L.	7365	Downing, Josie	3672
Donohoo, Lucile	8706	Downing, Joshua	3673
Don Carlos, Luther L.	8298	Downing, Sallie	3769
Don Carlos, William R.	8299	Downing, Sarah	3770
Don Carlos, Louis A.	10353	Downing, Eli	3771
Don Carlos, Frank L.	15486	Downing, Susan	3772
Donnelly, James	8472	Downing, Lucy	3773
Donnelly, Mattie A.	8473	Downing, Charles	4397
Donnelly, James O.	8474	Downing, Kate	5642
Donnelly, Mary E.	9111	Downing, Lucile	5643
Donnelly, Gladys	9112	Downing, Edward	5644
Donnelly, Mattie	9128	Downing, George	5645
Donnelly, Tom	9155	Downing, Maud	5646
Donnelly, William A.	9276	Downing, George	5678
Donnelly, Emma J.	24197	Downing, Jennie	5679
Donnelly, Emma	24198	Downing, George	7893
Donnelly, Paul	24199	Downing, George	7936
Donnelly, Ada	24200	Downing, Mollie	7937
Dooley, Margaret J.	12809	Downing, John	7938
Dooley, Myrtle	12810	Downing, Zuma	7939
Dooley, Earl N.	12811	Downing, Felix	7940
Dooley, Ruby E.	12812	Downing, Lizzie	7941
Doty, Sarah J. B.	8230	Downing, Nancy	7942
Doty, John E.	8231	Downing, Walter	9066
Doty, Sam D.	8232	Downing, Rachel	9067
Doty, Otis	8233	Downing, William	9099
Doty, Lula M.	8234	Downing, William	10879
Dotts, Beulah C.	27624	Downing, Richard	11092
Dotts, Daniel O.	27625	Downing, William H.	13166
Dotts, Bessie M.	27626	Downing, Lewis W.	13167
Doublehead, Bird	7852	Downing, Anna Louesa	13168
Doublehead, Blackbird	18380	Downing, Thomas B.	13744
Doublehead, Minnie	18381	Downing, Daniel	13789
Doublehead, Katie	18382	Downing, Martha	13790
Doublehead, Lulu	18383	Downing, William A.	13939
Doublehead, Joe	18384	Downing, Eliza J.	13940
Doublehead, Ailsy	18408	Downing, George G.	13941
Doublehead, Ada	19000	Downing, Carrie	13942
Doublehead, Isaac	20589	Downing, Samuel S.	13943
Doublehead, Jennie	20687	Downing, Nannie M.	13944
Doublehead, Lucinda	21299	Downing, Elodie V.	13945
Doublehead, John	25948	Downing, Ella V.	13946
Doublehead, Levi	28716	Downing, Elizabeth	13947
Doublehead, Bird	29321	Downing, William A. Jr.	13948
Doublehead, Filey E.	29322	Downing, David Monroe	13949
Doublehead, Clemmie T.	29323	Downing, Chester	13974
Doublehead, Peter	30527	Downing, Neppie	13983
Doublehead, Peggy	30528	Downing, Alex	13985
Doublehead, John	30529	Downing, Nancy	13986
Doublehead, Nancy	30530	Downing, Joel	13987
Doublehead, Carolina	30531	Downing, Katie	14149
Doublehead, Sallie	30623	Downing, Joseph	14561
Doublehead, Jennie	32773	Downing, Lewis	14562
Dougherty, Runabout	17950	Downing, Peggie	14563
Dougherty, Louella	17951	Downing, George	14564
Dougherty, Wat	17952	Downing, Drucilla	14565
Dougherty, Robin	17953	Downing, Thompson	14644
Dougherty, Anderson	17954	Downing, Sallie	14645
Dougherty, Annie	17955	Downing, Maggie	17116
Dougherty, John R. H.	27740	Downing, Jessie	17117
Dougherty, Mary	27741	Donwing, Thomas	17270
Douglas, Nancy J.	25034	Downing, Dora	17491
Douglas, Ella	25035	Downing, Benjamin	17508
Douglas, Walter C.	25036	Downing, Jesse	17534
Douglas, John A.	25037	Downing, William	17620
Douglas, Mollie J.	25038	Downing, Houston	17689
Douglas, Ida	25040	Downing, Elizabeth	17690
Douthitt, William D.	31870	Downing, Nancy	17691
Douthitt, Wanetta	31871	Downing, Mary	17692
Downing, Alice	119	Downing, Rebecca	17693
Downing, Luella	120	Downing, Hill	17694
Downing, Benjamin	121	Downing, Charles	17695
Downing, Caroline	898	Downing, Martha	14646
Downing, Katie	899	Downing, Polly	14647
Downing, Ned	1168	Downing, Lucy	14648
		Downing, Nancy	14649
		Downing, Joseph	14843

Name.	Roll No.	Name.	Roll No.
Downing, Nannie	14844	Downing, David	19513
Downing, Charlotte	14845	Downing, David	20073
Downing, Lizzie	14846	Downing, Jesse	20682
Downing, James	14963	Downing, Skaqua	20741
Downing, Emma	14964	Downing, Nancy	20742
Downing, Blue	14965	Downing, Ned	20764
Downing, Johnson	14966	Downing, Sallie	20765
Downing, Mollie	15165	Downing, Cull	20905
Downing, Ned	15166	Downing, George	21002
Downing, Cynthia	15167	Downing, Rachel	21388
Downing, Joel	15168	Downing, Dawes	21389
Downing, Lafayette	15169	Downing, Andy	21414
Downing, Mulberry	15381	Downing, Jennie	21415
Downing, Louis	15686	Downing, Dick	21455
Downing, Leo M.	15687	Downing, Becky	21456
Downing, Hazel I.	15688	Downing, Dick	21933
Downing, Ned	15879	Downing, Lidda	23564
Downing, Alex	15999	Downing, George B.	25066
Downing, Sarah	16219	Downing, James L.	25068
Downing, Lewis	16220	Downing, Effie O.	25069
Downing, Jennie	16494	Downing, William A.	25070
Downing, Susie	16495	Downing, Susan	25071
Downing, William P.	16518	Downing, Jesse	25073
Downing, Nancy J.	16519	Downing, Walter	25227
Downing, Susan B.	16520	Downing, Sallie	25296
Downing, James	16631	Downing, Wash	25794
Downing, Aley	16632	Downing, Elsie	25795
Downing, Mack	16690	Downing, Laura	25796
Downing, Sallie	16691	Downing, Lucy	25797
Downing, Cora	16692	Downing, Claud	25798
Downing, Robert	16693	Downing, Maud	25799
Downing, Eliza	17115	Downing, Eliza	25897
Downing, Charlotte	25898	Downing, Adam	31993
Downing, Joseph	25899	Downing, Charles	32021
Downing, Dole	25900	Downing, Belle	32291
Downing, Sam H.	25969	Downing, Mink	32632
Downing, Moses	26353	Downing, Annie	32865
Downing, John	26354	Dowell, Virtie A.	11578
Downing, Charles W.	26355	Dowell, Mammie	26369
Downing, Leroy	26635	Dowell, Ora L.	12125
Downing, Simpson	26636	Dowell, Henry H.	26370
Downing, Susie	26637	Dowell, Morgan A.	12126
Downing, Lydia	27451	Dowell, Bessie	26371
Downing, Susie	28303	Dowell, Claude E.	12127
Downing, Polly	28474	Dowell, Claud E.	26372
Downing, Henry	28544	Dowell, William E.	12128
Downing, David	28902	Dowell, Pressley P.	12129
Downing, Samuel	28903	Drake, Alethea	8364
Downing, Sissie	28904	Drake, Arizona M.	8365
Downing, Johnson	28907	Drake, Morland W.	8366
Downing, Jennie	28908	Drake, Clarence E.	8367
Downing, William	28909	Drake, Dora M.	8867
Downing, Lucy	29047	Drake, Nettie F.	8868
Downing, Sam	29048	Drake, Adelia M.	8869
Downing, Lucy	29520	Drake, William J.	8870
Downing, Maggie	29602	Drake, Emily J.	13106
Downing, Lewis	29603	Drake, Bessie W.	13107
Downing, George, Jr.	29604	Drake, John E.	13108
Downing, Samuel	29899	Drake, Emma L.	13109
Downing, Abraham	29900	Drake, Nannie E.	13110
Downing, Nayesah	29901	Drake, Emiline	32427
Downing, Chuwah-neeski	29902	Drake, Emma E.	32428
Downing, Ezekiel	29903	Drake, Raymond P.	32429
Downing, Susan	30259	Dragger, Lincoln	26092
Downing, Ed	30404	Dragger, Martha	26093
Downing, Nancy	30510	Dragger, Mary	26094
Downing, Hoolondake	30713	Dragger, Lewis	26407
Downing, Betsy	31967	Dragger, Nellie	26408
Downing, Jack	17796	Dragger, Charlotte	30727
Downing, James	17797	Dragger, Mariah	30728
Downing, Alice	17798	Drew, John T.	5149
Downing, Benjamin	17799	Drew, Mollie E.	5150
Downing, Jennie	17897	Drew, Maggie A.	5151
Downing, William	17898	Drew, Sarah E.	5152
Downing, Mike	17899	Drew, John T. Jr.	5153
Downing, Henry	18160	Drew, James M.	5154
Downing, Mary	18167	Drew, Mary E.	5155
Downing, Carrie	18168	Drew, Charlotte G.	5388
Downing, Dave	18224	Drew, George	6743
Downing, Scott	18223	Drew, Eugene H.	6744
Downing, Brice	18324	Drew, Richard E.	6745
Downing, Alex	18490	Drew, Unis P.	6746
Downing, Ella	18491	Drew, William H.	10118
Downing, Dave	18493	Drew, Ruby	10120
Downing, Takie	18494	Drew, Jamina	10121

Name.	Roll No.	Name.	Roll No.
Drew, Pearl	11415	Duckworth, Nevada	22336
Drew, William R.	11420	Duckworth, Effie	22337
Drew, Zada	22017	Duckworth, Nancy	22338
Drew, Jesse B.	24133	Duckworth, Gunter	22339
Drew, Pauline J.	24134	Duckworth, Robert	22340
Drew, Neva E.	24135	Duck, John	11782
Drew, William P.	28667	Duck, Lola	11783
Drew, Clara	30355	Duck, Tahnee	18036
Dreadfulwater, Wilson	18151	Duck, Jack	18037
Dreadfulwater, Celia	18152	Duck, Rachel	18038
Dreadfulwater, Andrew	18153	Duck, Linda	18039
Dreadfulwater, Nancy	18154	Duck, Mary	18094
Dreadfulwater, Willie	18155	Duck, George	19218
Dreadfulwater, John	18220	Duck, Lizzie	19219
Dreadfulwater, Nakie	18221	Duck, Tim	19220
Dreadfulwater, Henry	18390	Duck, Rachel	19221
Dreadfulwater, Peggy	18391	Duck, Jesse	20457
Dreadfulwater, John	18392	Duck, Yose	20458
Dreadfulwater, Ned	18834	Duck, William	20459
Dreadfulwater, Annie	18835	Duck, Richard	20470
Dreadfulwater, John	18836	Duck, Emeline	20471
Dreadfulwater, Lydia	21379	Duck, Nancy	20474
Dreadfulwater, John	21390	Duck, Lizzie	20475
Drowningbear, William	10934	Duck, Jennie	20492
Drum, Elizabeth	5936	Duck, Satarni	20493
Drum, Alex	8225	Duck, Charley	20494
Drum, Annie E.	11903	Duck, Nick	20495
Drum, Groundhog	20288	Duck, John	25947
Drum, Josie	30958	Duck, Lucy	29711
Drum, John	31284	Duck, Ollie	29712
Drum, Mamie	31285	Duck, Wah-ne-na-he	30662
Drum, Leslie Clyde	31286	Duck, Levi	32230
Drum, William	31319	Ducwah, Polly	24482
Drum, Jane	51320	Dugger, Polly	6189
Dry, Samuel	1226	Dugger, William	6190
Dry, Charlott	1227	Dugger, Daisy D.	6191
Dry, Mary	1228	Dudley, Mollie E.	1347
Dry, Ella	1229	Dudley, Fannie B.	1348
Dry, Jim	1230	Dudley, Jesse F.	1349
Dry, Annie	1231	Dudley, Maggie M.	1350
Dry, Daisy	9927	Dudley, Mamie G.	1351
Dry, Floyd A.	9928	Dudley, Nannie L.	2147
Dry, Johnnie Everett	9929	Dudley, William C.	2148
Dry, Phillip	18234	Dudley, Richard E.	2149
Dry, Darkey	18235	Dudley, Alfred	14279
Dry, Jumper,	18236	Dudley, Henry D.	14280
Dry, Lydia	18237	Dudley, Joseph A.	14281
Dry, Scraper	18238	Dudley, Annie	27648
Dry, Hunter	20242	Dudley, Ellen	27649
Dry, Celia	20243	Dudley, Samuel H.	27650
Dry, Johnson	20244	Duel, Emily	16534
Dry, Mattie	27865	Duel, Fay	16535
Dry, Barkie	27866	Duffield, Wallace	14391
Dry, Agnes	27867	Duffield, Everett R.	14392
Dry, John	27868	Duffield, Thomas W.	14393
Dry, Walter	27869	Duffield, Annie	16049
Dry, Jesse	30495	Duffield, George	16050
Drywater, Nancy	18676	Duffield, William H.	16051
Drywater, Samuel	18802	Duffield, Eli	16052
Drywater, Jennie	18803	Duff, Virginia C.	15341
Drywater, Jesse	18804	Duff, Bettie	15342
Dry, Susie	19758	Duff, Jennie B.	15343
Dry, Steve	19759	Duff, Linnie	15344
Drywater, John	20340	Dukes, Betsy	4784
Drywater, Mink	20365	Dukes, Hooley B.	23080
Drywater, Elsie	20366	Dukes, Beulah	23081
Drywater, Maria	20367	Duncan, Lizzie	1989
Drywater, Jesse	20908	Duncan, Clint	1990
Drywater, Lila	20909	Duncan, Mary L.	1991
Drywater, George	29876	Duncan, Cleo D.	1992
Drywater, Susie	30517	Duncan, Felix G.	1993
Drywater, Buck	30518	Duncan, Virner	1994
Drywater, Oo-ger-we-		Duncan, Josie Blair	1995
yah	30611	Duncan, Martha	4636
Drywater, Bunch	31979	Duncan, Thomas	6105
Drywater, Susan	31980	Duncan, John E.	6467
Drywater, Chu-nee-qua-		Duncan, Susie E.	6468
lee-skee	31981	Duncan, Ellis C.	6469
Dubois, William R.	7084	Duncan, Robert S.	6470
Dubois, Susan M.	7085	Duncan, Cathleen	6471
Dubois, Mavry J.	15545	Duncan, Albert C.	6472
Duckworth, Frank M.	11197	Duncan, Walter A.	6473
Duckworth, Lavinia A.	22335	Duncan, Johney Mac	6474

Name.	Roll No.	Name.	Roll No.
Duncan, Joanna C.	6680	Dunham, Muggie M.	15358
Duncan, Lucy A.	7155	Dunham, Vann	15359
Duncan, Lucy E.	7156	Dunagan, Cicero S.	17490
Duncan, Charles D.	7157	Dunagan, Georgia A.	25526
Duncan, James R.	7539	Dunagan, Mary O.	25527
Duncan, Susan	7540	Dunagan, Lula	25528
Duncan, DeWitt C.	7752	Dunagan, James B.	25529
Duncan, Joshua L.	8236	Dun-nee-wose	20362
Duncan, Charlotte P.	8237	Duniphin, Ellen F.	22221
Duncan, Dellen R.	8238	Duniphin, David N.	22222
Duncan, Charles T.	8239	Duniphin, May Eliza-	
Duncan, Lucy E.	8240	beth	22223
Duncan, Narcissus	8978	Dupree, Elmer	30760
Duncan, Nellie M.	8979	Dupree, Herbert	30761
Duncan, Allie V.	8980	Dupree, Emma	30762
Duncan, Carrie E.	8981	Dupree, Wright	30763
Duncan, Logan L.	8982	Dupree, William E.	30168
Duncan, Katie L.	8983	Dupree, Bessie	30169
Duncan, Louie E.	8984	Dupree, Fred	30170
Duncan, Alvie R.	8985	Dupree, Annie	30171
Duncan, Neoma I.	8986	Durall, Ada	9257
Duncan, Mary N.	9856	Durall, Harold	9258
Duncan, Frederick B.	9857	Durall, Edna E.	24254
Duncan, Catherine	11352	Durall, Benonia F.	24255
Duncan, Walter A.	14151	Durall, George R.	24256
Duncan, Walter E.	14152	Durkee, Elizabeth J.	13409
Duncan, John R.	14155	Durkee, George A.	13410
Duncan, Elizabeth S.	14718	Durkee, Laurah A.	13411
Duncan, Josie	15849	Durham, Nannie R.	13708
Duncan, John C.	15851	Durham, Wincie M.	13709
Duncan, James W.	18821	Durham, William	13710
Duncan, Lucinda B.	18822	Durham, Henry C.	13711
Duncan, Sammie V.	18823	Durham, Fred A.	13712
Duncan, Logan B.	18824	Dushane, Franklin	8954
Duncan, James N.	22244	Dushane, Simpson	8956
Duncan, Oran A.	22245	Dushane, Isaac	8957
Duncan, Nolan Lee	22246	Dushane, Dalbert J.	8958
Duncan, Oran W.	22247	DuShane, David C.	28725
Duncan, Claude E.	23571	DuVal, Fannie	3210
Duncan, Walter T.	24913	Duval, Samuel	19511
Duncan, Ethel M.	24915	Duval, William	19543
Duncan, Geneva I.	24916	Duval, Cora	19544
Duncan, Taylor	27139	Duval, Tom	19546
Duncan, Lydia	27140	Duval, Arch	19547
Duncan, John	27141	Duval, Peggie	19549
Duncan, Malinda	27142	Duval, Charlie	19550
Duncan, Nathaniel	27143	Duval, John	19551
Duncan, Hubert	27144	Duval, Isaac	21005
Duncan, Sally	27145	Duval, Benjamin	21190
Duncan, Emma	27146	Duval, Alice	21191
Duncan, Annie	27147	Duval, Richard	32350
Duncan, Felix	27148	Duvall, Mary R.	4724
Duncan, Charley	27149	DuVaul, Jesse J.	32346
Duncan, Joseph	27151	Dye, Minnie	14871
Duncan, James	27438	Dye, Olive G.	14873
Duncan, Maggie	27439	Dyer, Mathew	32127
Duncan, Lou	27440	Dykes, Arabella W.	111
Duncan, Willie	27523	Dykes, Mabel H.	112
Duncan, Martha	27524	Dykes, Nettie C.	113
Duncan, Andrew	27525	Dykes, Bunk	114
Duncan, Thomas	27526	Dykes, David A.	115
Duncan, Samuel G.	27527	Dykes, Tony R.	116
Duncan, Sarah L.	27528	Dykes, Walter V.	117
Duncan, Eva M.	27529	Dykes, Rocksey B.	118
Duncan, Sarah	27532	Dykes, Lou E.	13226
Duncan, Johnson	28363	Dykes, Julius O.	13227
Duncan, Leona	29045	Dykes, Chester J.	13228
Duncan, Nancy	29625	Dykes, Katie	18049
Duncan, Henry	31414	Dykes, Dawson	18050
Duncan, William W.	31973	Eagle, Rufus	4026
Dunback, Henrietta	5680	Eagle, Adam	4027
Dunback, Nancy	5692	Eagle, John	15011
Dunback, John	5693	Eagle, Annie	15012
Dunback, Effie	5694	Eagle, Henry	18306
Dunn, Fannie	10984	Eagle, Sallie	18309
Dunn, Virginia E.	10985	Eagle, Israel	18310
Dunn, Fannie P.	10986	Eagle, John	18791
Dunn, Thomas H.	10989	Eagle, Ida	18792
Dunn, Nancy	15526	Eagle, James	18793
Dunn, Maram P.	15534	Eagle, John A.	18794
Dunn, Ellen	15535	Eagle, Josiah	18795
Dunn, Amanda A.	21580	Eagle, William	18796
Dunn, Bettie	32564	Eagle, Ollie	18797
		Eagle, William	19939

Name.	Roll No.
Eagle, Peggie	19940
Eagle, Ida	19943
Eagle, George	19944
Eagle, Mary	27150
Eagle, Nancy	29714
Eagle, Susie	29931
Early, Martha A.	1525
Early, Dora	1526
Early, William	1527
Early, Mollie	1528
Early, Mattie L.	1529
Early, Robert R.	1530
Early, Ida B.	1531
Early, Malla E.	1532
Early, Susan A.	4483
Earnest, Ellen	3303
Earnest, Leroy	3304
Earnest, Albert N.	3305
Earp, Prissilla	15741
Earp, Cora	15742
Earp, Minnie L.	31965
Earp, Joe	31966
Earbob, Daky	15976
Earbob, Nancy	15980
Earbob, George	17497
Earbob, Mary	21856
Easky, Mary	1400
Easky, Mamie	6624
Easky, Eli	6625
Easky, Lula	6626
Easky, Caleb	17928
Easky, Patsy	17929
Easky, Joseph	17930
Easky, Andy	17931
Easky, Billie	17932
Easky, Wanonah	25571
Easky, Lenora	25572
Easky, Edward	25573
Easky, Lula	29521
Easly, Ida	30217
Eaton, Rebecca	1236
Eaton, Nancy J.	3887
Eaton, Ada G.	7012
Eaton, John E.	7013
Eaton, Taylor	7256
Eaton, Walter C.	7257
Eaton, Rose	9837
Eaton, John	9838
Eaton, James	9839
Eaton, Annie	10129
Eaton, Addie	10130
Eaton, Bryan W.	10131
Eaton, Samuel H.	10132
Eaton, James C.	11212
Eaton, Joel M.	11227
Eaton, Rachel C.	11376
Eaton, Martha P.	11377
Eaton, Ellis M.	11587
Eaton, Mollie	11588
Eaton, Lelia	11589
Eaton, Richard E.	11590
Eaton, William	11591
Eaton, Edgar W.	11592
Eaton, Walter R.	11784
Eaton, Maggie M.	11785
Eaton, Mary E.	11786
Eaton, Raleigh	11787
Eaton, Frank	11788
Eaton, Wallace Ross	21831
Eblen, Elizabeth L.	14034
Eckert, Louisa J.	4564
Eckert, Richard	4565
Eckert, Annie E.	4566
Eckert, Addie	4567
Eckert, Lula E.	4568
Eckert, Lydia F.	4569
Eckert, Lillie May	4570
Edens, Nancy	22203
Edens, Rena	22204
Edens, Frances	26087
Edgerton, Rollin McA.	29163
Edington, Betty	22133
Edington, Isabelle May	22134
Edmondson, James T.	670
Edmondson, Jula Ann	671
Edmondson, Augustus V.	672

Name.	Roll No.
Edmondson, Cherokee D.	7010
Edmondson, Florence E.	15726
Edmondson, Lugonia	15727
Edmondson, Beulah D.	15728
Edmondson, Lula	26649
Edmondson, Olive E.	26650
Edmondson, Laura H.	26651
Edmondson, Dora K.	26652
Edmondson, Nancy	27939
Edmonds, Frank	13429
Edmonds, Samuel T.	17134
Edmonds, Emma B.	25497
Edmonds, Hazel D.	25498
Edmonds, Bessie F.	25499
Edmonds, Bulah A.	25500
Edmonds, Henry	27862
Edmonds, Susanna	27863
Edmonds, William	27864
Edmiston, Elsa D.	21850
Edmiston, Jane E.	16183
Edwards, William	5635
Edwards, Belle	5636
Edwards, Stephen D. C.	7671
Edwards, Stephen	7673
Edwards, Emma	7674
Edwards, James	7675
Edwards, Susan M.	10336
Edwards, Mary L.	28678
Edwards, William P.	28679
Edwards, Esther E.	28680
Edwards, Grover C.	28681
Edwards, Franklin P.	28682
Edwards, Tennessee	28683
Edwards, Mattie	28684
Edwards, John B., Jr.	28685
Edwards, George D.	28686
Edwards, Rachel	32231
Eggleson, Julia L.	6826
Eggleson, Omer H.	6827
Eggleson, Zora A.	6828
Eggleson, Noah L.	6829
Eggleson, Jose M.	6830
Eggleson, Nellie A.	6831
Eggleson, Henry D.	6832
Eggleson, Callie V.	6833
Eiffert, Cecil E.	5321
Eiffert, Henry	5995
Eiffert, Sue	5996
Eiffert, Margaret E.	5997
Eiffert, Henry, Jr.	5999
Eiffert, Sally M.	6000
Elam, Lillie	13585
Elam, Clora E.	13587
Elan, Effie E.	9639
Eldridge, Jesse	4190
Eldridge, William J.	4191
Eldridge, Martin	11524
Eldridge, Taylor	11525
Eldridge, William J.	12727
Eldridge, Mable C.	12728
Eldridge, Andrew	27963
Eldridge, Ruth	27964
Eldridge, Pearl	27965
Eldridge, Alfred	27966
Eldridge, Rebecca	27967
Eldridge, Jesse	32558
Elders, George W.	27402
Elders, Alsie	27403
Elders, William	27404
Elders, George	27405
Elders, Thomas F.	27406
Ele, James G.	28672
Elgin, Fenton F.	3115
Elgin, Astor C.	3116
Eli, Taylor	18021
Eli, Jennie	18022
Eli, Nancy	18024
Eli, James	18025
Eli, Tom	20479
Eli, Lydia	20480
Eli, Eli	20481
Eli, Ibby	20482
Eli, George	20483
Eli, Sallie	20484
Eli, Jennie	20485
Eli, Mary Ellen	21901

Name.	Roll No.
Eli, Goldie	21902
Eli, Jennie	28465
Eli, Felix	29086
Elk, Sam	19291
Elk, Rachel	20530
Elk, Sealey	21007
Elk, Mary	21008
Elk, Rosa	21009
Elk, Lila	21010
Elk, William	25867
Elkins, Kate	28892
Elkins, Jim	28893
Elkins, Nora May	28894
Elkhair, Annie	31106
Elkhair, Rosa	31246
Elkhair, Sallie	31247
Elkhair, Jesse	31305
Ellis, Jackson W.	23
Ellis, Charlotte	24
Ellis, Nellie L.	25
Ellis, Jackson N.	26
Ellis, Richard	27
Ellis, Blair	28
Ellis, Mitchell	3394
Ellis, Henry	3395
Ellis, Robert R.	3396
Ellis, Mitchell, Jr.	3397
Ellis, Clara	3398
Ellis, Frances	4201
Ellis, Irene	4202
Ellis, Mildred R.	4203
Ellis, Lizzie	5177
Ellis, Junie M.	5178
Ellis, Martin O.	5179
Ellis, Houston	5180
Ellis, Melvina	8501
Ellis, May E.	8502
Ellis, John R.	8503
Ellis, Mary	8373
Ellis, Rachel	8504
Ellis, Lucy	10370
Ellis, Eli	10411
Ellis, Nancy	10512
Ellis, Fannie	10413
Ellis, William	10415
Ellis, Ethel B.	12690
Ellis, Hilrey O.	12691
Ellis, Nannie E.	25080
Ellis, Arthur T.	25081
Ellis, Walter C.	25082
Ellis, Ernest C.	25083
Ellis, George	26115
Ellis, Che-ga-yu	28511
Ellis, Lizzie	29122
Ellis, Charley	29525
Ellis, Weaver	31975
Elliott, Anna E.	126
Elliott, Mary	127
Elliott, Katie	5024
Elliott, Winfield S.	5025
Elliott, Robert	6013
Elliott, James	7978
Elliott, Maud	7979
Elliott, Georgia	7980
Elliott, Hiram	8422
Elliott, James H.	10758
Elliott, Emily	10759
Elliott, Edmund F.	10760
Elliott, Lida	10761
Elliott, Frank	10762
Elliott, Dora	10763
Elliott, Annie	12570
Elliott, William T.	17267
Elliott, Riley A.	17268
Elliott, Addie R.	17269
Elliott, Hiram, Jr.	24032
Elliott, Samuel T.	24033
Elliott, Vera M.	24034
Elliott, Lucullus	24035
Elliott, Lucien B.	24036
Elliott, Walter L.	30177
Elliott, Henry A.	30178
Elliott, Cordelia A.	30179
Elliott, Jessie M.	30180

Name.	Roll No.
Elliott, Georgia A.	30225
Elliott, John	32579
Elledge, Roy P.	9770
Elledge, Cena B.	9771
Ellick, Henry	13565
Ellick, Benjamin	13566
Ellick, Rebecca	13567
Ellick, Julia	31596
Elmore, Armstrong	18150
Elmore, Nancy	25582
Emmons, Theodore Pascal	32764
Emmons, Dallas Edwin	32765
Emmons, Vivian Herbert	32766
Emmons, Clarence Delbert	32767
Emmons, Warren Howard	32768
England, Lincoln	1384
England, Mattie	1385
England, Permelia	1386
England, Charlotte	1387
England, Betsy	1388
England, Benjamin C.	7660
England, Benjamin	7661
England, John	9144
England, Maud M.	9145
England, Harmon	9146
England, Joseph M.	9749
England, Sarah	9750
England, William L.	9751
England, Virgil	9752
England, Pauline	9753
England, William W.	11862
England, John Anna	11863
England, Samuel	11864
England, Susan L.	11865
England, George W.	12522
England, Flossa M.	12523
England, Lurie B.	12524
England, John	13287
England, Belle D.	13288
England, Lucy	13289
England, Joseph	13290
England, Frances	13291
England, Elvie	13292
England, Beulah	13293
England, Benjamin	13294
England, Emma	13295
England, McGlarthin	13296
England, Mattie	13297
England, Wash	17745
England, Katie	17746
England, Wilson	17747
England, Pigeon	17748
England, Betsy	17749
England, Andrew	17750
England, John	17751
England, Sallie	17754
England, Lucy J.	17778
England, Samuel	17919
England, Annie	17920
England, Madie	17921
England, William	17967
England, Nancy	17968
England, Tillman	18003
England, Mary	18004
England, Mattie	18005
England, James	18006
England, Claude	18007
England, Cullis	18008
England, Himon	18009
England, Ollie	19050
England, Dora	19051
England, Killey	19052
England, George	19053
England, Robin	19054
England, Killey	19055
England, Martin	19476
England, Charles	19980
England, Lucy	20080
England, Louvenia	20095

Name.	Roll No.	Name.	Roll No.
England, Dave	23631	Fair, Ellen	6754
England, Lydia	25575	Fair, Dora	6755
England, Peter	30521	Fair, Jake	6756
Epperson, Mary	28222	Fallen, Alexander	4782
Epperson, Oscar L.	28223	Fallen, Samuel	5085
Epperson, Benjamin F.	28224	Fallen, Jesse	11309
Epperson, Mary B.	29926	Fallen, Lucinda	11310
Epple, Annie	28647	Fallin, George	6066
Epple, Bessie	28648	Fallin, Malinda	6067
Epps, Laura	28720	Fallin, Nannie	6068
Erwin, Charles G.	13664	Fallin, Sarah	6069
Erwin, Mary I.	13665	Fallin, Susie	6070
Essex, Addie B.	13162	Falling, Jack	6445
Essex, Cole C.	13163	Falling, Nancy	6446
Essex, Susie I.	13164	Falling, Lizzie	6447
Essex, John S.	13165	Falling, Jennie	6450
Estes, Sarah	6699	Falling, Henry	7947
Ethridge, Ottamiza E.	11991	Falling, Johnson	8029
Ethridge, John	11992	Falling, Mary	8030
Etter, Lizzie	12571	Falling, Calvin E.	11280
Etter, Leonard A.	12572	Falling, Charley	11960
Etter, Birt E.	12644	Falling, John	12718
Etter, William E. A.	12645	Falling, Delilah	12719
Etter, Florence	12646	Falling, Delia R.	12720
Etter, Smurna	12647	Falling, Rider	18568
Eubanks, Roger R.	7015	Falling, Jennie	18569
Eubanks, William	16599	Falling, Jim	18602
Eubanks, Eliza C.	16600	Falling, Freddie	26492
Eubanks, Eugenia K.	16601	Falling, Maggie	26493
Eubanks, Ada A.	16602	Falling, Viola	26494
Eubanks, Samuel V.	16603	Falling, William L.	26495
Evans, Alice	124	Falling, Lila	32282
Evans, Walter A.	125	Falling, Bettie	32633
Evans, Annie	1135	Falling, Nick	32771
Evans, Robert H.	2277	Falling, Cah-na-loo-	
Evans, Effie M.	2278	lees-ky	32774
Evans, Walter N. Jr.	2279	Fallingpot, Grant	15411
Evans, Martha	8784	Fallingpot, Samantha	15412
Evans, Ola S.	10461	Fallingpot, Maudie	15413
Evans, Marie	10462	Fallingpot, Dobkin	16253
Evans, Leander K.	10463	Fallingpot, Betsy	32017
Evans, James P.	12247	Fallingwater, Jennie	20884
Evans, Catherine S.	16929	Fallleaf, John	31292
Evans, Susan	26780	Fallleaf, Ida	31293
Evans, Minnie	26783	Fallleaf, Fred	31294
Evans, Ruth B.	27887	Fargo, Charles A., Jr.	3560
Evans, Mattie	27888	Fargo, Narcissa	3561
Evans, Henry	27889	Fargo, Clarence	3562
Evans, Albert Lee	27891	Fargo, Charles A.	3579
Eversorts, Dave	19104	Fargo, Pearl	3580
Eversorts, Rhoda	19105	Fargo, Edna	3581
Everett, Ripley A.	31229	Fargo, Mabel	3582
Everett, William H.	31230	Fargo, Ina	3584
Everett, Florence A.	31231	Fargo, Delilah	3585
Everett, Martha M.	31601	Fargo, Myrtle	3586
Everett, Thomas H.	31602	Fargo, Joel B.	3587
Everett, Calvin, Jr.	31603	Fargo, Walter	3588
Ewers, Emmett	6206	Fargo, David R.	3589
Ewers, Lena E.	6207	Fargo, William L.	3639
Ewers, Charles E.	6208	Fargo, Cora	3640
Ewers, John T.	6210	Fargo, Saladen A.	3756
Ewers, Yuba D.	6211	Fargo, Olive	22886
Ewers, Ida H.	6222	Fargo, Benjamin	30063
Ewers, Eloise M.	6223	Fargo, Edward	31974
Ewers, William A.	6224	Farrar, Sallie M.	5558
Ewers, George Jr.	27836	Farrar, Jessie M.	5559
Ewers, Maland E.	27837	Farrar, Bruce	5560
Ewers, Tams Bixby	27838	Farrar, Oliver M.	13236
Ewers, Charles	27839	Farmer, Isabelle	5866
Ezell, Eva	26926	Farmer, Clara A.	5867
Ezell, Ethel	26927	Farmer, William L.	5868
Ezell, Albert	26928	Farmer, Grace L.	5869
Extine, Melvina S.	25075	Farmer, Leaty E.	5870
Fabors, Richard	8876	Farmer, Minnie M.	5871
Fabors, Susan L.	8877	Farmer, Sarah A.	8384
Factor, Margaret	14159	Farmer, Mintie	5872
Fagan, James A.	21519	Farmer, Robert A.	8385
Fagan, Joseph A.	12419	Farmer, Georgia	23286
Fagan, Luther	21520	Farbro, Sadie	10848
Fagan, William Henry	29611	Farbro, Clell	10849
Fain, Charlotte	2099	Farbro, Mary	13246
Fair, Rena	6325	Farbro, Tracy M.	13247
Fair, Bettie	6326	Farbro, Clara E.	13248

Name.	Roll No.
Farrington, Elizabeth V.	28039
Farrington, Columbus	28040
Farrington, Mary Belle	28041
Faulkner, David M.	2742
Faulkner, Lydia C.	2743
Faulkner, Bertha L.	2744
Faulkner, Henry I.	2745
Faulkner, Sallie M.	2746
Faulkner, Penelope A.	2747
Faulkner, LaFayette	3214
Faulkner, Lanora B.	3215
Faulkner, Benjamin F.	3288
Faulkner, George	3508
Faulkner, John	3511
Faulkner, Mary	3512
Faulkner, John	3513
Faulkner, Robert	3514
Faulkner, David	3515
Faulkner, Jennie	3516
Faulkner, Clem V.	3517
Faulkner, Mary	3518
Faulkner, Frank T.	3621
Faulkner, John W.	3682
Faulkner, David J.	3712
Faulkner, Charles	3723
Faulkner, Joseph V.	3724
Faulkner, Clayton	3775
Faulkner, Alva	3877
Faulkner, Jennie	3890
Faulkner, Elizabeth	3891
Faulkner, John F.	3892
Faulkner, Joseph	3893
Faulkner, William	5182
Faulkner, Jennie M.	11540
Faulkner, Emma	21732
Faulkner, Ollie B.	21733
Faulkner, Clarence	21734
Faulkner, Auda C.	21735
Faulkner, Roxie	21736
Faulkner, Josie A.	21737
Faulkner, Walter	22802
Faulkner, Leroy Franklin	22803
Faulkner, Lelah B.	22823
Faulkner, John S.	22824
Faulkner, Robert	22825
Faulkner, Minnie M.	29278
Faulkner, Janice M.	26677
Faulkner, Johnie	32409
Faucette, Mirah A.	32788
Fawling, Sarah J.	27354
Fawling, Andrew F.	27355
Fay, Frederick A.	30304
Feather, Mose	17804
Feather, Maggie	17805
Feather, Ketcher	17806
Feather, Robert	17808
Feather, Sallie	18030
Feather, Jesse	18375
Feather, Annie	18376
Feather, David	18801
Feather, Beckey	18924
Feather, Jennie	18926
Feather, George	18927
Feather, Scale	18928
Feather, Polly	19058
Feather, James	19071
Feather, Lillie	19072
Feather, Joseph	19138
Feather, John	19194
Feather, Nancy	20510
Feather, Joe	20895
Feather, Sallie	20896
Feather, Mary	22144
Feather, Zakrona	22145
Feather, Jack	25665
Feather, Joe	25682
Feather, Lizzie	25930
Feather, Jeremiah	29034
Feather, Margarett	29726
Feather, Linda	29842
Feeling, James	6313
Feeling, Samuel	6314

Name.	Roll No.
Feeling, Johnson	6547
Feeling, Ave	6548
Feeling, Eve	6549
Feeling, Susan	6550
Feeling, Mike	6551
Feeling, Maria	15222
Feeling, George	20262
Feeling, Lewis	20281
Feeling, Adam	21844
Feeling, Moses	25996
Feeling, Rachel	25997
Feeling, Annie	29645
Felton, George A. L.	7361
Feland, Margaret A.	11479
Feland, Minnie	11481
Feland, Joseph E. Jr.	11482
Feland, Rosa L.	11483
Feland, Lela B.	11484
Fence, George	17507
Fencer, Betsy	20263
Fencer, Anna	20582
Fencer, Dakie	30621
Fencer, Aggie	32513
Fencer, George	32775
Fents, Jane	22860
Ferguson, Annie	1887
Ferguson, Callie	1888
Ferguson, George G.	1889
Ferguson, Mamie	1890
Ferguson, Ruth	1891
Ferguson, Allie E.	2442
Ferguson, John W.	2443
Feuerstine, Rosa	7641
Feuerstine, Frank	7642
Fields, Chauncy	36
Fields, Richard	1120
Fields, John	1389
Fields, Nannie	1390
Fields, Florence	1391
Fields, Andrew	1471
Fields, Clarence S.	1473
Fields, Daniel	1962
Fields, Margaret	1963
Fields, Annie	2634
Fields, Betsy	2635
Fields, Lucy	3331
Fields, Squirrel	3367
Fields, James	3368
Fields, Wallace	3369
Fields, Charlotte E.	4380
Fields, Thomas F.	5422
Fields, Bushyhead	5423
Fields, Mary W.	5424
Fields, William S.	5425
Fields, Calvin L.	5426
Fields, Ella E.	5427
Fields, Rachel E.	5428
Fields, Ada	5429
Fields, Richard	5430
Fields, Walter G.	5431
Fields, Louvenia	5432
Fields, Joseph A.	5433
Fields, Cornelius B.	5436
Fields, Robert B.	5931
Fields, Samuel T.	5932
Fields, Betsy	5933
Fields, George B.	5934
Fields, Kiowa	5935
Fields, Mollie	6114
Fields, Ada W.	6419
Fields, Clarence R.	6420
Fields, James L.	6767
Fields, Henry R.	6768
Fields, Rachel	6769
Fields, Ruth	6770
Fields, Cherokee R.	6771
Fields, Walter L.	6843
Fields, Elmer	6941
Fields, Moses O.	7594
Fields, John L.	7595
Fields, James S.	7596
Fields, Caroline	7866
Fields, Benjamin F.	8649
Fields, Mathew	8789

Name.	Roll No.	Name.	Roll No.
Fields, Ruby M.	8790	Fields, George W. Jr.	17391
Fields, Thompson	8791	Fields, James F.	17392
Fields, Ezekiel	8797	Fields, Charles H.	17393
Fields, Ines L.	8798	Fields, Mattie M.	17394
Fields, Edna Ann	8799	Fields, Lucinda	17452
Fields, Samuel I.	9014	Fields, Teely	17453
Fields, Thomas J.	9015	Fields, Teemon	17454
Fields, Isa Cora	9016	Fields, Dick	17455
Fields, Thomas M., Sr	9418	Fields, Eliza	17626
Fields, Mary E.	9461	Fields, Walker	17666
Fields, Annie E.	9462	Fields, Annie	17670
Fields, William H.	9524	Fields, Cephus	17677
Fields, Roy	9525	Fields, Celia	20276
Fields, Arther C.	9526	Fields, Charles	20332
Fields, George W., Jr.	9720	Fields, Carrie	20333
Fields, Sabra E.	9754	Fields, Betsy	20334
Fields, Cora C.	9755	Fields, William	20335
Fields, Ezekiel	9782	Fields, James	20353
Fields, Ezekiel, Jr.	9783	Fields, Annie	20354
Fields, Ella Zoe	9784	Fields, Sam	20396
Fields, Maggie M.	9785	Fields, Bertha G.	21705
Fields, Lula P.	9786	Fields, Clyde E.	21706
Fields, Martha J.	9787	Fields, Birdie	22114
Fields, Richard A.	9791	Fields, William T.	22143
Fields, Arthur E.	9792	Fields, James W.	22537
Fields, George	9885	Fields, John S.	22538
Fields, Sarah	9886	Fields, Benjamin H.	22539
Fields, George Jr.	9887	Fields, Bashaba	23262
Fields, Laura	9888	Fields, Frank	23263
Fields, Samuel	9889	Fields, Frederick	23264
Fields, Bertha	9890	Fields, Alexander	23265
Fields, Jess	9891	Fields, Avi	23266
Fields, Minnie	9892	Fields, Kathryn	23267
Fields, Addie	9893	Fields, Henry F.	23583
Fields, Perry	9894	Fields, Carrie	23584
Fields, Albert	9895	Fields, Mable	23585
Fields, James M.	9970	Fields, Richard	23667
Fields, Timothy	9972	Fields, Strausie L.	24138
Fields, Saphronia E.	9973	Fields, Thomas M. Jr.	24284
Fields, James H.	9974	Fields, Esther M.	24285
Fields, Lee	9975	Fields, Luther T.	24286
Fields, Grant	9976	Fields, Dewey P.	24287
Fields, Ruth C.	9977	Fields, Nancy B.	24390
Fields, Virgil C.	9978	Fields, Alice	24391
Fields, Marshal P.	9979	Fields, Rufus	24392
Fields, Harvy E.	9980	Fields, Mary	24393
Fields, Pleasant	9992	Fields, Lulu	24394
Fields, William	9993	Fields, Ray	24395
Fields, Sarah E.	9994	Fields, John	24396
Fields, Irene M.	9995	Fields, Claude	24397
Fields, Nora	9996	Fields, Bessie E.	24408
Fields, Richard M.	10177	Fields, Stella V.	24409
Fields, Texanna	10178	Fields, William H.	24410
Fields, Claude	10179	Fields, George M.	24411
Fields, Charles	10180	Fields, Lillie E.	24412
Fields, Wirt	10181	Fields, James E.	24413
Fields, Jesse	10182	Fields, Thompson	25781
Fields, Pearce	10183	Fields, Lucy	25782
Fields, Patrick	10583	Fields, Linnie	25783
Fields, Mike	10584	Fields, Henry	26577
Fields, Stella	10585	Fields, Jefferson J.	26690
Fields, Louis	10695	Fields, Johnson	27657
Fields, Joel	10696	Fields, Victoria	27658
Fields, Lula P.	10697	Fields, George	27659
Fields, Mamie C.	10698	Fields, Rebecca	27660
Fields, Charles	10811	Fields, Wahlinne	28480
Fields, Charley	12786	Fields, Sam	29112
Fields, William J.	12787	Fields, Maggie	29113
Fields, George F.	12788	Fields, Jim	29114
Fields, Thomas J.	13570	Fields, Jincy	29115
Fields, Alva L.	13571	Fields, Betsy	29116
Fields, Earl	13572	Fields, Nancy	29117
Fields, William L.	13686	Fields, William W.	29191
Fields, John R.	14841	Fields, Jesse	29192
Fields, Robert W.	15525	Fields, Dora	29193
Fields, Richard	15897	Fields, Della	29194
Fields, Thomas R.	16937	Fields, Eugene	29195
Fields, James F.	17027	Fields, Howard E.	29196
Fields, Freeman	17290	Fields, Cledah	29197
Fields, William E.	17291	Fields, Louella	29198
Fields, Ella M.	17292	Fields, Edward	29199
Fields, Ethel	17293	Fields, Inez	29200
Fields, George W.	17389	Fields, Charlotte E.	29462
Fields, Mattie J.	17390		

Name.	Roll No.
Fields, Cora	29587
Fields, Fannie	29588
Fields, May	29589
Fields, Mary J.	29590
Fields, Maudie	29591
Fields, Robert R.	29592
Fields, Lula	29593
Fields, Nannie	29735
Fields, Wesley	30200
Fields, Lela B.	30201
Fields, Vaude E.	30202
Fields, Maggie Catherine	30203
Fields, Montgomery	30606
Fields, Catcher	30610
Fields, Tee-hu-yah	30617
Fields, Ora	31707
Fields, William H.	32399
Fields, George A.	32400
Fields, Lizzie	32401
Fields, William E.	32402
Fields, Howard	32403
Fields, Nora M.	32404
Filmore, George	23015
Filmore, Cherokee	23016
Filmore, Ella	23017
Filmore, Della	23018
Fincher, Sarah E.	7262
Fincher, James V.	7263
Fincher, Alvin R.	7265
Fincher, Luther M.	7266
Fincannon, Emma	9024
Fincannon, William A.	9025
Fincannon, Beulah N.	9026
Findley, Ruth E.	10964
Finley, Travers C.	13916
Finley, Viola D.	14618
Finley, George C.	14619
Finley, Gean	16285
Finley, Emma	16287
Finley, Annie	16288
Finley, Thomas	17357
Fish, Nellie	15071
Fish, Alice	15072
Fish, Nellie	15074
Fish, Joseph	16221
Fish, Fannie M. B.	16222
Fish, Ed	16673
Fish, Dennis	16674
Fish, Laura	26192
Fish, John	28407
Fisher, Ama Belle	5082
Fisher, Mary Ann	5083
Fisher, David	6181
Fisher, William	6182
Fisher, Lucrecia	6609
Fisher, Mattie E.	6610
Fisher, Bessie B.	6611
Fisher, Louetta	6612
Fisher, Daniel P.	6613
Fisher, Lela V.	6614
Fisher, Benjamin	6697
Fisher, Eliza	6698
Fisher, Anna	6700
Fisher, Jessie	6701
Fisher, Joseph	6702
Fisher, Eva	6703
Fisher, Isaac	12282
Fisher, Johnson	12285
Fisher, Elizabeth	12286
Fisher, Nancy	12287
Fisher, Moses	12288
Fisher, Stephen	17623
Fisher, Rufus	23436
Fisher, Charlotte	23437
Fisher, Maggie	23438
Fisher, Aggie	23439
Fisher, Viola	23440
Fisher, Foster W.	23441
Fishinghawk, Lydia	1732
Fishinghawk, Joseph	19267
Fishinghawk, Annie	19268
Fishinghawk, Chick-killa	19269

Name.	Roll No.
Fishinghawk, Sarah	19270
Fishinghawk, Jesse	19271
Fishinghawk, Dawes	19272
Fishinghawk, Jim	20109
Fishinghawk, Betsy	20110
Fisk, Minerva	15287
Fisk, Harry A.	15288
Fisk, Cora M.	15289
Fister, Martha A.	26267
Fister, Maggie M.	26268
Fister, Henry C.	26269
Fister, Nellie G.	26270
Fishback, Laverna A.	31872
Fishback, William A.	31873
Fishback, Annie B.	31874
Fishback, John E.	31878
Fite, Julia P.	45
Fite, William P.	46
Fite, Frances	47
Fite, F. Barto	48
Fite, Edward H.	49
Fite, Nannie K.	13920
Fite, Houston B.	13921
Fite, Augustus W.	13922
Fite, Sarah C.	13923
Fite, John W. S.	13924
Fite, Laura T.	13925
Fitzgerald, Catherine	4368
Fitzgerald, Katie	4369
Fitzgerald, Elnora	4370
Fitzgerald, Polly	4371
Fitzgerald, William R.	4372
Fitzgerald, John H.	4373
Fitzgerald, Martha J.	9437
Fitzgerald, Nora	9438
Fitzgerald, William R.	9439
Fitzgerald, Francis L.	9440
Fitzgerald, Josephine	32405
Fitzsimmons, Ida J.	10434
Fitzsimmons, John A.	10435
Fitzsimmons, Susan J.	10436
Fitzsimmons, Ettie E.	10437
Fitzsimmons, William P.	10438
Fitzsimmons, Girty M.	10439
Fitzsimmons, Mary E.	15482
Fitzsimmons, Mary J.	15483
Fitzsimmons, Charles C.	15484
Fitzsimmons, Robert E.	15485
Fivekiller, Joseph	2353
Fivekiller, Watte	2624
Fivekiller, Frost	5641
Fivekiller, Cleveland	22705
Fivekiller, Callie	22706
Fivekiller, Spencer	22707
Fivekiller, Annie	22708
Fivekiller, Anie	22709
Fixin, Nannie	28442
Fixin, Jesse	28443
Fixin, Blackbird	29099
Fixin, Alcy	29100
Fixin, Tom	29101
Flanders, Cynthia	10058
Flanders, Bessie R.	10059
Flanders, Floyd	10060
Flanders, Lyman G.	29769
Flanagan, William W.	10826
Flanagan, Charles A.	10827
Flanagan, Frank J.	10828
Flanagan, Mary E.	10829
Flanagan, Mike	10830
Flanagan, Trudie	10831
Flanagan, Rena I.	10832
Flanagan, Jessie B.	10933
Flanagan, Effie	22294
Flanagan, Orvel Huston	22299
Flanigan, Lula	31385
Flanigan, Rock C.	31386
Flanigan, Jennie E.	31387
Flanigan, Carmilita	31388
Flanigan, John H.	31389
Fleetwood, Melinda J.	2830
Fleetwood, Theodore	2831
Fleetwood, Thomas	2832

Name.	Roll No.	Name.	Roll No.
Fleetwood, Cleveland	2833	Flournoy, Walter G.	12965
Fleetwood, Redcloud	2834	Flournoy, May	12966
Fleetwood, Lee R.	2835	Flournoy, Laura M.	12967
Fleetwood, Jewel M.	2836	Flournoy, Mercer W.	12968
Fleetwood, Pearl I.	2837	Flournoy, Rollin D.	24945
Fleetwood, Eljerry	3519	Flournoy, Maude M.	24946
Fleetwood, Zelma	3520	Flournoy, Eldridge D. C.	24947
Fleetwood, William	3521	Flournoy, Bernice	24948
Fleetwood, Luvena	3522	Flournoy, Cherry M.	24949
Fleetwood, July	3523	Flournoy, Edgar	31858
Fleetwood, Eljerry Jr.	3524	Flournoy, Walter	31859
Fleetwood, Osey	3525	Flournoy, Alice	31860
Fleetwood, Henry F.	3526	Flournoy, Laura	31861
Fleetwood, Nancy G.	21756	Flournoy, Oscar	31862
Fleetwood, Edmund.	26813	Flournoy, Claude	31863
Fleming, Maria L.	26219	Flournoy, Edna	31864
Flesher, Lucinda	26260	Flower, Emeline	3709
Flesher, Viola M.	29261	Flower, William C.	3710
Flesher, Nora B.	29262	Flower, Polly V.	3711
Flesher, Eliza E.	29263	Floyd, Carrie W.	12773
Flesher, William H.	29264	Floyd, James D.	12774
Fletcher, John T.	813	Floyd, Dovey M.	12775
Fletcher, Junie M.	814	Floyd, Miller B.	12776
Fletcher, Dora M.	815	Floyd, George R.	12777
Fletcher, Nora	816	Floyd, Alvin L.	12778
Fletcher, Charlott	817	Floyd, Mary B.	12779
Fletcher, Benj. C.	818	Flute, Jesse	20201
Fletcher, Benjamin G.	1566	Flute, Sallie	20868
Fletcher, Mary H.	1567	Flute, Nannie	20869
Fletcher, Sarah E.	1568	Flute, Josie	20872
Fletcher, Calvin L.	1569	Flute, Charlotte	20873
Fletcher, Dora M.	1570	Flute, Aggie	20874
Fletcher, Eva	1571	Flute, Cynthia	20968
Fletcher, Jeanett L.	1572	Flute, Wilson	20969
Fletcher, Della J.	1573	Flute, John	25717
Fletcher, Ellis B.	1574	Flute, Esther	25718
Fletcher, Charlotte	1575	Flute, John Jr.	25719
Fletcher, Robert	1576	Flute, George	25720
Fletcher, Annie	1577	Flute, Lizzie	25721
Fletcher, James	1689	Flute, Jennie	28433
Fletcher, Josie	1690	Flute, Wat	28434
Fletcher, Ada	1691	Flute, Wash	28506
Fletcher, Ruth	1692	Flute, Hester	29909
Fletcher, Charlotte	1693	Flute, Thomas	29973
Fletcher, Josie	1694	Flute, Jensie	32396
Fletcher, Annie	11997	Fluke, Lou	9298
Fletcher, Martha	11998	Fluke, Lizzie	9299
Fletcher, Maggie	11999	Fluke, Andrew	9300
Fletcher, Mary	12000	Fluke, Edward	9301
Fletcher, Rachel Marindia	32441	Fluke, Henry	9302
		Fluke, Fred W.	9303
Fletcher, Mary Ann	32442	Fluke, Lula	9304
Fletcher, Thomas T.	32490	Fluke, George	24247
Flint, Joseph	7951	Flying, Jones P.	5624
Flint, Dona M.	8273	Flying, Neppie W.	5625
Flint, Delilah	8308	Flying, James L.	5626
Flint, William	8309	Flying, Linda A.	5627
Flint, Cora	8310	Flying, Jesse J.	5628
Flint, Charles	8311	Flying, John	5629
Flint, Nana	8312	Flying, Crawford D.	30426
Flint, Albert	8313	Fodder, Stephen	20013
Flint, Ballard	8314	Fodder, Betsy	20031
Flint, Opal	8315	Fodder, Katie	20126
Flint, Victoria A.	10449	Fodder, John	20277
Flint, Carroll W.	10450	Fodder, Mattie	20351
Flint, Amos V. Jr.	10451	Fodder, Susan	25847
Flint, Julia A.	10546	Fodder, Lena	25848
Flint, Sabra	11638	Fodder, Charlie	25885
Flint, William P.	11639	Fodder, Sallie	25886
Flint, Essie	11640	Fodder, Jennie	25887
Flint, Eva	11641	Fodder, Lizzie	30609
Flint, James E.	11642	Fodder, Susanna	32026
Flint, Susie	13545	Fodder, Smith	26346
Flint, Annie	28014	Fogg, Maggie	19073
Flint, Silas	28015	Fogg, Dick	19074
Flint, Samuel	31194	Fogg, Wakie	19075
Flint, Gertrude F.	32565	Fogg, William	19212
Flint, Su-ba-tah	32915	Fogg, Sarah	19213
Flippin, Mary L.	11390	Fogg, Nelson	19214
Flippin, Mary T.	11391	Fogg, Tu-na-wee	19215
Flippin, Ruth Aleene	11392	Fogg, Walice	19216
Flippin, Ella M.	11830	Fogg, Nannie	19217
Flournoy, Anna	11037	Fogg, Charles	19273

Name.	Roll No.	Name.	Roll No.
Fogg, Nancy	19274	Foreman, Sarah	3372
Fogg, Eli	19275	Foreman, Samuel S.	3399
Fogg, Lydia	19276	Foreman, Rufus L.	3400
Fogg, James	19277	Foreman, Saladen Watie	3401
Fogg, Susie	19278	Foreman, Sarah	3546
Fogg, John	20473	Foreman, William S.	4561
Fogg, Bird	27239	Foreman, William J.	5266
Fogg, John	28436	Foreman, Piercie J.	6088
Fogg, White	28437	Foreman, John	6692
Fogg, Nancy	28438	Foreman, Flora E.	7877
Fogg, Lucy	28439	Foreman, Austin W.	7879
Fogleman, Hattie O.	11439	Foreman, Ermina E.	7880
Fogleman, Clinton	11440	Foreman, George A.	7881
Fogleman, Hattie	11441	Foreman, Richard D.	7945
Fogleman, Rufus	11442	Foreman, Charles	8478
Fogleman, Lindon	11443	Foreman, William W.	11002
Fogleman, William P.	11444	Foreman, Belle L.	11003
Fogleman, Claud J.	11448	Foreman, James A.	11004
Fogleman, Minnie E.	11449	Foreman, Bessie J.	11005
Fogleman, Emmet D.	15462	Foreman, William Y. H.	12377
Fogleman, Len E.	15463	Foreman, Nancy	12378
Foley, Addie	4713	Foreman, John A.	12584
Foley, Maggie	4714	Foreman, John Ella	12585
Foley, Clarence	4716	Foreman, Leonard W.	12586
Foley, Lizzie	4717	Foreman, Laura A.	12603
Foley, Sarah	4718	Foreman, Ermina V.	12604
Foley, Lawrence	4719	Foreman, Taylor W.	12605
Foley, Roachman	4720	Foreman, Perry A.	12606
Foley, Cornelius	4721	Foreman, Nelson	13377
Folsom, Malvinia	675	Foreman, Nannie	13378
Folsom, Roxie A.	676	Foreman, Charles D.	13379
Folsom, William S.	677	Foreman, Essie E.	13380
Folsom, Joel	678	Foreman, Laura L.	13381
Folsom, Tandy W.	867	Foreman, Ellis W.	13382
Folsom, Mary A.	868	Foreman, James L.	13383
Folsom, Levi	1101	Foreman, Custis L.	13384
Folsom, Evaline	21533	Foreman, Randolph L.	13385
Fool, William	4889	Foreman, Nelson C.	13386
Fool, Bulah	4890	Foreman, Isabelle	13560
Fool, Charles Lee	32578	Foreman, Bluford W.	13703
Fooy, Evverett W.	16506	Foreman, Emiline	13704
Fooy, Susie L.	16507	Foreman, Emma M.	13705
Fooy, Maggie O.	16508	Foreman, Bluford W.	
Forbes, Ruth	15479	Jr.	13706
Forbes, Allice	15480	Foreman, Eliza L.	13707
Forbes, Eva	15481	Foreman, Thomas J.	13726
Forbes, Robert J.	21481	Foreman, Thomas W.	13728
Forbes, Ora	21482	Foreman, Cherokee	13729
Forbes, Rasmus	21483	Foreman, William E.	13730
Forbes, Ola Belle	21484	Foreman, Watie C.	13731
Forbes, Nancy E.	21529	Foreman, Thomas A.	13732
Forbes, William M.	21532	Foreman, William H.	14232
Foreman, William J.	756	Foreman, Letitia	14233
Foreman, John D.	888	Foreman, Florence	14234
Foreman, Edward D.	889	Foreman, John W.	14235
Foreman, Leander	890	Foreman, Minta R.	14635
Foreman, William	911	Foreman, Elias	14929
Foreman, Ellis	912	Foreman, Florence A.	14930
Foreman, Eddie	913	Foreman, Amos W.	14931
Foreman, Jesse R.	914	Foreman, William B.	15056
Foreman, Bertha	915	Foreman, Nellie	15057
Foreman, Thomas A.	920	Foreman, Mary	15241
Foreman, Elmer	1250	Foreman, Switch	16065
Foreman, Clint	1251	Foreman, Robert W.	15351
Foreman, Dennis	1252	Foreman, Lilla A.	16066
Foreman, Lydia	1295	Foreman, Maggie M.	16067
Foreman, Agnes	1296	Foreman, Mary E.	16068
Foreman, Susan	1297	Foreman, Effie G.	16069
Foreman, James E.	1411	Foreman, Nettie E.	16070
Foreman, Thomas	1412	Foreman, Jauneita	16124
Foreman, James E.	1413	Foreman, Samuel S.	16418
Foreman, Claudle C.	1414	Foreman, Minnie O.	16419
Foreman, William	1415	Foreman, Eveline	16420
Foreman, Dennis W.	1416	Foreman, Leroy	16421
Foreman, William P.	1426	Foreman, Ina	16932
Foreman, Nannie E.	3017	Foreman, William H.	17040
Foreman, Alexander	3018	Foreman, Thomas F.	17525
Foreman, Ada R.	3019	Foreman, Return	17537
Foreman, George D.	3020	Foreman, Samuel	17883
Foreman, Susan C.	3278	Foreman, Arch	19395
Foreman, Edward	3335	Foreman, Setahnie	19596
Foreman, John Timothy	3370	Foreman, Lila	19397
Foreman, Charles	3371	Foreman, Yerkenney	19399

Name.	Roll No.	Name.	Roll No.
Foreman, Peggy	19598	Fortner, Benjamin F.	6796
Foreman, Hugh	19767	Fortner, Samuel H.	6797
Foreman, Nellie	19768	Fortner, Ralph H.	6798
Foreman, Samuel	20439	Fortner, Grace	9184
Foreman, Lizzie	20440	Fortner, Lucy J.	23645
Foreman, Bluford	20441	Forkedtail, Jennie	19451
Foreman, Jennie	20442	Forkedtail, Ona	19452
Foreman, Jesse	20443	Foster, Peter	2481
Foreman, Elam	20558	Foster, Betsy	2482
Foreman, Nancy	20559	Foster, Mary	2483
Foreman, Katie	20560	Foster, John	2484
Foreman, Arch	20561	Foster, Sarah E.	8155
Foreman, Noah	20562	Foster, Cyrus W.	8156
Foreman, Luke	20752	Foster, Goldie M.	8157
Foreman, Martin	20802	Foster, Ruby L.	8158
Foreman, Charlie	21175	Foster, Elmer E.	8159
Foreman, Polly	21176	Foster, Belle	11082
Foreman, Ruthie	21177	Foster, Jane	11084
Foreman, Jennie	21178	Foster, Samuel C.	11231
Foreman, Thomas	21081	Foster, Mattie E.	11232
Foreman, Stephen	21616	Foster, Sylvia E.	11233
Foreman, Delilah E.	21754	Foster, John	11290
Foreman, George B.	21812	Foster, Susan	11291
Foreman, William	22057	Foster, Jane	11292
Foreman, Sallie F.	22105	Foster, Maggie	11293
Foreman, Thomas E.	22106	Foster, Annie	11294
Foreman, Susan A. E.	22157	Foster, James	11295
Foreman, John D. R.	22158	Foster, Thomas S.	11523
Foreman, Frank	22159	Foster, Artimissa	12838
Foreman, Venia	22476	Foster, Newton M.	12839
Foreman, Edward B.	22845	Foster, Mary M.	13796
Foreman, James	24609	Foster, Allen B.	13797
Foreman, Nellie M.	24611	Foster, Robert F.	13798
Foreman, Maud Ann	24612	Foster, William P.	13799
Foreman, James W.	24613	Foster, Thomas L.	13800
Foreman, Joseph T.	24614	Foster, Lelia	17004
Foreman, Henry J.	24615	Foster, Richard S.	17005
Foreman, Charles F.	24616	Foster, Jeff	17106
Foreman, John S.	24617	Foster, Blue	17107
Foreman, Rebecca J.	24618	Foster, Mary E.	17108
Foreman, William H. Jr.	25469	Foster, James	21182
Foreman, Susan A.	25470	Foster, Annie	21183
Foreman, Johnson	25471	Foster, Peter	21184
Foreman, Alice	25472	Foster, Ben	28341
Foreman, Frank	25473	Foster, Walter L.	29945
Foreman, Mary F.	25474	Foster, Mary	32349
Foreman, Walter H.	25475	Fouts, Maggie V.	2555
Foreman, Elizabeth	25963	Fouts, Jacob R.	2556
Foreman, Joseph A.	26019	Fouts, Richard L.	2557
Foreman, Steven	26020	Fouts, Mildred N.	2558
Foreman, Bessie	26021	Fouts, Ella	2559
Foreman, Maud	26022	Fouts, Amy	2560
Foreman, Thomas	26023	Fouts, Ruby	2561
Foreman, Jackson	26024	Fouts, Harriet E.	3423
Foreman, Oce	26025	Fouts, Irvin L.	3424
Foreman, Thomas	26318	Fouts, Maggie M.	3425
Foreman, Myrtle	26319	Fouts, Minnie	31315
Foreman, Johnson	27376	Foust, Rosa E.	8403
Foreman, Nancy E.	27377	Foust, Thomas J.	8404
Foreman, Charles H.	27378	Foust, Bertha	8405
Foreman, Jesse E.	27379	Foust, James M.	8406
Foreman, Susan A.	27380	Foust, Rebecca	8754
Foreman, Nannie E.	27381	Foust, John S.	8760
Foreman, Katie A.	27382	Fourkiller, Richard	19602
Foreman, Ada	29030	Fourkiller, Sarah	19603
Foreman, Charlotte	29434	Fourkiller, Grant	19606
Foreman, Charles	29717	Fourkiller Cloud	19607
Foreman, David M.	12679	Fourkiller, Dianna	19649
Foreman, Susan	29718	Fourkiller, Spade	19650
Foreman, William	29719	Fourkiller, Sampson	19675
Foreman, Joseph	29720	Fourkiller, Cicero	20940
Foreman, Lila	30574	Fourkiller, Maggie	20941
Foreman, Dawes	30575	Fourkiller, Charles	25776
Foreman, Nannie	32064	Fourkiller, Katie	25777
Foresythe, Jane L.	10764	Fourkiller, Larkin	25778
Foresythe, Sarah E.	10765	Fourkiller, William	25779
Foresythe, Lula L.	10766	Fourkiller, Charlotte	25780
Foresythe, Eren	10767	Fourkiller, Judge	30559
Foresythe, Elma I.	10468	Fowler, Ada E.	6328
Fortner, Norah	4496	Fowler, Bessie R.	6329
Fortner, Jack Jr.	4497	Fowlks, Laura	27411
Fortner, Annie W.	6795	Fowlks, Mamie	27415
		Fox, Jennie	8266

Name.	Roll No.
Fox, Thomas	8471
Fox, Susan	11902
Fox, Walter	14150
Fox, Jackson	14356
Fox, Joseph Jr.	15316
Fox, Pasy	17436
Fox, James	17739
Fox, Lillie	18040
Fox, George	19903
Fox, Annie	19904
Fox, Tenoowi	19905
Fox, Jennie	19906
Fox, Jinsey	19907
Fox, Nannie	19908
Fox, Dave	22052
Fox, Susie	22053
Fox, Lucinda	22054
Fox, Annie	25550
Fox, Emma	25551
Fox, Callie	25552
Fox, Darcus	25553
Fox, Joe	29033
Fox, Moses	32804
Foyil, Charlotte	11409
Foyil, Milo	11410
Frazier, Polly C.	457
Frazier, Claudy W.	458
Frazier, Mary M.	459
Frazier, John	4314
Frazier, Ethel	4315
Frazier, Evie	4316
Frazier, Daniel	4341
Frazier, Elizabeth	4342
Frazier, Serena	4343
Frazier, Daniel Jr.	4344
Frazier, Robert	4345
Frazier, Walter	4346
Frazier, Lucy	4347
Frazier, James	4348
Frazier, Peter	4349
Frazier, William	6017
Frazier, Ruth A.	7496
Frazier, Buck P.	7497
Frazier, Ira F.	4798
Frazier, Archie	7500
Frazier, Lela A.	11156
Frazier, Mattie E.	11157
Frazier, Charles	11158
Frazier, Bessie	23026
Frazier, Famous	23296
Frazier, Virgin	23297
Frazier, Benjamin	23298
Frazier, William T.	23299
Frazier, John	27322
Frazier, Bettie	27323
Frazier, John Jr.	27324
Frazier, Elizabeth	27325
Frazier, Ivy	27326
Frazier, Louis	27327
Frazier, Wilson	27328
Frazier, Ebbie	27329
Frazier, Peggie	27330
Frazier, Josephine	27332
Frazier, Sarah A.	29390
Frazier, Caldeen	29391
Frazier, Jessie	29392
Frazier, Grace	29393
Frayser, Emily B.	13421
Fratz, Emma S.	9381
Fratz, William F.	9382
Fratz, Martha J.	9383
Fratz, Louisa D.	9384
Fratz, Laura A.	9385
Francis, Nancy	11146
Francis, Carrie E.	11147
Franks, William W.	11416
Franks, Robert L.	11417
Franks, Carrie J.	11718
Franks, Collie	11419
Franks, Lillie R.	12084
Franks, Pearl	12086
Franks, Josephine	12087
Franks, Lula F.	12088

Name.	Roll No.
Franks, Charles E.	12089
Franks, Joel R.	12090
Franks, Myrtle	12091
Franks, Moses W.	12092
Franks, Virgil F.	12093
Franks, Carroll O.	12100
Franklin, Alexander B.	16961
Franklin, Jesse M.	16962
Franklin, John	16963
Franklin, John B.	16964
Franklin, Edgar E.	16965
Franklin, William	21963
Franklin, Francis M.	23934
Franklin, Willie K.	23935
Franklin, Fred	23936
Franklin, Bettie L.	23937
Franklin, John	23938
Franklin, Francis	23939
Franklin, Martin L.	23940
Franklin, George W.	31911
Franklin, George W. Jr.	31912
Franklin, Jessie M.	31914
Franklin, Basil W.	31915
Franklin, Dora M.	31916
Frakes, Annie L.	21971
Frakes, Winnie M.	21972
Free, Ruth C.	3569
Freeman, George J.	201
Freeman, Lula E.	202
Freeman, Carrie B.	203
Freeman, Willie D.	204
Freeman, Girlie L.	205
Freeman, Daniel W.	284
Freeman, William Clyde	285
Freeman, Cynthia L.	1660
Freeman, Naomi M.	1661
Freeman, William P.	1800
Freeman, Nancy E.	2225
Freeman, Alzira J.	2226
Freeman, John B.	2227
Freeman, Charley K.	2228
Freeman, George	4274
Freeman, Peggy	28034
Frellick, Mary	7248
Frellick, Jacob P.	7249
Frellick, Bertha E.	7250
Frellick, Francis	7251
Frellick, Rufus G.	7252
Frellick, Minnie I.	7253
French, Ola	2240
French, Dovey V.	2241
French, Curtis C.	2243
French, William	2436
French, Eliza	2437
French, Maud M.	5191
French, Fannie A.	5358
French, Joseph M.	5365
French, Myrtle	5366
French, Lewis	5367
French, Gipsie	5368
French, George	5369
French, Beulah	5370
French, Cabell V.	5371
French, Joseph M., Jr.	5372
French, John F.	5373
French, Thomas B.	11645
French, Lila	11646
French, Thomas F.	11647
French, George E.	12139
French, Henry C.	12140
French, Robert M.	13991
French, Jane A.	13992
French, Johnson T.	13993
French, Thomas F.	13994
French, Joseph A.	13995
French, Richard T.	13996
French, Eliza C.	13997
French, Marguerete	13998
French, William L.	14601
French, Nannie	15822
French, James	15823
French, Maggie	21792
French, Salina T.	23594

Name.	Roll No.	Name.	Roll No.
French, Joel B. M.	23595	Fugate, Bessie	31158
French, Henry J.	26103	Fuller, Rosa L.	5250
French, Maggie	28083	Fuller, Nellie R.	5251
French, Naked	32030	Fuller, James P.	5252
French, Charlotte	32031	Fuller, Robert W.	5253
Frenchman, Edward	31138	Fuller, James S.	23167
Frenchman, Effie L.	31139	Fuller, Robin V.	28194
Frenchman, Dennis W.	31140	Fuller, Willard S.	28195
Frenchman, Rosa M.	31141	Fulsom, Mary	2234
Frenchman, Charles	31221	Fulsom, John F.	17028
Frenchman, Willie	31222	Fulsom, Mary S.	31417
Fritz, Frances	8371	Fulsom, Rosa L.	31418
Fritz, Katie	8372	Fulton, James	15529
Frits, Edward	8613	Fulton, Joseph	15520
Fritz, Francis	24026	Fulton, Myrtle M.	15531
Fritz, Joseph P.	24058	Fulton, William	15532
Fritz, Charles F.	24059	Fulton, Fannie	15533
Frisley, Sallie	20226	Fults, Josephine A.	11413
Frizley, James	3656	Fults, Dorothy C.	11414
Frizley, Eliza	3657	Gabbert, Dora A.	9187
Frizley, George	3658	Gabbert, Winnie J.	9188
Frizley, Ben	3659	Gabbert, Mack O.	24233
Frog, Thompson	19056	Gabriel, Devere	13277
Frog, Susie	19057	Gabriel, Edna M.	13278
Frog, Sellout	20753	Gabriel, Clifford O.	13279
Frog, Alsie	25654	Galcatcher, Lee	11213
Frog, Daniel B.	25855	Galcatcher, Susan	11214
Frog, Cowan	32904	Galcatcher, Henry	11215
Frye, Charles O.	3097	Galcatcher, Mattie	11216
Frye, Sadie A.	3098	Galcatcher, Thomas	11217
Frye, Lee R.	3099	Galcatcher, Emma	15125
Frye, Argyle	3100	Galcatcher, Betsy	15211
Frye, Ramond	3101	Galcatcher, Wesley	15212
Frye, Charles O., Jr.	3102	Galcatcher, Maud	15213
Frye, Pliny S.	3103	Galcatcher, Ruth	15214
Frye, Catherine	3104	Galcatcher, Charles	17411
Frye, Mamie S.	3105	Galcatcher, Peggy	17412
Frye, Maggie	15930	Galcatcher, Lee	17413
Frye, George N.	15931	Galcatcher, Nancy	17414
Frye, Samuel M.	15932	Galcatcher, Lila	17415
Frye, Henry C.	15933	Galcatcher, Snowmaker	17416
Frye, Lillian F.	15934	Galcatcher, Allie	17417
Frye, Minnie S.	15935	Galcatcher, Margaret	17885
Frye, Mary M.	15936	Galcatcher, Tom	21365
Frye, Lewis	15937	Galcatcher, Lilly	25228
Frye, Joseph	15938	Galcatcher, Dawes	32631
Frye, Edward M.	17410	Gallagher, Thomas	12487
Frye, Dora	19284	Gallman, Mary A.	32205
Frye, Walter	19295	Gallman, Claud M.	32206
Frye, Mary	19296	Gallman, Rubie A.	32207
Frye, Eliza	29793	Gallman, Henrietta	32208
Frye, Edgar M.	29794	Galloway, Dollie E.	9759
Frye, Hattie M.	29795	Gamble, Louisa	8848
Fry, William H.	11551	Gamble, Archie A.	8849
Fry, Paul W.	11552	Gamble, Perry	8850
Fry, Robert E.	11553	Gamble, Lula B.	8851
Fry, Victorine C.	11554	Gamble, Chauncy	8852
Fry, Mary	11555	Gamble, Julia A.	9583
Fry, Amelia	12004	Gamble, Verdie A.	9584
Fry, Annie	12005	Gamble, Burnie	9585
Fry, Mary J.	12006	Gamble, Dudley	9586
Fry, Maxwell	12016	Gambel, Maudie E.	9587
Fry, Pearl	12017	Gamble, Mayjosy	9588
Fry, Merrett L.	12018	Gamble, Hester J.	9589
Fry, Cora Vivian	12019	Gamble, Goldie I.	9590
Fry, Cullie	12541	Gamble, Ott E.	9591
Fry, Gertrude	12542	Gamble, William C.	24141
Fry, Cecil R.	12543	Gambrell, Pearly M.	7832
Fry, Lettie M.	12544	Gann, Thomas	3178
Fry, Charlotte V.	24687	Gann, Charles H.	3342
Fry, William	24794	Gann, Nancy J.	3343
Fry, Zona	24796	Gann, Nora	3344
Fry, Pearl	30082	Gann, Robert	3345
Fry, Charles	32435	Gann, Leo	3346
Fryar, Voisie	32615	Gann, Vetorie	3347
Fryar, Andy	32616	Gann, Bessie	3348
Fryar, Archie S.	32617	Gann, George	3349
Fryar, Mary	32614	Gann, Henry	3350
Fugate, Lillie	31153	Gann, Augusta M.	3351
Fugate, George	31154	Gann, Elias	4174
Fugate, Pearl	31155	Gann, Rabbit	4175
Fugate, Stella	31156	Gann, Mintie	4176
Fugate, John	31157	Gann, Lizzie May	4177

Name.	Roll No.	Name.	Roll No.
Gann, J. Foxey	4178	Garroutt, Lillian O.	32597
Gann, Joe	20503	Garroutt, Daisy L.	32598
Gann, Jim	20504	Garbarino, Sarah A.	9125
Gann, Lydia	21867	Garbarino, Sarah J.	9126
Gann, Mary	25698	Garbarino, Martha L.	9172
Gann, George	22969	Gasaway, Nellie O.	25057
Gann, Mary	22859	Gasaway, Charlotte C.	25061
Gant, Edward	3899	Gassaway, Henry	11473
Garrett, Margarett	1872	Gassaway, Ina M.	11474
Garrett, John	1873	Gassaway, Neoma	11475
Garrett, Gracie	1874	Gasahele	28481
Garrett, Loy D.	1875	Gass, Lucy A.	6945
Garrett, Mary	13733	Gaskey, Laura K.	13235
Garrett, Allie	13734	Gaskey, John R.	13237
Garrett, Lola	13735	Gaut, Katie A.	12425
Garrett, Willie	13736	Gaut, Maggie	12426
Garrett, Thomas B.	13737	Gaut, William	12427
Garrett, Sim	14164	Gaut, Mattie	12428
Garrett, Bruce	14166	Gaut, Charles F.	12729
Garrett, George	22098	Gaylor, Lovena	12627
Garrett, Mary C.	26971	Gaylor, Thomas J.	12628
Garrett, Roy P.	26972	Gaylor, David H.	12629
Garrett, Earl	26973	Gaylor, Grover C.	12630
Garrett, Rachel C.	27674	Gaylor, Perry	12631
Garrett, Mattie B.	27675	Gear, Samuel	11165
Garrett, Robert M.	27676	Gentry, Maggie	8990
Garrett, Frank P.	27677	Gentry, Ralph R.	8991
Garrett, Susan F.	27678	Gentry, Blanche S.	8992
Garrett, Eva	27679	Gentry, Chris R.	8993
Garrett, Joseph B.	27680	Gentry, Gertrude W. D.	8994
Garrett, Frederick	30764	Gentry, Eva V.	9735
Garrett, Samuel F.	30765	Gentry, Wayne A.	9736
Garrett, Oren C.	30766	Gentry, Lelia V.	9737
Garrett, Bertha M.	30767	Gentry, Louisa	16111
Garrett, Clyde R.	30768	Gertie, Jennie	30111
Garrett, Claud L.	30769	Gettingdown, Charles	19284
Garrett, Homer L.	30770	Gettingdown, Lucy	19285
Garrett, Robert L.	31708	Gettingdown, Jesse	29092
Garrett, Robert L., Jr.	31709	Gettingdown, Betsy	29093
Garrett, Calvin C.	31710	Getup, Callie	27805
Garrett, Mary J.	32152	Geuy, Berley E.	32723
Garrett, Gracie D.	32153	Geuy, Charles	32724
Garrett, Ellis E.	32154	Ghormley, Thomas T.	1951
Garrett, Tilmon N. J.	32155	Ghormley, Charlotte	1952
Garetson, Ida A.	7759	Ghormley, John	1953
Garetson, Robert E.	7760	Ghormley, Ewing C.	8274
Garetson, James L.	7761	Ghormley, Ida	8275
Garetson, Morton F.	7762	Ghormley, Stella M.	8276
Garetson, Lucile	7763	Ghormley, Carrie E.	8277
Garrison, Betsy	6704	Ghormley, Beulah M.	8278
Garrison, Benjamin S.	6705	Ghormley, Hugh	8279
Garrison, Mollie A.	29414	Ghormley, Lillian J.	8280
Garrison, Nannie P.	29415	Ghormley, Ewing M.	8281
Garrison, Mollie V.	29416	Ghormley, Walter S.	14118
Garrison, Sallie M.	29417	Ghormley, Willeah M.	14119
Garrison, Vester P.	29418	Ghormley, Leola M.	14120
Garner, Virgil A.	3731	Ghormley, Walter F.	14121
Garner, Benjamin F.	3732	Ghormley, Sarah C.	14122
Garner, James E.	3733	Ghormley, Michael O.	14517
Garner, Perlymoy	3734	Ghormley, Michael A.	14519
Garvin, Benjamin F.	3244	Ghormley, Nancy	14518
Garvin, Eliza J.	3245	Ghormley, Lorenzo D.	14520
Garvin, Margaret	3246	Ghormley, Nancy J.	14521
Garvin, Walter A.	3247	Ghormley, Rachel C.	14522
Garvin, Ada C.	3248	Ghormley, Lilly M.	14523
Garvin, John F.	3249	Ghormley, Stephen N.	14524
Garvin, Mary E.	3250	Ghormley, William	14526
Garvin, Elizabeth C.	3251	Ghormley, Elizabeth	14527
Garvin, Benjamin R.	3252	Ghormley, Stella	14528
Garvin, Edward M.	3253	Ghormley, Sarah E.	14784
Garvin, Frances H.	30415	Ghormley, Anna E.	14791
Garvin, Ernest F.	30416	Ghormley, Don Carlos T.	14801
Garland, Frederick	13582	Ghormley, David V.	32678
Garland, William Clarance	13583	Ghormley, Mattie	32679
		Ghormley, William	32680
Garland, Elizabeth	13584	Gibbs, Bernice	4335
Garland, John	13586	Gibbs, Caroline	6615
Garland, Sallie T.	21942	Gibbs, Lillie O.	6616
Garard, Eva	21555	Gibbs, William P.	6617
Garard, Major	21557	Gibbs, Hettie E.	6618
Garard, Alpha	21558	Gibbs, Allen D.	6619
Garmany, Jane S.	32196	Gibbs, Lou A.	6620
Garroutt, Etta P.	32596	Gibbs, Gertrude	6621
		Gibbs, John T.	6622

Name.	Roll No.	Name.	Roll No.
Gibbs, Eliza	11634	Girty, Nancy	18709
Gibbs, Charles	11635	Girty, Jacob	18710
Gibbs, Joe S.	11636	Girty, Martha	18711
Gibbs, Edith	12329	Girty, Esther	18719
Gibbs, Thomas H.	12330	Girty, Mary	18720
Gibbs, James J.	12331	Girty, Alex	18724
Gibbs, Virgie	12332	Girty, Buck	18725
Gibbs, William	19971	Girty, Martin	18726
Giboney, Sarah J.	32443	Girty, Feggie	18736
Giboney, Laura M.	32444	Girty, Daniel	18739
Giboney, Russell	32445	Girty, Oscar	18740
Giboney, John William	32448	Girty, Susie	18741
Gibson, James	4322	Girty, McKinley	18742
Gibson, Minnie	4576	Girty, Nettie	18743
Gibson, James	4577	Girty, Maria	18745
Gibson, Ode	4578	Girty, Mintie	18747
Gibson, William M., Jr.	4679	Girty, Wilson	19514
Gibson, Hazel W.	4680	Girty, Ned	19525
Gibson, Marion W.	4709	Girty, Kate	19526
Gibson, James E.	4779	Girty, Tobacco	21042
Gibson, Nettie	5262	Girty, Eetsy	21228
Gibson, Eliza	10100	Girty, Daniel	29032
Gibson, Vivia O.	10101	Girty, Jennie	30535
Gibson, John	10444	Girty, Thomas	30558
Gibson, Lillie B.	11435	Gish, Lula	26563
Gibson, Mary	11436	Gish, Jesse F.	26564
Gibson, James	11437	Givens, Mary	14489
Gibson, Mallie D.	11438	Givens, John W.	14490
Gibson, Stan	19665	Givens, David L.	14491
Gibson, William	28794	Givens, Bertha L.	14492
Gibson, Dora	31218	Givens, Nancy J.	14493
Gibson, James R.	31219	Givens, Blancha O.	14494
Gibson, Emma	31224	Givens, George W.	14495
Gibson, Mary E.	32223	Givens, Jessie Ina	14496
Gibson, Ida F.	32532	Glad, Mary E.	23220
Gibson, John H.	7159	Glad, Frederick V.	23221
Gibson, Ary T.	7160	Glad, George M.	23222
Gibson, Quinton B.	7161	Glad, Lizzie	23223
Gibson, Mattie B.	7162	Glad, John A.	23224
Gibson, Mary L.	7163	Glad, Joseph B.	23225
Gibson, Jennie C.	7164	Glad, Frank E.	23226
Gibson, John L.	7165	Glad, Mollie	23227
Gifford, Lizzie E.	10317	Glad, Flora A.	23228
Gifford, John O.	10318	Glad, Barbara A.	23229
Gilbert. Kiamitia C.	10717	Glad, Minnie M.	23230
Gilbert, George	10923	Gladney, William J.	13586
Gilbert, Dennie B.	10924	Gladney, Elmira	13887
Gilbert, Esther	21739	Gladney, Annie	13888
Gillespie, William M.	10686	Gladney, Mary	13889
Gillespey, Vida B.	31402	Gladney, Henry	13890
Gillespey, Viola B.	31403	Gladney, Minnie B.	13891
Gilliam, William T.	26812	Gladney, Charlotte	13892
Gilliam, Eliza S.	29383	Gladney, Lizzie B.	13893
Gilliam, Robert N.	29384	Gladney, John R.	13894
Gilliam, Pearl E.	29386	Gladney, Joseph B.	14432
Gilliam, Minnie B.	29387	Gladney, Ellie A.	14433
Gillum, Myrtle	23654	Gladney, Essie	14434
Gillis, Mary E.	12739	Gladney, Joseph F.	16843
Gillis, William E.	12740	Glass, Annie	2107
Gilmore,Rachel C.	37	Glass, John	13255
Gilmore, Cyrus M.	38	Glass, Hawk	15361
Gilmore, Harry W.	39	Glass, Charles D.	17637
Gilmore, Nancy V.	40	Glass, Emma	17850
Gilmore, Donald B.	41	Glass, Peggie	18126
Gilmore, Lucile	42	Glass, Liza	18127
Gilstrap, Dempsey	10301	Glass, Eli	18128
Gilstrap, Nora E.	10302	Glass, Lydia	18129
Gilstrap, Albert L.	10303	Glass, Jennie	18130
Gilstrap, Robert D.	10304	Glass, Beckie	18131
Gilstrap, George A.	10305	Glass, Paul	18843
Gilstrap, Levi	10360	Glass, Louisa	18951
Gilstrap, Jennie	11069	Glass, Bettie	18952
Gilstrap, Louisa	23146	Glass, Mary	18953
Gilstrap, Louis	23147	Glass, Fannie	18954
Gilstrap, Horace	23148	Glass, Ada	18955
Gilstrap, Carrie L.	23149	Glass, Zeak	18956
Gilstrap, Earnest H.	23150	Glass, Emma	18957
Gilstrap, Clara O.	23152	Glass, Nancy	18958
Girty, James	17599	Glass, Sut	19302
Girty, Susie	17600	Glass, Charlie	19760
Girty, Mary	17601	Glass, Toonayi	19761
Girty, Pearl	17602	Glass, Ready	19848
Girty, Felix	17603	Glass, Bettie	20498
Girty, Thomas	17606	Glass, Cole	20499
Girty, Willie	18116	Glass, Thomas	21167
Girty, Snake	18708		

Name.	Roll No.	Name.	Roll No.
Glass, Nancy	21168	Goddard, Luticia E.	29305
Glass, Joshua	21185	Godfrey, Emma	22152
Glass, Annie	21186	Godfrey, Jeffie	22153
Glass, Lucy	22712	Godfrey, Clarence Frank-	
Glass, Mary	22713	lin	22154
Glass, Lula J.	25027	Goforth, Rachel M.	26507
Glass, Ella G.	25028	Goforth, Eulma	26508
Glass, Myrtle M.	25029	Goforth, Eulillie K.	26509
Glass, John D.	25030	Goforth, Lula B.	26510
Glass, Sallie	27161	Goforth, Alta	26511
Glass, William	27174	Goff, Nancy A.	27265
Glass, Cattawyu	27175	Goingtosleep, Looney	21236
Glass, Lizzie	27176	Goingtosleep, Polly	21237
Glass, John T.	27180	Goingsnake, Nah-she-	
Glass, Lewis	28163	yah	20390
Glass, Homer	28164	Goingsnake, Betsey	20391
Glass, Earnest	28165	Goingsnake, Thomas	20821
Glass, Willie	28475	Goingsnake, Nancy	20822
Glass, Susan	28940	Goingsnake, Nannie	30666
Glass, Peggie	29070	Goingwolfe, Sylvester	22530
Glass, Nancy	29071	Going Wolfe, Aaron	1440
Glass, Elizabeth	29225	Going Wolfe, Julia	1441
Glass, Cornelius	29226	Goins, Missouri R.	15593
Glass, Harvey	29227	Goins, Jeanette	15595
Glass, Dennis	29228	Goins, Lena	21658
Glass, Caswell	29229	Goins, Okley	21659
Glass, Tom	29790	Goings, Caroline	29147
Glass, Taylor	32362	Gonzales, John A.	2562
Glass, John	32431	Gonzales, Caleb	2563
Glenn, Nancy A.	7150	Gonzales, Frank	6034
Glenn, William H.	8335	Gonzales, Lucinda	6061
Glenn, Ethel M.	8336	Gonzales, Ancy	19553
Glenn, Franklin C.	8337	Gonzales, John	26396
Glenn, Jesse E., Jr.	8338	Gonzallis, Sarah	19036
Glenn, Daisy E.	10053	Gonzallis, Spencer	19037
Glenn, Richard F.	24382	Gonzallis, Jones	19038
Glenn, Nettie A.	24383	Gonzallis, Lizzie	19039
Glenn, Vinnie R.	24384	Gonzallis, Ollie	19040
Glenn, Charles R.	24385	Gonzalis, Maggie	20487
Glenn, Dottie	24386	Gonzalis, Ada	20488
Glenn, Thomas	24387	Gonzalis, Dave	20489
Glenn, Ross	24388	Gonzalis, John	20490
Glory, Nancy	18474	Gonzalis, Senora	20491
Glory, Joe	18475	Goodall, Lilie	28141
Glory, William	18480	Goodall, Caroline D.	28142
Glory, Fannie	18481	Goodall, Ida Ophelia	28143
Glory, Henry	19863	Goodall, Leora	28144
Glory, Charley	19864	Goodall, Elizabeth	28145
Glory, Mose	19865	Goodall, William Ed-	
Glory, Joe	19866	ward	28146
Glory, Richard	23051	Goodall, Robert J.	28147
Glory, Richard Jr.	23054	Goodall, Levi F.	28148
Glory, William P.	23053	Goodall, Elisha L.	28149
Glory, Elizabeth	23055	Goodman, Edward J.	10338
Glory, George W.	23056	Goodman, Jesse J.	10339
Goad, Eliza	17457	Goodman, Catherine B.	32475
Goad, Jesse	17458	Goodman, Ora M.	32476
Goad, Frank	17459	Goodman, Albert A.	32477
Goad, Grover	17460	Goodman, Susie J.	32478
Goad, Alice	17461	Goodman, Robert F.	32479
Goad, Pearl	17462	Goodman, Joseph F.	32480
Goad, Myrtle	17463	Goodwin, Rufus	4627
Goback, Lydia	2120	Goodwin, John	10206
Goback, Jesse	20862	Goodrich, Lydia	2019
Goback, Tooniye	25923	Goodrich, Martha	2020
Goddard, William	8091	Goodrich, John	5200
Goddard, William F.	8092	Goodrich, Jack	18372
Goddard, Charles J.	8093	Goodridge, George	19064
Goddard, Katy L.	8094	Goodmoney, Phoebe	29535
Goddard, Arey	8095	Goodmoney, Alonzo	29536
Goddard, William P.	8771	Goodmoney, Rider	19349
Goddard, Fleming L.	8772	Gooden, Doc.	8840
Goddard, Henry	9659	Gooden, Betsy	8841
Goddard, James I.	9660	Gooden, Lula	24462
Goddard, Henry M.	13014	Gooden, William	24463
Goddard, James	13393	Goodykoontz, Amanda H.	8383
Goddard, James W.	13394	Goodykoontz, Frank A.	9346
Goddard, Mary E.	22166	Goodtraveler, Fred R.	31512
Goddard, Babe	22167	Goo-yah, Soney	6281
Goddard, Elbert G.	28152	Goo-yah, Lizzie Soney	6282
Goddard, Stiles H.	28153	Gordon, Callie	2175
Goddard, Irene E.	28155	Gordon, Laura M.	2176
Goddard, Anna	28191	Gordon, John B.	2177

Name.	Roll No.	Name.	Roll No.
Gordon, Effie L.	2178	Gourd, Lydia R.	14359
Gordon, Dora A.	2182	Gourd, Katie R.	14360
Gordon, James C.	2183	Gourd, Frank R.	14512
Gordon, Dora A.	2182	Gourd, Cynthia R.	14513
Gordon, James C.	2183	Gourd, Ethel R.	14514
Gordon, Dora M.	2185	Gourd, Harris R.	14515
Gordon, Silas	3757	Gourd, Charles C. R.	14516
Gordon, Lucy	11833	Gourd, Carries S. R.	15850
Gordon, Clara M.	21654	Gourd, Ellis R.	16442
Gordon, George L.	21655	Gourd, Mattie R.	16443
Gordon, John A.	21656	Gourd, John E. R.	16444
Gordon, Amanda	21657	Gourd, William P. R.	16445
Gordon, Annie May	22912	Gourd, Lucinda R.	16446
Gordon, Noah	22913	Gourd, Walter R.	17961
Gordon, Martha J.	22914	Gourd, Maud R.	17962
Gordon, Mary E.	22915	Gourd, George R.	18316
Gordon, William H.	22916	Gourd, Columbia R.	18317
Gordon, Mary R.	28578	Gourd, Carrie R.	18322
Gordon, Elizabeth	28579	Gourd, Thomas R.	18335
Gore, Sallie	325	Gourd, Mariah R.	18336
Gore, Hattie	326	Gourd, Dave R.	18337
Gore, Johnathan, Jr.	327	Gourd, Sarah R.	18338
Gore, Nathaniel S.	329	Gourd, Eliza R.	18339
Gore, Henry B.	9360	Gourd, Thomas R. Jr.	18340
Gore, Goldie	9361	Gourd, Carrie R.	18341
Gore, Samuel M.	9362	Gourd, Susie R.	18342
Gore, Roberta	9363	Gourd, Nancy R.	18343
Gore, Johnathan	22251	Gourd, Alice R.	18344
Goree, Mariah	15886	Gourd, John R.	18385
Goree, Ellen A.	15888	Gourd, William R.	18441
Goss, Benjamin F.	1988	Gourd, Mollie R.	18442
Goss, Noah O.	2239	Gourd, Eli R.	18443
Goss, Jennie B.	2258	Gourd, Joe R.	18444
Goss, George O.	2259	Gourd, Charles R.	18825
Goss, George W.	6942	Gourd, Lydia R.	18826
Goss, Mary A.	6943	Gourd, Jim R.	18827
Goss, Benjamin F.	6944	Gourd, John R.	18828
Goss, Wiliam P.	15650	Gourd, Jesse R.	18829
Goss, Mamie J.	15651	Gourd, Susie R.	18830
Goss, Walter F.	15652	Gourd, Osie R.	18831
Gossett, George D.	7541	Gourd, Jim R.	18832
Gossett, William A.	7542	Gourd, Sam R.	18833
Gossett, Sturling O.	7543	Gourd, Toswell R.	21364
Gossett, James U.	7544	Gourd, Jack R.	21380
Gott, James W.	1695	Gourd, Nellie R.	21381
Gott, Ann	1696	Gourd, Looney R.	21382
Gott, Maggie	1697	Gourd, Daniel R.	27539
Gott, Pickens	1698	Gourd, Lulu R.	27540
Gott, James J.	1699	Gourd, Lewis B. R.	27541
Gott, Ruth	1700	Gourd, Kate R.	27542
Gott, Lucy E.	1701	Gourd, Terry R.	27543
Gott, William	1840	Gourd, Mary Jane R.	27544
Gott, Pearl	1841	Gourd, May	27545
Gott, Ruth	1842	Gourd, Catherine R.	28624
Gott, Ella	1843	Gourd, Jesse H. R.	30248
Gott, Kinnie	1844	Gourd, Alexander R.	30262
Gott, Alma	1845	Gourd, Artie R.	30263
Gott, John, Jr.	5267	Gourd, Andrew R.	30264
Gott, Susan E.	5268	Gourd, Susan R.	30265
Gott, John	5398	Gourd, Lizzie	32734
Gott, Susan E.	5399	Grace, Alcie C.	29526
Gott, Alfonso	5400	Grady, Ethel M.	2964
Gott, Laura	5401	Graham, William	160
Gott, James	5402	Graham, Bluford	161
Gott, Sophia A.	5403	Graham, Rosa B.	162
Gott, Mamie B.	5404	Graham, Mamie	4580
Gott, William H.	5405	Graham, Ora J.	13105
Gott, Nannie	5406	Graham, Katie	13272
Gott, Walter D.	5984	Graham, Alsie	25476
Gott, Susan T.	10825	Graham, Nancy J.	25477
Gott, Joseph M.	12853	Graham, Sarah	25478
Gott, George	12854	Graham, William A.	25479
Gott, Claude	12855	Graham, Barbary A.	25480
Gott, Mamie	12856	Graham, El Reno	25481
Gott, Jennie	12857	Graham, Elizabeth M.	28791
Gott, Walter	12858	Graham, Ellen Girtrude	28793
Gott, John W.	16412	Graham, Missouri	31799
Gourd, Elizabeth R.	5162	Graham, Tempa V.	31800
Gourd, James R.	12003	Graham, Robert L.	31801
Gourd, Elias R.	14071	Graham, Gideon	31802
Gourd, Sallie R.	14072	Graham, John W.	31803
Gourd, Allen E. R.	14073	Graham, Julius E.	31804
Gourd, Looney R.	14358	Graham, Francis W.	31805

Name.	Roll No.	Name.	Roll No.
Graham, Mary E.	31806	Grazier, Homer M.	9841
Graham, Jesse E.	31807	Grazier, Elmer	9842
Graham, Gracie M.	31808	Grazier, Luther	9843
Graham, Florence M.	31809	Grazier, Ora	9844
Graham, Joe E.	31820	Grazier, Alice	9845
Graham, William C.	31821	Grazier, Bertha	9846
Graham, John F.	31822	Grease, Will	21149
Graham, Edna M.	31823	Grease, Nancy	21150
Graham, Robert Lee	31824	Grease, John H.	28736
Graham, James M.	31826	Grease, Lottie E.	28737
Graham, Marion	31827	Greece, Betsy	14898
Graham, Maggie	31828	Greece, Charles	16408
Graham, Luther	31829	Greece, Nannie	16409
Graham, Floyd	31830	Greece, Margaret	16504
Grant, Freddie	1358	Greece, Elizabeth	18482
Grant, Don	27956	Greece, Isaac	18805
Grant, George O.	28166	Greece, George	20877
Grass, Jesse	6299	Greece, Wuttie	20878
Grass, Sarah	6300	Greece, Skake	20879
Grass, Rider	6544	Greece, Eliza	20880
Grass, Lucy	6545	Greece, Jennie	20881
Grass, Daniel	6546	Greece, Thomas	20974
Grass, William	14655	Greece, Nannie	20985
Grass, Tyannee	14656	Greece, Betsy	29937
Grass, James W.	14657	Green, Sallie	18717
Grass, Mollie	17964	Green, Mary J.	1055
Grass, Thomas	20674	Green, Sidney A.	1056
Grass, Betsy	20675	Green, Margaretta	1057
Grass, Vinnie M.	26258	Green, Jesse	1058
Grass, Minnie E.	26259	Green, Minnie E.	1059
Grass, Eveline	26260	Green, John R.	1060
Grass, Alice G.	27587	Green, Georgia	1061
Grass, Peggie	28052	Green, Preston D.	1062
Grass, Joseph	29741	Green, Jack	3779
Grass, Elizabeth	29742	Green, Ida	2780
Grass, David	29743	Green, Hannah C.	5002
Grass, Ida	29744	Green, Mary P.	5003
Grass, Thomas W.	29745	Green, Floyd C.	5004
Grass, Benjamin E.	29746	Green, Florence	5005
Grass, Benjamin C.	30255	Green, Paul W.	5006
Grass, Levi	30626	Green, Lenora	6371
Grasshopper, Jack	18844	Green, Frances	8999
Grasshopper, Nancy	32070	Green, Lucy	9000
Grasshopper, George	32232	Green, Louie	9030
Grapes, Mary	5465	Green, William L., Jr.	9143
Graves, Ida	4909	Green, Ralph S.	11730
Graves, Lillie M.	4910	Green, Evelyn V.	11735
Graves, Clarence	10876	Green, Laura B.	13089
Graves, Charles W.	10877	Green, Willie F.	13091
Graves, Fredrick E.	10878	Green, Emma	13092
Graves, Thomas	28362	Green, Fay F.	13852
Gravitt, James M.	12626	Green, Bertha M.	13853
Gravitt, Luther O.	12831	Green, Carlotta	13854
Gravitt, Ora B.	12832	Green, Lizzie J.	14062
Gravitt, Lillie P.	12833	Green, Earnestine L.	26566
Gravitt, Alice	12834	Green, Ethel R.	26567
Gravitt, Addie	12835	Green, Herbert Lee	26568
Gravitt, Eula	12836	Green, Louis F.	27441
Gravitt, Esther	12837	Green, Emma	28024
Gravitt, Jefferson M.	12840	Green, Hooley	28025
Gray, Josanna	7733	Green, McKinley	28026
Gray, William O.	7734	Green, Teddy	28029
Gray, Theodore B.	9922	Green, Bennett F.	29527
Gray, Walter A.	9933	Green, Emeline	30287
Gray, Francis E.	9934	Greenfeather, William	7949
Gray, Susie C.	13346	Greenfeather, Eliza	7950
Gray, Emmett W.	16994	Greenfeather, Jennie	9860
Gray, Susan	23835	Greenfeather, Lewis	9861
Gray, Elizabeth B.	23836	Greenfeather, Billy	9862
Gray, Emma	23971	Greenfeather, Alexander	9863
Gray, Thomas J.	27579	Greenfeather, Isaac	24076
Gray, Ann Eliza	28655	Greenfeather, John	26514
Gray, Jesse C.	29930	Greenfeather, Luther O.	26515
Gray, Hattie	30070	Greenfeather, Annie M.	26516
Gray, Oma	31897	Greenfeather, George	26517
Gray, Cecil	31898	Greenfeather, Laura	26518
Gray, Velton	31899	Greenwood, Della	31572
Grayson, Samuel	6533	Greenwood, Susie J.	4338
Grayson, Skimmer	18746	Greenwood, William F.	4339
Grayson, Watt	18748	Greenwood, Mary R.	4340
Grayson, Napoleon	29668	Greenwood, May B.	10213
Graybeard, Peter	15837	Greenwood, John M.	10214
Grazier, Martha	9840	Greenwood, Ola C.	10215

Name.	Roll No.	Name.	Roll No.
Greenwood, Lelia	10216	Gritts, George	18093
Greenwood, Martha E.	29423	Gritts, John	18386
Greenway, Alonzo	11103	Gritts, Lydie	18387
Greenway, Mary	11104	Gritts, John	18842
Greenway, Roberta	11105	Gritts, Rosa	18882
Greer, Eugenia O.	13387	Gritts, Runabout	19981
Greer, Mattie F.	13418	Gritts, Sarah	19982
Greer, Vera M.	13419	Gritts, Daniel	19983
Greer, Rufus Paris	13420	Gritts, Charles	19984
Gregory, Lawrence M.	1139	Gritts, Cahnundeski	19985
Gregory, Maggie J.	7501	Gritts, Tee-su-yah-kee	19986
Gregory, Rosie M.	7502	Gritts, Ned	20116
Gregory, Luther	7503	Gritts, Nannie	20117
Gregory, Mattie T.	10805	Gritts, Charlotte	20118
Gregory, Lee V.	10806	Gritts, Jenie	20119
Gregory, Mary M.	10807	Gritts, William	20761
Gregory, Charles T.	10808	Gritts, Daniel	20886
Gregory, Minnie B.	31039	Gritts, Peggie	20887
Gregory, Edith	31040	Gritts, Willie	20999
Gregory, William A.	31041	Gritts, James	21145
Grey, Tarleton	23840	Gritts, Wesley	21163
Grey, John C.	23970	Gritts, Thomas	25354
Griepenkirel, Mary L.	5647	Gritts, Agnes J.	25355
Grider, Margaret C.	6623	Gritts, Levi	25356
Grider, Mary	6627	Gritts, Maggie	25357
Grider, Harry	6628	Gritts, Charlotte P.	25358
Grider, Timothy	6629	Gritts, John B.	25359
Gribble, Barbara	13801	Gritts, Burney	25360
Gribble, Dollie	13802	Gritts, Stephen	25361
Gribble, Ida	13803	Gritts, Lillie	25362
Griffen, Raney E.	3144	Gritts, Lizzie A.	25363
Griffin, Jack 4039	4029	Gritts, Thomas Jr.	25364
Griffin, Gennetta	5086	Gritts, Thomas	28917
Griffin, Alice A.	5089	Gritts, Thomas Jr.	28918
Griffin, James D.	5846	Gritts, Jennie	28919
Griffin, Mary J.	5847	Gritts, Bird	28920
Griffin, James, Jr.	5849	Gritts, George	28921
Griffin, Nannie	5850	Gritts, George	28922
Griffin, Addie	5851	Gritts, Grabgrass	28923
Griffin, Lewis	5852	Gritts, Emma	28924
Griffin, John	5853	Gritts, Edna	28925
Griffin, Looney H.	5873	Gritts, James	28962
Griffin, Mary A.	5874	Gritts, Nannie	29265
Griffin, Lugie	5875	Gritts, Susan Q.	29756
Griffin, Eliza	5876	Gritts, Charlotte	29988
Griffin, Thomas	5877	Gritts, Rosa E.	31921
Griffin, Charles	5878	Gritts, Jennie	26089
Griffin, Joe	5880	Gritts, Alcie	26750
Griffin, Olive F.	16047	Gritts, Levi	26090
Griffin, Elizabeth	17266	Groves, Eliza	5651
Griffin, Nannie	21608	Groves, Ned	5652
Griffin, Clem	25341	Groves, Fannie	5653
Griffin, Richard	25342	Groves, Susie	5657
Griffin, Bettie	25343	Groves, Johnson	16312
Griffin, Robert	25344	Groves, Evans E.	16870
Griffin, Andrew	25345	Groves, James C.	16871
Griffin, Susan	25346	Groves, Lawrence M.	16872
Griffin, Charles	25535	Groves, John	18727
Griffin, Andrew J.	29378	Groom, Mollie	26137
Griffith, Martha J.	2825	Groom, Lucile	26138
Griffith, Mary F.	2826	Groom, Leeot	26139
Griffith, Bobe	8750	Groundhog, Joanna	25687
Griffith, Liddy Jewell	18034	Groundhog, Joe	26091
Grigsby, Daniel	1263	Grubb, Earl	27556
Grigsby, Emmons	1264	Grubb, Hiram	27557
Grigsby, James	1265	Grubb, Bertha	27558
Grigsby, Charlotte	1266	Grubb, Walter	27562
Grigsby, Henry C.	1267	Grubb, Charlotte	25208
Griggs, Colonel	24534	Grubb, Lillie M.	25209
Griggs, Frank	24535	Grubb, Ella B.	25210
Grimmit, Bill	18929	Grubb, Lydia	25211
Grimmit, Nancy	18931	Grubb, Joseph	25212
Grimmit, John	18932	Grubb, Rosa J.	25213
Grimmett, George	25754	Grubbs, Madenia	11660
Grimmett, Turner	28445	Grubbs, Naoma	11661
Grindstone, Stillian	21467	Grubbs, Monon	11662
Gritts, Franklin	5864	Grubbs, Marie	11663
Gritts, Dora	5865	Guess, Albert	26598
Gritts, Nancy	1659	Guess, Eliza	26599
Gritts, Nancy	14914	Guess, Susie	26600
Gritts, Levi	17924	Guess, George	16640
Gritts, Anderson	18091	Guess, Betsy	16641
Gritts, Lizzie	18092	Guess, Watie	18495

Name.	Roll No.	Name.	Roll No.
Guess, Susie	18496	Guthrie, Oscar	2478
Guess, Willie	18497	Guthrie, Margarett	2479
Guess, Sequoyah	28447	Guthrie, Florence A.	2480
Guess, Polly	28448	Guthrie, James	29465
Guess, Jessie M.	28449	Guthrie, Walter D.	14559
Guess, Victoria	30542	Guthrie, Loren P.	16500
Guess, George	19689	Guthrie, Myrtle	25379
Guineahead, Sallie	18682	Guthrie, William	25380
Guineahead, Levi	18683	Guthrie, Jacob	29569
Guineahead, Charlie	19303	Guthrie, Wade A.	29570
Guineahead, Alex	29877	Guthrie, Robert G.	29571
Guineahead, Annie	29878	Guthrie, Oscar	19132
Guineyhead, Emma	32611	Gwartney, Carrie J.	27807
Guinn, Ollie	5597	Gwartney, Mary A.	27808
Guinn, Leonard	5598	Gwartney, Dolly	27809
Guinn, Mary	14438	Gwartney, Stella E.	27810
Guinn, Beatrice	14439	Gwartney, Walter E.	27811
Guinn, Alma L.	14440	Habish, Louisa	9079
Guinn, Charles E.	14441	Habish, George E.	9391
Guinn, James L., Jr.	14442	Hacker, Frances L.	11892
Guinn, William I.	14443	Hacker, William McK.	11893
Guinn, Almon A.	14444	Hacker, Almon R.	32860
Guinn, Bessie	14445	Haddan, Elizabeth J.	6598
Guinn, Myrtle	14446	Haddan, Thomas E. F.	6599
Guinn, James D.	25297	Haden, Caldonia	23752
Guinn, Lu Ellen	30845	Haden, Wanita	26012
Guinn, Alice E.	25298	Haddock, Alfaretta	11260
Guinn, James D., Jr.	25299	Haddock, Charles W.	11261
Guinn, Mary E.	25300	Haddock, George W.	11262
Guinn, Susan	16018	Haddock, Edna O.	11263
Guinn, Lorim W.	16019	Haddock, Dewey W.	11264
Guinn, George W.	16020	Haddock, Myrtle M.	11265
Guinn, Lizzie E.	16021	Hadley, Stella L.	10728
Guinn, William P.	16022	Hadley, David L.	10730
Guinn, Addie B.	16023	Hadley, Georgia May	32511
Guinn, Lou E.	16024	Hadley, Willie Luvena	18052
Guinn, Walter F.	16025	Haegert, Rudolph	7383
Guinn, Bertha J.	16026	Haegert, Viola	30758
Guinn, Susie L.	32261	Haff, Sanford	30976
Guinn, Arthur L.	16027	Haff, Ray	30977
Guinn, Anna T.	25301	Haff, Sarah J.	30978
Guilliams, Carrie A.	13069	Haff, Sarah E.	30994
Guilliams, Barney W.	13070	Haff, Josephine J.	30995
Gulager, William M.	14295	Haff, Luella	31046
Gulager, Martha L.	14296	Haff, Eber H.	31047
Gulager, Mary E.	14297	Haff, Clara	31048
Gulager, Henry G.	14298	Haff, Benjamin F.	31059
Gulager, John D.	14299	Haff, Mary B.	31060
Gulager, Christian	16885	Haff, James R.	31061
Gunter, George	3648	Haff, Cassie A.	31062
Gunter, Oakly	3649	Hafford, Mary Virginia	32620
Gunter, James M.	3688	Hafford, Alice Aulika	32621
Gunter, George M.	3788	Hafford, Ottis O.	32622
Gunter, John E.	4140	Hafford, Curtis	32623
Gunter, Fannie F.	4141	Hagerty, Cora	9544
Gunter, Aurelia A.	4142	Hagerty, Gladys L.	9545
Gunter, Marvin J.	4143	Hail, George W.	2866
Gunter, Elba	4160	Hail, Eliza L.	2867
Gunter, John T.	24002	Hail, General M.	2868
Gunter, Mabel L.	24004	Hall, Alice M.	2869
Gunter, Agnes G.	24005	Hail, Mary E.	2870
Gunter, Jennie V.	24006	Hail, Maud M.	2871
Gunter, Luman	10569	Hail, George J.	2872
Gunter, Henry	12253	Hail, Joseph L.	14730
Gunter, John E.	30280	Hail, Zula L.	14731
Gunter, Cora	30281	Hail, George B.	14732
Gunter, Fannie R.	30282	Hail, Bessie M.	14733
Gunter, Etta	3689	Hail, Alla L.	14734
Gunter, Caldeen	32576	Hail, Eliza L.	14735
Gunter, Nancy	32195	Hail, James M.	14876
Gunter, George W.	29306	Hail, John G.	14877
Gustin, Charles E.	25076	Hail, Lillie B.	14878
Gustin, Melvina S.	25077	Hail, Elizabeth F.	14879
Guthrey, Ethel	28276	Hail, Amy	14880
Guthrey, Charles	28277	Hail, Kittie M.	14881
Guthrey, Emerson	28278	Hail, Oscar S.	14882
Guthrie, William P.	1203	Haines, Ida M.	30979
Guthrie, Martha J.	2070	Haines, Homer L.	30981
Guthrie, Jesse A.	2071	Hains, Nancy	8971
Guthrie, Lorenzo L.	2072	Hair, Walter	2638
Guthrie, Ora	2073	Hair, Betsy	2639
Guthrie, Calvin, Jr.	2476	Hair, Oscar	2640
Guthrie, Ruth	2477	Hair, James	2969

Name.	Roll No.	Name.	Roll No.
Hair, Andy	6142	Hall, Bessie A.	3120
Hair, Cherokee N.	23316	Hall, Alex E.	4655
Hair, Bessie P.	23317	Hall, Jesse	4656
Hair, Lucy J.	23318	Hall, Martha V.	7081
Hair, Nannie E.	23319	Hall, James R.	7082
Hair, Jesse J.	23320	Hall, Martha	7112
Hair, Maud Y.	23321	Hall, Benjamin	23616
Hair, Frank J.	23322	Hall, Robert	7806
Hair, Delilah	27957	Hall, Newton	7807
Hair, Nellie	26399	Hall, Maggie	7808
Hair, Dave	26400	Hall, Henry	7810
Hair, Nicholas	26401	Hall, Mary E.	8160
Hair, Jefferson	26402	Hall, Janie P.	8161
Hair, Jack	26403	Hall, Josephine	29474
Hair, Lizzie	26404	Hall, Annie	29475
Hair, George	26405	Hall, John R.	29476
Hair, Charlotte	26406	Hall, Maud	29477
Hair, David	6183	Hall, Sewell W.	24364
Hair, Sarah	6184	Hall, Bessie	24366
Hair, Josephine	30182	Hall, Edward L.	9824
Hair, Edward	11461	Hall, Walter	9825
Hair, Alexander C.	29947	Hall, Louis F.	9826
Hair, Nannie E.	29948	Hall, Jasper N.	9940
Hair, Rosa E.	29949	Hall, Abner	9941
Hair, William M.	17580	Hall, Jesse	9942
Hair, Sue Levina	23323	Hall, William O.	10040
Hair, John	18244	Hall, John W.	10041
Hair, Jennie	18245	Hall, Dora A.	10042
Hair, Oscar	18246	Hall, Lucy	10813
Hair, Chester	32272	Hall, Lu Ella	10814
Hair, Frederick	32273	Hall, Edward L.	7809
Hair, Maggie	18248	Hall, Frank	13155
Hair, Sarah	18287	Hall, Ollie	13156
Hair, Wilson	18288	Hall, Webster	13157
Hair, Lizzie	18247	Hall, Delora	13158
Hair, Andy	18325	Hall, Call W.	13159
Hair, Lizzie	18326	Hall, Frederick	13546
Hair, James	29699	Hall, Martha M.	13547
Hair, Jim	18904	Hall, William N.	13548
Hair, John	19157	Hall, Arthur L.	13549
Hair, Lucy	19158	Hall, Flora A.	15038
Hair, Alex	19159	Hall, Cincia	15039
Hair, Sarah	19160	Hall, Nellie	15040
Hair, Charles	19161	Hall, Mary	15041
Hair, Lucy	19169	Hall, Clara E.	15042
Hair, Henry	19170	Hall, J. Thomas, Jr.	15043
Hair, James	19238	Hall, Joseph R.	15044
Hair, Daniel	25888	Hall, Joseph Ann	27840
Hair, Charles	20710	Hall, James Eugene	27841
Hair, Daniel	21401	Hall, Mae Evelyn	27842
Hair, Maude	26003	Hall, Meda	32518
Hair, Watson	26004	Hall, Beatrice	9827
Hair, Sarah	30705	Hall, Bessie S.	10815
Halcomb, Richard	25509	Hall, Henry	31372
Halcomb, George	25510	Hall, Benjamin H.	31373
Halcomb, Charles	25511	Hall, Laura	31374
Halcomb, Mary	25512	Hall, Frank	31375
Hale, Nannie E.	2926	Hall, Jessie Mae	32125
Hale, Chulie	2927	Haller, John A.	14511
Hale, Myrtle	2928	Hallford, Ida J.	13283
Hale, Emma	2929	Hallford, William R.	13284
Hale, Nannie	2930	Hallford, James W.	13285
Haley, Nellie	4774	Hallum, Mary E.	7713
Haley, Arnee L.	4775	Hallum, Maud	7714
Haley, Albert J.	4776	Hallum, Mary M.	7818
Haley, Emma O.	4777	Hallum, Ora O.	7819
Haley, William W.	4778	Hallum, Ninnie	9308
Halfbreed, Lucy	27743	Halsell, Josie	23942
Halfbreed, Webster	17573	Halsell, Eva	23943
Halfmoon, Sadie	31142	Halsell, Clarence	23944
Halfmoon, Stella	31143	Halsell, Mary	23945
Halfmoon, Phoebe	31144	Halsell, Lucile	30175
Halfmoon, Frederick A.	31145	Halsell, Pauline F.	11289
Halfmoon, Thomas	31162	Halsell, Ewing	21903
Halfmoon, Freddie	31164	Ham, Betsy	25156
Halfmoon, Remie	31165	Ham, David H.	25157
Hall, Andrew Z.	973	Ham, Pearl	25158
Hall, William F.	2859	Ham, Dora	25159
Hall, Stella E.	2860	Ham, Jennie	25160
Hall, John W.	2861	Ham, Osie	25161
Hall, Esther	3117	Ham, Martha	25162
Hall, Samuel W.	3118	Ham, Wesley	25163
Hall, Floyd	3119	Hamil, Victoria	10534

Name.	Roll No.
Hamil, Elsie M.	10535
Hamil, Lester	10537
Hamilton, Lugenia	12675
Hamilton, Hugh M.	12676
Hamilton, Clarence W.	12677
Hamilton, Martha	32798
Hamilton, Susan C.	29171
Hamilton, Mary E.	29172
Hamilton, Waunett	29173
Hamilton, Jesse E.	29174
Hammer, Looney	23133
Hammer, Jennie	23134
Hammer, Josie	23135
Hammer, Eliza	23136
Hammer, Jane	23137
Hammer, James	23138
Hammer, Mary E.	23139
Hammer, Rider	18457
Hammer, Ailsey	18458
Hammer, Charlotte	18459
Hammer, Eli	18659
Hammer, Annie	18660
Hammer, Ginseng	18661
Hammer, Adam	20081
Hammer, John	20087
Hammer, Margaret	20088
Hammer, Ellen	20089
Hammer, Walter	20091
Hammett, Mary	11281
Hammett, Richard L.	11282
Hammett, Mary E.	11283
Hammett, Ethel C.	11284
Hammett, James E.	11285
Hampton, Jane E.	195
Hampton, Pearl	196
Hampton, Mary	197
Hampton, Dewitt	198
Hampton, Gracie	199
Hampton, Edgar	200
Hampton, George W.	2805
Hampton, Charlie S.	2806
Hampton, Mary E.	2807
Hampton, Walter A.	2808
Hampton, Sadie	2809
Hampton, John	4753
Hampton, Charley	4754
Hampton, Nettie	4755
Hampton, Walter H.	4756
Hampton, George Etta	30023
Hampton, Willie C.	30024
Hampton, Elizabeth	7297
Hampton, Andy W.	7299
Hampton, Mary S.	7300
Hampton, Lula	7301
Hampton, Dora A.	7302
Hampton, William C.	7312
Hampton, Floratta M.	7313
Hampton, Ritchie L.	7314
Hampton, Lon T.	9923
Hampton, Lula R.	9924
Hampton, Georgia	9925
Hampton, Jeannie	15107
Hampton, Burt	15108
Hampton, George T.	16435
Hampton, Mary	30412
Hampton, Fannie	21637
Hancock, Viola S.	6747
Hancock, Neva M.	6748
Hancock, Nina M.	6749
Hancock, William H.	6750
Hancock, Maggie C.	8002
Hancock, Louella	8003
Hancock, Jessie L.	8004
Hancock, Robert L.	8005
Hancock, Nellie I.	8006
Handle, Susie	18684
Handle, William	19355
Handle, Tom	19356
Handle, Ed	19358
Hand, Tom	19173
Haner, Lennie	25442
Handle, Dempsy	19357
Haner, Lucinda	25443

Name.	Roll No.
Haner, Thomas W.	25444
Haner, Nancy	25447
Hanes, Delilah A.	11511
Hanes, Nathan	11512
Hanes, Prudie G.	11513
Hanes, Charles E.	11514
Hanes, Anna V.	11515
Hanes, Sonora	11516
Hanes, Leroy	11517
Hanes, Arthur C.	11518
Hanes, Maud R.	11519
Hanes, Mary E.	11520
Hanes, Alger W.	11521
Haney, Roxie	12070
Haney, Jay T.	12075
Hanks, Calvin J.	3472
Hanks, Robert T.	5654
Hanks, Mary E.	5655
Hanks, Roberta	5656
Hanks, Calvin J.	25456
Hanks, Ora M.	25457
hanks, James O.	25458
Hanks, Maud K.	25459
Hanks, Grace	25460
Hanks, Fannie L.	25461
Hanks, Annie M.	25462
Hanks, Cora N.	25463
Hanks, Daisy	17456
Hanks, Bell	1664
Hanks, William	1666
Hankins, Dora B.	12859
Hankins, Curah D.	12860
Hankins, Mary L. B.	12861
Hanlin, Emma H.	32691
Hanna, Cleaveland	375
Hanna, Mary	1524
Hanna, Caledonia	1578
Hanna, John	29758
Hanna, Cora P.	28580
Hanna, Leota	9543
Hanna, Nancy	9699
Hanna, Claudie	9700
Hanna, Anna E.	9701
Hanna, Cora O.	9702
Hanna, Rosa A.	13430
Hanna, Robert O.	13431
Hanna, Mabel L.	13432
Hanna, Dennis R.	9638
Hanna, Eliza J.	9632
Hannah, Julia	1896
Hannah, Lee H.	1897
Hannah, William T.	1898
Hannah, Stella N.	1899
Hannah, Samuel A.	1900
Hannah, Cheese	1901
Hannah, Hooly	1902
Hannah, Georgie F.	2963
Hannah, William	26822
Hannah, May E.	26823
Hannah, Charles B.	26824
Hannon, Andrew	16334
Hannon, Jennie	16335
Hannon, Maggie	16336
Hannon, Edward	16337
Hannon, Mary	16338
Hannon, Gertrude	16339
Hannon, James	16340
Hannon, Frank	16341
Hannon, Watie	16342
Hannon, Maggie L.	5269
Hannon, Joseph E.	5270
Hannon, Newton E., Jr.	5271
Hannon, James T.	5272
Hannon, Roland H.	5273
Hannon, Levi E.	5274
Hannon, Wesley D.	5275
Hannon, Cherokee L.	5276
Hanson, Pigeon	9183
Hardbarger, Lila	18919
Hardbarger, Lewis	18920
Hardbarger, Johnson	18921
Hardbarger, John	19899
Hardbarger, Peggie	19900

Name.	Roll No.	Name.	Roll No.
Hardbarger, John Jr.	19901	Harlin, William L.	7870
Hardbarger, Sam	19902	Harlin, George W.	7871
Hardee, Katie	21575	Harlin, Nathan L.	8382
Harder, Willard H.	7690	Harlin, John H.	24432
Hardy, Anna	253	Harlin, Jessie	12554
Hardy, Jennie Ethel	254	Harlin, Nannie C.	22086
Hardy, Howard Lee	255	Harlin, Ezekiel	28799
Hardy, Mary E.	7421	Harlin, Miriam L.	24433
Hardy, John D.	7422	Harlin, John	28800
Hardy, Dudley R.	7423	Harlin, Mary	15629
Hardy, Myrty M.	7424	Harlin, Ellis C.	17569
Hardy, Henry W.	7425	Harlin, Jim	21540
Hardy, Mary A.	7426	Harlin, Willie	22026
Hardy, Lee	7427	Harlin, George	19999
Hardy, Della	7428	Harlin, Ned	30594
Hardy, Opel P.	7429	Harlin, Maria	30595
Hare, Bird	29052	Harlin, Carrie	30596
Hare, Ezekiel	21306	Harlin, Edgar L.	318
Hare, Mandy	32522	Harlin, Charles	7182
Hare, Jim	21307	Harless, Ophelia J.	26943
Hare, Frank	21308	Harless, Guye	26944
Hare, Addie	21309	Harless, Trenton	26945
Hare, Annie	21310	Harless, Elizabeth	26946
Harflich, Hettie	12290	Harless, Lola	1099
Hargis, Tooka A.	15788	Harless, Henry Luster	1124
Harland, Eli	18031	Harless, Annie	23424
Harlan, Albert W.	598	Harless, Rufus	23425
Harlan, Matilda	599	Harless, Warren R.	23426
Harlan, Ada	28540	Harless, Louisa	23427
Harlan, Silas F.	28541	Harlis, Harrison	6678
Harlan, Allie	28542	Harlow, Alabama	12710
Harlan, Charity D.	28543	Harlow, John	12711
Harlan, William	4752	Harlow, William S.	12712
Harlan, Clifford L.	28727	Harlow, Samuel T.	12713
Harlan, Bessie M.	10021	Harlow, Rosa I.	12714
Harlan, Daisy D.	10022	Harlow, Annie	13977
Harlan, Rubie V.	10023	Harlow, Peggie A.	29355
Harlan, John H.	13670	Harlow, Bertha	29356
Harlan, Harry W.	13671	Harlow, Walter	29357
Harlan, John G.	16094	Harlow, Alice	29358
Harlan, Eliza	16095	Harlow, James	29359
Harlan, Nannie J.	16096	Harlow, Joseph	29360
Harlan, Edna	16097	Harlow, Elick	29361
Harlan, Cherokee	16098	Harlow, Beulah M.	29362
Harlan, Sarah E.	16099	Harman, Henrietta	5967
Harlan, Eli	16100	Harmon, Joseph E.	29636
Harlan, Andrew O.	26769	Harmon, Jesse	2724
Harlan, Myrtle B.	26770	Harmon, Nancy	2725
Harlan, Nina E.	26771	Harmon, Willoby	2726
Harlan, Cliffton Alvarce	13672	Harmon, Fannie	2727
Harlen, Lydia	836	Harmon, Whitsett	2729
Harlen, George	837	Harmon, James	2730
Harlen, Caleb	838	Harmon, Amelia	2848
Harlen, Louisa J.	839	Harmon, John	4307
Harlen, Huey	840	Harmon, James	4439
Harlen, Ellis	841	Harmon, Cyntha	5950
Harlen, Annie B.	842	Harmon, McGilbry	5951
Harlin, John R.	22085	Harmon, Benjamin	5952
Harlin, David L.	309	Harmon, Lena	5953
Harlin, James R.	310	Harmon, Elizabeth	5968
Harlin, Delbert	312	Harmon, Vinnie M.	9277
Harlin, Cecil W.	313	Harmon, Thelma V.	9278
Harlin, Edgar C.	314	Harmon, James F.	9279
Harlin, Claud	315	Harmon, Jesse L.	17114
Harlin, Esther V.	316	Harmon, Mary	21372
Harlin, Luther A.	317	Harmon, Jack	2728
Harlin, Lewis S.	319	Harmon, Flora	31832
Harlin, Mary A.	373	Harmon, Lillie R.	31833
Harlin, James E.	650	Harmon, Claud	31834
Harlin, Nancy A.	651	Harmon, Dwight	31835
Harlin, Alviso V.	652	Harmon, William D.	31836
Harlin, Sallie K.	653	Harmon, Charlie	18767
Harlin, Jarrett B.	654	Harmon, Maggie	25613
Harlan, Silas	22531	Harmon, Edward	25614
Harlan, Mary	22532	Harmer, Katie	16582
Harlan, Lucinda	22533	Harmer, Emma M.	16583
Harlan, Ellis	22534	Harmer, Jessee	16584
Harlin, David L. Jr.	311	Harnage, William W.	5914
Harlin, Fannie	7181	Harnage, Richard	5915
Harlin, Oce	26459	Harnage, Charles D.	5916
Harlin, Jesse C.	26460	Harnage, Fannie C.	11055
Harlin, Callie	26461	Harnage, Emma R.	11066
Harlin, Ruth	26462	Harnage, Ezekiel S.	13251

Name.	Roll No.
Harnage, John G.	13769
Harnage, Jesse L.	14144
Harnage, William T.	16170
Harnage, Rosanna	16171
Harnage, William C.	16172
Harnage, Lena	16173
Harnage, Ruth B.	16174
Harnage, Custis L.	21740
Harnage, James Hall	11057
Harnar, Nellie M.	13578
Harnar, Eulailiah	13579
Harnar, Ralph R.	13580
Harnar, Claud R.	13581
Harp, Maggie	4180
Harp, Thomas L.	4181
Harp, Cynthia	4182
Harp, Ruth M	4183
Harp, Guy C.	4184
Harp, Ellis	4219
Harper, Elsie	28250
Harrell, Mary	30215
Harris, Collebert	26990
Harris, Joseph A.	4025
Harris, Charles	53
Harris, Daisy	54
Harris, Bird	55
Harris, Suenette	56
Harris, Charles D.	57
Harris, William B.	58
Harris, Chester H.	92
Harris, Wyley B.	93
Harris, Ward B.	94
Harris, Elizabeth	95
Harris, Sallie B.	99
Harris, Bonnie A.	100
Harris, Mollie L.	98
Harris, James S.	5297
Harris, Charlotte A.	5494
Harris, Jeannette	5495
Harris, Bettie V.	5496
Harris, Malinda	5498
Harris, Frank M.	5497
Harris, Niley	5499
Harris, Charlotte A.	5500
Harris, Parker C.	5831
Harris, Robert	5832
Harris, Colonel P.	5833
Harris, Emily	5834
Harris, James G.	5835
Harris, Sue L.	5836
Harris, Mary V.	5837
Harris, George	5838
Harris, Martha	5839
Harris, Thomas	5939
Harris, David	5940
Harris, Claude	5941
Harris, Cherokee	29432
Harris, Benjamin	27433
Harris, Thomas	6050
Harris, Dennis B.	6051
Harris, Matt	7617
Harris, Richard	7618
Harris, Willie	7619
Harris, Ida J.	8081
Harris, Flora M.	8082
Harris, Gertie N.	8083
Harris, Ulalah S.	8084
Harris, Roy C.	8085
Harris, John W., Jr.	8086
Harris, Mary J.	9023
Harris, Emma J.	10869
Harris, Susan T.	10870
Harris, Lou G.	10871
Harris, Alfred	10872
Harris, Minnie	10873
Harris, Charles J.	10874
Harris, Joseph	11047
Harris, James S.	11048
Harris, Othella	11049
Harris, Susan	11884
Harris, Mary J.	11885
Harris, Nancy D.	11886
Harris, Cora B.	11887

Name.	Roll No.
Harris, Ruby O.	11888
Harris, Colonel J.	14110
Harris, Mamie E.	14111
Harris, William R.	14112
Harris, Colonel J., Jr.	14113
Harris, Joel A.	14114
Harris, Mary E. C.	14115
Harris, Charles H.	14116
Harris, Joseph B.	16914
Harris, William	28331
Harris, Lucy	28332
Harris, John R.	17122
Harris, Thomas	17123
Harris, Philo H.	17244
Harris, Annie	28374
Harris, Martha L.	29397
Harris, Charles	29398
Harris, Johnnie A.	29399
Harris, Robert P.	29400
Harris, Nellie M.	29401
Harris, William M.	29402
Harris, Charlotta E.	26126
Harris, William B.	26127
Harris, Thomas M.	26128
Harris, John F.	26129
Harris, Prince H.	27434
Harris, Ida	5840
Harris, Edwin B.	14117
Harris, Claud	20984
Harrison, Celia	2680
Harrison, Claud	2681
Harrison, Benjamin	2682
Harrison, Jesse	2683
Harrison, Otto	2684
Harrison, Floyd	2685
Harrison, Oscar	2686
Harrison, Nannie D.	5855
Harrison, M. Rector	5856
Harrison, Bertha M.	5857
Harrison, Mattie E.	7320
Harrison, Mary E.	7321
Harrison, John T.	7322
Harrison, Samuel D.	7323
Harrison, Mary A.	8059
Harrison, Andrew P.	8906
Harrison, Nathan E.	8907
Harrison, Hannah E.	17570
Harrison, Jessie	17571
Harrison, Susan N.	2688
Harrison, Johnnie	5858
Harrison, Lella	17505
Harrison, Ray	17506
Harrison, Robert	21577
Harrison, Minnie	31573
Harrold, Rebecca M.	7729
Harrold, Maggie L.	7730
Harrold, William	7731
Harrold, Trevetta	7732
Harry, Taylor L.	8916
Hart, Sarah	4726
Hart, Joanna	5236
Hart, Maggie I.	24014
Hart, Robert E.	5237
Hart, Ollie E.	15808
Hart, Frances E.	15809
Hart, Eula B.	15810
Hart, William	16327
Hart, Lila	20028
Hart, John	32378
Hartgraves, William	13676
Hartness, Octavia	28197
Hartness, John	28198
Hartness, David	28199
Hartness, Allie	28200
Hartness, Katie	28201
Hartness, Josie	28202
Hartness, Edward	15478
Hartness, Erastus W.	16561
Hartness, George W.	16562
Hartness, Albert J.	16563
Hartness, Indianola	16564
Hartsock, Lizzie T.	16272
Hartsock, John Louis	16273

Name.	Roll No.	Name.	Roll No.
Harvey, Rosa	30218	Hawkins, Katie E.	24998
Harvey, James	30219	Hawkins, Pearl D.	24999
Harvey, Bertha	30220	Hawkins, Emma L.	25000
Harvey, Cleveland	30221	Hawkins, Maria L.	13764
Harvey, Robert	7952	Hawkins, Samuel F.	13781
Harvey, William	7966	Hawkins, Samuel S.	28181
Harvey, Nancy	7967	Hawkins, John A.	28182
Harvey, Alexander	7968	Hawkins, Quantrell G.	28183
Harvey, Rosa	7969	Hawkins, Della F.	28184
Harvey, Lucy	7970	Hawkins, Henry	17648
Harvey, Frank M.	7971	Hawkins, Mattie	17649
Harvey, John	8119	Hawkins, Hallie	17650
Harvey, Nannie	10949	Hawkins, Harry	17651
Harvey, Annie	21678	Hawkins, Dibrell	17652
Harvey, Stanfield	21808	Hawkins, Jessie	17653
Hastings, William W.	1788	Hawkins, Robie	17654
Hastings, Lulu M.	1789	Hawkins, Charlie	17655
Hastings, Lucile	1790	Hawkins, Peggie	18332
Hastings, Louisa J.	13938	Hawkins, Josiah	18404
Hastings, John R.	13961	Hawkins, Eva Belle	18405
Hastings, Elizabeth V.	14130	Hawkins, Mina	18406
Hastings, William W.		Hawkins, Eliza Jane.	18407
Jr.	14131	Hawkins, Joe	18430
Haston, Rosa	14321	Hawkins, Fannie	18431
Hatchet, Aggie	21344	Hawkins, Nancy	18432
Hatfield, Nannie	801	Hawkins, Jesse	18433
Hatfield, Winnie D.	802	Hawkins, Jim	18434
Hatfield, James R.	803	Hawkins, Nannie	18435
Hatfield, Margaret B.	4416	Hawkins, Alex	18445
Hatfield, Isaac	4417	Hawkins, Eve	18446
Hatfield, Hannah	4418	Hawkins, Lucy	18447
Hathcoat, Josie A.	14572	Hawkins, Nancy	26005
Hathcoat, Oma L.	14573	Hawkins, Jack	21441
Hathcoat, Nonie L.	14574	Hawkins, Lizzie	21442
Hathcock, Maude B.	5394	Hawkins, Susie	21443
Hathcock, Thomas R.	5395	Hawkins, Robert	21444
Hathcock, Charles M.	5396	Hawkins, John	26119
Hathcock, Edward T.	5397	Hawkins, Willie Joice	8470
Hatton, Agnes E.	8496	Haworth, Ida L.	8317
Hatton, Nathaniel M.	8497	Haworth, Lucile S.	8318
Hatton, Samuel	8498	Haworth, Perry E.	8319
Hause, Daniel M.	12209	Haworth, Edgar M.	8320
Hause, Lillie V.	12210	Haworth, Claude W.	8321
Hause, George W.	12211	Haworth, Grace	8322
Hause, Sarah R.	12212	Haworth, Owen H.	8323
Hause, Joseph M.	12213	Hayden, Rebecca C.	6201
Hause, Caleb W.	12214	Hayden, Ida M.	6202
Hause, Ruth E.	12215	Hayden, Lona	6203
Hause, Oliver	12216	Hayden, Lela	6204
Hause, Mabel E.	12217	Hayden, Essie	6205
Hause, Daniel M., Jr.	12218	Hayes, Charles J.	856
Hause, Maria V.	12219	Hayes, Vicie S.	4245
Hawk, Sarah	7180	Hayes, Pearl R.	4246
Hawk, Benjamin C.	27531	Hayes, Corrah F.	4247
Hawk, Lucy	28717	Hayes, Stella J.	4248
Hawk, Noah	8926	Hayes, Ethel	12878
Hawk, George	18311	Hayes, Richard W.	16771
Hawk, Mary	18925	Hayes, Eliza	16772
Hawk, Adam	20529	Hayes, Emma	16773
Hawk, Richard	32770	Hayes, J. Q.	21614
Hawkins, Myrtle	135	Hayes, Malinda E.	21709
Hawkins, Lundy	136	Hayes, Dewey	21710
Hawkins, Charles D.	8202	Hays, Sabra	6574
Hawkins, Ruth K.	8465	Hays, Bryan	6575
Hawkins, Roswell Drake	8466	Hays, Hugh M.	26909
Hawkins, Charles G.	8467	Hays, Curtis E.	26910
Hawkins, Thomas O.	8468	Hays, Craig C.	6579
Hawkins, Rhoda L.	8469	Hays, James E.	14035
Hawkins, Robert P.	8737	Haynes, Willie P.	9389
Hawkins, John I.	24154	Haynes, Oliver M.	9390
Hawkins, Biddie	9119	Hayney, Parthena	30258
Hawkins, George	9604	Hazlewood, Maude	13717
Hawkins, Elanor	10624	Hazlewood, Claude	13718
Hawkins, Walter H.	10625	Hazlewood, Winona	13719
Hawkins, Ralph	10626	Hazlewood, Mary A. F.	28938
Hawkins, Maud	10627	Head, Lucy A.	91
Hawkins, Samuel O.	10628	Head, Roosevelt	97
Hawkins, Edith	10629	Head, Etta L.	96
Hawkins, Ruby	10630	Headley, Elsie	32843
Hawkins, Abbie	24181	Headrick, William	4435
Hawkins, Ruth J.	24995	Headrick, Rose	4436
Hawkins, Glendwyn E.	24996	Headrick, Ruth	4437
Hawkins, May L.	24997	Headrick, Susan	4438

Name.	Roll No.	Name.	Roll No.
Headrick, Lucy	13476	Henderson, Lizzie	26550
Headrick, Michael P.	13477	Henderson, Ursey A.	26554
Headrick, Watie E.	13478	Hendrex, Annie	6815
Headricks, Sam	18678	Hendrex, Virgil F.	6816
Headricks, Claude	25610	Hendricks, Minerva	35
Headricks, Sophronia	25611	Hendricks, William H.	5332
Headricks, Jack	25612	Hendricks, Emma E.	5333
Headricks, Mary J.	18679	Hendricks, Annie E.	5489
Heady, Ella M.	8394	Hendricks, George	5490
Heady, Ella E.	31501	Hendricks, Richard F. B.	5491
Heady, Alva	31502	Hendricks, Louisa	28623
Heady, Frank	31503	Hendricks, John	18282
Heady, Ada M.	31504	Hendricks, Susie	18283
Heady, Leona	31505	Hendricks, Katie	18284
Heady, Oneida	31506	Hendricks, Daniel	18285
Heady, Clay	31507	Hendricks, Frank	28413
Heady, James E.	31508	Hendricks, Tece	27515
Heape, Lenora	10755	Hendricks, Robert M.	10675
Heape, Flora B.	10756	Hendricks, White McC.	10747
Heape, Hiram L.	10757	Hendricks, John	11974
Heape, Serrener	13540	Hendricks, Saphronia	11975
Heape, Edith	10822	Hendricks, Jesse L.	27759
Heape, Elizabeth M.	10817	Hendricks, Ruby E.	27760
Heape, Walter A.	13541	Hendricks, Cossie	32258
Heape, Clara E.	13542	Hendricks, Dennis	14539
Heape, George W.	13543	Hendricks, Eliza J.	14540
Heape, Richard E.	13544	Hendricks, Nelson	14541
Heard, Lula	4545	Hendricks, Mary A. F.	14542
Heard, Joseph S.	12919	Hendricks, Levi	14672
Heard, Willie	21852	Hendricks, Thomas	14962
Heath, Olive F.	21738	Hendricks, Alexander	15296
Heaton, Esther	3410	Hendricks, William	16053
Heaton, Charles	3411	Hendricks, Thomas	16496
Heaton, David	3412	Hendricks, Ellen	16497
Heaton, Calvin	3413	Hendricks, Thomas	29969
Heaton, Maggie	3414	Hendricks, Robert R.	29970
Heaven, Aki	20210	Hendricks, Clara M.	29971
Heaven, James	20211	Hendricks, Rufus	16622
Heaven, Steve	20212	Hendricks, Joseph	16623
Heaven, Lucy	20213	Hendricks, James K.	16624
Hedrick, Rebecca	10483	Hendricks, Wildie M.	16625
Hedrick, Minnie E.	10484	Hendricks, Marcus A.	16626
Hedrick, Joanna	10485	Hendricks, Jonas	16650
Hedrick, Morgan	10486	Hendricks, Nancy J.	16651
Hedrick, Asa Edward	10487	Hendricks, Lydia	16652
Hedricks, William	17245	Hendricks, Martha	16653
Hedricks, Joseph	17246	Hendricks, Frederick	16654
Hedricks, Mary	21109	Hendricks, George W.	16655
Hedricks, William C.	21110	Hendricks, Ada	16656
Heffernan, Joanna	26857	Hendricks, Flora	16657
Heffernan, Annie	26858	Hendricks, Nelly	16658
Heffernan, Pearl	26859	Hendricks, Charles R.	16659
Hefflefinger, Joseph E.	12365	Hendricks, Charley	17078
Hefflefinger, Pace G.	12366	Hendricks, Eleanor E. J.	32193
Hefflefinger, Elizabeth	12368	Hendricks, Zilph H.	32194
Hefflefinger, Vevi Josephine	12367	Hendricks, David	22127
		Hendricks, Mike	22128
Hefner, Lula M. J.	8048	Hendricks, James R.	29403
Hefner, Roy E.	8049	Hendricks, Sarah H.	29404
Hefner, Edith L.	8050	Hendricks, Isaac J.	29405
Hefner, Ruby	8051	Hendricks, Adam	21449
Heindselman, Sarah E.	24507	Hendricks, Tooka	21450
Heindselman, Ada E.	24508	Hendricks, Ellis	30719
Heindselman, William R.	24509	Hendricks, Infant	30720
		Hendricks, George	15297
Heinrichs, Kate E.	13960	Hendricks, Mary	22027
Heistand, Carrie A.	10562	Hendricks, Addie B.	16660
Heistand, Millard A.	10563	Hendryx, Eva M.	24046
Heistand, Bluford	10564	Hendryx, Bettie	7927
Heistand, Adam	10566	Hendrix, Sam	19676
Helterbrand, James	16352	Hendrix, Susie	19677
Helterbrand, John W.	16353	Henley, Clara E.	10198
Helum, Jesse	8879	Henley, Eddie	10199
Helvenston, Lucy A.	15695	Henley, Walter	10200
Helvenston, Mary E.	15696	Henley, Lelia M.	10201
Helvenston, Charles E.	15697	Henley, Ruth J.	10202
Helvenston, Ruth L. •	15698	Henley, Archie	10203
Helvenston, Claud	15699	Henley, Nannie Elizabeth	10204
Helvenston, Ethel	15700		
Henderson, James H.	8972	Henrichs, Henry	28196
Henderson, Ada	12319	Henry, Mary B.	23287
Henderson, Albert L.	12320	Henry, Jesse J.	23288
Henderson, Ophelia M.	12321	Henry, Oscar E.	23289

Name.	Roll No.	Name.	Roll No.
Henry, John	6196	Henson, Chili	11550
Henry, Almel	6197	Henson, Jesse	12181
Henry, Josiah	27968	Henson, Nellie	12182
Henry, Laura A.	27969	Henson, Laura	12183
Henry, Rosa J.	27970	Henson, Looney	12184
Henry, Rachel D.	27971	Henson, Richard	12185
Henry, Benjamin L.	27972	Henson, Charlotta	12337
Henry, Florence A.	27973	Henson, George E.	12338
Henry, Jesse	27473	Henson, Joseph	12648
Henry, Josiah	27474	Henson, James	15473
Henry, William E.	27475	Henson, Pearlie	15474
Henry, William A.	6947	Henson, Dulcemore	15475
Henry, Amelia D.	6948	Henson, Vestie	15476
Henry, Elsie A.	6949	Henson, Wash	28290
Henry, Mary B.	6950	Henson, May	28291
Henry, Agnes B.	6951	Henson, Hugh	15477
Henry, Viola	6952	Henson, Charles	15794
Henry, Alvin	6953	Henson, Peggy	15795
Henry, William M.	6954	Henson, Pearl	15796
Henry, Eva M.	6956	Henson, Charles, Jr.	15797
Henry, W. Gibbs	8809	Henson, Nancy	15798
Henry, Myrtle	8810	Henson, Susie	15800
Henry, DeWitt C.	8811	Henson, John C.	17199
Henry, Roy W.	8812	Henson, Cassie M.	17276
Henry, Walter N.	10278	Henson, Sixkiller	17277
Henry, Myrtle	10279	Henson, Nancy	27821
Henry, Effie	10280	Henson, Jesse T.	27822
Henry, Levi J.	11658	Henson, Powhatan	28364
Henry, Polly	11659	Henson, Maria	28365
Henry, Patrick	13197	Henson, James	17624
Henry, Marie	13198	Henson, Tom	17627
Henry, Bessie L.	13199	Henson, Annie	25541
Henry, Clarence R.	13200	Henson, Myrtie	25542
Henry, Catharine	13201	Henson, Lee	25543
Henry, Ada Bell	13202	Henson, Mary	25544
Henry, Albert G.	13488	Henson, Jim McK.	25545
Henry, Patrick D.	13504	Henson, Alice	22024
Henry, Odeyne	13505	Henson, Susan	26916
Henry, Archie L.	13506	Henson, Laura	26917
Henry, Joseph J.	28173	Henson, George L.	22048
Henry, Thomas	21954	Henson, George	32392
Henry, Hugh M.	21647	Henson, Pearline	32393
Henry, Wilbur W.	21648	Henson, Elizabeth	5990
Henry, Jerry	21649	Henson, Lottie Bell	5994
Henry, Ben	21411	Henson, Grover	27823
Henry, Sarah	21412	Henson, Ella E.	24515
Henry, Thomas	32727	Henson, Sam	21398
Henry, Ida	32728	Henson, Nancy	21399
Henry, Swimmer	32729	Henson, Ada	21400
Henry, Huburt	32892	Henson, James	32354
Henry, Robert	32893	Henson, Terrell	21402
Hensley, John W.	5036	Henson, Bettie	21403
Hensley, Samuel	5037	Henson, William	30706
Hensley, Houston	5038	Henson, Levi	12186
Hensley, James	5039	Henson, Dora	15799
Hensley, Joseph	5040	Herberger, Polly	85
Hensley, Minnie M.	32164	Herberger, Anna B.	86
Hensley, William W.	32165	Herberger, William M.	87
Hensley, Angie M.	32166	Herberger, Frances	88
Hensley, Ethel L.	21838	Herberger, Sallie	89
Hensley, Della G.	32167	Herberger, Hiram A.	90
Henson, Cherokee	149	Hereford, Joseph	4449
Henson, Bessie	150	Hereford, Saphronia	4450
Henson, Sarah J.	151	Hereford, Lennie B.	4451
Henson, Poss	1996	Hereford, James	4452
Henson, Jane	2395	Hereford, Robert	4453
Henson, Thomas	2396	Hereford, Jesse	4454
Henson, Sallie	2397	Hereford, Burk	4455
Henson, Johnnie A.	2398	Hereford, Mattie E.	4456
Henson, Charlotte	2399	Hereford, Ross B.	4457
Henson, John Nula	2519	Hereford, Golie	21759
Henson, Louis	3908	Hern, Florence M.	22362
Henson, Mary	3909	Hern, Minnie	22359
Henson, Clarence	3910	Hern, Helen	22361
Henson, Howard	3911	Hern, Margaret	730
Henson, Lucy	3912	Hern, Hellen	731
Henson, Elonzo	3913	Herran, Mattie C.	15628
Henson, Jesse	4060	Herrin, Paulina E.	21890
Henson, Richard	10314	Herrin, Walter H.	21891
Henson, Hattie M.	24512	Herrin, James A.	26751
Henson, Pearl J.	24513	Herrin, Harvey L.	26752
Henson, Martha I.	24514	Herrin, Fred W.	26753
Henson, Andrew J.	11549	Herrin, Bertha J.	26754

Name.	Roll No.	Name.	Roll No.
Herrin, Hattie M.	26755	Hicks, Sallie E.	7983
Herrin, Toy S.	26756	Hicks, Jennie	7984
Herod, Joel E.	7066	Hicks, Ada	7985
Herod, William M.	8742	Hicks, Maggie	7986
Herod, Charles O.	26527	Hicks, Emmett S.	7987
Herod, Beulah J.	26528	Hicks, Viola	7988
Herod, Jesse	26529	Hicks, Herbert W.	9956
Herod, Henry	26530	Hicks, Ethel I.	9957
Herod, Lillie M.	26531	Hicks, Homer W.	9958
Herod, Nellie M.	26532	Hicks, Clifton A.	9959
Herod, Ella G.	26533	Hicks, E. Ross	30249
Herod, Verna E.	21639	Hicks, William	30300
Herrod, Julian	28790	Hicks, Andrew J.	12926
Herron, Richard F.	16274	Hicks, Lonnie	12927
Hester, Hettie	27771	Hicks, Frank	12928
Hester, Alfred V.	27772	Hicks, Amelia	12929
Hewin, Levi	2381	Hicks, William	12930
Hewin, Spade	18377	Hicks, Eddie	13250
Hewing, Ruth	27162	Hicks, Edward D.	13804
Hewing, Narcissa	2516	Hicks, Lizzie	13805
Hiatt, Ellen	10776	Hicks, Jane S.	13806
Hiatt, Elsie M.	10777	Hicks, Joseph D.	13807
Hiatt, Edgar W.	10778	Hicks, Clara E.	13808
Hibbs, George M.	2653	Hicks, William P.	13809
Hibbs, Nancy M. J.	5107	Hicks, Edward	13810
Hibbs, John A.	5108	Hicks, Margeret E.	13811
Hibbs, David A.	5109	Hicks, John	25092
Hibbs, Emma M.	5110	Hicks, Emma	25093
Hibbs, Carl C.	5111	Hicks, Mary	28247
Hibbs, Viola	5112	Hicks, Ada	28248
Hibbs, Olley	5113	Hicks, Josiah	28249
Hibbs, James A.	31994	Hicks, Lillie	14596
Hibbs, Dennis B.	31995	Hicks, Jennie M.	14597
Hibbs, Laura E.	31996	Hicks, Nannie	15540
Hibbs, Bertha A.	31997	Hicks, Cora	16211
Hibbs, Maggie M.	31998	Hicks, Josiah	16275
Hibbs, Sarah I.	31999	Hicks, William H. H.	21625
Hibbs, Leonie E.	32000	Hicks, Lucy	21626
Hickey, Thomas P.	5349	Hicks, Austin	27849
Hickey, Lucinda	5350	Hicks, George W.	29549
Hickey, George H.	5351	Hicks, Almon A.	29550
Hickey, Nellie M.	5352	Hicks, Ruth H.	29551
Hickey, Rachel C. E.	5353	Hicks, Grace	29552
Hickey, William	5354	Hicks, Francis	29185
Hickey, John	5355	Hicks, Claude J.	32416
Hickey, Richard	5356	Hicks, Mary M.	32417
Hickey, Mary L.	5357	Hicks, Dave	26193
Hickey, Edna E.	6026	Hicks, George	26194
Hickey, Lawrence	6027	Hicks, Squirrel	26195
Hickle, Mary A.	3152	Hicks, Aaron	26196
Hickle, William R.	3153	Hicks, George	18132
Hickory, John	17617	Hicks, Jessie M.	25094
Hickox, Henry	190	Hicks, Maggie	25095
Hickox, Pauline	191	Hicks, Nelson	29072
Hicks, Taylor	2897	Hicks, Jeff	29073
Hicks, Lee M.	2898	Hicks, Henry	29074
Hicks, Mary M.	2899	Hicks, Ella	29075
Hicks, Annie L.	2900	Hicks, George	29076
Hicks, Taylor Jr.	2901	Hicks, Rhoda	29077
Hicks, Ranzia	2902	Hicks, Mary	18691
Hicks, Rosa L.	2903	Hicks, George	18692
Hicks, Henry T.	2904	Hicks, Ida	18693
Hicks, Nancy J.	2905	Hicks, Aaron	18694
Hicks, Benjamin F.	2966	Hicks, Nancy	21012
Hicks, Percy W.	5183	Hicks, Andy	21013
Hicks, Emma I.	5184	Hicks, Peggie	21084
Hicks, Nancy E.	5340	Hicks, Rachel	21127
Hicks, John	6162	Hicks, Alfred F.	30973
Hicks, John H.	23325	Hicks, Earnest	30974
Hicks, Guy	23326	Hicks, Esther B.	30975
Hicks, Arlie B.	23327	Hider, Nancy	1728
Hicks, Owen	23328	Hider, Tieaskie	1729
Hicks, Claud	23329	Hider, Rachel	27109
Hicks, Mina A.	23330	Hider, Joe	18504
Hicks, Etta M.	23331	Hider, Jennie	18505
Hicks, Nellie	6179	Hider, Ned	30500
Hicks, Arch	6180	Hider, Tom	28450
Hicks, Robert L.	6788	Hider, Ella	28451
Hicks, J. Ida	6789	Hider, Daniel	28452
Hicks, William	6790	Hider, Joshua	20581
Hicks, Robert	6791	Higgins, Lydia E.	4891
Hicks, Harvey I.	6773 5793	Higgins, Isabel	28618
Hicks, Millard F.	7982	Higgins, Paul	28619

Name.	Roll No.
Higgins, Lillie O.	12136
Higgins, Nettie M.	12137
Higgins, Robert J.	12138
High, Sarah E.	32673
High, Eddie C.	32674
High, William J.	32675
Highland, Nellie	21895
Highland, Sarah	21896
Highland, William	21897
Highland, Margaret	21904
Highland, Lucy	21032
Highland, Patrick	26140
Highland, James	22058
Highsmith, Mary F.	9347
Highsmith, Myrtle A.	9348
Highsmith, Roy B. L.	9349
Highsmith, Cora E.	9350
Highsmith, Stella H.	9351
Highsmith, Viola	9352
Highsmith, Minta Z.	9353
Hightman, Henry	28103
Hilburn, Maggie	9110
Hilburn, Bertha A.	31955
Hildebrand, Julia E.	22920
Hilderbrand, Robert	30050
Hilderbrand, John	3969
Hilderbrand, Maggie	3970
Hilderbrand, Rolin	3971
Hilderbrand, Jesse	3972
Hilderbrand, Sisie	3973
Hilderbrand, Jennie	28592
Hilderbrand, Joe	28593
Hilderbrand, Nettie	4358
Hilderbrand, George	4440
Hilderbrand, Emma	23012
Hilderbrand, Moses	23013
Hilderbrand, Emma	23014
Hilderbrand, Reece	4458
Hilderbrand, Lelia	4459
Hilderbrand, William	4460
Hilderbrand, Thomas	4461
Hilderbrand, John	4462
Hilderbrand, Annie	4463
Hilderbrand, Daniel	4783
Hilderbrand, Brice	5923
Hilderbrand, Stephen	5924
Hilderbrand, Hooley	5925
Hilderbrand, Bullett	5926
Hilderbrand, John	5948
Hilderbrand, John H., Jr.	26995
Hilderbrand, Peggie	26996
Hilderbrand, Mary	26997
Hilderbrand, Samuel	7846
Hilderbrand, Fannie L.	7847
Hilderbrand, Benjamin J.	26478
Hilderbrand, Laura	26479
Hilderbrand, Lucinda	26480
Hilderbrand, Ezra	26481
Hilderbrand, Rosa	26482
Hilderbrand, Cicero	26483
Hilderbrand, Laura M.	26484
Hilderbrand, Benjamin D.	26485
Hilderbrand, Gracie L.	26486
Hilderbrand, Joseph	28719
Hilderbrand, Wallace	8101
Hilderbrand, John W.	9815
Hilderbrand, Joe	10237
Hilderbrand, Cherokee	10320
Hilderbrand, John	13286
Hilderbrand, James Franklin	27778
Hilderbrand, John	27779
Hilderbrand, Wallace S.	9816
Hilderbrand, Joseph	25410
Hilderbrand, Tookah	25411
Hilderbrand, Josie	25412
Hilderbrand, Mary	25413
Hilderbrand, Thomas	25414
Hilderbrand, Mike	25415
Hilderbrand, Elijah	17801

Name.	Roll No.
Hilderbrand, Nancy	17802
Hilderbrand, John	28395
Hilderbrand, William	29300
Hilderbrand, Maggie	16765
Hilderbrand, Mary E.	8102
Hilderbrand, Arch	18514
Hilderbrand, Tyer	18515
Hilderbrand, Ida	18853
Hilderbrand, Katie	16762
Hilderbrand, Susie	18854
Hilderbrand, Betsy	29082
Hilderbrand, Jodie	18865
Hilderbrand, Lucy	18866
Hilderbrand, Joe	18867
Hilderbrand, Maggie	18868
Hilderbrand, Linda	29083
Hilderbrand, Karlardee	30541
Hilderbrand, Lucy	30556
Hilderbrand, Jim	30557
Hilderbrand, Jennie	32302
Hilderbrand, John	19740
Hilderbrand, Annie	19741
Hilderbrand, Infant	30571
Hilderbrand, Luella	19814
Hilderbrand, Lillian Agnes	7848
Hilderbrand, Charles	28493
Hilderbrand, Sallie	28494
Hilderbrand, Lem	28501
Hilderbrand, Lizzie	20827
Hilderbrand, Jim	26271
Hilderbrand, Elizabeth	8370
Hilderbrand, Nancy Louettie	26998
Hill, Daisy	5263
Hill, Laura L.	5264
Hill, Donzolean	27482
Hill, Helen A.	27483
Hill, Eliza A.	27530
Hill, Rollin R.	7245
Hill, Nannie May	32254
Hill, Clara M.	7246
Hill, Clyde R.	7247
Hill, John H.	26436
Hill, Luetta E.	30138
Hill, Mamie E.	26437
Hill, Mintie	26438
Hill, Oliver M.	7340
Hill, Elmer M.	7341
Hill, Rebecca	8349
Hill, Bessie L.	8350
Hill, Annie E.	8351
Hill, Ivey M.	8352
Hill, Walter H.	8353
Hill, Donna B.	8354
Hill, Rachel	8452
Hill, Davis	8457
Hill, Fannie E.	8458
Hill, George R.	8459
Hill, James J.	8460
Hill, William T.	8461
Hill, Rachel	8462
Hill, John R.	8463
Hill, Hattie M.	10751
Hill, Robert L.	11407
Hill, Rachel B.	11408
Hill, Matilda A.	2116
Hill, Wauneta B.	2117
Hill, Maggie S.	13753
Hill, Paul E.	7342
Hill, Martha	29296
Hill, Effie M.	32801
Hill, Clora E.	32802
Hill, William Jasper	5265
Hill, Maria A.	8464
Hill, James W.	31021
Hill, Albert T.	31248
Hill, Rosa M.	31393
Hill, Dixie A.	31394
Hill, Jacob	31610
Hill, Jane	31678
Hill, Alonzo T.	31679
Hillen, Samantha	22243

Name.	Roll No.
Hillis, Fannie M.	13054
Hilton, Maudie	21998
Hinds, Henry E.	2979
Hinds, Ida L.	2980
Hinds, Claude	2981
Hinds, Robert F.	3024
Hinds, Ellie G.	3025
Hinds, Ina M.	3026
Hinem, James P.	3894
Hines, Frank	28605
Hines, Henry W.	28606
Hines, Roxianna	28701
Hines, Joseph	28702
Hines, Mary B.	28703
Hinton, Henrietta J.	27794
Hinton, Henry R.	27795
Hinton, Emma A.	27796
Hinton, Herbert T.	27797
Hinton, Hattie F.	27798
Hinton, William C.	27799
Hinton, Gulielma.	27800
Hiser, Martha E.	15544
Hiser, Daniel A. J.	15546
Hiser, Okey M.	15547
Hiser, Hugh F.	15548
Hiser, Olive	15549
Hiser, James D.	15550
Hiseley, Thomas	5448
Hitchcock, Ireneus D.	29459
Hitchcock, Sarah E.	29460
Hitchcock, Osborn	29461
Hitchcock, Timothy B.	7643
Hitchcock, Lucy J.	7644
Hitchcock, Charles D.	7645
Hitchcock, Willam I.	7646
Hitchcock, Edward O.	7647
Hitchcock, Zoe Dimple	7648
Hitchens, Frank	10653
Hitcher, Quatie	18001
Hitcher, David	18858
Hitcher, Betsy	18859
Hitcher, John	18860
Hitcher, Wilson	29106
Hitcher, Ned	20065
Hitcher, Peggie	20066
Hitcher, Sallie	20067
Hitcher, Charley	20068
Hitcher, Annie	20069
Hitcher, Cora	25813
Hobbs, Malzerine	3427
Hobbs, Thomas A.	3430
Hobbs, Belle	10752
Hobbs, Voet	10753
Hobbs, Hista	10754
Hobbs, Walter J.	3431
Hobb, Missouri A.	10990
Hobb, Jesse P.	10995
Hodge, Annie	25031
Hodge, Earnest	25032
Hodge, Richard	25033
Hoffman, Ruth	10469
Hoffman, James	10470
Hoffman, Allen	10471
Hoffman, Minnie	10472
Hoffman, Charles	10473
Hoffman, Ralph	10474
Hoffman, Ellen	12485
Hoffman, Clark	12486
Hogan, Sarah	22458
Hogan, John Z.	26414
Hogan, Laura A.	26415
Hogan, Ruth M.	26416
Hogan, John C.	26417
Hogan, Margaret M.	23544
Hogan, Graham	23545
Hogan, Mabel	23546
Hogan, Bertha T.	21650
Hogan, Karl H.	26418
Hogg, Oliver	2976
Hogg, John	2977
Hogner, Lucy	1731
Hogner, William	19597
Hogner, John	19605

Name.	Roll No.
Hogner, George	19613
Hogner, Annie	19614
Hogner, Joseph	19615
Hogner, Nancy	19616
Hogner, Mary	19617
Hogner, Aggie	29102
Hogner, Lizzie	20045
Hogner, Writer	20046
Hogner, Charlotte	20047
Hogner, Adam	20048
Hogner, George	20049
Hogner, Chennasse	25815
Hogner, Nellie	20956
Hogner, Clem	20957
Hogshooter, Charles	28966
Hogshooter, Jesse	15962
Hogshooter, Peggie	15963
Hogshooter, Rachel	15964
Hogshooter, Polly	15965
Hogshooter, Maud	15966
Hogshooter, Young-beaver	18609
Hogshooter, Sarah	18610
Hogshooter, Watt	18611
Hogshooter, Ed	18612
Hogshooter, Lucy	20376
Hogshooter, James	32062
Hogshooter, Mary	32063
Hogshooter, Contaky	32315
Hogshooter, Oo-ker-we-you	32316
Hogshooter, Oo-cha-latah	32317
Hogshooter, William	32910
Hogshooter, Oce	20791
Hogshooter, Emma	20792
Hogshooter, Joseph	20793
Hogshooter, Ida	30651
Hogshooter, Ada	30652
Hogshooter	20796
Hogshooter, Rufus	20797
Hogtoater, Sunday	17826
Hogtoater, Ainsy	17827
Hogue, Mary E.	22011
Hogue, Joseph C.	22012
Hohenstein, Sam	13131
Holden, Delilah	28644
Holder, Amanda	22980
Holderman, Mary C.	9831
Holderman, Pearl	9832
Holderman, Cornelia E.	10031
Holderman, Curtis E.	17549
Holderman, Dorthy L.	17550
Holderman, Theodore G. E.	17551
Holderman, Henry C.	17553
Holderman, Mary A.	17554
Holderman, Hilda Marie	17552
Holland, Margaret E.	603
Holland, Mary	604
Hollanu, Lou	605
Holland, Walter	606
Holland, Henry	607
Holland, Ruth	608
Holland, Lelah P.	609
Holland, Pleasant H.	703
Holland, Nancy	704
Holland, Thomas L.	705
Holland, Dennis W.	706
Holland, Lugie	707
Holland, Nancy Ann	708
Holland, Richard S.	761
Holland, Laura	762
Holland, Flora L.	763
Holland, Nancy	765
Holland, Henry S.	1158
Holland, Mary L.	1159
Holland, Alice	1325
Holland, Hattie E.	1372
Holland, James B.	1373
Holland, Robert H. F.	1374
Holland, Henry D.	1375
Holland, Thomas R.	1376

Name.	Roll No.	Name.	Roll No.
Holland, Felix N.	1553	Holmes, Woster	32310
Holland, Thomas E.	1554	Holmes, Jim	20650
Holland, Maggie M.	1555	Holmes, Ellen	20651
Holland, John A.	1556	Holmes, Fog	20652
Holland, Mary C.	1557	Holmes, Pigeon	20653
Holland, John	1981	Holmes, Oolskuntney	20654
Holland, Lydia	2109	Holmes, Stonewall	26224
Holland, Flora S.	2111	Holson, Sallie	32789
Holland, Noah S.	2344	Holt, Mary	713
Holland, Georgia A.	2345	Holt, Evaline	714
Holland, Florence L.	2346	Holt, William L.	789
Holland, Grace	764	Holt, Olea E.	790
Holland, Noah S., Jr.	22701	Holt, Earl	916
Holland, Lizzie	22702	Holt, Pearl	917
Holland, Isaac J.	2348	Holt, Thomas B.	918
Holland, Charles B.	22703	Holt, Nellie	27286
Holland, Loretta	22704	Holt, William	27287
Holland, Manuel J.	5169	Holt, Minerva	27288
Holland, Virgie C.	5170	Holt, Annie	28079
Holalnd, Arther E.	5171	Holt, Frances	28080
Holland, Minnie L.	5172	Holt, Daniel	3940
Holland, Fannie E.	5173	Holt, Mary E.	22938
Holland, Robert B.	5174	Holt, Tuxie T.	22939
Holland, Horace S.	5175	Holt, Jacob D.	22940
Holland, Gracie G.	5176	Holt, Nora	6576
Holland, Josephine	7123	Holt, John	6577
Holland, Benjamin N.	7124	Holt, Charles	6578
Holland, James McK.	7125	Holt, Queen V.	7049
Holland, Julia A.	7126	Holt, Walter L.	7050
Holland, Louvenie J.	7127	Holt, Melvie	7051
Holland, Mabel A.	1160	Holt, John	7052
Holland, William G.	10416	Holt, Naoma E.	7053
Holland, Rachel	10417	Holt, Rubie M.	7054
Holland, Jesse W.	10418	Holt, Emma	30277
Holland, Robert L.	10419	Holt, Charles	17409
Holland, Mary E.	11433	Holt, Don Ragin	26513
Holland, William H.	11434	Holt, Pollie	30683
Holland, John A.	11643	Holt, Jennie	30684
Holland, Ada	11644	Holt, Diana	30685
Holland, James D.	12300	Holt, Sarah	30686
Holland, Viola M.	7128	Holt, Lizzie	26512
Holland, Laura C.	12301	Hood, John	4352
Holland, Ada F.	12302	Hood, Lena	4353
Holland, Fox	12303	Hood, Vanda	4354
Holland, James C.	12304	Hood, John	4441
Holland, Minnie B.	24842	Hood, Mary	4442
Holland, John W.	27786	Hood, Charley	4443
Holland, William	27787	Hood, Lizzie	4444
Holland, Leonard	27788	Hood, Jennie	4445
Holland, Robert	27789	Hiod, James	4446
Holland, Maggie	27790	Hood, Kitty	4447
Holland, Carrie	27791	Hood, Steven	4448
Holland, Dora A.	27792	Hood, Maud	5114
Holland, Nancy M.	27793	Hood, Sterling	5570
Holland, Robert J.	28899	Hood, David	5584
Holland, Pleasant Jr.	16414	Hood, William D.	30358
Holland, Walter	32543	Hood, Bessie L.	30359
Holland, Francis L.	32544	Hood, Susie	17099
Hollemon, Martha S.	6981	Hood, Dennis	25894
Hollemon, Bulah	6982	Hoid, Lizzie	25895
Hollemon, Charles J.	6983	Hood, Susan	26895
Hollemon, Harvey M.	6984	Hood, Radford G.	26896
Hollemon, Henry C.	6985	Hood, Benjamin H.	26897
Hollemon, Claud	6986	Hood, Lenettie	26898
Hollemon, Jesse D.	6987	Hood, Cyrus C.	26899
Hollemon, Lenna M.	6988	Hood, Oscar	26900
Holley, Dora M.	11359	Hood, Dollie	26901
Holly, Ethel A.	11861	Hood, Hettie E.	32085
Hollis, Elzora	9419	Hooper, Robert A.	26720
Hollis, Effie E.	9420	Hooper, Roxie	26721
Hollis, Edna L.	9421	Hooper, Dewey	26722
Holmes, William	2862	Hooper, Nancy	27306
Holmes, William S.	2863	Hooper, John	32023
Holmes, Susie	25525	Hooper, Turkey	26746
Holmes, Sallie	26221	Hooper, Ailey	26747
Holmes, Edward	26222	Hooper, Caroline	26748
Holmes, Frankie	26223	Hooper, Cornelius	26749
Holmes, Simon	29094	Hooper, Rabbit	30532
Holmes, Alsie	19838	Hooper, Lucy	20603
Holmes, Mary	19839	Hooper, George	20604
Holmes, David	19840	Hooper, Lewis	20605
Holmes, Christie	19841	Hooper, James	20606
Holmes, Tassel	32309	Hooper, John	20655

Name.	Roll No.	Name.	Roll No.
Hooper, Lizzie	20656	Horsefly, Nannie	7563
Hooper, Luke	20657	Horsefly, John	19447
Hooper, Jack	20658	Horseskin, Mary A.	1366
Hopkins, Maud S.	30141	Horseskin, John	17785
Hopkins; Thomas A.	30142	Horseskin, Jane	18940
Hopkins, Virgil A.	18072	Horsley, Martha E.	7560
Hopper, Jennie	29777	Horton, Rhoda A.	10110
Hopper, Lena	28581	Horton, Laura M.	10113
Hopper, Lucy	19882	Horton, Emmett L.	10114
Hopper, Martin	20413	Horton, William A.	10115
Hopper, Nellie	20414	Horton, Benjamin F.	10116
Hopper, Mary	20415	Horton, Nancy Alice	10117
Hopper, Dick	20416	Horton, James	31614
Hopper, George	20417	Hosey, Mollie L.	12757
Hopper, Tom	20418	Hosey, Mary W.	12758
Hopper, Nancy	20419	Hosey, Charley A.	12759
Hope, Maud	21589	Hosey, Cora J.	12760
Hope, Delbert	21590	Hosey, Ralph V.	12761
Hopson, Clara H.	9031	Hosey, Joseph	18178
Horn, Thomas	2370	Hosey, Katie	18179
Horn, Clyde	2371	Hosey, Timmie	18180
Horn, John	2372	Hosey, Anna	18181
Horn, Minnie	29781	Hosey, Maggie	18182
Horn, Callie	29782	Hosey, Alsie	18183
Horn, Maud	29783	Hosey, Dan	18184
Horn, Josephine	30051	Hoskin, Ned	8052
Horn, William	3389	Hoskin, Nellie	8053
Horn, Rachel	3390	Hoskin, Ned Jr.	23898
Horn, Louisa	4331	Hoskin, Elijah	8054
Horn, John	4414	Hoskin, Dennis	8055
Horn, Samuel	5069	Hosmer, John T.	27468
Horn, David	5070	Hosmer, Beulah E.	27469
Horn, Lafayette R.	5890	Hosmer, Solomon	21940
Horn, Charles W.	27428	Hothouse, Blue	25982
Horn, Thomas W.	27429	Hothouse, Sallie	25983
Horn, Mattie S.	27430	Hothouse. Lucinda	25984
Horn, Susan M.	27431	Hothouse, Lydia	25985
Horn, Eliza J.	8415	Hothouse, John	32353
Horn, Dora M.	8416	Hothouse, Oce	32077
Horn, Maggie	8417	Hothouse, Sarah	21447
Horn, Charles T.	8418	Hothouse, Samuel	32358
Horn, George H.	8419	House, Martha	10579
Horn, Emma	9618	House, Robert L.	10580
Horn, Melvine G.	9619	House, Effie M.	10581
Horn, Pearl G.	9620	Houseberg, Kizzie	19536
Horn, Ben A.	9621	Houseberg, Lydia	19537
Horn, Fannie M.	5683	Houseberg, Warren B.	19538
Horn, Thomas M.	5686	Houseberg, Dora M.	19539
Horn, Robert L.	22077	Houseberg, Jack	19540
Horn, Sammie R.	5891	Houseberg, John	21318
Horn, George	27110	Houseberg, Lizzie Bell	21319
Horn, Narcie	32298	Houseberg, Bettie	21320
Horn, Sarah	20129	Houseberg, Johnson	21321
Horn, Thomas	20727	Houseberg, Robert	21322
Horn, Mary	20728	Houseberg, Annie	21323
Horn, George	25998	Housebug, Henry	2574
Horn, Narnie	25999	Housebug, Callie	2575
Horn, John	3393	Housebug, Ellen	2576
Horn, Nannie	26000	Houser, Maud B.	29800
Horn, Florence	1360	Houser, William T.	29801
Horne, James A.	30112	Housley, Sallie	6356
Hornbuckle, Mabelle	11993	Housley, Ruth	6357
Hornbuckle, Lydia M.	11994	Housley, Sidney E.	8166
Hornbuckle, William L.	11995	Housley, Mary E.	8167
Hornbuckle, Nettie	11996	Housley, Louisa R.	8168
Hornbuckle, Rebecca J.	21755	Housley, John M.	8169
Hornbuckle, Lee M.	21757	Housley, Kennie C.	8170
Hornbuckle, Viola E.	21758	Houston, Mack	28872
Hornbuckle, Lucinda	21729	Houston, Jackson	28873
Hornbuckle, Mamie F.	21730	Houston, Alex	28874
Hornbuckle, Nellie E.	21731	Houston, George	28875
Horner, Laura A.	29906	Houston, Ola	17622
Horner, Lillie	29907	Houston, Annie	18286
Hornett, Lucy	16400	Houston, Tom	25590
Hornet, Thompson	17966	Houston, Isaac	21337
Hornett, Lucinda	16252	Houston, Annie	21338
Hornett, Daniel	16248	Houston, Nellie	30693
Hornett, Jennie	16249	Houston, Sallie	30694
Hornett, Charley	16250	Houston Charley	21404
Hornett, Sarah	16251	Houston, Jesse	21339
Hornett, Wilson	16399	Howard, George Anna	292
Horsefly, James	7561	Howard, George S.	293
Horsefly, Airey	7562	Howard, Clarence T.	294

Name.	Roll No.	Name.	Roll No.
Howard, Montie M.	295	Hubbard Thomas	14224
Howard, Emily	819	Hubbard, Allen	14225
Howard, Josephine L.	820	Hubbard, Corrilla	14226
Howard, Frank S.	1460	Hubbard, Sellar I.	14227
Howard, Katherine	1461	Hubbard, Craig T.	14228
Howard, Manila Dewey	1462	Hubbard, Moses	25182
Howard, Rebecca E.	2304	Hubbard, Ada	25183
Howard, George A.	4660	Hubbard, Daniel	25184
Howard, Walter L.	4661	Hubbard, Thomas	25185
Howard, Lydia M.	4662	Hubbard, Gracie	25186
Howard, William W.	4663	Hubbard, Nevermore	25187
Howard, Lillie M.	4664	Hubbard, Charlotte	16262
Howard, Enos Q.	4665	Hubbard, William	16263
Howard, John	4666	Hubbard Nancy J.	16264
Howard, Josephine	4667	Hubbard Thomas	16265
Howard, Mollie	4723	Huckleberry, Margaret	17247
Howard, Bernice M.	4915	Huckleberry, Margaret	
Howard, Anna M.	4916	C.	17248
Howard, Allie R.	29993	Huckleberry, Florence	17249
Howard, Bessie B.	29994	Huddlestun, Etta M.	13967
Howard, George A.	6146	Hudgpetch, Bertha	11880
Howard, Louie	6147	Hudgpetch, D. Floyd	11881
Howard, Nancy L.	296	Hudson, Mamie Z.	8388
Howard, Annie A.	297	Hudson, Etta M.	8389
Howard, Charles P.	12258	Hudson, Alpha B.	8390
Howard, Helen	12271	Hudson, Sylvanus B.	9708
Howard, Cicero J.	14598	Hudson, James S. P.	30208
Howard Russell R.	17287	Hudson, Lucy A.	30209
Howard, Percy P.	17485	Hudson, Lewis B.	13093
Howard, Emily	22088	Hudson, Amanda	13094
Howard, Corbett	22089	Hudson, Samuel W.	13229
Howard, Pearl	22090	Hudson Katie C.	13230
Howard, Charles F.	12259	Hudson, Norma E.	26718
Howard, Ella B.	26323	Hudson, Mabel R.	26719
Howard, Sallie E.	26324	Hudson, Stella E.	30364
Howard Lucil	21849	Hudson, Nancy M.	13231
Howdeshell, DeWitt C.	24172	Huey, Agnes	5756
Howdeshell, Jennie	24173	Huggins, Dora	30313
Howdeshell, DeWitt	24174	Huggins, Charley	30314
Howdeshell, William L.	9477	Huggins, William O.	30316
Howdeshell, Ralph	9479	Hughes, Maggie	123
Howdeshell, James T.	9480	Hughes, Grace A.	1639
Howdeshell, Grace	9481	Hughes, Louis C.	1640
Howdeshell, Minie J.	24175	Hughes, George H.	1641
Howdeshell, Mary	9482	Hughes Jennie L.	1642
Howe, Hattie	24313	Hughes, James H.	1643
Howe, Dora A.	24314	Hughes, Leroy S.	1650
Howe, Joseph O.	24315	Hughes, Henry	1651
Howe, Hugh	24316	Hughes, Ida	29621
Howell, Mary I.	3664	Hughes William C.	1819
Howell, Bessie	3665	Hughes, Mollie A.	1820
Howell, Carrie	3666	Hughes, William	3870
Howell, Prudie	3667	Hughes Nancy A.	3871
Howell, Lilly	3668	Hughes, Richard T.	3872
Howell, Eliza	8304	Hughes, Benjamin F.	3873
Howell, Charles M.	8724	Hughes, Monie	3874
Howdeshell, William H.		Hughes, Mary	3875
M.	9478	Hughes, Eliza	27452
Howell, Gracie P.	8725	Hughes, William	7026
Howell, Carl J.	8726	Hughes, Addie S.	14127
Howell, Flossie F.	8727	Hughes Jane	30337
Howell, Ella B.	10239	Hughes, George W.	30338
Howell, May	12038	Hughes, Eliza J.	30339
Howell, Rebecca	12043	Hughes, William P.	30340
Howell, Emmett L.	12044	Hughes, Annie M.	30341
Howell, James S.	10240	Hughes, George M.	14855
Howell, Herbert F.	3669	Hughes, Charles	15302
Howerton, Josephine	7692	Hughes, Ellen	15303
Howerton Did	7693	Hughes, Nathaniel	15304
Howerton, Levy	7694	Hughes, William	15305
Howerton, Sabra A.	7695	Hughes, James	15306
Howerton, Sarah J.	8561	Hughes, Rachel	15307
Howerton, Erva Otis	8570	Hughes, John	15308
Howie, Mary	8917	Hughes, John R.	15440
Howland Susan E.	4229	Hughes, Ellen	15621
Howland, William	4230	Hughes, Margaret	15622
Howland, Susan	4231	Hughes, Mattie	15623
Howland, John	16873	Hughes, David	16523
Hoyt, Florence	6247	Hughes, Carrie	16524
Hoyt, Sudie	6248	Hughes, Mary A.	17029
Hubbard, Thomas	5148	Hughes, Charles L.	17030
Hubbard Mary	5238	Hughes, Betsy	17031
Hubbard, Mose J.	6132	Hughes, George W.	17032

Name.	Roll No.
Hughes, Bryant	17625
Hughes, Jane	29053
Hughes, Lizzie	7024
Hughes, George	20363
Hughes, Linnie	20364
Hughes, Lewis	31686
Hughes, Clifford	31687
Hughes, Ada B.	31688
Hultt, Susan R.	29466
Hulbert, Susan E.	14624
Hulbert, Clarence E.	14625
Hulbert, Nannie R.	14626
Hulbert, Noris B.	14627
Hully, John	20513
Hully, Webster	32548
Hulsey, Josephine	8678
Humanstriker, William	20450
Humanstriker, Sakie	20451
Humanstriker, Lizzie	20452
Humanstriker, Margaret	20453
Humanstriker, Joe	20454
Humanstriker, Jennie	20469
Humanstriker, Mary	20476
Humanstriker, Kate	20477
Humberd, Margaret P.	4286
Hummingbird, Walter	27455
Hummingbird, Charlotte	27456
Hummingbird, Swimmer	27457
Hummingbird, Maggie	27458
Hummingbird, Stand	27459
Hummingbird, Jesse	27460
Hummingbird, Jacob	6303
Hummingbird, Lizzie	28640
Hummingbird, Richard	6304
Hummingbird, Dick	28012
Hummingbird, Mary	28013
Hummingbird, Flint	7442
Hummingbird, Susan	7443
Hummingbird, Annie	7444
Hummingbird, Daniel	32014
Hummingbird, Lucy	32015
Hummingbird, Annie	20192
Hummingbird, Nancy	26146
Hummingbird, Johnson	32016
Hummingbird, Randolph	17562
Hummingbird, Walter	17563
Hummingbird, George	17564
Hummingbird, Henry	17565
Hummingbird, Homer	17566
Hummingbird, Lester	17567
Hummingbird, Chester	17568
Hummingbird, Henry	26736
Hummingbird, Jacob	17934
Hummingbird, Jennie	17935
Hummingbird, Emma	17936
Hummingbird, Ella	17937
Hummingbird, Joshua	17938
Hummingbird, Lizzie	17939
Hummingbird, George	17940
Hummingbird, Wilson	17941
Hummingbird, Carrie	6305
Hummingbird, Gus	17942
Hummingbird, Isaac	19203
Hummingbird, Mandy	19204
Hummingbird, William	19205
Hummingbird, Rider	19206
Hummingbird, Josie	19207
Hummingbird, Stann	19208
Hummingbird, Rogers	19209
Hummingbird, Lizzie	19210
Hummingbird, Isaac, Jr.	19211
Hummingbird, Thompson	20188
Hummingbird, Nancy	20189
Hummingbird, Jim	20190
Hummingbird, Drinker	20191
Humphrey, David	10084
Humphrey, William	10085
Humphrey, John	10086
Humphrey, Fannie M	10087
Humphrey, David A.	10088
Humphrey, Artis G.	10089
Humphrey, Sadie E.	10090

Name.	Roll No.
Humphrey, James	11608
Humphrey, John	12488
Humphrey, Perry	12489
Humphrey, Eddie	12490
Humphrey, Ray	12491
Humphrey, Dora	21834
Humphry, Cora	21500
Humphry, William L.	21501
Humphry, Mattie C.	21502
Hungry, Soldier	18533
Hungry, Cahweyhawca	18534
Hungry, Betty	18535
Hungry, Sallie	18601
Hungry, Ben	21369
Hungry, Jennie	21370
Hungry, Peggie	21371
Hunt, Ruth	7414
Hunt, Nathaniel G.	7415
Hunt, Joseph T.	7416
Hunt, Nancy L.	7417
Hunt, Lucile M.	7418
Hunt, Charles J.	8787
Hunt, Bates J.	8788
Hunt, Daisy B.	9386
Hunt, Evan R.	9387
Hunt, Hellen E.	9388
Hunt, Laura M.	26694
Hunt, Mary E.	14378
Hunt, Julia B.	14379
Hunt, Etta	26757
Hunt, Lucile	26697
Hunter, Charles	21956
Hunter, Crecie L.	22074
Hunter, Lizzie	20478
Hunter, Lucretia G.	27860
Hunter, James S.	27861
Hunter, Maud	31700
Hunter, Florence I.	31701
Hunton, Julia A.	17110
Hunton, Lorena	17111
Hunton, Mary A.	17112
Hunton, John W.	17113
Hurd, George	24630
Hurd, Ivan	24632
Hurd, Leroy	24633
Hurd, Ethel W.	24634
Hurd, James F.	24635
Hurst, Sylvester	24468
Hurst, Walter E.	24469
Hurst, John W.	24470
Hurst, Annie M.	24471
Hurst, Maggie E.	24472
Hurst, Grace A.	24473
Hurst, Sarah E.	24474
Hurst, Nellie G.	24475
Hurst, John R.	11430
Hurst, Rachel	11431
Hurst, Albert J.	11432
Hussey, Clyde C.	32692
Hutchens, Edna M.	28275
Hutchings, Lydia	16979
Hutchins, Nettie	11254
Hutchins, Lou W.	11255
Hutchins, Bluford R.	11256
Hutchins, Ual R.	11257
Hutchins, Ethel D.	11258
Hutchins, Charlotte	25206
Hutchins, Daikie	30353
Hutchinson, Harry R.	22045
Hutchinson, Edith F.	22046
Hutton, Thomas	28338
Hyatt, Martha	25347
Hyatt, Lorena	25348
Hyatt, Erastus	25349
Hyatt, Edwin	25350
Hyatt, John V.	25351
Hyde, Charles M.	16317
Hyder, Sarah	17783
Hyder, Rachel	19989
Hyles, David	3694
Hyles, Maud	3695
Hyles, Alonzo	3696
Hyles, Ethel L.	3697
Hyles, Myrtle	3698
Ice, Robin	19339

Name.	Roll No.	Name.	Roll No.
Ice, Lewis	19833	Jack, Eliza	3869
Ice, Lucinda	19834	Jack, Nancy	4043
Ice, George	32340	Jackson, Emma L.	3638
Ice, Nannie	20864	Jackson, Cherokee J.	4325
Ice, Sullateskee	20865	Jackson, Walter W.	4326
Ice, Johnson	32732	Jackson, Mary	5469
Ickelbury, Nancy	27894	Jackson, Honor L.	5470
Ickelbury, Nellie	27895	Jackson, Lulu M.	5471
Ickelbury, Pearl	27899	Jackson, Henry	5472
Ingram, Albert T.	30124	Jackson, Cornelius	5473
Ingram, John M.	12693	Jackson, John	7205
Ingram, Amanda N.	12694	Jackson, Viola	7206
Ingram, Georgia L.	12695	Jackson, Bertha M.	7207
Ingram, Roy B.	12696	Jackson, James A.	7208
Ingram, John M., Jr.	12697	Jackson, Lillie M.	9441
Ingram, Anna L.	12698	Jackson, Lee R.	9442
Ingram, Ralph F.	12699	Jackson, Edith S.	9443
Ingram, David M.	13725	Jackson, Arminta J.	9669
Ingram, Emma L.	15265	Jackson, Hugh E.	9670
Ingram, Clue	15848	Jackson, Balma L.	9671
Inlow, Roy W.	28139	Jackson, Otto R.	9672
Inlow, William H.	13412	Jackson, Leona E.	9673
Inlow, Thomas J.	13413	Jackson, Pet	9882
Inlow, Elmira	25050	Jackson, Annie M.	17305
Inlow, Susan	25051	Jackson, Susan E.	17307
Inlow, Myrtle	25052	Jackson, Dora	18035
Inlow, William S.	25053	Jackson, Toshie A.	31837
Inlow, Carrie	25054	Jackson, Lela	9883
Inlow, Edgar	26905	Jackson, Bulah M.	9884
Inlow, Sylvester	26906	Jackson, Caroline	27711
Inlow, Henry H.	26907	Jackson, Lizzie	26579
Inlow, Nancy	26908	Jackson, Mary M.	10791
Irons, Minnie	17636	Jackson, George W.	10792
Ironside, Beverly	8912	Jackson, Edward W.	10793
Ironside, Eva	8913	Jackson, Bryant B.	11469
Ironside, Elmer	8914	Jackson, Julius L.	11869
Ironside, Robert	9045	Jackson, William B.	11870
Ironside, Birdie	9046	Jackson, Lila	11871
Ironside, Robert P.	9047	Jackson, Clara	2790
Ironside, Collin C.	9463	Jackson, Sarah L.	14205
Ironside, Harry T.	9464	Jackson, Charles C.	14206
Ironside, George R.	12983	Jackson, Mary M.	14207
Ironside, Charles T.	29413	Jackson, George A.	14208
Ironside, Bessie L.	8915	Jackson, Jesse	14209
Irvin, Carrie	4085	Jackson, Emma	14320
Irvin, Sedalia	4086	Jackson, Joe V.	14322
Irving, Joe	23121	Jackson, Mary	7209
Irving, Watie	23123	Jackson, Andrew	15690
Irving, Roy	23124	Jackson, Mattie I.	15691
Irving, Grover	23125	Jackson, Henrietta	17304
Irving, George	23127	Jackson, William E.	17306
Irving, Fannie	23128	Jackson, Flora	17713
Irving, Emery	23129	Jackson, Ella	31831
Irving, Stella	23130	Jackson, Osie	31838
Irving, William	23131	Jackson, Lizzie	31839
Irving, Samuel	23126	Jackson, Jessie	31840
Isaacs, William	29651	Jackson, Ray	31841
Isaacs, Agent	29652	Jackson, Clyde	31842
Isaac, John	21333	Jackson, Jesse C.	32535
Isbell, Jennie L.	8951	Jackson, Minnie L.	32536
Isbell, Ollie M.	8952	Jackson, Swimmer	17715
Isbell, Morris F.	9018	Jackson, Ruth	15692
Isbell, Charles T.	9019	Jackson, Esther R.	11873
Isbell, Levi P., Jr.	9020	Jackson, Ice	28491
Isbell, Thomas J.	16837	Jackson, Still	20769
Israel, Margarett	10332	Jackson, Minnie	25904
Israel, Walter	10333	Jackson, Jesse	25905
Israel, Della	10334	Jackson, Tom	25906
Irsael, Wiliam M.	14982	Jackson, John	25907
Israel, Sallie	14983	Jackson, Susie	25908
Israel, Roy	14984	Jackson, Walter	25909
Israel, Chester E.	14985	Jackson, Sarah	32067
Israel, Rufus R.	14986	Jackson, Arlie	32334
Israel, Ella	14987	Jackson, Mollie	32335
Israel, David	15775	Jackson, Mattie C.	9674
Israel, Bessie M.	15776	Jackson, Cleo A.	9444
Israel, John	28382	Jackson, Sarah A. E.	24920
Israel, Phillip	28383	Jackson, Willie	31163
Israel, Mary	28384	Jackson, John	31260
Israel, Sarah	32570	Jackson, Lillie	31261
Israel, Loyd	32571	Jackson, Walter	31263
Israel, Ada	10335	Jackson, Edward	31265
Isreal, William	28563	Jacobs, Joanna	3623
Ivey, Augustus E.	28878	Jacobs, Ida G.	3624
Ivey, Julia A.	28879	Jacobs, Isaac A.	3625
Ivey, Ada	16728	Jacobs, George F.	3626

Name.	Roll No.	Name.	Roll No.
Jacobs, Wenona	3627	Jeremiah, William A.	4112
Jacobs, Mary B.	3628	Jeremiah, Jesse J.	4113
Jacobs, Willis B.	3629	Jeremiah, Riley V.	4114
Jacobs, Lizzie M.	4133	Jeremiah, Claudie E.	4115
Jacobs, Bulah	4134	Jimison, Mary E.	4553
Jacobs, Isaac W.	4135	Jimison, Clarance	4554
Jairrels, Maggie	4327	John, Mary	19574
James, Calvin G.	159	Johns, Sidney	5503
James, Tennessee A.	266	Johns, Thomas L.	5504
James, Clara Dell	267	Johns, Ollie	5505
James, Lula Bell	268	Johns, Joseph	5506
James, Jesse Larmar	270	Johns, Ella	5507
James, Claud Frank	271	Johns, Jennie	13225
James, Lorenzo D.	274	Johnson, Peggie	1355
James, Flora Lee	275	Johnson, Cora	1463
James, Clara Bell	276	Johnson, Martha A.	1504
James, Albert B.	277	Johnson, James B.	1505
James, Lucinda	27930	Johnson, Minnie L.	1506
James, Cherokee M.	278	Johnson, John H.	1507
James, Opal I.	279	Johnson, Margaret E.	1508
James, Mattie E.	511	Johnson, Jesse	1509
James, Zula G.	512	Johnson, Annie B.	1510
Jackson, James	31262	Johnson, Lura R.	1511
Jackson, Pearl	31264	Johnson, William O.	1799
Jackson, Andrew	31266	Johnson, Maggie	1822
James, Lola E.	513	Johnson, Joseph R.	1895
James, Buna J.	514	Johnson, William	1961
James, Leland D.	515	Johnson, Rebecca	2030
James, Martha L.	516	Johnson, Clint	2031
James, Frank W.	517	Johnson, Hugh	2032
James, Mamie	23113	Johnson, John T.	2033
James, Jeter	23114	Johnson, Betsy	27166
James, Wilburn C.	23115	Johnson, James M.	2244
James, Suvrina L.	7366	Johnson, Julia A.	2246
James, John J.	7367	Johnson, Alicy A.	2245
James, Rex E.	7368	Johnson, Joseph T.	2251
James, Ray B.	7369	Johnson, Maud	2252
James, Ethel N.	7370	Johnson, Winnie V.	2253
James, Max A.	7371	Johnson, Lillie E.	2254
James, Ruth G.	7372	Johnson, Grady	2255
James, Fairy F.	7373	Johnson, Callie M.	2256
James, Mary E. A.	9909	Johnson, John W.	2257
James, Houston W.	9910	Johnson, Elony	22936
James, Jesse P.	9911	Johnson, Joseph	4045
James, William R.	28240	Johnson, Mary	4046
James, Irvin	16844	Johnson, Joseph Jr.	4047
James, Homer	21943	Johnson, Ninnie	4048
James, Calvin D.	280	Johnson, Luella	4049
James, Solkin	19685	Johnson, Charley	4050
James, Peter	19765	Johnson, Leonidas R.	28599
James, Lena	19766	Johnson, George W.	4087
James, Fallingblossom	32308	Johnson, Daisy P.	4088
James, Silas	25874	Johnson, James D.	4089
James, Frank Harold	21187	Johnson, Georgia L.	4090
James, Joe	26083	Johnson, Myer	5603
James, Sarah	25290	Johnson, Isaac	5604
James, Jesse L.	28957	Johnson, Patsy	6820
Jamison, Vida E.	5804	Johnson, Charlotte F.	7234
Jarvis, Georgie	22005	Johnson, John L.	7235
Jarvis, Ellen	22006	Johnson, Berry H.	7236
Jeffrey, Daniel H.	16478	Johnson, Charlotte T.	7237
Jeffrey, Samantha	16479	Johnson, Thomas	32452
Jenkins, Amanda	26468	Johnson, Martha E.	7346
Jenkins, Walter L.	26469	Johnson, Rachel	8258
Jenkins, Fannie M.	26470	Johnson, Everett H.	9002
Jenkins, John H.	26471	Johnson, Annie B.	32001
Jenkins, Elias H.	26472	Johnson, Bertha M.	32002
Jenkins, Lizzie	26473	Johnson, Frances C.	9689
Jenkins, Lula	26474	Johnson, Jennie	10217
Jenkins, Dollie	26475	Johnson, Frank M.	10218
Jenkins, Rufus	26476	Johnson, Edith M.	10219
Jenkins, Otis	26477	Johnson, Roy R.	10220
Jenkins, Henry	26892	Johnson, Flora D.	10221
Jenkins, Maud M.	26893	Johnson, William	10440
Jenkins, Ollie A.	26894	Johnson, Leo	10441
Jennings, Eloise	3334	Johnson, Frederick W.	10631
Jennings, Landrum C.	8040	Johnson, Josephine	11050
Jennings, Jananna	30159	Johnson, Florence E.	11051
Jennings, Clara M.	8041	Johnson, Claud M.	11052
Jennings, Sallie	14660	Johnson, Ada L.	11053
Jennings, Lizzie	14659	Johnson, Howard B.	11054
Jennings, Nellie	14661	Johnson, Mina M.	26638
Jennings, George B.	14662	Johnson, Morris S.	26639
Jennings, Andrew	14663		
Jennings, Caroline C.	8042		
Jeremiah, Robert E.	3759		

Name.	Roll No.	Name.	Roll No.
Johnson, John W.	26640	Johnson, Frank	16467
Johnson, Robert H.	26641	Johnson, Jennie	16530
Johnson, Mary E.	26642	Johnson, Elizabeth	16531
Johnson, Arthur T.	26643	Johnson, Lula	16532
Johnson, Nellie	13300	Johnson, Dudley	16627
Johnson, Claude V.	13301	Johnson, Jennie	17220
Johnson, Minnie M.	13302	Johnson, Tom	17222
Johnson, Earnest E.	13303	Johnson, Susie	17223
Johnson, William R.	13304	Johnson, Lizzie	25519
Johnson, Joseph	13335	Johnson, John W.	25520
Johnson, Ella	13336	Johnson, Martha E.	25521
Johnson, Jesse	13337	Johnson, Oscar E.	25522
Johnson, Edward	13338	Johnson, Dannie L.	25523
Johnson, Fannie	13339	Johnson, Roy W.	25524
Johnson, Mamie A.	13689	Johnson, William B.	17465
Johnson, Maude	12555	Johnson, John W.	30439
Johnson, Rebecca C.	13697	Johnson, Napoleon B.	30440
Johnson, Calvin	13698	Johnson, Richard W.	30441
Johnson, Margaret	13699	Johnson, Mary J.	30442
Johnson, Emma	13700	Johnson, Fannie F.	30443
Johnson, Henry	13701	Johnson, Samuel M.	30444
Johnson, Cicero	13746	Johnson, Samuel S.	17828
Johnson, Allen	13747	Johnson, Jennie	17829
Johnson, Mollie E.	13748	Johnson, Nannie	17830
Johnson, Thomas	13749	Johnson, Rachel	17831
Johnson, Alonzo	13750	Johnson, Annie	32669
Johnson, Henry	13751	Johnson, John Anna	32670
Johnson, Bell	13752	Johnson, Gracie Milli-	
Johnson, Benjamin	13812	gan	32671
Johnson, Theodore L.	29910	Johnson, George W.	29352
Johnson, John B.	29911	Johnson, George T.	29353
Johnson, Jacob E.	29912	Johnson, Joseph H.	29354
Johnson, Luella J.	29913	Johnson, John B.	32414
Johnson, Oliver W.	29914	Johnson, William	21793
Johnson, John H.	28212	Johnson, Annie E.	10223
Johnson, George W.	14022	Johnson, Lafayatte Lee	32672
Johnson, Cherokee C.	14023	Johnson, Little	18294
Johnson, Alta L.	26716	Johnson, James	29067
Johnson, Beulah M.	14024	Johnson, Mary	29068
Johnson, Bessie	14025	Johnson, Albert	17832
Johnson, Samuel M.	14026	Johnson, Jessie M.	14154
Johnson, Robert E.	14027	Johnson, Betsy	18695
Johnson, Cherrie E.	14028	Johnson, Davis	18817
Johnson, Martha N.	14153	Johnson, Andrew	18818
Johnson, Rebecca A.	14191	Johnson, Levi	18819
Johnson, William A.	14192	Johnson, John	19093
Johnson, Robert E.	14193	Johnson, White	20168
Johnson, George J.	14194	Johnson, Jennie	20169
Johnson, James Z.	14195	Johnson, John	25938
Johnson, Martha J.	14196	Johnson, Lizzie	25939
Johnson, Henry A.	14197	Johnson, Going-to-rain	30680
Johnson, Joseph F.	14198	Johnson, Se-wee	30681
Johnson, Charles P.	14199	Johnson, Frank	20995
Johnson, William I.	14748	Johnson, Redcloud	21146
Johnson, Cynthia	14749	Johnson, Nellie	21147
Johnson, Ellis	14750	Johnson, John	21312
Johnson, Rebecca	14920	Johnson, Lucy	21313
Johnson, Mary	15490	Johnson, Darkey	21314
Johnson, Thomas J.	15537	Johnson, Ella	21315
Johnson, Betsy	15539	Johnson, Peggie	21316
Johnson, Sherman	15566	Johnson, Arlie	32351
Johnson, William E.	15570	Johnson, Redbird	32352
Johnson, Lucy	15571	Johnson, Alex	21340
Johnson, Thomas E.	15572	Johnson, Peggie	25989
Johnson, John A.	15573	Johnson, Thomas	21341
Johnson, Mary B.	15574	Johnson, Mary	21342
Johnson, George H.	15575	Johnson, Nancy	21343
Johnson, William M.	15576	Johnson, Clem	30695
Johnson, Cicero L.	15577	Johnson, Ora	30696
Johnson, Venie	15578	Johnson, David	29143
Johnson, Samuel M.	15579	Johnson, Annie	29144
Johnson, Lewis	15580	Johnson, Charles	21448
Johnson, Samuel N.	28299	Johnson, Martin	18696
Johnson, Sam	15945	Johnson, Blue	18815
Johnson, Kate	15946	Johnson, Wilda	18816
Johnson, Nora	16229	Johnson, Ray	21721
Johnson, David	16230	Johnson, May	21722
Johnson, Viola	16231	Johnson, David L.	15581
Johnson, Stephen	15527	Johnson, Amanda	29146
Johnson, Claude	25370	Johnson, Dave	32591
Johnson, Albert M.	25371	Johnson, William	32521
Johnson, Oscar	16465	Johnson, Lee	32807
Johnson, Myrtie M.	16466	Johnson, Alcy	22151

Name.	Roll No.	Name.	Roll No.
Johnson, Henry	31448	Jones, Leroy	7293
Johnston, Eliza E.	13773	Jones, Nancy A.	7900
Johnston, Harriet B.	13774	Jones, Levi	8483
Johnston, Frances F.	13775	Jones, Charner	8679
Johnston, Edmond F.	13776	Jones, Agnes	8680
Johnston, William P.	13779	Jones, Carrie	8681
Johnston, Julia	16608	Jones, Judge	26547
Johnston, Mary L.	16609	Jones, Joana	9714
Johnston, Vivian W.	16610	Jones, Emma P.	9715
Johnston, William P.,		Jones, Myrtle J.	9716
Jr.	16611	Jones, James W.	9717
Johnston, Jimmie B.	16612	Jones, Magnolia	26644
Johnston, Frances	25699	Jones, Mary E.	11470
Johnston, Albert	25700	Jones, Thomas C.	11471
Johnston, Charley	25701	Jones, Frank	11472
Johnston, Lizzie	27259	Jones, Raymon B.	11476
Johnston, Shasta	32118	Jones, Carrie M.	11859
Johnston, Ouita	32119	Jones, Quatie	12081
Johnston, William L.	32120	Jones, Mary C.	12106
Johnston, Samuel L.	2935	Jones, William M.	12107
Johnston, Mary L.	2936	Jones, Sarah F.	12108
Johnson, Clifford	32386	Jones, Raymond	7294
Johnson, Ross	9690	Jones, Mary J.	12938
Johnson, Viola	13702	Jones, Annie	13256
Johnston, Horace	2937	Jones, Hattie	13257
Johnston, Sarah O.	2938	Jones, Thomas	13258
Johnston, Johnsie D. A.	2939	Jones, Cherokee	13259
Johnston, George H.	2942	Jones, Evert	13260
Johnston, Stonewall J.	27256	Jones, Herbert	13261
Johnston, Mary J.	27257	Jones, Nellie E.	13878
Johnston, Thomas	27258	Jones, James A.	282
Johnston, John E.	3590	Jones, Mabel	10190
Johnston, Sallie	3591	Jones, Myrtle	10186
Johnston, Nancy	3600	Jones, Mead Bertie	
Johnston, Samuel	2940	Stela	12082
Johnston, Mamie L.	11867	Jones, Cade ,R.	12109
Johnstone, Nellie V.	31084	Jones, Menerva	14167
Johnstone, Leo H.	31085	Jones, Ethel G.	14172
Jolley, Lucy A.	24576	Jones, Lizzie	14804
Jones, Zona	281	Jones, Jennie	14805
Jones, William H.	384	Jones, Charles D.	14847
Jones, Minnie Ellen	385	Jones, Mary	14848
Jones, Martha Ann-	386	Jones, Rufus C.	14849
Jones, Maggie Daw	387	Jones, Franklin P.	14850
Jones, Ophelia S.	388	Jones, Margaret B.	14851
Jones, Andrew J. A.	390	Jones, Mattie	15321
Jones, Thomas	431	Jones, James B.	15332
Jones, James H.	432	Jones, Celia	16613
Jones, Joel Thomas	433	Jones, James W. T.	16614
Jones, Arvilla	434	Jones, Andrew J.	16615
Jones, Leroy A.	435	Jones, Nancy T. E.	16616
Jones, James T.	436	Jones, Virgil A. S.	16617
Jones, John L.	439	Jones, Sophia	16703
Jones, Coleman F.	440	Jones, Lola	16705
Jones, Samuel E.	441	Jones, Elizabeth	16706
Jones, Emily M.	528	Jones, Eurine C.	16707
Jones, Jennie	1837	Jones, John L.	27819
Jones, Everet W.	4749	Jones, Claud W.	15323
Jones, Ella	23186	Jones, Clyde H.	15324
Jones, Jerry	23187	Jones, Miles C.	32373
Jones, Helen	23188	Jones, William	26177
Jones, Oscar	27435	Jones, Sarah	26178
Jones, Cooie	27436	Jones, Henrietta	11288
Jones, Jesse	27437	Jones, Mima A.	438
Jones, Mary	6358	Jones, Ida A.	30826
Jones, John E.	6359	Jones, Gracie	23189
Jones, George O.	6360	Jones, Freddie	11477
Jones, Perry	6361	Jones, Alie	29085
Jones, William A.	6362	Jones, Johnson	18998
Jones, Alma J.	6363	Jones, Smith	29845
Jones, Mora	6364	Jones, Reader	19108
Jones, Ada	6594	Jones, Rose	19109
Jones, Vera	6595	Jones, Cobb	19110
Jones, Jean	6596	Jones, John	19111
Jones, Mary	6597	Jones, Maggie	19112
Jones, Rachel	6806	Jones, Mariah	19113
Jones, Thomas B.	6807	Jones, Jesse	19114
Jones, Polk	6808	Jones, Sevenstarr	19115
Jones, McGranville	6809	Jones, Ellis	19116
Jones, Lula D.	7154	Jones, Josiah	19350
Jones, Nancy	27546	Jones, Oo-loo-che	19351
Jones, Theodore	7291	Jones, Joe	19352
Jones, McKinley	7292	Jones, Jim	19353
		Jones, Celia	19354
		Jones, Joe	20170

Name.	Roll No.	Name.	Roll No.
Jones, Sam	20235	Jordan, Walter B.	13224
Jones, William	20236	Jordan, Sallie	29289
Jones, Tom	32330	Journeycake, Eliza A.	10837
Jones, Bird	25912	Journeycake, Robert J.	10838
Jones, Thomas	30656	Journeycake, Jesse D.	10839
Jones, Eva Pauline	32375	Journeycake, Isaac, Jr.	10840
Jones, Jessie P.	27547	Journeycake, Buster B.	10841
Jones, Flora	21571	Journeycake, Samuel H.	31398
Jones, Robert E.	30828	Journeycake, Joseph F.	31399
Jones, Nellie J.	11287	Journeycake, Cora L.	31400
Jones, Mary F.	25207	Journeycake, Adula M.	31401
Jones, James	32121	Judge, William	18963
Jones, Estelle	32122	Judge	21250
Jordan, Alice	1560	Judge, Betsy	21251
Jordan, Bert	1561	Judge, Katie	21252
Jordan, Henry	1562	Julian, Susan J.	15709
Jordan, Bruce	1563	Julian, William B.	15710
Jordan, Fannie	1564	Julian, Eva M.	15711
Jordan, Fairy	1565	Julian, Etta P.	15712
Jordon, Takey	3145	Julian, Edwin C.	17335
Jordon, Columbus	30049	Julian, Robert W.	17527
Jordon, John	3148	Jumper, Jack	27260
Jordon, Maybell	3149	Jumper, Mary	27261
Jordon, Amelia	3150	Jumper, Nannie	27262
Jordan, Samantha I.	3243	Jumper, Nick	25608
Jordan, Perry	30083	Jumper, Jennie	25609
Jordan, Katie	30084	Jumper, Nannie	32283
Jordan, James A.	4954	Jumper, Lucy	32284
Jordan, Delia P.	27030	Jumper, Pheasant	19762
Jordan, Madison	27031	Jumper, Anna	19763
Jordan, John D.	27032	Jumper, Chelawnucha	19808
Jordan, Watie B.	27033	Jumper,	19807
Jordan, Carrie B.	9233	Jumper, Shellbroke	19809
Jordan, Nannie E.	26582	Jumper, Sargent	19810
Jordan, Victoria M.	26583	Jumper, Esiah	30585
Jordan, Lucy	26584	Jumper, Ooyostah	30586
Jordan, Daisy	26585	Jumper, Sam	19923
Jordan, John H.	26586	Jumper, Annie	19924
Jordan, Myrtle E.	26587	Jumper, Hunter	19925
Jordan, Ruby M.	10251	Jumper, Chaweeyuka	19926
Jordan, John D.	10383	Jumper, Jesse	20803
Jordan, Joseph H.	10384	Jumper, Cora	31982
Jordan, William S.	10385	Jumper, Charlie	21006
Jordan, Ellen	13222	Jumper, Agnes	25954
Jordan, Clara	13223	Jumper, Jennie	21432
Jordan, Susie	14263	Justus, Ella J.	14550
Jordan, Lola E.	14264	Justus, Eliza B.	15020
Jordan, Lester L.	14265	Justus, William R.	15021
Jordan, Stella B.	14266	Justice, Lydia	20062
Jordan, Gertrude M.	14267	Justice, Watt	20063
Jordan, Martin M.	14268	Justice, Mintie	20064
Jordan, Andrew V.	14429	Justice, Betsy	20612
Jordan, Alexander V.	16784	Justice, Ollie	20613
Jordan, Alexander	17065	Justice, John	20629
Jordan, Robert L.	17138	Justice, George	28512
Jordan, Charley	25501	Kaiser, Catherine	23982
Jordan, Myrtle	26781	Kaiser, Milton	23983
Jordan, Vannie	26782	Kaiser, Isaac H.	23984
Jordan, John W.	29346	Kaiser, Mary L.	23985
Jordan, Tennessee J.	29347	Kaiser, Catherine	23986
Jordan, Dixie M.	29348	Kaiser, William	23987
Jordan, John B.	29349	Kaiser, Lila	23988
Jordan, Daisy L.	29350	Kaiser, Jeannetta	23989
Jordan, Robert O.	29351	Kaiser, Charles I.	23990
Jordan, Thomas J.	29284	Karney, Annie	6173
Jordan, Felix	29285	Karney, Mary A.	6174
Jordan, Mollie	29286	Karney, Austin L.	6175
Jordan, Jessie	29287	Karney, Maggie	6176
Jordan, John W.	29288	Karney, Frank O. D.	6177
Jordan, Robert E. L.	29290	Karney, William B.	6178
Jordan, Hattie	29291	Kar-lo-yate	25629
Jordan, Lee O.	29292	Kate, Nancy E.	28882
Jordan, William P. A.	29293	Kate, Maud M.	28883
Jordan, Dennis B.	29294	Kay, Angie	28782
Jordan, John C.	29338	Kay, Ora L.	28786
Jordan, Herbert R.	29339	Kay, William E.	28787
Jordan, Roy C.	29340	Kay, Lula M.	28788
Jordan, William O.	29599	Kay, Emma B.	28789
Jordan, Ruthy M.	29600	Kearns, Sarah E.	5065
Jordan, Mary	29601	Kearns, Thomas J.	5066
Jordan, Sallie	21394	Kearns, Fannie E.	5067
Jordan, Joseph L.	21395	Kearns, Katie M.	5068
Jordan, Johnathan D.	21396	Kearns, Susan V.	22099
Jordan, Evelina	21397	Kearns, Rutha J.	22102
Jordan, Tom Magruder	16785	Kearns, Pearlie	22103
Jordan, Claud	21466		

Name.	Roll No.
Keck, Eva R.	2664
Keck, Dora M.	2665
Keck, Clarence R.	2666
Keck, Floretta E.	2667
Keck, Bona	2668
Keeler, Frank	10232
Keeler, Joseph C.	26590
Keeler, Albert	26591
Keeler, Fred	26592
Keeler, Maud	26593
Keeler, Lillie A.	26594
Keeler, Pearl	26595
Keeler, William	10354
Keeler, Lula	10355
Keeler, Lela B.	10356
Keeler, Charles R.	10427
Keeler, Majora	10428
Keen, Nancy A.	10664
Keen, Albert F.	10665
Keen, Arnold P.	10666
Keen, James H.	10667
Keen, Cora S.	10668
Keen, John R.	10669
Keen, Ross K.	10670
Keen, Joel L.	10671
Keen, William A.	21714
Keen, Wilma P.	21715
Keen, Dora Olive	21716
Keener, Thomas	6163
Keener, Aggie	6164
Keener, Emma	14137
Keener, Levi	16087
Keener, Annie	16088
Keener, Robert	16090
Keener, Samuel	16091
Keener, Ella	16092
Keener, Mirtle	16093
Keener, Joseph	16487
Keener, Lewis	28999
Keener, Jennie	29000
Keener, Daniel	29001
Keener, White	29002
Keener, Carrie	17971
Keener, Charles	21271
Keener, Lucinda	21272
Keener, Lulu	21273
Keener, Austin	21275
Keener, Walter	21276
Keener, Rufus	21277
Keener, Alsie	21278
Keener, Jack	21409
Keener, Lizzie	21410
Keener, Chow-we-yuke	30709
Keener, George	21425
Keener, Sarah	21426
Keener, Johnson	21427
Keener, Lillie	21428
Keener, Jeff	21429
Keener, Nick	21430
Keener, Richard	21431
Keener, Evans	26006
Keener, William	18467
Keener, Lizzie	18468
Keener, Heavy	29079
Keener, Thomas	18469
Keener, Jennie	18470
Keener, Betsy	18471
Keener, Lila	18472
Keener, Mary	18473
Keener, Emily	29080
Keener, Betsy	18329
Keener, Johnson	18330
Keg, Charlotte	21464
Keith, James	22653
Keith, Katie	1982
Keith, Johnson	1983
Keith, Soldier	1984
Keith, Annie	27138
Keith, Matthew	12587
Keith, William F.	12592
Keith, Albert M.	12593
Keith, Paul	12594
Keith, Pearlie L.	12595

Name.	Roll No.
Keith, Reuben M.	12596
Keith, James G.	12598
Keith, Joel A.	12599
Keith, Victoria	16879
Keith, Gertrude	16880
Keith, John A.	16881
Keith, Lossie	16882
Keith, Dewey	16883
Keith, Veror Azzeleen	12597
Keith, Eria	16884
Keller, Annie D.	28674
Kell, Charles L.	1417
Kell, Parry C. L.	1418
Kell, Louisa	5830
Kell, James L.	13388
Kell, Susan C.	13389
Kell, Lewis P.	13390
Kell, Emma E.	13391
Kell, Bud T.	22104
Kelleam, Mary Q.	18042
Kelleam, Fannin	18043
Kelleam, Robert	18044
Kelley, Sarah A.	2137
Kelley, Sarah C.	2138
Kelley, George W.	2139
Kelley, Nola	2140
Kelley, Addie R.	2141
Kelley, Lillie M.	2142
Kelley, Floyd	2143
Kelley, Gertie	2144
Kelley, Homer	2145
Kelley, Mary A.	27356
Kelley, John D.	5723
Kelley, D. Buffington	5724
Kelley, Joel F.	5725
Kelley, Biddy A.	5726
Kelley, Wiley E.	5727
Kelley, Jackson	5728
Kelley, Ellen	5729
Kelley, Mattie L.	5730
Kelley, Joanna	5731
Kelley, Nettie	5732
Kelley, Edna	27974
Kelley, Rosey M.	7419
Kelley, Margaret E.	26463
Kelley, Earnest H.	26464
Kelley, Fannie M.	26465
Kelley, Clyde B.	26466
Kelley, Claude C.	7532
Kelley, Thomas	7823
Kelley, Eva I.	7824
Kelley, Willard	7825
Kelley, Bessie	7826
Kelley, Sabra E.	26467
Kelley, James T.	8047
Kelley, Lula N.	8738
Kelley, Pauline G.	8739
Kelley, Fred L., Jr.	8740
Kelley, George S.	8741
Kelley, Laura E.	28738
Kelley, Mary I.	28739
Kelley, William P.	9289
Kelley, Fannie V.	9290
Kelley, Lizzie L.	9291
Kelley, Lucinda	12122
Kelley, Lillie M.	9292
Kelley, John	15655
Kelley, Susan	15656
Kelley, Charles	15657
Kelley, Tinsie	15658
Kelley, James L.	15659
Kelley, Joel	15660
Kelley, Mary	15661
Kelley, Maud	15662
Kelley, Theodore E.	30450
Kelly, Frances J.	26245
Kelly, Maggie M.	5733
Kelley, Flora	20150
Kelly, Myrtle A.	22231
Kelly, William H.	22232
Kelly, Mamie D.	22233
Kelly, Susan E.	22292
Kelly, Minnie M.	22295

Name.	Roll No.	Name.	Roll No.
Kelly, Nainah	22296	Ketcher, John	28915
Kelly, Joseph E.	22297	Ketcher, Lucinda	28916
Kelly, Alba	587	Ketcher, Rowena	15515
Kelly, Cora	588	Ketcher, Ellis	15814
Kelly, Nellie	1204	Ketcher, Ellis	28986
Kelly, Ellen	4860	Ketcher, Harvey	28987
Kendall, Mollie J.	13529	Ketcher, Ruth	28988
Kendall, Frankie	13551	Ketcher, Minnie	28989
Kendall, Frosty	13552	Ketcher, Aaron	16947
Kennedy, Peggie	19528	Ketcher, Susie	16948
Kennedy, William R.	19529	Ketcher, Jesse Albert	16949
Kenney, Charles D.	10043	Ketcher, Richard	16973
Kenney, Amanda C.	10044	Ketcher, Hattie	16974
Kenney, Emmett H.	10045	Ketcher, Ollie	16975
Kenworthy, Elizabeth	10007	Ketcher, Carrie E.	16976
Kenyon, Daniel C.	27716	Ketcher, John	30451
Kenyon, George A.	32698	Ketcher, Sarah	26735
Kephart, Ruth E.	24678	Ketcher, Andrew	17709
Kepler, Cynthia E.	23652	Ketcher, Johnson	17717
Kepler, Andrew H.	23653	Ketcher, Alice	17718
Kepler, Blueford	11989	Ketcher, Susie	17719
Kerr, Fred A.	4955	Ketcher, Lee	17720
Kerr, Jesse J.	4956	Ketcher, Nancy	17721
Kerr, Ida	4957	Ketcher, Celia	17722
Kerr, John E.	4958	Ketcher, Isaac	17723
Kerr, Ada	4959	Ketcher, John	17916
Kerr, Blanche	4960	Ketcher, Claudie	1637
Kerr, Sarilda	4961	Ketcher, Maudie	1638
Kerr, William W.	4962	Ketcher, Dollie V.	16977
Kerr, Amy R.	4963	Ketcher, Cornelius	25604
Kerr, Frank	27358	Ketcher, Lydia	25605
Kerr, Fannie	27359	Ketcher, Claude	25606
Kerr, Kate	27360	Ketcher, Lula	25607
Kerr, May	27361	Ketcher, Richard	20018
Kerr, Jane	27362	Ketcher, Maggie	20019
Kerr, Annie E.	27363	Ketcher, Susie	20020
Kerr, Simpson B.	27364	Ketcher, Martha	20070
Kerr, Frank Jr.	27365	Ketcher, Green	20563
Kerr, Frederick	27366	Ketcher, Lizzie	20564
Kerr, Susan T.	9220	Ketcher, Patsy	18327
Kerr, Ollie M.	9221	Ketcher, Josie	18328
Kerr, Neville C.	17054	Ketchum, Samuel	8653
Kerr, Lucinda	17055	Ketchum, Eva A.	30966
Kerr, George L.	17056	Ketchum, William T.	30967
Kerr, Albert S.	17057	Ketchum, Ludie N.	30968
Kerr, John L.	17058	Ketchum, James W.	30969
Kerr, Mamie E.	17059	Ketchum, Herbert	31532
Kerr, William W.	17066	Ketchum, Mary G.	31533
Kerr, Lanexa J.	9405	Ketchum, Charles C.	31534
Kerr, Willie	9408	Ketchum, Annie A.	31535
Kerr, Ellen Bean	17060	Ketchum, Abraham W. Jr.	31536
Kerr, Nannie Bean	17061	Ketchum, Enoch Wesley	31537
Ketcher, George	893	Ketchum, Daisy	31671
Ketcher, Lee	894	Ketchum, Bertha	31672
Ketcher, Henry	895	Ketchum, Elmer	31673
Ketcher, Willie	896	Ketchum, Earnest	31674
Ketcher, Cornelius	897	Ketchum, Charles E.	32219
Ketcher, Jeff	1631	Ketchum, James S.	32220
Ketcher, Benjamin	1632	Ketchum, Clarance R.	3221
Ketcher, Joseph	1633	Ketchum, Joseph B.	32222
Ketcher, Katie	1634	Ketchum, Solomon	32528
Ketcher, Ollie	1635	Ketchum, Lewis	32529
Ketcher, John	1636	Ketchum, Elizabeth	32530
Ketcher, Emma	1743	Ketchum, Roy Elmer	32808
Ketcher, Anderson	27093	Kettle, John	4884
Ketcher, Rachel	27094	Kettle, Jennie	4885
Ketcher, Thomas J.	27095	Keyes, Mary O.	15338
Ketcher, Alta V.	27096	Keys, Levi	129
Ketcher, Nancy	27097	Keys, Viola W.	130
Ketcher, Robert E. L.	27098	Keys, Carrie M.	131
Ketcher, Linnie	27099	Keys, Herbert G.	132
Ketcher, Elmira	27100	Keys, Lester	133
Ketcher, Ellis	1825	Keys, Mandy C.	1340
Ketcher, Lucy	1826	Keys, Lorenzo D.	1341
Ketcher, Richard	1827	Keys, Bertha A.	1342
Ketcher, Ezekiel	1828	Keys, Samuel J.	22668
Ketcher, Sallie	1829	Keys, Samuel L.	22670
Ketcher, Moses	3578	Keys, Robert L.	22671
Ketcher, Levi	29467	Keys, Laura E.	22672
Ketcher, Key	28911	Keys, William F.	22673
Ketcher, Betsy	28912	Keys, Nettie M.	22674
Ketcher, Dennis	28913	Keys, James M.	22675
Ketcher, Henry	28914		

Name.	Roll No.
Keys, Lorenzo D.	2100
Keys, Mike G.	2113
Keys, Willie M.	2114
Keys, Neoma	2115
Keys, Charles L.	2378
Keys, Theodore S.	2379
Keys, Wilson C.	2380
Keys, Charles	2577
Keys, John A.	2578
Keys, David R.	2579
Keys, Lewis K.	3155
Keys, Lawrence T.	3156
Keys, David H.	3157
Keys, George	6100
Keys, Jesse	6101
Keys, Henry	6102
Keys, James M.	6873
Keys, Nancy J.	6874
Keys, Bluford A.	6875
Keys, Lizzie C.	6876
Keys, Lucy L.	7465
Keys, Lewis S.	8859
Keys, Bettie	8860
Keys, Campbell T.	8861
Keys, Leroy H.	10244
Keys, Albert L.	10245
Keys, Pearl	10246
Keys, Raymond W.	10247
Keys, Olive M.	10248
Keys, Myrtle	10249
Keys, Samuel H.	10394
Keys, Mary J.	11038
Keys, Carrie	11040
Keys, Minnie	11041
Keys, Charles C.	11042
Keys, Joanna	12437
Keys, Victoria M.	12988
Keys, Hoolie	12989
Keys, Nellie	12990
Keys, Lizzie	12991
Keys, Lillie	12992
Keys, Samuel	12993
Keys, Maggie	30352
Keys, Minerva	14689
Keys, Oce	14709
Keys, Letitia B.	14710
Keys, LeRoy	14711
Keys, Lillie M.	14712
Keys, John L.	14713
Keys, Grover C.	14714
Keys, Clint E.	14715
Keys, Claud L.	14716
Keys, Susan R.	14717
Keys, Levi	14763
Keys, Elizabeth	14764
Keys, Riley	14812
Keys, William H.	14813
Keys, Addie R.	14814
Keys, Fannie L.	14815
Keys, George M.	14816
Keys, Riley V.	14817
Keys, James T.	15493
Keys, Margaret E.	15494
Keys, James M.	15495
Keys, Mary J.	15496
Keys, John D.	15497
Keys, Walter S.	15498
Keys, Levi H.	15499
Keys, Munroe A.	15729
Keys, Lucinda J.	16499
Keys, Dennis B.	16813
Keys, W. R. W. C.	21493
Keys, R. W. M.	21494
Keys, M. T. W.	21495
Keys, G. A. L.	21496
Keys, L. D.	21497
Keys, W. C.	21498
Keys, O. G.	21499
Keys, Colbert E.	27828
Keys, Tolbert M.	27829
Keys, Samuel H.	26924
Keys, Mary E.	18125
Keys, Jananthy	22651
Keys, Dick	22652
Key, Sam	20636
Key, Mollie	20637

Name.	Roll No.
Keys, Stuart	21857
Keys, James H.	31419
Kidd, Wilburn	6225
Kidd, Cora	6226
Kidd, James C.	6227
Kidd, Rocksey	6228
Kidd, Garfield	32736
Kidd, Monroe M.	32737
Kidd, Ida M.	32739
Kidd, Nancy	32740
Kidd, Felix	32741
Kidd, Oscar	32742
Kidd, Richard	32743
Kidd, Blanchia	32744
Kiddy, Fannie	29411
Kiddy, Maggie	21554
Kiddy, George B.	21559
Kidwell, William	22869
Kidwell, Rosa	22890
Kidwell, Norah	22891
Kiefer, Sarah C.	134
Kiefer, Elizabeth	137
Kiefer, Emma	138
Killah-nigi, Jennie	27228
Killah-nigi, Sarah	27229
Killah-nigi, Thomas	27230
Killah-nigi, Maggie	27231
Killer, Annie	18946
Killer, Sallie	29847
Killer, Dave	29848
Killer, Crawler	29849
Killer, Jackson	19084
Killer, Ellen	19085
Killer, Nancy	19086
Killer, Georgeanna	19087
Killer, Alice	19552
Killer, Starr	19849
Killer, Rolin	21114
Killey, John	20703
Kimbrough, John	17475
Kimbrough, John L.	17476
Kimbrough, William A.	17477
Kimbrough, Woody Ray	17478
Kincade, Robert L.	1811
Kincade, Samuel L.	1812
Kincaid, Edward	17782
Kincaide, Francis	13356
Kincaide, William R.	13361
Kincaide, Charles W.	13362
Kincaide, James L.	13364
Kincaide, Andrew M.	13363
Kincaide, Martha. L.	13365
Kindred, Ellen M.	26390
Kindred, William A.	26391
Kindred, Mary M.	26392
Kindred, Samuel H.	26393
Kindred, John	26394
Kindred, Ella L.	26395
King, Sophia	2934
King, Katie	4161
King, Robert	4162
King, Jackson	4163
King, Jennie	6781
King, Carrie	6782
King, Alma E.	6783
King, Joel B.	6784
King, Jessie	6785
King, Lillie P.	6786
King, Catherine	9225
King, James	9226
King, Annie E.	9227
King, Rosa	9228
King, Oliver D.	9229
King, Thomas	9230
King, Patrick H.	9253
King, Etta R.	9647
King, Nellie J.	9648
King, George	11836
King, Viola	11837
King, John	30275
King, Mary	30276
King, Richard W.	12670
King, Malvina	12671
King, Benjamin C.	12672
King, James W.	12674

Name.	Roll No.	Name.	Roll No.
King, Benjamin C.	28852	Kinnison, John A.	9683
King, Abbie	28853	Kinnison, Paschal B.	9684
King, Edward C.	14019	Kinnison, May B.	9685
King, Aggie	14020	Kinnison, Eva T.	9686
King, Benjamin W.	14021	Kinnison, Omer E.	26576
King, Elizabeth	30329	Kiper, Charlotte	15150
King, Mary E.	30330	Kiper, Jennie M.	15151
King, Zella M.	30331	Kiper, Hester M.	15152
King, James A.	14665	Kiper, Cassa E.	15153
King, William A.	14666	Kirk, John	22395
King, James A., Jr.	14667	Kirk, William	22396
King, Richard E.	14668	Kirk, William	792
King, Benjamin T.	14669	Kirk, Laura	793
King, Sarah J.	14671	Kirk, Samuel	794
King, Susie	15055	Kirk, Della	795
King, Ulysses S.	16396	Kirk, John	796
King, Parker C.	21521	Kirk, Rebecca	797
King, Francis	21522	Kirk, Rosa	798
King, James W.	29274	Kirk, Floyd	799
King, Rosa L.	29275	Kirk, Ruth K.	5886
King, Hallie D.	29276	Kirk, Cyrus R.	5917
King, Catherine	32803	Kirk, Semanthia E.	5918
King, Joseph W.	32189	Kirk, George J.	5919
Kingfisher, Annie	18191	Kirk, Quinn D.	5921
Kingfisher, Tooniah	18192	Kirk, Viola	5922
King, Charley	29679	Kirk, Susie	6897
King, Tom	29680	Kirk, John	12862
King, James	29681	Kirk, Maud	12863
King, Sam	29682	Kirk, Jesse	12864
King, Nancy	29683	Kirk, Bell	12865
King, Susie	29684	Kirk, Ellen	12866
King, Nancie	9231	Kirk, Francis M.	15722
King, Henry	6787	Kirk, Susanna	15839
King, Jane	31466	Kirk, Charlotte M.	15840
Kingfisher, West	6287	Kirk, Samuel	15842
Kingfisher, Car-lau-nur-		Kirk, Asbury	15844
ski	6289	Kirk, Ezekiel P.	15845
Kingfisher, Chulio	6290	Kirk, Albert	15846
Kingfisher, James	10149	Kirk, Robert	15841
Kingfisher, Lizzie	10150	Kirk, William P.	21581
Kingfisher, Blackfox	14337	Kirk, Francis M.	12867
Kingfisher, Polly	14338	Kirk, Jane	6899
Kingfisher, Israel	14339	Kirk, Isaac Jefferson	800
Kingfisher, Goingsnake	14340	Kirkscey, Irene	3935
Kingfisher, Susan	14341	Klaus, Alice	27021
Kingfisher, Nellie	14642	Klaus, Robert Jr.	27022
Kingfisher, Claud	14643	Klaus, Annie	27023
Kingfisher, John W.	17256	Klaus, William H.	26555
Kingfisher, Cora	17257	Klaus, Charlotte	26556
Kingfisher, Fannie	17258	Klaus, Jesse H.	26557
Kingfisher, Maggie	17259	Kneeland, Fannie R.	4911
Kingfisher, Willis	17260	Kneeland, Harry R.	4912
Kingfisher, Ida	17261	Kneeland, Louie G.	4913
Kingfisher, Susie	14342	Kneeland, Herbert	4914
Kingfisher, Tom	18656	Knight, Benjamin	27292
Kingfisher, Margaret	18657	Knight, Betsy	27293
Kingfisher, Louella	18658	Knight, Morris F.	8146
Kingfisher, Joe	18653	Knight, Thomas M.	8324
Kingfisher, Lizzie	18654	Knight, Robert D.	8519
Kingfisher, Polly	29837	Knight, Robert F.	8520
Kingfisher, Mary	29838	Knight, Grover C.	8521
Kingfisher, Clark	29839	Knight, William D.	8522
Kingfisher, Minnie	18655	Knight, Rachel J.	28728
Kingfisher, Nakie	29841	Knight, Fannie M.	28729
Kingfisher, Philip	19369	Knight, Joseph S.	9164
Kingfisher, Jennie	19370	Knight, Henry S.	9943
Kingfisher, Mary	19371	Knight, Herman	16760
Kingfisher, Joe	19372	Knight, Caroline	18305
Kingfisher, Lewis	19373	Knight, Benjamin	19972
Kingfisher, Frosty	30538	Knight, Arlie	19973
Kingfisher, Sam	30539	Knight, Starr	19974
Kingfisher, Watie	19484	Knight, Mary	19975
Kingfisher, Susan	19485	Knight, Susie	19976
Kingfisher, Mollie	19486	Knight, Bird	20014
Kingfisher, Skake	30464	Knight, Mary	20015
Kingfisher, James	32643	Knight, Gertrude	20016
Kinney, Eliza	31449	Knight, William	20074
Kinnison, Mary V.	9493	Knight, Walker	20075
Kinnison, Arthur B.	9495	Knight, Lila	20076
Kinnison, Austaphine C.	9679	Knight, Rosa	20077
Kinnison, Lenora A.	9680	Knight, Robin	20078
Kinnison, Joseph D.	9681	Knight, Benjamin	20121
Kinnison, Lizzie V.	9682	Knight, Aggie	20122

Name.	Roll No.	Name.	Roll No.
Knight, Ada	20123	Lacey, William D.	32920
Knight, Polly	20125	Lacey, Shelley M.	32921
Knighten, Cornelia J.	28205	Lacey, Miles L.	32922
Knighten, William C.	28206	Lacey, Ezekiel M.	32923
Knighten, Telitha L.	28207	Lacey, Jesse Franklin	32924
Knighten, Elsie J.	28208	Lacey, Martha E.	32925
Knightkiller, Zeke	17903	Lacy, Sam	18869
Knipe, Nellie	31178	Lacy, Nannie	18870
Knipe, Lila	31179	Lacy, Linnie	30522
Kobel, Corrie F.	2923	Lacy, Cornelius	28457
Koch, Annie E.	12551	Lacy, Nannie	20918
Koehler, John H.	5	Lacey, Lizzie	26159
Koehler, Annie E.	7	Lacy, Emma	25626
Koehler, Margaret	8	Ladd, Nettie	10133
Koehler, Elizabeth	9	Ladd, Percy H.	10134
Koehler, George W.	10	Ladd, Sadie D.	10135
Koehler, Alice	11	Ladd, Roy	10136
Koehler, William B.	12	Ladd, Essie M.	10137
Koehler, Charles R.	21587	Ladd, Grace	16825
Kolpin, Eliza	14056	Ladd, Delma O.	16826
Kolpin, Leon	14057	Ladd, Mary J.	26794
Kolpin, Augusta	14058	Ladd, Burnett A.	26795
Kolpin, John P.	29921	Ladd, Henry E.	26796
Krebs, Theresa C.	21680	Ladd, James D.	26797
Krebs, John R.	21681	Ladd, Tula M.	26798
Krigbaum, Jane	21780	Ladd, Clara L.	26799
Krigbaum, James A.	21781	Ladd, Mattie P.	26800
Kuder, Cora M.	24367	Ladd, Burris O.	26803
Kuder, Winrow E.	24368	Lafon, Sarah	9496
Kuder, Cora B.	24369	Lafon, Amos F.	9497
Kuhn, Eliza	9997	Lafon, Claud	9498
Kuhn, Clara M.	9998	Lafon, Flossie M.	9499
Kuhn, Rubie B.	9999	Lafon, Essie E.	9500
Kuhn, William L.	10000	Lafon, Mayes	9501
Kuhn, Mary Jane	13663	Lafon, Beverly	9503
Kumpe, John	2722	Lafalier, Ambrose	9504
Kumpe, Eliza	2723	Lafon, Clark	9502
Kumpe, Charlie A.	2732	Lafalier, Homer	9828
Kumpe, George C.	2849	Lafalier. Louis	9829
Kumpe, Carl B.	2850	Lafalier, John	9830
Kumpe, Mood E.	2851	Lahley, Mose	21060
Kumpe, Lyle T.	2852	Lahaley, Dakie	21061
Kyle, Addie R.	16734	Lain, Lydia M.	29927
Kyle, James H.	16735	Lain, Delpha O.	29928
Kyle, Maggie F.	16736	Lain, Rean	29929
Kyle, Charles F.	16737	Lamar, Mabel	152
Kyle, Daisy	16738	Lamar, Jessie	153
Kyle, Polly T.	16739	Lamar, Lucius	154
Kyle, Robert V.	16740	Lamar, Maud	155
Kyle, Burk	16741	Lamar, Nettie	156
Kyle, Enos B.	16742	Lamar, Mildred	157
LaBoyteaux, Mollie	542	Lamar, Frankie	158
LaBoyteaux, Willie Gray	543	Lamon, Mattie E.	5317
LaBoyteaux, Hutton	544	Lamon, Mary E.	5318
LaBarge, Ida M.	30106	Lamb, Frank A.	23216
LaBarge, Maud S.	30107	Lamb, Willie	23217
LaFallier, Clarence	27756	Lamb, Sylvannus K.	23218
LaFallier, Cora	28757	Lamb, May B.	25279
LaFallier, Frank J.	9931	Lamb, Andrew J.	25280
LaFallier, Harvey	9932	Lamb, Ella M.	25281
LaHay, Joseph M.	24655	Lamb, Ruth	25282
LeHay, John F.	24657	Lamb, William	25283
LaHay, Maggie R.	24658	Lamb, Mabel Jewel	25284
LaHay, Helen M.	24659	Lamm, Florence E.	32450
Lacie, Adam L.	1377	Lamm, Mary I.	32451
Lacie, Jennie A.	1378	Lamar, Jesse S.	7374
Lacie, Silas W.	1379	Lamar, Vivin U.	7375
Lacie, Rufus V.	1380	Lamar, Paden M.	7376
Lacie, Charlotte C.	1381	Lamar, James E.	8396
Lacie, Ellen L.	1382	Lamar, James R.	9954
Lacie, Iona	1383	Lamar, Charles E.	10005
Lacie, Mollie	15974	Lamar, Eddie	17757
Lacy, Addie	3898	Lamar, Annie E.	29186
Lacy, Mattie	29463	Lamar, Frank	29187
Lacy, Minnie	29464	Lamar, Vauda	29188
Lacey, Scott	8898	Lamar, Maudie	29189
Lacey, Ancy	8899	Lamar, James R.	29190
Lacie, Jennie	16417	Lamon, Malvina	5319
Lacey, James	26225	Lambert, John	10913
Lacey, Henry	26226	Lamascus, Annetta	17418
Lacey, Susan F.	26227	Lamascus, Bertha Ella	17419
Lacey, Jincy	18209	Lane, Henry	4098
Lacey, John D.	32918	Lane, Martha E.	225
Lacey, Josiah	18575	Lane, Henry Keefer	228

Name.	Roll No.	Name.	Roll No.
Lane, Goldie Myrtle	229	Landrum, William	8477
Lane, Rachel	22279	Landrum, Charles F.	8785
Lane, Alfred	22280	Landrum, Samuel	9074
Lane, Delora	22281	Landrum, Nellie	27627
Lane, Lenora	22282	Landrum, Edward	9093
Lane, Rosa M.	22283	Landrum, Johnson	9147
Langley, Lock	804	Landrum, Catherine	9148
Langley, Milly M.	22398	Landrum, Nellie J.	9149
Langley, Mary M.	22399	Landrum, Clifton L.	9150
Langley, Joseph H.	22400	Landrum, Stephen E.	9151
Langley, Alice A.	22401	Landrum, Mary I.	9152
Langley, John W. D.	951	Landrum, Ada M.	9153
Langley, Sarah R. L.	952	Landrum, Cicero M.	9160
Langley, Joseph O.	953	Landrum, Ada	9255
Langley, Minnie E.	904	Landrum, Elizabeth	9256
Langley, Jesse R. W.	955	Landrum, Hiram T.	10026
Langley, Robert R.	957	Landrum, Jesse V.	10027
Langley, Charley B.	958	Landrum, Roxie	10028
Langley, Western F.	959	Landrum, Susan	12474
Langley, Lock Jr.	961	Landrum, Elias Mc.	13837
Langley, Zachary T.	967	Landrum, Nana	13838
Langley, Charles O.	969	Landrum, David S.	13839
Langley, Susan J.	970	Landrum, Elias Mc. Jr.	13840
Langley, Marion J.	974	Landrum, Margaret M.	13841
Langley, Charles O.	975	Landrum, Charlotte J.	17556
Langley, Eva E.	976	Landrum, Hiram T.	17557
Langley, Samuel B.	27953	Landrum, Sallie G.	17558
Langley, Clarence B.	27954	Landrum, Alice W.	17559
Langley, William F.	22529	Landrum, James P.	17560
Langley, Ophelia W.	27076	Landrum, John A.	17561
Langley, Clarence F.	27077	Landrum, Janie	29230
Langley, Jesse H.	27078	Landrum, Lola M.	29231
Langley, William H.	27079	Landrum, Beulah A.	29232
Langley, Sidney J.	22577	Landrum, Arkansas C.	7122
Langley, Joseph	22578	Landrum, Osa L.	6825
Langley, Alice	22579	Lane, Narsona	8908
Langley, Lock	22580	Lane, Marsh C.	8909
Langley, Ollie	22581	Lane, Vernon W.	8910
Langley, William J.	22582	Lane, Maud	13515
Langley, Lillie J.	22583	Lane, Estella	13516
Langley, Amos	27281	Lane, Ethel L.	13517
Langley, Olly	27282	Lane, James G.	13518
Langley, Lizzie	27283	Lane, Lilian D.	12313
Langley, Ned	27284	Lane, George Floyd	32607
Langley, Levi	27285	Lane, Thomas L.	31592
Langley, James E.	5859	Lane, Rose E.	31593
Langley, Sallie	5860	Lane, Gordon F.	31594
Langley, Susie	5861	Lane, Andrew D.	31595
Langley, George	5862	Land, Deloid	9582
Langley, Ella	5863	Land, Joseph	9593
Langley, Jimmie	27555	Land, Houston E.	9594
Langley, John	28781	Land, William H.	9595
Langley, Charles T.	11398	Land, Susan E.	9596
Langley, Orin L.	27752	Land, Roxie M.	9597
Langley, Lucinda	12275	Land, Joseph G.	9598
Langley, Alexander	28797	Land, Pearl McC.	11421
Langley, Maggie	28798	Land, Stewart McC.	11422
Langley, Lot	30291	Lands, Dottie	30730
Langley, Kittie	30292	Lannom, Zora C.	10192
Langley, Zachery T.	977	Lannom, Camille	10193
Langley, Noah	28895	Lannom, Portia	10194
Langley, Hattie L.	28896	Lannom, Redcloud	10195
Langley, Audie E.	956	Lannom, Zora	10196
Langley, William J.	16628	Lanning, Ida M.	15925
Langley, Mary E.	960	Lanning, Lelia	15926
Langley, John C.	22584	Lansford, Nannie E.	17062
Landrum, Thomas	6794	Lansford, Rastie	17063
Landrum, Benjamin C.	6821	Langford, Caroline	18028
Landrum, Roxie M.	6822	Landers, Callie	21957
Landrum, Thomas E.	6823	Landers, Bertha	21958
Landrum, Bailey B.	6824	Landers, William H.	21959
Landrum, James K.	7120	Landers, Gracie	21960
Landrum, Hiram W.	7121	Largen, Sallie	1483
Landrum, Benjamin S.	23913	Largen, Mary E.	1484
Landrum, Pansy	23914	Largen, William J.	1485
Landrum, Serena M.	23915	Largen, John T.	1486
Landrum, Lonia O.	23916	Largent. Andrusha	21864
Landrum, Margaret E.	23917	Large, William C.	7820
Landrum, Benjamin S., Jr.	23918	Large, Eunice M.	23873
		Large, Grace L.	23874
Landrum, Cherokee	23919	Large, Benjamin F.	8031
Landrum, Allison	23920	Large, Claude A.	8032
Landrum, Clinton	23921	Large, Bert F.	8033

Name.	Roll No.	Name.	Roll No.
Larry, William	28656	Leach, Chulio	30689
Larry, Nellie	28657	Leach, Chuwee	30690
Larry, Cora	28658	Leach, David	29136
Larry, James	23491	Leach, Ella	29137
Larry, John	23492	Leaf, Jesse	29006
Larry, Luie	23493	Leaf, Sallie	29007
Larry, William	27488	Leaf, Nannie	29008
Lassley, Joanna	4136	Leaf, Jennie	29009
Lassley, Cecil Malcolm	4137	Leaf, Vennie	29010
Lasley, Nancy P.	11356	Leaf, John	16829
Lasley, Joseph V.	11358	Leaf, Jennie	19101
Lasley, Charles H.	21492	Leaf, Malinda	19306
Lasley, Sarah	19315	Leaf, Mary	19307
Lasley, Thomas J.	32894	Leaf, Peggie	25748
Lasley, Martha (now Smith)	32895	Leaf, Jim	19562
Laster, Nancy	27603	Leaf, John	19960
Latta, Felix	16849	Leaf, Nancy	19961
Latta, Mary F.	16850	Leaf, Lizzie	32311
Latta, Felix	25418	Leaf, Eli	32312
Lattimore, Mary	2749	Leaf, Peggy	19988
Lattimore, Calvin	2750	Leaf, Tom	20032
Lattimore, Samuel	2751	Leaf, Nancy	20033
Lattimore, Ezekiel S.	3130	Leaf, Getup	20034
Lattimore, Samuel M.	3131	Leaf, Ella	20035
Latty, Mary E.	30356	Leaf, Gaino	20036
Latty, Alice	30357	Leaf, Isaac	20037
Latty, Louvenia	22093	Leaf, Root	20038
Latty, Mary J.	22094	Leaf, Oolskawney	20039
Latty, Rachel	22095	Leaf, Nellie	20646
Latty, Betsy	22096	Leaf, Mary	20647
Latty, Fannie	22097	Leaf, Adam	20648
Laughlin, Nancy J.	11800	Leaf, Josiah	20683
Laughlin, James G.	11801	Leaf, Lydia	20684
Laurence, Rebecca J.	28693	Leader, Lucinda	17194
Laurence, Forest Lee	28694	Leader, Joe	17195
Laurence, Elbert R.	28695	Leader, David	17196
Lawrence, Lucy E.	23308	Leader, Ruth	17225
Lawrence, George C.	23309	Leader, Polly	17229
Lawrence, William A.	23310	Leader, Edward	17230
Lawrence, Bluie	13988	Leader, Peggy	17231
Lawrence, Augustus A.	28868	Leader, Andrew	17232
Lawrence, John Byas	32638	Leader, Charles	17233
Lawson, Roberta E.	31608	Leader, Jesse J.	28352
Lawrence, John W.	32917	Leader, Claud J.	28353
Layne, Eyou W.	13759	Leader, John	28354
Layne, Julian E.	13760	Leader, Joseph M.	28355
Layne, Viola C.	13761	Leader, William	17197
Layne, Laurinda E.	13762	Leader, Nancy Rebecca	28356
Layne, Bessie L. T.	13763	Leatherman, Lou	7534
Leach, Samuel	26970	Leatherman, Susan L.	7535
Leach, John R.	6137	Leatherman, Bessie O.	7536
Leach, Johanna R.	6138	Leatherman, Blanche M.	7537
Leach, William M.	6139	Leatherman, Wilmer A.	7538
Leach, Lee E.	6140	Leathers, Callie	28583
Leach, Ann	6141	Ledford, Saphronia	1547
Leach, Oo-ha-loo-gi	27993	Ledford, Samuel L.	1550
Leach, Cheyoker	27994	Lee, Lydia	1278
Leach, Arnela	27995	Lee, Levi	1279
Leach, John W.	11568	Lee, Addie	1280
Leach, Annie E.	11569	Lee, Mary M.	2198
Leach, Jemima	17145	Lee, Lela M.	2199
Leach, William B.	17146	Lee, Snowden L.	2200
Leach, Jefferson F.	17147	Lee, Ambrose E.	2201
Leach, Katie	17148	Lee, James A.	2202
Leach, John A.	17149	Lee, Oliver R.	2203
Leach, Peggie	17150	Lee, Beulah E.	2204
Leach, Mary	19581	Lee, Calvin,	2810
Leach, Ellen	19583	Lee, Martha	2811
Leach, Phillip	19979	Lee, Hannah	2812
Leach, Thompson	20182	Lee, Johnanna	2813
Leach, Oniwaki	20183	Lee, Robert	2814
Leach, Henry	20184	Lee, Walter	2815
Leach, Tom	20185	Lee, Lafayette	3391
Leach, Watt	20186	Lee, Leola	3392
Leach, Martin	20187	Lee, David M.	3552
Leach, French	21198	Lee, Mary E.	3553
Leach, Peggie	21199	Lee, Lizzie M.	3554
Leach, Ah-che-ner-ster	21200	Lee, Lou Emma	3555
Leach, Arleach	21201	Lee, Flossie E.	3556
Leach, Sampson	21202	Lee, Frank E.	3557
Leach, Takey	21203	Lee, Washington	3558
Leach, Cah-teh-yah	30688	Lee, Maudie M.	3559
		Lee, John	3406
		Lee, John Jr.	3407
		Lee, Walter	3408

Name.	Roll No.
Lee, Lizzie	3409
Lee, Robert E.	3707
Lee, Roy E. -	22909
Lee, Willie Z.	22910
Lee, Robert E.	3814
Lee, Lou V.	22924
Lee, Maude	22925
Lee, Audry E.	22926
Lee, Jewel	22927
Lee, Austin	3865
Lee, Amelia A.	5092
Lee, Ether	5093
Lee, Lawrence	5094
Lee, Willie	5095
Lee, Carrel E.	5843
Lee, Ola J.	5844
Lee, Lou	24017
Lee, Everet R.	24018
Lee, Laura A.	9325
Lee, Evert S.	9326
Lee, Montie L.	9327
Lee, Martin F.	9328
Lee, Rieff A.	9329
Lee, France Eller	9330
Lee, Daisy	12789
Lee, Lillie	28140
Lee, John F.	12790
Lee, Freddie E.	22928
Lee, Carrie	14375
Lee, Sallie	29753
Lee, Nellie	15179
Lee, Wayne	15180
Lee, Loyd	15181
Lee, Frances E.	16057
Lee, Almon	16058
Lee, Elizabeth	16468
Lee, Felix	17836
Lee, Walter	21717
Lee, Crossland	18138
Lee, Narcissa	18139
Lee, Clarence E.	14377
Lee, Mary	18965
Lee, Emma	18966
Lee, Lucinda	18989
Lee, Esther	25761
Lee, Isaac	19678
Lee, Luculla Lilian	17837
Lee, Julius P.	4320
Lee, Albert	21560
Lee, John	32889
Leerskov, Nancy	2466
Leerskov, Andreas	2467
Leerskov, Nelson N.	2468
Leerskov, William N.	2469
Leerskov, Jackson N.	2470
Leerskov, Mary N.	2471
Leerskov, Melvina N.	2472
Leerskov, Rachel N.	2473
Leerskov, John T.	16426
Leforce, Sallie	24184
Leforce, Emma G.	9100
Leforce, Fannie M.	9654
Leforce, James L.	9655
Leforce, Flossie M.	9656
Leforce, Sarah L.	9657
Leforce, Rachel A.	9658
Lehr, Mary	14008
Lehr, Queen	14010
Leigh, Rachel	14251
Leigh, Mamie	14252
Leigh, Arthur	14253
Leigh, Langford	14254
Leigh, Floyd	14255
Lemaster, Joseph	22235
Lemaster, Mary J.	22236
Lemaster, Fredrick G.	22237
Lemaster, Leo Alexander	22238
Lemaster, William	298
Lemaster, Narcissa	377
Lemaster, Curtis	378
Lemaster, Elizabeth	379
Lemaster, Alice May	380
Lemaster, Nelie	381
Lemaster, Jessie	382
Lemaster, Edward	610

Name.	Roll No.
Lemaster, Victoria E.	611
Lemaster, George E.	612
Lemaster, Oatha P.	613
Lemaster, John Adair	22239
Lemaster, Narcissa B.	21791
Lemons, Leslie W.	30113
Lemons, Roy V.	30114
Lenoir, Mary O.	13056
Lennon, Florence S.	29522
Lennon, Florence C.	29523
Lennon, John E. E.	29524
Lenox, Fannie	31843
Lenox, Birtie E.	31844
Lenox, Myrtle	31845
Lenowisha, Lizzie	31095
Leno, Rosie	31202
Leno, Grant	31309
Leoser, John H.	13795
Leoser, Callie	13813
Leoser, Walter S.	13823
Leoser, William T.	13871
Leoser, Susan	13872
Lephew, Robert E.	17109
Lephew, Henry	18226
Lephew, Charles	28342
Lerskove, Nellie	15053
Lester, Lula P.	16
Lesley, Fannie	2759
Lesley, Robert L.	2760
Lesley, Bertha L.	2761
Lesley, Elby F.	2762
Lesley, Ester C.	2763
Lesley, Julian W.	2764
Lesley, David E.	2765
Lesley, Bonnie M.	2766
Lessley, Thomas F.	2767
Lessley, Sarotha A.	3218
Lessley, Iantha P.	3219
Lessley, William E.	3220
Lessley, Burnell	3221
Lessley, Buena V.	3222
Lessley, Mollie F.	2768
Lester, Julia B.	11241
Lester, Alfred L.	11244
Lessley, Samuel C.	3223
Levi, Charley	25589
Levi, John	18436
Levi, Dianna	18437
Levi, William	32279
Levi, Adam	21053
Lewis, Amanda	4836
Lewis, Effie	4837
Lewis, George M.	23606
Lewis, Joanna	8017
Lewis, Lorena	8018
Lewis, Esther	13536
Lewis, Richard H.	13537
Lewis, Edward E.	13538
Lewis, Dena B.	29371
Lewis, Ida	29372
Lewis, Virginia N.	29373
Lewis, James	30858
Lewis, Nannie	30859
Lewis, Jefferson	30860
Lewis, Runabout	30861
Lewis, David	30862
Lewis, Bird	30863
Lewis, Thompson	30864
Lewis, Jacob	30865
Lewis, Jennie	30867
Lewis, John	30868
Lewis, Hattie	30869
Lewis, Frank H.	30866
Lewis, Margaret Elizabeth	21858
Lillard, Andrew J.	28974
Lillard, Zacariah	16071
Lillard, Ellen	16072
Lillard, William	16073
Lillard, Charles	16074
Lindsey, Nettie R.	662
Lindsey, Jesse H.	663
Lindsey, Johnnie	664
Lindsey, Thomas	665

Name.	Roll No.	Name.	Roll No.
Lindsey, Robert	666	Littlejohn, Charles J.	25504
Lindsey, Margarett A.	853	Littlejohn, John	18298
Lindsey, Jessie N.	854	Littlejohn, Benjamin	29138
Lindsey, Annie M.	855	Littlejohn	21238
Lindsey, Hattie	6098	Littlejohn, Jennie	21239
Lindsey, Edna	23345	Littlejohn, Levi	21240
Lindsey, Mariah L.	6665	Litle, Havana M.	7817
Lindsey, Gordon B.	6666	Little, Lucile	30160
Lindsey, Virginia L.	6667	Little, Elizabeth	8252
Lindsey, Clyde E.	6668	Little, Claudia J.	8253
Lindsey, Flora E.	6841	Little, Frank	8953
Lindsey, Annie R.	23468	Little, Joseph C.	27686
Lindsey, William A.	7814	Little, William M. Jr.	11664
Lindsey, Lizzie R.	7815	Littletom, Pete	30174
Lindsey, Rosa N.	27661	Little, Katie	31175
Lindsey, Laura I.	27662	Little, Ray	31176
Lindsey, Very M.	27663	Littledave, Ike	29688
Lindsey, Joe C.	11812	Littledave, Betsy	29689
Lindsey, Northrup H.	12045	Littledave, Isaac	29690
Lindsey, Mary	30417	Littledave, Alex	29691
Lindsey, William H.	30418	Littledave, Johnson	29692
Lindsey, Edward A.	30419	Littledave, Dick	29693
Lindsey, Ida L.	30420	Littledave, Eliza	29694
Lindsey, Frances J.	30421	Littledave, Annie	29695
Lindsey, James D.	30422	Littledave, Frank	18513
Lindsey, Henry G.	30423	Littledave, Dave	29508
Lindsey, Harris	30424	Littledave, William	29700
Lindsy, Elizabeth J.	5842	Littledave, Nancy	29701
Lincoln, Lela A.	22330	Littledave, Charley	29702
Lincoln, Florence K.	22331	Littledave, Emma	29703
Lincoln, Robert	18570	Littledeer, Sam	18379
Lincoln, Aggie	25602	Liver, Thomas	3358
Lincoln, Nannie	30508	Liver, Eliza	3359
Lincoln, Arcenie	30509	Liver, Lizzie	3360
Linder, Perine	22768	Liver, Felix	3361
Linder, Owen L.	22769	Liver, Susie	3362
Linder, Martha A.	15275	Liver, Martha	3363
Linder, Hiram V.	15377	Liver, Chulio	18366
Linder, Charlie W.	15378	Liver, Eliza	18367
Linder, John R.	15393	Liver, Taylor	18368
Linder, Julius C.	15394	Liver, Katie	18369
Linder, Hiram W.	15395	Liver, Emma	18370
Linder, Annie E.	15396	Liver, Mary	18371
Linder, William R.	15397	Liver, Jennie	18917
Linder, Cinderella	15398	Liver, John	19021
Linder, John R. Jr.	15399	Liver, Jackson	19028
Linder, Richard	16661	Liver, George	20404
Linder, Inez	16662	Liver, Bettie	25649
Linder, Ira A.	15380	Liver, Joe Martin	25650
Linder, Cairl R.	15400	Liver, John	27056
Linscott, Ellen	23550	Liver, Lydia	27057
Linscott, Odell	23551	Liver, Ben	27058
Linscott, Joseph A.	23552	Liver, Lula	27059
Linscott, Callie J.	23553	Liver, Lizzie	27060
Linscott, John W.	23554	Liver, John Jr.	27061
Linscott, Walter T.	23555	Liver, Thomas	27062
Linscott, Frank E.	23556	Liver, Blaine	30132
Linn, William T.	14633	Livingston, Sarah	12276
Linn, Bessie C.	14634	Livingston, Alfred	12278
Linn, Lucinda B.	21669	Livingston, Lonnie	12279
Linn, John W.	21670	Livingston, Robert	12280
Linn, Columbus G. W.	21011	Lizzard, Lizzie	19534
Lipe, John C.	10981	Lizzard, Susie	19532
Lipe, DeWitt	11274	Lloyd, Eliza J.	12492
Lipe, Mary E.	11275	Lloyd, Albert L.	12493
Lipe, Lola V.	11500	Lloyd, Robert L.	12494
Lipe, Nannie E.	11503	Lloyd, William T.	12495
Lipe, Maggie E.	11710	Lloyd, Maggie E.	12496
Lipe, Beulah	11711	Lloyd, Nancy R.	12497
Lipe, Clarke C. Jr.	11712	Lloyd, Hazel G.	12498
Lipe, Clarence	11713	Lloyd, Rachel M.	12504
Lipe, Herman V.	12063	Lloyd, Clarence L.	12505
Lipe, Mattie D.	12064	Lloyd, Laura B.	12506
Lipe, John G.	12177	Lloyd, Rosa B.	12507
Lipe, S. Lulu	12178	Lloyd, Pansy B.	12508
Lipe, Flora F.	12179	Locust, Sandy	27211
Lipe, Ada C.	12180	Locust, Henry	27212
Littlejohn, Narcena A.	1618	Locust, John	27213
Littlejohn, Felix E.	1619	Locust, Katie	27214
Littlejohn, Ella L.	2063	Locust, Maggie	3701
Littlejohn, Catherine	2753	Locust, Jesse	5618
Littlejohn, Charles P.	17255	Locust, Ocie	5619
Littlejohn, William J.	25503	Locust, Frank	5620

Name.	Roll No.	Name.	Roll No.
Locust, Martha E.	5621	Longbird, John	28898
Locust, William	5622	Longbird, Fannie	28573
Locust, Mike	5623	Longtail, Abraham	7622
Locust, Ida	17848	Longtail, Amanda	7623
Locust, Minnie	17851	Longtail, Albert	7624
Locust, Jackson	19260	Longtail, Annie	7625
Locust, Susie	19261	Longtail, Rebecca	7626
Locust, Abraham	19262	Longtail, Charles	7627
Locust, Ross	19263	Longtail, Sophronia	7628
Locust, Luke	19264	Longtail, Ninnie	7629
Locust, Johnson	20437	Longtail, Josephine	7630
Locust, Susie	20438	Longtail, Minnie	7361
Locust, James	21054	Longtail, Barney	7845
Locust, George	21112	Longtail, Willie	7632
Locust, Jess	21164	Longbone, Willie	31172
Locust, Lewis	29316	Longbone, Anna	31173
Locust, John	32823	Longbone, Emmett	31174
Locust, Jennie	32824	Longbone, Silas	31197
Locut, Fish	25751	Longhone, Caroline	31198
Locut, Quakie	25752	Longbone, George	31199
Locut, Ned	25753	Longbone, Roy	31200
Locut, Peggie	19533	Longbone, Jesse	31201
Locut, William	20532	Longbone, Ray	31316
Locker, Richard M.	30772	Longbone, James P.	31404
Locker, Lola R.	30773	Longbone, Stella E.	31405
Locker, Dallas C.	30774	Longbone, Susie	31406
Locker, John S.	30775	Longbone, Frank	31575
Loflin, Charles M.	12898	Longbone, Susan	31576
Loflin, Rebecca J.	14906	Looney, Henry	23047
Loflin, Vaul D.	14908	Looney, Walter P.	23049
Loflin, Chester C.	14909	Looney, Emmett J.	23050
Loflin, Harris A., Jr.	14910	Looney, John	20003
Loflin, Clarence R.	14911	Looney, John Jr.	31978
Loflin, Oscar M.	14912	Looney, William	4684
Logsdon, Bessie B.	24897	Looking, Arch	32009
Logsdon, Albert I.	24898	Loudermilk, Stonewall	1908
Logsdon, Everet E.	24899	Lovett, John	4192
Long, Robert H.	299	Lovett, James	5063
Long, Ivan	300	Lovett, Irene	5064
Long, Mary C.	301	Lovett, Richard	30349
Long, Lucinda	302	Lovett, Rachel	30350
Long, Lemuel D.	22248	Lovett, Eliza	30351
Long, Manda A.	307	Lovett, John J.	18699
Long, Flossie	308	Lovett, William	29546
Long, Akey	1491	Lovett, Elmira	29547
Long, Minnie	1492	Lovett, Rosa	29548
Long, Jackson A.	1493	Lovett, George	20621
Long, Bird	2644	Lovett, John J.	20620
Long, Jennie	2645	Lovett, Lydia	21031
Long, Martha	2646	Love, Alexander	30116
Long, Mollie	2647	Love, Elizabeth	25445
Long, Samuel	2648	Love, Richard	25446
Long, Sallie	2649	Love, Ben	29154
Long, Annie	2650	Love, Susan	31420
Long, Jack	28582	Love, Maggie	31421
Long, Smith	2651	Love, Benjamin J.	31538
Long, Isaiah H.	8154	Love, Lorenzo	31539
Long, Eliza	29478	Love, Minnie	31540
Long, Ralph	303	Love, Carrie	31541
Long, Katie	25250	Love, Blanton D.	31591
Long, Columbus Jr.	25251	Love, Charles H.	31643
Long, Henry H.	21675	Lowery, Elsie	44
Long, Francis L.	21676	Lowery, Ellen M.	5339
Long, Flora A.	21677	Lowery, William P.	11027
Long, Eugenia	25252	Lowery, Mary	11028
Long, Charles K.	31518	Lowery, Katie E.	11029
Long, Charles E.	31519	Lowery, Paul	11030
Long, William A.	31520	Lowery, Ned	28237
Long, Irvin D.	31521	Lowery, Ida	28238
Long, Felix E.	31522	Lowery, Andrew	14462
Long, Mauda	32242	Lowery, James B.	14463
Long, Ida	32243	Lowery, Mary	14464
Long, Thomas	32244	Lowery, Daniel V.	14465
Long, Alberta	32840	Lowery, Charles A.	14466
Long, Elmer L.	32841	Lowery, Jenette S.	14467
Long, William Lucien	32842	Lowery, Andrew, Jr.,	14468
Londagin, Timmie	15407	Lowery, George H.	14469
Londagin, Kate	25067	Lowery, Lucy	14470
Londagin, Margaret P.	25072	Lowery, Switzler	15240
Longcrier, Frances	17464	Lowry, John J.	3060
Longcrier, Rosie B.	17466	Lowry, Charlotte E.	27367
Longcrier, Minnie	17467	Lowry, Sarah	27368
Longbird, Edward	28897	Lowry, Bettie	14256
		Lowry, Samuel C.	14257
		Lowry, Minnie O.	14258

Name.	Roll No.	Name.	Roll No.
Lowry, Return J.	16853	Lowe, James	31846
Lowry, Jack	16854	Lowe, May	31847
Lowry, Josephine E.	12013	Lowe, Zelma	31848
Lowry, Beulah	12015	Lowe, Roberta	31849
Lowrey, Daniel W.	4946	Lowe, Rosa	31850
Lowrey, Ellen	4947	Lowrance, Edith M.	31634
Lowrey, Florence	4948	Lowrance, Arthur L.	31635
Lowrey, George	4949	Lowrance, Addie L.	31636
Lowrey, Richard	4950	Luckey, Martha	23593
Lowrey, James	4951	Lucky, Sarah F.	7715
Lowrey, John	4952	Lucky, Sabrina L.	7747
Lowrey, Dora	4953	Lucky, Jackie M.	7748
Lowrey, William	5023	Lucas, John	14497
Lowrey, John	5071	Lucas, Frank	14498
Lowrey, Ellis	5097	Lucas, Sarah	20252
Lowrey, Johnson	5098	Lucas, Annie	30960
Lowrey, William W.	5164	Lucas, Jacob	31564
Lowrey, Lou	29904	Lucas, Joseph	31565
Lowrey, Henry	5408	Luke, Mary J.	17377
Lowrey, Joanna	5409	Luke, Elzora	17382
Lowrey, John A	5410	Lulie, Eliza	24062
Lowrey, Oma	27412	Lulie, Susie	24063
Lowrey, Jeter B.	27413	Lunsford, Ellen	5360
Lowrey, Charles	27414	Lunsford, Jesse	5361
Lowrey, John	10184	Lunsford, Lucy	5362
Lowrey, Thomas J.	10185	Lunsford, Mary	5363
Lowrey, Nannie	10187	Lunday, Josephine	30034
Lowrey, John, Jr.	10188	Lunday, Lewis	30916
Lowrey, Willia	10189	Lunday, Rosa	30917
Lowrey, William A.	10743	Lunday, Maud J.	30961
Lowrey, Randolph	10744	Lunday, Leander	31001
Lowrey, Lizzie	25690	Lunday, Martha L.	31002
Lowrey, Austia	10745	Lunday, Frank F.	31003
Lowrey, Louisa M.	11935	Lunday, Florence L.	31004
Lowrey, Fannie P.	5165	Lunday, Cleora A.	31006
Lowrey, Anderson	28843	Lunday, Robert L.	31026
Lowrey, Lucy	28844	Lunday, Robert H.	31027
Lowrey, Raphael	27818	Lunday, William E.	31028
Lowrey, Eliza	17169	Lunday, Mark	31029
Lowrey, James M.	17171	Lusk, Lorenzo J.	2506
Lowrey, Susan	17172	Lusk, James S.	2507
Lowrey, Mary	17173	Luton, Rebecca L.	11323
Lowrey, James Jr.	17174	Luton, Lewis C.	11324
Lowrey, Minnie	17175	Luton, William E.	11325
Lowrey, Susie	17176	Luton, Samuel F.	11326
Lowrey, Jennie	17177	Luton, Dempsey A.	11327
Lowrey, Andrew	17178	Luton, Ruth A.	11328
Lowrey, Henry C.	17179	Luton, Joseph M.	11329
Lowrey, George	26739	Luton, Jesse A.	11330
Lowrey, Ellis	26740	Lutes, Rachel	12076
Lowrey, Emma	26741	Lutz, Mary T.	29916
Lowrey, Henry	26742	Lutz, Leo C.	29917
Lowrey, Carrie	26743	Luton, Alice R.	11331
Lowrey, Moses	26744	Lyman, James	7316
Lowrey, George	25689	Lyman, Joseph	7317
Lowrey, Charlie	25691	Lyman, Martha	7318
Lowrey, Emma	25692	Lyman, Callie	7319
Lowrey, Lydia	25693	Lyman, Mary	10432
Lowrey, Linda	25694	Lyman, Mary P.	12097
Lowrey, Joe	25695	Lyman, Patrick	12098
Lowrey, Annie	25931	Lyman, Lewis	29484
Lowrey, Dollie	25932	Lyman, Elmira	29485
Lowe, Mary	27024	Lyman, Levi	29486
Lowe, William S.	27025	Lyman, Lewis A.	29487
Lowe, Flossie	27026	Lyman, Nora	29488
Lowe, Ralph	27027	Lyman, John L.	14087
Lowe, Louie	27028	Lyman, Nancy	14088
Lowe, James W.	27029	Lyman, Bertha S.	14168
Lowrimore, Katie B.	11031	Lyman, Ada A.	14169
Lowrimore, Flona May	11032	Lyman, Beulah M.	14170
Lowrimore, Bessie	4297	Lyman, Savola R.	14171
Lowrimore, J. Arley	4301	Lyman, Johnson	27835
Lowther, Josephine	11353	Lyman, James	26915
Lowther, Grover	11354	Lyman, Jackson	25937
Lowther, William A.	11355	Lyman, William	21104
Lowther, Leroy G.	24736	Lyman, Susie	21105
Lowther, Katie L.	24737	Lyman, Lucy	21106
Lowther, Matthew	24738	Lyman, Nancy	21107
Lowther, Wayne Scott	24739	Lynch, Cicero L.	2101
Lowther, Lem M.	24740	Lynch, Nancy E.	2102
Lowther, Watson B.	11686	Lynch, Joseph M.	2103
Lowther, Eugene W.	26274	Lynch, John B.	2354
Lowther, Jennie L.	26275	Lynch, Cicero L. Jr.	2355
Lowther, Sammie	26276		
Lowther, Willie Eugene	26277		

Name.	Roll No.
Lynch, Susan F.	3021
Lynch, Nannie B.	3022
Lynch, Jeter	3023
Lynch, Joseph J.	5907
Lynoh, Susan	27580
Lynch, Cynthia	31968
Lynch, Earl C.	31969
Lynch, Emma O.	31971
Lynch, Bert W.	31972
Lynch, Edward B.	32573
Lynch, Fannie B.	12700
Lynch, Pricie G.	12701
Lynch, Isla M.	12702
Lynn, Eliza	18020
Lynch, Lucy	18071
Lynch, Herbert L.	12703
Lynch, Ruth B.	30735
Lynch, John	30736
Lynch, Cynthia	30737
Lynch, Claude	30738
Lynch, Rosa M.	30739
Lynch, Willis	30740
Lynch, John B.	31033
Lynch, Ada J.	31034
Lynch, Mary E.	31035
Lynch, Benjamin H.	31036
Lynch, Sarah F.	31037
Lynch, Charles W. A.	31038
Lynch, Lucile	31715
Lyons, Anna E.	31942
Mabry, Sallie B.	5528
Mabry, John E.	5529
Mabry, Ethel M.	5530
Mabry, William H.	5531
Mabry, Edna	31897
Mabry, Roby	31880
Mabry, Charley	31881
Maberry, Charles E.	31574
Macy, Lorena E.	8766
Macy, Vera W.	8767
Macy, Roena G.	8768
Maddin, Daisy	5659
Maddin, Letitia A.	26053
Maddin, Arthur B.	26054
Maddin, Marcus E.	26055
Maddin, Otto L.	26056
Madden, Emily	5881
Madden, Victor E.	5882
Madden, Leo B.	5883
Madden, Thomas R.	5884
Madden, Nellie	9003
Madden, Eunice M.	9004
Madden, Thomas R.	9005
Madden, Constance	9006
Madden, Annie	28234
Madden, Clarence	28235
Madden, Jack	32018
Madden, Howard	32019
Madden, Ora	21974
Madden, Amanda	31488
Madden, Alice C.	31489
Madden, Leonard C.	31490
Madden, Glady O.	31491
Madison, Lydia	9103
Madison, Robert P.	9104
Madison, Beulah	9105
Madison, Cornelia	9106
Madison, Nannie E.	12232
Madison, Virgie	12233
Madison, Pigin	12234
Madison, Jesse	12235
Madison, Missouri P.	12236
Madison, Ninya Jane	9102
Madison, Dabner L.	9107
Maddox, Lucinda	8656
Maddox, Lucien B.	24117
Maddox, Eliza B.	24118
Maddox, Robert	24119
Maher, Elvira	16966
Maher, Henry	16967
Maher, David	16968
Maher, Jesse	16969
Maher, Frank	16970
Maher, Jennie	16971
Maher, Mary	16972

Name.	Roll No.
Maher, William	17364
Maher, Minnie A.	17365
Maine, Florence	12001
Maine, William O.	12002
Majors, Nellie	21704
Mallen, Elizabeth	10925
Mallen, Jesse	10936
Mallen, William	10938
Mallen, Barbara	10939
Malone, Myrtle C.	8988
Malone, Annie P.	12051
Malone, Alvah V.	12057
Maloney, Ida L.	8710
Maloney, Scott C.	8711
Maloney, Nellie G.	8712
Maloney, Clara V.	8713
Mann, Pauline	11360
Mann, Lola	11361
Mann, David S.	29747
Mann, Elizabeth	29748
Mann, Pleasanton R.	29749
Mann, DeWitt R.	29750
Mann, Bertha C.	29751
Mann, Robert J.	14243
Mann, Narcissa	14244
Mann, Robert L.	14245
Mann, Charlotte G.	14246
Mann, Ruth L.	14247
Mann, Gertrude E.	14248
Mann, John D.	14249
Mann, Effa V.	14250
Mann, Bertha E.	14318
Mann, Sarah E.	14319
Mann, Richard C.	14367
Mann, Henderson L.	14368
Mann, Laura E.	14369
Mann, Henderson	21795
Manning, Lucy	12873
Manning, Peggy	16953
Manning, Johnson	16954
Manning, Johnson	17628
Manning, Nancy	17629
Manning, Ellis	17630
Manning, Sallie	17631
Manning, Wilson	17790
Manning, Jessie M.	25556
Manley, Minnie W.	12625
Manley, Lawrence	28122
Mantooth, Mary E.	24217
Mantooth, Mary E.	24212
Mantooth, Edna E.	24213
Mantooth, Catherine G.	24214
Mantooth, Sarah W.	24215
Mantooth, Susan	24216
Mantooth, Elizabeth L.	9944
Mantooth, Demi L.	9945
Manifee, Victoria B.	13209
Manifee, Leah	13210
Manahan, Henry A.	11111
Manahan, Samuel C.	11112
Manahan, Emma	11113
Manahan, Mary F.	11114
Manahan, Frank	11115
Manahan, Viola	11116
Manahan, Charles	11117
Manahan, William McK.	11118
Manus, Aggie	18996
Manus, Jennie	19162
Manus, Annie	19163
Manus, William	19164
Manus, Jesse	19165
Manus, George	19166
Manus, Simon	19167
Manus, Nannie	19168
Manus, Richard	19265
Manus, Josiah	32642
Manus, Maggie	20775
Manus, Wuttie	20882
Manus, Dick	20883
Manus, Nellie	25946
Manus, Clabron	28262
Manus, Polly	28263
Manus, Samuel	15104
Manus, Mary	15105
Manus, Maggie	15106
Manus, Joseph L.	15427

Name.	Roll No.	Name.	Roll No.
Manus, Sallie	15209	Martin, Minnie	23371
Manus, Edna M.	25240	Martin, Amie M.	23372
Manus, Dorothy I.	25241	Martin, John S.	23373
Manus, Alison	25242	Martin, Charles D.	23374
Manus, John	28945	Martin, William H.	6365
Manus, Annie	28946	Martin, Henry A.	6366
Mankiller, Thomas	16490	Martin, Lenora A.	6367
Mankiller, Beacher	16491	Martin, Jennie E.	6377
Mankiller, Jack	28366	Martin, Hernando	6459
Mankiller, Maud	19098	Martin, Birdie M.	6460
Mankiller, George	19099	Martin, Johnanna	6461
Mankiller, May	19100	Martin, DeWitt	6462
Mankiller, Jake	25669	Martin, Rebecca	30119
Mankiller, Susie	25670	Martin, Granville A.	6722
Mankiller, John	25671	Martin, Callie	27982
Mankiller, Lizzie	25672	Martin, Benjamin F.	27983
Mankiller, Jennie	25673	Martin, George A.	27984
Mankiller, Nakie	25674	Martin, Willie V.	23477
Mankiller, Colson	25675	Martin, Lizzie E.	23633
Mankiller, Richard	25676	Martin, Thomas D.	23634
Mankiller, Lucy	19179	Martin, Julian C.	23635
Mankiller, William	19181	Martin, Walter	23636
Mankiller, Nancy	19182	Martin, Richard L.	7710
Mankiller, Cynthia	19183	Martin, Flora B.	7711
Mankiller, Bessie	19184	Martin, Rosa M.	7794
Mankiller, Polly	29859	Martin, Andrew J.	8140
Mankiller, Arch	29860	Martin, Myrtle I.	8141
Mankiller, Warlice	20861	Martin, Hassie I.	8142
Mankiller, Mary	25677	Martin, Idus A.	8143
Mannon, John	20278	Martin, Cassie L.	8144
Mannon, Jennie	32061	Martin, Opal R.	8145
Mannon, Nick	25849	Martin, Nellie L.	9309
Mannon, Michael	25850	Martin, Lucile McG.	9310
Mannon, Nellie	25851	Martin, Florence	9372
Mannon, Dianna	25852	Martin, Lycurgus C.	9373
Mannon, Johnson	32314	Martin, Allen J.	9374
Maples, Bettie H.	2986	Martin, Frayser D.	9375
Maples, Cynthia M.	28721	Martin, Howard P.	9376
Maples, Harvey S.	21674	Martin, Robert McC.	9377
Martin, Mary G.	1147	Martin, Joysoline	9378
Martin, Sevenia G.	22461	Martin, Mary E.	9379
Martin, Lucinda	1257	Martin, Mabel	28747
Martin, Abraham	1258	Martin, William A.	28763
Martin, Susan J.	4430	Martin, Willie A.	10456
Martin, Amanda P.	4431	Martin, George W.	24544
Martin, Levi T.	4432	Martin, James N.	24546
Martin, George W.	4433	Martin, Morris R.	24547
Martin, David E.	4434	Martin, George W.	24550
Martin, Richard	4648	Martin, Eben C.	24551
Martin, Walter A.	4649	Martin, Sarah E.	10488
Martin, William A. H.	4650	Martin, William P.	10489
Martin, Sirena	4651	Martin, Joel T.	26609
Martin, Octavia	4652	Martin, James R.	10503
Martin, Richard B.	4653	Martin, John A.	27722
Martin, Sanford M.	4654	Martin, Rosa C	27723
Martin, William H.	4936	Martin, William H.	27724
Martin, Jennie	4937	Martin, Rebecca E.	27725
Martin, Frank G.	4938	Martin, Annie E.	27726
Martin, Eugene	4939	Martin, Amanda	10709
Martin, Henry	4940	Martin, Polly	10710
Martin, Susie L.	4941	Martin, Thomas A.	10731
Martin, Josephine	4942	Martin, James A.	10737
Martin, Cordelia	4943	Martin, Lelia E.	10738
Martin, Jennie	4944	Martin, William H.	10739
Martin, Sequoyah R.	4945	Martin, Josephine I.	10740
Martin, Lizzie	5447	Martin, Flora L.	10741
Martin, Warren	5734	Martin, William P.	10948
Martin, Mary J.	5735	Martin, George A.	10952
Martin, Leroy	5736	Martin, Jewell E.	10953
Martin, Lewis A.	26389	Martin, Roy D.	10954
Martin, Eliza J.	5785	Martin, Samuel J.	10955
Martin, Annie	5786	Martin, Austin	26630
Martin, Callie	27443	Martin, Cora	26631
Martin, Mary	6238	Martin, John M.	11108
Martin, Harriett C.	6239	Martin, Rosa	11164
Martin, Clara May	6240	Martin, Allmon	11504
Martin, William R.	6242	Martin, Allmon, Jr.	11507
Martin, Grover	6241	Martin, Henry C.	11505
Martin, Richard T.	6243	Martin, Olive	11508
Martin, Lizzie	6244	Martin, Iva	11509
Martin, Rosa	6245	Martin, Peter	25505
Martin, Susie J.	23369	Martin, Cora	17403
Martin, Susie J.	23370	Martin, John A., Jr.	17404

Name.	Roll No.
Martin, George D.	17405
Martin, Addie B.	17406
Martin, Charles J.	17407
Martin, James	30445
Martin, Nancy	30446
Martin, Daniel	17589
Martin, Clarinda	26738
Martin, David F.	26745
Martin, Charlotte C.	30757
Martin, John S., Jr.	30759
Martin, Enos Q.	32703
Martin, John W.	29175
Martin, Mamie	29179
Martin, Harry	29180
Martin, Walter	29181
Martin, Gracy	29182
Martin, Charles N.	29184
Martin, Cora E.	29201
Martin, John Deloss	32701
Martin, Dora Melissa	32702
Martin, Cora D.	25834
Martin, George M.	25835
Martin, Ingram C.	25836
Martin, William P.	11510
Martin, John W	12289
Martin, William A.	30274
Martin, Clarence F.	8482
Martin, Arthur	23639
Martin, Ola P.	14064
Martin, Mintie B.	14617
Martin, Nancy L.	14861
Martin, Gertrude	14865
Martin, Mary A.	15766
Martin, Dora J	15768
Martin, Hurmon S.	15769
Martin, Ilo L.	15770
Martin, Martha A.	15771
Martin, Mary E.	15772
Martin, Frederick	15773
Martin, Margaret A.	15767
Martin, Dollie	16343
Martin, Hercules	16344
Martin, Mary	16345
Martin, Matilda	16346
Martin, Edgar	16347
Martin, Calvin	16348
Martin, William	16904
Martin, Ivy M.	16905
Martin, Zella	16906
Martin, Margaret J.	16907
Martin, Cynthia U.	16908
Martin, Annie	16957
Martin, Jennie	16958
Martin, Thomas	16959
Martin, James	16960
Martin, William	17262
Martin, Lawrence W.	17263
Martin, Roxie B.	26855
Martin, Thomas	32367
Martin, Lora	32368
Martin, Nelly	29183
Martin, Pearly Emiline	6369
Martin, Rhoda May	15774
Martin, Jessie S.	22837
Martin, Caledona	22836
Martin, Mack McK.	27986
Martin, Hattie M.	31913
Martin, Lula	14866
Martin, Annie	18698
Martin, Katie	20916
Martin, Lillie May	17408
Martin, Lollie Lee	25837
Martin, John B.	26856
Martin, A. L	32600
Martin, Charlie	32668
Martin, Harvey	32700
Martin, Josephus	32863
Martin, Nancy	31338
Martin, Mamie	31339
Martin, Annie M.	31668
Martin, Clara F.	31732
Martindale, Sarah	3962
Martindale, Lula	3963

Name.	Roll No.
Marshall, Julia	4188
Marshall, Irving Jr.	4189
Marshall, Martha J. R.	24828
Marshall, William B.	24829
Marshall, Ethel	24830
Marshall, Paul	24831
Marshall, Fannie	24832
Marshall, Myrtle	24833
Marshall, Charles E.	24834
Marshall, Hazel M.	24835
Marshall, Cornelia	17543
Marshall, Ettea F.	30729
Marshall, Andrew	31543
Marshall, James J.	31544
Marshall, Annie	31545
Marsh, Rosa	4579
Marsh, Clarence	4581
Marsh, Frederick W.	15765
Marlow, Carrie E.	5032
Marlow, Minnie	5033
Marlow, Edna	5034
Marlow, Ida	5035
Marker, Robert J.	30158
Marker, Grace A.	24132
Marker, Laura A.	24131
Marker, Charles J.	30918
Marker, John B.	30936
Marker, Clayton L.	30937
Marker, Gracie L.	30938
Marker, Annie L.	30939
Marion, James S.	6370
Marrs, Amanda Olivia	8533
Marrs, Edgar C.	8534
Marrs, John D.	8535
Marrs, Augustus G.	8536
Marrs, Olivia	8537
Marrs, William C.	8538
Marrs, Barney	8539
Marrs, Manton L.	8540
Marrs, David M., Jr.	8541
Marrs, Myrtle	8542
Marrs, Arkansas D.	15430
Marrs, Ivey N.	15431
Marrs, Harrison	21579
Marrs, Charles	29831
Marrs, David	29832
Marrs, Katie	29834
Marrs, Richard	29833
Marrs, Sallie	29835
Marrs, Lucinda	29836
Marks, Fannie E.	8133
Marks, Albert B.	8134
Marks, Walter R.	8135
Marks, Majora M.	8136
Markham, Charlotte	8618
Markham, Walter A.	15562
Markham, Ella V.	15563
Markham, Helen G.	15564
Markham, Carter D.	15757
Markham, Eliza A.	15758
Markham, Fortner	15759
Markham, Beatrice	15760
Markham, DeWitt	15761
Markham, Hogan	15762
Markham, Earl	15763
Markham, Lucile	15764
Markham, Allen	28297
Markham, Piercy	28298
Markham, Ewing	28300
Markham, Clarence	28301
Markham, James	28302
Markham, Burk	30414
Markham, John	16898
Markham, Cicero	30891
Marcus, Lucius	29297
Massey, Rachel	6710
Massey, James P.	6711
Massey, Ellen	6712
Massey, Clorinda	6713
Massey, William G.	6714
Massey, Nannie	6715
Massey, Minnie	6716
Mason, Ava C.	24120

Name.	Roll No.
Mason, Charles L.	24121
Mason, Willis	28792
Masterson, Ruby L.	8964
Masterson, Mildred C.	8965
Masterson, Aldon M.	8966
Masingale, Nancy	30856
Mathis, Janie	521
Mathis, Eda	522
Mathis, Eliza	523
Mathis, Ollie	524
Mathis, Lottie	525
Mathis, Nancy	3402
Matheson, Maud	5673
Matheson, Floyd	5674
Matheson, Richard T.	5675
Matheson, Alexander R.	5676
Matheson, Ida McKinley	5677
Matteson, Eliza E.	10649
Matteson, Walter W.	10650
Matteson, Leo V.	10651
Matteson, Cora H.	10652
Matteson, William	21924
Matteson, Albertus Hester	10654
Matthews, Madeline	13530
Matthews, Addie	26804
Matthews, Mary L.	26805
Matthews, William L.	26806
Matthews, Joseph T.	26807
Matthews, Jessie M.	26808
Mathews, , Mary H.	28662
Matney, Mamie	29394
Matney, Albert J.	29393
Matney, Louis F.	29396
Matoy, Lewis	25659
Matoy, Maggie	25660
Matoy, Sarah	25661
Matoy, William	25662
Maupin, Carrie L.	1008
Maupin, Bessie B.	1009
Maupin, Alma	1010
Maupin, Maggie L.	13414
Maupin, Walter G.	13415
Maupin, Flossie M.	13416
Mauck, Sarah E.	12432
Mauck, Lora D.	12433
Mauck, Jacob T.	12434
Mauck, Bessie L.	12435
Maxwell, Jenetta A.	4780
Maxwell, Alcie E.	4781
Maxwell, Charles L.	28617
Maxwell, Armstead B.	10139
Maxwell, Nancy	10140
Maxwell, Leonard F.	28765
Maxwell, Charles	10141
Maxwell, Christopher C.	10142
Maxwell, Marcus	32422
Maxwell, Benjamin F.	30813
Maxwell, Alfred L.	30814
Maxwell, Blanche A.	30815
Maxwell, Clyde B.	30816
Maxwell, Florence E.	30817
Maxwell, Mary G.	30818
Maxfield, Albert G.	17993
Maxfield, Stephen G.	26903
Maxfield, Gracie	26904
Mayfield, Charles H.	32605
Mayfield, Orlando	32606
Mayfield, John B.	3741
Mayfield, Trixy V.	3742
Mayfield, Jessie H.	5260
Mayfield, Watie L.	5261
Mayfield, Lena U.	9533
Mayfield, Ellison L.	9534
Mayfield, Alma N.	9535
Mayfield, Luther C.	9536
Mayfield, Orley B.	9537
Mayfield, Edna P.	9538
Mayfield, Carl R.	9539
Mayfield, Nannie	28748
Mayfield, Michael F.	10982
Mayfield, Thomas N.	10983
Mayfield, Sarah	11145

Name.	Roll No.
Mayfield, William R.	11896
Mayfield, Francis M.	12661
Mayfield, John T.	12662
Mayfield, Elizabeth	12663
Mayfield, Frederick	12664
Mayfield, Julia	12665
Mayfield, Frank	12666
Mayfield, Leonard	12667
Mayfield, John R.	30369
Mayfield, Ross G.	30370
Mayfield, Gretchen	30371
Mayfield, Blanche	30372
Mayfield, Isaac H., Jr.	15748
Mayfield, Ray	15749
Mayfield, Isaac H., Sr.	16109
Mayfield, Mary M.	16110
Mayfield, William W.	23902
Mayfield, Ella	26109
Mayfield, Noah	26110
Mayfield, Watie	26785
Mayfield, Nettie	12668
Mayfield, Nellie M.	11897
Mayfield, Charles Leland	28749
Mayfield, Beaula Vivian	9540
Mayfield, Joseph M.	32719
Mayfield, Mary	32720
Mayes, John T.	1767
Mayes, Cynthia P.	2056
Mayes, William L.	6693
Mayes, George W.	6717
Mayes, Susie E.	6718
Mayes, Edward T.	6719
Mayes, Richard C.	6720
Mayes, George W., Jr.	6721
Mayes, Ella	28645
Mayes, Jefferson E.	28646
Mayes, Wilson C.	28649
Mayes, William H.	23432
Mayes, Joel B.	23433
Mayes, Pixie A.	23467
Mayes, Walter A.	6850
Mayes, Nannie R.	6851
Mayes, Hall	6852
Mayes, Washington	6853
Mayes, Mamie D.	6854
Mayes, Jesse E.	6855
Mayes, Mary D.	23496
Mayes, Samuel H.	23497
Mayes, Martha E.	23498
Mayes, Carrie M.	23499
Mayes, Adeline	23501
Mayes, Joseph F.	23509
Mayes, Sime	6927
Mayes, Wiley B.	6966
Mayes, Ermina	6967
Mayes, Sallie A.	23539
Mayes, Beatrice	23540
Mayes, Isabel	23541
Mayes, Julia	23542
Mayes, Cherokee	7000
Mayes, Mary T.	23597
Mayes, Cooie D.	23598
Mayes, William P.	9239
Mayes, Annie H.	9240
Mayes, Nellie M.	9241
Mayes, Joel B.	9242
Mayes, Lizzie B.	9243
Mayes, Ridge P.	9244
Mayes, Mary H.	9245
Mayes, Joel B.	11792
Mayes, Mary	12882
Mayes, Georgia V.	12883
Mayes, Tip C.	13713
Mayes, Charles T.	14968
Mayes, Jack	14969
Mayes, Cherry W.	14970
Mayes, Adair	14997
Mayes, Soggie	14996
Mayes, Lindsay	14998
Mayes, William	15955
Mayes, Eliza	15956
Mayes, Lola	16175
Mayes, Johnson	16276

Name.	Roll No.	Name.	Roll No.
Mayes, Jesse	16278	Meigs, Charles R.	15828
Mayes, George	16279	Meigs, Elinor B.	15829
Mayes, John H.	16280	Meigs, John C.	15830
Mayes, Samuel H., Jr.	25432	Meigs, Mary E.	27814
Mayes, Charlotte	25433	Meigs, Cooie	27815
Mayes, Pearl	25434	Meigs, Benjamin F.	15855
Mayes, Ruth	25435	Meigs, Florence S.	15856
Mayes, Sara	25436	Meigs, John W.	15857
Mayes, George	21384	Meigs, Elizabeth G.	15858
Mayes, Mike	21385	Meigs, Return R.	15975
Mayes, Charles	21386	Meigs, James R.	25303
Mayes, Gladis M.	12884	Meigs, Silas D.	25304
Mayes, Mary L.	28650	Meigs, Robert E.	25305
Mayes, Martha L.	28651	Meigs, Fannie J.	25306
Mays, Susie	7072	Meigs, Elizabeth G.	25307
Mays, William	7073	Meigs, Florein N.	16031
Mays, Joseph	7074	Meigs, Mollie C.	16032
Mays, Josie	7075	Meigs, Josephine E.	25308
Mays, Gertie	7076	Meigs, Daniel B.	16048
Mays, Bertha	7077	Meigs, Return J.	16060
Mays, Jesse	7078	Meigs, Robert H.	17075
Mays, Leroy	7080	Melton, Simpson F.	182
Mayor, Ida	6669	Melton, Isabelle	183
Mayor, William	6670	Melton, Narcissa	184
Mayor, Ida	6671	Melton, George A.	185
Mayor, Leander	6672	Melton, Rosa Belle	186
Mayor, Samuel H.	6673	Melton, Maudy May	187
Mayor, Joseph H.	6674	Melton, Simpson Jr.	188
Mayor, Oliver D.	6675	Melton, Wiley J.	331
Mayor, Helen M.	6676	Melton, Ella	332
Mayor, Mable C.	6677	Melton, John H.	333
May, Joanna	24582	Melton, Lucien	335
May, George H.	24583	Melton, Elizabeth	336
Mayberry, Beatrice	11160	Melton, Florence	337
Mayberry, Maude V.	11161	Melton, Mollie	334
Mayberry, Perry	11162	Melton, Mary Ann	409
Mayberry, Floyd	11163	Melton, David	28659
Mayo, Jessie V.	2704	Melton, William H.	28661
Mayo, Richard W.	20954	Melton, Rebecca A.	28663
Maytum, Minnie E.,	12978	Melton, Julia	28664
Maytum, Amos	12982	Melton, William T.	7094
Mead, Sarah	2770	Melton, Louisa B.	7095
Meadows, Leonard L.	26419	Melton, Cora M.	7096
Meadows, Lola M.	26420	Melton, Clara E.	7097
Meadows, Emma E.	26421	Melton, Annie M.	7098
Means, Amanda	7821	Melton, Ethel E.	7099
Means, Mary E.	7822	Melton, Otto V.	7100
Measles, Minner	5662	Melton, Louisa B.	7101
Measles, Ellis	5663	Melton, John Q.	7102
Measles, Algia	5664	Melton, Charles F.	7202
Measles, Barney	5665	Melton, Narcissa	7203
Measles, Blanche	5666	Melton, Charles W. E.	7204
Measles, Beulah	5667	Melton, Mattie J.	30032
Measles, Leonard	5668	Melton, Lee	13674
Measles, Emily B.	10749	Melton, James	13675
Meek, William A.	8829	Melton, Opal May	30459
Meek, Sabra E.	8830	Melton, Gertrude	22293
Meek, Mary J.	15638	Melton, Emma B.	22298
Meek, Walter G. A.	15639	Mellowbug, Betsy	20382
Meek, Mary F. V.	15640	Mellowbug, Wilson	20383
Meek, Myrtle E.	29330	Mellowbug, Joe	20384
Meek, Ethel R.	29331	Mellowbug, Esiah	20392
Meeks, Willie	7556	Mellowbug, Carrie	20393
Meeks, Norman W.	7557	Mellowbug, Whirlwind	30616
Meeks, William	14173	Mellowbug, Smith	20804
Meeks, Charles	18768	Mellowbug, Tarnie	20805
Meeks, Mary Ann	18769	Mellowbug, Teh-gar-tlu-gar	30641
Meeks, Polly	18770	Merryman, May	5286
Meeks, William	18771	Merryman, Earl	5287
Meeker, George	23269	Merryman, Ruth S.	5288
Megg, Anderson	29713	Merrell, John T.	8475
Megg, Annie	20686	Merrell, Joe Annie	8476
Mehlin, Elizabeth	10801	Merrell, Della G.	24083
Mehlin, Charles H.	26693	Merrell, Gretchen J.	24084
Mehlin, Ida	31391	Merrell, Dewey W.	24085
Mehlin, Nadle Lee	31392	Merrell, William P.	9068
Meigs, Henry C.	6106	Merrell, Mary	9069
Meigs, James M.	6107	Merrell, Lillie	9070
Meigs, Alice M.	6108	Merrell, Corinthia C.	9331
Meigs, Josephine	6109	Merrell, Luverna	9332
Meigs, John H.	15825	Merrell, Lola	9333
Meigs, Elinor M.	15826	Merrell, Dollie	13450
Meigs, Carrie M.	15827	Merrell, Ethel W.	13451
		Merrell, Fay M.	13452

Name.	Roll No.	Name.	Roll No.
Merrell, William Press-		Miller, Hettie M.	3477
ley	9334	Miller, Peggie B.	3478
Merrett, Nora	27481	Miller, Maud D.	3479
Merritt, Elmer P.	31633	Miller, Florence	3539
Merchant, Carrie M.	14098	Miller, Hettie 'L.	3540
Merchant, Mattie E.	14099	Miller, William J. J.	3541
Merchant, Eulalia	14100	Miller, Thomas F.	3542
Messer, Nannie	1393	Miller, Ida I.	3543
Messer, George P.	1394	Miller, William W.	3700
Messer, Ruth R.	1395	Miller, William	3803
Messer, Charles A.	1396	Miller, Nancy	3804
Messer, Elizabeth M.	1397	Miller, Martha	30061
Messer, Lucinda	1398	Miller, Mary C.	30071
Messer, John H.	1892	Miller, Cora	4619
Messer, Raymond D.	26339	Miller, Chute	4620
Messer, Clarence C.	26340	Miller, Charles	4621
Messer, Paul Virgil	26341	Miller, Lucinda	5293
Metzner, Mary	31546	Miller, John H.	30110
Metzner, Herbert	31547	Miller, Foreman	27427
Meyers, Mary	15018	Miller, Sallie	6848
Meyers, Andrew	15019	Miller, Benjamin	6849
Micco, Lorinda	32779	Miller, Martin	7062
Micco, Jim	62780	Miller, Daniel D.	7063
Micco, Mariah	32887	Miller, Nannie G.	7064
Middlestriker, Jack	22918	Miller, John M.	28688
Middlestriker, Moses	22919	Miller, Lucinda	28689
Middlestriker, John	3774	Miller, Cornelius B.	28690
Middlestriker, Lizzie	3805	Miller, John J.	28691
Mike, Robin	19800	Miller, Joseph	28692
Mike, Susie	19801	Miller, Andrew J.	23732
Mike, Lila	19802	Miller, Mahana	23734
Mike, Maggie	19803	Miller, Robert L.	23735
Mike, Scott	30582	Miller, Mamie J.	23736
Mike, Ganah	30583	Miller, Sallie E.	23737
Milligan, Saphronia	556	Miller, Andrew J., Jr.	23738
Miller, Joe	26952	Miller, Pearl	23739
Miller, Nannie	26953	Miller, Dawes	23740
Miller, Josie	26954	Miller, Myrtle T.	23741
Miller, Mariah	26955	Miller, Mary E.	7474
Miller, Annie	1665	Miller, Felix F.	7475
Miller, Nancy	1749	Miller, Emma M.	7476
Miller, John H.	1750	Miller, James C.	7477
Miller, Joseph M.	1751	Miller, William E.	7478
Miller, George J.	1752	Miller, William P.	7598
Miller, Nancy A.	1753	Miller, Mary E.	7738
Miller, James L.	1754	Miller, Guy E.	7739
Miller, William	1817	Miller, Jesse	9917
Miller, Charley	2016	Miller, Robert L.	9930
Miller, Julia	2017	Miller, William W.	26657
Miller, Ida	2018	Miller, Charles W.	26658
Miller, Henry	2021	Miller, Henry M.	26659
Miller, Rufus	27152	Miller, Joseph C.	26660
Miller, Mary	27153	Miller, David A.	26661
Miller, Ida	27154	Miller, Matilda A.	26662
Miller, Alfred	2075	Miller, John B.	26663
Miller, Cornelius S.	2403	Miller, Willis L.	24713
Miller, John	2404	Miller, Nan J.	24714
Miller, Nora B.	2405	Miller, Mary L.	24715
Miller, George	2406	Miller, Chloe	24716
Miller, Oatha	2407	Miller, Marion A., Jr.	24717
Miller, John W.	2444	Miller, Joe L.	24718
Miller, Louvinia	2445	Miller, Cassey B.	7065
Miller, William H.	2446	Miller, Neppie A.	12843
Miller, Joseph S.	2447	Miller, Monnie	12844
Miller, Ute B.	2448	Miller, Homer	12845
Miller, Franklin S.	2449	Miller, Nellie	12846
Miller, Mary A.	2450	Miller, Pearlie M.	7740
Miller, James J.	3205	Miller, Mattie L.	7741
Miller, Charles	3206	Miller, Roxie L.	7742
Miller, Louis	3207	Miller, Idella J.	7743
Miller, Jackson	3208	Miller, John L.	8548
Miller, Thomas	3306	Miller, Cynthia	8549
Miller, Sarah	3307	Miller, Annis	8550
Miller, John H.	22835	Miller, Ida M.	8573
Miller, George L. W.	3352	Miller, Ida M.	8818
Miller, William H.	3353	Miller, Mary H.	8819
Miller, George R.	3354	Miller, Martha F.	8820
Miller, Sarah F.	3355	Miller, Tulla	8821
Miller, Lena M.	3356	Miller, George	8822
Miller, Pleasant H.	3381	Miller, Christina	8823
Miller, Frances E.	3382	Miller, Hattie	8824
Miller, Ethe M.	3383	Miller, Myrtle	8825
Miller, George W.	3384	Miller, Caroline	26549
Miller, Louisa	3385	Miller, Lillie	26551
Miller, John T.	3386	Miller, Jesse T.	26552
Miller, Jane	3476	Miller, Stan	9370

Name.	Roll No.	Name.	Roll No.
Miller, Malvina	24270	Miller, Rozella	28156
Miller, Charles M.	24271	Miller, Everet	28157
Miller, Dona E.	24272	Miller, Thomas H.	14762
Miller, John E.	24273	Miller, Nannie	18615
Miller, Manerva	24274	Miller, Jennie	18616
Miller, Lillie M.	24275	Miller, Katie	18617
Miller, Sevola B.	24276	Miller, Steve	18618
Miller, Ellen H.	9393	Miller, Ray E.	1818
Miller, William R.	9394	Miller, William	19321
Miller, Alta R.	9395	Miller, Martha	19322
Miller, Howard K.	9396	Miller, Lizzie	19323
Miller, Warren A.	9541	Miller, Andrew	19324
Miller, Lillie	9542	Miller, Emma	19413
Miller, Thomas	12847	Miller, Alfred	20238
Miller, Beryl	12848	Miller, Aggie	20239
Miller, Rose	12849	Miller, Susan	20240
Miller, William H.	13177	Miller, Annie	30593
Miller, Thomas H.	13178	Miller, George	20241
Miller, George W.	13179	Miller, James Coody	17351
Miller, Charles H.	13180	Miller, Ella	26956
Miller, Joseph P.	13181	Miller, Andy	29886
Miller, William E.	13182	Miller, Sallie	29887
Miller, Stand W.	13183	Miller, Lee	29888
Miller, Elizabeth	13184	Miller, Henry	29889
Miller, Richard A.	13185	Miller, Dave	29890
Miller, Oce C.	13186	Miller, Lillie	29891
Miller, Nannie E.	13305	Miller, Susie	20668
Miller, Ray F.	13306	Miller, John	25896
Miller, Avery M.	13371	Miller, John	32640
Miller, Virgil A.	13372	Miller, Betsy	32641
Miller, Calvin T.	13373	Miller, Ollie	21125
Miller, Delilah	13833	Miller, Willie	21126
Miller, Clara K.	13834	Miller, Joseph	21232
Miller, Suake L.	28230	Miller, Lydia	21233
Miller, Minnie L.	28231	Miller, Waiter	21234
Miller, Dicie G.	28232	Miller, Richard	21235
Miller, Henry S.	28233	Miller, Lizzie E.	23814
Miller, Della	14009	Miller, Willie L.	23817
Miller, Darthula	14759	Miller, Willie Walter	1755
Miller, Mary J.	14760	Miller, Dalvy	3357
Miller, William J.	14761	Miller, Lester Riah	26013
Miller, Allie E.	15197	Miller, Raymond	21836
Miller, Dora E.	15198	Miller, Pearl Lee	21868
Miller, James W.	15199	Miller, Gladys	21846
Miller, Florence	15200	Miller, George W.	32539
Miller, Mae Bell	15201	Miller, John W.	32540
Miller, Martin	16217	Miller, Robert D.	32541
Miller, Alice	16218	Miller, Jacob	31203
Miller, Andrew J.	25352	Miller, Duncan	31204
Miller, Mattie E.	25353	Miller, Elizabeth	31205
Miller, Archibald	16987	Miller, Urban	31225
Miller, Noah	17128	Miller, Cornelius	31233
Miller, Nettie	17129	Miller, Rosie	31234
Miller, Mattie	17130	Miller, Rosa	31381
Miller, Edith	17131	Miller, Mamie A.	31382
Miller, Elizabeth	17132	Miller, Ida P.	31384
Miller, Admiral D.	17133	Miller, Catherine	31467
Miller, William B.	17170	Miller, Edward	31468
Miller, Samuel W.	17350	Miller, Eva	31469
Miller, Mary	17526	Miller, Ida	31470
Miller, Bertha	17803	Miller, Sadie	31471
Miller, Rufus	26231	Miller, Stephen A., Jr.	31472
Miller, Joshua D.	26232	Miller, Joseph	31682
Miller, Sarah	26233	Miller, Benjamin	32098
Miller, Elizabeth	26234	Milink, Lizzie J.	22863
Miller, William A.	26235	Milink, Eliza	22864
Miller, Roy	26553	Milink, John L.	22865
Miller, John H.	21899	Milink, Elizabeth	22866
Miller, Noma E.	21900	Miles, Eliza	4710
Miller, Ruthie May	13835	Miles, Annie E.	4711
Miller, Martha	21797	Miles, Lucy D.	9425
Miller, Charles E.	21798	Miles, Benedict F.	9426
Miller, Julia B.	21803	Miles, Elizabeth	9427
Miller, Leonard	21804	Miles, Jessie E.	4712
Miller, Moses	21814	Miles, Nancy A.	14063
Miller, William L.	22049	Miles, Louisa	14545
Miller, America A.	22050	Miles, Bettie C.	14546
Miller, Louis M.	22051	Mills, Jennie	6923
Miller, Dora	26866	Mills, Jesse L.	6924
Miller, Finey S.	3480	Mills, Cynthia E.	6925
Miller, Mary A.	6074	Mills, Samuel H.	6926
Miller, Myrtle M.	6079	Mills, Abraham	24291
Miller, Grayson N.	3544	Mills, Eliza	9432
Miller, Charles H.	7744	Mills, Frank H.	9719
Miller, Belmont	3387	Mills, William F.	24353
		Mills, Loyal H.	24354

Name.	Roll No.	Name.	Roll No.
Mills, Auburn E.	24355	Mitchell, George W. Jr.	27694
Mills, Laura H.	24356	Mitchell, Sallie A.	9793
Mills, Cyrus	9721	Mitchell, Don	9794
Mills, Cindarella	9722	Mitchell, Robert L.	10011
Mills, Kenneth B.	9723	Mitchell, William D.	26648
Mills, David G.	9724	Mitchell, Franklin P.	11386
Mills, Theodore R.	9725	Mitchell, Bertie	11387
Mills, Tessie E.	9726	Mitchell, Bruce	11388
Mills, Elsie M.	9727	Mitchell, Reese B.	11389
Mills, William E.	10012	Mitchell, Susan	14940
Mills, James	11779	Mitchell, Toy	14941
Mills, George	12341	Mitchell, Joseph	14942
Mills, Looney	12342	Mitchell, Esther	14943
Mills, William R.	24922	Mitchell, Levie L.	15109
Mills, James E.	24924	Mitchell, John	16588
Mills, Benjamin A.	13594	Mitchell, Nancy E.	16716
Mills, John A.	13631	Mitchell, Isaac G.	16717
Mills, Vinnie E.	13632	Mitchell, Jasper L.	16718
Mills, Floyd A.	13633	Mitchell, Earl	16719
Mills, Dora R.	13634	Mitchell, Posey H.	16720
Mills, James L.	16938	Mitchell, Opel H.	16721
Mills, Clarence A.	24357	Mitchell, Walker	16804
Mills, Lizzie	29090	Mitchell, Mary A.	16805
Millner, John	12012	Mitchell, Myrtle	16806
Millhollon, Sarah F.	12905	Mitchell, Joanna	32506
Millhollon, John D.	12906	Mitchell, Lela	32507
Milam, Sarah E.	24951	Mitchell, Maggie	32508
Milam, James E.	24952	Mitchell, Franklin R.	29424
Milam, Jesse B.	24953	Mitchell, Mattie J.	21927
Milam, Allie	24954	Mitchell, Ott W.	21928
Milam, Noolie	24955	Mitchell, Lee A.	21929
Milam, Viola	24956	Mitchell, Ross B.	27695
Milam, Charles	24957	Mitchell, Floyd	22487
Milam, William W.	24958	Mitchell, Rachel	20311
Milam, Annie W.	24959	Mitchell, Sissa	20312
Milam, Gladys M.	24960	Mitchell, Dora	20313
Milligan, Caleb H.	15610	Mitchell, Infant	30600
Milligan, Gracie V.	15611	Mitchell, Trilby	
Milligan, Franklin	15612	Trissie	29425
Minis, Mary	8878	Mitchell, Claud O.	21930
Minor, Minnie L.	13141	Mixwater, Alex	19978
Minor, Delbert L.	13142	Mixwater, George	20705
Minor, Beulah A.	13143	Mixwater, Betsy	25925
Mink, Nellie	16941	Mixwater, Daniel	25926
Mink, Sa-ta-ka	19078	Mixwater, Mary	25927
Mink, Mary	29881	Mizer, Sarah	10567
Mink, Margaret	29882	Mizer, Sheridan	10568
Mink, Sallie	32058	Mizer, Mary E.	12984
Mink, Candy	20405	Mizer, Lelia	13005
Mink, Sallie	20406	Mizer, John W.	13006
Mink, Martha	20407	Mizer, Cora	13007
Mink, Eve	20408	Mizer, Nellie R.	32259
Mink, Lizzie	20409	Mock, Nannie J.	11187
Mink, Linda	20410	Mocker, Ben	20264
Mink, Manda	20411	Mocker, Mary	20266
Mink, Ellen	20412	Mocker, Polly	20265
Mink, Runabout	21192	Mockicin, Bird	32084
Minshall, Eliza A.	30920	Mode, Serena	62
Minshall, Mary E.	30921	Mode, Floyd	71
Minshall, Walter T.	30922	Mode, Sarah	7599
Minshall, Joseph P.	30923	Mode, Frances M.	7600
Minshall, Margaret M.	30924	Mode, Maud M.	7601
Mitchell, Mike H.	1298	Mode, William E.	7602
Mitchell, Joseph A.	1336	Mode, Henry D.	7603
Mitchell, Arvel	22485	Mode, Georgia	7604
Mitchell, Dovie	22486	Mode, Viola	7605
Mitchell, Thaddeus	2669	Mode, John R.	8977
Mitchell, Mary J.	2670	Mohr, Lucinda	5031
Mitchell, Cora E.	2671	Monroe, Thomas J.	452
Mitchell, Irene	2672	Monroe, Charles S.	453
Mitchell, Callie	22736	Monroe, Maggie S.	454
Mitchell, David	22737	Monroe, Nola A.	455
Mitchell, Della	22738	Monroe, Bertha F.	456
Mitchell, Altie	22739	Monroe, Muta A.	571
Mitchell, Ben	22740	Monroe, Beulah	572
Mitchell, Thomas P.	2881	Monroe, Grover C.	573
Mitchell, Mary E.	26424	Montgomery, Clara P.	8448
Mitchell, Mary J.	26425	Montgomery, Silvia V.	8449
Mitchell, Hugh	22741	Montgomery, Frederick	
Mitchell, Martha J.	27687	O.	8450
Mitchell, Savola L.	27688	Montgomery, James W.	15807
Mitchell, Claud S.	27689	Montgomery, Minnie	15806
Mitchell, Lee R.	27690	Moore, Henry W.	3197
Mitchell, Joseph F.	27691	Moore, Mary E.	6688
Mitchell, Clay A.	27692	Moore, Walter F.	6689
Mitchell, Beulah V.	27693	Moore, Alice	23418

Name.	Roll No.	Name.	Roll No.
Moore, Charles E.	23419	Morton, Milam	4186
Moore, Jesse J.	23420	Morton, Jennie O.	10285
Moore, Dora B.	23421	Morton, Cartherine G.	10286
Moore, Clarence	23422	Morton, Joel J.	26308
Moore, John	6751	Morton, Robert L.	26309
Moore, Carrie	6752	Morton, Grover C.	26310
Moore, William	6810	Morton, William H.	26311
Moore, Susie	6811	Morton, Mary B.	26312
Moore, John	6812	Morton, Newton	18295
Moore, David	6813	Morton, George	18296
Moore, Mary	7483	Morton, Clara E.	4187
Moore, Elijah	7878	Morton, Flossie	26313
Moore, Bettie	8120	Morton, Noah	31713
Moore, Sammie	8121	Morton, Babe	31714
Moore, Josie	8123	Morris, Frances E.	769
Moore, Johnie	8124	Morris, Thomas R.	770
Moore, Mary	8125	Morris, Virge C.	857
Moore, Lewis, Jr.	8126	Morris, Mary	858
Moore, Fred	8127	Morris, Lou	859
Moore, Stein S.	8128	Morris, Willie	860
Moore, William H.	8172	Morris, Minnie	861
Moore, Ellis	24149	Morris, Arthur	862
Moore, Eliza J.	24151	Morris, Richard	863
Moore, Lee R.	10037	Morris, Sophia	864
Moore, Thomas D.	11166	Morris, Gabe	865
Moore, Thomas J.	11411	Morris, Glove	874
Moore, Cora A.	27753	Morris, Gatsy	875
Moore, William M.	27754	Morris, Nick B.	876
Moore, John F.	27755	Morris, Artie	877
Moore, Etta	11952	Morris, Roxie	878
Moore, Lucinda	28117	Morris, Charles L.	881
Moore, Daniel E.	28118	Morris, James L.	882
Moore, Dovey E.	28119	Morris, Bessie	883
Moore, Charles	28120	Morris, Benjamin A.	884
Moore, Lucinda E.	28121	Morris, Grace P.	885
Moore, Carl	23423	Morris, Goldie M.	886
Moore, Louisa	30288	Morris, Henry	1080
Moore, Jesse A.	30289	Morris, Pollie	1081
Moore, Evangeline	30290	Morris, Fannie	1082
Moore, Jesse J.	12934	Morris, George	1083
Moore, Fannie L.	12935	Morris, Jeff	1084
Moore, Fannie	28254	Morris, Stella	1085
Moore, Mary H.	28255	Morris, John B.	1609
Moore, Albert S.	28256	Morris, Fannie	1610
Moore, Katie E.	28257	Morris, Fred	1611
Moore, Edwin C.	28258	Morris, Benjamin	1612
Moore, Callie A.	28259	Morris, Bert	1613
Moore, Grover C.	28260	Morris, Sadie B.	1614
Moore, Sallie A.	28261	Morris, Kate	1615
Moore, William A.	15075	Morris, Frankie	1616
Moore, Charles T.	15082	Morris, Levia	1617
Moore, Jesse	15594	Morris, Joseph H.	2057
Moore, Mary E.	17152	Morris, Marcus D.	2058
Moore, Pearl M.	17153	Morris, Minnie E.	2059
Moore, Eliza	15242	Morris, William A.	2060
Moore, Annie	15243	Morris, Cornelia A.	2061
Moore, Isabell U.	21549	Morris, John A.	2062
Moore, Howard W.	30782	Morris, Wilson E.	2077
Moore, Maggie M.	21611	Morris, Polly E.	2078
Moore, Lizzie	27489	Morris, Robert L.	2079
Moore, Wannetta	8173	Morris, Osceola	2080
Moore, Luella	32505	Morris, Pearl M.	2081
Moore, Myrtle	32509	Morris, John A.	2082
Moore, Bessie	30781	Morris, Jesse E.	2083
Moore, Mollie	31792	Morris, Margaret A.	2084
Moore, Nora	31793	Morris, Landon C.	2085
Moore, Walter	31794	Morris, Parker	2301
Moore, Clara	31795	Morris, Phoebe	2302
Moore, Ora	31796	Morris, Jennie	2303
Moore, James W.	31797	Morris, Edna	2304
Moore, Edna Edith	31798	Morris, Mary J.	2305
Morton, John W.	749	Morris, Eleanor	2907
Morton, Bessie	750	Morris, Susie I.	2908
Morton, Cherokee	15957	Morris, Bonnie T.	2909
Morton, Edna A.	15958	Morris, Enoley	4220
Morton, Maud M.	15959	Morris, Eliza	7925
Morton, Lock	15960	Morris, William	7926
Morton, George	15961	Morris, Jordan	10529
Morton, Rebecca	27082	Morris, Fay	10530
Morton, Take	2029	Morris, Irene	10531
Morton, Mary A.	3715	Morris, Don	10532
Morton, Clara	3716	Morris, John	10557
Morton, Edna	3717	Morris, William O.	10558
Morton, Edward	4091	Morris, Dosa A.	10559
Morton, Drew	4179	Morris, Bessie J.	10560
Morton, Lewis	4185	Morris, Ruby	10561

Name.	Roll No.	Name.	Roll No.
Morris, Jumbo	10570	Morgan, Jessie E.	14947
Morris, Jennie	30229	Morgan, Elmira	14948
Morris, Bessie R.	27731	Morgan, James	14949
Morris, Dallas	27732	Morgan, Leslie	14950
Morris, Augusta	11024	Morgan, John	14951
Morris, Maggie	11607	Morgan, Beverly M.	14952
Morris, Horra N.	11866	Morgan, Effie	14953
Morris, Thaddeus M.	12322	Morgan, Josephine	14954
Morris, Dee	24844	Morgan, Louie	14955
Morris, Lila	24845	Morgan, Sarah	15514
Morris, Minnie	24846	Morgan, Mark	17067
Morris, Myrtle	24847	Morgan, Sophronia	17068
Morris, Eliza J.	24848	Morgan, Susan E.	17310
Morris, John	24849	Morgan, James L.	17311
Morris, Henry	12824	Morgan, Eli	17312
Morris, Joanna	12825	Morgan, Bettie	17313
Morris, Dennis	866	Morgan, Florence	31875
Morris, Sarah	880	Morgan, Alice A.	31877
Morris, Ellen F.	14031	Morgan, Bertha B.	28880
Morris, Mary T.	14032	Morgan, Gideon I.	28881
Morris, Thomas F.	14033	Morgan, John J.	21885
Morris, Silas R.	14364	Moreland, Sarah J.	2133
Morris, Hugh M.	14616	Moreland, C. McDonald	2134
Morris, E. Loyd	15157	Moreland, Jessie M.	2135
Morris, John	15158	Moreland, Martha J.	2136
Morris, William	15159	Moreland Nancy M.	2137
Morris, Nolan	15160	Moreland, Ella	13028
Morris, Mollie	15161	Moreland, Robert H.	13029
Morris, Ella	15162	Moreland, Thomas M.	13030
Morris, Ella	16815	Moreland, William R.	13031
Morris, Lydia	16816	Morrison, Annie E.	7579
Morris, Stand Watie	16817	Morrison, Elsie L.	7580
Morris, Harry	16818	Morrison, Ruth	7581
Morris, Carrie	16819	Morrison, Bessie	7582
Morris, Loyal	16820	Morrison, Henry C.	7583
Morris, Rebecca J.	16821	Morrison, Leroy C.	7584
Morris, Charles T.	16822	Morrison, Susan K.	10322
Morris, John	17818	Morrison, Mary M.	10323
Morris, George	17819	Morrison, Maggie V.	10324
Morris, Sallie	17820	Morrison, Robert T., Jr.	10325
Morris, Rufus	17821	Morrison, Delila L.	10326
Morris, Joseph	17822	Morrison, Ellen C.	10327
Morris, Elizabeth	17823	Morrison, Claud A.	10328
Morris, Savannah	30803	Morrison, Angie L.	10329
Morris, Mary J.	26041	Morrison, Dora V.	10330
Morris, Nancy J.	26042	Morrison, John	10331
Morris, Sarah C.	26043	Morrison, Susanna	12607
Morris, John W.	26044	Morrison, William E.	12608
Morris, Charles T.	26045	Morrison, James E.	21859
Morris, Della M.	26046	Morrison, Blanch E. H.	32126
Morris, Myrtle	26047	Morrow, Maggie L.	7998
Morris, Jesse M.	26048	Morrow, James C.	7999
Morris, Anna L.	26049	Morrow, Frederick L.	8000
Morris, Bertha L.	26050	Morrow, Leo	8001
Morris, Clarence Emery	11025	Morrow, Nancy	17076
Morris, Dallas	10533	Moretz, Clara S.	15290
Morris, George	19509	Morehouse, Katie May	26820
Morris, Mary	19510	Morehouse, Nora	26817
Morris, Joe	25776	Morehouse, Helen	26818
Morris, Houston	32303	Morehouse, Clarence A.	26819
Morris, John	19530	Mosier, Neva	13015
Morris, Lucy	19531	Mosier, Grace M.	13016
Morris, Jim	28520	Mosier, Iva L.	13017
Morris, Lincoln	16823	Mosier, Chester S.	13018
Morris, Claude Daniel	26051	Moss, Lonia	17369
Morris, Maud C.	26052	Mose, September	20853
Morgan, Frank M.	22516	Mose, Lizzie	20854
Morgan, Minnie	22518	Mose, Jennie	20855
Morgan, Olney S.	4735	Mose, Charles	20856
Morgan, Samuel S.	4736	Mose, Sallie	20857
Morgan, Malinda J.	5575	Mose, Thomas	20858
Morgan, Maud M.	5576	Mosier, Esther	13019
Morgan, Lou J.	5577	Moton, John H.	3568
Morgan, Dora D.	6571	Moton, William H.	3571
Morgan, William L.	6572	Moton, Lou E.	3572
Morgan, Gideon	6761	Moton, Ollie May	3573
Morgan, Martha L.	6762	Moton, Gatsy	3574
Morgan, Margaret E. A.	6763	Moton, Frank	3575
Morgan, Amanda P.	6764	Moton, Fred R.	3576
Morgan, Sallie M.	6765	Moton, Clem C.	3845
Morgan, Ellen P. M.	6766	Moton, Jesse E.	3846
Morgan, Houston M.	13822	Moton, Willie E.	3847
Morgan, Lulu	13850	Moton, Andy M.	3848
Morgan, Taylet	14944	Moton, Bertie M.	3849
Morgan, Ruth	14945	Moton, Mary E.	22930
Morgan, Flora A.	14946	Mothershed, Lulu	4122

Name.	Roll No.	Name.	Roll No.
Moten, John W.	4051	Murphy, John	2522
Moten, Oscar	4052	Murphy, Lugie	2523
Moten, Bessie	4053	Murphy, William	2524
Moten, Joseph	4054	Murphy, Amy	2525
Motte, William R.	21950	Murphy, Jennie	2583
Motte, Emma	21951	Murphy, Charles	32609
Motte, Joseph H.	21952	Murphy, Nellie	32610
Motte, Rebecca A.	21953	Murphy, Pearlie	32250
Motte, Mattie B.	21955	Murphy, Minnie	32251
Mounts, Ruth	4593	Murphy, Edna	32252
Mounts, Robert E. L.	4594	Murphy, Maggie F.	1131
Mounts, John T.	5670	Murphy, Thomas	6007
Mounts, Teddy R.	5671	Murphy, Amanda	6008
Mounts, David H.	5672	Murphy, Sallie	6009
Mouse, Watt	8892	Murphy, Looney	6010
Mouse, Nancy	8893	Murphy, Jesse	6011
Mouse, Blossom	9457	Murphy, Blue	6404
Mouse, Johnson	9458	Murphy, Emma C.	7384
Mouse, Sapsucker	9459	Murphy, Andrew	7385
Mouse, Lewis	10083	Murphy, Cora	7386
Mouse, Nancy	10093	Murphy, Henry	7387
Mouse, John R.	14537	Murphy, Thomas	7388
Mouse, Mary	14538	Murphy, Nola	7389
Mouse, Cornelius	28900	Murphy, Lula	7390
Mouse, Darcus	28901	Murphy, David	24093
Mouse, Tony	29013	Murphy, Gertrude	24094
Mouse, Charlotte	29014	Murphy, Joel	24095
Mouse, Price	29015	Murphy, William	24096
Mouse Roll	29016	Murphy, Jessie C.	24721
Mouse, Olkin	29017	Murphy, Augustus	24722
Mouse, Sallie	29018	Murphy, Iris	24723
Mouse, Lucy	29019	Murphy, Byna	24724
Mouse, Peggy	16710	Murphy, Lilla	24725
Mouse, Aggie	8894	Murphy, Oliver	24726
Mouse, Degane	19474	Murphy, Wyche	24727
Mouse, Abraham	19769	Murphy, Sue	24728
Mouse, Olkin	19770	Murphy, James L.	16878
Mouse, Chicoowee	30576	Murphy, Lizzie	28323
Mouse, Lila	30577	Murphy, Sarah R.	26821
Mouse, Sahnahna	20587	Murphy, Canary J.	6012
Mouse, Gahyawhi	20588	Murphy, Jennie	18318
Mouse, Tookah	32874	Murphy, Maria M.	18319
Mouse, Hominy	32875	Murphy, Sophia	18320
Mouse, George	32876	Murphy, Robert	18321
Mount, Emma L.	9788	Murphy, Sallie	29884
Mount, Mike E.	9789	Murphy, Mack	19883
Mount, Leta P.	9790	Murphy, Annie	19889
Mounce, Rosanna	25109	Murphy, Ned	19890
Mounce, Thomas	25110	Murphy, Celie	19891
Mounce, Ellis	25111	Murphy, Lucy	19892
Mounce, Martha J.	31954	Murphy, Nelson	20718
Mulkey, John R.	4284	Murphy, Jackson	20910
Mulkey, John R.	4285	Murphy, Betsy	20911
Mulkey, Lewis A.	4669	Murphy, Willie	20912
Mulkey, Jack R.	23058	Murphy, John	20913
Mulkey, Julia	23059	Murphy, Lizzie	20914
Mulkey, Wiley R.	5493	Murphy, Thomas	20915
Mulkey, Lettie V.	23252	Murphy, Ellen	21334
Mulkey, Alonzo S.	5509	Murphy, Eve	21335
Mulkey, Jonathan D.	5515	Murphy, Polly	21420
Mulkey, Eliza J.	5516	Murphy, Robert Linzey	24097
Mulkey, Rose E. C.	5517	Murphey, Annie H.	12683
Mulkey, Lewis W.	5519	Murray, Elmo	11796
Mulkey, James D.	5763	Murray, Lee	11798
Mulkey, James E.	5764	Murray, Ross	11799
Mulkey, Earnest	5765	Murray, Sarah E.	12375
Mulkey, Nat	5766	Murray, Annie	12376
Mulkey, Eva E.	5767	Murray, Catharine	25214
Mulkey, Ennis	5768	Murray, Robert N.	25215
Mulkey, James D.	16860	Murray, Lindley L.	25216
Mulkey, Richard J.	16865	Murray, Mildred I.	25217
Mulkey, Charles A.	26216	Murray, James	27871
Mulkey, Clara Edith	26217	Murray, Jennie	27872
Mulkey, John R.	5769	Murray, Malcomb	27875
Mullens, Sallie	8397	Murray, Nannie	27874
Mulcare, Minnie	9625	Murray, John	27876
Mulcare, Nova	9626	Murray, Lizzie	27873
Mulcare, Sterling P.	9627	Muskrat, Joseph D.	367
Mulcare, Ella	9628	Muskrat, Nina P.	369
Mulcare, Frederick	9629	Muskrat, Ira Dee	370
Mulcare, Thomas E.	11953	Muskrat, Ruby E.	371
Mulley, Ella	21066	Muskrat, Dorcas	2003
Munroe, Dora A.	29519	Muskrat, Lucy	3090
Murphy, Sallie	1129	Muskrat, Jake J.	28634
Murphy, Martha M.	1130	Muskrat, Daniel	7218
Murphy, Lydia	2521	Muskrat, James	23717

Name.	Roll No.
Muskrat, Joseph A.	23718
Muskrat, Lee R.	23719
Muskrat, Clyde	23720
Muskrat, Nellie M.	23721
Muskrat, George D.	23722
Muskrat, James W.	23723
Muskrat, James	9991
Muskrat, Maudie	24435
Muskrat, Claudie	24436
Muskrat, Harvey B.	24437
Muskrat, Ruth M.	24438
Muskrat, Ruby	24439
Muskrat, Arch	28244
Muskrat, Nancy	25419
Muskrat, Jack	25420
Muskrat, Joe	25421
Muskrat, Becky	25422
Muskrat, Thomas	25423
Muskrat, Malinda	17079
Muskrat, Wilson	17080
Muskrat, Sallie	17081
Muskrat, Eliza	17082
Muskrat, Katie E.	17086
Muskrat, Thomas J.	30452
Muskrat, Thompson	17764
Muskrat, Henry	17894
Muskrat, Charlotte	18023
Muskrat, Thelma	24440
Muskrat, Roseborough	372
Muskrat, Dave	18351
Muskrat, Polly	18352
Muskrat, Calhoun	18728
Muskrat, Susie	18729
Muskrat, Annie	18730
Muskrat, Georgia	18731
Muskrat, Dawes	18732
Muskrat, Nancy	20107
Muskrat, Charley	20108
Muskrat, John	20455
Muskrat, Mary	20456
Muskrat, Joe	20704
Muskrat, Katie	32585
Mush, Lucy	26147
Mush, Mollie	26148
Musgrove, William A.	11899
Musgrove, Clara E.	12420
Musgrove, Clem R.	12421
Musgrove, Franklin F.	12422
Musgrove, Andrew L.	12423
Musgrove, Cassie V.	12869
Myers, George W.	22225
Myers, Francis M.	22227
Myers, Edith	22228
Myers, Georgia	22229
Myers, Lelia A.	22230
Myers, Isaac H.	32432
Myers, Mary A.	32433
Myers, George E.	32434
Myers, Wilella	29165
McAfee, Mary J.	3829
McAfee, Johnnie E.	3830
McAfee, Frances Elizabeth	3831
McAffrey, Andrew	8583
McAffrey, Ollie C.	8584
McAffrey, Aldona	8585
McAffrey, Fannie	8625
McAffrey, James A.	8626
McAffrey, Hugh, Jr.	8627
McAffrey, Napoleon	8628
McAffrey, Walter T.	8629
McAffrey, Rhoda S.	8630
McAffrey, John	8632
McAffrey, William M.	8633
McAffrey, Joseph L.	8635
McAffrey, Loran R.	8631
McAllister, John W., Jr.	5306
McAllister, John W.	5305
McAllister, Joe William	5307
McAnally, Sallie	10996
McAnally, Robert E.	11023
McAndrews, Ellen	12169
McAndrews, Nora E.	12170
McAndrews, Mike C.	12171
McAndrews, David R.	12172
McAndrews, John F.	12173

Name.	Roll No.
McBride, Mary J.	15264
McBroom, Effie	27353
McCabe, Elizabeth	30062
McCaffree, Czarina V.	11925
McCaffree, Bradley Doras	11926
McCaleb, Addison F.	10614
McCaleb, Charles G.	10616
McCamish, Richard W. C.	31022
McCamish, Jim	31023
McCamish, Ben	31024
McCarty, Lydia F.	11218
McCarty, Reuben C.	11219
McCarty, Moses	11220
McCarty, John	11221
McCarty, Nancy	11222
McCarty, Frederick	11399
McCarty, Frank	11400
McCarty, Thomas	11401
McCarty, Charlsey F.	11402
McCarter, Joe	18388
McCarter, Watt	18389
McCarter, Clem	18898
McCarter, Susie	18899
McCarter, Polly	32286
McCarter, Sallie	21311
McCarter, Eyuste	32380
McCarter, Lula	32577
McCartlin, William	31238
McCartlin, Albert	31239
McCartlin, James	31240
McCartlin, Nona	31241
McCauley, Bertha	22101
McCausland, Mary M.	7060
McCay, Alfred	30040
McCay, John B.	30042
McCay, Evaline D.	30043
McCay, Alfred A.	30044
McCay, William C.	30045
McCay, James J.	30046
McCay, John S.	11850
McCay, Jessie	11851
McCay, William L.	11852
McCay, Claude R.	11853
McCay, Mary J.	11855
McCay, Benjamin F.	12220
McCay, Charles C.	12221
McCay, Jesse L.	12222
McCay, William H., Jr.	13348
McCay, Charlotte	14790
McCay, Watson B.	11854
McClain, Susie	5412
McClain, Minnie E.	22408
McClain, Mattie May	22409
McClain, Mollie A.	22410
McClain, Maudie L.	22411
McClain, William E.	21851
McClain, Hattie J.	24788
McClain, Sarah V.	27756
McClain, William	12780
McClain, Delilah B.	12781
McClain, Robert	12782
McClain, Addie	12783
McClaren, Neppie	17890
McClanahan, Zoa Z.	4366
McClanahan, Leonard L.	4367
McClellan, Margaret P.	5304
McClellan, Rachel L.	11370
McClellan, Edward W.	11371
McClellan, William A.	11372
McClellan, Charles T.	11373
McClellan, Mary E.	11423
McClellan, John F.	12442
McClellan, Charles W.	12443
McClellan, Jennie L.	12444
McClellan, Susan	12445
McClellan, Stephen L.	12446
McClellan, Lela G.	12447
McClure, Kate	5524
McClure, Henry B.	5798
McClure, James E.	5799
McClure, Kathryn	5800
McClure, Thomas	5801
McClure, Minnie F.	5802
McClure, Hazel	5803

Name.	Roll No.	Name.	Roll No.
McClure, Robert L.	5805	McCoy, James Willis	32423
McClure, Charles J.	5813	McCoy, William M.	32424
McClure, Edwin	5814	McCoy, Lela F.	32425
McClure, Francis	5815	McCoy, Sina A.	32426
McClure, Della	5816	McCoy, Alex	18081
McClure, Hattie	5817	McCoy, Saphronia	18082
McClure, Douglas	5818	McCoy, Tom	18083
McClure, William J.	17069	McCoy, Zeke	18084
McClure, John	17070	McCoy, Lilah	18085
McClure, Fannie F.	26879	McCoy, Sam	18086
McClure, Slater L.	26880	McCoy, Cherokee	18087
McClure, Roy M.	26881	McCoy, Ellen	18088
McClure, William L.	26882	McCoy, Levi	18089
McClure, Hugh C.	26883	McCoy, Leaf	18090
McClure, Marguerite J.	26884	McCoy, Looney	18148
McClure, Elizabeth L.	26885	McCoy, Sadie	18149
McClure, Eulala	26886	McCoy, Charles	19312
McClure, Eva Pauline	26887	McCoy, Stand	19328
McClure, Rhoda K.	31362	McCoy, Lizzie	19341
McClure, Lewis L.	31363	McCoy, Betsy	19342
McClure, William E.	31364	McCoy, Sam	19343
McClure, Leroy T.	31365	McCoy, Jeff D.	19555
McClure, Mary V.	31444	McCoy, Mayes	19556
McClure, Bertha F.	31445	McCoy, Grover	19557
McClure, Orion J.	31446	McCoy, Mary	19558
McClure, Edward F.	31447	McCoy, Clement	19559
McCombs, Elizabeth	8399	McCoy, Laura	19560
McCombs, John W.	8400	McCoy, Fanny	19561
McCombs, Birdie	8401	McCoy, Esther	20514
McCombs, Clara V.	8402	McCoy, Sarah	20713
McConnell, Mary	3336	McCoy, Ned	20715
McConnell, Lizzie	11061	McCoy, Dick	21077
McConnell, Ida	11063	McCoy, Alex, Jr.	21117
McConnell, Jerry	11064	McCoy, Yahni	21118
McConnell, Lillie May	11065	McCoy, Levi	21119
McCorkle, Emma	5156	McCoy, Eve	21120
McCorkle, David W.	17594	McCoy, Lucy J.	9576
McCorkle, Mary C.	17595	McCoy, Hattie	26331
McCorkle, Joseph L.	17596	McCrady, Eliza A.	2738
McCorkle, James M.	17598	McCrady, Young M.	2739
McCormic, Isabella C.	31930	McCrady, Foster	2740
McCormic, Bonnie C.	31931	McCrady, Beulah	2741
McCormic, Earl	31932	McCracken, William E.	3919
McCormic, John B.	31933	McCracken, Walker	28084
McCormic, Rosa M.	31934	McCracken, Rufus W.	23270
McCoy, George W.	22447	McCracken, Mary	29998
McCoy, Ida R. V.	22248	McCracken, Joseph L.	6337
McCoy, Lela H.	22449	McCrary, James R.	7621
McCoy, Elsey A.	22450	McCrary, Sterling P.	23877
McCoy, William B.	22451	McCrary, Louisa	7943
McCoy, Tom	1427	McCrary, William	7944
McCoy, Rosanna	1428	McCrary, William C.	8800
McCoy, Ida	1429	McCrary, Willie A.	8801
McCoy, Ellen	3388	McCrary, David E.	8802
McCoy, James L.	26989	McCrary, Jack W.	21672
McCoy, John W.	6389	McCracken, Oneida	24586
McCoy, John W. Jr.	6390	McCracken, Lillian	24587
McCoy, Martha	6392	McCracken, Horace L.	24588
McCoy, Lillie A.	6393	McCracken, Mary	29998
McCoy, Lem L.	6394	McCracken, James T.	30278
McCoy, Vina	6395	McCracken, Russell L.	30279
McCoy, George	6396	McCracken, John W.	31390
McCoy, Mary A.	25809	McCuen, George	2608
McCoy, Chester F.	9570	McCuen, Jane	2609
McCoy, John M.	9571	McCuen, Lewis	2610
McCoy, Minnie V.	9572	McCuen, Katie	2611
McCoy, Robert L.	9573	McCuen, Mary	2612
McCoy, Fredonia I.	9574	McCues, Virgie E.	2613
McCoy, Charles R.	11296	McCuen, William B.	2614
McCoy, Archibald B.	11595	McCuen, Sarah	2615
McCoy, Archibald C.	11596	McCulloch, Lula M.	8034
McCoy, Claud S.	11597	McCullough, James F.	22199
McCoy, Emily	10684	McCullough, Mattie L.	22200
McCoy, Freddie	10685	McCullough, Lelia	22201
McCoy, Maggie	14560	McCullough, Ardath E.	22202
McCoy, Waddy T.	15362	McCullough, John W.	286
McCoy, Albert	15363	McCullough, Rachel J.	287
McCoy, Myrtle	15364	McCullough, Milton J.	288
McCoy, Watt W.	15365	McCullough, Ora	289
McCoy, Edward	16943	McCullough, Oma	290
McCoy, Lela G.	16944	McCullough, Venie	291
McCoy, Charles	28357	McCullough, George E.	7696
McCoy, Sallie	28358	McCullough, Milton H.	7697
McCoy, Edward E.	28359	McCullough, Luther A.	7698
McCoy, Peachie	28360	McCullough, William P.	24334
McCoy, George	17511		

Name.	Roll No.
McCullough, Lillian M.	24336
McCullough, Milton M.	24337
McCullough, Joseph H.	9666
McCullough, Eva C.	9667
McCullough, Rachel J.	9687
McCullough, Charles H.	9688
McCullough, Pete	30296
McCullough, Maggie J.	30297
McCullough, Winnie D.	30298
McCullough, Rex J.	30299
McCullough, George E.	7699
McCullough, William E.	24338
McCullough, Cleva O.	9668
McCutchen, Florence E.	11831
McCutchen, Gracie I.	11832
McDaniel, Thomas	4409
McDaniel, Willis N.	4410
McDaniel, Lonard T.	4411
McDaniel, Stella	30077
McDaniel, Mary	4757
McDaniel, Daniel	4850
McDaniel, Georgia	5418
McDaniel, Jimy	5419
McDaniel, Rosie	5420
McDaniel, Nelson	28654
MeDaniel, Calvin	6834
McDaniel, William	6835
McDaniel, Robert	6836
McDaniel, David	6837
McDaniel, Frederick	10148
McDaniel, Fannie	30222
McDaniel, Charley	10639
McDaniel, Mary	10902
McDaniel, Minnie M.	10903
McDaniel, John R.	10904
McDaniel, Martin	11857
McDaniel, Willie	24769
McDaniel, Bessie	24770
McDaniel, Alexander L.	24783
McDaniel, Robert	24784
McDaniel, Kate	24785
McDaniel, Nellie	24786
McDaniel, Alexander L. Jr.	24787
McDaniel, Andrew J.	28050
McDaniel, Arthur L.	28051
McDaniel, Jesse	11963
McDaniel, Ross	11964
McDaniel, Rosa	28221
McDaniel, Martha H.	14132
McDaniel, Luna M.	14133
McDaniel, Tommie I.	14134
McDaniel, Martha S.	14135
McDaniel, Susan A.	14136
McDaniel, Joseph T.	14238
McDaniel, Lewis	25270
McDaniel, Olla	25271
McDaniel, Bertha	25272
McDaniel, William	25273
McDaniel, Leonard	25274
McDaniel, Albert	25275
McDaniel, Etta F.	25276
McDaniel, Sarah M.	25277
McDaniel, Jefferson	25278
McDaniel, Wilson H.	15812
McDaniel, Sarah	15813
McDaniel, Nancy	16787
McDaniel, Eliza	16869
McDaniel, George B.	17118
McDaniel, Ella	17183
McDaniel, Ida	15815
McDaniel, Kin	6838
McDonald, Ray	9601
McDonald, George W.	5007
McDonald, William C.	5008
McDonald, Narcina M.	5009
McDonald, Edward L.	5010
McDonald, Charles S.	5189
McDonald, Charley C.	5190
McDonald, Theodore	6085
McDonald, Isaac N.	9599
McDonald, Roy	9600
McDonald, Ralph C.	9602

Name.	Roll No.
McDonald, George B.	11137
McDonald, Matilda	11834
McDonald, Vina	11835
McDonald, Mary A.	11918
McDonald, Minnie M.	11919
McDonald, Virgie T.	16254
McDonald, Robert R.	25317
McDonald, Essie V.	25318
McDonald, Earnest C.	25319
McDonald, Garland	22160
McDonald, Mattie C.	22161
McDonald, Jessie M.	28741
McDowell, Joe	9170
McDowell, Jessie M.	24219
McDowell, Dewy R.	24220
McDowell, Martha	30847
McDowell, Ivy M.	30850
McEachin, Maggie	2957
McEachin, Martha	2958
McElhaney, Mary E.	26292
McElhaney, Charles A.	26293
McElhaney, William J.	26294
McElhaney, John H.	26295
McElhaney, George S. L.	26296
McElmeel, Elizabeth	16847
McElmeel, Elizabeth	16848
McElreath, William M.	6539
McElreath, Thomas M.	6540
McElreath, Anna G.	6541
McElreath, Elizabeth	6542
McElreath, Mary B.	6543
McEnery, Lizzie	2209
McEnery, Ruth S.	2210
McEnery, Hazel	23070
McEnery, Fred B.	32022
McEwin, Joseph	31127
McEwin, Charles	31128
McEwin, Lizzie	31129
McEwin, Frank	31130
McFall, Eugenia	9695
McFall, Frankie R.	24344
McFall, Eddie J.	24345
McFall, Wiley W.	9696
McFall, William J.	9697
McFall, Lizzie M.	10399
McFall, John U.	10400
McFall, Edward L.	10401
McFall, Louisa M.	10402
McFall, Ella L.	10403
McFall, Richard S.	10404
McFarland, Mary L.	10080
McFarland, Jessie	10081
McFarland, Willie	10082
McGee, Thomas J., Sr.	582
McGee, Cleroe	583
McGee, Saladin C.	584
McGee, Joseph F.	585
McGee, Quilliki	586
McGee, Susan	8494
McGhee, Samuel B.	27651
McGhee, Belle	27652
McGhee, Bertie O.	27653
McGhee, Buena Vista	27654
McGhee, Richard J.	27655
McGhee, Edith I.	27656
McGhee, David A.	9630
McGhee, Dennis B.	9631
McGhee, John R.	9633
McGhee, Elizabeth B.	9634
McGhee, Esther L.	9635
McGhee, Florence E.	9636
McGhee, Ambrose	9637
McGhee, John H.	9649
McGhee, Ambrose H.	9650
McGhee, Elizabeth	9651
McGhee, Jasper H.	9652
McGhee, Byrl H.	9653
McGhee, David A.	27681
McGhee, Marium	27682
McGhee, Warren A.	27683
McGhee, James M.	28750
McGhee, Martha A.	28751
McGhee, Robert J.	28752

Name.	Roll No.	Name.	Roll No.
McGhee, Thomas O.	28753	McKinney, Dennis B.	4170
McGhee, Walter C.	28754	McKinney, Mary	4171
McGhee, Thomas J. Jr.	10055	McKinney, Stella M.	4172
McGhee, Rondal E.	10056	McKinney, Almira J.	12877
McGhee, Eula B.	10057	McKinney, Amanda E.	12879
McGhee, Albert V.	26621	McKinney, John L.	14872
McGhee, Nellie J.	26622	McKinney, Johnson P.	18046
McGhee, Sarah A.	26623	McKinney, Ida B.	4173
McGhee, Clarettie	26624	McKinney, Myrtle	3787
McGhee, Rosa M.	26625	McKinzey, Simon	28396
McGhee, Bluford	26626	McKinzey, Minnie	28397
McGhee, Martha E.	28755	McKinzey, Benjamin	23574
McGinnis, William T.	30270	McKinzey, Annie	26120
McGinnis, Elizabeth C.	30271	McKnight, Susie	13435
McGinnis, Charles C.	30272	McKnight, Jessie M.	13436
McGlamery, Rosa B.	29379	McKnight, Joe	13437
McGlamery, Felix G.	29380	McKnight, George L.	13438
McGlamery, Esther C.	29381	McKnight, Cora L.	13439
McGlamery, John S.	29382	McKnight, Mattie E.	29243
McGrath, Amanda	10812	McKnight, Addie L.	29244
McHenry, Lucinda	16362	McKnight, Ruth	29245
McHenry, Henry	16363	McKnight, Laura M.	29246
McHenry, Harriet	16364	McLain, Jesse	27344
McHenry, John	16365	McLain, Maggie	27345
McInerney, Joe	3474	McLain, Frank	27346
McIntosh, James	26578	McLain, Nannie	27347
McIntosh, John	10340	McLain, Samuel H.	27348
McIntosh, Kay-haw-ka	24520	McLain, Calvin C.	27349
McIntosh, John R.	13008	McLain, Eliza	27350
McIntosh, Maria L.	13009	McLain, George W.	27351
McIntosh, Beatrice N.	13010	McLain, Charlotte	27352
McIntosh, Frank	29685	McLain, Joseph	27370
McIntosh, Mary	29686	McLain, Thomas	27371
McIntosh, Richard	29687	McLain, Jesse	5518
McIntosh, John	18345	McLain, John	5520
McIntosh, Myrtle	18346	McLain, James	5521
McIntosh, Huling	24521	McLain, Edward	5902
McIntosh, Louisa	32555	McLain, Luney	6405
McInerney, Pinkie A.	15724	McLain, Rachel	23377
McKay, Nellie	18331	McLain, Ellis	23378
McKay, Joe	21255	McLain, Calvin	23379
McKay, Wilson	25990	McLain, Lillie	23330
McKay, Eliza	25991	McLain, Josie	7612
McKeehan, Minnie M.	11932	McLain, Myra	11465
McKeehan, Laura V.	11933	McLain, Martha A.	11936
McKeehan, Verna B.	11934	McLain, Levi L.	11937
McKee, William R.	16037	McLain, Cora N.	11938
McKee, Mary J.	16038	McLain, Nannie R.	11939
McKee, Joseph R.	16042	McLain, James	12020
McKee, Lizzie	16043	McLain, Henry	15444
McKee, Alphonso	16044	McLain, Earl	15445
McKee, Theodore C.	16045	McLain, William	15596
McKee, Alfred C.	16488	McLain, Jesse J.	15597
McKee, William J.	16525	McLain, Callie	15598
McKee, George D.	16526	McLain, Delilah	15599
McKee, John T.	16527	McLain, Josie	15600
McKee, Pearl A.	16528	McLain, William F.	15601
McKee, Cadet A.	16529	McLain, Ethel	15602
McKeehan, Elizabeth	11362	McLain, Floyd	17314
McKee, Sequoyah	18772	McLain, Beulah M.	26305
McKee, Florian M.	16039	McLain, Charlie M.	26306
McKee, Joseph R., Jr.	16046	McLain, Ella M.	21818
McKelvey, Johnsana D.	30909	McLain, Myra M.	27372
McKelvey, Edna A.	30911	McLain, John	19962
McKenzie, Mary	9356	McLain, Ella	19963
McKenzie, Lucile	9357	McLain, Cynthia	19964
McKenzie, Jonathan G.	9358	McLain, Henry	19965
McKenzie, Wilbur H.	9359	McLain, Bullett	19966
McKenney, Hattie J.	11826	McLain, Ned	19967
McKenney, Alvertie G.	11827	McLane, Edward	9577
McKenney, James O.	11828	McLane, Minnie B.	11499
McKenney, Mary	11829	McLane, Austin	12347
McKinney, Alexander F.	3781	McLane, Lou	12348
McKinney, Ida	3782	McLane, Jessie H.	12350
McKinney, Emma	3783	McLane, Sarah F.	12351
McKinney, Lonzo	3784	McLane, John A.	12352
McKinney, May	3785	McLane, Clyde	12353
McKinney, Mary	3786	McLane, Ellen C.	12349
McKinney, Lucy	4165	McLane, Rachel	12354
McKinney, Cora	4166	McLaughlin, Willie	376
McKinney, Jessie	4167	McLaughlin, Francis	27396
McKinney, Luella P.	4168	McLaughlin, David C.	6691
McKinney, Dennis	4169	McLaughlin, Joshua E.	7633

Name.	Roll No.
McLaughlin, Carrie	7634
McLaughlin, Ila	7635
McLaughlin, Maggie M.	23810
McLaughlin, William C.	7636
McLaughlin, George	7909
McLaughlin, Fannie	7910
McLaughlin, William T.	7911
McLaughlin, Annie	7912
McLaughlin, Joseph F.	9546
McLaughlin, Carrie E.	24306
McLaughlin, George F.	24307
McLaughlin, William	9661
McLaughlin, Anna E.	9847
McLaughlin, Louisa I.	9848
McLaughlin, Susie	9849
McLaughlin, Frank J.	7913
McLaughlin, Frederick	27633
McLaughlin, Minnie M.	27634
McLemore, Julia	28074
McLemore, Chester	28075
McLemore, Robert	28076
McLemore, Lizzie	28077
McLemore, John	28078
McLemore, William	1937
McLemore, Eliza	1938
McLemore, Annie	1939
McLemore, Tom	1940
McLemore, Lee	1941
McLemore, Wattie	1942
McLemore, Dick	1943
McLemore, George W.	2451
McLemore, Lizzie	2452
McLemore, Lucinda	2453
McLemore, Augustus	2454
McLemore, Emmet	2455
McLemore, Thomas	2586
McLemore, Thomas	18893
McLemore, Robert	18894
McLemore, Samuel	20214
McLemore, Margaret	20215
McLemore, Robert	20216
McLemore, Ollie	20227
McLemore, Louisa J.	20228
McLemore, Joe	21140
McMains, Sallie	11008
McMains, James A.	11009
McMains, Ota F.	11010
McMakin, Savannah	22169
McMakin, Eula J.	22170
McMakin, Susan K.	22171
McMakin, Andrew J.	22172
McMakin, Charles	22173
McMurray, Eliza J.	16982
McMurtrey, Louisa E.	26104
McMurtrey, Bertie B.	26105
McMurtrey, Jessie Edward	26106
McMullens, Susan	9123
McMullens, Minnie M.	9124
McNabb, Mary E.	21922
McNabb, Clifford S.	21923
McNair, Edward B.	6723
McNair, Nicholas B.	6817
McNair, Oscar	6818
McNair, Clem	6819
McNair, Nannie	23455
McNair, William G.	23456
McNair, Benjamin F.	23457
McNair, Nancy S.	6844
McNair, Owen F.	6845
McNair, Dennis	6846
McNair, Callie	6847
McNair, Etta	23500
McNair, William	10423
McNair, James P.	23458
McNairn, Louisa	30993
McPhearson, William R.	1748
McPhearson, John T.	5421
McPherson, Polly	1907
McPhearson, John V.	1909
McPherson, Julia	4001
McPherson, David	4002
McPherson, Jackson	23454
McPherson, Robert	25253
McPherson, Willis	25254

Name.	Roll No.
McPherson, Carlos V.	16543
McPherson, Lewis	16544
McPherson, Beatrice	16545
McPherson, John W.	16546
McPherson, Harriett B.	16978
McPherson, Mary	21819
McPherson, Jennie	21820
McPherson, Joanna	21821
McPhearson, Louisa A.	21936
McSpadden, R. Vance	9734
McSpadden, Florence E.	12940
McSpadden, Thomas B.	12941
McSpadden, Ella B.	12942
McSpadden, Elizabeth P.	12943
McSpadden, Maude H.	12944
McSpadden, Forest K.	12945
McSpadden, Theodore R.	12946
McSpadden, Oscar L.	12947
McSpadden, Serena	13032
McSpadden, Zoe	13033
McSpadden, Floyd C.	13034
McSpadden, Roscoe C.	13035
McSpadden, Zella C.	13036
McSpadden, Alma	13037
McSpadden, Sallie C.	13071
McSpadden, Clem M.	13072
McSpadden, May	13073
McSpadden, Herbert T.	13074
McSpadden, Maud I.	13075
McSpadden, Helen	13076
McSpadden, Pauline	13077
McSpadden, Ellen E.	13739
McSpadden, Mary J.	13740
McSpadden, James W., Jr.	13741
McSpadden, Cherrie A.	13742
McSpadden, Helen I.	13743
McSpadden, Cora	13814
McSpadden, Theodore B.	13815
McSpadden, Nellie E.	13816
McSpadden, Gertrude	13817
McSpadden, Captola V.	16302
McSpadden, Madeleine W.	16303
Nading, Pearl	9645
Nading, Ethel M.	9646
Nading, Nancy	31068
Nading, Virgil	31069
Nairn, James	31348
Nairn, William Jr.	31349
Nairn, Ettie	31350
Nairn, Eva	31351
Nakedhead, Harlan	27204
Nakedhead, Lizzie	27205
Nakedhead, Thomas	27206
Nakedhead, John	27207
Nakedhead, Jack	22711
Nakedhead, Charles	3641
Nakedhead, John	17854
Nakedhead, Lizzie	18216
Nakedhead, Sammie	18217
Nakedhead, James	18307
Nakedhead, Joe	18308
Nakedhead, Jennie	4018
Nakedhead, Oscar	32033
Nall, Joella	8360
Nall, Dora E.	8361
Nall, Josie E.	8362
Nall, Sarah	27684
Nall, Morris L.	27685
Nall, Georgia	8363
Nall, John L.	30950
Nall, Mary E.	30951
Nance, Sarah A.	7466
Nance, John F.	7468
Nance, Lula M.	7469
Nance, Claude W.	7470
Nance, James E.	7471
Nance, Mary J.	7472

Name.	Roll No.	Name.	Roll No.
Nance, William M.	7473	Nelson, Wesley	3964
Nance, Walter S.	21584	Nelson, Lewis	3965
Nash, Lucy M.	4241	Nelson, Henry	3966
Nash, Corinne	4242	Nelson, Jessie	5770
Nash, Hilda	4243	Nelson, Dehison S.	5771
Nash, Edwin O.	4244	Nelson, Ella	23802
Nash, Francis A.	4258	Nelson, Ruby A.	23803
Nash, Florian H., Jr.	4259	Nelson, Polly A.	23804
Nash, Ida V.	4260	Nelson, Effie J.	23805
Nash, Fanny E.	4261	Nelson, James C.	23806
Nash, Lewis R.	4279	Nelson, Edward J.	32619
Nash, Fairy F.	4280	Nelson, Martha	8307
Nash, Edgar R.	4281	Nelson, Jessie D.	3967
Nash, Dorothy M.	4282	Nelson, Mary	30374
Nash, Tookah	4505	Nelson, Esther	25506
Nash, Clara A.	4506	Nelson, Effie O.	21875
Nash, Bertha M.	4507	Nelson, Jesse	21876
Nash, W. Carol	4508	Nelson, Ethel	21877
Nave, Walter	11462	Nelson, Ereah	21878
Nave, Joseph	11945	Nelson, Mariam West-	
Nave, Alsie	11946	ley	21879
Nave, Joseph Jr.	11948	Nelson, Arthur	32725
Nave, Alfred	11949	Nelson, Myrtle E.	32726
Nave, Andy R.	16281	Nelson, Sarah B.	4064
Nave, Ella C.	25327	Nellis, Nancy	22457
Nave, Andy R., Jr.	25328	Nely, Smith	27163
Nave, George F.	25329	Nely, Lucinda	27164
Nave, Joanna G.	25330	Nely, James	27165
Nave, Fannie B.	25331	Nelms, Sarah	8574
Nave, Ida M.	25332	Nelms, Arch	12448
Nave, Susie M.	25333	Nelms, Ibbie	12449
Nave, Henry D.	16301	Nelms, Jennie	12450
Nave, Thomas	15336	Nelms, Victoria	12451
Nave, Louis E.	25337	Nelms, Ellen	12452
Nave, Jennie	25338	Nelms, Rachel	12453
Nave, Robert	29968	Nelms, Luke	12454
Nave, Anna C.	16744	Nelems, Felix	13331
Nave, Julia	21935	Nelms, Adam	17892
Nazworthy, Hannah A.	21695	Nelms, John	17906
Neal, Annie	2584	Nertahweyah	17889
Neal, Laura	2585	Nettles, Ruth	4071
Neal, Dick	5927	Nettles, Charles C.	4072
Neal, Richard, Jr.	5928	Nettles, Leona H.	4073
Neal, James	5929	Nettles, Frederick M.	4074
Neal, Polly	5930	Neugin, Jack	1316
Neal, Nannie	5947	Neugin, Emiline	1317
Neal, Samuel H.	17026	Neugin, Sarah	1318
Neal, James	28336	Neugin, Cornelius	1319
Neal, Richard, Jr.	28337	Neugin, Millard	1320
Neal, Joe Willie	31825	Neugin, Nelson	1321
Ned, Nellie	21055	Neugin, Franklin	1322
Ned, John	19299	Neugin, Jack, Jr.	1323
Ned, Liza	19300	Neugin, Maggie L.	1324
Nedson, Leach	25881	Neugin, Neal	15008
Nedson, Annie	32750	Neugin, Jennie	15009
Needles, Amanda	30059	Neugin, Susie	15010
Needles, Jug	30060	Neugin, Joseph	15013
Neese, Winona	10452	Neugin, Henry	15065
Needham, Martha E.	7827	Neugin, David	15097
Needham, John S.	7828	Neugin, Titus	15098
Needham, Sallie M.	7829	Neugin, Rebecca	28284
Needham, Fannie P.	7830	Neugin, Rachel	28934
Needham, Jesse G.	7831	Neville, Rosa L.	23776
Needham, Valentine W.	10794	Neville, Helen G.	23777
Needham, Allie A.	10795	Neville, James Carroll	23778
Neff, William	3068	Newman, Namie	1457
Neff, Mattie	3069	Newman, William T.	1458
Neff, Hooley P.	3070	Newman, Nora M.	1459
Neff, Ezra	3071	Newman, Sallie F.	12875
Neff, America	3072	Newman, Luther C.	20104
Neff, Arizona	3073	Newman, Katie	31762
Neff, Olen L.	3074	New, Josephine	10013
Neff, Sarah F.	16144	New, Ezra E.	10014
Neff, James M.	16145	New, Isaac	10015
Ney, Mary B.	16146	New, Nancy A.	10016
Neff, Ada L.	16147	New, Sarah	10017
Neff, Thomas E.	16148	Newton, Elizabeth	25201
Neighbours, Isaac	30057	Newton, Emma D.	25202
Neighbours, James W.	7457	Newton, Josie E.	25203
Neighbours, Lourine L.	9758	Newton, Mack J.	25204
Neighbours, Lucy F.	9763	Newton, Laura A.	15182
Neilson, Nonie	32225	Newton, Clifford	15183
Neilson, Ella M.	32534	Newton, Oscar	15184

Name.	Roll No.
Newton, Edgar	15185
Newton, Sidney	15918
Newton, Dellie	15919
Newton, Rhuby	15920
Newton, Walter	15921
Newton, William	15922
Newton, Lizzie	15923
Newton, Ida L.	16795
Newton, Urvin C.	16796
Newton, Clyde	16798
Newton, Charlotte	32898
Newcomb, Solomon	31456
Newcomb, Robert F.	31474
Newcomb, Edward T.	31644
Newcomb, Polly M.	32100
Newcomb, Otmus A.	32101
Nicholson, Henry F.	6118
Nicholson, Willie	6119
Nicholson, David L.	6120
Nicholson, Cornelia	6121
Nicholson, Leo B.	6122
Nicholson, Sallie B.	28626
Nicholson, Daniel G.	24562
Nicholson, Henry	24563
Nicholson, Lettie M.	24564
Nicholson, Sim	24565
Nicholson, Richard H.	11102
Nicholson, Richard	11572
Nicholson, Edward E.	12263
Nicholson, Thomas K.	12264
Nicholson, Gracie L.	12265
Nicholson, James P.	12266
Nicholson, Edward V.	13045
Nicholson, Leah G.	13046
Nicholson, Lula M.	29375
Nicholson, Eliza D.	29376
Nicholson, Eva E.	13047
Nicholson, Roy Preston	11573
Nicholson, Samuel Jasper	29377
Nicholas, Murta A.	8270
Nicholas, Alice R.	8271
Nicholas, William E.	31526
Nichols, Josephine	6740
Nichols, Frank L.	6741
Nichols, Nettie M.	6742
Nichols, Augustus B.	8174
Nichols, Lucy M.	8175
Nichols, Thomas W.	8176
Nichols, Claude D.	8177
Nichols, Clifford C.	8178
Nichols, Maud I.	8179
Nichols, James L.	8447
Nichols, Henrietta	9086
Nichols, Frank	30230
Nidiffer, Samuel	172
Nidiffer, Emma	173
Nidiffer, Ezekiel	175
Nidiffer, Henry	177
Nidiffer, George	178
Nidiffer, Rufus	179
Nidiffer, Samuel, Jr.	174
Nidiffer, Claud	180
Nidiffer, Connally	181
Nidiffer, Isaac	349
Nidiffer, Beulah	350
Nidiffer, Doyle	351
Nidiffer, Nancy	7339
Nidiffer, Annie L.	8019
Nidiffer, Henrietta E.	8020
Nidiffer, Martha M.	8021
Nidiffer, John R.	8022
Nidiffer, George W.	8023
Nidiffer, Freeman E.	8024
Nidiffer, Mamie L.	8025
Nidiffer, Freeman	8203
Nidiffer, Charles	9422
Nidiffer, Wesley I.	9423
Nidiffer, Otis Ellsworth	9424
Nidiffer, George	23955
Nidiffer, Minnie G.	23957
Nidiffer, Jessie .G	23958
Nidiffer, Lucile F.	23959

Name.	Roll No.
Nidiffer, Mary D.	30953
Nidiffer, Ella E.	30954
Nidiffer, Robert H.	30955
Nidiffer, Eula M.	30956
Nidiffer, Edward O.	32110
Nidiffer, Louisa E.	32111
Niemeyer, William W.	26214
Niemeyer, Alfred C.	26215
Niemeyer, Sarah E.	30825
Neimeyer, Chas. H.	30827
Night, Lunie	20924
Ning-go-mah-le-com-in	31571
Nipp, Joseph	9428
Nipp, Ella	9429
Nipp, Henry E.	9430
Nipp, Joseph F.	9431
Nipp, Cora	26519
Nipper, Robert W.	11307
Nitts, Nakie	32681
Nivens, Julia	5720
Nix, John S.	6439
Nix, Sabina	9137
Nix, James O.	9138
Nix, Frank E.	9139
Nix, Maude E.	9140
Nix, William I.	9141
Nix, George F.	9142
Nix, Sarah E.	9392
Nix, Robert F.	14961
Nix, Elsie	19416
Nix, Nancy	19417
Nix, Chu-nu-lu-hunski	19418
Nix, Peter	20566
Nix, Rachel	20567
Nix, Lucy	20568
Nix, Houston	20569
Nix, Cloyeeker	20570
Nix, Cohtahgawie	32318
Nix, Jennie	32319
Noah, Georgia A.	4266
Noah, Elija	4267
Noah, Nathaniel	4268
Noah, Josephine	4733
Nobles, Nathaniel C.	9873
Nobles, William R.	9874
Nobles, Joel B. M.	9875
Nobles, Eula R.	9876
Noblett, Newton A.	9811
Noblett, James E.	9812
Nofflett, Mary	9224
Nofire, Lizzie	1948
Nofire, Polly	1949
Nofire, Jack	1950
Nofire, Joshua	18787
Nofire, Margaret	18788
Nofire, Mary	18789
Nofire, Sequoyah	18790
Nofire, Jane	20607
Nofire, Andy	20608
Nofire, Jim	20609
Nofire, Nancy	20610
Nofire, Anter	20611
Nofire, Allen	20745
Nofire, John	20746
Nofire, John	25746
Noisewater, Betsy	27114
Noisewater, Nancy	2119
Noisewater, John	28431
Noisewater, Jennie	19045
Noisewater, Pigeon	28432
Noisewater, Nancy	19046
Noisey, Mack	19934
Noisey, Susie	19935
Noisey, John	19936
Noisey, Thomas	21035
Noisey, Wakie	21036
Noisey, Polly	21037
Noisey, Thomas Jr.	29123
Nolen, James A.	27600
Nolen, Henry N.	27601
Nolen, Nancy	27454
Norrid, Mahulda E.	2853
Norrid, Serena E.	2854

Name.	Roll No.	Name.	Roll No.
Norrid, Willie B.	2855	Olson, Lewis A.	7572
Norrid, David	2856	Olson, Denny F.	7573
Norrid, Adda R.	26349	Olson, Richard F.	7574
Norrid, Myrtle M.	26350	Olson, Andrew B.	7575
Norton, Jennette	26345	Olson, James F.	7576
Norton, Cora	12583	Olson, Oliver R.	7578
Norman, James A.	5259	Oneal, Lieu A.	13216
Norman, Martha J.	5739	Oneal, Georgia B.	13217
Norman, Cyrus W.	5809	Oneal, William C.	13218
Norman, Carlton W.	5810	Oneal, Robert E.	13219
Norman, Albert C.	5985	Oneal, James E.	13220
Norman, Mary J.	6724	Oneal, Lieu A.	13221
Norman, James R.	6727	Onelasa, Dober	28458
Norman, Levi	6728	Onelasa, Lucy	28459
Norman, Ollie B.	5812	On-the-hill, Steve	7890
Norman, Mary J.	5986	On-the-hill, Celia	7891
Norman, Albert C.	5987	On-the-hill, John	7892
Norman, Linn A.	21839	Oodeleda, John	15309
Norris, Lucy	12909	Oodeleda, Jennie	15310
Noyes, Mary A.	26121	Oodeleda, Ross	15311
Noyes, Benjamin F.	26122	Oodeleda, Polly	15312
Noyes, Henry E.	26123	Oodeleda, Sallie	15313
Noyes, Roger L.	26124	Oodelda, Emma	15315
Noyes, Georgia May	26125	Oolahnahsteski, Sallie	29976
Nuckolls, Emma J.	7144	Oo-so-wee, Sarah	8921
Nuckolls, Jennie F.	7145	Oo-so-wee, Jack	8922
Nuckolls, Ollie M.	7146	Oo-so-wee, Ona	8923
Nuckolls, James S.	7147	Oo-so-wee, Annie	28740
Nuckolls, Susan E.	22275	Oo-sah-we, Mary	25992
Nuckolls, Opal	7148	Oo-sah-we, Stephen	25993
Nuckolls, Lula M.	22276	Oo-sah-we, Maggie	25994
Nunnallee, Mary E.	7194	Oo-sah-we, Josiah	25995
Nunnallee, John H.	7195	Oo-yu-sut-tah, John	20398
Nunnallee, Walter S.	7196	Oo-yu-sut-tah, Sarah	20399
Nunnallee, Annie M.	7197	Oo-yu-sut-tah, Jerry	20400
Nunnallee, Katie E.	7198	Oo-yu-sut-tah, Hester	20401
Nunnallee, Tennessee	7298	Oo-yu-sut-tah, Swim-	
Nunnallee, Minnie D.	30137	mer	20402
Oakball, Betsy	18905	Oo-yu-sut-tah, Joe	20403
Oakball, John	20337	Oo-so-sutta, Rufus	25913
Oakball, Jennie	20338	Orchard, Jeremiah	22142
Oakball, Skiyosty	20339	Orterlifter, Andrew	20233
Oakball, Ah-no-he	30607	Orterlifter, Susie	20234
Oakball, Cull	30608	Osage, Vina	15003
Oakball, White	30673	Osage, Sallie	15004
Oakball, Susan	30674	Osage, Stephen	15262
Oakball, Fallingpot	30675	Osage, Phillip Jr.	15263
Oakley, William F.	32574	Osage, Phillip	15786
Oborn, Willie M.	30009	Osage, Nancy J.	15787
Odell, Margarett	10424	Osage, Eben E.	15789
Odle, Etta	22523	Osage, Mary E.	15790
Odle, Margaret M. A.	22525	Osage, Hooly B.	15791
Odle, James	22526	Osage, Charlie	20669
Odle, William Jr.	22527	Osage, Jeff	21291
Odle, Sallie	29614	Osage, Minnie	21292
Odle, Alvin	29615	Osage, Osage	21293
Odle, Bessie	29616	Osage, Mandy	21294
Odle, Louisa	22524	Osage, Mary	29515
Oer, Polly	2627	Osage, Jack	21387
Oer, John	2628	Osborn, Fanny	26923
Oer, Belle	2629	Oskison, William M.	28726
Oer, Nannie	2630	Oskison, Richard	9252
Oer, Nora	2631	Oskison, John	29433
Oer, Sarah	2632	Overley, Myrtle B.	518
Oer, Eva	2633	Overley, Forest W.	519
Oglesby, Oakley	16161	Overley, Paul K.	520
Oglesby, James M.	17855	Overtaker, James D.	2689
Oglesby, Ruth	17856	Overtaker, Nellie M.	2690
Oglesby, John	17857	Overtaker, Fannie	29607
Oglesby, Lee May	17858	Overtaker, Maggie	29608
Oglesby, Eldee	17859	Overlees, Earl R.	31191
Oliver, Kate	3675	Overlees, Willie E.	31192
Oliver, Maud	3676	Overlees, Milo H.	31193
Oliver, Albert	3677	Owen, Gracie	4498
Oliver, Graysey E.	3678	Owen, William O.	8707
Oliver, Mary S.	10632	Owen, Booth	8708
Oliver, William F.	10633	Owen, Robert L.	13433
Oliver, Martha J.	10634	Owen, Dorothea	13434
Oliver, Maudie E.	10635	Owen, William O.	32495
Oliver, Pickcie	10636	Owen, William O. C.	32496
Oliver, Hattie	10637	Owen, Narcissa C.	28172
Oliver, James M.	12895	Owen, Henry	21599
Olson, Lydia	7571	Owen, William	22084

Name.	Roll No.	Name.	Roll No.
Owen, Caledonia	31922	O'Reilly, Mary Ellis	16981
Owen, Alice L.	32891	Pack, Laura	1069
Owens, Samuel	4571	Pack, Fred	1070
Owens, Eugene	4704	Pack, Ella	1071
Owens, Mary	5482	Pack, Clayton	1072
Owens, Malzreen	28652	Pack, Mary A.	2193
Owens, Martin	18063	Pack, Nellie	2194
Owens, Charles	19697	Pack, Zeke	2195
Owens, Susan	19698	Pack, Abraham	2196
Owens, Jim	19699	Pack, Charles W., Jr.	2197
Owens, Maggie	19700	Pack, William S.	3448
Owens, Betsy	19701	Pack, Ariminta	3449
Owens, Jennie	19702	Pack, Allie J.	3450
Owens, Seladin	19725	Pack, Lee	1073
Owens, Laille	19726	Pack, Arminda B.	15528
Owens, Joe	19727	Pack, Lila	15536
Owens, Ida	19728	Pack, Nelson	21030
Owens, Sallie	19729	Pace, Etta E.	6344
Owens, Dave	20583	Pace, Minnie G.	6345
Owens, Gahneyawah	20584	Pace, Joseph C.	6346
Owens, Annie	20585	Pace, Annie L.	9773
Owens, Jesse	20586	Pace, Elbert E.	9774
Owens, Lucy	28492	Pace, Hayden A.	9775
Owens, Esther	30564	Pace, Minnie	13340
Owens, Skaklelawski	30565	Pace, Lora	13341
Owens, Oolootsa	30570	Pace, Leonard	13342
Owens, Akey	30622	Pace, Rosa L.	13343
Owl, Nancy	1856	Pace, James W.	13345
Owl, Charlie	1857	Pace, Elva M.	6347
Owl, Lewis	15565	Paden, James	163
Owl, Sam	28421	Paden, Lucy J.	164
Owl, Alice	28422	Paden, Howard	165
Owl, Charlie	28423	Paden, Maggie	166
Owl, Joe	28424	Paden, Homer	167
Owl, Cat	28425	Paden, James	168
Ownbey, Raymond S.	24100	Paden, Coffee W.	169
Ownbey, Mary A.	24101	Paden, Jesse J.	170
Ownbey, Margarett E.	24102	Paden, Mary	171
Ownbey, James L.	24103	Paden, Andrew T.	1558
O'Brien, Martha	15472	Paden, Martha J.	1559
O'Brien, Etta	26014	Paden, Mark L.	1662
O'Fields, Lillie	30120	Paden, John H.	1663
O'Fields, Samuel	27563	Paden, Robert E. L.	1838
O'Fields, Moses	8885	Paden, Zachery T.	1910
O'Fields, Jennie	8886	Paden, George W.	1004
O'Fields, Lila	8887	Paden, Charles B.	2005
O'Fields, James	8888	Paden, Jackson T.	2006
O'Fields, Ninnie	8889	Paden, Lucinda	2118
O'Fields, Eve	12455	Paden, Benjamin F.	2382
O'Fields, David	14690	Paden, Lucinda	2383
O'Fields, Emma	14691	Paden, Jennie M.	2384
O'Fields, James	14692	Paden, Margaret A.	2385
O'Fields, Charlott	14694	Paden, Lucinda	2386
O'Fields, Polly	14803	Paden, Benjamin F., Jr.	2387
O'Fields, Robert	17779	Paden, Susan A.	2388
O'Fields, Cintha	8890	Paden, Mary L.	22565
O'Fields, Ben	18619	Paden, Harrison J.	22612
O'Fields, Annie	18620	Paden, Laura J.	22613
O'Fields, Bushyhead	18621	Paden, Nora L.	22656
O'Fields, Bettie	18622	Paden, Cliff E.	22657
O'Fields, Sallie	18623	Paden, John B.	27168
O'Fields, Sam	18624	Paden, Maud A.	27169
O'Fields, Fannie	18625	Paden, Charles L.	27170
O'Fields, Joe	18626	Paden, Lucinda R.	27171
O'Field, Austin	26443	Paden, Colbert H.	27172
O'Field, Alsie	26444	Paden, Taylor J.	23660
O'Field, Rosa	26445	Paden, William R.	23661
O'Field, Eldorado	26446	Paden, Maud J.	23662
O'Field, Dick	19400	Paden, Russell R.	23663
O'Field, Lizzie	19401	Paden, Kittie	23664
O'Field, Charley	19716	Paden, Riley R.	23665
O'Field, Nellie	19717	Paden, Benjamin R.	23666
O'Field, Jim	19718	Paden, Lewis D.	9578
O'Field, Lee	19719	Paden, John B.	9579
O'Field, George	19720	Paden, Richard B.	9580
O'Field, Mollie	19721	Paden, John H.	9603
O'Field, Sallie	19722	Paden, John E.	24321
O'Field, Lizzie	19723	Paden, George T.	24322
O'Field, Noah	19724	Paden, Claude E.	24323
O'Field, Maggie	30568	Paden, Beuna J.	24324
O'Field, Abel	30569	Paden, Zachrah R.	24325
O'Leary, James	10987	Paden, Thomas J.	13951
O'Leary, Jerry	10988	Paden, Martha J.	13952
O'Reilly, Mary	16980	Paden, Susan E.	13953
		Paden, Van	13954

Name.	Roll No.	Name.	Roll No.
Paden, Nannie E.	13955	Panter, Ben	2286
Paden, Lucy	13956	Panther, Sequoyah	3378
Paden, Thomas A.	15952	Panther, James	3379
Paden, Thomas A.	16688	Panther, Rachel	15916
Paden, Sophia M.	28471	Panther, Martha	19568
Paden, Alec Anderson	9581	Panther, John	19569
Paden, Ethel O.	22653	Panther, Alice	19570
Padget, George	4350	Panther, Tom	19571
Padget, Eliza	16367	Panther, Josiah	21422
Padget, Jacob	16368	Panther, Lydia	30714
Padget, Maria	16369	Panther, Eliza	31936
Padget, Annie	16370	Panther, Thomas	31937
Padget, Jesse	16371	Panther, John	32907
Padget, Robert	16372	Pann, Richard	16255
Padget, Luke	16373	Pann, Susan	16256
Padget, Perry	16374	Pann, James	17641
Padgett, Charlie	2074	Pann, Nannie	17642
Paget, Ella L.	14324	Pann, Lewis	17645
Painter, LaVerna A.	31810	Pann, Alsey	17646
Painter, Ada R.	31811	Pann, Richard	17644
Painter, Eva P.	31812	Pann, Mariah	29153
Painter, John W.	31813	Pann, Peter	21439
Painter, Ray D.	31814	Pan, Robin	17638
Painter, Roberta A.	31815	Pan, Jennie	17639
Painter, Roy V.	31816	Parker, Ruth D.	30090
Palone, Mary	673	Parker, Lizzie	32612
Palone, John	674	Parker, Jesse J.	32613
Palone, Fred	687	Parker, Ludie S.	23951
Palone, John D.	688	Parker, Lizzie	8728
Palone, Richard	689	Parker, Claud J.	8729
Palone, Clarence C.	10565	Parker, John N.	8730
Palone, Thomas	10571	Parker, Mack R.	8731
Palone, Clara	10572	Parker, Grace	8732
Palone, Cleveland	10573	Parker, Edna	8733
Palone, Fred E.	690	Parker, Benjamin F.	8734
Palone, Wilsòn	29036	Parker, Joseph R.	8735
Palone, Jincy	29037	Parker, Laura	32782
Palone, Andrew	25854	Parker, Josephine	30231
Palone, Nannie	20786	Parker, Emma J.	30232
Palone, Andrew Jr.	30647	Parker, John Y. Y.	30233
Palone, Frank	27047	Parker, Minnie	30234
Palone, Mary	27048	Parker, William	30235
Palone, Stephen	27049	Parker, Sarah	28265
Palone, Jesse	27050	Parker, Bertha M.	28266
Palone, Charles	27051	Parker, Frederick	28267
Palone, Lizzie	27052	Parker, Annie	30824
Palone, Tom	27053	Parker, Walter	8736
Palone, Ruth	27054	Parker, Ella M.	30236
Palmer, Margaret D.	15467	Parker, Marvin D.	28268
Palmer, Arthur	15468	Parker, Joseph	27850
Palmer, Edgar	15469	Parker, David	27851
Palmer, Thede	15470	Parker, Dora	27852
Palmer, Luella	3292	Parker, Harrison G.	27853
Palmer, Nancy J.	31358	Parker, Mary L.	31133
Palmer, Alonzo A.	31359	Parker, Geneva Blanche	31136
Palmer, Jennte	31360	Parker, Charles F.	31317
Palmour, David S.	13595	Parker, Millie M.	31318
Palmour, Emily E.	13596	Parker, Dennis B.	31325
Palmour, John R.	13597	Parker, Lillie	31637
Palmour, Fannie A.	13598	Parker, Carrie	31638
Palmour, James A.	14094	Parker, John W.	31639
Palmour, Charles F.	25828	Parker, Minnie	31640
Palmour, Ina	25829	Parker, Elmer	31641
Palmour, Asa	25830	Parker, Bertha	31642
Palmour, Newton D.	25831	Parsons, Rebecca A.	6055
Palmour, Paul A.	25832	Parsons, Mary	6056
Palmour, Roe E.	25833	Parsons, Henry F.	10391
Palmour, Benjamin F.	30884	Parsons, Oscar W.	10393
Palmour, John D.	30885	Parsons, Josie Farel	10392
Palmour, Bessie	30886	Parris, Malachi	679
Palmour, Robert	30887	Parris, Jesse R.	941
Palmour, Mary L.	30888	Parris, Frances	942
Palmour, Sarah	30889	Parris, Fannie	943
Palmour, Hugh A.	30890	Parris, Elizabeth	944
Panter, Eliza L.	1584	Parris, Maggie	1156
Panter, James A.	1585	Parris, Ella M.	3444
Panter, John D.	1586	Parris, Unie C.	3445
Panter, Alfred N.	1587	Parris, Moses	3446
Panter, Nancy R.	2281	Parris, James	6511
Panter, Lelia	2282	Parris, Nancy	6512
Panter, Susan	2283	Parris, Margaret E.	6513
Panter, George	2284	Parris, Mary	6514
Panter, Tom	2285	Parris, Robert E.	9624

Name.	Roll No.
Parris, William	12272,
Parris, John F.	12517
Parris, Wilbern	13691
Parris, Ezekiel P.	29494
Parris, Susan E.	29495
Parris, Betsy	13770
Parris, Albion	13771
Parris, Betsy	13777
Parris, Wikerson H.	13824
Parris, Jane	13825
Parris, Jackson	13826
Parris, Charlotte	13827
Parris, George W.	29497
Parris, Annie K.	29498
Parris, Susan L.	29499
Parris, Thomas J.	28861
Parris, Emiline	28862
Parris, Johnson	28863
Parris, Jesse H.	28864
Parris, Bettie	28865
Parris, Anna	28866
Parris, Moses E.	28867
Parris, Noah	14201
Parris, Noah L.	14202
Parris, Sallie	14203
Parris, William B.	14204
Parris, Myrtle E.	29925
Parris, Jesse J.	31962
Parris, William	14293
Parris, Andy	14310
Parris, Moses	14311
Parris, John H.	14312
Parris, Fannie	14313
Parris, George Bud	14452
Parris, Johnanna	14453
Parris, Cynthia	14454
Parris, Martin	14455
Parris, Richard	14456
Parris, Drift	14457
Parris, Nannie	14458
Parris, George Bud, Jr.	14459
Parris, Mantie	14614
Parris, Loring	30346
Parris, Thomas	14897
Parris, Moses	15034
Parris, Loonie	15054
Parris, Charley R.	15366
Parris, Nellie	15392
Parris, Minnie	15847
Parris, Edward	16163
Parris, Elvie	16164
Parris, Allen R.	16165
Parris, Flossie	16166
Parris, Robert B.	16167
Parris, Theodore	16168
Parris, Henry C.	16226
Parris, James	16234
Parris, Margaret	16235
Parris, Janeanna	16236
Parris, Taylor	16238
Parris, Susan	16239
Parris, Matilda	16240
Parris, Samantha	16241
Parris, William	16286
Parris, James K.	16296
Parris, Ranson	16571
Parris, Seley	16572
Parris, Eliza	16573
Parris, Ellen C.	16574
Parris, Malinda	16575
Parris, Sarah J.	16576
Parris, Ezekiel	16577
Parris, Hick	16578
Parris, Ellen	16579
Parris, George	16580
Parris, Richard J.	16827
Parris, William	21534
Parris, William H.	21726
Parris, Sadie	21727
Parris, Ezekiel	21775
Parris, Roscoe	21776
Parris, Jack	26262
Parris, Joan	26263
Parris, Brunette	26264
Parris, Rosey	26265

Name.	Roll No.
Parris, Buster	26266
Parris, Mable A.	16297
Parris, Josie B.	945
Parris, Flora E.	21728
Parriss, Curtis	21833
Parris, John Weaver	32359
Parris, Samantha	32878
Parnell, Mary	4262
Parnell, Annie	4263
Parris, Grover C.	4264
Parnell, Wallace	4265
Parnell, Celia	4269
Parnell, Samuel	4271
Parnell, Benjamin	4272
Parnell, Jesse	15883
Partain, Lydia	6170
Partain, Rose M.	6171
Partin, Susie	6501
Parkhurst, Mary C.	7270
Parkhurst, Maggie	7271
Parkhurst, Jesse	7272
Parkhurst, Mary	26433
Parkhurst, John	26434
Parkhurst, Martha	26435
Parkhurst, Mary Eva	25581
Parkhurst, Mattie Jane	7273
Parrish, George	7955
Parrish, Mary	7956
Parrish, Nancy J.	7957
Parrish, Charles W.	7958
Parrish, Ada	8044
Parrish, Eveline	8045
Parrish, Annie	8046
Parrish, Orron	8069
Parrish, Alice	8070
Parrish, Jennie	8072
Parrish, Isaac	8071
Parrish, Joseph D.	10590
Parrish, George L.	10591
Parrish, John M.	10592
Parrish, James L.	10593
Parrish, Alvin H.	10680
Parrish, Claud H.	10681
Parrish, Thomas L.	10682
Parrish, Gracie F.	10683
Parrish, Walter S.	10691
Parrish, Bessie	10692
Parrish, William T.	30226
Parrish, William T., Jr.	30227
Parrish, Sadie B.	30228
Parrish, Polly J.	7959
Parks, Johnson C.	23960
Parks, Irene	23962
Parks, James W.	23963
Parks, Missouri	23964
Parks, Lula A.	23965
Parks, Samuel F.	8616
Parks, Alberta	8617
Parks, Jennie	8619
Parks, Melvin C.	9081
Parks, James G.	9201
Parks, Margaret J.	9704
Parrish, Samuel C.	8043
Parks, John	9705
Parks, Ora A.	9706
Parks, Owen B.	9707
Parks, Annie	26588
Parks, Martha S.	26589
Parks, Charles	11739
Parks, Robert C.	13023
Parks, Robert C., Jr.	13024
Parks, John R. B.	13025
Parks, Milton B.	13026
Parks, Alexander B.	13027
Parks, George B.	13187
Parks, Richard B.	13234
Parks, Maggie M.	13326
Parks, Ruth E.	13330
Parks, Sterling P.	13602
Parks, Lou A.	13603
Parks, Rosa E.	13604
Parks, Amanda A.	13605
Parks, Richard H.	13606
Parks, Johnny C.	13607
Parks, Susie	13608
Parks, Thaddeous T.	13630

Name.	Roll No.	Name.	Roll No.
Parks, Jeff T.	16289	Pardo, Charlie	21093
Parks, Etta	16290	Pardo, Susie	21094
Parks, Clarence J.	16291	Paradee, Talesphor L.	31287
Parks, Ruth A.	16292	Paradee, Georgia A.	31288
Parks, Mildred J.	16293	Paradee, Elsie	31289
Parks, Cynthia	17448	Paschal, Annie	27572
Parks, Claud	17449	Paschal, Ridge	14615
Parks, Emit	17451	Pate, Albert N.	479
Parks, Joseph	21908	Pate, Laura R.	480
Parks, James A. T.	29529	Pate, Gracie F.	481
Parks, John C.	22003	Pate, Joseph E.	482
Parks, Elizabeth Mai	8620	Pate, William C.	483
Parks, Cora B.	10523	Pate, Sallie M.	22267
Parks, Lewis	10528	Pate, Joseph B.	22268
Parks, James W.	13609	Pate, Mary A.	22269
Parks, Oliver R.	31302	Pate, Sybbil D.	22270
Parks, Jacob	31303	Pate, Alethea A.	27934
Parks, Harrison	31304	Pathkiller, John	27036
Parks, George	31306	Pathkiller, Fannie	27037
Parks, James	31307	Pathkiller, William	27038
Parks, Rosa	32533	Pathkiller, Johnson	16319
Parkison, Ada R.	9662	Pathkiller, John R.	16320
Parkison, Henry B.	9663	Pathkiller, Sarah E.	16321
Parkison, Beulah J.	9664	Pathkiller, Laura B.	16322
Parkison, Louie R.	9665	Pathkiller, Jennette	16323
Paris, Annie E.	10069	Pathkiller, Cora L.	16324
Paris, Frank	10070	Pathkiller, William E.	16325
Paris, John C.	10071	Pathkiller, James M.	16326
Paris, Delbert C.	10072	Pathkiller, Jennie	29879
Paris, Marion	10073	Pathkiller, John	29880
Paris, Susiè	10074	Patton, Ada	1915
Paris, William F.	13271	Patton, Frank N.	1916
Paris, Cora	13273	Patton, Ruth	1917
Paris, Mattie	13274	Patton, Catherine M.	2054
Paris, Fay	13275	Patton, George H.	2055
Paris, Nina	13276	Patton, Turner B.	4040
Paris, Lemuel	13395	Patton, Delta	4041
Paris, Archibald	13396	Patton, Elizabeth	4055
Partin, Nina M.	10341	Patton, DuMont	4056
Partin, Everett T.	10342	Patton, William D.	4057
Parsley, Nannie	11332	Patton, Helen L.	4058
Parsley, Pauline	11333	Patton, Robert B.	4150
Parsley, Cora E.	11334	Patton, Charlotte	4151
Parsley, Fred	11335	Patton, William S.	4152
Parsley, Sallie	11336	Patton, Susan J.	4153
Parkes, Richard T.	13323	Patton, Robert E.	4154
Parkes, Oscar W.	13324	Patton, Lucy M.	4155
Parkes, Sarah E.	13325	Patton, Charles F.	4156
Parham, Emma E.	25261	Patton, Caleb F.	4157
Parham, Claude C.	25262	Patton, Minnie M.	4158
Parham, Clarence W.	25263	Patton, Leola	1918
Parham, Ada E.	25264	Patton, Gideon	27296
Parson, Cicero	15885	Patton, Marie	27297
Parson, Lula	4270	Patton, William M.	27298
Parson, Mary H.	4273	Patton, Charles H.	10802
Parson, Agnes	21023	Patton, Pansy	10803
Parson, Johnson	14658	Patton, Arminta F.	10816
Parkinson, Addie M.	25448	Patton, John H. Jr.	10818
Parkinson, Rachel M.	25449	Patton, Emma	10819
Parkinson, Ruth	25450	Patton, Luella	10820
Parkinson, Joe T.	25451	Patton, Robert J.	10821
Parkinson, Isabel J.	25452	Patton, William W.	10899
Parkinson, Addie F.	25453	Patton, Jane	13554
Parkinson, Bruce C.	25454	Patton, Robert I.	4042
Parkinson, Evaline	25455	Patton, Myrtle	21773
Parkhill, Jennie	32559	Patton, Amous W.	10900
Parkhill, Emma	32560	Patton, Silas Corneilus	10804
Parkhill, Nan	32561	Patton, Clifton B.	21582
Parr, Mollie E.	29429	Patton, Ruth M.	32124
Parr, John R.	29430	Patterson, John A.	2190
Parchmeal, John	20677	Patterson, Joseph	2191
Parchmeal, Susie	20678	Patterson, William P.	2349
Parchmeal, Walker	20679	Patterson, Mary L.	2350
Parchmeal, Gohene	30627	Patterson, Lucy J.	2351
Parchmeal, Betsy	30628	Patterson, Isabel	3931
Parchmeal, Lucy	20681	Patterson, Grover C.	3932
Parchcorn, Price	20690	Patterson, Lillie M.	3933
Parchcorn, Nancy	20691	Patterson, Lucy M.	3934
Parchcorn, Ezekiel	20692	Patterson, Lillian D.	29779
Parchcorn, Senost	20693	Patterson, Homer L.	29780
Parchcorn, Catawyah	20694	Patterson, Annie L.	2352
Parchcorn, Bear	32328	Patterson, Mary	28801
Parchcorn, Chenaust	32329	Patterson, Frank	28805
Pardo, Dick	20826		

Name.	Roll No.	Name.	Roll No.
Patterson, Edna M.	28806	Payne, Charlotte E.	12659
Patterson, Charles W.	13357	Payne, Lizzie	14123
Patterson, Joseph A.	15649	Payne, Edward	14126
Patterson, Leonard B.	17074	Payne, Florence	30335
Patterson, Zona	31724	Payne, Frank S.	14314
Patterson, Sarah A.	31725	Payne, Albert	14315
Patterson, Martha A.	31726	Payne, Mary	14316
Patterson, Claud A.	31727	Payne, Frederick	14317
Patterson, Edgar D.	31728	Payne, Susie D.	14829
Patterson, Thomas M.	31729	Payne, Silas B.	14830
Patterson, Virgil V.	31730	Payne, Charles C.	14831
Patrick, James	5163	Payne, Mary E.	15090
Patrick, Almira	5695	Payne, James M.	15091
Patrick, John J.	5722	Payne, Maggie D.	15092
Patrick, Mike	10255	Payne, Lena E.	15093
Patrick, Jane E.	10256	Payne, William B.	15094
Patrick, John	10257	Payne, Edith B.	15095
Patrick, Herald B.	10258	Payne, Etta	15876
Patrick, George W.	10264	Payne, Mary A.	30898
Patrick, John	10265	Payne, Silas D.	30899
Patrick, Ida	10266	Payne, Mary E.	32618
Patrick, Alic	10267	Payne, Andrew J.	21367
Patrick, Eliza	12096	Payne, Charles H.	31943
Patrick, William	28308	Payne, Floy G.	31944
Patrick, Mary	28309	Payton, Charlotte	7504
Patrick, Florence	30393	Payton, Lee	7505
Patrick, John	16886	Payton, Emma A.	14553
Patrick, Flossie	16887	Payton, Freddie F.	14554
Patrick, Lela E.	16888	Payton, John M.	14555
Patrick, Addie	16889	Payton, Fannie E.	14556
Patrick, Laura	21887	Payton, Maude F.	14557
Patrick, Bertha	21888	Payton, Garland S.	14558
Patrick, Annie	21889	Payton, Ida	8657
Patrick, Rachel	26297	Payton, Coleman	8660
Patrick, Eliza	26298	Payton, Ray	8658
Patrick, Lucy	26299	Payton, Ream	8659
Patrick, Fannie	26300	Pearce, Hazel M.	29446
Patrick, Maggie L.	21999	Peak, Stephen W.	6279
Patrick, Cleveland M.	29257	Peak, Connelly	6280
Patrick, James Joshua	10268	Peak, Edward W.	27548
Patrick, Grover C.	29612	Peak, Thomas S.	27549
Pation, Sarah O.	30839	Peak, William	29038
Pation, Minnie M.	30840	Peak, Lillie M.	19815
Patterson, Ada V.	29776	Peak, James	25876
Patzol, Rollan	24346	Peak, Checonala	25877
Patzol, Vinnie M.	24347	Peak, Maud	15947
Payne, Bell	22360	Peak, Charles Curtis	15948
Payne, George E.	1894	Peach, Birdie	9186
Payne, Belle D.	3632	Pearson, Ola	10699
Payne, Mabel C.	3633	Pearson, Lena H.	10700
Payne, Howard A.	3634	Pearson, George W.	10701
Payne, Gerald L.	3635	Pearse, Jackson K.	12440
Payne, Myra L.	3636	Pearse, Bertie S.	12441
Payne, Houston C.	3637	Pease, Jessie	12468
Payne, Sallie A.	3650	Pease, Volney	12469
Payne, John H.	3651	Peacheater, Nellie	15210
Payne, Robert	3652	Peacock, James	22139
Payne, Claudius G.	3653	Peacock, Rosie	31329
Payne, Harrold B.	3654	Pecan, John	24813
Payne, Lee R.	3655	Peck, Eliza C.	3000
Payne, Julius C.	6534	Peck, Matilda	3015
Payne, Julia M.	6535	Peck, Ben A.	3016
Payne, Willie W.	6536	Peck, Mary	12010
Payne, Eva H.	6537	Peck, Charles E.	12011
Payne, Jonathan R.	7042	Peck, Jesse B.	12014
Payne, Nina	7518	Peek, Susan E.	27931
Payne, Sarah L.	7519	Peek, Dolly M.	11149
Payne, Anzia M.	26496	Peek, Henry C.	11150
Payne, Louis L.	26497	Peek, Grace O.	11151
Payne, Joseph E.	26498	Peek, Jesse J.	11152
Payne, Glessnor	26499	Peek, Susie A.	11153
Payne, William C.	26500	Peek, Richard T.	11154
Payne, Laura E.	24139	Peek, Edna E.	11155
Payne, Rosa E.	12370	Peebles, James L.	14473
Payne, Winona M.	12371	Peebles, Nannie	14474
Payne, Floyd B.	12372	Peebles, Joseph L.	14475
Payne, Ruth A.	12373	Peebles, James S.	14476
Payne, Gus E.	12374	Peebles, Lottie M.	14477
Payne, Henry	28132	Peebles, Edgar V.	14478
Payne, Alfred W.	28134	Pegg, Thomas	27989
Payne, Claud L.	28135	Pegg, Nancy	27990
Payne, William P.	12657	Pegg, Swimmer	27991
Payne, Pearl J.	12658	Pegg, Watt	27992

Name.	Roll No.	Name.	Roll No.
Pegg, Susie	27996	Petit, Ruth	2428
Pelone, Nancy	16516	Petitt, Thomas	2652
Pelsue, Ethel R.	10281	Petitt, John R.	5462
Pelsue, Sarah I.	10282	Petitt, Rufus R.	5463
Pelsue, Owen E.	10283	Pettitt, Richard M,	5464
Pemberton, Mary A.	3620	Petitt, William	12900
Pemberton, Oliver P.	3921	Petitt, Mary J.	12901
Pemberton, Jackson	4013	Petitt, Pearl	12902
Pemberton, Lewis	4014	Petitt, Bertha	12903
Pemberton, Rilla M.	31083	Petitt, Floyd H.	12904
Pemberton, Lillie J.	31086	Petitt, George W.	15276
Pennel, Dora	5908	Petitt, Cherokee	15277
Pennel, Alice	5909	Petitt, Elsie	15278
Pennel, Thomas W.	5910	Petitt, Thomas	15279
Pennel, Charles	5911	Petitt, Frank	15280
Pennel, James	5912	Petitt, Susan	15281
Pennel, Moses H.	5913	Petitt, Adna H.	15282
Pennington, Julia P.	24941	Petitt, Martin	15283
Pennington, Julian D.	24942	Petitt, Jennie	15284
Pennington, Mary N.	24943	Petitt, Sadie E.	15285
Pennington, Jessie E.	24944	Petitt, Eliza	15853
Pendleton, Sallie G.	30325	Petitt, Thomas J.	15863
Pendleton, Lucy I.	15551	Petitt, Mack	28310
Pendleton, Earnest T.	15552	Petitt, Charles	16112
Pendleton, Ruby M.	15553	Petitt, Timothy	17098
Perry, Sion M.	352	Petitt, Rachel	28340
Perry, Floyd L .	353	Petit, Lala	17100
Perry, Earl	354	Peters, Annie A.	2987
Perry, Almeda	355	Peters, Thomas L.	2988
Perry, Theodore W.	2673	Peters, Viola E.	2989
Perry, Kate P.	2674	Peters, Bessie E.	2990
Perry, Ezekiel H.	28534	Peters, Lorenzo M.	2991
Perry, Ezekiel S.	28535	Peters, Minnie S.	2992
Perry, Stella	28536	Peters, Nora A.	2993
Perry, Earnest B.	7190	Peters, Iantha S.	2994
Perry, Effie D.	7191	Peters, Plumie	2995
Perry, Myrtle	7192	Peters, Cynthia	16855
Perry, Oliver H.	7193	Peters, John	20352
Perry, Artemus J.	7482	Peters, Mary	28478
Perry, Columbus H.	7662	Peters, Joe	25860
Perry, Pearl	7663	Peters, John, Jr.	25861
Perry, Kineth B.	7664	Peter, George	20673
Perry, Mariah	32474	Pettit, Oscar D.	4222
Perry, Samuel	10600	Pettit, Emma	4223
Perry, Amanda	10601	Pettit, Ruth E.	4224
Perry, Saphronia	14956	Pettit, Maud E.	4225
Perry, Samuel A.	10603	Pettit, Jessie B.	4226
Perry, Ida	10604	Pettit, Marion J.	4227
Perry, Daisy	10605	Pettit, Floyd E.	4228
Perry, Helen	12130	Pettit, Jane	4804
Perry, John F.	12131	Pettit, Cynthia	4805
Perry, Lizzie J.	12132	Pettit, Guy	4806
Perry, Della	12133	Pettit, Robert B.	4807
Perry, Effy	12134	Pettit, Mary	4808
Perry, Mary J.	12135	Pettit, Joseph	4810
Perry, Nathan M.	25491	Pettit, Frank J.	4811
Perry, James R.	25492	Pettit, Alvin D.	4812
Perry, Lewis L.	25493	Pettit, Marie	4813
Perry, Elizabeth K.	25494	Pettit, Lizzie	4814
Perry, Robert L.	25495	Pettit, Joseph	28607
Perry, Morris G.	25496	Pettit, Dollie	5019
Perry, Ernest G.	26278	Pettit, Richard	5020
Perry, Mary G.	26279	Pettit, Emma	5021
Perry, Josie	31102	Pettit, Watie	23151
Perry, Adam	31208	Pettit, Roberta	4809
Perry, William	31209	Pettit, Nicholas	14811
Perry, Elizabeth H.	32914	Pettit, Nancy ·	15543
Perkins, Mary A.	5255	Pettit, Edward	28959
Perdue, James S.	14357	Pettit, Eliza	28960
Perlon, Lacie R.	12513	Pettit, Lizzie	28961
Perlon, Nona B.	12514	Pettit, Lorinda	32379
Petty, Vetoria	1883	Pettit, Beulah	18062
Petty, Sarah L.	1884	Pettit, William	25703
Petty, Ida M.	1885	Pettit, John	30534
Petty, Charlotte E.	14956	Pettit, Jack	29867
Petty, Mike G.	14957	Pettit, Lucy	29868
Petty, James S.	14958	Pettit, Jack, Jr.,	29869
Petty, William C.	14959	Pettit, Tom	29870
Petty, Carl C.	14960	Pettit, Wolf	29871
Petty, John T.	16891	Pettit, Esther	29872
Petty, Clarence F.	21667	Pettit, Lillie	29873
Petty, George R.	21668	Pettit, Ida	29874
Petty, George W.	22055	Pettit, John S.	29875
Petty, Rachel Mayes	22056	Pettit, Wahcene	28453
Petty, Rosella C.	1885	Pettit. Annie	19573
		Petiett, Lafella	7586

Name.	Roll No.	Name.	Roll No.
Petiett, Andrew	7587	Phillips, Mamie E.	15820
Pevehouse, Sanora A.	11494	Phillips, John M.	25293
Pevehouse, William A.	11495	Phillips, John R.	25294
Pevehouse, Sarah E.	11496	Phillips, Mary M.	25295
Pevehouse, Prudence E.	24889	Phillips, William	16075
Pfannkuche, Agnes P.	7333	Phillips, Martha	16076
Pfannkuche, Charles C.	7334	Phillips, Lizzie	16077
Phariss, Agnes	12660	Phillips, Ada B.	16078
Phariss, Pleasant H.	12819	Phillips, Laura A.	16079
Phariss, Selvert	12820	Phillips, Henry	25396
Phariss, Jackson L.	12822	Phillips, James F.	17181
Phariss, Clinton L.	12823	Phillips, Bettie	17182
Phariss, John B.	17077	Phillips, Jesse	17184
Phariss, Ada B.	12821	Phillips, Nancy	17185
Phariss, Farle	29530	Phillips, Ida	17186
Phariss, Allen	29531	Phillips, Laura	17187
Phariss, Amy A.	29532	Phillips, Rachel	17188
Pheasant, Phoebe	20424	Phillips, Walter L.	17189
Pheasant, Thomas M.	12407	Phillips, Elmer L.	17217
Pheasant, Lucy	29011	Phillips, Roxie E.	17218
Pheasant, George	16845	Phillips, Henry C.	17219
Pheasant, Dick	18516	Phillips, Hughey P.	17591
Pheasant, Annie	18517	Phillips, Audie J.	15821
Pheasant, Charles	19635	Phillips, Robert	29081
Pheasant, Sarah J.	19636	Phillips, Jennie	19541
Pheasant, Nellie	30560	Phillips, Caroline	19542
Pheasant, Abraham	20026	Phillips, Polly	19959
Pheasant, Alex	20040	Phillips, Jim	20614
Pheasant, Jim	20041	Phillips, Lizzie	20615
Pheasant, Lula	20042	Phillips, Nellie	20616
Pheasant, Jenanna	20044	Phillips, Joe	20617
Pheasant, Lizzie	20421	Phillips, Tom	20618
Pheasant, George	1030	Phillips, Nellie	25922
Phillipps, Moses	22345	Phillips, Joe	28515
Phillipps, Robert	27940	Phillips, Eliza	21033
Phillips, Jennie	27941	Phillips, Arch	29124
Phillips, James	27942	Phillips, Nancy	29125
Phillipps, Sallie	27943	Phillips, Johnson	29126
Phillipps, Jeff	27944	Phillips, John	29127
Phillipps, Alice	27945	Phillips, Jim	29128
Phillips, Martha	1148	Phillips, Ahama	29129
Phillips, Rufus	919	Phillips, Lucy	29130
Phillips, Mary M.	26327	Phillips, Peggie	29131
Phillips, James H.	26328	Phillips, George	29132
Phillips, Barney	26329	Phillips, Betsy	21148
Phillips, Jennie	1149	Phillipps, Mabel I.	27946
Phillips, Andrew	1399	Phillips, Lucy	3327
Phillips, William	2104	Phillips, Daniel James	3329
Phillips, Betsy	2105	Phillips, John	21034
Phillips, Walter E.	2106	Phillips, Ula Maud	11134
Phillips, Walter	4471	Phipps, Mattie	4545
Phillips, May	4472	Phipps, Amanda	4981
Phillips, William L.	4473	Phipps, Bettie	4982
Phillips, Cordelia	4474	Phipps, John	4983
Phillips, Calvin C.	4475	Phipps, Carrie	4984
Phillips, Claud	5750	Phipps, Joe	4985
Phillips, Emma	5751	Phipps, Beulah M.	4986
Phillips, Flora R.	6022	Phipps, Lulu P.	4987
Phillips, Julious	23417	Phipps, Ella B.	4988
Phillips, James H.	6694	Phipps, Alberta	4989
Phillips, Harvey	27016	Philips, Hattie	16489
Phillips, Delia M.	27017	Philips, James W.	16492
Phillips, Elvie	27018	Picaman, Susanna M.	11343
Phillips, Charles	6695	Picaman, Clara M.	11344
Phillips, Clintie	6696	Picaman, Clarence M.	11345
Phillips, Alice	6725	Picaman, Jennie	11346
Phillips, William	6726	Picaman, Augustus	11347
Phillips, William P.	9850	Picaman, Julius W.	11348
Phillips, Jane A.	9851	Picaman, Dewey M.	11349
Phillips, Lula B.	9852	Picaman, Caroline S.	11350
Phillips, Dewey	9853	Pickard, Mary E.	26828
Phillips, Penn	9854	Pickard, William H.	26829
Phillips, Etta	10337	Pickard, Narcissa J.	26830
Phillips, Susan P.	10905	Pickard, Robert B.	26831
Phillips, Grace	27730	Pickard, Dewey C.	26832
Phillips, Josephine V.	10967	Pickard, Maude M.	26833
Phillips, Micajah H. Jr.	10969	Pickup, Dick	18204
Phillips, Spencer	10968	Pickup, George	18205
Phillips, Josephine V.	10970	Pickup, Sallie	18206
Phillips, Frank	11131	Pickup, Joe	32512
Phillips, Spencer O.	11132	Pickup, Jim	18414
Phillips, Ewell	11133	Pickup, Moses	18512
Phillips, Nancy J.	15818	Pickup, Simon	18668
Phillips, Bird H.	15819		

Name.	Roll No.	Name.	Roll No.
Pickup, Sallie	18669	Pitcher, Horace G.	13475
Pickup, Polly	19487	Plank, Marsilla	7277
Pickup, Ned	32545	Plank, Florence L.	7278
Pickup, Julia	32546	Plank, Russell W.	7279
Pierce, John	1004	Plank, Norris B.	7280
Pierce, Willie	1005	Plank, Berthey I.	7281
Pierce, Moses	1006	Plank, Uziel S.	7282
Pierce, Richard	1017	Pogue, Nancy	16828
Pierce, Nannie B.	1018	Pogue, James	16831
Pierce, Walter H.	1019	Pogue, Jesse	16830
Pierce, Roxie	1020	Poindexter, Maggie	5960
Pierce, Harve	1021	Poindexter, William	5961
Pierce, Ada	1022	Poindexter, Benjamin	5962
Pierce, Ella	1023	Poindexter, Paralee	5963
Pierce, Ida	1024	Poindexter, Ellen	5964
Pierce, Bessie	1007	Poindexter, Lucinda	5965
Pierce, Nancy J.	4844	Poindexter, Louisa	5966
Pierce, Gerty	4845	Pointer, Samuel J.	23567
Pierce, Mark	4846	Pointer, Patsy	23566
Pierce, James C.	4847	Polone, James N.	10640
Pierce, Nannie	5211	Polone, Lizzie	10641
Pierce, Cornelius	5212	Polone, Dove	10642
Pierce, Susan	5213	Polone, Herbert	10643
Pierce, Effie	5214	Polone, Lovvie	10644
Pierce, Charles P.	5215	Polone, Mary	10645
Pierce, Claud	5216	Polone, Myrtle	10646
Pierce, Ruth	5217	Polone, P. V.	10647
Pierce, Edna	5218	Polone, Ray	10648
Pierce, Stella	5219	Polecat, Cornelius	3961
Pierce, May	5220	Polecat, Walter	3994
Pierce, Helen E.	26134	Polecat, Lucy	3995
Pierce, Mary E.	26135	Polecat, Betsy	3996
Pierce, Athelstan R.	26136	Polecat, Isaac	3997
Pierce, Robert	31893	Polecat, Levi	3998
Pierce, Myrtle	31894	Polecat, Sarah A.	3999
Pierce, Arthur	31895	Polecat, Andrew	26359
Pierce, Charles E.	31896	Polecat, Wilburn	26360
Pigeon, Looney	13639	Polecat, Celey	26361
Pigeon, Lilly	13640	Polson, William D.	29456
Pigeon, Lula	17979	Polson, Ridge	29457
Pigeon, Lugenia	17980	Polson, Lue	11816
Pigeon, Robert	17981	Polson, John M.	11817
Pigeon, Carrie	18160	Polson, Eddie	11818
Pigeon, Sallie	18499	Polson, Freddie	13467
Pigeon, Jesse	18355	Polson, Jasper L.	13468
Pigeon, Callie	18356	Polson, James D.	13469
Pigeon, Ella	18357	Polson, William R.	13470
Pigeon, Sarah	18358	Polson, Nellie	21984
Pigeon, Jesse Jr.	32276	Polson, Martin	21985
Pigeon, John	20369	Polson, Mattie	21986
Pigeon, John R.	20739	Polson, Earl	21987
Pigeon, Nannie	20740	Polson, Margaret Francis	18073
Pigeon, Ookilli	30632	Polson, Marie Almedia	29458
Pigeon, William	25903	Poorboy, George C.	12416
Pigeon, Millie	20866	Poorboy, Thomas	14978
Pigeon, Richard	20927	Poorboy, Watie I.	28958
Pigeon, Thomas	20932	Poorboy, Israel	21799
Pigeon, Annie	28513	Poorboy, Jeff	21800
Pigeon, George	21133	Poorboy, Bird	20260
Pigeon, Nannie	21134	Poorboy, Jack	28476
Pigeon, Maggie	21135	Poole, Charles W.	24978
Pigeon, Charlotte	21136	Poole, Walton	24980
Pigeon, Wasa-lou-kee	26001	Poole, Carlisle	24981
Pigeon, George	26002	Poole, Scott O.	24982
Pigeon, Susie	26149	Poole, Gladys C.	24983
Pigeon, Charles	32376	Poorbear, Famy	14651
Pigeon, Lydia	32377	Pope, Georgie	4873
Pinner, John	23637	Pope, Clem W.	4874
Pinner, Pearl	23638	Pope, Robert S.	4875
Pinkney, William H.	14471	Pope, Madalyn K.	4876
Pittit, Frank	28706	Pope, James	5989
Pittit, Alex	17632	Pope, James M.	5988
Pittit, Lizzie	17633	Pope, Sidney	5991
Pittit, Jennie	17634	Pope, Jane B.	5992
Pittit, Susan	17635	Pope, Andrew A.	5993
Pitts, Cora	3630	Poplin, Catharine O.	7718
Pitts, Clarence N.	3631	Poplin, Annie J.	7719
Pittsenberger, Annie E.	27773	Poplin, Ora A.	7720
Pittensbarger, Lillie H.	31666	Poplin, Gaither O.	7721
Pitcher, Viola D.	13471	Poplin, Margarett	7722
Pitcher, George B.	13472	Poplin, Rosebud	7723
Pitcher, Ida P.	13473	Poplin, Nellie	7724
Pitcher, Charles P.	13474		

Name.	Roll No.	Name.	Roll No.
Porter, James M.	27247	Prater, Mable Clare	21824
Porter, Nana M.	7043	Prather, Caroline C.	9698
Porter, Mildred M.	7044	Prather, Howard L.	9738
Porter, Jim	25715	Prather, Frances F.	9739
Porter, Lucy	25716	Prather, Lee B.	9740
Porter, Dick	19333	Prather, Annie O.	9741
Porter, William	19334	Prather, Minnie O.	9742
Porter, Wolfe	19335	Prather, Fannie D.	9743
Porter, Sarah	19336	Prather, Martha E.	9744
Porter, Myrtle	27248	Prather, Alvie M.	9745
Porter, Sallie	32699	Prather, Charilla C.	9746
Post, Carrie E.	5563	Prather, James F.	9747
Post, William T.	5564	Prather, Bertha R.	9748
Post, Margaret	5565	Prather, Thomas W.	24359
Post, Andrew	5566	Prather, Charles D.	24361
Post, Maude A.	5567	Prather, Wesley L.	24362
Post, Charles	5568	Prather, Vinita B.	24363
Post, Daniel	5569	Prather, John E.	13818
Potts, Richard H.	27932	Prather, George E.	13819
Potts, Mary B.	27933	Prather, Elizabeth B.	13820
Potts, Lyda A.	5483	Prather, Josephine	13821
Potts, Hugh A.	5484	Prather, Caroline	14569
Potts, Mont E.	5485	Prather, Richard L.	14570
Potts, Virgie L.	5486	Prather, Sam Houston	29540
Potts, Amy F.	5487	Prather, Maggie	29541
Potts, Campbell L.	5488	Prather, Jesse Q.	29516
Potts, Thomas	27444	Prather, Eva L.	12256
Potts, Lucy	27445	Prather, James L.	12257
Potts, Louella	27446	Preston, Zacariah	226
Potts, William	27447	Preston, Willie M.	227
Potts, Samuel S.	27448	Price, Fannie	76
Potts, John W.	27449	Price, Marshall	77
Potts, Sallie	27450	Price, Gracie	78
Potts, Annie	28935	Price, Bessie	79
Potts, Arthur N.	28936	Price, Alma	80
Potts, Carrie	28937	Price, James H.	2368
Potter, Jesse J.	7709	Price, Joseph W.	2369
Potter, Ray	29768	Price, Joel S.	2616
Potter, Hester	7703	Price, Mack E.	2819
Potter, George	7704	Prnce, Undeen	2820
Potter, Florence E.	7705	Price, George W.	2821
Potter, Mary L.	7706	Price, Mary L.	2822
Potter, Robert D.	7707	Price, Charles E.	2823
Potter, John W.	7708	Price, William T.	2824
Potter, Eliza A.	25113	Price, Susie	3040
Potter, Edward	25114	Price, John W., Jr.	3042
Potter, Joel	25115	Price, Mary E.	3041
Potter, Laura E.	25116	Price, Annie	3043
Potter, Susie M.	25117	Price, Sarah L.	3044
Potter, Green	25118	Price, Charlie T.	3045
Potato, George	20336	Price, Reece B.	3062
Potato, Ned	20472	Price, William	3123
Potato, George	30710	Price, Narcissus J.	5753
Potato, Lucinda	30711	Price, Ella	5754
Potato, Carrie	30712	Price, Looney	5807
Powell, Richard W.	555	Price, Sarah	5808
Powell, Lillie M.	2791	Price, Daniel C.	11744
Powell, Beckey J.	2792	Price, Annie B.	11745
Powell, Julia	2793	Price, Looney D.	11806
Powell, Joseph	3191	Price, Charley C.	12470
Powell, Sarah L.	3192	Price, Daisy E.	12471
Powell, Mary E.	7670	Price, Charley B.	12472
Powell, Ivey N.	8109	Price, James	12515
Powell, Victoria	8110	Price, Ruthie E.	16356
Powell, James W.	8111	Price, Mary	13447
Powell, Richard W.	8112	Price, James S.	14725
Powell, Robert L.	8113	Price, Sidney W.	14726
Powell, Dora	8114	Price, Shory A.	16395
Powell, Luvina	8115	Price, John R.	16473
Powell, Fannie	15681	Price, Katie	16474
Powell, William H. H.	21816	Price, Samuel	16475
Powell, James F.	21817	Price, Loto	16476
Powell, Minnie J.	15680	Price, Addie E.	17162
Powell, Sam	15682	Price, Maggie J.	17163
Powell, Joseph	31659	Price, Clarence M.	17164
Powhatan, Norma P.	2221	Price, Henry P.	17165
Powhatan, Cordelia A.	2222	Price, Mary K.	17166
Powhatan, Sarah L.	2223	Price, Ila I.	17167
Prater, Mattie C.	6648	Price, George M.	27927
Prater, David G.	6649	Price, William S.	27928
Prater, William E.	6650	Price, Henry L.	27929
Prater, Mary C.	6651	Price, Cecil Dewey	13448
Prater, Henry L. D.	6652	Price, Essie Lucille	17168

Name.	Roll No.
Price, Clarence Thurston	12473
Price, Arley G.	18115
Price, Eddie	3046
Price, Clarie	3063
Price, Ottus	20863
Price, Ida	11947
Price, Georgia Belle	81
Price, Alcie Annie	11950
Price, Cora Bell	11807
Pritchett, George	4078
Pritchett, Bettie	29819
Pritchett, Curtis	26368
Pritchett, Jennie	16155
Pritchett, Charles	16156
Pritchett, James	16157
Pritchett, Henry	16158
Pritchett, Samuel J.	16480
Pritchett, Jackson	16481
Pritchett, Edward	16482
Pritchett, Charles D.	16483
Pritchett, Nancy	18312
Pritchett, Charley	30486
Pritchett, Laura	30487
Pritchett, Jennie	30488
Pritchett, Tony	30489
Pritchett, Bird	30490
Pritchett, Jane Anna	30491
Pritchett, Rufus	30492
Pritchett, Willie	18776
Pritchett, Tom	25615
Pritchett, Jennie	25616
Pritchett, Liza	25618
Pritchett, Joe	25619
Pritchett, Jonn	25620
Pritchett, Martha	25621
Pritchett, Red	19139
Pritchett, Fannie	19140
Pritchett, Johnanna	19141
Pritchett, Felix	19142
Pritchett, Jesse	19143
Pritchett, Hiyan	19870
Pritchett, Nellie	19871
Pritchett, Lucy	20134
Pritchett, William	30682
Pritchett, Annie	25617
Pritchard, Laura Narcissa	32769
Pritchet, Thomas	1433
Pritchet, Jesse	27069
Privat, Louisa	22185
Prim, Annie E.	10238
Prince, Taylor	21188
Prince, Jennie	21189
Proctor, Ezekiel Jr.	1181
Proctor, Sallie	1182
Proctor, Sam M.	1183
Proctor, Eli	1184
Proctor, William C.	1185
Proctor, Walter	1186
Proctor, Mary J.	1187
Proctor, Charlie J.	1188
Proctor, Ezekiel	1212
Proctor, William R.	1213
Proctor, Joseph	1521
Proctor, Katie	1523
Proctor, Sallie M.	1522
Proctor, Nelson	3075
Proctor, Lydia	3076
Proctor, Charlie	3077
Proctor, Watt	3078
Proctor, Thomas	2509
Proctor, Sallie	3510
Proctor, Nannie	3674
Proctor, Polly	29810
Proctor, Joseph	29811
Proctor, Bird	26999
Proctor, Lola	27000
Proctor, Wyly	27001
Proctor, Dakie	27002
Proctor, Cornsilk	27003
Proctor, Nancy	27004
Proctor, Alexander	23332

Name.	Roll No.
Proctor, Sarah	2333
Proctor, Eliza	23334
Proctor, Columbus	23335
Proctor, Nancy H.	23685
Proctor, Alex	26447
Proctor, Toowat	26448
Proctor, Avie	27559
Proctor, Hunter	26449
Proctor, Caroline	26450
Proctor, Betsy	26451
Proctor, Thomas	26452
Proctor, Lucy	26453
Proctor, Walker	7453
Proctor, Cumming	26455
Proctor, Nellie	26456
Proctor, Charlotte	26457
Proctor, Willie	26458
Proctor, Ezekiel	29496
Proctor, Ed	27005
Proctor, Margaret	14165
Proctor, Eliza	29659
Proctor, Lucy	14461
Proctor, Mike	28311
Proctor, Nancy	18670
Proctor, Bell	18900
Proctor, Willie Bell	25628
Proctor, George	32287
Proctor, Sallie	32388
Proctor, Isaac	32389
Proctor, Crawler	20151
Proctor, Nancy	20152
Proctor, Joe	20153
Proctor, Rachel	20154
Proctor, Adam	20766
Proctor, William	30648
Proctor, Mary	21102
Proctor, Daniel	21103
Propp, Mary E.	7255
Prophet, William	29282
Pruitt, Litt	5557
Pruett, George	12872
Puckett, Pechey E.	12415
Puckett, Joseph L.	12417
Puckett, Bee I.	12418
Puller, Robbin	21303
Puller, Lizzie	21304
Puller, Arleach	21305
Pumpkin, Frank	6275
Pumpkin, George	23510
Pumpkin, Peggy	6922
Pumpkin, George	28969
Pumpkin, Lizzie	32020
Pumpkin, Thomas	18878
Pumpkin, Mary	18879
Pumpkin, Jenanna	18880
Pumpkin, Annie	18881
Pumpkin, James	18884
Pumpkin, Mary	18885
Pumpkin, Richard	18886
Pumpkin, Eli	18887
Pumpkin, George	21468
Puppy, Sallie	30524
Puppy, Ned	30525
Puppy, Doll	30526
Purcell, Charles H.	7653
Purcell, Troy N.	7654
Purcell, Minnie	7655
Purcell, Dealtha	7656
Purcell, Edith E.	7657
Purcell, Charles H.	7658
Purcell, John W.	7785
Purcell, Squire L.	10657
Purcell, Carl B.	26272
Purcell, Milford C.	26273
Purcell, Scroggs R.	26161
Purcell, Hattie E.	26162
Purcell, Harry W.	26163
Purcell, Charles H.	26164
Purcell, Ada M.	26165
Purcell, Julia E.	26166
Purcell, James C.	26167
Purcell, Mary H.	26168
Puryear, Lucy	15613

Name.	Roll No.	Name.	Roll No.
Puryear, Ernest	15614	Rafferty, Vina L.	7608
Purdue, Elizabeth	32652;	Rafferty, Lester	7609
Purdue, William Henry	32653	Rafferty, Dewey R.	7610
Purkey, Effie	30910	Rafferty, Hattie	7611
Putnam, Katie	4858	Ragsdale, Riley	1470
Putnam, Samuel	4859	Ragsdale, Isaac H.	3437
Putnam, Josie I.	6348	Ragsdale, Johnsanna	3438
Putnam, Jesse V.	6349	Ragsdale, Susan N.	3439
Pyburn, Earnest C.	11480	Ragsdale, Mary V.	3440
Pyeatt, Bessie L.	11497	Ragsdale, Charles O.	3441
Pyeatt, Margie E.	11498	Ragsdale, John A.	3442
Pyeatt, Annie M.	15022	Ragsdale, Robert	3443
Pyeatt, Cherry E.	15023	Ragsdale, Joseph	29798
Pyeatt, Aaron D.	15024	Ragsdale, John H.	29799
Pyeatt, Charley R.	15025	Ragsdale, Florence V.	3475
Pyeatt, Willie L.	15026	Ragsdale, George	3601
Pyeatt, Martha M.	15027	Ragsdale, Grover C.	3750
Quarles, Carrie E.	747	Ragsdale, Ellen	3751
Quallote, John	12748	Ragsdale, May	3752
Quallote, Houston	12749	Ragsdale, Sadie	3753
Qualls, Maggie F.	14628	Ragsdale, Willard	3754
Qualls, Romulus A.	14629	Ragsdale, Thomas	5136
Qualls, James F.	14630	Ragsdale, Lucinda	5137
Qualls, William R.	14631	Ragsdale, Willie A.	5188
Qualls, Dudley A.	14632	Ragsdale, John	27407
Qualls, Leona F.	21550	Ragsdale, Jennie	27408
Quesenbury, Harriett B.	2589	Ragsdale, Alice	27409
Quesenbury, Lucy	2590	Ragsdale, Margaret	27410
Queen, Joe	8500	Ragsdale, Lucy	23300
Queen, George R.	12397	Ragsdale, Benjamin	6035
Quinton, George	2474	Ragsdale, Sarah	6052
Quinton, Lydia	2475	Ragsdale, David W.	6886
Quinton, Charlotte	22717	Ragsdale, Rutha	6887
Quinton, Sequoyah	22718	Ragsdale, Maggie	6888
Quinton, Lewis	3132	Ragsdale, David	6889
Quinton, Letha	3133	Ragsdale, Nancy	6890
Quinton, James	3134	Ragsdale, Claude	6891
Quinton, Johnson	3135	Ragsdale, Muggie	6898
Quinton, Lewis	3136	Ragsdale, Ezekiel	3755
Quinton, David	3137	Raincrow, Sarah	6448
Quinton, Nancy L.	3692	Raincrow, Susan	6449
Quinton, Clara	6166	Raincrow, Rachel	15208
Quinton, Cornelius	6167	Raincrow, Jesse	16008
Quinton, Noah	6168	Raincrow, Lacie	16009
Quinton, Nannie M.	6169	Raincrow, Charles	16228
Quinton, Ethel M.	12071	Raincrow, Joseph	21016
Quinton, Isaac S.	12072	Raincrow, Mary	21017
Quinton, Nancy E.	12073	Raincrow, Ida	21018
Quinton, Marietta	12074	Raincrow, Cornelius	21019
Quinton, Mack	14585	Raincrow, Alsie	21020
Quinton, Emily	14586	Raincrow, Katie	21021
Quinton, Jackoline A.	14587	Raincrow, Rachel	21022
Quinton, Joseph	14588	Rainey, Janie L.	8339
Quinton, Jack	25536	Rainey, Homer	8340
Quinton, Cornelius	25537	Raines, Viola	9007
Quinton, Jesse	25538	Raines, George M.	9008
Quinton, John Henry	32537	Raines, William H.	9009
Quinton, Willie	32538	Raines, Gordon B.	9010
Quinton, Sarah E.	22076	Raines, Hita E.	9011
Quinton, Myrtle C.	3693	Raines, Mary	9012
Quinton, Jeff	19301	Raines, Jennings D.	9013
Quinton, John	25731	Rains, Nancy A.	26834
Quinton, Frank	20506	Rains, Ollie M.	26835
Quinn, Lenora A.	31605	Rains, John H.	26836
Quinn, Edward S.	31606	Rains, Roy A.	26837
Quinn, Thomas L.	31607	Raley, Mary L.	3683
Rabbit, Andy	12528	Raley, Nancy J.	10702
Rabbit, Sallie	12529	Raley, William L.	10703
Rabbit, Maggie	12530	Raley, Bertha P.	10704
Rabbit, Ida	12531	Raley, Jesse M.	10705
Rabbit, Alcy	12532	Raley, Thomas L.	10706
Rabbit, William R.	12533	Raley, Ida M.	10707
Rabbit, Rosa	12534	Raley, Martha	11766
Rabbit, Jack	12535	Raley, Oliver W.	11767
Rabbit, Thomas	17707	Raley, Oscar C.	11768
Rabbit, Arch	20735	Raley, William H.	11769
Rabbit, Rachel	20736	Raley, George W.	11770
Rabbit, Keller	32331	Raley, James M.	11771
Rackleff, George	15128	Raley, Harriett J.	10708
Rackleff, Johnie	15129	Ralston, James D.	21679
Rachel	28499	Rame, Fred	23892
Rafferty, Caldonia	7606	Randolph, Eliza	3721
Rafferty, Myrtle L.	7607	Randolph, Pinkey M.	3722

Name.	Roll No.	Name.	Roll No.
Randolph, Joel	30115	Ratler, Mary	17824
Randolph, Malderine E.	13446	Rattlingourd, Thomas	23192
Rankin, Ellen	9872	Rattlingourd, Lizzie	23194
Randall, William P.	30857	Rattlingourd, Nancy	23195
Randall, Viola M.	26302	Rattlingourd, James	23196
Randall, Lolena L.	31377	Rattlingourd, Esther	23197
Randall, Frank H., Jr.	31378	Rattlingourd, Thomas	
Randall, Arthur S.	31379	Jr.	23198
Randall, Lambert K.	31380	Rattlingourd, Susan	6018
Randall, Minnie V.	31422	Rattlingourd, George	6020
Randall, James	31423	Rattlingourd, Ellen	6021
Randall, Samuel B.	31424	Rattling Gourd, Arte-	
Randall, Flora	31425	miss	11621
Randall, Nora	31426	Rattling Gourd, Charles	
Randall, Fay	31427	A.	11622
Raper, Charles	4535	Rattling Gourd, Nora	11623
Raper, Moses	4978	Rattling Gourd, Gertie	11624
Raper, Ross	4979	Rattlingourd, Henry	12268
Raper, Louella	23214	Rattlingourd, Sarah	12269
Raper, Sam	29654	Rattlingourd, James E.	12270
Raper, Vida	29655	Rattlingourd, Daniel	12801
Raper, Margaret	29656	Rattlingourd, Edward	12802
Raper, John A.	6378	Rattlingourd, Taylor	12803
Raper, John A.	23383	Rattlingourd, Jack	12804
Raper, Mary	6892	Rattlingourd, George	12805
Raper, Benjamin	6893	Rattlingourd, Calvin	12806
Raper, Laura	6894	Rattlingourd, Sister	12807
Raper, Nellie	30148	Rattlingourd, James	14289
Raper, Joseph	32461	Rattlingourd, Henry	14900
Raper, John H.	9410	Rattlingourd, Morgan	14901
Raper, Sarah E.	9411	Rattlingourd, Lila	17945
Raper, Mary E.	9412	Rattlingourd, Susie	
Raper, Sarah J.	9413	Ann	32267
Raper, Willie	9414	Ratt, Addie	17974
Raper, George G.	9415	Rattlingourd, Mollie	20079
Raper, Rosa G.	9416	Rat, Taki	20130
Raper, Essie M.	9417	Rat, James	20147
Raper, Charles	11043	Rat, Jennie	20148
Raper, Young	11044	Rat, Polly	20149
Raper, John	11045	Rat, Sarah	20177
Raper, William T.	11673	Rat, Ella	20178
Raper, William P.	12567	Rattlingourd, Nancy	21212
Raper, Alvin F.	12568	Rattlingourd, Jennie	21214
Raper, Jess McK.	12569	Rattlingourd, John	21215
Raper, Mary E.	11046	Rattlingourd, Nick	32246
Raper, Lewis	15442	Rattlinggourd, James	5602
Raper, James	16509	Rattlinggourd, Looney	11930
Raper, Martha J.	16510	Rattlinggourd, Sarah	26680
Raper, George W.	32463	Rattlinggourd, Tecum-	
Raper, Martin	21932	seh	26681
Raper, George	7524	Rattlinggourd, Jeter	26682
Raper, Nancy	20729	Rattlinggourd, Dorothy	26683
Raper, David Washing-		Rattlinggourd, John	17484
ton	32462	Rattlinggourd, Vura	26152
Raper, Jennie	4980	Rattlinggourd, Lorin C.	26153
Rasmus, Josephine C.	15891	Ratlingourd, Charles	16780
Rasmus, Bascom P.	16783	Ratlingourd, David	16781
Rasmus, Beuna Vista	29020	Ratlingourd, Sarah	20664
Rasmus, Nancy E.	25416	Ratlingourd, Bertha	20665
Rasmus, Norma E.	25417	Ratliff, Richard	15519
Ratcliff, Rachel	1136	Ratliff, Lizzie M.	15520
Ratcliff, Eliza	1137	Ratliff, Mary A.	15521
Ratcliff, Ella	1138	Ratliff, John	15522
Ratcliff, Eva E.	9728	Ratliff, Houston	15647
Ratcliff, Frederick F.	9729	Ratliff, Robbin S.	15648
Ratcliff, James W.	9730	Rattler, Rider	25502
Ratcliff, Finis R.	9731	Rattler, Lizzie	17210
Ratcliff, Mary E.	9732	Rattler, Lilly	17211
Ratcliff, Norville	9733	Rattler, Nora	17212
Ratcliff, Daniel	15811	Rattler, William	18301
Ratley, Lona M.	30053	Rattler, Annie	18302
Ratley, Pearl	30054	Rattler, Lizzie	18303
Ratley, Rosa	27511	Rattler, Cahena	18304
Ratliff, Nettie	27512	Rat, Mary	19879
Ratley, Charley	27513	Rattler, Jeff	20925
Ratley, Frank	27514	Rattler, Susan	20926
Ratley, Moses J.	25424	Rat, James	25942
Ratley, Lawrence	25425	Rat, Susie	25943
Ratley, Beulah	25426	Rat, Arlie	25944
Ratley, Wallace	17427	Rat, Polly	25945
Ratley, Sarah	17429	Rat, John	20947
Ratler, Nancy	27294	Raven, Albert	5446
Ratler, Lucy A.	27295	Raven, Ella	27510

Name.	Roll No.	Name.	Roll No.
Raven, Fox	23908	Redbird, Jackson	21218
Raven, John	23909	Redbird, Eliza Jane	21219
Raven, Lucy	32029	Redbird, Johnson	21220
Raven, Bony	19381	Redbird, Jack	21465
Raven, Wahsinni	19382	Redinger, Mary A.	17278
Raven, Jeremiah	19383	Redinger, Henry F.	17279
Raven, George	20314	Reese, Joseph	995
Raven, Mary	20315	Reese, Ida	996
Raven, Mary	21421	Reese, Charles	997
Raven, William	32382	Reese, Andy	998
Ray, Joella	2708	Reese, Jesse	999
Ray, James R.	2711	Reese, Ellis	1000
Ray, Asa	3092	Reese, Nancy J.	1361
Ray, Pearl	3093	Reese, Susan E.	22513
Ray, Bud	3094	Reese, Ellen	1362
Reed, Mary J.	29605	Reese, John	1363
Reed, Frederick W.	29606	Reese, Ellis	1474
Reed, Emily J.	23680	Reese, Richard	27084
Reed, Joseph H.	23681	Reese, Annie	27085
Reed, Ellen	23682	Reese, Betsy	27086
Reed, Rufus	23683	Reese, Charles	28560
Reed, Valina	7659	Reese, Arley	28561
Reed, Nancy M.	9060	Reese, Roddy A.	4515
Reed, Etta	9061	Reese, Martha	4516
Reed, John	9062	Reese, Henry D.	27335
Reed, Pearl	9063	Reese, Eloise	4517
Reed, Luna	9274	Reese, Charles	4518
Reed, Lizzie	1040	Reese, Rora	4519
Reed, John R.	1041	Reese, Inez	5186
Reed, Andrew	10420	Reese, Tuxie O.	6133
Reed, Samuel	1042	Reese, Thomas	14395
Reed, Mollie E.	11119	Reese, Levi	14398
Reed, Myrtle B.	11120	Reese, James G.	15887
Reed, Walter S.	11121	Reese, Joseph	28312
Reed, Jennie	11122	Reese, Sarah	28313
Reed, Cynthia A.	11665	Reese, White	28314
Reed, Thomas L.	11666	Reese, Lizzie	28315
Reed, Claude P.	11667	Reese, Annie	28316
Reed, Noama A.	11668	Reese, Maggie	28317
Reed, Clarence R.	11669	Reese, Nellie	16832
Reed, Clyde O.	11670	Reese, President C.	16833
Reed, Linna I.	29563	Reese, Charles Jr.	16834
Reed, Nancy A.	29564	Reese, Charley	16930
Reed, Philetus L. A.	29565	Reese, Felix	16931
Reed, Ala M.	29566	Reese, Noah	21925
Reed, Alice L. V.	29567	Reese, Stad Dawson	21926
Reed, Harley Monroe	9275	Reed, Paralee	12800
Reed, Anna F.	1043	Reed, John	12808
Reed, David A.	29568	Reese, Emma	27087
Reed, Sarah F.	2260	Reeves, Martha E.	1974
Reed, Annie	28042	Reeves, Stella	1975
Reed, Lucy	28043	Reeves, John	1977
Reed, Celia	28045	Reeves, Lawson M.	1978
Reece, Annie	28704	Reeves, Theodore H.	1979
Reeve, Arlie	16722	Reeves, Margaret Alida	27461
Reeve, Nettie	16723	Reeves, Hogan T.	6327
Reeve, Bertha	16724	Reeves, Nancy M.	13360
Reeve, Edward	16725	Reeves, Mary E.	15433
Reeve, Ida	16726	Ray, Jessie	3095
Reid, Francis A.	15046	Ray, Mylie	3096
Reid, Clarence A.	15047	Ray, Jennie A.	28092
Reid, Leola	15048	Ray, Cassonia E.	28097
Reid, Whitelaw E.	15049	Raymond, Carrie	4526
Reid, Bertha M.	15050	Raymond, Ada	4527
Reid, Grace M.	15051	Raymond, Sue N.	4528
Reid, Rubie M.	15052	Raymond, Amanda J.	7479
Reid, Cleo T.	31683	Raymond, John	12526
Reid, Thompson	31684	Raymond, Oscar	19712
Remsen, Julia E.	7132	Ray, George W.	21683
Remsen, Alvie M.	7133	Reaves, Angie	5139
Renfrow, Emma	27586	Reaves, Lettie	5141
Reneckar, Sarah	15860	Reaves, Dimer W.	6054
Reneckar, Robert R.	15861	Reaves, John A.	29420
Reneckar, Andrew J.	15862	Reaves, Charles B.	29431
Reneckar, Bettie J.	15863	Reaves, Effie M.	29432
Renfro, Arbazena	31019	Reagan, Lydia A.	13935
Renfro, Reno B.	31020	Reagan, Arthur G.	13936
Redbird, Jesse	20507	Reagan, Austin G.	13937
Redbird, Betsy	20508	Redden, Lou E.	3792
Redbird, Sam	28482	Redden, James Z.	3793
Redbird, Chewooan	20571	Redden, Moses O.	3794
Redbird, Josie	30618	Redden, John	3795
Redbird, Guntakee	30619	Redden, William H.	3796
		Redden, Nealy M.	3797

Name.	Roll No.	Name.	Roll No.
Redden, Hugh M.	3798	Rich, Vera V.	2676
Redden, Charles O.	3799	Rich, Mae	11705
Redden, Sarah Ada	3800	Rich, Russell E.	11706
Redington, Isabelle	29445	Rich, Beuna	11707
Redmond, Malinda	13267	Rich, Fred	16800
Redding, Eliza C.	29364	Rich, Bertha	16801
Redding, Samuel	29365	Rich, Onie T.	11708
Redding, Amanda L.	29366	Rich, Donie C.	11709
Redding, Jessie M.	29367	Rice, Violet	30004
Redding, Isaac E.	29368	Rice, Mantie	27504
Redbird, Daniel	18348	Rice, Ruby M.	27505
Redbird, Annie	18349	Rice, Emma	13012
Redbird, Joseph	18350	Rice, Dorothy	13013
Redbird, Nathaniel	19239	Rice, Sarah	28991
Redbird, Mary	19240	Rice, James A. Jr.	29757
Redbird, Sarah	19241	Rice, Della M.	24964
Redbird, Lizzie	19242	Rice, Charles F.	31206
Redbird, John L.	19243	Rice, Nora E.	31207
Redbird, Mary	19244	Riceman, Martha	7961
Redbird, George	25685	Riceman, John	7962
Redbird, Peggie	25686	Riceman, Dandy	7963
Redbird,	19445	Rider, Minda L. H. C.	972
Redbird, Sarah	19446	Rider, Joseph	1970
Redbird, Henry	19664	Rider, Sarah	29788
Redbird, White	20004	Rider, Sally	1971
Redbird, Quatie	20005	Rider, Lila	1972
Redbird, Ketcher	20006	Rider, Elizabeth	2007
Redbird, Will	20007	Rider, Myrtle M.	2008
Redbird, Betsy	20008	Rider, Viola	2009
Redbird, Jackson	20050	Rider, Jack W.	22795
Redbird, Nancy	20051	Rider, Austin W.	22797
Redbird, Jim	20052	Rider, Tip P.	22798
Rex, Alfred	7907	Rider, C. Augustus	22799
Rex, Eliza M.	27812	Rider, Thomas Needles	22800
Rex, Mary Ama	27813	Rider, Jack B.	3374
Reynolds, Lulu E.	732	Rider, Samuel	3375
Reynolds, Lois T.	733	Rider, Benjamin F.	3376
Reynolds, William A.	5222	Rider, Josephine	4257
Reynolds, Ellen	5449	Rider, Carrie	4747
Reynolds, Jesse	5450	Rider, Nancy J.	5596
Reynolds, Minnie	5451	Rider, Charles R.	23515
Reynolds, George	5452	Rider, Clarence A.	24080
Reynolds, Alice M.	9548	Rider, Clarence A.	24081
Reynolds, Harry L.	9549	Rider, William P.	24552
Reynolds, Annie P.	10823	Rider, Charles	10711
Reynolds, William J.	28816	Rider, Delilah	10712
Reynolds, Bessie L.	28817	Rider, Charles M.	10713
Reynolds, Cinderella	17420	Rider, Susanna	10714
Reynolds, Maude E.	9550	Rider, Stand W.	10715
Reynolds, Vera	734	Rider, Austin	11093
Reynolds, Eva A.	22100	Rider, James H.	11228
Rhodes, Nellie	14037	Rider, William	11424
Rhodes, Edward	30804	Rider, Louisa	11425
Rhomar, May	17271	Rider, Emma	11426
Rhomar, Emma N.	17272	Rider, Caroline	11427
Rhomar, May F.	17273	Rider, Blueford W.	13111
Rhomar, Maggie B.	17274	Rider, Lydia	13112
Rhomar, Fannie C.	17275	Rider, Samuel H.	13113
Ribbon, Jack	18523	Rider, Percival	13114
Ribbon, Lucy	25599	Rider, John G.	13483
Richards, Susan M.	1514	Rider, Wilson	25079
Richards, Sarah M. J.	1515	Rider, Thomas L.	15418
Richards, Joseph C.	1516	Rider, Mary A.	15419
Richards, Mary F.	1517	Rider, Ruth B.	15420
Richards, Nora B.	1518	Rider, Phoebe	15421
Richards, Lelia H.	8087	Rider, Mittie E.	15422
Richards, Beatrice	8088	Rider, Roscoe C.	15423
Richards, Earl	8089	Rider, Milton L.	15424
Richards, Carrolton M.	8090	Rider, Iva J.	15425
Richards, Mary	13720	Rider, Cherokee A.	15426
Richards, Sim B.	13721	Rider, Mary	16153
Richards, Roddie	13722	Rider, Weata	16154
Richards, Ella Q.	13723	Rider, Wilson	16619
Richards, Mary W.	13724	Rider, Mahala	16620
Richardson, Nancy E.	22725	Rider, Julia	16621
Richardson, Mary E.	5199	Rider, Luvinia	16856
Richardson, Emma	6913	Rider, Henry	16857
Richardson, Nannie V.	6914	Rider, Jefferson Davis	10716
Richardson, Alma E.	6915	Rider, Alice	18233
Richardson, Kittie	31855	Rider, Charlotte	1973
Richardson, Delia F.	31856	Rider, George	28435
Richardson, Finis T.	31857	Rider, Ada	19065
Richardson, Zora I.	22726	Rider, Bertha	19066
Richardson, Jasper Cecil	21865	Rider, John	25680
Rich, Minnie B.	2675	Rider, Mollie	19144

Name.	Roll No.
Rider, Lizzie	19145
Rider, Eli	19193
Rider, John	32666
Rider, Sadie	32256
Rider, Nancy	32667
Rider, Tom	32260
Ridge, Andrew	4204
Ridge, Susan	29740
Ridge, Beaver	8891
Ridge, Adam	8895
Ridge, Jennie	8896
Ridge, Cull	8897
Ridge, John	12527
Ridge, Moses	14535
Ridge, Awa	14536
Ridge, Nancy	14551
Ridge, Nellie	14552
Ridge, John	14808
Ridge, Sarah	30381
Ridge, John	17498
Ridge, Jeremiah	17499
Ridge, Polly	17500
Ridge, Peter	17501
Ridge, Annie	17893
Ridge, Callie	22018
Ridge, Fannie	22019
Ridge, Joseph	22020
Ridge, Jesse	22021
Ridge, Nannie	22022
Ridge, Myrtle	22023
Ridge, Ben	20271
Ridge, Jane	20272
Ridge, Oce	20273
Ridge, Frank B.	32897
Riddle, Louisa E.	7526
Riddle, Giles H.	7527
Riddle, Lula May	7528
Riddle, Fannie J.	7991
Riddle, Ida J.	7992
Riddle, Frederick F.	7993
Riddle, Fannie M.	7994
Riddle, Dewey L.	7995
Riddle, Lilliam R.	7996
Riddle, Henry	17882
Riddle, Frace Thomas	7997
Riddle, Edna Lee	7529
Ridenour, Elizabeth	29553
Ridenour, Charles C.	29554
Ridenour, Elmer O.	29555
Rienhardt, Sarah	10911
Reinhardt, Charles	10912
Reinhardt, Mary	29203
Rigsby, Hannah	3028
Rigsby, James	3029
Rigsby, Jessie	3030
Rigsby, Tiny	3031
Riggs, Mattie A. M.	11927
Riggs, William E.	11928
Riggs, Rollie L.	11929
Riggs, Eliza	13152
Riggs, Noula E.	13317
Riggs, Frank S.	13318
Riggs, Nadia E.	13319
Riggs, Glenn L.	13320
Riggs, Alf. E.	13321
Riggs, Harvey D.	13322
Riley, Webster	501
Riley, James T.	545
Riley, Bertha A.	546
Riley, Francis M.	547
Riley, William T.	548
Riley, Charles R.	549
Riley, Joseph H.	550
Riley, Mary	3867
Riley, John M.	4840
Riley, Sarah	5445
Riley, Downing	29644
Riley, John M.	6475
Riley, Nannie E.	6476
Riley, Mattie	6477
Riley, Cherry	6478
Riley, Nannie E.	6479
Riley, Wilder	6480
Riley, Owen	6481
Riley, Mamie	6482

Name.	Roll No.
Riley, John Jr.	6483
Riley, John R.	27518
Riley, Eddie L.	27519
Riley, Orville K.	27520
Riley, Thomas T.	27521
Riley, Mary J.	7086
Riley, Edward E.	7087
Riley, Pearlie C.	7088
Riley, Lewis P.	10594
Riley, John W.	10595
Riley, Cora	10596
Riley, Lewis W.	10597
Riley, Rufus	10598
Riley, Mary E.	10599
Riley, Atwood T.	10607
Riley, Minnie	24602
Riley, Elizabeth	24603
Riley, Celia L.	26627
Riley, James	10850
Riley, Raymond	10851
Riley, Thomas M.	10852
Riley, James E.	10853
Riley, Jennie F.	10854
Riley, Rufus R.	27727
Riley, Samuel R.	10901
Riley, Mary E.	10235
Riley, Nancy J.	14059
Riley, Johnson	21884
Riley, George W.	21973
Riley, John H.	30805
Riley, Ruth P.	30806
Riley, Mamie A.	30807
Riley, Richard	29419
Riley, Rufus Randolph	10236
Riley, Richard	32599
Riley, Ed	26304
Riley, Thomas	32790
Riley, Susan A.	32791
Riley, Mabel	30808
Ringo, Lucy A.	10783
Ringo, Charles C.	10784
Ringo, George G.	10785
Riley, Nona F.	10786
Ringo, William P., Jr.	10787
Ringo, Libbie M.	10788
Ringo, Ethel D.	10789
Ringo, Alfred V.	10790
Rinehardt, Cassie	10796
Rinehardt, Henry H.	10797
Rinehardt, Ada	10798
Rinehardt, Willie L. L.	10799
Rinehardt, Augusta	10800
Rippetoe, Rebecca J.	9776
Rippetoe, Martha B.	9777
Rippetoe, Cora E.	9778
Rippetoe, Bessie M.	9779
Rippetoe, Lee	9780
Rippetoe, Laura Pearl	9781
Risingfawn, Joseph S.	7558
Risingfawn, Joseph T.	23773
Risingfawn, Stella M.	23774
Risingfawn, Ada Lee	23775
Ritchson, Lillie M.	11736
Ritchson, Inthe E.	11737
Ritchson, Biddie L.	11738
Ritchie, Anderson	16438
Ritchie, Mary A.	17348
Ritchie, Alice L.	17349
Ritter, Martha E.	21593
Ritter, Bessie M.	21594
Ritter, Editha	31703
Ritter, Howell W.	31704
Ritter, Ada E.	31705
Ritter, Willie C. W.	31706
Rivet, Lurena	11526
Roastingear, Joe	3791
Roastingear, John	3975
Roastingear, Katie	3976
Roastingear, Charlotte	3977
Roastingear, Jennie	3978
Roastingear, William	3979
Roastingear, Allie	3980
Roach, Mattie	8137

Name.	Roll No.	Name.	Roll No.
Roach, Charles	8138	Robbins, James C.	16581
Roach, Thomas N.	8139	Robbins, Claud E.	29004
Roach, Annie B.	9364	Robbins, William L.	29005
Roach, Mable	9365	Robbins, William H.	4590
Roach, George W.	13464	Robbins, Jessie	8803
Roach, Olive R.	13465	Robbins, Lottie	32899
Roach, Minnie M.	13466	Robinson, Joseph M.	29759
Roach, Thomas	14742	Robinson, Emma	5157
Roach, Emma	14743	Robinson, Nancy	23207
Roach, Maggie	14744	Robinson, Eliza	23208
Roach, Joshua W.	14745	Robinson, John Jr.	23210
Roach, Nancy	14746	Robinson, Elizabeth M.	23703
Roach, John	30394	Robinson, Charles	23704
Roach, Nellie	30395	Robinson, Fannie E.	23705
Roach, Callie	30396	Robinson, Josie	9087
Roach, Charles	30397	Robinson, Jesse	9088
Roach, Sarah	30398	Robinson, Effie	9089
Roach, James	30399	Robinson, George E.	28036
Roach, Polly	30400	Robinson, Le Ella F.	28037
Roach, Tandy	30401	Robinson, Sarah F.	13122
Roach, Annie	30402	Robinson, Willie H.	13123
Roach, Elmira	30403	Robinson, Annie	13124
Roach, George	16422	Robinson, Samuel R.	13125
Roach, Sarah	16423	Robinson, Thelma M.	13126
Roach, Thomas	16424	Robinson, Irvin	30315
Roach, George, Jr.	16425	Robinson, Laura	13679
Roach, Thomas	16592	Robinson, Richard	13680
Roach, Tennessee	21523	Robinson, Sarah E.	13681
Roach, Thomas E.	14747	Robinson, Pearl E.	13682
Roach, Nancy	28414	Robinson, Walter S.	13683
Roach, Jesse	18845	Robinson, William H.,	
Roach, Frankie C.	9366	Jr.	13684
Robertson, Sarah C.	625	Robinson, John C.	17421
Robertson, Bethena M.	626	Robinson, Joseph F.	17422
Robertson, William T.	627	Robinson, Charles	17468
Robertson, Grace	628	Robinson, Lucy	17469
Robertson, Bessie	629	Robinson, Samuel	17470
Robertson, Minnie H.	630	Robinson, Rebia	17471
Robertson, Robert F.	631	Robinson, Rachel J.	17529
Robertson, Andrew J.	5778	Robinson, John	17530
Robertson, Biddy A.	5779	Robinson, Ella F.	17616
Robertson, Nellie	5780	Robinson, Ella M.	18041
Robertson, Fannie	5781	Robinson, Cynthia E.	21712
Robertson, Nancy	5782	Robinson, Mary J.	21713
Robertson, Jefferson	5820	Robinson, Dora	17531
Robertson, William A.	5821	Robinson, Carleton	28038
Robertson, Mary E.	5822	Robinson, William E.	6656
Robertson, Fannie	5823	Robinson, Ina Bell	21862
Robertson, Joseph F.	5824	Robinson, Joseph Nel-	
Robertson, Rebecca	5829	son	13127
Robertson, Evans P.	14832	Robbs, Mary E.	23176
Robertson, Sarah E.	14833	Robbs, Lucinda	23177
Robertson, Watie E.	14834	Roberts, Esther S.	22646
Robertson, Arthur E.	14835	Roberts, Martha E.	22647
Robertson, Albion S.	14836	Roberts, Stephen S.	27160
Robertson, Lella E.	14837	Roberts, Johnnie A.	29626
Robertson, William C.	14838	Roberts, Mary E.	2816
Robertson, Annie	28321	Roberts, Pearl M.	2817
Robertson, Emeline	28322	Roberts, Callie ·	6355
Robertson, Elzemar	23876	Roberts, George W.	9085
Robertson, Hattie	23878	Roberts, Agnes	9833
Robertson, George Ann	5783	Roberts, May	9834
Robertson, Richard	5825	Roberts, John	9835
Roberts, Margarett E. A.	1681	Roberts, Mary E.	10880
Roberts, Samuel W.	1912	Roberts, William E., Jr.	10882
Roberts, Ruby	1913	Roberts, Charles A.	10883
Roberts, Roy	1914	Roberts, Floyd B.	10884
Roberts, Hubert A.	1933	Roberts, James T.	10881
Roberts, Laura E.	1934	Roberts, Henry G.	13003
Robbins, Shubie W.	27738	Roberts, Fannie R.	13004
Robbins, Ollie M.	27739	Roberts, Anna	13062
Robbins, Levi W.	11138	Roberts, Marion	13063
Robbins, Myrtle M.	11139	Roberts, John H.	13064
Robbins, Emma	11140	Roberts, Earl L.	13065
Robbins, Lonie Lee	11141	Roberts, Arthur S.	13066
Robbins, Dora L.	11142	Roberts, Mary	13067
Robbins, William O.	12623	Roberts, Lenoir	13068
Robbins, Doc	29940	Roberts, Lydia V. S.	14210
Robbins, Nancy J.	15032	Roberts, Leroy	14211
Robbins, William	15033	Roberts, Comodore P.	14212
Robbins, Henry	28285	Roberts, Maurice R.	14213
Robbins, Joseph	16389	Roberts, Arthur L.	14214
Robbins, Johnson	16390	Roberts, Vinny L.	14215

Name.	Roll No.	Name.	Roll No.
Roberts, Alexander	26695	Roe, Polly	4536
Roberts, Paul	26696	Roe, James F.	4537
Roberts, Murray E.	17396	Roe, Grace A.	4538
Roberts, Joseph	17483	Roe, Minnie M.	4539
Roberts, Oriville	9836	Rogers, George W.	614
Roberts, Della M.	31428	Rogers, Gertrude	615
Roberts, Joseph E.	31429	Rogers, Samuel M.	22686
Robber, Joseph	4038	Rogers, William M.	22687
Robber, Elizabeth	32682	Rogers, Thomas Z.	22688
Robison, Annie	4100	Rogers, Andrew W. G.	22689
Robison, Lizzie M.	4101	Rogers, Buland F.	22690
Robison, William H.	4102	Rogers, William P.	2827
Robison, Emma R.	4103	Rogers, Charles H.	2828
Robison, Elzina	6352	Rogers, George W.	2829
Robison, Zada	6353	Rogers, Bessie E.	3547
Robison, Bertha M.	6534	Rogers, Beulah E.	3548
Robison, Manervy	12976	Rogers, Jack	3859
Robison, Rosella	12977	Rogers, Andrew J.	4144
Robison, Samuel L.	12979	Rogers, Caroline	4145
Robison, Charles W.	12980	Rogers, Lula	4146
Robison, George W.	12981	Rogers, Winnie D.	4147
Robison, Annie Jose-		Rogers, Emma M.	4359
phine	4104	Rogers, Claud	4360
Robbins, Richard B.	4588	Rogers, Maude	4361
Robbins, Eva J.	4589	Rogers, Rebecka I.	4362
Robbins, Benjamin F.	27733	Rogers, Katie	4374
Robbins, Henry	27734	Rogers, Peggy	4375
Robbins, Charles	27735	Rogers, Phoena	4376
Robbins, Claud	27736	Rogers, Joseph	4377
Robbins, Cora	27737	Rogers, Peggy M.	4378
Robins, Milo T.	5639	Rogers, Mary	4412
Robins, William B.	5640	Rogers, Gertrude W.	4509
Robins, Thomas	20776	Rogers, Lewis B.	23032
Robins, Annie	20777	Rogers, Howard C.	23033
Robins, Henry	20823	Rogers, John	4511
Robins, Sallie	20824	Rogers, Emma	23034
Robins, Chulio	20285	Rogers, Charles	4512
Robins, Jane	32908	Rogers, Cynthia	4513
Robards, Christopher		Rogers, Laura	4514
C.	12649	Rogers, Sirrisia	4972
Robards, Myrtle	12650	Rogers, Eliza	4973
Robards, Edna	12651	Rogers, Georgia A.	4974
Robards, Amy	12652	Rogers, Sirrisia	4975
Robards, Herbert E.	12653	Rogers, William	4976
Robards, Cree	12654	Rogers, Charley	4977
Robards, Tarvis	12655	Rogers, Clifford	5168
Roberson, Esther	24967	Rogers, John L.	5296
Roberson, Katie	24968	Rogers, Annie	23178
Roberson, Jasper C.	24969	Rogers, Artemus W.	23179
Roberson, DeWitt	24970	Rogers, Alma J.	23180
Roberson, Clara N.	24971	Rogers, Sadie	23181
Roberson, Jack S.	24972	Rogers, Cherokee A.	5389
Roberson, Mary	24973	Rogers, Andrew L.	5392
Roberson, Dewey	24974	Rogers, David	5806
Roberson, Pickens B.	16790	Rogers, Hugh M.	5973
Roberson, Caleb S.	16791	Rogers, Walter S.	29763
Roberson, Paralee A.	16792	Rogers, Walter P.	29764
Roberson, Beulah I.	16793	Rogers, John H.	29765
Roberson, Susie G.	16794	Rogers, Philip O.	29766
Roberson, William C.	30413	Rogers, Charles C.	29767
Roberson, Evans	26108	Rogers, Sampson	28630
Robin, Eli	28385	Rogers, Lizzie	28631
Robin, Ollie	28386	Rogers, Frank	28632
Robin, Eli Jr.	28387	Rogers, Andrew J.	23346
Robin, Price	28388	Rogers, Henry B.	23348
Robbin, Sparrow	21245	Rogers, Levi H.	23349
Robbin, Lydia	21246	Rogers, Nannie	23350
Robbin, George	21247	Rogers, John	23351
Rock, John	16933	Rogers, George L.	23352
Rock, Jennie	16934	Rogers, Sallie	6580
Rock, Daniel	16935	Rogers, Pearl	6581
Rock, Lee	16936	Rogers, Frank	6582
Rock, Ketcher	21267	Rogers, Hugh	6583
Rock, Sallie	21268	Rogers, Terry	6584
Rock, Mary	32365	Rogers, Ethel	6585
Rodecker, Emma L.	4922	Rogers, Charles A.	6917
Rodecker, Brant L.	4923	Rogers, Nancy E.	6918
Rodecker, Lulu Minnie	4924	Rogers, Catherine	6919
Rodman, George H.	30206	Rogers, Knox	6920
Rodgers, Lizzie	32655	Rogers, Eva	6921
Rodgers, Charles F.	32656	Rogers, Berrilla S.	7089
Rodgers, Lillie Ann	32657	Rogers, Robert L.	7091
Rodgers, William D.	32658	Rogers, Minnie V.	7092

Name.	Roll No.	Name.	Roll No.
Rogers, Thomas J.	7254	Rogers, William C., Jr.	14782
Rogers, Thomas T.	23695	Rogers, Lucile	14783
Rogers, Rollie E.	23697	Rogers, David	15123
Rogers, Zilpha E.	23698	Rogers, Lucinda	15124
Rogers, William E.	23699	Rogers, Sarah A.	15954
Rogers, Laura A.	7491	Rogers, Charles H.	17544
Rogers, Tipton	7492	Rogers, Frederick E.	21997
Rogers, William H.	28707	Rogers, Wellington	32415
Rogers, Athelstan	7872	Rogers, Ruby L.	32418
Rogers, Roy	7873	Rogers, John G.	26840
Rogers, Homer	7874	Rogers, Eula C.	22009
Rogers, Edrie	7875	Rogers, Nickolas R.	22010
Rogers, Nannie Q.	7876	Rogers, Florence S.	26844
Rogers, Rebecca	27575	Rogers, Connell	4510
Rogers, Belle	8116	Rogers, Kate A.	23029
Rogers, Ella K.	8117	Rogers, Ella C.	23030
Rogers, James F.	8198	Rogers, Marion S.	23031
Rogers, Henry F. A.	8264	Rogers, Gabe	21941
Rogers, Rosella	8265	Rogers, Essie D.	11633
Rogers, Lewis	24075	Rogers, Sarah J.	18118
Rogers, Rachel	9101	Rogers, Peter	18189
Rogers, Thomas J.	9517	Rogers, Nahyesah	18190
Rogers, Alva M.	9518	Rogers, Leo Hastings	4363
Rogers, Lewis D.	9519	Rogers, Ruth A.	26608
Rogers, Mary E.	9520	Rogers, Andrew	23353
Rogers, Ira T.	24302	Rogers, Camille	32489
Rogers, Laura A.	9920	Rogers, John L., Jr.	23182
Rogers, William G.	10205	Rogers, Rosa	18425
Rogers, Joseph R.	26601	Rogers, Lovely	19520
Rogers, Victoria R.	26602	Rogers, William	21015
Rogers, Oscar L.	26603	Rogers, George	25957
Rogers, Robert·R.	26604	Rogers, Nellie	25958
Rogers, Gabriel M.	26605	Rogers, Katie	25959
Rogers, Guy R.	26606	Rogers, Bettie	25960
Rogers, Joseph R.	26607	Rogers, Lovely	25961
Rogers, Jennie H.	10455	Rogers, Wilson	21090
Rogers, Jackson	11020	Rogers, Susan	21091
Rogers, Linnie	11021	Rogers, Gahni	21092
Rogers, Pearl E.	11022	Rogers, Charles	32651
Rogers, Edward	11086	Rogers, Lizzie	21113
Rogers, Frank W.	11087	Rogers, Lucy	21179
Rogers, Nora M.	11088	Rogers, Sophie	21180
Rogers, Flora S.	11089	Rogers, Wilson	21454
Rogers, Dubie R.	11090	Rogers, Susie	32078
Rogers, Belle B.	11091	Rogers, Jess	26011
Rogers, William O.	11159	Rogers, Cephas	29315
Rogers, Clement V.	11383	Rogers, Mary V.	28124
Rogers, William P.	11384	Rogers, Louis	28220
Rogers, Gilbert L.	8118	Rogers, Flora E.	30919
Rogers, Lewis H.	11630	Rogers, Thomas	30934
Rogers, John K.	11631	Rogers, Josephine	30946
Rogers, Nettie E.	11632	Rogers, James F.	30947
Rogers, Walter S.	32488	Rogers, Nellie B.	30948
Rogers, Iola	11780	Rogers, Mary J.	30949
Rogers, George L.	11781	Rogers, Lillie	31109
Rogers, Charles H.	12281	Rogers, Lula M.	31110
Rogers, Levi T.	12380	Rogers, William E.	31111
Rogers, Susie	12381	Rogers, Rilla B.	31112
Rogers, James	12382	Rogers, Eliza J.	31113
Rogers, Emma	12383	Rogers, Arthur M.	31114
Rogers, George	12384	Rogers, Augustus L.	32811
Rogers, Eula M.	6586	Rogers, Mary May	32812
Rogers, Sarah	12456	Rogers, John W.	32813
Rogers, John L.	12573	Rogers, Louise E.	32814
Rogers, John L., Jr.	12574	Rogers, Ruth A.	32815
Rogers, Rosa	12575	Rogers, Robert C.	32816
Rogers, Ella A.	12576	Rogers, James C.	32817
Rogers, Maud S.	616	Rohr, Lula	11681
Rogers, Katie	12764	Rohr, Viola A.	11682
Rogers, Ruth E.	12986	Rohr, Walter H.	11683
Rogers, Maude E.	12987	Rolston, Louis	617
Rogers, William R.	13038	Rolston, John	618
Rogers, Sarah B.	13039	Rolland, Martha J.	4795
Rogers, Mary K.	13232	Rolland, Emma L.	4796
Rogers, Louisa P.	13233	Rolland, John E.	4797
Rogers, David M.	13355	Rolland, Susetta	4798
Rogers, Love	13403	Rolland, Maud E.	4799
Rogers, Thomas L.	13635	Rolland, Elijah	4800
Rogers, Mamie E.	13636	Rollens, Elmina	11931
Rogers, Malt L.	13637	Rollens, Annie	12114
Rogers, Sylvester A.	13638	Rollens, William P.	12115
Rogers, John O.	13828	Rollens, Joseph L.	12116
Rogers, William C.	14781	Rollens, Rufus M.	12117

Name.	Roll No.	Name.	Roll No.
Rollens, Emma D.	12118	Ross, Lewis W.	28924
Rollens, Jerry, Jr.	12119	Ross, Maud W.	11078
Rollens, Automeo	12120	Ross, Sadie B.	11079
Rollens, John C.	12121	Ross, Frank	7045
Rollens, Bulah	12123	Ross, Ella	7046
Rook, Bessie F.	5545	Ross, Allie N. C.	7047
Rooster, Maggie	19584	Ross, Cherry	7048
Rooster, James	25800	Ross, George F.	9870
Rooster, Lizzie	25801	Ross, Gunter	11081
Rooster, Sallie	25802	Ross, Edward G.	11101
Rooster, Dobson	25803	Ross, Leonara	11672
Ross, Bullet	3660	Ross, Nellie C.	11750
Ross, Kye	3661	Ross, Wayne McL.	11751
Ross, Joshua	128	Ross, Roy V.	11752
Ross, Sealy	1846	Ross, Ollie F.	11860
Ross, Nellie	1847	Ross, Gilbert R.	12077
Ross, Sallie	1848	Ross, Robert	12078
Ross, Penelope	2231	Ross, Rufus	12079
Ross, Lucinda	2232	Ross, James R.	12080
Ross, Albert	2377	Ross, Maggie	12324
Ross, Maud	3662	Ross, Orville V.	12325
Ross, Ollie	18026	Ross, Oma V.	12326
Ross, McDuff	18057	Ross, Walter L.	13425
Ross, Jackson	18169	Ross, Clarence S.	13426
Ross, Lewis	18170	Ross, Charles R.	13427
Ross, Sarah	18171	Ross, Mary E.	13428
Ross, Jodie	18172	Ross, John	13768
Ross, Anna	18173	Ross, Leonidas C.	13780
Ross, Joseph	18174	Ross, George	13968
Ross, Jack	18175	Ross, Comodore	13969
Ross, Betsy	18176	Ross, Lugie J.	13971
Ross, Celia	18677	Ross, Ora V.	13972
Ross, Lewis	18780	Ross, William W.	14719
Ross, Polly	18781	Ross, Lila J.	14720
Ross, Lizzie	18782	Ross, Allen C.	14721
Ross, Nannie	18783	Ross, Lizzie V.	14722
Ross, Josie	18784	Ross, Jane S.	14723
Ross, Martha	18947	Ross, Wallace C.	14724
Ross, John	18948	Ross, John	14741
Ross, Tom	18949	Ross, Nellie P.	14824
Ross, Will	18950	Ross, Lewis A.	14825
Ross, Lucinda	20635	Ross, Wirt	14826
Ross, Maggie	20762	Ross, Daniel H.	14827
Ross, Charles	20763	Ross, Shorey	15035
Ross, William	20933	Ross, William P.	15036
Ross, George	20948	Ross, Sarah	15037
Ross, Rachel	20958	Ross, Eliza	15251
Ross, Jennie	20959	Ross, Samuel	15417
Ross, Mary Ann	21513	Ross, Robert B.	16354
Ross, Thomas	21514	Ross, Fannie D.	16355
Ross, Mollie	21515	Ross, Lulu V.	16356
Ross, Grover C.	21516	Ross, Fannie V.	16357
Ross, Ollie	21517	Ross, Jennie F.	16358
Ross, Malissa	21743	Ross, Susan M.	16359
Ross, Allie J.	22149	Ross, Robert B., Jr.	16360
Ross, Altie E.	22150	Ross, Anna P.	16361
Ross, Wasker L.	22770	Ross, Lelia	16704
Ross, Alvin	22771	Ross, Tookah	16835
Ross, Alvah	22772	Ross, Raymond	16836
Ross, Henry	25224	Ross, Lizzie	17139
Ross, Eck	25508	Ross, Fannie V.	17140
Ross, John	25583	Ross, Zona	17141
Ross, Nancy	25584	Ross, Nancy	17144
Ross, Ida	25750	Ross, Silas D.	17343
Ross, William Jr.	25940	Ross, Nancy	17344
Ross, Betsy	25941	Ross, George	17345
Ross, Jessie C.	26189	Ross, Ioney	17346
Ross, Susie	26190	Ross, Nannie	17800
Ross, Jack	26191	Ross, Celia	2485
Ross, Edward	26787	Ross, William H.	2692
Ross, James L.	26789	Ross, Lizzie	2693
Ross, Mary L.	26790	Ross, Osa	2694
Ross, Jennie P.	26791	Ross, Johnsie	2695
Ross, Susie Jane	26792	Ross, Alex	2882
Ross, William W. Jr.	27843	Ross, Mary E.	2891
Ross, Bettie	27890	Ross, Claude	2892
Ross, William	27921	Ross, Blue	2893
Ross, Francis M.	27922	Ross, Cherokee	2894
Ross, George	27923	Ross, Daniel C.	2895
Ross, Annie	27924	Ross, Martin	2931
Ross, Margaret V.	27925	Ross, Flora J.	2932
Ross, Joanna	28022	Ross, John	2933
Ross, Willie	28023	Ross, Jesse T.	2970

Name.	Roll No.	Name.	Roll No.
Ross, Cora	2971	Rose, Pearl	5572
Ross, Carrie	2972	Rose, Joseph	5573
Ross, Nora	2973	Rose, Henrietta	5574
Ross, Lora L.	2974	Rose, George	14383
Ross, Tim	2975	Rose, Addie	17088
Ross, George B.	3108	Rose, Bushyhead	17089
Ross, James W.	3109	Rose, Eliza	21794
Ross, Cora F.	3110	Roseborough, Lucy G.	8409
Ross, William T.	3415	Roseborough, Sarah L.	8410
Ross, Wesley W.	3416	Roseborough, Jesse F.	8411
Ross, Katie M.	3417	Roseborough, Claud	8412
Ross, Moses	3681	Roscopf, Phoebe E.	11648
Ross, Charles L.	3922	Rosenthal, Nancy H.	11856
Ross, Maggie	3923	Rosin, Swimmer	25764
Ross, David W.	3924	Rosin, Lizzie	25765
Ross, Daisy M.	3925	Rosin, Annie	25766
Ross, Midget	3926	Rosin, Comingdeer	25866
Ross, Annie L.	3927	Rounds, Alice C.	17087
Ross, Robert F.	4289	Round, Jack	18603
Ross, Ara E.	4290	Round, Annie	18604
Ross, Robert S.	4291	Rowsey, Eva E.	493
Ross, Charles F.	4292	Rowsey, Paul E.	494
Ross, Pearl E.	4293	Rowe, May B.	4787
Ross, Lena E.	4294	Rowe, Napoleon B.	6155
Ross, William D.	4722	Rowe, Leatha	6156
Ross, Hubbard	4729	Rowe, Joseph D.	6157
Ross, Marjorie	4730	Rowe, Sallie	6158
Ross, Mary J.	4731	Rowe, Mattie	6159
Ross, Emma L.	4732	Rowe, Pearl	6160
Ross, James	4908	Rowe, Davie	6161
Ross, Belle	4917	Rowe, Sallie	6321
Ross, Emma	5588	Rowe, Felix	6322
Ross, Susie	5589	Rowe, Martin M.	6340
Ross, Annie	5590	Rowe, Emma A.	9484
Ross, William H.	5797	Rowe, Charles K.	9485
Ross, Dannie H.	6019	Rowe, Clarence M.	9486
Ross, Daniel	6148	Rowe, Benjamin	9487
Ross, Ruth C.	6149	Rowe, Andrew	12850
Ross, Florence E.	6150	Rowe, Thomas	12851
Ross, Maggie M.	6151	Rowe, James	12852
Ross, Cornelius	6152	Rowe, Jack	15143
Ross, Carrie E.	6153	Rowe, Taylor	17612
Ross, Daniel W.	6154	Rowe, Lydia	17965
Ross, John H.	6515	Rowe, Joseph	18158
Ross, Ray P.	6516	Rowe, Charles	18159
Ross, Daisy M.	6517	Rowe, Lydia	20426
Ross, Henry C.	6528	Rowe, Emma	21329
Ross, Josephine	6529	Rowe, Linda	21330
Ross, Joseph M., Jr.	6530	Rowe, Maudie	21331
Ross, Felix H.	6531	Rowe, Ella	21332
Ross, Mary J.	6532	Rowe, David V.	21823
Ross, William P.	11077	Rowe, Thomas	21938
Ross, Mollie A.	28295	Rowe, Dick	21939
Ross, Polly	28514	Rowe, Nellie	22091
Ross, Charles M.	28839	Rowe, Neda	22092
Ross, Susie E.	28840	Rowe, Joanna	25688
Ross, Edwin B.	28841	Rowe, Nancy	26150
Ross, Susie H.	28842	Rowe, Lula	26573
Ross, Rufus D.	28992	Rowe, Ruby	26575
Ross, Sallie	29234	Rowe, David C.	27006
Ross, Harriett	29258	Rowe, Eliza E.	27007
Ross, Alice	29277	Rowe, Clem V.	27008
Ross, Dora F.	29279	Rowe, Grover C.	27009
Ross, Stella	29280	Rowe, Maggie E.	27010
Ross, Andrew E.	29500	Rowe, Lydia E.	27011
Ross, Rufus	29657	Rowe, Etta M.	27012
Ross, McKinley	29658	Rowe, Benjamin D.	27013
Ross, Akey	30055	Rowe, Laureen	27014
Ross, Nannie	30260	Rowe, Sam Mayse	27015
Ross, Dot	30799	Rowe, James	27816
Ross, Kit	30800	Rose, Betsy	27817
Ross, Lola	30801	Rowe, Frank	29773
Ross, McKinley	30802	Rowe, Sadie	29774
Ross, William	32059	Rowe, Hazic	29775
Ross, Ora O.	32255	Rowe, Red	30016
Ross, Cucumber	32320	Rowe, Katie	30386
Ross, Rhoda	32321	Rowe, Irnus Lee	30387
Ross, Nerva	32322	Rowland, Emily	11593
Ross, Annie	32323	Rowland, Addie B.	13485
Ross, John	32324	Rowland, Samuel W.	13486
Ross, Rachel	32325	Rowland, Robert F.	13487
Ross, Gracie	32525	Rowland, Pruea L.	26303
Rosser, Minnie	5026	Rowley, Ida M.	28773
Rosser, Kipling	28614	Rowley, Clarence R.	28774
Rosser, Ada	28615	Rowden, Luevader	30250
Rose, Jennie	5571	Rowden, Amon	30251

Name.	Roll No.	Name.	Roll No.
Rowden, Emma	30252	Russell, Cornelius W.	13527
Rucker, May D.	29214	Russell, Mark R.	13528
Rucker, Earnest L.	29215	Russell, Kate	13668
Rucker, Maybel M.	29216	Russell, Ollie	13669
Rucker, Frank M., Jr.	29217	Russell, George B.	15542
Rucker, John Marshal	29218	Russell, Sam	19686
Ruddles, Norris	12318	Russell, Dave	19736
Ruddles, Jesse L.	21746	Russell, Diana	19737
Ruddles, Jesse F.	21747	Russell, James	20245
Ruddles, Clara I.	21748	Russell, Daniel	20246
Ruddles, Charley	21749	Russell, Darius	20247
Rule, Jennie E.	9614	Russell, Joseph	20248
Rule, George E.	9615	Russell, Lydia	20249
Rule, Richard O.	9616	Russell, John	20250
Rule, Charles O.	9617	Russell, Annie	21843
Runyon, Evaline	4598	Russell, Charley	22137
Runyon, Minnie	4599	Russell, Frank	22138
Runyon, Sarah	4600	Russell, Joseph M.	22403
Runyon, Jessie	4601	Russell, Alice I.	22404
Runyon, Nettie	4602	Russell, Ollie M.	22405
Runyon, Lawson	4603	Russell, Pearl F.	22406
Runyon, Thomas J.	4843	Russell, George	22952
Runyon, William W.	16398	Russell, Lucinda	26888
Runyan, Robert	5030	Russell, Lucy C.	26889
Runyan, Katie	10224	Russell, Frank	26890
Runyan, Elma	10225	Russell, David C.	26891
Runyan, Samuel	10226	Russell, James	29661
Runyan, Esther E.	10227	Russell, Oatha P.	29662
Runyan, Frank C.	10228	Russell, Jessie N.	29663
Runyan, Nancy	14599	Russell, Vivian	29664
Runabout, Blue	14240	Russell, Connie	30447
Runabout, Charlotte	14239	Russell, Carl	30448
Runabout, James	14241	Russell, Christopher	30449
Runabout, White	14242	Russel, Dave	32336
Runabout, Dianna	15225	Russel, Washington	32337
Runabout, Linnie	28495	Russell, Alonzo	32517
Runels, John	16202	Rush, Ida	3126
Runels, Anderson	16203	Ruch, Maude	3127
Runels, Floyd	16204	Ruch, Benjamin A.	3128
Runels, Lizzie	16205	Rush, Mary Alpha	3129
Runels, Kizzie	16206	Rush, Isabelle	4839
Runels, Johnnie Jr.	16207	Ruch, Nancy E.	5090
Runels, China	16208	Rush, Sibley	5091
Runels, Minervia	16209	Rusk, Joseph	14223
Runels, Wirt	16210	Rusk, Ella	30332
Runaway, Hunter	19414	Rusk, Ned	30333
Runaway, William	28035	Rusk, Roscoe	30334
Runaway, Will	28044	Rusk, Ada	30336
Runningbear, Betsy	25738	Russel, Jack	30038
Russell, James B.	805	Russel, Wuttie	30039
Russell, Paul	806	Rutherford, Bettie	1487
Russell, Frances E.	807	Rutherford, Edna	5378
Russell, Joseph L.	808	Rutherford, Susan E.	5379
Russell, Charles F.	809	Rutherford, Mary P.	5380
Russell, Berry A.	810	Ryan, John	1343
Russell, Clara M.	811	Ryan, Martha A.	1344
Russell, Ellen I.	812	Ryan, Emmett	1345
Russel, Watt	1232	Ryan, Calvin	1346
Russell, Arlly	1233	Ryan, William H.	17922
Russell, Richard	1234	Ryals, Mary J.	25188
Russell, William	2150	Ryals, Charles L.	25189
Russell, Lucy	2151	Ryals, Lettie M.	25190
Russell, William L.	2152	Ryals, Melvin	25191
Russell, Robert	3048	Ryals, Simmie I.	25192
Russell, Ethel M.	3049	Ryals, Ida L.	25193
Russell, Andrew	3254	Ryals, William Mc-	
Russell, Polly	3255	Kinley	25194
Russell, Daniel	3325	Ryder, Thomas	15466
Russell, Drucella	3326	Sack, Jack	18186
Russell, Ida	3328	Sack, Rachel	18187
Russell, Jane	3904	Sack, Doctor	29670
Russell, Pollie	3905	Sack, Gatayah	29671
Russell, Carrie	3906	Sager, Amelia A.	257
Russell, Walker Jr.	3907	Sager, Lewis H.	258
Russell, May	4044	Sager, James F.	259
Russell, Robert L.	11172	Sager, Ollie Myrtle	260
Russell, Maud M.	11173	Sager, Sarah J.	8747
Russell, Gus	11174	Sager, Lucile	8748
Russell, Inola	11175	Sager, Henry	23611
Russell, Floyd	11176	Sager, Nancy C.	26942
Russell, Ada	11177	Sage, Ada B.	28807
Russell, William H.	11618	Sage, Eva O.	28808
Russell, Ed W.	11619	Sage, Georgia	28809
Russell, Maggie M.	13526		

Name.	Roll No.	Name.	Roll No.
Sahni, Creek	32879	Sanders, Jenkins	3501
Sallee, Callie A.	11547	Sanders, Ellis B.	3502
Sallee, Minnie R.	11548	Sanders, George O.	3503
Salley, Sarah B.	11609	Sanders, William S.	3504
Salley, Florence M. B.	11611	Sanders, Frank	3974
Salley, George O. D.	11613	Sanders, Rachel	3981
Samuel, Carrie	767	Sanders, Walter Levi	3982
Samuel, Minnie	6195	Sanders, Walter	4017
Samuel, Florence	6342	Sanders, William F.	4419
Samuel, Vance R.	6343	Sanders, Myrtle	4562
Samuels, Robert E.	3708	Sanders, Hughie L.	4563
Samuels, George P.	3713	Sanders, George O.	5231
Samuels, Nannie	3714	Sanders, Lizzie A.	5232
Samuels, Jesse C.	26347	Sanders, Thomas	5299
Samuels, Lutetia	26348	Sanders, Susie	6332
Sam, Sulteesky	1998	Sanders, Della M.	6333
Sam, Nancy	1999	Sanders, John L.	6334
Sam, Levi	2000	Sanders, William A.	6335
Sam, Josiah,	2001	Sanders, Jasey E.	6336
Sam, Annie	2002	Sanders, Nicholas L.	6939
Sam, Jacob	2041	Sanders, Irene	6940
Sam, Alec	17986	Sanders, Susie	7041
Sam, Linda	17987	Sanders, Martha J.	9071
Sam, Betsy	17988	Sanders, Martha L.	9072
Sam, Creek	19937	Sanders, Cornelius	10475
Sam, Whitetobacco	19938	Sanders, Maude	10476
Sam, Charlie	21044	Sanders, Clyde	10477
Sam, Nakie	21045	Sanders, Corene	10478
Sam, Martin	21047	Sanders, Nannie	10479
Sam, Nannie	21048	Sanders, Mattie	11015
Sam, Mabel	21049	Sanders, Sequoyah	11016
Sam, Susan	21050	Sanders, Pigeon	11017
Sam, Watt	21162	Sanders, Joseph	11018
Sam, John	25577	Sanders, John	11493
Sam, Emma	32877	Sanders, Clem	11570
Sampson, Austin	21707	Sanders, Walter Lee	11571
Sanders, Peggie	1496	Sanders, Charles	11973
Sanders, Margaret C.	1588	Sanders, William E.	11977
Sanders, Flarra M.	1589	Sanders, Etta J.	11978
Sanders, John B.	1590	Sanders, John G.	11979
Sanders, James	2108	Sanders, William E., Jr.	11980
Sanders, Thomas	2292	Sanders, DeWitt C.	11981
Sanders, Bettie	2293	Sanders, George F.	11982
Sanders, Mary	2294	Sanders, Joseph	12141
Sanders, James M.	2295	Sanders, Frances	12142
Sanders, Lydia	2296	Sanders, Berry	12143
Sanders, Lula	2297	Sanders, Rat	12189
Sanders, Felix	2298	Sanders, Annie	12190
Sanders, French	2299	Sanders, John M.	12385
Sanders, Maggie L.	2300	Sanders, James R.	13599
Sanders, Lizzie	2307	Sanders, Ose O.	13600
Sanders, Isaac	2400	Sanders, Madison	14408
Sanders, Isabelle	2401	Sanders, Louisa	14409
Sanders, Charley W.	2402	Sanders, Thomas	14410
Sanders, Thomas, Jr.	2422	Sanders, Elizabeth	14411
Sanders, Maud H.	2425	Sanders, John H.	14412
Sanders, Cena	2426	Sanders, Geneva	14413
Sanders, David, Jr.	2424	Sanders, Carl	14414
Sanders, Jesse	2427	Sanders, Maggie D.	14415
Sanders, Susie	2431	Sanders, James	14417
Sanders, John C.	2496	Sanders, Moses F.	15127
Sanders, Sallie J.	2497	Sanders, Armine	15615
Sanders, Jim M.	2498	Sanders, Samuel L.	15733
Sanders, Robert L.	2499	Sanders, Jesse	15816
Sanders, George	2500	Sanders, Floyd	15817
Sanders, Willie A.	2501	Sanders, Arthur	15889
Sanders, Eddie R.	2502	Sanders, Jesse	15927
Sanders, John W.	2503	Sanders, George	16006
Sanders, Walter	2656	Sanders, Caroline	16007
Sanders, Robert	3216	Sanders, Samuel S.	16113
Sanders, Mary	3282	Sanders, Elizabeth	16114
Sanders, Sadie B.	3283	Sanders, Katie A.	16116
Sanders, Charlotte	3284	Sanders, John	16133
Sanders, Hooley B.	3285	Sanders, Callie	16134
Sanders, Edward	3286	Sanders, Polly M.	16135
Sanders, Henry H.	3289	Sanders, Mahala	16136
Sanders, Charlotte E.	3290	Sanders, Nick	16137
Sanders, Samuel	3291	Sanders, Watt	16138
Sanders, Katie	3403	Sanders, Diana M.	16227
Sanders, Oklahoma	3404	Sanders, Samuel	16258
Sanders, Dexter	3498	Sanders, , Jessie B.	16259
Sanders, Teezhee	3499	Sanders, Charles	16260
Sanders, Beatrice	3500	Sanders, Pearl E.	16261

Name.	Roll No.	Name.	Roll No.
Sanders, Thomas	16397	Sanders, Florence	27202
Sanders, Samuel	16498	Sanders, George M.	27203
Sanders, Florence W.	16547	Sanders, Lewis	27398
Sanders, Laura W.	16548	Sanders, Maud	27399
Sanders, Samuel G.	16549	Sanders, Thomas J.	27400
Sanders, Fannie M.	16550	Sanders, Charlotte.M.	27401
Sanders, James A.	16551	Sanders, Arther T.	27769
Sanders, Sarah E.	16552	Sanders, Lucinda	27770
Sanders, Jananna	16598	Sanders, Eliza	28466
Sanders, David	16915	Sanders, Jesse	29221
Sanders, Caroline	16916	Sanders, John	29501
Sanders, Arthur	16917	Sanders, Ida .	29502
Sanders, Sallie	17376	Sanders, Soggy	29641
Sanders, James	18773	Sanders, James	29642
Sanders, Stephen	18774	Sanders, Jennie	29643
Sanders, Lila	18775	Sanders, John	29646
Sanders, Lewis	18786	Sanders, Mary	29647
Sanders, Eli	19090	Sanders, Nicholas	29648
Sanders, Eliza	19091	Sanders, Annie	29649
Sanders, Ada	19092	Sanders, Jennie	29650
Sanders, Emma	19094	Sanders, Sarah	29653
Sanders, Steve	19340	Sanders, David	29850
Sanders, Watson	19398	Sanders, Betsy	29851
Sanders, Mary	19599	Sanders, Washington	29852
Sanders, William	19673	Sanders, Tim	29853
Sanders, Charlie	19854	Sanders, Ellis	29854
Sanders, Hooley	19860	Sanders, Robert	29855
Sanders, Mary	19861	Sanders, Pigeon	29856
Sanders, Mose	19862	Sanders, Jennie	29857
Sanders, Naki	19869	Sanders, Slick	29858
Sanders, Jennie	19872	Sanders, Ellen M.	30069
Sanders, Wat	19888	Sanders, Elizabeth	30385
Sanders, Samuel Oscar	19987	Sanders, Nannie	30497
Sanders, Charles	20105	Sanders, Laura	32290
Sanders, James	20747	Sanders, Ellis	32297
Sanders, Rachel	20748	Sangster, Elsie J.	4595
Sanders, Charlie E.	20749	Sangster, Maggie	4596
Sanders, Elizabeth	20750	Sangster, Katie	12899
Sanders, Mary Bell	20751	Santafe, Lydia	17264
Sanders, Carl S.	21772	Sand, John	19631
Sanders, Nellie	21860	Sand, Noah	20318
Sanders, William	22036	Sand, William	20319
Sanders, John D.	22116	Sand, Stephen	30601
Sanders, John	22730	Sand, Betty	30602
Sanders, Mattie	22804	Sand, James	30603
Sanders, Daisy M.	22805	Sand, Charlotte	30604
Sanders, Claude	22806	Sand, William	30605
Sanders, Clifford	22807	Sandige, Jane	32861
Sanders, Clyde	22808	Sapsucker, Levi	19375
Sanders, Edward B.	22809	Sapsucker, Yeh-kin-nie	19376
Sanders, Vera	22810	Sapsucker, Henry	19377
Sanders, Celia	22943	Sapsucker, Davison	19378
Sanders, DeWitt	23004	Sapsucker, Als-ah	19379
Sanders, Jane Anna	23005	Sapsucker, Jensie	19380
Sanders, Frankie	23006	Sapsucker, Luke	25530
Sanders, Andrew	23168	Supsucker, Lena	25531
Sanders, Jesse	23590	Sapsucker, Sissie	25532
Sanders, Clara	23864	Sapsucker, Edna	25533
Sanders, Pearl	23591	Sapsucker, Sallie	25534
Sanders, Frank	24865	Sapsucker, John	29023
Sanders, Ed	24866	Sapsucker, Susie	29024
Sanders, Linn	24867	Sapsucker, Price	29026
Sanders, Eli B.	24868	Sapsucker, Nancy	29027
Sanders, Leva	24869	Sapsucker, George	29028
Sanders, John	25574	Sapsucker, Cochran	29029
Sanders, George	25739	Sarver, Victoria	10453
Sanders, Daniel	25740	Sarver, Amos V.	10454
Sanders, Lizzie	25741	Sartain, Lucinda J.	13975
Sanders, John	25819	Sartain, Gilbert C.	13976
Sanders, Jennie	25820	Sarcoxie, Lucy	31100
Sanders, Jesse	26160	Sarcoxie, Elizabeth L.	31103
Sanders, Mollie	26629	Sarcoxie, Reuben	31125
Sanders, Clinton F.	26675	Sarcoxie, Roy L.	31126
Sanders, Lena	26784	Sarcoxie, Charley	31321
Sanders, Carrie	26851	Sarcoxie, Willie	31322
Sanders, Nicholas	26852	Sarcoxie, Mary	31323
Sanders, Delilah	27080	Sarcoxie, Minnie	31324
Sanders, James	27081	Sarahas, Polly H.	32792
Sanders, Benjamin	27167	Sarahas, Frank	32839
Sanders, John M.	27198	Saterfield, Susan	4108
Sanders, James P.	27199	Saterfield, Henry M.	4109
Sanders, Lucinda	27200	Saterfield, Oscar	4110
Sanders, Lizzie	27201	Saterfield, William	4111

Name.	Roll No.	Name.	Roll No.
Satterfield, James L.	4121	Schrimsher, Mattie B.	16874
Satterfield, Andrew W.	32604	Schrimsher, Jasper N.	26911
Satterwhite, Elizabeth	4323	Schrimsher, Josephine	26912
Saunders, Charles L.	5344	Schrimsher, Marie	26913
Saunders, Franklin L.	5345	Schrimsher, Nellie P.	26914
Saunders, Minnie E.	5345	Schuth, Vinnie M.	9711
Saunders, Mary	32229	Schuth, Elizabeth I.	9712
Sawney, Tickaneeski	1643	Schuth, Ruby E.	9713
Sawney, Sallie	1649	Schuth, Eva S.	26571
Sawney, Columbus	1955	Scott, George W.	110
Sawney, Jennie	1956	Scott, Ida L.	102
Sawney, John	1957	Scott, Lee R.	103
Sawney, Peter	1958	Scott, Chester A.	104
Sawney, Laura	1959	Scott, Chorena C.	105
Sawney, Susan	1960	Scott, Patterson M.	106
Sawney, Sarah	2122	Scott, Lucy A.	107
Sawney, Robert	2123	Scott, Helen M.	108
Sawney, Roy	2124	Scott, Naomi	109
Sawney, Celia	2127	Scott, Jennie	1031
Sawney, Johnanna	2128	Scott, Henry	1032
Sawney, Moses	2129	Scott, Dennis	1033
Sawney, Annie	2130	Scott, Ella	1034
Sawney, Eliza	2131	Scott, Susan	1035
Sawney, Charlotte	2132	Scott, Thomas	1036
Sawney, Lucy	18941	Scott, Rufus	1037
Sawney, Annie	18942	Scott, Margaret	1038
Sawney, Lizzie	18943	Scott, Fannie B.	1039
Sawney, Jack	19022	Scott, Huckleberry	1476
Sawney, Susie	19023	Scott, Katie	1477
Sawney, Springston	19024	Scott, Emma	1478
Sawney, Lydia	19025	Scott, Mary A.	1479
Sawney, Joe	19026	Scott, John O. L.	1480
Sawney, Annie	19027	Scott, Beulah	1481
Sawney, William	25683	Scott, Daniel	1488
Sawney, Lizzie	25684	Scott, Annie	1489
Sawney, Samuel	27219	Scott, Lincoln	1490
Sawney, Alex	28570	Scott, Pollie	1727
Sawney, Lizzie	28571	Scott, Peggy	1730
Sawney, Mike	28572	Scott, Robert	2236
Sawney, Loula	32245	Scott, Kate	2520
Sawney, Annie	32294	Scott, Richard J.	2959
Sawney, Cay-hu-ka	32295	Scott, Susie F.	2960
Sawney, Goh-he-neh	32296	Scott, Carrie E.	2961
Sayers, William T.	27959	Scott, Susie	2962
Sayers, Cora A.	27960	Scott, Willie	3009
Sayers, William T.	21898	Scott, Sue	3008
Scales, Mattie	1140	Scott, Belle	3010
Scales, Ethel	1141	Scott, Claude	3011
Scales, Grover	1142	Scott, Earnest B.	3012
Scales, Joseph	1143	Scott, Jesse	3013
Scales, Lillie	1144	Scott, Jennie	3027
Scales, Louisa	1145	Scott, William	3718
Scales, George	1146	Scott, Sarah	3719
Scales, Sophia J.	4275	Scott, Minnie	3720
Scales, Joseph A., Jr.	4276	Scott, Belle H.	4484
Scales, Frank V.	4277	Scott, Emma H.	4485
Scales, Amanda P.	4278	Scott, John S.	4486
Scacewater, James	2069	Scott, Allen H.	4487
Scacewater, Lucian B.	22663	Scott, Gibson R.	4491
Scacewater, Murtie M.	27155	Scott, Nann	4529
Scarcewater, Ross	3340	Scott, Elizabeth O.	4585
Scarcewater, Jimmie	3341	Scott, Delilah	4591
Schrader, Susan A.	646	Scott, John T.	4592
Schrader, Josephine E.	649	Scott, Georgia A.	4703
Schaublin, Julia	5057	Scott, Moses J.	6099
Scharble, Joseph O.	21937	Scott, Cherokee	6989
Schell, Tennessee	23117	Scott, Jesse	6990
Schell, Irven Earl	28616	Scott, William	6991
Schoonover, Thomas J.	6075	Scott, David	6992
Schoonover, Stonewall		Scott, Looney	6993
J.	6076	Scott, Anna	6994
Schoonover, Grover C.	6077	Scott, Cornelius	6995
Schoonover, Victoria	6078	Scott, Gertie	6996
Schoonover, Frank	6086	Scott, William	6997
Schoonover, Vesta V.	6087	Scott, Myrtie	6998
Schliecker, Lucy C.	30952	Scott, Nannie	6999
Schliecker, August F.	30957	Scott, Lena C.	8215
Schrimsher, Juliette M.	11758	Scott, Gladys M.	8216
Schrimsher, Earnest B.	11900	Scott, Edith	8217
Schrimsher, John G.	12391	Scott, Joseph P., Jr.	8218
Schrimsher, Juliette M.	12392	Scott, Thomas A.	8254
Schrimsher, Elizabeth		Scott, Amanda C.	8507
B.	12431	Scott, George W.	8508

Name.	Roll No.	Name.	Roll No.
Scott, James W.	8509	Scott, Egnew	30894
Scott, Charles D.	8510	Scott, Delilah	32046
Scott, Willard B.	8524	Scott, Adam	32305
Scott, Helena	8523	Scott, Charlotte	32630
Scott, Winnie M.	8525	Scobey, Mary	12545
Scott, Velma D.	8526	Scobey, Floyd L.	12546
Scott, Lula	8831	Scoggins, Lucy J.	21990
Scott, Ethel N.	8832	Scoggins, Effie	21991
Scott, George E.	8833	Scoggins, Omer	21992
Scott, James A.	8834	Scoggins, Lola	21993
Scott, Myrtle	8835	Scoggins, Jesse E.	21994
Scott, Marion	8836	Scoggins, Una	21995
Scott, Polly	10029	Scoggins, Willie	21996
Scott, Arminda	10030	Scoville, Leona J.	31335
Scott, Sabrina	13962	Scraper, Rebecca	19880
Scott, William T.	13963	Scraper, Ellen	19881
Scott, Susan V.	13964	Scraper, Thomas	16117
Scott, Mattie E.	13965	Scraper, Sallie	16118
Scott, Calvin C.	15443	Scraper, Paulina	16119
Scott, Mary E.	15981	Scraper, Malinda	16120
Scott, Theodore E.	15982	Scraper, Nancy	16121
Scott, Mary F.	15983	Scraper, Louis	16122
Scott, Grover H.	15984	Scraper, William	16689
Scott, Martin B.	16867	Scraper, Charles	18501
Scott, Bonnie C.	16868	Scraper, Fields	19029
Scott, Alfred A.	17254	Scraper, Lucy	19030
Scott, Charley	18103	Scraper, Jennie	19031
Scott, Nancy	18104	Scraper, John	19033
Scott, Dora	18105	Scraper, Jesse	19032
Scott, Ned	18106	Scraper, Anewake	19034
Scott, Charley	18107	Scraper, Nannie	19035
Scott, Maud	18108	Scraper, Nannie	19874
Scott, Peter	18596	Scraper, Dick	19884
Scott, Betsy	18597	Scraper, Sallie E.	22502
Scott, Gaw-ye-na-ey	18598	Scraper, Archie	26325
Scott, Louella	19327	Scraper, James	26326
Scott, Eli	19604	Scraper, Bettie	27088
Scott, John	20217	Scraper, Oliver	27089
Scott, George	20219	Scraper, John	27090
Scott, Laura	20218	Scraper, Henry	28981
Scott, George	20427	Scraper, Lydia	28982
Scott, Lucinda	20428	Scraper, Elijah	29983
Scott, John	20429	Scraper, Fannie	28984
Scott, Emeline	20430	Scraper, Earnest	28985
Scott, Lilly	20431	Scraper, Lulu	29012
Scott, Coming	20432	Scraper, Ned	29888
Scott, William	20433	Scraper, Susie	29089
Scott, Dick	20434	Scraper, Ben	29091
Scott, Martin	20435	Scraper, Nellie	29883
Scott, Eli	20436	Scruggs, Red Cloud	9801
Scott, Linnie	20770	Scruggs, Dave	9802
Scott, John Wesley	20772	Scruggs, John G.	11167
Scott, Wahlaneetah	21056	Scruggs, Lincoln	13090
Scott, Elmyra	21478	Scruggs, Cora	30204
Scott, Orville E.	21479	Scruggs, Charlie	32563
Scott, Clarence Reed	21480	Scroggins, Martha	27476
Scott, Eura	22047	Scroggins, Freddie	27477
Scott, Caroline	22648	Screechowl, Thompson	32880
Scott, Nellie	25804	Screechowl, Dick	32831
Scott, Riley	25805	Screechowl, Mintie	32882
Scott, Elsie	25806	Screechowl, Rosa	32883
Scott, Jennie	22649	Screechowl, Isaac	32884
Scott, Nannie	22650	Screechowl, Sallie	32885
Scott, Marion M.	23548	Screechowl, Annie	32886
Scott, Roxie A.	23558	Scullawl, Joseph	10151
Scott, Noly	23559	Seullawl, John	10171
Scott, George	23560	Scullawl, Jennie	10172
Scott, Buster	23561	Scullawl, Mary	10173
Scott, Edna	23562	Scullawl, William	10174
Scott, Evie	23563	Scullawl, Richard	10175
Scott, Susan	25772	Scullawl, William	26116
Scott, John B.	27597	Scullawl, Caroline	26117
Scott, Charles F.	27598	Scullawl, Bear	27715
Scott, George	27705	Scudder, Jacob Mc.	17160
Scott, Ella N.	29950	Scudder, Herman G.	17161
Scott, Amy M.	29951	Scudder, William H. H.	24929
Scott, Walter	29991	Scudder, Gordon H.	24930
Scott, William N.	30388	Scudder, Newton G.	24931
Scott, Francis M.	30389	Scudder, Maggie L.	24932
Scott, James S.	30390	Scudder, Nellie V.	24933
Scott, Hazel I.	30391	Scudder, Annie C.	24934
Scott, French	30892	Scudder, William H. H.	
Scott, Joseph	30893	Jr.	24935

Name.	Roll No.	Name.	Roll No.
Scudder, Julia I.	24936	Sears, David	6387
Scudder, Lewis B.	24937	Sears, Joel	6388
Scudder, Ida J.	24938	Sears, Peggie	28245
Scudder, Cherokee G.	5159	Sears, Ella	28246
Scudder, Lewis B.	5158	Seabourn, Sadie L.	7151
Scudder, Alfred B.	5160	Seabourn, Joy C.	7152
Scudder, Maggie B.	5161	Seabourn, Joseph D.	7153
Scuggin, Aggie	25827	Secondine, Malinda	7964
Scuggin, Lacy	26534	Secondine, Harrison	7965
Scuggin, Eliza	26535	Secondine, Nannie	27667
Scuggin, Samuel	26536	Secondine, Susanna	27668
Scuggin, Walker	26537	Secondine, Victoria	27669
Scuggin, Mollie	26538	Secondine, Tecumseh	27670
Scuggin, Wyly	26539	Secondine, Delaware	27671
Scuggin, Charity	26540	Secondine, Clarence	27672
Scuggin, Grape	27620	Secondine, Filmore W.	30246
Seabolt, Christopher C.	2842	Secondine, Esther	30247
Seabolt, James	2844	Secondine, Katie	30935
Seabolt, Thomas L.	2845	Secondine, Jacob	30972
Seabolt, Dovie	2846	Secondyne, Anderson	31049
Seabolt, Lizzie	3067	Secondine, Laura	31473
Seabolt, Jeremiah M.	3079	Secondine, Annie E.	31513
Seabolt, Penelope	3080	Secondine, Eliza J.	31514
Seabolt, Mary	3081	Secondine, Bessie	31515
Seabolt, Scott	3545	Secondine, Charles	31567
Seabolt, Luna	3686	Secondine, Matilda	31568
Seabolt, Sarah E.	3687	Secondine, Lucinda	31569
Seabolt, John E.	3690	Secondine, Andrew	31570
Seabolt, Elvira	3691	Secondine, Edna M.	31578
Seabolt, James	3776	Secondine, Joseph	31645
Seabolt, Albert	3778	Secondine, Isaac	32112
Seabolt, Nancy	3821	Secondi, Cornelius	19313
Seabolt, Polly	3835	Secondi, Emma	19314
Seabolt, William	3850	Secondi, Lydia	19316
Seabolt, Beatrice	3851	Secondyne, Rosa	24330
Seabolt, Eliza	3852	Secondyne, Emeline	24331
Seabolt, William	3853	Secrest, John O.	5906
Seabolt, King	3878	Seekings, Dannie	16788
Seabolt, Betsy	3879	Seekings, William T.	16789
Seabolt, Akie	3880	Seigel, Anna J.	32102
Seabolt, Alfred P.	3953	Seigel, Ada	32103
Seabolt, Alfred L.	3954	Seigel, Charles J.	32104
Seabolt, Ottoway	3955	Seigel, Leslie M.	32105
Seabolt, Martin L.	3956	Seigel, James A.	32106
Seabolt, Robert E.	3957	Seigel, Eva G.	32107
Seabolt, Benjamin	4003	Seigel, Anna R.	32108
Seabolt, Victoria	4004	Seigel, Henry E.	32109
Seabolt, John	4022	Selvidge, John B.	14343
Seabolt, Stephen	4028	Selvidge, Goldie S.	14344
Seabolt, James M.	4062	Selvidge, Percy L.	14345
Seabolt, Olly	4063	Selvidge, Katie	14346
Seabolt, George W.	4065	Selvidge, Dolpha	14347
Seabolt, Lucy	4066	Seller, Henry	19172
Seabolt, Bertha A.	4067	Sellers, Chickaleelee	29862
Seabolt, Levi D.	4068	Sellers, Peggie	29863
Seabolt, Mary E.	4069	Sellers, Richard	29864
Seabolt, Claton M.	4070	Sellers, Mark	29865
Seabolt, Timothy E.	4205	Sellers, Maud	29866
Seabolt, Mamie L.	4206	Sequoyah, Stute	12284
Seabolt, Ora	21528	Sequoyah, Tom	20723
Seabolt, Susanna	21591	Sequoyah, Sarah	20724
Seabolt, Vealie	21592	Sequoyah, Lucy	20725
Seabolt, Ida Margret		Sequoyah, Ella	20726
Ann	21837	Sequoyah, Daniel	21317
Seabolt, Josiah	22953	Sequoyah, Dick	21416
Seabolt, Minnie M.	22954	Sequoyah, Lucy	21417
Seabolt, Charles E.	22955	Sequoyah, Betsy	21418
Seabolt, Nancy A.	22956	Sequoyah, Sarah	30267
Seabolt, Trilby L.	22957	Sequichie, Joseph R.	13153
Seabolt, Joseph M.	22958	Sequichie, Marion L.	13154
Seabolt, Anderson	22961	Sequichie, Arch	13573
Seabolt, Lizzie	26351	Sequichie, Arch Jr.	13574
Seabolt, Charles	26352	Sequichie, Nina K.	13575
Seabolt, John M.	26357	Sequichie, Alma	13576
Seabolt, Loy H.	26358	Sequichie, Squirrel	25878
Seabolt, Sally	27263	Sequichie, Bettie	25879
Seabolt, Choowee	28440	Sequichie, Jackson	25880
Seabolt, Georgia A.	29544	Sequichie, Annie L.	26692
Seabolt, Sam H.	29545	Sequichie, Emma	32519
Seabolt, Lucy	29807	Settle, Martha J.	11940
Seabolt, Bean	32013	Settle, Louan	11941
Sears, Stephen	6385	Settle, Eugene	11942
Sears, Samuel	6386	Settle, Martha H.	11943

Name.	Roll No.
Settle, Charles A.	11944
Settle, Randolph	12022
Settle, Lee	12113
Setser, Martha	14543
Setser, Francis M.	28269
Setser, Walter M.	28270
Setser, Martha J.	28271
Setser, William F.	28272
Setser, Waneta M.	28273
Setser, Albert A.	28274
Setser, Annah M.	30829
Setser, Jane A.	30830
Setser, Maud L.	30831
Setser, Ella M.	30832
Setser, David F.	30833
Setser, Lillie E.	30834
Severs, Samuel B.	31983
Severs, Bessie	31985
Severs, Emma	31986
Severs, Charles J.	31987
Severs, Samuel B., Jr.	31988
Severs, Barto F.	31989
Sevier, Jack	2841
Sevier, James J.	14770
Sevier, Callie O.	14771
Sevier, Anna E.	14772
Sevier, Jerry A.	14773
Sevier, James C.	14774
Sevier, Alice K.	14775
Sevier, Charles F.	14776
Sevier, Leo E.	14777
Sevier, Nelson A. M.	14778
Sevier, Joseph B.	14779
Sevier, Susie	14780
Sevier, William P.	14894
Sevier, Ida E.	14895
Sevier, Maud	14896
Sevier, Daniel	16477
Sevier, May	23312
Sevier, John C.	23313
Sevier, Jesse	28236
Sevens, Joseph S.	15803
Seven, Rufus	32381
Sevenstar, Larken	18360
Sevenstar, Sawnie	29809
Sevenstarr, Cynthia	18438
Sevenstarr, Ella	18439
Shafer, Annie	265
Shackelford, Martha F.	1407
Shackelford, Effie	1409
Shackelford, Ollie	1408
Shackelford, Charles L.	1410
Shackleford, Cora A.	6135
Shackleford, Carlotta	6136
Shamblin, Rebecca E.	2570
Shamblin, Susan	10608
Shamblin, Bessie B.	10609
Shamblin, Pleas F.	10610
Shamblin, Stephen D.	10611
Shamblin, Bert A.	10612
Shamblin, Annie E.	10613
Shamblin, George W.	29259
Sharp, Fannie	4328
Sharp, Mike	4329
Sharp, Danniel	4330
Sharp, John W.	8751
Sharp, Charlotte	8752
Sharp, Richard H.	8753
Sharp, John	8755
Sharp, Albert	8756
Sharp, Caroline	8757
Sharp, Grover	8758
Sharp, George W.	8761
Sharp, Edward L.	9718
Sharp, Frog	19423
Sharp, Nancy	19424
Sharp, William	19425
Sharp, Ga-yah-hi	19426
Sharp, Rattler	19437
Sharp, Oosquina	19438
Sharp, Chigayn	19439
Sharp, John	21436
Sharp, Clifford	21822

Name.	Roll No.
Sharp, Mary	27637
Sharp, Sarah	30548
Sharp, Lewis	30549
Sharp, Nancy A.	31624
Sharp, Mary E.	31625
Sharp, William C.	31626
Sharp, Burr W.	31627
Sharp, Peggie	32871
Shanahan, Charlotte E.	9234
Shanahan, Winnie	9235
Shanahan, Ellen	9236
Shanahan, Julia	9237
Shanahan, Leo Nelson	9238
Shanahan, Jennie	9280
Shanahan, Maggie C.	9281
Shanahan, Jennie	9282
Shanahan, Timothy	9283
Shaw, Bertha M.	12936
Shaw, Bessie B.	12937
Shaw, Mary P.	13245
Shaw, Thomas P.	14756
Shaw, Lena A.	14757
Shaw, William E.	14758
Shaw, Susan	23950
Sharyer, Lulu	12973
Sharyer, Lulu L.	12974
Shade, Joseph	14146
Shade, Peggy	14147
Shade, Adam	15066
Shade, Isaac	15083
Shade, Lucy	15084
Shade, John	15085
Shade, Elizabeth	15086
Shade, Coon	15087
Shade, Isaac Jr.	15088
Shade, Henry	15096
Shade, Thomas, Jr.	16678
Shade, Betsy	16679
Shade, Lille	16680
Shade, Joseph Jr.	16681
Shade, Bushyhead	20731
Shade, Ollie	20732
Shade, Josie	20733
Shade, Betsy	20734
Shade, Maggie	21249
Shade, Thomas	28905
Shade, Peggie	28906
Shade, Major	28976
Shade, Albert	28977
Shade, Ruth	28978
Shade, Sallie	29363
Shailer, William R.	31251
Shailer, James E.	31252
Shailer, John N.	31253
Shailer, Ivy P.	31254
Shailer, Roy F.	31255
Shailer, Ruby A.	31256
Shailer, Edward	31669
Shakingbush, George	27276
Shakingbush, Susie	27277
Shakingbush, Aggie	27278
Shakingbush, Lela	27279
Shakingbush, Levi	27280
Shanks, Jesse J.	28345
Shanks, Nannie E.	28346
Shanks, Narcissa	28347
Shanks, John E.	28348
Shay, Minnie	28524
Shay, Jessie L.	28525
Shadix, Sarah	29166
Shawnee, Francis	30154
Shawnee, William	30155
Shawnee, Ida	30156
Shawnee, Ada	30157
Shawnee, Louis	30933
Shawnee, Charles	31122
Shawnee, Mary	31123
Shawnee, William	31124
Sheffield, Marnie C.	1174
Sheffield, Beulah I.	1175
Sheffield, Walter J.	1176
Sheffield, Mary I.	1177
Sheffield, Katie	1178

Name.	Roll No.	Name.	Roll No.
Sheffield, Isom N.	1179	Sheldon, Walter M.	8807
Sheffield, Mark C.	1180	Sheldon, Willie M.	8808
Shell, James	1222	Sherley, Amanda	15582
Shell, Mary E.	1223	Sherley, Willie W.	15583
Shell, Susan E.	1224	Sherley, Annie B.	15584
Shell, Eunice V.	1225	Sherley, Maggie L.	15585
Shell, Laura	1773	Shirley, John L.	15587
Shell, William	1920	Shirley, Eliza	15588
Shell, Nancy J.	1921	Shirley, Lovey	15589
Shell, David	1922	Shirley, Annie	15591
Shell, John	1923	Shetley, Eliza	26252
Shell, Cindy	2456	Shetley, Nancy	26253
Shell, James	2458	Shetley, Susan	26254
Shell, Sallie	18798	Shelly, Lucy	25096
Shell, Lila	18002	Shelly, Mary L.	25097
Shell, Emma	18799	Shelly, Oscar R.	25098
Shell, Arch	18800	Shelly, Maggie N.	25099
Shell, Sam	18906	Shelly, Ollie	25100
Shell, Lucy	18907	Shelly, Fay	25101
Shell, Huckleberry	18908	Shelly, Rosa E.	25102
Shell, Jack	18909	Shelly, Maudena	25103
Shell, Luke	18910	Shelly, Rosa A.	32497
Shell, Charlie	18911	Shelly, William D.	32498
Shell, Charles	19252	Shelly, Thomas J.	32499
Shell, Rebecca	19253	Shearer, Ella	26723
Shell, Lula	19254	Shearer, Laura S.	26724
Shell, Susie	19255	Sheshey, William W.	31063
Shell, Nannie	19256	Shinn, Marion R.	4306
Shell, Charlotte	19257	Shinn, Columbus M.	17397
Shell, Tash	22599	Shinn, Mary J.	17398
Shell, Jennie	22600	Shinn, Jesse J.	17399
Shell, Susan	22601	Shinn, Frank J.	17400
Shell, Ada	22602	Shinn, Alexander	17401
Shell, Johnanna	22603	Shinn, John J.	17482
Shell, Jesse	22604	Shipley, Jennie B.	7199
Shell, Florence M.	22605	Shipley, John R. P.	7200
Shell, Elmer Clyde	22642	Shipley, William P.	7201
Shell, Charlotte	25811	Shimp, Louisa J.	13490
Shell, Jennie	27189	Shimp, Bernice R.	13491
Shell, Richard	27190	Shimp, George B.	13492
Shell, Grassy	32360	Shimp, Louisa P.	13493
Shepard, Jack	3085	Shirley, Nannie	15630
Shepard, Joe	3086	Shirley, Mattie	16331
Shepard, Oscar	3087	Shirley, James W.	29298
Shepard, Emma	3088	Shirley, John W.	29299
Shepard, Meda	3089	Short, Guess	3337
Shepard, Mollie	4727	Short, Joe	3338
Shepard, Elizabeth	4728	Short, Houston	3339
Sheppard, George W.	5224	Shook, Euretter	3506
Sheppard, Charles	5225	Shook, Jessie	3507
Sheppard, Edward	5226	Shook, Minnie O.	30197
Sheppard, Pearl	5227	Shook, Clarence Ray	30199
Sheppard, Jackson	5228	Shook, John B.	32818
Sheppard, Richard A.	16899	Shook, Amos	32819
Sheppard, William E.	28349	Shook, Lillie	32820
Sheppard, Bessie	28350	Shook, William T.	32821
Sherman, Mary J.	6907	Shoemaker, Rachel	6372
Sherman, Albert M.	6908	Shoemaker, Nora Ann	6373
Sheehan, Annie E.	8015	Shoemaker, John W.	6374
Sheehan, William D.	8016	Shoemaker, Franklin C.	6375
Sheehan, John E.	8268	Shoemaker, David W.	6376
Sheehan, James	8269	Shoemake, James	12401
Sheehan, Ellen	23999	Shoemake, Nancy B.	17581
Shelton, Claude S.	8762	Shoemake, Carrie	17582
Shelton, Mary Z.	8763	Shoemake, Clifton B.	17584
Shelton, Johnnie B.	8764	Shoemake, William H.	32130
Shelton, Ann B.	9080	Shoemake, Lula B.	32131
Shelton, Mary J.	14128	Shoemake, Mary E.	32132
Shelton, James A.	14577	Shoemake, John W.	32133
Shelton, Harvey W. C.	16313	Shoemake, Calvin B.	32134
Shelton, Mary J.	14578	Shoemake, Luda G.	32135
Shelton, Mary A. E.	16314	Shoemake, Claude	32136
Shelton, Harvey W. C. Jr.	16315	Shoemake, Maude	32137
Shelton, Norman B.	22125	Shoemake, Maggie M.	32138
Shelton, Mayme Lorine	22126	Shoemake, Effie	32139
Shelton, Spencer	28226	Shoemake, William M.	32140
Shelton, Susan	28227	Shoemake, Georgia A.	32141
Shelton, Robert L.	28228	Shoemake, Clem	32142
Shelton, Spencer Jr.	28229	Shoemake, Pigeon	32143
Shelton, Raymon S.	30785	Shoemake, John W.	32147
Sheldon, William T.	8805	Shoemake, James	32146
Sheldon, Debora	8806	Shoemake, William A.	32148
		Shoemake, Grace L.	32149

Name.	Roll No.
Shoemake, James N.	32150
Shoemake, Harmon A.	32157
Shoemake, Rose Anna	32158
Shoemake, James W.	32159
Shoemake, Noah H.	32160
Shoemake, Mattie M.	32161
Shoemake, Rexie L.	32162
Shoemake, Ella	32163
Shoemake, Jesse E.	32168
Shoemake, Oscar	32169
Shoemake, Maud	32170
Shoemake, Hugh	32171
Shoemake, Walsie L.	32172
Shoemake, Della	32173
Shoemake, Ninna	32174
Shoemake, Grace	32175
Shoemake, Charles F.	32176
Shoemake, Minnie M.	32177
Shoemake, Bobbie	32178
Shoemake, Walter	32179
Shoemake, Cherokee G.	32180
Shoemake, Mary I.	32181
Shoemake, Richard W.	32182
Shoemake, Ada	32183
Shoemake, Ira	32184
Shoemake, Thomas H.	32185
Shoemake, Hugh A.	32187
Shoemake, Alta M.	32188
Shouse, Henry L.	9075
Shouse, Lottie M.	9076
Shouse, Clarence	9077
Shouse, Louisa	9222
Shouse, Ada	9223
Shouse, Nimrod	9271
Shouse, Harry	9272
Shouse, Howard Athen	28746
Shotpouch, Betsy	19384
Shotpouch, Byrd	30540
Shoap, Mary J.	23708
Showers, Mary J.	30176
Showers, William P.	30181
Shufeldt, Ross F.	11070
Shufeldt, John H.	11106
Shufeldt, Ethel M.	11107
Shufeldt, Percy A.	21966
Shufeldt, Zoe E.	21967
Shufeldt, Benjamin C.	21968
Shufeldt, Markham W.	21970
Shultz, Susan	17124
Shutt, John W.	26876
Shutt, Georgia	26877
Shutt, Virginia	26878
Shutt, Clementine W.	30780
Silk, George W.	3314
Silk, Susan C.	3315
Silk, Rosa L.	3316
Silk, Samuel	3317
Silk, Ezekiel	3861
Silk, Levi	11278
Silk, Melvina	11279
Silk, William	11316
Silk, Pearl	11317
Silk, Nancy	11889
Silk, Katie	12306
Silk, Sophia	15202
Silk, Nellie	15203
Silk, Johnson	15204
Silk, Charles	15205
Silk, Susan	15206
Silk, Jennie	15207
Silk, John	17373
Silk, Nellie	17374
Silk, Louanna	17375
Silk, Nellie	20524
Silk, Lizzie	20525
Silk, Aggie	27249
Silk, George	27301
Silk, Lucy	27302
Silk, Katie	27303
Silk, Betsy	27304
Silk, Sarah	30435
Silversmith, John	7171
Silversmith, Katie	7172
Silversmith, Rachel	7173

Name.	Roll No.
Silversmith, Bettie	7174
Silversmith, Manda	7175
Silversmith, Mary	7176
Silversmith, Steve	7177
Silversmith, Earnest	7178
Silversmith, Sarah	7179
Silversmith, Bettie	24389
Silversmith, Adolphus	30205
Silverheel, John	19202
Silverheel, George	30183
Silcox, Jim	20253
Silcox, Susie	20254
Silcox, Eliza	20255
Silcox, Jack	20256
Simco, Lutitia	27255
Simmons, Nancy	1432
Simmons, Samuel	2549
Simmons, Lewis D.	2941
Simmons, Thomas B.	6113
Simmons, Mary E.	13252
Simmons, Elmer A.	13253
Simmons, John A.	13254
Simmons, Aggie	20516
Simmons, Alex	20542
Simmons, Susie	20543
Simmons, Sadie	22761
Simmons, Walter C.	22762
Simmons, James F.	22763
Simmons, Callie E.	22764
Simmons, Johnson	27068
Simmons, George	29754
Simmons, Stand	32065
Simmons, Maggie	32446
Simmons, Columbus	32447
Simmons, Stealer	32685
Simons, Steve	18994
Simon, David	7452
Simon, May	7523
Simerson, Lorena	9001
Simerson, Cora E.	13654
Simerson, Elva B.	13655
Simerson, William J.	13656
Simerson, Sarah	19365
Simerson, John	30537
Simerton, Patsy	27479
Simlin, Wilson	28970
Simlin, Rachel	28971
Simpson, Oma	3930
Simpson, Undine	4318
Simpson, Fannie C.	4319
Simpson, Walter L.	10729
Simpson, Kate	13507
Simpson, James A.	13508
Simpson, Mary F.	13509
Simpson, Hugh	13510
Simpson, Grover	13511
Simpson, Minnie	13512
Simpson, John	13513
Simpson, George	13514
Simpson, Polly	22885
Simpson, Eliza	30373
Simpson, Nelson	30375
Sims, Mary T.	2978
Sims, Jesse C.	2982
Sims, Lonnie L.	2983
Sims, Ethel E.	2984
Sims, Oscar H.	2985
Simms, Sarah	9185
Simco, Josephus	26991
Simco, Ralph	26992
Simco, Alia	26993
Singleton, Annie	26772
Singleton, Dolly	26773
Singleton, Frank	26774
Singleton, Henry	26775
Singleton, John	26776
Singleton, Dock	26777
Singleton, Rosa	26778
Singleton, Charley	26779
Sisson, Charles H.	6053
Sisson, Lady	22606
Sisson, Hattie N.	22607
Sisson, Charles H., Jr.	23303
Sisson, Jessie M.	23304
Sisson, Sue	23305
Sisson, Mary	23306

Name.	Roll No.	Name.	Roll No.
Sittingdown, Nancy	2136	Sixkiller, Samuel	20061
Sittingdown, William	25634	Sixkiller, Bluford	20267
Sittingdown, Stephen	26362	Sixkiller, Annie	20268
Sittingdown, James	26363	Sixkiller, Maud	23599
Sittingdown, Thadius	26364	Sixkiller, Lola	23600
Sittingdown, Minnie	26365	Sixkiller, Blanche	23601
Sittingdown, Agnes	26366	Sixkiller, Mabel	23602
Sittingdown, Edgar	26367	Sixkiller, Henry	23603
Sittingdown, Ella	29820	Sixkiller, Mary A.	23604
Sitsler, George W.	30135	Sixkiller, Linnie	25562
Sitsler, James Lewis	30136	Sixkiller, Young Wolfe	25563
Sitten, Naomi A.	31698	Sixkiller, Mintie	25763
Sitten, Theodore L.	31699	Sixkiller, Hattie	26937
Sixkiller, Glover	768	Sixkiller, John B.	27220
Sixkiller, Nancy	1357	Sixkiller, Cicero	27221
Sixkiller, Sam	2316	Sixkiller, Dora	27222
Sixkiller, Nancy	2317	Sixkiller, Joseph	27470
Sixkiller, Lynch	2318	Sixkiller, Lucy	27471
Sixkiller, George	2319	Sixkiller, Gracie	27472
Sixkiller, Emma	2320	Sixkiller, Bertha	28556
Sixkiller, Ned	2321	Sixkiller, Carrie B.	28730
Sixkiller, Delia	2322	Sixkiller, Jennie	29721
Sixkiller, Walter	2323	Sixkiller, Peggie	29722
Sixkiller, Julia	2324	Sixkiller, Henry	32313
Sixkiller, Martha	2325	Six, John W.	6368
Sixkiller, Henry	2326	Six, Ida	17773
Sixkiller, Narcissa	2327	Six, Enoch	17772
Sixkiller, Frank	2328	Six, John	17807
Sixkiller, Stella	2329	Six, Groundhog	30551
Sixkiller, Arch	2418	Six, Humphrey	30552
Sixkiller, Walter R.	2330	Six, Tincup	30553
Sixkiller, Joshua	2547	Skaggs, Myrtle A.	11457
Sixkiller, Johnie	2548	Skaggs, Roy	11458
Sixkiller, Luke	7397	Skaloll, James	21290
Sixkiller, Emma	7398	Skelley, Cora	32247
Sixkiller, James	10732	Skelley, Charles	32248
Sixkiller, Nancy	10733	Skelley, Joseph	32249
Sixkiller, Carrie	10734	Skinner, Thomas F.	7545
Sixkiller, Pearl	10735	Skinner, Morgan D.	7546
Sixkiller, Joseph	10736	Skinner, Galuga T.	7547
Sixkiller, Henry	11223	Skinner, Bettie A.	7548
Sixkiller, Linnie M.	11224	Skinneer, Mary A.	7549
Sixkiller, William F.	11225	Skinner, Laura C.	26558
Sixkiller, Artemecie M.	11226	Skinner, John	28810
Sixkiller, Charles	12339	Skinner, Ray N.	28811
Sixkiller, Martin	12340	Skillman, Sarah E.	9210
Sixkiller, Hooley	12885	Skillman, Bessie D.	9211
Sixkiller, Jesse M.	12886	Skillman, John O.	9212
Sixkiller, James T.	13397	Skitt, Patsey	19663
Sixkiller, Claude L.	13398	Skitt, Martha	20137
Sixkiller, Robert M.	13399	Skitt, Sam	20138
Sixkiller, Ida M.	13400	Skitt, Nancy	20139
Sixkiller, Pleasant T.	13401	Skitt, Ben	20140
Sixkiller, Jesse	14348	Skitt, Ella	20141
Sixkiller, Sarah	14349	Skitt, Alice	20142
Sixkiller, Katie	14350	Skitt, Mattie	20143
Sixkiller, Ethel	14351	Skitt, Calvin	20144
Sixkiller, Josie	14967	Skitt, Margaret	22788
Sixkiller, Fannie	16040	Skitt, Lucy	25821
Sixkiller, Samuel R.	16877	Skidmore, Annie F.	21764
Sixkiller, Sallie	18313	Skidmore, Eugene O.	21765
Sixkiller, Charlie	18605	Skidmore, Otis T.	21766
Sixkiller, Eliza	18606	Skidmore, Elizabeth A.	21767
Sixkiller, Rufus	18607	Skidmore, Henry C.	21768
Sixkiller, Sampson	18608	Skidmore, Letitia F.	21769
Sixkiller, Charlotte	18913	Skidmore, Benjamin F.	21770
Sixkiller, George	18914	Sleeper, Cricket N.	15249
Sixkiller, Sam	18915	Sleeper, Nannie I.	15250
Sixkiller, Annie	19002	Sleeper, Minnie	17352
Sixkiller, John	19067	Sleeper, Julia	17353
Sixkiller, Winnie	19068	Sleeper, Gideon D., Jr.	17354
Sixkiller, Ora	19069	Sleeper, Walter J.	17355
Sixkiller, Nannie	19070	Sleeper, Mattie	17356
Sixkiller, Gafford	19245	Slack, Olive A.	31499
Sixkiller, Susie	19246	Slack, Edith	31500
Sixkiller, Nellie	19248	Slagle, Minnie H.	24377
Sixkiller, Laura	19249	Slagle, Gordon	24378
Sixkiller, Abraham	19666	Slagle, Dennis	24379
Sixkiller, Margaret	19667	Slagle, Hattie F.	24380
Sixkiller, Dennis	19668	Slagle, Ellsworth	24381
Sixkiller, Sarah	19669	Sloan, Mary E.	887
Sixkiller, Kate	19670	Sloan, Alexander G.	5116
Sixkiller, Lincoln	19671	Sloan, Nora C.	5117
Sixkiller, Retta	19672	Sloan, Lizzie H.	5118
Sixkiller, Johnson	20059	Sloan, Cora E.	5119
Sixkiller, Lula	20060	Sloan, Robert D.	7210

Name.	Roll No.	Name.	Roll No.
Sloan, Edward E.	9605	Smith, Samuel	4828
Sloan, Mary D.	9606	Smith, Juney	4826
Sloan, Minnie E.	9607	Smith, Samuel L.	5076
Sloan, Annie M.	9608	Smith, Elmira	5077
Sloan, Samuel J.	9609	Smith, Sirrissia	5078
Sloan, Eva L.	9610	Smith, Edith H.	5185
Sloan, James E.	9611	Smith, Lydia	5320
Sloan, Nina P.	9612	Smith, Callie	5637
Sloan, Florence C.	9613	Smith, Callie M.	5638
Sloan, William A.	13648	Smith, McCoy	5700
Sloan, Thomas A.	15725	Smith, Jennie	5701
Sloan, Floreda	27892	Smith, Walter	5702
Sloan, Jesse L.	27893	Smith, Juliette	5703
Smallwood, Katie	1368	Smith, Wilson	5704
Smallwood, William	5127	Smith, Mannie	5705
Smallwood, Mary L.	5128	Smith, May	5706
Smallwood, David E.	16267	Smith, Junie	5707
Smallwood, Louisa	16268	Smith, Jennie, Jr.	5708
Smallwood, Samuel M.	16269	Smith, James	5892
Smallwood, Patsie E.	16270	Smith, Mary	5893
Smallwood, Samuel	17097	Smith, Charles	5894
Smallwood, Lila	18997	Smith, Mattie	5895
Smalley, Susan	11110	Smith, Edward	6023
Smartt, Daisy P.	23947	Smith, Lutitia	6024
Smartt, Susan H.	23948	Smith, William	6025
Smartt, Jack A.	23949	Smith, Edward B.	6029
Smart, Henry	25427	Smith, Sarah	6060
Smart, Nelson	25428	Smith, Dennis	6062
Smart, William H.	25429	Smith, Lee	6063
Smart, James F.	25430	Smith, Archie	6064
Smart, Hattie E.	25431	Smith, Mattie	6065
Smedley, Jack	16743	Smith, Sylvester S.	6257
Smedley, Richard	29517	Smith, Logan	6258
Smedley, John	29518	Smith, Harrison	6259
Smith, Elizabeth	256	Smith, Lydia	6260
Smith, Othie A.	320	Smith, Josephine	6391
Smith, Florence	321	Smith, James Wesley	6397
Smith, Lee B.	322	Smith, George W.	6492
Smith, Lellia L.	223	Smith, Nannie B.	6493
Smith, Ruby E.	224	Smith, Walter	6494
Smith, Eulalia C.	504	Smith, James	6495
Smith, Willie A.	505	Smith, Rosetta	6496
Smith, Amos F.	506	Smith, Narcissie	6497
Smith, Rhoda C.	527	Smith, Scott	6498
Smith, Jay P.	529	Smith, Elizabeth J.	7324
Smith, Maude E.	530	Smith, Martha V.	7325
Smith, Willis H.	531	Smith, Susie	7327
Smith, Audry A.	532	Smith, Mamie E.	7328
Smith, Wyannetta	533	Smith, John R., Jr.	7329
Smith, Walter E.	574	Smith, Minnie J.	7392
Smith, Mildred B.	575	Smith, Hugh E.	7393
Smith, Avery	576	Smith, William E.	7394
Smith, Sarah P.	636	Smith, Eliza V.	7395
Smith, Walter F.	637	Smith, Sidney L.	7396
Smith, Nathaniel D.	638	Smith, Walter	7433
Smith, Homer L.	639	Smith, Susan	7434
Smith, Sarah	1063	Smith, Datus	7435
Smith, Walter D.	1064	Smith, Mary E.	7436
Smith, Grover C.	1065	Smith, Amanda A.	7437
Smith, Lucy L.	1066	Smith, Rachel	7438
Smith, Floy L.	1067	Smith, Callcayah	7439
Smith, Rebecca E.	1068	Smith, Isaac	7440
Smith, George W.	1824	Smith, Maggie	7441
Smith, Rosa A.	1954	Smith, Lucy	7780
Smith, George S.	2408	Smith, Lucy F.	7781
Smith, Tilden	2414	Smith, William L.	7782
Smith, Esther	2460	Smith, Lewis E.	7783
Smith, John	2461	Smith, David C.	7784
Smith, Huckleberry	2465	Smith, Kitty J.	8208
Smith, Maria	2504	Smith, Martha M.	8209
Smith, Lovely	3882	Smith, Clearcy	8292
Smith, Anderson	3883	Smith, Cora P.	8293
Smith, Pearl E.	3884	Smith, Ruth L.	8294
Smith, Elizabeth G.	4381	Smith, Bertha B.	8295
Smith, Simmie	4382	Smith, James L.	8296
Smith, Adelia	4383	Smith, Sallie	10742
Smith, John	4384	Smith, Emma	8491
Smith, Minnie	4385	Smith, Ivy N.	8492
Smith, Julius	4386	Smith, Oscar C.	8493
Smith, Bewlie	4389	Smith, Lizzie	8918
Smith, Salol	4740	Smith, Fred E.	8919
Smith, Martha	4822	Smith, Richard L.	8920
Smith, Kiahua	4823	Smith, Josie A.	9406
Smith, Elizabeth	4824	Smith, Lenora	9407
Smith, Famous	4825	Smith, James W.	9558
Smith, William H.	4827	Smith, Mahala	10207

Name.	Roll No.	Name.	Roll No.
Smith, William	10208	Smith, Tom	18099
Smith, James	10209	Smith, George	18100
Smith, Elizabeth	10210	Smith, Kiah	18101
Smith, Catherine	10211	Smith, Stoke	18102
Smith, Theodore	10242	Smith, Oo-la-wha-tee	18210
Smith, Beulah M.	10746	Smith, Dick	18518
Smith, Jack	10863	Smith, Willie	18583
Smith, George W.	10915	Smith, Lila	18584
Smith, James O.	11033	Smith, Lizzie	18585
Smith, Ola J.	11034	Smith, Bessie	18586
Smith, Shelly K.	11035	Smith, Annie	18587
Smith, Betty	11036	Smith, Fannie	18588
Smith, Mary J.	11235	Smith, Peter	18589
Smith, John A.	11236	Smith, Charley	18671
Smith, Elizabeth R.	11237	Smith, Susan	18672
Smith, Ada M.	11238	Smith, James	18673
Smith, Elmer T.	11239	Smith, Lillie	18674
Smith, Clarence B.	11240	Smith, Peggie	19319
Smith, Sarah J.	11276	Smith, Susan	19325
Smith, Laura K.	11277	Smith, John	19326
Smith, Eliza	11598	Smith, John	19777
Smith, Louis C.	11604	Smith, Lydia	19778
Smith, James R.	11605	Smith, Samuel	19779
Smith, William L.	12333	Smith, Lucy	19780
Smith, Saphronia P.	12334	Smith, Jennie	19781
Smith, Oma L.	12335	Smith, Jim	19931
Smith, John W. B.	12336	Smith, Richard	19955
Smith, John Q. A.	12414	Smith, Sam	19957
Smith, Nancy	12602	Smith, John	19958
Smith, John N.	12939	Smith, William	20385
Smith, Lillie	13206	Smith, Eli	20386
Smith, Julius	13207	Smith, Stan Watie	20387
Smith, Susan C.	13244	Smith, Dave	20388
Smith, James	13270	Smith, John	20942
Smith, Lula B.	13550	Smith, Jennie	20943
Smith, Wallace M.	13553	Smith, Annie	20944
Smith, George	13783	Smith, Josie	20945
Smith, Betsy	13784	Smith, Polly	21253
Smith, Sallie	13785	Smith, Susie	21254
Smith, Johnson	13786	Smith, James	21258
Smith, Daniel	13787	Smith, Nellie	21259
Smith, Levi	13788	Smith, Lizzie	21260
Smith, Thomas	13979	Smith, Rachel	21262
Smith, Polly	13980	Smith, Lydia	21261
Smith, Mary	13981	Smith, Joseph E.	21366
Smith, Emma	13982	Smith, Mintie A.	21638
Smith, Narcissa E.	14090	Smith, Sarah E.	21689
Smith, Lula E.	14091	Smith, Olive	21690
Smith, Jesse W.	14092	Smith, Cora L.	21691
Smith, John M., Jr.	14093	Smith, Maud	21692
Smith, Wilson	14148	Smith, Eliza	21693
Smith, Eugene C.	14216	Smith, Jimmie	21694
Smith, Lamech	14371	Smith, Hattie F.	21701
Smith, Nellie	14372	Smith, Alma I.	21702
Smith, Fitzhugh L.	14373	Smith, Homer	21703
Smith, Bryan	14374	Smith, Henry B.	21750
Smith, Sarah	15441	Smith, Lelia C.	21751
Smith, John B.	15778	Smith, Mary A. B.	21752
Smith, Maggie	15779	Smith, Francis Brooke	21753
Smith, Annie B.	15780	Smith, Jessie	21854
Smith, James	15781	Smith, Artha D.	21905
Smith, Thomas	15782	Smith, Ethel	21906
Smith, Elzena	16232	Smith, William L. E.	21907
Smith, Nuner Bell	16233	Smith, Clarence L.	22013
Smith, Ida R.	16407	Smith, Maude A.	22014
Smith, James G.	16406	Smith, Freeman C.	22015
Smith, James J.	16413	Smith, William L.	22316
Smith, Lutie L.	16983	Smith, Pearl H.	22317
Smith, Louise	16984	Smith, Florence C.	22327
Smith, Florence F.	16985	Smith, Emmet B.	22328
Smith, Mittie	16986	Smith, Margaret E.	22332
Smith, Famous	17033	Smith, Lizzie	22661
Smith, Eliza	17034	Smith, Emma	23073
Smith, Nannie	17035	Smith, Juliette	23072
Smith, Frank	17036	Smith, Salol Jr.	23074
Smith, David	17037	Smith, Lucy	24669
Smith, Cherry	17038	Smith, Walter A.	24670
Smith, Joseph W.	17039	Smith, Mary C.	25078
Smith, Mont	17402	Smith, Charles	25403
Smith, Emma	17810	Smith, Lizzie	25598
Smith, Jesse J.	17811	Smith, Sam	25975
Smith, Jennie	17812	Smith, James	25977
Smith, William	17813	Smith, Nancy	25978
Smith, Vernon S.	18061		
Smith, Redbird	18097		
Smith, Lucy	18098		

Name.	Roll No.	Name.	Roll No.
Smith, William	25979	Smith, Nina M.	31442
Smith, Tom	25980	Smith, William T.	31443
Smith, Lewis	25981	Smith, Lillie	31452
Smith, Richard	26381	Smith, Henry	31453
Smith, May B.	26382	Smith, Samuel	31454
Smith, Willie E.	26383	Smith, William B.	31523
Smith, Elizabeth	26384	Smith, Mark F.	31524
Smith, Fred B. F.	26548	Smith, Thomas C.	31525
Smith, William A.	26572	Smith, Alice	31964
Smith, Milam C.	26809	Smith, Lee	32343
Smith, Charles	26962	Smith, Ellen	32344
Smith, Eliza	26963	Smith, Mose	32523
Smith, Lucinda	26964	Smith, Dave	32556
Smith, Eli	26965	Smith, Martha	32895
Smith, Adeline	26966	Smith, Thomas F.	32896
Smith, Nellie	26967	Smith, Wilson	32911
Smith, Kate	26968	Smoke, Looney	19764
Smith, Henry	26969	Smoke, Lewis	25600
Smith, William	27133	Smoke, Grant	30494
Smith, Annie	27134	Smoke, Lucy	32051
Smith, Lizzie	27135	Smoke, Buck	32278
Smith, Betsy	27136	Smoke, Budding	32307
Smith, Walter F.	27373	Smoke, Lewis	32745
Smith, Jesse E.	27374	Smoke, Polly	32746
Smith, Willie N.	27375	Smoke, Cha-wa-yu-ga	32747
Smith, Eliza	27467	Smoke, Oo-yu-ty	32748
Smith, Harry	27502	Smoker, Spade	30058
Smith, Hiram R.	28104	Smoker, Nancy	32608
Smith, Beulah	28105	Smyth, Sallie	1533
Smith, Frank E.	28106	Snail, Walker	30629
Smith, John	28239	Snail, Joshua	19756
Smith, Henry J.	28526	Snail, Lydia	19757
Smith, Myrtie I.	28527	Snail, John	20695
Smith, Willie M.	28528	Snail, Annie	20696
Smith, Robert Lee	28529	Snail, Looney	20697
Smith, Percy W.	28530	Snake, Thomas	20356
Smith, Margaret R.	28531	Snake, Nancy	20357
Smith, Alice D.	28532	Snake, Ezekiel	20358
Smith, Jessie H.	28533	Snaketail, Quatie	2051
Smith, Nancy	28567	Snake Wolfe, Jackson	17900
Smith, Daniel	28568	Snake Wolfe, Lila	17901
Smith, Lucy	28569	Snake Wolfe, Polly	26255
Smith, Lizzie	28622	Snell, Coming	1237
Smith, John	28625	Snell, Anna	1238
Smith, Dennis	28673	Snell, Lyda	1239
Smith, Emma S.	28675	Snell, Bertha	1240
Smith, Laura L.	28676	Snell, Annie	8132
Smith, Jasper N.	28677	Snell, Ooyostah	17755
Smith, John	28724	Snell, Squirrel	17756
Smith, Charles	28941	Snell, Katie	17759
Smith, Annie	28942	Snell, Charles	17760
Smith, Jim	29103	Snell, Alexander	17761
Smith, John Jr.	29120	Snell, Nona	17762
Smith, Jennie	29140	Snell, Nannie	17763
Smith, Lizzie	29141	Snell, Coon	17769
Smith, Frank	29311	Snell, Susie	17770
Smith, Edward	30000	Snell, Nora	17771
Smith, Benjamin	30149	Snell, Eli	18846
Smith, Samuel	30150	Snell, Katie	18847
Smith, Joseph	30151	Snell, Alice	18848
Smith, Zella	30207	Snell, Charley	20257
Smith, Thomas F.	30427	Snell, Ina	20258
Smith, Nannie	30428	Snell, Eli	20279
Smith, Emma C.	30429	Snell, Ben	20280
Smith, Samuel	30430	Snell, Sam	20291
Smith, Roach Y.	30432	Snell, Maria	20292
Smith, Susan	30431	Snell, Nellie	20293
Smith, Annie	30433	Snell, Nancy	20294
Smith, Jennie	30434	Snell, Gilbert	20767
Smith, Dave	30578	Snell, Susan	20768
Smith, Elula G.	31007	Snell, Jennie	25408
Smith, Ruby I.	31008	Snell, Sarah	25409
Smith, Jasper E.	31009	Snell, George	25858
Smith, Margaret L.	31010	Snell, Sarah	27035
Smith, Ella C.	31011	Snell, Fannie	28477
Smith, Jessie	31013	Snell, Swimmer	30634
Smith, Alma E.	31014	Snell, Rachel	30635
Smith, Della	31015	Snider, Annie B.	13040
Smith, Lewyn	31016	Snider, Thomas B.	13041
Smith, William A.	31017	Snider, Perry E.	13042
Smith, Mary L.	31439	Snider, Jerry R.	13043
Smith, Irving L.	31440	Snider, Walton I.	13044
Smith, John T.	31441	Snider, Jacob A.	15170
		Snider, James F.	15171

Name.	Roll No.	Name.	Roll No.
Snider, Roy C.	15172	Sourjohn, Nancy	32580
Snider, Cecil F.	15173	Sourjohn, Jennie	32581
Snider, Alice	16802	Sourjohn, Lewis	32582
Snider, Celia D.	25229	Sourjohn, Lizzie	32583
Snider, Laura R.	25230	Sourjohn, Levi	32584
Snider, Minnie L.	25231	Sourjohn, Silk	32650
Snider, Darry R.	25232	Sourjohn, James	32778
Snider, Mac E.	25233	Spade, Johnson	1430
Snider, Hopi H.	25234	Spade, Rachel	1431
Snip, Nick	27040	Spade, John	16501
Snip, Susan	27041	Spade, Leonard	18267
Snip, Charles	27042	Spade, Arley	18268
Snip, Nancy	27043	Spade, White	18269
Snip, Josie	27044	Spade, Grape	18270
Snip, Rufus	27045	Spade, Lula	18271
Snip, Bessie	27046	Spade, Emma	18272
Snow, Mary A.	2340	Spade, Sam	20001
Snodgrass, Lydia B.	6485	Spade, Nellie	20394
Soap, Jack	18855	Spade, Rachel	20395
Soap, Betsy	18856	Spade, John	20794
Soap, Katie	18857	Spade, Eliza	20795
Soap, Bob	19059	Spade, Ella	20806
Soap, Tom	19152	Spade, Sagie	20807
Soap, Johnson	19153	Spade, Jane	20808
Soap, Sulteeskie	19154	Spade, Takie	20809
Soap, Cornelius	19155	Spade, Maria	20810
Soap, Katie	19156	Spade, Sarah	20811
Soap, Rachel	19185	Spade, Nannie	25381
Soap, Eva	19258	Spade, Jennie	25382
Soap, Ancy	19259	Spade, Watt	25383
Soap, Johnson	20444	Spade, James	27063
Soap, Nick	20445	Spade, Jennie	27064
Soap, Nellie	20446	Spade, Robert	27065
Soap, Willie	20447	Spade, Charles	27066
Soap, Charley	20448	Spade, Ruskey	27067
Soap, William	20936	Spade, Robert	27516
Soap, Mary	20937	Spade, William	28468
Soap, Sah-ne	20938	Spade, Watson	28564
Soap, George	26084	Spade, Johnson	28565
Soap, Mollie	26085	Spade, Josie	29003
Soap, Na-na-thla	29087	Spade, Annie	29105
Soap, Jennie	29846	Spade, Robert	30646
Soap, Walter	30725	Spade, Nannie	30653
Soap, Redbird	30726	Sparks, Johnsie A.	3193
Soap, Moses	32285	Sparks, William	3194
Soldier, Taylor	6315	Sparks, John R.	3195
Soldier, Nancy	6316	Spaniard, Jack	18064
Soldier, Annie	6317	Spaniard, Emma	19506
Soldier, Martha-	6318	Spaniard, Lizzie	19507
Soldier, Peter	7932	Spaniard, Lydia	19508
Soldier, Susan	7933	Spaniard, Ezekiel	20229
Soldier, Whitaker	7934	Spaniard, Sarah	20230
Soldier, Julia	7935	Spaniard, Mose	20231
Soldier, Oce	20685	Spaniard, Richard	21368
Sootawakeky, John	21085	Spaniard, William	29021
Sootawakeky, Iyanstah	21086	Spaniard, Teacher	29022
Sootawakeky, Lizzie	21087	Spaniard, Hazel	31692
Sootawakeky, Charlie	21088	Sparrowhawk, Joseph	20987
Sootawakeky, Watie	21089	Sparrowhawk, Lydia	20988
Sootawawkeky, Kahorkah		Sparrowhawk, Annie	20989
	32348	Sparrowhawk, Betsy	20990
Sookey,	28430	Sparrowhawk, Maggie	20991
Southerlin, Earnest	5342	Sparrowhawk, Fish	20992
Southerlin, Jesse	5343	Sparrowhawk, Peggie	20993
Southerland, Arebella	9397	Sparrowhawk, Polly	29975
South, Kate	12765	Spears, Lydia	8598
South, Ellen	12766	Spears, Josephine	8599
South, Charley C.	12767	Spears, Mollie	8600
South, Wilson C.	12768	Spears, William	8601
South, Kate	12769	Spears, Calvin	8602
South, Rebecca	12770	Spears, Ada	8603
South, Constance	12771	Spears, Minnie Isabel	8606
South, Susie	26922	Spears, Amos	12521
Souther, Minnie V.	13867	Spears, Stephen	13877
Sourjohn, Mary	18410	Spears, Mary J.	14218
Sourjohn, Susie	18411	Spears, Dennie S.	14219
Sourjohn, Willie	18412	Spears, John	14220
Sourjohn, Eli	18413	Spears, Lizzie	14221
Sourjohn, Nellie	18814	Spears, James	14222
Sourjohn, Isaac	20282	Spears, Lizzie	14786
Sourjohn, Albert	21038	Spears, Polly	14922
Sourjohn, Ooliyey	21039	Spears, Robert	15992
Sourjohn, Levi	21040	Spears, Lizzie	15993
Sourjohn, Anderson	21041	Spears, Minnie	15995
Sourjohn, Sarah	25316	Spears, Arthur	15994

Name.	Roll No.
Spears, Dora	15996
Spears, Charles	15997
Spears, Crossly	15998
Spears, Arch	16590
Spears, Albion B.	16591
Spears, Walter	18810
Spears, Eli D.	28004
Spencer, Allen	11039
Spencer, Mary C.	14544
Spencer, John T.	26632
Spencer, Samuel T.	28137
Spencer, Nancy J.	32011
Spencer, Gonia V.	32012
Speaker, Ben	15870
Speaker, Nancy	15871
Speaker, Eli	15872
Speaker, Samuel	15873
Speaker, Dick	15874
Speaker, Joseph	15875
Speaker, Arch	19842
Speaker, Sunday	19843
Speaker, Susie	19844
Speaker, Lydia	19845
Speaker, Hattie	19846
Speaker, Jennie	20928
Speaker, Tahtiye	20931
Spickerman, Ella L.	31721
Spickerman, Hellen J.	31722
Spickerman, William Glenn	31723
Splitnose, Charley	17336
Splitnose, Thomas	17337
Splitnose, Susan	17338
Splitnose, Henry	17339
Splitnose, Jennie	17340
Splitnose, Nannie	30065
Splitnose, Rosa	30066
Spoon, William	12187
Spoon, Sarah	12188
Spoon, Joshua	20531
Spring-water, Susan	3209
Springwater, Minnie A.	3881
Springwater, Troy H.	3886
Springwater, Emma J.	4149
Springwater, Jennie	18933
Springwater, Lizzie	18934
Springwater, Ida	19595
Springwater, Levi	19885
Springwater, Lula	19886
Springwater, John	19887
Springwater, Johnson	25726
Springwater, Amanda	25727
Springwater, Warlena	25728
Springwater, Columbus	25742
Springwater, Katie	25743
Springwater, Lucy	25770
Springwater, Will	28418
Springwater, Dennis B.	28444
Springwater, Cold	28460
Springston, John L.	15339
Springston, William P. B.	15340
Soriggs, Alexander A.	15701
Spriggs, John B.	15702
Spriggs, Annie B.	15703
Spriggs, Mamie P.	15704
Spriggs, Henry A.	15705
Soriggs, Judge L.	15706
Spriggs, Seaburn P.	15707
Spriggs, Lucy L.	15708
Springer, Nina W.	21602
Springer, Gertrude	21603
Sourlock, Hardin H.	21696
Sourlock, Louis P.	21697
Spybuck, Susie	31577
Spybuck, Bushyhead	31579
Spybuck, Peter	9877
Spybuck, Henry	10410
Spybuck, Mary	10724
Spybuck, Elizabeth	30153
Spybuck, George	30172
Spybuck, Mary	30173
Spybuck, Annie	31268
Spybuck, Frank	31269

Name.	Roll No.
Spybuck, Minnie	31270
Spybuck, William	31271
Spybuck, Jessie	31272
Squirrel, Jack F.	6200
Squirrel, Martin	15149
Squirrel, Mitchel	15163
Squirrel, Rosella	15164
Squirrel, Jack	17765
Squirrel, Watt	18218
Squirrel, Jennie	18219
Squirrel, Charles T.	18595
Squirrel, Jim	18651
Squirrel, Nar-ye-cear	18652
Squirrel, Benjamin	19230
Squirrel, Lucy	19231
Squirrel, Sarah	19232
Squirrel, Jennie	19233
Squirrel, Alex	19234
Squirrel, Jim	19235
Squirrel, Charlie	19470
Squirrel, Peter	19687
Squirrel, Betsy	19688
Squirrel, George	19748
Squirrel, Jesse	20344
Squirrel, Daniel	20345
Squirrel, Moses	20377
Squirrel, Mary	20378
Squirrel, Linnie	20379
Squirrel, Sequichie	20593
Squirrel, Darkey	20738
Squirrel, Willie	25554
Squirrel, Peter A.	25555
Squirrel, Sam	25603
Squirrel, Gur-you-chey	25859
Squirrel, Mose	27573
Squirrel, Isaac	27574
Squirrel, Charles	27714
Squirrel, Lillie	30613
Squirrel, Jim	30614
Squirrel, Dave	30633
Stand, Robin B.	1667
Stand, Lucy	1668
Stand, Peggy	1669
Stand, Sallie	1670
Stand, Richard C.	1671
Stand, Taylor B.	1672
Stand, Katie	1673
Stansill, Hill	1044
Stansill, Jennie	1045
Stansill, Archilla	1046
Stansill, Bertha	1047
Stansill, John	1454
Stansill, William R.	1455
Stansill, Joel B. M.	1456
Stanley, Nannie	21588
Stanley, Annie	7725
Stanley, Bessie A.	7726
Stanley, Jefferson H.	7727
Stanley, Mabell	7728
Staller, James	6414
Staller, Windy	6415
Staller, Jesse	6416
Staller, Samuel	6417
Staller, Looney	6418
Starr, Samuel J.	1830
Starr, Sarah R.	1831
Starr, George E.	1832
Starr, Martin C.	1833
Starr, Joseph	1834
Starr, Ezekiel E.	1876
Starr, Eldorado	1877
Starr, Mary Bell	1878
Starr, Joel B. M.	1879
Starr, Callie	1880
Starr, Jananna R.	1881
Starr, Ezekiel	1882
Starr, Caleb E.	2308
Starr, Floyd	2309
Starr, Samuel	2310
Starr, Charlie	2311
Starr, Louvenia	2312
Starr, Hooley	2314

Name.	Roll No.	Name.	Roll No.
Starr, Nancy	2315	Starr, William	18852
Starr, Emmet	2423	Starr, Fannie	18959
Starr, Ellis	2601	Starr, Bettie	18960
Starr, Martha	2602	Starr, Callie	18961
Starr, Lucy	2603	Starr, Mary	19320
Starr, Florence B.	2604	Starr, Nancy	19566
Starr, Charley C.	2605	Starr, Joe	19565
Starr, Hulda	2606	Starr, Susie	19567
Starr, Daisy	2607	Starr, Rachel	19742
Starr, George W.	3267	Starr, Ezekiel	21111
Starr, Florence E.	3268	Starr, John	21598
Starr, David R.	3269	Starr, Georgia A.	21886
Starr, Washington H.	3270	Starr, Emma	22273
Starr, Lugie	3332	Starr, Ezekiel	22274
Starr, Clem R.	3333	Starr, Nancy	22503
Starr, Georgia	3405	Starr, Delilah	22504
Starr, Kate	3679	Starr, Jessie	22505
Starr, George	4076	Starr, Alice	22506
Starr, Rachel	4077	Starr, Maggie E.	22637
Starr, Samuel S.	4232	Starr, Watt	24729
Starr, Henry	4233	Starr, George C.	24730
Starr, Katie	4234	Starr, Mary B.	24731
Starr, James	4235	Starr, Lettie B.	24732
Starr, Lucy	4236	Starr, Joseph M.	24733
Starr, Sophie	4237	Starr, Nancy J.	27734
Starr, Laura	4238	Starr, Caleb L.	24735
Starr, Rachel	4239	Starr, Charles C.	24820
Starr, Jack	4240	Starr, Orange W.	24821
Starr, Fannie C.	4249	Starr, Glenn	24822
Starr, Thomas	4250	Starr, Jessie M.	24823
Starr, Mary B.	4251	Starr, Lizzie	25663
Starr, Cherokee	4252	Starr, Rufus	25664
Starr, Margaret	4253	Starr, Tarney	25812
Starr, E. Cassie	4623	Starr, Mary	26187
Starr, Laura	4715	Starr, Jennie	27291
Starr, Ellis	5229	Starr, James	28060
Starr, Charles	5794	Starr, Saphronia	28061
Starr, Pochahontas	5795	Starr, Jack	28062
Starr, Junita	5796	Starr, Tobe	28063
Starr, Jennie L.	5826	Starr, Hattie	28064
Starr, Henry	5827	Starr, Katie	28065
Starr, Jesse	7735	Starr, Lilly	28066
Starr, Jennie	7736	Starr, Charley	28067
Starr, John C.	9178	Starr, Yute	28068
Starr, Jessie B.	9179	Starr, Agnes	28069
Starr, James C.	9180	Starr, Caleb	28070
Starr, Arch	12457	Starr, Lola	28071
Starr, Andy T.	12458	Starr, Etta	28327
Starr, Tony B.	12459	Starr, Henry G.	29572
Starr, Maud M.	12460	Starr, Caleb S. Jr.	29640
Starr, Ida M.	12868	Starr William	29732
Starr, Joe	14460	Starr, Katie	29733
Starr, Jennie	14603	Starr, Carl M.	29734
Starr, Tom	14602	Starr, Charles	30068
Starr, Charles L.	15694	Starr, Nancy	30590
Starr, Jacqueline	16115	Starr, Albert	30591
Starr, Caleb W.	16266	Starr, Bluford W.	12254
Starr, Isabel	16808	Starnes, John	5239
Starr, Milo	16809	Starnes, Thomas	5240
Starr, Polly	16810	Starnes, Mary E.	5241
Starr, Richard	16811	Starnes, Emma	5242
Starr, Alice	16918	Starnes, Bessie	5243
Starr, Cooey	16919	Starnes, Lelia	5244
Starr, Tuxie	16920	Starnes, Maggie	6338
Starr, Caleb	16921	Starnes, Jessie	6339
Starr, John	17663	Stalsworth, Lena	10694
Starr, Lucinda	17664	Stallcup, Sarah K.	22038
Starr, Rufus	17665	Stallcup, Florence	22039
Starr, Ailsy	17737	Stallcup, Mary A.	22040
Starr, Cora	17738	Stallcup, Dicy D.	22041
Starr, William	17923	Stallcup, Cullice	22042
Starr, Lizzie	18613	Stallcup, Sealy	22043
Starr, Thomas	18700	Stalk, Sever	23891
Starr, Ruth	18701	Stalk, Henry	26491
Starr, Elmira	18702	Stalk	28016
Starr, Rosa	18703	Standingwater, William	21433
Starr, Cooper	18704	Standingwater, Charlotte	21434
Starr, Eliza	18705	Standingwater, Dave	21435
Starr, Katie	18706	Standingdoor, Goose	18483
Starr, Molsie	18707	Standingdoor, Ailsey	30496
Starr, Tuxie	18749	Starbuck, Goldie	10351
Starr, Sam	18759		

Name.	Roll No.	Name.	Roll No.
Starbuck, Earnest G.	10352	Stephens, Cynthia B.	5593
Starkey, Sarah E.	11340	Stephens, George D.	5594
Starkey, Willie	11341	Stephens, Lee M.	5595
Starkey, Henry	11342	Stephens, Spencer S.	5760
Starkey, Jennie	30253	Stephens, Sarah R.	5761
Stark, Mattie S.	17309	Stephens, Nancy M.	11969
Stapler, John B.	13846	Stephens, Allie M.	11970
Stapler, Ellie M.	13847	Stephens, Willie D.	11971
Stapler, Nellie M.	13848	Stephens, Thelmer G.	11972
Stapler, John B. Jr.	13849	Stephens, Spencer A.	12509
Stapler, James S.	14580	Stephens, Spencer F.	12510
Stapler, Lorena O.	14581	Stephens, Ola E.	12511
Stapler, Anna P.	14582	Stephens, Leona I.	12512
Stapler, Otway H.	14583	Stephens, Ernest L.	12614
Stapler, John W.	14584	Stephens, Spencer H.	12615
Statham, Nancy J.	3432	Stephens, Ernest L. Jr.	12616
Statham, Donia E.	3433	Stephens, Thomas F.	14620
Statham, Leonadis A.	3434	Stephens, James E.	14621
Statham, Edmund R.	3435.	Stephens, Taylor C.	14622
Statham, Cleo B.	3436	Stephens, Albert	14623
Stattler, Minnie M.	4075	Stephens, William H. Jr.	16223
Standingdeer, Jackson	32648	Stephens, John H.	16225
Standingdeer, Davis	25955	Stephens, Leona L.	24876
Standingdeer, Annie	32649	Stephens, William L.	28944
Starkweather, Martha J.	28193	Stephens, Nellie	19338
Stanclift, Lillie G.	29385	Stevens, Flora	507
Stand, Edward	32265	Stevens, William E.	509
Stayathome, John	19195	Stevens, Rubbie M.	510
Stayathome, Sarah	19196	Stevens, Lucy	15880
Stayathome, Nancy	19197	Stevens, Mary J.	23586
Stayathome, Ned	19198	Stevens, Joe M.	23587
Stayathome, Choweenka	19199	Stevens, David Lesley	23588
Stayathome,' Alie	20859	Stevens, Elmira	25287
Stayathome, William	20860	Stevens, Elizabeth	25288
Stayathome, Joe	20861	Stevens, Stephen	25289
Stealer, Lewis	17963	Stevens, Fannie	25291
Stealer, Sallie	18215	Stevens, Marshal C.	27589
Stealer, Ned	18563	Stevens, Laura	27590
Stealer, Charlotte	18564	Stevens, Carrie L.	27591
Stealer, Bettie	18918	Stevens, Mary E.	27592
Stealer, George	18971	Stevenson, Daisy E.	3111
Stealer, Katie	18972	Stevenson, Margaret	3112
Stealer, Wm. Angell	18973	Stevenson, Emma	3113
Stealer, Thomas	21782	Stevenson, Dorothy B.	3114
Stealer, Jennie	21783	Stevenson, William F.	14529
Stealer, Mariah	21784	Stevenson, Mary E.	16307
Stealer, David	21785	Stevenson, John A.	16308
Stealer, John	27896	Stevenson, William C.	16309
Stealer, William	27897	Stevenson, Clemmie R.	28252
Stealer, Myrtle	27898	Stevenson, Mary P.	28253
Stealer, Anna	28242	Stephenson, Rosa L.	30970
Stealer, Wilson	28408	Stephenson, Mary A.	30971
Stealer, Jim	28409	Stephenson, Fannie F.	32202
Stealer, Lizzie	28410	Stephenson, Freddie	32203
Stealer, Sarah	28411	Stephenson, Walter	32204
Stealer, Lewis	30506	Stephenson, John H.	32211
Stealer, Thompson	30507	Sterling, Ella	26246
Stealer, Cum-skoo-wee	32686	Sterling, Lillie E.	26247
Steele, James	8035	Sterling, Nellie	26248
Steele, Ollie	26925	Sterling, Ethel M.	26249
Steele, Robert V.	32008	Stewart, Catherine	3211
Steele, John	32867	Stewart, John T.	3212
Steele, Eva	32868	Stewart, David C.	3213
Steele, Lena	32869	Stewart, Rachel	3897
Steele, Minnie	32870	Stewart, Tony	3900
Steel, Polly	29135	Stewart, Thenia	3901
Steere, Sarah	11094	Stewart, Omie	3902
Steere, Annie	11095	Stewart, Eller	4991
Steere, Minnie	11096	Stewart, Newton	4992
Step, Charles	29627	Stewart, Settie L.	4993
Step, Polly	29628	Stewart, William H.	5434
Step, Lizzie	29629	Stewart, Annie M.	5435
Step, Annie	29630	Stewart, James O.	7564
Step, Chulio	29631	Stewart, George A.	7565
Step, Jennie	29632	Stewart, William A.	7566
Step, Ellis	29633	Stewart, Ralph M.	7567
Stepp, Laura A.	11625	Stewart, Mina	12031
Stepp, George C.	11626	Stewart, John I.	12032
Stepp, Earnest L.	11627	Stewart, Della I.	12033
Stepp, Leonard	11628	Stewart, Minnie B.	12034
Stepp, Charles B.	11629	Stewart, William C. Jr.	12035
Stephens, Ophelia B.	2220	Stewart, Charles A.	12036
Stephens, Betsy	5592	Stewart, Hubert H.	12037

Name.	Roll No.	Name.	Roll No.
Stewart, John H.	12826	Still, Ezekiel	27997
Stewart, Max	12827	Still, Mollie E.	27998
Stewart, William N. Jr.	12828	Still, Frank J.	27999
Stewart, Celina K.	17370	Still, May E.	28000
Stewart, Margaret A.	22129	Still, Clem L.	28001
Stewart, James A.	22130	Still, Flora G.	28002
Stewart, John W.	22131	Still, Pochahantus	28003
Stewart, Nancy J.	22132	Still, Mary	28441
Stewart, George W.	26734	Still, Edward	28833
Stewart, Sallie B.	30047	Still, Ned	28835
Stewart, Eva L.	30048	Still, Sallie	28836
Stewart, Florence	31030	Still, Green	29752
Stewart, William M.	31031	Still, James	32361
Stewart, Samuel	31032	Still, May	32500
Steward, Barbara A.	11245	Still, Geneva	32501
Steward, Cornelius B.	11246	Still, Clyde	32502
Steward, Sidney T.	11247	Still, James	32542
Steward, James L.	11248	Stiles, Charlotte E.	6216
Steward, Mary L.	11249	Stiles, Emma J.	6217
Steward, Lydia M.	11250	Stiles, Clerinda M.	6218
Steward, Sarah M.	11251	Stick, Eli	19796
Steward, Charles J.	11252	Stick, Joe	19811
Steward, Minnie O.	11253	Stick, Caroline	19812
Stiles, Eva	12637	Stick, Spade	19813
Stiles, Susie A.	12638	Stick, Emily	25875
Stiles, Samuel M.	12639	Stick, Takey	30587
Still, Clarence	82	Stick, Jack	30588
Still, Beulah	83	Stiffness, Susie	20833
Still, William	84	Stiffness, Kahheetah	20834
Still, Tom	843	Stillé, Levi	30846
Still, Lucy	844	Stille, Ida	30848
Still, Betsy	845	Stille, Elias	30849
Still, Sam	846	Stine, May	11696
Still, Tom	847	Stine, Joanna	4364
Still, Addie	848	Stine, Edward J.	11698
Still, Willie	949	Stinger, Louisa	9799
Still, Mary	1534	Stinger, Albert	9800
Still, Maggie	1535	Stinson, Lena M.	13479
Still, Johnana	1536	Stinson, Willie M.	13480
Still, David	4398	Stinson, Violet V.	13481
Still, Lucy	6323	Stilley, Ora B.	30210
Still, Enos	6324	Stilley, Cora D.	30211
Still, Asia	7295	Stovall, Susie	6212
Still, Chester	7296	Stovall, Keekee Tehee	6213
Still, Cook	14217	Stovall, Luberdie	6214
Still, James L.	14323	Stovall, Elmer	6215
Still, George	14327	Stockton, Clara	10350
Still, Mary E.	14328	Stockton, Sarah	21596
Still, Emma A.	14365	Stockton, Ada	21597
Still, Lewis L.	14366	Stockton, Effie May	32524
Still, Susan	14430	Stokes, Mattie B.	7347
Still, Jonas	15076	Stokes, Georgia A.	10344
Still, William J.	15077	Stokes, Olive M.	10345
Still, Laura	15078	Stokes, Gretta E.	10346
Still, Emma	15079	Stokes, Minnie V.	11378
Still, Ollie	15080	Stokes, Annie L.	11379
Still, Thomas J.	15081	Stokes, Mary M.	11307
Still, John N.	16682	Stokes, Ewing M.	11308
Still, Cook	16683	Stokes, Herschel V.	13309
Still, Bertha	16684	Stokes, William T.	13310
Still, Ella M.	16685	Stokes, Maude M.	13311
Still, Curtis	16686	Stokes, Robert Y.	13312
Still, Chester	16687	Stokes, Jennie E.	13313
Still, James	16698	Stokes, Carl N.	13314
Still, John	16875	Stoneberger, Rose May	3505
Still, Emet	16876	Stone, Mary E.	10096
Still, Sampson	17428	Stone, Oral M.	10097
Still, John	17585	Stone, Pearl	10098
Still, Dick	18777	Stone, William F.	10099
Still, Eliza	18778	Stone, Lelia	29307
Still, Horn	18779	Stone, Foster	29308
Still, Jack	18867	Stone, Elizabeth E.	28633
Still, Ester	18995	Stool, Sam	18982
Still, John	19151	Stop, Darkey	19286
Still, William	20274	Stop, Caniyah	19287
Still, Corneleous	21826	Stop, Caneetah	19288
Still, Henry	22993	Stop, Jennie	20010
Still, Luella	22994	Stop, Johnson	26009
Still, James	25404	Stop, Sallie	28998
Still, Mary E.	25405	Stop, Adam	29148
Still, Nellie	25681	Stop, Charlotte	29149
Still, Louisa M.	26317	Stop, Sarah	29150
Still, General	27985	Stop, Gilbert	29637

Name.	Roll No.	Name.	Roll No.
Stop, Mary	29638	Stroup, Johnnie L.	11535
Stop, Flora	29639	Strout, Eliza A.	8975
Stop, Samuel	29784	Stuart, Riley W.	8129
Stop, Sallie	29785	Stuart, Albert E.	8130
Stop, Bluford	32079	Stuart, Mabel M.	8131
Stop, Che-cor-na-lah	32080	Stuart, Edward	13685
Stop, Abraham	32363	Stucker, Pearl I.	8066
Stop, Littlebird	32364	Stucker, Ruth A.	8067
Stopp, Sallie	32044	Stubbs, John S.	7861
Storey, Martha A.	21965	Stubbs, Sama E.	32233
Storts, Margaret	30342	Stubblefield, Mary C.	26762
Storts, Beulah	30343	Stubblefield, Myrtle I.	26763
Storts, Clara M.	30344	Stubblefield, Lena V.	26764
Storts, Lydia	30345	Sturdivant, Martin B.	7167
Stout, Martha	12293	Sturdivant, Richard	7168
Stout, Russell S.	12294	Sturdivant, John	7351
Stout, Mary A.	30091	Sturdivant, Arron	7430
Stout, Louisa J.	30092	Sturdivant, Preston	7431
Stout, Emma E.	30093	Sturdivant, Alvia C.	7432
Stout, Susan M.	30094	Sturdivant, Joseph	8516
Stout, Samuel J.	30095	Sturdivant, John	15138
Stout, James W.	30096	Sturdivant, Elizabeth	15439
Stout, John H.	30097	Sturdivant, Nancy	17780
Stout, Abram	31462	Sturdivant, Mollie L.	17781
Stout, Frank	31463	Suagee, Stand	7445
Stout, Mamie	31464	Suagee, Robert	7446
Stout, Edward	31465	Suagee, Dennis	7447
Stover, Lewis	1259	Suagee, Thomas	7448
Stover, William R.	14269	Suagee, Watie	7449
Stover, Edith L.	14270	Suagee, May	7450
Stover, Roger Q.	14271	Suagee, Roy L.	7451
Stover, William A.	14272	Suagee, Louisa	7506
Stover, Ralph B.	14273	Suagee, Marcus D. L.	7508
Stover, Ola	14274	Suagee, Thomas W.	7509
Stover, Lizzie	14326	Suagee, Louisa A.	7510
Stover, Jennie	27870	Suagee, Maud D.	7511
Stover, Medicine	28286	Suagee, Laura I.	9409
Stowers, Bessie	32902	Suagee, Joel	9819
Strange, Mary R.	12975	Suagee, Evaline	9820
Strange, Mary B.	13456	Suagee, Floyd	9821
Strange, Mary E.	13457	Suagee, David	9822
Strange, John D.	13458	Suagee, Peter C.	13482
Strange, Janie A.	13459	Suagee, Sam	16711
Strange, Ella	13460	Suagee, Nellie	25406
Strainer, Aggie	29509	Suagee, Henry	25407
Stranks, Emily J.	21610	Sua-gee, Stand	32912
Stratton, Ada	14180	Sua-gee, York-sie	32913
Stratton, Myrtle M.	14181	Suake, Swimmer	20812
Stratton, Samuel T.	14182	Suake, Katie	20813
Stratton, John M. Jr.	14183	Suake, Jim	20814
Stratton, Jesse H.	14184	Suake, Jane	20815
Stratton, Willie W.	14185	Suake, Ahno-he	30663
Street, Jacob	10363	Suake, Lillie	30664
Strickland, Sarah C.	22162	Suake, Mary	30665
Strickland, Kate C.	22163	Sudderth, Louisa	10658
Strickland, Elizabeth L.	22164	Sudderth, Hallie B.	10659
Strickland, Rogers	22165	Sudderth, Delia F.	10660
Strickler, Maggie	32387	Sudderth, Theodore B.	10661
Strickler, Fred	32388	Sudderth, Edgar S.	10662
Strickler, Alie	32389	Sudderth, Lloyd W.	10663
Strickler, Frank	32390	Sugar, Henry	25914
Strickler, Leander	32391	Sugar, Sallie	29724
Strong, Augustus C.	10957	Sullateskee	18547
Strong, Phillips	10958	Sullateskee, Annikee	18548
Strong, Susan V.	10959	Sullateskee, Charlotte	18549
Strong, Ross	10960	Sullateskee, Chewaney	18550
Strong, Dewey	10961	Sullateskee, George	21266
Strong, Koto A.	10962	Sullateskee, Watt	21348
Strong, Willie Vlana	10963	Sullateskee, Eliza	21349
Strong, Lula	21882	Sullateskee, Annie	21446
Strong, Tom	25956	Sullateskee, Neryutaie	30639
Strole, Ellen G.	27635	Sullateskee, Ailey	30640
Strother, Barbara K.	31527	Sullateskee, Oo-stay-lah	30700
Strother, Dwight Lynn	31528	Sullateskee, George	30701
Stroud, Nora M.	24243	Sulteesky, John	30436
Stroud, Joseph Robert	24244	Sulletaskee, Oo-yusk	32332
Stroup, Clara B.	11528	Sultzer, Sparrow	18849
Stroup, Elward L.	11529	Sultzer, Lucinda	18850
Stroup, Earl R.	11530	Sultzer, Wilburn	18851
Stroup, Theo P.	11531	Sullivan, James B.	32253
Stroup, Jessie	11532	Sullivan, William P.	6452
Stroup, Ruby	11533	Sullivan, Willis S.	6466
Stroup, Willie	11534	Sullivan, Jefferson D.	6630

Name.	Roll No.	Name.	Roll No.
Sullivan, George T.	6631	Sunday, Laura	15224
Sullivan, Arther E.	6632	Sunday, James	16212
Sullivan, Maud E.	6633	Sunday, Katie	16213
Sullivan, Maggie M.	6634	Sunday, David	16214
Sullivan, Ira J.	6635	Sunday, Nicholas	16215
Sullivan, James R.	6636	Sunday, Betsey	16216
Sullivan, Frank	6653	Sunday, Charles	16505
Sullivan, Sarah	15367	Sunday, Thomas	17202
Sullivan, Susan	15368	Sunday, Malinda	17203
Sullivan, Ellis	15369	Sunday, George	17204
Sullivan, Mary	23385	Sunday, James	17205
Sullivan,, George	23386	Sunday, Izora	17206
Sullivan, Annie	23387	Sunday, Evy	17207
Sullivan, John L.	23388	Sunday, Kelley	17208
Sullivan, Robert	23390	Sunday, Katie	17209
Sullivan, Eliza	23389	Sunday, William	17538
Sullivan, Jefferson D.	24850	Sunday, William	18119
Sullivan, William J.	24851	Sunday, Neppie	18120
Sullivan, Emma M.	24852	Sunday, Jake	18121
Sullivan, Charles F.	24853	Sunday, Ellis	18122
Sullivan, Florane	24854	Sunday, Leroy	18123
Sullivan, Peggie	27975	Sunday, Jessey D.	18124
Sullivan, Conrad	29324	Sunday, Dick	21270
Sullivan, Orval E.	29325	Sunday, Peggie	21279
Sullivan, William H.	29326	Sunday, William	21282
Sullivan, Willis S.	29327	Sunday, William	24700
Sullivan, Melvin	29328	Sunday, Edward	24698
Sullivan, Raymond P.	29329	Sunday, Edward Jr.	24701
Summers, Joseph P.	6946	Sunday, Ellen	24702
Summers, Andrew	9622	Sunday, Silas	25384
Summers, Mary	9623	Sunday, Molly	25588
Summers, Arthur	10008	Sunday, Louella	25862
Summers, Calvin	10009	Sunday, John	28243
Summers, Frederick	10010	Sunday, Andy	28993
Summers, George C.	11671	Sunday, Mary	28994
Summers, Caroline	21651	Sunday, Elva	28995
Summerfield, Isaac	8769	Sunday, Eliza	30015
Summerfield, Daky	8770	Sunshine, Ollie	19200
Summerfield, Sam	19799	Sunshine, Mary	19201
Summerfield, Awy	25868	Sunagoowi, Bullette	21046
Summerfield, Jesse	25569	Sutherland, George Jr.	15674
Summerfield, Swimmer	25870	Sutherland, Lula	15675
Summerfield, Becky	25871	Sutherland, Sequoyah V.	15676
Summerfield, Oowati	25872	Sutherland, Alby M.	17587
Summerfield, Aggie	25873	Sutherlin, Pollie	13144
Summerfield, Jack	27605	Sutherlin, Allie B.	13145
Summerfield, Samantha	27606	Sutherlin, Samuel A.	13146
Summerfield, Joseph	27607	Sutherlin, Leroy	13147
Summerfield, Clem	27608	Sutherlin, Herbert F.	13148
Summerfield, Malinda	27609	Sutherlin, Jesse E.	13149
Summerfield, Mary	32027	Sutherlin, William O.	13150
Summerfield, Scott	32028	Sutherlin, Alice L. D.	13151
Summerfield, Kahsunny	32052	Sutteer, George	25768
Summerfield, Leora	32053	Sutteer, Maud	25769
Summerfield, Celia	32054	Sutton, Joseph S.	2591
Summerfield, Ridge	32055	Sutton, Bettie	3602
Summerfield, Ahseny	32056	Sutton, Willis J.	3603
Summerlin, Georgia L.	15616	Sutton, Pearley	3605
Summerset	18571	Sutton, Joel E.	3606
Summerset, Alsie	18572	Sutton, Sallie	3604
Summerset, Lena	18573	Sutton, Esther F.	3607
Summerset, Wilson	18574	Sutton, Anna L.	3608
Summerset, Sarah	28415	Sutton, Bettie E.	3609
Summerhill, Burton D.	22874	Sutton, William H.	7137
Sumter, Georgian	4638	Sutton, David H.	7138
Sumter, Thomas R.	4639	Sutton, Edward A.	7139
Sumter, Belle	4640	Sutton, John A.	7140
Sumter, Labanie	4641	Sutton, Hattie M.	7141
Sumter, Mattie	4642	Sutton, Claud	7142
Sumter, Susie	4643	Sutton, Bertha	7143
Sumter, Callie	4644	Sutton, Alexander	10718
Sumter, George Maryland	4645	Sutton, John S.	11380
Sumpter, Caldonia S.	21567	Sutton, George F.	11381
Sumpter, Altie M.	21568	Sutton, John R.	11382
Sumpter, Raymond L.	21569	Sutton, Ottis W.	20565
Sumpter, Cecil Victor	21570	Sutton, Lucy C.	32006
Sunday, Jane	12738	Suwat, William	17733
Sunday, Nancy	14353	Suwat, Easter	17734
Sunday, Levi	14354	Suwat, West	17735
Sunday, Annie	15058	Suwat, Oliver	17736
Sunday, Lizzie	15220	Suwat, Margaret	25049
Sunday, Jane	15221	Suwat, Beulah	25055
Sunday, Susan	15223		

Name.	Roll No.
Suwat, Thomas	26737
Suwake, James	19658
Suwake, Elizabeth	19659
Suwake, Mary	19660
Suwake, Lawyer	19661
Suwake, David	21325
Swallow, Sarah	7129
Swallow, William J.	7130
Swallow, Elizabeth M.	7131
Swaggerty, Lucy G.	7531
Swain, Rebecca M.	8699
Swan, Susan	13423
Swan, Paul	13424
Swanock, James	31185
Swanock, Ida M.	31186
Swanock, Bessie Marie	31187
Sweeten, Phillip G.	12632
Sweeten, Emma P.	12633
Sweeten, Clem	12634
Sweeten, Samuel M. Jr.	12635
Sweeten, Roy Cleophas	12636
Sweatman, Mattie J.	7857
Sweatman, Mamie M.	7858
Sweatman, Bessie A.	7859
Sweatman, Ola D.	7860
Sweetwater, William	19366
Sweetwater, John	32634
Sweetwater, Gelda	32635
Sweetwater, Viola	32636
Swift, Frank T.	26758
Swift, Crystie	26759
Swift, Frank B. Jr.	26760
Swift, Mabel	26761
Swift, James F.	26793
Swims, Hannah	4357
Swimm, Mary E.	11579
Swimm, Sarah A.	11580
Swimm, John L.	11620
Swimmer, William	3163
Swimmer, Joseph	3164
Swimmer, James S.	3165
Swimmer, Mary J.	4138
Swimmer, George L.	4139
Swimmer, John	17946
Swimmer, Oowahnenah	17947
Swimmer, Martha	17948
Swimmer, Nancy	17994
Swimmer, Flora	18252
Swimmer, Adam	18361
Swimmer, Ellen	18362
Swimmer, Nellie	18363
Swimmer, Arch	18364
Swimmer, James	18365
Swimmer, Stealer	18399
Swimmer, Sarah	18400
Swimmer, Frank	18402
Swimmer, Jesse Lee	18403
Swimmer, Lizzie	20136
Swimmer, Thomas	20328
Swimmer, Snake	20341
Swimmer, Lilly	20342
Swimmer, William	20638
Swimmer, Susie	20639
Swimmer, Lydia	20640
Swimmer, Nannie	20641
Swimmer, Ollie	20642
Swimmer, Alex	20643
Swimmer, Ella	20711
Swimmer, John	20712
Swimmer, William	25744
Swimmer, William Jr.	25745
Swimmer, Henry	25882
Swimmer, Thomas	26079
Swimmer, Jennie	26080
Swimmer, Eve	26081
Swimmer, Nancy	26082
Swimmer, Lizzie	28405
Swimmer, Edward	28406
Swimmer, George	28487
Swimmer, Lou	28488
Swimmer, Annie	28489
Swimmer, Tom	28490
Swimmer, Coleman	28562

Name.	Roll No.
Swimmer, Wash	28635
Swimmer, Betsy	28636
Swimmer, Cull	28637
Swimmer, Louisa	28638
Swimmer, Jennie	28639
Swimmer, Annie	29727
Swimmer, Charles	30470
Swimmer, Lizzie	32024
Swimmer, Bettie	32025
Swimmer, Lizzie	32227
Sykes, Frederick	5937
Sykes, Alexander	5969
Sykes, Bertie A.	5970
Sykes, Leander	5971
Sykes, Bertha O.	5889
Tabaccowill, Atsie	27305
Tabler, Letha	7490
Tackett, Bert A.	6454
Tackett, Maud P.	6455
Tackett, Walter E.	6456
Tacket, Sarah	15325
Tadpole, Tiger	6269
Tadpole, Sallie	6270
Tadpole, Annie	6271
Tadpole, Rufus	15805
Tadpole, Thomas J.	16283
Tadpole, Commodore P.	16284
Tadpole, Lydia	23358
Tadpole, Cataruy	23359
Tadpole, Polly	23360
Tadpole, Grover	25285
Tadpole, Elmer	25286
Tadpole, Eli	25309
Tadpole, Dorcas	25310
Tadpole, Okla	25311
Tadpole, Lelia	25312
Tadpole, Emma	25313
Tadpole, William H.	25314
Tadpole, Annie	25315
Taft, Clarence A.	31923
Taft, Austin K.	31924
Taft, Asa S.	31925
Taft, Nellie H.	31926
Taft, Sherman W.	31927
Taft, Stanley B.	31928
Taft, Daniel E.	31929
Tague, Nancy J.	12715
Tagg, Sam	18506
Tagg, Sallie	18627
Tagg, John	29696
Tagg, Esther	29697
Tagg, Dutch	29698
Tagg, Maud	32280
Tagg, Arlie	32281
Tagg, Gundeckky	32547
Tahla, Johnson	20449
Tah-la-lah, Checoowah	25910
Tahquette, Annie	18251
Tail, Sallie	20389
Tail, Amos	20540
Tail, French	20773
Tail, Lucy	20774
Tail, Lizzie	20965
Tail, Henry	20966
Tail, Sallie	20967
Tail, George	28479
Tail, Ezekiel	30636
Take, Bluford	18232
Talbott, Thorton S.	7267
Talbott, Sarah F.	7268
Talbott, James A.	7269
Talbott, John W.	14336
Talbert, Abbie E.	11267
Talbert, Anna	11268
Talbert, Mary	11269
Talbert, Ellen	11270
Talbert, Carrie	11271
Talbert, Georgia	11272
Talbert, Grover	11273
Talbert, Mary A.	11843
Talbert, Cora E.	11844
Talbert, Ethel	11845
Talbert, Rosa	11846

Name.	Roll No.	Name.	Roll No.
Talbert, Terry	11847	Tarepen, Lizzie	19654
Talbert, Ivory	11848	Tarepen, Gabriel	19655
Talbert, Bert F.	11849	Tarepen, Betsy	19656
Talbert, Annie	11965	Tarepen, Che-nah-ye	19657
Talbert, Roscoe	11966	Tarripin, Susan C.	14416
Talbert, Otto	11967	Tarksehagee, Nake	29078
Talbert, Jennie	11968	Tar-ske-yah-ke, Lizzie	25807
Talley, Eliza	16484	Tar-ske-yah-ke, George	25808
Talley, Johnie	16485	Tassel, Whitewater	28796
Talley, Artemiss	16486	Tatum, Alice	3319
Talley, Mary J.	26228	Tatum, Lula	3320
Talley, Della R.	26229	Tatum, Sitting Bull	3321
Talley, Ida B.	26230	Tatum, Thomas.	3322
Talley, James W.	22087	Tatum, Jay	3323
Tally, Betsy	4725	Tatum, Dock	3324
Tally, Andrew	4934	Tatum, Earl	21724
Tally, Maggie	4935	Tate, William J.	10721
Tally, Benjamin	14002	Tau-unea-cie, Daniel	9189
Tally, Cynthia	14003	Tau-unea-cie, Jeffie	9190
Tally, Walter E.	14004	Tau-unea-cie, Ollie	9191
Tally, Flora M.	14005	Tau-unea-cie, Lewis	9192
Tally, Rachel	14006	Tau-unea-cie, Jane	17700
Tally, DeWitt C.	14007	Taylor, Jessie	283
Tallow, John	19481	Taylor, Rachel L.	1599
Tallow, Annie	19482	Taylor, Maggie	1600
Tallow, Soggie	19483	Taylor, Nannie C.	1601
Tanner, Nancy	7888	Taylor, Annie A.	1602
Tanner, Peter	7889	Taylor, Mary A.	1603
Tanner, Thomas	9460	Taylor, Susie B.	1604
Tanner, Jennie	11894	Taylor, Richard L. Jr.	1605
Tanner, Verra C.	11895	Taylor, William B.	1606
Tanner, Pheasant	14867	Taylor, Martha	1607
Tanner, Betsy	14868	Taylor, Peggy	1620
Tanner, Minnie	14869	Taylor, Nacissa	2510
Tanner, Scott	14870	Taylor, Minnie E.	3036
Tanner, Samuel	15944	Taylor, Nancy I.	3037
Tanner, Charles	17740	Taylor, Mary A.	3038
Tanner, Betsey	17741	Taylor, John	3050
Tanner, Sarah	17742	Taylor, Nancy R.	3051
Tanner, Lena	17743	Taylor, Theodore	3052
Tanner, Laura	17744	Taylor, John C.	3053
Tanner, Sequoyah	20676	Taylor, Myrtle G.	3054
Tanner, Rachel	26307	Taylor, James F.	3055
Tanner, James	26541	Taylor, Juanita	3056
Tanner, Annie	26542	Taylor, Mary H.	3057
Tanner, Annie Jr.	26543	Taylor, Soper B.	3058
Tanner, Mary	26544	Taylor, Clifton Breckin-	
Tanner, James Jr.	26545	ridge	3059
Tanner, Ollie	26546	Taylor, John M.	3743
Tanner, Maggie A.	26565	Taylor, Juliette L.	4466
Tanner, Sabra L.	26569	Taylor, George	5022
Tanner, Willie W.	26570	Taylor, Charles F.	5277
Tanner, Taylor	28963	Taylor, Jennette	5885
Tanner, Allen	28964	Taylor, Sarah E.	6115
Tanner, Stacy	28965	Taylor, Conney M.	6116
Tanner, Ada M.	31115	Taylor, William F.	6117
Tanner, Frank N.	31116	Taylor, William F.	6554
Tanner, Albert E.	31117	Taylor, Hermas J.	6555
Tanner, Lillie E.	31118	Taylor, Julia M.	6556
Tanner, Clyde V.	31119	Taylor, Zacariah	6557
Tanner, Zoma L.	31120	Taylor, Columbus W.	6558
Tanner, James N.	31361	Taylor, Frank J.	6559
Tanner, Lily	31531	Taylor, Rachel G.	6560
Tanksley, Ella	12669	Taylor, Wiley	6779
Tankersley, Egbert	16952	Taylor, James L.	6877
Tankersley, Augustus		Taylor, Nellie B.	6878
H.	25265	Taylor, Alice M.	6879
Tankersley, Maggie	25266	Taylor, Margarette	6880
Tankersley, Henry A.	25267	Taylor, Cynthia J.	7833
Tankersley, Alexander	25268	Taylor, Robert L.	7834
Tankersley, Jane L.	25269	Taylor, Bertie	7835
Tankersley, John A.	26919	Taylor, Gertie	7836
Tannehill, Lillie M.	9259	Taylor, Surse	7837
Tannehill, Andrew P.	9260	Taylor, Hubert	7838
Tannehill, Dewey	9261	Taylor, Jemima W.	7839
Tannehill, Minnie	9262	Taylor, Chester	8249
Tapp, Elnora	4927	Taylor, Mary A.	8250
Tapp, James	5029	Taylor, Emma C.	8251
Tarapin, Ollie	16493	Taylor, Thomas	9078
Tarepen, Jesse	18466	Taylor, Lydia K.	9510
Tarepen, Joe	18873	Taylor, Alma L.	9511
Tarepen, Wildy	18874	Taylor, Campbell H.	11071
Tarepen, Ellen	18875	Taylor, Stacy B.	11072

Name.	Roll No.	Name.	Roll No.
Taylor, Campbell H. Jr.	11073	Taylor, John	17532
Taylor, George A. M.	11074	Taylor, Mariah	17533
Taylor, Grayson F.	11075	Taylor, Eliza	17943
Taylor, Regina	11076	Taylor, James	20509
Taylor, Mary E.	11308	Taylor, Will	21051
Taylor, John O.	11687	Taylor, Nancy	21052
Taylor, William T.	11693	Taylor, Charlotte T.	21671
Taylor, Beulah M.	11694	Taylor, Arbra F.	21840
Taylor, Lelah M.	11695	Taylor, Henry	22111
Taylor, James E.	11714	Taylor, Moses	22113
Taylor, Lenora M.	11715	Taylor, Katie	23069
Taylor, Dora J.	11716	Taylor, Martha	23712
Taylor, Samuel C.	11717	Taylor, Robert O.	23713
Taylor, Clyde E.	11718	Taylor, Georgia M.	23714
Taylor, Zeunafron E.	11719	Taylor, Frank R.	23715
Taylor, Bertha B.	11720	Taylor, William H.	23716
Taylor, Emma I.	11721	Taylor, John N.	24206
Taylor, Walter A.	11722	Taylor, Roy S.	24208
Taylor, Mary I.	11723	Taylor, Creed N.	24209
Taylor, Thomas D.	12261	Taylor, Anna L.	24210
Taylor, Daniel O.	12262	Taylor, Alfred	25014
Taylor, Lizzie	12519	Taylor, Gertie-	25016
Taylor, David	12772	Taylor, Pearl	25017
Taylor, Edward	13132	Taylor, Callie	25018
Taylor, Cornelia	13133	Taylor, David	25019
Taylor, Roy	13134	Taylor, Carl	25020
Taylor, Mabel	13135	Taylor, Sallie	25021
Taylor, Edward C.	13136	Taylor, Herbert	25022
Taylor, Jesse F.	13137	Taylor, Mattie	25023
Taylor, Mary E.	13138	Taylor, William B.	25024
Taylor, Sarah	13139	Taylor, Grace	25025
Taylor, Flora C.	13140	Taylor, Maud D.	25026
Taylor, John F.	13171	Taylor, Annie	25630
Taylor, James M.	13172	Taylor, Columbus	25631
Taylor, Albert	13173	Taylor, Mary	25632
Taylor, Richard L.	13174	Taylor, Mack	26839
Taylor, Fred E.	13175	Taylor, William	27191
Taylor, Anna E.	13176	Taylor, Sarah	27192
Taylor, Laura E.	13203	Taylor, William Jr.	27193
Taylor, William M.	13204	Taylor, Jackson	27194
Taylor, David Sr.	13205	Taylor, Jennie	27195
Taylor, Robert	13208	Taylor, John S.	27196
Taylor, Edward	13265	Taylor, Eliza	27197
Taylor, James	13266	Taylor, Caldonia C.	27900
Taylor, Alma R.	13347	Taylor, Gussie B.	27901
Taylor, Maggie S.	13778	Taylor, Delta L.	27902
Taylor, William H.	14525	Taylor, Jack	27903
Taylor, Jennie C.	14785	Taylor, Mattie	27904
Taylor, Mina	14787	Taylor, Maggie	27905
Taylor, Bessie	14788	Taylor, George D.	27906
Taylor, Zachy	14789	Taylor, Isaac	28047
Taylor, John B.	14842	Taylor, Thomas J.	28225
Taylor, Albert A.	14856	Taylor, Tryphinia	28307
Taylor, Allie B.	14857	Taylor, Eva	28390
Taylor, Susie P.	14858	Taylor, Rider	28391
Taylor, Malcolm L.	14859	Taylor, Shadock	28393
Taylor, Albert A. Jr.	14860	Taylor, Mary	28392
Taylor, Kate	14932	Taylor, Betsy	28394
Taylor, Mary E.	14933	Taylor, Mary E.	28589
Taylor, Thomas W.	14934	Taylor, James G.	28590
Taylor, Martha A.	14935	Taylor, Joseph W.	28591
Taylor, Henry	14936	Taylor, John M. Jr.	28758
Taylor, Lucinda	14937	Taylor, Eva	28759
Taylor, Andrew J.	14938	Taylor, John M. Jr.	29406
Taylor, Cherry L.	14939	Taylor, Blaine S.	29407
Taylor, Joseph M.	15030	Taylor, Murel	29408
Taylor, John D.	15459	Taylor, Robert C.	29409
Taylor, Wiley A.	15460	Taylor, Florence Thelma	29410
Taylor, Andrew C.	15461	Taylor, Ross	30052
Taylor, Amanda	15859	Taylor, Timothy W.	30146
Taylor, Nancy	16188	Taylor, Flossie G.	30147
Taylor, George	16189	Taylor, Ellen	30161
Taylor, Flora	16190	Taylor, Mary	30162
Taylor, Effie	16191	Taylor, Laura E.	32010
Taylor, Henry	16192	Taylor, Henry E.	32234
Taylor, Delora	16193	Taylor, Georgia L.	32235
Taylor, Bettie	16194	Taylor, Isom	32557
Taylor, John	16195	Taylor, James	32716
Taylor, Joseph	16196	Teague, Rosella	2857
Taylor, Fred	16197	Teague, Murttle	2858
Taylor, Campbell H.	16310	Teague, Mary J.	6433
Taylor, Robert R.	16311	Teague, Frances J.	6434
Taylor, Thomas F.	16318	Teague, Cora A.	6435

Name.	Roll No.	Name.	Roll No.
Teague, Mary E.	6436	Teel, Etha	6685
Teague, Benjamin F.	6437	Teel, George	6686
Teague, Henry A.	6438	Teel, John	6687
Tecumseh, Lucy	25863	Teel, Carrie A.	14420
Tecumseh, Dick	25864	Tell, Sarah E.	6568
Tecumseh, Robert	25865	Tell, Alice C.	6570
Teehee, Susie B.	6520	Tell, Charles K.	26422
Teehee, Annie N.	6521	Ten Brook, Mattie G.	206
Teehee, Oscar E.	6522	Ten Brook, Earling	207
Teehee, Felix M.	6523	Ten Brook, Ida J.	208
Teehee, Moody M.	6525	Tenkiller, Nancy	20838
Teehee, Christian G.	6526	Tenkiller, Della	20839
Teehee, Margaret	6538	Tenkiller, Chicaleelee	20840
Teehee, Houston B.	14727	Tenkiller, Layyah	20841
Teehee, Peggy	15977	Tennison, Lizzie	32776
Teehee, Jesse	15978	Terrell, Elizabeth	1444
Teehee, Charles	15979	Terrell, Sarah	1445
Teehee, Lizzie	27466	Terrell, Charles	1446
Teehee, Lee	30453	Terrell, William	1447
Teehee, Henry	30454	Terrell, Dennis	1448
Teehee, Moses	30455	Terrell, Lucinda	1449
Teehee, Colbert	30456	Terrell, Jennie	1450
Tehee, Charles	16000	Terrell, William R.	5477
Tehee, Lizzie	16001	Terrell, Ross Fred Jr.	6840
Tehee, Florence	16002	Terrell, Dora	11083
Tehee, Ada	16003	Terrell, Ruby B.	11085
Tehee, Hoke	16004	Terrell, Thomas H.	11492
Tehee, Maggie	16005	Terrell, Betsy	13262
Tehee, Stephen B. Jr.	16618	Terrell, Polly	13915
Tehee, Nelson	17849	Terrell, James	14579
Tehee, John	18465	Terrell, Annie	15664
Tehee, Eli	19771	Terrell, John	15666
Tehee, Olsey	19772	Terrell, Joseph	15667
Tehee, Nellie	19773	Terrell, Richard	15668
Tehee, George	19774	Terrell, Samuel	15669
Tehee, Grant	19775	Terrell, Cynthia	15670
Tehee, Elsie	19776	Terrell, Samuel	15721
Tehee, Charlie	20347	Terrell, William	16080
Tehee, Lizzie	20348	Terrell, Elizabeth	16081
Tehee, Mary	20349	Terrell, Katie	16082
Tehee, George	20350	Terrell, Joseph	16083
Tehee, Jim	20680	Terrell, Ella	16084
Tehee, Jim	21207	Terrell, Susan	16085
Tehee, Jack	21208	Terrell, Viola	16086
Tehee, Betsy	21209	Terrell, John	16454
Tehee, Tatiah	21210	Terrell, Samantha	16455
Tehee, Nancy	21211	Terrell, Albert	16456
Tehee, Jess	21226	Terrell, Julia	16457
Tehee, Dora	21227	Terrell, Mary	16458
Tehee, Susie	21229	Terrell, Ellis	16459
Tehee, Nannie	21230	Terrell, Jackson	16460
Tehee, Polly	21231	Terrell, Green	17886
Tehee, Charlie	21451	Terrell, Aaron	17887
Tehee, Nancy	21452	Terrell, William	21363
Tehee, Little Bird	21453	Terrell, Robert M.	22123
Tehee, Rosabelle	23215	Terrell, Emma	22124
Tehee, Stephen	25387	Terrell, Bean	31976
Tehee, Martin	25388	Terrell, Albert	31977
Tehee, Schofield	25389	Terrill, Albert P.	12791
Tehee, Lizzie	25390	Terrill, Willie E.	12792
Tehee, Munroe	25391	Terrill, Una L.	12793
Tehee, Levi	25392	Terrill, May	12794
Tehee, Sequoyah	25393	Terrill, Pearl R.	12795
Tehee, Davis	25394	Terrill, Edward M. Jr.	12796
Tehee, Tildon	25976	Terrill, Rossor	12797
Tehee, Susan	28305	Terrill, Fannie O.	12798
Tehee, Eliza	28306	Terrill, Noah L.	12799
Tehee, Alex	30676	Terrill, John G.	22997
Tehee, Kaheta	30677	Terrill, Eulah	22999
Tehee, David	32586	Terrill, Hazel	23000
Tehee, Charles	32772	Terrill, Mamie	23001
Teekahlanneesky, Jack	19824	Terrill, Edmon J.	23002
Teekahneyeskee, John	1001	Terrill, Carl	23003
Teekahneyeskee, Jim	1002	Terrapin, Charlie	20934
Teekahneyeskee, George	1003	Terrapin, Callie	20935
Tekahoo-geesky,	19448	Terrapin, Abraham	20952
Tekahoo-geesky, Ainsey	19449	Terrapin, Betsy	20953
Tekahnawheel, Olsie	26954	Terrapin, James	27706
Tekahnawheel, Ollie	30630	Terrapin, Betsy	27707
Teel, Lafayette	6681	Terrapin, Mollie	27708
Teel, William L.	6682	Terrapin, Lydia	27709
Teel, John H.	6683	Terrapin, Sallie	27710
Teel, Nannie	6684	Terrapin, Charles	29505

Name.	Roll No.	Name.	Roll No.
Terrapin, Polly	29506	Thomas, William B.	14640
Terrapin, Wakie	32345	Thomas, Mable	14641
Terrapin, Thomas	32566	Thomas, Lucius F.	14990
Terrapin, Jennie	32567	Thomas, John B.	14991
Terrapin, Lydia	32568	Thomas, Rachel	15665
Terrapin, Charlie	32569	Thomas, Annie	15672
Terrepinhead, Kate	19517	Thomas, Mary M.	18033
Terrepinhead, Nancy	19518	Thomas, Samuel	21578
Terrepinhead, John	19519	Thomas, Arch W.	21663
Tesquantmee	20572	Thomas, Fred	21664
Tesquantmee, Rachel	20573	Thomas, Laura J.	21665
Teter, Alice	7017	Thomas, Lillie B.	21666
Teter, Clara	7018	Thomas, Job	31665
Teter, Myrtle	7019	Thomas, Blue	13484
Teter, Walter,	7020	Thomas, Lydia	28154
Teter, Edna	7021	Thomason, Maggie B.	850
Teter, Goldie E.	7022	Thomason, Daniel W.	851
Thatcher, Sarah E.	32217	Thomason, Freddie D.	852
Thatcher, Joel M.	32218	Thompson, Louisa	72
Thatcher, Mary L.	32527	Thompson, Katherine J.	73
Theurer, Alta	31938	Thompson, Claude A.	75
Theurer, Mary E.	31939	Thompson, Gilbert S.	22035
Theurer, Lena	31940	Thompson, Milton K.	74
Theurer, Alta	31941	Thompson, Daltòn A.	667
Thirsty, William	18530	Thompson, Eernest J.	668
Thirsty, Susie	19409	Thompson, Peggy	680
Thirsty, Ollie	19410	Thompson, Will	681
Thirsty, Jennie	19783	Thompson, Flora	683
Thirsty,	19782	Thompson, Joel	684
Thirsty, Nancy	19784	Thompson, Lena	685
Thirsty, Nahyesah	19785	Thompson, Rachel	1714
Thirsty, Goodmoney	19816	Thompson, Ella A.	1715
Thirsty, Annie	19817	Thompson, Joseph C. Jr.	1716
Thirsty, Darkie	30579	Thompson, William C.	1717
Thirsty, Infant	30589	Thompson, Susie	1718
Thomas, Thomas C.	338	Thompson, Calvin H.	1719
Thomas, Charlie	339	Thompson, Andrew J.	1720
Thomas, Henry	340	Thompson, Jesse	3298
Thomas, Myrtle	341	Thompson, Emma	3299
Thomas, Thomas J.	342	Thompson, Geneva B.	3300
Thomas, Daisy	343	Thompson, William M.	3418
Thomas, Martha E.	344	Thompson, Mary	3789
Thomas, James A.	345	Thompson, Margy May	3790
Thomas, Mary H.	346	Thompson, Elizabeth A.	5669
Thomas, Claud	347	Thompson, Louisa T.	6458
Thomas, Eliza G.	1925	Thompson, James W.	6463
Thomas, George F.	1926	Thompson, Lewis	6464
Thomas, Jimmy T.	1930	Thompson, Carrie	6465
Thomas, Menarva T.	2035	Thompson, Clara C.	6552
Thomas, George E.	2494	Thompson, Stella R.	6553
Thomas, Lettie L.	2495	Thompson, Eugenie M.	7014
Thomas, Lizzie	3447	Thompson, Walter A	7016
Thomas, Martha J.	6640	Thompson, Robert	7420
Thomas, George W.	6641	Thompson, Myrtle	8065
Thomas, Beulah B.	6642	Thompson, Mary B. B.	8068
Thomas, John P.	6643	Thompson, Flora B.	8106
Thomas, Beart A.	6644	Thompson, Glena M.	8107
Thomas, James	6645	Thompson, James A.	8147
Thomas, Joseph	6646	Thompson, Sarah	8148
Thomas, Ira F.	6647	Thompson, Lewis K.	8553
Thomas, Lettie J.	6805	Thompson, James R.	8555
Thomas, Johnanna	7406	Thompson, Thomas F.	8571
Thomas, Henry R.	7407	Thompson, Susan C.	8572
Thomas, Napoleon F.	7408	Thomason, Rachel F.	8880
Thomas, Jessie A.	7409	Thomason, Bertha E.	8881
Thomas, John L.	7410	Thomason, George L.	8882
Thomas, Thura	7411	Thompson, Maggie L.	9181
Thomas, Ellis	7412	Thompson, Albert L.	9182
Thomas, Elizabeth	7413	Thompson, Rachel	9454
Thomas, Jimmie	8122	Thompson, Hallie	9703
Thomas, Thomas C.	8621	Thompson, Eador J.	10942
Thomas, Vera L.	8622	Thompson, Roda F.	10944
Thomas, Nicholas	8677	Thompson, Ada G.	10945
Thomas, Oscar	10725	Thompson, Ruby M.	10946
Thomas, Stella S.	10943	Thompson, James P.	10971
Thomas, William E.	10947	Thompson, Youless	10972
Thomas, Eugenia	12750	Thompson, Earl	10973
Thomas, Viola B.	12751	Thompson, Reuben C.	11541
Thomas, George H.	12752	Thompsqn, Ollie R.	11542
Thomas, Arvol V.	12753	Thompson, George A.	11543
Thomas, Threon T.	12754	Thompson, Floyd O.	11544
Thomas, Mary L.	14638	Thompson, Lottie M.	11545
Thomas, Southey E.	14639	Thompson, Jessie S.	11546

Name.	Roll No.
Thompson, Mary E.	11911
Thompson, Letitia V.	11912
Thompson, Mary A.	11913
Thompson, Francis L.	11914
Thompson, Joseph H.	11915
Thompson, William C.	12124
Thompson, Hooley D.	13332
Thompson, Alice E.	13333
Thompson, John M.	13334
Thompson, James P.	13917
Thompson, Maggie M.	13918
Thompson, James M.	13919
Thompson, Joseph M.	13930
Thompson, Lula	13931
Thompson, Anna C.	13932
Thompson, Edward H.	13933
Thompson, Mamie L.	13934
Thompson, Robert J.	14018
Thompson, Caleb S.	14036
Thompson, Lihu F.	14200
Thompson, John F.	14282
Thompson, John N.	14283
Thompson, Mary S.	14284
Thompson, Nellie	14285
Thompson, Margaret L.	14286
Thompson, Jesse C.	14287
Thompson, William W. L.	14288
Thompson, David L.	14290
Thompson, George W	14291
Thompson, John H.	14292
Thompson, Jesse D.	14380
Thompson, James W.	14421
Thompson, James M.	14422
Thompson, Lilly C.	14423
Thompson, Daniel G.	14424
Thompson, Bertha L.	14425
Thompson, Della M.	14426
Thompson, William E.	14451
Thompson, Hiram A.	14472
Thompson, John M.	14479
Thompson, Caleb A.	14499
Thompson, John D.	14500
Thompson, Sarah A.	14501
Thompson, Florence L.	14502
Thompson, Gertrude M.	14503
Thompson, Jesse C.	14504
Thompson, Gracie L.	14505
Thompson, James A.	14506
Thompson, William J.	14507
Thompson, Francis B.	14508
Thompson, Richard L.	14509
Thompson, Alfred D.	14510
Thompson, Ollie	14693
Thompson, Rose	14902
Thompson, Eloise	14903
Thompson, Ida F.	14904
Thompson, Narcissa	15739
Thompson, Ethel	15740
Thompson, Clem	15804
Thompson, Julia A.	15910
Thompson, John G.	15911
Thompson, Benjamin R.	15912
Thompson, Mary A.	15913
Thompson, Joseph D.	15914
Thompson, Ray H.	15915
Thompson, George R.	15917
Thompson, Felix	15953
Thompson, Malinda L.	17280
Thompson, Florence E.	17281
Thompson, Nora B.	17282
Thompson, Nellie F.	17283
Thompson, Ira	17284
Thompson, Ella. M.	17285
Thompson, Mary Malinda	17286
Thompson, Charles	17619
Thompson, Henry	18507
Thompson, Sarah	18508
Thompson, Judge	18509
Thompson, Ellen	18510
Thompson, Lacey	18511
Thompson, Henry	19755

Name.	Roll No.
Thompson, Weakie	20528
Thompson, John	20688
Thompson, Aggie	20689
Thompson, Arch	21405
Thompson, Annie	21406
Thompson, Nancy	21408
Thompson, Lucy M.	21931
Thompson, Cherokee C.	22148
Thompson, Frank	22850
Thompson, Nannie	22851
Thompson, Donnie	22852
Thompson, Lillian	22853
Thompson, Sallie	22854
Thompson, Willie	22855
Thompson, Charley	22856
Thompson, John R.	22857
Thompson, Joseph L.	23974
Thompson, Alice	23976
Thomposn, Ada	23977
Thompson, Ollie V.	23978
Thompson, Annie K.	23979
Thompson, William P.	23991
Thompson, Elizabeth C.	23992
Thompson, Sadie P.	23993
Thompson, Elizabeth C. Jr.	23994
Thompson, Georgia	25104
Thompson, Katie M.	25105
Thompson, William C.	25106
Thompson, Robert H.	25134
Thompson, William F.	25135
Thompson, Louis A.	25136
Thompson, John	25137
Thompson, Mary A.	25138
Thompson, Jesse C.	25139
Thompson, Albert Troy	25165
Thompson, Helen	25302
Thompson, William	25917
Thompson, Eve	25918
Thompson, Joseph	25919
Thompson, George	25920
Thompson, Robert F.	26032
Thompson, James W.	26033
Thompson, Lark A.	26034
Thompson, John Lewis	26035
Thompson, Laura	26301
Thompson, Thomas L.	26410
Thompson, Mamie O.	26411
Thompson, Minnie O.	26412
Thompson, David W.	26413
Thompson, Jennie	26580
Thompson, Joseph	32482
Thompson, Susie	32783
Thompson, Martha	32888
Thompson, Newton	26581
Thompson, Jessie	26730
Thompson, John L.	26765
Thompson, Oliver N.	26766
Thompson, Nathaniel A.	26767
Thompson, Clarence E.	26768
Thompson, Narcissa	27340
Thompson, William B.	27341
Thompson, Gracie	27342
Thompson, Katie	27343
Thompson, Lorena	27480
Thompson, Robert H.	30376
Thompson, Ethel	30377
Thompson, Etta M.	30378
Thompson, Robert L.	30379
Thompson, Mary E.	30380
Thompson, James C.	30612
Thompson, Che-ga-yu	30667
Thompson, Drunken	30707
Thompson, Gilbert T. Sr.	30744
Thompson, Gilbert T. Jr.	30745
Thompson, Matthew	30746
Thompson, Allison	30747
Thompson, Ernest W.	30748
Thompson, Mamie	30749
Thompson. Allison Archibald	30750
Thompson, James K.	30751
Thompson, Joseph G.	30752

Name.	Roll No.
Thompson, Ernest	30753
Thompson, Allison G.	30754
Thompson, Ernest T.	30755
Thompson, Hugh C.	30756
Thompson, Jane A.	31042
Thompson, Clara M.	31043
Thompson, George L. G.	31044
Thompson, James C.	31045
Thompson, James H:	31214
Thompson, Sarah	31215
Thompson, Jesse	31216
Thompson, Emily J.	23572
Thompson, Joseph F.	23453
Thome, Lucy	5601
Thorne, Cull	13905
Thorne, Elias C.	13904
Thorne, Julia A.	13906
Thorne, Caleb	13907
Thorne, Jaennette	13908
Thorne, John	13909
Thorne, Cull Jr.	13910
Thorne, William	13911
Thorne, Oscar	13912
Thorne, Arthur	13913
Thorne, Cherokee L.	13914
Thorne, William P.	15099
Thorne, Maude E.	15100
Thorne, Clifford	15101
Thorne, Anna M.	15102
Thorne, Percy A.	15103
Thorne, Everts	16633
Thorne, Charles	16634
Thorne, William	16635
Thorne, Maggie	16636
Thorne, Esther	16637
Thorne, Arthur	16638
Thorne, Alonzo	16639
Thorne, Ephraim	22069
Thorne, William R.	22070
Thorne, Louella	22071
Thorne, Jacob H.	25225
Thorne, Walter	25226
Thornton, William I.	495
Thornton, Amanda M.	496
Thornton, Alice	497
Thornton, Thomas J.	498
Thornton, Reese	1025
Thornton, Mike	1026
Thornton, John W.	1027
Thornton, James	1303
Thornton, Jesse J.	1304
Thornton, Joseph	1781
Thornton, Peggie	1782
Thornton, Lila	1783
Thornton, Jesse	1784
Thornton, Wiley	1785
Thornton, William	1786
Thornton, Eli	1787
Thornton, Smith	2967
Thornton, William	2968
Thornton, Mary	3189
Thornton, Hermon	3190
Thornton, Wallace	3308
Thornton, Minnie	3309
Thornton, Wallace Jr.	3310
Thornton, Joseph	3311
Thornton, Walter	3312
Thornton, John K.	3313
Thornton, William	3699
Thornton, Flora A.	4502
Thornton, Owen F.	4503
Thornton, Charles A.	4871
Thornton, Guy E.	5245
Thornton, Nancy	5346
Thornton, Lucile	5247
Thornton, Thomas J.	5248
Thornton, Flora	5249
Thornton, Lewis R.	5347
Thornton, Ellen S.	5348
Thornton, George W.	9193
Thornton, Percy M.	9042
Thornton, Ora J.	9194
Thornton, Nellie E.	9195

Name.	Roll No.
Thornton, Mary M.	9196
Thornton, Nora V.	9197
Thornton, Lucy G.	9198
Thornton, George R.	9199
Thornton, Blanchie E.	9200
Thornton, Lizzie	10518
Thornton, Henry J.	10520
Thornton, Murrell H.	12762
Thornton, Gladys M.	12763
Thornton, Polly	20011
Thornton, Nellie	20090
Thornton, Johnson	20124
Thornton, Sallie	20533
Thornton, Tookah	20534
Thornton, Arch	20535
Thornton, Thomas	20536
Thornton, Minnie	20923
Thornton, Cherokee	21883
Thornton, Archie A.	22147
Thornton, Susan E.	22641
Thornton, Lizzie	22893
Thornton, Mary E.	22894
Thornton, Minnie L.	22895
Thornton, Ellen S.	23099
Thornton, Carrie	26386
Thornton, William L.	28772
Thornton, William H.	28990
Thornton, Orville E.	30152
Thornton, Josie M.	11610
Thornton, Clement Y.	5721
Thornbrugh, Hortense D.	10550
Threekiller, Joseph	1243
Threekiller, Mary	1244
Threekiller, James	1245
Threekiller, Jennie	1246
Threekiller, Chenarse	1247
Threekiller, Kayah	1248
Threekiller, Johnson	1249
Threekiller, Thomas	19674
Thrower, Ella	19835
Thrower, Nancy	19836
Thrower, Charlie	25786
Thurman, Belle	6706
Thurman, Lula E.	6707
Thurman, Willie J.	6708
Thurman, Levi R.	6709
Thurman, Della	11452
Thurman, Virginia A.	11453
Thurman, Ida B.	21476
Thurman, Ada	21477
Thurman, Ada	21741
Thurman, Elizabeth	21742
Thurman, Mary C.	22391
Thurman, Lillie	22392
Thurman, Salina	22393
Thurman, Finis	22394
Tiblow, Obediah	10176
Tiblow, Charles	10362
Tiblow, Bertha	10367
Tiblow, Charles	10368
Tiblow, William S.	10405
Tiblow, Lulu	10406
Tiblow, Beatrice	10407
Tiblow, Mary A.	32201
Tiblow, George W.	32481
Tickeater, Cahseelouee	13601
Tickeater, Boudinot	17867
Tickeater, Alley	17868
Tickeater, John	17869
Tickneskey, John	14740
Tickneskey, Sarah	21470
Tickaneesky, Sarah	17975
Tidwell, John	1503
Tidwell, Charner	1548
Tidwell, John W.	1549
Tidwell, Versanoy	1551
Tidwell, Cella E.	1552
Tidwell, Beulah	6123
Tidwell, James M.	6124
Tidwell, Pleasant H.	14687
Tidwell, James P.	14688
Tidwell, Minor L.	22407

Name.	Roll No.	Name.	Roll No.
Tidwell, Ada M.	27951	Tipton, John L.	16463
Tidwell, Robert G.	27952	Tipton, Cora A.	16464
Tidmore, Emma	16713	Tipton, Lonie	21845
Tidmore, Loy H.	16714	Tipton, Robert W.	25195
Tidmore, Laura M.	16715	Tipton, Fannie	25196
Tieaskie, Elizabeth	1494	Tipton, William	25197
Tieskie, George	20071	Tipton, Oscar	25198
Tieskie, Elias	20072	Tipton, Frank	25199
Tieskie, Annie	21760	Tipton, Annie	25200
Tiffany, Wallace	27497	Tipton, Eugene E.	25397
Tiffany, Andrew	27498	Tipton, John H.	25398
Tiffany, Alex	27499	Tipton, Minerva J.	25399
Tiger, William J.	8866	Tipton, Myrtle	25400
Tiger, Thomas	9380	Tipton, Laura	25401
Tiger, Lizzie	11574	Tipton, Samuel	25402
Tiger, George	11575	Tipton, Fannie	28854
Tiger, Mary	11576	Tipton, George L.	28855
Tiger, Lillie	11577	Tipton, Albert M.	28856
Tiger, Emma	18056	Tipton, Cora A.	28857
Tiger, Nellie	18528	Titsworth, Nannie	5140
Tiger, Hettie	18529	Titsworth, Reaves S.	5142
Tiger, John	19364	Titsworth, Kate	30086
Tiger, Flora	32268	Titsworth, Eugene	30088
Tilden, Tyler	6441	Titsworth, Speer	30089
Tilden, Eliza	6442	Tittle, James M.	8061
Tilden, Peter	6443	Tittle, Effie C.	8062
Tilden, Daniel	16201	Tittle, Henry C.	9232
Tiley, William A.	11724	Tittle, Robert W.	9246
Tiley, Etta O.	11725	Tittle, Ottis W.	9247
Tiley, Abel R.	11726	Tittle, Hugh T. E.	9248
Tiley, Lottie M.	11727	Tittle, Mary A.	9249
Tiley, Ida B.	11729	Tittle, Robert W. J.	9250
Tiley, Mary G.	24745	Tittle, Elizabeth.	25147
Timmons, Minnie E.	3141	Tittle, Golie M.	25148
Timmons, Elizabeth	12297	Tittle, Clyde L.	25149
Timmons, Viola	12298	Tittle, Omer A.	25150
Timmons, Dott	12299	Tittle, Bessie	25151
Timmons, Thestar M.	21825	Tittle, Lelia	25152
Timms, Mattie	16436	Tittle, Frederick	26841
Timms, William A.	16437	Tittle, Vera	26842
Timson, John	4572	Tittle, Emery E.	26843
Timson, Maud	4573	Tittle, James D.	28019
Timson, John	4574	Tittle, Daniel J.	28020
Timson, Neppie	5757	Tittle, William C.	28021
Timpson, Susan	7914	Todd, John	12743
Timpson, Samuel	7915	Todd, Mary M.	12744
Timpson, Nancy	7916	Todd, Florence E.	12745
Timpson, Kate	7917	Todd, Lois L.	12746
Timberlake, Margarett	9120	Todd, Susie	30268
Timberlake, Jennie	9592	Toffelmire, Bettie	27522
Timberlake, William R.	11790	Tolen, Soldier	18074
Timberlake, John A.	29222	Tolen, Rachel	18075
Timberlake, Florence N.	29223	Tolen, Watt	18077
Tinney, Lydia	3841	Tolen, Jack	18078
Tinney, Laura M.	3843	Tolen, Sallie	19337
Tiner, William J.	28292	Toney, Eli	16434
Tiner, Willie C.	28293	Toney, Levi	17008
Tincup, James	6230	Toney, Susan	17009
Tincup, Lucinda	6231	Toney, Calvin H.	17010
Tincup, Henry	6232	Toney, Cicero D.	17011
Tincup, James	6233	Toney, Bettie	17012
Tincup, Florence	6234	Toney, Katie	17013
Tincup, Mary	6235	Toney, Sallie	17014
Tincup, Edmond	6236	Toney, John	18750
Tincup, Austin	6237	Toney, Jennie	18751
Tincup, William W.	29448	Toney, Thomas	18752
Tincup, May	29449	Toney, Nancy	18753
Tincup, Joseph E.	29450	Toney, Mary	18754
Tincup, Jesse W.	29451	Toney, George	18755
Tindle, Annie	15554	Toney, Jesse	18756
Tindle, Julia	15555	Toney, Famous	18757
Tindle, Wallie	15556	Toney, Lee	18758
Tindle, Henry C.	15557	Toney, John	22107
Tindle, Alexander	15558	Toney, Susie	22108
Tindle, Ginsie	15559	Toney, Jennie	22109
Tindle, Jeff	15560	Toney, George	22110
Tinoowie, Ooyatuck	19619	Toolate, Oolawcut	19743
Tinoowie, Nannie	19620	Toolate, Ahnie	19744
Tinoowie, Jennie	19621	Toolate, Aily	19745
Tinoowie, Mary	19622	Toolate, Davis	19746
Tinoowie, Quahleyuke	19623	Toolate, Nelson	19747
Tipton, Rufus	13879	Toolate, Warcester	19749
Tipton, William L.	14611	Toolate, Buck	25785

Name.	Roll No.	Name.	Roll No.
Tooley, William	28722	Treuman, Benjamin O.	1423
Too-noo-wee, Sally	17151	Trickett, Mary E.	426
Too noo-wee, Nancy	19171	Trickett, Johnnie M.	427
Tootle, Rachel	25153	Trickett, Leora A.	428
Tootle, Harry	25154	Trickey, Mary E.	26921
Tootle, Charles	25155	Trimble, Elizabeth	26786
Tooniye	25787	Trippard, James R.	5079
Too-su-wah-lah-tah,		Trippard, Annie	5080
Swimmer	18557	Triplet, Anna	15126
Too-su-wah-lah-tah,		Triplett, Ollie	16010
Jennie	18558	Triplett, William	16011
Too-su-wah-lah-tah,		Triplett, Charlotte	16012
Lucy	25825	Triplett, Daniel	16013
Too-su-wah-lah-tah,		Triplett, Evert	16014
Dirteater	25826	Triplett, William Jr.	16015
Torbett, Walter T.	7901	Triplett, John C.	16016
Torbett, William G.	9926	Triplett, Susan	16017
Torrey, Carrie	30305	Triplettt, Thomas W.	16452
Tovey, Anna M.	24038	Triplett, Lizzie	16453
Tovey, Thomas W.	24039	Triplett, Mary A.	16995
Tovey, Bella M.	24040	Triplett, Edward D.	28328
Tovey, Annie L.	24041	Triplett, Lucy E.	28329
Tovey, Frank L.	24042	Triplett, Mary P.	28330
Tovey, Hooley B.	24043	Tritthart, Minerva	8645
Tovey, Ruby D.	24044	Tritthart, Henry	8646
Tovey, Novel W. J.	24045	Tritthart, James	8647
Tower, Jane	25376	Tritthart, Robert Ray	8648
Tower, Isaac	26188	Tritthart, Lorena	24107
Towers, Clem R.	27462	Trott, James	2965
Towers, Charlotte J.	27463	Trott, James C.	7352
Towers, Maud L.	27464	Trott, Dora	7353
Towers, James E.	27465	Trott, Willie	7354
Towey, John	28456	Trott, William L.	8480
Towie, Jeff	18079	Trott, Dot F.	8481
Towie, Polly	18080	Trott, William H.	9251
Towie, Lou	18500	Trott, Eugene H.	26520
Towie, Wilson	18527	Trott, Hardin H.	27560
Towie, Samuel	28955	Trott, May	27594
Towler, Josephine	5525	Trott, Belle	27595
Towler, Cinderella	5526	Trott, Clarence E.	30087
Townsend, Charlotte	6383	Trott, John R.	30851
Townsend, Charlotte	6384	Trott, William O.	30883
Townsend, Jesse	16712	Trotter, Luella	3760
Townsend, George	29956	Trotter, Bessie L.	3761
Townsend, Laura	29957	Trotter, Louie E.	3762
Townsend, Addie	29958	Trotter, Minnie B.	8010
Townsend, Walter	29959	Trotter, Lula B.	8011
Townsend, Jesse	29960	Trotter, Hardin H.	8012
Towry, Emma C.	3377	Trotter, Sarah M.	8013
Towser, Charles	11412	Troglin, John S.	11445
Trammel, Annie	3454	Troglin, Louisa	11446
Trammel, Rossie I.	3455	Troglin, Wesley S.	11447
Trammel, Earle E.	3456	Troglin, James H.	11460
Trammel, Lizzie W.	3457	Troglin, Elihu M.	11463
Trammel, Dennis W.	3458	Troglin. Isaac M.	11464
Trammel, Elba T.	3459	Troth, Susan E.	24010
Trammel. Teddy R.	3460	Troth, Mary M.	24011
Trammell, Lue Emma	3862	Troth, Beuna V.	24012
Trammell, Charles L.	3863	Troth, Vera L.	24013
Trammell, Elmer	3864	Troth, Viola Essie	24015
Trammell. Thomas	3866	Trottingwolf, Lincoln	10159
Trainor, Walter E.	16649	Trottingwolf, Susan	10160
Trainor, Leonard E.	11654	Trottingwolf, Nelson	10161
Trainor, May	11655	Trottingwolf, Sequoyah	10162
Trainor, Clifford R.	11656	Trottingwolf, Clarence	10163
Trainor, Emmett Hunter	11657	Trout, George W.	9202
Trainor, Hattie C.	14102	Trout, Mattie A.	9203
Trainor, Nevermore	17253	Trout, James M.	9204
Trainor, John T.	30392	Trout, Henry	9205
Trapp, Joseph	12393	Trout, Isaac D.	9206
Treasurer, Clem	20737	Trout, Georgia	9207
Treasurer, Cornelius	28496	Trout, Creed	9208
Treasurer. Nancy	28497	Trout, Samuel	8105
Trent, Mollie	4877	Trout, Andrew M.	23780
Trent, Richard	4878	Trout, James	23782
Trent, Martin	4879	Trout, William	23783
Trent, Thomas	4880	Trout, Ethel	23784
Trent, Jefferson	12908	Trout, Newton	23785
Trent, Edward A.	16838	Trout, Wyley B.	23786
Trent, Sarah M.	16839	Trout, Valena V.	23904
Trent, Mary E.	16840	Trout, Mary Irene	23905
Treuman, Mary	1419	Trout, Logan	24021
Treuman, Samuel O.	1422	Trout, George W.	24023

Name.	Roll No.	Name.	Roll No.
Trout, Buford L.	24024	Turnham, Harrold H.	3567
Trout, Edith M.	24025	Turner, Minnie E.	8959
Trout, Cornelia E.	27582	Turner, Ruby	8960
Truitt, Mamie H.	4036	Turner, Pearl	8961
Tucker, Marcus L.	1652	Turner, James B.	8962
Tucker, Adolphus L.	1653	Turner, Ray	8963
Tucker, Newell E.	1654	Turner, Mary E.	10191
Tucker, Luer C.	1655	Turner, William	15939
Tucker, Felix A.	1656	Turner, Nellie	15940
Tucker, Luther C.	1657	Turner, Daniel	15941
Tucker, Estell G.	1658	Turner, Iva	15942
Tucker, William	7764	Turner, Isaac	15943
Tucker, Ella	8288	Turner, Annie	15987
Tucker, Mary F.	8289	Turner, Anna L.	15988
Tucker, Annie M.	8290	Turner, Susie	15989
Tucker, John M. Jr.	8514	Turner, Jesse	16448
Tucker, Samuel L.	8515	Turner, Josephine	16449
Tucker, Logan	8714	Turner, John	16450
Tucker, Martha	9293	Turner, Nancy	16451
Tucker, Cornelia B.	9294	Turner, Annie	18614
Tucker, Edith M.	9295	Turner, Martha	19415
Tucker, Inez L.	9296	Turner, Mary	20919
Tucker, Beulah F.	9297	Turner, Susan	20920
Tucker, John M.	10357	Turner, Louisa	21274
Tucker, Annie	10358	Turner, John W.	24761
Tucker, Edith	10359	Turner, Edith A.	24762
Tucker, Blanche	10361	Turner, Daniel W.	24763
Tucker, Daniel	10442	Turner, Galena M.	24764
Tucker, John S.	11813	Turner, William D.	26130
Tucker, Guy	11814	Turner, Jessie M.	30283
Tucker, Evlyn	11815	Turner, William B.	30284
Tucker, Charles	16536	Turner, Henry F.	30285
Tucker, Betty	16537	Turner, Saladin W.	30286
Tucker, Alice	16540	Turn, Sallie	15985
Tucker, Fannie	16541	Turn, Alex	15986
Tucker, Thompson	16542	Turn, William	25810
Tucker, David,	17492	Turn, Henry	25814
Tucker, Susan	17493	Turley, Mary	11793
Tucker, George	17496	Turley, William B.	11794
Tucker, Johnson	17503	Turley, Laura Bell	11795
Tucker, Dudley H.	17512	Turtle, Ned	19018
Tucker, Charles D.	17513	Turtle, Margaret	20270
Tucker, Sallie	18448	Turtle, Arch	20320
Tucker, Jennie	18820	Turtle, Fannie	20321
Tucker, Isaac	18838	Turtle, Charlotte	20322
Tucker, Thomas	18839	Turtle, Charley	20323
Tucker, Rachel	18840	Turtle, Adam	20324
Tucker, Ezekiel	21000	Turtle, William	20325
Tucker, Lizzie	21001	Turtle, Emma	20326
Tucker, Lucinda	21003	Turtle, Joe	20327
Tucker, Levi	21295	Turtle, William	20787
Tucker, Annie	21296	Turtle, Sallie	20788
Tucker, Ollie	21297	Turtle, Charles	20789
Tucker, William	21298	Turtle, Susan	20790
Tucker, Jennie	21445	Turtle, Cah-neh-ee	30649
Tucker, Calvin	21711	Turtle, Takie	30650
Tucker, George	21761	Turnover, Margarett	4351
Tucker, George H.	21762	Tweedle, Florence M.	4084
Tucker, William	21763	Tweedle, Susan Frances	32822
Tucker, Thomas F.	22117	Twist, Noah A.	2794
Tucker, Walter W.	22118	Twist, Katie V.	2795
Tucker, Nellie	22119	Twist, Della D.	2796
Tucker, Hilliard M.	22120	Twist, Jesse C.	2797
Tucker, Viola	22121	Twist, Robert E. L.	2798
Tucker, Esther	22122	Twist, Noah F.	2799
Tucker, John	26007	Twist, Dovela	2800
Tucker, Betsy	26008	Twist, William J.	12503
Tucker, Mary	26118	Twist, William G.	12499
Tucker, Joshua	26526	Twist, Albert T.	12500
Tucker, Coon	29069	Twist, Jessie L.	12501
Tucker, George C.	29303	Twist, Edward C.	12502
Tucker, Lillie Mable	29304	Twist, Tony	14636
Tucker, Cora	30498	Twist, Sarah C.	14637
Tucker, Susie	30691	Twist, Albert W.	16102
Tucker, Sallie	30692	Twist, John W.	16382
Tulk, Irene	17101	Twist, Felix A.	16383
Tully, Morris C.	32890	Twist, Ethel	16384
Tulsa, Lizzie	17853	Twist, Gracie B.	16385
Tunnell, Cora	12058	Twist, Katie E.	16386
Turnham, Jennie	3563	Twist, Isaac	19176
Turnham, Ira K.	3564	Twist, Abraham	22596
Turnham, Della G.	3565	Twist, John	22597
Turnham, Geneva	3566	Twist, Bertha	22598

Name.	Roll No.	Name.	Roll No.
Twist, Teesie	28455	Tyner, Daniel W.	30841
Twist, Jennie	29622	Tyner, Ella E.	31935
Twist, George	32629	Tyner, Bushyhead	32004
Twister, Levi	25856	Tyner, Canzadia	32763
Twister, Annie	25857	Tyner, Lewis	32844
Twitty, Lydia	11858	Tyner, Martha Elizabeth	32845
Twilley, Lucy J.	14275	Tyner, Robert Lee	32846
Twilley, William D.	14276	Tyner, Sarah Delilah	32847
Twilley, Lillie M.	14277	Tyner, Mattie Emaline	32848
Tygor, Eugene	26522	Tyner, William Demp-	
Tygor, Frances	26523	sey	32849
Tygor, Blanche	26524	Tyner, John Lewis	32850
Tyler, Ruth A.	8692	Tyner, Ben Lafayette	32851
Tyler, Clara E.	8693	Tynon, Ora	8722
Tyler, William O.	8694	Tynon, Lillie B.	8723
Tyler, Charles N.	8695	Tynon, Andrew	24128
Tyler, Frederick E.	8696	Tynon, Ara	8715
Tyler, George H.	8697	Tynon, William	8716
Tyler, Essie M.	8698	Tynon, John	8718
Tyner, Nancy	2042	Tynon, Thomas	8719
Tyner, Mary	2043	Tynon, Rufus	8720
Tyner, George	2044	Tynon, Joe	8721
Tyner, James	2045	Ulteeskee, Akey	30216
Tyner, Jenana	2046	Ummerteskee, William	21413
Tyner, Frank	2047	Ummerteskee, William	21437
Tyner, Alice	2048	Ummerteskee, Lizzie	21438
Tyner, Carrie	2049	Ummerteskee, Peggie	30660
Tyner, Suella	2050	Ummerteskee, Watt	30661
Tyner, John W.	2636	Ummerteskee, Darkey	30718
Tyner, Lula	10229	Ummarteskee, Runabout	25915
Tyner, Weaver	10260	Ummarteskee, Nellie	25916
Tyner, Laura	10261	Underwood, Margaret A.	7343
Tyner, Maud	10262	Underwood, Willis	7344
Tyner, George W.	10306	Underwood, Cora	7345
Tyner, Clem C.	10307	Underwood, Janie	19266
Tyner, John C.	10308	Underwood, Charles	27935
Tyner, George A.	10309	Underwood, Henry	27936
Tyner, Fannie A.	10310	Underwood, Agnes	27937
Tyner, Mollie L.	10311	Underwood, Margaret	32738
Tyner, Letitia A.	10312	Ussrey, Samuel	2715
Tyner, Lo Sitah	10313	Ussrey, Margaret A.	2716
Tyner, George E.	10343	Ussrey, Claud	2717
Tyner, Leonard P.	10347	Ussrey, Samuel	15693
Tyner, Frazier McL	10348	Ussrey, George W.	15723
Tyner, Susan	10366	Ussrey, John	17435
Tyner, Cordelia	10369	Ussrey, Luvena	3121
Tyner, James F.	10371	Ussrey, Ezekiel	3122
Tyner, Quaty	10372	Uhles, Ruby	6896
Tyner, Delilah	10373	Vann, William	101
Tyner, Aaron	10374	Vann, David W.	589
Tyner, James F., Jr.	10375	Vann, Pearl R.	590
Tyner, Ralph	10376	Vann, John H.	591
Tyner, Minnie	10377	Vann, Fannie M.	592
Tyner, Thomas J.	10409	Vann, Floy E.	593
Tyner, Jefferson	10617	Vann, Fay	594
Tyner, Clinton A.	15878	Vann, Martha O.	595
Tyner, Lydia	17574	Vann, David W.	596
Tyner, Lillie M.	17575	Vann, James G.	597
Tyner, Mary E.	17576	Vann, Betsy	2121
Tyner, Hugh	17577	Vann, Dora	2125
Tyner, Willie A.	17578	Vann, John	2126
Tyner, Oscar	17579	Vann, Robert P.	2913
Tyner, Carter B.	24490	Vann, Coowie	2914
Tyner, Carter B., Jr.	24492	Vann, Nannie	2915
Tyner, Mary E.	24493	Vann, Joseph B.	2916
Tyner, William H.	24494	Vann, Frank J.	2917
Tyner, Lewis F.	24495	Vann, Mittie	2918
Tyner, Ada Bell	24496	Vann, Edward F.	2919
Tyner, John	24529	Vann, Robert P., Jr.	2920
Tyner, Rachel	24530	Vann, Lizzie T.	2921
Tyner, Davis	24531	Vann, Connie G.	2922
Tyner, Linda	24532	Vann, Ephriam	3082
Tyner, Reuben	26610	Vann, Martha	3084
Tyner, Roxie A.	26611	Vann, William	3091
Tyner, Mary E.	26612	Vann, Joseph C.	3318
Tyner, George W.	26613	Vann, Richard	3421
Tyner, Beatrice	26614	Vann, Annie	3422
Tyner, Cena	26615	Vann, Betsy	3766
Tyner, Maudie M.	26616	Vann, Julia	3767
Tyner, Grace	26617	Vann, James W.	3768
Tyner, Clinton E.	29202	Vann, Arcene	3807
Tyner, Minnie E.	29421	Vann, Henry	4023
Tyner, John W., Jr.	29422	Vann, Susie	4024

Name.	Roll No.	Name.	Roll No.
Vann, Cornelius	4148	Vann, Jesse	19590
Vann, Fred	4355	Vann, Eliza	19591
Vann, Nancy	4356	Vann, Jack	19592
Vann, Herman J.	4670	Vann, Rose	19593
Vann, Lizzie	4671	Vann, Josiah	19594
Vann, Clem	4672	Vann, Charles	19827
Vann, Joseph	4673	Vann, Dirtthrower	19828
Vann, William	4674	Vann, Mary	19829
Vann, Sophia	4675	Vann, Bearpaw	19830
Vann, Lola	4676	Vann, James	19831
Vann, Elnora	4677	Vann, Patsie	19832
Vann, Daisy	4678	Vann, Nancy	19873
Vann, James W.	5012	Vann, Mack	20181
Vann, Florence	5013	Vann, Young Wolfe	20202
Vann, Mary E.	5014	Vann, Allen	20204
Vann, Charlott A.	5015	Vann, Charles	20329
Vann, Wade H.	5294	Vann, Nelson	20330
Vann, Morter	5585	Vann, Joe	20371
Vann, Minerva	5586	Vann, Nancy	20372
Vann, Ida	5587	Vann, Linnie	20373
Vann, William	6031	Vann, Lydia	20374
Vann, Charles E.	6071	Vann, Will	20375
Vann, Ada	6072	Vann, Lee	20526
Vann, John S.	6073	Vann, Hickory	20699
Vann, John F.	6110	Vann, French	21241
Vann, Daniel W.	6561	Vann, Nannie	21242
Vann, Clerinda	6562	Vann, Joe	21243
Vann, Ada	6563	Vann, Arch	21244
Vann, David W.	6564	Vann, Jesse	21248
Vann, Clerinda A.	6565	Vann, Katie	21744
Vann, William C.	6566	Vann, George B. M.	23089
Vann, Emma E.	6567	Vann, Holmes	23091
Vann, Susie	6842	Vann, Perry I.	23092
Vann, James T.	6900	Vann, Mertie	23093
Vann, Nannie E.	6901	Vann, Cora L.	23094
Vann, Bertha A. L.	6902	Vann, George F.	23095
Vann, Oscar T.	6903	Vann, Clement I.	23527
Vann, Lula M.	6904	Vann, Emma	23528
Vann, Ivy J.	6905	Vann, Carrie B.	23529
Vann, Jessie J.	6906	Vann, Martha E.	23530
Vann, Joe	11746	Vann, Clement M.	23531
Vann, Lizzie D.	11747	Vann, Sina	25637
Vann, Clem N.	11748	Vann, White	25638
Vann, Jesse E.	11749	Vann, Nancy	25678
Vann, Jesse H.	12147	Vann, Aleck	25679
Vann, Skillie	14074	Vann, Andrew	25844
Vann, Rachel	14075	Vann, Samuel	26256
Vann, Johnson	14076	Vann, Elizabeth	26257
Vann, Lilah	14077	Vann, Alcie	27177
Vann, Katie	14078	Vann, Jesse	27178
Vann, Dick	14079	Vann, Scott	27179
Vann, Jesse	14080	Vann, Ada	27269
Vann, George	16512	Vann, Nannie Ruth	27275
Vann, Sallie	16513	Vann, John R.	27289
Vann, Walter	16517	Vann, Flora	27290
Vann, Joseph	16694	Vann, Joanna	27642
Vann, Cynthia	16695	Vann, Ralph J.	27643
Vann, Elizabeth	16696	Vann, William W.	27644
Vann, Gid	16697	Vann, Carrie M.	27645
Vann, Sallie	17135	Vann, Callie	27646
Vann, Daisy	17136	Vann, Lucullus E.	27961
Vann, Mary	17198	Vann, Mary L.	27962
Vann, Arch	18058	Vann, Lucullus	28264
Vann, Jennie	18059	Vann, Alice	28339
Vann, Ada	18060	Vann, Katie	28575
Vann, Amos	18297	Vann, John C.	28770
Vann, George	18489	Vann, Napoleon B.	28771
Vann, Akie	18944	Vann, Thomas	28952
Vann, Nancy	18945	Vann, Jennie	28953
Vann, Noname	18999	Vann, Ada	28956
Vann, Heavy	19123	Vann, Elizabeth	29031
Vann, Ellis	19188	Vann, Nellie	29507
Vann, Hunter	19308	Vann, Mary	29805
Vann, Linda	19309	Vann, Stephen	29961
Vann, French	19310	Vann, Sarah	29962
Vann, Jess	19311	Vann, Tipton	29963
Vann, George	19501	Vann, Harris	29964
Vann, Ellen	19502	Vann, Thomas	29965
Vann, Rachel	19503	Vann, Betsy	29966
Vann, George Byers	19504	Vann, Josephine	29967
Vann, Mandy	19527	Vann, Fisher	30462
Vann, Ida	19554	Vann, Jennie	30463

Name.	Roll No.	Name.	Roll No.
Vann, Silk	32060	Wade, Churchill	8559
Vann, Isaac	32081	Wafford, Joseph	6209
Vann, Sarah	32082	Wagnon, Martha E.	968
Vann, Augustus	32083	Wagnon, Julian M.	971
Vann, Cornelius	32271	Wagnon, Thomas F.	14038
Vann, Quaty	32553	Wagnon, Lucinda	14039
Vann, Oo-kil-lah	32554	Wagnon, Emma J.	14040
Vann, Tom	32572	Wagnon, Maude M.	14041
Vann, Kinny	32592	Wagnon, James F.	14042
Van Antwerp, Avis	14654	Wagnon, Thomas J.	14043
Vanmatre, Martha	22460	Wagnon, Ada	14044
Vanmatre, John T.	22462	Wagnon, Millard A.	14045
Vanmatre, James C.	22463	Wagnon, Marshall J.	14055
Vanmatre, Bessie M.	22464	Wagon, Freddie A.	23301
Vandever, Mattie J.	28687	Wagon, Kate	31101
Vasbinder, Annie	27719	Wahlasky, Willie	19402
Vasbinder, Walter C.	27720	Wahlasky, Wahleah	19403
Vasbinder, James K.	27721	Wahler, Takey	21373
Vaughn, Charles	11920	Wahler, Akie	21374
Vaught, Junie	4415	Wahler, Peggie	21375
Vaught, Lucinda	4425	Wahler, Jennie	21376
Vaught, Josephh	4426	Wahler, Levi	21377
Vaught, John	4427	Wahler, Lydia	21378
Vaught, Johnanna	4428	Wakefield, Virginia	10122
Victor, Delilah C.	238	Walden, Minnie	7027
Victor, Octa Lucile	239	Walden, James	7028
Victor, Fred Samuel	240	Walden, Nora	7029
Victor, James Y.	241	Walden, Thomas	7030
Victor, Sadie	242	Walden, Una	7031
Victor, Gladys	243	Walden, Nancy	13673
Victory, John	28107	Walden, Samuel	13677
Victory, Henry	28109	Walden, Elzie E.	13678
Victory, Tensy	28110	Walden, Ida M.	24755
Victory, Samuel	28111	Walden, Mary L.	24756
Victory, Charles	28112	Walden, Laura B.	24757
Victory, Susan	28113	Walden, William G.	24758
Victory, Andrew	28114	Walden, Robert F.	24759
Victory, Anna A.	28115	Walker, James L.	2264
Victory, Donney	28116	Walker, Lillie A.	2265
Vickery, James N.	4193	Walker, Lelia E.	2266
Vickery, John W.	4524	Walker, Esther J.	2267
Vickery, John W. Jr.	4525	Walker, Grover H.	2268
Vickery, Lillie E.	4530	Walker, Minerva	2269
Vickery, Nettie M.	4532	Walker, Josie V.	2270
Vickery, Martha E.	21869	Walker, Nellie	1235
Vickery, Mary A.	21870	Walker, Susan B.	3469
Vickery, Mattie A.	21871	Walker, Myrtle M.	3470
Vickery, Charlotte M.	21872	Walker, Mary	4061
Vickery, Charles L.	21873	Walker, Richard M.	6080
Vickery, William P.	21874	Walker, Elizabeth	6081
Vickrey, Frank	1464	Walker, Bessie	6082
Vickrey, Maggie A.	1465	Walker, Rosa	6083
Vickrey, Saphronia M.	1466	Walker, Ollie	6084
Vickrey, Caledonia	1467	Walker, Elizabeth N.	6093
Vickrey, Leona	1468	Walker, Emma M.	6094
Vickrey, Odie B.	1469	Walker, Edmond	6111
Vickry, Charles	3061	Walker, Jack	6128
Vickry, John H.	22778	Walker, Susan A.	6129
Vickry, William P.	22780	Walker, Timothy M.	6130
Vickry, Sarah	22781	Walker, Henry C.	6131
Vickry, Florence	22782	Walker, Suzanna	6451
Vickry, Cora	22783	Walker, Lizzie	7689
Vickry, Richard	22784	Walker, James Jr.	7691
Vickry, Ruthie	22785	Walker, Jennie	7922
Vinita, Albert	10622	Walker, Blossom	7923
Vinita, Dero T.	10623	Walker, Susan	7924
Vinita, Laura E.	10720	Walker, Daniel H.	8842
Vinita, John	13616	Walker, John F.	8843
Vinyard, Frances E.	32370	Walker, Lenora L.	8844
Vinyard, John	32371	Walker, Mathew R.	9315
Vinyard, Chelsea	32372	Walker, Reginald B.	9316
Vore, Frank	5954	Walker, Waller W.	9317
Vore, Charles F.	5955	Walker, Malcom B.	9318
Vore, Frank N.	5956	Walker, Jo Percy	9319
Vore, Mary	5958	Walker, Percy L.	9337
Vore, Thomas S.	5959	Walker, Mary M.	9338
Wade, Clara	4748	Walker, Narcissa O.	9339
Wade, Berenice	4851	Walker, Earle P.	9340
Wade, James M.	5187	Walker, Gleason	9341
Wade, Raymond J.	5188	Walker, Nannie L.	9465
Wade, Ida M.	8556	Walker, Jennie M.	9466
Wade, Preston P.	8557	Walker, James T.	9467
Wade, Emily D.	8558	Walker, John A.	9468

Name.	Roll No.	Name.	Roll No.
Walker, Leonard A.	9469	Walker, Estella	29557
Walker, William J.	9470	Walker, Mabel	29558
Walker, Anna L.	9471	Walker, Callie E.	29559
Walker, George W.	9489	Walker, Samuel L.	29560
Walker, Lewis	9490	Walker, Emery F.	29561
Walker, Henry	9491	Walker, Blanche	29562
Walker, Anna	9528	Walker, James A. Jr.	30185
Walker, Beulah	9529	Walker, William	31613
Walker, Claudine	9530	Walker, James	32068
Walker, James	10426	Walker, Addie	32472
Walker, Frank T.	10466	Walker, Bessie M.	32473
Walker, Annie B.	10467	Walkingstick, Cecil	1354
Walker, William J.	10490	Walkingstick, Calvin	1353
Walker, Watt	10491	Walkingstick, Peggy	1442
Walker, Mary E.	10492	Walkingstick, Edward	1443
Walker, James G.	10493	Walkingstick, James M.	1688
Walker, Charles	10606	Walkingstick, Malinda D.	1980
Walker, James F.	10929	Walkingstick, Mary J.	3032
Walker, Arminta L.	10930	Walkingstick, Lucy R.	3033
Walker, Areta J.	10931	Walkingstick, Lewis D.	3034
Walker, Etta E.	10932	Walkingstick, Ethel	15154
Walker, Mary E.	11026	Walkingstick, Irene	15156
Walker, William J.	11811	Walkingstick, Edward	16181
Walker, Katie	13618	Walkingstick, Benjamin	16182
Walker, Susie	13619	Walkingstick, John R.	16184
Walker, Thompson	13620	Walkingstick, Katie	16185
Walker, Jack	13621	Walkingstick, Simon R.	16593
Walker, Rosa	13622	Walkingstick, Ada S.	16594
Walker, Nannie	13623	Walkingstick, Simon	
Walker, John	13624	R. Jr.	16595
Walker, Martha L.	14427	Walkingstick, Celeter	16596
Walker, Willard L.	14428	Walkingstick, Bruce	16597
Walker, Frederick L.	15734	Walkingstick, Leona	17846
Walker, India O.	15735	Walkingstick, Christina	17847
Walker, Lillie E.	15736	Walkingstick, Ben	18032
Walker, William H.	16176	Walkingstick, Mack	18990
Walker, Robert W.	16178	Walkingstick, Charles	18991
Walker, Frank L.	16179	Walkingstick, Bettie	18992
Walker, John W.	16180	Walkingstick, Jennie	18993
Walker, Edward A.	17234	Walkingstick, Steven	19505
Walker, Katie	17235	Walkingstick, Daniel	20017
Walker, Eliza	17236	Walkingstick, Henry	20054
Walker, Florence W.	17238	Walkingstick, Betsy	20055
Walker, John L.	17239	Walkingstick, Charlotte	20056
Walker, Jennie	17240	Walkingstick, Isaac	20057
Walker, Jack O. Jr.	17241	Walkingstick, Lydia	
Walker, Susie	17242	Ann	20092
Walker, Lydia	17510	Walkingstick, Jane	20093
Walker, Rachel	17917	Walkingstick, Frances	20094
Walker, Lucy	18559	Walkingstick, Susan	20127
Walker, Joe	18560	Walkingstick, Huey M.	21934
Walker, Backwater	18561	Walkingstick, Jennie	25166
Walker, Watt	18562	Walkingstick, Jesse	25167
Walker, James	19545	Walkingstick, Susan E.	26725
Walker, William	20193	Walkingstick, Nina M.	26726
Walker, Mary	20194	Walkingstick, Bettie C.	26727
Walker, Sallie	20195	Walkingstick, Callie L.	26728
Walker, Maggie	20196	Walkingstick, Ezekiel	27055
Walker, Ell	20744	Walkingstick, Maggie	27453
Walker, Richard	20949	Walkingstick, Lydia	29043
Walker, Eliza	20950	Walkingstick, Wilson	2486
Walker, Annie	20951	Walkingstick, Nancy C.	2487
Walker, Walker	20955	Walkingstick, John C.	2488
Walker, Jack	21213	Walkingstick, Ada J.	2489
Walker, Mary S.	24190	Walkingstick, Dora	2490
Walker, Alma W.	24191	Walkingstick, Mary C.	2491
Walker, Marth J.	24192	Walkingstick, Thomas L.	2492
Walker, James E.	24193	Walkingstick, James W.	2493
Walker, James A.	24258	Wallace, Mamie	4481
Walker, Nannie	25666	Wallace, Clarence	4482
Walker, Itaskia	26931	Wallace, Lillie	5283
Walker, Ollie	26932	Wallace, Jennie	5284
Walker, Nellie	26933	Wallace, Florence	5285
Walker, William T.	26934	Wallace, William B. Jr.	10974
Walker, Jessie	26935	Wallace, Ruby	10975
Walker, Ernest	26936	Wallace, Thomas C.	11557
Walker, Katie	28017	Wallace, Marion	11558
Walker, Sissie	28018	Wallace, Julia	14174
Walker, Ida T.	28280	Wallace, Lulu	14175
Walker, James L.	28281	Wallace, Grace	14176
Walker, Goldie E.	28282	Wallace, Martha	14177
Walker, Johnie E.	28283	Wallace, Julius M.	14178
Walker, Mary	29556	Wallace, Alice E.	14179

Name.	Roll No.
Wallace, Martin DeWitt	14612
Wallace, Ollief J.	14613
Wallace, Emma	16130
Wallace, Floyd C.	16131
Wallace, Glenn O.	16132
Wallace, Ada	31483
Wallace, Pearl	31484
Walkabout, Henry	14081
Walkabout, Hettie	14082
Walkabout, Joseph	14083
Walkabout, Henry Jr.	14084
Walkabout, Levi	14085
Walkabout, John	14086
Walkley, George	11266
Walkley, Celia M.	11306
Walkley, Henry C.	11374
Walkley, Mary A.	26654
Walkley, Ruby L.	26655
Walkley, William S.	26656
Wall, Lula B.	9268
Wall, John M.	9269
Wall, Jack	21617
Walls, Richard	16332
Walls, Ed	23589
Walls, Nancy	26112
Walls, Samuel	26113
Walls, Lizzie	26114
Wallis, Richard N.	12609
Wallis, Clarence A.	12610
Wallis, Bertha A.	12611
Wallis, Jency W.	12612
Wallis, Florence E.	12613
Waller, Susie L.	13057
Waller, Cole B.	13058
Waller, Goldie J.	13059
Waller, William T. H.	13060
Waller, Bertha M.	13061
Wallen, Rosanna	26439
Wallen, Stuvie	26440
Wallen, Clyde	26441
Wallen, Alta F.	26442
Walters, Lillie	4208
Walters, Zack	4209
Walters, Zeff	4210
Walters, Pearl	4211
Walters, Harry	4212
Walters, Vada	4213
Walters, Clara	4214
Walters, Ollie	4215
Walters, James	14376
Walton, George O.	13868
Walton, Thomas W.	13869
Walton, Minnie Eva	32420
Waltrip, Elmira	17696
Waltrip, James J.	17697
Waltrip, Rachel	17698
Waltrip, James W.	17699
Wann, Rosa L.	11124
Wann, Opal	11125
Wann, Willie	11126
Wann, Jessie	11127
Wann, John M.	11128
Wann, Maggie M.	11129
Ward, John L.	230
Ward, Lura	231
Ward, Leola	232
Ward, Cornelia J.	233
Ward, Winnie D.	234
Ward, Adda D.	235
Ward, John D.	236
Ward, Daniel M.	1132
Ward, Thomas M.	1133
Ward, George	1134
Ward, Yell C.	1268
Ward, Nancy A.	1269
Ward, John	1270
Ward, George	1271
Ward, Susie A.	1272
Ward, Caldeen	1273
Ward, Margaret Ann	1871
Ward, George O.	3174
Ward, Nina	3175
Ward, Victoria	3176

Name.	Roll No.
Ward, Essie M.	3177
Ward, John F.	6134
Ward, Joseph L.	6380
Ward, W. Mae	6381
Ward, Martha L.	6382
Ward, Mollie E.	7158
Ward, Louisa J.	7183
Ward, Joseph McC	7184
Ward, Hugh T.	7185
Ward, Rosa V.	7186
Ward, Lillie D.	7187
Ward, Beulah B.	7188
Ward, Delena	7189
Ward, John E.	7378
Ward, Minnie	7379
Ward, William W.	8551
Ward, Henry H.	8552
Ward, William	8654
Ward, Isabelle R.	9129
Ward, Lela M.	9130
Ward, Genobie A.	9131
Ward, Aletha B.	9132
Ward, Carrie M.	9133
Ward, Lena N.	9134
Ward, Ida B. V.	9135
Ward, Robert E. L.	9136
Ward, Minneola	9164
Ward, James O.	9981
Ward, Leonorah	10864
Ward, Violet	10865
Ward, Thomas C.	11144
Ward, George W.	11181
Ward, Amos F.	11182
Ward, William R.	11183
Ward, Margaret C.	11184
Ward, Nathaniel	11185
Ward, Pearl	11186
Ward, Joel B.	11485
Ward, Florence A.	11486
Ward, Minnie A.	11487
Ward, Clem A.	11488
Ward, Lena E.	11489
Ward, Finies	11490
Ward, Eveline	11753
Ward, Joel B. C.	11772
Ward, Minnie	11773
Ward, William R.	11774
Ward, Ellis B.	11775
Ward, Charles R.	11776
Ward, Caldeen	11789
Ward, William H.	11868
Ward, Jay H.	11916
Ward, James M.	12191
Ward, Basil W.	12192
Ward, Thomas C.	12193
Ward, Estella J.	12194
Ward, Joel R.	12195
Ward, Arthur D.	12196
Ward, Wert McD.	12197
Ward, Lorena R.	12198
Ward, Moses H. Jr.	12273
Ward, Clarence V.	12842
Ward, Ada B.	13053
Ward, Darius E.	13855
Ward, James D.	13856
Ward, Hinman H.	13857
Ward, Sidney R.	13858
Ward, Gertrude I.	13859
Ward, Ruth E.	13860
Ward, Martha A.	13861
Ward, Rebecka L.	13862
Ward, James	15471
Ward, Joel	15523
Ward, Bryant	15524
Ward, Lucinda	15890
Ward, Francis A.	15899
Ward, Marion W. S.	15900
Ward, George D.	15901
Ward, Nettie A.	15902
Ward, Mary E.	15903
Ward, John R.	15904
Ward, James F.	15905
Ward, John D.	20983

Name.	Roll No.
Ward, William W.	22206
Ward, Lola	22207
Ward, Laura E.	22208
Ward, Alta J.	22209
Ward, Maude M.	22210
Ward, George M.	22211
Ward, Martha J.	22212
Ward, Fannie F.	23504
Ward, John H. L.	23505
Ward, Bessie	23506
Ward, Cora D.	23507
Ward, Lily	23508
Ward, George D.	23787
Ward, Ethlynne	23789
Ward, Vann	23796
Ward, Thomas F.	24688
Ward, James M.	24689
Ward, Bertha M.	24690
Ward, John F.	24691
Ward, Ella N.	24692
Ward, James O.	24751
Ward, Karl E.	24752
Ward, Henry J.	26708
Ward, Samuel J.	26709
Ward, Ethel M.	26710
Ward, Sarah R.	26711
Ward, James H.	27566
Ward, Mary Ann	27567
Ward, George V.	27568
Ward, James L.	27584
Ward, Sabra C.	28287
Ward, Charles E.	28288
Ward, Jasper	28779
Ward, John G. S.	28780
Ward, Myrtle B.	29533
Ward, Marvin Jefferson	29534
Ward, Alexander G.	29573
Ward, Lucy F.	29574
Ward, George	29575
Ward, Roxie M.	29576
Ward, William M.	29577
Ward, Joe M.	29578
Ward, Joel C.	29579
Ward, Samuel H.	29623
Ward, Louella	30017
Ward, Luela O.	30018
Ward, William W.	30306
Ward, Minnie B.	30307
Ward, Walter M.	30308
Ward, Manerva E.	30309
Ward, Tennie	30310
Ward, Effie E.	30311
Ward, Leona	30312
Ward, Lucinda	31074
Ward, Cassie A.	31075
Ward, Elizabeth	31076
Ward, Lena M.	31077
Ward, Corah B.	32781
Warneke, Annie	3158
Warneke, Katie	3159
Warneke, Mary	3160
Warneke, Edgar	3161
Warneke, Maud	3162
Warneke, Irene	3166
Ware, Hattie A.	14566
Ware, Goldie A.	14567
Ware, Bulah	14568
Ware, Edgar I.	14571
Ware, Mary J.	16469
Ware, George F.	16470
Ware, Josephine M.	16471
Ware, Ada A.	21630
Warner, Martha J.	1165
Warner, Rachel E.	1166
Warner, Mary I.	1167
Warner, Cora E.	18837
Warner, Ivan L.	26212
Warner, Bertha M.	26213
Warner, Eliza	30986
Warner, Jennie M.	30987
Marner, Maud A.	30988
Warner, Henry C.	30989
Warner, Rosy A.	30990

Name.	Roll No.
Warner, Clara B.	30991
Warner, Edna	30992
Warren, Ida J.	7067
Warren, Nolson G.	7068
Warren, Jessie M.	7069
Warren, Lydia	7070
Warren, Vera	7071
Warren, Arthur	27564
Warren, Mary Olive	27565
Warren, James Fannie	32659
Warren, John Henry	32660
Warren, Willie Demoris	32661
Warseat, George	20630
Warseat, Lucy	20631
Warseat, Dave	20632
Warseat, Levi	20633
Warseat, Ellis	20634
Warseat, Isaac	20666
Warseat, Nellie	20667
Warwick, Jacob M.	15713
Warwick, George F.	15714
Warwick, Elbert S.	15715
Warwick, William L	15716
Warwick, Alice C.	15717
Warwick, Frances M.	15718
Warwick, Leroy	15719
Warwick, Thomas A.	15720
Warwick, Lena L.	17064
Washington, George	4029
Washington, Georgia Ann	4030
Washington, Nancy	4031
Washington, Susan	4032
Washington, Luke	4033
Washington, Rufus	4034
Washington, Bertha	4035
Washington, George	8453
Washington, Saphronia	8454
Washington, Annie	8455
Washington, Lewis	8456
Washington, Charley L.	15237
Washington, Edward T.	15238
Washington, Mary E.	15239
Washington, Rosa	17794
Washington, Martha Axe	17795
Washington, George	19516
Washington, George	21151
Washington, Lizzie	21152
Washington, Peggie	21153
Washington, Red	21154
Washington, Blue	21155
Washington, James	21156
Washington, Cherokee	21157
Washington, John	30072
Washington, Mary	30073
Washington, Robert	30074
Washington, Bettie	30075
Washington, Emmet L.	30076
Washington, Albert	30912
Washington, George	31025
Washington, Joe	31226
Washington, George M.	31652
Washington, John W.	32113
Washington, Louis	32114
Washington, Ethel W.	32115
Washington, Hannah S.	32116
Washington, Gertrude	32117
Washington, Rosa	10284
Washington, Elizabeth	15235
Washington, Sallie M.	15236
Washbourne, Claude L.	7348
Washbourne, Joy L.	7349
Washbourne, Rollin R.	7350
Washbourne, Washington W.	9336
Washbourne, Edward N.	13880
Washbourne, Carrie L.	13881
Washbourne, Clyde L.	13882
Washbourne, Ruth C.	13883
Washborune, Bert	13950
Washbourne, Percy H.	25168

Name.	Roll No.	Name.	Roll No.
Washbourne, Claud L. Jr.,	25169	Waters, Annie	13129
		Waters, Sarah	13130
Washbourne, Myra M.	25170	Waters, Andrew	17367
Washbourne, Roscoe C.	25171	Waters, Mary	17368
Washbourne, Noble P.	25172	Waters, Dekeney	18109
Washbourne, Percy H.,		Waters, Johnson	19917
Jr.	25173	Waters, Sarah	19918
Washbourne, William		Waters, George	19919
J. B.	25174	Waters, Tom	19920
Washburn, Lilly	10937	Waters, Nellie	19921
Washburn, Leroy L.	10941	Waters, Lydia	19922
Washam, Mary A.	12048	Waters, John	20644
Washam, Rufus O.	12049	Waters, Susie	20645
Washam, Robert E.	12050	Waters, Maudie	22416
Washam, Martha E.	23575	Waters, Cora May	22423
Wassom, Maggie M.	23232	Waters, Kerens	22608
Wassom, Blaine W.	23233	Waters, Florence M.	22812
Wassom, Mattie	23234	Waters, John Jr.	22813
Wassom, John	23235	Waters, Saphronia	22814
Wasson, Catherine	27622	Waters, Sam	22815
Wasson, Nettie M.	27623	Waters, George	22828
Watkins, John	1	Waters, Mary C.	22829
Watkins, Lucy	2	Waters, Mose W.	22830
Watkins, Alice	4	Waters, Grover C.	22831
Watkins, Minnie M.	5687	Waters, Nannie M.	22832
Watkins, Thomas S.	5688	Waters, Gertrude	22833
Watkins, Susan	5689	Waters, Eulalah V.	22834
Watkins, Fannie	5690	Waters, Sylvester	27317
Watkins, William	5691	Waters, William	27318
Watkins, Samuel	6002	Waters, Mary A.	27319
Watkins, Nancy D.	6003	Waters, Andrew	27320
Watkins, Alexander	6004	Waters, Deacon	28446
Watkins, Samuel, Jr.	6005	Waters, Lydia	28595
Watkins, Grover L.	6006	Waters, Joe	29118
Watkins, Lillie C.	14680	Waters, Hattie	29119
Watkins, Bertha M.	14681	Waters, Richard	29121
Watkins, William G.	14682	Waters, George Jr.	29737
Watkins, Elizabeth E.	14683	Waters, Richard	32326
Watkins, Jessie L.	14684	Waters, Eliza	32327
Watkins, Berley W.	14685	Watie, Charlott	17618
Watkins, Henry A.	14686	Watie, John	17621
Watkins, Sarah J.	14883	Watie, Nancy	19041
Watkins, Gideon M.	14884	Watie, Polly	19042
Watkins, Dallas R.	14885	Watie, Johnson	19403
Watkins, Franklin S.	14886	Watie, Mary	19404
Watkins, Bessie M.	14887	Watie, Lillie	28344
Watkins, Mary E.	14888	Watie, Sallie	29715
Watkins, Ollie L.	14889	Watie, Luella	31689
Watkins, Clyde O.	14890	Watie, Pearl	31690
Watkins, Lidie S. M.	21640	Watie, Albert	31691
Watkins, Mary A.	21641	Watt, Johnson	1519
Watkins, John F.	21642	Watt, Walter	1520
Watkins, William P.	21643	Watt, Charles T.	11230
Watkins, George A.	21644	Watt, Charles	17819
Watkins, Joseph	21645	Watt, Eliza	19633
Watkins, De Witt T.	21646	Watt, Noname	19634
Watkins, Amanda E.	29211	Watt, Henry	19640
Watkins, Myrta E.	29212	Watt, Louisa	19641
Watkins, Harley V.	29213	Watt, Arlie	19642
Waters, Vina E.	1813	Watt, Caroline	19643
Waters, Gertrude A.	1814	Watt, Lydia	19644
Waters, Eva M.	1815	Watt, William	19679
Waters, Florence W.	1816	Watt, Stephen	19680
Waters, John	3217	Watt, Linnie	19681
Waters, L. Florence	3330	Watt, Jackson	19683
Waters, Charles	3983	Watt, Emily	19684
Waters, Mary	3984	Watt, Jonas	20897
Waters, Sallie	3985	Watt, Maud	20898
Waters, James	3986	Watt, Luke	20899
Waters, Richard	3987	Watt, Daniel	20921
Waters, Lucy	3988	Watt, Nancy	20922
Waters, Jennie	3089	Watt, Susan	26095
Waters, Mike	3990	Watt, Mush	26096
Waters, Annie	3991	Watt, Coh-tah-ga-wie	26097
Waters, Charles Jr.	3992	Watt, Elizabeth	26098
Waters, William	3993	Watt, Jennie	26099
Waters, Albert	4194	Watt, Wilson	26100
Waters, Belle	4195	Watt, Henry	26101
Waters, Ella	4196	Watt, Chewey	26102
Waters, Sarah A.	4197	Watts, William T.	26197
Waters, George	4198	Watt, William	28653
Waters, George McK.	4200	Watt, Youngbeaver	20111
Waters, Mary	13128	Watt, Mary	30561

Name.	Roll No.
Watt, John	20002
Watt, Edna	20012
Watts, Jacob	59
Watts, Elizabeth	60
Watts, Richard	66
Watts, Minnie	67
Watts, Nannie	68
Watts, Mary	69
Watts, John	70
Watts, Lucy	4832
Watts, Thomas	16922
Watts, Louvenia	16923
Watts, Eddie	23083
Watts, Zoe A.	28203
Watts, Mildred W.	28204
Watts, Louisa J.	4221
Waterdown, Nellie	19945
Waterdown, Diana	19946
Waterdown, Ahnawake	19947
Waterdown, Joe	19948
Waterdown, Ellis	19949
Waterdown, Steve	19950
Waterdown, Lynch	25788
Waterdown, Lizzie	25789
Waterdown, Julia	25790
Waterdown, Susie	25791
Waterdown, Bettie	25792
Waterdown, Baxter	25793
Waterfallen, Jennie	7055
Waterfallen, Nancy	7056
Waterfallen, Sarah	7057
Waterfallen, Levi	7058
Waterfallen, Lillie	7059
Waterfallen, James	25970
Waterfallen, Eliza	25971
Waterfallen, Eli	25972
Waterfallen, Annie	25973
Waterfallen, Bessie	25974
Waterfalling, Mike	18484
Waterkiller, Ellis	4551
Watermelon, Charles	19690
Watermelon, Lila	19691
Watermelon, Polly	19692
Watermelon, John	20698
Watermelon, Chutiakey	30562
Watson, Addie C.	15
Watson, Addie	17
Watson, Lucy	18
Watson, Drucilla	19
Watson, Nathaniel D.	20
Watson, Bessie	21
Watson, Jessie	22
Watson, Charles W.	551
Watson, John C.	552
Watson, Floyd	554
Watson, Frank	553
Watson, Idelia	12065
Watson, Charles M.	12066
Watson, Clarence K.	12067
Watson, Lola M.	12068
Watson, Robert S.	12069
Wauseet, Charles	7960
Waybourn, Oma	6379
Waybourn, Levi W.	26131
Waybourn, David L.	26132
Waybourn, Liddie	26133
Waybourn, Lawson T.	26872
Waybourn, Pearl	26873
Waybourn, William D.	26874
Waybourn, Alton	26875
Waybourn, Wilson L.	29336
Waybourn, Edna	29337
Waybourn, Robert L.	31693
Waybourn, Oscar	31694
Waybourn, Reana M.	31695
Waybourn, Henry W.	31696
Waybourn, William F.	31697
Wayne, John	22528
Wayne, Charles	32342
Wayner, William	20486
Wayner, Ice	32639
Weavel, Willie	19060
Weavel, Tawney	19061

Name.	Roll No.
Weavel, Lizzie	19062
Weavel, Chowin	19076
Weavel, Oo-ti-yah	19077
Weavel, Wuttie	19106
Weavel, Rider	19124
Weavel, Nancy	19125
Weavel, Katie	19855
Weavel, Bettie	19856
Weavel, Dick	19857
Weavel, John	19858
Weavel, Lucy	20128
Weavel, Miller	25639
Weavel, Caroline	25640
Weavel, Nancy	25641
Weavel, Betsey	25642
Weavel, Albert	25643
Weavel, Noah	25644
Weavel, Nannie	32909
Weaver, Hettie	1074
Weaver, Joanna	1075
Weaver, Mary	1076
Weaver, Anise	1077
Weaver, Katie	1078
Weaver, Thomas	1079
Weaver, John	1096
Weaver, Mary E.	1097
Weaver, John W.	1098
Weaver, Joseph	1102
Weaver, Jane	4094
Weaver, Mary	4096
Weaver, Bonnie	4097
Weaver, Alice	4308
Weaver, Felix	4309
Weaver, Nancy	4310
Weaver, William F.	4311
Weaver, Freddie	4312
Weaver, James F.	4313
Weaver, Florence D.	12148
Weaver, Herman	12149
Weaver, Laura B.	12150
Weaver, Fannie	12151
Weaver, Maude J.	12152
Weaver, Rose P.	12153
Weaver, Jennie	12735
Weaver, Baby	12736
Weaver, Joseph	12737
Weaver, Samantha	23339
Weaver, Claudie W.	23340
Weaver, Robert L.	23341
Weaver, Lucy Ann	23342
Weaver, Nellie	29821
Weaver, Luge	29822
Weaver, Margret E.	29823
Weaver, James	29824
Weaver, David M.	30925
Weaver, John Q.	30926
Weaver, Basil	30927
Weaver, Arnetta	30928
Weaver, George H.	30929
Weaver, Rosella	30930
Weast, Ethel	32257
Webb, Jennie D.	27673
Webber, William	19927
Webber, Sallie	19928
Webber, John	19929
Webber, Ollie	19930
Webber, Squirrel	19932
Webber, Wahleah	19933
Webber, Charlie	21081
Webber, Odie	21082
Webber, Adam	21083
Webber, Richard	21807
Webber, James C.	31516
Webber, Ida M.	31517
Webber, Almira C.	31662
Webber, Albert E.	31663
Webber, Alonzo	31664
Weber, Emma	31107
Weber, Rosa	31108
Webster, Alcy	2052
Webster, Arthur	15144
Webster, Charles	15145
Webster, Silas	15146

Name.	Roll No.	Name.	Roll No.
Webster, Hubbard	15147	Welch, Jackoline	2169
Webster, Henry	21813	Welch, John B.	2170
Webster, Nora A.	26814	Welch, Carnie	2171
Webster, Sallie J.	26815	Welch, Frank	2172
Webster, John Hamilton	26816	Welch, Emma	2173
Weddells, Mary E.	27880	Welch, Cherokee	2174
Weddells, George N.	27881	Welch, Thomas	2237
Weddells, Beulah	27882	Welch, David	3802
Weddle, Lula P.	31866	Welch, Mary	3832
Weddle, Curtis	31867	Welch, Ned	3833
Weddle, Morris O.	31868	Welch, Looney	3834
Weddle, Roy	31869	Welch, John P.	6143
Weeley, Nelson	20961	Welch, Annie	6144
Weeley, Nancy	20962	Welch, Samuel S.	6145
Weeley, Jay C.	20963	Welch, George T.	6776
Weeley, Mary J.	20964	Welch, Francis B.	6863
Weeley, Joseph	20970	Welch, John C.	8780
Weeley, Tehooyah	20977	Welch, Ailsey	8781
Weeley, Chenasah	20978	Welch, Cora	8782
Weeley, Thomas	20979	Welch, Ausley	8783
Weeley, William	20980	Welch, Annie	11014
Weeley, Wakie	20981	Welch, Phoeba Irene	11019
Weeley, Cynthia	20982	Welch, Mack E.	13610
Weeley, Nancy	20986	Welch, Richard L.	13612
Weeley, Polly	29932	Welch, Polly	13613
Weeley, William	29953	Welch, Leroy	13614
Weeley, Susan	29974	Welch, Thomas	
Weeley, Grapes	32564	Didimus	13615
Weems, Jennie	28876	Welch, Marshall N.	14370
Weigand, Lucy	5658	Welch, James	14419
Weinberg, Rachel A.	9878	Welch, John D.	16387
Weinberg, Catherine	9879	Welch, Edward	16803
Weinberg, Henry S.	9880	Welch, Thomas J.	17090
Weinberg, Susan F.	9881	Welch, Fannie	17091
Weir, Nathaniel B.	410	Welch, Maud G.	17092
Weir, Mary E.	411	Welch, Samuel B.	17093
Weir, May Ellen	412	Welch, Thomas R.	17094
Weir, Rexie James	413	Welch, John	17095
Weir, Charles S.	414	Welch, Loice	17096
Weir, Ruth Ada	415	Welch, Caroline	17784
Weir, Mary Pearl	416	Welch, Nancy	18241
Weir, Samuel K.	7485	Welch, Anna	19475
Weir, Early F.	7486	Welch, Eve	19495
Weir, William D.	7487	Welch, Nenahwi	19496
Weir, Daniel W.	7981	Welch, John D.	19497
Weir, William A.	8813	Welch, Mary	19498
Weir, Webster W.	23812	Welch, Wayne	19499
Weir, Sabra	23813	Welch, Anna	19500
Weir, Brack C.	23815	Welch, Sam	21630
Weir, Joseph H.	23816	Welch, John	21391
Weir, John W.	24230	Welch, Nancy	21392
Weir, Lillie M.	24232	Welch, Luke	21393
Weiss, Rebecca J.	30041	Welch, Veda E.	21687
Welch, Cyntha A.	374	Welch, Eva A.	21688
Welch, John	726	Welch, Dovie D.	22373
Welch, Franklin	727	Welch, Harry	22379
Welch, Iva	728	Welch, John L.	25129
Welch, Robert	729	Welch, Minnie C.	25130
Welch, Mack	929	Welch, Emma M.	25131
Welch, Emma	930	Welch, Link W.	25132
Welch, Esther	931	Welch, Hattie A.	25133
Welch, Myrtle	932	Welch, Maud	25164
Welch, Georgie	933	Welch, Virgel L.	25339
Welch, Ethel	934	Welch, Cherokee R.	25340
Welch, Moses	935	Welch, John E.	25372
Welch, Bruce	937	Welch, Charley	25373
Welch, Mollie	938	Welch, Jesse	25374
Welch, Nay	939	Welch, Hoolie	25375
Welch, Lee	940	Welch, William L.	25823
Welch, Scott	946	Welch, Elizabeth	25824
Welch, Elizabeth	947	Welch, David	27550
Welch, Mary	948	Welch, Hester	27551
Welch, Charlott	949	Welch, Nancy	27552
Welch, Johnnie	950	Welch, Celia	27553
Welch, James Mack	1048	Welch, David Jr.	27554
Welch, Cleo	1049	Welch, Alexander	28594
Welch, Frank J.	1726	Welch, Maggie	28596
Welch, Alfred G.	2163	Welch, Polly	28597
Welch, Robert	2166	Welch, Thomas S.	28598
Welch, Mary	2164	Welch, Joseph V.	29162
Welch, Mary	2165	Welch, Cornelius	30704
Welch, Joseph	2167	Welch, Hester	30835
Welch, George	2168	Welch, Susan	30836

Name.	Roll No.	Name.	Roll No.
Welch, Jesse	30837	West, Hester I.	8700
Welch, Thomas J.	30838	West, James C.	8845
Wells, Lucy Jane	442	West, Lester H.	8846
Wells, Milo C.	443	West, Ray	8847
Wells, William P.	2709	West, John H.	8968
Wells, James H.	10504	West, Harold A.	8969
Wells, John R.	10506	West, Ruth Elene	8970
Wells, Julia	10507	West, Clementine	13349
Wells, Edgar G.	10508	West, Mahala M.	13350
Wells, Adam B.	10509	West, Nola A.	13351
Wells, John R. Jr.	10510	West, Tooker B.	13352
Wells, Frederick C.	10914	West, Willie J.	13353
Wells, Emma E.	12461	West, Bertha J.	13354
Wells, Effie	12462	West, Lizzie V.	14229
Wells, Archie	12463	West, Leroy	14230
Wells, Bessie	12464	West, Minnie W.	14231
Wells, N. L.	12465	West, Addie	14405
Wells, Burl	12466	West, Dolly	14406
Wells, Emma	12467	West, Sandy	14407
Wells, James M.	12617	West, Richard	15743
Wells, Charles H.	12618	West, Leuella	16663
Wells, Malinda A.	12620	West, Burrell	16664
Wells, Lutitia	17378	West, Albert	16665
Wells, Joseph J.	17379	West, John C.	16766
Wells, Bessie D.	17380	West, Margaret E.	16767
Wells, Joseph A.	17381	West, Frank	16768
Wells, George W.	23617	West, Mary	16769
Wells, James R.	23619	West, Nannie	16770
Wells, John R.	23620	West, Laura B.	16812
Wells, Laura A.	27614	West, Richard F.	17041
Wells, William	27615	West, Dubert E.	17042
Wells, Samuel B.	27616	West, John A.	17043
Wells, Nannie B.	30079	West, Ellis C.	17044
Wells, Thomas D.	30080	West, Vera M.	17045
Wells, Ama R.	30081	West, Robbie Lee	17046
Wellbaum, Susanah	20619	West, George H.	17444
Welter, Cilla J.	29369	West, Bertha M.	17445
Welter, Nicholas T.	29370	West, Alvie Thomas	18055
Welter, Samuel L.	29374	West, John D.	23459
Welty, Lydia F.	4881	West, Nannie	23460
Werther, Lucy	10890	West, Lillie	23461
Werther, Charles	10891	West, Jasper N.	23462
Werther, Minnie	10892	West, Ora	23463
Werther, Oliver	10893	West, Bert	23464
Werther, Ollie	10894	West, Ruth	23465
Werther, Edward	10895	West, Walter A.	23513
Werther, Clarence	10896	West, William N.	26788
Werther, Ida	10897	West, John B.	28296
Werther, Lucille K.	10898	West, Thomas C.	28333
West, Sallie	1369	West, Tecumseh	28334
West, Alice P.	1370	West, Rufus B.	32436
West, Bettie	1371	West, George M.	32437
West, Alice	1542	West, Henry B.	32438
West, Sarah K.	1543	West, Charles H.	32439
West, James M.	1544	West, Morgan	32440
West, Augustus W.	1545	Westover, Willard W.	11599
West, Ella R.	1546	Westover, Thomas H.	11600
West, John H.	4396	Westover, Lelia E.	11601
West, Clifton P.	5133	Westover, Josephine	11602
West, Pearl	5134	Westover, Warren F.	11603
West, Ethel	5135	Westenhaver, Flora	13461
West, James P.	5441	Westenhaver, Bertha M.	13462
West, William R.	5442	Westenhaver, George	
West, John	5443	Baxter	13463
West, Jeff	5444	Wesson, Catherine	22059
West, Robert E.	5896	Wesson, David	22060
West, William E.	5897	Wesson, George N.	22061
West, Walter T.	5898	Wesson, Virgil	22062
West, Martin	5899	Wesson, Virginia	22063
West, Elizabeth D.	5900	Wetzel, Sarah L.	7737
West, Valeria E.	5901	Wetzel, Martha	23711
West, Calvin	6032	Wetzel, Claud C.	32457
West, Polk	6033	Wetzel, Ida May	32458
West, William D.	7109	Wetzel, Oliver K.	32459
West, Leona C.	7110	Wetzel, Edwin	32460
West, Walter A.	7111	Whale, Cinda	18744
West, James B.	7113	Whaler, Henry	18888
West, Josephine L.	7114	Whaler, Polly	18889
West, Culliciah D.	7115	Whaler, Eliza	18890
West, Sequoyah B.	7116	Whaler, Jennie	18891
West, Calvin C.	7117	Whaler, Eli	18892
West, Josephine C.	7118	Whaler, Canutch	30523
West, Joseph A.	7119	Whaler, Daniel	30721

Name.	Roll No.
Whaler, Kayukah	30722
Whelchel, Mary E.	692
Whelchel, Luella.	693
Whelchel, Stella	694
Whelchel, Fannie	695
Whelchel, James O.	696
Whelchel, Francis Earl	697
Wheeler, William W.	2703
Wheeler, Carnall	2705
Wheeler, Theodore	2706
Wheeler, Will W.	2733
Wheeler, John P.	2924
Wheeler, Nancy	2925
Wheeler, Fannie M.	3106
Wheeler, Tolbert	9795
Wheeler, Mary J.	9796
Wheeler, Jennie O.	9797
Wheeler, Olden Everett	9798
Wheeler, Rebecca N.	27019
Wheeler, William Robert	27020
Wheeler, Edward	31134
Wheeler, Bryant	31135
Wheeler, John	31648
Wheeler, Beauford A.	32757
Wheeler, Kate	32758
Wheeler, Samuel	32810
Wheatley, Eddie	26810
Wheatley, Claude E.	26811
Whitaker, William T.	6502
Whitaker, William J.	6503
Whitaker, Emma D.	6504
Whitaker, Maggie R.	6505
Whitaker, Charley	6506
Whitaker, Ella O.	6507
Whitaker, Claud	6508
Whitaker, Clarence	6509
Whitaker, Edna M.	6510
Whitaker, Victor	6775
Whitaker, Austin	6758
Whitaker, Virgil O.	6759
Whitaker, Eldie E.	6760
Whitaker, James E.	21631
Whitaker, David L.	26169
Whitaker, Joshua W.	32688
Whitaker, Stephen	32689
Whitaker, Eger J.	32690
White, Thomas	1791
White, Aggie	1792
White, James	1804
White, Jennie	1805
White, Tom	1806
White, Sunday	1807
White, Annie	1808
White, George	1809
White, Watt	1810
White, Florence	4994
White, Charles E.	4995
White, Flossie E.	4996
White, Lillian	4997
White, James E.	7258
White, Hooley C.	7259
White, Polly A.	7260
White, Lula E.	7261
White, Nancy	7853
White, Hill	7886
White, Lucy	7887
White, William H.	8007
White, David	8008
White, Devee	8009
White, Nancy	8325
White, Amos	9643
White, Nancy	9644
White, Peter	9813
White, Emma	9814
White, Thomas	10293
White, Reuben	10321
White, Nannie J.	11097
White, Mary M.	11098
White, Ruth E.	11099
White, Fabean V.	11100
White, Annie E.	11286
White, Helen D.	11961

Name.	Roll No.
White, Beuna V.	11962
White, Joseph	13563
White, Mollie	13564
White, Josiah	15653
White, Irvin	15654
White, Kate	17494
White, Rosa	17495
White, James	17714
White, Henry	17766
White, Mary	17767
White, Nancy	17768
White, George	18633
White, Martha	18634
White, Alex	18635
White, Sager	18636
White, Ookali	18637
White, Tom	18638
White, Mary	21561
White, Lewis R.	21562
White, Mary P.	21563
White, William J.	21564
White, Thomas J.	21565
White, James A.	21572
White, Willie G.	21573
White, George W.	21574
White, Martin	21855
White, Bertha	22031
White, Donavan	22032
White, Ursley P.	26179
White, Sarah M.	29426
White, Ida M.	29427
White, Clarence S.	29428
White, Rosa	31121
White, Silas	31257
White, Samuel	31258
White, Martha	31340
White, Minnie M.	31341
White, Anderson	31342
White, Susan A.	31343
White, Forest R.	31344
Whiteday, Charles	7493
Whiteday, William	26501
Whiteday, Susan	26502
Whiteday, Dora	26503
Whiteday, Julia	26504
Whiteday, Bennie	26505
Whiteday, Nellie	26506
Whitedeer, Abbie C.	9157
Whitedeer, Cora J.	9158
Whitedeer, Paul	9159
Whitefeather, Charles	11130
Whitefeather, Isaac	31455
Whiteturkey, Rosa E.	31182
Whiteturkey, Nannie V.	31183
Whiteturkey, Lizzie	31244
Whiteturkey, Dennis	31245
Whiteturkey, George	31277
Whiteturkey, Katie	31278
Whiteturkey, Denny	31279
Whiteturkey, May	31280
Whiteturkey, Hattie	31281
Whiteturkey, Jenette	31282
Whiteturkey, Ettie	31283
Whiteturkey, Fred	31296
Whiteturkey, Phoebe	31297
Whiteturkey, Mamie	31298
Whiteturkey, Guy	31299
Whiteturkey, Eva May	31300
Whitekiller, Buffalo	15067
Whitekiller, Eliza	15068
Whitekiller, Birdchopper	15069
Whitekiller, Susie	15070
Whitekiller, Maggie	16538
Whitekiller, William	16539
Whitekiller, David	21098
Whitekiller, Sallie	21099
Whitekiller, Mary	21100
Whitekiller, Charlie	21101
Whitewater, Bird	12408
Whitewater, Willee	12295
Whitewater, Allen	21137
Whitewater, Sallie	21138

Name.	Roll No.	Name.	Roll No.
Whitewater, Mary	21139	Whisenhunt, Luther	17489
Whitewater, Famous	21160	Whisenhunt, Johanna	25482
Whitewater, George	21161	Whisenhunt, Mary A.	25483
Whitewater, Ellen	21165	Whisenhunt, Charles E.	25484
Whitewater, Jim	21166	Whisenhunt, Wiley	25485
Whitewater, David	61	Whisenhunt, Noah	25486
Whitewater, Cabin	63	Whisenhunt, Effie	25487
Whitewater, Thomas	64	Whisenhunt, Telee	25488
Whitewater, Archie	65	Whisenhunt, Fred	25489
Whitfield, Hulda	2505	Whisenhunt,Dyton B.	25490
Whitfield, John D.	2508	Whisenhunt, Andrew B.	28370
Whitfield, Luke	21551	Whisenhunt,	
Whitfield, Benjamin	21552	Jefferson B.	28371
Whitmire, Charley	986	Whisenhunt, Emily H.	28372
Whitmire, Palmyra	987	Whisenhunt, Winnie D.	28373
Whitmire, Andy	988	Whisenhunt, Ruth W.	30104
Whitmire, James W.	989	Whirlwind, Lewis	12343
Whitmire, Noah	990	Whirlwind, Susie L.	12344
Whitmire, Jack	991	Whirlwind, Lola A.	12345
Whitmire, Willie	992	Whirlwind, Rosa A.	12346
Whitmire, Eli H.	1205	Whirlwind, Ketcher	18647
Whitmire, George C.	1206	Whirlwind, Elsie	18648
Whitmire, Mary L.	1207	Whirlwind, Wahlesa	18649
Whitmire, Mary L.	1475	Whirlwind, Cawheny	18650
Whitmire, Henry R.	1646	Whirlwind, Lewis	30514
Whitmire, White	6587	Whipple, Andrew J.	27583
Whitmire, Annie	6588	Whitney, Louella E.	9805
Whitmire, William	6589	Whitney, Mack W.	9806
Whitmire, Walter	6590	Whitney, Frederick C.	9807
Whitmire, Joseph	6591	Whitney, Mary E.	9808
Whitmire, Stephen	6592	Whitney, Bertha J.	9809
Whitmire, John	6593	Whitsett, William E. Jr.	3272
Whitmire, Maude	15155	Whitsett, Charles T.	3274
Whitmire, Edward	16282	Whitsett, Joseph H.	3275
Whitmire, Jonathan	16560	Whitsett, Hayden	3276
Whitmire, George G.	17522	Whitsett, Flora	3277
Whitmire, Lydia	17523	Whitsett, Charles B.	3287
Whitmire, George V.	17524	Whitsett, Susan M.	22820
Whitmire, Margaret	17976	Whitsett, Foreman	26342
Whitmire, Johnson	19645	Whitsett, Lilian	26343
Whitmire, George	19646	Whittinton, Cornelius	1103
Whitmire, George	21981	Whittinton, Jessie	1104
Wihtmire, Bettie	21982	Whittinton, John	1105
Whitmire, Johnson	21983	Whittinton, Jim	1106
Whitmire, Nannie	22453	Whittinton, Annie	1107
Whitmire, Roy C.	27034	Whittinton, George L.	1108
Whitmire, Walter S.	28053	Whittinton, Cynthia	1109
Whitmire, William	28054	Whooper, Youngsquirrel	19682
Whitmire, James	28055	Whooper, Charles	32749
Whitmire, Denis	28056	Wicked, Maria	2515
Whitmire, Thomas	28057	Wicked, Lemuel	5081
Whitmire, Johnathan	28058	Wicked, Albert	5084
Whitmire, Nellie	28059	Wicked, John N.	5099
Whitmire, George W.	28289	Wicked, Jessie	5100
Whitmire, Charles	28417	Wicked, Johnnie	5101
Whitmire, Peggy	32900	Wicked, Newton	5120
Whitmire, Ruth E.	31970	Wicked, Mary	5121
Whisenhunt, Brunett	1086	Wicked, Nettie G.	5122
Whisenhunt, William	1087	Wicked, Ola	5123
Whisenhunt, Benjamin	1088	Wicked, Lillie	5549
Whisenhunt, Mary	1089	Wicked, Vaden	21698
Whisenhunt, Josie	1090	Wicked, Ruth	21880
Whisenhunt, Joseph	1091	Wicked, Alpha O.	21881
Whisenhunt, John L.	1092	Wicked, Annie L.	23141
Whisenhunt, James	1093	Wicked, Lem I.	23142
Whisenhunt, Pearl P.	1094	Wicket, Charles	19575
Whisenhunt, Annie B.	1095	Wicket, Mary E.	25580
Whisenhunt, Thomas J.	12023	Wickett, Webster	28005
Whisenhunt, Eliza V.	12024	Wickett, Sarah	28006
Whisenhunt, Lillie A.	12025	Wickett, Richard	28007
Whisenhunt,		Wickett, Lottie	28008
William W.	12026	Wickett, Edith	28009
Whisenhunt, Andrew J.	12027	Wickett, Lurena	28010
Whisenhunt, Robert L.	12028	Wickett, Lucy	28011
Whisenhunt, John E.	12029	Wicket, Emma	32552
Whisenhunt, Henrietta	12030	Wickett, William	3151
Whisenhunt, Robert L.	12039	Wickett, James P.	3224
Whisenhunt, Homer L.	12040	Wickett, Docia M.	3225
Whisenhunt, Fay	12041	Wicket, Jesse	3419
Whisenhunt, Janie E.	12042	Wicket, Edna E.	3420
Whisenhunt, Nancy J.	17486	Wickett, Submit	16041
Whisenhunt, Frederick	17487	Wickliffe, Samuel	6172
Whisenhunt, Young E.	17488	Wickliffe, Nancy	20888

Name.	Roll No.	Name.	Roll No.
Wickliffe, John	20889	Wilkerson, George W.	15509
Wickliffe, Thomas	20890	Wilkerson, Cora	15510
Wickliffe, John Jr.	20891	Wilkerson, Austin	15511
Wickliffe, Lewis	21350	Wilkerson, Maggie	15512
Wickliffe, Ella	21351	Wilkerson, Maud	15513
Wickliffe, Annie	21352	Wilkerson, William D.	15603
Wickliffe, Alsie	21353	Wilkerson, Susie	17226
Wickliffe, Joe	21354	Wilkerson, Nancy	17227
Wickliffe, Jennie	30702	Wilkerson, Katie	17424
Wickliffe, Takey	30703	Wilkerson, Walter	17425
Wickliffe, Charles	29510	Wilkerson, John	17426
Wickliffe, Charlotte	29511	Wilkerson, Eliza	17535
Wickliffe, James	29512	Wilkerson, Ollie	17536
Wickliffe, James	29513	Wilkerson, Frost	17608
Wickliffe, Anna	29514	Wilkerson, Leonard	17613
Wicks, George Albert	28609	Wilkerson, Eva	17614
Wicks, John A.	28610	Wilkerson, Minnie	17615
Wicks, Nancy J.	28611	Wilkerson, John	11210
Wicks, Joseph	28612	Wilkerson, Louie	11363
Wicks, Benjamin	28613	Wilkerson, Rachel	26653
Wilbur, Sarah H.	8149	Wilkerson, Lizzie	27742
Wilbur, Lloyd W.	8150	Wilkerson, George	28351
Wilbur, Fred B.	8151	Wilkerson, Abraham	28461
Wilbur, Thomas G.	8152	Wilkerson, Ellen	28584
Wilder, Charlotte B.	6484	Wilkerson, Daniel	28585
Wilder, Clem V.	6486	Wilkerson, Ora	28586
Wildcat, Jennie	18883	Wilkerson, Lillie	28587
Wildcat, William	21069	Wilkerson, Lena	28588
Wildcat, Arniwakie	21070	Wilkerson, Mary E.	29345
Wildcat, Geyaraha	21071	Wilkerson, Oscar	32602
Wildcat, French	21072	Wilkie, George W.	739
Wildcat, Alex	21073	Wilkie, Sidney M.	740
Wildcat, Charlotte	21074	Wilkie, May Bell	741
Wildcat, Charldee	21075	Wilkie, John	742
Wildcat, Walker	21076	Wilkie, Nancy T.	743
Wildcat, Bennie	21078	Wilkie, David	744
Wildcat, Tuff	21079	Wilkie, Louisa J.	745
Wildcat, Louisa	21080	Wilkie, Jesse L.	746
Wildcat, Goround	21122	Wilkie, David	962
Wildcat, Nellie	21123	Wilkie, John W.	963
Wildcat, Jackson	21124	Wilkie, Ollie L.	964
Wildcat, Alcy	21128	Wilkie, George W.	965
Wildcat, Spade	21129	Wilkie, David L.	966
Wildcat, Coleston	21130	Wilkie, Jesse W.	1125
Wildcat, Nancy	28521	Wilkie, John W.	1126
Wiley, Worcester	17358	Wilkie, Samuel D.	1127
Wiley, Charles W.	23040	Wilkie, Walter D.	1128
Wiley, Davis	25729	Wilkie, John M.	1339
Wiley, Nannie	25730	Wilkie, John W.	1424
Wiley, Mouse	28030	Wilkie, George H.	1425
Wiley, Nancy	28031	Wilkie, Margaret E.	22507
Wiley, Annie	28032	Wilkie, Laura J.	22508
Wiley, Linnie	28033	Wilkie, Nancy M.	22509
Wiley, Rachel	32510	Wilkie, Leli L.	22510
Wilkerson, Asa	2883	Wilkie, Sidney E.	28550
Wilkerson, Margarett	2884	Wilkins, Fannie	33
Wilkerson, Robert	2885	Wilkins, Nannie	34
Wilkerson, Daniel	2886	Wilkins, George W.	9113
Wilkerson, Lester	2887	Wilkins, Rachel	31070
Wilkerson, Margarett	2888	Wilkins, William H.	31071
Wilkerson, Colbert	2889	Wilkins, Robert C.	31072
Wilkerson, Sarah	4547	Wilkins, Martha Jane	31073
Wilkerson, Ruth	4548	Wilkins, Ethel	24187
Wilkerson, Mary	4549	Wilkinson, Rebecca A.	10676
Wilkerson, Ellen	4550	Wilkinson, Iva E.	10677
Wilkerson, Richard	12386	Wilkinson, Lottie E.	10678
Wilkerson, Annie	12387	Wilkinson, Louisa J.	11527
Wilkerson, Ella M.	12388	Wilkinson, Clara M.	13500
Wilkerson, Katie	12389	Wilkinson, John F.	13501
Wilkerson, Oliver C.	12390	Willey, Milo J.	4520
Wilkerson, Esther L.	14089	Willey, Myrtle	4522
Wilkerson, James	15253	Willey, Addie	4523
Wilkerson, Martha	15254	Willey, Mary	4604
Wilkerson, Leeler	15255	Willey, Rosanna	31561
Wilkerson, Andrew J.	15256	Willey, Lena	31562
Wilkerson, George W.	15257	Willey, Viola M.	31563
Wilkerson, Linzie H.	15258	Willey, Lottie	31566
Wilkerson, Lewis E.	15259	Williams, Alice	29
Wilkerson, Hattie	15261	Williams, Magdalena	30
Wilkerson, Eliza C.	15298	Williams, Walter L.	31
Wilkerson, John O.	15299	Williams, Robert C.	32
Wilkerson, Barney L.	15300	Williams, William D.	735
Wilkerson, Mattie E.	15301	Williams, John L. W. Jr.	736

Name.	Roll No.
Williams, Minnie M.	737
Williams, George A. Jr.	738
Williams, William W.	921
Williams, Lizzie L.	922
Williams, Blanche	923
Williams, Robert H.	924
Williams, Ima	925
Williams, Thomas E.	926
Williams, Robert B.	927
Williams, Ellis	1100
Williams, Lee	1121
Williams, Maude L.	1122
Williams, Frank E.	1123
Williams, Martha J.	1150
Williams, Ellen	1151
Williams, Fred	1152
Williams, Charles M.	1286
Williams, Mary M.	4693
Williams, George C.	4694
Williams, Edward B.	4695
Williams, Nannie K.	4696
Williams, Barbara B.	4697
Williams, Nancy	5334
Williams, Robert E.	5542
Williams, Henry C.	5543
Williams, Herbert A.	5544
Williams, Isaac E.	5546
Williams, Sue	6246
Williams, David B.	6250
Williams, Minnie	6251
Williams, DeWitt T.	6252
Williams, Mattie	6253
Williams, Sue	6254
Williams, Anna	6256
Williams, Elizabeth	6398
Williams, Charley	6399
Williams, Pearl	6400
Williams, Hattie M.	6401
Williams, Clem	6402
Williams, John	6403
Williams, Vera F.	6965
Williams, Mary	6977
Williams, Clem	6978
Williams, Viola	6979
Williams, Kittie	6980
Williams, Malinda N.	7103
Williams, Mattie L.	7104
Williams, Allie B.	7105
Williams, Andrew W. M.	7106
Williams, Charlotte C.	7107
Williams, Arthur R.	7108
Williams, Joseph L.	7800
Williams, Elenor M.	7801
Williams, Nellie L.	7802
Williams, Timothy E.	7803
Williams, Hazel A.	7804
Williams, Carlos E.	7805
Williams, William A.	8190
Williams, Jennie	8543
Williams, Claud	8544
Williams, Newton	8591
Williams, Laura E.	8592
Williams, Addie M.	8593
Williams, Lottie	8594
Williams, Davie S.	8595
Williams, Maggie	8596
Williams, William P.	8597
Williams, Mattie	8655
Williams, Joel M.	8837
Williams, Jennie M.	8838
Williams, Joe F.	8839
Williams, Lewis L.	8943
Williams, Elsie E.	8944
Williams, Gamaliel B.	9209
Williams, Elgin M.	9434
Williams, Ira E.	9435
Williams, Ionia	9436
Williams, Alonzo	10018
Williams, Levenia	10940
Williams, Belle	11808
Williams, James S. Jr.	11809
Williams, Leroy H.	11810
Williams, Jennie	12363

Name.	Roll No.
Williams, Harrison	13121
Williams, Charles	13366
Williams, Sallie	13367
Williams, Jack	13539
Williams, Nancy	14302
Williams, Thomas	14650
Williams, Watie	15568
Williams, Clarence	15569
Williams, George A.	15929
Williams, Alexander	16589
Williams, John	18485
Williams, Jesse	18486
Williams, Arley	18807
Williams, Charley	18808
Williams, Betsy	18809
Williams, William Walter	21469
Williams, Maggie A.	22004
Williams, Emma S.	22007
Williams, Harrison Jr.	22008
Williams, Blanche I.	23236
Williams, Robert A.	23237
Williams, Clara M.	23238
Williams, Samuel C.	23742
Williams, Ethel	23744
Williams, John B.	24236
Williams, Harriett	24237
Williams, Grace	24238
Williams, Pearl E.	24451
Williams, Roy M.	24452
Williams, Gertie S.	24453
Williams, Mary E.	24454
Williams, Sarah A.	24856
Williams, Willie J.	24857
Williams, Annie G.	24858
Williams, Guy	26280
Williams, Anna	26281
Williams, Lizzie	26388
Williams, George W.	26691
Williams, Clara M.	27599
Williams, Ruth	28416
Williams, James L.	28557
Williams, Lois	28558
Williams, Ralph E.	28559
Williams, William G.	28709
Williams, Clara	28710
Williams, Thomas	28711
Williams, Sarelda	28712
Williams, Matilda	28713
Williams, Rosanna	28714
Williams, Thomas W.	28814
Williams, Fannie	28815
Williams, Leonard W.	29452
Williams, Tuxie	29453
Williams, Charles P.	29468
Williams, Walter M.	29469
Williams, Claude A.	29470
Williams, Myrtle L.	29471
Williams, Charles L.	29472
Williams, Clarence P.	29473
Williams, Nervie	30273
Williams, Lillie	31104
Williams, Nannie	31105
Williams, George	31223
Williams, Sarah	31235
Williams, Fred	31236
Williams, Minnie Bell	32491
Williams, Andrew N.	32492
Williams, Clarence E.	32493
Williams, Raleigh	32494
Willis, Hester	698
Willis, George G.	699
Willis, Clauda C.	700
Willis, Lula	701
Willis, Thula E.	702
Willis, Jesse R.	1155
Willis, Florence A.	1721
Willis, Nora M.	1722
Willis, Robert H.	1723
Willis, Oma	1724
Willis, Hazel M.	1725
Willis, Thomas J.	7023
Willis, Charles	7025

Name.	Roll No.	Name.	Roll No.
Willis, Jerry	10054	Wilson, Polly M.	13959
Willis, Ollie S.	12601	Wilson, Mary E.	14399
Willis, John W.	14592	Wilson, Amanda L.	14400
Willis, Hugh W.	14593	Wilson, James M.	14401
Willis, Minnie	14595	Wilson, Samuel S.	14402
Willis, William B.	14874	Wilson, Eva E.	14402
Willis, Effie	14875	Wilson, William D. L.	14404
Willis, John P.	14905	Wilson, John F.	15402
Willis, Rogina	15017	Wilson, John M.	15403
Willis, Nathaniel D.	16257	Wilson, Joseph A.	15404
Willis, Claud M.	22984	Wilson, Frederick C.	15405
Willis, Bessie E.	22985	Wilson, Albert	15447
Willis, Armour A.	22986	Wilson, Mattie M.	15448
Willis, Walter B.	22987	Wilson, Gilbert A.	15449
Willis, William W.	22988	Wilson, Jesse T.	15450
Willis, Leander	23706	Wilson, William C.	15451
Willis, James E.	25320	Wilson, George	15838
Willis, Charlie	25321	Wilson, Charlotte	15924
Willis, Annie M.	25322	Wilson, Darcus	15928
Willis, Thomas E.	25323	Wilson, Youngpigeon	16699
Willis, Robert L.	25324	Wilson, Ridge	16700
Willison, Mary J.	26170	Wilson, Oo-kilee	16701
Willits, Lucy	31311	Wilson, Ahquas	16702
Willits, Minnie	31314	Wilson, Melvina	17190
Williamson, Leon L.	9547	Wilson, Ada L.	17191
Williamson, Frank E.	28967	Wilson, Felix	17192
Williamson, Mary D.	28968	Wilson, James W.	17193
Wills, Katie	9561	Wilson, Jim	18207
Wills, Clarence R.	9562	Wilson, Fannie	17502
Wills, John B.	9563	Wilson, Runabout	17969
Wilson, Mary Ann	429	Wilson, Rachel	17970
Wilson, Bertha L.	430	Wilson, Lydia	18208
Wilson, Rebecca V.	600	Wilson, Lila	18249
Wilson, James R.	601	Wilson, Selsie	18250
Wilson, Cora	602	Wilson, Dianna	18903
Wilson, Martha J.	2333	Wilson, Hickory	20590
Wilson, James W.	3167	Wilson, Emily	21471
Wilson, Albert M.	3168	Wilson, Sarah S.	21472
Wilson, Sallie B.	3169	Wilson, Daniel M.	21473
Wilson, Ida F.	3170	Wilson, Georgiaann S.	21474
Wilson, Robert	3171	Wilson, Oscar	21475
Wilson, Sue	3172	Wilson, Fred B.	21790
Wilson, Viola	3173	Wilson, Armindie	22037
Wilson, Finnie	3489	Wilson, Ella	22867
Wilson, Ora	3583	Wilson, William	22868
Wilson, John H.	3815	Wilson, Oma	22869
Wilson, William H.	3816	Wilson, Finny Jr.	22870
Wilson, Lucy E.	3817	Wilson, Minnie	22871
Wilson, Lelia O.	3818	Wilson, Rory	22967
Wilson, Iva G.	3819	Wilson, Rory Sequoyah	22968
Wilson, John B.	3820	Wilson, Susannah	25218
Wilson, Mary E.	5027	Wilson, Annie V.	25219
Wilson, Ethel	5028	Wilson, Minerva	25220
Wilson, Emma	5309	Wilson, Josephine	25221
Wilson, Robert	5310	Wilson, Elizabeth	25222
Wilson, Gilbert B.	5311	Wilson, Susan	25223
Wilson, Lovely R.	5312	Wilson, Lizzie	25292
Wilson, William T.	5648	Wilson, Magnolia	26929
Wilson, Jessie L.	5649	Wilson, Vernon	26930
Wilson, Charles A.	5650	Wilson, DeWitt C.	28176
Wilson, Alice	5762	Wilson, Ella M.	28177
Wilson, Hope E.	6792	Wilson, Lelia S.	22178
Wilson, George O.	6931	Wilson, Clinton A.	28179
Wilson, Mary B.	6932	Wilson, Nancy	28519
Wilson, Vincent A.	6933	Wilson, James D.	28818
Wilson, Martha J.	8817	Wilson, Enoch	28972
Wilson, Robert L.	8826	Wilson, Mary	28973
Wilson, James D.	8828	Wilson, Ned	29049
Wilson, Homer A.	8827	Wilson, Samuel R.	29803
Wilson, Martha E.	9264	Wilson, Georgia E.	29804
Wilson, Elgin D.	9265	Wilson, Chudahagi	30592
Wilson, Martha E.	9266	Wilson, James	30668
Wilson, Clare E.	9267	Wilson, Elizebeth	30669
Wilson, Donithan A.	9270	Wilson, Stealer	30670
Wilson, May	9488	Wilson, Wilson	30671
Wilson, Lula	11890	Wilson, Nancy	30672
Wilson, Mary E.	12549	Wilson, Minnie	31092
Wilson, Nora	12550	Wilson, Charles	31093
Wilson, Nancy C.	12915	Wilson, Lillie	31094
Wilson, John H.	12916	Wilson, Rosa	31131
Wilson, Janie	12917	Wilson, Lula	31132
Wilson, Benjamin F.	13957	Wilson, Joseph	31177
Wilson, Louaner	13958	Wilson, James A.	31210

Name.	Roll No.	Name.	Roll No.
Wilson, Pearl M.	31211	Witt, Gladys R.	4495
Wilson, Edna D.	31212	Witt, Jane	7649
Wilson, Della	31213	Witt, Allie	7650
Wilson, Frank	31220	Witt, Tipton	7051
Wilson, Jacob	31250	Witt, Dee	7652
Wilson, Cornelius	31259	Witt, Michiel O.	7677
Wilson, Lillie	31273	Witt, David T.	8103
Wilson, Thomas	31274	Witt, Hugh F.	8104
Wilson, Walter	31275	Witt, Abe	12918
Wilson, Reuben	31276	Witt, William F.	15352
Wilson, Anderson	31457	Witt, Elmer L.	15353
Wilson, Ida	31458	Witt, Della J.	15354
Wilson, Watton	31459	Witt, Bert E.	15355
Wilson, Reed	31680	Witt, Mary E.	15356
Wilson, Dennis F.	31681	Witt, William M.	15357
Wilson, George W.	32410	Witt, John W.	15730
Wilson, William	32411	Witt, Naoma	15731
Wilson, Pearlie	32412	Witt, Rufus	15732
Wilson, Nancy	32099	Wofford, Jeneva	1495
Wilson, Lizzie	32338	Wofford, Frank	4741
Wilson, Annie	32503	Wofford, Clarence	4742
Wilson, Letitia M.	28819	Wofford, Rogers	4743
Wiltshire, Abbie	3642	Wofford, Harry	4744
Wiltshire, Ida J.	3643	Wofford, Emmett	4745
Wiltshire, Annie	3644	Wofford, Fannie	4746
Wiltshire, Mary	3645	Wofford, Mary	4907
Wiltshire, Duke	3646	Wofford, Bluford W.	11375
Wiltshire, Henry H.	3647	Wofford, William M.	11502
Wimer, Susan J.	8499	Wofford, Joseph V.	12244
Wimer, Rebecca D.	31917	Wofford, John C.	12245
Wimer, Jacob F.	31918	Wofford, Fay	12246
Wimer, Permelia E.	31919	Wofford, George A.	14014
Winget, Nannie A.	15244	Wofford, Sarah	14015
Winget, Charles M.	15245	Wofford, Callie B.	14016
Winget, Tedie M.	15246	Wofford, George N.	14017
Winget, Hannah P.	15247	Wofford, Amanda M.	14138
Winget, Jesse	15248	Wofford, Martha J.	14431
Winget, Myrtle L.	21853	Wofford, Lydia	15641
Winkler, Susan M.	10378	Wofford, Jesse	15642
Winkler, Losson	10279	Wofford, Jennie	15643
Winkler, Beulah	10380	Wofford, Ruth	16028
Winkler, Annie B.	10381	Wofford, Maggie	16029
Winkler, Mary Violet	10382	Wofford, Alexander	16030
Wingfield, Henry E.	9306	Wofford, Than	18502
Wingfield, William		Wofford, Taylor	18841
Edward	9307	Wofford, Josie	19047
Wingfield, Robert O.	24280	Wofford, Jesse	19048
Wingfield, Ella	24281	Wofford, Ned	19715
Wingfield, Henry R.	24282	Wofford, William	19730
Wingfield, Peter L.	24283	Wofford, Alma	19731
Wing, Otis	24604	Wofford, John	19732
Winn, Nannie E.	2944	Wofford, Ridge	19733
Winn, Clem	31290	Wofford, Ben	19734
Winn, Mary I.	2945	Wofford, Jim	19735
Winn, James	31295	Wofford, Nancy	20304
Winn, Levin H.	2946	Wofford, Charles	20592
Winn, Lila G.	2947	Wofford, James	21347
Winn, Nellie E.	2948	Wofford, Levi	27264
Winstead, Ada A.	14907	Wofford, Elizabeth E.	27611
Winstead, Florence E.	14913	Wofford, Jackson E.	27612
Winpeglar, Stella	3014	Wofford, Pearl	27613
Winton, Fagin	1012	Wofford, James M.	27745
Winton, Thomas	1013	Wofford, Clara M.	27746
Winton, Dee	1014	Wofford, Susie	28483
Winton, Rolen	1015	Wofford, Annie	28484
Winton, Martha E.	1016	Wofford, Mary	28485
Winton, Edith	5289	Wofford, Sarah	28486
Winton, Moses C.	5290	Wofford, George	29840
Winton, Audie	5291	Wofford, Charles	30406
Winton, Carl	5292	Wofford, Sampson	30598
Winton, Lloyd	5552	Wofford, David	30599
Winton, Dolly	5553	Wofford, Samuel	31711
Winton, Lillie B.	5554	Wofford, Linnie	32048
Winton, Dock L.	5556	Wofford, Ed	32905
Winton, Mansfield	5617	Wofford, Homer	32906
Winton, Ola P.	27883	Wolf, Eli	1215
Winton, Clarence	27884	Wolf, Caroline	1216
Winton, Leonard	27885	Wolf, Sallie	1217
Winton, Minnie Belle	27886	Wolf, Henry	1218
Wiswell, Susie	23009	Wolf, Richard	1219
Wiswell, Myrtle F.	23010	Wolf, Jennie	1220
Wiswell, Dee E.	23011	Wolf, Doney	1221
Witt, Eula L.	4494	Wolf, Louisa	1359

Name.	Roll No.	Name.	Roll No.
Wolf, Jack	1434	Wolfe, Jack	20976
Wolf, Katy	1435	Wolfe, Henry Wimer	21725
Wolf, Sarah	1436	Wolfe, Joseph	22540
Wolf, Richard	1437	Wolfe, William	22542
Wolf, Cynthia	1438	Wolfe, Avola M.	23754
Wolf, Humingbird	1439	Wolfe, Thomas	25539
Wolf, Peter	18536	Wolfe, Johnnie	25540
Wolf, Rosie	18662	Wolfe, Sarah	25747
Wolf, Jennie	18663	Wolfe, Mary	26330
Wolf, Arch	18664	Wolfe, Jennie	27092
Wolf, Sarah	18665	Wolfe, Jackson	27101
Wolf, Katie	18666	Wolfe, Betsy	27102
Wolf, Sam	18667	Wolfe, Eliza	27103
Wolf, Hider	20115	Wolfe, Maggie	27104
Wolf, David	27070	Wolfe, Ella	27105
Wolf, Hughes	27071	Wolfe, Henry	27106
Wolf, Monroe	27072	Wolfe, George	27107
Wolf, Redcloud	27073	Wolfe, James	27137
Wolf, Henry	27074	Wolfe, Katie	28566
Wolf, Annie	27075	Wolfe, Mollie	28708
Wolf, Mary	29987	Wolfe, John W.	28858
Wolfe, Elnora	261	Wolfe, Thomas L.	28859
Wolfe, Helena E.	262	Wolfe, Lena	28860
Wolfe, Jennie M.	263	Wolfe, Minnie	29155
Wolfe, Dora A.	264	Wolfe, Richard	29156
Wolfe, Susan A.	1299	Wolfe, Walter	29710
Wolfe, Mitchell	1300	Wolfe, Scott	29954
Wolfe, Alice	1301	Wolfe, Mary	29955
Wolfe, Thomas	1302	Wolfe, Elizabeth C.	30293
Wolfe, Elizabeth	1451	Wolfe, Mabel A.	30294
Wolfe, Charles	1452	Wolfe, Lena M.	30295
Wolfe, Lincoln	1453	Wolfe, Pickup	30679
Wolfe, Katie	1733	Wolfe, Loyal B.	31078
Wolfe, Arch	2040	Wolfe, Frances J.	31079
Wolfe, Jackson	6188	Wolfe, Winnie L.	31080
Wolfe, Jane Y.	6199	Wolfe, Bennie W.	31081
Wolfe, Lewis	6219	Wolfe, Lottie S.	31082
Wolfe, Louie	6220	Wolfe, Eliza	32069
Wolfe, Richard	6221	Wolfe, Melton	32341
Wolfe, William R.	7484	Wood, William H.	141
Wolfe, Kate T.	9114	Wood, Acenith	142
Wolfe, Paul T.	9115	Wood, Lewis E.	143
Wolfe, Ralph R.	9116	Wood, Lucy B.	144
Wolfe, Gordon B.	9117	Wood, Harriett T.	145
Wolfe, Margarett L.	9118	Wood, William O.	146
Wolfe, Foster L.	9367	Wood, Maudie May	147
Wolfe, Addie L.	9368	Wood, Bertha Ethel	148
Wolfe, Samuel W.	9369	Wood, Foster E.	6330
Wolfe, Frank	13577	Wood, William C.	6331
Wolfe, Addie	13984	Wood, Wyly E.	6518
Wolfe, William	15949	Wood, Marion F.	7681
Wolfe, Ben	15950	Wood, William H. C.	8381
Wolfe, Tom	15951	Wood, Henry C.	13020
Wolfe, Richard M.	16394	Wood, Ora	13021
Wolfe, Thomas P.	16472	Wood, Roxie M.	13649
Wolfe, Peter	16675	Wood, Auslem T.	13650
Wolfe, Eva	16676	Wood, Donas O.	13652
Wolfe, William B.	17590	Wood, Frederick T.	13651
Wolfe, William	19126	Wood, Rosa	13765
Wolfe, Jennie	19127	Wood, Wincie	13766
Wolfe, Nancy	19128	Wood, Henry H.	13767
Wolfe, Polly	19129	Wood, William H. Jr.	13884
Wolfe, Ezekiel	19130	Wood, Lillie P.	13885
Wolfe, Cealie	19131	Wood, John J.	14186
Wolfe, Willie	19180	Wood, Susan	14187
Wolfe, Lacy	19611	Wood, Frank	14188
Wolfe, Polly	19612	Wood, Jesse J.	14189
Wolfe, John	20269	Wood, John H.	14190
Wolfe, Thomas	20359	Wood, William C.	14381
Wolfe, Nannie	20360	Wood, Josephine A.	15045
Wolfe, John	20754	Wood, Frank	15110
Wolfe, Nancy	20755	Wood, Addie	15111
Wolfe, Lucy	20756	Wood, Bushyhead	15112
Wolfe, Alsie	20757	Wood, Minnie B.	15113
Wolfe, John	20758	Wood, Martha A.	15114
Wolfe, Charlotte	20759	Wood, Cherrie Z.	15115
Wolfe, Polly	20760	Wood, Stella E.	15116
Wolfe, Dick	20816	Wood, Robert O.	15117
Wolfe, Ike	20817	Wood, Lizzie V.	15118
Wolfe, De-saw-gue-la-sky	20818	Wood, Rosa E.	15119
Wolfe, Stop	20819	Wood, Martin C.	15414
Wolfe, Car-we-ge-ula	20820	Wood, Gracie E.	15415
		Wood, Nora E.	15416

Name.	Roll No.
Wood, Henry P.	22189
Wood, Samantha	22190
Wood, Houston	22191
Wood, Viella	22192
Wood, Tempy	22193
Wood, Sherman	22194
Wood, Minnie	22195
Wood, Hemp	22196
Wood, James F.	23669
Wood, James N.	23671
Wood, Columbus	23672
Wood, Bennie V.	23673
Wood, Frankie Ola	23674
Wood, Bessie M.	23675
Wood, Myrtle I.	23676
Wood, Lillie	23822
Wood, Earnest	23823
Wood, Roy	23824
Wood, Joda	23825
Wood, Josephine	23826
Wood, Clara L.	23827
Wood, Walter	23828
Wood, George G.	26286
Wood, Leonard C.	26287
Wood, Zollie E.	26288
Wood, Rollin M.	27490
Wood, William	28192
Wood, Amanda	30786
Wood, Susan H.	31492
Wood, Edward	31493
Woods, John	5904
Woods, Laura	5905
Woods, Amanda	7489
Woods, Lizzie	12409
Woods, Georgia A.	12410
Woods, Annie	12411
Woods, Mary	12412
Woods, Beulah	12413
Woods, Anna M.	21600
Woods, Amos Richard	21601
Woods, Margaret	26261
Woods, Charles W.	27698
Woods, James M.	27699
Woods, Louis E.	27700
Woods, Terry W.	27701
Woods, Mamie E.	27702
Woods, Elbert B.	27703
Woods, Charles A.	27704
Woodall, Stand W.	8248
Woodall, William C.	8305
Woodall, Leander	8306
Woodall, Lewis	8333
Woodall, James T.	8342
Woodall, Bettie	8343
Woodall, Ira	8344
Woodall, Isaac	8345
Woodall, James	8346
Woodall, Oceola	8347
Woodall, Effie B.	8348
Woodall, Walter	8414
Woodall, Nolen	8667
Woodall, Cora A.	8668
Woodall, Mabel C.	8669
Woodall, Fleeta E.	8670
Woodall, Maxine	8671
Woodall, John P.	8672
Woodall, Maggie E.	9433
Woodall, George W.	9912
Woodall, Susan	9913
Woodall, John D.	9914
Woodall, Nancy	9915
Woodall, William B.	9955
Woodall, Sarah A.	14751
Woodall, George	14752
Woodall, Maggie	14753
Woodall, Beulah	14754
Woodall, Ellen	14755
Woodall, Loonie	16299
Woodall, Hiram	17555
Woodall, Callie	20960
Woodall, Lola	21723
Woodall, Nannie	23021
Woodall, James B.	23852

Name.	Roll No.
Woodall, Anna M.	23853
Woodall, Frank F.	23854
Woodall, Jefferson A.	23855
Woodall, Benjamin J.	23856
Woodall, Mary E.	23857
Woodall, Lucy A.	23858
Woodall, Alee A.	23859
Woodall, Clara	27091
Woodall, Lucien	27576
Woodall, Anna	27577
Woodall, Amanda	27578
Woodall, George	28621
Woodall, Lucy A.	30328
Woodall, James	30437
Woodall, Sarah E.	30962
Woodall, Ida W.	30963
Woodall, Stand W.	30964
Woodall, Vera M.	30965
Woodall, William C.	499
Woodall, Margaret E.	500
Woodall, Rozie A.	821
Woodall, Katie	822
Woodall, Emma	823
Woodall, Thomas	824
Woodall, Watie	825
Woodall, James	826
Woodall, Charles	827
Woodall, Margarett A.	1835
Woodall, Buna Vista	1836
Woodall, Thomas F.	4476
Woodall, Emma V.	4477
Woodall, Mamie	4478
Woodall, Mary	4480
Woodall, Robert	5501
Woodall, Bertha E.	5502
Woodall, Daniel	5510
Woodall, Emaline	5511
Woodall, Oscar D.	5512
Woodall, Albert D.	5513
Woodall, Cora E.	5514
Woodall, Margaret	5551
Woodall, William	5561
Woodall, Henry H.	5562
Woodall, Maggie F.	6028
Woodall, John	6030
Woodall, Thomas	18213
Woodall, Richard	18214
Woodard, William	4637
Woodard, George	5129
Woodard, Viola	5130
Woodard, Edwin	5131
Woodard, Mary	5132
Woodard, William	7904
Woodard, Hannah E.	7905
Woodard, David B.	7906
Woodard, John S.	13738
Woodard, Martha	16861
Woodard, Eliza	16862
Woodard, Cowesta	16863
Woodard, Ollie	16864
Woodard, John	16866
Woodard, Sarah	16945
Woodard, Annie	16946
Woodard, Ann Eliza	17905
Woodard, William	21362
Woodard, Margaret A.	25008
Woodard, James O.	25009
Woodard, Zachariah	25010
Woodard, Nellie E.	25011
Woodard, Albert	25012
Woodard, Bert	25013
Woodard, Joseph	28820
Woodard, Nannie	28821
Woodard, Mary	28822
Woodard, Henry	28823
Woodard, Jackson	28824
Woodard, Martha	28825
Woodard, Bunch	28826
Woodard, Nannie F.	28827
Woodard, Daniel	28828
Woodard, Allen	28829
Woodard, Looney O.	28830
Woodard, Minnie E.	28831

Name.	Roll No.	Name.	Roll No.
Woodard, Della	28832	Wright, Annie	17705
Woodward, Janie	4095	Wright, Lizzie	17706
Woodward, Edwin H.	4099	Wright, Loony	19494
Woodworth, Nancy A.	30326	Wright, Ellis	21832
Woodworth, Ora	30327	Wright, Charlotte	22472
Woody, Ida M.	11058	Wright, Johnathan	22473
Woody, Eunice A.	11059	Wright, Jack	22474
Woody, Inez M.	11060	Wright, Sallie	22475
Woolley, Texana	31851	Wright, Jesse V.	22615
Woolley, Irene W.	31852	Wright, Eli	22617
Woolley, Wilburn E.	31853	Wright, Jesse J.	22618
Worfford, Joseph	5201	Wright, Mary A.	22619
Worfford, Nannie	5202	Wright, John H.	22620
Worfford, William	5203	Wright, Mertle D.	22621
Worfford, Charles	5204	Wright, Ellis B.	23479
Worfford, Troy	5205	Wright, William E.	23480
Worfford, Mary	5206	Wright, F. Otto	23481
Worfford, Jesse	5207	Wright, C. Mayes	23482
Worfford, Martha	5208	Wright, J. Bryan	23483
Worfford, Monnett	5209	Wright, Ida L.	23484
Worfford, Lewis	5210	Wright, Jack L.	23485
Work, Charles	7789	Wright, Ruth	23486
Work, Eliza	7790	Wright, William W.	27744
Work, John	7791	Wright, Tilmon	29435
Work, Jesse	7792	Wright, George W.	29436
Work, William	7793	Wright, Cornelius	29437
Work, Maggie	23209	Wright, Benjamin F.	29617
Work, Edith	23211	Wright, Belle	29618
Wren, George H.	4646	Wright, Willie E.	29619
Wren, Charles R.	4647	Wright, Julia A.	29620
Wright, Caleb	1893	Wyche, Robert D.	6046
Wright, Jacob C.	2801	Wyche, Effie	6047
Wright, Lizzie	3725	Wyche, Jessie C.	6048
Wright, William C.	3726	Wyche, Bernice M.	6049
Wright, George	3727	Wyche, John W.	11703
Wright, Nettie M.	3728	Wyche, Willie M.	11704
Wright, Mark C.	3729	Wyly, William B.	3663
Wright, Grace L.	3730	Wyly, Robert L.	13772
Wright, Annie	6193	Wyly, Oliver L.	13873
Wright, William R.	6194	Wyly, Betsy	13874
Wright, Ethel J.	6527	Wyly, Robert M.	13875
Wright, Jesse E.	6637	Wyly, Albert S.	16401
Wright, Mary E.	6638	Wyly, Wilson	19049
Wright, Willie C.	6639	Wyly, Alice	22347
Wright, Nancy	7948	Wyly, William E.	22348
Wright, Lizzie	8326	Wyly, Robert	22349
Wright, Bessie	8327	Wyly, John E.	22350
Wright, Emma	8328	Wyly, George	25889
Wright, Maurice K.	8329	Wyly, Nannie	25890
Wright, Joe B.	8330	Wyly, John D.	25891
Wright, Minnie E.	8331	Wyly, Elijah	25892
Wright, Maggie E.	8374	Wyly, Frank	25893
Wright, Mabel	8375	Wyly, Percy	26712
Wright, Dora	8376	Wyly, Robert J.	26713
Wright, Benge	8377	Wyly, Leah	26714
Wright, Willie E.	8378	Wyly, Thurman	26715
Wright, Tony M.	8379	Wyly, Lydia	28304
Wright, Pauline	8380	Wyly, Cora A.	29739
Wright, Mollie J.	9691	Wyly, Steeler	32049
Wright, Fannie M.	9692	Wyly, Nelsinny	32050
Wright, Samuel D.	9693	Yaholah, Dave	20517
Wright, Gurtrude	9694	Yaholah, Lydia	20518
Wright, Jackson W.	10779	Yaholah, John	20519
Wright, Katie	10780	Yaholah, Alex	20520
Wright, Shelly K.	10781	Yaholah, Rock	20521
Wright, William		Yaholah, Jack	20522
Jackson	10782	Yaholah, Sam	20523
Wright, William W.	14674	Yaholah, Jennie	20537
Wright, Mollie	14675	Yaholah, Johnson	29107
Wright, Jesse	14676	Yaholah, Nellie	29109
Wright, Colbert	14677	Yaholah, Polly	29108
Wright, William	14678	Yaholah, Heavy	29110
Wright, Ada	14679	Yaholah, Kahorkah	29111
Wright, Ellis S.	15328	Yaholah, Wuttie	20828
Wright, Ella W.	15329	Yaholah, Jack	20829
Wright, Alexander D.	15458	Yaholah, Ehhyoikah	20832
Wright, Jackson	17685	Yaholah, Daniel	20847
Wright, Annie	17686	Yaholah, Lewis	21058
Wright, Lucinda	17687	Yaholah, Nannie	28517
Wright, James	17701	Yahn, Rebecca	11685
Wright, Sarah	17702	Yarborough, Lizzie	4751
Wright, Thomas	17703	Yarborough, Miner-	
Wright, Josie	17704	va W.	29594

Name.	Roll No.	Name.	Roll No.
Yarborough, Samuel A.	29595	Young, James	17289
Yarborough, Minerva	29596	Young, Tom	17814
Yarborough, Bessie	29597	Young, Cynthia	17815
Yarborough, Roy	29598	Young, William	17817
Yarter, Clem	18806	Young, Joseph	17833
Yates, Ellen	4737	Young, Peggie	17834
Yates, Edith	4739	Young, George	17835
Yates, George	4750	Young, Lewis	17876
Yeargain, Mary J.	560	Young, Mary	17877
Yeargain, Turner A.	561	Young, Alice	17878
Yeargain, Robert P.	562	Young, Simon	17879
Yeargain, Scott A.	29237	Young, John W.	17881
Yeargain, Majorie C.	29238	Young, Jack	17888
Yeargain, Joseph D.	29239	Young, Amanda	21919
Yearger, Nannie I.	557	Young, Viola	17880
Yearger, Laura V.	558	Young, Lucy	29233
Yearger, Claud W.	559	Young, Oo-yastah	29235
Yellowbird, Sallie	19512	Young, Will	29236
Yellow-bird	19515	Young, DeWitt W.	9859
Yocum, John V.	11697	Young, Bird Alie	18300
York, Lillie B.	13558	Young, Mamie E.	11406
York, Vera Maud	13359	Young, Della	14143
Yost, Catherine	8651	Young, Thomas Straugh	5282
Yost, Ella	8652	Young, Alcy	25635
Young, Charles	2036	Young, Lyda	20232
Young, Betsy	2037	Young, Willie	16125
Young, Callie	2038	Young, James	25962
Young, Silas	2039	Young, Tassel	21355
Young, Roach Jr.	2112	Young, Sallie	21356
Young, Lillie M.	2874	Young, Steps	21357
Young, William	2875	Young, Jency	21358
Young, Esther	2876	Young, Ned	21359
Young, Thomas	2877	Young, Annie	16123
Young, Eli	2878	Young, Nathan	31087
Young, Houston	2879	Young, Edward	31188
Young, John	2880	Young, Mary E.	31660
Young, Roach	3198	Young, Emma L.	31661
Young, Nancy	3199	Youngbird, Isaac	18462
Young, Richard	3200	Youngbird, Nancy	18463
Young, Louisa	5233	Youngbird, Lucy	18464
Young, Daniel Jr.	5234	Youngbird, Nancy	25749
Young, Jessie	5235	Youngbird, White	28462
Young, Thomas F.	5278	Youngbird, Aggie	28463
Young, Lilietta	5279	Youngbird, Annie	28464
Young, Commillious	5280	Youngbird, Charlotte	30572
Young, Camie M.	5281	Youngdeer,	20892
Young, Joshua	6291	Youngdeer, Nannie	20893
Young, Richard	6292	Youngdeer, Reuben	20894
Young, Roy V.	30125	Youngduck, Cah-tay-ah	18811
Young, Carrie E.	29787	Youngduck, Noah	18812
Young, Robert A.	7274	Youngduck, Joe	20900
Young, James L.	8786	Youngduck, Stacy	20901
Young, Eva B.	9355	Youngduck, Keller	25933
Young, Malinda	9855	Youngduck, Susan	20904
Young, John W.	9858	Youngduck, Nancy	28509
Young, Frank L.	9921	Youngduck, Nepie	28510
Young, Mary L.	10833	Youngpig, Arch	18861
Young, Cornelia B.	10834	Youngpig, French	18864
Young, Clara E.	10835	Youngpig, Betsy	18862
Young, James E.	10836	Youngpuppy, Eunuch	30657
Young, Mary H.	11403	Youngpuppy, Jennie	30658
Young, Otto A.	11404	Youngpuppy, John	30659
Young, Hattie	11405	Youngwolf, Dave	20024
Young, Samantha J.	28869	Youngwolf, Mary	20025
Young, Nellie M.	28870	Youngwolf, Sallie	20027
Young, Bessie B.	28871	Yount, Sarah	13417
Young, Pressha S.	28214	Zane, Jefferson	10693
Young, Grace B.	28215	Zane, Etha	31383
Young, Oshen P.	28216	Zane, Arizona L.	31410
Young, Ollie M.	28217	Zeigler, Samuel	31479
Young, William J.	28218	Zeigler, Nancy	31480
Young, Mary	28219	Zeigler, Jeremiah	31481
Young, America	14139	Zeigler, Charlotte	31482
Young, Ludeny	14140	Zelgar, Sarah E.	10687
Young, Oscar F.	14141	Zelgar, Mary	10688
Young, Maggie	14142	Zelgar, Josie E.	10689
Young, Mary	14921	Zelgar, Elva	10690
Young, Henry L.	14923	Zeno, Maud	7458
Young, Richard	14924	Zinn, Melvina J.	7275
Young, Robert	14925	Zinn, William H. F.	7276
Young, Eva	14926	Zufall, Nannie J.	25464
Young, Dewey B.	14927	Zufall, Roy E.	25465
Young, Eva	17288	Zufall, John	25466

Name.	Roll No.	Name.	Roll No.
Zufall, Irene	25467	Zufall, Marion R.	27919
Zufall, Mattie	25468	Zufall, Eva	27920
Zufall, Maggie	27910	Zulkey, Rhoda I.	31616
Zufall, Pearl E.	27911	Zulkey, Charles W.	31617
Zufall, Oscar O.	27912	Zulkey, Alexander	31618
Zufall, Maggie	27913	Zulkey, Leroy H.	31619
Zufall, Benjamin H.	27914	Zulkey, Minnie M.	31620
Zufall, Grace A.	27915	Zulkey, Ada A.	31621
Zufall, Herbert	27916	Zulkey, Oliver C.	31622
Zufall, George Jr.	27917	Zulkey, Mark L.	31623
Zufall, Lewis E.	27918		

INDEX TO
MINOR CHEROKEES BY BLOOD

Name.	Roll No.
Arrington, Thomas Aubrey	1127
Arrowood, Roy	2785
Arterberry, Ruth	2147
Arterberry, Florence L.	2148
Arwood, Jimmie Allen	473
Arwood, Mary Pearl	474
Ashes, Katie	3990
Ashley, Elsie Lee	3920
Atkins, Mable M.	969
Atkins, Jack H.	961
Atkisson, Royce A.	3988
Atkisson, Ada M.	3989
Backwater, Polly Ann	4830
Badger, Joseph	4003
Badger, Hattie	4004
Badger, Alice	4005
Bailey, Robert L.	135
Bailey, Columbus	2604
Bailey, John Adam	2605
Bailey, Goldie Grace	1548
Bailey, Lilian	1549
Bailey, Theodore Roosevelt	1732
Baird, Lessie M.	1620
Baker, Vera	1419
Baker, Opal Fay	2048
Baker, Arphie Ray	2189
Baker, Matt R.	2332
Baker, Oliver Raymond	2463
Baker, Donald	4118
Baker, Gladys V.	4119
Baker, Oliver C.	1042
Baker, Ray	1357
Baker, Mary Maria	1358
Baldridge, David Rogers	683
Baldridge, Millard Curtis	684
Baldridge, Lizzie	2151
Baldridge, Jackson A.	3605
Baldridge, Rose E.	3606
Baldridge, Ollie	3996
Ballard, William H. Jr.	10
Ballard, Freeman Stokes	1795
Ballard, Mary Wilmer	913
Ballard, Jenevieve	914
Ballard, Geesquantnee S.	1136
Ballard, George W.	1556
Ballard, Cherokee Elmiria	2190
Ballard, Fannie Elizabeth	2191
Ballard, Lucien Keith	2427
Ballard, Frona	2742
Ballard, Jack	2743
Ballard, Capitola L.	2828
Ballard, Thomas	3874
Ballew, Kermit	3801
Ballew, Ellen J.	3924
Ballinger, Maiva C.	3189
Balloue, James	611
Bandy, Melvan G.	780
Bandy, Meala R.	781
Bankhead, Nelie Leona	4066
Barber, Pearl May	1604
Barger, Claude	243
Barger, Joseph S.	3406
Barger, William E.	607
Barger, Jesse R.	608
Barger, Bernice Ina	616
Barger, Edward Raymond	617
Barger, Cora	2519
Barke, Lemie Lavicie	2037
Bark, Betsie	2043
Barks, Mathew Miles	1133
Barker, John Curtis	513
Barker, Bertha Burnice	2266
Barnes, Bessie	2291
Barnes, Virgil T.	2041
Barnes, Lafayette F.	2042
Barnes, Bonnie Lee	2928
Barnes, Cleo	2929
Barnes, Mary Beatrice	4353
Barnes, Eula May	3897

Name.	Roll No.
Barnes, Pheba	832
Barnes, Phema	833
Barlow, Robert Lee	4411
Barnett, Flora M.	118
Barnett, Raymond L.	119
Barnett, Lloyd Eugene	501
Barnett, Alma A.	3508
Barnett, Arlis D.	3509
Barnett, Bertha M.	3349
Barnett, Lenora	3223
Barnett, Jessie McDonald	4213
Barnoskie, Lizzie	4730
Barr, Ota E.	4179
Barr, Thelma	4701
Barrett, Jack	101
Barrett, Hilda Jessie	1505
Barrick, Bessie	56
Barry, Emmie Gertrude	2740
Baskins, Leroy	3959
Bass, Harold E.	499
Bat, Earthy	2566
Bat, Daniel	2567
Bates, Christol Iva	3336
Batt, Charles	1286
Batt, Daylight	2187
Batt, Lucy	2188
Batt, Richard W.	3537
Batt, Isaac N.	3538
Batt, William A.	3539
Batt, Anna Clyde	4214
Battenfield, Frantz	478
Baughman, Nannie Lewellan	2870
Baughman, Dora E.	2871
Bazzell, Fay	1503
Bazzell, Leroy	1504
Beamer, Lola May	1541
Bean, Henry M.	533
Bean, Ora	1292
Bean, Eli	1293
Bean, Madge	1762
Bean, James Clifford	2786
Bean, Sidney C.	3694
Bean, Webster	4483
Bean, Lizzie	3875
Bean, Gladys Dee	3732
Beanstick, Grant	4558
Beanstick, Susannah	4559
Bearpaw, George	2493
Bearpaw, Stand Watie	3991
Bearpaw, Nancy	3992
Bearpaw, Ka-na-gee	4120
Bearpaw, Shaker	4121
Bearpaw, Emiline	4721
Bearpaw, John Waner	4722
Beaubien, Goldie J.	1787
Beaver, Maud	2789
Beaver, Nancy	4215
Beaver, Linnie	4216
Beaver, Eliza	4862
Beaver, Wilson	4738
Beavert, Tomie	827
Beck, Lillie B.	46
Beck, Frank	203
Beck, Ellis Elija	4511
Beck, Richard W.	1603
Beck, Joe R.	2345
Beck, Lotta Ann	2954
Beck, Fannie Leona	3299
Beck, Nettie M.	3612
Beck, Kermit	3348
Beck, Sarah I.	3668
Beck, Cliff	3669
Beck, Carl D.	3079
Beck, Arlie Lee	3733
Beck, Willie Oren	4389
Beck, Susie S.	4578
Beets, Nancy A.	779
Bell, Van Swanigan	477
Bell, Daisey	496
Bell, Irene	999
Bell, Mary	2044
Belt, Nancy	3649

Name.	Roll No.
Bell, Dee A.	3703
Bell, Laura	4243
Bell, George Jr.	4244
Bell, Jesse	1735
Bell, John Davis	1736
Bendabout, John	3993
Bendure, Charley E.	1056
Bendure, John B. Jr.	1057
Benge, Ritchard	393
Benge, Mitchell	394
Benge, Jeff M.	1362
Benge, Thelma	1407
Benge, Robert	1408
Benge, George Ross	1409
Benge, Maggie	2572
Benge, Ross	2573
Benge, Edna Lee	2863
Benge, Addie	4575
Benge, Dreivie H.	3608
Benge, Eva	3896
Benge, Jesse L.	3997
Bennett, Leroy	1359
Bennett, Dyton, Jr.	3695
Berd, Evlyn	1521
Berner, Ovel R.	613
Berner, Goldia M.	614
Berry, Albert King Jr.	1058
Berry, Clyde A.	1555
Berry, Minnie	4000
Berry, John Henry	4242
Berry, Zim L.	1738
Berryhill, Cora Lee	4507
Bethel, David Franklin	1989
Beveart, Lucy S.	1414
Bible, Lettie Ethel	4329
Bible, Jessie James	1017
Bibles, Clara Catharine	984
Bice, Latha J.	3029
Bice, Lillie L.	3030
Bickford, Charles Henry	995
Bickford, William Freddie	996
Bickford, Lizzie	997
Bigbey, Fred J.	4603
Bigbey, Teetsey Ora	2930
Bigbey, Marvin A.	2931
Bigby, Jessie Z.	3376
Bigby, Claude D.	3377
Bigby, Gladys D.	3994
Bigby, Mary C.	3995
Biggers, J. George	674
Bigfeather, Jennie	2868
Bigfeather, Annie	2869
Bigknife, Ogle N.	612
Billings, John Harvey	2665
Bingham, Kermit	1745
Bingham, Charles Winston	1746
Birchfield, Cecil F.	1130
Bird, Mary	610
Bird, Felix P.	1524
Bird, Florence H.	1525
Bird, Joseph	3923
Bird, John	4727
Bird, Eloise	4889
Bishop, Selma Erskin	113
Bishop, Madrid Orine	114
Bishop, Lillian Lucile	1055
Bishop, Eva Lucille	3480
Bishop, Ora May	1880
Bishop, Ruby Cathorine	1887
Bitting, Jackson	2822
Bitting, Mary	2823
Bivins, Gussie Bell	3737
Bivins, Thomas Lee	3738
Black, Nellie	1401
Black, Mary L.	2568
Black, Marian E.	2934
Black, Mary Tina	3080
Blackard, Vida Ruth	1403
Blackard, William Hormer	3481
Blackbird, William	4739

Name.	Roll No.
Blackbear, Gateyah	4868
Blackbear, Tsigeni	4848
Blackfish, William Vernie	354
Blackfox, Eliza	4939
Blackstone, Theodoria	1792
Blackstone, Alta	1793
Blackstone, Venia	1794
Blackstone, Nora	4780
Blackwood, Nancy Gladys	1607
Blackwood, Youngbird	3790
Blackwood, Margaret	3791
Blackwood, George	4014
Blackwood, Nathaniel H.	4269
Blair, Jewell	127
Blair, George R.	681
Blair, Viola	682
Blair, Ruby B.	4480
Blair, Katie	3921
Blair, Nellie	3922
Blasingame, Denis O.	526
Blasingame, Gladis P.	527
Blakemore, Susanna Margaret	2322
Blake, Mabel Heber	776
Blake, Hester Keet	777
Blalock, Ozeta Cecelia	4890
Bledsoe, Fannie Gray	116
Bledsoe, Bessie M.	2194
Bledsoe, Everet Barney	2195
Blevins, Rosa	1022
Blevins, Mollie	3465
Blevins, Fred	1400
Blevins, Lily May	2656
Blevins, Jabe	3611
Bliss, Vern A.	678
Bliss, Lawrence E.	679
Bliss, Luria V.	2652
Blossom, Lizzie	1356
Blossom, Sam	1411
Blossom, Phillipps	2196
Blossom, Emmie	2344
Blossom, Agnes	4491
Bluebird, Lizzie	2428
Bluebird, Johnson	4811
Bluejacket, Dana	208
Bluejacket, Jessie M. Lee	2292
Blythe, Mattie A.	831
Blythe, Cornelius	4147
Boatman, Ocie E.	1733
Boatman, Dovie L.	1734
Bob, Mary	4949
Bogle, Clifford	1405
Bogle, Josephene Susan	1406
Bolin, Mabel Edna	3584
Bolin, Ross Markham	3585
Bolin, Jack	4802
Bond, Porter W.	1968
Bond, Clifton T.	1969
Bond, Siddie S.	3149
Boney, Galesgewe	4847
Boon, Louria Booth	53
Booth, John H.	1291
Boswell, Lillie M.	620
Boswell, Sarah Elizabeth	2429
Boswell, Hooley Reuben	2651
Boudinot, Rachel C.	998
Bowen, Othel M.	274
Bowen, Iva May	2574
Bowen, Lillie J.	2575
Bowers, Ulah Agnes	58
Bowers, Deloss Harrison	59
Bowles, Riley	3789
Bowling, Liddy	2981
Bowman, Hubert Pond Creek	1131
Bowman, Samuel James Rosewell	1132
Boyd, Albert C.	2650
Boydstun, Gracie	618
Boydstun, Indiaola	619
Boyles, Lydia Irene	2829
Boyles, Buela Jane	2830
Brackett, Carroll M.	136

Name.	Roll No.
Brackett, Vernie J.	442
Brackett, Voil	1803
Brackett, Martha	2046
Brackett, Nancy	2047
Brackett, Rosa	4490
Brackett, Willie E.	3943
Bradburn, Charles Providence	4669
Bradley, Edna Cherokee	1353
Bradshaw, James Theodore	196
Bradshaw, James Kennaw	3164
Bradshaw, Ford Allen	3165
Bradshaw, Julia	3378
Bradshaw, Berthie Lee	3379
Bradshaw, John Luther	3025
Bradshaw, Chester	3026
Bradshaw, Clayton	510
Brady, John Davis	2425
Brady, Vernon C.	3998
Brady, Clella E.	3999
Branan, Virgil C.	49
Branan, George F.	50
Brannon, Lawrence A.	1608
Brannon, Jesse E.	1609
Branson, John E.	1739
Branum, Delia P.	3027
Branum, Victor A.	3028
Brassfield, Clarence Raymond	3788
Bratcher, Earnest	3300
Bray, Charles	1134
Bray, Bertie	1135
Breeden, Joseph A.	272
Breeden, Charles A.	273
Breeden, Velmer M.	680
Breeden, Mary Elizabeth	778
Breeden, Mary Annie	2569
Breeden, Lena Allie	2570
Breedlove, Jack Thompson	743
Breedlove, William Curtis	744
Brehmn, Sam Mayse	4001
Brehmn, Amos Rogers	4002
Breuninger, Louis D.	3224
Brewer, William S.	162
Brewer, George H.	1412
Brewer, John B.	2045
Brewer, Alice A.	2464
Brewer, Nannie McCracken	2865
Brice, Sarah Elnora	3178
Brice, Winnie Jane	3179
Brickey, Burnice Cathline	2741
Bridge, Susie	1970
Briece, Thelma M.	223
Briggs, Perdie	2826
Bright, John W.	1404
Bright, Gatsie H.	1413
Bright, Hirum	1606
Bright, Jewel	2461
Briley, Lela Elizabeth	3898
Brimage, Harvy	2257
Brimage, Mary	2258
Brimage, Christie	4798
Broaddus, Burnell	621
Brock, James C.	4212
Brockman, Pauline	2744
Brodie, Theo	138
Brooks, Eunice Geneva	3876
Brown, Eloise Caroline	240
Brown, Hamer E.	241
Brown, Henry L.	242
Brown, George Ann	500
Brown, May Irene	676
Brown, Bessie Glenn	391
Brown, Mary L.	392
Brown, Geneva Adrin	1268
Brown, Frederick C.	1269
Brown, Herbert Reed	775
Brown, Annie L.	4515
Brown, Noreana	4516
Brown, Jewel E.	808
Brown, Cecil E.	809

Name.	Roll No.
Brown, Robert Benton	815
Brown, Melinda A.	828
Brown, Fannie Elizabeth	829
Brown, Covie	915
Brown, Eben	962
Brown, Lella Emily	993
Brown, Joseph	994
Brown, Jess Lee	1360
Brown, Arthur	1361
Brown, Fern	4420
Brown, Fay	4421
Brown, Ruth May	4427
Brown, Bertha	2522
Brown, Ada	1605
Brown, Patty Ruth	3482
Brown, Lillian	3483
Brown, Akie	2040
Brown, Delora A.	2681
Brown, Isaac A.	2864
Brown, Maggie May	2956
Brown, Roosevelt	4468
Brown, Mary	3180
Brown, Nellie I.	3181
Brown, Leslie L.	3188
Brown, Vear	4173
Brown, George Fenton Carl Curtis	3686
Brown, Harvey Cecil	3
Browning, Thelma L.	422
Browning, Lawford L.	423
Bruner, Samuel L.	2551
Bruner, Gertrude C.	3734
Bruner, Allie M.	3735
Bruton, Jessie B.	911
Bruton, Bonnie D.	912
Bryan, Joseph Lucullus	81
Bryan, Mamie Alexander	82
Bryan, Clement	1250
Bryan, William Austin	3081
Bryant, Martha V.	4566
Bryant, Margarette D.	2426
Bryant, Eleanor	2667
Bryant, Hazel C.	2668
Buchanan, Martha	2049
Buckhorn, Arch	4663
Buckmaster, Ethel May	1200
Buck, Polly	2666
Buck, Gun-ni-da	2787
Buckner, Wales Spencer	350
Buckskin, Emily	2645
Buffalo, Florence	355
Buffalo, Henry Thomas	356
Buffington, Marie	1552
Buffington, Margueriet	1553
Buffington, Garret W.	3479
Buffington, Jesse A.	1601
Buffington, Claton D.	1602
Buffington, Bruce G.	3666
Buffington, Pink	3667
Buffington, Jessie May	3961
Buffington, Susan Nellie	3962
Bullette, Maudie	1364
Bullette, Fannie	4481
Bullette, Louis	4482
Bullock, Rosy Elizabeth	3960
Bumgarner, Rufus Keys	4293
Bump, Lillian E.	1417
Bump, Lawrance DeWitt	1418
Bunch, Betsey	1355
Bunch, Richard	4851
Bunch, Samuel	1737
Burchett, Leo Benjamin	2149
Burchett, Susie Bethel	2150
Burckhalter, Tom Churchill	1554
Burgess, George L.	1415
Burgess, Cooie E.	1416
Burgess, Eva Florence	2739
Burgess, Garnett	3613
Burnes, Bob	1137
Burnett, William James	3841
Burnett, Arche Cordelia	3952
Burr, Cordelia	236

Name.	Roll No.
Burr, Glaydis Pearl	4409
Burr, Myrtle	4410
Burr, Andy	3221
Burr, Lillie May	3222
Burr, Eva	3925
Burrows, Lela	609
Burrows, Lawrence Edward	615
Burrows, Eva Catherine	1000
Burrow, Susie May	1354
Burrows, William Reece	1363
Burton, Nolia L.	2788
Buse, Sherman B.	2907
Bush, Hallie	2192
Bush, Wheeler	2193
Bush, Nancy	4860
Bush, Easter	4861
Bushyhead, Jesse C.	4503
Bushyhead, Dennis W.	4504
Bushyhead, Louisa	2404
Bushyhead, Virgil Lee	2462
Bussey, Charles Pickens	677
Bussey, Earl William	1870
Buster, Roda	4416
Buster, George	4720
Buster, Mollie	4844
Butler, Roland F.	675
Butler, George Alva	2197
Butler, Birtha	2346
Button, Ruth Elliott	2198
Butts, Goldie May	735
Butz, Helen Rebecca	194
Butz, Emily Elizabeth	195
Buxton, Ollie	1890
Buxton, Mary Emiline	1889
Buzzard, Lon	4752
Buzzard, Nancy	4877
Buzzard, Loyd	4982
Buzzard, Elmer	4275
Byers, Georgia M.	3736
Byrd, Katherine E.	3280
Byrd, Grace T.	3281
Byrd, Claris Clementine	2682
Byrd, Bulah Bell	3706
Byrd, Thomas	3707
Byrd, Robert	4913
Byrd, Ruth N.	4914
Byrd, Edna May	2683
Caldwell, Annie	2211
Callahan, Cora M.	3842
Callison, Walter C.	4085
Calvert, Iola B.	2260
Calvert, Fount W.	1719
Calvert, Jasper F.	2063
Campbell, Alluwee	624
Campbell, Bessie Gertrude	395
Campbell, Flora	1796
Campbell, George Lowery Jr.	1797
Campbell, Taplin B.	886
Campbell, Earl B.	887
Campbell, Joseph M.	1001
Campbell, Clarence Ray	1815
Campbell, Ellis	2509
Campbell, Sam	2510
Campbell, Henry E.	2689
Campbell, Nannie Ethel	4021
Campbell, Charles	3650
Campbell, Nancy	4665
Campbell, Lucy	4666
Cannon, Spence W.	1247
Cannon, Florence Wilma	1248
Cannon, Fred	538
Cannon, Tilden	841
Cannon, Price	842
Cannon, James D.	1972
Cannon, Alvin A.	2445
Cannon, Effie L.	2790
Cannon, Fannie	3678
Cannon, James Leonard	4219
Canoo, Charles	3710
Canoe, Wyly	4659
Cantrell, Floyd Leslie	2709

Name.	Roll No.
Cantrell, John F.	2750
Cantrell, Hiram J.	2751
Carden, Maud M.	630
Carey, Thomas	916
Carey, Joseph S.	917
Carey, Dollie	2872
Carey, Emma	4926
Carey, Robert	2209
Cargill, Cecil W.	3877
Carlile, Senareste	685
Carlile, Noland E.	1393
Carlile, Minta Ellen	1394
Carlile, Emma Alma	4577
Carlile, Dollie Josie	3636
Carlile, Homer E.	3062
Carlile, Thomas Sydney	3193
Carlile, Levi	3194
Carlock, Jewell J.	1420
Carman, Lawrence	1820
Carman, Camuel Clarance	1821
Carnes, Dorthy M.	3582
Carnes, Aubrey	4347
Carnes, Hazel A. T.	2952
Carpenter, Lenard	2470
Carpenter, Mamie	2471
Carpenter, Evelyn G.	2984
Carrick, Thomas Ray	2791
Carrick, Ella Beatrice	2792
Carroll, Julia	1977
Carroll, Charlotte C.	2412
Carroll, Jensine E.	2413
Carselowey, Leverna G.	2053
Carter, Charles Walter	144
Carter, Ora B.	145
Carter, Joel E.	784
Carter, Houston	2495
Carter, John E. Jr.	2496
Carter, Sarah Elizabeth	3722
Carver, Bessie	209
Carver, Emma	2206
Casey, Herschell Everette	1515
Cason, Jessie	3005
Cason, Leethier	3006
Cass, Joseph H.	1059
Cass, Paul	1978
Cass, Lewis Porter	2241
Catcher, George	3458
Catcher, Losier	3459
Catcher, John Henry	2747
Catcher, Vance	2748
Catcher, A. A.	4599
Catcher, Ore L.	4600
Cates, Raymond	1765
Catron, Mary	4713
Catron, John Emma	4714
Catron, Loryetta J.	4972
Caulk, William M.	1242
Cavalier, Walter A.	2348
Caywood, Walter	238
Caywood, Lafayette	3350
Caywood, Jessie A.	3351
Cearley, Opal Modelle	4089
Chair, Cora M.	840
Chambers, Hurt Caldeen	4505
Chambers, Florence Velma	4403
Chambers, Henry Franklin	504
Chambers, Jennie Pauline	505
Chambers, Harold J. T.	458
Chamberlain, William Orvel	2985
Chance, Tilman G.	1421
Chance, Arthur	4010
Chance, Jasper Owen	4011
Chancellor, John C.	3393
Chandler, Thelma	1140
Chandler, Rebecca C.	1974
Chandler, Susie Catherine	2062
Chandler, Lillian	2793
Chandler, Frances	4294

Name.	Roll No.	Name.	Roll No.
Chandler, John	4295	Clark, Emma O.	2240
Chaney, Leona C.	456	Clark, Owen Blake	2797
Chanley, Ralph	2745	Clark, Peachie	2798
Chanley, Mary Edith	3383	Clark, Levi Scott	3926
Chapman, Harold Martin	2875	Clark, Ellis	3932
Charles, Mary Alice	4123	Clarke, Clement Cobb	4278
Charles, Annie	4893	Clawson, Lucile	42
Charles, Cha-lee-dee	4894	Clay, Bessie	4301
Charley, William C.	4390	Clay, Pearl Claire	4302
Charley, Athia Lucile	4391	Clay, Abraham L.	3381
Chastain, Rholan	1979	Clayton, Eldryce	
Chastain, John Jr.	3195	Wahneta	4124
Chastain, James B.	3196	Cleland, Wheeler	
Chaudoin, Johnnie	1929	Bancroft	3583
Chaudoin, Della	3197	Cleveland, Cathaleene H.	1138
Chaudoin, Curtis	3198	Clifton, Alice	2690
Cheek, Seba L.	125	Cline, Lella L.	2050
Cherry, Jessie Hilda	3928	Cline, Ross A.	2051
Cherry, Edith Gurtrue	3929	Cline, Anna Marria	2795
Chicken, Galoladi	4827	Cloud, Annie Lee	3602
Childers, Claud Franklin	9	Cloud, Riley H.	2472
Childers, Mervin Cleveland	14	Cloud, Lucile	2473
Childers, Ivy C.	15	Cloud, Joseph C.	3572
Childers, John Howard	16	Cloud, Embra Marie	2746
Childers, Vera Esta	1789	Cloud, Joeanna	2775
Childers, Minnie M.	3150	Cloud, Claucine	2794
Childers, Charles C.	3151	Clyne, Jennie E.	4433
Childress, Alma Allen	2205	Clyne, Sallie E.	4434
Chisholm, Chauncy	3742	Coast, Clara Bell	3228
Chisholm, Enes	3743	Coast, Albert Franklin	3229
Choate, James Anderson	2873	Coats, Louis H.	468
Choate, Juanita	4088	Coats, Capitolia W.	2293
Choate, Georgia Velma	4090	Coats, Lula May	2294
Chouteau, William Grant	1828	Coats, Bessie	2520
Chrisman, Audery Stella	2710	Coats, Lillie May	2503
Chrismon, Preston James	1980	Coats, Lillie M.	2653
Chrismon, Earl Gilbert	2199	Coats, Mary J.	2686
Chrismon, Louis Preston	2200	Coats, William P.	2687
Christian, James W.	4706	Coats, Robert P.	3343
Christian, Orlando O.	4707	Cobb, Onas R.	1002
Christie, May C.	1060	Cobb, Preston L.	1003
Christie, Lydia	3474	Cobb, Carolyn Elizabeth	2056
Christie, Annie E.	1622	Cobb, Ruth Isabel	2057
Christie, Blanch	2688	Cobb, Thomas	2552
Christie, William Jr.	3652	Cobb, Theodore Richard	2203
Christie, Dianne	4891	Cobb, Florence Lillie	2204
Christie, Kate	4892	Cobb, Harry Franklin	4597
Christie, Greece	4936	Cobb, Kedzie Pharr	4598
Christie, Amos	4887	Cobstill, Bessie	688
Chronister, Ella	4197	Cobstill, Bettie	689
Chuculate, Samuel C.	686	Cochran, Jay	244
Chuculate, Emma Lucile	1423	Cochran, Lethie M.	245
Chuculate, Nancy	2478	Cochran, Lucy	1614
Chuculate, Francis	2479	Cochran, Joe	1615
Chuculate, Robert	3278	Cochran, Walker	2208
Chuculate, Lizzie	3226	Cochran, Lucy	3139
Chuculate, Henry	3227	Cochran, Rose Lee	3020
Chuculate, Nellie	3792	Cochran, Price	3382
Chuculate, Ella May	3793	Cochran, Lula May	3060
Chuculate, Hyde	4086	Cochran, Eliza	3061
Chuculate, Oscar	4087	Cochran, Jack	3873
Chucuerlate, Lewis	4122	Cochran, Alec	4500
Chulio, Margaret	1971	Cochran, William	1894
Chulio, John W.	3499	Cochran, Ora May	4143
Chunestudy, John Davis	4950	Cockrell, Francis M.	3740
Chuwalooky, Steve	2669	Cockrell, Hilda	3741
Chu-wa-looky, Mary	2446	Cockrum, James A.	1270
Chu-wa-looky, Polly	3304	Cochrum, Grover	1613
Clapp, Bettie Ray	3095	Cockrum, Aleck	4148
Clapp, Dovie D.	3096	Coffee, Lincoln B. N.	3171
Clapper, Carl E.	454	Coffman, Sequichie E.	1621
Clapper, Arthur H.	455	Coker, Claud O.	4506
Clark, William H., Jr.	147	Coker, Milley L.	150
Clark, Ansie	625	Coker, George E.	2017
Clark, Lester Wayne	626	Coker, Alma E.	3614
Clark, William A., Jr.	1061	Coker, Mettie Irene	3082
Clark, Lillie B., Jr.	1062	Coker, Dora M.	4431
Clark, Velma Lee	1819	Cole, Mitchel	2052
Clark, Charles Henry	1513	Cole, Pearl C.	2207
Clark, Paunee	3484	Coleman, Alex Columbus	1804
Clark, George W.	2058	Coleman, Myrtle Delora	1805
Clark, Nancy Iola	2059	Coleman, Tom	4740
Clark, Myrtle	2239	Collier, Harmon	179

Name.	Roll No.
Collier, Eliza E.	1004
Collier, Lulu B.	1005
Collier, Mattie	4645
Collins, William R.	107
Collins, Caroline	108
Collins, Thomas Jefferson	166
Collins, Maggie D.	519
Collins, Rosa P.	520
Collins, Ivey G.	785
Collins, Susie A.	786
Collins, John Edgar	837
Collins, Sallie S.	1422
Collins, John Robert	2465
Collins, Nora E.	4006
Collins, Nannie M.	4007
Collins, Gazelle	4008
Collins, Allmon Andrew	4009
Collins, Columbia	4188
Collins, Robert Warren	4189
Collins, Houston	4678
Collipriest, Gertrude Ruby	2210
Comer, Sadie E.	148
Comer, Susie	149
Comfort, Bertha May	1612
Coming, Berry	3651
Condreay, Sadie	3466
Condry, Monte LaFayette	2468
Conklin, Carlis Allen	834
Conley, Fannie	536
Conley, Modie	537
Conley, Nancy	3905
Connally, Clarence William	3267
Conner, Marvin R.	275
Conner, Millard L.	276
Conner, Earl Loyd	1611
Conseen, Pliny	2061
Coodey, Andrew M.	517
Coodey, Sequoyah	518
Coody, Bessey Deliah	1788
Coody, Alice	1366
Coody, Samuel	3676
Coody, Joseph	3677
Coody, Susie	4012
Cook, Glen	2878
Cooley, Curtis B.	1973
Cooper, Floyd J.	2466
Cooper, John M.	2467
Coon, Claude Otto	528
Coon, Eva	529
Coon, Turtle	3964
Copeland, Lorena	838
Copeland, Theodore E.	839
Coram, Sarah	1616
Cordray, Letha M.	1829
Cordray, James Andrew	3404
Cordray, Bertha May	3405
Cordreay, James Benjamin	4697
Cordrey, Kerney	4878
Cordrey, Annie	4879
Cordon, Catherine Blount	38
Cormicle, Eva	1506
Corn, Anna Evelyn	1557
Corn, Dwight S.	1558
Cornatzer, Clarence D.	1043
Cornatzer, Nita T.	1044
Cornatzer, Rachel L.	2064
Cornatzer, Warner B.	2065
Cornsilk, Rosa	1514
Corntassell, Bertha	4376
Correll, Perry	3700
Couch, Lula E.	2152
Couch, Leon	2153
Couch, Christopher G.	2154
Couch, Leola	3794
Couch, Curtis Forman	3795
Couch, Alfred Buffington	239
Couch, William	515
Couch, Ruth C.	525
Coughran, Malinda	687

Name.	Roll No.
Coughran, Bessie	2749
Countryman, Scott	3467
Countryman, Florence	3468
Countryman, Arthur Wayne	4276
Countryman, Ralph	4277
Countryman, Velva Irene	1748
Countryman, Thomas Franklin	1749
Countryman, Oliver	1893
Covey, Tena M.	736
Cowan, Margaret Elizabeth	3248
Cowand, Henry Jefferson	782
Cowart, Martha E.	2060
Cowden, Fay Modie Marrie	2155
Cowles, Beaulah May	1139
Cowles, Silvia Rose	2497
Cowles, Elvia A.	2498
Cox, Sarah Vinitta	1623
Cox, Dilliard	1976
Cox, Isaac Leroy	2469
Cox, Ailem Wimer	2867
Coyne, Caroline	2347
Coyne, Catharine A.	2922
Crabtree, Clarence C.	3032
Craft, Flora Belle	4218
Craig, Thomas	1294
Craig, Lizzie	1295
Craig, Hugh Carl	3444
Craig, Burley	2702
Craig, Florence J.	4978
Craig, Callie P. V.	4979
Crail, Leonard	2156
Crail, Lewis	2157
Crain, Floyd Levi	260
Crain, Richard	1426
Crain, William Luther	1427
Cramp, John	3170
Crane, Etter	1276
Crane, Eva May	1277
Crane, Eula	4154
Crawford, Jessie	1046
Crawford, Carl Francis	1424
Crawford, Charley Lester	2654
Crawford, Emma Bell	4198
Crawford, Alice Leeola	1425
Cripps, Helen C.	2054
Cripps, Amy L.	2055
Crittenden, Eddie Andrew	627
Crittenden, Lena E.	964
Crittenden, Clyde	1212
Crittenden, Jennie M.	2576
Crittenden, Mary S.	2577
Crittenden, Susan Ailey	2494
Crittenden, Willis	2876
Crittenden, John	4399
Crittenden, Beatrice	1891
Crittenden, Forest	1892
Crocker, Alfred L.	1617
Crocker, Ella M.	1618
Crocker, Simeon W.	1619
Crocket, Winston G.	2158
Crossland, Myrtle M.	2670
Crossland, Dora	3190
Crossland, Emmett	3191
Crossland, Walter	3192
Crotzer, Iva J.	535
Crotzer, Willie I.	475
Crouch, Mary Lucile	2611
Crow, Lou	622
Crow, William	623
Crowder, Louner M.	2277
Crowder, Culvin	2278
Crowder, Robert Lee	3536
Crutchfield, Joseph Martin	1750
Culley, Thelma	628
Culley, Ira	629
Culver, Bluford	2752
Cumiford, John E.	835

Name.	Roll No.	Name.	Roll No.
Cumiford, Zeta	836	Dawes, Loyd	1516
Cummings, Albert	1184	Dawes, Edith Burnell	1517
Cummings, Willie C.	4217	Dawson, William Elbert	488
Cumpton, Ruth	3403	Dawson, Oowaluki	540
Cunningham, John		Dawson, Herbert Clinton	502
Calhoun	1365	Dawson, Uva Beatrice	503
Cunningham, Jeter		Dawson, Lorene M.	1283
Thompson	2986	Dawson, Opal	843
Cunningham, James		Dawson, Velma L.	3427
Oliver	2987	Dawson, Arthur Floyd	1006
Cunningham, Royal W.	3268	Dawson, Zola Ada	1007
Cunningham, David B.	3269	Dawson, Elbert	2282
Curry, Earl	783	Dawson, Edna May	2283
Czarnikow, J. Warren	3279	Dawson, Jewel P.	2499
Daggett, Lois	358	Dawson, Bessie J.	3088
Daggett, Jessie Ray	359	Dawson, Nora E.	3089
Daley, James M.	4778	Dawson, William Arthur	3933
Dameron, Martha	696	Day, Bennie Weaver	522
Dameron, Feby	697	Day, Lois Evelyn	523
Dancer, Stella May	4485	Dayton, Charles E.	986
Daniel, Eathel L.	541	DeLozier, Elsie Bell	965
Daniel, Leon R.	844	DeLozier, Joseph Wade	2212
Daniel, Samuel J.	845	DeShane, Leetho	1986
Daniel, Opal Ray	3421	DeVaughn, Lillie A.	2286
Daniel, Brewer	1201	Deal, Sadio May	830
Daniel, Peachie	1202	Deal, Callie	985
Daniels, William R.	634	Deal, Margarett A.	1428
Daniels, Opal Violet	1430	Deal, Joseph A.	1429
Daniels, Homer Lee	1431	Dean, James E.	2881
Daniels, Mary	3797	Deatherage, Callie M.	2069
Daniels, Willie	2530	Deatherage, Clara E.	2070
Dannenberg, Okla	191	Deerinwater, Chewie	4724
Dannenberg, Susie	230	Deese, Hugh John	2691
Dannenberg, Robert O.	693	Deitrick, Leora	2264
Dannenberg, Opal		Deitrick, Beulah	2279
Carmen	1141	Deitrick, Evelyn	2280
Dannenberg, Madgie N.	1142	Delgado, Delphia	3307
Darnell, Charles Luther	1159	Delozier, Clara J.	633
Dassler, Robert	3521	Demott, Fay	3152
Daugherty, Thomas W.	636	Demott, Emery Ray	3153
Daugherty, Joshua	4546	Dempsey, Jackson	539
Daugherty, Charley	2301	Denbo, Bertha O.	1255
Daugherty, Lulu	2066	Denbo, James Raymond	787
Daugherty, Katie	2213	Denbo, Milton D.	2215
Daugherty, Lila	2946	Denbo, Ida M.	2216
Daugerty, Mary	2947	Dennis, Basil B.	1559
Daugherty, Blue	3231	Dennis, Harold J.	1560
Daugherty, Jeff	3232	Denny, Ralph V.	4428
Daugherty, Dorthy D.	4199	Denny, Eromlys Nathan	1895
Daugherty, Elizabeth A.	4200	Denton, Edward F.	98
Daugherty, Thomas Jr.	4688	Denton, Virgie	1519
Davidson, Marvin Wayne	1271	Denton, Hurste	1520
Davidson, Robert Donnel	1272	Denton, Floyd	1624
Davidson, Athelene	4608	Denton, Tete M.	1625
Davis, Ella	2245	Devine, George Otis	2067
Davis, Anna D.	269	Devine, Robert Lee	2068
Davis, Margaret	424	Dial, Robert Lee	690
Davis, James	737	Dial, Isaac	2351
Davis, Edith M.	738	Dick, Eura	4619
Davis, Janie Bell	745	Dick, Verna	4620
Davis, Mary Aileene	1157	Dick, Arvil Luis	3557
Davis, Jewell Neal	1158	Dick, George	2989
Davis, Beula M.	1627	Dick, Margrett	3744
Davis, Nancy M.	1628	Dick, Jessie Taylor	3745
Davis, Sidney Cicero	2523	Dick, Henry	4812
Davis, Kattie	1985	Dick, Calvin	1898
Davis, William Theodore	3019	Dick, Mazel	1899
Davis, Richard Jefferson	4452	Dick, William	1900
Davis, Will	3308	Dickerson, Lee Ray	2612
Davis, William Andrew	4453	Dickson, Cleva Latitia	1790
Davis, John T.	3373	Dickson, Lucile	1791
Davis, James A.	3084	Dildine, Anna May	2799
Davis, Rutha May	3085	Dirteater, Sarah	2990
Davis, Ray Allen	3712	Dirteater, Jack	2991
Davis, Jessie James	3713	Disney, Minnie May	3064
Davis, Ellen E.	4807	Dixon, George W. Jr.	846
Davis, Willie	3845	Dixon, Samuel Paul	847
Davis, Cherry	3846	Dixon, Rubie M.	3286
Davis, George Anna	4013	Dobkins, Juanita C.	1802
Davis, Robert S.	4015	Dodge, Clifton Rogers	1984
Davis, Roberson C.	4091	Dodge, Arthur	4220
Davis, Kate Lois	4499	Dodge, Charles Vance	4373
Davis, Johnson	4886	Dodge, Russell	4374

Name.	Roll No.
Doherty, Clarisa J.	353
Doherty, Maimie T.	3562
Doherty, Robert R.	3563
Doherty, Roger E.	3843
Doherty, Anna B.	3844
Donaldson, William Henry	1896
Donnelly, Ray Edgar	2548
Dotson, Lewis B.	3294
Dotson, Chas.	3295
Doublehead, Lettie Francis	3437
Doublehead, Henry	3063
Dougherty, Tom	695
Downing, Maggie	4753
Downing, Noyah	1561
Downing, Fannie	2334
Downing, Jesse W.	2335
Downing, George	2349
Downing, Louisa	2350
Downing, Tommie	4442
Downing, Henry	2474
Downing, Owen Brady	2475
Downing, Thomas B.	2880
Downing, Mary	4803
Downing, Joannie	4804
Downing, Pearl	4625
Downing, Levi	3653
Downing, Mollie	3199
Downing, Alex	3200
Downing, Steve	3086
Downing, Maggie	3087
Downing, Stacy	4125
Downing, Nancy	4180
Downing, Lizzie	4946
Downing, Mose	4900
Downing, Robert L.	4392
Drake, James F.	2341
Drake, Mary A. M.	2342
Drake, Nora M. C.	2343
Drake, Fred John	4204
Drake, Seymour B.	4279
Dreadfulwater, Joel	2214
Dreadfulwater, Charley	3654
Drum, Flold Edward	4508
Dry, Willie	4819
Dry, Lucy	2800
Dry, Robert L.	1897
Drywater, Dick	3201
Dubois, James	469
Duboise, Fairry Marie	918
Duck, Ola	3401
Duck, Tom	3305
Duck, Davis	3306
Duck, Frank	3384
Duckworth, Helen Nanette	635
Dudley, Mattie E.	1629
Dudley, Edith M.	1630
Dudley, Ninnie	2217
Dudley, Hazel	2833
Dugger, Bessie Ethel	120
Dugger, Samuel E.	534
Duncan, Inola Josephine	1254
Duncan, Puna	1160
Duncan, Lena	1161
Duncan, Thelma M.	1518
Duncan, Charlie David	1432
Duncan, William, Francis	1433
Duncan, Ruth P.	1626
Duncan, Heman C.	1981
Duncan, Charles Dugger	2879
Duncan, Mary Nettie	3965
Dunham, Addie Ethel	2923
Duniphin, Marion L.	1982
Duniphin, Samantha J.	1983
Dunn, Myra	357
Dunn, Rosa Lee F.	1203
Dupree Eleanor	3522
Durall, Hugh Allen	691
Durall, George Marvin	692
Durham, Amanda L.	3083

Name.	Roll No.
Durkee, Emery C.	1011
Duval, Logan	3796
Duval, Mach	4907
Duval, Coleman	4908
Dykes, Henry Jackson	3934
Dye, Susan Bell	2832
Dyer, J. Blair	631
Dyer, Sell Word	632
Eagle, Jennie	2754
Eagle, Walter S.	4633
Eagle, Kee-Kee	4897
Eagle, Charley	4898
Eads, Emmet	2957
Earl, Susie	637
Earl, Reece	638
Early, Dovie	788
Earp, Hattie	361
Earp, Mattie	362
Earp, John L.	3123
Earp, Oscar L.	2711
Earp, Jay B.	3385
Earp, Josh William	3386
Easky, James	2992
Eaton, Charley	398
Eckert, Sarah Jane	1635
Edens, George W.	2476
Edmonds, William Henry	2531
Edmonds, Mertle Pearl	2532
Edmonds, Mary Catharine	4726
Edmondson, Hugh Allen	704
Eggleson, Mamie D.	1633
Eggleson, Lola B.	1634
Eibing, George Snyder	4973
Eibing, Frank August	4974
Elam, James Earl	3936
Elders, Charlie R.	1987
Eldridge, Harold Everette	2579
Eldridge, Jewell D.	2580
Elkins, Gladys	3318
Ellick, William	1631
Ellick, McNeer	1632
Ellington, Elmo Watts	192
Ellington, Marie	193
Elliott, Francis Lee	163
Elliott, Sadie M.	1705
Elliott, Ruth	3031
Ellis, William H.	167
Ellis, Gladys W.	399
Ellis, Nathaniel B.	3429
Ellis, Gracie L.	4334
Ellis, Maggie F.	4335
Ellis, Tommie	4576
Ellis, Vinton M.	2242
Ellis, Harvey Nathaniel	4016
Ellis, Minnie M.	1926
Elrod, Russell C.	2993
England, Dudley	1434
England, Henry	1435
England, Beulah L.	3523
England, Myrtle V.	2352
England, Cora E.	2353
England, Alex	2701
England, Georgie	3110
England, Opel V.	2882
England, Mary	3746
Epperson, Arthur R.	506
Epperson, Alec Leonard	700
Epperson, Lola May	701
Epperson, Willie C.	702
Epperson, Lowern F.	703
Ervin, Eva Eviline	4280
Essex, Paul R.	1636
Estes, Bertha L.	360
Etter, Howard	3109
Evans, Mary	747
Evans, Katie Mayree	3804
Ewers, Alice M.	2071
Ewers, Ethel M.	2072
Ewers, George P.	2073
Ewers, Veva Lee	3558

Name.	Roll No.
Ewers, Roscoe Glenn	3935
Fair, Clide	2078
Fain, Stella Xinzy	2994
Fallleaf, George	3847
Fallin, Maybelle	1837
Falling, Oo-chah-le-tah	3433
Falling, Jess	2382
Falling, Gilbert	4552
Falling, Henry Edward	4553
Falling, George	3524
Fallingpot, Lacy	4551
Farbro, William Carl	3968
Fargo, Joe W.	1757
Fargo, May E.	425
Fargo Benjamin E.	426
Fargo, Murphy	3798
Farmer, Frankie Oleta	1287
Farrington, Abram	363
Faulkner, Alice Ruby	126
Faulkner, Willie R.	639
Faulkner, Winnie L.	640
Faulkner, Hastings M.	641
Faulkner, James Tillman	642
Faulkner, Lavina H.	1638
Faulkner, Frank Foreman	1639
Faulkner, Oma	2075
Faulkner, Ivie Irene	2076
Faulkner, Allie L.	2354
Faulkner, Olga M.	2095
Faulkner, Alice	3310
Faulkner, Jennie May	3752
Faulkner, Bessie	4361
Fausett, Florence	2080
Feeling, Jeff	3540
Feeling, Andrew	3541
Feeling, Rachel	4696
Feland, Bernice	989
Fencer, Dick.	4901
Ferguson, Cookson	2593
Ferguson, Grace	2801
Fields, William McK.	4
Fields, Sylvia C.	1018
Fields, Mildred B.	1019
Fields, Lewis B.	919
Fields, Freda M.	966
Fields, Mable Pearl	3901
Fields, John Thomas	1122
Fields, Edna Serena	4413
Fields, Charles N.	1823
Fields, Viola	1824
Fields, Rosa	3445
Fields, Alpha	3446
Fields, James E.	1163
Fields, Edna Irene	3486
Fields, Owen G.	2074
Fields, Jackson T.	3525
Fields, Bertha Jaunita	2623
Fields, Lillian	2505
Fields, Ollie	3543
Fields, Mamie L.	1798
Fields, George E.	1799
Fields, Thelma	3124
Fields, William	1878
Fields, Charley	3938
Fields, Catcher	4864
Fields, Nannie	4865
Fields, Susie	4682
Fields, Fanny	4686
Fields, Ross	4687
Filmore, Della	4789
Filmore, James	4790
Filmore, Millard	4791
Fine, Calvin D.	121
Fine, Indaola	122
Fish, Joe	4681
Fisher, William Elzie	364
Fisher, Ivy Marinda	365
Fisher, North L.	706
Fisher, Carrie	1206
Fisher, Louise Chandler	2305
Fisher, Mose Wiley	4128
Fisher, Lillie	4129

Name.	Roll No.
Fite, Denman Wyly	228
Fitzgerald, Jessie E.	249
Fitzsimmons, Grace F.	2218
Fitzsimmons, Cecil P.	3166
Flanagan, Ruby May	1143
Flanagan, Ruth Alta	1144
Flanagan, Robert E.	2077
Flanigan, Frank P.	3392
Fleetwood, Clifford	1162
Fleetwood, Rosie Nellie	4763
Fleming, Mary E.	790
Fleming, Annie May	791
Fletcher, Willie H.	1637
Flint, Daphne	849
Flint, Lillian E.	3302
Flint, Herold W.	3303
Flint, Hazel Leah	3749
Flint, Adrain Leon	3750
Flint, Jessie Juanita	1902
Flippin, Rebecca Lane	99
Flournoy, Yula C.	789
Flournoy, James F.	967
Flournoy, Leo Clinton	968
Flournoy, Dennis	4281
Flournoy, Clifton D.	4282
Fluke, Fransis M.	792
Fluke, Annie B.	793
Fluke, Susan	3878
Fodder, William	4221
Fogg, Lena	3751
Fogg, Gibb	4076
Fogg, Annie	4077
Fogle, Opal	2885
Fogleman, Jossie L.	2477
Fogleman, Maggie E.	2402
Fogleman, Beulah	2403
Folsom, Violie R.	1438
Folsom, John D.	1439
Folsom, Opal	3714
Folsom, William Gill	3715
Fool, Richard	402
Fool, Bessie	403
Fooy, Madaline L.	2219
Forbes, Albin	2995
Forbes, Fannie	4632
Ford, Virginia	1836
Foreman, Ruth	185
Foreman, Cherokee	186
Foreman, Jewel M.	4602
Foreman, Leo E.	705
Foreman, Margaret Edith	400
Foreman, Jesse	990
Foreman, John Jefferson	2032
Foreman, Lilla A.	2958
Foreman, Richard	2959
Foreman, George Clifton	3309
Foreman, Andy Joe	3747
Foreman, Charley E.	3748
Foreman, Jack T.	4245
Foreman, Lee Roy	4270
Foreman, Daniel	4970
Foreman, Dee-gin	4971
Foreman, Callie	4870
Forsythe, Ellen A.	1903
Foster, Denver J.	268
Foster, Harvey Bennett	229
Foster, Joseph	507
Foster, Emmett Herold	643
Foster, William N.	848
Fourkiller, Dee-da-noo-ski	4969
Fourkiller, John	4741
Fourkiller, Sequoyah	4742
Foust, Mamie May	1436
Foust, Minnie O.	1437
Fouts, Eula	1284
Fouts, Nellie	1285
Fowler, Eva Lou	1640
Fowlks, Anna	2755
Fowlks, George William	2756
Fox, James F.	2553
Fox, Sarah	4834
Franklin, Ella K.	401

Name.	Roll No.
Franklin, Hellen Ruth	1563
Franklin, Margaret M.	4340
Franks, Johney Preston	3485
Frazier, Rosa	1
Frazier, Lillian	2079
Frazier, Gracie	3940
Free, Clarence R.	3966
Free, Maggie M.	3967
Freeman, Howard E.	258
Freeman, Calvin	3548
Freeman, Henry Perry	2883
Freeman, Jack Alven	2884
French, Leona Mattie May	987
French, John H.	988
French, Walter Paul	1988
French, Nina	2081
French, Walter Inman	2082
French, Maud	2251
Frenchman, Adam F.	850
Frenchman, Earnest	4034
Fritz, Lena May	1562
Frog, John	4092
Fry, Robert Lawrence	3500
Frye, Harriett B.	111
Fryar, Vance	920
Fulton, Frank A.	4655
Funk, Rovilla M.	41
Gabriel, Tracy Ethel	2757
Gabriel, Loyd Elzeworth	2758
Gaffney, Robert	460
Gaines, Willie Juanita	1838
Galcatcher, Mollie	1642
Galcatcher, Tuxie	2159
Galcatcher, Nannie	2160
Gamble, Edgar William	921
Gamble, Bodly I.	1641
Gann, Mary	644
Gann, Sue	2902
Gann, George	2296
Gann, Floyd	3941
Gann, Cynthia	1904
Gardenhire, William Thomas	2355
Gardenhire, George Martin	2356
Garner, Roy	651
Garner, William Hood	4621
Garnes, Elva May	3573
Garnes, Earl Wilson	3574
Garrett, Kathleen Butler	406
Garrett, Edna	798
Garrett, Edward Ottis	4018
Garrett, Annie E.	2960
Garrett, Tedy R.	2961
Garrett, Millie R.	2962
Garrison, Susie	1564
Garrison, L. P.	1565
Garroutte, Robert Anderson	3125
Garroutt, Edith May	3090
Garroutt. Ealinor S.	3091
Jarvin, Elmer C.	508
Jasaway, Ruby F.	1993
Jaylor, Emma Fay	3160
Jaylor, Agnes Elizabeth	3161
Jaylor, Elizabeth	3879
Jentry, Hearst T.	2085
Jertie, Stan Gray	3314
Jhormley, Maurice	1164
Jhormley, Connell Rogers	1165
Jhormley, Janice F.	2431
Jhormley, Ahniwake	2658
Jhormley, Georgia B.	2659
Jibbs, Leonard Andrew	794
Jibbs, Ezra F.	795
Jibbs, Mary D.	2511
Jibbs, Edward H.	2512
Jibbs, Nellie	3033
Jibbs, Preston F.	3034
Jiboney, Mary Elizabeth	2357
Jibson, John A.	796
Jibson, Maggie	797

Name.	Roll No.
Gibson, Lin Otho	816
Gibson, Mary Louise	1648
Gibson, Clausine	4033
Gibson, Lulu May	4205
Gilbert, Charles Lester	142
Gilbert, Florence	484
Gilbert, Allen	485
Gilbert, Betsy Ann	2835
Gillespey, Joseph F.	2221
Gilliam, Robert Hershall	1443
Gilliam, Alma May	4025
Gilstrap, Harry	2084
Gilstrap, Alva	4858
Gipson, Finney Dovie	1646
Gipson, Fannie Laura	1647
Gipson, Austin Edward	3559
Girty, Nora	4299
Girty, Henry D.	4300
Gish, Earl	1643
Gish, Ada	1644
Givens, Marvin Nicholas	1952
Givens, Martha Lee	1953
Glad, Frank	3035
Glad, Joe H.	3036
Glass, Franklin	4709
Glass, Lizzie B.	3469
Glass, Mary J.	4446
Glory, Martin	3203
Glory, Annie	3270
Goad, Arthur	4096
Goddard, Walter T.	3526
Goddard, John H.	4253
Goddard, Oren E.	4254
Godfrey, Ernest Powell	2948
Goforth, Mary E.	1166
Goingsnake, Royal	4246
Goingsnake, Lizzie	4247
Goins, Ezra	542
Goins, Ethel	4155
Golden, D.	3312
Golden, James	3313
Gonzallis, Jackoline	3387
Goodall, Samuel A.	2927
Goodman, Master B.	1990
Goodman, Joseph P.	1991
Goodman, Kathryn E.	3549
Goodrich, Edith	851
Gordon, Raymond D.	546
Gordon, Lucy Belle	4604
Gordon, James Grover	4605
Gordon, Russell	2924
Gordon, Dora E.	2834
Gordon, William F.	4093
Gordon, Odie M.	4094
Gore, Elda B.	4523
Gore, Heber B.	4524
Goss, Otis W.	1441
Goss, Owen A.	1442
Goss, William T.	3580
Gott, William	646
Gott, Moses	4513
Gott, Joseph	4514
Gott, Alice Pauline	991
Gott, Lola Bell	4716
Gourd, Lee R.	1992
Gourd, Rufus R.	2973
Gourd, Roy E. R.	3680
Graham, Lenord Frances	1146
Graham, Elmer Andrew	1147
Graham, Carl C.	4019
Graham, Franklin A.	4020
Graham, Josie	4438
Graham, Marvin	4439
Graham, William C.	4767
Graham, Joseph A.	3154
Graham, Alexander Travis	3701
Graham, Sallie May	3702
Grass, Levi	2249
Graves, Clarence, Jr.	3530
Graves, Helen E.	4156
Gravitt, Oma L.	32
Grayson, Annie	3803

Name.	Roll No.	Name.	Roll No.
Grayson, Emma	4030	Hall, Charles Oliver	802
Grazier, Joseph	4842	Hall, Bessie May	461
Grazier, Homer M.	4843	Hall, Gilbert Spencer	2810
Greathouse, George		Hall, Laura Esther	2811
Edward	4131	Hall, Jessie Gladys	4535
Greece, Bert	3202	Hall, John Bright	1845
Green, Harden H., Jr.	1251	Hall, Gracie	4554
Green, Margurrete S.	1252	Hall, Martha E.	2309
Green, Marion F.	123	Hall, Joseph N.	4805
Green, James F.	124	Hall, Elsa Maree	2996
Green, Carl Edward	490	Hall, Eugene	3753
Green, Oliver L.	2988	Hall, Kittie	4248
Green, Velma	557	Hallford, John Arthur	1910
Green, Geneva	992	Hallford, Nellie Edith	1911
Green, Oscar R.	1649	Hallmark, Pleasant	4132
Green, James W.	2613	Hallmark, Allen	4133
Green, John A.	2614	Hallum, Willie O.	817
Green, Muree	3408	Hallum, Eliza May	1912
Green, Willie	3409	Hamil, Mabel Jane	1067
Green, Wiley Ray	3311	Hamil, George Edward	1068
Green, Tamsie Ada	3848	Hamilton, James R.	172
Green, Clara May	4283	Hamilton, George T.	173
Greenfeather, Ross J.	1167	Hamilton, Joseph R.	656
Greenwood, Dwight Paul	922	Hamilton, Lynn Boyd, Jr.	2584
Greenwood, Hassie F.	1145	Hamilton, Ralph	3112
Greer, Jennie Florence	543	Hamilton, Lester	3113
Greer, Alice Edna	544	Hammer, Minnie	652
Greer, Rufus Franklin	1645	Hammer, Ury	3317
Gregory, Luther N.	969	Hampton, George Samuel	366
Gregory, Ida May	2248	Hampton, Henry	1656
Grey, Clara Lucille	551	Hampton, Otto	1657
Griffin, William Hale	2220	Hampton, Maxine	1849
Griffin, Boon C.	4781	Hampton, Webb	3805
Griffith, Perry G.	649	Han, Mattie J.	2615
Griffith, Bonnie May	650	Han, Dora M.	2616
Griffith, William W.	3799	Hancock, Mabel Fenola	3881
Griffith, Mary May	3800	Hancock, Maggie Lewis	3882
Grimes, Alice Irene	3126	Handle, Betcie	4984
Grimmett, De-yoh-li-	4872	Hanes, William E.	1063
Grisham, Claud	2432	Haney, Cloyd May	1813
Grisham, Eva	2433	Haney, Floyd	1812
Grisham, Clifford	2692	Haney, Matttie F.	4398
Grisham, Lucile	2693	Hankins, Icee Lennes	1841
Gritts, Nicholas	4031	Hanks, Emma Ruth	237
Gritts, Nancy	4032	Hann, Russell L.	4169
Groom, Lessie	647	Hanna, John R.	2359
Groom, Leatha	648	Hannah, Daniel	2086
Groves, Bird	4095	Hannah, Cherokee	4296
Grubb, John	2774	Hansen, Reta	2926
Guess, Lena	4751	Hannon, Emmet	
Guilliams, Bessie Mary	4026	Franklin	1008
Guinn, Ida Gertrude	1440	Hannon, Florence M.	1009
Guinn, Maze	4631	Hannon, Lawrence J.	1010
Gunter, Addie	214	Hanson, Rossie Lee	1994
Gunter, Ola	215	Hardbarger, Annie	4097
Gunter, Lois Fern	4149	Hardy, Jennie M.	328
Guthrie, Lora V.	2083	Hardy, Claud	2254
Guthrie, Maudie May	4648	Hardy, John R.	2255
Guthrie, Odie Bell	4649	Hardy, Earl S.	3412
Habich, Dorathy	1999	Hare, Pearl	1155
Hacker, Alexander G.	4394	Harflich, Heimenn V.	822
Hacker, Frank	4395	Harlan, Homer Ransom	1843
Haddan, Marie S.	750	Harlan, Opal A.	1844
Haff, Oliver Lee	657	Harlan, Leola F.	4190
Haff, John W.	658	Harless, Robert	2360
Haff, Lynas	1176	Harless, Carr	3236
Haff, Claud	1177	Harlin, Richard G.	4671
Hafford, Hazel	709	Harlin, Ellis Sequoyah	4502
Hagerty, Cora B.	218	Harlin, Grace Leota	2093
Haglund, Marie Melba	3235	Harlin, Mary E.	2521
Hail, Nina May	659	Harmer, Charlie	547
Hail, Jada J.	2582	Harmer, Olin	548
Haines, Robert M.	1569	Harmon, Riley R.	2295
Hair, Susie	4534	Harmon, Manda	4567
Hair, Betsy	4736	Harmon, Annie	4568
Hair, Nannie	4932	Harnage, Nannie	
Hair, William	4933	Pauline	1663
Haley, Emmett Clyde	803	Harnar, Rendall D.	2999
Halfbreed, Thomas C.	3850	Harper, Cherokee	2087
Halfmoon, Opal	2268	Harris, Dewitt	168
Hall, Jeff R.	1262	Harris, Frank	210
Hall, Frank Hearn	662	Harris, Jesse	211
Hall, Floyed Edward	801	Harris, Roy	1031

Name.	Roll No.	Name.	Roll No.
Harris, Troy	1032	Hendricks, Nina	2
Harris, George	1171	Hendricks, Albert	655
Harris, Violet	1172	Hendricks, Nelson L.	443
Harris, Kate	4422	Hendricks, Lonie C.	1148
Harris, Dovie May	4718	Hendricks, Mamie E.	1149
Harris, Walter	4038	Hendricks, Arretta M.	1150
Harris, Martha	4039	Hendricks, Andy	3065
Harris, William		Hendricks, Charles	2997
Christofer	4595	Hendricks, Cora May	4927
Harrison, Hazel Leon	39	Hendricks, Harvey S.	1913
Harrison, Loyd C.	40	Hendricks, Viola	2535
Harrison, Laura Bell	63	Hendricks, Thelma Golda	2536
Harrison, Wm. Preston	64	Hendryx, Lorena	1451
Harrison, Marguerite E.	1776	Hendryx, Evan Morris	1452
Harrison, Vivian M.	852	Henegar, Charles A.	2618
Harrison, Maud Ellen	1181	Henley, Rachel Ella	4975
Harrison, Harry	3233	Henry, Warren D.	1830
Harrison, Mary	4222	Henry, Martin	4882
Harrison, Edward	1239	Henry, Opal L.	1673
Harrod, Geneva	3390	Henry, Clemie	1997
Harrod, Willie W.	3391	Henry, Myra	229
Harrold, Jay L.	1846	Hensley, William L., Jr.	21
Harry, May O.	4343	Hensley, Cleston L.	2226
Harry, Offe E.	4344	Hensley, A. V.	4473
Hart, Elmer C.	1651	Henson, Claude W.	1444
Hart, John H.	3204	Henson, Amy	3550
Hart, Helen G.	3205	Henson, Eliza	1882
Hart, Charley	3230	Henson, Washington	4396
Hartman, Louis L.	4770	Hereford, Blanchie May	2537
Hartman, Theodore R.	4771	Hern, William Herburt	1655
Hartness, Mineola	3673	Herod, William M., Jr.	4317
Hartness, Buster	3674	Herod, Ray	4318
Hartsock, Tedie	2524	Herod, Gracie	4319
Harvey, Irena	4852	Herrin, Clara C.	3687
Harvey, Mamie Irene	4579	Herrin, James R.	3688
Hastings, Mayme Starr	1064	Hester, Russell Porter	1072
Hastings, Suewayne		Hewin, Nancy	1665
Louise	1169	Hewin, Snow	3591
Hastings, John Rogers,		Hiatt, Everett Burton	973
Jr.	1170	Hibbs, Marion Lester	2534
Hathcoat, Floyd E.	1153	Hibbs, Edna May	2533
Hathcoat, Thadeous L.	1154	Hickey, Lula M.	3883
Hathcoat, Horrace		Hicks, Daniel Arthur	284
Cailtor	2480	Hicks, Floyd	2267
Hattton, Mauda	231	Hicks, Fay Carrol	748
Hatton, Bessie	232	Hicks, Vivian Alfreda	749
Hause, Benjamin F.	512	Hicks, Mary	3422
Hawk, Martha	3140	Hicks, Dovey	3438
Hawk, Tom	4941	Hicks, Mary Bell	1175
Hawkins, William E.	799	Hicks, Willard M.	1996
Hawkins, Bertha S.	800	Hicks, Viola	2336
Hawkins, Ada Opal	2388	Hicks, Ralph C.	2657
Hayes, Nellie Ruth	974	Hicks, Beatrice I.	2660
Hayes, Roy R.	3575	Hicks, George E.	2661
Hayes, Thomas F.	3576	Hicks, Alva Lee	3711
Hayse, Glover Franklin	4435	Hicks, Walter	3930
Haze, Clyde	1650	Hider, Lewis	2726
Head, Mary W.	1066	Hider, Jesse	2727
Headrick, Annie	4772	Higgins, Vinita	435
Headrick, Charlie T.	4773	Higgins, William Lee	436
Heady, Blanch	65	Highsmith, Georgia M.	2090
Heady, Ruth	66	Hightower, Harvey	3001
Heape, Dollie	1069	Hilderbrand, Willie	4316
Heape, Josie May	1070	Hilderbrand, Francis	
Heape, Lizzie M.	1071	Joseph	1178
Heard, Ethel Belle	1774	Hilderbrand, Cherokee	
Heard, Bessie	1775	Delilah	1179
Heard, Clifton	888	Hilderbrand, Samuel J.	4332
Heath, Eva Elizabeth	970	Hilderbrand, Wallace A.	4333
Heath, Henry Franklin	971	Hilderbrand, Lura Pixie	1570
Hedrick, Ida Alice	4369	Hilderbrand, Dennis D.	1571
Hedrick, Lena E.	4370	Hilderbrand, Walter	2963
Hedrick, David N.	4371	Hilderbrand, Lucion	4954
Hedricks, Mark	4676	Hill, Tresha Alice	853
Heindselman, Leon E.	2998	Hill, John E.	1029
Heistand, Oscar	1975	Hill, Pauline	1030
Helms, Essie May	1664	Hill, Mammie E.	751
Henderson, Herbert C.	2903	Hill, George M.	752
Hendren, Beulah	3632	Hill, Alfred Dodge	1455
Hendren, Nina	3633	Hill, Mildred	1456
Hendren, Lonie O.	3037	Hill, Francis Elizabeth	1567
Hendrex, William		Hill, Mary Davis	1568
Harrison	1023	Hill, Aaron Bryant	1666

Name.	Roll No.
Hill, Mary A.	1995
Hill, Elvin May	1907
Hill, Dessa L.	1771
Hinds, Lillie R.	1204
Hinds, Lewis R.	1205
Hinds, Walter F.	4555
Hinds, Ira L.	4556
Hinds, Carolyn Ruth	3237
Hines, Letha	1257
Hines, Mose	1258
Hinman, Vinita F.	4475
Hinshaw, Gaylord Adolphus	2586
Hitchcock, Clayburn M.	2925
Hixson, Jessie O.	407
Hodge, George	1842
Hoffman, Christine	1152
Hoffman, John Willie	2978
Hoffman, Lelie L.	2979
Hogan, James Philip	1847
Hogner, May B.	1174
Hogner, Levi	1652
Hogner, Ellen	3802
Hogshooter, Narcisser	4943
Hogue, Candray Lea D.	550
Hohenstein, Lena	2272
Hohenstein, Lyle	2273
Holden, Verdie Florence	2306
Holden, Ethel Goldie	2307
Holderman, Lena Violet	1658
Holderman, Marion S.	4341
Holderman, Covel S.	4342
Holland, Birdie	1267
Holland, Elizabeth	804
Holland, Celia Jane	1151
Holland, Charles T.	2361
Holland, Florence M.	2362
Holland, Bertha	2363
Holland, Clyde V.	2364
Holland, Beulah B.	3127
Holland, Albert J.	3128
Holland, Gladys A.	3141
Holland, Clarice I.	3142
Holland, Franklin Harmon	3754
Holland, Daisy Adline	4134
Holley, Hazel Elizabeth	134
Hollis, Lawrence P.	1905
Hollis, Perry D.	1906
Holmes, Lillie	2308
Holmes, Patrick Mathias	2671
Holmes, Callie	4037
Holt, Cunnie Dolton	5
Holt, Preston Reed	4304
Holt, Ella Blanche	4305
Holt, Marcus Alonzo Hanna	660
Holt, Delmar Dee	661
Holt, William Henseley	1661
Holt, Lucy Dale	1662
Holt, Sylvia Ree	3155
Holt, Joel	4464
Homan, James E.	2619
Homan, Addie Reba	2620
Honeysuckle, Samuel David	1045
Hood, Ida S.	1446
Hood, Tokay E.	4863
Hood, Gladys Pearl	1915
Hood, Ida May	1914
Hooper, Jensey	3038
Hooper, Ah-woo-stee	4723
Hopkins, Opal M.	1156
Hopper, Gussie	3039
Horn, Cassie M.	29
Horn, Andy	3447
Horn, Ophelia	3448
Horn, Jess	3449
Horn, Lizzie	1445
Horn, Florence L.	3849
Horn, Laura E.	4644
Hornbuckle, Andy Columbus	877

Name.	Roll No.
Hornbuckle, Stella May	1296
Hornbuckle, Curtis	1297
Hornbuckle, Isaac	1908
Hornbuckle, Pocahontas	1909
Horner, Annie	4956
Horner, Willie	3316
Hornet, Nannie B.	3679
Horrell, Mary T.	2698
Horton, Delpha D.	2250
Hosey, Ella	2980
Hosey, Dick	1998
Hoskin, Neal	1566
Hosmer, Zoue Dell	653
Houseberg, Cullus	2753
Houser, Andrew D.	2712
Houser, Leroy	2713
Houser, Loy H.	2714
Housley, William M.	4174
Housley, Jessie E.	4175
Howard, Charles	202
Howard, Wretha May	972
Howard, Theodore Roosevelt	2222
Howard, Arthur R.	2223
Howard, Pearley May	3589
Howard, Eva Nell	3590
Howard, Della May	3670
Howard, Ida Jane	3641
Howard, Lelan S.	3806
Howdeshell, Annie	1660
Howe, Richard	553
Howell, Leora V.	707
Howell, Earl E.	708
Howell, Hazel	1012
Howland, Ira Lee	1173
Hubbard, Bessie	1273
Hubbard, Beulah	3615
Huckleberry, Louise	1065
Hudgpetch, Nellie L.	552
Hudson, Louis	4401
Hudson, Orvale L.	3554
Hudson, Refa N.	3555
Hudson, Sylvanus B.	3730
Huggins, J. Shink	1653
Huggins, Robert L. Jr.	1654
Hughes, Alma L.	1447
Hughes, Viola R.	1448
Hughes, Arnold C.	1449
Hughes, Robert V.	1450
Hughes, Willie F.	2227
Hughes, Icie V.	2228
Hughes, Jesse A.	3655
Hughes, Maud E.	3656
Hughes, Carrie V.	3969
Hughes, Orville M.	4035
Hughes, Flossie B.	4036
Hughes, Milburn C.	4135
Hughes, May	4959
Hulbert, Carlton M.	2358
Humanstriker, Bob	1453
Humanstriker, Dick	1554
Hummingbird, Dennis	4497
Hummingbird, Eugene D.	4498
Hummingbird, Dick	4078
Hummingbird, Charles	4079
Hummingbird, William	4157
Hummingbird, Lila	4733
Hummingbird, Katie	4689
Humphrey, Jesse E.	4417
Hunt, Nettie Lucille	2091
Hunt, Anna Ruth	2092
Hunt, Roy Edwin	3234
Hunter, Grace	4404
Hurd, Ruth Iona	3111
Hurst, Emma S.	491
Hurst, James C.	492
Hurst, Coydie C.	495
Hutchens, Agnes Pearl	1833
Hutchens, Corthel Olden	1834
Hutchins, Willard Beatrice	1659
Hyatt, Bertha May	2594
Hyatt, Clara Elizabeth	2595

Name.	Roll No.	Name.	Roll No.
Hyatt, Clifford A.	3206	Johnston, Carrie L.	4494
Hyatt, Lilly May	3207	Johnson, Elizabeth	3939
Hider, Daniel	4831	Johnson, Josie	4657
Hyles, David Jr.	4440	Johnson, Otis	1916
Ickelbury, Lieu	554	Johnston, Winnie E.	1182
Ickelbury, Max	555	Jones, Sally L.	47
Inglis, Burl Davenport	493	Jones,'. Pearlie Inez	159
Ingram, Waunita	4040	Jones, Mollie Rosetti	556
Inlow, George O.	4306	Jones, Ray E.	1278
Inlow, Laura J.	4542	Jones, Warren	1279
Ironside, Bertha Vinita	4430	Jones, Lillia L.	1024
Irvin, Essie	3182	Jones, Nancy Lenora	923
Irvin, Bessie	3183	Jones, Maggie Margarete	924
Irvin, Otis	3184	Jones, Hellen Estella	4921
Irving, Renie	2000	Jones, Hazel E.	4922
Irving, Venie	2001	Jones, Patsey R.	1461
Isaacs, Mary Malinda	854	Jones, Francis	1462
Isbell, Harrold 'Cleo	3475	Jones, Maybee Lee	1572
Isbell, Clifford LeRoy	3476	Jones, Otta May	1573
Isbell, Thomas Pascal	4429	Jones, Cornelious	1574
Israel, Minnie	4027	Jones, Roy	3739
Israel, Toy R.	4136	Jones, Dennis	2002
Ivey, Augustus E. Jr.	271	Jones, Nola	2003
Jackson, Gussie F.	396	Jones, Willard	2005
Jackson, Addie	367	Jones, Vinita G.	2094
Jackson, Zella Minervia	1027	Jones, Perrilla M.	2715
Jackson, John Evert	1028	Jones, Clarence J.	4448
Jackson, Mary Jewel	2281	Jones, Jesse H.	4449
Jackson, Neely	3450	Jones, Reader	4801
Jackson, Winnie I.	1667	Jones, Harry	3162
Jackson, Reese F.	4601	Jones, Flossie May	3319
Jackson, Minnie	1806	Jones, Charles Elvin	3040
Jackson, John F.	3353	Jones, Thelma L.	4980
Jackson, Henry D.	3354	Jones, Ida May	3807
Jackson, Jas. Cleo	4041	Jones, Mitchell	3808
Jackson, Willie B.	4042	Jones, Daisy	3809
Jackson, Johnnie Bryant	4043	Jones, Ellen May	3851
Jackson, Emmett Dalton	4820	Jones, Archie	4637
James, Euchalata	404	Jones, Arlington	4638
James, Houston R.	405	Jones, Louis	3942
James, Clara E.	2096	Jones, Laura	4044
James, Mildred Irene	2836	Jones, Edgar	4656
James, Llena Allanna	2837	Jones, Maggy A.	2585
Jenkins, Grover	2004	Jones, Thomas R.	1917
Jenkins, Theodore	2230	Jones, Arthur	3163
Jennings, Louie W.	710	Jordan, George W.	160
Jeremiah, Annie	1458	Jordan, Bright D.	161
Jeremiah, Clarice	1459	Jordan, Charles Bambridg	479
Jeremiah, Robert A.	1460	Jordan, Vannie. M.	480
Jeremiah, Watie	3266	Jordan, David W.	397
Jiles, Alvin Guy	427	Jordan, Myrtle M.	429
Jiles, Lena Opal	428	Jordan, William L.	430
Jimison, Hurshell	3544	Jordan, Mabel	1885
John, Maggie	4098	Jordan, Mary Emma	3352
Johns, Richard, Garvey	85	Jordan, Winnie Davis	3272
Johns, Delora	86	Jumper, Louis Chee-Chee	3238
Johnson, Paul	183	Jumper, Bettie	4691
Johnson, Lela O.	4916	Justus, William I.	1457
Johnson, Catherine A.	4917	Justus, Claud R.	2886
Johnson, Frankie	753	Kaiser, Thomas Jackson	1831
Johnson, Cordie	1816	Kate, Jasper W.	2716
Johnson, Louis C.	2006	Kate, James N.	2717
Johnson, Percy L.	2007	Kay, Elizabeth	445
Johnson, Mary Blanche	1707	Kaywood, Sarah	4964
Johnson, Carl F.	4560	Kaywood, Tom	4965
Johnson, Andrew A.	2161	Kearns, John Wesley	2167
Johnson, Roy C.	2162	Kearns, Barbary A.	2538
Johnson, Robert L.	2163	Keefer, Frederick	
Johnson, Lulel W.	4563	Charles	184
Johnson, Truman	2434	Keefer, Lewis J.	187
Johnson, John Doss	3105	Keeling, Lois Mary	1674
Johnson, Tribble Byrum	3106	Keen, Albert	2904
Johnson, James R.	3114	Keen, Wiley Anderson	2905
Johnson, Lafayette	2035	Keen, Hazel Fern	3143
Johnson, Lilley L.	1839	Keener, Lilia	3592
Johnson, Rosevelt	1840	Keener, Aggie	3389
Johnson, Emma May	3371	Keener, Joe W.	3210
Johnson, Susie	3372	Keener, William R. R.	3211
Johnson, Elcy	3388	Keener, Ben	4354
Johnson, Martha	3208	Keith, Eldon	1379
Johnson, Bettie	3271	Keith, William	3487
Johnson, Tommy	4484	Keith, Beula Bell	3488
Johnston, Flora L.	4493	Keith, Viola R.	3531

Name.	Roll No.	Name.	Roll No.
Keith, James R.	3532	Kinney, Clifford E.	3411
Keith, Hugh Yeager	3239	Kinnison, Amanda Naoma	30
Kell, Kermit Kelley	1740	Kinnison, Lieura Norma	31
Kell, Edith E.	4466	Kinnison, Mary Ruth	91
Kelleam, Margaret		Kinzer, Willie C.	36
Francis	137	Kirk, Ora Ethel	549
Keller, George	754	Kirk, George E.	2700
Keller, Pearl	4045	Kirk, Minnie	3129
Kelley, Loney A.	1298	Kirk, Bennie	3130
Kelley, Lee W.	1669	Kirk, Maggie	3577
Kelley, Howard A.	1871	Kirk, Freddie	4981
Kelley, John A.	4664	Kirk, Christial	3810
Kelley, Grace E.	4206	Kirk, Susan May	4099
Kelly, Laurie Marie	925	Kirk, Lottie Allice	4100
Kelly, Norval Ray	2699	Klaus, Anna Mae	1575
Kendrick, Seldon A.	2703	Klaus, Everett Arlos	1670
Kennedy, John Lee	857	Kneeland, Ross Murrell	224
Kent, Margaret C.	2908	Knight, Ru Ennis	494
Kepler, Neva Winona	3637	Knight, Laura	3811
Kerr, William R.	444	Knight, Mary L.	3812
Kerr, Edgar D.	756	Knight, Bill	4942
Kerr, Edmond B.	757	Knight, Henry	4297
Kerr, Earl Sequoyah	758	Knighten, Susie A.	3290
Kerr, Tildia B.	3428	Koehler, John Leroy	165
Kerr, Luella	2776	Krigbaum, Nettie Olene	4685
Ketcher, Levi	481	Kuder, James Albert	2676
Ketcher, Cora	4324	Kuder, Charles Francis	2677
Ketcher, Bert	855	Kumpe, Fannie Pearl	1463
Ketcher, David	856	Kumpe, Allyn V.	1675
Ketcher, Fayloney	4757	Kumpe, Ethel Belle	3209
Ketcher, Ruth Vivian	2008	Kyle, Kittie E.	858
Ketcher, Leonard		Kyle, Mariah A.	4046
Lavelle	2009	Kyle, Flora I.	4047
Ketcher, Sarah	2164	Lacey, Joseph Adam	711
Ketcher, Davis	2165	Lackey, Harvey H.	1678
Ketcher, Bettie	2266	Lacy, Nancy	4821
Ketcher, Willie	4841	Lacy, Rose	4822
Ketcher, Flossie D.	2694	Ladd, Clifford	1305
Ketcher, Ned Roosevelt	2695	Ladd, Ethel	2302
Ketcher, Frank	3755	LaFalier, Esther	2011
Ketcher, Noah	4476	Lafalier, Ruby	3527
Ketchum, Lena	3430	Lafalier, Homer	3528
Ketchum, James L.	3460	Lain, Ida M.	2773
Ketchum, Maver L.	4557	Lamar, Essie D.	2232
Key, Jesse	3872	Lamar, Ada Marie	3172
Keys, Cleo May	4423	Lamar, J. Sims	3593
Keys, Cora Elaine	3470	Lamascus, Ruby M.	71
Keys, Lelia J.	1668	Lamb, Charles Dorsey	247
Keys, Jorden Lindsey	3586	Lamon, Katherine Wise	221
Keys, Rodgers	3167	Lamon, Helen	222
Keys, Alford C.	2838	Landrum, Lois Stewart	129
Keys, Clyde P.	4574	Landrum, Morya Clifford	462
Keys, John R.	4465	Landrum, Waunetta T.	1465
Keys, Verlie	3394	Landrum, Helena B.	1466
Keys, Paul	3395	Landrum, Pearl M.	4191
Keys, Hazel	4728	Landrum, Alice J.	4672
Kidd, Lester	4418	Lane, Lasca Gazelle	1078
Kidd, Captain	4419	Lane, Thomas A. G.	1467
Kiddy, Lorene	1073	Lane, William V.	2316
Kidwell, Clella	2888	Landers, George	4050
Killer, James	4923	Langley, Katherine	90
Killer, Rollin	4224	Langley, Maudie L. P.	2259
Kimbrough, Gladys Iona	3413	Langley, Joseph A.	1025
Kincade, Batia Elmer	4414	Langley, Francis E.	1026
Kindred, Jesse Columbus	2097	Langley, William C.	1079
King, Dora	441	Langley, Homer L.	1464
King, Freddie	956	Langley, Andrew J.	2366
King, George Walker	1074	Langley, Fannie L.	2435
King, Pauline Margaret	1075	Langley, Manerva L.	2436
King, Clifford W.	2887	Langley, Noah R.	3131
King, Agnes	2915	Langley, Mary J. E.	3756
King, Julius Elles	2916	Langley, Gladys D.	3757
King, Essie Aurela	3186	Lansford, Loula	1299
King, Velma	3852	Lansford, Eugene	1300
King, Addie M.	3853	Langton, Bertha	1963
King, Dollie	4223	Langton, Mary	1964
Kingfisher, Nancy	2964	Large, William C.	4543
Kingfisher, Susie	3634	Largent, Ida May	823
Kingfisher, Jesse	3635	Largent, William Arch	824
Kingfisher, Joe	2910	Larman, Perry A.	4159
Kingfisher, Stella	2913	Larry, Gracie	1303
Kingfisher, Nancy	4985	Lattimore, Carrie M.	4271
Kinney, Flold V.	3410	Laughlin, Betty Marie	1468

Name.	Roll No.
Laughlin, Mary Lee	1469
Lawhead, Ollie	2664
Lawrence, Gilbert Shelton	190
Lawrence, Lena Gertrude	3451
Lawrence, Albert Beauregard	4249
Lawson, Edward C.	663
Layne, John W.	1860
Layne, Marie A.	1861
Leach, Hattie	4813
Leader, Ed	1253
Leaf, Lucy	4225
Leaf, Charley	4226
Leafer, Johnnie	4375
Leafer, Laurence	4376
Leathers, Lillian True	1191
Leathers, Irene Bently	1192
Leathers, Flint	3884
Leathers, Roy Lee	3885
Ledford, Emma	1304
Lee, Thelma Claudia	666
Lee, William P.	1076
Lee, Robert E.	1183
Lee, Myrtle	1188
Lee, Felix Helen	1189
Lee, Carl	2168
Lee, Mary Marie	2410
Lee, Charles H.	2411
Lee, Audry Dortell	2805
Lee, Adrain Dorothy	2806
Lee, Jackson L.	2839
Lee, Lucian G.	2840
Lee, Hazel E.	1957
Lee, Oral Evaline	3320
Lee, Spi Jim	3321
Lee, Daisy	4355
Lee, Jess	3945
Lee, Bertha Easter	4048
Leforce, Charles William	665
Leforce, Ora B.	1679
Lemaster, Robert Sylvester	3240
Lemons, Eunice Velma	3970
Lemons, Wallace Edward	3971
Lessley, Lula Caldonie	560
Lesley, Rufus Wesley	466
Lessley, Icie Rebecca	467
Levi, Redbird	4814
Levi, Fred	1928
Levson, Juliett	3564
Lewis, Charles Walter	975
Lewis, William Henry	976
Lewis, Elsie	4529
Lewis, Nellie May	2430
Lewis, Arthur G.	3489
Lewis, Grace E.	2243
Lewis, Ira A.	2244
Lewis, Lizzie	2596
Lewis, Vittum Fite	2965
Linder, Geaniever	3115
Linder, Voldy, Aline	3116
Linder, Hiram F.	3724
Linder, Roco B.	3813
Lindsey, Mamie May	859
Lindsey, Edna Lee	860
Lindsey, James E.	2169
Linn, James R.	3356
Linn, Goldie M.	2914
Linscott, Beatrice Josephine	561
Lipe, DeWitt	664
Littledave, Betsy	2010
Littledave, Miner	1752
Littledave, Andrew	2909
Little, Ramona D.	2437
Littlejohn, Thomas F.	596
Littlejohn, James S.	597
Littletom, Ida	4924
Littrell, Alford Jesse	1301
Liver, Theodore R.	1187

Name.	Roll No.
Liver, Lydia	3854
Liver, Eliza	1919
Locker, Edward Van	2246
Locust, Peter H.	1190
Locust, Thomas J.	4850
Locust, May	2889
Locust, Ester	4698
Locust, Walker	4793
Lee, Sadie E.	2231
Lofton, Clifford	1123
Logsdon,Nora May	755
Longbone, Jacob L.	559
Longbone, Frankie	926
Longbird, Betsy	2481
Longcrier, Henry Beecher	1676
Longcrier, Howard	1677
Londagin, Robert B.	2202
Longtail, Henry	1747
Long, Simpson N.	112
Long, Zelma Irena	3461
Long, Lenord Columbus	3462
Long, Pearl B.	2098
Long, Roy R.	2099
Long, Cornelius	2866
Long, Lucile	4809
Long, Georgia	4810
Long, James	4049
Looney, Benjamin A.	3551
Looney, James E.	4137
Loux, John Raymond	409
Love, Samuel Drake	1077
Love, John S.	4393
Lovett, Ina Bell	4748
Lowe, Nina	35
Lowrey, Wanetta	225
Lowrey, Raymond B.	226
Lowrey, Howard R.	450
Lowrey, James Fite	459
Lowrey, Gladdis I.	3491
Lowrey, Vance	3510
Lowrey, Eugene	3944
Lowrey, Cora Lee	4101
Lowrey, Floridan Hariden	4102
Lowrey, Henry C.	4662
Lowry, Charley	4544
Lowry, Emett	4545
Lowry, Maggie N.	2719
Lowry, John W.	2720
Lowery, Silas C.	4436
Lowery, George	4977
Lowery, Johnnie B.	4192
Lowther, Clifford W.	69
Lowther, Laura Ethel	4754
Lowther, Viola Fay	4755
Lowrimore,Vera L.	1302
Lowrimore, William H.	1918
Lucas, Raymon Soper	2966
Luke, Elmer Lemon	3273
Lunday, Elmer L.	1047
Luton, David E., Jr.	4158
Lutz, Herman A.	1185
Lutz, Frederick A.	1186
Lynch, Alice F.	368
Lynch, Nancy Esther	2718
Madden, Mamie M.	3490
Madden, Vera B.	2320
Maddin, Letitia A.	2105
Madison, Joseph F.	861
Maher, James T.	2447
Maine, Sigsbee	2707
Majors, Robert R.	4207
Majors, Forrest	4208
Maloney, Bessie V.	2482
Manar, Walter Jefferson	2103
Manley, Kizzie	2636
Mankiller, Wuttie	4161
Manifee, George Mitchell	1081
Mann, Homer E.	2100
Mann, Robert F.	1967
Mann, Ida L.	4459
Mann,William H.	4460

Name.	Roll No.	Name.	Roll No.
Mann, Bessie	4274	Meigs, Return J.	3066
Manor, Berl	1686	Meigs, Jane Ever	4285
Manus, Vivian Ellice	4564	Meigs, Mary A.	4286
Manus, Celestia Elaine	4565	Melton, Ora Nay	348
Marion, John F.	2761	Melton, Esse	349
Marker, John D.	930	Melton, Hubert S.	927
Markham, Mary M.	2725	Melton, Graydon D.	928
Marlow, Ruby	1927	Merchant, John D. Jr.	3912
Marsh, Thelma	1288	Merrell, Please C.	1037
Marsh, Herbert S.	1289	Merrell, Presley E.	1580
Marrs, Rutha M.	2312	Merrell, Charles Loy	1581
Marshall, Jessie	4053	Merryman, Claude B.	1311
Martin, Howard L.	19	Merryman, Clarence J.	1312
Martin, Charles H.	20	Messer, William	
Martin, Pauline B.	175	Woodcock	4647
Martin, George Walter	4915	Metzner, George	
Martin, Clarence M.	372	Frederick	562
Martin, Marie	373	Metzner, Amelia	563
Martin, Lewis V.	2269	Meyer, Elijah Samuel	1777
Martin, Willie	2270	Micco, Bessie	4845
Martin, Andy	1034	Mickle, Hoyt	171
Martin, Edward	1035	Miller, Mamie Lee	1245
Martin, Joseph C.	1036	Miller, Margarette J.	1246
Martin, Minta	933	Miller, Clifford	78
Martin, Harney C.	3423	Miller, Alma L.	152
Martin, Finnie E.	3424	Miller, Clarence R.	153
Martin, Wayne Holly	3455	Miller, Julia Elizabeth	482
Martin, Fred C.	1402	Miller, Edna	4703
Martin, Joseph Edward	1479	Miller, Tip Bluefoot	280
Martin, Mary Majdaline	3512	Miller, Sherman	369
Martin, Felix Authur	2104	Miller, Johnie	4326
Martin, Nell Bertie	2233	Miller, Esther	1817
Martin, Elvira	2370	Miller, Lusena	1818
Martin, Paul Revere	2673	Miller, Thomas	1195
Martin, Dorothy L.	3138	Miller, Bluie	1196
Martin, Ouida Rae	3607	Miller, Mary Ellen	1197
Martin, Walter Ervin	3357	Miller, Alfred A.	1470
Martin, Nettie B.	3358	Miller, Wade S.	1577
Martin, Fay	2504	Miller, Mary Caroline	1680
Martin, Jesse R.	3067	Miller, Jacob William	1681
Martin, Samuel B.	3758	Miller, Birdie M.	2012
Martin, Nora V.	3759	Miller, Ollie Bell	4441
Martin, Phronie	4364	Miller, Dovie Ollie	2587
Martin, Sarah Edith	3972	Miller, Susan	2369
Martin, Jacob Wheeler	4104	Miller, Cherokee	4573
Martin, Dottie B.	4160	Miller, John Alven	3565
Martin, William E.	4379	Miller, Bessie Z.	3566
Martin, Neevie L.	1924	Miller, Carrie Ellen	3567
Martin, Edger L.	1925	Miller, Birdie	2968
Mathis, John	139	Miller, Johnie	3657
Mathews, Carl	564	Miller, Clarence R.	3658
Maupin, Joe Shelbey	713	Miller, Waitie H.	3856
Maupin, James W.	1307	Miller, James Rosco	4138
Maupin, Claud	1308	Miller, Edyth Era	4139
Maxfield, Cora	818	Miller, Susie	4823
Maxfield, Pauline	819	Mills, William, Sanford	531
Maxwell, Irene Ora	3547	Mills, Cassie N.	1814
Maxwell, Mary Ruth	3042	Mills, Emma L.	1687
Mayberry, Marie	1085	Mills, Cyrus B.	1688
May, Vera	977	Mills, Mary D.	2525
Mays, Freddie	715	Millnk, Mamie	805
Mays, Robert A.	716	Miles, Emily May	864
Mayo, Francis Willie	2704	Miles, Guy	2944
Mayo, Virginia Dale	2705	Millner, James Bassman	1854
Mayo, Bessie	2706	Minor, Robert E.	447
Mayes, Wanda	4708	Minor, Clara B.	862
Mayes, Joseph M.	2762	Minor, Ray C.	863
Mayes, Cherie	4181	Mitchell, Foreman Drew	712
Mayturn, Minerva C.	1850	Mitchell, Inez	1472
Meadows, Leonard		Mitchell, Bessie Lola	1473
Phillip	2287	Mitchell, Lovel	4548
Meadows, Russell Milton	2288	Mitchell, Mamie	2372
Means, Alex V.	1280	Mitchell, Chloede	2373
Means, Lelia M.	1281	Mitchell, Delilah	
Meeden, Charles Samuel	3696	Josephene	2634
Meeker, Reece	4051	Mitchell, Nora Belle	4777
Meeks, Clyde Ledrew	24	Mitchell, Sarah Ella	4641
Meeks, Galuga Morgan	25	Mitchell, Opal M.	4284
Meeks, Charles Jr.	2760	Mizer, Ada B.	2418
Mehlin, Elizabeth		Mode, Bernice	714
Katherine	2303	Mode, Louie R.	733
Mehlin, Edna May	2304	Montgomery, Irene	1578
Meigs, George McKee	3398	Montgomery, Mary	

Name.	Roll No.	Name.	Roll No.
Maulcie	1579	Mouse, Mattie	4983
Montgomery, Mildred	1683	Mulcare, George	
Montgomery, Vera	1684	Franklin	3552
Moon, Clarice Ervet	2911	Mulkey, Ruby C.	1689
Moon, Florence Alphalee	2912	Mulkey, Mannon	4588
Moore, William, Adair	408	Mulkey, Mary	4589
Moore, Bertie L.	865	Mulkey, Cora Winona	3517
Moore, Ada P.	866	Mulkey, Nina Inez	3518
Moore, Veta C.	867	Mulkey, Dennis E.	3601
Moore, Robert L.	2235	Murray, Charles William	2367
Moore, Monsieur	2415	Murray, John Wiseman	2368
Moore, Clark S.	2416	Murray, Myrtle Belle	3132
Moore, Eli	3118	Murray, Cleona	2737
Moore, Willie	3119	Murray, Zora	3886
Moore, Malcolm	2796	Murphy, Mattie Louise	102
Moore, Rennie	2804	Murphy, Robert Hays	1198
Moore, James R.	2891	Murphy, Thomas J.	1697
Moore, Horace Adair	2917	Murphy, Willie Clyde	2438
Moore, Emmett Togo	2918	Murphy, James Houston	2484
Moore, Florence	3243	Murphy, Claud M.	3323
Moore, Mary Ola	3244	Murphy, Otis	3619
Moore, Lonnie Maxin	4856	Murphy, Floyd	3620
Morgan, Houston L.	169	Murphy, Verna	3242
Morgan, Velma E. F.	1476	Murphy, Charles	
Morgan, George		Thomas	4368
Franklin	4126	Murphy, Esther	4873
Morgan, Mary Caroline	4127	Muskrat, Truman	929
Morgan, John Duffey	3168	Muskrat, John	980
Morgan, Arthur F.	1922	Muskrat, Steve	2485
Morris, Earle	1015	Muskrat, Odessa Alice	4250
Morris, Lucile	1016	Myers, Ruth	2107
Morris, Pearl Leo	734	McAfee, Robert W.	1851
Morris, Lowen B.	1033	McAffrey, Bula E.	3902
Morris, Thomas P.	1306	McAffrey, William H.	1243
Morris, Linnie I.	1475	McAffrey, Cleora I.	1244
Morris, Charley G.	1685	McAffrey, Katie O.	3454
Morris, Theodore R.	3511	McAlister, Lawrence S.	3453
Morris, Oweda	4469	McAllister, Mary Ellen	278
Morris, John	4580	McAnally, Mark F.	3274
Morris, Claud	4581	McAndrews, Mary M.	1855
Morris, Balma D.	4103	McBee, Carrie	4582
Morris, Lulu	4859	McBee, Leona	4583
Morris, Carl	4227	McCaffree, Barton A.	3396
Morris, Justice	4228	McCaffree, Laura V.	3397
Morris, Annie E.	4229	McCamish, Calvin	670
Morris, Gertrude	4674	McCarty, Della	2405
Morris, Clyde	1923	McCarty, Velmar	2234
Morrison, Cherry O.	565	McCausland, Fannie Bell	3241
Morrison, Sherman W.	566	McCay, Ivera J.	4520
Morrison, Minnie C.	446	McCay, Charles B.	4756
Morrow, Otto	931	McCay, Florence J.	759
Morrow, Roscoe	932	McCay, Ruth Gladys	2371
Morrow, Ruby L.	2759	McClure, Ella	4517
Moreland, Ray Harvey	3452	McCullough, Esta Z.	3604
Moreland, Joe Wade	1875	McCollum, Flora R.	4232
Moreland, Mary		McCombs, Charles H.	1576
Elizabeth	1876	McCoy, Earl	1856
Morton, William Henry	4769	McCoy, Pauline A.	1735
Morton, Dortha May	4356	McCoy, Orlbie	1168
Morton, Walter E.	4357	McCoy, Cherokee	2311
Morton, Junia C.	3814	McCoy, Bulah A.	3906
Morton, Maudie Alice	3815	McCoy, Hugh R.	3907
Morton, Johney E.	4646	McCoy, Vernon T.	2802
Morton, Mary E.	4052	McCoy, Chester C.	2803
Morton, Cherokee I.	4474	McCoy, Fannie	4774
Morton, Bessie A.	4683	McCoy, Walter	4775
Morton, Sterling L.	4684	McCoy, Jessie L.	4380
Most, Susan Grace	1083	McCoy, Ester	4881
Mosier, John A. Jr.	2106	McCoy, Emma	4835
Moton, Edgar Maze	3716	McCoy, Sadie	4836
Moton, Golden Okla	3717	McCracken, Eldee	279
Moten, Gracie	4783	McCracken, Zona Belle	3002
Motte, William R. Jr.	4405	McCracken, Irene	3003
Motte, Lillie May	4406	McCrary, Ella	516
Mount, John Richard	667	McCullough, Zelma C.	178
Mount, Grace A. G.	934	McCulloch, Robert	
Mount, Chrystal Clark	3041	Armstrong	668
Mounts, Thelma		McCullough, Bernice L.	1474
Josephine	1199	McCullough, James W.	2108
Mouse, Lydia	1682	McCullough, Gladys M.	2417
Mouse, Jefferson	2561	McCullough, Reba O.	3617
Mouse, John	2562	McCullough, John H.	3618
Mouse, Babie	3133	McCullough, Peter C.	1921

Name.	Roll No.	Name.	Roll No.
McDaniel, Clifford	1764	Neely, Iva Florence	935
McDaniel, Earl	978	Neel, Ola May	3659
McDaniel, Merrel	979	Neff, Inola	2109
McDaniel, Annie L.	4530	Neff, Watie E.	2110
McDaniel, Joseph J.	1207	Neff, Jessie E.	2111
McDaniel, Rogers	3594	Neighbors, William Oscar	3595
McDaniel, Noah Oland	4928	Neighbors, Arthur Frank-	
McDaniel, Mona Mae	4381	lin	3596
McDaniel, Archie	4382	Nelson, Watie Z.	825
McDonald, Thomas J.	669	Nelson, Sarah Adele	2637
McDonald, Paul		Nelson, Ernest Price	2638
Alexander	3058	Nelson, George D.	3899
McDonald, Claud	4591	Nelson, Clara M.	3900
McDowell, Dora		Nelson, Jesse	4934
Kathleen	2285	Nelson, Charles	4935
McElhaney, Fay	3117	Neugin, Bark	3760
McElreath, Daisy A.	4937	Neville, Oliver Crayton	870
McFadden, John Herbert	384	New, William Denny	2419
McFarland, Gertrude	437	Newman, Virgil K.	868
McFarland, Homer G.	1309	Newton, Laura Miriam	374
McGee, Mable C.	1832	Newton, Mary	4920
McGhee, James A.	1193	Newton, Walter 'Lee	2777
McGhee, Pauline	1852	Newton, Johnnie	3718
McGhee, Lucile	1853	Newton, Claudy	3719
McGhee, Lorena M.	1471	Newton, Carl	3212
McGhee, Linal. B.	2101	Newton, Jesse	3213
McGhee, Hazel Marie	2102	Nicholson, Henry, Jr.	68
McGinnis, Christine G.	2949	Nicholson, Edgar Russell	463
McGlamery, Georgia	2276	Nicholson, Clara Hestella	2458
McInerney, Mary	3904	Nicholson, Eva Lorene	3501
McIntosh, Bertha	1780	Nicholson, Ralph Clifford	4432
McIntosh, Ethel R.	1080	Nichols, Glenn F.	1313
McKeehan, Norean J.	27	Nichols, Elmer Ewell	1857
McKeehan, James I.	267	Nichols, Raymond	
McKee, Freeman	4230	Eugene	1858
McKee, Pearlie E.	4231	Nichols, Cleao	2708
McKenzie, Lacy L.	2554	Nichols, Annie Victoria	3043
McKinney, John E.	1477	Nidiffer, Rollin	3417
McKinney, Rebecca Susan	3546	Nidiffer, Grover B.	1315
McKinney, John Gladney	4162	Nidiffer, Ray O.	4287
McKinzey, Lola D.	1478	Nipp, Nora Maxene	4426
McKnight, Lola State	1084	Nix, Lucile I.	1314
McLain, Susie A.	197	Nix, Roger F.	1208
McLain, Isaac	198	Nix, John Knight	4496
McLain, Oda B.	199	Nix, Bessie	4826
McLain, Wat Mayes	717	Noah, Benjamine F. V.	1086
McLain, Harley	1310	Noel, Augusta May	2608
McLain, Louis	2488	Nofflett, Joseph	2374
McLain, Elmer	2721	Nofire, Nannie	3816
McLain, Arthur	2722	Nofire, Mary Jane	4699
McLane, Mary Stella Lee	2967	Noisey, Geh-hue-gah	4700
McLaughlin, Neal	151	Noisey, Oo-gee-ghutt	4609
McLemore, Ko-hene	4799	Norman, Alice May	4840
McLemore, Jess	4800	Norman, Louis Edward	4345
McLemore, Cicero L.	4725	Norman, Howard Owen	4346
McMains, Delva May	1901	Noris, Florence	2621
McNabb, Anna G.	2723	Nuckolls, Gladys Fay	3245
McNabb, Mary E.	2724	Odle, Cora	3621
McNair, Philip Pink	4522	Odle, Ada	3622
McNair, Opal K.	3616	Odle, Renie	3360
McNair, Henry	3322	Odle, Jack	3361
McPherson, Herbert D.	448	Oer, Emma May	470
McSpadden, William Fair,		Oglesby, Gladys	3173
Jr.	370	Oliver, Charles Leonard	464
McSpadden, Clinton	371	Oliver, Cassie 'B.	2375
McSpadden, Maurice		Omstead, Waneeta	3857
Rogers	1082	Oneal, Frona E.	375
Nading, Ralph	252	Osage, Martha	3156
Nading, Flosa May	253	Osage, Bety	3157
Nading, Glenn A.	718	Osage, Susie	2894
Nading, Irene L.	719	Osborn, Ruby Dale	2439
Nail, Minnie Ellen	1256	Osborne, Orville O.	2330
Nakedhead, Jim	2314	Osborne, Edwin V.	2331
Nakedhead, Rachel	3134	Oskison, Sadie L.	2778
Nall, Mildred E.	250	Oskison, Leona M.	2779
Nall, William E.	251	Oskison, Helen Day	3761
Nash, Clarence Evelyne	1764	Otting, Opal	2588
Nave, Leon S.	2528	Overley, Fern Lucile	3399
Nave, Ruby M.	2529	Overley, Rossie Ellen	3400
Nave, John Mack	2841	Overtaker, Carnell	4940
Neal, James C.	4501	Owen, Gertie Mable	936
Neal, Florence Ethel	3246	Owens, Chester Alba	227
Needham, Thomas B.	869	Owens, Samuel P.	1316

Name.	Roll No.
Owens, Arnold Adelbert	3568
Owens, Florence	3855
Owens, Ike	4857
Owens, Siquani	4895
Owl, Daniel	3946
Owl, Washington	3947
O'Dell Samuel Lawson	2625
O'Fields, Janana	2807
O'Fields, Jeff	2808
O'Fields, Ina	2892
O'Fields, Lillie	2893
O'Fields, Smith	3973
O'Fields, Ella May	3974
O'Harrow, George E.	2583
O'Reilly, James Philip	2969
Pace, Louis C.	2506
Pace, Joel S.	2507
Pace, Lauraette L.	2508
Pace, Carry May	2500
Pace, Thomas Jefferson	2501
Pack, Ida	1694
Pack, Anna	1695
Pack, Lilley	2261
Pack, Emma	3895
Paden, John B.	760
Paden, Mamie B.	4424
Paden, Ina A.	4425
Paden, Gean D.	4549
Paden, Cora A.	2113
Paden, Lewis D., Jr.	4451
Paden, Mattie	3325
Paden, Cloyd	3326
Paden, Arthur H.	4140
Padget, Taylor	3764
Painter, Donald Leo	806
Palmer, Sarah Myrtle	1770
Palmer, Ocie	1781
Palmer, Vella	1782
Palmer, Vada	1783
Palmer, Cherry May	4106
Palmer, Elizabeth Hazel	4107
Palone, Cora	4536
Palone, Grover	4537
Palone, Ora May	4538
Palone, Henry Franklin	1862
Palone, Nancy	1863
Palone, Gussie Franklin	1864
Palone, Arvie	1865
Palone, Floyd	1320
Palone, Mary Ethel	1321
Pann, Walter	2780
Panter, Louie N.	2970
Paris, Lamoin	6
Paris, Varna Alice	1088
Paris, Jewell	4372
Parris, Susan C.	1807
Parris, Green L.	1690
Parris, Elizabeth	1691
Parris, Lavina Bertha	2672
Parris, Lee	2896
Parris, Violet	2897
Parris, William C.	3660
Parris, Eloise M.	4358
Parrish, Winnie May	1020
Parrish, Tommie G.	1585
Parrish, Asaneth	1586
Parrish, Berley E.	2628
Parrish, George H.	2629
Parrish, Albert Logan	2333
Parrish, Irene May	3560
Parrish, Tressa Eva	3561
Parr, Lonnie Fite	206
Parks, Myrtle C.	567
Parks, Bertha E.	568
Parks, Mary Jane	957
Parks, Ruth	1087
Parks, Cara M.	4758
Parks, Alfred E.	4759
Parks, Ruby Lee	1507
Parks, Margarette	1508
Parks, Byron D.	2406
Parks, Wahlelle T.	3661
Parks, Charles	4667

Name.	Roll No.
Parker, Lillie E.	4525
Parker, George	937
Parker, Edward J.	938
Parker, Leona M.	939
Parker, Omer	1322
Parker, Lake	1323
Parker, Ether	1209
Parker, Williard Lee	1547
Parker, Ida O.	2607
Parker, Stella S.	4450
Parnell, Myrtle Ethel	3672
Parsley, Robert	282
Parsons, John H.	37
Parsons, Alpha	4362
Parson, Myrtle	1480
Parson, Carl	2842
Parson, William Larence	2843
Parson, Aggie	1481
Partain, Charles H. T.	2172
Partain, Milly E.	2173
Partain, Verell Everett	3979
Parkinson, James	1210
Parkhurst, Mabel B.	1211
Parkhurst, Henry	2850
Patillo, Andy E.	2763
Patillo, Eva May	2764
Patrick, Clara	410
Patrick, David	4437
Patrick, Mary E.	3671
Patterson, Rosco S.	26
Patterson, Kinney V.	3513
Patterson, Aurthur L.	2176
Patterson, Flora C.	2236
Patterson, Amelia	1930
Patton, William 'Watie	1089
Patton, Gideon Jay	1859
Patton, Roy Gideon	3463
Patton, Joseph A. Jr.	1692
Patton, Herbert Nelson	2898
Patton, Robert S.	3762
Patton, Grace Lee	4734
Paul, Bertha	4384
Payne, Ellen O.	874
Payne, Fred	1213
Payne, Luttie A.	1584
Payne, Ollie Golden	2112
Payne, Nettie	4765
Payne, Maggie A.	3247
Payne, Ruby G.	3697
Payton, Nora May	2174
Payton, Horace	4454
Payton, Bessie	1931
Payton, Elizabeth	1932
Pearce, Lewis G.	2265
Pearce, Herbert Eugene	2284
Pearse, Lue E.	891
Pearse, John W.	892
Peak, Jess	3763
Peak, Homer	4966
Pearson, Walter, Everet	571
Pearson, John Alvis	3858
Peck, Lafe	1482
Peck, Beaulah	1483
Peebles, George D.	2376
Peebles, Vera E.	2377
Peek, Dew M. W.	3948
Peek, Russel	2731
Pelsue, Florence R.	958
Pemberton, William C.	7
Pemberton, Roy W.	8
Pemberton, Eliza	2729
Pemberton, Mable Lee	2730
Pendergraft, Ira R.	158
Pendergraft, Oswald	4336
Pendleton, Juanita	2378
Pennel, Bernice C.	2175
Pennington, Allie Maxine	1373
Penoi, Una Josephine	3327
Perry, Vinita	739
Perry, Susan Marie	411
Perry, Theodore C.	2513

Name.	Roll No.	Name.	Roll No.
Perry, Orvill Lee	2114	Prater, Robbie	873
Perdue, Daniel W.	2115	Prather, Roberet Daniel	259
Peters, Flora Anna	871	Prather, Flora M.	2237
Peters, Teddy Wesley	872	Preston, Halle	1866
Petterson, Emma	216	Preston, Dixie Ione	1867
Petterson, Lizzie	217	Preston, Gouldie Agnes	4470
Pettit, Joseph	4314	Preston, Herman J. D.	4471
Pettit, Amelia	4315	Price, Florence Lillian	48
Pettit, Nancy	3817	Price, Lena	109
Pettit, Cora	4743	Price, Beverly Joe	164
Petitt, William		Price, John J.	283
Percivill	1825	Price, Ross A.	3275
Petitt, Mazie Opal	1826	Price, Samuel W.	3276
Petitt, Hearsel	2971	Price, Cordelia Maud	2899
Petty, Juel Edna Jane	3441	Price, Samuel Floyd	2900
Petty, John Columbus	3442	Price, Mira L.	3324
Petty, Sarah Marie	2526	Price, Mary Ann	3249
Petty, Leona	2728	Price, Vida O.	3887
Phariss, Elmus Gertrude	465	Price, James F.	4080
Pheasant, Tams	740	Prim, Lawrence Duncan	820
Phillips, Ola May	43	Pritchett, Steve	3045
Phillips, Vergia	4310	Pritchett, Ollie	3949
Phillips, George William	720	Pritchett, Isiac	3975
Phillips, Joel Arthur	1090	Pritchett, Lillie	3976
Phillips, Henry	1319	Pritchett, Kattie	3977
Phillips, Allice	1214	Pritchett, Sallie	3978
Phillips, Roy	1215	Proctor, Feather	1693
Phillips, Zoe	1238	Proctor, Mollie	2448
Phillips, Jesse	3473	Proctor, Abraham	2449
Phillips, Cecil	1696	Proctor, Aggie	2450
Phillips, Lizzie	2563	Provence, Cumming	
Phillips, James William	3556	Christine	2626
Phillips, Fred T.	3185	Provence, Barto Rogers	2627
Phillips, Senora M. B.	3689	Pruitt, Sherman	3638
Phillips, Archie	3859	Pumpkin, Charley	3913
Phillips, John	4679	Pumpkin, Joh n	4056
Phillips, Clarence	4680	Purcell, Wilbur	1582
Phillipps, Opel M.	3643	Purcell, Asa G.	1583
Pickard, Gracie A.	1484	Purcell, Coleman R.	4613
Pickard, Warnetta	2597	Purcell, Zola Beatrice	4054
Pickard, Onnie J.	2598	Qualls, Mary J.	2365
Pickup, James Gorden	1041	Queen, Tilda Vilena	3287
Pickup, John	2170	Queen, Alton J. H.	3288
Pickup, Lucy	2171	Quinley, Martin	2379
Pickup, Jennie	4055	Quinton, Zelma	3860
Pierce, Hazel	761	Quinton, Wiona	3861
Pierce, Earl Boyd	2609	Ragsdale, Vera	1329
Pierce, Mollie	4596	Ragsdale, Cherokee	1330
Pigeon, Vann	3514	Ragsdale, Rease	1698
Pigeon, George Jr.	4815	Rains, Francis Carl	4407
Pigeon, Alisa	4874	Rains, Hellen Tsisqua	4408
Pigeon, Ga-du-u-eh	4885	Rains, Jessie	1490
Pigeon, Tom	4896	Rainey, Annie Catherine	3640
Pigeon, Elsie	4750	Raley, John D.	200
Pinkney, Lily M.	2539	Raley, Clara B.	201
Pitts, Alma E.	54	Ramsey, James William	60
Pitts, Pauline Elizabeth	204	Ramsey, Rufus Earl	61
Pitts, William Virgil	205	Ramey, Maurice Earl	248
Pitts, Gladys	3296	Randall, Joseph U.	4057
Plank, Garnett	281	Randall, Peter T.	4058
Pointer, Pauline Marie	2589	Randolph, Tim G.	3819
Polecat, Bethel	3914	Randolph, James H.	3820
Polecat, Ethel	3915	Randolph, Robert C.	3821
Polecat, John	4782	Raper, William J.	288
Polone, Tiff	889	Raper, Mary Jane	4628
Polone, Lillie May	890	Rasmus, Josephine F.	1489
Polson, Cornelius V.	821	Ratliff, Maggie Lulu	2901
Polson, John W.	1091	Ratliff, Kale	3950
Polson, Charlie	1092	Ratliff, Vann	3951
Polson, Marjorie	3431	Rattler, Josie	3981
Polson, Willie E.	1317	Rattler, Charlie	3982
Polson, Jewell	1318	Rattler, Timothy	4059
Poorboy, Willie	3144	Rattler, Luke	4060
Porter, Charles	3502	Rattler, Nannie	4866
Potter, Mary	3370	Rattler, Walter	4867
Potter, Cloe E.	4383	Rattlingourd, Judy	376
Potts, Mary	4105	Rattlingourd, Veta M.	1093
Potts, Burnard C.	4251	Rattlingourd, Cherokee	
Potts, Earnest M.	4252	A.	1094
Powell, Mary May	44	Rattlingourd, Martin	2877
Powell, Ochelata	45	Rattlingourd, Carl	3024
Powell, Katy Belle	569	Rattlingourd, Kenefick	3214
Powell, Avious	570	Rattlingourd, James T.	4960

Name.	Roll No.	Name.	Roll No.
Ravin, Abe	4952	Robber, Leona	4976
Ravin, Sarah	4953	Robber, George	3046
Ray, Gladdys A.	2514	Roberts, Harry Gilmor	295
Ray, Bertha Z.	3888	Roberts, Jessie J.	1221
Ray, Susie	4141	Roberts, Silas	1222
Reaves, Johnnie Winnie	4330	Roberts, Verna M.	1709
Reaves, Clem Burks	4331	Roberts, Zelma A.	1710
Redbird, Hooley Bell	4061	Roberts, Frank	4455
Redden, Maudie May	1223	Roberts, Mamie	4456
Redinger, Laurence B.	2555	Robertson, Clem	2317
Reece, George		Robertson, Ethel	2459
Washington	4669	Robertson, Andrew J.	3068
Reed, Lou Otta	575	Robertson, Rhoda	
Reed, Tressie Althia	1699	Matilda	4108
Reed, Vurnis	1700	Roberson, Ralph	
Reed, Glen Blackburn	4623	Raymond	1325
Reed, Edith Alta	4624	Roberson, Bertie Lucian	1326
Reed, Cleo F.	1755	Roberson, Minnie Jane	2972
Reed, Irena B.	1756	Robbins, Guss C.	17
Reese, William R.	285	Robbins, Beuna J.	18
Reese, Chief Hannaw	286	Robbins, Goldie Cathrine	573
Reese, Ada	1706	Robbins, Viola Valintine	574
Reese, Johnson	2571	Robbins, Robert Calvin	1327
Reese, Roy	3047	Robbins, Cecil Alva	1328
Reeves, Jessie W.	412	Robbins, Ida M.	1216
Reeves, Edmond Harvey	2116	Robbins, Margaret A.	1217
Reid, Mary Cleo	293	Robbins, Joseph Wade	1868
Rex, Norma L.	645	Robbins, Larson Wesley	2420
Reynolds, Gertrude	1324	Robbins, William	
Reynolds, Albert T.	2642	Thomas	2421
Reynolds, Miles	3720	Robins, Cherokee	449
Reynolds, Stella	3721	Robison, Mary Jane	1240
Reynolds, Jessie M.	4255	Robison, Andy	1241
Reynolds, George W.	4256	Robison, Della Edna	4443
Rhea, Cecil May	438	Robison, Clara O'Dean	3542
Rhoads, Nettie M.	3493	Robinson, Thomas	
Rhodes, Minnie E.	3443	Carlile	654
Rhodes, Cecil Edward	3766	Robinson, Watie	289
Richards, Kanzada	2380	Robinson, Edgar D.	724
Richardson, William R.	3623	Robinson, David	3010
Richardson, John Elmer	4182	Robinson, Nomie C.	3011
Richardson, Mattie Viola	4183	Robinson, LeRoy	
Riddle, Mabel F.	1869	Prather	1589
Riddle, George William	1708	Robinson, Clarence	
Rider, Violet	290	Roosevelt	1704
Rider, Jennie May	291	Robinson, Margaret	2486
Rider, L. Dee	296	Robinson, Cornelius	2487
Rider, Abraham	721	Robinson, Ross L.	3145
Rider, Jessie Gunter	981	Robinson, Elizabeth F.	3146
Rider, Stanwatie	1098	Robinson, Hubert	
Rider, Anna	4614	Spencer	1048
Rider, Jack C.	3822	Rodden, Bula Lea	4288
Rider, Elva Iona	1937	Rodgers, James Vittum	746
Rider, Anna Leona	1938	Rodecker, Adda Maud	141
Ridge, Daniel	4445	Rodman, Allen Hugh	2274
Ridgway, Beulah	3048	Roe, Dorris Ellen	2014
Rienhardt, Lennie May	1096	Rogers, Joseph Earl	572
Rienhardt, Alma Fay	1097	Rogers, Katharyn	581
Rigsby Mary Luvinia	1263	Rogers, Bear	292
Riggs, Author J.	4150	Rogers, Clem	
Riley, Helen	132	Huckleberry	1021
Riley, Opal	133	Rogers, Mary N.	1021
Riley, Printice	1800	Rogers, Ramona S.	1332
Riley, Eula	4606	Rogers, David M.	1218
Riley, George W. Jr.	1065	Rogers, Edmond	1485
Riley, Minerva E.	4415	Rogers, Clint D.	1587
Riley, Neva	2639	Rogers, Anna B.	1588
Riley, Evalyn	4786	Rogers, Kenneth Scott	2831
Riley, Richard Wilson	4787	Rogers, Ople	4561
Ringo, Robert B.	1224	Rogers, William Penn	2684
Rinehardt, Everett R.	1872	Rogers, Alta Elizabeth	2685
Rinehardt, Earl	3158	Rogers, Edward Jr.	4201
Rinehardt, Vernnen	3159	Rogers, Joel Mays	4202
Riner, Marjory	3250	Rogers, Robbie Myrtle	4203
Rippetoe, Beulah	1936	Rogers, Damon E.	2765
Risingfawn, Myrtle E.	2117	Rogers, Lucinda	2781
Ritchie, Gracy Jane	4363	Rogers, Annie L.	2809
Ritchson, Walcie A.	1486	Rogers, Charlie	2825
Ritchson, Andrew J.	1487	Rogers, Sequoyah	3174
Roach, Zana	4233	Rogers, William Edward	3328
Roach, Georgia C.	1933	Rogers, Thomas Nelson	3818
Roastingear, Dora	3767	Rogers, Bessie	4692
Roastingear, Arther	3768	Rogers, Mary	4794

Name.	Roll No.	Name.	Roll No.
Rogers, Robert W.	1934	Samuels, May	3691
Rogers, Winona	1935	Sam, Eli	4668
Rohr, Otis D.	76	Sandifer, William	
Rohr, Roxie Thelma	77	Franklin	486
Rolland, Mary A.	3175	Sandifer,Robert Lee	487
Rolland, Elmer	3176	Sanders, Lucinda Jane	4402
Rollens, Paralee	875	Sanders, Sarah S.	762
Rollens, Verona	876	Sanders, Henry T.	4325
Rolston, Vera B.	140	Sanders, Leland A.	941
Rooster, Bettie	4365	Sanders, Lester	3432
Rose, George	2674	Sanders, Nancy J.	1225
Rose, Jesse W.	2624	Sanders, Allen G.	1226
Ross, Andrew J.	143	Sanders, Harris	3520
Ross, Mamie Elizabeth	156	Sanders, Edward	2118
Ross, Jennie Pocahontas	157	Sanders, Jessie C.	2119
Ross, Margret M.	545	Sanders, Abraham	2201
Ross, Silas McDonald	287	Sanders, Mamie H.	2337
Ross, Jessie James	722	Sanders, Hazel C.	2338
Ross, Paulean Leuiza	723	Sanders, Joe	2391
Ross, Gazelle	807	Sanders, Lizzie Ruth	3571
Ross, Francis Curtis	1049	Sanders, Allen	3147
Ross, Eda	3492	Sanders, Samuel O.	2812
Ross, Neoma	2178	Sanders, Eli	2895
Ross, Henry Pigeon	2179	Sanders, Thomas W.	3329
Ross, Adam	2451	Sanders, Matt	3069
Ross, Lucille	2452	Sanders, Caroline May	3070
Ross, Nancy	2453	Sanders, Mamie Etta	3071
Ross, Field	3004	Sanders, Mollie	3257
Ross, Joe	2732	Sanders, Mary	3258
Ross, Lucinda	2733	Sanders, Sam	3823
Ross, Frank	2932	Sanders, George	3824
Ross, Mildred F.	3639	Sanders, Mary L.	3827
Ross, Lulu Carmen	3251	Sanders, Bessie E. B.	3863
Ross, Lois	3252	Sanders, Marie	3889
Ross, Joseph E.	3980	Sanders, Jesse	3931
Ross, Nelton	4654	Sanders, Adeline	4062
Rosser, Eddy W.	3215	Sanders, John Hubert	4063
Rosser, Charles Y. Jr.	3216	Sanders, Murrell	4237
Rowe, Joe	2488	Sanders, Charley	4238
Rowe, Watt M.	2890	Sanders, Samuel S. Jr.	4387
Rowe, Alice	4163	Sapsucker, Josie	4788
Rowland, Ivey V.	3471	Sarcoxie, Byveian	577
Rowland, Macie B.	1488	Sarcoxie, Henry	380
Rowland, Minnie C.	1701	Sartain, Ella Adair	694
Rowland, Marry Opal	1702	Satterfield, Earle Ethel	4109
Rowland, Mary	3862	Satterfield, Ada Vaney	4110
Rudd, Louie Gladney	4634	Sawney, Jim	3472
Rule, Rosa L.	256	Sawney, Nannie	3515
Rule, Leo	257	Sawney, Nancy	3516
Runels, Evaline	4808	Sawney, Thomas	2120
Runyan, Robert C.	2640	Sawney, Stand	3626
Runyan, Thomas J.	2641	Scales, Ann L.	2813
Russell, David Lee	51	Scales, Mary E.	2814
Russell, Alice Ola	52	Scacewater, Clara E.	2847
Russell, Lela	75	Scacewater, Jack	2848
Russell, Ruby P.	810	Schaublin, John R.	900
Russell, Flossie	1331	Schell, Margarett V.	584
Russell, Ellis B.	1220	Schoonover, Annie R.	79
Russell, John D.	4710	Schoonover, Frank M.	80
Russell, Jennie	4711	Schliecker, Herman A.	2556
Russell, Paul H.	2527	Schrimsher, Loletia	1228
Russell, Girtie L.	4458	Schrimsher, Maxine	1229
Russell, Lucy	2313	Schrimsher, John G.	1230
Russell, Flaucy M.	3765	Schrader, Frederick	
Russell, Franklin		Wm.	3984
Charles	4670	Schrader, Charles F.	3985
Russell, Clem	4385	Schuth, Gladys Ermina	297
Russel, Emma	4824	Schuth, Walter Jay	813
Rutherford, Samuel E.	377	Scoggins, Louis	313
Ryals, Sadie C.	3662	Scoggins, Florence	
Ryder, Wilson	3217	Pearl	381
Rye, Robert Lee	174	Scoggins, Clarence	
Sage, Ruby	763	Edward	382
Sager, Eddy A.	698	Scoggins, Veva Bee	383
Sager, Ella M.	699	Scoggins, Marion	2407
Sager, L. D.	942	Scott, Lena	70
Sallee, William Jennings	764	Scott, Fite B.	188
Sallee, Leo Eldridge	765	Scott, Ida Nola	189
Salley, Glorah V.	2489	Scott, Florence Evelyn	302
Samson, Ruth E.	2133	Scott, Arthur Lee	304
Samuel, Maurine	1712	Scott, George Sanders	305
Samuel, Charles F.	2408	Scott, Gladys H.	3008
Samuels, Florence W.	3690	Scott, Gibson, R., Jr.	3009

Name.	Roll No.
Scott, Laura Vivian	1266
Scott, Cora	379
Scott, Ollie	4705
Scott, Bertha Evaline	811
Scott, Hickey	379
Scott, David E.	1102
Scott, Ida	1873
Scott, Rena	1874
Scott, Eva Ruth	1590
Scott, Margaret Fay	1591
Scott, Gertrude Vaughan	1592
Scott, Lillie Beaulah	2018
Scott, Theodore A.	2132
Scott, Ruth A.	2319
Scott, Millard E.	3016
Scott, Iva L.	3017
Scott, Milo B.	3253
Scott, Reginald Aurther	3916
Scott, Gus Coble	3917
Scott, Ananias	4064
Scott, Beutice H. Young	4257
Scott, Robert Mays	4258
Scott, Nancy	4729
Scott, Cheese	4745
Scott, Lacie	4746
Scott, Riley	1944
Scott, Lucresie	1945
Scraper, Alice	3579
Scraper, Ice	4694
Scraper, Robert	4747
Scroggins, Bertha Bell	1741
Scroggins, George	1742
Scruggs, Jack	898
Scruggs, Revord	899
Scruggs, Julia M.	4187
Scudder, Clifford Harrison	1751
Scullawl, Dare	521
Seabolt, Minnie	312
Seabolt, Vera M.	2974
Seabolt, Ura E.	2975
Seabolt, Nancy	3333
Seabolt, Daniel H.	4776
Seabolt, Ella May	3049
Seabolt, Tennie Emma	3050
Seabolt, Raymond G.	3775
Seabolt, Willie L.	3776
Seabolt, Dewey D.	4186
Seabolt, Carrie M.	4236
Seals, John	3256
Sears, Henrietta	4918
Sears, Joseph H.	4919
Secondine, Henry A.	1493
Seccondi, Tom	2845
Secondyne, Edward	1940
Seekings, Nancy Jane	23
Selgel, George A.	2121
Seiler, Kathleen, Ione	3681
Sellers, Ruth	1877
Sequichie, J. Oris	4151
Sequichie, Jennie	4660
Sequichie, Eliza	4661
Sequichie, Nellie L.	3903
Setser, Lillieann M.	3692
Setser, Thomas W.	3693
Sevens, Georgia N.	1522
Sevens, Deward L.	1523
Sevier, Alma E.	3773
Sevier, Thompson C.	3774
Sevier, Joseph Eugene	4184
Sevier, Carrol Laverne	4185
Sevenstar, Mary	2950
Shackelford, Aurielee	265
Shackelford, Robert Estell	3890
Shamblin, Dock H.	725
Shamblin, George Clark	897
Shamblin, Emma May	2122
Shannon, Jesse W.	3625
Shakingbush, William	3723
Sharp, Cora N.	310
Sharp, Rebecca L.	311
Sharp, Alma Thay	1227

Name.	Roll No.
Sharp, Franklin Brewster	3569
Sharyer, Stella	1716
Sharyer, Mary Jane	2766
Shay, Minnie T.	413
Shearer, John M.	1232
Shearer, Joseph T.	1233
Shearhart, Cale M.	4165
Sheehan, Eva	2386
Shell, Thompson	3494
Shell, William E.	1509
Shell, Pearl E.	1510
Shell, Lucinda	2123
Shell, Charley	2124
Shell, Emma	2578
Shell, Stan	3331
Shell, Howe L.	3332
Shell, Columbus L.	4962
Shell, Callie Myrtle	4400
Shelly, Effie Grace	3771
Shelly, John Robert	3772
Shelly, Jewell	3983
Shelton, Sadie M.	2643
Sherley, Flossie M.	2383
Sherley, James E.	2384
Shetley, Sarah	1337
Shimp, Mary Agness	72
Shimp, Lydia Ester	73
Shinn, Emma	2393
Shinn, Arthur	2394
Shinn, Ralph	3102
Shinn, Gladis Lee	3259
Shipley, Mary A.	117
Shirley, James P.	4164
Shirley, Viola	4261
Shoemake, Oscar Lee	4311
Shoemake, Lola	4312
Shoemake, Alice Bertha	1494
Shoemake, Mildred R.	4550
Shoemake, Fred	4629
Shoemake, Syrena H.	3682
Shoemaker, Herbert Norman	583
Shoemake, Maggie May	4320
Shoemake, Ira Dell	4321
Shook, Ethel	4142
Shook, John R.	2125
Shouse, Joe Harry	1249
Shotpouch, Sarah	4855
Shufeldt, Mabel Francis	303
Shufeldt, Violet A.	3597
Silcox, Dollie	4925
Silk, Edna	585
Silk, George W. Jr.	4486
Silversmith, Lizzie	1942
Silversmith, Pearl	1943
Simco, John	3953
Simon, Anna	3439
Simon, Frosty	3440
Simmons, Ida Bell	3708
Simmons, Lyda	3709
Simmons, All-li-gah	4837
Simpson, Thomas A.	1264
Simpson, Joseph R.	1265
Singleton, Lucy	307
Sisson, Pauline	4327
Sisson, Tom W.	2817
Sisson, Dave	2818
Sitten, Jeanie I.	2128
Sittingdown, Emma Geneva May	4784
Sixkiller, Hallie M.	1500
Sixkiller, Rutha L.	2126
Sixkiller, Cherokee	2127
Sixkiller, Houston	2414
Sixkiller, Sadie	2767
Sixkiller, Felix	3148
Sixkiller, William	3864
Sixkiller, Mary	4911
Sixkiller, Ganer	4912
Sixkiller, Lula M.	1949
Skinner, Robert Emmett	878
Skinner, Mary Pauline	1715

Name.	Roll No.
Skitt, Thomas	4650
Slape, Evert E.	3581
Slagle, Velma J.	4386
Slaughter, Tommey	94
Slaughter, Sidney Estelle	95
Slaughter, Oscar	3464
Sleeper, Margaret Lucille	579
Sleeper, Lewis Gardner	580
Sloan, Bonnie C.	128
Sloan, Naomia C.	3769
Sloan, James E.	3770
Smallwood, Annie	3098
Smallwood, Richard	3099
Smart, Cora B.	3416
Smith, Bonnie Kathleen	11
Smith, Thelma Florence	12
Smith, Nathaniel DeWitt	181
Smith, Floyd	576
Smith, Wayne Monroe	298
Smith, Samson	3407
Smith, Anton N.	1801
Smith, Ben R.	766
Smith, Wade H.	767
Smith, Owen	812
Smith, Franklin S.	3414
Smith, Gladys	3418
Smith, George Clinton	896
Smith, Doris Palmer	940
Smith, Joe V.	1050
Smith, Richard Edwin	1099
Smith, Texanna	1124
Smith, Albert Carlisle	1219
Smith, George W.	1237
Smith, Theresa	3094
Smith, Grover P.	2016
Smith, Mary Jeanette	2622
Smith, Charley	2318
Smith, Hugh W.	2590
Smith, Arthur O.	4444
Smith, Jesse	2389
Smith, Julian	2395
Smith, George J.	2675
Smith, Flossie	2630
Smith, Evylin	4572
Smith, Earl F.	2815
Smith, Daniel	2844
Smith, James Lafayette	3177
Smith, Ruthie May	3330
Smith, Emmett	4350
Smith, Emma	3254
Smith, Ray	3255
Smith, Hazel Madge	4477
Smith, Richard E.	3777
Smith, Nola	3778
Smith, Walter	4495
Smith, Jennie	4166
Smith, Fannie	4167
Smith, Nancy	4695
Smith, Lillie	4869
Smith, Spear	4986
Smith, Redflag	4875
Smith, Alec	4978
Smith, Kun-scuw-wi	4744
Smith, Jennie Eveline	1939
Smoke, Ellen	4899
Snell, Budd	1714
Snell, Jennie	3362
Snell, Bertha	3363
Snell, Lizzie	4825
Snider, Vivid O.	2768
Snip, Kinnie	2846
Snyder, Clarence	3780
Soap, John	4675
Soap, Sallie	4795
Sootawakeky, Key-ho-gah	4909
Sootawakeky, Eh-daw-leh-hi	4910
Sortore, Mable Clair	1336
Sosbee, Juanita	57
South, Edwin Clifford	2019
Spade, Rosa	2440

Name.	Roll No.
Spade, Susie	4833
Spaniard, Buck Richard	3609
Spaniard, Lila	4693
Sparkman, Pansy Jenett	2224
Sparks, Letty H.	2130
Sparks, James P.	2131
Spears, Sadie	300
Spears, Walter E.	301
Spears, John Alvin	1671
Spears, Daniel Eli	1672
Spears, Edward Z. T.	3624
Spears, Mary	3779
Spears, Laura Cecil	4176
Spears, Floid	4177
Spears, Mary Eva	4178
Splitnose, Martha	893
Springer, Owen	3578
Springwater, Eliza	1234
Springwater, William R.	1368
Springwater, Arthur	2315
Squirrel, Watt	100
Squirrel, Joseph	4615
Squirrel, Nancy	4616
Squirrel, Walter	4626
Squirrel, Susie	4884
Squirrel, Sukie	4871
Staller, Lizzie	3434
Stallcup, Ida	2454
Stanclift, William Henry	270
Stalk, Claude	1236
Stanley, Barney	3364
Stanley, Alva	3365
Starr, Edwin B.	97
Starr, Rena	1235
Starr, Nellie	2549
Starr, Elizabeth	2550
Starr, Lillie	2696
Starr, Felix	2697
Starr, Roosevelt Q.	3570
Starr, Cherry	3260
Starr, Ezekiel	3261
Starr, Lulu	3262
Starr, Jack Raymond	3826
Starr, Ernest W.	4234
Starr, Gee-stun-nah	4737
Starr, Eugene F.	1947
Starr, Mary B.	1948
Stansill, Minnie J.	1946
Starnes, Margie	2644
Starks, Cynthia Angia	586
Starks, Alfred George	587
Stayathome, Bird	4168
Stealer, Molley	4715
Stealer, Celie	2390
Steele, Ollie M.	233
Steele, Paul Vernest	582
Steele, Tomie D.	509
Steele, Leila M.	1367
Stephens, Sarah M.	1767
Stephens, Cherokee	1768
Stephens, Ruth	943
Stephens, Lewis Granville	944
Stephens, Sarah R.	1335
Stephens, Bertha	3051
Stephens, Clyde	3052
Stephens, Eugene L.	1950
Stephens, Homer	1951
Stephenson, Mary	306
Stephenson, Salestie	431
Stephenson, Roxie M.	1051
Sterling, Ada B.	2238
Stevens, Claudie W.	309
Stevens, Jessie Jewel	2617
Stevens, Floyd	3315
Stevenson, Daisy Edgar	3825
Steer, Jaunita	4210
Stewart, James	308
Stewart, Pauline	451
Stewart, Oneida Grace	452
Stewart, Ruth	453
Stewart, Ewing V.	1333

Name.	Roll No.
Stewart, Thomas R.	1334
Stewart, Ross	1499
Stewart, Myrtie May	2129
Stewart, Land J.	2381
Stewart, Teautla	3865
Still, Laura Ellen	1231
Still, Noble	4298
Still, Lela May	3291
Still, Mary	2655
Still, Tobe	2444
Still, James	2782
Still, Joe Ivey	2783
Still, Mack Edna	2784
Still, Polly	2874
Still, Louie L.	2933
Still, John T.	3828
Still, Pearl	4491
Still, Rugie	4235
Stiles, Elsie Josephine	299
Stine, Mattie Lane	2422
Stockton, Bernice	578
Stockton, Roy	2392
Stokes, Nannie Ruth	67
Stokes, Nona J.	894
Stokes, Nora A.	895
Stogsdill, Earnest	2275
Stone, Fay	4259
Stone, Lucile	4260
Stop, William	4883
Stover, Samuel Louis	1100
Stover, Mattie Elizabeth	1101
Stover, Bessie	2953
Stover, Carrie H.	1822
Storts, Ada Vesta	1743
Storts, George F.	1744
Strange, Lula Euphemia	378
Strong, Ahniwake	1941
Stratton, Thomas D.	2816
Stroud, Earl DeLoss	33
Stroud, Johnnie Roy	34
Stroup, Freddie B.	4193
Stubblefield, Paschal P.	2919
Sturdivant, Eva E.	1495
Sturdivant, Carl T.	1496
Suagee, Madeline M.	182
Suagee, Cella J.	901
Suagee, Gladys W.	902
Suagee, Estella May	1497
Sudderth, Evlyn M.	2015
Sullivan, Charles Leroy	1779
Sullivan, Elva Vestor	1259
Sult, Elmer D.	1711
Summers, John H.	13
Summers, Wynemer Lee	1594
Summerfield, Nancy	4339
Summerfield, Ollie	4947
Summerfield, Edd	4948
Summerlin, Edna May	1498
Summerlin, Noah C.	4366
Summerlin, Virgil D.	4367
Sunday, Louis	1762
Sunday, Laura	1763
Sunday, Frank	3366
Sunday, William	4289
Surrell, Mildred D.	3725
Surrell, John R.	3726
Suskey, Mattie	471
Suskey, Cleeo	472
Sutherland, Mary Helen	2605
Sutherlin, James Marion	1713
Suwat, Zada	1491
Suwat, Ruth	1492
Sweatman, Milford	1593
Sweeten, Jessie Leona	1778
Sweeten, Samuel J.	4592
Swimmer, Lucy V.	2225
Swimmer, Sundy	2385
Swimmer, Cull	2397
Swimmer, Lucy	3359
Sykes, Delilah	2601
Tagg, Arch	2853
Tagg, Henry	2854

Name.	Roll No.
Tail, Lewis	4642
Tail, Cusarnee	4643
Tail, Nancy	4849
Tail, Nellie	4846
Talbert, Hazel A.	1344
Talbert, Fay Leona	1345
Talbert, Alice Lula	1346
Talkington, Clement Horrace	3100
Talkington, Welton Collins	3101
Talkington, Olin	4067
Talley, Fred	2180
Talley, Jessey Bryan	2851
Talley, Esther Mae	2852
Tally, Ethel May	2181
Tally, Rosetta	3987
Tankersley, Lee Austin	945
Tannehill, Loid	1954
Tanner, Olan Roscoe	1883
Tanner, Jesse Harold	1884
Tanner, Allen	2455
Tanner, John	2456
Tanner, Clark	2920
Tanner, Jennie	2819
Tanner, Lucy	2820
Tanner, Eucha	4478
Tarepen, Dollie	4944
Tarepen, Ollie	4945
Tate, Roy L.	2540
Tate, Sarah M.	2541
Tau-unea-cie, Lexie	4531
Taylor, McCutcheon	4303
Taylor, Stacy Ann	4308
Taylor, Mitchell Turner	4309
Taylor, William James	532
Taylor, Ruth M.	316
Taylor, Rachel M.	317
Taylor, William E.	4313
Taylor, Shelly K.	770
Taylor, Gilbert Thompson	771
Taylor, Clint Roger	3435
Taylor, Sequoyah G.	3436
Taylor, Laura A.	4540
Taylor, Bernard	3285
Taylor, Mandy M.	4337
Taylor, Eda Malinda	4338
Taylor, Roy	3495
Taylor, Hazel May	3496
Taylor, Mattie A.	2134
Taylor, George	2135
Taylor, Robert Drake	2321
Taylor, Neta	2632
Taylor, James F.	2581
Taylor, Ufern B.	2769
Taylor, Walter	2770
Taylor, Thomas Vivan	4467
Taylor, John	3830
Taylor, Mildred B.	3867
Taylor, Millard Brown	3868
Taylor, Laura Beatrice	4651
Taylor, Elwyn F.	4539
Teague, Lewis O.	768
Teague, Theodore L.	769
Teel, Ollie	4322
Teel, Pleney	4113
Teekahneyeskee, Fred L.	3301
Tehee, Mary	3013
Tehee, Dewey	4963
Tell, Benjamin Goss	1526
Tennison, Jessie Victoria	4262
Tennison, George Walter	4263
Tennison, Sallie Ann	4264
Terrapin, Wilson	1372
Terrell, George	3072
Terrell, Leonard	3073
Terrell, Charles L.	4652
Terrell, Etta	4653
Terrell, Anna	3014
Terrill, John Jennings	4532
Tevebaugh, Lowell B.	3367
Tharp, Raymond	4267

Name.	Roll No.	Name.	Roll No.
Tharp, Ruby	4268	Thornton, Rogers	4265
Thirsty, Webster	4903	Thornton, Nick	4266
Thomas, Nellie	264	Thrasher, Ella	277
Thomas, Lenard Raymond	1784	Thurman, Mary Alice	74
Thomas, Gladys Macil	1785	Thurman, William E.	1107
Thomas, Lydia E.	880	Thurman, Samie	1108
Thomas, Willie Wade	1880	Thurman, Winchester	1879
Thomas, Sequoyah B.	1881	Tibbs, George R.	3368
Thomas, Clarence Houston	1886	Tibbs, Effie A.	3369
Thomas, William Ray	4760	Tidmore, Andrew	2339
Thomas, Clyde	4761	Tidmore, Ruby Lee	2340
Thomas, Louise	2139	Tiger, Rebecca R.	1596
Thomas, Annie M.	3533	Tilden, Donnie	4170
Thomas, Lucius S.	2591	Tiley, Minnie P.	2517
Thomas, George L.	2592	Tiley, Edward S.	2518
Thomas, Roswell Eugene	2502	Timberlake, John Dick	3059
Thomas, Clarence	3891	Timberlake, Cuscia Albertia	4239
Thomas, Maggie	4712	Timmons, Welchie A.	2027
Thompson, Frances Pauline	22	Timson, Agnes	2738
Thompson, Claude E.	55	Timms, Dora	4111
Thompson, Thomas R.	3402	Timms, Amy	4112
Thompson, Louise Elizabeth	110	Tincup, Gracie Mildred	1103
Thompson, Edward	588	Tincup, Cyrus Raymond	1104
Thompson, Guy	2262	Tincup, Jessie Lee	4611
Thompson, Trilby Hays	2263	Tincup, Sidney	4612
Thompson, Albert Andrew	1769	Tindle, Nancy Allen	2136
Thompson, John	1052	Tindell, Arnom Lee	1720
Thompson, James Roy	1339	Tiner, Era Mae	2662
Thompson, Oma	1340	Tinnin, Lucile Brown	314
Thompson, Ola	1341	Tinney, Walter Hamilton	2557
Thompson, Leatha	1342	Tinney, Nathan Franklin	3781
Thompson, Leala	1343	Tipton, Andrew	3908
Thompson, Lewis L.	2409	Tipton, Jessie	4806
Thompson, Maurice Clifton	3284	Tittle, Willie V.	4377
Thompson, Harley C.	1595	Tittle, Thelma	4378
Thompson, Vera Dez	1597	Titsworth, Addie Bell	1374
Thompson, Ruble M.	2024	Titsworth, Marietta	2423
Thompson, Marvin J.	2441	Todd, Robert S.	2020
Thompson, William	2442	Todd, Fredrick P.	2021
Thompson, Mamie Ethel	4766	Todd, George W.	2022
Thompson, Baunia Vista	2602	Todd, Waldemar Dwight	3519
Thompson, Bonnie Lee	2603	Toney, Annie	2515
Thompson, Emmit G.	2247	Toney, Lucy	2516
Thompson, Harvy F.	3097	Tooley, Dennis	4764
Thompson, Clarence E.	3021	Tovey, Mamie L.	3627
Thompson, Opal F.	3022	Tovey, Thomas S.	3628
Thompson, Norma Viola	3135	Towler, Herma A.	4152
Thompson, Thomas	2821	Towler, Thomas Aubrey	4153
Thompson, Thomas F.	2938	Townsend, Thomas R.	4144
Thompson, Ada M.	4627	Trainor, Lydia Lucile	1105
Thompson, Ivy May	4461	Trapp, William R.	2023
Thompson, George William	3355	Trammell, James W.	3120
Thompson, Bud Edward	4472	Trammel, Wendrell	3829
Thompson, Mary Ellen	3727	Trent, Edith	4447
Thompson, Fredie A.	3866	Trickett, James William	1848
Thompson, Travis	3963	Trippard, James Raymond	1260
Thompson, William B.	4130	Tritthart, George William	814
Thompson, Elbert	4194	Troth, Mabel Ethel Eunice	4272
Thompson, Blank	4967	Troglin, James Russel	2396
Thorne, Georgia E.	170	Troglin, Thomas Jefferson	1106
Thorne, Edith I.	315	Trott, Henry Moore	4990
Thorne, Lula	2935	Trotter, Fannie E.	1380
Thorne, Opal	2936	Trottingwolf, Nellie	589
Thornton, Susie May	590	Trout, Jesse V.	1375
Thornton, Wilbur J.	414	Trout, Thomas L.	4547
Thornton, Susie J.	415	Trout, Thomas	4938
Thornton, Lewis R.	1369	Tucker, Thelma Don Tilla	1721
Thornton, Richard A.	1370	Tucker, Floyd C.	2030
Thornton, May	1717	Tucker, Davis H.	2137
Thornton, Fannie	1718	Tucker, Jessie L.	2138
Thornton, Nannie May	2025	Tucker, Edith M.	2631
Thornton, William Jessie	2026	Tucker, Osborn R.	3121
Thornton, Vivian	2028	Tucker, Eliza	2937
Thornton, Dwight H.	2029	Tucker, Sallie	2977
		Tucker, Edward	3044
		Turley, Willard Lee	1338

Name.	Roll No.
Turn, Jennie Ann	4065
Turnham, Clinton	3698
Turner, Marion Lowrey	483
Turner, Ada B.	904
Turner, Floyd	946
Turner, Opal	947
Turtle, Linnda	4968
Twist, Kuroki	1772
Twist, Darias	3334
Twist, Dollie May	3335
Tyner, Clara Belle	4853
Tyner, Myrtle Irene	4854
Tyner, George Blueford	385
Tyner, Leo D.	439
Tyner, Leonard	440
Tyner, Reuben B. Jr.	903
Tyner, Luella Mamie	4328
Tyner, Cora May	948
Tyner, William Walter	949
Tyner, Zeno	3053
Tynon, Willa Fay	1371
Underwood, Ora Alma	1722
Ussrey, Mellie Elsie	2271
Uto, Pearl B.	2982
Uto, Claud	2983
Vandagriff, Tokio	318
Vandagriff, Sarah Fern	3103
Van Hoefen, Harry S.	3122
Vanausdall, Howard	4388
Vanmatre, Dennie	2855
Vann, William W.	1382
Vann, Ezekel	1410
Vann, George	3015
Vann, Jack	2310
Vann, Susie	2633
Vann, James T.	3598
Vann, John F.	2939
Vann, George	2976
Vann, Rachel	3337
Vann, Bill	3338
Vann, Nellie A.	3729
Vann, Elias	3831
Vann, Martha	3832
Vann, Lester D.	3869
Vann, Rosella	3986
Vann, Joseph Cunningham	4240
Vann, Alberta Sarah	4241
Vann, Jess	4838
Vann, Lizzie	4839
Vaughn, Thelma Lucile	416
Vaughan, Lillian V.	950
Vickery, Florine	4462
Vickery, Grant Lee Fate	4463
Vickery, Edgar Fay	3728
Vincent, Clausine R.	234
Vincent, Robert B.	235
Vinyard, Gus	1109
Vise, Marguerite Thelma	1125
Voglemann, Zelma J.	4068
Vowell, Howell Carlile	255
Vowell, Eva	4290
Wade, Meigs Jr.	511
Walkabout, Jennie	2564
Walker, Hazel Josephine	87
Walker, Velma Nadine	88
Walker, Lillian L.	1760
Walker, Clover B.	1761
Walker, Ray	432
Walker, Ruby V.	433
Walker, Robert C.	728
Walker, Robert L.	905
Walker, Eunice Ruth	1053
Walker, Minnie Opal	2183
Walker, Dama Sybil	2398
Walker, Paul T.	3603
Walker, Cornelius	3137
Walker, Arthur J.	3007
Walker, L. Ladd	2858
Walker, Inez J.	3704
Walker, Neal C.	3705
Walker, Bluie G.	3263
Walker, Robert	3893

Name.	Roll No.
Walker, Esther	4073
Walker, Frankie	4145
Walkingstick, Benjamin T.	420
Walkingstick, Mattie E.	2140
Walkingstick, Rosa A.	2141
Walkingstick, Sallie	2401
Walkingstick, Alice	3169
Walkingstick, George	4929
Wall, Cyril L.	3599
Wall, Eva B.	3600
Waller, Bessie O. W.	254
Wallen, Jewell	3000
Wallace, James E.	1116
Wallace, Lucille	2326
Wallace, Thomas	2545
Wallace, Margie V.	2546
Wallis, Austin Homer	1808
Wallis, Myrtle Beatrice	1809
Walton, Clara Lee	3292
Walton, Ethel Estora	3293
Walters, Robert C.	593
Walters, Mamie R.	594
Walters, Guy	4071
Walters, Wilbur	4291
Waltrip, Georgie M.	2827
Waltrip, Cecil	3380
Wann, Robert Lee	4209
Ward, James Virgil	340
Ward, Bertha A.	341
Ward, Lucile E.	342
Ward, Rholand V.	343
Ward, Rubia O.	344
Ward, Grace L.	345
Ward, Lee O.	885
Ward, Robert F. K.	4528
Ward, Wille Lois	4412
Ward, Leatrice L.	1388
Ward, Paul Howell	1389
Ward, Daphne Alone	1390
Ward, Lottie Lorinia	1531
Ward, Samuel J.	2142
Ward, George Herbert	2145
Ward, Lula Edith	3534
Ward, Charles Edgar	3535
Ward, Dortha Ludema	2424
Ward, John S.	2856
Ward, James O.	4487
Ward, Carrie E.	4488
Ward, Charles F.	3870
Ward, William L.	1261
Ware, Thelma	339
Ware, Mary May	982
Warfield, Robert Henry	3477
Warner, Flossie	741
Warner, Jewel	742
Warner, John T.	3277
Warneke, Elizabeth	3683
Warneke, Louis	3684
Warren, Helen L.	28
Warseat, Gracie	3954
Washburn, David Deloss	321
Washburn, Dealia Harlett	322
Washam, Garrett Henderson	908
Washington, Christopher	600
Washington, Clifford	601
Washington, Freddie	4017
Washington, Rachel	951
Washington, William	3909
Washington, John	3910
Washington, Oaley	4586
Washington, Noley	4587
Washington, William	4816
Wassom, George Washington	1113
Waters, John W.	326
Waters, Berlia	327
Waters, Georgia	4768
Waters, Arthur	2945
Waters, Lydia	4070
Waters, Rosella	4829
Waters, Mary	4955

Name.	Roll No.	Name.	Roll No.
Waters, Alpha E.	3506	West, Jess	2543
Waters, Clara M.	3507	Westenhaver, Henry	
Waters, Okla Lee	2544	Ray	1727
Waters, Julia Saalee	599	Wheatley, Fadelia M. E.	130
Waters, Eva	325	Wheatley, Hubert	131
Watkins, Goldie May	2298	Whelchel, Mary B.	1534
Watkins, Effa Glyas	1835	Wheeler, Abraham	
Watkins, Flora J.	1542	Theodore	337
Watkins, Bud	1543	Wheeler, John P. Jr.	3833
Watkins, Callie May	1729	Wheeler, Lucy	3955
Watkins, Omie Gertrude	219	White, Golda Edith	1013
Watkins, Clarence		White, William Otto	1014
Newton	220	White, Jewell Clyde	595
Watson, Minnie J.	338	White, Tennie	331
Waterdown, Bow	4988	White, George	1038
Watt, Rosa	4702	White, Ila	1039
Watt, Ada	3342	White, Marvel LeRoy	952
Watt, Hazel	4792	White, Dora D.	953
Watt, Clara	4930	White, Lee	1610
Watt, Little Beaver	4931	White, Ona	3289
Watt, Lila	4796	White, Louise M.	2599
Watts, Mary A.	89	White, Lila	2678
Watt, Peggie	4690	White, Luna	2921
Waybourn, Eva	1282	White, Macie	3136
Waybourn, John J.	3456	White, Eva Maloy	3648
Waybourn, Sarah F.	4351	White, Charles H.	1960
Weavel, Least	2324	Whiteday, Morris B.	418
Weavel, Polly	2325	Whiteday, Francis D.	419
Weavel, Levi	4114	Whitfield, Roy L.	3341
Weaver, Lavada	3419	Whitmire, White	2857
Weaver, Lewis R.	4074	Whitmire, William F.	2943
Weaver, Florence	1961	Whitmire, Regnald H.	4022
Weaver, Minnie	1962	Whitmire, Golda E.	3834
Weaver, Nancy	3504	Whitekiller, Willie	2648
Weaver, Charolette	3505	Whitekiller, Alice	2649
Webb, Georgia	3782	Whitsett, Clara	103
Webb, Emmett Phelps	3685	Whitsett, Paul G.	104
Webber, Clinton Newton	1110	Whitsett, James	115
Webber, Maudry	4117	Whitsett, Gladis M.	1810
Webster, Harris B.	884	Whitsett, Francis	1811
Weddel, Rubie L.	434	Whisenhunt, Sidney	332
Weddells, Ora Ethel	2735	Whisenhunt, Mary Bulah	333
Weir, Vinita F.	4607	Whisenhunt, Jesse B.	4527
Weir, Raymond G.	4639	Whisenhunt, Cooper	1385
Weir, Dorothy L.	4640	Whisenhunt, Ruth	1386
Weiss, Alfred B.	906	Whisenhunt, Hazel	1387
Welch, Esther May	4797	Whisenhunt, Myrtle	2771
Welch, Lorene	1527	Whisenhunt, Linnie	2772
Welch, Mary	1528	Whiteturkey, Cloyd	4510
Welch, Emmet D.	1529	Whiteturkey, Beulah	
Welch, Mirty	2635	May	2297
Welch, Cecil	3545	Whittington, Cornelus	
Welch, George	4617	Jr.	3646
Welch, Ollie	4618	Whittington, Eli	3647
Welch, Mandy May	4717	Whitewater, Lizzie	4817
Welch, Roy D.	2646	Whitewater, Ross	4818
Welch, Irra C.	2647	Wickett, Oma L.	1786
Welch, Nettie	4570	Wickett, John	3075
Welch, George	4571	Wicket, Stella	2036
Welch, Annie	4622	Wicked, Elnora M.	2399
Welch, Sadie	3958	Wicked, Claud Charles	1544
Wells, Daisy Bell	881	Wicked, Clide Virgel	1545
Wells, William Evart	882	Wickliffe, Willie	4828
Wells, Lillian May	1290	Wickliffe Ben	4904
Werther, Emil	386	Wickliffe, Tom	4905
West, Lucy E.	1350	Wickliffe, Charley	4906
West, Dora E.	1376	Wilkins, Rubby E.	346
West, Claud Otto	3457	Wilkins, Ruthie	347
West, Clyrl Clinton	3012	Wilkins, Mary	731
West, Robert Irvin	1539	Wilkins, Bertha	2182
West, Richard Eugene	1540	Wilkie, Lizzie	524
West, Frances Marie	1703	Wilkie, Jeese H.	1535
West, Emma E.	3282	Wilkie, Stella	1725
West, Emmet S.	3283	Wilkie, Clinton	1726
West, James Edward	2679	Wilkie, Myrtle L.	2323
West, Ella May	2680	Wilkie, Margarett	4779
West, Laura Annie	2955	Wilkie, Mason T.	1958
West, William C.	4349	Wilkerson, William	324
West, William J. B.	3835	Wilkerson, Addie May	729
West, Mollie P..	3892	Wilkerson, John L.	1383
West, William Horrice	4902	Wilkerson, Tom	1384
West, Henry L.	4785	Wilkerson, Jesse W.	4457
West, Rosa	2542	Wilkerson, Hadaner	4115

Name.	Roll No.
Wilkerson, Ranle M.	1955
Wilkerson, Wyly F.	1956
Wilkerson, Jay Hugh	2088
Wilkerson, Vera May	2089
Wilkinson, Lucile	1117
Wilkinson, Blanche Josaphine	1728
Willits, Eunice Archie	591
Wildcat, Yah-hoo-lah	4888
Wiley, Bertha	2560
Willey, Theodore R.	180
Willey, Madalene	963
Willey, Lena	2299
Willey, Dora Dean	2300
Williams, Jessd Arthur	3092
Williams, Laura Junita	3093
Williams, Arthur F.	489
Williams, Mary Leona	592
Williams, Everett	598
Williams, Sid	330
Williams, James L.	772
Williams, Melvin Ross	3420
Williams, Leonard D.	1114
Williams, Amanda S.	1115
Williams, Opal Nute	1348
Williams, Ruby Victoria	1349
Williams, Marguirite	1381
Williams, Julia	2031
Williams, Annie	2143
Williams, Flora	2329
Williams, Newton A.	3553
Williams, Virgie	2490
Williams, Terry	2491
Williams, John H.	3587
Williams, Harmon	3588
Williams, Charlie G.	2940
Williams, Jennie C.	3631
Williams, Carl A.	3644
Williams, Edgar R.	3645
Williams, Percy F.	3225
Williams, Rosa Ella	4116
Williams, Butha May	3497
Williams, Hilda Opal	3498
Williams, Fred M.	3503
Williamson, William F.	154
Williamson, Mary Nettie	155
Willis, Louise	959
Willis, Gracie	1536
Wilson, Marion	176
Wilson, Claud Roy	207
Wilson, Keener C.	558
Wilson, Naomi R.	323
Wilson, Alta M.	334
Wilson, Ella M.	388
Wilson, Thomas S.	726
Wilson, Mary M.	727
Wilson, Lizzie Ella	1378
Wilson, Emma	1391
Wilson, Dovie Lillie Timpson	1392
Wilson, Thomas J. C.	1537
Wilson, Wilmer W.	1538
Wilson, John A.	1723
Wilson, Fay Ella	1724
Wilson, Wade C.	2610
Wilson, Grace	4989
Wilson, Henry	2327
Wilson, Lonnie	2328
Wilson, Frank E.	2663
Wilson, Floyd R.	2941
Wilson, Rubbie F.	3023
Wilson, Josephene	3340
Wilson, Clemie B.	3344
Wilson, Nellie	3345
Wilson, Minnie E.	3055
Wilson, Ruby Harry	3074
Wilson, Nannie	4359
Wilson, Bertha	4072
Wilson, Clyde C.	4146
Wilson, Permelia A.	4195
Wilson, Urban	4961
Windham, Fleeta Mae	1965

Name.	Roll No.
Windham, Cherokee Elizabeth	1966
Winget, Nono E.	2400
Wingfield, Andrew Evert	2734
Wingfield, Edith Ann	3610
Winkler, Frank W.	1118
Winkler, Blanch D.	1119
Winstead, Herbert H.	1827
Winton, Rena B.	4509
Winton, Neva Irene	4533
Wiswell, James F.	3871
Witt, Maud Marie	3630
Witt, Phillip	4585
Wofford, James C.	262
Wofford, Georgie L.	263
Wofford, Lizana	329
Wofford, Robert T.	4512
Wofford, Walter Floyd	4951
Wofford, Edward Lee	1120
Wofford, Mary Gertrude	2033
Wofford, Ira Eugene	2034
Wofford, Onanugotsa	4731
Wofford, Polly	4732
Wofford, Char-wah-you-ka	4957
Wolfe, Muttie J.	4307
Wolfe, Ruby Daisy	319
Wolfe, Thomas Leroy	320
Wolfe, Hasting	4526
Wolfe, Katherine	1180
Wolfe, Leo F.	1530
Wolfe, Fannie	3529
Wolfe, Ophelia	2558
Wolfe, Lincoln	2559
Wolfe, Lewis A.	4562
Wolfe, Ethel Mae	2736
Wolfe, John C.	3339
Wolfe, William R.	3629
Wolfe, Cliff	3699
Wolfe, Jesse	3836
Wolfe, Nan	3837
Wolfe, Lena Elizabeth R.	4171
Wolfe, Clyde	1959
Wolf, Jessie	4958
Wolf, Rider	4489
Wolf, Tsoliowa	4880
Wolf, Ned	4735
Wood, Clara B.	387
Wood, Lea E.	3415
Wood, Madaline	4521
Wood, Foster J.	907
Wood, Theron	1347
Wood, Barnett Rogers	2547
Wood, McRay	2824
Wood, Ruby L.	2942
Wood, Bernard	4348
Wood, Leroy	3642
Wood, Buster Brown	4360
Wood, Artie Evert	4590
Wood, Joe	4075
Woodall, Charles Washington	146
Woodall, Nolen S.	335
Woodall, Lelia	336
Woodall, Annie E.	1351
Woodall, Ruby E.	1352
Woodall, Caroline	1377
Woodall, Mary D.	1395
Woodall, Susie	3911
Woodall, Bert Vance	3675
Woodall, Jim	4397
Woodard, Joeellar	2951
Woodard, Eula May	3663
Woodard, Ethel	3264
Woodard, Clyde	3265
Woodard, Erna Lee	4028
Woodard, Lay Mabell	4029
Woods, Emma F.	1111
Woods, Ruth V.	2859
Woods, Cornelius Mchew	3894
Woods, John Henry	3957
Woods, Vestia Eugenia	4273

Name.	Roll No.	Name.	Roll No.
Wooley, Joe Elmer	3054	Yates, Ray C.	3018
Worfford, Leatha	2144	Yelton, Madaleen	2146
Woolery, Mark O.	476	York, George Eaton	92
Work, Able	212	York, James Mooring	93
Work, Gracie	213	York, Mary I.	732
Work, Ruby	954	Young, John	2256
Work, Ludie	955	Young, John S.	671
Work, Ralph	1532	Young, Luella	730
Work, Rachel	1533	Young, Lealer Missouri	2565
Worthington, Marshall		Young, Lewis	2460
G.	530	Young, Evaline	3297
Wright, Bessie R.	672	Young, Johnie	3298
Wright, Caddo M.	417	Young, George E.	3056
Wright, Buster B.	1598	Young, Neomia B.	3057
Wright, Sallie Undine	2457	Young, Ella M.	3218
Wright, Bessie	2252	Young, Johnie C.	3219
Wright, Andy	2253	Young, Johnson R.	3838
Wright, Jack	4635	Young, Mary C. W.	4492
Wright, Claud	4636	Young, Fannie	3918
Wright, Frank J.	3956	Young, Jessie A.	4658
Wright, Curtis	4069	Youngbird, Agatiya	4832
Wright, Gertrude		Younger, Daisy Ellen	351
Frances	4081	Younger, Mattie Adia	352
Wright, Caleb P.	4082	Youngwolf, Ellis	3783
Wyche, Thomas George	1112	Youngwolf, Lucy	3839
Wyly, Lucien B.	883	Zufall, Dorothy Eva	4610
Yadon, Emmitt A.	96		

INDEX TO
DELAWARE CHEROKEES

Name.	Roll No.
Peterson, Eliza	37
Pom-mah-pun-aqua	80
Qua-tuck-a-che	148
Randall, Frank H.	127
Randall, James T.	138
Roberts, Luella C.	139
Sarcoxie, Mary D.	69
Sarcoxie, John	119
Sarcoxie, Jefferson D.	189
Secondine, John	24
Secondine, Filmore	168
Secondine, Simon	171
Secondine, Ruth	172
Shailer, William H.	100
Shaw, James	187
Smith, Sarah	18
Smith, Sallie O.	141
Smith, William C.	142
Smith, George F.	160
Spybuck, Mary	104
Stout, John W.	144
Stout, Eliza	145
Stout, John R.	150
Stout, Susie	151
Swanock, Martha	72
Swannock, Jonas	90
Tanner, Charles V.	43
Tanner, Ida F.	44
Thursday, Mary	41
Walker, John	196
Washington, James	1
Washington, Edson	21
Washington, Mrs. Thomas	66
Washington, William	77
Washington, George	115

Name.	Roll No.
Washington, Mary	116
Washington, Cyrus	188
Weaver, Mary	5
Webber, Hannah	159
Wheeler, Robert	89
White, Mary	46
White, Mary	47
White, William	92
Whiteturkey, Albert	42
Whiteturkey, Robert	64
Whiteturkey, Josephine	65
Whiteturkey, Dutch	96
Whiteturkey, Widow	107
Whiteturkey, Samuel	109
Willey, John R.	167
Williams, Samuel	32
Williams, Mrs. Samuel	33
Wilson, Nancy	71
Wilson, Mary	34
Wilson, James	82
Wilson, Lizzie	83
Wilson, William	106
Wilson, Joshua	183
Wilson, Jane	184
Wilson, Thomas	185
Win-da-la-a-qua	60
Wolfe, Henry	28
Yellowjacket, John	86
Yellowjacket, Ora	87
Yellowleaf, Sarah	125
Young, John	29
Young, Ora	30
Zane, Matilda	129
Zeigler, Henry W.	157

CHEROKEES BY INTERMARRIAGE

Name.	Roll No.
Jordan, Sarah A.	249
Jeffrey, Nancy	270
Johnson, John W.	63
Jackson, James A.	157
Kelley, Valeria A.	159
Keeler, George B.	161
Kelley, Martha	187
Kolpin, Charles W.	188
Knight, Martha L.	262
Kelly, Joel	273
Lewis, Rowland M.	22
Loflin, Harris A.	53
Littlejohn, Napoleon B.	151
Lindsey, Riley W.	155
Lee, Lizzie	152
Linsy, Harvy	168
Lamar, Mary	180
Lemaster, John	181
Littlejohn, William N.	195
Luckey, Napoleon B.	232
McGhee, Mary C.	36
McAllister, Nancy H.	25
McLeod, Murdoch	46
McCrary, Jemima	77
McAnally, William H.	93
McCarty, John H .	95
McSpadden, John T.	175
McDaniel, Thomas B.	190
McElmell, Peter	191
McClellan, Charles M.	192
McCullough, Milton H.	224
McSpadden, James W.	230
McAlister, Louisa	271
McAffrey, Hugh	202
Miller, Martha A.	29
Martin, William	40
Mehlin, James G.	44
Mann, Charlotte C.	52
Morgan, Mary L.	55
Mode, Isaac M.	75
Mitchell, Bettie A.	94
Martin, James	124
Morrow, James T.	147
Mitchell, George W.	173
Miller, French	186
Meek, Abram	193
Miller, Robert C.	218
Miller, Rebecca	227
Mulcare, Michael	257
Morris, Ellen E.	258
Moore, Lewis	261
Mann, Marshall	283
Nix, Robert K.	84
Nicholson, Mary H.	130
Norwood, Andrew H.	236
Nash, Florian H.	66
Pemberton, James K.	16
Parrish, Holland L.	43
Parks, John	88
Patterson, Charles	112
Phillips, Micajah H.	143
Phillips. Sarah	177
Perry, Stacy E.	170
Pheasant, Martha	255
Perdue, Dollie	269
Prather, Robert A.	281
Price, James M.	288
Price, Sarah L.	62
Quarles, William R.	133
Quesenbury, Argyle	134
Rider, Jane	61
Raley, James M.	65
Rogers, Nancy E.	73
Rollens, Joseph	99
Robbins, Rebecca C.	110
Rasmus, William F.	113
Rider, Nancy J.	116
Riley, Polly Ann	131
Raymond, Alfred C.	171
Riley, Elizabeth	205
Roberts, Solon H.	213
Remsen, Tredwell S.	217

Name.	Roll No.
Ross, Elzina	219
Reed, Joseph (W.)	229
Randolph, Martha	252
Raper, Mary A.	254
Rogers, Woods B.	256
Ratley, Elvira	266
Reaves, Martha A.	272
Ross, Annie	276
Sager, Augustus C.	3
Samuels, Charles R.	15
Sanders, Nancy J.	207
Saunders, Lemuel S.	58
Scott, John T.	82
Scott, John	211
Skinner, Frank	201
Sloan, Naoma A.	87
Southerland, Enoch S.	85
Smith, Lee B.	7
Smith, John D.	9
Smith, Frank N.	24
Smith, John A.	50
Smith, Peter	91
Smith, Hueston	149
Smith, John J.	246
Smith, John M.	267
Smith, Gaines C.	274
Stephens, Elijah	108
Stevens, William H.	189
Stewart, William N.	148
Sturdivant, Matilda	72
Trott, Louisa J.	31
Tittle, Mary S.	34
Tyner, Almyra V.	39
Thornbrugh. James	42
Thornton, Diophantus D.	132
Taylor, Robert R.	78
Taylor, Elzada	279
Thompson, David G.	139
Thompson, Mary J.	234
Thompson, Robert H. F.	250
Tipton, David	145
Thomas, Jesse A.	28
Vann, Rosanna J.	150
Vanhoy, John F.	153
Vestal, Jerry H.	214
Wallace, Martin A.	51
Walker, Annie	209
Walker, Mary J.	286
Ward, Alice N.	69
Ward, Eliza F.	74
Ward, Mary	120
Ward, Catherine J.	125
Ward, Lizzie	126
Washbourne, Cynthia A.	164
Wasson, Fleming H.	54
Welch, Lucinda	220
Welch, E. A.	251
Wetzel, Daniel K.	278
Wilkerson, Rebecca	129
Wheeler, Emma C.	64
Whisenhunt, Noah	178
Wilder, William L.	197
Willey, Charles E.	18
Williams, Robert B,	154
Williams, Jennie	32
Williams, George W.	68
Williams, George W.	169
Wilson, Minta	275
Winton, Nancy	21
Wood, Henry G.	210
Wooddall, Margaret M.	172
Wolfe, Maggie J.	115
Wolfe, Nancy	244
Wren, Edwin	19
Wright, Hattie	237
Wyly, Robert F.	265
Yeargain, James C.	6
Young, Daniel	137
Zufall, George	179

Name.	Roll No.
Anderson, Sarah	1882
Anderson, Mary	1883
Anderson, Octa E.	3209
Anderson, Hattie M.	2233
Anderson, Amanda	2291
Anderson, Thomas	2739
Anderson, Angeline	2687
Alberty, Josie	4240
Alberty, Easter	4241
Alberty, Jane	3705
Alberty, William	3506
Arnsby, Lewis	1116
Arnsby, Benson	2728
Armstrong, Lulu	1801
Arnold, Louisa	3343
Austin, Robert	3178
Austin, Hannibal	3179
Austin, Lula	3180
Austin, Frank	3181
Austin, Elizabeth	3182
Austin, Cornelius	1779
Baker, Thomas	20
Barker, Harrison	639
Barker, Reedy	640
Barker, Henrietta	641
Baldridge, Wheat	787
Baldridge, Ellen	2815
Barden, Louis	804
Barden, Luny	805
Barden, Oscar	806
Barnes, Pollie	909
Barnes, McKinley	910
Barker, Billie	978
Baker, Melinda	1054
Baker, Willie	1058
Baker, Sallie	1502
Barnett, Mary	3309
Barlow, Mintie	1931
Baldridge, Jack	2010
Baldridge, Minnie	2011
Baldridge, Dick	2012
Baldridge, John	2013
Baldridge, Charles	2014
Baldridge, Phoebe	2015
Baldridge, Solomon	2016
Barker, Susie	2301
Barker, William H. Jr.	2302
Barker, Earnest N.	2303
Barker, Clarence	2304
Barnes, Sarah	3779
Barnes, Jennie	3780
Barnes, Samuel	3781
Barnes, Nola	3782
Barnes, Robert	3783
Baldridge, Rose E.	3450
Baldridge, Izetta M.	3451
Baldridge, William A. D.	3452
Baldridge, Parthena	3453
Baldridge, Chudie	3454
Baldridge, Charley	3455
Baldridge, John	3457
Baldridge, Russell	3458
Barnes, Lizzie	3670
Baldridge, John Jr.	3459
Baldridge, Jessie	3460
Baldridge, Anderson	3461
Baldridge, Columbus	3462
Baldridge, Inola	3463
Barnett, Jesse	4325
Ballard, Jennie	3706
Ballard, Malcolm	3707
Ballard, Spivey	3709
Ballard, Anna	3710
Barnes, Clara	3839
Barnes, Jane	3840
Barnes, William	3841
Barnes, Precillar	3842
Baker, Maggie	395
Bean, William	169
Bean, Charlotte	170
Bean, Peggie	171
Berry, Charles	429
Bean, Walter	545

Name.	Roll No.
Beck, Nathan	689
Benton, Viola	693
Bean, Minnie	755
Bean, Louisa	763
Bean, Malinda	764
Bean, Thomas	765
Bean, Murphy	766
Bean, John	767
Benge, Will	772
Beck, Amanda	3136
Benton, Amanda	841
Benton, Isaiah	842
Benton, Aaron	843
Benton, William	844
Benton, Claude	4051
Bell, Ora	885
Beck, Jim	911
Beck, Addie	912
Beck, Gertie	913
Benton, James G.	916
Benton, Thomas	917
Bean, Patum	920
Bean, Eartha	921
Bean, Louie	922
Bean, Clara	923
Bean, Emma	924
Bean, Ira	925
Bean, Frances	953
Bean, Anderson	954
Bean, Amanda J.	955
Bean, Bertha A.	956
Beck, Jennie	962
Beck, William	1031
Beck, Jane	1032
Beck, Sadie M.	1033
Beck, Joseph H.	1034
Benge, Isaac	1061
Benge, Jennie	1062
Benge, Annie	1063
Benge, Katie	1064
Benge, James	1065
Benge, Emma	1066
Benge, Roger L.	1067
Benge, Charles	1087
Benge, Henrietta	1088
Bean, William	2830
Bean, Dock	1184
Berlone, Mary	1262
Bean, Dennis	1463
Bethel, Fannie	1516
Benge, Samuel	1632
Bean, Joseph	1784
Bean, Hattie	1785
Bean, Isaac	1786
Bean, Ethel	1787
Bean, Amy	1794
Bean, Susan	1795
Bean, Rosella	1796
Bean, Alexander	1797
Bean, William	1798
Bean, Evylon	1799
Bean, Thomas	1802
Bean, Lewis	1815
Bean, James A.	1816
Bean, Clifton	1817
Bean, Sevier	1818
Bean, Frank C.	1819
Bean, Joshua	1832
Bean, Lucinda	1837
Bean, Lillie	1838
Bean, Phyllis	1848
Bean, William	1849
Bean, Sephenia	1850
Bean, Eliza J.	1898
Bean, Ida	1932
Bean, John	1952
Bean, Malinda	1994
Bean, Harvey	1996
Beck, Mary J.	2026
Bean, George	2171
Beck, Minnie	2251
Beck, Eliza	2253
Beeson, Susan	2328

Name.	Roll No.
Beck, Nelson	3851
Bean, Henry	3815
Bean, Debbie W.	3619
Bean, Tobias	3773
Bean, Arthur	3774
Bean, Arthur	3883
Bean, Joseph	3884
Bean, Ruby	3529
Bean, Lucy	4106
Bean, Mary	4107
Bean, William	4108
Bean, Samuel	4109
Bean, Leander	3386
Bean, Alsea	3947
Bean, Dovie	3951
Bean, Effie	3952
Bean, Ernest	3953
Bean, Mary	3954
Bean, Viola	3955
Beck, Benjamin	3690
Beck, Josephine	3692
Beck, John	3693
Bean, Emma	3599
Bean, Henrietta	3600
Beck, Samuel	4163
Beck, Luquittie	4164
Bean, Ellen	4326
Beck, Fanny	3817
Beck, James	3818
Beck, Hattie	3819
Beck, Florence	3820
Beck, Nelson Jr.	3821
Beck, Dempsey	3822
Beck, Viola	3823
Beck, Lewis	3824
Beck, Cora	3825
Beck, Maryland	3832
Beck, Ida	3833
Beck, Harvey	3834
Beck, Ida	3816
Beck, Dallas	3830
Beeson, Malinda	4218
Beck, Benjamin	3835
Beeson, Roxie	3687
Bean, Andrew	3887
Bean, Sandy	3888
Bean, Lottie	3889
Bean, Rector	3890
Beck, Beulah	1571
Bean, Lula	3482
Rell, Annie	3788
Bird, Joanna	2884
Bird, Jesse	3262
Bird, Ella	3263
Bird, George	3264
Bird, Benjamin	3265
Bird, Arthur	3266
Bird, Henry	2608
Birdson, Bessie	3946
Bland, Mary	47
Blake, Sallie	149
Blackwell, Rebecca	496
Blackwell, Cynthia	638
Blackhawk, Stephen	1068
Blunt, Maude	1693
Blunt, Belle	1694
Blair, Squire	1789
Blythe, Monroe	1803
Blythe, Lucy	1975
Blunt, Ella	2636
Bolen, Addie	912
Bolin, Luther	1409
Bolin, Eliza	1566
Bolin, Klee	1567
Bolin, Harrison	1568
Boudinot Jennie	1667
Booker, Ethel	2457
Bowles, Susan	2541
Boudinot, Alexander	3066
Boone, Mary	3494
Boyd, Polly	4010
Bowlin, Elizabeth	3989
Bowlin, Henrietta	3990

Name.	Roll No.
Bowlin, William Henry	3991
Bowlin, Eunice Cornelius	3992
Bowlin, Helen F.	3993
Bowlin, Doda C.	3994
Bowlin, Leonard Elmer	3995
Bowlin, Sophia A.	3996
Boudinot, Mariah	4222
Boudinot, Alexander Jr.	3673
Brewer, Rab	24
Brewer, Sallie	25
Brewer, Ezekiel	26
Brewer, Dennis	27
Brewer, Clara	28
Brown, Maud	2752
Brown, Julia	241
Brown, Clark	257
Brewer, Samuel	499
Brady, Barney	520
Brown, Clarence	581
Brown, Herbert	601
Brown, Sallie	506
Bruner, Emma	632
Bruner, Isabel	635
Bruner, Annie	636
Brewer, Ezekiel	678
Brewer, Louisa	679
Brewer, Kemp	680
Brown, Jennie	827
Brown, Lewis	828
Brown, Charles	829
Brown, Julia	830
Brown, Alex	831
Brown, Mollie	832
Brown, Gracie	833
Brown, Sarah A.	834
Brown, Amelia	835
Brown, Julia	836
Brown, Jeff	837
Brown, Jesse	2818
Brown, James	2819
Brown, Henry	838
Brown, John	839
Brown, William	840
Brown, Katie	871
Brown, William H.	892
Brown, Birt M.	893
Brown, Emma	894
Brown, Anna	902
Brown, Charles	963
Bruce, Dora	3005
Bruce, Ella	3006
Brown, David	997
Brown, Florence	998
Brown, Lydie	999
Brown, Mary	1000
Brown, Peggie	2828
Brewer, Jackson	1081
Brown, John	1082
Brown, Richard	1083
Brown, Julie Ann	1084
Brown, Gertrude	1249
Brown, Marcus	1250
Brewer, Seenie	1269
Brown, Henry	1321
Brown, Jane	1322
Brown, Emma	1323
Brown, George	1324
Brown, Lillie	1325
Brown, Eli	1326
Brown, Samuel	1328
Brown, Savilla	1355
Brown, Elizabeth	1356
Brown, Ethel	1357
Brown, Lillie	1391
Brown, Marie	1392
Brannon, Henrietta	1436
Brannon, Ophelia	1437
Brannon, Arena	1438
Brannon, Mattie	1439
Brown, Joseph	2734
Brown, Dee	2841
Brown, Milton	2842

Name.	Roll No.	Name.	Roll No.
Brown, Joe	2843	Butler, Ella J.	37
Brown, Joe	1535	Butler, Elizabeth	38
Brown, Enious	1713	Butler, Joseph H.	39
Brown, Rhoda	1714	Butler, Alice E.	40
Brewer, Charlotte	1721	Butler, Lillie V.	41
Brewer, Rose E.	1722	Butler, Annie B.	42
Bryant, Sophia	1881	Buckler, Eliza J.	180
Breakbill, Sophia J.	1967	Butler, Mary	3927
Breakbill, Louie	1968	Buffington, William	293
Breakbill, Stella	1969	Burgess, John	320
Breakbill, Isaac	1970	Burgess, Jennie	321
Breakbill, Mary	1971	Burgess, Mattie	322
Bryant, Rosa	2036	Burgess, Ola	323
Brown, Minnie	3216	Burgess, Elizabeth	324
Brown, Floyd	3217	Burgess, Carrie	325
Brown, Sylvester	3218	Burgess, Cora	326
Brown, Ellen	2064	Burgess, Johnnie	327
Brown, Annie E.	2065	Buffington, Ambrose	410
Brown, May A.	2066	Buffington, Dorcas	690
Brown, Dunk	2067	Buffington, Ambrose	3058
Brown, Charlie	2068	Burton, Kiamitia	2715
Brown, John P.	2923	Burton, Nancy	2716
Brown, Polly A.	2388	Butler, Lone	2833
Brown, William	2389	Butler, Sam	2834
Brown, Aseney	2390	Buffington, Nancy	1352
Brown, Richard	2391	Buffington, Harry	1353
Brown, Rhoda	2392	Butler, Jerry B.	1675
Brown, Phillip	2393	Burgess, Charley	1688
Brown, Anderson	2409	Burgess, Lola	1689
Brown, Jesse, Jr.	2430	Burgess, Annie	1690
Brown, Bettie	2930	Burgess, Gilbert	1691
Bradford, Fannie	2434	Buffington, Augustus	1734
Bradford, Tessie	2435	Buffington, Mary	1735
Bradford, Jennetta	2436	Buford, Jennie	1790
Bradford, Malissa	2437	Buford, Johnson	1791
Bradford, Deatrus	2438	Buford, Walter	1792
Bradford, Frances	2439	Buffington, John	1859
Bradford, Tola	2440	Buffington, Mary	1860
Bradford, Lula	2441	Buffington, Frank	1861
Brown, Sarah	2931	Buffington, Walter	1862
Brown, Luther	2932	Buffington, Clarence	1863
Brown, Clyde	2933	Buffington, Jesse	1864
Brown, Mahala	2456	Buffington, Stella	1865
Brown, Ethel	2457	Buffington, Bert	1866
Brown, Isreal	2462	Buffington, Aldrick	1867
Brown, Silas H.	2467	Buffington, Ernest	1999
Brown, Willie	2935	Buffington, Saphronia	2000
Brown, George	2936	Buffington, Albert	2001
Brown, Viola	2937	Buffington, Augustus	2002
Brown, Pearl	2468	Butler, John L.	2085
Brown, Amanda	2487	Burney, James	2564
Brown, Minnie	2488	Burney, Mariah	2565
Brown, Beulah	2489	Burney, Willie	2566
Brown, Cora	4060	Burney, Cora	2567
Brown, Rebecca A.	2578	Buffington, Ruth	2589
Brown, Ada	2579	Buffington, Ella	3025
Brown, Cora	3963	Burney, Louisa	4185
Brown, Jesse	3493	Buckner, Lizzie	3471
Brown, Edward	3581	Buckner, Horace	3472
Bryant, Mandy	2959	Buckner, Willie	3473
Bryant, Malinda	2960	Buckner, Walter	3474
Bryant, Oscar	2961	Bursby, Eliza J.	3809
Brown, Jonas	3941	Bursby, Lela	3810
Brown, Henry	3582	Bursby, Pleas	3811
Brown, Stella	3583	Bursby, Earnest	3812
Brown, Laura	3584	Burkhardt, Nora	3403
Brown, Lettie	4033	Burl, Sarah	4145
Brown, Howard	4037	Byrd, Susie	1230
Bryant, Ella	4189	Byrd, Henrietta	1231
Brown, Nellie	3591	Byrd, Amanda	1232
Brown, Roxie	3592	Byrd, John	1233
Brown, Moses	3593	Byrd, Rose	1234
Brown, Jennie	3594	Byrd, Malissa	1235
Brown, William	3595	Byrd, Emma	1236
Brown, Michael	3596	Byrd, Susie	1237
Brown, Margaret	2585	Byrd, Lawrence	1238
Brown, Lillie	3658	Byrd, Castella	1239
Brown, Julia	820	Campbell, Charles, Jr.	54
Buffington, Henry	8	Campbell, Lillie E.	55
Buffington, Daisey	9	Cates, Lucy	329
Butler, Samuel	35	Cates, Henrietta	330
Butler, Cynthia	36	Cates, Ernest	331

Name.	Roll No.	Name.	Roll No.
Cates, Dora	332	Campbell, Mary E.	2890
Cates, Maud	333	Campbell, Hannah	2342
Cates, Clarence	334	Campbell, Clara	2343
Carter, Joseph	533	Canard, Annie	3720
Carter, Angeline	534	Casey, Carrie	2754
Carter, Lila	535	Carter, Minnie	3359
Carter, Cornelius	536	Castleberry, Ida	3867
Carter, Frances	537	Carlington, Laura	3475
Cates, Thomas	600	Chase, Maria	430
Campbell, Alena	845	Chase, Henry	431
Campbell, Amanda	846	Chase, Fannie	432
Campbell, Dora	847	Chase, Anna	521
Campbell, Elijah	848	Charles, Caroline	918
Campbell, Joseph	933	Choate, Greely	1292
Campbell, Jackson	934	Choate, Sherman	1293
Carr, Ellis	3156	Chase, Ruth A.	1384
Carr, Milton T.	3157	Chase, Arthur	1385
Carter, Mose	1157	Chase, Charles	1386
Carter, Oma	1158	Chouteau, Martha	1499
Carter, Peggie	1159	Chouteau, William	1671
Carter, Jesse	1160	Chouteau, Rose	1672
Carter, Jennetta	1161	Chouteau, Ellen	1673
Carter, Frances	1162	Chouteau, Carrie	1674
Caldwell, Corrine	1259	Chambers, William	2198
Caldwell, Sallie	1260	Chambers, Ed	2256
Calvin, Sarah	1368	Chambers, Meriland R.	2257
Calvin, Earl	1369	Chambers, Matt	2258
Calvin, Pearl M.	1370	Chambers, Leroy	2259
Calvin, Lillian	1371	Chambers, Oliver J.	2260
Carter, Andy	1395	Chambers, Caroline	2283
Carter, Florence	1396	Chambers, Dora	2423
Carter, Elnora	1397	Chambers, Minnie	2424
Carter, Andy	1398	Chambers, Frances	2485
Carter, William	1399	Chambers, Emanuel	2607
Carter, David	1400	Chambers, Elnora	2742
Carter, Mary	1401	Chambers, Grant	3353
Carter, John	3303	Chouteau, John	2683
Carter, Fred	3304	Chouteau, Eli	2685
Campbell, Susie	1440	Childers, Rocky	3521
Campbell, Peggie	1441	Choteau, Samuel	3513
Campbell, Octavia	1442	Choteau, Louisa	3514
Campbell, Osa	1443	Chouteau, William	3488
Campbell, Ora	1444	Chouteau, Joshua	3490
Carter, Luke	1505	Chouteau, Cornelius	3491
Carter, Minnie	1538	Chambers, Charles C., Jr	3019
Campbell, Mary	1643	Chatman, Sarah	4145
Carter, Arch, Sr.	1657	Chatman, Jim	4148
Carter, Sarah	1658	Chatman, Julia	4149
Carter, Johnson	1659	Chatman, Nannie	4150
Carter, Matilda	1660	Chambers, Dick	3653
Carter, Arch, Jr.	1661	Chambers, Henry	3899
Campbell, Alfred	3314	Chambers, Ella	3414
Campbell, Edna	1894	Chouteau, Tobe	2958
Campbell, James	2019	Chambers, Jack	4006
Campbell, Jessie	2344	Chukelate, Susie	3942
Cabbell, Annie H.	3234	Chouteau, Mary	484
Cabbell, Sophronia	3235	Clifton, Anthony	988
Cabbell, Earnest	3236	Clark, Menty	1410
Carson, Laura	2591	Clay, Rachel	2124
Carson, Nona	2592	Claggett, Ruth	3248
Campbell, George	2628	Claggett, Millie J.	3249
Carter, Nelson	2699	Claggett, Tessie M.	3250
Caesar, Mary	3511	Claggett, Ralph N.	3251
Carson, Lillie	3021	Claggett, Charles A.	3252
Carson, Lourena	3022	Clark, Beatrice	3502
Ceasar, Henry	4147	Clark, Ocie F.	3503
Carter, Lydia	3604	Clark, Jettie	3504
Carbin, Eliza	3758	Clark, Appelina	3505
Carbin, Hattie	3761	Clinch, Richard	4036
Carbin, Henry	3762	Claggett, Nancy	3689
Carbin, Ruby	3763	Claggett, Willie	3640
Carter, Henry	3500	Claggett, Elizabeth	3641
Carson, Mary	3827	Claggett, Isabell	3642
Campbell, Viva	2879	Claggett, Mariah	3643
Campbell, Grace	2880	Claggett, Alexander	3644
Campbell, Edward	2881	Claggett, Nancy J.	3645
Campbell, Martha	2882	Claggett, Josie M.	3646
Campbell, Charles	2885	Claggett, Jane	3837
Campbell, Emma	2886	Claggett, Rose E.	3838
Campbell, Walter	2887	Collins, Abraham	73
Campbell, John	2888	Collins, Frank	74
Campbell, Albert	2889	Collins, Martha	75

Name.	Roll No.	Name.	Roll No.
Coody, Joseph	3072	Crossland, Henry	2691
Coody, Elijah	296	Crossland, George, Jr.	3507
Coody, Henry	297	Crittenden, Anthony	4156
Cotton, Cynthia	619	Crittenden, Josie	4157
Cotton, Taylor	620	Crittenden, William	4158
Cotton, Wisdom	621	Crittenden, Lucy	4159
Cotton, Elizabeth	622	Crittenden, Steve	4160
Cotton, Jesse	623	Crittenden, John	4161
Cotton, Bessie	624	Crittenden, Mary	3495
Cotton, Killring	625	Crossland, Joseph	3508
Cornish, Addie	786	Crippin, Alice	3864
Cooper, William	888	Curtis, Louisa	1853
Collins, Blanche	907	Cunningham, Polly	2115
Cooper, Leon	974	Curtis, Addie	3411
Coody, Alex	1119	Curtis, Leander	3413
Coody, Katie	1120	Curls, Julius	4299
Coody, William	1133	Curls, Riley	4300
Cordrey, Rufus A.	2854	Curls, Willie	4301
Cordrey, Eddie	2855	Curls, Edward	4302
Cordrey, Toby	2856	Curls, James	4303
Cordrey, Jeffie	2857	Curls, George	4304
Coleman, Rosie	2042	Curls, Stephenia	4305
Coody, Josephine	2413	Curls, Clarence	4306
Coody, James	2414	Curls, Beatrice	4307
Cox, Sarah	2514	Davis, Sarah	128
Cox, Lizzie	2522	Davis, Alice	291
Cox, Annie	2523	Dandridge, Mattie	322
Cox, Dora	2524	Dalton, Narcissa	328
Coody, William, Jr.	3528	Davis, Lucy	329
Colbert, Rosa	3388	Daniels, Mish	397
Colbert, Maggie	4104	Daniels, Nannie	2779
Colbert, Dan	4105	Daniels, Abe	420
Coody, Susan	3696	Daniels, Fannie	421
Coker, Bunk	3481	Daniels, Mary	422
Colbert, Jennie	2977	Daniels, John	423
Colbert, Elzora	2978	Daniels, Jennie	424
Colbert, Louisa	2979	Daniels, Susan	425
Colbert, Annie	2980	Daniels, Fannie	426
Colbert, McKinley	2981	Daniels, Julia	427
Colbert, Kizer	2982	Dansby, Charles	3108
Coats, Saphronia	2994	Dansby, Walter	372
Crawford, Beatrice	81	Davis, Phillis	3060
Crockett, Lydia	148	Davis, Rachel	1011
Crossland, Lewis	575	Davis, Isaac	3175
Crossland, John	3096	Davis, Napoleon	3176
Crossland, Willie	3097	Davis, Mamie	1899
Crossland, Martha	3098	Davis, Elizabeth	1900
Crossland, George	3099	Daniels, Frank	3326
Crossland, Lila	3104	Daniels, Willie	3327
Crapo, Jacob	602	Daniels, Lewis D.	2104
Crapo, Judy	603	Daniels, Patsy	2105
Crapo, Daisy	3109	Daniels, William H.	2108
Crapo, Diley	604	Davis, Emma	2262
Crutchfield, Frank	616	Davis, Joseph	2263
Crossley, Jane	634	Davis, William, Jr.	2264
Crawford, Lena	2793	Davis, Bertie	2265
Crawford, Jessie	2795	Davis, Chester	2266
Crawford, John	2796	Davis, Julia	2267
Crawford, Thomas	2797	Davis, Jennette	2268
Crawford, Frank	2798	Davis, Henry	2269
Crawford, Annie	2799	Davis, Oscar	2270
Crawford, David	2800	Davis, Carrie	2271
Crossland, George	736	Davis, Lottie	2272
Crossland, Gracie	737	Davis, Lovie	2293
Crossland, Simon	746	Davis, Peggy	2445
Crossland, Andy	1051	Davis, Coren	2446
Crossland, Samuel	875	Daniels, Jesse	2458
Crossland, Andrew	1090	Daniels, Alberty	2459
Crossland, Fannie	1091	Dawn, Mary	3032
Cravens, Lucinda	1358	Daniels, George	3879
Cravens, Addison	1359	Daniels, Frances	3880
Cravens, Lela M.	1360	Daniels, Nathan	3881
Cravens, Roland	1361	Daniels, Henry	3882
Cravens, Harvey	1362	Daniels, Enoch	3906
Crossland, Isaac	1453	Daniels, Ralph	3908
Crossland, Elmira	1454	Daniels, Marshall	3909
Crossland, Samuel	1455	Davis, Joe	3389
Crossland, Rosanna	1456	Davis, Sadie	3390
Crossland, Elena	1457	Davis, Willie	3391
Crossland, Leota	1458	Davis, Thomas	3392
Crossland, Lincoln	1459	Davis, Joseph	3393
Crossland, Jonas	1670	Davis, Dan C.	3394

Name.	Roll No.	Name.	Roll No.
Davis, Carl	3395	Downing, John	2165
Davis, Charles	3396	Downing, Joel	2166
Davis, John L.	3397	Downing, Cora	2168
Davis, John L., Jr.	3398	Downing, Asa	2169
Davis, James	3399	Dotson, Angeline	2338
Davis, Lizzie	3400	Downing, Susan E.	2588
Daniels, Ibbie	3636	Downing, Thomas	2712
Daniels, Frank	3637	Downing, Mary E.	4110
Daniels, Martha A.	3638	Downing, Mary L.	4111
Daniels, Lucinda	3647	Downing, Hurbert	4224
Daniels, Thomas	3648	Downing, Mary	3665
Daniels, Josephine	3649	Downing, Leegustus	3666
Daniels, Lewis	3650	Downing, Inez L.	4044
Daniels, Charles	3651	Downing, Caldonia	2954
Daniels, Jonas	3652	Drew, Jennie	3081
Day, Andrew	3476	Drew, Sallie	495
Day, Ella	3477	Drew, Isaac	566
Day, Lena	3478	Drew, Luella C.	567
Day, Clarence	3479	Drew, John	1012
Daniels, Nellie J.	2702	Drew, James	1117
Daniels, Amanda	359	Drew, Benjamin	1200
Davis, Annie	3703	Drew, Cornelia	3297
Davis, Henrietta	3990	Drew, Amanda	3298
Dennis, Ada	92	Drew, Thomas	1299
Dennis, Junius	119	Drew, Ruth	1300
Delwood, Fannie	242	Drew, Nip	1301
Delwood, Maggie	243	Drew, Sallie	1302
Delwood, Richard	244	Drew, Gano	1303
Delwood, Wren	245	Drew, Katie	1304
Dennis, Bertha	357	Drew, Henrietta	1305
Dennis, Rosa	1495	Drew, George	1306
Dennis, Fannie	1496	Drew, Lottie	1307
Deckman, Amanda	2033	Drew, Charlie	1308
Deckman, Charles W.	2034	Drew, Jesse	1309
Dennis, James	2316	Drew, Lewis	1310
Dennis, Annie	2317	Drew, Jane	1311
Dennis, John	2318	Drew, Lem	1312
Derrick, Lucian	2839	Drew, Lucy	3177
DeMumber, Patsy	3740	Drew, James	1315
Dean, Charley	3982	Drew, Ida	2835
Derrick, Josie	2701	Drew, Jimmie	2836
Derrick, Jennie A.	2703	Drew, Delia	2837
Derrick, Katie	2704	Drew, Lena	2838
Derrick, Henrietta	2705	Drew, Hester	1316
Rerrick, Eddie	2706	Drew, Annie	1317
Derrick, William H.	2707	Drew, Colbert	3009
Derrick, Charley B.	2708	Drew, Dinah	4052
Derrick, Minnie Overo	2709	Drew, Joshua	1597
Denumber, Cora	4205	Drew, Susan	1598
Dickson, Mattie J.	436	Drew, Rosa	1599
Dickson, Eustace F.	437	Drew, Leo	1600
Dixon, Nathaniel	518	Drew, Maria	1601
Dixon, Clem	519	Drew, Minnie	1602
Diges, William	2727	Drew, Lucy	1603
Dixon, Letha	2877	Drew, Mary	1604
Dixon, Wiley	2878	Drew, Peachie	1605
Dickson, Julia	2482	Drew, Moses	1630
Dickson, Effie	2484	Drew, Louisa	3189
Dotson, Susan	3134	Drew, DeWitt	3190
Dotson, Eliza	1279	Drew, Ethel	3512
Dotson, Creed	1282	Drew, Mat	3026
Dotson, Cathaline	1283	Drew, Malissa	3027
Dotson, Nora	1284	Drew, Aginora	3028
Dotson, Frances A.	1285	Drew, Cassie	3029
Dotson, Mary	1448	Drew, Beulah	3030
Dotson, John I.	1449	Duncan, Ella	1506
Dotson, Dewey	1450	Duncan, Tilden	1596
Dotson, Nathaniel	1451	Duncan, Ella	3239
Downing, Zebidee	1914	Duncan, Ida	3240
Downing, Jennie	1915	Duncan, James	3241
Downing, Emanuel	1916	Duncan, Luvenia	3242
Downing, Maggie	1917	Duncan, George	3243
Downing, Lydia	1918	Eagle, Charles	1203
Downing, Luvinia	1919	Eagle, Pauline	1204
Downing, Dorothea	1920	Eaton, Tom	1742
Downing, Walter	1921	Eaton, Stephen	2846
Downing, Henry	2868	Eaton, Johnanna	2847
Downing, Martha A.	2003	Eaton, Nina	2848
Downing, Oliver	2007	Eaton, Phil.	2849
Downing, Maudie	2008	Eastman, Eliza	3608
Downing, Georgie	2009	Eastman, Lee	3609
Downing, Judie	2164	Eastman, Lewis	3610

Name.	Roll No.	Name.	Roll No.
Eastman, Pearl	3611	Foye, Cynthia	159
Eastman, Ollie	3612	Foreman, Caroline	230
Eastman, Mary	3613	Ford, Willie	3075
Eastman, Roberta	3614	Foster, Carrie	240
Ebb, Madeline	3456	Foreman, Julia	249
Edwards, Mollie	3059	Foreman, Albert	250
Elliott, Annie	592	Foreman, Caroline	251
Elliott, Pennie K.	593	Foreman, Eddie	252
Elliott, Wiliam Harlin	594	Foreman, Maude	253
Ellis, Augustus	1492	Foreman, Grover C.	254
Elliott, Mary	1612	Ford, Luther	268
Elliott, Robert	1615	Foster, Amanda	290
Elliott, George	1616	Ford, Lutetia	366
Elliott, Amelia	447	Ford, Bessie	367
Escoe, Dora	4103	Ford, John	368
Evans, Malinda	1278	Foreman, Gus	3079
Evans, Henry	1330	Foreman, Aaron	3110
Evans, Mary	1331	Foreman, Floyd	713
Evans, David	1332	Foreman, Jesse	735
Evans, Fannie	1333	Ford, Daniel	3128
Evans, Martha J.	1334	Ford, Bessie	3129
Evans, William	1513	Ford, Mary M.	3130
Evans, Jennie	2127	Ford, Virgin Mary	3131
Evans, Henrietta	2128	Ford, William McK.	3132
Evans, James	2129	Foreman, Zack	788
Faber, Lottie	4255	Foreman, Sheridan	789
Fields, Bertha	448	Foreman, Roscoe W.	790
Fields, Mike	598	Foreman, Zack, Jr.	791
Fields, Oma V.	599	Foreman, Rhoda B.	792
Fields, Kate	694	Foreman, Dewey	793
Fields, Frank	695	Foreman, Allen	799
Fields, James	696	Foreman, Alfronie	800
Fields, Ernest	697	Foreman, Jerry	801
Fields, Emma	995	Foreman, Antone	802
Fields, James	1013	Foreman, Jerry	811
Fields, Rockwell	1014	Foreman, Kizzie	812
Fields, Lydia	1015	Foreman, Jackson	813
Fields, Keller	1016	Foreman, Carrie	814
Fields, Samuel	1017	Foreman, Nancy	815
Fields, Adda	1018	Foreman, Sarah B.	816
Fields, Charles	1019	Foreman, Willie C.	817
Fields, Mike	1167	Foreman, Richard	860
Fields, Carrie	1168	Foreman, Sallie	861
Fields, Jeta	1169	Foreman, Jane	862
Fields, Anna	1170	Foreman, Mattie	863
Fields, Ross	1171	Foreman, Nora	864
Fields, Willie	1172	Foreman, Freeland	865
Fields, Clyde	1173	Foreman, Lela	866
Fields, Ab	1373	Foreman, Birdie	867
Fields, Diana	1375	Foreman, Benjamin	870
Fields, Joab	1376	Foreman, Zachariah	915
Fields, Lydia	1377	Foreman, Clora	1038
Fields, John	1378	Foreman, Wesley	2729
Fields, Lula	1379	Foreman, Abe	1179
Fields, Archie	1380	Foreman, James	1226
Fields, Mose	1381	Foreman, John	1247
Fields, Turner	1382	Foreman, Georgia E.	1248
Fields, Levi	4090	Foreman, Jesse	1383
Fields, John Sr.	1711	Foreman, Benjamin	1460
Fields, Vinnie	1715	Foreman, Jacob	1622
Fields, Willie S.	1716	Foreman, Leah	1623
Fields, Nellie	1717	Foreman, Lillie	1624
Fields, Edward	1718	Foreman, Lela	1625
Fields, Kella	1719	Foreman, Andrew	1626
Fields, Green	1720	Foreman, Albert	1627
Fields, Jerry	2698	Foreman, Addie	1628
Fields, Maggie	3013	Foreman, Robert	1629
Fields, John, Jr.	3014	Foreman, Robert	2206
Fields, Mary	3015	Folsom, Eliza	1953
Fisher, Rocky	3521	Foster, George	2025
Fleeks, Mary	255	Foreman, Linnie	2208
Fletcher, Mattie	863	Foreman, Dennis	3934
Flowers, Alice	3223	Foreman, Harrison	2216
Flowers, Viola	3224	Foreman, Caroline	2217
Flynn, Sarah	4347	Foreman, Zack	2218
Flynn, Oliver	4348	Foster, Edward	2395
Flynn, Joseph	4349	Foster, Jennie	2396
Flynn, Fannie	4350	Foster, Lillie	2397
Flynn, Serena	4351	Foster, Stella	2398
Flynn, Nettie	4352	Foster, Pearlie	2399
Flynn, Castella	4353	Foster, Clem	2400
Flynn, Gracie	4354	Foster, Idella	2401

Name.	Roll No.	Name.	Roll No.
Foster, Quinnie	2402	Gaskins, Lola	3349
Foster, Jerry	2405	Gaskins, Minnie	3350
Foster, Malissa	2411	Gains, Eliza	3530
Foster, Percy	2412	Garrett, Eliza	3530
Foster, John	2416	Garrett, Maud	3704
Foster, Clara	2418	Garlington, Laura	3475
Foster, Maude	2419	Gentry, Carrie	1607
Foster, James	2420	Gentry, George	1609
Foster, John	2421	Givens, Ella	1390
Foster, Charles	2425	Gibson, Susie	2072
Foster, Frank	2426	Gibson, Clifford	2073
Foster, Phillip	3226	Gibson, Roy	2074
Foster, George W.	3227	Gibson, Reed	2075
Foster, Walter	3228	Gibson, Lena	2349
Foster, Arthur	3229	Gibson, Sarah	2526
Foster, Asa	3230	Gibson, Harvey	2527
Foreman, Minnie	2500	Gibson, Ada	2528
Foster, Thomas	3341	Gibson, Pearlie	2529
Foster, James	3342	Gibson, Sedalia	2530
Foster, Sarah	3351	Gibson, Myrtle	2531
Ford, Ollie	2741	Gibson, Cynthia	2532
Ford, Florence	2968	Gibson, Carrie	4293
Ford, Henry	2969	Gilds, John G.	4074
Ford, Fannie	2970	Glass, Bettie	1096
Ford, Clarence	2971	Glass, Austin	1097
Foreman, William L.	3016	Glass, Joseph, Jr.	1098
Foreman, Charles	3672	Glass, Eli	1099
Foster, Louis	3759	Glass, Bertha	1100
Foster, John	3760	Glass, Ellen	1110
Foster, Sarah	4217	Glass, Fox	1123
Foster, Clara	3858	Glass, Lucy	1124
Foster, Clarence	3859	Glass, John	1125
Foster, Carrie	3860	Glass, Minnie	1126
Foster, Cora	3861	Glass, Katie	1127
Foster, George	4013	Glass, Marthy	1128
Foster, Armstead	3419	Glass, Neal	1227
Foster, Annie	3813	Glass, Samuel	1228
Foster, John	3367	Glass, Fannie	1229
Foreman, Benjamin	4092	Glass, Philip	1294
Foreman, Mattie	3724	Glass, Joseph	1514
Foreman, Silvester	3717	Glass, Susie	2339
Foreman, Etha	3718	Glass, Robert	2346
Ford, Nona	3919	Glass, Elizabeth	2347
Ford, Jackson	3920	Glass, Douglas	2348
Frye, Rosa	1469	Glass, Lena	2349
French, James	1613	Glass, Nancy	2350
French, Thomas	1614	Glass, Luvina	2351
Fry, Andy	1960	Glass, Ida	2352
Fry, Milly	1961	Glass, Henry	2353
Fry, Henrietta	1962	Glass, Randall	2562
Frye, Leander	1991	Glass, John	2563
French, Eli	2245	Glass, Lewis	2632
French, David	2410	Glass, Louis	3913
Francis, Jack	2480	Gnash, Lonie	3436
Francis, Beatrice	2481	Goldsby, Clarence	2751
French, Wash	2669	Goff, Matilda	701
French, William	2670	Goldsby, Luther	2172
French, Aleck	2671	Goldsby, Nina	3931
French, David	2672	Goldsby, Roberta	3932
French, Easter	2673	Grimmet, Clark	2753
French, Clara	2676	Grimmett, Willie	2758
French, Charles W.	2677	Grimmett, Mary	210
Franklin, Annie	2974	Grimmett, Richard	213
Frye, Andrew L.	3732	Grimmett, Henderson	3050
Frances, Peggie	3498	Grimmett, Philip	214
French, Walter	3509	Grimmet, John	503
French, Emeline	4121	Grimmet, Mary	3039
French, James	3480	Green, Rosetta	692
Freeman, Mariah	4234	Green, Easter	770
Frazier, Bessie	3616	Green, Georgia F.	3283
Funkhauser, Julia	898	Green, Charlie	3284
Funkhauser, Lee	1240	Green, Clarence	3285
Fulsom, Jess	4045	Green, Aleck	1049
Fulsom, Charley	4046	Griffin, Nathan	1196
Fulsom, Allie	4047	Griffin, Betsie	1197
Fulsom, Girtie	4048	Griffin, Josie	1198
Garnett, Willie	718	Gray, Susie	1364
Gaskins, Louisa	3343	Gray, Lucinda	1366
Gaskins, Joella	3344	Gray, Delia	1367
Gaskins, John	3346	Grimmett, Benjamin, Jr.	1464
Gaskins, Ida	3347	Grimmett, Ben	2236
Gaskins, Levi	3348	Groves, Mary	2315

Name.	Roll No.	Name.	Roll No.
Groves, Carrie	2319	Hale, Ellis	1113
Grimmett, Squirrel	2634	Harlin, Harry	1241
Grimmett, Henderson	2644	Haddox, Beulah	3928
Grimmett, Evans	2645	Hamilton, Annie	1253
Grimmett, Ethel	2646	Hamilton, Roswell	1254
Grimmett, Frank	2647	Hamilton, Squirrel	1255
Grimmett, George	2648	Hamilton, Nanie	1256
Grimmett, Mamie	2649	Hayes, Euna	1528
Grimmett, Ellis	2674	Harlin, Solomon	1553
Grimmett, Ellis, Jr.	2648	Harlin, Sarah	1554
Grimmett, William	3267	Harlin, Levi	1555
Grimmett, Peggie	2972	Harlin, Walter	1556
Grimmett, Sandy	2973	Harlin, Solomon, Jr.	1557
Grimmett, Frances	3464	Harlin, Thomas	1678
Grimmett, Susan B.	3465	Harlin, Jane	1634
Grooms, Martha	3563	Harlin, Kizzie	1679
Grooms, Dona	3564	Harlin, Nelson	3068
Grooms, Peter W.	3565	Harlin, Kinney	3069
Grooms, Leuretha	3566	Harlin, Benjamin	1682
Groomer, Willie	4025	Harlin, Howard	1683
Groomer, John Delma	4026	Harlan, Neely	1684
Grayson, Callie	3721	Harlan, Caroline	1685
Graves, Chaney	3654	Harlan, Willie	1686
Graves, Harry	3655	Hardrick, Cella	1751
Graves, Nellie	3656	Hardick, Perry	1752
Graves, Andy	3657	Hardrick, James	1753
Graves, Lillie	3658	Hardick, Rosa	1754
Graves, Fred	3659	Hardick, Julia	1755
Graves, Martha	3660	Hardrick, Lewis	1756
Graves, Georgia	3661	Harris, Julia M.	1911
Graves, Eli	3663	Hardrick, Rosanna	1922
Graves, Mabel	3664	Harris, Minerva	2473
Grimmett, Harry	4094	Hardman, Joseph	2740
Graves, Jefferson	3938	Hardman, Effie I.	3259
Graves, Fannie	4350	Harris, Carrie	3569
Gunter, Rachel	1102	Haris, Delilah	3570
Gunter, Lewis, Jr.	1103	Hardick, Mary	3805
Gunter, Myrtle	1104	Hardrick, Precilla	3808
Gunter, Lucy	1105	Harper, Robert	3607
Gunter, Rosa	1515	Harper, Jordon	4359
Gunter, Fannie	1516	Harris, Thomas H.	4005
Gunter, Alice	1517	Harrison, Susie	4063
Gunter, Tuxie	1518	Harrison, Johnnie	4065
Gunter, Rosanna	1519	Hanks, Lena	3711
Gunter, Jesse	1520	Hailstock, Charley	3625
Gunter, John	1521	Harrison, Freeman	4064
Gunter, Richard	1522	Henderson, Emma	2543
Gunter, Lewis	3358	Henderson, Lennie E.	2544
Gunter, Henry	3417	Henderson, Russell	4112
Gunter, Isaac	3418	Henderson, Birt	3726
Gunter, John	4226	Henry, Charlotte	3846
Harris, William	21	Henderson, Henry	3828
Harris, John	22	Hicks, Howard	571
Harlin, Samuel	43	Hicks, Ora	572
Harland, Eulia	181	Hill, Mary	3038
Hall, Josephine	3071	Hicks, Wash	699
Hall, Jennie	3073	Hicks, Mary	700
Hall, Georgianna	3074	Hill, Martha	1388
Harlin, Bass	278	Hill, Harrison	1534
Harlin, Georgian	2763	Hill, Nancy	3194
Harlin, Clem	280	Hill, Perlien	3195
Harlin, Mitchell	2764	Hill, Thomas	3196
Harlin, Eddy	2765	Hicks, Robert	1724
Harlin, John	476	Hicks, Martha	1725
Harlin, Mary	477	Hicks, William H.	1726
Hall, Elizabeth	540	Hicks, Clarence	1727
Harris, Sallie	583	Hicks, Robert A.	1728
Harris, Eddie C.	584	Hicks, Ella	1729
Harris, Willie	585	Hicks, Jesse	1730
Harlin, Charlotte	657	Hicks, Albert	1731
Harris, Carrie	712	Hill, Lucy	2442
Harlin, Joseph	2810	Hill, Cynthia	3233
Harlin, Charlotte	2811	Hill, Pauline	4129
Harlin, William	2812	Hill, Jesse	4130
Harlin, Leanna	2813	Hight, Fannie	3694
Harlin, Myrtle	2814	Hill, Lucinda	3948
Hall, John	2717	Hill, Alsea	3949
Hall, Lizzie	1092	Hill, Isaac	3950
Hall, Josie	1093	Hill, Donie	3620
Hall, Dave	1094	Hickey, Peggy	4068
Hale, Richard	1111	Hill, Amanda	4330
Hale, David	1112	Hill, Della	4331

Name.	Roll No.
Hill, Flossie	4332
Hill, Sadie	4333
Hill, James Harrison	3943
Holt, Ibby	408
Holt, Lucy	992
Holt, James	993
Howell, Sarah	3164
Holt, Edmond	1339
Holt, George	1593
Holt, Alexander	1646
Holmes, Jesse	2945
Hopkins, Randolph	2653
Howell, Maria	2986
Howell, Georgeann	2987
Howell, Mary	2988
Howell, Beulah	2989
Howell, Iola	2990
Howell, Emma	2991
Howell, Beatrice	2992
Hopkins, Delilah	3959
Hopkins, Florence B.	3960
Hopkins, Ira	3961
Hopkins, Lucinda	3962
Hopkins, Gussie	3963
Hopkins, Johnnie	3964
Hopkins, Nancy	3965
Hopkins, Alfred	3966
Hopkins, Lena	3967
Hopkins, Charlie	3968
Howard, Anna	3710
Hudson, William	295
Hudson, Peggie	392
Hudson, Fannie	393
Hudson, Annie	394
Hudson, Maggie	395
Hudson, Frank H.	439
Humphrey, James	613
Humphrey, Peggie	614
Humphrey, Phillip	615
Humphries, Emily	649
Hudson, Susan	781
Humphrey, Jerry	1431
Humphrey, Susie	1432
Humphrey, Ida	1433
Huston, Troy	1434
Humphrey, Johnanna	1435
Humphrey, Altha	1447
Humphreys, Julia	1618
Hunter, Mary	1884
Hunter, Roosevelt	1887
Hudson, Susan	2146
Hughes, Martha	2329
Hughes, Arthur	2330
Hughes, Lee	2331
Hughes, John	2332
Hughes, Luella	2333
Hughes, Lola	2334
Hughes, Emmett	2335
Hughes, Calvin	2336
Humes, Ella	3571
Hughes, Charles	3621
Hughes, Walter	3622
Hudson, Peter	3674
Hudson, William	3675
Hudson, Emmett	3676
Hudson, Levi	3677
Hudson, Wilburn	3678
Hudson, Ida	3679
Hudson, Ivory	3680
Huff, Pearl	3691
Humphreys, Sallie	4119
Humphreys, Ada	4120
Huston, Susie	1432
Irons, John	67
Irons, Martha	68
Irons, Will	69
Irons, Robert	70
Irons, Albert	71
Irons, Joanna	72
Irons, Emma	76
Irons, Lydia A.	377
Irons, Mary	378

Name.	Roll No.
Irons, Etha	379
Irons, Johnnie	380
Ireland, Henry	399
Ireland, Harry	400
Ireland, Mattie	401
Irons, Jenanna	668
Irons, Susie	669
Irons, Ned	756
Irons, Julia	757
Irons, Alice	758
Irons, Emma	759
Irons, Pollie	760
Irons, Jeff	761
Irons, Henderson	762
Irons, Andy	1079
Irons, Josie	1080
Irvin, Mamie	3843
Irvin, Richard	3844
Irvin, Minerva	3845
Ivory, Minnie	3077
Jamison, Gabriel	3112
Jackson, Fannie	873
Jackson, John A.	874
Jackson, Mary	2654
James, Benjamin	3517
James, Allen	3522
James, John A.	3523
James, Reuben	3524
James, Archie	3525
Jamison, William	2984
Jenkins, Margaret	337
Jenkins, Dollie	338
Jenkins, Johnnie	339
Jenkins, Glennie	340
Jenkins, Mamie	341
Jenkins, Maybel	342
Jenkins, Patsey	1903
Jimison, Evaline	4146
Johnson, Joseph	2750
Johnson, Tobe	3033
Johnson, Patsy	91
Johnson, Samuel	3034
Johnson, Maggie	3035
Johnson, Viola	3036
Johnson, Sandy	3010
Johnson, Malinda	3011
Johnson, Moses	161
Johnson, Julia	162
Johnson, Moses, Jr.	163
Johnson, Mary	164
Johnson, Louisa	165
Johnson, Sandy	166
Johnson, Toby	167
Johnson, Sarah	168
Johnson, Cy	231
Johnson, Lucinda	232
Johnson, Toby	233
Johnson, Harry	234
Johnson, Ada	235
Johnson, Dora	236
Johnson, Cy, Jr.	237
Johnson, Sarah	238
Jones, Alice	291
Johnson, Albert	315
Johnson, Leander	2771
Johnson, Benjamin	2772
Johnson, Mary Etta	2773
Johnson, Lewis	343
Johnson, James	344
Johnson, Louella	345
Johnson, Sanford	346
Johnson, Lewis, Jr.	347
Johnson, John	375
Johnson, John H. C.	376
Johnson, Charlotte H.	383
Johnson, Frank	418
Johnson, Leander	419
Johnson, Nettie	2780
Johnson, William R.	493
Johnson, Elizabeth	561
Johnson, Hattie	562
Johnson, Della	563

Name.	Roll No.	Name.	Roll No.
Johnson, Murrell	605	Johnson, Nola	4282
Johnson, Annie	659	Johnson, Della	4283
Johnson, Henry	698	Johnson, Ella	4284
Jones, Eliza	2816	Johnson, Harrison	4285
Johnson, Martha	903	Johnson, Lottie	4286
Johnson, George	904	Johnson, Rebecca	4287
Jones, Reedy	908	Johnson, Luford	4288
Johnson, Fog	970	Johnson, Wilbert	4289
Johnson, Harriett	971	Johnson, Arch	4290
Johnson, Clara	972	Jones, Rachael	3420
Johnson, Walter	1035	Jones, Cynthia	3421
Johnson, Nathan	1039	Jones, Laura	3422
Johnson, Martha	1040	Jones, Sophia	3402
Johnson, Laurie	1041	Jones, Nora	3403
Johnson, Ernest	1042	Jones, Henry	3404
Johnson, Leon	1043	Jones, Ola	3405
Johnson, John	1044	Jones, Timothy	3406
Johnson, Joseph	1045	Jones, Helen	3407
Johnson, Henry	1046	Jones, Willie	3408
Jones, Jack	1047	Jones, Lorena	3409
Jones, Callis	1048	Johnson, Amanda	3429
Johnson, Dinah	1130	Johnson, Catherine	3430
Johnson, Andrew	1181	Johnson, Hallie M.	3431
Johnson, Nicey	1182	Johnson, Nettie	3432
Johnson, Minnie	1193	Johnson, Reuben	3433
Johnson, Joanna B.	1194	Johnson, Zilla A.	3434
Johnson, Lillybelle	1195	Johnson, Simuel	3435
Johnson, Emmett	2831	Johnson, Minnie	3359
Jones, Charles	1258	Johnson, Frank	2360
Jones, Andrew	1263	Johnson, Jay	3361
Jones, William	1264	Johnson, Fannie	3362
Johnson, Ben	1394	Johnson, Ethel	3363
Johnson, Alsie	1462	Johnson, Hattie	3364
Johnson, John	1479	Johnson, Arthur	3365
Jones, Owens	1501	Jones, Lula	3482
Johnson, Susan	1828	Jones, Anna	3483
Johnson, Amanda	1839	Johnson, David	3999
Jones, Alice	1840	Johnson, Laura	4007
Jones, Oscar	1841	Johnson, George	4008
Jones, Willie	1842	Johnson, Nancy	4009
Johnson, Evan	1846	Johnson, Admiral D. G.	4002
Johnson, Murrell	2867	Johnson, Lila	883
Johnson, Andy	1891	Keys, Frank	3133
Jones, Eva B.	2883	Keys, Martha	2718
Johnson, Seymour	2041	Keys, Susan	3134
Jones, Mary	2087	Keys, Alice	3135
Jones, Harriet	2088	Keys, Elnora	2719
Johnson, Sarah	2907	Kemp, Alexander	1341
Johnson, James	2908	Kemp, Christie	1342
Johnson, Hannah	2162	Kemp, Willie	1343
Johnson, Pearl	2163	Kemp, Florence	1344
Johnson, Benjamin	3268	Kemp, Clarence	2732
Johnson, Harvey	3269	Keys, Maria	1402
Jones, George Ann	2585	Keys, Mary	1403
Jones, Lettie	2586	Keys, Lou	1404
Jones, Bettie	3357	Keys, Rosella	1405
Johnson, Hannah	3852	Keys, Callie	1406
Johnson, Zadie	3853	Keys, Annie	1407
Jones, Georgia	3539	Keys, Bettie	1408
Jones, John H.	3540	Keys, Jonas	3062
Jones, Ellen	3541	Keys, George	3184
Jones, Charlie	3542	Keys, Lizzie	3186
Jones, Susie	3543	Keys, Florence	3188
Jones, Walter	3544	Keys, Henry	1644
Jones, Roxie	3545	Keys, Ellen	3191
Jones, McKinley	3546	Keys, Ananias	3192
Jones, Centralia	3547	Keys, John	3310
Johnson, Malinda	3553	Keys, Abraham	2089
Johnson, Lottie	3554	Keys, Willie	2090
Johnson, Lizzie	3555	Keys, John	2091
Johnson, Belle	3556	Keys, Ella	2092
Johnson, Eva	3557	Keys, John	2320
Johnson, Annie	3558	Keys, Minnie	2321
Johnson, Peter McKinley	3559	Keys, Stella	2322
Johnson, Reuben	3560	Keys, Johnetha	2323
Johnson, Lewis	3561	Keys, Charles	2324
Johnson, Julia	3562	Keys, Hannah	2325
Johnson, Deliliah	4277	Keys, Lillie	2326
Johnson, Allie	4278	Keys, Jessie	2327
Johnson, Luman	4279	Keys, Charles	3238
Johnson, Jesse	4280	Kell, Katie	3384
Johnson, Alfred	4281	Kernel, Katie	3829

Name.	Roll No.	Name.	Roll No.
Kelley, Mary E.	2953	Lane, George	2417
Kirby, Rhoda	131	Landrum, Lone	4095
Kirby, Benjamin H.	132	Landrum, Cherry	4096
Kirby, Mary J.	133	Landrum, Jesse	4097
Kirby, Peggy	134	Landrum, Reed	4098
Kirby, Susanna	135	Landrum, Minnie	4099
Kircum, Maud	905	Landrum, Pearl	4100
Kircum, William M.	906	Landrum, George	4101
King, Mary	1594	Landrum, Mamie	4102
King, Willie	1595	Landrum, Celia V.	3986
Kirk, Silas	2308	Landrum, James	4176
Kirk, Ruth	2309	Lane, Mary C.	4038
Kirk, Nora	2310	Lane, Millie	4043
Kirk, Cora	2311	Lane, James A. G.	3878
Kirk, Edwin	2312	Lasley, John	4001
Kirk, Gertie	2313	Lasley, Lula	3635
Kirk, Herbert	2314	Landrum, Joseph	3728
King, Florence	2503	Lee, Alzie	129
Kilpatrick, Ada	4230	Lewis, Jacob	481
Kilpatrick, Ivy	4231	Lewis, Sylva	482
Kilpatrick, Warren	4232	Lewis, Pearl	483
Kilpatrick, Easter	4233	Lewis, Mary	484
Kirk, Thomas	4335	Lewis, Dollie	485
Landrum, Daniel	7	Lewis, Nellie	486
Lasley, Columbus	44	Lewis, Pearl	3106
Lasley, Peggy	45	Lewis, Emma	821
Lasley, Charles	46	Lewis, George	824
Lasley, Mary	47	Lewis, Annie	825
Lasley, Florence	48	Lewis, Addie	826
Lasley, Ola	49	Lewis, Moses	1001
Lasley, Columbus Jr.	50	Lee, Jesse	3161
Lasley,, Nellie	51	Lee, Maggie	3162
Lasley, Hannah	52	Lee, Millie A.	3163
Lasley, William	56	Lewis, Edna	1114
Lasley, Lucy	440	Lewis, Estella	1115
Lasley, Edward	441	Lee, Clarence	1338
Lasley, John	442	Ledman, Eliza	1868
Lasley, Frank	443	Ledman, James	1869
Lasley, James	444	Ledman, Roy	1870
Langston, Eliza	479	Ledman, Josephine	1871
Lasley, Lewis	574	Ledman, John	1872
Lasley, Zola	3057	Ledman, Hannah	1873
Laflace, Robert	919	Ledman, Viola	1874
Landrum, William	1242	Ledman, Charley	1875
Landrum, Charity	1243	Ledman, Mary	1876
Landrum, Benjamin	1244	Lett, Annie B.	3206
Landrum, Cassie	1245	LeFlore, Alfred	1995
Lang, Minnie	1387	Leek, Henry	2299
Landrum, Arch	3317	Lett, Rebecca	2394
Landrum, Winnie	1743	Leek, Elizabeth	3244
Landrum, Sherman	1774	Lett, Minerva	2557
Landrum, Alice	1775	Lett, Odie	2558
Landrum, Lavina	1776	Lett, Leona	2559
Landrum, Cicero	1777	Lett, Eddie	2560
Landrum, John	1778	Leek, Ed	3352
Lane, Florence	1824	Lephfew, Frank	3041
Lane, Della	1825	Lephfew, Liddie	3042
Landrum, Spencer	1831	Lephfew, Lizzie	3043
Landrum, Albert	2863	Lewis, Richard	3487
Landrum, Obee	2864	Lewis, Ida B.	3376
Landrum, Gertie M.	2865	Lewis, William E.	3377
Landrum, Caroline	1843	Leek, Samuel	3939
Landrum, Jincy	1877	Leek, Solomon	3945
Landrum, Lovie	1892	Leflore, Lovie	1892
Landrum, Odoth	1893	Linsey, Thomas	725
Lane, Susan B.	2027	Lipe, Mary	1393
Landrum, Major	2032	Little, Mary	2621
Landrum, William L.	2103	Little, George	2622
Landrum, John	2109	Little, Martha E.	2623
Landrum, Mary	2110	Little, Albert	2624
Landrum, George	2111	Lowrey, Nelson,	29
Landrum, Nelson	2112	Lowrey, Ella	30
Landrum, Betsy	2113	Lowrey, Jessie	31
Landrum, Benjamin	2114	Lowrey, Ruth C.	32
Landrum, Lon	3328	Lowrey, Mary	33
Landrum, Eva	3329	Lowrey, Elias C.	34
Landrum, Polly	2115	Lott, Jennie	670
Landrum, Sam	2170	Lott, William	671
Landrum, Harry	2360	Lovely, James	3160
Lasley, Jane	2380	Logan, Nancy	1257
Lasley, Logan	2381	Lowe, Carrie	1468
Lasley, Cynthia	2382	Lorens, Simpson	1619
Lane, Lucinda	2415		

Name.	Roll No.	Name.	Roll No.
Lorens, Lula	1620	Mayfield, Betsy	530
Lowrey, Jesse	3849	Mayfield, Luke	531
Lowe, Eda	1964	Mackey, Ned	576
Lowrey, Augustus	3237	Mackey, William	577
Lowe, Leroy	2483	Mackey, Emma	578
Lowrey, Ellen	2540	Mackey, Sampson	579
Love, Anna	2616	Mackey, Sallie	2785
Love, Earnest	2617	Mackey, Ned Jr.	2786
Love, Lillie	2618	Mayberry, Ellen	586
Love, Emma	2619	Mayberry, Thomas	587
Love, Della	2620	Mayberry,Zora	588
Lowrey, George	2633	Mayberry, Willie	589
Love, Flora	3467	Mayberry, Charlie	590
Lonien, Rebecca	3806	Mayberry, George	591
Luther, Jack	1280	Mayo, Mary	611
Luther, Anna	1662	Mayes, Willie	643
Luther, Ada	1663	Mayes, Robert	644
Luckey, Harriett	2975	Mayes, Joshua	645
Luckey, Geneva	2976	Mayes, Samuel	646
Lynch, Ellen	101	Mackey, Ellis	3118
Lynch, Amy	1210	Mackey, George	3119
Lynch, Nancy	1211	Mackey, Battice	3120
Lynch, Elzira	3004	Mackey, Nancy	3121
Lynch, Allen	1741	Mackey, Anna	3122
Lynch, Mary	1762	Mackey, Martha	3123
Lynch, Josephine	1763	Mackey, Columbus	3124
Lynch, Simon	1764	Mackey, Sallie	3125
Lynch, Edey	1765	Mackey, Ernestine	3126
Lynch, Lewis	1766	Mackey, Mary	3127
Lynch, Ibbie	1767	Martin, Alex	2803
Lynch, Anderson	1768	Martin, Dinah	2804
Lynch, Williard	1769	Martin, Gracie	2805
Lynch, Charles J.	1782	Martin, Peggie	2806
Lynch, William	1793	Martin, Joseph	2807
Lynch, Maria	2851	Martin, Lucy	2808
Lynch, William Jr.	2852	Martin, Sarah	2809
Lynch, Corine	2853	Mackey, Mulsie	738
Lynch, Evans	1800	Mackey, Bertha	739
Lynch, James W.	1805	Mackey, Perry	753
Lynch, Spicie	1806	Mackey, Dinah	754
Lynch, Simon Jr.	1827	Martin, Thomas	768
Lynch, Tobe	1880	Marshall, Susan	794
Lynch, Anderson	1933	Mayfield, Amanda	3147
Lyons, Nancy	1934	Mayfield, Curry	3148
Lyons, Delsie	1935	Mackey, Mary	3155
Lyons, James E.	1936	Mackey, Emma	3158
Lyons, Mahala L.	1937	Mackey, Dennis	975
Lyons, Katie	1938	Martin, Johnson W.	1178
Lynch, William	1993	Mackey, Rufus	1180
Lynch, John	2018	Martin, Helen	1208
Lynch, Matilda	2919	Mackey, Nan	1251
Lynch, Florence "	2921	Mackey, Eva	1252
Lynch, Iola B. M.	2922	Malven, Peggie	2832
Lynch, Andrew	3428	Mackey, Roswell	3302
Lynch, Margaret	2985	Markham, Oscar	1340
Lynch, Early	4199	Martin, Lucy	1389
Lynch, Calvin	4200	Markham, Sig	1411
Lynch, Neatie	3885	Markham, Nancy	1415
Lynch, Garfield	3671	Markham, Ethel	1416
Lynch, Martha	4034	Markham, William	1417
Lynch, George	3497	Markham, Myra	1418
Lynch, Emily B.	3307	Markham, Nealy	1419
Lynch, Amanda	3308	Markham, Jesse	1420
Lynch, Elmer	3499	Mackey, Lula	1541
Mayfield, George	5	Markham, William	1569
Mackey, Roswell	125	Markham, Cora	1570
Mackey, Eli	126	Markham, Beulah	1571
Mackey, Roswell Jr.	127	Markham, Mattie	1572
Mathews, Samie M.	156	Markham, Clarence	1573
Martin, Jerry	223	Markham, Legus	1574
Martin, Willie	2760	Markham, Callie	1575
Martin, Annie	225	Markham, Clementine	1576
Mackey, Jane	271	Mackey, John	1696
Mackey, Mary	272	Martin, Frank	1732
Mackey, Eli	273	Martin, Clara E.	1733
Mackey, Kate	274	Martin, James	1736
Mayes, Katie	348	Martin, Luberta	1737
Mayes, Gippy	349	Martin, Isaac	1770
Mayes, Mack	350	Martin, Bessie	2850
Mayfield, Sallie	354	Martin, Mary	1771
Mayfield, Joana	369	Martin, Lora	1772
Mayfield, Clarietta	370	Martin, Rule	1773
Mayfield, Cleveland	371	Martin, Fred	4053

Name.	Roll No.	Name.	Roll No.
Martin, Nelson	4054	Martin, Nannie	3757
Martin, Solomon	4055	Martin, July	3893
Martin, Sylvester	4056	Martin, Queen	3894
Martin, Prisilla	4057	Martin, Carrie	3895
Martin, Lola	4058	Martin, Annie	3896
Martin, James	4059	Martin, Wesley	3897
Madden, Malinda	1807	Martin, Betsy	3898
Mayfield, Nicey	1814	Martin, John	4198
Martin, Arthur	1823	Manley, Kate	4135
Martin, Joseph	1836	Manley, Ida	4136
Martin, Clarence	2866	Manley, Frank	4137
Martin, Carrie	1844	Manley, Sarah	4138
Martin, Katy	1851	Manley, Lela	4139
Martin, Lee	1852	Manley, Joseph, Jr.	4140
Martin, Carrie	1888	Manley, Willie	4141
Martin, Frances	1889	Manley, Daisy	4142
Martin, Lucy	1895	Martin, Myrtle	4039
Martin, Della	1896	Martin, Jessie	4040
Martin, Sedalia	1897	Martin, Susan	4041
Martin, Ida	1924	Martin, Ora	4042
Martin, Luvenia	1925	Martin, Clem	3598
Martin, Henrietta	1926	Martin, Cora	4205
Martin, Ray	1927	Martin, Allen	4336
Martin, Andrew	1928	Mayfield, Charles	3798
Martin, Bennie	1929	Mayfield, Emanuel	3799
Martin, Frances	2869	Mayfield, Beulah	3800
Martin, Nealey	2870	Mayfield, Royal	3801
Martin, Phoebe	2871	Mayfield, McKinley	3802
Martin, Nathaniel	1930	Mayfield, Nathaniel	3803
Martin, Nicey	1946	Mayfield, Bennie	3804
Martin, Nancy	1947	Mackey, Minnie	4070
Martin, Juno	1965	Mackey, Tommie	4071
Martin, James L.	2017	Martin, Pearlie	3892
Macum, Stephen	2176	Martin, Jacob	3751
Maken, Thomas	2214	Martin, Lady	3752
Maken, Rosaline	2215	Mathews, Florence	153
Martin, Gracie	2220	Martin, Israel	3585
Martin, Ada	2221	Martin, Lizzie	3586
Martin, Claude	2222	Martin, Maggie	3587
Martin, Oscar	2223	Martin, Louis	3588
Martin, Augustus	2224	Martin, Laura	3589
Madden, John	2237	Martin, Lottie	3590
Madden, William O.	2238	Martin, William	3836
Madden, Barney	2239	Meadows, Florenee	153
Madden, John Jr.	2240	Meadows, Joseph	154
Madden, Myrtle	2241	Meadows, Julia	155
Madden, William Jr.	2244	Melton, John	435
Mayfield, Johnnie	2711	Meigs, Samuel	1134
Mackey, Peggie	2962	Meigs, Ida	1135
Markham, John	4220	Meigs, Robert	1136
Markham, Joe	4221	Meigs, Anna	1137
Mackey, James	3918	Meigs, Christine	1138
Martin, General Blunt	2910	Meigs, Johnson	1139
Martin, Felix	2911	Meigs, Ellen	1140
Mabry, Mary	3532	Meigs, Cora	1141
Mabry, Frank	3533	Meigs, Minnie	1142
Martin, Michael	3573	Meigs, Rebecca	1143
Martin, George	3574	Meigs, Leroy	1144
Martin, Alice	3575	Meigs, James	1145
Martin, Martha	3576	Meigs, Stephen	1146
Martin, Clifton	3577	Melton, Nathan	1426
Martin, Ethel	3578	Melton, Lillie	2840
Martin, Jane	3579	Melton, Nathan	1445
Martin, Joshua	3580	Melton, Rosanna	1446
Martin, Sarah A.	3738	Melton, Rosetta	3183
Martin, Ocie	3739	Melton, Leve	1712
Martin, John	3741	Meigs, Mattie	2159
Martin, Aaron, Jr.	3742	Meigs, Lee Ella	2161
Martin, John	3743	Melton, Henry	2183
Martin, Jerome	3744	Melton, Minta	2184
Martin, Susan	3745	Melton, Steve	2185
Martin, Catherine	3746	Melton, Sallie	2186
Martin, Frank	3747	Merrell, George	2918
Martin, Joshua Sr.	4075	Melton, George	2431
Martin, Julia	4076	Melton, Amanda	2432
Martin, Herman	4077	Melton, George, Jr.	2433
Martin, Hester	4078	Melton, Victoria	2534
Martin, Joe	3886	Melton, Judy	2535
Martin, Sam	3753	Melton, Willie	3278
Martin, Mose	3754	Melton, Elizabeth	4297
Martin, Caroline	3755	Melton, Elnora	4298
Martin, Patsy	3756	Melton, Peter	3416

Name.	Roll No.	Name.	Roll No.
Merrell, Mattie	4113	Mundis, Arrell	2229
Merrell, Willie	4114	Mundis, Lydia Josaphine	2230
Merrell, Sadie	4115	Munson, Josie	2252
Merrell, Ethel	4116	Murrell, Jenetta	2354
Merrell, Cora	4117	Musgrove, Rider	2924
Merrell, Charles	4118	Musgrove, Leoda	2925
Melton, Bessie	3764	Musgrove, Mary	2926
Melton, Joe	3765	Musgrove, Alex	2927
Melton, Iola	3766	Musgrove, George	2928
Meigs, Florence	3820	Musgrove, Lula	2929
Milam, Mike	3107	Musgrove, George	3231
Miller, Jennie	987	Musgrove, Rebecca	3232
Milam, Rosella	989	Musgrove, Susie	2552
Milam, Effie	991	Musgrove, Annie	2554
Midleton, Tobe	3198	Musgrove, William	2555
Midleton, Neal	3199	Musgrove, Judy	2556
Midleton, Delana	3200	Murrell, Flora	3311
Mitchell, Kittie	1878	Musgrove, Ella	3914
Mitchell, Mildred	1879	Musgrove, Willie	3980
Miller, Lula	2909	McIntosh, William	114
Miller, Frank	2686	McIntosh, Robert	115
Miller, Gular	2710	McNack, Frances	190
Miller, Dora	4201	McNack, Wallace	3274
Miller, Vine	4202	McNack, Fannie	3275
Miller, Clarence	4203	McNack, Bertha	3276
Miller, Jerald	4204	McNack, Charles	3277
Miller, Charles Wesley	4274	McNack, David	191
Minsy, Albert	3662	McNack, Lewis	192
Miller, Mary E.	4062	McNack, Jessie	193
Moore, Frank	433	McNack, Adam	194
Morris, Alice	702	McNack, Jerry	195
Morris, Susan	703	McDade, Mollie	275
Morris, Charles	704	McDade, Frank	276
Morris, William	705	McDade, Luster	277
Morris, Callie	706	McDaniels, Sophie	633
Morris, Maggie	707	McDaniels, Peggie	637
Morris, Joshua	708	McWaters, Hannah	642
Morris, Sarah	709	McWaters, Ernon	647
Morris, Rosa	710	McWaters, Sherman	648
Morgan, Lucy	1948	McConnell, Sallie	715
Morgan, Oscar	1949	McConnell, Elnora	716
Morgan, Ella	1950	McCoy, Cornelius	724
Morgan, Annie	1951	McClure, Ibby	803
Moore, Nelson	1973	McClure, Cornelius	807
Moore, Rosa	1974	McClure, Henry W.	808
Moore, Lucy	1975	McClure, Ary	809
Moore, Ella	1976	McClure, Leo	810
Moore, Sophia	1977	McCracken, Andrew	1060
Moore, Thomas H.	1978	McCoy, Waddie	1205
Moore, John E. D.	1979	McCoy, Carrie	1206
Moore, Alexander	1980	McCoy, Viola	1207
Moore, Emily J.	1981	McCoy, Austin	1209
Moore, Herbert L.	1982	McCullough, Bessie	1503
Moore, Helen	1983	McConnell, Betsy	1692
Moore, Lewis	1984	McNair, Columbus	1738
Moore, Feriby L.	1997	McNair, Morris	1739
Morris, Sarah	3208	McConnell, Violet	2078
Morris, Octa E.	3209	McConnell, Pearlie	2079
Morris, David C.	3210	McIntosh, Dice	2949
Morris, Koolie B.	3211	McIntosh, Will	2950
Morris, Crowder	3212	McCoy, John	3940
Morris, Louisa	3213	McLain, Nellie	3784
Morris, Wy Jay	3214	McLain, Leo	3785
Morris, April	3215	McLain, Maxie	3786
Morris, Readus	2081	McLain, Cassie M.	3787
Morris, Emma	2082	McQueen, Sabra	4144
Morris, Delbert C.	2083	McNair, Mattie	4175
Morris, Mary	2210	McElroy, Allie	3605
Morris, John Q.	2211	McNair, Sarah	3466
Morris, Elinor	2212	McNair, Dinah	3469
Morris, Eliza	2387	McGilbrey, Jane	3401
Morgan, Susan E.	2588	McCurtain, Samuel	3826
Monday, Katie	2749	McLain, Rosa	3865
Morris, Charlie	3695	McClendon, Fannie	421
Moore, Thomas H.	4004	McDaniel, Jake	3470
Muck, Katie	1064	Nave, Will	2761
Musgrove, Eddie	1529	Nave, Mattie	2762
Munson, Emma	2122	Nave, Edward	2766
Munson, Lewis	2123	Nave, Lily	384
Muldrow, Aggie	2142	Nave, Cornelius	411
Mundis, Sarah	2226	Nave, Florence	412
Mundis, Nellie	2227	Nave, Thomas G.	413
Mundis, Carl W.	2228	Nave, Dora E.	414

Name.	Roll No.	Name.	Roll No.
Nave, Charles	415	Nivens, June	99
Nave, William	416	Nivins, Amelia	100
Nave, Margaret O.	417	Nivins, Richard	102
Nalls, Sarah	1089	Nivins, Annie	103
Nave, Benjamin	2738	Nivins, Josie	104
Nave, Charity C.	1986	Nivins, Flora	105
Nave, Jordan	2174	Nivins, Sada	106
Nave, Albert	2404	Nivins, Callis	107
Nave, Artie	2934	Nivins, Emma	108
Nave, Frances	2475	Nivins, Dewey	109
Nave, Luella	2476	Nivins, Nellie	110
Nave, Ulysses	2536	Nivens, Clifford	111
Nave, Maggie	2537	Nivens, Isaac	335
Nave, Gertie	2538	Nivens, Henry	336
Nave, Velmafey	2539	Nivens, July	361
Nave, John	2551	Nivens, Lila	2774
Nave, Amanda	2944	Nivens, Jessie	2775
Nave, George F.	4091	Nivens, Hanson	2776
Nave, Lewis A.	3260	Nivens, Webb	2777
Nave, Ellen	2568	Nivens, Dennis	2778
Nave, George	2569	Nivens, Harrison	489
Nave, Kellar	2570	Nivens, Bertie	653
Nave, Laura	2571	Nivens, Rufus	1487
Nave, Mariah	2572	Nickels, Lizzie	3115
Nave, John N.	2573	Nivens, Thomas	1539
Nave, Evaline	2574	Nolen, Queen	3894
Nave, Emmet	2575	Oats, Gracie	2805
Nave, Sherman	2576	Oliver, Lena	2793
Nave, Peggie	2577	Owens, Lizzie	2656
Nave, Eli	2602	Owens, Livius	2657
Nave, Jane	2603	Owens, Ernest	2658
Nave, Harvey	2946	Owens, Susan M.	2659
Nave, Ellis	2610	Owens, Lloyd	2660
Nave, Mary	2611	Owens, Zelia	2661
Nave, Ethel	2612	Owens, Erman	2662
Nave, Aleck	2613	Owens, Charles S.	2663
Nave, Elnora	2614	Owens, Rebecca	3806
Nave, Myrtle	2615	Owens, Susie	3807
Nash, Julia	3538	Parker, Samantha	198
Nash, John H.	3548	Parker, Leonard	199
Nash, Allie	3549	Pack, Henry	303
Nash, Jesse H.	3550	Pack, Frank	2767
Nash, Ollie	3551	Pack, Lizzie	2768
Nash, Lucy	3552	Pack, Addie	2769
Nash, Berry	3567	Pack, Okla	2770
Nash, Edward	3568	Parks, Bass	544
Nave, Wash, Jr.	3734	Parks, Laura	654
Nave, Dave	3735	Paden, Jennie	938
Nave, Reuben	3736	Paine, Jackson	942
Nave, George F.	3737	Parris, Robert	1002
Nave, Lena	3626	Parris, Patsy	1003
Nave, Osie P.	3627	Parris, John	1004
Nave, Willie	3628	Parris, Felix	1005
Nave, Ella	3629	Parris, Mertie	1006
Nave, Georgia	3630	Pack, William H.	1027
Nave, Henrietta	3632	Parris, James	1028
Nave, Clem	3633	Parris, Sarina	1029
Nave, Sherman	3634	Parris, Thomas	1030
Nave, Arthur	3031	Parris, William	1118
Nelson, Idella	226	Pack, Martha	1174
Nero, Rosa	683	Parris, David	1186
Nero, Willie	684	Parris, Fannie	1187
Nero, Nancy	685	Parris, Jane	1188
Nero, Clifford	686	Parris, Ada	1189
Nero, Sarah	1266	Parris, Bertha	1190
Nero, Roger H.	1267	Parris, David Jr.	1191
Nero, Jesse Corine	1268	Parris, Lillie	1192
Nelson, Jennie	2057	Parker, Malinda	1527
Nelson, Zacharia D.	2058	Parker, Nona	1530
Nelson, Cora F.	2059	Parker, Spain	1531
Nelson, Elizabeth R.	2060	Parker, Ola	1532
Nelson, Eddie	2061	Parris, Anthony	1559
Nelson, Lola M.	2062	Parris, Laura	1560
Nelson, William McK.	2063	Parris, Aleck	1561
Neal, Ellen	2666	Parris, William	1562
Nelson, Henrietta	1231	Parris, Earl	1563
Nivens, Alexander	93	Parris, Cora	1564
Nivens, Mary	94	Parris, Madie	1565
Nivens, Samuel	95	Parris, Caleb	1640
Nivens, Charles	96	Pack, George D.	1281
Nivens, John	97	Patterson, Frances	2029
Nivens, Wheeler	98	Patterson, Arthur	2030

Name.	Roll No.	Name.	Roll No.
Patterson, York A.	2031	Reynolds, Nellie	174
Pack, Joseph	2695	Reynolds, Laura	175
Payne, James	3020	Reynolds, Lilbun	176
Pack, Lottie	3831	Reynolds, Henry	177
Petitt, George	298	Reynolds, Bessie	178
Petitt, Philies	299	Reynolds, Henry	451
Petitt, Sophie	300	Reynolds, Maggie	452
Petitt, Annie	301	Reynolds, Martha	450
Petitt, Henry	302	Reynolds, Sheridan	453
Petit, Samuel	364	Reynolds, Columbus	454
Pettit, Ibby	408	Reynolds, Harrison	492
Perry, Ann	769	Richardson, Chaney	396
Penn, Sarah	882	Rider, Reed	1085
Penn, Lila	883	Rider, Jess	1086
Penn, Anna	884	Rider, Jerry	1471
Perryman, Patsie	1265	Rider, Annie	1472
Pennington, Rachel	2474	Rider, Rose	1473
Pennington, Mahala	2477	Rider, Betsie	1474
Pennington, Melissa	2478	Rider, Ella	1475
Pennington, Rachel	2479	Rider, Sarah R.	1496
Pee, Susan	4032	Rider, Sam	1483
Perry, Levie Thomas	342	Rider, John H.	1542
Phillips, Eva	1252	Rider, Thomas	2735
Pinder, Nancy	2716	Rider, Frank	1558
Pinder, Daniel	3018	Richardson, Lizzie	
Pitts, Luversa	2902	Blanche	4219
Powell, Luvanda	500	Rider, James	1577
Powell, Alexander	1923	Rider, Clem	1578
Porter, Ellen	1110	Rider, Luther	1579
Porter, Nan	2731	Rider, Jesse	1580
Porter, Ernest	1421	Rider, Leonard	1581
Porter, Douglas	1422	Rider, Angeline	1582
Porter, Edna	1423	Rider, Ellen	1583
Porter, Maudy	1424	Rider, William	1676
Porter, Willie	1425	Rider, Edie	1677
Powell, Rilda	2679	Rider, Lige	1783
Porlar, Richard	1621	Rider, Robert	1939
Porlar, Ellen	3985	Rider, Sarah	2037
Pool, Lewis A.	3944	Rider, Georgia	2038
Poorboy, Belle	887	Rider, Mariah	2469
Price, Emma	943	Rider, Charlie	2470
Price, Louisa	944	Rider, Lovely	2952
Price, Minerva	945	Rider, George	4239
Price, Matilda	946	Rider, Henry	4235
Price, John	947	Rider, Carlos	4236
Price, Perry	948	Rider, Flora B.	4237
Price, Louvenia	3299	Rider, Leullen	4238
Price, Savannah	3300	Rider, Bertha	3923
Price, Jennie	3301	Rider, Buck	3979
Purtle, Emma	4319	Rider, Bertha	1587
Ray, Jane	658	Riley, Jefferson	565
Ray, Lewis	660	Riley, Robin	726
Ragsdale, Jonas	1912	Riley, Emma	727
Ragsdale, Annie	1913	Riley, Nannie	728
Ragsdale, Willie	2289	Riley, Frank	729
Rainey, Pearl	2163	Riley, Alex	731
Ratliff, Edith	3332	Riley, McKinley	732
Ratliff, Henry	3333	Riley, Sarah	733
Ratliff, Edna	3334	Riley, Esther	771
Ratcliff, Myrtle	2947	Riley, Stephen	795
Reed, Frank	474	Riley, Emiline	796
Reed, Sarah	1095	Riley, Sallie	3166
Reed, Bethel	1101	Riley, Moses	3167
Reed, Harriet	2136	Riley, Carrie	3168
Reed, Henry	2137	Riley, Andy	3169
Reed, George Jr.	2138	Riley, Georgia	3170
Reed, Lee	2139	Riley, Florence Ella	1902
Reed, Mabel	2140	Riley, Moses	4242
Reed, Millie	2345	Riley, Lillie	4243
Reed, Sylvester	2920	Riley, Andrew	4244
Reese, Jesse	1749	Riley, Nathaniel	4245
Reese, Betsy	1750	Riley, Jesse	4246
Reese, James	1757	Riley, Joseph	4247
Reese, Anderson	1758	Riley, Ollie	4248
Reese, Ben	1759	Riley, Viola	4249
Reese, Amanda	1760	Riley, Mabel	4250
Reese, Beatrice	1761	Riley, Elnora	4251
Reese, Sarah	2173	Riley, Ideller	4252
Reid, Mollie	3526	Riley, Luther D.	4253
Reid, Daniel	3527	Riley, Frank	4254
Reeves, Winnie	3697	Riley, Lottie	4255
Reynolds, Nancy	172	Riley, Fannie	4256
Reynolds, Mary	173	Riley, James	4257

Name.	Roll No.	Name.	Roll No.
Riley, Ralph	4258	Ross, Alexander	1150
Riley, Arizona	4259	Ross, James	1151
Riley, Inola	4260	Ross, Rosanna	1152
Riley, Earl E.	4261	Ross, Clarence	1153
Riley, Clarence	4262	Ross, Lizzie	1154
Riley, Jerry	4263	Ross, Samuel	1155
Riley, Samuel	4264	Ross, Motto	1156
Riley, James E.	4265	Ross, Moses	1163
Riley, Amanda	4266	Ross, Mary	1164
Riley, Mariah	4267	Ross, Lula	1165
Riley, Maggie	4268	Ross, Percy	1166
Riley, Calvin	4269	Ross, Lewis	2730
Riley, Bertha	4270	Ross, Austin	1183
Riley, Ada	4271	Ross, Aaron	1461
Riley, Leona	4272	Ross, Caroline	1635
Riley, Arthur	4296	Ross, James	1636
Riley, Lenora Odine	4291	Ross, Ada	1637
Riley, John C.	4329	Ross, Louis	1638
Riley, William	4292	Ross, Jessie L.	1639
Riley, Ed	4342	Ross, Maggie	1641
Riley, Matt	4343	Ross, Lee	3070
Riley, Jessie	4344	Ross, Minnie	3316
Riley, Howard	4345	Ross, Martha	1909
Riley, Annie	4346	Ross, Watie	3325
Riley, Richard	4355	Ross, George	2876
Riley, Willie	4356	Ross, John Henry	1992
Riley, Mary	4357	Ross, Frank	2125
Riley, Fred	4358	Ross, Frank Jr.	2126
Riley, Henry B.	3891	Ross, Josie	3219
Ross, John H.	1	Ross, Jessie	3220
Ross, John H. Jr.	2	Ross, Lovetta	2143
Ross, Elnora	3	Ross, Henrietta	2144
Ross, Edward	66	Ross, Nathan	2145
Ross, Joseph	89	Ross, William	2422
Ross, Jane	3045	Ross, Mariah	2580
Ross, Stephen	3046	Ross, Jesse	2584
Ross, Jessie	3047	Ross, Perry	2590
Ross, Mamie	3048	Ross, George	2606
Ross, Ethel	3049	Ross, Edmond	2630
Ross, Henry	146	Ross, Etta J.	2631
Ross, Polly	147	Ross, Tom	2684
Ross, Hannah	3012	Ross, Rebecca	3496
Ross, Sarah	387	Ross, John, Jr.	4360
Ross, Bessie	388	Ross, Mary	3486
Ross, Robert	389	Ross, Joe	4162
Ross, Richard	390	Ross, Samuel	3366
Ross, Alberty	391	Ross, Rachel	4184
Ross, Moses	403	Ross, Minnie	3623
Ross, Maria	404	Roach, Daniel	123
Ross, Ishmael	405	Roach, Jesse	124
Ross, Louis	406	Roach, Joseph	4050
Ross, Moses Jr.	407	Roach, Samuel	818
Ross, Tomy	409	Roach, Julia	820
Ross, Polly	564	Roach, Lovely	822
Ross, Moses	687	Roach, Maud	823
Ross, Lena	691	Roach, Robert	876
Ross, Sarah	886	Robertson, Jemima	316
Ross, Stephen	889	Robertson, Lucinda	351
Ross, Carrie	890	Robertson, Anna	352
Ross, Stick	895	Robertson, Fayette	353
Ross, Nancy	896	Roberson, Calvin	356
Ross, Malcolm	897	Roberson, Bertha	357
Ross, Julia	898	Roberson, Watie	358
Ross, Amanda	899	Roberson, Amanda	359
Ross, Patsie	900	Roberson, Arthur	360
Ross, Clem	901	Rogers, Joseph	650
Ross, Martha	957	Rogers, Sylva	651
Ross, Jackson	958	Rogers, Gabe	2788
Ross, Kate	959	Rogers, Malinda	656
Ross, Addie	960	Roach, Henry	964
Ross, Peggie	961	Roach, Rebecca	965
Ross, Lawrence	973	Roach, Patsie	966
Ross, Ned	2821	Roach, Joseph H.	967
Ross, Isaac	2822	Roach, Elmira	968
Ross, Nannie	2823	Roach, Conway	969
Ross, Edward	2824	Robinson, Belle	1107
Ross, Sarah	1055	Robinson, Katie	1108
Ross, Henry Jr.	1056	Robinson, Roberta	1109
Ross, Etta	1057	Roach, Joseph	1212
Ross, Lawrence T.	1131	Roach, Patsie	1214
Ross, Rhoda	1132	Roach, Maggie	1215
Ross, Jodie	2829	Roach, Leroy	1216
Ross, Joseph	1149		

Name.	Roll No.	Name.	Roll No.
Roach, Florence	1217	Rogers, Willis	2504
Roach, Lillie	1218	Rogers, Sarah	2505
Roach, Tuxie	1219	Rogers, Sim	2938
Roach, Ella	1220	Rogers, Aggie	2939
Roach, Stella	1221	Rogers, Sallie	2940
Roach, Oscar	1222	Rogers, Leonard	2941
Roach, Muggie	1223	Rogers, Rosa	2942
Roach, Bertha	1224	Rogers, Sharp	2943
Roach, Laura	3291	Rogers, Rufus O.	3261
Roach, Ollie	3295	Rogers, Rosie	2625
Roe, Cassie	1337	Rogers, Clem	2627
Rogers, George	1349	Rogers, Jasper	2629
Rogers, Rose	1350	Rogers, Eli	2643
Rogers, Jesse	1351	Robinson, Arthur	2694
Rogers, Pompey	1363	Rogers, Charley	2696
Rogers, Daniel	2733	Rogers, Sam	2697
Rogers, William	1470	Rogers, Ellis	4128
Rogers, Willie Lee	1477	Rogers, Jack	2956
Rogers, Henrietta	1478	Rogers, Pompey	3425
Rogers, Betsy	1544	Rowe, Alexander	4049
Rogers, Ella	1545	Robinson, Bettie	3312
Rogers, Fred	1546	Robinson, Rosa	3748
Roland, Sarah	1687	Robinson, Nody	3749
Rowe, Jesse	1746	Robinson, Melly	3750
Rowe, Lutitia	1747	Rogers, William	4123
Rowe, Daniel	1748	Rogers, Mary	4124
Rogers, Reuben	1945	Rowe, John	3727
Rowe, Laura	1985	Rogers, Eliza	4154
Rogers, Eliza	1990	Rogers, Augustus	4127
Rowe, Ada	2004	Rodgers, Willie	4228
Rowe, Washington	2005	Rogers, Sam	4125
Rowe, Viola	2006	Rogers, Ella	3025
Rowe, Perry	2020	Sanders, Anderson	77
Rowe, Jesse	2021	Sanders, Sarah	78
Rogers, Ethel J.	2051	Sanders, David	79
Rogers, Ray	2052	Sanders, Carrie	80
Rogers, Roy McK.	2053	Sanders, Fannie	82
Rogers, Nelson V.	2055	Sanders, Lucy	267
Rogers, Cooey V.	2056	Sanders, Matilda	609
Rowe, Luther G.	3933	Sanders, Robert	677
Rogers, Florence	2286	Sanders, Allen	2789
Rogers, Nellie	2287	Sanders, Andy	2790
Rogers, Walter	2288	Sanders, John	2791
Rogers, Houston, Sr.	2305	Sanders, Martha	2792
Rogers, Bud	2306	Sanders, Anderson	935
Rogers, Anderson	2307	Sanders, Sarah	936
Roach, Lucy J.	2365	Sanders, Joe	979
Roach, Earnest	2366	Sanders, Emma	990
Roach, Denis	2367	Sanders, Alexander	1052
Robinson, Lizzie	2368	Sanders, Frances	1053
Robinson, Frederick	2369	Sango, Alice	1261
Robinson, Nora	2370	Sanders, Tuxie	1287
Robinson, George	2371	Sanders, Willie	1288
Robinson, Lola	2372	Sanders, Ben	1413
Robinson, Della	2373	Sanders, Sam	1550
Robinson, Tolly	2374	Sanders, Maria	1606
Robinson, Hannah	2375	Sanders, Elvie	1608
Robinson, Parine	2376	Sanders, Margaret	3063
Roach, Maggie	2403	Sanders, Lewis	1645
Rowe, Hayward	2447	Sanders, Vina	3193
Rowe, Lucinda	2448	Sanders, Ann	2095
Rowe, Charles	2449	Sanders, Belle	2096
Rowe, Ella	2450	Sanders, Benjamin	2097
Rowe, Perry	2451	Sanders, Jennette	2098
Rowe, Louis	2452	Sanders, Ben	2130
Rowe, Albert	2453	Sanders, Lizzie	2131
Rowe, Rachel	2454	Sanders, Aleck	2132
Rowe, Aggie	2455	Sanders, Jesse	2133
Rogers, Rab	2460	Sanders, George	2134
Rogers, Rhoda	3935	Sanders, Mark	2135
Rogers, Lucy	3337	Sanders, Clyde	2148
Rogers, Isaac	3338	Sanders, Charley R.	2149
Rogers, Grace	3339	Sanders, Reuben	2152
Rogers, Margaret	3340	Sanders, Alice G.	2153
Rogers, Houston, Jr.	2461	Sanders, Alice C.	2154
Rose, Eliza	2463	Sanders, Pearl	2155
Rose, Frank	2464	Sanders, Rugartha L.	2156
Rose, George	2465	Sanders, Bessie M.	2157
Rose, John	2466	Sanders, James H.	2158
Robinson, Annie	2486	Sales, Pleas	2160
Rogers, Allen	2501	Sanders, Malinda	3330
Rogers, Gratt D.	2502	Sanders, Josephine	3331

Name.	Roll No.	Name.	Roll No.
Sanders, Tim	2337	Sheppard, Nathaniel	3412
Sanders, Michael M.	2506	Shields, Mary	4072
Sanders, Daniel, Jr.	2525	Silk, Anderson	672
Sanders, George	2533	Silk, Annie	673
Sanders, Benjamin	2655	Silk, Lillie	674
Sanders, Daniel	2664	Silk, Josephine	675
Sanders, Malinda	2665	Silk, Squire	676
Sanders, Ellen	2666	Silk, John	1122
Sanders, Ethel	2667	Simmons, Janie	3624
Sanders, Ed	2668	Skates, Harriet	246
Sales, Lillie S.	2745	Skates, John	247
Sales, Peter L.	2746	Skates, Henry	248
Sales, Ulysses S.	2747	Slater, Lula	1275
Sales, Robert R.	2748	Slater, Jethel	1276
Sales, Ira G.	3936	Slater, Elizabeth	1277
Sales, Annie E.	3937	Smith, Robert, Jr.	4
Sanders, Rosa	2692	Smith, Lucy	267
Sanders, Rubetta	2693	Smith, Ollie	270
Sanders, Louisa	3484	Smith, Amie	501
Sanders, Willie	3485	Smith, James	525
Sanders, John	4003	Smith, Pearl	3089
Sanders, Fannie	3869	Smith, Henry	3090
Schrimsher, Sophie	189	Smith, Gilbert	3091
Schrimsher, Edward	211	Smith, John	3092
Schrimsher, Frank	212	Smith, Sarah	3093
Scarborough, Narcissus	3139	Smith, Ruth E.	3094
Schrimsher, Willie	891	Smith, July	3095
Scarborough, Laura	1201	Smith, Flora	607
Scarborough, Emma	1202	Smith, David	608
Schrimsher, Esther	1543	Smith, Alice	612
Schrimsher, John	1547	Smith, Dora	617
Schrimsher, Sadie	1548	Smith, Thomas	618
Schrimsher, Ruth	1549	Smith, Rosa	740
Scales, Vinay	2141	Smith, Preston	741
Scott, Rutha	2175	Smith, Keller	1016
Scott, Dutch	2177	Smith, Bob	3171
Scott, Lizzie	2178	Smith, Melinda	3172
Scott, Martha	2179	Smith, Willie	3173
Scott, Millie	2180	Smith, Maria	1270
Scott, James	2295	Smith, Willie	1271
Scott, Henry	2297	Smith, Jimmie	1272
Schaefer, Myra	2383	Smith, Joe	1273
Scales, Mary	3225	Smith, Luther	1274
Schrimsher, Henry	3424	Smith, Sarah V.	1427
Scott, Bell	3723	Smith, Luther I.	1428
Scott, Fannie	4273	Smith, Aurillia	1430
Scott, Bessie	4275	Smith, Helen	2076
Scott, Jimmie	4276	Smith, Belle	2096
Scott, Mary	3722	Smith, Keller	2570
Schrimsher, Lela	3426	Smith, Charley	2951
Sheppard, Morris	116	Smith, Zora	3355
Sheppard, Josephine	113	Smith, Benjamin	3356
Sheppard, Etha	117	Smith, Katie	3385
Sheppard, Edna	118	Smith, Charley	3905
Sheppard, Simon	434	Smith, Sonney	3971
Sheppard, Coffee	455	Smith, Flora	3972
Sheppard, Nancy	511	Smith, David	3973
Sheppard, Fannie	512	Smith, Thomas	3974
Sheppard, Emma	513	Smith, Neely	3975
Sheppard, Annie	514	Smith, Gladys	3976
Sheppard, Thomas	515	Smith, Floyd	3977
Sheppard, Claud	516	Smith, Carrie	3978
Sheppard, Willie M.	517	Smith, Joseph	3987
Sheppard, Clem	2784	Smith, Alpha	4309
Sheppard, Lula	522	Smith, Ella	3914
Sheppard, Henry	523	Snow, Daniel	3082
Sheppard, Delmer	524	Snow, Ruth	3083
Sheppard, Gunter	2787	Snow, Jane	3084
Shepard, Siegel	950	Sorrell, Ida	4136
Shepard, Elizabeth	951	Spight, Delilah	877
Shepard, Barney	952	Spight, Rachel	878
Sheppard, Clementine	1286	Spight, Katie	879
Sheppard, Mary	1327	Starr, Oliver	130
Sheppard, Mary E.	1372	Starr, Harry	304
Sheppard, Meuty	1410	Starr, Martha	305
Shannon, Roosevelt	1507	Starr, Daniel	306
Shankling, Mary	2872	Starr, Linniebell	307
Shankling, Della	2873	Starr, Sallie	308
Shankling, Cornelius	2874	Starr, Harretora	309
Shankling, Nelson	2875	Starr, Caroline	310
Sheppard, Nancy	3516	Starr, Harry Jr.	311
Sheppard, Morris	3492	Starr, Anise	312

Name.	Roll No.	Name.	Roll No.
Starr, Luther	313	Thompson, Hayes	259
Starr, Emma	314	Thompson, Annie	260
Stanton, Lucy	398	Thompson, Harrison	261
Stanton, Emma	402	Thompson, Grant	262
Starr, Samuel	480	Thompson, Emmett	263
Starr, Pearl	580	Thompson, Johnnie	365
Starr, Willie M.	582	Thompson, Levi	3080
Starr, Florence	595	Thompson, Joseph	428
Starr, Juliet	596	Thompson, Cora	2781
Starr, Willie L.	597	Thornton, Dollie	457
Stidman, Lizzie	717	Thornton, Thomas	458
Starr, Sarah	743	Thornton, Salina	459
Starr, Andy	977	Thompson, William	550
Starr, Julia	1129	Thompson, Victoria	551
Starr, John	1246	Thompson, Jordan	552
Stidman, Charles	1488	Thompson Steven	553
Stidmon, Samuel	1551	Thompson, Lillie	554
Stidmon, Mary	1552	Thompson, Ellis	555
Still, Harry	4206	Thompson, Jesse	556
Starr, Georgia	2246	Thompson, Coleman	557
Starr, Walter	2247	Thompson, Turner	558
Starr, Herbert	2248	Thompson, Dora	559
Starr, Earmy	2249	Thompson, Jesse	3105
Starr, Mark	2250	Thompson, Cynthia	610
Starr, Isabelle	2700	Thompson, Alfred	682
Starr, Samuel H.	3775	Theodore, Edith	2801
Starr, Sallie	3776	Theodore, Idella	2802
Starr, Lillie	3777	Thomas, Fannie	730
Starr, Leona	3778	Thompson, Henry	747
Starr, Annie	3788	Thompson, Lucinda	748
Starr, George	3789	Thompson, Pompey	749
Starr, Turner	3790	Thompson, Clarence	750
Starr, Henry	3794	Thompson, Houston	752
Starr, Henrietta	3795	Thompson, Richard	2720
Starr. Jessie	3796	Thompson, Edward	2721
Starr, Harry	3797	Thompson, Susan	2722
Still, Della	4024	Thompson, Jeff	2723
Starr, Hannah	4014	Thompson, Susie	2724
Starr, Minerva	4015	Thompson, Bessie	2725
Starr, Theodore	4016	Thompson, Emanuel	2726
Starr, Mabel	4017	Thompson, Jeff	819
Starr, Leone	4018	Thomas, Hannah	1007
Starr, Leota	4019	Thomas, Freddie	1008
Starr, George	3730	Thomas, Gracie	1009
Starr, Arthur	3731	Thomas, Florence	1010
Starr, Viola	4069	Thompson, John	1074
Starr, George, Jr.	3733	Thompson, Sarah	1075
Starr, Nancy	3336	Thompson, Hayes	1076
Sumpter, Mary	152	Thompson, Jeter	1077
Sutton, Joseph	1781	Thompson, Henrietta	1121
Sumner, Bennie	3698	Thompson, Sylvia	1411
Sumner, Charlie	3699	Thomas, Willie	1320
Sumner, Estella	2700	Thompson, Bertha	3305
Sumner, Sylvester	3701	Thompson, Leander	1485
Swan, Peggie	742	Thompson, Bart	1489
Swepston, Jane	1706	Thompson, Egypt	1490
Swepston, Lelia	1707	Thompson, Aaron	1491
Swepston, Lena	1708	Thompson, Carrie	1494
Swepston, Joanna	1709	Thornton, Henrietta	1504
Swepston, Vann	1710	Thompson, Charles	1508
Sykes, Della	3998	Thompson, Alex	1509
Tatum, Gonie	850	Thompson, Laura	1510
Tatum, Anderson, Jr.	2820	Thompson, Harry	1511
Taylor, Judy	3061	Thompson, Richard	1512
Taylor, Willie	1319	Thompson, William	1617
Taylor, Katie	2099	Thompson, Etha L. J.	3306
Taylor, William	2298	Thompson, Frank	2844
Taylor, Lewis	2690	Thompson, Maloy	1642
Taylor, James	4000	Thomas, Mattie	1668
Taylor, Henry	3729	Thomas, Sammie C.	1669
Taylor, Etta	3606	Thompson, Pompey	1680
Tabb, Martha	2718	Thompson, Louisa	1681
Terry, Eliza	1898	Thompson, Albert	1698
Terry, Corether Belle	3207	Thompson, Laura	1699
Thompson, Jonas	120	Thompson, Willie	1700
Thompson, Ida	121	Thompson, June	1701
Thompson, Annie	122	Thompson, Nannie	1702
Thompson, Henry	196	Thompson, Alsey	1788
Thompson, Robert	221	Thompson, Walter	1829
Thompson, Lydia	222	Thompson, Ethel	1830
Thompson, Sarah	256	Thompson, Jordan	1890
Thompson, Lillie	258	Thompson, Willis	3037

Name.	Roll No.	Name.	Roll No.
Thompson, Cealy	1987	Tyner, Prince	372
Thompson, Elyard	1988	Tyner, Martha	373
Thompson, Rachel	1989	Tyner, Willie	374
Thompson, Vicia	1885	Tyner, John H.	386
Thompson, Martha J.	1886	Tyner, Annie	2317
Thomas, John	2508	Upchurch, Caroline	1723
Thomas, Laura	2509	Vann, Frank	3924
Thompson, Eliza	2635	Vann, Lonnie	3925
Thompson, Luther	2638	Vann, Jesse	3926
Thompson, Ollie	2639	Vann, Daniel	10
Thompson, Rena	2640	Vann, Henry	11
Thompson, Bessie	2641	Vann, Lorena	12
Thompson, Albert	2642	Vann, Martha	13
Thomas, Mattie	2963	Vann, Ellen	14
Thomas, Adelbert	2964	Vann, Major R.	23
Thomas, Donald	2965	Vann, Sank	57
Thomas, Leonard	2966	Vann, Fannie	58
Thompson, Annie	3369	Vann, James	59
Thompson, Emma	3368	Vann, Proctor	60
Thompson, Peggie	3370	Vann, Mary	61
Thompson, Rebecca	3371	Vann, Lillie	62
Thompson, Bessie	3372	Vann, Rachel	63
Thompson, Grant	3373	Vann, Gertrude	64
Thompson, Clarence	3374	Vann, Jesse	65
Thompson, Lewis	3375	Vann, Eli	88
Thompson, Blue	3615	Vann, Ellis	90
Thompson, Ada	3617	Vann, Sarah	141
Thompson, Edward	3618	Vann, Melinda	142
Thompson, Emily	3922	Vann, William	143
Thompson, Robin	3510	Vann, Cora	144
Thompson, Simon	2993	Vann, Stella	145
Thompson, Berry	3534	Vann, Cynthia	159
Thompson, Elmer	3535	Vann, Carrey	160
Thompson, Leo	3536	Vann, Moses	188
Thompson, Morrison	3537	Vann, Mabel	2759
Thomas, Etta	4020	Vann, Martha	197
Thompson, Clyde	4021	Vann, Simon	228
Thomas, Albert	4022	Vann, Susan	2996
Thomas, Earl	4023	Vann, Willie	2997
Thompson, Ophelia	4308	Vann, Samuel	229
Thompson, Libbie	4310	Vann, Catherine	269
Thompson, Hirschel	4311	Vann, Emanuel	281
Thompson, Harvey	4312	Vann, Martha	285
Thompson, Clyde	4313	Vann, Clara	286
Thompson, Alpha	4309	Vann, Arie	287
Thompson, Nelson	3387	Vann, Maria	362
Thornton, Georganna	3988	Vann, Anois	363
Thornton, Rhoda	3847	Vann, George	460
Thompson, Bell	4227	Vann, Sylvester	461
Thornton, Robert	3921	Vann, Susan	462
Thompson, Stella	4012	Vann, Minnie	463
Thompson, William	4011	Vann, James	464
Thompson, Lelia	183	Vann, Reed	465
Thompson, Emma	759	Vann, Mary	466
Titsworth, Lillie	1624	Vann, Lillie	467
Towers, John	3423	Vann, Clark	468
Townsend, Mollie	4314	Vann, Garfield	469
Townsend, Rosa	4315	Vann, Jesse	470
Townsend, George	4316	Vann, Lincoln	471
Townsend, Arthur	4317	Vann, Lila	472
Townsend, Ethel	4318	Vann, Reed Jr.	473
Tucker, Cynthia	151	Vann, Louis	475
Tucker, Lewis	1486	Vann, Ruth	487
Tucker, Maria	2089	Vann, Clifton	488
Turner, Maude	2419	Vann, Samuel	3085
Tucker, Albert	2561	Vann, Jacob	3086
Tucker, Eliza	2743	Vann, Zeb	3087
Tucker, Lee	2741	Vann, John	3088
Tucker, William	3017	Vann, Edie	491
Tucker, William	4207	Vann, Annie	494
Tucker, Harriett	3597	Vann, Daniel Jr.	506
Tucker, George	3601	Vann, Ida	507
Tucker, Floyd	3602	Vann, Spiberry	508
Tucker, Sarah M.	3603	Vann, Ellis	509
Tyner, Ada	150	Vann, Henry	510
Tyner, Tessie	216	Vann, Lillie	554
Tyner, Andrew	217	Vann, Martha	558
Tyner, Daniel	218	Vann, Ella	569
Tyner, Charlotte	219	Vann, George	570
Tyner, William	220	Vann, John	573
Tyner, Sarah	264	Vann, Eddie	3100
Tyner, Della	265	Vann, Myrtle	3101
Tyner, Daniel	266	Vann, Oma	3102

Name.	Roll No.	Name.	Roll No.
Vann, Johnnie	3103	Vann, William Jr.	1647
Vann, Roswell	3111	Vann, Sarah	1648
Vann, Henry	714	Vann, Beatrice	1649
Vann, Dan	780	Vann, Augustine	1650
Vann, Cato	3137	Vann, Jessie A.	1651
Vann, Roand	3138	Vann, Harrison	1652
Vann, Narcissus	3139	Vann, Daniel O.	1653
Vann, Thursday	3140	Vann, Thomas	1654
Vann, Ella	3141	Vann, Marie	1655
Vann, Nannie	3142	Vann, Martha·	1656
Vann, Annie	3143	Vann, James	2845
Vann, Rebecca	3144	Vann, Thomas	3197
Vann, Estella	3145	Vann, James N.	4337
Vann, George	3146	Vann, William	4338
Vann, Minerva	852	Vann, George	4339
Vann, Viola	853	Vann, Cleveland	4340
Vann, Lucy	854	Vann, Clora	1703
Vann, Charles	855	Vann, James	1704
Vann, Katie	856	Vann, Andrew	1705
Vann, Carrie	857	Vann, Caroline	1723
Vann, Thomas	858	Vann, George West	1740
Vann, Joseph	859	Vann, Ben	3201
Vann, Jerry	937	Vann, Cooley	1820
Vann, Jennie	938	Vann, Alexander	1821
Vann, Luella	939	Vann, Arreano	1822
Vann, Jessie M.	940	Vann, Lillie	2736
Vann, Johnnie A.	941	Vann, Cullis	2737
Vann, Jesse	3984	Vann, Samuel	1826
Vann, Mary J.	3149	Vann, Dennis	2858
Vann, Frank	3150	Vann, Lula	2859
Vann, Jerry	3151	Vann, Ulysses	2860
Vann, Jesse Jr.	3152	Vann, Bruce	2861
Vann, Estella M.	3279	Vann, Nolan	2862
Vann, Tressie	3153	Vann, Johnson	1833
Vann, Albert	3154	Vann, Daisy	1834
Vann, Rufus	980	Vann, Juanita	1835
Vann, Sallie	981	Vann, George	1847
Vann, Ardelia	982	Vann, Matilda	1910
Vann, Willis	983	Vann, Ben	1940
Vann, Alford	984	Vann, Sarah	1941
Vann, John	986	Vann, Lydia	1942
Vann, Emma	3159	Vann, Laura	1943
Van Zant, Rockwell	1021	Vann, James M.	1944
Van Zant, Maggie	1020	Vann, James	1954
Van Zant, Lillie	1022	Vann, Ave	1963
Van Zant, Sarah	1023	Vann, Stanford	1966
Vann, Alice	1036	Vann, Ellis	1972
Vann, Della	1037	Vann, Cunnigan	1998
Vann, Alexander	1050	Vann, Johnson Jr.	2039
Vann, Jesse	1072	Vann, Steve	2040
Vann, Sophia	1073	Vann, Ellen	2891
Vann, Sophie	1106	Vann, Birt	2892
Vann, James	1175	Vann, Walter	2893
Vann, Floyd	1176	Vann, Fredonia	2894
Vann, John	1177	Vann, Elia	2895
Vann, James	1185	Vann, Elder	2896
Vann, Jack	1295	Vann, Dunk	2043
Vann, Rosa	1296	Vann, Chick	2044
Vann, Lovely	1297	Vann, Eli	2045
Vann, Dara	1298	Vann, Patsie	2046
Vann, Alex	1314	Vann, Watt	2047
Vann, Susan	1336	Vann, Ben	2048
Vann, Lottie	1465	Vann, Jim	2086
Vann, Bishop	1466	Vann, Luversa	2902
Vann, Hettie	1467	Vann, Esther	2903
Vann, Lula	1492	Vann, Virgil	2904
Vann, Willie	1493	Vann, George	2905
Vann, Samuel	1523	Vann, Lucinda	2906
Vann, David	1524	Vann, Benjamin	2093
Vann, Willie	1525	Vann, Grace	2094
Vann, Mamie	1526	Vann, Katie	2099
Vann, Dave	1584	Vann, Mary	2100
Vann, Sarah	1585	Vann, Katie	2101
Vann, Robert	1586	Vann, Jettie	2102
Vann, Bertha	1587	Vann, Alex	2106
Vann, Lewis	1588	Vann, Nealy	2107
Vann, Willie	1589	Vann, Edmond	2188
Vann, Eddie	1590	Vann, Dinah	2189
Vann, Maggie E.	1591	Vann, Eli	2285
Vann, Mattie	1592	Vann, William	2290
Vann, Anna M.	3186	Vann, Amanda	2291
Vann, Priscilla	3187	Vann, Lewis	2292
Vann, Edmond	1610	Vann, Jennetta	2296

Name.	Roll No.	Name.	Roll No.
Vann, Joseph	2300	Vernon, Maggie	2403
Vann, Fred	2340	Walker, Peggie	16
Vann, Julia	2341	Walker, Moses	53
Vann, Henry	2355	Walker, Thomas H.	83
Vann, Callie	2356	Walker, Dinah	84
Vann, Pearlie	2357	Walker, Frank	85
Vann, John H.	2358	Walker, Edward	86
Vann, Jess D.	2359	Walker, Charlotte	87
Vann, William	2384	Watkins, Nannie	157
Vann, Victoria	2385	Watkins, Lona H.	158
Vann, Eli	2386	Watie, Thomas	3051
Vann, Gilbert	3065	Watie, Minta	3052
Vann, George	2406	Watie, Everett	3053
Vann, Carrie	2407	Watie, Mary	3054
Vann, Jesse L.	2408	Watie, Nannie	3055
Vann, David	2427	Watie, Leona	3056
Vann, Wiley	2428	Walker, Ambrose	355
Vann, Sterling P.	2429	Watie, Walter	385
Vann, Jane	2471	Walker, Clark	3078
Vann, Frank	2472	Walker, Isaac J.	532
Vann, Reed	2515	Watie, David	538
Vann, Joseph	2516	Watie, Amanda	539
Vann, Lilah	2517	Walker, Elizabeth	540
Vann, Lula	2518	Walker, Paul	541
Vann, Johnnie	2519	Walker, Rosabella	542
Vann, Bert	2520	Walker, Violet	543
Vann, Charlie	2521	Ward, Sylvester	2794
Vann, George	3245	Ward, Rachel	775
Vann, Magdaline	3246	Ward, Cora	779
Vann, Maude I.	3247	Walker, Susan	781
Vann, Arthur	2542	Walker, Pearl	782
Vann, Rosa	2609	Walker, Rowena	784
Vann, Blue	2626	Walker, Lewis	785
Vann, Elmer	2637	Watie, Joseph	797
Vann, Nancy	2688	Watie, Martha	798
Vann, James	2689	Watson, Sarah	2825
Vann, McKinley	3023	Walker, Nancy	1078
Vann, Garfield	3024	Watson, Maggie	1147
Vann, George	3917	Watson, Minnie B.	1148
Vann, Pansy	3688	Walker, Lizzie	3174
Vann, Herbert	3689	Walker, Fannie	1289
Vann, Josh	4027	Walker, Mary	1329
Vann, George	4028	Walker, Alice	1631
Vann, James	4029	Walker, May	1633
Vann, Cull	4030	Wallace, Elma	3202
Vann, Eva	4031	Wallace, Oliver	3203
Vann, Charles	3969	Washington, Nancy	2035
Vann, Willie	3970	Ward, Iva	2077
Vann, Walter	4327	Ward, Nancy	2199
Vann, Waneta	4328	Ward, Elmira	2200
Vann, Dennis	4155	Ward, Luther	2201
Vann, Gilbert	3410	Ward, Henry	2202
Vann, Ollie	4035	Ward, Hattie	2203
Vann, Phillis Ann	3854	Warren, Maggie	2362
Vann, Mary J.	3855	Walker, Rachel	2507
Vann, Bessie	3856	Walker, Elnora	2510
Vann, Tollie	3857	Walker, Walter H.	2511
Vann, Ellis	3354	Walker, William W.	2512
Vann, Rolla	3814	Walker, Clarence	2513
Vann, Isabell	3468	Walker, Daniel	2593
Vann, Alice	3929	Walker, Aggie	2594
Vann, Mattie	3712	Walker, Mack	2595
Vann, Eli	3713	Walker, Della	2596
Vann, Ora	3714	Walker, Effie	2597
Vann, Jennie	3715	Walker, May	2598
Vann, Lindsey	3515	Walker, Jesse	2599
Vann, Sallie	4093	Walker, Eddie	2600
Vann, Giptor	3915	Walker, Lonie	2601
Vann, Buster	3916	Walker, Charlotte	2604
Vann, Frank	4320	Walker, Luther	2605
Vann, Riley	4321	Watson, Eliza	3040
Vann, Lieutenant	3716	Watson, David	3044
Vann, Minnie	755	Walker, Frances	3518
Vann, Mary	4066	Walker, David	3519
Vann, Harry	4067	Walker, Willis	3520
Vann, Rufus	4341	Washington, Ritta	3501
Vann, Arthur	3983	Wallace, Dora	3437
Vann, Hannah	3702	Wagoner, Cora J.	4294
Vann, Annie	3703	Wagoner, Oval	4295
Vann, Dewey	3930	Warren, Matilda	3997
Vann, Julia	4225	Ward, Sarah	3681
Vann, Lovat	4322	Ward, Vannie	3682
Vann, Bessie	3946		

Name.	Roll No.	Name.	Roll No.
Ward, Martha	3683	West, George, Jr.	3873
Ward, Neal	3684	West, Jessie	3874
Ward, Myrtle	3685	West, Albertha	3875
Ward, Lena	3686	West, Callis	3876
Wade, Rodia	3981	West, Callis	3877
Walton, Judie	2164	Webber, Andrew	3900
Webber, Katie	19	Webber, Levi	4174
Welch, Henry	294	Weaver, Emily	4334
Wear, Dora	661	Webber, Hallie M.	3431
Wear, Mamie	662	Whitmire, Mary	490
Wear, Conway	663	Whitmire, Mattison	2817
Wear, Williams	664	Whitmire, Charles	926
Wear, McKinley	665	Whitmire, Maggie	927
Wear, Zandora	666	Whitmire, Leroy	928
Wear, Edward L.	667	Whitmire, Frances C.	929
Webber, Samuel	719	Whitmire, Sam	930
Webber, Judy	720	Whitmire, Austin	931
Webber, Johnson	721	Whitmire, Lucy	932
Webber, George	722	Whitmire, James	3165
Webber, Alice	723	White, Lydia	949
Webber, Frank	734	White, Louisa	1853
Welch, Sadie	2827	White, Frank	1854
Welch, Daniel	1069	White, Stella	1855
Welch, Walter	1070	White, Ray	1856
Welch, Lula	1071	White, Willie	1857
Welch, Lone	1412	White, Della	1858
Welch, Eunice	1484	White, Fannie	2190
Webber, Clarence	2028	Whitmire, Jacob	3204
Webber, Ellen	2147	Whitmire, Albert	3205
Webber, Boyd	2150	Whitmire, Joe	2049
Webber, Nelia	2151	Whitmire, Fannie F. C. B.	2054
Welch, Frank	2443	Whitmire, Maria	2069
Welch, Louis.	2444	Whitmire, Maudie	2070
Webber, Aaron	2545	Whitmire, Elmer	2071
Webber, Annie	2546	Whitmire, Helen	2076
Webber, Ola	2547	Whitmire, William	2080
Webber, Minnie	2548	Whitmire, Zeke	2084
Webber, Nora	2549	Whitmire, William	2897
Webber, Johnie	2550	Whitmire, Lettie	2898
Webber, Ada	3345	Whitmire, Mose	2899
Webber, David	2675	Whitmire, Edward	2900
Webber, Samuel	3270	Whitmire, Sequoyah	2901
Webber, Sarah	3271	Whitmire, Lewis	2116
Webber, Eliza	3272	Whitmire, Betsy	2117
Webber, Thomas	3273	Whitmire, Ruth	2118
Webber, George	2678	Whitmire, Mary E.	2119
West, Garfield	2680	Whitmire, Aleck	2120
West, Jesse	2681	Whitmire, Eliza	2181
Weaver, Lewis	2995	Whitemire, Aaron, Jr.	2182
Welcome, Amanda	2983	Whitmire, James	2187
Webb, Jane	3531	White, Alice	2191
West, Henry	4079	Whitmire, Clora	2192
West, Callis, Jr.	4080	Whitmire, Winona	2193
West, Cornelius	4081	White, Melissa	2194
West, Charlie	4082	Whitmire, Rachel M.	2195
West, Carrie	4083	Whitmire, Clayborn	2196
West, Ella	4084	White, Serena	2197
West, Watie	4085	Whitmire, Gertie	2205
West, Walter	4086	Whitmire, Aaron	2219
West, Sadie	4087	Whitmire, Needham	2914
West, Martha	4088	Whitmire, George A.	2915
West, Vinita	4089	Whitmire, Walter	2225
West, Sidney	4143	Whitmire, Louisa	2231
Webber, Robert	4131	Whitmire, Eva	2232
Webber, Sam	4132	Whitmire, Hattie M.	2233
Webber, Julia	4152	Whitmire, Dora	2234
Webber, Samuel	4153	Whitmire, Charles	2235
Webber, Josh	4133	Whitmire, Charles	2916
Webber, Mary A.	3901	Whitmire, Emma	2917
Webber, Rachel	3902	Whitmire, Looney	2273
Webber, Andy	3903	Whitmire, Lena	2275
Webber, Aaron	4173	Whitmire, Mary	2274
Webber, Katie	3904	Whitmire, Looney, Jr.	2276
Webber, William	3725	Whitmire, Hubbard	2277
Webber, Andy	4229	Whitmire, Ella	2278
West, Houston	3866	Whitmire, Crawford	2279
West, Ida	3867	Whitmire, Georgia	2280
West, Nancy	3868	Whitmire, Hattie	2281
West, Fannie	3869	Whitmire, Johney	2282
West, Georgia	3870	Whitmire, Angeline	2338
West, William	3871	White, Nathaniel	2294
West, George	3872	Whitmire, Joe	3848

Name.	Roll No.	Name.	Roll No.
Whitmire, Moses, Sr.	2361	Willis, Frank	1335
Whitmire, Thomas	2363	Winters, Rachel	1533
Whitmire, Dennis	2364	Winters, Fannie	1536
Whitmire, Mary	3335	Winters, Hannah	1537
Whitmire, Isaac	2379	Williams, Carrie	1611
Whitmire, Dick	3253	Wilson, Henry	1664
Whitmire, Joseph	3254	Wilson, Lizzie	3313
Whitmire, Jeff	3255	Wilson, John	1665
Whitmire, Rosella	3256	Wilson, Anna M.	1666
Whitmire, Daniel	3257	Wilson, Florence	3315
Whitmire, Sanford	3258	Williams, Augustus	2998
Whitmire, Ida	2553	Williams, Mary	2999
Whitmire, Gettie	2582	Williams, Alexander	3000
Whitmire, Mamie	2583	Williams, Ellis	3001
Whitmire, Dave	2587	Williams, Arthur	3002
Whitmire, Nathan	2650	Williams, Martha	3003
Whitmire, Nancy	2651	Williams, Peter	1744
Whitmire, Blanche	2652	Wright, Sallie	1808
Whitmire, Ann	2967	Williams, Flossie	1845
Whitmire, Ella	4134	Williams, Peggy	2121
Whitmire, Susie	4151	Williams, George	2204
Whitmire, Samuel	3318	Williams, Easter	2242
Whitmire, Earnest	3319	Williams, Sylvia	2243
Whitmire, Levi	3320	Wilson, Victoria	2534
Whitmire, Benjamin	3321	Wilson, Frances	3791
Whitmire, Harvey	3322	Wilson, William B.	3792
Whitmire, Blanche	3323	Wilson, Ernest	3793
Whitmire, Bookher	3324	Wilson, Clarence	3489
Whitmire, Jane	3296	Wickliff, Cynthia J.	3910
Whitmire, Sarah	4122	Wickliff, William	3911
Whitmire, Patsy	4126	Wickliff, George C.	3912
Whitmire, Frank	4186	Williams, Martha	3850
Whitmire, Jesse	4187	Williams, Alf	2957
Whitmire, Ada	4188	Williams, Elizabeth	3719
Whitmire, George	4190	Wilson, Blanche	3956
Whitmire, Bessie	4191	Wilson, Winnie	3957
Whitmire, Austin	4192	Wilson, Emma	3958
Whitmire, Cora	4193	Williams, Melvina	4073
Whitmire, Mineola	4194	Williams, Amanda	3429
Whitmire, Josephine	4195	Workman, Jennie	284
Whitmire, Arthur	4196	Workman, Henry	288
Whitmire, Lela	4177	Workman, Rosa	289
Whitmire, Nelson	4197	Wofford, Napoleon	681
Whitmire, Annie	4223	Wofford, Sherley	3113
Whitmire, Rosa	3438	Wofford, Wallace	3114
White, Florence	140	Wofford, Lizzie	3115
Whitmire, Allie	4278	Wofford, Ellis	3116
Wilson, Rachel	136	Wofford, Alice	3117
Wilson, Frederick	137	Wofford, Walter	985
Wilson, Amanda	138	Wofford, Alma	1199
Wilson, Isaac	139	Wofford, Amanda	3007
Wilson, Florence	140	Wofford, Cooey	3008
Wilson, Sarah	182	Woodard, Charles	2213
Wilson, Lelia	183	Woodard, Ella	3221
Wilson, Thomas	184	Woodard, John	3222
Wilson, Bertha	185	Woods, Annie	2682
Wilson, Allie	186	Wolfe, Solomon	3668
Wilson, Robert	187	Wolfe, Ola	3669
Williams, Matilda	282	Wolfe, Charles	3667
Williams, Belle	283	Wolfe, Grant	3767
Willis, Eva	292	Wolfe, Robert	3768
Wilson, Reed	381	Wolfe, Lilah	3769
Wiggins, Peggie	438	Wolfe, Jesse	3770
Williams, Henry	456	Wolfe, Charlie	3771
Williams, Dollie	485	Wolfe, Elnora	3772
Wilson, Rebecca	496	Woodall, Chess	3427
Wilson, Fannie	497	Woodall, Rachel	4061
Wilson, Ada	498	Wright, Richard	711
Wilson, Manuel	526	Wright, Hannah	744
Wilson, Frances	527	Wright, Rosetta	745
Wilson, Thomas	528	Wright, Edward	3292
Wilson, Griggs	529	Wright, Frank	3293
Wilson, Katie	626	Wright, John	3294
Wilson, Cora	627	Wright, Charlie	1225
Wilson, Elizabeth	628	Wright, Robert	1313
Wilson, Myrtle	629	Wright, Sallie	1808
Wilson, Kittie	630	Wright, Thomas	2912
Wilson, Barto	631	Wright, Rosevelt	2913
Williams, Fannie	1024	Wright, George	2284
Williams, Evaline	1025	Young, Polly	15
Williams, Lewis	1059	Young, Peggy	16
Williams, Sarah	1354	Young, Rosa	17

Name.	Roll No.	Name.	Roll No.
Young, Frank	18	Young, Ella	869
Young, Jacob	227	Youngblood, Reedy	880
Youngblood, Savina	849	Youngblood, Oakley	881
Youngblood, Gonie	850	Young, Bethel	1026
Youngblood, Clayton	851	Young, Nellie	3415
Young, Lucinda	868		

Name.	Roll No.	Name.	Roll No.
Crossland, Hattie	284	Harris, Dora	42
Crossland, Susie Anne	383	Harris, Berdena	288
Crossland, Rennie	384	Harris, Luther	410
Crittenden, Henry	553	Harris, Cal	428
Curls, Julious	595	Harrison, Robert J.	95
Davis, Emma	67	Harlin, Lene	110
Davis, Thlemer	179	Harlin, Terry	111
Davis, Marcia Mae	242	Harlin, Creola	389
Davis, Richard Downing	243	Harlin, Millard	390
Davis, Lawrence A.	538	Harlin, Lula	409
Day, Addie	147	Harlin, Ernesteen	286
Day, Charley	148	Harlan, Alleena	287
Day, Janie	149	Hall, Clarenda	544
Daniels, Clifford Elvira	180	Herrel, Clayford	345
Daniels, Katherine	218	Hill, Lagus	152
Daniels, Dorthy M.	219	Holt, Alex Cravens	504
Daniels, Alice	220	Holt, Jacob	526
Deckman, Joseph A.	56	Holmes, Clarence	230
Deckman, John W.	57	Holmes, Mary	231
Dennis, Shannon	82	Hopkins, Ollie	481
Dehart, Dora	191	Hopkins, Kizzie	482
Delwood, Geneva	479	Hopkins, Pleasant	483
Delwood, Foreman	480	Hopkins, Edward	547
Dickson, Henry W.	337	Howard, Irene	108
Dickson, Letitia	338	Howard, Elizabeth	109
Dickson, Leslie M.	339	Howell, Ben Junior	380
Dotson, Zack	103	Hudson, Elmer	135
Dotson, Theola	104	Hudson, Mercy	136
Downing, Roy	175	Huff, Newell	183
Downing, Hooley	176	Huff, Lucile	184
Downing, Henryetta May	177	Huff, Esterie	361
Downing, Elmirah	178	Humphry, John	619
Downing, Theodore R.	516	Hunter, Noris	271
Downing, Emmet	280	Irons, Careoline	247
Downing, Willie	359	Irons, Joe	346
Downing, Sophia	360	Irons, Roseburn	347
Drew, Richard	17	Irons, Williard	
Drew, Willie	102	Roosevelt	404
Drew, Bessie	385	Irons, Charley Henry	550
Drew, Jake	386	Irven, Henry H.	508
Drew, Robt.	533	Irven, Clarence A.	509
Drew, Paul	546	Jackson, Willie	112
Duncan, Jake	542	Jackson, Bertha	453
Duncan, Mary	543	Jackson, Charlie	454
Elliott, Calella	387	Jackson, Tom	455
Elliott, Frank	388	James, Leolia	506
Elliott, William	490	James, Henry	507
Fields, Ollie	107	Jamison, Leon	187
Fields, Charley	376	Jenkins, Irena	403
Fields, Addie	572	Johnson, Lucile	134
Ford, Myrtle M.	599	Johnson, At	153
Ford, Sammie	244	Johnson, Carrie	185
Ford, Willie	373	Johnson, Mamie	186
Foreman, Lillian A.	412	Johnson, Mary	512
Frye, Florence H.	576	Johnson, Ellen	513
Frye, Edgar N.	577	Johnson, Raymond	232
French, Eugene	618	Johnson, Frank	248
Funkhouser, Sallie E.	165	Johnson, Catherine	249
Funkhouser, Wallace R.	106	Johnson, Jessie	250
Gaines, Florence	405	Johnson, Clarence	252
Gibson, Glennie	182	Johnson, Nelson	251
Gibson, Ramond	228	Johnson, Ross	317
Gibson, Odesia	229	Johnson, Frankie B.	318
Glass, Cynthia	181	Johnson, McKinley	534
Glass, Polly	269	Johnson, Leroy	535
Glass, Ethel	41	Johnson, Lacey	587
Grimmett, Solomon	68	Jones, Roosevelt	290
Grimmett, Otha	150	Jones, Charley	45
Grimmett, Sam	151	Jones, Harry	289
Grimmett, Luther	245	Keys, Dane	154
Grimmett, Sadie	246	Keys, John Henry	188
Hardrick, Jefferson	356	Keys, Clarence	233
Hardrick, Roy Fanchaw	1	Keys, Watie	234
Hardrick, Ruthie Adla	2	Kelley, Louisa	491
Hardrick, Flossie		King, Lizzie	10
Morine	3	King, George Jr.	11
Hardrick, Samuel	357	Lasley, Clifford	374
Harris, Arthur	20	Laflace, Walter	563
Harris, Armon	21	Laflace, Zelius	564
Harris, Arthur W.	27	Laflace, Archie	565
Harris, James M.	28	Landrum, Paralee	529
Harris, Lawrence	34	Landrum, Lillie	530
Harris, Ambrose	35	Landrum, Joseph	531

Name.	Roll No.	Name.	Roll No.
Landrum, Russell	471	McClendon, Abe	237
Ledman, Georgie	189	McGunder, Rosena	117
Leek, Elizabeth	281	McGunder, Minnie Ola	118
Lett, Stella	69	McDaniels, Isaac	335
Lewis, William	235	McMullan, Thelma	523
Lewis, Robert	236	McNack, Bertha	422
Lewis, Bethel	319	McNack, Edgar	539
Liggins, Jessie	494	McWaters, Clyde	477
Lonien, William	101	McWaters, Clara	478
Love, Toles	429	Nash, Henry L.	24
Love, Bessie	430	Nash, Alfred	25
Luther, Flora	354	Nave, Lewis	556
Lynch, Roosevelt	573	Nave, Robert Arthur	266
Lynch, Tilman	190	Nave, Cullus	282
Lynch, Sammie	408	Nalls, Mathew	363
Lynch, Lonnie Lee	528	Nalls, Allen	364
Maynard, William	22	Nelson, Albertie	162
Mabry, Malinda J.	26	Newton, Willis F.	276
Mackey, Naomi	85	Neal, Marrea	365
Mackey, Eli	391	Neal, Pasco	366
Mackey, Oscar	392	Neal, Castella	367
Mackey, Enlas	600	Nero, Carrie	552
Mackey, Lorena	601	Nivens, Nola	71
Mackey, Mattie	597	Nivens, Roseville	72
Maken, Clarence	115	Nivens, Nannie	73
Maken, Roy	116	Nivens, Douglas	74
Malone, Alice	536	Nivens, Berry	614
Madden, Edith Wilder	263	Nivens, Becky	615
Madden, Elmer Dorsey	264	Nivins, Callis	334
Martin, Jennie	119	Oates, Alexander	122
Martin, George	157	Oates, Ora	123
Martin, Oscar	158	Owens, John F.	438
Martin, Elvaloyd	193	Patterson, Clifton	310
Martin, Josephine	194	Parker, Ella	393
Martin, Viola	514	Parker, Robin	394
Martin, Gertha	608	Parris, Charlotte	415
Martin, Loved	609	Parris, Eddie	604
Martin, Israel Jr.	610	Payne, James	603
Martin, Lottie	362	Perry, Levie Thomas	342
Martin, Cordia	578	Phillips, Clemtory	197
Martin, Gladdis	492	Pitts, Wellington	450
Martin, Joy	493	Pitts, Louisa R.	451
Markham, Hattie May	120	Pinder, Anna Luther	613
Markham, Eulalah	121	Porter, Dewy	413
Markham, William	238	Porter, Violet	414
Markham, Fleta	239	Price, Stella	554
Mathews, Frankie	58	Rainey, Walter Lee	270
Mathews, Helen	272	Ray, Johnie	349
Mayes, Emma	331	Reed, David	18
Mayes, Clem	330	Reed, Susie B.	19
Mayberry, Louanna	348	Reed, Myrtle	138
Mayfield, Ora	59	Reynolds, Eli	201
Mayfield, Lucinda	60	Reynolds, Blanchie	291
Mayfield, Annie	426	Reynolds, Kathrine	292
Mayfield, Adam	427	Reynolds, Robert	464
Mayfield, Maria	486	Reynolds, Vice	465
Mayfield, Artice	575	Rhea, Willard	62
Maxey, Reyburn	340	Rider, James Austin	61
Maxey, Floyd	341	Rider, Emma	303
Meigs, Rosevelt	83	Riley, Homer E.	497
Meigs, Clementine	113	Riley, Ethel	498
Meigs, Viola	114	Riley, Alice	593
Merrell, Birtle	160	Riley, Morris C.	617
Merrell, Elnora	431	Riley, Jesse	594
Merrell, Lucinda A.	432	Riley, Flossie Maybell	616
Moore, Everett Leon	84	Roach, Crawford	198
Moore, Garland	195	Roach, Henry	293
Moore, Octava Delora	196	Roach, Glover	294
Moore, Alfred	475	Robinson, William	14
Moore, Drew Sella V.	476	Robinson, Rachel	15
Morris, John Henry	192	Robinson, Mady May	321
Morris, Schuylor	302	Robinson, Betty Ann	322
Muck, William R.	16	Robinson, Opel	395
Mundis, Ralph C.	411	Rogers, Edna	202
Musgrove, Leona	375	Rogers, Clarence	203
McLain, Julus	86	Rogers, Katie	
McLain, Mack	496	Catharine	261
McClane, Cornelius	161	Rogers, Leroy	377
McConnell, Theodore		Rogers, Stella	406
Roosevelt	137	Rogers, Henry	416
McCoy, Henry	301	Rogers, Ida Myrtle	417
McClure, Natholean	155	Rogers, George	418
McClure, Mary Willie	156	Rogers, Alma M.	551

Name.	Roll No.	Name.	Roll No.
Ross, Willie	36	Thompson, Alex	439
Ross, Trim	87	Thompson, Clifford	440
Ross, Leroy	590	Thompson, Eddie	441
Ross, Georgia	591	Thompson, Clyde	485
Ross, Ann Allie	124	Thornton, Lottie	75
Ross, Janie	199	Tucker, Lucy	313
Ross, Thelma A.	351	Turner, Evrett	129
Ross, Tommy	378	Turner, Clara	130
Ross, Christian	495	Turner, Leon Eugene	131
Ross, Sadie	586	Tyner, Minnie May	350
Ross, Ewing	13	Tyner, Zevelena	569
Rose, Creola	320	Tyson, Garnett	38
Rowe, Lewis	571	Vann, Emma Lenora	39
Rouse, Jesse	23	Vann, Lorena	40
Sanders, Annie	127	Vann, William F.	65
Sanders, Napolian	128	Vann, Georgia	76
Sanders, Willard	139	Vann, Lena	77
Sanders, Florence	140	Vann, Heriel L.	132
Sanders, Pearl A.	208	Vann, Charley	211
Sanders, Alberty	325	Vann, Ruth	515
Sanders, Leona	326	Vann, Clyde	212
Sanders, Fannie	525	Vann, Jessie	213
Sanders, Theodore	466	Vann, Maude E.	567
Sanders, Ray	467	Vann, Willie	557
Scarborough, Mabelle	46	Vann, Rosella	304
Scarborough, Alberta	47	Vann, Rena	305
Sheppard, Clem	205	Vann, Victoria	524
Shankling, Willie Aaron	267	Vann, Joseph Willard	
Shields, Hazel May	540	Anthony	328
Shields, Olander	541	Vann, Fannie	329
Simmons, Augustus	37	Vann, Larneil	368
Silk, Jim	89	Vann, Gladys	369
Silk, William	419	Vann, Willa	370
Silk, Annie	420	Vann, Homer Preston	532
Silk, Alice	421	Vann, Lenard	570
Sissle, Minerva	487	Vann, Lillie	407
Smith, Conday	126	Vann, Elmore	596
Smith, Raymond	163	Vann, Ella	611
Smith, Sarbra	164	Vann, Ardella	612
Smith, Sylvester	204	Vann, Josie Phene	442
Smith, Lingo	206	Vann, Lottie	579
Smith, Morea	207	Vann, Tommy C.	580
Smith, Beulah May	257	Vann, Hanner	581
Smith, Thelma	258	Vann, Emma	462
Smith, Loyd W.	295	Vann, Buddie	463
Smith, Sarah Kattie	296	Vann, Clara	468
Smith, Lucy	518	Vann, Frank	469
Smith, Willie	519	Vann, Bennie	472
Smith, Ibbie	333	Walker, George	9
Smith, Maggie	433	Walker, Walter	66
Sorril, Ruby	43	Walker, Elizabeth	142
Sorril, Eva	44	Walker, Girtrue	143
Spight, Bernice	125	Walker, Smith Elliott	308
Stanton, Norris	501	Walker, Nancy Melvina	309
Stanton, Robert	502	Watkins, Booker T.	381
Stephens, Lula Nancy	63	Watkins, Julius	
Stidmon, Ollie	254	Augustus	382
Starr, Luthor	90	Wagoner, Oak Leon	592
Starr, Lawnie C.	91	Waitie, Alice	558
Starr, Viola	240	Webber, Ellie Malinda	560
Starr, Baby Robert	241	Webber, Leander	144
Starr, Emma	255	Webber, Melvine	145
Starr, Loley	256	Webber, Beatrice	297
Starr, Marion	323	Webber, James Roy	448
Starr, Floyd	324	Webber, Jossieline	449
Starr, Agatha	379	Whitmire, Flora	92
Starr, Dannie	559	Whitmire, Teddie R.	93
Starr, Gertrude	484	Whitmire, Lawrence	606
Summer, Pearlie	141	Whitmire, Elnora	607
Swepston, Clover	88	Whitmire, Silvertia	214
Taylor, Herman	568	Whitmire, Ernest	215
Taylor, Elijah	327	Whitmire, Mariton	396
Terry, Margie Luceil	209	Whitmire, Arthur B.	602
Terry, Leonetta	210	Wickliffe, Louie E. L.	221
Thomas, Jerry	500	Wickliffe, Guthrie	222
Thompson, Julius	64	Williams, Arthur Homer	470
Thompson, Teetsy	259	Williams, Rockwell	488
Thompson, Jesse	260	Winters, Frank	352
Thompson, Louie	583	Winters, Carrie E.	353
Thompson, Abbie	584	Wilson, Rhoberta	306
Thompson, Oliver	307	Wilson, Samuel	371
Thompson, Georgie	314	Wilson, Teddy	372
Thompson, Amy	315	Wolfe, Oatas	598

Name.	Roll No.	Name.	Roll No.
Wofford, Henryetta	200	Young, Willie	133
Workman, Samuel	298	Young, Uzella	397
Woods, Eliza	435	Young, Augusta	398

Name.	Roll No.
Alexander, Lizzie	8018
Alexander, Nancy	9851
Alexander, Robert	9974
Alexander	10181
Albert	5375
Albert, Prince	7160
Albert, Jackson	7161
Albert, Watty	7162
Albert, David	7163
Alex, F. G.	6101
Alex, Elizabeth	6102
Alex, Mary	9982
"Alecher"	8309
Amos	5114
Amy	7891
Amster, Susana	8321
Anderson, Phoebe	776
Anderson, William	2816
Anderson, Cilla	2817
Anderson, Walter	2818
Anderson, Andrew	2819
Anderson, Susan	3108
Anderson, Austin	3111
Anderson, Lucy	3112
Anderson, Ruth	3113
Anderson, Solomon	3151
Anderson, Emma	3152
Anderson, Emmett A.	3153
Anderson, Beatrice	3154
Anderson, Sam Clarence	3155
Anderson, Earnest	3156
Anderson, David V.	3942
Anderson, Lizzie M.	3943
Anderson, Robert	3944
Anderson, George W.	3945
Anderson, Tifney	4684
Anderson, Narto	4685
Anderson, Simon	4686
Anderson, Amos	4687
Anderson, Leah	5298
Anderson, Minnie	5496
Anderson, Sampson	5527
Anderson, Tyler	5528
Anderson, Willie	5529
Anderson, Millie	5721
Anderson, Phoebe	5722
Anderson, Martha	6520
Anderson, Alma	6522
Anderson, Annie	6521
Anderson, Ella	6618
Anderson, Emma	6619
Anderson, Richmond	6620
Anderson, Mose	7471
Anderson, Lucy	7472
Anderson, Timmie	7703
Anderson, Charles	7886
Anderson, Billie	8997
Anderson, Lottie	9075
Anderson, Norman	9217
Anderson, Samuel	9218
Anderson, Thomas	9515
Anderson, Augusta	9549
Anderson, Thomas	10106
Ansill, Samuel E.	1406
Ansill, Daisy	1407
Ansill, Sallie	1408
Ansill, Wm. Oscar	1409
Ansill, John Lee	9843
Ansiel, James F.	2140
Ansiel, Arnecie	2623
Ansiel, Charley D.	2624
Ansiel, John G.	4277
Ansiel, Robert L.	6335
Ansiel, William W.	6336
Ansiel, Charles A.	6337
Ansiel, Jennie M.	9665
Annie	4007
Annie	4943
Annie	8451
Annie	8664
Andy, Cornelius	5937
"Angie"	9256

Name.	Roll No.
Apueka, William	238
Apueka, Nancy	239
Apueka, Willie	240
Apueka, Tooka	241
Apueka, Nathaniel	242
Apueka, Setty	243
Apueka, Jemima	244
Applegeet, Orvill B.	9526
Artusse, Annie	2049
Artusse, John	3739
Artusse, Mary	6827
Arnett, Maggie	2609
Arnett, Iona	2610
Arnett, Fred	2611
Arch, John	10132
Arch, Sarwike	10131
Arch, Dick	10133
Arch, Hokte	10134
Arlie	5382
Arhalokoche	6162
Arkalokoche, Sofa	6163
Arhalokoche, Winey	6164
Arhalokoche, George	6165
Arhalokoche, Maggie	6166
Arhalokoche, Lewis	6167
Arhalokoche, Maxey	6168
Arhalokoche, Rosanna	6169
Arpinculikee	6550
Arsoyalee, Lovina	7084
Arpoika, George	7416
Arpoika, Sissie	7417
Ar-tar-kin-nay	7920
Arssee, Albert	8339
Arlike	8455
Arbuckle, Betsey	8462
Arbuckle, Napsey	8463
Arbuckle, Battle	8464
Arbuckle, Fanny	8465
Arbuckle, Louisa	8466
Arbuckle, Millie	8467
Arbuckle, Tommy	8468
Arbuckle, Salinee	10095
"Arfulka"	9238
Arbor, Henderson	9612
Arbor, Caney	9613
Asbury, Moses	109
Asbury, Lucy	110
Asbury, Rhoda	111
Asbury, Louina	112
Asbury, Francis	1142
Asbury, Jennetta	1143
Asbury, Eliza	1144
Asbury, Anderson	1479
Asbury, Thomas	3436
Asbury, Joshua	4442
Asbury, Miley	4443
Asbury, Rosie	4444
Asbury, George T.	4445
Asbury, Josephine	4446
Asbury, James	4447
Asbury, Siah E.	4448
Asbury, Jim	6207
Asbury, Wisey	6208
Asbury, Mary	7602
Asbury, John	7604
Asbury, Thomas	7605
Asbury, Wesley	8783
Ashley, Isabel Jane	200
Ashley, John R.	201
Ashley, Amanda S.	202
Ashley, Hettie E.	203
Ashley, James T.	204
Ashley, Daniel	205
Ashley, Adolphus K.	206
Ashley, George S.	207
Ashley, Emma	208
Asbell, Emma	4289
Asbell, Glen	4290
Asbell, Wallace	4291
Asbill, Sarah A.	5603
Asbill, Edna	5604
Asbill, Brina	5605

Name.	Roll No.	Name.	Roll No.
Atkins, Thomas	45	Barnett, Sandy	3128
Atkins, Tommy	46	Barnett, Chillie	3129
Atkins, Billy	615	Barnett, Joe	3267
Atkins, Susan	616	Barnett, Wanney	3268
Atkins, Mary	617	Barnett, Annie	3269
Atkins, Daniel	618	Barnett, Sallie	3421
Atkins, Annie	619	Barnett, Ellen	3989
Atkins, Thomas	620	Barnett, James	4418
Atkins, Janie	621	Barnett, Mehote	4419
Atkins, Elmira	622	Barnett, Winey	4420
Atkins, Billy	826	Barnett, Kogee	4450
Atkins, Salina	827	Barnett, Nancy	4487
Atkins, Anderson	828	Barnett, Losana	4488
Atkins, Jane	966	Barnett, Joseph	4489
Atkins, Alice	3566	Barnett, George	4490
Atkins, Charles	3567	Barnett, Helie	4491
Atkins, Hellen C.	3568	Barnett, Mollie	4494
Atkins, Robert D.	3569	Barnett, Nancy	4496
Atkins, Mary	5159	Barnett, Jimmy	4497
Atkins, Nancy	6292	Barnett, Nellie	4498
Atkins, Thomas	7913	Barnett, Robert	4499
Atkins, John	8371	Barnett, George	4500
Atkins, Louisa C.	9472	Barnett, Ida	4501
Atkins, John H.	9806	Barnett, Tom	4502
Atkins, James A.	9807	Barnett, Himer	4503
Atkins, Nathaniel	9808	Barnett, Mary	4506
Atkins, Annanias A.	9809	Barnett, Jackson	4524
Atkins, Naoma	9810	Barnett, Jumsey	4534
Atkins, Leola	9811	Barnett, Katie	4535
Atkins, Bertie	9812	Barnett, Soocer	4552
Atkins, William Sherman	10075	Barnett, Adline	4554
Austin, Taylor	7122	Barnett, Daniel	4593
Austin, Daniel	2270	Barnett, Eliza	4594
Audd, Joseph McDonald	9447	Barnett, Tochee	4601
Audd, Flora R.	2429	Barnett, Palmer	4602
Audd, Coodey L.	2430	Barnett, Sampson	4603
Audd, Clarence Y.	2431	Barnett, Jackson	4617
Audd, Oma M.	2432	Barnett, Phoebe	4618
Audd, Clyde B.	2433	Barnett, David	4951
Audd, Ellen M.	2434	Barnett, Patty	4952
Audd, Leonard G.	2435	Barnett, Melviney	4953
Aubrey, Samuel	9660	Barnett, Hettie	4954
Aubrey, Millie	4170	Barnett, Wesley	4955
Aubrey, Olla	4173	Barnett, Amos	4956
Aultman, Benjamin	431	Barnett, Tucker	4979
Aultman, Frank B.	678	Barnett, Cilla	4980
Aultman, Jessie M.	679	Barnett, Hannah	4981
Aultman, James	680	Barnett, Winey	4982
Ayers, Gussie	1434	Barnett, Samochee	5053
Ayers, Lester	1435	Barnett, Ellie	5078
Ayers, Walter	9973	Barnett, William	5081
Barnett, Susanne	1	Barnett, Jonas	5723
Barnett, George	184	Barnett, Louisa	5724
Barnett, Cita	185	Barnett, Harley	5725
Barnett, Moses	186	Barnett, Jonas	5749
Barnett, Johnson	187	Barnett, Morris	5750
Barnett, Jeanetta	188	Barnett, Lillie	5751
Barnett, Louisa	189	Barnett, Hannah	5752
Barnett, Melissa	190	Barnett, Charles	5765
Barnett, William	281	Barnett, Jennie	5766
Barnett, Linda	282	Barnett, Samuel	5767
Barnett, William A. Jr.	283	Barnett, George	5768
Barnett, Mary	284	Barnett, Leah	5769
Barnett, Martha	285	Barnett, Roman	5770
Barnett, Benache	286	Barnett, Ella	5771
Barnett, Susannah	287	Barnett, Toney	6065
Barnett, Pompey	288	Barnett, Dave	6066
Barnett, Yah la we	289	Barnett, Polly	6067
Barnett, Wesley	324	Barnett, Mary Alice	6068
Barnett, Thomas	788	Barnett, Daniel W.	6069
Barnett, Jackson	789	Barnett, Mary	6073
Barnett, Malissa	790	Barnett, Tim	6075
Barnett, Frank	791	Barnett, Tarhinner	6076
Barnett, Joe	1361	Barnett, Wash	6077
Barnett, Sallie	1417	Barnett, Thomas	6078
Barnett, Daniel	2128	Barnett, Louisa	6079
Barnett, Samara	2129	Barnett, Albert	6080
Barnett, Sarah	2130	Barnett, Bennie	6081
Barnett, Elizabeth	3123	Barnett, Dennis	6082
Barnett, Scipio	3124	Barnett, George	6129
Barnett, Austin	3125	Barnett, Columbus R.	6130
Barnett, Dock	3126	Barnett, Ada P.	6131
Barnett, Pollie	3127	Barnett, William	6825

Name.	Roll No.	Name.	Roll No.
Barnett, Lucy	6826	Baysinger, William	1759
Barnett, Wesley	7128	Bard, Daniel L.	2131
Barnett, Tom	7378	Bard, William J. B.	2132
Barnett, Louisiana	7386	Barr, Emma	2444
Barnett, Sukey	7858	Barr, Laura	2445
Barnett, William	7888	Backbun, Duffy A.	9522
Barnett, Edmond	8047	Benson, David M.	63
Barnett, Samuel	8048	Benson, Lena E.	64
Barnett, Thomas	8049	Benson, William	65
Barnett, Lucy	8277	Benson, Lillie M.	66
Barnett, Austin	8320	Benson, Hattie	67
Barnett, Mahala	8405	Benson, Haney	4538
Barnett, Louis	8406	Benson, James	7670
Barnett, Timothy W.	8750	Benson, Silpie	7671
Barnett, Mary Ann	8835	Benson, Annie	7672
Barnett, Lydia	8845	Benson, Waley	7673
Barnett, Lonie	9667	Benson, Sallie	7674
Barnett, Nancy	9770	Benson, Katie	7675
Barnett, George	9772	Benson, Matilda	8029
Barnett, Minnie	9871	Benson, Kokey	8030
Barnett, Johnny	9873	Benson, Johnson	8311
Barnett, Tom	9874	Berryhill, Joseph	85
Barnett, Lucy	9899	Berryhill, Susie	93
Barnett, Salina	9990	Berryhill, David L.	103
Barnett, Millie	10005	Berryhill, Peggy	104
Barnett, David	10006	Berryhill, Numan	105
Barnett, Annanias	10062	Berryhill, Pleasant	117
Barnette, Wm.	1338	Berryhill, Sarah Lee	118
Barnette, Lizzie	1339	Berryhill, Sam	119
Barnette, Alex	1340	Berryhill, Oscar	120
Barnette, Polly	1341	Berryhill, Josephine	121
Barnette, Susie	1342	Berryhill, Clarence	122
Barnette, Judie	1343	Berryhill, Effie L.	123
Barnette, James	1344	Berryhill, Alec	130
Barnette, Martha	1345	Berryhill, Annie	131
Barnette, Wesley	1346	Berryhill, David L.	132
Barnette, Benjamin	1347	Berryhill, Susannah C.	307
Barnette, John	1348	Berryhill, Isabenda	308
Barnette, Lucy	1349	Berryhill, Henrietta	640
Bailey, Mattie	76	Berryhill, William	797
Bailey, Joseph Martin	77	Berryhill, Jennie	798
Bailey, Charles	2537	Berryhill, Konsie	1079
Bailey, George Ella	2645	Berryhill, Harrison	1157
Bailey, Georgie Ella	2646	Berryhill, Bettie	1158
Bailey, Howard L.	2647	Berryhill, William	1159
Bailey, Lonie Lee	2648	Berryhill, Elizabeth	1160
Baily, Moses	1288	Berryhill, Lucy	1161
Baker, Annie	577	Berryhill, Eliza	1214
Baker, Henry	578	Berryhill, Zachariah T.	1545
Baker, John	5022	Berryhill, Ida Belle	1546
Baker, Mentie	5023	Berryhill, Andrew J.	1734
Baker, Tarsey	5024	Berryhill, Buford O.	1735
Baker, Wiley	5025	Berryhill, Altie May	1736
Baker, Sunday	5064	Berryhill, Walter Ray	1737
Baker, Lasley	5065	Berryhill, John	2031
Baker, Rebecca J.	5833	Berryhill, Hokosy	2032
Baker, Eldo	5834	Berryhill, Houston	2033
Baker, Butler	5835	Berryhill, Lucinda	2034
Baker, Maud Anna	5836	Berryhill, Martha	2035
Baker, Clara Belle	5837	Berryhill, Columbus	2101
Baker, Benjamin W.	5838	Berryhill, Emma	2102
Baker, Ella B.	9079	Berryhill, John H.	2103
Baker, George K.	9523	Berryhill, David	2104
Baker, John	9997	Berryhill, William	2105
Barber, John C.	880	Berryhill, Albert	2106
Barber, Robert T.	881	Berryhill, Daniel B.	2107
Barber, Robert T.	3413	Berryhill, Columbus D.	2108
Barber, John W.	3414	Berryhill, Ara Ann	2109
Barber, Lula F.	3415	Berryhill, Wm. T.	2483
Barber, Minnie P.	3416	Berryhill, Jake (A. J.)	2500
Barber, Walter C.	3417	Berryhill, James	2501
Barber, Dovie E.	3418	Berryhill, Rachael	2502
Barber, Shellie L.	3419	Berryhill, Gertrude	2503
Barbee, Sarah M.	1884	Berryhill, Bessie	2504
Baughman, Fannie	9504	Berryhill, Lee	2505
Barnwell, David	1600	Berryhill, William	2511
Barnwell, Katie	1601	Berryhill, Joseph F.	2512
Barnwell, John	3946	Berryhill, Nevada	2513
Barnwell, Jane	3947	Berryhill, Theodore	2519
Barnwell, Joe	5581	Berryhill, Lony Love	2520
Baysinger, Eliza	1756	Berryhill, Jackson G.	2521
Baysinger, Columbus	1757	Berryhill, Ollie	2522
Baysinger, Nellie	1758	Berryhill, Thomas H.	2582

Name.	Roll No.	Name.	Roll No.
Berryhill, Theodore F.	2583	Beaver, Wilson	7425
Berryhill, John P.	2584	Beaver, Levina	7426
Berryhill, Cora F.	2585	Beaver, Nausoche	7427
Berryhill, William T.	2586	Beaver, Williamsee	7428
Berryhill, Della I.	2587	Beaver, Daniel	7429
Berryhill, Stanford	2736	Beaver, Party	7538
Berryhill, Jessie L.	2737	Beaver, Lucy	7539
Berryhill, Bluford W.	2738	Beaver, Nicey	7541
Berryhill, George F.	2739	Beaver, Barney	7825
Berryhill, Carl C.	2740	Beaver, Lousanna	8427
Berryhill, Charles		Beaver, Byer	8693
Lawson	2741	Beaver, Mulsey.	8694
Berryhill, Oliver P.	2766	Beaver, Roman	8695
Berryhill, Roby B.	2971	Beaver, Roley	8696
Berryhill, Thomas J.	3329	Beaver, Colbert	8697
Berryhill, Sam	3837	Beaver, Turner	8698
Berryhill, Sophie	3838	Beaver, Annie	8882
Berryhill, Maudie	3839	Beaver, Sanger	9118
Berryhill, Louisa	3840	Beaver, Elsa	9119
Berryhill, Anderson	4352	Beaver, Nellie	9120
Berryhill, Albert	4595	Beaver, Willie	9344
Berryhill, Louisa	4775	Beaver, Annie	9345
Berryhill, Charlie	4776	Beaver, George	9585
Berryhill, Susanna	4777	Beaver, Joe	9890
Berryhill, Joseph	4820	Bean, Rhoda	671
Berryhill, Sallie	4821	Bear, Walter	1966
Berryhill, Annie	4822	Bear, Polly	1967
Berryhill, Emma	4823	Bear, Katie	3923
Berryhill, John	4824	Bear, Marche	3924
Berryhill, Anderson	4825	Bear, Juda	3925
Berryhill, Louisa	4826	Bear, Hannah	3926
Berryhill, Richard	5670	Bear, Paro	3927
Berryhill, Josephine	5671	Bear, Munnie	4155
Berryhill, Willie	6418	Bear, Cinda	4327
Berryhill, Geo. Franklin	7912	Bear, Little	4329
Berryhill, Peter	8237	Bear, Sarley	4330
Berryhill, Emma	8238	Bear, Senie	4331
Berryhill, Lizzie	8239	Bear, Pinar	4332
Berryhill, Hepsey	8240	Bear, Sampson	4333
Berryhill, Eveline	9174	Bear, Johnson	4334
Berryhill, Mildred E.	9434	Bear, Sammie	4335
Berryhill, Littleton	9506	Bear, Lonie	4336
Berryhill, Gracie I.	9560	Bear, Sarah	6857
Berryhill, Andrew J.	9622	Bear, Rhina	6939
Berryhill, Peggie	9670	Bear, Hilly	6976
Berryhill, Martha	9671	Bear, Nocos Elle.	7195
Berryhill, Rosa Lee	9993	Bear, Ulsar	7196
Beaver, Wilson	559	Bear, Joseph	7197
Beaver, Emma	560	Bear, Samuel	7198
Beaver, Tiller	739	Bear, Bennie	7199
Beaver, Beckey	740	Bear, Lucinda	7200
Beaver, Harry	741	Bear, Alexander	7201
Beaver, Cora	1294	Bear, Polar	7393
Beaver, Lucy	1295	Bear, Mannie	7394
Beaver, Frank	1296	Bear, Lewis	7720
Beaver, Rosa	1493	Bear, Yarner	8117
Beaver, Martha	1750	Bear, Tinor	8233
Beaver, Daniel	1751	Bear, Susanna	8235
Beaver, Wattie	2026	Bear, Fannie	8357
Beaver, David	2632	Bear, Harty	8394
Beaver, Samuel	3551	Bear, Bamma	8395
Beaver, Viola	3552	Bear, Lottie	8415
Beaver, Fred	3797	Bear, Ryder	8419
Beaver, Joe	4146	Bear, Hepsey	8420
Beaver, Lela	4147	Bear, Louis	8557
Beaver, John	4148	Bear, John	8686
Beaver, Jimsey	5085	Bear, Jakey	8687
Beaver, Tiner	5086	Bear, Taylor	8730
Beaver, Riley	5087	Bear, Kizzie	8731
Beaver, Thomas	5088	Bear, Caesar	8732
Beaver, Sam	5108	Bear, Sunthape	8733
Beaver, Peter	5451	Bear, Roman	8734
Beaver, Babie	5452	Bear, Jessie	8735
Beaver, Simmer	5453	Bear, Edward	8879
Beaver, John	5924	Bear, Thomas	8986
Beaver, Halleyamson	6384	Bear, David	9261
Beaver, Jennie	7174	Bear, Harry	9444
Beaver, Alex	7175	Belcher, Simon	799
Beaver, Marty	7176	Belcher, Christopher C.	3511
Beaver, Lizzie	7177	Belcher, Tobe	7294
Beaver, Lou Ella	7178	Belcher, Martha	7295
Beaver, Mollie	7395	Belcher, Bessie	7296
Beaver, Oklow	7396	Belcher, Emma	7297

Name.	Roll No.	Name.	Roll No.
Belcher, Sunny	7298	Beck, Fannie	6974
Belcher, Jennie	9543	Betsey	8069
Berry, Louisa	1262	"Betsey"	9139
Berry, Louise A.	5972	Benjamin, Timmie	7326
Berry, Anna Marie	5973	Bean, Monday	8250
Berry, Frances	9160	Bean, Sabena	9765
Berry, Adesta	9161	Bean, Okfuske	9766
Berry, Josephine	9162	Bettie	8292
Berry, Spire McIntosh	9163	Bellen, Nellie	8379
Berry, Louise	9164	Beartail, John	9315
Bellsted, Tookah	1625	Beartail, Louisa	9316
Bellstedt, Lula	4454	Beartail, Lydia	9724
Bell, Eli	2311	Bethel, Howard R.	9455
Bell, Silby	2312	Benham, Willie	9477
Bell, Silla	2313	Bird, Moses	259
Bell, Cornelius	2314	Bird, Sallie	260
Bell, Willie	2315	Bird, Amanda	261
Bell, James	2894	Bird, Louisa	262
Bell, Jasper	3062	Bird, Ellis	263
Bell, George	3110	Bird, Nannie	264
Bell, Aaron	9532	Bird, Upler	623
Bertholf, Amanda J.	2781	Bird, Margaret	624
Bertholf, Alice K.	2782	Bird, Eliza	625
Bertholf, Emma H.	2783	Bird, Annie	626
Bertholf, Myrtle M.	2784	Bird, Nancy	627
Bertholf, Dewitt T.	2785	Bird, Joanna	628
Bertholf, Bettie L.	2786	Bird, Charlie	629
Bertholf, Ruble Cherokee	2787	Bird, Eva	630
Beef, Jim	2912	Bird, Lewis	809
Beef, Kizzie	2913	Bird, Walter	810
Behen	3036	Bird, Hughey Elmer	1323
Behen, Micco	3037	Bird, Susie	3498
Behen, Chefargee	3038	Bird, Jimmie	4998
Behen, Walie	3039	Bird, Annie	4999
Behen, Helay	3040	Bird, Charlie	5794
Behen, Asa	9464	Bird, Katie	5795
Bennett, Lou Ellen	3099	Bird, Hullie	5796
Bennett, Gertrude	7921	Bird, Willie	5797
Bennett, Lonie	7922	Bird, Edmund	5798
Bennett, Leo E.	7923	Bird, Albert	5799
Bemo, Myrtle L.	3932	Bird, James	6474
Bemo, Alexander	8632	Bird, Nelsie	6475
Bemo, Leon	8795	Bird, Willie	6476
Beams, Mitchell	3933	Bird, Malinda	6477
Beams, Annie	4504	Bird, Stella	6540
Beams, Isom	4505	Bird, Melissa	6566
Beams, Lilly	9896	Bird, Nellie	7194
Beams, Jacob	10070	Bird, Polly	7219
Beshers, Mary	4169	Bird, Sissie	8123
Ben, Big	4565	Bird, Hannah	9390
Ben, Martha	4566	Bible, Lewis	942
Ben, John	4567	Bible, Mulsie	943
Ben, Willie	4568	Bible, Lewis Jr.	944
Ben, Wicey	4569	Bible, Emmet	946
Ben, Robert	9886	Bigpond, Susanna	1807
Benden, Louis	5194	Bigpond, Daniel	1838
Benden, Dicey	5195	Bigpond, Nancy	1839
Benden, Anna	5197	Bigpond, Shackleford	1840
Benden, Jeff	5198	Bigpond, Joseph	1841
Benden, George	5199	Bigpond, Johnson	3254
Benden, Joseph	5543	Bigpond, Lucy	3255
Benden, Jonas	5544	Bigpond, John	3432
Benton, Louisa	5416	Bigpond, Albert	3828
Benton, Lewis	7635	Bigpond, John	3885
Benton, Robert	8070	Bigpond, Rachel	3886
Benton, Jennie	8367	Bigpond, Sam	3887
Benton, Mary	8368	Bigpond, Lallo	3888
Benton, Daniel	10148	Bigpond, Lallie	3889
Beddoe, Virona	5737	Bigpond, Jackson	3890
Beddoe, Morellis R.	5738	Bigpond, Sissie	5389
Beddoe, Hettie R.	5739	Bigpond, Ella	5390
Beddoe, Lonzo A.	5740	Bigpond, James	6488
Beddoe, Malvina P.	5741	Bigpond, Gosse	6489
Bearhead, Robison	6779	Bigpond, Odie	6490
Bearhead, Louisa	6780	Bigpond, William	6491
Bearhead, Barney	7996	Bigpond, James Jr.	6492
Bearhead, Betsey	7998	Bigpond, Uconthla	6493
Bearhead, Polly	7999	Big-pond, Charley	7018
Bearhead, Yanah	10142	Big-pond, Louisa	7019
Bearhead, Mollie	10143	Bigpond, Sophia	8613
Beck, Odus	6971	Bigpond, Martha	8614
Beck, Gerty	6972	Bigpond, Albert	9460
Beck, Otto	6973	Big Pond, James	7016

Name.	Roll No.	Name.	Roll No.
Big Pond, Sarah	7017	Blackgrass, Wisey	7735
Bighead, Stanwaitie	1855	Blake, Simon	8721
Bighead, Millie	1856	Blake, Louisa	8722
Bighead, Sallie	1857	Blake, Phema	8723
Bighead, Konzie	1858	Blake, Peter	9947
Bighead, Addie	1859	Bluford, Fickey	8782
Bighead, Nancy	1860	Blunt, Philip	8966
Bighead, Sampsey	3371	Blunt, Joe	9286
Bighead, Salina	3372	Bowers, Fred	391
Bighead, John	3373	Bowers, Harold	392
Bighead, Lizzie	7519	Bowers, Edith	9719
Bighead, Lottie	7520	Bowers, Frederick	9720
Bighead, Jimmie	7521	Boudinot, Cornelius	643
Bighead, Nancy	7522	Boudinot, Susanna	644
Bighead, Jack	9530	Boudinot, Jessie	645
Biggs, Susanna	2457	Boudinot, Belfoure	646
Biggs, William	5250	Boles, Mattie	1332
Biggs, George C.	9058	Boles, James	1333
Biggs, Jeannetta	9059	Boles, Jennie P.	9035
Biggs, Sinda	9060	Boles, Fred	9036
Biggs, Susan	9061	Boles, Holland	9037
Biggs, Robert	9062	Boles, Pearl	9038
Biggs, Homer	9063	Boles, Cherokee	9039
Bittle, Jacob	3146	Boles, Ruby	9040
Bittle, William	6033	Boles, Laura H.	9041
Bittle, Muskogee Essie	8568	Boles, Charlie O.	9467
Bird-Creek, Jesse	4623	Boone, Charley	1565
Bird-Creek, Mandy	4624	Boone, Zenus	1566
Bird-Creek, Peggie	4625	Boone, Ural	1567
Bird-Creek, Moses	4626	Boone, Thomas	3355
Bird-Creek, Timmie	4627	Boone, Imy	3356
Bird-Creek, Stanley	4628	Boone, Newman	3357
Bird-Creek, Belcher	4629	Boone, Josephine	3358
Billiy, Billiy	5055	Boone, Daniel	3359
Billy, William	5056	Boone, Belle	8611
Billy, Minnechar	5057	Boone, Blanche	8612
Billy, Hannah	5058	Boone, Madge	9484
Billy, Millisey	5059	Boulton, Etta C.	3535
Billy, Sinnie	5061	Boulton, Howard H.	3536
Billy, Simon	8752	Boulton, Etta Marie	3537
Billy, Emma	8753	Boulton, Noco C.	3538
Billy, Annie	9167	Bosen, Sam	4656
Billy, Emma	9168	Bosen, George	5100
Billy, Lumber	9748	Bosen, Mary	6430
Billy, Nancy	9749	Boling, Martha F.	5916
Billy, William	9750	Boling, Sophia O.	5917
Billy, David	9751	Boling, Connie M.	9592
Billy, Susan	9752	Boling, John R.	9902
Billy, Tookah	9753	Boatmun, Laura	6833
Billy, Eliza	9835	Bowlegs, Lulu	7466
Billie, Emma	5944	Bowlegs, Florence	7467
Billie, Jonas	5945	Bowlegs, Ethel	7468
Billie, Lina	5946	Bowlegs, Lulu Winnie	7469
Billey, John	9148	Bonbee	7930
Billey, Pilot	9149	Boney, James	8144
Birdhead, Lucy	7421	Bruner, John	55
Birdhead, Sinda	7430	Bruner, Pamela	56
Birdhead, Meloche	7431	Bruner, Benj.	57
Birdhead, Robison	7432	Bruner, May Bell	59
Birdhead, Willochee	7433	Bruner, Mamie	374
Big William, Hannah	8429	Bruner, Megually	375
Big Mosquito	1904	Bruner, Willie	376
Big Mosquito, Jensey	1905	Bruner, Jensy	1920
Big Mosquito, Albert	1906	Bruner, Richard R.	2007
Big Mosquitto,		Bruner, Harriet	2008
Ta-co-con-wee	1907	Bruner, Pinkey	2009
Big Mosquito,		Bruner, Eliza Jane	2010
Co-yon-fo-lany	1908	Bruner, Henry	2013
Big Mosquito, Agnes	9685	Bruner, Billy	2086
Big Mosquito,		Bruner, Adaline	2087
Care-co-con-thlana	9821	Bruner, Iona	2088
Blue, Sampson	94	Bruner, Bessie	2089
Blackwell, Tecumseh	1532	Bruner, Lilly	2090
Blackwell, Thomas	1533	Bruner, Loney	2091
Blackwell, Lucy	6379	Bruner, Nellie	2092
Blackston, Albert	1599	Bruner, William	2093
Bland, Sue A.	3559	Bruner, Lyman	2094
Bland, Vera	3560	Bruner, Miller	2154
Bland, Era	3561	Bruner, Lucy	2155
Bland, Owen W.	3562	Bruner, Fannie	2156
Bland, Hazel M.	3563	Bruner, Edward	2157
Bland, John C.	3564	Bruner, Lee	2158
Blend, Roley	5656	Bruner, Emma	2159

Name.	Roll No.	Name.	Roll No.
Bruner, Charles Eberle	2160	Bruner, Jesse	7269
Bruner, Grace	2196	Bruner, Rentie	7366
Bruner, Thomas	2230	Bruner, Susie	7367
Bruner, Arlinger	2329	Bruner, Robertson	7371
Bruner, Patty	2330	Bruner, Millie	7372
Bruner, Richmond	2385	Bruner, Minnie	7373
Bruner, Bettie	2386	Bruner, Nola	7374
Bruner, Daniel	2462	Bruner, Roman	7375
Bruner, Bettie	2463	Bruner, John	7403
Bruner, Mattie	2464	Bruner, Sallie	7404
Bruner, Mahala	2465	Bruner, Lizzie	7405
Bruner, Overton	2466	Bruner, Dewey	7445
Bruner, Link	2467	Bruner, James	7475
Bruner, Freeland	2821	Bruner, Togy	7476
Bruner, Rhoda	2822	Bruner, Arthur	7477
Bruner, Mitchell	2823	Bruner, William	7530
Bruner, Joe	2885	Bruner, Ida	7531
Bruner, Dave	2919	Bruner, Wego	7542
Bruner, Josie	2920	Bruner, Taylor	7640
Bruner, Archie	2990	Bruner, Nancy	7641
Bruner, Mary	2991	Bruner, Joe	7644
Bruner, Maggie	2992	Bruner, Annie	7645
Bruner, Annie	2993	Bruner, Hannah	7704
Bruner, Joseph	3142	Bruner, Louis	7705
Bruner, Lucy	3143	Bruner, Mary	7706
Bruner, Nathan	3185	Bruner, John	7826
Bruner, Rider F.	3190	Bruner, Sallie	7827
Bruner, Katie	3191	Bruner, Yoapka	7880
Bruner, Amanda	3192	Bruner, David	8432
Bruner, Thompson	3452	Bruner, Jackson	8509
Bruner, Charley	3460	Bruner, Lucinda	8918
Bruner, Sam	3695	Bruner, Nellie	8999
Bruner, Sindoche	3696	Bruner, John	9216
Bruner, Sulda	4161	Bruner, Esther	9514
Bruner, Lucy	4162	Bruner, Benjamin	9567
Bruner, Emma	4164	Bruner, Cassie	9569
Bruner, Charley	4479	Bruner, Siah	9581
Bruner, Jesse	4544	Bruner, Willie	9611
Bruner, Jennetta	4646	Bruner, Dewey	9636
Bruner, John	4647	Bruner, Dick	9789
Bruner, Miller	4893	Bruner, Millie	9867
Bruner, Liza	4894	Bruner, David	9870
Bruner, Abney	5054	Brown, Younger	834
Bruner, Berry	5200	Brown, Martha	835
Bruner, Polly	5201	Brown, Dick	836
Bruner, Eddie	5202	Brown, Pilot	837
Bruner, Mattie L.	5203	Brown, William C.	179
Bruner, Mindle H.	5204	Brown, Samuel	421
Bruner, Dave	5205	Brown, Dewey	672
Bruner, Louisa	5260	Brown, Nora	757
Bruner, Eddie	5448	Brown, Ella	792
Bruner, Lizzie	5449	Brown, Taylor	829
Bruner, Richard	5571	Brown, Julia	1180
Bruner, Sarah	5572	Brown, John	1181
Bruner, Drefus	5573	Brown, Charity	1182
Bruner, Winfield	5576	Brown, Charles	1183
Bruner, Mary	5731	Brown, Elwood	1184
Bruner, Emmett	5732	Brown, Rose	1185
Bruner, George E.	5733	Brown, Madison	1186
Bruner, Georgia	5734	Brown, Minnie	1187
Bruner, William G.	5813	Brown, Carrie C.	1525
Bruner, Jennie	5814	Brown, Tussekiehutkie	1526
Bruner, Emanuel	5815	Brown, Thomas	1815
Bruner, Lewis	5816	Brown, Timmie	1947
Bruner, Tom	6128	Brown, Jake	1963
Bruner, Wash	6198	Brown, Sallie	1964
Bruner, Judy	6226	Brown, Jennette	1965
Bruner, Suther	6227	Brown, Larry	1983
Bruner, Thomas	6510	Brown, Hardin	1984
Bruner, Mekey	6511	Brown, Buster	1985
Bruner, Losanna	6512	Brown, Robert	1986
Bruner, John	6830	Brown, Bessie	1987
Bruner, Nicey	6831	Brown, Eliza	2053
Bruner, Maggie	6856	Brown, Oliver	2054
Bruner, Jackson	6975	Brown, Myrtle	2055
Bruner, Barney	7055	Brown, Ralph	2056
Bruner, Jackson	7100	Brown, Flora	2057
Bruner, Robert	7182	Brown, George A.	2058
Bruner, David	7185	Brown, Nathaniel	2244
Bruner, Ilsey	7186	Brown, Sparhechar	2487
Bruner, Lillie	7187	Brown, Sinnie	2488
Bruner, Jemime	7188	Brown, Joseph, Wm.	2578
Bruner, Hyman	7205		

Name.	Roll No.	Name.	Roll No.
Brown, Elmer Wesley	2579	Brown, Tah-sa-con-	
Brown, Geraldine	2580	thle-ney	9201
Brown, Joanna	2767	Brown, Cah-ka-le-co-	
Brown, Willie	2768	con-thla	9202
Brown, James	2868	Brown, Tah-con-fah	9203
Brown, Conthlany	2869	Brown, Yah-la-ne	9204
Brown, Samuel W.	2958	Brown, Da-ke-sah-co-	
Brown, Jennie E.	2959	con-ta-ney	9205
Brown, Bessie	2960	Brown, Alice	9404
Brown, Alice	2961	Brown, Addie	9445
Brown, Susan	2962	Brown, Lorena M.	9648
Brown, Samuel W., Jr.	2963	Brown, William J.	9756
Brown, Neosho P.	2964	Bray, Vicey	569
Brown, Jennie	2967	Bray, Mary	570
Brown, Rosannah	3148	Bradley, Lewis	1066
Brown, Echoluste	3150	Bradley, Sam	1067
Brown, Frances	3392	Bright, Nannie	1387
Brown, Peter	3393	Bright, John	6560
Brown, Joe	3394	Bright, Rhoda	6564
Brown, Lucinda	3395	Bright, Lumber	7101
Brown, Charlie	3396	Bright, Leon De Witt	9588
Brown, Willie	3540	Brady, Lucinda	1641
Brown, Julia	3541	Brady, Albert	5475
Brown, George	3823	Brady, Dora	5476
Brown, Legus	3824	Brady, Foil M.	9191
Brown, Lalley	3974	Brady, Charley	9192
Brown, Lucy	3975	Brady, Sam R.	9193
Brown, Nellie	3976	Brady, Martha	9830
Brown, Madison H.	4088	Bristor, Sudom	1669
Brown, Cilla	4089	Brockman, Mary E.	2882
Brown, Esther M.	4090	Brinton, Samuel	2948
Brown, Sammie	4091	Brinton, Sussie	2949
Brown, Nettie	4092	Brinton, Carrie	2950
Brown, Roland	4403	Brinton, Sarney	2951
Brown, Lizzie	4404	Brinton, Edith	2952
Brown, Julia	4425	Brinton, Tilda	7516
Brown, Melia	4426	Brinton, Ruth	9395
Brown, Bertha	4427	Broadnax, Nannie	3426
Brown, James C.	4428	Brummet, Anna	3677
Brown, Francis	4429	Breeding, Eliza	4778
Brown, Willie	4606	Breeding, Dick Bland	4782
Brown, Melinda	4607	Brooks, George	5162
Brown, Flora A.	4779	Brooks, Widey	5163
Brown, Lilly	4780	Brooks, Lucinda	5164
Brown, Bernard	5196	Brooks, Eddie	5165
Brown, Ada J.	5232	Brooks, Mona	5166
Brown, Athalene	5233	Brooks, Joe	7770
Brown, Claud W.	5234	Brooks, Annie	7771
Brown, Banner	5297	Brooks, Emma	7772
Brown, Mollie	5299	Brook, Jennetta A.	6138
Brown, Chailey	5418	Brook, Jennetta L.	6139
Brown, Nannie	5938	Brook, Lillie	6140
Brown, Bettie	6013	Brook, John	6141
Brown, Lou	6181	Brook, Lucile E.	6142
Brown, Elizabeth A.	6263	Brook, Nina T.	8570
Brown, Alice	6264	Brook, Nina	8569
Brown, Josephine	6265	Brook, Frederick H.	9958
Brown, Jackson	6266	Brewer, Jessie	5939
Brown, Louis	6267	Broyles, Ida B.	5966
Brown, Zora	6268	Brimer, Wilbert	7782
Brown, James	6269	Bunner,	14
Brown, Jennie	6274	Bunner, Losie	15
Brown, Nancy	6275	Bunner, Martha	16
Brown, Jackson	6286	Bunner, Indie	17
Brown, Clarence W.	6451	Bunner, Mosey	18
Brown, Wilson	6807	Bunner, Fenie	19
Brown, Joseph	6882	Bunner, Miley	20
Brown, Albert	7078	Bunner, Masaner	21
Brown, Lou	7578	Bunner, Nancy	23
Brown, Josiah	7680	Bunner, Barney	25
Brown, Lizzie	7681	Bunner, Addie	9394
Brown, Katie	7682	Bullet, James	589
Brown, Lydia	8079	Bullet, Lucy	590
Brown, Cosaye	8314	Bullet, Arthur	591
Brown, Zenie	8671	Bullet, Nellie	592
Brown, Ollie B.	8672	Bullet, Johnnie	593
Brown, Ellen	8673	Bullet, Annie	594
Brown, Neilson	8674	Bullet, Ben	595
Brown, Samuel B.	8675	Bullet, Mary Ann	9540
Brown, Mabel	8676	Bullet, Sam	10104
Brown, Con-pe-sin-ney	9199	Bullett, Millie	8658
Brown, Loda	9200	Bullett, Soloman	8663

Name.	Roll No.	Name.	Roll No.
Bullett, John	8776	Buckley, Sam	4709
Bullett, Jennie	9762	Buckley, Liza	4710
Bullett, Jemima	10116	Buckley, Henry	4711
Butler, Sam	681	Buckley, Sallie	4712
Butler, Jim	1468	Buckley, Solomon	4713
Butler, Mollie	3361	Buckley, James	4714
Butler, Manny G.	6215	Buckley, George	4715
Butler, Elizabeth	6216	Buckley, Lucinda	4716
Butler, Fount G.	6217	Buckley, Rufus	4717
Butler, Sammie	6218	Buckley, Ceasar	5112
Butler, Pusler	6389	Buckley, Betsey	5113
Butler, Legus	7029	Buckley, Emma	9692
Butler, John	8948	Burdett, Sudie M.	5292
Butler, Emma	8949	Burton, Robert O.	5460
Butler, Delpha	9571	Burton, Samuel	5461
Buslar, James	715	Burton, Abi L.	5462
Burgess, Lee	813	Burton, Minnie Ola	5463
Burgess, Cumseh	814	Burton, Mary E.	5464
Burgess, Alice	853	Burton, Mary	6809
Burgess, Malissa	874	Burton, Mack	8596
Burgess, Hettie	875	Burton, Lydia	8597
Burgess, Mattie	876	Bucktrot,	7860
Burgess, Sarah	877	Bucktrot, Madie (Wydie)	7861
Burgess, Ida	1042	Bucktrot, Lucy	7862
Burgess, Ellen	1043	Bucktrot, Wysena	7863
Burgess, Dave	1109	Bucktrot, Sam Green	7864
Burgess, Jane	1219	Bucktrot, Conzey	7865
Burgess, Ben	1220	Bucktrot, Angee	7866
Burgess, Lee	3078	Buckner, Samuel	7897
Burgess, Tyler	4226	Buckner, Lizzie	8338
Burgess, James	5638	Buckner, Wiley	8541
Burgess, Susanna	5639	Buckner, Susie	8542
Burgess, Senora	5640	Buckner, Scott	8543
Burgess, Ellis	5641	Buckner, Nancy	8544
Burgess, Emma	5642	Buckner, Mannie	9932
Burgess, Albert	5643	Bunny, George	7972
Burgess, Yarna	5644	Bunny, Jeannetta	7973
Burgess, Edward	5645	Bush, Hattie	8424
Burgess, Riley	5646	Bush, Jessie	8425
Burgess, Mary E.	5647	Burns, Alvin	9175
Burgess, Barney	5648	Burns, Isaac	9176
Burgess, Edmond	5668	Bushyhead, Cleveland	9282
Burgess, Benjamin E.	6327	Byrd, Annie C.	3512
Burgess, May	6328	Byrd, Leah	5080
Burgess, Walter	6329	Byrd, Louisa	5083
Burgess, Ethel	6330	Byrd, Lucinda	5123
Burgess, Gussie	6331	Byrd, Chiska	5124
Burgess, James, Jr.	9817	Byrd, Mary	5229
Buffalo, George	1227	Byrd, Melissee	5230
Buffalo, Yana	1228	Byrd, James	6380
Burke, Maggie J.	1569	Byrd, Judy	6381
Burke, John Thomas	1570	Byrd, Jennetta	6382
Buck, John	1891	Byrd, Lucy Ann	7054
Buck, Rosa	1892	Byrd, Nellie	7838
Buck, Reuben	1893	Byrd, Thomas	7876
Buck, Sillibee	1894	Byrd, Felix	7877
Buck, Annie	1915	Byrd, Dudie	7878
Buck, Perryman	1916	Byrd, Coleman	7879
Buck, Joe	4904	Byrd, Sandy (Leader)	8856
Buck, Simpson	5690	Cane, Charlie R.	39
Buck, Joseph	5780	Cane, Minnie P.	40
Buck, Annie	5781	Cane, Hattie N.	41
Buck, Roman	5782	Cain, Daniel	5726
Buck, Daniel	5951	Cain, Nisey	5727
Buck, Mary	5952	Cain, Roman	5728
Buck, Toney	5953	Cain, Allie	5729
Buck, Roley	5954	Cain, Polly	5730
Buck, William	5956	Cain, Ottawa	7453
Buck, Lottie	6921	Cain, Mary J.	7454
Burnett (nee Hodges), Mary Jane	2227	Cain, Sildy	7456
Burnette, Myrtle	9419	Cain, Legey	10177
Burrow, Thomas R.	2531	Cain, Marsey	10178
Burrow, John D.	2532	Carr, Robert	232
Bunger, William	2685	Carr, Bettie	233
Bunger, John	3972	Carr, Addie	234
Bunger, Enoch	3973	Carr, Ida	235
Burt, Eliza	3207	Carr, Lulu	236
Butcher, Norfer	4312	Carr, Annis	237
Butcher, Mussy	4313	Carr, Cornelius	815
Butcher, Edmond	4394	Carr, Nancy	938
Buckley, Polly	4708	Carr, Alex	1450
		Carr, Annie	1451

Name.	Roll No.	Name.	Roll No.
Carr, John	1452	Canard, Rosanna	4969
Carr, Susanna	1453	Canard, Cogee	6059
Carr, Sallie	1454	Canard, Susan	6657
Carr, Nicey	1494	Canard, Malinda	6658
Carr, Hepsey	1495	Canard, Katie	6742
Carr, Albert	2377	Canard, Susanna	6743
Carr, Thomas	2378	Canard, Louisa	7251
Carr, Severs	2379	Canard, James	9396
Carr, Frank	2380	Canard, Stephen	9408
Carr, William H.	2625	Carthlony	1851
Carr, William	2686	Carthlony, Tahsalay	1852
Carr, Willie	2985	Cahwee, Peter	1949
Carr, Leaster	4350	Cahwee, Ekalarney	3066
Carr, Eunice	4521	Casey, Julia	2210
Carr, Limbo	5826	Casey, Nellie	2211
Carr, Millie	5827	Casey, John Jr.	2212
Carr, Bessie	5828	Casey, Salie	7385
Carr, Salina	5829	Casey, Joseph	9977
Carr, Ellen	5830	Carvy, Lewis	2955
Carr, Nellie	6032	Campbell, Susan	3011
Carr, Addie	6346	Campbell, William	3012
Carr, George	7153	Campbell, Fannie	3013
Carr, Willie	7632	Campbell, Willie	4276
Carr, Archie	8491	Campbell, Frank	9950
Carr, Sallie	8492	Cahkokethlon, Agie	3046
Carr, Etta	9229	Cah co ke thlon	7919
Carr, Mabel	9230	Cates, Joseph	6366
Carr, Harley	9910	Calile, Bessie	3456
Cable, Mary Isabel	1133	Carlile, Ora	3457
Cable, John Henry	1134	Carbage, Monky	3493
Cable, Cora E.	1135	Casteel, Sammie	3697
Carruth, Lewis	1248	Cat, Matilda	4271
Carruth, Dicey	1249	Cat, Annie	4273
Carruth, Katie	1250	Cat, John	4274
Carter, Sarah	1420	Cat, Lou	4275
Carter, Rufus M.	1423	Cahtahwon, Willie	6706
Carter, John Calvin	1424	Cahtahwon, Minnie	6707
Carter, Millie C.	2289	Cahtahwon, Maggie	6708
Carter, Sally	2290	Cahtahwon, Lucinda	9701
Carter, Rosa	2291	Cah-tah-won	7762
Carter, Annie	3582	Carey, Jessie	7625
Carter, Ethel Lee	3583	Caesar, Sissie	7718
Carter, Henry	3650	Caesar, Samego	8823
Carter, Annie	3651	Caesar, Rachael	8824
Carter, Fred	3652	Caesar, Sowikee	8892
Carter, Jim	8963	Caesar, George	8893
Carter, Minnie Lou	9668	Carney, Fulsom	8317
Callahan, Jas. O.	1425	Carney, Wallace Jr.	9639
Callahan, Eula	1426	Cato, Ben	9280
Callahan, Samuel B.	1535	Cato, Rhoda	10144
Callahan, Evelyn	1536	Catch, Willie	9357
Callahan, Gipsie	1537	Castello, Nora	9469
Callahan, Walter K.	1538	Canawa, Missie	10097
Callahan, Benton	1746	Cedar, Susan	6878
Callahan, James W.	1747	Checotah, Martin,	99
Callahan, Muskogee J.	1748	Checotah, Louisiana	100
Callahan, Homer Bryan	1749	Checotah, Millie	1093
Callahan, Mary Alice	9733	Checote, Samuel J.	245
Callahan, Ruby	9951	Checote, Annie	246
Call, Pearl	1557	Checote, Martin L.	247
Call, Gracie	1558	Checote, Samuel J. Jr.	248
Call, Nellie	1559	Checote, George W.	249
Call, Archibald	1560	Checote, Emma	1229
Carnard, Samuel	1773	Chully, Taylor	126
Canard, Sallie	4572	Chully, Millie	127
Canard, David	4573	Chully, Mulsey	128
Canard, Hannah	4574	Chully, Jimboy	129
Canard, Samuel	4668	Chissoe, Austin	325
Canard, Judy	4669	Chissoe, Elnora	326
Canard, Sophia	4670	Chissoe, Sally	327
Canard, Nancy	4671	Chissoe, Taylor	328
Canard, Felix	4842	Chissoe, Dora	330
Canard, Jeff	4843	Chissoe, Taylor	336
Canard, Simmer	4844	Chissoe, William	337
Canard, Rachael	4845	Chissoe, Sadie	338
Canard, Roly	4846	Chissoe, Newton B.	339
Canard, Pusley	4890	Chissoe, Hazel	340
Canard, Billy	4964	Chissoe, Sam	449
Canard, Katie	4965	Chissoe, Lena E.	450
Canard, Lucy	4966	Chissoe, William	451
Canard, Joseph	4967	Chissoe, Willie	641
Canard, Narburg	4968	Chissoe, Mary	642

Name.	Roll No.	Name.	Roll No.
Chissoe, Theodore S.	9411	Chockley, Sebon	701
Chissoe, Sarah	9866	Chockley, Billie	702
Chapman, Mary Lu	515	Cho, Hachoche	8173
Childers, Robert	607	Chupco, Joney	727
Childers, Hattie	608	Chupco, Mary	728
Childers, Sam	609	Chupco, Mistaley	729
Childers, Benjamin	650	Chupco, Barnoche	730
Childers, Annie	651	Chupco, Hennehah	924
Childers, Alice	652	Chupco, Spatker	4355
Childers, Red Eagle	653	Chupco, John	4541
Childers, Lizzie	654	Chupco, Rosanna	4542
Childers, Emma	720	Chupco, Katie	4917
Childers, Chisso	783	Chupco, Toney	4918
Childers, Millie	784	Chupco, James 'C.	4919
Childers, Lena	785	Chupco, Amos	4920
Childers, Emmet	786	Chupco, Moser	4921
Childers, Ida	787	Chupco, Joseph	4922
Childers, Googee	811	Chupco, Tomy	4923
Childers, Lewis C.	816	Chupco, Dinah	7845
Childers, Mahaley ~	817	Chupco, Johnson Taylor	10074
Childers, Amos	818	Chupko, Sarkarye	3354
Childers, Susanna	819	Chupko, Misley	5856
Childers, Silas	878	Chupko, Martha	5857
Childers, Robert	879	Chupko, Major	7714
Childers, Sauce	959	Chupko, Katcha	8003
Childers, Mary	960	Chupko, Betsey	9799
Childers, Bowman	961	Chisholm, Anderson	844
Childers, John	962	Chisholm, Rosa	845
Childers, Ellis	963	Chisholm, Louisa	956
Childers, Edward	964	Chisholm, Nancy	1046
Childers, Tackie	965	Chisholm, Samuel	1194
Childers, Lewis	967	Chisholm, Mose	1325
Childers, Sarah	968	Chisholm, Sophie	1326
Childers, Sauce No. 2	969	Chisholm, Fannie	1327
Childers, James	1003	Chisholm, Shawnee	1433
Childers, Garfield	1004	Chisholm, Mary	2304
Childers, Susie	1005	Chisholm, George	3380
Childers, Pearlie	1006	Chisholm, Lucy	3381
Childers, William	1055	Chisholm, March	3961
Childers, Annie	1056	Chisholm, Sallie	5351
Childers, Mary	1057	Chisholm, William	5352
Childers, Winfield	1058	Chisholm, Polly	6021
Childers, Robert Jr.	2006	Chisholm, James	6022
Childers, Hattie	2441	Chisholm, Mary	6023
Childers, Effie	2442	Chisholm, Polly	6024
Childers, Cooie	2535	Chisholm, Lizzie	6025
Childers, Hubert	2536	Chisholm, Henry S.	6026
Childers, Lydia	2612	Chisholm, Grover C.	6027
Childers, James	2613	Chisholm, William	6028
Childers, Joe	2614	Chisholm, Ida	6029
Childers, Pratt	2615	Chisholm, Mattie	6144
Childers, Paul	2616	Chisholm, George	6145
Childers, Daniel	2708	Chisholm, Bettie	6146
Childers, Mildred	2709	Chisholm, Jackson	6147
Childers, Clarence Wm.	2710	Chisholm, Lena	6148
Childers, N. B.	2791	Chisholm, John	6197
Childers, Susan K.	2792	Chisholm, Jesse	6332
Childers, Ellis B.	3741	Chisholm, Nellie	6333
Childers, Walter A.	3742	Chisholm, Lucy	6334
Childers, Irene	3743	Chisholm, James	7157
Childers, Rachael	3833	Chisholm, Henry	9188
Childers, Maggie	3834	Chisholm, Tom	9267
Childers, Anderson	3970	Chisholm, Pauline	9474
Childers, Lydia	3971	Chisholm, John	9999
Childers, Joe	5958	Charles, Ellen	1052
Childers, James E.	6182	Charles, Gustavus A.	1053
Childers, Susie May C.	6183	Charles, Reuben	1054
Childers, William	6984	Charles, Sukey	8475
Childers, Samuel	8517	Charles, James	8476
Childers, Daisy	9235	Charles, Ellen	8477
Childers, Jim	9430	Charles, Lousannah	8865
Childers, Richard	9452	Charles, Sam	8866
Childers, Arthur	9471	Charles,· Louisa	8867
Childers, Thomas	9494	Charles, Lucinda	8868
Childers, Edward	9561	Charles, Thomas	8869
Childers, Quincy	9575	Charles, David	8870
Childers, Stella	9590	Chalakee, Jimsey	1102
Childers, Tilda	9746	Chalakee, Louvina	1103
Chenewee, Joe	660	Chalakee, Nicey	1104
Chenewee, Ella	661	Chalakee, Thomas	1105
Chenewee, Rider	662	Chalakee, Jimmy	1106
Chockley, Pusler	699	Chalakee, Johnny	1107
Chockley, Mollie	700		

Name.	Roll No.	Name.	Roll No.
Chalakee, Daniel	1108	Coachman, Nancy	3352
Chartie, Washington	1210	Coachman, Mattie	4809
Chamberlain, Susie	1307	Coachman, Ward	5109
Chamberlain, Charlie		Coachman, George	5110
Leroy	1308	Coachman, Lizzie	5111
Chamberlain, Ruth		Coachman, Charles	5365
Hazel	9705	Coachman, Anna	5366
Chambers, Lewis	2619	Coachman, Gussie	5367
Chenosky	4180	Coachman, Guy	5368
Chemarye	4349	Coachman, Aggie	5369
Chamela	5036	Coachman, C. Hobson	5370
Cheek, Levia	5391	Coachman, J. Bryan	5371
Charley, Stella	6523	Cousins, Mattie	269
Chotkey, Nancy	8434	Cousin, Thompson	648
Chotkey, Addie	8436	Coon, Sam	543
Chotkey, Mahala	8437	Coon, Munner	544
Charlochee	6611	Coon, Narlie	545
Charlochee	7419	Coon, Simer	546
Chiye	6727	Coon, Lizzie	547
Char-co-te-ten-na	6891	Coon, Taylor	548
Char-co-te-ten-na,		Coon, Wotka	549
Polly	6892	Coon, Sallie	2373
Char-co-te-ten-na,		Coon, Roy	2374
Katie	6893	Coon, Charles	2375
Char-co-te-ten-na,		Coon, Freddie Carr	2376
Elder	6894	Coon, William	4063
Charlesey, Ellen	7059	Coon, Sealey	4064
Charlesey, Jennie	9625	Coon, Kaney	4065
Charlesey, Lizzie	9626	Coon, Cumpsy	4066
Cho-elle	8184	Coon, Tobler	4067
Cho fo lo che	8380	Coon, Suckie	5694
Cheparney	8400	Coon, Lader	7513
Cheparney	8454	Coon, Lumsey	8280
Charity, Lady	8758	Coon, Gracie Amber	9489
Charity, Christie	8759	Collins, Linda	579
Chardy, Susie	8911	Collins, Lila	580
Chief, Wilburn	8940	Collins, Jinnie	581
Chief, Reuben	9745	Collins, Ned	601
Che-qua-wa	9785	Collins, Lewis	1365
"Cinda"	8307	Collins, Sophie	1366
Cinda	8519	Collins, Jennie	1367
Cloud, Eliza	1007	Collins, Roman	1368
Cloud, Nancy	3428	Collins, John	2381
Cloud, David	3429	Collins, Arcelia	2382
Cloud, Mary P.	4872	Collins, Jacob M.	2411
Cloud, Barney	5417	Collins, Aurora	4409
Cloud, Sophia	8520	Collins, Wynema	4410
Cloud, Dora	8521	Collins, Shannon R.	4411
Cloud, Stephen	8846	Collins, Orvid L.	4412
Cloud, Laslie	9287	Collins, Emma L.	4413
Cloud, Lizzie	9288	Collins, Howard R.	4414
Cloud, Charles	9289	Collins, Bryan S.	4415
Cloud, Mary	9290	Collins, Norma	4416
Cloud, Jennie	9291	Collins, Cora L.	4417
Cloud, Dave	9887	Collins, Wash	6393
Cloud, Miley	9888	Collins, Jennie	6394
Clinton, Sallie	1874	Collins, Willie	6395
Clinton, Rosa	2075	Collins, Addie	6396
Clinton, Louise	3082	Collins, Wash Jr.	6397
Clinton, Vera	3083	Collins, Sunday	8796
Clinton, Paul	3084	Collins, Dora	9453
Clinton, Lee	3085	Collins, Susanna	9594
Clinton, Walton S.	3086	Collins, Nancy D.	9763
Clinton, Celia	3087	Cox, Lydia	778
Clinton, Billie	3422	Cox, Isparhecher	781
Clinton, Willie	3423	Cox, Wm. McKinley	782
Clinton, Elsie	3424	Cox, John	2729
Clinton, Wilson	3425	Cox, Annie	7555
Clinton, Fred S.	3565	Cox, Maggie	7556
Clinton, Willis	4085	Cox, Nancy	7557
Clinton, George	7010	Cox, Sarah	8078
Clinton, Sallie	7011	Cox, Cheparnie	8080
Clinton, Motey	7012	Cox, Kullar	8081
Clinton, Lee	7013	Cox, Ludie	9502
Clinton, Lynch	7014	Cox, Jennie	9628
Clinton, George	8253	Cox, Daniel	2730
Clayton, Bessie	9425	Cooper, Annie	931
Cornelius, Elias	27	Cooper, Emma	932
Cornelius, George	5851	Cooper, Albert	1953
Cornelius, Millie	5852	Cooper, John	1954
Coachman, Josephine	58	Cooper, Sam	1955
Coachman, Peter	3351	Cooper, Stella	9912

Name.	Roll No.	Name.	Roll No.
Cooper, Sarah	9552	Colbert, Bettie	9642
Cowans, Thompson	1318	Coffee, Willie	3654
Cowans, Austin	1319	Coffee, Effie	3656
Cowans, Katie	1320	Coffee, Micco	3657
Coser, Annie	1456	Coffee, Polly	3658
Coser, Nancy	1457	Coffee, Jimmy	3666
Coser, Nutetsa	3685	Coffee, John	7763
Coser, Lizzie	3686	Coffee, Lucy	9792
Coser, Nancy	3687	Cotanny	3829
Coser, Annie	8494	Coker, Lewis	4783
Coser, Mattie	8495	Coker, David	5096
Cosar, Tom	5210	Coker, Wisey	8470
Cosar, Jennie	5211	Coker, Emma	8514
Cosar, Beeker	5213	Coker, London	8773
Cosar, Lydia	5214	Coker, Polly	8912
Cosar, Mack	5490	Coker, Colbert	8913
Cosar, Sissie	5491	Coker, Jipsey	8914
Cosar, Lillie	5492	Coker, Lucy	8915
Cosar, Willie	7362	Coker, Thomas	9054
Cosar, George	8769	Coker, Charley	9371
Cosar, Lucinda	8770	Coker, Leah	9372
Cosar, Melissa	8771	Coker, Ober	9373
Cosar, Chester	8772	Coker, Gibson	9374
Cosar, Sam	9601	Coker, Richmond	9823
Combs, Katie	1617	Coker, Cheparney	9927
Combs, Joseph	1618	Coker, William	5245
Combs, Rena	1619	Coney, Moses	4832
Combs, Birl	1620	Coney, Liza	4833
Covey, Mary J.	1752	Coney, Tom	4834
Covey, John	1753	Colonel, Agnes	4861
Covey, Marcus William	1754	Cornells, Emma	4863
Covey, Byron L.	1755	Cornells, Melissey	4865
Coonhead, Hannah	2076	Cornell, Willie	5454
Coonhead, Nicey	2077	Cornell, Manie	5455
Coonhead, Willie	7985	Cornell, Benjamin	5456
Coonhead, Nessie	7986	Cornell, Annie	5457
Coonhead, Joshua	9328	Cornell, Moses	9578
Cook, Zachariah	2282	Cowe, Sarty	4891
Cook, Daniel	2283	Cowe, Annie	7642
Cook, Wallace	2284	Cowe, Samuel	7643
Cook, Joseph	2285	Cowe, Porter	9159
Cook, Reuben	2286	Cowee, Ella	10023
Cook, Louisa	2287	Compier, Mitchell	5240
Cook, Jesse	2288	Co-den-ny	5593
Cook, Leah	6371	Conpethloney	6483
Cook, Hammond	9401	Cotetan	6487
Cohn, Joe	9983	Comie, Thomas	6570
Cochran, Rockey F.	2305	Colmon, Nettie G.	6746
Cochran, Walter Lee	9459	Colmon, Dollie C.	6747
Coodey, William S.	2422	Colmon, William E.	6748
Coodey, Minnie	2423	Co-co-tah-la-ney	7007
Coodey, Amanda	2424	Conley, William	7398
Coodey, Sarah J.	7154	Conner, Adam	7785
Colbert, Louvina	3464	Conner, Lucy	7786
Colbert, Ella	3465	Conner, Thomas	8593
Colbert, George	3466	Conner, Abbie	9210
Colbert, Benjamin	3467	Conner, Nettie	9211
Colbert, Joe	6276	Conner, Willie	9212
Colbert, Semondy	6277	Conner, John	9213
Colbert, Jackson	6278	Conner, Amey	7990
Colbert, Charley	6279	Co ah	7915
Colbert, Lizzie	5616	"Co-yar-kah"	7926
Colbert, Robert	5617	Com me see	7932
Colbert, Joe	5618	Company, Daniel	8037
Colbert, Mary	5619	Company, Garrett	8038
Colbert, Willie	5620	Company, Sam	8039
Colbert, William	6777	Co ah la lo tu ney	8104
Colbert, Mahala	6778	Co-pah-tan-ney	8525
Colbert, Daniel	7843	Co-nei-sen-ney	8526
Colbert, Lucy	7844	Co-nah-ke	8777
Colbert, Dick	8447	Couch, Roy L.	9427
Colbert, Thompson	8546	Crowell, Edw.	42
Colbert, Ellen	8547	Crowell, Edward L., Jr.	43
Colbert, Sam	8563	Crowell, Robert A.	44
Colbert, Matilda	8605	Crowell, Benj. F.	47
Colbert, Louis	8606	Crowell, Thos. J.	54
Colbert, Walter	8607	Crosby, Mary A.	1110
Colbert, Malissa	8737	Crosby, Charles E.	1112
Colbert, Leemon	8738	Crosby, Elizabeth A.	1113
Colbert, Kizzie	8739	Crosby, Mary Elizabeth	1114
Colbert, Nellie	9284	Crosby, Ellis Charles	1115
Colbert, Linda	9431	Crow, Ah-la-co-hon-ny	1297

Name.	Roll No.	Name.	Roll No.
Crow, Babie	1298	Davis, Hilly	655
Crow, Mollie	1299	Davis, Martha	656
Crow, James	6285	Davis, Cheparnee	657
Crow, Melissa	9262	Davis, Annie	658
Crow, Cinda	9263	Davis, Lucy	659
Crow, Sarnie	9264	Davis, Tommie	759
Crow, Mary	9265	Davis, John	1064
Crow, Sina	10026	Davis, Celina	1065
Crow, Susie	10027	Davis, Sampson	1384
Crosslin, Martha	1615	Davis, Betty	1385
Criswell, Mary J.	2190	Davis, Yoman	1386
Crabtree, Gertie	2384	Davis, Amanda S.	1438
Crabtree, George	2805	Davis, Lewis H.	1571
Crabtree, William F. Sr.	2807	Davis, Florence M.	1572
Crabtree, Elizabeth	2808	Davis, Nancy W.	2125
Crabtree, Hattie H.	2809	Davis, Amos	2126
Crabtree, William F. Jr.	2810	Davis, Lena	2127
Crabtree, Sue Anna	2811	Davis, Ellen	2418
Crabtree, Dollie	3484	Davis, Oliver	2630
Crabtree, Leotia	3553	Davis, Samuel C.	2769
Crabtree, James		Davis, Ethel Irene	2770
Walrond	3554	Davis, Martin	3063
Crabtree, Braxton B.	4357	Davis, Minnah	3064
Crabtree, Malinda	4358	Davis, Joseph	3065
Crabtree, Bessie	4359	Davis, John	3463
Crabtree, Gabriel B.	4360	Davis, Joe	3767
Crabtree, William B.	4861	Davis, Kogee	3768
Crabtree, Lynn	4362	Davis, William	3769
Crabtree, James C.	5806	Davis, Sartie	3770
Crabtree, Shelton B.	5807	Davis, Munna	3771
Crabtree, Lurline R.	5808	Davis, March	3772
Crawford, Henry	5888	Davis, Sallie	3826
Cross, Moses	6918	Davis, Jesse	3904
Crowels, Annie	8152	Davis, Allie	4105
Crowels, Jonah	8153	Davis, Karneyoh	4227
Crowels, Freeman	8154	Davis, Phoebe	4236
Crowels, Katie	8155	Davis, Benjamin	4507
Cumseh, Charley	745	Davis, Milley	4553
Cumseh, Sissie	746	Davis, Sam	4588
Cumseh, John	747	Davis, Necos	4810
Cumseh, Myer	748	Davis, Polly	4811
Cumseh, Annie	749	Davis, John	4812
Cumseh, Thomas	750	Davis, George	4813
Cumseh	5376	Davis, Sissie	4814
Cumseh, Parnoskey	8951	Davis, John	4815
Cumseh, Manie	8952	Davis, Polly	4816
Cumsey, Lewis	3167	Davis, Turner	4817
Cumsey, Emma	3168	Davis, Jack	4818
Cumsey, Vinita	6691	Davis, Peggie	4819
Curtain, Richard	2072	Davis, John	4936
Curtain, Lewis	5044	Davis, Susan	4937
Cummings, Lonie	4441	Davis, Annie	4938
Cummings, David	6818	Davis, Joslin	4957
Cummings, Louisa	6819	Davis, Eliza	4958
Cummings, Benjamin	6820	Davis, James	4959
Cummings, Rufus	6821	Davis, Esther	4960
Cummings, Thomas R.	6822	Davis, Ella	5875
Cummings, Howard	6823	Davis, Willie	5876
Cummings, Boyd	6824	Davis, Selina	5997
Culler, Thomas	4786	Davis, Eli	6056
Culler, Mary	4787	Davis, Jesse	6091
Culler, Major	4788	Davis, Wisey	6092
Culler, Jimmie	4789	Davis, Cokey	6094
Culler, David	4790	Davis, Emma	6241
Culler, Johnny	4791	Davis, John	6689
Culler, Annie	4792	Davis, Selina	6964
Culler, Yarner	4793	Davis, James	6965
Culler, Susie	4794	Davis, Millie	6966
Cubbie, Jacob	4989	Davis, Katie	6967
Cubbie, Rhoda	4990	Davis, Jimmie	7529
Cubbie, John J.	4991	Davis, Dochee	7783
"Culbert"	5779	Davis, Sam B.	7855
Culley, Albert	7415	Davis, Ilsey	8894
Cuffee, Bunnie	7854	Davis, Charlotte	8967
Davis, John	60	Davis, Dennis	8973
Davis, Benjamin	61	Davis, Hannah	8974
Davis, Rebecca	62	Davis, Siney	8975
Davis, Alex	90	Davis, Jeff	8976
Davis, Josiah	91	Davis, Eli	8977
Davis, George	92	Davis, Emma	8978
Davis, Annie C.	162	Davis, Moody	8979
Davis, Noah	256	Davis, Bettie	8980
Davis, Kizzie	613		

Name.	Roll No.	Name.	Roll No.
Davis, Cathie	8983	Deere, Bessie	7498
Davis, Jesse	9246	Deere, Katie	7499
Davis, Joseph	9281	Deere, Annie	7537
Davis, Roy Edgar	9432	Deere, John	7546
Davis, Pete	9503	Deere, Thompson	7626
Davis, Lillie	9537	Deere, Sarah	7627
Davis, Marshall	9584	Deere, Newman	7628
Davis, James O.	9606	Deere, Joseph	7629
Davis, Billy	9608	Deere, Lewis	7630
Davis, Cheparney	9609	Deere, Henry	7631
Davis, Cherokee	9735	Deere, Hunter	8001
Davis, Gooty	9736	Deere, Noah	8553
Davis, Susan	9793	Deere, Mary	8554
Davis, Billie	9854	Deere, Millie	8555
Davis, Lizzie	10004	Deere, Hence	8556
Davis, Ollie	10119	Deere, John	8689
Daniel, Unah	353	Deere, Silla	8761
Daniel, Mary	354	Deere, Sinah	8987
Daniel, John	355	Deere, Ben	8992
Daniel, Annie	366	Deere, Lucy	9155
Daniel, Lusanna	3433	Deere, Isaac	9424
Daniel, Sallie	4160	Deere, Mindy	10058
Daniel, Lizzie	6738	Deere, Mary	10059
Daniel, Martin	6739	Deere, Ruth	10113
Daniel, Thompson	9215	Deer, Jonas	941
Daniel, Annie	9410	Deer, Elizabeth	1862
Daniels, Saloma	1913	Deer, Charles	1863
Daniels, Jasper	1914	Deer, Silas	2207
Daniels, Mollie	1973	Deer, Wesley	2208
Daniels, Sanford	1974	Deer, Lizzie	3766
Daniels, Lemus	1975	Deer, Thomas	3993
Davison, David	1235	Deer, Mary	3994
Davison, Dicey	1236	Deer, Bettie	3995
Davison, John	1237	Deer, George	3996
Dan, Siah	1616	Deer, Louis	3997
Dan, Amy	1664	Deer, Huldy	3998
Dan, Tena	1665	Deer, Daniel	3999
Dan, Billy	1666	Deer, Joe	4042
Dan, Benjamin	1667	Deer, Yarnar	4043
Dansby, Vicy	1968	Deer, Lucy	4044
Dansby, Ella	1969	Deer, Daniel	4045
Dansby, Martha	1970	Deer, Lawyer	4468
Dansby, Andy	1971	Deer, Hepsey	4469
Dansby, Bertha	1972	Deer, Willie	4470
Day, Vinita	3850	Deer, William	4471
Day, Roy L.	3851	Deer, Walter	4472
Day, Lena	4464	Deer, Amos	4473
Day, Henry	8825	Deer, Butler	4474
Danly, Hittie	4673	Deer, Isaac	4577
Dacon, Sardy	5017	Deer, Sarforcher	4578
Dacon, Harney	5018	Deer, Willie	4676
Dacon, Lina	5019	Deer, Mabel	4862
Dacon, Chilly	5020	Deer, Ben	4939
Dacon, Sandy	5021	Deer, Moses	5007
Dacon, Nannie	9232	Deer, Ellen	5008
Dawson, Willie	5817	Deer, Enos	5009
Dawson, Alice	5818	Deer, Jimsey	5284
Dawson, Martha	5819	Deer, Pinky	6178
Dasher, Louisa	6403	Deer, Nora	6282
Dasher, Annie Zora	6404	Deer, James	7060
Dasher, Ida Belle	6405	Deer, Lucy	7061
Damet, Eliza	6901	Deer, Edmond	7062
Davy, Wantay	8512	Deer, Mary A.	7063
Dale, Mabel	9703	Deer, Nellie	7064
Deere, Melanie	557	Deer, Isreal	7304
Deere, Isaac	2695	Deer, Joe	7358
Deere, Louis	3249	Deer, Mary	7359
Deere, Jennie	3250	Deer, Challie	7360
Deere, Thomas	3251	Deer, Wash	7903
Deere, Albert	3252	Deer, Sparny	8042
Deere, Hannah	3253	Deer, Sophia	8043
Deere, Tecumseh	3598	Deer, Alfred	8044
Deere, Nancy	3599	Deer, Ella	8045
Deere, Noah	3600	Deer, Jim	8195
Deere, Mose	4195	Deer, Daniel	8216
Deere, Eliza	4196	Deer, Lucy	8217
Deere, Hullie	4200	Deer, Lydia	8218
Deere, Wesley	4328	Deer, Jackson	8219
Deere, Wisey	4892	Deer, Alice	8575
Deere, Wysie	5227	Deer, Romsey	9359
Deere, Peter	6959	Deer, Munna	9360
Deere, Betty	6960	Deer, Ellen	9361
Deere, Albert	7231		

Name.	Roll No.
Deer, Barney	9362
Deer, Nancy	9363
Deer, Philip	9399
Deer, Eddie	9402
Deer, John	9623
Deer, Thomas	10120
Derrisaw, Cooper	1363
Derrisaw, Polly	3300
Derrisaw, Sissy	3301
Derrisaw, Millie	3302
Derrisaw, Barney	7243
Derrisaw, Toche	7244
Derrisaw, William	7245
Derrisaw, Emma	7246
Derrisaw, Susie	7247
Derrisaw, Polly	7248
Derrisaw, Mattie	7249
Derrisaw, Oscar	7250
Derrisaw, Sarah	7266
Derrisaw, Fannie	7267
Derrisaw, Beeley	7268
Derrisaw, Jimmie	9883
Derisaw, Hettie	1488
Derisaw, David	3180
Derisaw, Sarah	3181
Derisaw, John	4369
Derisaw, Liza	4370
Derisaw, Ben	8828
Depriest, Cordie	1561
Depriest, Nicey	1562
Depriest, Jeff	1563
Depriest, Thompson	2257
Depriest, James	2452
Depriest, Emily	2453
Depriest, Bettie	2454
Depriest, Rufert	2455
Depriest, Franklin	2526
Depriest, Patience	2937
"De-con-sac"	7909
Deo, Nasa	8201
Deo, Thomas	8202
Deo, Sa ki ye	8203
Deo, Jennie	8204
Deo, John	8205
Deo, Thompson	8206
Deo, Kogee	10016
"Dewochee"	9271
Deerhead, Jennie	9989
Dixon, Lela	4667
Dixon, Jonas	9015
Dice, Dove	5361
Dickson, Chicken	6699
Dickson, Nancy	6700
Dickson, Linda	6701
Dickson, Wilson	6702
Dickson, Anna	10114
Dick, Timmie	8416
Dick, Joe	8710
Dick, Lucy	8711
Dick, Junie	8712
Dick, Janatta	8713
Doyle, George	682
Doyle, Sam H. Sr.	988
Doyle, Seaborn J.	989
Doyle, Pearl	990
Doyle, Mary	991
Doyle, George S.	992
Doyle, Nimrod N.	3052
Doyle, Albert	3053
Doyle, Arthur	3054
Doyle, Burris	3055
Doyle, William	3056
Doyle, Roy	3057
Doyle, Myrtle	3058
Doyle, Lee	3059
Doyle, Sarah A.	3577
Doyle, Thomas E.	3578
Doyle, John N.	3609
Doyle, Wallace	5971
Doyle, Tyler	6504
Doyle, Sam H., Jr.	6784
Doyle, Cora	6968
Doyle, Laura	9564

Name.	Roll No.
Doyle, Mable	9675
Downing, Watley	2272
Downing, Toche	2273
Downing, Sanford	2274
Downing, Nannie	2275
Downing, Bessie	2276
Downing, Miley	6090
Doughty, Gertrude	3669
Doughty, Daisy	3670
Dorsey, Alice	7087
Dorsey, Katie	7088
Dorsey, Joseph	7089
Dorsey, Emma	8229
Dolly	8268
Donaldson, Bernie	9857
Donaldson, Sallie	9858
Drew, Emmet	698
Drew, Maggie	713
Drew, Alice	714
Drew, Ella	1679
Drew, Charley	1730
Drew, Emma	2173
Drew, Rachel F.	2174
Drew, Dave	2175
Drew, Amos	2495
Drew, Nettie	2496
Drew, Daniel	2497
Drew, Legus C.	6548
Drew, Mont	9470
Dryden, Mattie B.	2001
Dryden, Lucy	2002
Dryden, Leona	2003
Dryden, Rosella	2004
Dryden, William	2005
Drake, Benjamin H.	6983
Dunn, Tupper	8
Dunn, Susie	9
Dunn, Harry	10
Dunn, Nannie	11
Dunn, Reubon	12
Dunn, Thomas	299
Dunn, Beulah	300
Dunn, Jennie	4456
Dunn, Noah	9299
Durant, Nancy	1213
Durant, Otho	1603
Durant, Belle	1604
Durant, Inez P.	1605
Durant, Robert	3856
Durant, Dicey	3855
Durant, Thos. J.	3884
Durant, Adam	7491
Dunson, Thomas	1547
Dunson, Andy	2027
Dunson, Hokty	2028
Dunson, Edmond	2029
Dunson, Luna E.	2036
Dunson, Lewis	2037
Dunson, Lucy	2038
Dunson, Jemima	2039
Dunson, Mattie	2040
Dunson, Alice	2041
Dunson, David	2339
Dunzy, Jackson	3201
Dunzy, Lucinda	3202
Dunzy, Louis	3203
Dunzy, Dallas	3204
Dunzy, Nathan	3205
Dunzy, Joseph	3206
Dunzy, Philip	4672
Dunzy, Sahweheche	8590
Du Bois, B. R.	6753
Du Bois, Mildred	7173
Duckworth, Cecil	9832
Dyer, Eliza	3981
Dyer, Sarah	3982
Dyer, Amanda	3983
Dyer, Abbie	3984
Dyer, Rebecca	3985
Dyer, Francis	3986
Dyer, William McKinley	9704
Eagle, Ullie	4338

Name.	Roll No.	Name.	Roll No.
Edwards, Sarah C.	1842	Evans, Laura	3611
Edmond, Ben	8241	Evans, Florence	3612
Ekar, Echo	6772	Evans, Mary	3613
Ekar, Amey	6773	Evans, Minnie	3614
Ekar, Dickey	6774	Evans, Alexander	3615
Ekoconney	6868	Evans, Thomas	3616
Ellis, Hannah	4278	Evans, Cora	3617
Ellis, Emma C.	4279	Evans, Ida	3618
Ellis, Hattie B.	4280	Evans, Arch N.	3619
Ellis, Maud	4281	Evans, Lettie	3624
Ellis, Amos	6494	Evans, Wiley	3625
Ellis, Lizzie	6593	Evans, James	3626
Ellis, Nellie	6594	Evans, Richard	3627
Ellis, Minnie	6595	Evans, Charlie	3628
Ellis, Jack	7508	Evans, Savanah	3629
Ellis, Willie	8760	Evans, Dora	3630
Ellis, Martha	9003	Evans, Clarence	3631
Elissy	5378	Evans, Alta	3632
Elle, Nocus	7967	Evans, Clemm	3633
Elle, Nocus	8243	Evans, Lee	3634
Emery, Melissa B.	2745	Evans, Rex Dewey	3635
Emery, Byron Posey	2746	Evans, Vina	5881
Emery, Jones Gladstone	2747	Evans, Mary A.	5882
Emarthla, Tulmarsy	4305	Evans, Minnie	5883
Emarthla, Millie	4306	Evans, Newton	5884
"Emarthla"	6874	Evans, Lona	5885
Emarthla, Jimhoker	6875	Evans, Harrison	5886
Emarthla, Hattie	6876	Evans, Lena	5887
Emarthla, Gabriel	6877	Evans, Lela	9614
Emarthla, Okchum	7558	Evans, Myrtle G.	9689
Emarthla, Selina	7559	Ewing, Peter R.	3218
Emarthla, Tom	7748	Ewing, Susan A.	3219
Emarthla, Micco	7760	Ewing, Arthur E.	3220
Emarthla, Sallie	7761	Ewing, Orie	3221
Emarthla, Echo	9276	Farrill, Sarah	95
Emarthla, Karpetcher	9346	Farrill, Katie	96
Emarthla, Hotulke	9954	Farrill, Henry	97
Emarthlochee, Yarhar	4391	Farrill, May	98
Emarthlochee, Numsy	4392	Farrell, Fred	5720
Emarthlochee, Maudie	4393	Fatt, Dick	271
Emarthlocke, Henehe	7044	Fatt, Hannah	272
Emarthlocke, Hepsey	7045	Fat, John	1491
Emarthlocke, Osirra	7046	Fat, Lucinda	1492
Emarthloche, Daniel	9253	Fat, Bettie	7739
Emarthloche, Sampson	9368	Fat, Sammy	9558
"Emay"	8160	Farmer, Liza	1885
English, Bessie E.	1155	Farmer, Nellie W.	1886
English, Frederick S.	1156	Fair, Hannah	3145
England, Susannah	3597	Factor, Nancy	5412
Erwin, Mary	2412	Factor, Sarah	5413
Escoe, Charlie J.	908	Factor, Harry	5414
Escoe, Zelmo	909	Factor, Keneth J.	9488
Escoe, James	910	Factor, Jakey	7330
Escoe, Tommie	911	Factor, Liza	7331
Escoe, Jean	912	Factor, Peggy	7332
Escoe, Isaiah	913	Factor, Herbert	7333
Escoe, Hattie	914	Factor, Youthlechee	7707
Escoe, John C.	2217	Factor, Sissie	7708
Escoe, Mary	2218	Factor, John	7709
Escoe, Edward	3727	Factor, Lillie	7710
Escoe, Wiley T.	3952	Factor, Fannie	7713
Escoe, Walter J.	3953	Factor, Billy	7716
Escoe, Charlie J.	3954	Farnie	7081
Escoe, John H.	3955	Far lo con we ney	8103
Escoe, Ida Maude	3956	Fayeche	8133
Escoe, Ethel May	3957	Fah-co-con-we-ney	8527
Escoe, Leona Francis	3958	Feeley, Charles	9743
Escoe, Earnest B.	3959	Fife, Elijah L.	393
Escoe, Ella Mabel	3960	Fife, Millie	394
Escoe, Anna	6251	Fife, Nancy	395
Escoe, Johnnie	9706	Fife, Nellie	396
Escoe, Luther	9707	Fife, Lena	397
Escoe, Bessie	9863	Fife, Sillar	398
Estes, Kizzie	3310	Fife, July	1460
Estes, Ollie Caroline	3311	Fife, Sissie	1461
Estes, Joseph Elmer	3312	Fife, Samuel	1462
Estes, Julius Benny	3313	Fife, Chapman	1463
Estes, William D.	3314	Fife, Gibson	1464
Estes, Clarence Davis	3315	Fife, Soda	2972
Estepe	8212	Fife, Molea	2973
Eufaula, Eliza	6710	Fife, Amy	2974
Eufaula, William	8513	Fife, Bessie	2975
Euchee, Billy	7001	Fife, Robert	3135

Name.	Roll No.	Name.	Roll No.
Fife, Timmie	4653	Fish, Katie	4750
Fife, Sarah	4654	Fish, Frazier	4751
Fife, Jessie	4657	Fish, Milley	4752
Fife, Susan	4658	Fish, Billy	4753
Fife, Jennie	4666	Fish, Eliza	4754
Fife, Nixey	4699	Fish, Jonas	5130
Fife, Jacob	4700	Fish, Morleyar	5131
Fife, Nellie	4701	Fish, Annie	7183
Fife, Sukey	4702	Fish, Bessie	7184
Fife, Betsy	4703	Fish, Peter	7299
Fife, Robert	4704	Fish, Lucinda	7300
Fife, Liza	4705	Fish, Robert	7535
Fife, Jimmie	6437	Fish, Arnikee	7536
Fife, Lucinda	6438	Fish, Weleya	7742
Fife, Timmie	6439	Fish, Nellie	7743
Fife, Parsutta	7484	Fish, Willie	7744
Fife, Lizzie	7485	Fish, Daniel	7745
Fife, Narhela	7780	Fish, Jackson	7746
Fife, Sandy	7971	Fish, Okachie	7755
Fife, Allie Ola	8040	Fish, Wattie	7799
Fife, Melinda	8041	Fish, Wisey	8312
Fife, Nixie	8430	Fish, Elson	8325
Fife, Minnie	9285	Fish, Rose	8336
Fife, Levina	9366	Fish, Lewis	8337
Fife, Bixby	9441	Fish, Jennie	8778
Fife, Una	9813	Fish, Jimsey	8779
Fife, William	9906	Fish, Jimsey	8813
Fife, Willie	9940	Fish, Hannah	8814
Fife, Mammie	9941	Fish, Peter	8815
Fields, Ponsey	550	Fish, Nicey	8816
Fields, Cinda	551	Fish, Wiley	8817
Fields, Lartie	552	Fish, Jennie	8819
Fields, John	553	Fish, Thomas	9490
Fields, Lucy	3842	Fish, Sam	9774
Fields, Legus	3843	Fish, Elsie	9924
Fields, Tilda	4107	Fish, Eliza	9992
Fields, Simon	4619	Fish, John	10124
Fields, Nellie	4721	Fixico, Yarhar	734
Fields, Mitchell	4767	Fixico, Cholar	1820
Fields, Artus	4940	Fixico, John	3217
Fields, Waitie	4941	Fixico, Wegus	3934
Fields, Lasley	4945	Fixico, Lettif	4003
Fields, Mitchell	8426	Fixico, Hinny	4004
Fields, William	9548	Fixico, Pefeny	4123
Fields, Jobe	9803	Fixico, Locher	4135
Fields, Solomon	9804	Fixico, Hotulke	4143
Field, Nellie	9342	Fixico, Hebsey	4144
Field, Washington	9352	Fixico, Hulberta	4230
Field, Annie	9353	Fixico, Loisoche	4231
Field, Lydia	9369	Fixico, Angie	4235
Field, Thomas	1352	Fixico, Cheyamy	4298
Field, Lunder	1353	Fixico, Sinhejeschee	4339
Field, David	1364	Fixico, Benjamin	4341
Field, Lucy	4563	Fixico, Cheparney	4342
Field, Punskee	4564	Fixico, Chular	4377
Field, Eblo	4727	Fixico, Sallie	4378
Field, Jesse	4728	Fixico, Sewika	4380
Field, William	6709	Fixico, Liddie	4381
Field, Harper	7067	Fixico, Thomas	4382
Field, Mahala	7068	Fixico, Bastie	4579
Field, Lucy	7069	Fixico, Sunny	4580
Field, Millie	7070	Fixico, Tagie	4531
Field, Kogee	7071	Fixico, Oscoce	4596
Field, Isom	7072	Fixico, Semarhichkar	4597
Field, Frank	7073	Fixico, Willie	4598
Field, Ablow	7689	Fixico, Ilba	4599
Field, Lydia	7690	Fixico, Linda	4677
Field, Walter	7691	Fixico, Fushutche	5079
Field, John	7692	Fixico, Cosar	5216
Field, Taylor	8270	Fixico, Maley	5217
Field, Mattie	9952	Fixico, Emma	5218
Fish, Jack	558	Fixico, Nupsey	5219
Fish, Wo-thlar-sha	1302	Fixico, Mapetta	5223
Fish, Joseph	2232	Fixico, Neha	6687
Fish, Nancy	2235	Fixico, Tulmochuss	6692
Fish, Tom	2921	Fixico, Sallie	6693
Fish, Josiah	4005	Fixico, Barney	6694
Fish, Janie	4075	Fixico, Daley	6695
Fish, Willie	4078	Fixico, Martha	6696
Fish, Elmer	4719	Fixico, Minta	6697
Fish, Little	4747	Fixico, Roman	6698
Fish, Winey	4748	Fixico, Nocus	6934
Fish, Mehaley	4749		

Name.	Roll No.	Name.	Roll No.
Fixico, Cotcha	7234	Fipps, William B.	1520
Fixico, Samson	7235	Fipps, Pearl	1521
Fixico, Sparney	8252	Fipps, Gertie E.	1522
Fixico, Choela	8381	Fipps, Aaron	1523
Fixico, Nocus	8740	Fipps, Vernie	9674
Fixico, Sallie	8741	Finniegan, Onie	2206
Fixico, Benoche	9156	Fier, Dick	5143
Fixico, Ben	9239	Fier, Elizabeth	5144
Fixico, Nellie	9400	Fier, Emma	5145
Fixico, Sampson	9550	Fine, Charity	6210
Fixico, Katie	9595	Fine, Edna Albert	6211
Fixico, Cinda	9855	Fine, Gertie Elbertha	6212
Fixico, Annie	9856	Flack, Cornelia	1611
Fixico, Susan	10030	Flack, Mattie	1612
Fixico, Hully	10032	Falck, John	1613
Fixico, Cheparney	10033	Flanley, William	758
Fixico, Jenatte	10034	Flint, Lizzie	2690
Fixico, Sarna	10035	Flint, Brown	2691
Fixico, Henehoche	10036	Flint, Morris	2692
Fixico, Mina	10037	Flippin, Mary Jane	1217
Fixeco, Pahose	4706	Flippin, Jerome	1218
Fixico, Edward	4707	Flowers, John	6293
Fixeco, Anderson	6941	Flowers, Susan	6294
Fixeco, Betsey	7747	Flowers, Mattie	6295
Fixeco, Katcha	7840	Flowers, Joseph	6296
Fixeco, Ar-ha-loc	7898	Flowers, Lewis	6900
Fixeco, Karwassat	8054	Flowers, Mintie	9837
Fixeco, Katcha	8126	Flowers, Johnny	9928
Fixeco, Salina	8127	Foshee, Mary A.	302
Fixeco, Yahola	8194	Foshee, Sarah	304
Fixeco, Yarhola	8209	Foshee, Walter A.	305
Fixeco, Heneha	8215	Foshee, Andrew Jackson	306
Fixeco, Fushutche	8226	Foshee, William R.	309
Fixeco, Nocus	8334	Foshee, Dewey McKinley	9529
Fixeco, Willie	8587	Foster, Sandy	474
Fixeco, Cano	8921	Foster, Millie	475
Fixeco, Parhos	8932	Foster, Gabriel	476
Fixeco, Mollie	9051	Foster, Noah	477
Fixeco, Tommy	9166	Foster, Moses	478
Fixeco, Dicey	9178	Foster, Samuel	1621
Fixeco, Chippie	9679	Foster, Jennie	1622
Fixseko, Cusseta	10002	Foster, Abe W.	2292
Fixoco, Cho	8013	Foster, Sallie	2293
Fisher, Henry C.	998	Foster, Ira P.	2447
Fisher, Lucy B.	999	Foster, Mattie L.	2448
Fisher, Carrie	1000	Foster, William	3176
Fisher, Ollie C.	1001	Foster, Cora	3177
Fisher, Eloise B.	1002	Foster, Mary E.	3297
Fisher, Joe	1726	Foster, Edna Earle	3298
Fisher, Nancy	1727	Foster, Mary	4582
Fisher, Alice	1728	Foster, Chotka	4583
Fisher, Yarner	1729	Foster, Edward	5215
Fisher, William	2151	Foster, Eliza	5285
Fisher, Sarah	2152	Foster, William C.	5286
Fisher, Sam	2449	Foster, Ida M.	5287
Fisher, Louis Henry	2450	Foster, Claude C.	5288
Fisher, Freida Chenena	2451	Foster, Walter S.	5289
Fisher, Sam	2824	Foster, Robert H.	5290
Fisher, Albert	4422	Foster, Charles E.	5291
Fisher, Amos	4423	Foster, Henry	5975
Fisher, James	4512	Foster, Janie	5976
Fisher, Hannah	4513	Foster, Robinson	5977
Fisher, William	4514	Foster, Lucy	6238
Fisher, Mariah	4515	Foster, Caroline	6345
Fisher, Lewis	4516	Foster, David	6637
Fisher, Seaborn	4517	Foster, Meleny	6638
Fisher, Sarah A.	5682	Foster, Me-se-ley	6683
Fisher, Barney	6816	Foster, Kinder	6685
Fisher, George	6817	Foster, Wolley	6786
Fisher, Daniel	8159	Foster, Turner	6787
Fisher, Lucy	8227	Foster, Betsey	8857
Fisher, Billie	8228	Foster, Adam	8858
Fisher, Mikey	8515	Foster, Sukey	8859
Fisher, Amos	8810	Foster, Charles	8860
Fisher, Aggie	8811	Foster, Lizzie	8861
Fisher, Cheparney	8812	Foster, Malinda	9681
Fisher, Timmie	9903	Foster, Martha	9693
Fisher, Elsie	9907	Foster, Summer	9814
Fisher, Willie	9933	Foster, Willie Frances	9844
Fipps, Alice M.	1517	Foster, George	10031
Fipps, Myrta May	1518	Fox, Nellie	1637
Fipps, Beulah E.	1519	Fox, Sutar	1638

Name.	Roll No.	Name.	Roll No.
Fox, Yarner	1639	Francis, Millie	158
Fox, Alice	1640	Francis, Emma	159
Fox, Luke	1816	Francis, Locha	160
Fox, Maggie	1817	Francis, Martha	161
Fox, Mary	1818	Francis, William	399
Fox, Henry	1819	Francis, Minkey	400
Fox, Charlie	1821	Francis, Thomas	401
Fox, Andewe	1822	Francis, Lena	402
Fox, Sakena	1823	Francis, Leah	403
Fox, William	1887	Francis, Minnie	404
Fox, Sukey	1888	Francis, Mitchell	443
Fox, William Jr.	1889	Francis, Manerva	444
Fox, Sarah	2777	Francis, Mary	445
Fox, Eliza	2778	Francis, Lizzie	446
Fox, Jennie	3505	Francis, Hattie	447
Fox, John	4265	Francis, Garfield	448
Fox, Lena	4266	Francis, Jeff	452
Fox, Cumsey	4267	Francis, Mack	453
Fox, Katy	4268	Francis, William	460
Fox, William	4269	Francis, Jackson	4522
Fox, Lucy	4270	Francis, Sukey	4523
Fox, Willie	5156	Francis, Robert	6202
Fox, Wash	5157	Francis, Millie	6203
Fox, Hearney	5158	Francis, Martha	6323
Fox, Martha	6636	Francis, Mack	7086
Fox, Winey	7579	Francis, Christie	7388
Fox, Jimmie	8699	Francis, Annie	8304
Fox, Addie	8700	Francis, Martha	9496
Fox, Ada	9391	Francis, John	9582
Fox, Jennetty	10057	Francis, Louis	9727
Fox, Ada	916	Francis, Elizabeth	10060
For-lee-yer	5300	Francis, Amos	10061
Foley, William	6113	Freeman, John	432
Foley, Amey	6114	Freeman, Louis	433
Foley, John	6116	Freeman, William	434
Foley, Kissie	6117	Freeman, John	435
Foley, Lonie	6118	Freeman, Mary	756
Foley, Minnie	6119	Freeman, Celia	1489
Foley, Eliza	7834	Freeman, Columbus	1642
Foley, Kizzie	7835	Freeman, Major	2316
Foley, Taylor	7836	Freeman, John	5209
Foluthoker	7881	Freeman, Sudie	5621
Forty-four, Billy	9840	Freeman, Lloyd C.	9090
Foreman, George E.	9710	Freeman, Emma J.	9091
Foreman, Maggie Belle	9711	Freeman, Joseph L.	9103
Foreman, Jeremiah E.	9712	Freeman, Josephene	9105
Foreman, Sarah C.	9713	Freeman, Theodore O.	9106
Foreman, Minnie E.	9714	Freeman, Carlyle D.	9107
Foreman, Annie	9715	Freeman, Lynne S.	9108
Foreman, Stephen S.	9716	Freeman, Estella E.	9109
Foloppa, Sam	9819	Freeman, Rhoda	9248
Frank, Barney	32	Franklin, Lena	3048
Frank, Liddy	33	Franklin, James E.	3049
Frank, Tingo	34	Franklin, Samuel B.	3050
Frank, Amanda	35	Franklin, Ethel May	3051
Frank, Joseph	36	Franklin, Frank	6338
Frank, Norah	37	Franklin, Dave	6339
Frank, Henry	38	Franklin, Harriett	6340
Frank, Short	1830	Franklin, Polly	6341
Frank, Bettie	1831	Franklin, Judy	6342
Frank, Josie	1832	Franklin, Billie	6343
Frank, Leah	1868	Franklin, William Penn	9718
Frank, Hitchete	5911	Fry, Susie	1149
Frank, John	6070	Fry, Robert	1427
Frank, Sallie	6071	Fry, Dema	1428
Frank, Katie	6072	Fry, Lawrence	1429
Frank, Thomas	6097	Fry, Leona	1430
Frank, Ella	6471	Fry, Lottie	1431
Frank, William	7024	Fry, Milly	1432
Frank, Jane	7133	Fry, Sam	8488
Frank, Jimmie	7134	Friday, Jennie	5582
Frank, Dave	7135	Friday, Lewis	7465
Frank, Sammie	7136	Frazier, Nettie	6478
Frank, Austin	7155	Frazier, Alice	8919
Frank, Lucy	7156	Fulsom, William	329
Frank, Addie	7317	Fulsom, George	1301
Frank, Harry	8562	Fulsom, Thomas	3916
Frank, Noah	8853	Fulsom, Louisa	3917
Frank, Levina	8854	Fulsom, Thomas	7277
Frank, Jennie	8855	Fulsom, Millie	7278
Frank, Lizzie	9931	Fulsom, Joe	7279
Frank, Louis	9948	Fulsom, Robert	7286
Francis, John	157		

Name.	Roll No.	Name.	Roll No.
Fulsom, Willie	7287	Gibson, Leonard	5753
Fulsom, Sarah	7288	Gibson, Dicey	5754
Fulsom, Sam	7289	Gibson, Charles	6902
Fulsom, Salo	7290	Gibson, John	8157
Fulsom, Pan-te-ney	8804	Gibson, Wilson	8208
Fulsom, Wicey	9602	Gibson, Elsie	8688
Fulsom, Emma	9945	Gibson, Micco	8829
Fulotka	1035	Gibson, Isparhecher	8830
Fulotka, Susan	1036	Gibson, Daisy	8831
Fulotka, Oscar	1037	Gibson, May Della	8832
Fulotka, Nellie	1038	Gibson, Pearl	8833
Furr, Jude	3522	Gibson, Irene	8834
Furr, William G.	3523	Gibson, Milder	9557
Furr, Benjamin C.	3524	Gibson, Lizzie	9998
Furr, Samuel	3525	Gilcrease, Lizzie	1504
Furr, Perry	3526	Gilcrease, Thomas	1505
Furr, Mamie	3527	Gilcrease, Eddie	1506
Furr, Arthur B.	3528	Gilcrease, Ben	1507
Furr, Archie D.	3529	Gilcrease, Lena	1508
Fulton, Friday	5942	Gilcrease, Florence	1509
Fuswa, Mary	8573	Givens, Choctaw	6797
Gaither, Alice M.	177	Givens, Kizzie	6798
Gaither, Woolery L. F.	178	Givens, Robert	6799
Gambler, Miley	350	Givens, Sam	6800
Gambler, Tommie	351	Givens, William	8055
Gambler, Lizzie	352	Givens, Eddie	8056
Gambler, Wallace	8594	Givens, Charley	9726
Gambler, John	8595	Givens, Hepsey	9731
Gaines, Willie	721	Given, George	9984
Garner, Susan L.	882	Gillis, Taylor A.	9512
Garner, John L.	883	Glenn, Ida E.	2968
Garner, Willie B.	884	Glenn, Mabel C.	2969
Garner, Robert T.	3420	Glenn, Gracie	2970
Gant, Cordelia	1274	Glenn, Elmer	9776
Garrett, Mary	2347	Glass, Neller	5903
Gamble, Willie S.	3286	Gooden, Toney	509
Gamble, Robert Lee	3287	Gooden, John	3133
Garland, Tookah	5097	Gooden, Sagone	3134
Garland, Louis	5098	Gooden, Henderson	3345
Garland, Libbie M.	5099	Gooden, Mary	3692
Garland, David M.	5100	Gooden, Nancy	3744
Garland, Floyd	5101	Gooden, Bessie	3749
Gaino, Yabe	6754	Gooden, Edward	3853
Gaino, Sallie	6755	Gooden, Susan	3854
Gaino, Aggie	6756	Gooden, Jacob	6992
Gaino, Amanda	6757	Gooden, Louisa	6993
Gano, Winnie	8000	Gooden, Nellie	6994
Ganò, Harriet	9964	Gooden, Tontah	6999
Gaddis, Eliza	9651	Gooden, William	7109
George, Long	793	Gooden, Sordie	7110
George, Jensie	794	Gooden, Lizzie	7111
George, John	7002	Gooden, Daniel	7112
George, Millie	7004	Gooden, Annie	7113
George, Lizzie	7005	Gooden, George	7473
George, Alexander	7006	Gooden, David	7474
Gentry, R. J.	1643	Gooden, Chauker	7856
Gentry, Lizzie	1644	Gooden, Daniel	9055
Gentry, Pearl	1645	Gooden, Frank	9605
Gentry, Robert J. Jr.	1646	Gooden, Hoplin	10028
Gentry, William E.	1653	Gordon, Vinita	1322
Gentry, Sallie D.	1654	Gotts, Lucy R.	2814
Gentry, Caroline	1655	Gotts, Harry	2815
Gentry, Mary E.	1656	Goober, Nicey	4540
Gentry, Sallie P.	1657	Goat, John R.	5477
Gentry, Robert L.	1658	Goat, Angeline	5478
Gentry, Bluford M.	1659	Goat, Roman	5479
Gentry, Rachael J.	1660	Goat, Martin	5480
Gentry, Boyd E.	1661	Goat, Peggy	5481
Gentry, Scott	1853	Goat, Katie	5482
Gentry, Abbie	1854	Goat, Wardley	5483
Geneva, Sallie	5231	Goat, Susie	5484
Gibson, Joseph	106	Goat, Wisey	5485
Gibson, Martha	107	Goat, Alfred	5487
Gibson, Gilbert	108	Goat, Rachael	5488
Gibson, Josephine	2721	Goat, Sallie	10009
Gibson, Jerusha	3570	Gouge, Daisy	5695
Gibson, William S.	3571	Gouge, Earnest	8497
Gibson, John E.	3572	Gouge, Jack	8498
Gibson, Joseph A.	3573	Gooch, Henry	6213
Gibson, James T.	3574	Gooch, George	6214
Gibson, Silas B.	3575	Gooch, Ed	7773
Gibson, Mary E.	3576	Gooch, Dollie	7774
Gibson, Montie	3610	Gooch, Arthur	7775

Name.	Roll No.	Name.	Roll No.
Goodman, Sah-con-cah-ny	6654	Grayson, Kate M.	6052
		Grayson, Sunday	6058
Goodman, Ah-ha-co-can-ny	6655	Grayson, Willie	6095
		Grayson, Addie	6098
Goodman, Ta-tah-la-co-con-thla	6656	Grayson, Winey	6283
		Grayson, Mollie	6284
Goody, Jim	9258	Grayson, Mary	7114
Grayson, Sophia	166	Grayson, James	7140
Grayson, Colbert	250	Grayson, Wiley	7141
Grayson, Ben	296	Grayson, Jeannetta	7144
Grayson, Mary	297	Grayson, Buck	7145
Grayson, Christina	298	Grayson, Dickie	7146
Grayson, James L.	870	Grayson, Janie	7147
Grayson, Ben	871	Grayson, Menene	7301
Grayson, Jennie	903	Grayson, Ellis	7859
Grayson, Sam	945	Grayson, Jennie	7991
Grayson, Pete	1078	Grayson, Chimker	7992
Grayson, Robert	1189	Grayson, Foster	8142
Grayson, Willie	1190	Grayson, Martha	8143
Grayson, Isaac	1652	Grayson, Susan	8428
Grayson, Josephine	1674	Grayson, Roley	8581
Grayson, Jim	1890	Grayson, Katie	8582
Grayson, Robert	2097	Grayson, Cecil W.	8669
Grayson, James	2098	Grayson, Wiley	8808
Grayson, David	2099	Grayson, Amy	8809
Grayson, Emma	2100	Grayson, Daniel	8849
Grayson, Dick	2138	Grayson, Rina	9358
Grayson, Jenetta	2153	Grayson, Webster	9437
Grayson, Eli	2202	Grayson, Clarence	9446
Grayson, Katie	2203	Grayson, Thomas	9596
Grayson, Edmond	2204	Grayson, Adeline	9610
Grayson, Henry	2205	Grayson, Lealah	9822
Grayson, Charley	2489	Grayson, Johnson	10063
Grayson, Agnes P.	2490	Grayson, Annie	10064
Grayson, Van	2508	Grayson, Jimson	1725
Grayson, Nannie	2617	Grissom, Maggie J.	169
Grayson, Ellen	2870	Grissom, Myrtle M.	170
Grayson, Eli	2871	Grissom, John F.	171
Grayson, Cora	2872	Grossom, James H.	172
Grayson, Parthena	2873	Grissom, Joseph M.	173
Grayson, Annie	2939	Grissom, Thomas B.	174
Grayson, Robert	2940	Grissom, Fred M.	175
Grayson, Ben	2941	Grissom Viola	176
Grayson, Mahala	3008	Gray, Amy	321
Grayson, Sam	3495	Gray, Louina	322
Grayson, Joe	3496	Gray, Sandy	323
Grayson, Dave	3497	Gray, Lizzie	1096
Grayson, Emma	3649	Gray, Louis,	2387
Grayson, Joe	3707	Gray, Nancy	2388
Grayson, Robert	3758	Gray, Miley	2389
Grayson, Lena	3760	Gray, Louisa	2390
Grayson, Henry	3775	Gray, Louisa	2674
Grayson, Lilly	3776	Gray, Isaac	2750
Grayson, Alice	3844	Gray, Susan	2751
Grayson, Vinnie Ree	3845	Gray, Amos	2880
Grayson, Lyna	3852	Gray, Louina	2881
Grayson, Samuel	3911	Gray, Mary	4400
Grayson, Watty	3969	Gray, Louisa	5357
Grayson, Robert	4023	Gray, Jackson	5358
Grayson, Louisa	4024	Gray, Lee	5359
Grayson, Robert Jr.	4025	Gray, Walter	6414
Grayson, Emma	4026	Gray, Annie	6415
Grayson, Billy	4027	Gray, Annie	6431
Grayson, Nancy	4449	Gray, Siah	6530
Grayson, Walter C.	4773	Gray, Mary	6531
Grayson, Lenore	4774	Gray, Thomas	6532
Grayson, George W.	5189	Gray, Emma	6533
Grayson, Annie	5190	Gray, Edmond	6534
Grayson, Washington	5191	Gray, Jobie	6535
Grayson, Tsianina	5192	Gray, Lucinda	6536
Grayson, William	5235	Gray, Nancy	6537
Grayson, Nancy	5236	Gray, Nettie	6538
Grayson, John	5237	Gray, Willie	7225
Grayson, Annie	3759	Gray, Silanie	7302
Grayson, Della E.	5433	Gray, Eliza	7497
Grayson, Charles C.	5458	Gray, Neteche	7510
Grayson, Cleveland	5459	Gray, Dosey	7511
Grayson, John	5714	Gray, Cemme	7512
Grayson, Rose	5936	Gray, Ben	8279
Grayson, Sam	6048	Gray, James L.	8373
Grayson, Claude R.	6049	Gray, Belle	8374
Grayson, Jennie May	6050	Gray, Mildred	8375
Grayson, Vinnie	6051		

Name.	Roll No.	Name.	Roll No.
Gray, James	8622	Gully, Lizzie	812
Gray, Walter	8623	Guinn, William Ivory	6703
Gray, Louisa	8624	Hardridge, Julia	101
Gray, Barney	8625	Hardridge, Lona	102
Gray, Lena	8626	Hardridge, Goldie	461
Gray, Moses	9663	Hardridge, Joe	462
Gray, Henry	9836	Hardridge, Ella	1012
Gregory, James R.	454	Hardridge, Adam	2095
Gregory, Annie	455	Hardridge, Lizzie	2096
Gregory, Gilbert R.	456	Hardridge, Taylor	2905
Gregory, Albert R.	457	Hardridge, Eli E.	3507
Gregory, Archie A.	458	Hardridge, Millie	3508
Gregory, Arthur V.	459	Hardridge, Lucy	3521
Gregory, Noah	2333	Hardridge, Edmond	4555
Gregory, Carrie E.	2334	Hardridge, Solomon	5772
Gregory, Ara N.	2335	Hardridge, Helen	9599
Gregory, Jesse L.	2336	Haynie, Jeff	270
Gregory, Asa B.	2337	Haynie, Andy	343
Gregory, Foster L.	2338	Haynie, March	344
Gregory, Emma A.	3021	Haynie, Edward	345
Gregory, Andie Lee	3022	Haynie, Minnie May	346
Gregory, Clemmie R.	9643	Haynie, Felix	726
Greenleaf, Sarah	493	Hawkins, Samuel	492
Greenleaf, Annie	494	Hawkins, Sunday	2061
Greenleaf, Ida	495	Hawkins, Sarah	2062
Greenleaf, Malissa	496	Hawkins, Fannie	2063
Greenleaf, Taylor	497	Hawkins, Lucy	2064
Greenleaf, Nellie	498	Hawkins, Winey	2065
Greenleaf, Hullyanda	7452	Hawkins, Daniel	3841
Green, Charley	708	Hawkins, Jammie	5710
Green, Martha	1662	Hawkins, Millie	5788
Green, Stepney	1663	Hawkins, Simpson	6273
Green, John	2195	Hawkins, Wizey	6776
Green, Leah	6060	Hawkins, Eliza	6851
Green, James	6062	Hawkins, Katie	6852
Green, Taylor	6255	Hawkins, Amanda	6853
Green, Tecumseh	6425	Hawkins, Jonas	6854
Green, Jimmy	6426	Hawkins, Wiley	6855
Green, Nicey	6427	Hawkins, Okla Hosta	6860
Green, Jesse	6795	Hawkins, Bunny	7056
Green, Louisanna	6796	Hawkins, Sepile	7085
Green, Fred	6981	Hawkins, John	7280
Green, Alexander	7102	Hawkins, Pink	7281
Green, Nancy	7103	Hawkins, Jackson	7319
Green, Wesley	7439	Hawkins, Nicey	7351
Green, John	7440	Hawkins, Bunnie	7389
Green, Kizzie	7443	Hawkins, Turner	7677
Green, Ena	7444	Hawkins, Mack	7678
Green, Barney	7502	Hawkins, Lucinda	8057
Green, Celia	7503	Hawkins, Susan	8273
Green, Cinda	7506	Hawkins, Corner	8274
Green, David	7507	Hawkins, Billy	8275
Green, Absey	7694	Hawkins, Susie	8501
Green, Hagie	7727	Hawkins, Lizzie	8703
Green, Simpson	7808	Hawkins, Sarah	8704
Green, Caesar	7809	Hawkins, Johnnie	8705
Green, Mary	7810	Hawkins, Katie	8706
Green, Lucy	8361	Hawkins, James	8774
Green, Sarlarka	8567	Harvison, George D.	561
Green, Louisa	9327	Harvison, Lula E.	562
Grace, John	1602	Harvison, Nellie May	563
Grant, U. S.	1824	Harvison, Thomas C.	2762
Grant, Assie	1825	Harvison, Reese	3506
Grant, Sam Miller	1826	Harvison, Dollie	8504
Grant, Timmie	1827	Harvison, Floyd	8505
Grant, Lucy	1828	Harvison, Irene	8506
Grant, Frank	1829	Harvison, Clifford	8507
Grant, Niffey	5661	Harvison, Marie	8508
Grant, Meley	5662	Harvison, Thelma B.	9389
Grant, Billie	5663	Harris, Thomas	565
Grant, Minnie	5664	Harris, Cheasquah	2180
Grant, Stella	9583	Harris, Buena Vista	2181
Graves, Leona	2543	Harris, Mabel Anna	2182
Graves, Bonnie Gertrude	2544	Harris, Walter	3636
Ground, Willie	3847	Harris, Ellen	4433
Grimes, Willie	6605	Harris, Charles	4434
Grimes, Susannah	6995	Harris, William R.	4480
Grammar, Charles	7560	Harris, Johnson E.	4481
Greenwood, Hannah	8493	Harris, Ella	4482
Greenwood, Lewis	8634	Harris, Bird	4483
Greenwood, Dick	9157	Harris, Su Anna	4484
Greenwood, Alice	9591	Harris, Isparhecher	4485

Name.	Roll No.	Name.	Roll No.
Harris, Mehele	5993	Harjo, Abbie	4759
Harris, Willie	5994	Harjo, Chapley	4766
Harris, Lula	10014	Harjo, Wacus	4802
Harris, Red Bird	10017	Harjo, Millie	4803
Harjo, Chenubbe	572	Harjo, Nancy	4804
Harjo, Sartupe	573	Harjo, Addie	4805
Harjo, Arley	574	Harjo, Lillie	4806
Harjo, Mollea	575	Harjo, Bunny	4807
Harjo, Susan	576	Harjo, Lucy	4808
Harjo, Yahola	668	Harjo, Lumka	4827
Harjo, Jennetta	1240	Harjo, Kissie	4828
Harjo, Willie	1279	Harjo, Nargie	4829
Harjo, Henry M.	1795	Harjo, Annie	4830
Harjo, Katie	1796	Harjo, Seyada	4831
Harjo, Naomi	1797	Harjo, Mehaley	4858
Harjo, Lillie May	1798	Harjo, Linda	4906
Harjo, Bennie	2030	Harjo, Sunday	4907
Harjo, Mattie	2050	Harjo, Jenna	4908
Harjo, Minda	2051	Harjo, Cheparney	4909
Harjo, Tommy	2052	Harjo, Thompson	4910
Harjo, Littiff	2161	Harjo, Edmund	4911
Harjo, Mary	2162	Harjo, Marsey	4912
Harjo, Ben	2163	Harjo, Cho-co-te	4913
Harjo, Salina	2164	Harjo, Annie	4914
Harjo, Cinda	2165	Harjo, Fushutche	5000
Harjo, Buzzie	2166	Harjo, Eliza	5001
Harjo, Sarah	2167	Harjo, Sunday	5002
Harjo, Wilyarmy	2413	Harjo, Sampson	5003
Harjo, Susie	2414	Harjo, James	5004
Harjo, Jackson	3248	Harjo, Joseph	5005
Harjo, Aharlok	3303	Harjo, Jonas	5006
Harjo, Jockey	3304	Harjo, Melosia	5026
Harjo, Woxey	3363	Harjo, Connuggy	5115
Harjo, Hepsey	3364	Harjo, Polly	5116
Harjo, Peter	3365	Harjo, Minar	5117
Harjo, Rosanna	3366	Harjo, Mussey	5118
Harjo, Nathan	3367	Harjo, Joseph	5119
Harjo, Obie	3368	Harjo, Johnson	5129
Harjo, Joe	3369	Harjo, Edmond	5175
Harjo, Louvina	3370	Harjo, Newman	5176
Harjo, Lizzie	3501	Harjo, Nancy	5241
Harjo, Johnson	3502	Harjo, Bennie	5244
Harjo, Liza	3725	Harjo, Willie	5276
Harjo, Oscar	3726	Harjo, Tilda	5277
Harjo, Moser	3787	Harjo, Hagie	5278
Harjo, Mahaley	3788	Harjo, Sunduller	5301
Harjo, Sulphur	3900	Harjo, Susie	5302
Harjo, Lizzie	3901	Harjo, Peter	5303
Harjo, Leosta	3902	Harjo, Bunny	5526
Harjo, Louisa	3903	Harjo, Toney	5530
Harjo, Kogee	3905	Harjo, Jimsey	5553
Harjo, Melinhoda	4053	Harjo, Sulka	5554
Harjo, Millyanna	4054	Harjo, Joshua	5555
Harjo, Thaneda	4055	Harjo, Jack	5557
Harjo, Hutchenubbe	4056	Harjo, Katie	5558
Harjo, Silbie	4057	Harjo, Mollie	5559
Harjo, Oklossie	4058	Harjo, Maggie	5588
Harjo, Samson	4059	Harjo, Emarthla	5589
Harjo, Nancy	4060	Harjo, Beasley	5822
Harjo, Nekie	4061	Harjo, Lumsey	5845
Harjo, Mulley	4062	Harjo, Lilla	5918
Harjo, Annie	4103	Harjo, Rhoda	5919
Harjo, Missey	4106	Harjo, Lizzie	6225
Harjo, Nannie	4126	Harjo, Lucinda	6228
Harjo, Willie	4127	Harjo, Anna	6229
Harjo, Johnson	4131	Harjo, Betty	6230
Harjo, Jane	4132	Harjo, Wotko	6239
Harjo, Louvina	4133	Harjo, Millie	6240
Harjo, Chofolop	4181	Harjo, Shanco	6398
Harjo, Lucy	4182	Harjo, Maudie	6399
Harjo, Lody	4183	Harjo, Sandy	6400
Harjo, Annoche	4186	Harjo, Willie	6408
Harjo, Hotulke	4232	Harjo, Charley	6409
Harjo, Hannah	4233	Harjo, Cowe	6440
Harjo, Tulmochus	4258	Harjo, Peggy	6441
Harjo, Chemona	4259	Harjo, Alex	6469
Harjo, Ochees	4310	Harjo, Nancy	6470
Harjo, Mitchie	4311	Harjo, Albert	6472
Harjo, Wattie	4340	Harjo, Martha	6473
Harjo, Joseph	4698	Harjo, Aharluck	6502
Harjo, Waxie	4755	Harjo, Tommie	6503
Harjo, Suwerneryeche	4756	Harjo, Eufaula	6554
Harjo, Ceasar	4757	Harjo, Sulsey	6555

Name.	Roll No.	Name.	Roll No.
Harjo, Nancy	6556	Harjo, Lewis	8254
Harjo, Lewey	6557	Harjo, Eufaula	8258
Harjo, Israel	6558	Harjo, Hillis	8264
Harjo, Henry	6559	Harjo, Cinda	8271
Harjo, Turpus	6571	Harjo, Joker	8272
Harjo, Sar-wak-ho-che	6572	Harjo, Kutchussee	8286
Harjo, Lucy	6573	Harjo, Whynie	8287
Harjo, William	6574	Harjo, Haleya	8288
Harjo, Annie	6575	Harjo, Charley	8289
Harjo, James	6576	Harjo, Noah	8290
Harjo, Belle	6577	Harjo, Yarkinha	8313
Harjo, Marsey	6579	Harjo, Woxie	
Harjo, Folohkee	6580	Emarthla	8322
Harjo, Willie	6589	Harjo, Millie	8323
Harjo, Lowiney	6590	Harjo, Simon	8324
Harjo, Billy	6606	Harjo, Shawnee	8332
Harjo, Kizzie	6607	Harjo, Contah	8333
Harjo, Mary	6609	Harjo, Its has	8350
Harjo, Amos	6635	Harjo, Liger	8372
Harjo, Amos	6717	Harjo	8574
Harjo, Tulsa	6720	Harjo, Keper	8583
Harjo, Ebner	6721	Harjo, Sophia	8589
Harjo, Josiah	6722	Harjo, Tulmochus	8591
Harjo, Nocus	6954	Harjo, Jennie	8652
Harjo, Moleyar	6955	Harjo, Chinee	8653
Harjo, Selina	6956	Harjo, Polly	8651
Harjo, Chelokke	7049	Harjo, Taylor	8655
Harjo, Ka-pet-cha	7082	Harjo, Cheparnoche	8850
Harjo, Nellie	7083	Harjo, Yarma	8851
Harjo, Jimsey	7150	Harjo, Melene	8852
Harjo, Daniel	7151	Harjo, Nancy	8878
Harjo, Susie	7152	Harjo, Tulsa	8899
Harjo, Itshas	7179	Harjo, Sookey	8900
Harjo, Pin	7220	Harjo, George	8901
Harjo, Miloche	7221	Harjo, Jemima	8902
Harjo, Alec Little	7222	Harjo, Josiah	8903
Harjo, Polly	7223	Harjo, Noah	8916
Harjo, Peter	7224	Harjo, Susie	8917
Harjo, John	7226	Harjo, Eliza	8922
Harjo, Jennie	7227	Harjo, Lucinda	8923
Harjo, Noah	7228	Harjo, Thomas	8924
Harjo, Addie	7229	Harjo, Lilly	8925
Harjo, Leah	7230	Harjo, Totkis	8926
Harjo, Kepsy	7270	Harjo, Susie	8927
Harjo, Nocus	7325	Harjo, Chotkee	8928
Harjo, Muska	7361	Harjo, Rhoda	8929
Harjo, Yar-teh-ka	7387	Harjo, Seaver	8930
Harjo, Talof	7501	Harjo, Tommoche	8931
Harjo, Sophia	7509	Harjo, Thlathlo	8936
Harjo, Alex	7567	Harjo, Stephen	8938
Harjo, Nancy	7611	Harjo, Kogee	8939
Harjo, Yarner	7612	Harjo, Louisa	8953
Harjo, Hillis	7650	Harjo, Linda	8954
Harjo, Mary	7651	Harjo, John	8955
Harjo, George	7652	Harjo, Hannah	8956
Harjo, Willie	7653	Harjo, Frank	8957
Harjo, Louisa	7654	Harjo, Joe Tiger	8958
Harjo, Poley	7655	Harjo, Nocus	9026
Harjo, Malinda	7656	Harjo, Tilla	9027
Harjo, Kussie	7737	Harjo, Missie	9034
Harjo, Lucy	7740	Harjo, Cheparney	9076
Harjo, Cono	7802	Harjo, Effie	9133
Harjo, Yahola	7803	Harjo, Houston	9134
Harjo, Lucy	7804	Harjo, Millie	9135
Harjo, James Larney	7805	Harjo, Sallie	9136
Harjo, Okfuske	7816	Harjo, Segar	9137
Harjo, Choe ka	7889	Harjo, Neha Thlocco	9231
Harjo, Chitto	7934	Harjo, Dave	9237
Harjo, Wotko	8022	Harjo, Cinnie	9242
Harjo, Tarkosar	8052	Harjo, Huntie	9243
Harjo, Jeannetta	8093	Harjo, Legus	9268
Harjo, Willie	8094	Harjo, Ispokoke	9298
Harjo, Buddie	8095	Harjo, Kuncheya	9317
Harjo, Jennie	8096	Harjo, Marsey	9318
Harjo, Tuckabatchee	8166	Harjo, Jimmie	9329
Harjo, Woxie	8180	Harjo, Leah	9348
Harjo, Estonahe	8181	Harjo, Yarkinhar	9349
Harjo, Jonas	8182	Harjo, Kosapa	9376
Harjo, Tarsee	8183	Harjo, Needa	9377
Harjo, Sawonoke	8190	Harjo, Maleya	9378
Harjo, Mary	8191	Harjo, Lumsey	9379
Harjo, Milley	8192	Harjo, Mamie	9481
Harjo, Hotulke	8193	Harjo, Alice	9485

Name.	Roll No.
Harjo, Minnie	9491
Harjo, Amos	9539
Harjo, Kina	9680
Harjo, Jessie	9929
Harjo, Aholak	9980
Harjo, Sallie	10021
Harjo, Thluc-pol-i-key	10022
Harjo, Mitchell	10076
Harjo, Mona	10093
Harjo, Lizzie	10105
Harjo, Maria	10108
Harjo, Jessie	10109
Harjo, Rina	10110
Harjo, Chuckaleesa·	10111
Harjo, Pen	10118
Haney, William	614
Haney, Narchker	8456
Haney, Lena	8457
Haney, Leah	8458
Haney, Emma	8754
Haikey, Frank,	696
Haikey, Nancy	697
Haikey, Sukey	716
Haikey, Eliza	717
Haikey, Susanna	718
Haikey, Ella	719
Haikey, Ben, Jr.	947
Haikey, Ben	950
Haikey, Jennetta	951
Haikey, Dave	952
Haikey, Ellis	953
Haikey, John	954
Haikey, Edward	955
Haikey, Malissa	1459
Haikey, Maymie	9407
Haikey, Kono	9942
Haynes, Lasley	724
Haynes, Lizzie	725
Haynes, Laslie	3144
Haynes, Samuel J.	5683
Haynes, Sarah	5684
Haynes, Stella J.	5685
Haynes, John	5686
Haynes, Elijah	5687
Haynes, Joseph	5715
Haynes, Dicey	5716
Haynes, James	5925
Haynes, Martha	5926
Haynes, Thomas	926
Haynes, Tochee	927
Haynes, Thomas Jr.	928
Haynes, Liddie	933
Harrison, Eli	1080
Harrison, Ellen	1081
Harrison, Jimmy	1082
Harrison, Lizzie	1083
Harrison, Nero	1085
Harrison, Benjamin	1087
Harrison, Mamie	1903
Harrison, Keltie	3117
Harrison, William	3462
Harrison, Charles	5338
Harrison, Harvey	5339
Harrison, Napoleon	5497
Harrison, Susan	5498
Harrison, Peter	5499
Harrison, Lena	5500
Harrison, Lucy	5501
Harrison, John	5502
Harrison, Emma	9533
Harper, Albert	1291
Harper, Jennie	1292
Harper, Alfred	1293
Harper, Ida	6726
Harper, Marfe	8129
Harper, Peggie	8130
Harper, Pettie	8131
Harper, Jim	8134
Harper, Koke	8135
Harper, Peggie	8136
Harper, Somaye	8137
Harper, Shawnee	8413
Harper, Mary	8414

Name.	Roll No.
Harper, John	8461
Harper, Lizzie	9461
Harper, Mattie	9462
Harper, Simon	9732
Harmon, Dan A.	1337
Harmon, Ben T.	2498
Harmon, Will S.	2499
Harman, Laura A.	9442
Harry Simon	1635
Harry, Rebecca	1636
Harry, John	2883
Harry, Mary	2884
Harry, Willie	2886
Harry, Edmond	3331
Harry, Sartarpeka	3332
Harry, Ella	3333
Harry, Shawnee	3334
Harry, Willie	3335
Harry, Robert.	3818
Harry, Sally	3819
Harry, Albert	3830
Harry, Dick,	3831
Harry, Cornelius	3832
Harry, David	3857
Harry, Martha	3858
Harry, Nora	3859
Harry, Luke	3860
Harry, Legus	3861
Harry, Peggie	3862
Harry, Henry	3864
Harry, Micey	3865
Harry, Aggie	3866
Harry, Jackson	3867
Harry, August	3868
Harry, Tony	3869
Harry, Nellie	3870
Harry, Eddie	3871
Harry, Robert	3872
Harry, Rufus	3874
Harry, Wheaton	6998
Harry, Caroline	8993
Harry, Martha	7297
Harry, Roy	9517
Harwell, Mary L.	2256
Harwell, Walter B.	9845
Harwell, Lilla M.	9846
Harwell, Lena M.	9847
Harwell, Nina P.	9848
Harrington, Amanda	2565
Harrington, Lucy	2566
Hamilton, Pearly	2618
Hamilton, Peter	2748
Hamilton, Rose	2749
Hamilton. Alex	9476
Harner, Ella·	2633
Harner, Leo George	2634
Hammer, Louis	8433
Hance, Jennie	2835
Hance, Elzonie	2836
Hance, William W.	2837
Hance, Bessie	9466
Hallford, Emaline	3162
Hallford, Ross	3164
Hallford, Annie Belle	3165
Hallford, Anoma	3166
Har-ka-wa-tlflany	3227
Hagie, Ben	3260
Hall, James	3620
Hall, Sandy	3621
Hall, David	3622
Hall, George	3623
Hall, Hannah E.	4112
Hall, Alvie	4113
Hall, Melburn	4114
Hall, Lena	6429
Hall, Nora	8369
Hall, George	9553
Hall, Louis S.	9635
Hannah,·	2891
Harjochee, Isparney	4049
Harjochee, Amanda	4050
Harjochee, Amos	4051

Name.	Roll No.	Name.	Roll No.
Harjochee, Joseph	4192	Herrick, Juanita	1204
Harjochee, Losana	4220	Herrick, Willie J.	9656
Harjochee, Jimmie	4221	Herrod, Samuel	1410
Harjochee, Harper	4222	Herrod, Cilla	1411
Harjochee, Sas-ho-ye	9392	Herrod, Maria	1412
Harjoche, Yarteka	4343	Herrod, Mary	1413
Harjoche, Charfeny	4344	Herrod, Mary L.	2137
Harjoche, Nity	4346	Herrod, Sophia	3238
Harjoche, Keseathor	4347	Herrod, Andy	5467
Harjoche, Nokos	6758	Herrod, Rosanna	7252
Harjoche, Melosey	6759	Herrod, Rosanna	7614
Harjoche, Lizzie	6760	Herrod, Liza	7767
Harjoche, Hulbutta	8649	Herrod, Nettie	7768
Harjoche, Mahwe	8650	Herrod, Lena	7769
Harjoche, Lena	9801	Herrod, David	8996
Harjoche,,Lottie	10146	Hendrickson, Eliza	3399
Harchoche, Tulwar	4301	Hendrickson, Frank	3400
Harchoche, Finar	4302	Hendrickson, Thomas	9654
Harchoche, Lydia	4303	Henry, Lucy	3545
Harchoche, Dicey	4304	Henry, Estella May	3546
Halley, Hosa	4405	Henry, Louise	3547
Halley, Taylor	9747	Henry, Lula	3548
Hammonds, Jennie	4431	Henry, Beulah	3549
Hammonds, Embry	4432	Henry, Jessie	3550
Hailey, Melissa	4590	Henry, Hugh	3641
Hailey, Lony	4591	Henry, Luella	3642
Hays, Henry	4655	Henry, Patrick	3643
Hayes, Marchie	6661	Henry, Mack	3644
Hayes, Parhie	6662	Henry, Annie May	3645
Hay, John	6895	Henry, Woodson	3646
Hay, Egie	6896	Henry, Hettie	3647
Hay, Deshalecoweney	6897	Henry, Hugh, Jr.	3648
Hay, Johnson	9587	Henry, Frank	3883
Hale, Summer	4838	Henry, James	4430
Hale, Lucy	4839	Henry, Thomas	5905
Hale, Mabel	4840	Henry, Mary	5906
Hale, Ollie	8046	Henry, Francis	5907
Hale, Jasper	8635	Henry, Walter	5908
Hardage, Lewis	5168	Henry, Peggy	8633
Hardage, Rebecca	5169	Henry, James	9343
Hardage, Ruth E.	5170	Henry, Edmond	10123
Hardage, Joseph H.	5171	Hennehughee, Watley	4215
Hardage, Hannah	5172	Hennehughee, Hene	4216
Hardage, May	5173	Hennehughee, Roney	4217
Hardage, Lucy	6157	Henehochee, Miny	4314
Harley, Samson	7406	Henehochee, Beenie	4315
Harley, Jennie	7407	Henecochee, Engie	4316
Harley, Alex	9786	Henehochee, Lena	4317
Harrod, Sarah	8020	Henehochee, Hopoeth	9838
Harjoge, Hulputta	8088	Hen, Betsey	4493
Harjoge, Marfey	8089	Hen, Willie	4570
Harjoge, Frank	8090	Henshaw, Thomas	4849
Harjoge, Chagee	8091	Hetahcoweney	6485
Hart, Lucy	6344	Hettie	7734
Har-no-gee	5402	Hemer, Louie	8165
Har lar char	6871	Hengst, Emma J.	9084
Hayne, Annie	8301	Hengst, William H.	9085
Hayne, Mollie	8302	Hengst, Virginia P.	9086
Haines, David W.	8561	Hengst, Frankfort	9087
Harge, George	8648	Hengst, Arena Marie	9088
Hamby, Dora	9994	Hennehuchee, Hardy	9273
Hamby, Myrtle	9995	He-tah-co-co-tan	9957
Hamby, Archie	9996	Hill, George W.	48
Harriott, Nettie	10170	Hill, Lucy	49
Harriott, Amos W	10171	Hill, William McKinley	50
Harriott, Louisa M.	10172	Hill, Amanda	51
Harriott, Joseph F.	10173	Hill, Walter,	52
Hennehah, Eli	554	Hill, Melissa	53
Hennehah, Lucinda	555	Hill, Ada	1111
Heneha, Lena	568	Hill, Lucy	2662
Heneha, Eannah	4080	Hill, David	3447
Heneha, Artussee	7392	Hill, Jennie	3448
Heneha, Janie	7610	Hill, John	3449
Heneha, Chukchat	8207	Hill, Lilly	3450
Heneha, Matup	8211	Hill, Jackson	3451
Heneha, Mary	9839	Hill, Cilla	4659
Heneha, Lussie	9840	Hill, Charley	4663
Heneha,Osa	10089	Hill, James H.	4664
Helton, Lonie	665	Hill, Emma	4731
Helton, Jesse Newman	9908	Hill, Belcher	4732
Herrick, Mary	1202	Hill, William	5027
Herrick, Leo, Jr.	1203	Hill, Lena	5028

Name.	Roll No.	Name.	Roll No.
Hill, Jesse	5029	Hodge, Alvin T.	2225
Hill, Tony	5030	Hodge, Mary Jane	2226
Hill, Johnston	5031	Hodge, Mary Jane	2227
Hill, Sunday	5033	Hodge, Dav Mc.	2228
Hill, Hannah	5034	Hodge, May	2229
Hill, Mitchell	5789	Hodge, Lula M.	2267
Hill, David	6242	Hodge, Horace	2523
Hill, Millie	6243	Hodge, Green	2764
Hill, Minnie	6244	Hodge, David M.	3378
Hill, James	6373	Hodge, Susan	3379
Hill, Polly	6374	Hodge, Johnson F.	5569
Hill, Luella	6375	Hodge, Mary	5570
Hill, Kate	6376	Hodge, John N.	5978
Hill, Leah	6377	Hodge, Ethel	5979
Hill, Fanny	6378	Hodge, Oma M.	5980
Hill, Arney	6446	Hodge, Lela	6360
Hill, Ida	6447	Hodge, Virginia	9375
Hill, Elmer	6524	Hodges, Green F.	6156
Hill, Dave	6632	Horn, Nellie	1334
Hill, Sallie	6633	Horn, Nellie	1334
Hill, Tobe	7165	Horn, Minnie E.	1335
Hill, Nigee	7166	Horn, Mattie E.	1336
Hill, Mollie	7167	Horn, Sam	1580
Hill, Lizzie	7168	Holman, Dora	1794
Hill, Willie	7169	Holden, Thomas	1895
Hill, Annie	7170	Holden, Kate	1896
Hill, Tiller	7171	Hood, Sarah	2357
Hill, Munna	7172	Hood, Henry	2358
Hill, Wunche	7181	Hood, Jackson	2359
Hill, Louisa	7232	Hood, William	2360
Hill, Lucy	7446	Hood, John	2361
Hill, Jesse	7447	Hood, James	2362
Hill, Hettie	7448	Hood, Joe	9629
Hill, Lizzie	7449	Houston, Eva C.	2480
Hill, Houston	7450	Houston, Carrie	2481
Hill, Sampson	7451	Houston, Lucien A.	2482
Hill, Soma	8318	Houston, Turner	9292
Hill, John	8319	Houston, George	9293
Hill, Jacob	8756	Houston, Jesse	9294
Hill, John	8757	Hosey, Harriet	2524
Hill, Cinda	8863	Hosey, Lee	2525
Hill, Jesse	9380	Hosey, John B.	2527
Hill, Jefferson	9767	Hosey, Orlando	2528
Hill, Nancy	10066	Hosey, Isaac	2529
Hill, Amy	10067	Hosey, Nora F.	9586
Hill, Jesse	10141	Hosmer, Susie	2719
Hicks, George	917	Hosmer, Frank	2720
Hicks, Elsie	918	Hosmer, Fannie	2722
Hicks, Bunner	919	Howell, Lee	2743
Hicks, Johnson	920	Howell, Annie	2744
Hicks, Robert	921	Holt, Abbie	2799
Hicks, George	3242	Holt, Henry	2801
Hicks, Dicey	3243	Holt, Emanuel	2802
Hicks, Bunny	3244	Holt, Sarah Jane	2803
Hicks, Henry	3245	Holt, Mattie	2804
Hicks, Louana	3246	Holleyman, Maggie G.	2847
Hicks, Joe	3247	Holleyman, Delila	2848
Hicks, Wesley	4118	Holleyman, Myrtle V.	2849
Hightower, Lydia A.	1033	Holleyman, Herman O.	2850
Hightower, William S.	1034	Holleyman, Homer A.	2851
Hickory, Joe	1676	Holleyman, Thomas J.	9351
Hickory, Thomas	3963	Hopwood, George W.	3178
Hickory, Jennie	3964	Hopwood, Mary L.	3179
Hickory, Lucinda	3965	Hopwood, Kellem F.	3182
Hickory, Addie	7057	Hopwood, John L.	3183
Hickory, Amos	7058	Hopwood, Edgar Denton	3184
Hinneha, Eny	4145	Hopwood, Ira Homer	9421
Hinneha, Daniel	4197	Homer, Henry	3660
Hinneha, Noah	4198	Homer, Alex	6428
Hinneha, Peter	4199	Homer, John	9000
Hinneha, Jonas	4201	Holahta, Che-parn	3688
Higgins, Josephine	5810	Holahta, Lucy	3689
Hickman, Jack	5949	Holahta, Hettie	6916
Hickman, Eliza	5950	Holahta, Nocus	9144
Hillie	6944	Holahta, Arlinda	9145
Howard, Abbie Lee	521	Holahta, Larnee	9146
Howard, Benjamin F.	522	Holahta, John	9147
Howard, Polly Lue	523	Holahta, Martha	9885
Hoktee	667	Holata, Susey	9011
Hokto	7051	Holata, Willie	9012
Hodge, Katie	1193	Holata, Wileya	9986
Hodge, Elum B.	1216	Hooks, Alice	3997
Hodge, Pearl	1503	Hooks, Ruby Mildred	3998

Name.	Roll No.	Name.	Roll No.
Hooks, Ruth	3992	Hully, Baby	5531
Hooks, Rudie	9450	Hully, Annie	5532
Hope, Sharper	4323	Hully, Wesley	5533
Hope, Robert	6728	Hully, Arnie	5534
Hope, Henry	6729	Hully, Ida	5535
Hope, Millie	6730	Hully, Lucy	5536
Hope, Rebecca	8034	Hully,	7108
Hope, Sanford	8230	Hummecher, Joseph	5438
Hope, Willie	8231	Hummecher, Wynie	5439
Hotulkoce	4733	Hulsey, George	6614
Holmes, Hully	5132	Hulsey, Mack	6615
Hopiye, Isparney	5900	Hulsey, Sophia	6616
Hopiye, Jennie	5901	Hulsey, Lizzie	6617
Hopiye, Edmond	5902	Hutke, Mary	6621
Hopiye, Sam	8775	Hulputta, Thomas	7698
Hopaye, Ahalek	6468	Hutkey, Missie	7839
House, Lottie	6910	Hutkey, Kizzie	9207
Holder, John	7009	Hulsa, Ross	8864
Holder, Washington	8802	Hulma	9943
Homahte, Watko	8196	Hutchee, Nocus	9991
Homahte, Nochiheche	8197	Is-ka-wa-pee	564
Homahte, Lena	8198	Island, Joe	753
Homahte, Cothca	7236	Island, Sallie	754
Homahte, Harnoche	7237	Island, Mamie	777
Homahite	8167	Island, Lizzie	1260
Homahta, Hane	8185	Island, George	3157
Homahta, Thomas	8186	Island, Callie	3158
Homahta, Mesela	8188	Island, Eliza	3159
Hopsey	7801	Island, Jim	3160
"Hopiyoche"	7899	Island, Boney	5565
Holuby, Cooper	8071	Island, Bessie M.	5566
Holuby, Nettie	8072	Island, Ben	5595
Holuby, Turner	8073	Island, Haymen	5755
Holuby, Sally	8074	Island, Hettie	5756
Holuby, Nora	8075	Island, Henry	6745
Holuby, Mollie	8076	Island, Sunday	9449
Holuby, Hattie	9780	Isparhecher	1225
Holen, David	8242	Isparhecher, Cindochee	1226
Holupe, George	8370	Isaac, Louis	2419
Hobia, Isaac	8935	Isaac, Lena o	2420
Holden, Sarah	9795	Isaac, Lydia	2421
Honechike	10127	Ishmael, James M.	2558
Hughes, Jimmie P.	295	Ishmael, Fannie	8959
Hughes, Robert	1581	Ishmael, Maggie	8960
Hughes, Willie	1582	Ishmael, Mary	8961
Hughes, Melvina	1588	Ireland, Susan	3208
Hughes, Loonie	1589	Ireland, Mildred	3209
Hughes, Amos	1590	Ireland, Susan	3210
Hughes, John	1591	Ireland, John	3211
Hughes, Lena	1592	Inscho, Hattie	3637
Hughes, James	1593	Inscho, Ruth	3638
Hunter, Ellis	410	Inscho, Willie	3639
Hutton, Annie	885	Inscho, Claburn	3640
Hutton, Bessie	886	Ispocogee, Belcher	6149
Hutton, Sedalia	887	Ispocogee, Jennie	6150
Hutton, Salina	888	Ispocogee, Topley	7574
Hutton, Alex	889	Ingram, John F.	6184
Hutton, Robert	890	Ingram, David C.	6185
Hutton, Billy	891	Ingram, Mary A.	6186
Hutton, Houston	892	Ingram, Thomas J.	6187
Hutton, Louisa	3475	Ingram, Janetta	6188
Hutton, Tooka	3476	Ingram, David P.	6189
Hutton, Rebella	3477	Ingram, Eliza J.	6190
Hutton, Sarah	3478	Ingram, Mary Ella	6191
Hutton, Lizzie	3479	Ingram, Lotta C.	6192
Hutton, Jeff	3480	Israel, Ella	8677
Hutton, Lucy	3481	"Imly"	9269
Hutton, Fannie	3482	Isbell, Catherine C.	9673
Hutton, Ben	3483	Ingley, Columbus F.	9737
Hutton, James	9122	I-che-ney	9904
Hutton, Gracie	9465	Iswihhohke	7050
Hutton, Essie	10047	Jacobs, Frank D.	273
Huckaby, Elsie	1195	Jacobs, Jennie C.	274
Huckaby, William	1199	Jacobs, Newman F.	275
Huckaby, Aaron	1200	Jacobs, Sarah	276
Huckaby, Andrew	9409	Jacobs, Josie	277
Huffstetler, Mary L.	2530	Jacobs, Willie	278
Hully, Tom	5011	Jacobs, Louis	279
Hully, Betsy	5012	Jacobs, Della	3362
Hully, Wisey	5013	Jacobs, John A.	5093
Hully, Betty	5014	Jacobs, Frank	5094
Hully, Kogee	5015	Jacobs, Lizzie	5095
Hully, Emma	5016	Jacobs, Joseph	6781

Name.	Roll No.	Name.	Roll No.
Jacobs, Stephen	6782	Jessie, Billy	1392
Jacobs, Jennie	6783	Jessie, Mary	1393
Jacobs, Sampson	7982	Jessie, Emma	1394
Jacobs, Thomas	8017	Jessie, Susan	1395
Jacobs, Cinda	8822	Jessie, Lillie	5805
Jacob, Pilot	3921	Jessie, Katie	6322
Jacob, Charles	4585	Jesse, Eliza	7271
Jacob, Nancy	4586	Jesse, Massie	7272
Jacob, Hully	4587	Jesse, Bunnie	7273
Jacob, Sam	8149	Jesse, Jennetta	7274
Jacob, George	9794	Jesse, Willie	7275
Jackson, Chowa	379	Jesse, Timmie	7276
Jackson, Susie	380	Jennetta	3719
Jackson, Susanna	381	Jennetta	7391
Jackson, Matilda	2443	Jeannetta	8450
Jackson, Lou	2678	Jefley, Thomas	4679
Jackson, Ella	2679	Jefley, Cogee	4680
Jackson, Thomas	2680	Jefley, Willie	4681
Jackson, William	2681	Jefley, John	4682
Jackson, James	2682	Jefley, Tewee	4683
Jackson, Henry	2683	Jennie	5052
Jackson, Susie	2684	Jennie	6943
Jackson, Lilly	4835	Jenkins, Henrietta	7042
Jackson, Saber	5853	Jenkins, Thomas DeWitt	7043
Jackson, Nancy	5854	Jenkins, Buna E. M.	9624
Jackson, Sallie	6087	Jimboy, Hepsie	1606
Jackson, George	6354	Jimboy, William	1712
Jackson, Lucy	6951	Jimboy, Mahala	1713
Jackson, Ceasar	6952	Jimboy, Wiley	1714
Jackson, Wiley	6953	Jimboy, Lucy	1715
Jackson, Barney	8063	Jimboy, Willie	1716
Jackson, Eliza	8064	Jimboy, Reuben	1717
Jackson, Johnson	8065	Jimboy, Newton	1718
Jackson, Malinda	8066	Jimboy, Fannie	1719
Jackson, Bunnie	8067	Jimboy, Amos	1720
Jackson, Johnnie	8068	Jimboy, Lizzie	1721
Jackson, Will	8403	Jimboy, Alex	1722
Jackson, Sallie	8780	Jimboy, J. S. Lamar	1723
Jackson, Billie	8981	Jimboy, Amanda	1724
Jackson, Amy	8982	Jimboy, Fuller	5262
Jackson, Louis	9138	Jimboy, Mollie	5263
Jackson, Lurena	9545	Jimboy, Addie	5264
Jackson, Martha	9615	Jimboy, Thomas	9350
Jackson, Simon	10025	Jims, Holee	4345
Jack, Eddie	2733	Jimmie	7107
Jack, Alice	2788	Jim, Sissy	7303
Jack, Alice Luvina	2790	Jim, Tom	8510
Jack, Wallace	3434	Jim, Louisianna	8511
Jack, Phillip	6903	Jimsey, Jeannetta	8122
Jack, Sam	6904	Jimsey,	8263
Jack, Jennie	6905	Jimsey, Hannah	8837
Jack, Chapley	7129	Jimsey, Canoe	8838
Jack, Lena	7130	Jimsey, Unah	8839
Jack, Nero	7779	Jourdan, Mason F.	31
Jack, Big	8291	Jones, Charlie	372
Jack, Kernal	8842	Jones, Pearl D.	598
Jack, Parney	8843	Jones, Napoleon	1490
Jack, Jackson	9078	Jones, Thomas	1583
James, Edward	4351	Jones, Lila	1584
James, Morris	6223	Jones, Louiney	1585
James, Chotkey	7021	Jones, Martha	1586
James, Millie	7022	Jones, Taylor	2693
James, Nancy	7023	Jones, Betsey	2694
James, Geo.	7896	Jones, Kawee	3045
James, Martha	8499	Jones, Benjamin	4584
James, Billie	8500	Jones, Jemima	4690
James, Gibson	8502	Jones, Goliah	5522
Jameson, Hepsey	4406	Jones, Mikey	5523
Jackey	7126	Jones, Lucy	5524
Ja-tah-ko-con-cah-ney	7910	Jones, William	5525
Jefferson, Lena	735	Jones, Willie	5667
Jefferson, Moses	736	Jones, Lucinda	5867
Jefferson, Thomas	737	Jones, Emma	5868
Jefferson, Walter	738	Jones, John	5869
Jefferson, Manuel	1165	Jones, Lillie	5870
Jefferson, Jane	1166	Jones, Louisa	7534
Jefferson, John	1447	Jones, Martin	7548
Jefferson, Silas	3694	Jones, Hannah	7549
Jefferson, Manuel	4457	Jones, Sallie	7550
Jefferson, Prince	8516	Jones, Pollie	7551
Jerry, Louis	795	Jones, Hattie	7553
Jemima	1246	Jones, Nancy	7636

Name.	Roll No.	Name.	Roll No.
Jones, Lizzie	7719	Johnson, Alex	6805
Jones, Mollie	7721	Johnson, Louis	6858
Jones, Levina	7818	Johnson, Walter	7099
Jones, Sulloly	7819	Johnson, Ceasar	7340
Jones, Annie	7820	Johnson, Eliza	7341
Jones, George	7821	Johnson, Wesley	7342
Jones, William	7822	Johnson, Sandy	8120
Jones, Nellie	7823	Johnson, Jinnie	8121
Jones, Albert	8023	Johnson, Susan	8423
Jones, Legus	8024	Johnson, Robert	8681
Jones, Salina	8025	Johnson, Judy	8682
Jones, Thomas	8026	Johnson, Polly	8683
Jones, Maxey	8027	Johnson, Susie	8684
Jones, Loney	8220	Johnson, Coweta	8685
Jones, Haikey	8397	Johnson, Sam	8724
Jones, William	9022	Johnson, Lydia	8725
Jones, Mary	9023	Johnson, Sallie	8726
Jones, Maude Cox	9574	Johnson, Edmond	8727
Jones, Ella	9759	Johnson, Youman	8728
Johnson, Colbert	378	Johnson, Sallie	8729
Johnson, Fred	510	Johnson, Cooper	8933
Johnson, Wisey	511	Johnson, Judy	8934
Johnson, Noah	534	Johnson, Jinney	9024
Johnson, Peter	535	Johnson, Taylor	9025
Johnosn, Isaac	709	Johnson, Mollie	9130
Johnson, Nicey	710	Johnson, Daniel	9131
Johnson, Annie	711	Johnson, Susie	9279
Johnson, Robert F.	722	Johnson, Alice	9414
Johnson, Ella	723	Johnson, Mollie	9426
Johnosn, Sophia	977	Johnson, Katie	9468
Johnson, Clay	978	Johnson, Katie	9475
Johnosn, Todd	979	Johnson, Oda Casey	9520
Johnson, Daniel	1070	Johnson, Unah	9788
Johnson, Chutkee	1071	Johnson, Yuna	9944
Johnson, Wiley	1072	Johnson, Lucy	10015
Johnson, Samuel	1234	Jobe, Louis N. B.	1205
Johnson, Harry	1436	Jobe, Cherokee Mary	1206
Johnson, Ruth	1499	Jobe, Gertrude	1207
Johnosn, Peter	1564	Jobe, Florence	1208
Johnson, John	1573	Jobe, Eliza M.	1209
Johnson, Ida	1786	Josie	1247
Johnson, Andrew	1835	Jo-be-la-fah-ny	1978
Johnson, Eliza	1836	Jo-be-la-fah-ny, Mary	1979
Johnson, Anderson	1837	Jo-be-la-fah-ny, Sarah	1980
Johnson, Miley	1861	Jo-be-la-fah-ny, Wesley	1981
Johnson, Lorena	3678	Jordan, Emma	3034
Johnson, Keeper	3906	Jonasee, Parcilla	4299
Johnson, Jennette	3907	Jonasie	8097
Johnson, Susie	3908	John, McCully	5992
Johnson, Harber	3909	John, Short	7189
Johnson, Jacob	4028	John, Winey	7190
Johnson, Nannie	4029	John, Johny	7191
Johnson, Yarner	4030	John, Louisa	7192
Johnson, Colberson W.	4031	John, Katie	7193
Johnson, Millie	4032	John	8261
Johnson, Joseph	4033	John, Wosey	9546
Johnson, Miller	4093	Joseph, Kittie	7637
Johnson, Halley	4094	Joseph, George	8788
Johnson, Maggie	4095	Joseph, Jeannatta	8789
Johnson, Willie	4096	Joseph, Jemima	10090
Johnson, Chenowee	4097	Jonah, Louisiana	2129
Johnson, Cullie	4098	Joney, Milley	9208
Johnson, Mahaley	4099	Jo-con-fah	7955
Johnson, Lena	4100	Jo-con-fah, Po-con-we-ney	7956
Johnson, Sunny	4101	Jo-con-far, Melissa	7957
Johnson, Missaley	4102	July, Louisa	319
Johnson, Samuel	4134	July, Turner	320
Johnson, Miley	4223	Kanard, Thomas J.	226
Johnson, Adam	4224	Kanard, Eliza	227
Johnson, Sango	4367	Kanard, Annie	228
Johnson, Linar	4368	Kanard, Polly	229
Johnson, Hannah	5265	Kanard, Louis	230
Johnson, Polly	5266	Kanard, Louisa	231
Johnson, Emmett	5267	Kanard, James	1230
Johnson, Ada	5268	Kanard, Annie	1231
Johnson, Nathan	5269	Kanard, William	1232
Johnson, Little Tom	5372	Kanard, Nellie	1233
Johnson, Ellie	5373	Kanard, Washington	2658
Johnson, Albert	5374	Kanard, Washington	6525
Johnson, Lydia	6435		
Johnson, Mahala	6436		
Johnson, Robert	6804		

Name.	Roll No.	Name.	Roll No.
Kanard, Fannie	6526	Kelley, Ida	605
Kanard, Bettie	6528	Kelley, Marsey	606
Kanard, Lizzie	7090	Kelley, Tobey	1059
Kanard, George	7212	Kelley, Wesley	1060
Kanard, Rosana	7213	Kelley, Eliza	1061
Kanard, Lumber	7214	Kelley, Emma	1062
Kanard, Annie	7215	Kelley, Sukey	1063
Kanard, Susan	7216	Kelley, Edna	3109
Kanard, Tilda	7217	Kelley, Robert	3174
Kanard, Jennie	8826	Kelley, Wilson	3458
Kanard, Melissa	8827	Kelley, Mary	3459
Kanard, Josiah	9277	Kelley, Lonie	3461
Kanard, Thomas B.	9381	Kelley, Wiley	7052
Kanard, Judy	9397	Kelly, Ferdinand	905
Kanard, Hully	9486	Kelly, Wadly	1275
Kanard, Eliza	9769	Kelly, Mahaley	1276
Kanard, Albert	9815	Kelly, Jackson	1277
Kannard, Joseph	4383	Kelly, David	1278
Kannard, Onida	4384	Kelly, Newman	2150
Kannard, Joanna	4385	Kelly, John	3789
Kannard, Martin	4388	Kelly, Albert	7047
Kay, Thomas	3336	Kelly, John	7048
Kay, Sina	3337	Kelly, Levina	7974
Kay, John	3338	Kelly, John	9150
Kay, Betsy	3339	Kelly, Sallie	9151
Kay, James	3340	Kelly, James	9152
Kay, Eli	3341	Kelly, Sarah	9153
Kay, Willie	3342	Kelly, Johnnie	9154
Kay, Chisso	3343	Kelly, Sam	4549
Kay, Lucy	3344	Kelly, Mary	2604
Karlarney	6628	Kelly, Louina	2605
Karlarney, Lydia	6629	Kelly, Reuben	2606
Karlarney, Isom	6630	Kelly, Mary	2607
Karlarney, Alex	6631	Kelly, Thomas	2608
Karselarney	7438	Kenerd, Martin	695
Ka-co-quan-ney	8114	Kenard, Nicey	929
Katie	8199	Kennard, George	2723
Kalaney	8267	Kennard, William	2724
Kano, Marker	8278	Keeny, Joe	4111
Kano, Jonas	8281	Kenny, George	8247
Kano, Thomas	8351	Kernal, Louis	4282
Kano, Missie	8360	Kernal, Aggie	4283
Kano, Bird Creek	8389	Kernal, Charlie	4284
Kano, John	8390	Kernal, Isaac	4285
Kano, Louisa	8391	Kernal, Amey	4286
Kano, Jannie	8392	Kernal, Sam	4287
Kano, Barney	8393	Kernal, Johnson	4288
Karny, Lizzie	8315	Kernall, Mose	4374
Ka-ko-con-ney	8806	Kernall, Sallie	4375
Ka-la-wee	8848	Kernall, Cheparney	4376
Kernells, Temiye	331	Kernal, Chotka	4874
Kernells, Sissie	332	Kernal, Winey	4875
Kernells, Nettie	333	Kernal, Mary	4876
Kernells, Amanda	334	Kernal, Louis	4877
Kernells, Annie	335	Kernal, Nellie	4878
Kernells, Martha	744	Kernal, Louisa	4879
Kernell, Lucinda	3510	Kernal, Lucy	8909
Kernell, Dixon	5995	Kernal, Loske	9864
Kernell, Ida	5996	Kemarye	4401
Kernell, Sam	6517	King, William	367
Kernel, George	8942	King, Nancy	499
Kernels, Johnson	9849	King, Ludie	500
Key, Thomas	542	King, Hully	501
Key, Ety	4110	King, Albert	502
Key, Naggy	8646	King, Johnson	1388
Key, Katy	8647	King, Millie	1389
Keys, Edward	2506	King, John Emmet	1390
Keys, James	2507	King, Lizzie	1391
Keys, Sam R.	5791	King, Jackson	1465
Keys, Jesse	5792	King, Jennie	1466
Keys, Pearl	5793	King, Wiley	1467
Keys, Sarah	6204	King, Louisa	1469
Keys, Ella	6205	King, Peter	1470
Keys, Ada	6206	King, Cogee	1471
Keys, Richard	8801	King, Robert	3427
Keys, Lee	4022	King, Sylvia	3474
Keys, Charley	4046	King, Annie	4386
Keys, Semarhetchkar	4047	King, Her-lert-hoy-e	4620
Keys, Lesta	4048	King, John	4622
Kelley, Annie	602	King, Saline	5279
Kelley, Lucy	603	King, Peter	5280
Kelley, Minnie	604	King, Robert	5974

Name.	Roll No.	Name.	Roll No.
King, Elizabeth	5998	Larney, Tommy	70
King, Jack	6170	Larney, Lydia	71
King, Annie	6171	Larney, David	72
King, Wilson	6172	Larney, Harrison	73
King, Sarah	6173	Larney, Jackson	74
King, Joseph	6174	Larney, Minnie	75
King, Hepsey	6175	Larney, Jimmy	930
King, Chotkey	6176	Larney, Thompson	1731
King, Louisa	6177	Larney, Betsy	1732
King, Dick	6245	Larney, Mitchell	1733
King, Emina	6246	Larney, Jack	3041
King, Amos	6479	Larney, Cilla	3042
King, Simondy	6480	Larney, William	4575
King, Louis	6481	Larney, Maner	4576
King, Harney	6482	Larney, Thompsey	5138
King, Haney	6565	Larney, Fannie	5139
King, Millie	6686	Larney, Mary	5224
King, Billy	7079	Larney, Annie	5225
King, Sam	7080	Larney, Moses	5226
King, Kogee	7646	Larney, Jennie	5785
King, Annie	7978	Larney, Lucinda	5891
King, Peter	7979	Larney, Pollie	5892
King, Lily	7980	Larney, Eddie	5893
King, Edmond	7981	Larney, Dick	5894
King, Peter	9435	Larney, Sarkerparcher	5895
King, Maxsey	9483	Larney, Martha	7787
King, Lillian Beatrice	9702	Larney, Polly	8943
Kiefer, Martha Lee	2514	Larney, Daniel	9641
Kiefer, Annie E.	2515	Laslie, John	310
Kiefer, Leroy R.	2516	Laslie, Fannie	311
Kiefer, John D.	2517	Laslie, Ella	312
Kiefer, George D.	2518	Laslie	8028
Kiefer, Stella F.	9686	Laslie, Lewis	8335
Kite, Jemima	3891	Lasley, Jim	3530
Kite, William Foley	3892	Lasley, Lizzie	3531
Kite, Abe L., Jr.	3893	Lasley, Bob	3532
Kizzie	4154	Lasley, Minnie	3533
Kizzie	9104	Lasley, Sam	3534
Kizzie	8296	Lasley, Roman	5060
Killer, Caesar	6785	Lasley, Colbert	5133
Kinha, Chotkey	7726	Lasley, Winey	5134
Kinney, Chowey	8251	Lasley, Dickey	7831
Kiyer, Annie	8736	Lasley, Thompson	7832
Killcrease, Wade	9326	Lasley, Sukey	7833
Knight, Thomas	518	Lasley, Tobey	8008
Knight, Robert	519	Lasley, Yunah	8009
Knight, Mary	520	Lasley, Sam	8221
Knight, Ramsey	532	Lasley, Wisey	8222
Knight, Amy	533	Lasley, Liza	8223
Knight, Jacob	536	Lasley, Alec	8224
Knight, James	537	Lasley, Moses	8225
Knight, London	538	Lasley, William	8385
Knight, Susan	539	Lasley, Louisa	9356
Knight, Walter	540	Lasley, Tewe	9364
Knight, Lucy	541	Lasley, Nancy	9365
Knight, Jacob	860	La-Faror, Saladen	1587
Knight, Malinda	861	Land, Joseph Henry	1695
Knight, David	4136	Land, Salina	1696
Knight, Jackson	5657	Land, Paul	1697
Knight, Mollie A.	5658	Land, Job A.	1698
Knight, Peter	5659	Land, Alvin G.	1699
Knight, Lena	5660	Land, Willie	1700
Knight, Wilson	5839	Laport, Jennie	2306
Knight, Haney	5840	Laporte, William J.	2307
Knight, Tochee	5841	Lakey, Thomas	7139
Knight, Mary	5842	Lakey, Mollie	7736
Knight, Misley	5843	Lakey, Jimmie	10091
Knight, Georgie	5846	"Lar-we-saw"	7928
Knight, David	5862	Lannan, Jennie	9196
Knight, Nicey	5863	Lannan, Mary	9197
Knight, Fuller	5991	Lannan, Maggie	9198
Knight, Boston	6256	Lannan, Jennie	9687
Knight, Dochee	6257	Lee, Barney	1129
Knight, Katie	6688	Lee, Gano	1701
Knight, Jasper	9463	Lee, Cinda	1702
Knight, Annie	9755	Lee, Albert	1703
Knoll, Sally	2731	Lee, Sallie	1704
Knoll, Dora	2732	Lee, Willie	1705
Kochokhey, Henehar	8051	Lee, Lucy	1706
Kolvin, Lete	8092	Lee, Nicey	6424
Konahe	8168	Lee, David	9278
Ko-chuk-ne, Nocus	9556	Lerblance, Alice	1651

Name.	Roll No.	Name.	Roll No.
Lerblance, Jennie	5896	Lindsey, Freeland	8059
Lerblance, Ellen	5897	Lindsey, Lydia	8060
Lerblance, Jeannetta	5898	Lindsey, Kizzie	8061
Lerblance, Harriet	5899	Lindsey, Lewis	8062
Lerblance, Frank H.	5967	Lindsey, Silla	8386
Lerblance, Addie L.	5968	Lindsey, Roley	8387
Lerblance, Howard P.	5969	Lindsey, Dorsey	8388
Lerblance, Lizzie	5970	Lindsey, Tosa	10179
Lerblance, Andrew	6083	Littlehead, Cowee	796
Lerblance, Willie	6084	Littlehead, Nancy	1950
Lerblance, Nora	6085	Littlehead, Wesley	1951
Lerblance, Lillian	9696	Littlehead, Tom	1952
Lerblance, Pearl	9697	Littlehead, William	6723
Leath, Louisa	1997	Littlehead, Willie	7958
Leath, John Henry	1998	Littlehead, Nannie	7959
Leath, Thomas J.	1999	Littlehead, Sarah	7960
Leath, Wm. Bogle	2000	Littlehead, Whiteman	7961
Leath, Thomas F.	9659	Littlehead, Hannah	9652
Lewis, Thomas	2486	Littlehead, Leslie	10020
Lewis, Lizzie	2796	Litka, Martha	1448
Lewis, Ruth Oneita	2797	Litka, Lucy	1449
Lewis, Holly	3655	Litka, Arma	1649
Lewis, Jack	4014	Litka, Charley	7582
Lewis, Delilah	4015	Litka, John	9473
Lewis, John	4016	Lieber, Dora	2188
Lewis, Lucy	4250	Lieber, James Howard	2189
Lewis, John	4762	Livingston, Lillious	3028
Lewis, Manna	4763	Linton, Pauline B.	4371
Lewis, Edmond	4764	Linton, Shannon R.	4372
Lewis, Fannie	4765	Linton, Pauline E.	4373
Lewis, Mary	5909	Likowski, Sarah A.	5679
Lewis, Kizey	5921	Likowski, Herman A.	5680
Lewis, Jane	6030	Likowski, William H.	5681
Lewis, Francis	6031	Likowski, Senora E.	6505
Lewis, Jackson	7131	Likowski, Joseph	6506
Lewis, Nancy	7132	Likowski, Lydia Lucile	6507
Lewis, Jackson	7500	Likowski, James B.	6508
Lewis, Thomas	8422	Likowski, Frank, Jr.	6509
Lewis, Ellis J.	8440	Little, Thomas	6927
Lewis, Frazier	8441	Little, Sallie	6928
Lewis, Daniel	8485	Little, Sam	6929
Lewis, Polly	8486	Little, Standon	6930
Lewis, Benjamin	8487	Little, Susanna	6931
Lewis, Maxey	8751	Little, John	9728
Lewis, Johnson	8765	Lissar	7613
Lewis, Lucinda	8766	"Lizzie"	8118
Lewis, Colman	8767	Lizzie-pe	8236
Lewis, Dollie	8768	Lipscomb, Mattie R.	8797
Lewis, Thompson	9367	Lipscomb, Helen V.	8798
Lewis, David	9566	Lipscomb, Lillian L.	8799
Lewis, Nellie	10071	Litia	10117
Leader, John	2932	Lovett, George	252
Leader, Sussie	2933	Lovett, Annie	253
Leader, Joshua	2934	Lovett, Wisey	254
Leader, Eliza	2935	Lovett, Lucy	255
Leader, Sam	2936	Lovett, Lizzie	257
Leader, Barney	6802	Lovett, Kizzie	268
Leader, Tilda	6803	Lovett, Pilot	703
Leader, Emma	6949	Lovett, Lawrence	704
Leader, Nancy	6950	Lovett, Austin	2936
Leader, Hepsie	7397	Loney, Major	427
Leader, David	7470	Loney, Lucy	428
Leader, Thomas	9961	Loney, Annie	3130
Leecher, Mutter	4307	Loney, Sam	8564
Leetcher	7883	Loney, Leah	9644
Leverett, Kogee	2655	Looney, Josiah	1681
Lena, Hettie	4634	Looney, Fannie	1682
Lena, Peter	5871	Looney, George Barney	1683
Lena, Bessie	5872	Looney, Charles William	1684
Lena, John	5873	Lowe, Katie	755
Lena, Betsey	5874	Lowe, Louie	772
Leno, Robert	9831	Lowe, Susie	1196
Lewallen, Louisa	6281	Lowe, Nancy	1197
Lewallen, Lillie	9695	Lowe, Lizzie	1198
"Leider"	7954	Lowe, Missouri	2348
Lindsey, Lila D.	411	Lowe, Gertrude	2349
Lindsey, Amos	4905	Lowe, Eliza	4571
Lindsey, Samantha	5552	Lowe, Comma	4801
Lindsey, Walter	6460	Lowe, Canuky	4902
Lindsey, Mulka	6466	Lowe, Toche	4903
Lindsey, Minnie	6467	Lowe, William	4961
Lindsey, Phillip	8058	Lowe, Sally	4962

Name.	Roll No.	Name.	Roll No.
Lowe, Tutler	4963	Long, Lucy	8007
Lowe, Alex	4976	Long, Sallie	8077
Lowe, Martha	4977	Long, Henry	8106
Lowe, Sally	4978	Long, Lizzie	8107
Lowe, John	5343	Long, Bob	8108
Lowe, Lizzie	5495	Long, Lewis	8109
Lowe, Mack	5507	Long, Lannie	8110
Lowe, Lizzie	5508	Long, Harry	8111
Lowe, Tobler	5545	Long, Sawena	8112
Lowe, Sallie	5546	Long, Jimmie	8113
Lowe, Jackson	5800	Long, Sak-quanny	8522
Lowe, Lena	5801	Long, Matilda	9016
Lowe, Joanna	5802	Long, Richmond	9403
Lowe, Washington	6600	Long, Wewoka John	9721
Lowe, Liza	6601	Long, Mattie	9841
Lowe, Amos	6602	Long, Peter	9842
Lowe, Nicey	6603	Long, Selena	9914
Lowe, Josie	6604	Long, Ella	10048
Lowe, Levina	7437	Love, Jonas	1304
Lowe, Columbus	7441	Love, Willie	1305
Lowe, Mary	7442	Logan, Samuel	3410
Lowe, Willie	8249	Logan, Mary	3411
Lowe, Samuel	8343	Logan, Bessie	3412
Lowe, Mahaley	8344	Logan, Stella	3950
Lowe, Johnson	8345	Logan, Sallie	4545
Lowe, John	8346	London, Betsy	5665
Lowe, Nancy	8347	London, Ellen	7633
Lowe, Jennie	8348	London, Ollie	7634
Lowe, Lena	8349	Lotka	6836
Lowe, Leona	8355	Lotka, Supsie	6837
Iowe, Liza	8356	Louiney	7106
Lowe, Sallie	9589	Lott, Thomas	7379
Lowe, Abbie	517	Lott, Lena	7380
Low, Louisa	8031	Lott, Nancy	7381
Low, Taylor	8032	Lott, Annie	7382
Low, Annie	8033	Lott, Millie	7383
Low, Susie	8358	Lott, Willie	7384
Low, Kizzie	8818	Lott, Losie	9775
Low, Cinda	9067	Louisiana	7813
Loler, Kizzie	851	Louisiana	9142
Loler, Maggie	854	Loskey	9073
Loler, Lewis	2266	Longbread, Nannie	10125
Long, Yusie	862	Longbread, Lyddie	10126
Long, Israel	863	Looma	10137
Long, Jacob	4635	Lumkin, Barney	948
Long, Thomas	4880	Lumkin, Homer	6011
Long, Sindy	4881	Lunsford, John C.	3383
Long, Noah	4882	Lundsford, Martha	3384
Long, Susie	4883	Lunsford, Thomas	3385
Long, Betsy	4884	Lunsford, William	3386
Long, Taylor	4885	Lunsford, Lula	3387
Long, David	4886	Lunsford, John	3388
Long, Thomas	4887	Lunsford, Paul	3389
Long, Susanna	4915	Lunsford, Ben	3390
Long, Bunny	4916	Lunsford, Winnie	9438
Long, Ben	5167	Lunsford, Charley	9439
Long, Bessie	5242	"Lucy"	3653
Long, Carcharty	5243	Lucy	4017
Long, Selver	5283	Lucy	4600
Long, Henry	5318	"Lucy"	5776
Long, Martha	5319	"Lucy"	8308
Long, Milton	5320	Lucy	8327
Long, Jesse	5321	"Lucinda"	5777
Long, Annie	5322	Lucinda	7778
Long, Washington	5340	Lucinda	8294
Long, Martha	5341	Lucinda	8643
Long, George	5342	Lucas, Sallie	6567
Long, Sam	5509	Lucas, Bettie	6568
Long, Kizzie	5510	Lucas, Amos	6569
Long, Joshway	5511	Lucas, Susan	6578
Lonk, Loday	5512	Lucas, Mary	6582
Long, Hannah	5513	Lucas, Famous	6583
Long, Thomas	5514	Lucas, Mollie	7884
Long, Coley	5515	Lucas, Sam	7885
Long, Daniel A.	5735	Lynch, Joe	465
Long, Lucy B.	5736	Lynch, Yanah	466
Long, Mesulta	6348	Lynch, Isparhecher	467
Long, Tom	7504	Lynch, Wesley R.	1084
Long, Judy	7505	Lynch, Hannah	1086
Long, Jessie	8004	Lynch, James H.	1173
Long, John	8005	Lynch, Dolly	1174
Long, Kizzie	8006	Lynch, James H., Jr.	1175

Name.	Roll No.	Name.	Roll No.
Lynch, John T.	1176	Manley, Linda	7076
Lynch, Bessie	1179	Manley, Lena	7077
Lynch, Cora	9143	Manley, David	8719
Lynch, Sarah	1130	Manley, Eliza	8720
Lyden, Susanna	1614	Manley, Mary	8840
Lydia	7814	Manley, Louis	8988
Lydia	10140	Manley, Mary	8989
Marshall, Lizzie	22	Manley, Jack	8990
Marshall, Rufus	409	Manley, Thomas	9008
Marshall, Lewis	415	Manley, Isaac	9092
Marshall, Elsie	416	Manley, Adam	9259
Marshall, Thomas	437	Manley, Leeda	9260
Marshall, Rachel	438	Manley, Bunnie	9634
Marshall, James	439	Manley, Dicey	9797
Marshall, Waitie	440	Manly, Levi	6074
Marshall, Mattie	441	Manly, Fannie	7869
Marshall, Ida	442	Martin, Anna	180
Marshall, Lafayette	1010	Martin, James	181
Marshall, Mattie	1011	Martin, Etta Elmory	182
Marshall, Choatkey	1362	Martin, Ida May	183
Marshall, Benjamin	1942	Martin, Johnson	842
Marshall, Beauregard	1943	Martin, Evaline	3505
Marshall, Anna E.	1944	Martin, Henry	4674
Marshall, Alva Ruth	1945	Martin, Betsy	4675
Marshall, Gertrude Belle	1946	Martin, Dave	5212
Marshall, Dinah	2136	Martin, Samuel	7517
Marshall, David	2302	Madison, John	779
Marshall, Hildred	2303	Madison, Alice	780
Marshall, Sallie	2351	Manuel, Mary	807
Marshall, Tip	2758	Manuel, Lucy	3330
Marshall, Arthur	2759	Manuel, Sam	3542
Marshall, Nettie	2760	Manuel, Robert	3784
Marshall, Nora	2761	Mantooth, Annie	1029
Marshall, Charles	3229	Mantooth, Laura	1032
Marshall, Phillip	3499	Marsey, Dave	1251
Marshall, David	3500	Marsey, Sam	4156
Marshall, Eliza	3503	Marsey, Louisa	4157
Marshall, Timmie	3504	Marsey, Sam, Jr.	4158
Marshall, John	3690	Marsey, Katie	4159
Marshall, Jim	3752	Marsey, Mike	4984
Marshall, Liley	3753	Marsey, Lumsey	4985
Marshall, Aggie	3754	Marsey, Katie	4986
Marshall, Billie	3755	Marsey, Wisey	4987
Marshall, Judy	3756	Marsey, Intey	4988
Marshall, Londo	3757	Marsey, Thomas	5136
Marshall, Mary	3774	Marsey, Winey	5137
Marshall, Susanah	3825	Mann, Sarah E.	2113
Marshall, Nitty	4001	Mann, Addie B.	2114
Marshall, Hepsey	4002	Mann, Thomas E.	2115
Marshall, Barney	4052	Mann, Hazel	2116
Marshall, Philip	4795	Mann, William	2117
Marshall, Aggie	4796	Mann, Manila	2118
Marshall, Molsie	4797	Malone, Hepsey	2484
Marshall, Susie	4798	Marston, Nannie	2308
Marshall, Watie	4799	Marston, May Malinda	2309
Marshall, Johnny	4800	Marston, John	2310
Marshall, George	5757	Maxwell, John C.	2590
Marshall, Violet	5758	Maxwell, Jessie L.	2591
Marshall, Walter	5823	Maxwell, Laura E.	2592
Marshall, Thomas J.	5855	Maxwell, Maude P.	2593
Marshall, Louisa	6123	Maxwell, John B.	2594
Marshall, Elvina	6124	Maxwell, Colbert J.	2595
Marshall, Nora	6297	Maxwell, Rollie C.	2596
Marshall, Leonidas	6401	Maxwell, Leona V.	2597
Marshall, Tucker	6561	Maxwell, Joseph L.	9661
Marshall, Sam	8690	Maloney, Annie C.	2812
Marshall, Aggie	8691	Maloney, Ruby	2813
Marshall, James	8692	Maloney, Annie	7159
Marshall, Lizzie	8803	Manwarring, Melita	2987
Marshall, Mollie	10088	Manwarring, Silver	2988
Manley, Siah	68	Manwarring, Melita Grace	2989
Manley, Jonas	69		
Manley, Joseph	5912	Mayes, Martha	3322
Manley, Sunny	5913	Mayes, Thomas	3323
Manley, Samuel	5914	Mayes, James	9300
Manley, Sarah	5915	Marcum, Rose	3513
Manley, Tom	6347	Marcum, Sarah	3514
Manley, Lofa	6843	Marts, Daisy	3728
Manley, Lizzie	6844	Marweoly	3762
Manley, Hallie	6845	"Marwole"	8119
Manley, Pompey	7074	Marpiyecher	4013
Manley, Martha	7075	Marlow, Ellen	4086

Name.	Roll No.	Name.	Roll No.
Marlow, Ruth	4087	Miller, Louis	5040
Marhoyee	4260	Miller, Lizzie	5041
Mason, Polly	4387	Miller, Lizzie	5042
Marks, Martha	5037	Miller, Otto	5043
Marks, Thomas J.	5038	Miller, Samuel H.	5585
Marks, Samuel	5039	Miller, Mollie	5586
Marks, Annie	6584	Miller, Sam	5984
Marks, Lizzie	6585	Miller, Lizzie	5985
Marks, Charles B.	6586	Miller, Louisa	5986
Marks, John	7518	Miller, Jennie	5987
Marks, John B.	9570	Miller, Joney	5988
Mathewson, Phoebe B.	5415	Miller, Nessey	5989
Matoy, Charles	5889	Miller, Reuben J.	6194
Matoy, Lydia	7679	Miller, Thomas	6326
Mahala	6942	Miller, John	6932
Manawa, Bunnie	6989	Miller, Jim	6933
Manawa, Lydia	6990	Miller, Lizzie M.	6970
Manawa, George	6991	Miller, Johnson	7577
Marseya	7092	Miller, Lewis	8844
Major, Loby	7096	Miller, Annie	9240
Major, Sallie	7097	Miller, Susie	9241
Major, Ida	7098	Miller, Polly	9632
Mannie	7554	Miller, Charles L.	9722
Marye, Hothle	7658	Micco, Robert	865
Martha	7994	Micco, Parfena	1073
Martha	8528	Micco, Lucy	1092
Martha	9909	Micco, Mannie	1272
Martie	8164	Micco, Okfusky	4009
March, Willie H.	10053	Micco, Hoye	4010
March, Nicholas	10054	Micco, Henry	4011
March, Gracie	10055	Micco, Thompson	4012
March, Lloyd	10056	Micco, Sarkinnarne	4128
Marley	10128	Micco, Katie	4129
Meagher, Isabelle	2	Micco, Charley	4130
Meagher, Sarah	3	Micco, Johnson	4249
Meagher, Edward	4	Micco, Concharty	4318
Meagher, Walter	5	Micco, Kintar	4319
Meagher, John S.	6	Micco, Katie	5281
Meagher, Thomas F.	7	Micco, Mary	5590
Melton, Edward	688	Micco, Hully	6386
Meyers, Martha	3288	Micco, Okchiye	7091
Meyers, Mabel	3289	Micco, Yarkinha	7329
Meyers, Joseph	3290	Micco, Cosar	7543
Merrell, Josie C.	6325	Micco, Lucy	7544
Melar	7314	Micco, Chona	7545
Mesala	7882	Micco, Yahola	7806
Meliah	7989	Micco, Polly	7975
Melinda	8210	Micco, Billie	7976
Melia (Nellie)	8214	Micco, David	7977
Mechiskoche	8282	Micco, Seber	8087
Mehate	8376	Micco, Aktiyarchee	8890
"Melosa"	9385	Micco, Kapitche	9672
Michiley	26	Micco, Willie Tulwar	9981
Milker, Lucy	133	Micco, Mullie	10107
"Milker"	7983	Miles, Rosalie	906
Minter, Millie	209	Miles, Louise	907
Minter, Harry	210	Minton, Ida Amelia	1022
Minter, Rupert	211	Minton, Nona	1023
Minter, John	212	Minton, Malven	1024
Minter, Douglas	213	Minton, Jarritt O.	1025
Minter, Coachman	214	Mingo, Joseph	2699
Minter, Mark	215	Mingo, Louisiana	2700
Miller, Robert	479	Mingo, Carie	2701
Miller, Katie	504	Mingo, Louella	2702
Miller, Wilson	633	Mingo, Warnie	2703
Miller, Seborn	1738	Mingo, Robert J.	2704
Miller, Effa	1739	Mingo, Irene	2705
Miller, Tobias	1740	Mingo, Youpehake	2706
Miller, Bluford	2119	Mingo, Narhe	2986
Miller, Lizzie A.	2120	Mingo, Joseph	5717
Miller, Florence A.	2121	Mingo, Aggie	5718
Miller, Ida T.	2122	Mingo, Monroe	5719
Miller, Mary M.	2123	Mingo, John	8991
Miller, Bluford W.	2124	Missouri, Davis	3222
Miller, Jennie	2779	Mitchell, Levi	3929
Miller, Zela	2780	Mitchell, Sally	3930
Miller, Nancy	3141	Mitchell, Albert	3931
Miller, Charles H.	3186	Mitchell, Severs	4163
Miller, Ambrose	3187	Mitchell, Enoch	4379
Miller, Taylor	3897	Mitchell, Addie	4407
Miller, Betty	3898	Mitchell, Monroe	4408
Miller, Emma	4781	Mitchell, Hannah	4530

Name.	Roll No.	Name.	Roll No.
Mitchell, Rachael	4531	Morton, Austin A.	318
Mitchell, Mintie	4532	Morton, Tucker W.	1626
Mitchell, Sissie	7121	Morton, Martha L.	1627
Mitchell, Sam	7741	Morton, Richard L.	1628
Mitchell, Mandy	7984	Morton, William V.	1629
Mitchell, Selina	7987	Morton, Oscar M.	1630
Mitchell, Emma	7988	Morton, Stanton R.	1631
Mitchell, Nancy	8283	Morton, Roy H.	1632
Mitchell, Bunnie	8284	Morton, Osborn A.	1741
Mitchell, Louvina	8285	Morton, Joan	3663
Mitchell, Lewis	8481	Morton, George F.	3664
Mitchell, Billie	8482	Morton, Airy Ethel	3665
Mitchell, Moses	8483	Morton, William P.	3928
Mitchell, Soloman	8484	Morton, Mossie	4261
Mitchell, Aggie	8670	Morton, Delilah	4395
Mitchell, Hannah	9760	Morton, Ellis	4396
Mitchell, Sissie	10012	Morton, Clarence	4397
Mitchell, Cheparney	10013	Morton, Lelora	4398
Mikey, Silwar	4151	Morton, Walter W.	4399
Mikey, Amy	4152	Morton, Perry K.	5151
Mikey, Lizzie	4153	Morton, Annie	5152
Mikey, Simon	4187	Morton, Irene	5153
Mikey, Marfy	4189	Monnie	377
Mikey, Ollie	4348	Morey, Jacob	647
Mikey, Louie	8667	Morey, Calley D.	2237
Mikey, Bessie	8668	Morey, Samuel	2238
Mikey, Lizzie	9249	Morey, Tally D.	2239
Mikey, Magnolia	9250	Morey, George W.	2240
Mikey, Robinson	9251	Morey, Anson	2243
Mickens, Margie	4451	Morgan, Chilly W.	767
Mickens, Oscar	4452	Morgan, Ranny M.	768
Mickens, Walter	4453	Morgan, Edith M.	769
Milam, Laura T.	5560	Morgan, Florence	770
Milam, Kate W.	5561	Morgan, Lawrence	771
Milam, Charles A.	5562	Morgan, Leona P.	6199
Milam, Arthelus M.	5563	Morgan, Fannie	6200
Minugh, Alice V.	6252	Morgan, Luther F.	6201
Minugh, Daisy Lee	6253	Morrison, Jeremiah C.	846
"Millie"	8128	Morrison, Mary	847
Millie	8262	Morrison, Henry	848
Millie	8645	Morrison, Bessie.	849
Milloche	8156	Morrison, Bluford	850
"Missie"	9141	Morrison, Anannias R.	855
Mitchelly	8162	Morrison, Henry	856
Mickey	8050	Morrison, Sallie	857
Mickey, Palmer	8576	Morrison, Jerry	858
Mickey, Mollie	8577	Morrison, Duffey	859
Mickey, Sandy	8578	Morrison, John Sr.	2649
Moore, Napoleon B.	225	Morrison, Louisa	2650
Moore, Lola	742	Morrison, Manny	2651
Moore, Noah	743	Morrison, Mary	2652
Moore, Wm. N.	1088	Morrison, Major	2653
Moore, Lizzie	1089	Morrison, John Jr.	2654
Moore, Wright	1090	Morrison, Hence	3068
Moore, John R.	1091	Morrison, Luke	3069
Moore, Lizzie	1487	Morrison, Waitie	4324
Moore, Mamie	1534	Morrison, Eliza	4325
Moore, Thomas	1574	Morrison, Ellen	4326
Moore, Mattie	1575	Morrison, Lily	9649
Moore, Linney	1576	Morrison, Felix G.	9666
Moore, Julia	1577	Morrison, Louisa	9976
Moore, Moses	1578	Morrison, Addie	5935
Moore, Limon	1579	Montgomery, Bessie	981
Moore, Albert	1867	Montgomery, George	982
Moore, Robert	4239	Montgomery, Eliza	983
Moore, Robert Lee	4240	Montgomery, Thomson	984
Moore, Ada V.	4241	Montgomery, Josie Belle	985
Moore, Georgiana	4242	Montgomery, Hattie	986
Moore, Oliver Lee	4243	Montgomery, Alfred	9562
Moore, Verna Ellen	4244	Montgomery, Henry	9563
Moore, Thomas J.	4245	Monday, Jackson Louis	1094
Moore, Heney	6314	Monday, McKinley	1095
Moore, Bessie	6315	Monday, March	2874
Moore, Phillip	6316	Monday, Jennetta	2875
Moore, Sallie	6848	Monday, Martin	2876
Moore, James	9559	Monday, Haga	7561
Molone, Louisa	2197	Morris, Susan	1125
Molone, Billy	2198	Morris, Emma	1126
Morton, Mattie	313	Morris, Ollie May	8678
Morton, William Arthur	314	Morris, Pearl Garland	8679
Morton, Benjamin H.	315	Montgall, Lizzie E.	2559
Morton, Joseph L.	316	Moonie, Sallie	3827
Morton, Minnie May	317	Monahwee, Minnie	5489

Name.	Roll No.	Name.	Roll No.
Monahwee, Ella	6250	McCoy, Robert	3296
Monahwee, John	6736	McCoy, Barney	6646
Monahwee, Cynda	6737	McCoy, Susan	6647
Monahwee, David	6740	McCoy, Ruthie May	9405
Monahwee, Sambo	6741	McCoy, Minnie	9197
Moffer, Waitie	8124	McCoy, Israel	9498
Moses, Willie	8276	McCoy, Lina	9802
Mollie	8503	McCaughan, L. Elizabeth	2999
"Monarye"	9169	McCaughan, Thomas	3000
Moffit, Annie	9247	McCaughan, Nellie	3001
Murphy, Conny	217	McCaughan, Ninon	3002
Murphy, Conny Jr.	218	McCaslin, Jennie	3515
Murphy, Mattie	219	McCaslin, May	3516
Murphy, Robert	220	McCaslin, Nettie	3517
Murphy, Augustus	221	McCaslin, Myrtle	3518
Murphy, Sallie	222	McCaslin, Jessie	3519
Murphy, Eliza Jane	223	McClosky, Mamie M.	4424
Murphy, Eliza J.	2460	McCalvey, Margaret	4435
Murphy, William S.	2461	McCalvey, Edward,	4436
Murphy, N. P.	6136	McCalvey, Everett	4437
Murphy, Richard L.	9708	McCalvey, Joseph	4438
Murphy, Catherine	9709	McCalvey, Lucy	4439
Murrell, Lucy	1607	McCalvey, Cornelius	4440
Murrell, Sambo	1608	McCosar, Katie	5160
Murrell, Crawford	1609	McCosar, Bunnie	7115
Murrell, Louisa	1610	McCosar, Elliott	7116
Murray, Martha	2539	McCosar, Eliza	7117
Murray, Jesse	2540	McCosar, Ida	7118
Murray, Ada	2541	McCosar, Bettie	7119
Murray, Clarence Lee	2542	McCosar, Bessie	7120
Murray, Charles E.	2620	McCray, Otto	5362
Murray, Wiliam A.	2621	McCulla, Tulmarsey	8904
Murray, Gertie May	2622	McCulla, Mary	8905
Murray, Helen	9319	McCulla, Thomas	8906
Murray, John	9320	McCulla, George	8907
Murray, Whig	9321	McCulla, Cheparney	8908
Murray, Ruth	9322	McCulla, Nancy	8910
Murray, William	9323	McDermott, Jesse	1263
Murray, Nettie Belle	9669	McDermit, Henry	2509
Mullen, Celestie	2581	McDermit, Ella Grace	2510
Muskogee	2774	McDermott, Walter	9516
Mukes, Maggie	3805	McDuff, Rachael	2707
Mukes, Alice	3806	McElroy, Jennie H.	4108
Mukes, Alex	3808	McElroy, Oma G.	4109
Mukes, Joseph	9694	McElroy, Joanna	6120
Mulgussie, Lucy	6761	McElroy, Clarence	6121
Mullie	8598	McElroy, Emmett	6122
Mullie, Sam	8599	McFarland, Sarah	7320
Mullie, Siah	8600	McFarland, David	7321
Mullie, Sallie	8601	McFarland, Lilly	7322
Mullie, Phenie	8602	McFarland, Lena	7323
Mullie, Willie	8603	McFarland, James	7324
Mulkusee, Sente	8651	McGilbray, Farsey	666
Mutte Loke, Willie	7015	McGilbray, Linda	669
Myers, Betsey	2995	McGilbray, Jennie	670
Myers, Minnie L.	2996	McGilbray, Rose	673
Myers, Jefferson M.	2997	McGilbray, John	674
Myers, Caroline	5336	McGilbray, Haley	687
Myers, Lizzie	5337	McGilbray, Captain	934
Myers, Sallie	7696	McGilbray, Lizzie	935
Myers, Willie Frances	9757	McGilbray, Minnie	936
McCombs, Mollie	1331	McGilbray, Katie	937
McCombs, David	5622	McGilbray, Louisa	940
McCombs, Millie	5623	McGilbray, Lizzie	1396
McCombs, Tom	5624	McGilbray, Jackson	1397
McCombs, Lena	5625	McGilbray, Wisey	1398
McCombs, Pollie	5626	McGilbray, Hepsey	1399
McCombs, Leah	5627	McGilbray, George	1524
McCombs, Bessie	5628	McGilbray, Polly	2660
McCombs, William	5629	McGilbray, Walter	2663
McCombs, Sallie	5630	McGilbray, Rosanna	5356
McCombs, Tooker	5631	McGilbray, Abbie	9547
McCombs, Bettie	5632	McGilbra, Lewis	5398
McCombs, George W.	5633	McGilbra, Cinda	5399
McCombs, William P.	5634	McGilbra, Joseph	5400
McCombs, Joseph	5636	McGilbra, Solomon	5401
McCombs, James	5637	McGilbra, Lettie	7907
McCombs, Sarah	8082	McGilbra, Annie	7908
McComb, Joseph	6444	McGilbra, Hepsey	8019
McCoy, Henry	1982	McGilbra, Barney	8469
McCoy, Mary	2906	McGilbra, Amie	6291
McCoy, Delphia	3009	McGee, John W.	2771
McCoy, Lemuel	3010	McGee, Tamar Belle	2772

Name.	Roll No.	Name.	Roll No.
McGee, Mary	3014	McIntosh, Ben	2825
McGee, Walter	3015	McIntosh, Lizzie	2826
McGee, Nancy	3016	McIntosh, Mattie	2827
McGee, Clarence	3017	McIntosh, David H.	2828
McGee, Sudie	3018	McIntosh, John D.	2829
McGee, Frank	3019	McIntosh, Sadie	2830
McGee, Cornelia	3020	McIntosh, Grace	2831
McGertt, John	4888	McIntosh, William C.	2832
McGertt, Linda	4889	McIntosh, Bertha	2833
McGirtt, Billy	5045	McIntosh, Ben R.	2834
McGirtt, Dora	5046	McIntosh, Freeland B.	2877
McGirtt, Sophia	5047	McIntosh, Eulala	2878
McGirt, Jackson	5309	McIntosh, Rufus C.	2879
McGirt, Lincoln	5310	McIntosh, Sanubure	3035
McGirt, Buckner	5325	McIntosh, Kate,	3193
McGirt, Linda	5326	McIntosh, John	3194
McGirt, Robert	5327	McIntosh, Julia	3195
McGirt, Alex	5328	McIntosh, Bettie	3196
McGirt, Mongy	5547	McIntosh, Jewel	3197
McGirt, John	5548	McIntosh, Roy	3198
McGirt, Isaac	6057	McIntosh, Thomas	3199
McGirt, William	6423	McIntosh, Martha	3299
McGirt, Hepsie	6465	McIntosh, Charles	3470
McGirt, Soloman	7282	McIntosh, Katie	3471
McGirt, Hattie	7283	McIntosh, Ben Dave	3472
McGirt, Lonnie	7284	McIntosh, Charles Lee	3473
McGirt, Jimmie	7285	McIntosh, George	3555
McGirt, Aaron	8579	McIntosh, Winnie	5228
McGirt, Dick	8586	McIntosh, Luke G.	5743
McGirt, Jim	8941	McIntosh, Leona	5744
McGeeley, Timmie	5403	McIntosh, Lucius G.	5745
McGirth, Houston	6007	McIntosh, Jennetta	5746
McHenry, Lewis	634	McIntosh, Minnie	5747
McHenry, Silla	635	McIntosh, Dessie Lee	5748
McHenry, Lewis Jr.	636	McIntosh, Bunnie	6258
McHenry, Jesse	637	McIntosh, Leah	6259
McHenry, David	638	McIntosh, May	6260
McHenry, Greely	639	McIntosh, Roley	6261
McHenry, James	8518	McIntosh, Mildred	6262
McIntosh, John	418	McIntosh, John	6300
McIntosh, Susan	419	McIntosh, Mary	6301
McIntosh, Annetta	422	McIntosh, Minerola	6302
McIntosh, Etta	423	McIntosh, Job	6303
McIntosh, Jennetto	516	McIntoosh, Morie	6422
McIntosh, Alex	760	McIntosh, Louis	6711
McIntosh, Martha	761	McIntosh, Leah	6712
McIntosh, Solomon	762	McIntosh, Kogee	6744
McIntosh, Newman	763	McIntosh, Roley	6977
McIntosh, Cora	764	McIntosh, Ellen	6978
McIntosh, Lucy	765	McIntosh, Thomas	6979
McIntosh, William	766	McIntosh, John	6982
McIntosh, Thomas	1675	McIntosh, Greely	7253
McIntosh, Roley C.	1766	McIntosh, John	7615
McIntosh, Fannie	1767	McIntosh, Lyddia	7616
McIntosh, Roley C. Jr.	1768	McIntosh, Hepsey	7617
McIntosh, Hector	1769	McIntosh, Lizzie	7618
McIntosh, Mamie	1770	McIntosh, Leah	7619
McIntosh, Monodese	1774	McIntosh, David	7620
McIntosh, Lula N.	1775	McIntosh, Henry	7621
McIntosh, William Yancy	1776	McIntosh, Tokka	7724
		McIntosh, Ella	8820
McIntosh, Zolena Kaniah	1777	McIntosh, Abraham	9056
McIntosh, Xenophon	1778	McIntosh, Martha	9057
McIntosh, Amos	2183	McIntosh, Miley	9089
McIntosh, Louina	2184	McIntosh, A. G.	9093
McIntosh, Walley	2185	McIntosh, Freeland	9094
McIntosh, John	2186	McIntosh, Van A.	9095
McIntosh, Tayola	2187	McIntosh, Daniel N.	9096
McIntosh, Commodore	2547	McIntosh, Waldoe E.	9097
McIntosh, Arsyno	2548	McIntosh, Lucile	9182
McIntosh, Maggie	2549	McIntosh, John R.	9301
McIntosh, Lizzie	2550	McIntosh, Lula T.	9429
McIntosh, Edna	2551	McIntosh, Tiger	9453
McIntosh, Iona	2552	McIntosh, Willie	9505
McIntosh, Della	2553	McIntosh, Lula	9604
McIntosh, Wm. R.	2554	McIntosh, Vera Thelma	9723
McIntosh, Annie	2555	McIntosh, Lewis	9778
McIntosh, Sarah	2556	McKellop, Albert P.	405
McIntosh, Viola	2557	McKellop, Annie	406
McIntosh, D. N. Jr.	2711	McKellop, Barney	407
McIntosh, Hannah Vera	2712	McKellop, Arthur A.	408
McIntosh, Virgie May	2713	McKellop, Eliza	712
		McKellop, Peter	800

Name.	Roll No.	Name.	Roll No.
McKellop, Wilson	801	McNevins, Andrew S.	4650
McKellop, Minnie	864	McNevins, George Dewey	4651
McKellop, Almarine E.	4165	McPerryman	7489
McKellop, Ruth A.	4166	McPerryman, Celia	7490
McKellop, James E.	4167	McQueen, James	2533
McKellopp, Grace	4168	McQueen, Sarah	2534
McKellop, Joseph M.	4930	McQueen, Willie	7781
McKellop, Sallie	4931	McQueen, Nancy	10039
McKellop, Cherokee	4932	McQuarie, Ray Lee	9165
McKellop, Effie	4933	McRay, Bellzora	3520
McKellopp, Thomas	4934	McWilliams, Thomas	5783
McKellop, Betsey	7757	McWilliams, Miley	5784
McKellop, Wilson	9493	Nail, James	2401
McKellop, Alice	9597	Nail, Cornelius	3149
McKellup, Lucinda	4636	Nail, Joe	3795
McKim, William A.	2014	Nave, Alice	2477
McKim, Hattie	2015	Nave, Ethel	2478
McKim, Robert A.	3060	Nave, Eva	2479
McKim, Robert M.	3061	Nave, Laura	9440
McKim, Fannie Maree	9554	Narcóme, Sunday	6626
McKinney, Hepsey	5146	Narcome, John	6627
McKinney, Roley	5147	Narcome, Lizzie	3491
McKinney, Susie	5148	Narcome, Dinah	6704
McKinney, Unah	5149	Narcome, Sunday	3492
McKan, John	5238	Narcome, Johnson	5506
McKan, Hepsey	5239	Narcome, Simpson	6019
McKane, William	9978	Narcome, Lizzie	6020
McKinney, Albert	5518	Narcome, Eliza	6624
McKinney, John A.	5519	Naharkey, Moses	4363
McKinney, Sadie C.	5520	Naharkey, Millie	4364
McLish, Sailie	3494	Naharkey, Sammie	4365
McMinn, Annie	2277	Naharkey, Wehiley	4366
McNac, Julia	488	Narcomey, Daniel	4477
McNac, Robert	503	Narcomay, Thomas	6581
McNac, Alex	1016	Nancy	5377
McNac, Mary	1017	Nancy	8015
McNac, Alice	1018	"Nancy"	8306
McNac, Myrtie	1019	Nancy	9014
McNac, Albert	1020	Narchubby, Sallie	8146
McNac, Mary	1021	Narchubby, Ellis	8147
McNac, Peter	1268	Narchubby, Sissy	8148
McNac, Lousanna	1269	"Navey"	9270
McNac, Parney	1270	Nar-wal-le-pe-sec	9781
McNac, Tommie	1271	Narchechar	9897
McNac, Martha	1273	Nelson, Eli	156
McNac, Wallace C.	5742	Nelson, Amos	3169
McNac, Lena	5809	Nelson, Sallie	3170
McNac, Susie	6788	Nelson, Mahala	3171
McNac, Mulsey	6915	Nelson, Nora	3172
McNac, Peter	6917	Nelson, John	3173
McNac, Phillip	7123	Nelson, Mary S.	4308
McNac, Nannie	7124	Nelson, Eula May	4309
McNac, Johnny	7125	Nelson, Frankie L.	9603
McNac, John	7478	Nelson, William	10121
McNac, Dave	8984	Nero, Mose	368
McNac, William McKin-		Nero, Zedrick	3863
ley	9417	Nero, Jack	6063
McNack, Dicey	2659	Nero, Louisa	6064
McNack, Berry	3798	Nero, Joseph	7020
McNack, Alex	3799	Nero, Nancy	7025
McNack, Caroline	3800	Nero, Governor	7026
McNack, Charley	3801	Nero, William	7027
McNack, Rosana	3802	Newton, Sarah Eliza-	
McNack, Shawnee	3803	beth	2572
McNack, Stella	3804	Newton, Valley Ruth	2573
McNack, Aaron	3822	Newton, Ruby E.	2574
McNack, Charley	7053	Newton, Samantha E.	9935
McNulty, Cherokee	1875	Newton, Connie O.	9936
McNulty, Lena	1876	Newton, Ollin	9937
McNulty, George W.	1877	Newton, Vera S.	9938
McNulty, Maude M.	1878	Newton, John P.	9939
McNulty, Annie	1879	Newberry, Jeannetta	2714
McNulty, Beulah	1880	Newberry, Lulu	2715
McNulty, Thomas J.	1881	Newberry, Maud A.	2716
McNulty, Wanney	1882	Newberry, Millard F.	2717
McNulty, John	1883	Newberry, Carl	2718
McNally, Cassie	4630	Nevey, Annie	5981
McNally, Samuel	4631	Nevey, John	5982
McNally, Susan	4632	Nevey, Johnie	5983
McNally, Mack	4633	Nevy, Moseley	8656
McNevins, Lee	4648	Nettie	7917
McNevins, Nancy	4649	"Nellie"	7927

Name.	Roll No.
Nivens, Willie	5811
Nivens, Jessie	5812
"Nicey"	7911
Nicey	8293
Nidy	8265
Nichols, Emma	8608
Nichols, William B.	8609
Nichols, Grace Alva	9443
Notchee	24
Nolan, Sarah Jane	582
Nolan, Thomas Jefferson	583
Nolan, Martha Ann Eliz	584
Nolan, Isaac	585
Nolan, James	586
Nolen, Lucy	3291
Nolen, Jesse	3292
Nolen, Samuel	3293
Nolen, William	3294
Nolen, Lee	3295
Noon, Jim	4292
Noon, Sophie	4293
Noon, Nathan	4294
Noon, Martha	5221
Noon, Fisher	5222
Noon, Palmer	5220
Noon, Wiley	5282
Noon, Alex	9487
Noble, Annie V.	5353
Noble, Lucile	5354
Noble, Myrtle	5355
Noble, Minnie	6196
Noble, Mariah	6290
Noble, Wesley	8255
Noble, Susan	8256
Nocus eka	8002
Nokeche	8244
Norman, Rosa Alabama	9225
Norbe,	9824
Nuk-mel-lee- Meshaney	3401
Nuk-mel-lee Willie	3402
Nuk-mel-lee- Rosa	3403
Nukmellee	3404
Nubbie, George W.	4354
Nubbie, Wilson	9893
Nubbie, Malissa	9894
O'Brien, Albert Victor	869
Owens, Mary	1496
Owens, Martha	9738
Owens, Elva	9739
Owens, Addie	9740
Owens, Ollie M.	9741
Owens, Albert Poage	9742
Owen, Mary Severs	2689
Owen, Samuel	5419
Owen, Pearl	5420
Owen, Myrtle	5421
Owen, Clarence	10029
Orcutt, Adaline	1808
Orcutt, Annie	1809
Orcutt, Alvin	1810
Orcutt, Elam	1811
Orcutt, David	1812
Orcutt, Ollie	1813
Orcutt, Christina	1814
Orcutt, Annie B.	4174
Orcutt, William A.	4175
Orcutt, Homer A.	4176
Orcutt, Pleasant E.	4177
Orcutt, Archibald M.	4178
Orcutt, William McKinley	9418
Orcutt, Lela M.	9573
Oswalt, Marion W.	2436
Oswalt, William M.	2437
Offutt, Minnie	3846
Offutt, Bessie	3848
Offutt, Raymond	3849
Osah, Solomon	5957
Okfuskee. Leah	8950
Partridge, Lucinda	373
Partridge, Sam	1047
Partridge, Jemima	2994
Partridge, Reuben L.	3777

Name.	Roll No.
Partridge, Leonard C.	3778
Partridge, Ruby M	3779
Partridge, Toby	6416
Partridge, Mary	6417
Partridge, Amos	6419
Partridge, Ollie	6420
Partridge, Alice	6421
Payne, Charley	1031
Paine, Eliza	7857
Parkinson, Jim	1939
Parhosey, Jemima	4104
Palmer, Watty A.	5174
Palmer, Malinda	7722
Palmer, David	9513
Palmer, Mary	6898
Palmer, Jennie	6899
Parlie	5383
Panter, Jemima	5551
Patton, Emma	5567
Pakoska, Lucy	5701
Pakoska, Lewis	5702
Pakoska, Noah	5703
Pakoska, Liza	5704
Panoske, Daniel	6764
Panoske, Melsey	6765
Panoske, Susan	6766
Panoske, Andy	6767
Painkiller, Peter	6883
Pah-co-quah	7003
Pahoseyahola, Josie	7399
Pahoseyahola, Soatka	7400
Pahoseyahola, Lodie	7401
Pahoseyahola, John	7402
Parnosky, Willie	7479
Parnosky, Salina	7480
Parnosky, Noah	7481
Parnosky, Minnie	7482
Parnosky	7483
Parnoskey, Sarah	8877
Parnoskie, Barnoge	8657
Par-tah-ka-zo-lee	8533
Pah-cah-ney	8534
Parks, Margaret Atkins	9805
Parks, Fronie	9859
Parks, Fannie	9860
Parks, Julius	9861
Parks, Chaney	9862
Parker, Martha	10122
Perryman, Ellen	571
Perryman, Enos	773
Perryman, Dora	774
Perryman, Lillian	775
Perryman, Nicey	993
Perryman, Willie	994
Perryman, William	1074
Perryman, Lucy	1075
Perryman, Emma	1076
Perryman, Eddie	1077
Perryman, Wm.	1131
Perryman, Mary	1132
Perryman, Hattie	1140
Perryman, Martha	1321
Perryman, Noble	1480
Perryman, Susanna	1481
Perryman, Hattie	1482
Perryman, Phoebe	1483
Perryman, Enos	1484
Perryman, George R.	1498
Perryman, Lydia	1500
Perryman, Annie	1501
Perryman, Mary	1502
Perryman, Clarissa	2219
Perryman, Nathaniel	2220
Perryman, Addie	2221
Perryman, Mary	2222
Perryman, Flossie	2223
Perryman, John W.	2224
Perryman, John T.	2241
Perryman, Washington L.	2242
Perryman, Cornelius B.	2245
Perryman, Sanford	2258

Name.	Roll No.	Name.	Roll No.
Perryman, Robert L.	2567	Pelah	6484
Perryman, Lucy	2568	Peeper, Mary	6880
Perryman, Joseph	2569	Peeper, Everett	6881
Perryman, Ralph	2570	Peeper, Clarence	9598
Perryman, Eliza	2571	Petelle	7950
Perryman, Rachel	2626	Pehoye	8200
Perryman, Ab	2627	Perkins, Gus	8793
Perryman, Mamie	2628	"Peloche"	9275
Perryman, George B.	2629	Phillips, Tecumseh	893
Perryman, George B.	2631	Phillips, Coosie	894
Perryman, Moses	2636	Phillips, Thomas	895
Perryman, Rachel H.	2637	Phillips, Sarah	896
Perryman, Cosetta	2638	Phillips, Eliza	897
Perryman, Sam	2793	Phillips, Bettie	898
Perryman, Mollie	2794	Phillips, Jennetta	899
Perryman, Mamie	2795	Phillips, Hattie	900
Perryman, Legus C.	2943	Phillips, Joe	901
Perryman, Arparye	2944	Phillips, Walter	902
Perryman, Henry W.	2945	Phillips, John	915
Perryman, Homer	2946	Phillips, Lewis E.	1623
Perryman, Katie	3435	Phillips, Johnson	6304
Perryman, Ben	3978	Phillips, Hettie	6305
Perryman, Martha	3979	Phillips, Ben	6306
Perryman, Frances E.	3980	Phillips, Betsie	6307
Perryman, Millie	4761	Phillips, Wallace	6308
Perryman, Benjamin	5102	Phillips, Daniel	6309
Perryman, John	5331	Phillips, Betsey	6713
Perryman, Silla	5332	Phillips, Louisa	6714
Perryman, William	5333	Phillips, Taylor	6715
Perryman, Martha	5334	Phillips, Abbie	6716
Perryman, Edmond	5904	Phillips, Mattie	8083
Perryman, Ellen	6219	Phillips, Billy	8084
Perryman, John W.	6612	Phillips, Jennie	8085
Perryman, Tecumseh	6613	Phelama)	8245
Perryman, Thomas W.	6749	Pigeon, Lizzie	124
Perryman, Thomas L.	6750	Pigeon, Robert	125
Perryman, Arthur R.	6751	Pigeon, Dave	5344
Perryman, Walter L.	6752	Pigeon, Nancy	5345
Perryman, Hamor C.	7008	Pigeon, Tiger	5346
Perryman, Philip	7142	Pigeon, Peggy	5347
Perryman, Leah	7143	Pigeon, Lesbee	6634
Perryman, Legus	7717	Pigeon, Mate	7260
Perryman, Louis	9017	Pigeon, Jonas	7261
Perryman, Georgia R.	9428	Pigeon, Lena	7262
Perryman, Susie	9448	Pigeon, Joseph	7263
Perryman, Edith M.	9538	Jigeon, Jakeman	7264
Pemberton, Charity R.	2016	Pigeon, John	7265
Pemberton, William T.	2017	Pigeon, Cemelane	9053
Pemberton, John C.	2018	Pigeon, Misser	9313
Pemberton, James A.	2019	Pidgeon, Jesse	1478
Pemberton, Washington		Piegon, Leetchee	5955
L.	2020	Pike, Albert	705
Pemberton, Viola C.	2021	Pike, Joseph	706
Pemberton, Wilton	2022	Pike, George	707
Pemberton, Ida L.	2023	Pinehill, Sarah	1146
Perry, Maud	2734	Pinehill, Lasley	2907
Perry, Charles Owen	2735	Pinehill, Sally	2908
Penaka	2773	Pinehill, Leo	2909
Peters, Simon	2938	Pickett, Daniel	1799
Peters, Betsey	3233	Pickett, Malinda	1800
Peters, Ellen	3234	Pickett, Jennie	1801
Peters, Ben	3235	Pickett, Jennetta	1802
Peters, Kizzie	3236	Pickett, Louisa	1803
Peters, Cilla	3237	Pickett, Ella	1804
Peters, Isom	5503	Pickett, Lucy	1805
Peters, Louisa	5504	Pickett, Ada	1806
Peters, Lula	5505	Pickett, Albert	2112
Peters, Ellen	7158	Pickett, Johnson,	3043
Peter, Lizzie	6563	Pickett, Arlaquinny	3044
Peter, Jennie	7514	Pitman, Lucinda	1833
Peter, Louisa	7515	Pitman, Rowie Elizabeth	1834
Peter, Little	7524	Pitman, Rosanna	3729
Peter, Millie	7525	Pitman, Lewis	3730
Peter, Sallie	7528	Pitman, Edward	3731
Peter, Joseph	8680	Pitman, Laurl	3732
Peter, Locahull	9347	Pitman, Homer	3733
Peter, John	9963	Pitman, Walter	3734
Penn, William	6461	Pitman, Rosella	3735
Penn, Miley	6462	Pitman, Mary	3736
Penn, Annie	6463	Pitman, Arthur	3737
Penn, Sharpsey	6464	Pitman, Sammie	3738
Penn, Mary	9979	Pitman, Cecil	9456

Name.	Roll No.	Name.	Roll No.
Pittman, Celia	6588	Posey, Nora S.	9114
Pittman, Jennie	6587	Posey, Kennie	9115
Pitts, Emma	2278	Posey, Boyce W.	9116
Pitts, Pearlie	2279	Posey, T. C.	9479
Pitts, David Franklin	2280	Posey, Homer H.	9593
Pitts, William R.	2281	Postoak, Rachel	2231
Pierce, Jacob	3074	Postoak, Bettie	2233
Pierce, Sallie	3075	Postoak, George	2236
Pierce, Jennetta	3076	Postoak, Lincoln	2324
Pierce, Silla	3077	Postoak, Lilly	2325
Pinky, Willie	3724	Postoak, Tecumseh	2326
Porter, Susan	167	Postoak, Gracie	2327
Porter, Katie May	168	Postoak, Nannie	2328
Porter, Lewis	417	Post, Thomas	2755
Porter, William A.	1527	Post, John	2756
Porter, Pleasant, Jr.	1528	Post, Cornelius	2757
Porter, Will	1529	Post, Homer	5890
Porter, Stockton	1530	Post, William	6158
Porter, Edward B.	2407	Polk, Thomas K.	6310
Porter, Ben E.	2408	Polk, Lucinda	6311
Porter, Misey	4076	Polk, Sarshoye	6312
Porter, Sallie	4077	Polk, Benjamin	6355
Porter, Ochee	4079	Polk, Comfort	6356
Porter, James	4193	Polk, Dililah	6357
Porter, Nancy	4194	Polk, Delilah	6358
Porter, Hager	4389	Polk, Walter	6359
Porter, March	4390	Polk, Daniel W.	6846
Porter, Ben	5583	Polk, Katie	6847
Porter, Lena	5584	Polk, Mose	7211
"Porter,"	5778	Polk, Silla	7837
Porter, Pleasant	6220	Polk, Winey	9637
Porter, Annetta Mary	6221	Polakaconthla	6869
Porter, Leonora E.	6222	Powell, Carline	7218
Porter, Nellie	7408	Powell, Pesaka	8011
Porter, Tobie	7568	Powell, Elizabeth	8012
Porter, Isom	8755	Powell, Hannah	8874
Posey, Walter	1742	Powell, Cinda	9128
Posey, Laura S.	1743	Powell, Hannah	9132
Posey, Ola B.	1744	Powell, Sammie	9226
Posey, George A.	2024	Powell, Pearl	9227
Posey, Edward U.	2025	Powell, Park	9228
Posey, Frank	2199	Poloke, Sam	7569
Posey, Emma	2200	Poloke, Lucy	7570
Posey, Gertrude	2201	Po-char-ney	8615
Posey, Robert A.	2425	Polokee, Tom	8746
Posey, Lee A.	2426	Polokee, Susie	8747
Posey, Mary E.	2427	Polokee, Esal	8748
Posey, William A.	2428	Polokee, Ludie	8749
Posey, Henry	2494	Polecat, Sa-pe-sa	9124
Posey, John M.	2639	Polecat, Pah-la-tha-	
Posey, Annie L.	2640	shee-nay	9126
Posey, John W.	2641	Polecat, Ka-no-chee-	
Posey, Jim H.	2642	shu-mar	9127
Posey, Walter A.	2643	"Polly"	9140
Posey, Ruby	2644	Price, Lelia	971
Posey, Lewis H.	2896	Price, Oscar	972
Posey, Nancy	2897	Price, Owen	973
Posey, John	2898	Price, Benny	974
Posey, Mattie	2899	Price, Sallie	2331
Posey, Conny	2900	Price, James Lawrence	2332
Posey, Horace	2901	Price, Susan	2854
Posey, Darwin	2902	Price, Lucy	2855
Posey, Ella	2903	Price, James Jr.	2856
Posey, Mendum	2904	Price, Pleasant Porter	2857
Posey, William	2910	Price, Louvina	6254
Posey, Edith	3163	Presley, Mary M.	1309
Posey, Alexander L.	3671	Presley, Rosetta	1310
Posey, Irving	3672	Presley, Arthur	1311
Posey, Kipling	3673	Presley, Smith	1312
Posey, M. A.	6806	Presley, Louisa	1313
Posey, Albert W.	6813	Presley, Lillie	1314
Posey, Leonard Earle	6814	Presley, Farilla	1315
Posey, Elmer Carl	6815	Presley, Harrison E.	1316
Posey, Richard T.	9004	Presley, Thomas	
Posey, Dennis	9005	Jefferson	1317
Posey, Jonathan R.	9006	Proctor, Toney E.	2575
Posey, Beatrice	9007	Proctor, Susan	2576
Posey, William A.	9009	Proctor, Mabel	2577
Posey, James S.	9110	Proctor, Lewis	3711
Posey, Andy W.	9111	Proctor, Schokah	3712
Posey, Thomas U.	9112	Proctor, Ellen	3713
Posey, Lena L.	9113	Proctor, Nancy	3714

Name.	Roll No.	Name.	Roll No.
Proctor, Susie	3715	Reed, Jennie	5049
Proctor, Johnson	3716	Reed, Ella	5050
Proctor, Billie	3717	Reed, Leister	5051
Proctor, Alex	5450	Reed, John	5089
Proctor, Sallie	5666	Reed, Rachel	5090
Proctor, Nicey	5910	Reed, Judie	5091
Proctor, Timmie H.	6053	Reed, Martha	5177
Proctor, Nellie	6054	Reed, Johnson	5920
Proctor, Monroe	6055	Reed, Andrew	7202
Proctor, Washington	6096	Reed, Walter	7203
Proctor, Kelly	7815	Reed, Leah	7204
Proctor, Harry	7828	Reed, Benjamin J.	7455
Proctor, David	7841	Reed, Lucy	8794
Proctor, Manda	7842	Reynolds, Anty	2752
Proctor, Tom	7867	Reynolds, Ellis	2753
Proctor, Chaeller	7868	Reynolds, Leona	2754
Proctor, Caesar	7901	Reynolds, Silas	3556
Proctor, Huethlego	7902	Reynolds, Lucy	3557
Proctor, Leber	8175	Reynolds, Elsey	3558
Proctor, Lumber	8792	Reynolds, Lewis	6790
Proctor, Jeannetta	9236	Reynolds, Dave	6791
Proctor, Sampson	9779	Reynolds, Jerry	6792
Proctor, Mahala	9800	Reynolds, Eliza	6793
Proctor, Myrtle	9895	Reynolds, Susie	6794
Proctor, Sarah	10003	Reynolds, Ariadne	7461
Provence, Mary	3585	Reynolds, Annie	7462
Provence, Bertie	3586	Reynolds, Laura	7463
Provence, Mathew	3587	Reynolds, William E.	7464
Provence, Ruth	3588	Renfro, Bettie	5878
Pumpkin, Deconthla	1948	Renfro, Willie	5879
Pumpkin, Thomas	9534	Renfro, Roy Tillman	5880
Pussey, Sarah	4202	Red, Martha	8138
Puntka, Cinda	8885	Red, Foxie	8139
Puntka, Eliza	8886	Red, Thomas	8496
Puntka, Mikey	8887	Red, Leah	10073
Puntka, Jimsey	8888	Rhodes, Martha Ella	2976
Puntka, Lucy	8889	Rhodes, Leona Dee	2977
Ralston, Electa J.	2895	Rhodes, Annie May	2978
Ralston, Nancy	10149	Rhodes, John P.	2979
Ralston, Allen W.	10150	Rhyne, Elizabeth	3667
Ralston, Charles C.	10151	Rhyne, Altus	3668
Ralston, Benjamin F.	10152	"Rhoda"	9386
Ralston, Joseph W.	10153	Riley, Barney	1369
Ralston, Benjamin		Riley, Nancy	1370
F. Jr.	10154	Riley, Thomas	1371
Ralston, Roy P.	10155	Riley, Bunner	1372
Ralston, Mary B.	10156	Riley, Moses	1373
Ralston, John F.	10157	Riley, Suter	1374
Ralston, Ella E.	10158	Riley, Peter	1375
Ralston, John F.	10164	Riley, Easma	1376
Ralston, Sadie Pearl	10165	Riley, James	1377
Ralston, Nancy Jane	10166	Riley, Alice	3067
Raabe, Ida May	3454	Riley, Micco	3088
Raabe, Rosa Pearl	3455	Riley, Annie E.	3089
Randall, Bony	4320	Riley, Horace R.	3090
Randall, Timmie	4321	Riley, Mary Elizabeth	3091
Randall, Lizzie	4322	Riley, Isaih	3092
Randall, Sam	4742	Riley, Marzell	3093
Randall, Dicy	4743	Riley, Francis	3094
Randall, Emma	4744	Riley, Cleveland	3659
Randall, Ida	4745	Riley, Cheesie	4536
Randall, Amy	4746	Riley, Maley	4537
Randall, Thomas	5651	Riley, Warnie	4543
Randall, Elsie	5698	Riley, Washington	4546
Randall, Mollie	5699	Riley, Annie	4547
Randall, Peter	5700	Riley, Amosee	4548
Rawson, Susan	4691	Riley, Moese	6353
Raiford, Arthur E.	5691	Riley, Tiger	8473
Raiford, Jannetta	5692	Riley, Boone P.	8665
Raiford, Ferdinand	5693	Riley, Chatman	8714
Raiford, Ossie	5696	Riley, John	8715
Rabbit, Amos	7457	Riley, Minnie	8716
Rabbit, James	7458	Riley, George	8717
Rabbit, Sakoyike	7459	Riley, Johnson	8785
Rabbit, Edmond	7460	Riley, Jas.	8786
Rabbit, Jack	10135	Riley, Parfna	8787
Rabbit, Sissie	10136	Riley, Willie	9021
Reddy, Kizziah	468	Riley, Lewis	9324
Reddy, Maggie	469	Riley, Lucy	9325
Rentie, Susan	866	Riley, Unus	10094
Reed, Jim	2085	Richard, Mary	2144
Reed, Stephen	4992	Richard, Jasper	2671
Reed, Porter	5048	Richard, Minnie	2672

Name.	Roll No.	Name.	Roll No.
Richard, Sam	6088	Roberts, James	7370
Richard, Wesley	6089	Roberts, Mahala	7752
Richard, Kogee	6383	Roberts, Noah	7753
Richard, Eastman	7664	Roberts, Hannah Tyler	7754
Richard, Yarna	7665	Roberts, Josie	8257
Richard, Jennetta	7666	Roberts, Annie.	9829
Richard, Jemima	7667	Roberts, Millie	9925
Richard, Samuel	7668	Roberts, Millie	10145
Richard, Sallie	9535	Robison, William	2268
Ricketts, Robert J.	2438	Robison, Cherokee	2269
Ricketts, Malinda Ann	2439	Robison, Elizabeth	2271
Ricketts, Margaret A.	2440	Robison, Thomas	4556
Riddle, Tokie	5607	Robison, Louisa	4612
Riddle, Sam	5608	Robison, Benjamin	4613
Riddle, Fibbie	5609	Robison, Holmes	4614
Riddle, Rafert	5610	Robison, Josephus	4615
Riddle, Cub	5611	Robison, Eddie A.	4616
Riddle, William	5612	Robison, Lizzie	4660
Riddle, Gertie	5613	Robinson, Mariah	4661
Riddle, Rufus	9631	Robison, Arline	4662
Richmond	4179	Robison, Amos R.	4665
Richardson, Lina	9074	Robison, Maggie	4983
Rogers, Wm. P.	89	Robison, Barney C.	5256
Rogers, Kate D.	596	Robison, Ida B.	5257
Rogers, Mary R.	597	Robison, George E.	5258
Rogers, W. B.	599	Robison, Fannie	5259
Rogers, Caesar	2697	Robison, Alexander Wt	5261
Rogers, Mollie	2698	Robison, Leah	5273
Rogers, Chepon	3118	Robison, Clem	5274
Rogers, Johnnie	3119	Robison, Susie	5275
Rogers, Robert	3120	Robison, Sophia	5441
Rogers, Melvina	5947	Robison, Monkey	5442
Rogers, Viola	5948	Robison, Hilley	5443
Rogers, Susan M.	7624	Robison, Annie	5444
Rogers, Annie	9768	Robison, Daniel	5445
Rodgers, Mack Albert	9525	Robison, Lona	5446
Rothhammer, Louisa J.	148	Robison, Celia	5447
Rothhammer, Willie A.	149	Robison, Mattie	6003
Rothhammer, Lillie E.	150	Robison, William R.	6004
Rothhammer, Joseph		Robison, George H.	6005
H. Jr.	151	Robison, Rufus M.	6006
Rolland, Amos	191	Robison, Joe S.	6008
Rolland, Jacob	192	Robison, Lizzie	6009
Rolland, Peter	193	Robison, William R.	6179
Rolland, Master	1897	Robison, Augusta	6180
Rolland, Annie	1898	Robison, George F.	9190
Rolland, Susie	1899	Robison, James Abner	9388
Rolland, Wilson	1900	Robison, Sekice	9688
Rolland, Temarye	1901	Root, Jennie	2956
Rolland, Rufus	10115	Root, Martha May	2957
Rowley, Charles	980	Robin, Lulu	3807
Rowley, Josie	987	Robins, Johnson	3873
Rowley, Eveline X.	9565	Robertson, Myer	4771
Robinson, George	1306	Roberson, Mary	6231
Robinson, Addie	3228	Roberson, Amos	6232
Robinson, Annie	6125	Rulison, Ruth L.	28
Robinson, George	6126	Rulison, Edgar R. Jr.	29
Robinson, Henry	6127	Rulison, Irving M.	30
Robinson, Ida	9679	Russell, Mary A.	1221
Robinson, Willie	9865	Russell, Earl C.	1222
Ross, Muskogee	1400	Russell, Estle I.	1223
Ross, Susie	1401	Russell, Leva	1224
Ross, J. Ewing	1402	Rucker, Mary M.	2139
Ross, John Y.	1403	Rumsey, Louisa	3317
Ross, Jennie P.	1404	Rumsey, Mitchell	3318
Ross, Frank Leslie	1405	Rumsey, Jennie	3319
Roberts, William J.	1708	Rumsey, Napoleon	3320
Roberts, Maud	1709	Rumsey, Pink	3321
Roberts, Ethel	1710	Rumsey, Della	3346
Roberts, Edward L.	1711	Rumsey, Sam J.	3347
Roberts, George	3223	Rumsey, Alonzo	3348
Roberts, Weleyar	4205	Rumsey, Edmond	3349
Roberts, Warley	4206	Rumsey, Daniel	3350
Roberts, Mitchell	4207	Runner, Susan	3948
Roberts, Wisey	4208	Runner, Bunnie	3949
Roberts, Joe	4209	Ryan, Eliza	80
Roberts, Cholichar	4210	Ryal, Annie	6542
Roberts, Arnie	4211	Ryal, Emma	6543
Roberts, Louisa	4212	Ryal, John B.	6544
Roberts, Kendall	4295	Ryal, Grover	6545
Roberts, Mary	4296	Ryal, Hallie	6546
Roberts, Johnson	4297	Ryal, Lewis J.	6547
Roberts, Annie	6879	Sarty, Googan	290

Name.	Roll No.	Name.	Roll No.
Sarty, Susan	291	Sango, Bertha	3544
Sarty, Abbie	292	Sango, Thomas	3021
Sarty, Jenette	293	Sarwarhie	3718
Sarty, Pokar	294	Sarwarhie, Isparhecher	3720
Sarty, Ned	436	Sarwarhie, Willie	4402
Sarty, Elsie	808	Sarsar.	3761
Sarty, Herbert	830	Sarls, Jennie	4492
Sarty, Jasper	831	Sammy, Lucinda	4850
Sarty, Lizzie	832	Sand, Hully	4928
Sarty, Wesley	838	Sands, Phillip	5674
Sarty, Hattie	839	Sands, Martha	5675
Sarty, Austin	840	Sands, Stella	5676
Sarty, Thomas	841	Sands, Roley	5844
Sarty, Sarah	842	Sands, Daniel	5847
Sarty, Roman	843	Sands, Robert	5848
Sarty, Rollie	3285	Sands, Miley	5849
Sarte, Suma	7571	Sands, Moley	5858
Sartie	10078	Sands, Emma	5859
Sapulpa, Elizabeth	1690	Sands, John	5860
Sapulpa, Esther	664	Sands, Amous	5861
Sapulpa, William A.	3281	Sands, Taylor	5864
Sapulpa, Harrison	3282	Sands, Annie	5865
Sapulpa, George A.	3283	Sands, Ella	5866
Sapulpa, Phoebe	3284	Sands, Albert	9798
Sapulpa, James	6442	Sands, Lena	10049
Sapulpa, Lizzie B.	6443	Sandy, Jacob	5125
Sapulpa, Rosa	6445	Sandy, Sophia	5126
Sartoris, Martha	867	Sandy, Malinda	5127
Sampson, Martha	1328	Sarhilla	4942
Sampson, Washington	1329	Sarkache, Feney	5943
Sampson, Thomas	1330	Sartolumka	6789
Sampson, Lucy	2176	Sak-ka-senny	6906
Sampson, Rhoda	2177	Sallie	7105
Sampson, Walter	2178	Sallie	7993
Sampson, John	2179	Sallie	8260
Sampson	2209	Sarterpeye	7418
Sampson, Mary	2391	Sarkahche, Tuchie	7572
Sampson, Ophelia	2392	Sam, Kizzie	7638
Sampson, Joseph	2393	Sa he pah ke	7759
Sampson, Bonnie A.	2394	Sar ye che	7824
Sampson, Lee	2395	"San-nor-ka"	7929
Sampson, George	2396	Sah-cah-jah-thla	8116
Sampson, Elsie	4218	Sak-yo-thli-ke	8125
Sampson, Johnson	4219	Salmer	8572
Sampson, John	5592	Salumba, Peggie	8701
Sampson, Vina	9013	Salumba, Lucy	8702
Sampson, David J.	9158	Sarwanoke, Mitchell	8707
Sampson, Burleigh R.	9650	Sarwanoke, Nancy	8708
Sanders, Sarah E.	2402	Sarwanoke, Mary	8709
Sanders, Edna	2403	Sar-yo-kiche	8784
Sanders, Elizabeth	2404	Sarkecher	8985
Sanders, Maud	2405	Sarhoseker	6193
Sanders, Millard	2406	Sah-ta-quan-ney	9065
Sanger, Clemmie H.	2545	Sarnie, Annie	9121
Sanger, George N.	2546	"Sannah"	9221
Sanger, Stephen	3391	"Sarthle poche"	9233
Sanger, Lena	4873	"Sar wo li che"	9340
Sanger, Amanda	6911	Scott, Thomas	152
Sanger, Joseph C.	6912	Scott, Mulley	153
Sanger, Fannie E.	6913	Scott, Sookie	154
Sanger, Walter G.	6914	Scott, Kizzie	155
Sanger, Claude	9677	Scott, Willie	163
Sanger, alias Tiger,		Scott, Betty	164
Stella	5193	Scott, Lou M.	216
Sanger, George H.	5253	Scott, James	265
Sanger, Mabel M.	5254	Scott, Lucy	922
Samuel, Abraham Pin	3161	Scott, Amos	1145
Samuel, Ben	5388	Scott, Bosie	1167
Samuel, Jennie	5941	Scott, Willie	1168
Samuel, Monie	9266	Scott, Annie	1169
Sawyer, Alice	3490	Scott, Vollie	1170
Sawyer, Wesley	4836	Scott, Fuller	1171
Sawyer, Ellen	4837	Scott, Wallace	1172
Sawyer, Moses A.	4924	Scott, James N.	1177
Sawyer, Polly	4925	Scott, Buck	1178
Sawyer, Amanda	4926	Scott, Philip	1238
Sawyer, Yokum	4927	Scott, James	1239
Sawyer, Minda	4929	Scott, Nicey	1241
Sawyer, Solomon	5062	Scott, Josephine	1242
Sawyer, Sukey	5063	Scott, Sanford	1243
Sawyer, Minnie	8421	Scott, Miller	1421
Sango, Millie	3539	Scott, Ella	1422
Sango, Edward	3543	Scott, Ellis	1455

Name.	Roll No.	Name.	Roll No.
Scott, Samuel	1779	Scott, Lillie	6608
Scott, Nancy	1780	Scott, Sunday	6872
Scott, Daniel	1781	Scott, Narchie	6873
Scott, John	1782	Scott, Noble	7035
Scott, Bennie	1783	Scott, Judy	7036
Scott, Daniel N.	2042	Scott, Ella	7037
Scott, Emma	2043	Scott, Jackson	7038
Scott, Kiamish	2044	Scott, Sallie	7039
Scott, Gertrude	2045	Scott, Polly	7040
Scott, Roy Edward	2046	Scott, Lona	7041
Scott, Thomas H.	2047	Scott, Jennie	7363
Scott, Jim Ben	2048	Scott, Boya	7364
Scott, George W.	2491	Scott, Mesale	7365
Scott, James G.	2492	Scott, Ben	7591
Scott, Fred Y.	2493	Scott, Kizzie	7592
Scott, Peggy	3140	Scott, Sallie	7593
Scott, Bennie	3353	Scott, Wisey	7593
Scott, Pigeon	3764	Scott, Emma	7595
Scott, Hannah	3765	Scott, Matilda	7661
Scott, Charles	3820	Scott, Minnie	7662
Scott, Julia	3821	Scott, Alex	7758
Scott, Alick	3882	Scott, Haney	8158
Scott, Tullemarsey	3899	Scott, Alec	8305
Scott, Samuel	3918	Scott, Wiley	8310
Scott, Nancy	3919	Scott, Louisa	8448
Scott, Wicey	3920	Scott, Lizzie	8460
Scott, James	3922	Scott, Annie	8471
Scott, Andy	3966	Scott, George	8472
Scott, Nora	3967	Scott, Edward	8535
Scott, Lou	3968	Scott, Tena	8536
Scott, Louis	4018	Scott, Katie	8537
Scott, Nicey	4019	Scott, Lizzie	8538
Scott, Sampson	4020	Scott, Cheparney	8539
Scott, Peer	4021	Scott, Agnes	8551
Scott, Hunter	4150	Scott, Liza	8571
Scott, Tulmars	4184	Scott, Sammie	8659
Scott, Kochetly	4185	Scott, Hattie	8660
Scott, Thomas	4190	Scott, Frank	8661
Scott, Louisa	4191	Scott, Martha	8662
Scott, Lambert	4604	Scott, Annie	8764
Scott, Lucy	4605	Scott, Winey	8880
Scott, Frazier	4608	Scott, James	8881
Scott, Martha	4609	Scott, George Wash-	
Scott, Jane	4610	ington	9180
Scott, Pearlie	4611	Scott, Daisy	9181
Scott, Winchley	4678	Scott, Annie	9406
Scott, Turner	4722	Scott, Ida	9423
Scott, Lucinda	4723	Scott, Setepakee	10147
Scott, Lucy	4724	Schrimsher, Edward L.	1647
Scott, Henry	4760	Schrimsher, Gertrude	1648
Scott, Annie	4854	Schrimsher, George	7697
Scott, Roman	4855	Sevier, Vicey	480
Scott, Silas	4856	Sevier, Kizzie	481
Scott, Nancy	4857	Sevier, Lena	482
Scott, Litka	4860	Sevier, Emma	483
Scott, James	4864	Sevier, Fannie	484
Scott, Sukey	5105	Sevier, Joseph	485
Scott, Sally	5106	Sevier, Martha	3316
Scott, Winey	5959	Sevier, Louis	5689
Scott, Alec	5960	Sevier, Mary	4421
Scott, Lucinda	5961	Severs, Frederick B.	1162
Scott, Marcy	5962	Severs, Annie A.	1163
Scott, Harper	5963	Severs, Annie E.	1164
Scott, Sampson	5965	Severs, Shawnee	4737
Scott, Louisa	6135	Severs, William	4738
Scott, Albert	6151	Sever, George	8474
Scott, Bettie	6152	Seagro, Chepahnoche	751
Scott, Bessie	6153	Seagro, Susan	752
Scott, Ether	6154	Segro, Tom	6529
Scott, Peter	6155	Self, Mid T.	1211
Scott, William	6387	Self, W. B.	1212
Scott, Mahoye	6388	Self, James B.	1844
Scott, Billie	6406	Self, James H.	1845
Scott, Losanna	6407	Self, Della	1846
Scott, Sowitee	6410	Self, Sam	1847
Scott, Kissie	6411	Self, Ruben	1848
Scott, Annie	6412	Self, Lelah	1849
Scott, Wiley	6454	Self, Millie	1850
Scott, Rosanna	6455	Self, William Buck	2446
Scott, Sukey	6456	Self, James A.	3023
Scott, Mary	6457	Self, Henry A.	3024
Scott, Daniel	6458	Self, Louvina L.	3025
Scott, Betsey	6459	Self, Ethel Lee	3026

Name.	Roll No.	Name.	Roll No.
Self, Bertha May	3027	Shannon, Sally H.	6801
Self, Lula T.	3029	Shawnego, Stella	6247
Self, Blanche C.	3030	Shawnego, John	6248
Self, Cordella A.	3031	Shawnego, Lucy	6592
Self, John H.	3032	Shawnego, Henry	6596
Self, Plezzie Lee	3033	Shawnego, Sisle	6597
Self, John R.	3405	Sharlin, Katie	7623
Self, John C.	3406	Shicar	7648
Self, William J.	3579	She qua bee	7931
Self, Vessie E.	3580	Shar-shon-tey	7933
Self, William L.	3581	Shelly, Tom	8418
Self, Samuel C.	3584	Shwinogee, Winey	9206
Self, Mattie	3594	Shreffner, Mary E.	10167
Self, Mary J.	5759	Shreffner, Joseph W.	10168
Self, Callie M.	5760	Shreffner, David W.	10169
Self, Homer J.	5761	Simms, Maxey	266
Self, Roxy Anna	5762	Simms, Bunner	267
Self, Katie	5763	Simms, Louisa	9790
Self, Grover	5764	Simmer, Sammy	349
Self, James R.	9234	Simmer, John	3212
Self, John B. Jr.	9330	Simmer, Lena	3213
Self, Ira B.	9531	Simmer, Hattie	3214
Self, Duffie Le Roy	9684	Simmer, Alex	3215
Self, Elsie Ray	9700	Simmer, Lucinda	3216
Self, John B.	9777	Simmer, John	4234
Semikee	1245	Simmer, John	4739
Sewel, Parney	3809	Simmer, Selie	4740
Sewel, Sinda	3810	Simmer, Kogee	4741
Sewel, Ben	3811	Simmer	6159
Sewel, Thomas	3812	Simmer, Arch	6160
Sewel, Waddie	3813	Simmer, Sallie	6161
Sewel, Laslie	3814	Simmer, Charley	9170
Sewel, Liza	3815	Simmer, Kizzie	9171
Sewel, Loney	3816	Simmer, Joseph	9172
Sewel, Noah	3817	Simmer, Emma	9173
Sewell, Washington	4639	Simmer, Samuel	9331
Sewell, Sophia	4640	Simmer, Louinie	9869
Sewell, Ben	4641	Simmer, Jesse	10010
Sewell, George	4642	Simer, Moonie	5711
Sewell, Anna	4643	Simer, Millie	5712
Sewell, Amanda	4644	Simmons, Charley	382
Sewell, Edmond	4645	Simmons, Martin	566
Sewell, Willie	6724	Simmons, Esther	2409
Sewell, Nancy	6725	Simmons, Clara	2456
Sewell, Frank	7254	Simmons, Emma	2927
Sewell, Angeline	7255	Simmons, Ella	2928
Sewell, Anderson	7256	Simons, Viola	2929
Sewell, Sophia	7257	Simmons, Peggie	4119
Sewell, Nellie	7258	Simmons, Mary	4120
Sewell, Lizzie	7259	Simmons, Bettie	4121
Sewell, Thomas	8871	Simmons, Scott	4122
Sewell, Frank	8872	Simmons, Benhakka	4124
Sewell, Robert	10092	Simmons, Fannie	4125
Seber, Sampson	3962	Simmons, Joe	4486
Sealie	4337	Simmons, Charley	5564
Seaborn, Joe	4510	Simmons, Charley	7791
Seaborn, Stella	4511	Simmons, Jennie	7792
Secrow, Bettie	5335	Simmons, Annie	7793
Semarte	5379	Simmons, Lona	7794
Selumber, Robert	7532	Simmons, Charley	7829
Selumber, Winey	7533	Simmons, Dochee	7830
Se-yo-ke	7669	Simmons, Moses	7871
Selina	7784	Simmons, Lucy	7872
Sena	8213	Simmons, Walter	7873
Semi-hoye	8449	Simmons, Dorsey	7874
Seper, Joseph	8548	Simmons, Louisa	7875
"Selvina"	9254	Simmons, Sandy	8174
"Setehme"	9274	Simmons, George	8340
Sharp, Lewis E.	1437	Simmons, Martha	8341
Sharp, Johnnie	1497	Simmons, Samuel	8342
Sharp, Noah	2012	Simmons, Jeff	8627
Sharp, Frances	4784	Simmons, Mary	8800
Sharp, Culberson	4785	Simmons, John	9019
Sherrill, Mattie M.	1764	Simmons, John (or Tissie)	10138
Shepherd, Annie	3835		
Shepherd, Hannah	3836	Simmons, George (or Hothkoper or Hoe Kapo)	10139
Shepherd, Addie M.	6810		
Shepherd, Maud	6811	Simon, Sam	632
Shepherd, Oscar Lee	6812	Simon, Joe	2078
Shepherd, Elisha	9551	Simon, Sophie	2079
Shannon, Floyd	5773	Simon, Caesar	2080
Shannon, Daisy	5774		
Shannon, Lucy H.	5775		

Name.	Roll No.	Name.	Roll No.
Simon, Mandy	2081	Smith, Joseph	2696
Simon, George	2082	Smith, James Ross	2953
Simon, Peter	2083	Smith, Allen	3047
Simon, Ida	2084	Smith, Thomas M.	3104
Simon, Joe	3374	Smith, Martin W.	3105
Simon, Frank	3375	Smith, Martin C.	3106
Simon, Rater	3376	Smith, Phatimma	3107
Simon, Simon	3377	Smith, Martha	3270
Simon, Robert	5311	Smith, Maria E.	3360
Simon, Lena	5312	Smith, Charles S.	4458
Simon, Granville	5313	Smith, Louisa B.	4459
Simon, Jennie	5314	Smith, Jay G.	4460
Sinhoethar	923	Smith, Horace Greeley	4461
Simpson, Robert L.	1188	Smith, Walter C.	4462
Simpson, Susan A.	4141	Smith, Lucile	4463
Simpson, James H.	4142	Smith, Louis N.	4465
Simpson, John C.	4550	Smith, Rashie C.	4466
Simpson, John Francis	4551	Smith, Zular M.	4467
Simpson, Mary U.	6313	Smith, Martha	5395
Simpson, Hattie M.	6838	Smith, Anna Belle	5396
Simpson, Shelby	9028	Smith, Louisa	5397
Simpson, Archie	9029	Smith, Martin	5577
Simpson, Joe	9030	Smith, Isaac	5578
Simpson, Malinda	9031	Smith, Mollie	5579
Simpson, Susie	9032	Smith, Ida	5580
Simpson, Tahahke	9033	Smith, Grace	5697
Sizemore, Stephen	1668	Smith, Seper	5803
Sizemore, William	8962	Smith, Napka	5804
Sizemore, Nicey	9064	Smith, Charity	5824
Silpee	3721	Smith, Willie G.	5825
Sipley, Jim	5304	Smith, Frank	5877
Sipley, Co-cha-gee	5305	Smith, John	5990
Sipley, Timmy	5306	Smith, Joe	6041
Sipley, William	5307	Smith, Rose	6042
Sipley, Emma	5308	Smith, Kogee	6043
Siah	7104	Smith, Annie	6044
Siah, Mary	7164	Smith, Katie	6046
Siah	8644	Smith, Wesley	6317
Siah, John	9901	Smith, Louina	6318
Sin-ki-ye	7676	Smith, Anna Eliza	6319
Sim hoye	8014	Smith, William	6676
Sim a poka	8378	Smith, Winey	6677
Skeen, Julia	1787	Smith, Orrey	6678
Skeeter, Willie	6111	Smith, Ella	6679
Sleep, Tom	5516	Smith, John	6718
Sleep, Saheche	5517	Smith, Mary	6719
"Slumker"	7900	Smith, Belcher	6762
Sloan, Jemima	9640	Smith, Sarah	6763
Sloane, Sallie	9987	Smith, Wiley	6861
Sloane, Sampson	9988	Smith, Rhoda	6862
Smith, Daniel B.	135	Smith, Lena	6863
Smith, Mary I.	136	Smith, Jim	6864
Smith, Pearl	137	Smith, Lizzie	6865
Smith, Alfred C.	138	Smith, Sallie	6866
Smith, William S.	139	Smith, Matilda	7093
Smith, Albert L.	140	Smith, Rosa	7180
Smith, Franklin M.	141	Smith, James	7368
Smith, Mose	412	Smith, Mollie	7369
Smith, Lizzie	413	Smith, Aggie	7523
Smith, Sallie	414	Smith, Micky	7526
Smith, Nina	1116	Smith, Lydia	7527
Smith, Daniel B. No. 2	1117	Smith, George	7562
Smith, Marsey	1264	Smith, Tildy	7563
Smith, Lewis	1265	Smith, Dinah	7564
Smith, Emma	1266	Smith, Joe	7565
Smith, Matilda	1472	Smith, William	7566
Smith, Hattie	1531	Smith, George	7895
Smith, John F.	1988	Smith, Eliza	8035
Smith, Rannie	1989	Smith, Emma	8086
Smith, Lewis	1990	Smith, Emily	8248
Smith, Ella	1991	Smith, Sarney	8299
Smith, Edna	1992	Smith, Annie	8352
Smith, Lawrence	1993	Smith, Segomaha	8382
Smith, Guy	1994	Smith, Ella	8383
Smith, Pearl	1995	Smith, Sarty	8384
Smith, Willis	1996	Smith, Chatman	8438
Smith, Stephen	2246	Smith, Martin	8439
Smith, Arthur Ray	2247	Smith, Jeffrey	8584
Smith, Anna A.	2248	Smith, Miley	8585
Smith, George W.	2295	Smith, Mary	8621
Smith, Lucinda A.	2458	Smith, Joe	8718
Smith, Shelton	2459	Smith, Freeman	8821
Smith, Janie	2560	Smith, John Jr.	9184

Name.	Roll No.
Smith, Leo	9283
Smith, Hinty	9370
Smith, Grace	9478
Smith, Willie	9482
Smith, Clarence N.	9492
Smith, Sam	9913
Smith, Betsy	9953
Smock, Eloise Grayson	6137
Smiley, Lottie	6907
Smiley, Earnest	6908
Smiley, Allen	6909
Sneed, Artra	371
Sneed, Charley	1026
Sneed, Peoria	1027
Sneed, Almorene	1028
Sneed, Frank	3271
Sneed, William	9500
Sneed, George	9825
Sneed, George Everett	9826
Sneed, Maron	9827
Sneed, Leonard	9828
Sneed, John	9850
Sneed, John	10079
Sneed, Sue Willie	10080
Sneed, Charles Jr.	10081
Sneed, Ernest	10082
Snake, Cotahyar	631
Snakeya, David	1254
Snakeya, Molleanna	1255
Snakeya, Mary	1256
Snakeya, Abram	1257
Snakeya, Gabriel	1258
Snakeya, Onie	1259
Snakeya, Tobe	9398
Snap, James	1300
Snapp, Amanda	4272
Snow, Martha	6109
Snow, Jessie	6110
Snow, Ca-pah-ny	6648
Snow, Yar-la-co-we-ny	6649
Snow, Louisa	6650
Snow, Wesley	6651
Snow, Harthlee	6652
Snow, Tecumseh	6653
Soffie, John	1843
Sookey, Wiley	2133
Sookey, Boney	2134
Sookey, Martha	2135
Sone, Dickey	3468
Sone, Sallie	3469
Sorrell, Dorothy	3895
Sorrell, Julia	3896
Sorrell, Lillie	9544
Soweka, Lewis	4638
Sorbe, Susan	5472
Sorbe, Mary E.	5473
Sorbe, Anna Belle	5474
Socer	6143
Solomon, Lahtah	6449
Solomon, Celey	6450
Solomon, Roley	7749
Soloman, Wisey	6985
Soloman, Susie	6986
Soloman, Johnson	6987
Soloman, Sam	6988
So-con-thla-ney	6705
Sohkuekar	6775
Solander, Minnie	7065
Solander, Hettie L.	7066
Soldier, Robert	7575
So har ho ye	7997
Sooktey	8328
Soc-con-tay	8805
Soffeeney	9956
Spaulding, Josephine	1439
Spaulding, Samuel B.	1440
Spaulding, Lelia A.	1441
Spaulding, Homer O.	1442
Spaulding, Grace B.	1443
Spaulding, Etta	1444
Spaulding, Thomas L.	1445
Spaulding, James S.	1446
Spaulding, Sophia	3147

Name.	Roll No.
Spaulding, Edith	6367
Spaulding, George W.	9355
Spaniard, James	7343
Spaniard, Malinda	7344
Spaniard, Alice	7345
Spaniard, Misselda	7346
Spaniard, Jemima	7347
Spaniard, Joe	7348
Spaniard, Simon	7349
Spaniard, Annie	7350
Spaniard, Henry	7492
Spaniard, Louisa	7493
Spaniard, Chiler	7494
Spaniard, Chotie	7495
Spaniard, Martha	7496
Spaniard, John	9052
Spocogee, Polly	9020
Squire, John	1930
Squire, A-la-sho-o-con-co-nay	1931
Squire, Candy	1956
Squire, Beckie	1957
Squire, John	1958
Squire, Hannah	1959
Squire, Noah	1960
Squire, Te-ke-co-co-nay	1961
Squire, Delia	1962
Stidham, Wilson	301
Stidham, Theodore E.	1191
Stidham, Geo. W. Sr.	2259
Stidham, Ottie	2260
Stidham, Lela	2261
Stidham, Kittie	2262
Stidham, Geo. W., Jr.	2263
Stidham, Albert L.	2264
Stidham, Marie Oleta	2265
Stidham, Leonidas G.	5652
Stidham, Leola May	5653
Stidham, Georgiana	5654
Stidham, Eloita	5655
Stidham, Leah	6093
Stidham, Rose	6645
Stidham, Timmie	7352
Stidham, Eliza	7353
Stidham, Polly	7354
Stidham, George	7355
Stidham, Edward	7356
Stidham, John	7357
Stidham, Clifford	7924
Stidham, Albert P.	7925
Stidham, Buckner Lawrence	8862
Stidham, Nellie	9183
Stidham, Ben	9717
Stidham, William	9962
Stake, Lizzie	470
Stake, Joseph	471
Stake, Salina	472
Stake, James	473
Stake, Albert	1414
Stake, Sallie	1415
Stake, Jennie	1416
Stake, Ellen	1418
Stake, Jeffie	1419
Stake, Eliza	1477
Stake, Winey	5713
Steele, Edward	949
Steele, Tula	2011
Steele, Samuel Edward	2965
Steele, Lena N.	2966
Steele, Catherine C.	4455
Steele, Manie	7969
Steele, Susan	7970
Steele, Mary	9833
Starr, Miley	1691
Starr, Robert	5596
Starr, Lillie	5597
Starr, Ella	5598
Starr, Thomas	5599
Starr, Lydia	5600
Starr, Lena	5601
Starr, Lona	5602

Name.	Roll No.	Name.	Roll No.
Starr, Daniel	5672	Stubblefield, Ida	6518
Starr, Louisa	5773	Stubblefield, Ella M.	6519
Starr, Chesley	6361	Stubblefield, Joseph S.	9577
Starr, Katie	6362	"Standwaitie"	5384
Starr, Martha	6363	Standwaite, Toady	5385
Starr, Chipley	6551	Standwaitie, Joseph	5386
Starr, Nancy	6552	Standwaitie, Wilson	5387
Starr, Reuben	6553	Stepney, Sissie	8329
Starr, Sallie	7766	Stepney, Liley	8330
Starr, James	7936	Stepney, Thompson	8331
Starr, Pulhokey	7937	Stand, Phillip	8404
Starr, Edward	7938	Stand, Thomas	9758
Starr, Lewis	7939	Stevenson, Mamie	9296
Starr, Nellie	7940	Stephens, Vadie	9572
Starr, Annie	7941	Steen, Robert	9898
Starr, Lizzie	7942	Stanley, Mattie E.	10159
Starr, Melissa	7943	Stanley, Earl A.	10160
Starr, Annie	8807	Stanley, Pearl A.	10161
Starr, Adam	9761	Stanley, Joseph C.	10162
Starr, Emma	9868	Stanley, Pleasant	10163
Starr, Cora Ellis	10100	Sullivan, Hattie	13
Starr, Henry	10101	Sullivan, Annie	86
Starr, Annie	10102	Sullivan, Obey	87
Starr, Gertrude	10103	Sullivan, Helen	88
Starr, Moses	4946	Sullivan, William	1252
Starr, Susie	4947	Sullivan, Louina	1253
Starr, Hebsey	4948	Sullivan, Ellen	1685
Starr, Minnie	4949	Sullivan, Wiliam	1688
Starr, Nina	4950	Sullivan, Kizzie	1689
Stewart, John	1902	Sullivan, Mary Ann	4000
Stewart, America	3589	Sullivan, Minnie	4897
Stewart, Annie	3590	Sullivan, Jimmie	4901
Stewart, Effie	3591	Sullivan, William	7622
Stewart, Alice	3592	Sullivan, Willie	8140
Stewart, Ruthie Pearl	3593	Sullivan, Thomas	8141
Stewart, Robert W.	4475	Sullivan, Lucy	9252
Stewart, Lucy	4476	Sullivan, George	9519
Stewart, Noah	4478	Sullivan, Sulphur	9911
Stewart, Albert P.	5434	Sunday, Edmund	420
Stewart, Louisa	5435	Sunday, Anderson	995
Stewart, Clyde	5436	Sunday, Alex	996
Stewart, Annie	5437	Sunday, Ellen	997
Stewart, Thomas A.	5440	Sunday, Tilda	6045
Stewart, George E.	9501	Sunday, Mattie	7817
Stewart, Edna	9690	Sugar, Wesley	424
Staley, John	1909	Sugar, Togy	425
Staley, Sak-co-ta	1910	Sugar, Armster	426
Staley, Eu-con-co-con- thla	1911	Sugar, Thomas	689
		Sugar, James	2168
Staley, Tar-sa-co-con- thla	1912	Sugar, Helen	2169
Storm, Lou	2353	Sugar, Kizzie	2170
Storm, Annie	2354	Sugar, Yarner	2171
Storm, Eliza	2355	Sugar, Pilot	2172
Storm, Parelee	2356	Sugar, Joseph	2931
Storm, Gladys	9678	Sugar, Sam	5574
Stoddard, William	2858	Sugar, Eddie	5575
Stoddard, Lousanna	2859	Sugar, James, Jr.	9627
Stoddard, Mamie	2860	Sutton, Mollie	1594
Stoddard, Jesse	2861	Sutton, James D.	1595
Stratton, Louisa	2862	Sutton, Samuel Jesse	1596
Stover, Daniel	3261	Sutton, Lorena	1597
Stover, Lavina	3262	Sutton, Loretta	1598
Stover, Lillie	3263	Summers, Clinton P.	2838
Stover, Eli	3264	Summers, Thomas	2839
Stover, Wasa	3265	Summers, James	2840
Stover, Willie	3266	Summers, Dee	2841
Stover, Reuben	9415	Summers, Ada	2842
Stevens, Idella M.	3324	Summers, Frank	2843
Stevens, Myrtle M.	3325	Summers, Cordia	2844
Stevens, Stella I.	3326	Summers, Mary	2845
Stevens, Pearl V.	3327	Summers, Pet	2846
Stevens, Mary	3397	Summers, Fannie	9655
Stevens, Bryan	3398	Sulphur, James	2863
Stevens, Clarence O.	9542	Sulphur, Kizzie	2864
Stevens, Sarah	10044	Sulphur, Edmond	2865
Stevens, Wiley	10045	Sulphur, Kizzie	2866
Stevens, Mose	10046	Sulphur, George	2867
Stephenson, Polly	5103	Sulphur, Hattie	10040
Stephenson, Augusta	5104	Sulphur, Alex	9621
Stephenson, Nancy	7695	Sunny, Walter	3987
Stubblefield, Lousanna	5360	Sunny, Mary	3988
		Sunny, Peggie	4356

Name.	Roll No.	Name.	Roll No.
Sutor, Robert	4006	Taylor, Albert	9309
Suka	4237	Taylor, Cub	9310
Sumehcha	4248	Taylor, Jennie	9339
Sumka, Willie	4637	Tarvin, Marion E.	1147
Sumka,	5615	Tarvin, Rita	1148
Susanna	8377	Tarvin, Beauregard C.	1150
"Sumsey"	5786	Tarvin, Pleasant F.	9098
Sumsey, Sissie	5787	Tarvin, Marion	9099
Suder, Lobla	681	Tarvin, Randon	9100
Suder, Bunny	6682	Tarvin, Fannie	9101
Suder, Choatkey	10024	Tarvin, Sehoy M.	9102
Sukey	7390	Tarvin, Theresa	9413
Sukey	8453	Tarvin, Mary B.	10018
Sucky	7733	Tah-co-we-nay	2110
Sutherland, Lol	8549	Tah-co-we-nay, Jennetta	2111
Sutherland, Earnest	8550	Tahladege, Chepan	2914
Susanna	9001	Tahladege, Mary	2915
Sudcharkey, Sampson	10038	Tahledege, Millie	2916
Swingle, Levi	9457	Tahledege, Wattie	2917
"Sylla"	9383	Tahledege, Cable	2918
Tarpeliche	356	Taryole	4188
Tarpalechee, Miller	1101	Taryolie, Turner	9930
Taylor, Melvina L.	675	Tamochee, Patsy	4229
Taylor, William	676	Tate, Mary	5255
Taylor, Royal B.	677	Tate, Mary	9872
Taylor, Teperke	939	Tate, Twintilla	9875
Taylor, Rosa	1013	Tate, Maty	9876
Taylor, Pearl	1014	Tarkey	5380
Taylor, Harry C.	1015	Ta-co-ney	7000
Taylor, Solomon	1771	Tarpley, Jacob	7573
Taylor, Fred	1772	Talomase, Dickey	7811
Taylor, Frank	3328	Talomase, Eliza	7812
Taylor, Nancy	3595	Tah-ka-ney	7849
Taylor, Barney	3596	Tahkaney, Tah-pan-far	7850
Taylor, Abraham	3708	Tahkaney, Marsie	7851
Taylor, Lilia	3709	Tahkaney, Dillie	7852
Taylor, Sammy	3710	Tahkaney, Connee	7853
Taylor, Turner F.	3722	Tar lo shaw	7952
Taylor, Sissie	3723	Taye	8354
Taylor, Cub	3773	Tar-chom	8531
Taylor, Tom	4238	"Tayoposka"	9272
Taylor, Sunda	4300	Tapp, Marie	9420
Taylor, Frank	6014	Taborn, Nancy Atkins	10085
Taylor, Maria	6015	Taborn, Susie Atkins	10086
Taylor, Lewis	6016	Tahkee	10129
Taylor, Emma	6017	Terrell, Mary E.	463
Taylor, Kizzie	6018	Terrell, Henry	464
Taylor, Monny	6768	Tecumseh, Tecumseh	2468
Taylor, Mollie	6769	Tecumseh, Ellis	2469
Taylor, Silla	6770	Tecumseh, Eliza	2470
Taylor, Jonas	6771	Tecumseh, Alec	2471
Taylor, Lucy	6969	Tecumseh, Nicey	2472
Taylor,	7306	Tecumseh, Austin	2473
Taylor, Jo-lo-lon-fah	7307	Tecumseh, Nero	2474
Taylor, Timmie	7308	Tecumseh, Willie	2475
Taylor, Eliza	7309	Tecumseh, Eddie	2476
Taylor, Ada	7310	Tecumsey	8295
Taylor, Milea	7583	Techarna, Jackson	2980
Taylor, Isaac	7584	Techarna, Eliza	2981
Taylor, Lucinda	7585	Techarna, Lochar	2982
Taylor, Emma	7586	Techarna, Louisa	2983
Taylor, Hardy	7596	Techarna, Malissa	2984
Taylor, Sarpsey	7597	Teke	4149
Taylor, Jemima	7598	Tea, Thomas	5422
Taylor, Susie	7599	Tea, Judy	5423
Taylor, Eliza	7600	Tea, Anna	5424
Taylor, Jacob	7601	Tea, Lucy	5425
Taylor, Taylor	7606	Tea, Nancy	5426
Taylor, Lizzie	7607	Tea, Amos	5427
Taylor, Marchie	7608	Tea, Ellen	5428
Taylor, Dumsey	7609	Tea, Emma	5429
Taylor, Mary	7953	Tell, Amos	5940
Taylor, Leechie	8442	Tell, Addie	9528
Taylor, Eliza	8459	Templin, Benjamin A.	7094
Taylor, John W.	9117	Temahee	7732
Taylor, Mannie	9255	Te yo hee	7750
Taylor, Roley	9303	Temunthlahpe, George	7892
Taylor, Nellie	9304	Tehunthlahpe, Nellie	7893
Taylor, Leah	9305	Temunthlahpe, Tina	7894
Taylor, Soma	9306	Temunthlahpe, Tiger	10050
Taylor, Ellis	9307	Temunthlahpe, Dollie	10051
Taylor, Sarah	9308	Temunthlahpe, Prince	10052

Name.	Roll No.	Name.	Roll No.
Tebe, Wisey	8944	Thomas, Sam	1924
Tebe, Willie	8945	Thomas, Sophia	1925
Tebe, Yarner	8946	Thomas, Emma	1926
Tebe, Tarbie	8947	Thomas, William	1927
Tebe, Jennie	9764	Thomas, Johnson	1928
Terry, Annettie Joseph-		Thomas, Lizzie	1938
ine	10174	Thomas, Melesse	2383
Thompson, Alex	251	Thomas, Mollie E.	3070
Thompson, March	258	Thomas, George W.	3071
Thompson, Willie	833	Thomas, Mary Ellen	3072
Thompson, Betty	1486	Thomas, Douglass	3073
Thompson, Robert	1633	Thomas, John	4246
Thompson, Hepsey	1634	Thomas, Bettie	4247
Thompson, Jackson	2806	Thomas, Parnosky	4251
Thompson, Mary	2820	Thomas, Adam	4252
Thompson, Simmer	3230	Thomas, Kaley	4253
Thompson, Misey	3231	Thomas, Amos	4895
Thompson, Phoebee	3232	Thomas, Bepsey	4896
Thompson, Haga	3257	Thomas, Milly	4898
Thompson, Tauchie	3258	Thomas, Emma	4899
Thompson, Newman	3259	Thomas, Bettie	4900
Thompson, March	3277	Thomas, Aggie	6132
Thompson, Silby	3278	Thomas, James C.	6133
Thompson, Manuel	3279	Thomas, Lizzie Lou	6134
Thompson, George	3280	Thomas, Waitie	7137
Thompson, Ella	4652	Thomas, John	7138
Thompson, Alice	5430	Thomas, Katie	7587
Thompson, Ellen	5431	Thomas, Linda	7588
Thompson, Victoria	5432	Thomas, Louisa	7589
Thompson, Thomas	5677	Thomas, Millie	7590
Thompson, Rose	5678	Thomas, Bettie	7807
Thompson, Rose	5790	Thomas, Willie	8150
Thompson, Tom	5927	Thomas, Dick	8161
Thompson, Nicey	5928	Thomas, Albert	8443
Thompson, Captain	5929	Thomas, Tumsey	8762
Thompson, Rosa	5930	Thomas, Kate	9002
Thompson, Sonny	5931	Thomas, Willie	9527
Thompson, Sam	5932	Thomas, Harley	9617
Thompson, Hully	5933	Thomas, Lydia	9618
Thompson, Sarah	5934	Thomas, Lena	9619
Thompson, Legus	6287	Thomas, Eliza	9620
Thompson, Lena	6288	Thomas, Leaster	9884
Thompson, Legus, Jr.	6289	Thomas, Emily	10096
Thompson, Josephine	6390	Thomas	10130
Thompson, Henry	6391	Throckmorton, James W.	2059
Thompson, Riley	6392	Throckmorton, Ida	2060
Thompson, Susanna	6541	Throckmorton, Natura E.	2066
Thompson, Roman	6549	Throckmorton, Eva B.	9576
Thompson, Me-li-sa	6684	Thurman, Alice	2635
Thompson, Nancy	6731	Thurman, Silas	2947
Thompson, Charlie	6732	Thorpe, Fannie	5688
Thompson, Robert	6733	Thlocco, Toche	6598
Thompson, Amanda	6734	Thlocco, Fus	9959
Thompson, Lucy	6735	Thomasoche	7420
Thompson, James	6980	Thornsberry, Annie	9877
Thompson, Susan	7318	Thornsberry, John	9878
Thompson, Lizzie	7723	Thornsberry, Lena	9879
Thompson, Caesar	7728	Thornsberry, Rachael	9880
Thompson, Melinda	7729	Thornsberry, Willie	9881
Thompson, Leah	7730	Thornsberry, Wynema	9882
Thompson, Henry	8036	Thluppa (or Thloppie)	10041
Thompson, Ben	8489	Tiger, Motey	78
Thompson, Jeannetta	8490	Tiger, Kissie	79
Thompson, Minnie	8552	Tiger, Amos	81
Thompson, Otie	8642	Tiger, George W.	142
Thompson, Thomas	8791	Tiger, Susan	143
Thompson, Alex	8836	Tiger, Adolphus	144
Thompson, Little	8937	Tiger, Luther	145
Thompson, Billy	8964	Tiger, Oscar	146
Thompson, Lettie	8965	Tiger, Minnie	147
Thompson, Cinda	8968	Tiger, Johnson E.	224
Thompson, Nellie	8969	Tiger, Annie	567
Thompson, Thomas	9244	Tiger, Nellie	663
Thompson, Lucy	9245	Tiger, Billy	690
Thompson, Russell	9393	Tiger, Lilah	691
Thompson, Mussie	9820	Tiger, Eliza	692
Thatcher, Nancy	872	Tiger, Thomas	693
Thatcher, John Douglas	873	Tiger, Lyman	694
Thatcher, Edmond	9518	Tiger, Eliza	731
Thomas, Mack	1921	Tiger, Niloge	732
Thomas, Sarah	1922	Tiger, Selina	733
Thomas, Philip	1923	Tiger, Thomas	820

Name.	Roll No.	Name.	Roll No.
Tiger, Martha	821	Tiger, Jinalee	4726
Tiger, Leaster	822	Tiger, Mattie	4729
Tiger, Ben	823	Tiger, Billy	5032
Tiger, Jim	824	Tiger, Lumyer	5035
Tiger, Martha	1039	Tiger, Catchochee	5066
Tiger, Leaster	822	Tiger, Lucinda	5067
Tiger, Ben	823	Tiger, Jesse	5068
Tiger, Jim	824	Tiger, Jeanetta	5069
Tiger, Martha	1039	Tiger, Miller	5070
Tiger, Sam	1040	Tiger, Hettie	5071
Tiger, Lydia	1041	Tiger, Dave	5150
Tiger, Louisa	1044	Tiger, Barney	5183
Tiger, Marchie	1045	Tiger, Katie	5184
Tiger, Ben	1118	Tiger, George	5185
Tiger, Mary	1119	Tiger, Charley	5186
Tiger, Manday	1120	Tiger, Leona	5187
Tiger, Rosie	1121	Tiger, Fannie	5188
Tiger, Jim	1122	Tiger, Louis	5270
Tiger, Nancy	1123	Tiger, Joseph	5271
Tiger, Amy	1124	Tiger, Nettie	5272
Tiger, John	1127	Tiger, Tobe	5315
Tiger, Dave	1136	Tiger, Susan	5317
Tiger, Neosho	1137	Tiger, Jeff	5537
Tiger, Willie	1138	Tiger, Kogee	5538
Tiger, Cotsar	1139	Tiger, Dave	5541
Tiger, Lucy	1267	Tiger, Coge	5542
Tiger, Jack	1283	Tiger, Chapley	5549
Tiger, Jennetta	1284	Tiger, Nancy	5550
Tiger, Lucy	1285	Tiger, Mickey	5556
Tiger, Walter	1286	Tiger, Alberd	5587
Tiger, Siller	1287	Tiger, George	5591
Tiger, Eliza	1290	Tiger, Louisa	5964
Tiger, Simpson	1378	Tiger, Louisa	6012
Tiger, Jennie	1379	Tiger, George W.	6034
Tiger, Sallie	1380	Tiger, Susan H.	6035
Tiger, Lena	1381	Tiger, Ada M.	6036
Tiger, Albert	1382	Tiger, Ida R.	6037
Tiger, Lovey	1383	Tiger, Eugene M.	6038
Tiger, Lydia	1624	Tiger, Dewitt T.	6039
Tiger, John	1680	Tiger, Matilda	6099
Tiger, Stanwaitie	1935	Tiger, Con-san-na	6103
Tiger, Jesse	1936	Tiger, Timmie	6104
Tiger, Minnie	1937	Tiger, Salina	6105
Tiger, Lodie	1940	Tiger, Noah	6106
Tiger, Dollie	1941	Tiger, Saloma	6107
Tiger, Isaac	2073	Tiger, Lucy	6108
Tiger, Mary	2074	Tiger, William	6320
Tiger, Johnson	2661	Tiger, Nancy	6321
Tiger, Amanda	2892	Tiger, Thloppie	6413
Tiger, John	2893	Tiger, Pinar	6495
Tiger, Conzie	3100	Tiger, Turner	6496
Tiger, Fancy	3101	Tiger, Sissy	6497
Tiger, Aney	3102	Tiger, George	6498
Tiger, Betsey	3103	Tiger, Philip	6499
Tiger, Tecumseh	3131	Tiger, Lodie	6500
Tiger, Judy	3132	Tiger, Tasharlacoconthla	6501
Tiger, John	3136	Tiger, Joseph	6513
Tiger, Winey	3137	Tiger, Dosie	6514
Tiger, Jacob	3138	Tiger, Lillie	6515
Tiger, Samuel	3139	Tiger, Katie	6516
Tiger, John	3224	Tiger, Annie	6539
Tiger, Millie	3225	Tiger, Roley	6591
Tiger, Casey	3226	Tiger, Coody	6659
Tiger, George	3239	Tiger, Jumbo	6663
Tiger, Willie	3240	Tiger, Ka-ka-ney	6664
Tiger, Lucy	3241	Tiger, John	6665
Tiger, John	3763	Tiger, Willie	6666
Tiger, John	3794	Tiger, Jim	6667
Tiger, Pufney	3875	Tiger, Sam	6690
Tiger, Winey	3876	Tiger, Robert	6808
Tiger, Mary	3877	Tiger, George	6832
Tiger, Susie	3878	Tiger, John	6839
Tiger, Roman	3879	Tiger, David	6840
Tiger, Daniel	3880	Tiger, John	6850
Tiger, Malinda	3881	Tiger, Polly	6997
Tiger, Daniel	3935	Tiger, Sukey	7028
Tiger, Sarah	3936	Tiger, Sophia	7030
Tiger, Palmer	3937	Tiger, Hapsey	7031
Tiger, David	3938	Tiger, Tommie	7032
Tiger, Medelia	3939	Tiger, Taylor	7033
Tiger, Lonie	3940	Tiger, Annie	7034
Tiger, Bessie	3941	Tiger, Tamer	7148
Tiger, Lietka	4725		

Name.	Roll No.	Name.	Roll No.
Tiger, Mesaley	7149	Tilly, Christie	5178
Tiger, Lizzie	7233	Tilly, Myrtle	5179
Tiger, Willie	7238	Tilly, Nannie E.	5180
Tiger, George	7239	Tilly, Anna	5181
Tiger, Eliza	7240	Tilly, Ina	5182
Tiger, Kizzie	7422	Tikoche	6233
Tiger, Benny	7423	Tiller, John	6452
Tiger, Annie	7424	Tiller, Loodie	6453
Tiger, Minerva	7576	Tiller, Noah	6622
Tiger, Leah	7580	Timothy, Taylor	7684
Tiger, Louis	7581	Timothy, John	7685
Tiger, Albert	7657	Timothy, Ella	7686
Tiger, Cinda	7711	Timothy, Turner	7687
Tiger, Louis	7712	Timothy, Warsey	7688
Tiger, Hannah	7765	Timothy, Noah	9311
Tiger, Nicey	7870	Timothy, Eliza	9312
Tiger, Lilly	7944	Timothy, Sandy	9314
Tiger, Amos	7945	Timothy, Wesley	9725
Tiger, Salina	7946	Town, James	2887
Tiger, Jeannetta	7947	Town, Sallie	2888
Tiger, Tom	7948	Town, James, Jr.	2889
Tiger, George	7951	Town, Emma	2890
Tiger, Wilson	7962	Topartheche	3453
Tiger, Eliza	7963	Todd, Katie	5206
Tiger, Addie	7964	Todd, Jesse J.	5207
Tiger, Wesley	7965	Todd, Lela E.	5208
Tiger, Nancy	7966	Toskey, Ned	5705
Tiger, Jacob	7968	Toskey, Cinda	5706
Tiger, John	8053	Toskey, Susana	5707
Tiger, Thomas	8297	Toskey, Lucy	5708
Tiger, Wattie	8298	Toskey, Eli	5709
Tiger, Archie	8444	Toskey	7127
Tiger, James	8445	Tom, Euchee	6432
Tiger, Silvia	8446	Tom, Louanna	10180
Tiger, Mollie	8523	Tommie, Hulpata	6660
Tiger, Malinda	8524	Tok hah ke	7887
Tiger, Wesley	8610	Toney, Rogers	8435
Tiger, Jim	8616	Toney, Lizzie	8540
Tiger, Co-ke-ther-ney	8617	Toot-chee	8452
Tiger, Char-ko-char-ney	8618	Tobler, Maria	8558
Tiger, Pa-sak-ta	8619	Tobler, Paulina	8559
Tiger, Ke-e-co-ka-ney	8620	Tobler, Alvan	8560
Tiger, Louis	8873	Toot-ho-ye	8920
Tiger, Hully	8875	Trusler, Lucile Frances	9754
Tiger, Joseley	8876	Trent, Chaney	9916
Tiger, Sophia	8896	Trent, Frank	9917
Tiger, Noah	8897	Trent, Mary	9918
Tiger, Rhoda	8898	Trent, Will	9919
Tiger, Sah- co po chuny	9214	Trent, Susie	9920
Tiger, Lucinda	9220	Trent, Lee Drew	9921
Tiger, Goody	9257	Trent, Bennie	9922
Tiger, Jackson	9354	Trent, Fannie C.	9923
Tiger, William	9412	Turner, Fannie X.	194
Tiger, Mary	9499	Turner, Hattie	195
Tiger, Edward B.	9524	Turner, Annie	196
Tiger, Helen May	9536	Turner, George P. M.	197
Tiger, Turner	9568	Turner, Hammer G., Jr.	198
Tiger, Philip	9579	Turner, Marguerite Estel-	
Tiger, Louisa	9638	la	199
Tiger, Tah-per-scoy-ka	9647	Turner, Tookah B.	1048
Tiger, John	9729	Turner, Tookah K.	1049
Tiger, Louisa	9730	Turner, Clarence W., Jr.	1050
Tiger, Martha	9787	Turner, Marion	1051
Tiger, Cotala	9852	Turk, George	429
Tiger, Elba	9853	Turk, Nepsey	430
Tiger, Jessley	9889	Turk, Frank	1350
Tiger, John	9892	Turk, Peggie	1351
Tiger, Nancy	9985	Turk, Lucinda	1354
Tiger, John	10000	Turk, Benjamin	9219
Tiger, Johnson	10001	Turk, Jerry	9645
Tiger, Louisa	10098	Tulsa, Emma	1458
Tiger, Anna	10099	Tulsa, Joe	8566
Tiger, He-con-con-thla	10112	Tulsa, Willie	8790
Tiner, Tecumseh	1692	Turnham, Curley	1788
Tiner, Katie	1693	Turnham, William R.	1789
Tiner, John	1694	Turnham, Violet	1790
Tiner, Martha	6112	Tuttle, Mary Ann	2296
Timmunichee, Taylor	1864	Tuttle, Lura Lee	2297
Timmunichee, Mollie	1865	Tuttle, Lilly May	2298
Timmunichee, Mary	1866	Tucker, Hettie	2742
Tiplow, John	4847	Turkey, Colbert	6209
Tiplow, Susan	4848	Tuckabatchee, Ned	7095

Name.	Roll No.	Name.	Roll No.
Tuckabache	8300	Washington, Sukey	7291
Tuffer	8169	Washington, Colbert	7292
Tuffer, Sene	8170	Washington, Emma	7293
Tuffer, Mary	8171	Washington, Marchie	7487
Tuffer, Lizzie	8172	Washington, Waitie	7488
Tustunukoche	8266	Washington, Liza	7647
Tustenuggy, Takoser	8891	Washington, Kogee	7776
Tyler, Joe	6829	Washington, Minnie	7777
Tyler, Cinda	7788	Washington, Thomas	8151
Tyler, Lucy	7789	Washington, George	8353
Tyler, Kate	7800	Washington, John	9066
Tyler, John	8010	"Washington"	9177
Tyhoka	7540	Washington, Brutus	9433
U-par-har-ha	5128	Washington, Thomas	9580
Unussee, Barnossee	7935	Washington, Mary	9782
U-la-ah-con-tay-na	8847	Washington, Walter	9783
Vann, John	957	Washington, Willie	9784
Vann, Dicey	958	Washington, Thomas	9900
Vann, Katie	1303	Washington, Walter	9949
Vann, Watlie	3200	Walker, Mary	487
Vann, James S.	9186	Walker, Jim	587
Vann, Sarah Heland	9187	Walker, Lucy	588
Vanderslice, Roxan	2067	Walker, William Walter	868
Vanderslice, Isaac	2068	Walker, Josephine	1030
Vanderslice, Harvey L.	2069	Walker, Minnie	1068
Vanderslice, Harriet	2070	Walker, Nettie	1069
Vanderslice, Ida Jane	2071	Walker, William	1485
Vanderslice, Patience	2725	Walker, Izora E.	3188
Vanderslice, Thomas J.	2726	Walker, Edward H.	3407
Vanderslice, Bertha May	2727	Walker, Eula	3408
Vanderslice, Annie Maud	2728	Walker, Mary	3409
Vanderslice, Mary Ann	9451	Walker, Dick	3740
Vance, Mary E.	2340	Walker, George	4509
Vance, Joseph	2341	Walker, Benjamin	6061
Vance, George William	2342	Walker, Mary	4692
Vance, Samuel E.	2343	Walker, Eddie	4693
Vance, Florence A.	2344	Walker, George W.	4694
Vance, Benjamin	2345	Walker, Ellen	4695
Vance, Ollie May	2346	Walker, William	4696
Vance, William	9555	Walker, Susan	4697
Vannest, Grace O.	2397	Walker, Martha Jane	5521
Vannest, Annie M.	2398	Walker, Bettie	7207
Vannest, Harry L.	2399	Walker, Louis	7208
Vannest, Ada E.	2400	Walker, Wisey	7209
Vandivew, James	5614	Walker, Isaac	7210
Vowell, Martha	1510	Walker, Mabel	8588
Vowell, Tom	1511	Walker, Mineola	9657
Vowell, John	1512	Walker, Liza	9926
Vowell, Rena	1513	Watson, Kate	802
Vowell, Casie	1514	Watson, Milburn L.	803
Vowell, Leroy	1515	Watson, Annie L.	804
Vowell, Jesse	1516	Watson, Jane	805
Vowell, Sam	2588	Watson, Young	806
Vowell, Floyd	2589	Watson, Homer	1324
Vowell, Joseph Le Roy	9699	Watson, Mahala A.	1568
Vore, Lizzie	2852	Watson, Fanny Anna	1765
Vore, Fred	2853	Watson, Ellen	2249
Vore, Tewohley	5251	Watson, Robert	2250
Washington, Rhoda	383	Watson, George	2251
Washington, Winey	384	Watson, John	2252
Washington, Casinie	385	Watson, Nellie	2253
Washington, Peter	386	Watson, Louisa	2254
Washington, George	387	Watson, Annie	2255
Washington, Austin	388	Watson, Katie	4518
Washington, Wesley	389	Watson, Bessie	4519
Washington, Peter	390	Watson, George	4520
Washington, Willie	925	Watson, Daniel	4539
Washington, William	2149	Watson, Josiah	4557
Washington, Willie	5493	Watson, Yarner	4558
Washington, Waitie	5494	Watson, Hettie	4559
Washington, Isaac	5635	Watson, Webster	4560
Washington, Catherine	6298	Watson, Fannie	4561
Washington, Marion M.	6299	Watson, Jane	4562
Washington, Watson	6349	Watson, Ida	5082
Washington, Lucy	6350	Watson, Louisa	5084
Washington, Ida	6351	Watson, Eddie	5107
Washington, Minnie	6352	Watson, Amos	6527
Washington, Moses	6364	Watson, Parnoska	7241
Washington, Linda	6365	Watson, Chammy	7242
Washington, Dixon	6385	Watson, Bella	7377
Washington, Dave	6849	Watson, Santy	7659
Washington, Walter	6867	Watson, Sallie	7660

Name.	Roll No.	Name.	Roll No.
Watson, David C.	7663	Weldon, Viola	114
Watson, Daniel	8316	Weldon, Robert Lee	115
Watson, John	9077	West, Arabella W.	116
Watson, Fannie	7206	West, Sue Hettie	134
Wadsworth, Ben	1192	West, Polly	514
Wardsworth, Mattie	1869	West, Thomas	600
Wadsworth, Irene	1870	West, Lizzie	1686
Wadsworth, John	1871	West, Rosie	1687
Wadsworth, William	1872	West, Louisa	3691
Wadsworth, Newman	1873	West, Cogee	3693
Wadsworth, Caddo	3977	West, Sally	3745
Wadsworth, Mitchell	6195	West, Eliza	3746
Wadsworth, Lussie	7764	West, Kizzie	3747
Wadsworth, Eliza	8628	West, George	3748
Wadsworth, Annie	8629	West, Thomas	3750
Wadsworth, Richard	8630	West, Lucy	3751
Wadsworth, Daniel	8631	West, George	4115
Wadsworth, Thomas	9946	West, Siker	4116
Ware, Lula	1791	West, Ledie	4117
Ware, Oren	1792	West, Waddie	4137
Ware, Ivy	1793	West, Sissy	4138
Wallow, Lucy	2677	West, Williamsee	4139
Wallow, Sallie	7699	West, Milochee	4140
Wallow, Nellie	7700	West, Robert	4254
Wallow, Simmer	7701	West, Sarnie	4255
Wallow, Peter	7702	West, Katie	4256
Ward, Effie	2763	West, Ella	4257
Ward, Charlie	2765	West, Pompey	4508
Warner, Rosa L.	2954	West, Billy	4525
Warlecy	3079	West, Louisa	4526
Warlecy, Nancy	3080	West, Daniel	4527
Warlecy, James	3081	West, Louisa	4528
Wallace, Ella	3114	West, Susan	4529
Wallace, Tula	3115	West, Thomas	4533
Wallace, Albert	3116	West, Parsinder	4589
Wallace, Janison	6249	West, Feny	4592
Way, Vida M.	3189	West, Losanna	4621
Watkins, U. S. Grant	4172	West, Lumsey	4944
Warden, Coy	5329	West, Nellie	9891
Warden, Hugh	5330	West, Johnnie	9905
Watts, Anna H.	5348	West, Hettie	10008
Watts, Mary Etta	5349	Wesley, Jimsey	165
Watts, Robert L.	5350	Wesley, John Lowe	2299
Watts, Mary	9222	Wesley, Bettie May	2300
Warnarkee, Silla	6433	Wesley, Roley	2301
Warnarkee, Wicey	6434	Wesley, Bella	2675
Warnarkee, Winnie	10007	Wesley, Daniel	2676
Wattie	6486	Wesley, Charley	4495
Wattie, Parnie	8176	Wesley, Joe	5922
Wattie, Thomas	8177	Wesley, Kentucky	5923
Warlesee	6680	Wesley, John	6224
Wa ta she	6884	Wesley, Polly	6448
Watashe, Rosa	6885	Wesley, Victor	6668
Watashe, Celia	6886	Wesley, Elsie	6669
Watashe, Barney	6887	Wesley, Louis	6670
Watashe, Wiley	6888	Wesley, John	6671
Watashe, Eliza	6889	Wesley, Bessie	6672
Watashe, Lofahye	6890	Wesley, Thomas	6673
"War-co-che"	7731	Wesley, Rhoda	6674
"Wa-co-che"	9042	Wesley, Lizzie	6675
Wa-co-che, Lotta	9043	Wesley, Keeper	8098
Wa-co-che, Isaac	9044	Wesley, Leah	8099
Wa-co-che, Benjamin	9045	Wesley, Louisa	8100
Wa-co-che, Johnson	9046	Wesley, Eddie	8101
Wa-co-che, Jimmie	9047	Wesley, Major	8480
Wa-co-che, Alex	9048	Wesley, Nettie	9773
Wa-co-che, Aggie	9049	Wesley, Cogee	10068
Wa-co-che, Eliza	9050	Weaver, Emma	486
Warrior, Lydia	8410	Weaver, Mary	489
Warrior, Dave	8411	Weaver, Edward	490
Warrior, John	8412	Weaver, Georgia	491
Waitie, Osie	8841	Weaver, Rena	9223
Waspee	9010	Weaver, Helen R.	9224
Walter, Isaac	9791	Weaver, Etta May	9683
Wanakee, Lizzie	9934	Weatherspoon, Vicey	2352
Webster, Edward	82	Wells, Lydia	2363
Webster, Betsey	83	Wells, Ellen	2364
Webster, Albert	84	Wells, Martha	2365
Webster, Jefferson	4688	Wells, Joseph	2366
Webster, Mattie	4689	Wells, Lizzie	2367
Webster, Bunner	9915	Wells, Loyal	2368
Weldon, Mrs. Ruby D.	113	Wells, Watie	2369
		Wells, Walter	2370

Name.	Roll No.	Name.	Roll No.
Wells, Lee	2371	Williams, Charles '	5465
Wells, Viola	2372	Williams, Emma	5466
Welakoche	8763	Williams, Abbie	5468
White, Mose	1128	Williams, Rose Ann	5469
White, Tellie	1153	Williams, Mary Ann	5470
White, Malissa	1154	Williams, Clara May	5471
White, Tennessee	2687	Williams, Nellie	6599
White, Everett B.	2688	Williams, Nathan	6639
White, Phenia	3674	Williams, Lillie D.	6640
White, Maud Annie	3675	Williams, Hannah	6641
White, Rosella	3676	Williams, Susie	6642
White, Susie	435ɔ	Williams, Jennie	6643
White, James	4935	Williams, Martha	6644
White, Ben	6280	Williams, Annie	7305
White, Barney	73ʑ	Williams, Luster	7434
White, Peter	7328	Williams, Sally	7435
White, George	7715	Williams, Richard	7436
White, George	8359	Williams, Sinthe	7796
White, William	9607	Williams, Lucy	7797
Whitlow, David	1201	Williams, Taner	7798
Whitlow, David B.	167	Williams, Jane	9018
Whitlow, Cleveland	1678	Williams, Ellen	9302
Whitlow, William	2141	Williams, Thomas	9341
Whitlow, Leo	2142	Williams, Tamer	9521
Whitlow, Ralph	2143	Williams, Walter E.	9646
Whitlow, Edmond	8016	Williams, Willie	9834
Whitlow, Edward	9955	William, Doctor	6623
Whetstone, James	2318	William	7649
Whetstone, Edward	2319	Willingham, Doc	1355
Whetstone, Carrie	2320	Willingham, Nisey	1356
Whetstone, Charlie	2321	Willingham, Mary	1357
Whetstone, Alvin	2322	Willingham, Rachael	1358
Whetstone, Mary Ella	2323	Willingham, Lizzie	1359
Whetstone, Presley	2673	Willingham, Bettie	1360
Whetstone, Nancy C.	10065	Wills, John J.	1539
Whitten, Willie	2350	Wills, Louis Leroy	1540
Whitfield, Millie	3661	Wills, Mollie L.	1541
Whitfield, Rachel	3662	Wills, Bluford	1542
Whaley, Fannie	4262	Wills, Buford	1543
Whaley, Rufus M., Jr.	4263	Wills, Theodore Dewey	1544
Whaley, Elizabeth D.	4264	Wills, Henry F.	2191
Wisner, Annie D.	341	Wills, Dottie Ruth	2192
Wisener, Ben J.	2294	Wills, William H.	2598
Wisener, Joe	3430	Wills, Albert G.	2599
Wisener, Katie	3431	Wills, Bonnie	2600
Wiley, Nettie	610	Wills, Joe B.	2601
Wiley, Angie	611	Wills, John S.	3951
Wiley, Benny	612	Wills, Joseph	8970
Wiley, Walter	904	Wills, Eliza	8971
Wiley, Lizzie	1008	Wills, Thomas	8972
Wiley, Louisa	1009	Wills, Buck H.	9682
Wiley, Malissa	1097	Wilson, Jesse	1141
Wiley, Cinda	1098	Wilson, John Emmet	1670
Wiley, Major	1099	Wilson, Hattie L.	1671
Wiley, Martha	1100	Wilson, Margaret A.	1672
Wiley, Andrew	1473	Wilson, Earnest C.	1673
Wiley, Annie	1474	Wilson, Thomas	2193
Wiley, Susie	1475	Wilson, Manana	2194
Wiley, Mary	1476	Wilson, Hettie	2656
Wiley, James	2410	Wilson, Verbena	2657
Wiley, Dickson	3894	Wilson, Martha	2942
Wiley, Moses	7683	Wilson, Emily	3485
Wiley, Jennie	8431	Wilson, Kate	3486
Wiley, Adam	8565	Wilson, Lillie	3487
Wiley, Lizzie	9600	Wilson, Harvey	3488
Wineblood, Mary E.	970	Wilson, William	3489
Wineblood, Laura	975	Wilson, Della	4171
Wineblood, Eva	976	Wilson, Mahala	5246
Williams, George	1151	Wilson, Noonley	5247
Williams, Daniel	1152	Wilson, Simon J.	5248
Williams, Eddie	1215	Wilson, Abbey	5249
Williams, Thomas	1261	Wilson, Solomon	5252
Williams, Vina	1553	Wilson, George	7552
Williams, Alex.	1554	Wilson, Bettie	7904
Williams, Emma	1555	Wilson, Jasper	7905
Williams, Naoma	1556	Wilson, Toney	7906
Williams, Nora	2234	Wilson, Thomas	8478
Williams, Sarah E.	2775	Wilson, Charley	8479
Williams, Sadie May	2776	Wilson, Robert B.	9454
Williams, Eli	2911	Wilson, Annie	9698
Williams, Elizabeth	3706	Wilson, Nora	10069
Williams, Rena	3910	Wilson, Mary E.	10083

Name.	Roll No.	Name.	Roll No.
Willie, Sam	1244	Wolf, Lucy	8362
Willie	8402	Wolf, Janie	8363
Wicey	2485	Wolf, George	6859
Wicey	8246	Wolf, Susie	8364
Withers, Maggie	2538	Wolf, Mary	8365
Withers, Lydia	2602	Wolf, Francis	8366
Withers, Loney Ethel	2603	Wolf, Annie	8666
Withers, Joseph A.	9616	Wolf, Roley	8742
Winters, Nelson	2922	Wolf, Levina	8743
Winters, Ed	2923	Wolf, Mandy	8744
Winters, Rosa	2924	Wolf, Sam	8745
Winters, Mary	2925	Wolf, Birdie	9422
Winters, William	2926	Wolf, Lee	9653
Winters, Leether	9495	Wolf, Amy	9734
Willis, Kogee	3121	Wolf, Kimbo	10072
Willis, Wesley	3122	Wolf, Bertha	10087
Wildcat, Willie	4730	Wolfe, Ellen	7486
Wildcat, Sandy	5072	Wolfe, John	9416
Wildcat, Losanna	5073	Woodard, Mollie	2800
Wildcat, Aleck	5074	Woods, Eliza	3601
Wildcat, Annie	5075	Woods, Claude	3602
Wildcat, George	5077	Woods, Florence Lillian	3603
Wildcat, Jim	8102	Woods, John R.	3604
Wildcat, John	9194	Woods, Cora	6047
Wildcat, Albert	9195	Woods, Ralph M.	9541
Wildcat, Maxey	9662	Wotkoche	8178
Wildcat, Jesse	9796	Wolke	8781
Wind, Fanny	4734	Wright, Walter D.	1548
Wind, David	4735	Wright, Charles F.	1549
Wind, James	4736	Wright, Maysie A.	1550
Wind, George	4768	Wright, Lela S.	1551
Wind, Milly	4769	Wright, Annie E.	1552
Wind, Susie	4770	Wright, Cora Adeline	4083
Wind, Job	9691	Wright, Judge William	4084
Winey	5381	Wright, Clida Owen	9630
Wilcox, Ella	6040	Wray, Claud	2561
Willior, Peggy	6961	Wray, Benjamin	2562
Willior, Lena	6962	Wray, Lillie	2563
iWillior, Seper	6963	Wray, Lee	2564
Wisey	6996	Wynn, Lizzie	4718
Wisey	8401	Wynn, Pearl L.	4720
Wistochee	7639	Yahola, Billey	524
"Wilumpka"	7795	Yahola, Winey	525
Wiggie	7995	Yahola, Katie	526
Wikey	8145	Yahola, Addie	527
Widy	8399	Yahola, Mollie	528
Wiker, Yarhola	8407	Yahola, Sadie	529
Wiker, Marley	8408	Yahola, Mary	530
Wiker, Belloche	8409	Yahola, Loper	531
Willison, Irene	9080	Yahola, Arbeka	1280
Willison, James M.	9081	Yahola, Rhoda	1281
Willison, Helen	9082	Yahola, Willie	1282
Willison, Howard D.	9083	Yahola, Charfukner	2415
"Wilyumka"	9382	Yahola, Wattey	2416
"Williamochee'	9387	Yahola, Nancy	2417
Winn, Geneva Atkins	10084	Yahola, Sallie	3382
Woodward, Pollie	1784	Yahola, Conip	3912
Woodward, Clarence	1785	Yahola, Cinda	3913
Woodward, Nellie E.	2213	Yahola, Woxie	4008
Woodward, Helen M.	2214	Yahola, Wotko	4069
Woodward, Hazel D.	2215	Yahola, Kowockkochi	4070
Woodward, Grace E.	2216	Yahola, Nelly	4071
Wolf, John	1976	Yahola, Sunday	4072
Wolf, Lucy	1977	Yahola, Linda	4073
Wolf, George	2664	Yahola, Wanchee	4074
Wolf, Nannie	2665	Yahola, Jackson	5293
Wolf, Kizzie	2666	Yahola, Celia	5294
Wolf, Josie	2667	Yahola, Parnogee	5295
Wolf, Linda	2668	Yahola, Henry	5323
Wolf, Mattie	2669	Yahola, Barney	5820
Wolf, Buck	2670	Yahola, Kizzie	5821
Wolf, Isla	3914	Yahola, Rhoda	6115
Wolf, Ebla	3915	Yahola, Parhose	6919
Wolf, Nancy	6234	Yahola, Mawokike	6920
Wolf, Ella	6235	Yahola, Lila	6922
Wolf, Freeland	6236	Yahola, Lowe	6923
Wolf, Motey	6237	Yahola, Lizzie	6924
Wolf, William	7410	Yahola, Nellie	6925
Wolf, Bettie	7411	Yahola, Rhoda	6926
Wolf, Enoch	7412	Yahola, Karpitcher	7334
Wolf, Martha	7413	Yahola, Loda	7335
Wolf, John	7414	Yahola, Elder	7336

Name.	Roll No.	Name.	Roll No.
Yahola, Katie	7337	Yardy, Willie	1650
Yahola, Ida	7338	Yah-pon-na	1289
Yahola, Mannie	7339	Yargee, Elizabeth	2789
Yahola, Tommy	7376	Yargee, James	3698
Yahola, Neha	7409	Yargee, Mandy	3699
Yahola, Mollie	7738	Yargee, Rhody	3700
Yahola, Lena	7751	Yargee, Lizzie	3701
Yahola, Tulmas	7790	Yargee, John	3702
Yahola, Addie	7848	Yargee, Walter	3703
Yahola, Wiley	7847	Yargee, Cordelia	3704
Yahola, Emarthla	8132	Yargee, Jennie	4772
Yahola, Nocus	8232	Yargee, John I.	4866
Yahola, Thomas	8636	Yargee, Nancy	4867
Yahola, Lizzie	8637	Yargee, Nathaniel V.	4868
Yahola, James	8638	Yargee, Pleasant	4869
Yahola, Bessey	8639	Yargee, Charley	4871
Yahola, Lucinda	8640	Yargee, Hattie L.	4870
Yahola, Willie	8641	Yargee, Dave	5010
Yahola, Dora	8883	Yargee, George	5092
Yahola, Pollie	8884	Yargee, Hannah	5296
Yahola, Eliza	9179	Yargee, Annie	5392
Yahola, Bettie	9744	Yargee, Wynie	5393
Yahola, Polly	9818	Yargee, Culley	5394
Yarhola, Osuchee	4203	Yargee, Hattie	5539
Yarhola, Arsfolechar	4204	Yargee, Alvey	5540
Yarhola, Nokos	4213	Yargee, William	5606
Yarhola, Judy	4214	Yargee, Mitchell	5649
Yarhola, Aaron	4225	Yargee, Mariah	5650
Yarhola, Lucy	4228	Yargee, John	6324
Yarhola, Magie	4758	Yargee, Sam	6402
Yarhola, Cussehta	4970	Yargee, Cullie	6610
Yarhola, Linda	4971	Yargee, Monday	7846
Yarhola, Maley	4972	Yargee, John	8530
Yarhola, Nancy	4973	Yargee, Willie	8604
Yarhola, Billy	4974	Yargee, Alexander	9633
Yarhola, Lessey	4975	Yargee, Millie	7547
Yarhola, Fushutche	4993	Yellowhead, Folsom	3272
Yarhola, Mary	4994	Yellowhead, Tahcowee	3273
Yarhola, Willie	4995	Yellowhead, Lucinda	3274
Yarhola, Malinda	4996	Yellowhead, Kelley	3275
Yarhola, Kizzie	4997	Yellowhead, Jonah	3276
Yarhola, George	5135	Yellowhead, Saloma	10019
Yarhola, Tuskeheneha	5140	Yarbrough, John	3606
Yarhola, Polhoya	5141	Yarbrough, Betsey	3607
Yarhola, Simochee	5142	Yarbrough, Thomas	3608
Yarhola, Joe	5363	Yarbrough, James	5850
Yarhola, Yarner	5364	Young, Adeline	3679
Yarhola, Sampson	7311	Young, Harry	3680
Yarhola, Sarah	7312	Young, Polly	3681
Yarhola, Jemima	7313	Young, Katie	3682
Yarhola, Martha C.	9436	Young, Mary Ella	3683
Yarholar, Chapley	4851	Young, Fay	3684
Yarholar, Wisey	4852	Youbartka	4841
Yarholar, Lizzie	4853	"Yarner"	5076
Yarholar, Stella	4859	Yarmer, Kizzie	7315
Yarholar, Ok ta yah che	9068	Yarmer, Mitchie	7316
Yarholar, Annie	9069	You-con-co-con-thla-	
Yarholar, Lena	9070	nay	5594
Yarholar, Amos	9071	Yonder, Polly	6562
Yarholar, Aney	9072	Yetekahajo, Wisey	6828
Yaholar, Josey	5120	York, James	7603
Yaholar, Betsey	5121	Yon ho ye	7890
Yaholar, Lucy	5122	Yar star co con thla ney	7916
Yaholar, Thomas	6368	Yar char ney	8105
Yaholar, Mary	6369	Yu-pa-ha-ke	8179
Yaholar, Roman	6370	Yaffie	8998
Yaholar, Louis	6372	"Ya ma hike"	9185
Yardy, Thomas	683	You-co-tah-lar-ney	9958
Yardy, Wisey	684	Yohola, Hardy	8234
Yardy, Joseph	685	Zon-keo-tee-tay	9816
Yardy, Thomas, Jr.	686		

INDEX TO
NEW BORN CREEKS BY BLOOD

Name.	Roll No.
Bighead, Lizzie	60
Bighead, Sam	1118
Bighead, Pa-thlum-ka	1230
Biggs, Martha	1239
Big Mosquito, Jennie	737
Bigpond, Susie	240
Bigpond, Anderson	241
Bigpond, Louis	939
Bigpond, Wilson	33
Bird, Kizzie	990
Birdhead, Yanah	546
Bland, Davis M.	802
Bland, Arlie S.	803
Boles, Pearl Amy	857
Boling, Walter Gilmore	903
Boling, Dixie Self	1128
Boon, Ikey	811
Boon, Isaac	812
Boone, Ladossa Fredre	828
Bosen, Pearlie	978
Boudinot, Mitchel	224
Bough, Willie E.	201
Bough, Henry	246
Bough, Ethel	247
Brian, John William	63
Brian, Mary Ellen	64
Bright, Thelma Beatrice	169
Bright, Reubin	720
Bright, Lafa	721
Brightman, Lyeman	679
Brink, Lizzie	750
Brook, Annetta May	179
Brooks, Thomas Clifford	315
Brown, Daniel W.	139
Brown, Ada	313
Brown, Sandy	314
Brown, Thomas Jefferson	495
Brown, Ruth	604
Brown, John William	605
Brown, Eva May	616
Brown, Alex	672
Brown, Edward S.	687
Brown, Cleller	713
Brown, Henry	761
Brown, Lula	850
Brown, Thomas	918
Brown, Georgia	971
Brown, McKinley	1029
Brown, Hettie	1030
Brown, Willie	1087
Brown, John	1088
Bruce, Browder F.	140
Bruner, J., Esther	12
Bruner, Richard Douglas	62
Bruner, Meneffie	73
Bruner, Flora	152
Bruner, Iva M.	451
Bruner, Lewis	533
Bruner, Bertha	759
Bruner, Maggie	760
Bruner, Lady Beatrice	810
Bruner, Pearl	904
Bruner, Bunnie	936
Bruner, Thomas	937
Bruner, Archie	999
Bruner, Bettie	1000
Bruner, Jessie	1001
Bruner, Bessie	1002
Bruner, Willie	1034
Bruner, Minnie	1085
Buck, Sarah	707
Buck, Sappho	947
Buckley, Cora	1276
Buckner, Jack	863
Bucktrot, Sagie	852
Bullett, Chitto Harjo	1140
Bullett, Bailey	1163
Bullett, Jacob	1240
Bunner, Susie	1247
Burgess, Ruby	161
Burgess, Daniel	826
Burgess, Bird	827

Name.	Roll No.
Burgess, Roman	1075
Burgess, Raymond B.	1222
Burnett, Joseph L.	675
Burnette, Moses	80
Burton, Ethel V.	67
Burton, Wynema Owen	68
Burton, Charles Checotah	172
Burton, Rufus Cheestell	173
Butcher, Lela	1028
Butler, Eddie	1186
Byrd, Yahdeka	633
Byrd, Jemima	634
Cable, Virgie Plimmer	77
Caesar, Moser	551
Caesar, Hannah	550
Caesar, Panuggee	1130
Call, Charles	764
Callahan, Mary Elizabeth	71
Callahan, Etta Sybil	72
Callahan, Sam	75
Callahan, Jesephine Nevada	167
Campbell, Tine Winburn	113
Canard, Lena	147
Canard, Lizzie	215
Canard, Millie	921
Canard, Louisa	1105
Cane, Robert Carl	227
Cane, William R.	228
Carr, Verna Vinita	357
Carr, Cecil Raymond	755
Carr, Washington	948
Carter, Susie	48
Carter, Jennie	49
Carter, William Thomas	820
Casey, Vera Irene	639
Casey, Alvro Edgar	640
Casey, Eli	641
Castillo, Mabel	203
Cates, Governor	1005
Chamberlain, Dewey	982
Chamberlain, Ruby	983
Char-co-te-ten-na, Ella	1181
Charles, Sophia	424
Charles, Ellis Buffington	425
Charlesey, Flora	665
Charlesey, Martha	666
Chenubia, Martha	193
Cherry, Colona Blanche	363
Cherry, Francis Doyle	364
Childers, Stella	306
Childers, Ruthie	323
Childers, Mose	324
Childers, Ruby Mildred	387
Childers, Maria	431
Childers, Emmet	433
Childers, Virgie	515
Childers, Effie	1122
Chisholm, Minnie	443
Chissoe, Please S.	673
Chissoe, Sam, Jr.	744
Chotky, William	1171
Chupco, Cilla	1054
Churchill, Ethel May	682
Clark, Alex	642
Clarkston, Raymond	601
Clayton, Ernest	830
Clayton, William McKinley	831
Clinton, Nexie	263
Clinton, Rachel	966
Cloud, Hattie	938
Cobb, Johnnie	322
Coker, London	506
Coker, Sallo	1178
Coker, Ella	1179
Colbert, William	888
Colbert, Kizzie	1059
Collins, Noah	718

Name.	Roll No.	Name.	Roll No.
Collins, Roy	1112	Derisaw, Willie	968
Colmon, Nettie Alice	573	Derrisaw, Carrie	736
Colmon, Gladdys Leuna	574	Derrisaw, Tuxey	1280
Combs, John Boyd	694	Dice, Freddie James	218
Combs, Pearl	230	Dice, Liza Jane	219
Comie, Larley	1004	Dillsaver, Orvel Dean	129
Compier, Willie	1162	Dillsaver, Robert Lowe	130
Coodey, Walter Lee	657	Ditzler, James Albert	367
Coon, Oda M.	144	Ditzler, Fannie Ann	501
Coonhead, John	1284	Dixon, Ethel Lulee	606
Cooper, Wheeler	55	Dixon, Henry Jefferson	607
Cooper, Effie	56	Douglas, Duard C.	823
Cooper, Florence	158	Downing, Jesse	1050
Cooper, Nellie	476	Doyle, Eva	234
Coppedge, Velma G.	28	Doyle, Walter	235
Corey, Cordelia	745	Doyle, Cecil Lee	683
Corey, Tom	1061	Doyle, Susie Lee	700
Cornell, David	572	Doyle, Minnie May	701
Cosar, Galvos	977	Doyle, Clarinda	702
Cosar, Lena	485	Doyle, Leo	961
Couch, Gertie May	99	Doyle, Beulah	989
Couch, Allie B.	100	Doyle, Clarrance William	1115
Cowe, Effa	78	Doyle, Mose	1116
Crabtree, Rebecca	817	Drew, Clarence	53
Crabtree, Hattie	818	Drew, Sarl E.	198
Crosby, Berry Martin	596	Drew, Roy W.	199
Crosby, Ferdinand Wilber	597	Drew, Moses Warrner	632
Crow, Tommy	637	Drew, Madella E.	898
Crowell, Otis Buel	699	DuBois, Elizabeth Gladys	170
Crowell, Francis Willard	1183	Duckworth, Vera Oma	656
Cubbie, Liza	1202	Dunson, Millie	539
Cubbie, Daniel	1203	Dunson, Raymond	965
Culler, Leah	1044	Dunzy, Velma	346
Cummings, Susie	29	Dyer, Lotta	842
Cumsey, Lena	1072	Dyer, Emmett	1082
Cumsey, Annie	1073	Easley, John Pickard	530
Cunningham, William Leo	437	Ellis, James	775
Daily, Margaret Willison	259	Emarthla, Walter	1252
Dale, Charles Henry	89	Enrigues, William	276
Damet, Susan	95	Escoe, William Albert	65
Damet, William F.	96	Escoe, Leo Bennett	970
Daniel, Unah Jr.	44	Eubanks, William Albert	447
Daniel, Robert	1083	Evans, Phidelta Lee	142
Dansby, Lucinda	813	Evans, James, Jr.	143
Davis, Lizzie	175	Evans, Nettie	421
Davis, Ross	319	Ewing, Eulelia	730
Davis, Eugene	320	Ewing, Ethel	731
Davis, Elizabeth E.	345	Factor, Cogee	516
Davis, Annie	394	Factor, George	517
Davis, Alice	417	Farmer, Natalie	5
Davis, Fanny	582	Field, Ida	1148
Davis, Minnie	583	Field, Sonnie	1225
Davis, Nora	631	Fields, Legus	911
Davis, Mack	749	Fife, Dawes	157
Davis, Clarence B.	846	Fife, Exie	851
Davis, Harvie L.	847	Fife, James	371
Davis, Hattie Johnson	984	Fife, Josey	525
Davis, Nicey	1079	Fipps, Eva	297
Davis, Tom	1089	Fish, Posey	906
Davis, Mattie	1169	Fish, George	1110
Davis, Samuel	1286	Fish, Nache	1111
Dawson, Dessie Lee	124	Fish, Lizzie	1154
Day, Beatrice	770	Fish, George	1291
Day, Robert, Jr.	771	Fisher, Lizzie	756
Deer, Ellen	356	Fisher, Bertha	757
Deer, Sealy	446	Fisher, Aubrey	758
Deer, Minnie	486	Fisher, Bettie	1099
Deer, Minnie	1106	Fixeco, Joseph	1243
Deer, Edmund	1200	Fixico, Icey	51
Deer, Jessie	1274	Fixico, Willie	418
Deer, Lula	1282	Fixico, Robert	435
Deere, Raymond	328	Fixico, Winey	741
Deere, Willey	1066	Fixico, Jeffy	742
Deere, Annie	1267	Fixico, Roley	1058
Deere, Lumsey	1278	Fixico, California	295
Deere, Charlie	1279	Fleet, John J.	524
Deo, Amos	1144	Flowers, Willie Eva	565
Deo, Susie	1145	Foley, Arney	1244
Depriest, Luther	729	Foshee, Henry C.	1043
Derisaw, Lila	967	Foster, John W.	250
		Foster, Oceola	299
		Foster, Jimmie	300

Name.	Roll No.
Foster, Lula B.	479
Foster, Mary Josephine	677
Foster, Susie Mills	781
Foster, George Cameron	922
Foster, Henry	1039
Foster, Lula	1040
Foster, Lowiney	1150
Fox, Katie	392
Fox, Elzie	469
Fox, Sandy	1263
Francis, Bettie	251
Francis, Jeff	252
Francis, Roley	274
Francis, Samuel	275
Francis, Susie	594
Francis, Freeland	1070
Frank, Leah	294
Frank, William	370
Frank, Neddie	411
Frank, Mahala	412
Frank, Vera	797
Frank, Austin	953
Frank, Johnson,	1051
Freeman, Theodore R.	166
Freeman, Hovah Monroe	710
Frick, Jay	1237
Frick, William	1238
Friday, Willie	1092
Fry, Clarence	1226
Fry, Sandy	1258
Fry, Sarty	1259
Fulsom, Ladee	748
Fulsom, Rhoda	798
Futrell, Jimmie	339
Futrell, Pearlie	340
Gaither, Maggie Emily	186
Gambler, Martin	1056
Gatlin, Helen	366
Gibson, Verna Marie	181
Gibson, Charles Counterman	182
Gibson, Joseph B.	534
Gibson, Martha	991
Gilbert, Jeniry	1013
Gilcrease, Elmer Lee	84
Gilcrease, Mabel	85
Gilcrease, Bessie	86
Gillis, Elmer	880
Givens, Minnie	623
Givens, Lonie	624
Givens, Harper	649
Glenn, Elma	808
Goat, Eddielinie	651
Goat, Angeline	659
Goat, Alice Sukey	660
Gooch, Maudie	466
Gooch, Claudie	467
Goode, Rowena	145
Gooden, Carrie	456
Gooden, Charley	691
Gown, Sarah	457
Graham, Sissie	1003
Granberry, Alma Dee	860
Grant, Lena	338
Gray, Johnson	32
Gray, Addie	264
Gray, Roley	489
Gray, Fannie	835
Gray, Susie	836
Gray, Johnnie	1288
Gray, Mandy	1289
Grayson, Pearl	61
Grayson, Samson	282
Grayson, Mamie	669
Grayson, Gertrude	780
Grayson, Ollie	815
Grayson, Lillie	816
Grayson, Sarah	834
Grayson, Panzie May	934
Greenwood, Effie Belle	739
Gregory, Frank Lee	226
Gregory, Rose Ida	236

Name.	Roll No.
Gregory, Fletcher Raymond	793
Haikey, Bertha	18
Haikey, Sissie	19
Haikey, Jessie	54
Haikey, Burney	188
Hale, Billy	1199
Haley, George Elmer	824
Hall, Mollie	194
Hall, Alta	454
Hallford, Nathan	497
Hallford, Lynn	498
Hamilton, Mary	959
Hancock, Lizzie	676
Harjo, Johnnie	187
Harjo, Nettie	221
Harjo, Lizzie	267
Harjo, Melissa	268
Harjo, Roman	291
Harjo, Mord	292
Harjo, Wilson	532
Harjo, Amos	548
Harjo, Una-see	549
Harjo, Alice	560
Harjo, Alfred	663
Harjo, Nancy	664
Harjo, Ella Ruth	897
Harjo, Sunday	943
Harjo, Fanny	946
Harjo, Lilley	1020
Harjo, Sallie	1024
Harjo, Susie	1025
Harjo, Roller	1036
Harjo, Winey	1060
Harjo, Lesta	1108
Harjo, Emma	1109
Harjo, Ethal	1114
Harjo, Bennie	1126
Harjo, Ida	1160
Harjo, Hannah	1214
Harjo, Robert	1215
Harjo, George	1257
Harjo, Philliby	1266
Harjo, Jimmie	1275
Harjo, Fred	1283
Harjoche, Martha	1248
Harjoche, Adam	1249
Harley, Joseph	1068
Harmon, Lonie	919
Harris, Charlie	6
Harris, Mary J.	24
Harris, Winnie Davis	34
Harris, Cora	406
Harris, Lulu May	458
Harris, Theodore Quincy	459
Harrison, Bettie	1049
Harry, Wilson	684
Harry, Jessie	685
Harry, Liza	805
Harry, Susie	806
Harry, Bunch	807
Hart, Florence E.	41
Hawkins, Kate	587
Hawkins, Melissa	588
Hawkins, Louis	1046
Hawkins, Pink	1097
Hawkins, Nellie	1098
Hay, Modie	853
Haynes, Roley	929
Haynie, Felix Jr.	359
Hays, Sallie Willison	36
Hellet, Adam	1198
Helton, Ruthia Ellen	333
Helton, Romie Robert	334
Hendrickson, Elijah	344
Hendrickson, Sarah Jane	567
Hendrickson, Peter	692
Heneha, Roy	1018
Heneha, Ralph	1019
Hengst, Joseph A.	790
Hengst, Charles Augustus	791
Henry, Howard H.	248

Name.	Roll No.	Name.	Roll No.
Henry, Edith Clair	249	Kelley, Rosella	963
Henry, Hillibe Micco	318	Kelly, Elizabeth	301
Henry, Eugene Rolley	331	Kelly, Roland E.	302
Henry, Willie Jackson	332	Kelly, Roman	427
Henry, Tchinina	335	Kelly, Alabama	428
Henry, James Pier	386	Kelly, Perry	714
Herrod, Tarpie	1196	Kelly, Marshall	1120
Hewlett, Myrtle	383	Kelly, Amy	1210
Hickory, Louina	655	Kelly, Sallie	1260
Highland, Patrick, Jr.	128	Kelly, David	1261
Hill, Lucy	229	Kernel, Freeman	1052
Hill, Mandy	347	Kernel, Harry	1157
Hill, Arney	391	Kerr, Commodore Jr.	111
Hill, George	526	Kerr, Ethel	695
Hill, Nettie	1096	Key, Hugh Benjamin	317
Hill, Lumsey	1192	Keys, James	995
Hinneha, John	217	Kiefer, Clarance Ebert	825
Hodge, Gusta A.	213	King, Jessie	185
Hogan, Willie D.	1007	King, Lucy	262
Holleyman, Marcellus	993	King, Claudy J.	561
Holleyman, Marcella	494	King, Berry W.	562
Hood, Reid Lee	377	King, Luther Lewis	563
Hooks, Richard Roy	473	King, Henry Lee	768
Hope, Beaden	1067	King, John B.	769
Hoplye, Lucindy	1095	King, Caesar	861
Hopwood, Ora Pearle	115	King, Sallie	1151
Horn, Jessie	916	King, Janelly	1246
Horn, Fannie Lee	917	King, Luila	1262
Howard, Myrtle May	26	Kite, Lucy May	609
Howard, Maxie	104	Knight, Leaster	389
Howell, Samuel Webster	753	Knight, Jenetta	400
Huckaby, Ora	992	Knight, Wiley	779
Hughes, Lena Ethel	106	Land, Helen	197
Huston, Thomas Adison	821	Larney, Almarine	444
Hutton, Iola	307	Larney, Cheparney	1287
Ingram, Sudie	964	Lasley, Lizzie	1241
Ishmael, James L.	207	Lasley, Sam	1242
Ishmael, Eva J.	208	Leader, Lizzie	519
Island, Luvena	472	Leader, Allice	520
Island, Lizzie	610	Leader, Jennie	547
Island, Leggues	611	Leader, Absalom	784
Island, Louisa	1041	Leader, Edward	785
Ispocogee, Noah	854	Leath, Jessie May	336
Ispocogee, Sam	889	Leath, James Henry	337
Jack, Mandy Amy	638	Letts, Oscar Lovick	878
Jackson, Diamond	518	Leverett, Bessie	751
Jacob, John	1127	Lewallen, Lucy	653
Jacob, Nicey	1264	Lewis, Frank Turner	375
Jacobs, William R.	132	Lewis, John David	376
Jacobs, Elsie B.	212	Lewis, Jimmy	471
Jefferson, Senora	627	Lewis, Mosey	568
Jimboy, Peggy	225	Lewis, Lillie	569
Jobe, Leo J.	81	Lewis, Eddie	570
John, Albert	312	Lewis, Ella	595
John, Lena	536	Lewis, Lulu	726
Johnson, Viola	27	Lewis, Emma	754
Johnson, Miley	150	Lewis, Albert	876
Johnson, George	164	Lewis, John	877
Johnson, Leora	308	Lewis, Billy	907
Johnson, Ella	309	Lewis, Mattie	958
Johnson, Bessie	590	Lindsey, Addie	997
Johnson, Winey	690	Lindsey, Columbia	1182
Johnson, Floyd Ila	766	Lindsey, Sarah	1191
Johnson, Amandy	843	Litka, Newman	409
Johnson, Hotulke	865	Littlehead, Ada	804
Johnson, Ulter	949	Loney, James	652
Johnson, Martin	980	Long, Newman	706
Johnson, Emma	981	Long, Anna	708
Johnson, Nora	1090	Long, Roley	1134
Johnson, Carr Raymond	1136	Long, Wallace	1149
Johnson, Emma	1201	Long, Sa-ke	1086
Johnson, Harpley	1216	Looney, Sullivan	202
Johnson, Rena	1227	Looney, Forest Leonard	388
Johnson, Susanna	1255	Looney, Della May	402
Johnson, Onate	1256	Lott, Lucy	1101
Jones, Caddo	870	Lott, Jennie	1102
Jones, Clarence	913	Lowe, Joe	809
Josie, Jennie	1026	Lowe, Jennie	1155
Kanard, Cilla	1078	Lowry, Amos	507
Kannard, Melissa	996	Lucas, Rufus	397
Kano, Nicey	1253	Lucas, Frank	398
Kano, Katy	1254	Lucas, Josephine	399

Name.	Roll No.
Lucus, Tony	924
Lunsford, Hattie	579
Mackey, Bessie Adella	767
Maloney, Lena	613
Manley, Peepsie	858
Manley, Arthur	956
Manley, Lindy Isaac	727
Manley, Melah	728
Mantooth, Isabella	795
Marks, George	508
Marshall, Benjamin Jr.	22
Marshall, George Freeman	23
Marshall, Lena May	190
Marshall, Henry	884
Martin, Loney	74
Martin, Leona	108
Martin, Jesse	231
Matoy, Annie	1167
Maxey, Eugene Willie	119
Maxey, Simeon C.	120
Mayes, Martha Jr.	372
Mayes, Marry	373
Meyers, Herbert	626
Micco, Lucy	426
Mikey, Lewis	123
Mikey, Enos Vey	840
Miles, Jennie Murrell	116
Miles, Vivian	117
Miller, Eugene	112
Miller, Samuel H. Jr.	133
Miller, George Thomas	272
Miller, James Franklin	273
Miller, Sarah	844
Miller, Malvin H.	1037
Miller, Cecil	1038
Mingo, Bessie	711
Mingo, Joseph	985
Minter, Thelma Agnes	97
Minton, Ada	114
Minugh, Jesse L.	740
Mitchell, Morris	859
Mitchell, Albert	1132
Mitchell, Joseph	1133
Moffer, Wilson	912
Monahwee, Ella	1166
Monday, Edna	1212
Monday, Annie	1213
Moore, Susie	358
Moore, John	379
Moore, Jessie Susan	1231
Morrison, Ernest	643
Morrison, Hettie Jane	644
Morrison, Hettie Ola	717
Morrison, Mary	839
Morrison, Lula Mildred	972
Morrison, Stan Watie	973
Morrow, Elva	413
Morton, Roy Ray	214
Morton, Claude S.	405
Morton, Okland	499
Morton, Leo Britt	602
Morton, Ellis M.	696
Mosquito, Kattie	382
Mukes, Hattie	777
Mukes, Ada	778
Murphy, Eva Dorcas	50
Murphy, Blanch	189
Murray, Helen M.	625
Murrell, Wiley	310
Musgrove, Herold D.	296
Myers, Oscar D.	890
Myers, Laura M.	891
McBirney, Dorothy Vera	271
McCalvey, Joseph Hiram	341
McCalvey, Emmit	743
McCombs, Nathaniel H.	17
McCosar, Arthur	688
McCoy, Ollie	171
McCoy, Nettie	527
McCoy, Robert Elihu	528
McDermott, Helen	1
McDermott, Lizzie	452

Name.	Roll No.
McDermott, Charlie	453
McDonald, Edward Ray	283
McFarland, Ned	856
McFarland, Yancy	960
McGilbra, Sanford	674
McGilbray, Melissa	598
McGilbray, George	1234
McGilbry, George L.	678
McGirt, John	941
McGirtt, George	719
McGuire, Marcus Wilson	40
McHenry, Abbie	90
McHenry, Bettie	91
McIntosh, Edith Edna	92
McIntosh, Vivian	93
McIntosh, Edith Louise	107
McIntosh, Annie Lila	127
McIntosh, Cheesie	176
McIntosh, Sequoah	177
McIntosh, Isaiah J.	531
McIntosh, Ida	540
McIntosh, Jeanetta	593
McIntosh, Ida M.	612
McIntosh, Maudy Van	773
McIntosh, Malissa Christa	774
McIntosh, Charles Curtis	1015
McIntosh, John Granville	1069
McIntosh, Nathaniel	1131
McKan, George	1045
McKellop, Louisa	98
McKim, Willie Byno	432
McKinnon, Lila Belle	209
McNac, Charley	82
McNac, Marcy	83
McNac, Flossie	407
McNac, Bettie	902
McNac, Tullie	1076
McNevins, Willie Clay	557
McNevins, Flora	558
McPerryman, Lewis	554
McPerryman, Eli	555
Naharkey, Millie	126
Narcomay, Alice	538
Nave, Nara	541
Nave, Otha	542
Nelson, David Jefferson	619
Nero, Fannie	1174
Newberry, Buford	321
Newton, Ewell Durant	462
Newton, Guy Jackson	463
Nichols, Leo Carlton	30
Noon, Lucinda	697
Nubbie, Robert	957
Nubbie, George	1235
Oliver, Louis	216
Orcutt, Guy B.	11
Pahoseyahola, Bennie	1273
Pakoska, Winford	1119
Palmer, James W.	195
Palmer, Daniel B.	196
Palmer, Ella	564
Parnosky, Cindy	1103
Parnosky, Cheparney	1104
Parker, Charles Edward	151
Parks, Dora Ellen	290
Patton, Lora	892
Patton, Dora	893
Patton, Leo Ora	894
Peeper, Viney May	801
Pemberton, Reacy Adeline	969
Pense, Alice	566
Perryman, Okema	149
Perryman, Montie	325
Perryman, Leah	1093
Phillips, Lydia	20
Pigeon, Nache	1193
Pike, Fay	155
Pinehill, Mary	1185
Pitman, Vonnie	608
Pitman, Robert, Jr.	794

Name.	Roll No.
Pitman, Moses	848
Pitts, Drannan	667
Pitts, Burrell H.	668
Pitts, Major Barbee	1014
Polk, Ethel	747
Porter, Mildred	7
Porter, Pleasant	102
Porter, McKinley	103
Porter, L. Ray	210
Porter, Edith P.	211
Porter, Benjamin	401
Posey, Wynema Torrans	4
Posey, Terry O.	153
Posey, Hugh F.	156
Posey, Thomas Owen	470
Posey, Lola Colesta	483
Posey, William Edward	512
Posey, Eloise	686
Posey, Nina E.	976
Post, Samantha	620
Post, El Louisa	621
Postoak, Arthur E.	599
Postoak, Hattie L.	600
Postoak, Julia	900
Postoak, Jennie	901
Postoak, Eli	979
Powell, John	395
Pressgrove, Joseph	125
Price, Minnie May	1009
Proctor, Lillie	455
Proctor, Stella	481
Proctor, Sam	482
Proctor, Dennis Flinn	905
Proctor, Sam	1187
Proctor, Lydie	1188
Puntka, Josie	1158
Puntka, Winey	1159
Puryear, William H.	146
Raabe, Stella	134
Raabe, Celia	135
Raiford, Jaunetta	885
Raiford, Pearl	1194
Railford, Lena	1195
Randall, Roman	1100
Reed, John	581
Renfro, Elza Tillman	191
Renfro, Alef Adelaide	192
Rentie, Lucreesey	866
Reynolds, Oscar Lee	238
Reynolds, Arthur Leroy	326
Reynolds, Lizzie	327
Reynolds, Clarence Andrew	716
Reynolds, Ernest	752
Richard, Albert	35
Richard, Annie	438
Richard, Minnie	1211
Ricketts, Clarence Francis	278
Ricketts, Goldie Ardell	279
Riley, Martha	496
Riley, Claud	704
Riley, Henry Earl	705
Riley, Tootie	950
Riley, Leah	951
Roberson, Leo	575
Roberson, Ellen	576
Roberson, Clarence	1233
Roberts, Tura E.	9
Roberts, Walter H.	10
Roberts, Cainey	762
Roberts, Joseph	874
Roberts, Indie	1065
Roberts, Sister	1250
Robertson, Andrew Jackson	681
Robins, Thomas	783
Robinson, Myrtice A.	662
Robinson, Nelson	925
Robinson, Louisa	926
Robison, Adeline Belle	121
Robison, Newman Joseph	122
Robison, Christie	448

Name.	Roll No.
Robison, Richard Chisholm	449
Rogers, Woods Cooper	136
Rogers, John	137
Rogers, Lucy	1006
Ross, Lena M.	25
Rothhammer, Ernest Ralph	289
Russell, Clemmie	105
Ryal, Willie B.	864
Salt, Edward	1147
Saltsman, Gordon P.	16
Sampson, Wiley	868
Sands, Nettie	580
Sandy, Stella	316
Sanger, Wah-nah-ka	635
Sanger, Jaunitta	855
Sarty, Mamie	79
Sarty, Manuel	141
Sarwanokee, Fannie	1272
Sawyer, Almon	1223
Sawyer, Samuel	1224
Scott, Christie Annie	222
Scott, John	223
Scott, Lillian	360
Scott, Hepsey	622
Scott, Billie	974
Scott, Bessie	1135
Scott, Lumb	1206
Scott, Rufus	1207
Seber, Jimmie	1217
Self, Ivory Bell	439
Self, Nellie E.	440
Self, William K.	441
Self, Edward N.	442
Self, Maggie Ophelia	577
Self, Golie Ray	578
Self, Jackson C.	782
Selvidge, Clarence	788
Sevier, Tom	1080
Sevier, Lena	1081
Sewel, Ellen	930
Sewel, Elliott	931
Shepherd, May	617
Shepherd, Maggie	618
Shepherd, Sammie	849
Sherrill, Gracie	47
Simmer, Hinney	537
Simmer, Andy	1152
Simmons, Samuel	362
Simmons, Emma	862
Simmons, William	923
Simms, Lucinda	975
Simon, George	200
Simon, Peyton	493
Simon, Levada	494
Simpson, Mary Elizabeth	434
Simpson, Catherine Elizabeth	654
Skeeter, Fred	31
Sladen, Sam	1265
Smith, Terry Steven	70
Smith, Ruth	76
Smith, Oliver Russell	206
Smith, Gladdis G.	393
Smith, Albert K.	415
Smith, Edna	592
Smith, Ester	698
Smith, Estella	920
Smock, Anna Louise	45
Snakeya, Heness	998
Snap, Andy	1008
Sneed, Susie Rose	1010
Sneed, Larzar	1011
Snow, Ada	1084
Sookey, Josephine	689
Spencer, Lanah	1021
Spencer, Loma	1022
Squire, Sarah	288
Stake, Missie	352
Staley, Nellie	789
Starr, Jesse J.	1271

Name.	Roll No.	Name.	Roll No.
Stephens, Willie	342	Vance, William Mellette	571
Stephens, Johnnie	343	Vann, Lydia	952
Stephenson, Siney	396	Wadsworth, Mary	269
Stepney, Lizzie	1251	Wadsworth, James	628
Stewart, Floyd Lee	589	Wadsworth, Jessie	
Stidham, Thomas		Eulalie	680
Edward	2	Wadsworth, Leo E.	871
Stidham, Cleo	3	Wadsworth, Elle E.	872
Stidham, Mattie	867	Walker, George	
Stidham, Johnny	1197	Washington	614
Stoddard, Joseph	460	Walker, Edith	615
Storm, Bertha	419	Walker, Johnson	646
Storm, Pocahontas	420	Walker, Annie	647
Strouvelle, Charles		Wallace, Tully Mae	131
Edward Jr.	58	Ware, Ima	875
Strouvelle, Alice Kendall	59	Washington, George	354
Staley, Kissie	1071	Washington, Sadie	355
Stubblefield, McAffee	559	Washington, Claud	490
Stubblefield, Minnie	584	Washington, Melah	734
Stubblefield, Johnnie	585	Washington, Mandy	735
Sudduth, Rosetta	1042	Washington, Sue	776
Swingle, Hattie	445	Washington, Lillie	927
Tar lo shaw, Louisa	1168	Washington, Lizzie	1229
Tarvin, Marie Louisa	384	Washington, Ralph	1285
Taryole, Frank	553	Wa ta she, Joe	535
Tate, Joseph	543	Watson, Lela	477
Tate, Anie May	799	Watson, Minnie	653
Tate, Flora Ada	800	Watson, Nora	715
Taylor, Lucile	829	Watson, Ellen	873
Taylor, Eli	1047	Watson, Dave	935
Taylor, Judy	1205	Watson, Dave	1031
Tebe, Arthur	670	Watson, Johnny	1153
Tebe, Nellie	671	Watts, William T. Jr.	648
Tecumseh, Mary	962	Watts, Minnie	733
Tecumseh, Effie	1062	Weaver, Lois Alleen	280
Tecumseh, Edward	1063	Weaver, Bert Leo	281
Thatcher, Charley Dee L.	899	Weaver, May	285
Thompson, Ollie	712	Weaver, Billie	286
Thompson, Nora	869	Weaver, Amos	287
Thompson, Isreal	1177	Webb, Ethel Samantha	38
Throckmorton, William		Webb Ettie Jane	39
D.	180	Webster, Seeley	94
Tiger, Ethan Allen H.	66	Wesley, Peter	261
Tiger, Ewnah J.	148	Wesley, Tiger	353
Tiger, Edward	162	Wesley, Ida	1139
Tiger, George	163	West, Elsie	1074
Tiger, Mary	168	West, Robert	1141
Tiger, Aby	183	West, William	1142
Tiger, Waxin	184	Whetstone, Eula Pearl	1094
Tiger, Hettie	220	White, Romie Loundine	468
Tiger, Phillip	266	White, Clara	772
Tiger, Jefferson	311	White, Laura	1064
Tiger, Ada	390	White, Lizzie	1236
Tiger, Robert	487	Whitlow, Sissie	374
Tiger, Josie	488	Whitlow, John	1138
Tiger, Nancy	629	Wilcox, John	37
Tiger, Emma	709	Wildcat, Peter	1143
Tiger, Martha	763	Wildcat, Bessie	1176
Tiger, Porter	792	Wiley, Haley	478
Tiger, Susannah	841	Wiley, Charlie	480
Tiger, Lousanna	1027	Williams, Charley	52
Tiger, Selanie	1048	Williams, John F.	239
Tiger, Nina	1053	Williams, Henryetta	351
Tiger, Bryan	1107	Williams, Davis	491
Tiger, Nancy	1121	Williams, Viola	492
Tiger, Eli	1146	Williams, John	
Tiger, Roman	1156	Randolph	942
Tiger, Melah	1204	Williams, John	1012
Tiger, Joanna	1228	Williams, Bettie	1189
Tilley, Frank	1124	Williams, Baby	1190
Tilley, Laura May	1125	Williams, John	1221
Timothy, Eliza	1281	Williford, Joe Brown	101
Tobler, Pleasant	1017	Wills, William H.	408
Todd, Bertha	544	Wills, Hazel Irene	522
Todd, Arthur Lee	545	Wills, Lilly	529
Toney, Foley	1129	Wills, Arthur Rex	746
Toney, Wiley	1220	Wilson, Ida	42
Turnbow, James Henry	159	Wilson, Otto	43
Turnbow, Charlie	160	Wilson, Oleta	69
Turnham, Lillie May	822	Wilson, Bennie	410
Trent, Jesse	165	Wilson, Raymond	422
Trusler, Fred	258	Wilson, Sarah Jane	423
Unussee, Mardie	368	Wilson, Robert Henry	703

Name.	Roll No.	Name.	Roll No.
Wilson, Wisey	1032	Woodward, Edith	436
Wilson, Minnie	1033	Wright, Olive A.	378
Wilson, Bessie	1137	Wright, Ynema B.	932
Wilson, Enus	1218	Wright, Ava E.	933
Wilson, Annie	1219	Yahola, Jennetta	57
Wind, Jesse	603	Yahola, Roman	348
Winters, Elijah	484	Yahola, Houston	349
Wiseman, Harry	284	Yahola, Abraham	461
Wisener, Bessie	887	Yahola, Minnie	1268
Wisener, Minnie	1117	Yaholar, Jimmie	914
Withers, Oliver Lee	87	Yaholar, Della	1245
Wofford, Jackson	265	.Yardy, Hettie	429
Wolf, Seaner	298	Yardy, Dock	430
Wolf, Timmie Barnett	650	Yargee, Amos	940
Wolf, Jennie	1232	Yarhola, Jefferson	1170
Wolf, Matilda	1290	Yarholar, Clarence	915
Woods, Lillie Rosell	630	Young, Lucius	732
Woods, Argethel	1057		

INDEX TO
MINOR CREEKS BY BLOOD

Name.	Roll No.	Name.	Roll No.
Depriest, Theodore R.	49	Harjo, Alva	417
Derrisaw, Lydia	69	Harjo, Minnie	418
Dice, Elmer	204	Harjo, Martha	444
Douglas, Raymond R.	124	Harjo, Macel	482
Doyle, John Henry	21	Harjo, Lillie	484
Doyle, Blanche	54	Harmon, Benjamin T.	46
Doyle, Seaborn	302	Harris, Naoma	314
Dunn, Ralph	193	Harvison, Hazel Vivian	23
Dunson, Hettie	135	Hasley, Josephine	164
Ellis, Fred	160	Hawkins, Jennie	252
Emarthla, Joseph	474	Hays, Mary Shannon	8
Enriguee, Winnie	90	Hellet, Aman	346
Ernest, Anna Lee	35	Helton, George Thomas	284
Escoe, Leona G.	10	Hendrickson, Joe	241
Escoe, Myrtle Josephine	213	Henry, James Harvey	218
Escoe, Lindsey	353	Herrod, Robert Andrew	268
Evans, Savannah	220	Hickman, Alva	130
Evans, Alva Arizona	355	Higland, Leroy	61
Fellows, Leona	77	Hill, Jacob	181
Field, Frank	129	Hill, Sallie	352
Field, Butler	405	Hockett, Agnes Diana	238
Field, Sunday	407	Hodge, Nathaniel	217
Fife, Hannah	106	Hodge, Major Benjimen	271
Fife, Lena	127	Hooks, Virgie	270
Fife, Dixon	306	Huckaby, Mary Alice	103
Fife, Andrew	468	Hulsey, John Henry	172
Fipps, Effie	109	Hutton, Sally	59
Fish, Johnson	152	Ingley, Gladys G.	362
Fisher, Fillisee Norene	52	Inman, Naomi	376
Fisher, Ben	137	Isaac, John	394
Fisher, Eddie	138	Island, Laurence	68
Fisher, Elsie	380	Jackson, Birtha	94
Fixico, Sulter	81	Jacobs, Emma	454
Fixico, Yana	170	Jacobs, Johnny	475
Foshee, Ernest	151	Jefferson, McDora	210
Foshee, Homer L.	198	Jimboy, Nannie	136
Foster, Lewis E.	84	Jimboy, Mary	257
Francis, May Della	86	Johnson, Sissie	399
Frank, Stella	215	Johnson, Weetsie	443
Frank, George	267	Jones, Lizzie	67
Franklin, Polly	370	Jones, Adzel	76
Fulsom, Henry	18	Jones, Wesley	133
Fulsom, Wiley	318	Kalaney, Chepon	192
Furr, Albert Clinton	223	Kernal, Lilly	442
Gaither, Myrtle Washington	39	Kernells, Minnie	329
Gibson, Frankie	65	King, Pearl Leverh	323
Goode, Annie Elderrein	254	King, George	390
Goodwin, Reese	256	Kite, Edna Bettie	25
Gouge, Chunna	478	Knight, Jessie	315
Gouge, Pewter	489	Knight, Iola	391
Gouge, Sam	490	Land, Knaustaway	224
Gouge, Suckcho	491	Lannan, Ora	259
Gouge, Casawka	492	Lannan, Nora	260
Gray, Carl	79	Lasley, Sallie	410
Grayson, Lela	107	Lasley, Jackson	411
Grayson, Hellen	200	Leath, Muskogee	392
Grayson, Ella	273	Lee, Robert E.	297
Grayson, Roosevelt	381	Letts, Vernon Milford	88
Grayson, Nochey	493	Letts, Vera May	89
Green, Nancy	264	Leverett, Fanny	29
Green, Kizzie	265	Lewis, Washie	34
Green, Barney	455	Lewis, Eula Velma	186
Gregory, Nina Crete	117	Lewis, Nut-te-che	255
Gregory, Delila May	219	Lewis, Micco	26
Grissom, John Edward Franklin	233	Lieber, Albert Leon	5
Haikey, Masey	92	Lindsey, Noah	366
Haley, Kizzie	197	Littlehead, La-sa-wee	235
Hall, Cleo C.	336	Littlehead, Maggie	236
Hall, Sunnie	341	Littlehead, Joe	294
Hall, Manima	356	Loney, Ellen	345
Hallford, Esther	433	Long, Bettie	180
Hamilton, James M.	119	Long, Ah-la-co-ga-nay	377
Hamilton, Mahala	312	Looney, Beckie Lena	134
Hardridge, Clarence	47	Lott, Addie	404
Hardridge, Jasper	53	Lovett, Loran Alfred	415
Harjo, Joe	123	Lowe, Albert Chastain	413
Harjo, Samuel	144	Lowe, William	175
Harjo, Mollie	179	Lowry, Ama C.	188
Harjo, Lucy	245	Lucas, Delphine	307
Harjo, Freeda	288	Lunsford, Ida	278
		Mann, Hazel May	212
		March, Edith	459

Name.	Roll No.	Name.	Roll No.
March, William K.	460	Roberts, Annie	343
Marshall, Mamie	332	Robison, Samuel	20
Martin, March	1	Rogers, Legus	299
Martin, Joe Ross	11	Ross, J. E. Jr.	12
Martin, Henry	113	Rowley, Henry Stevens	379
Matoy, Gertrude	73	Sampson, Jessie D.	27
Mayes, Minnie	205	Sanger, Pauline	99
Meagher, Katherine		Sarnie, Joe	209
Frances	330	Sarty, Joe	96
Micco, Iseral	494	Sarty, Lena	429
Mikey, Helen	206	Sarwanoke, Turner	347
Miller, James A.	176	Sarwanoke, Bessie	348
Miller, Samuel	279	Scott, Lizzie	372
Mitchell, Hettie	349	Scott, Lelia	373
Mitchell, Firsey	350	Scott, Lola	324
Mitchell, Selanie	351	Scott, Adam	340
Mitchell, Amy	471	Sewel, Willie	157
Moore, Carr Orlando	95	Sewel, Louisa	331
Moore, Elizza	389	Sewell, Willie	458
Moore, Winnie Mary	396	Simmer, Peter	141
Morrison, Tully	30	Simmer, Lillie	159
Morrison, Andrew		Simmer, Aggie	449
Jackson	32	Simmons, Lena	333
Morrow, Jesse	359	Simmons, Sadie	382
Morrow, Lester	360	Simmons, Ida	406
Morton, Thomas Allen	229	Sloan, Albert	485
Mosquito, Ira	287	Sloan, Lillie	486
Murray, Margaret Mary	82	Sloan, Loney	487
McCann, William C.	243	Smith, Ruth	383
McCosar, Alice	158	Smith, Margaret Ellen	388
McCosar, Solomon	190	Smith, Martin	408
McFarland, Leah	479	Smith, Violet Elizabeth	319
McGee, Princess Aline	31	Snakeya, Amos	274
McGertt, Nathan	480	Snakeya, Nora	275
McGirt, Bessie	189	Snow, John	310
McGuire, Oscar H.	13	Stake, Louisa	300
McKellop, Lydia	234	Starr, Walter	342
McIntosh, Kitty	33	Starr, Lena	448
McIntosh, Wanda		Statham, Elizabeth	227
Wynona	60	Steen, John Howard	246
McNac, Katie	397	Stephenson, Eddie	62
McNac, Hallie	428	Stevens, Ida Bell	239
McNac, Joseph	447	Stevens, Lenon	240
McNac, Lizzie	481	Stoddard, Stella	317
Narcomay, Lizzie	162	Stout, Ethel	161
Nash, Ora	398	Stover, Daniel Jr.	72
Nelson, Lizzie	277	Stubblefield, Ross	
Nero, Samuel	378	Marion	174
Okchunpulla	477	Sullins, Gladys May	187
Orcutt, Pearlie	83	Sullivan, Emma	424
Orcutt, Winnie M.	266	Sullivan, John	425
Owens, Nellie	434	Sulphur, Andrew	57
Palmer, Jack Frost	167	Sumka, Henry	191
Panoske, Lydia	450	Swingle, Alice	231
Panoskie, Penie	451	Taborn, Albert	374
Parks, Rosetta	293	Taborn, Gertrude	375
Partridge, Jonas	387	Talomase, Emma	412
Penn, Emoney	222	Tarloshaw, Mista	339
Perryman, Sarah Ann	303	Tarvin, B. C. Jr.	467
Phillips, Nancy	50	Taryole, Tupper	445
Pinky, Lizzie	338	Tate, Elmer	173
Pitman, Clarence	70	Tate, Jesse	298
Pitman, Edith Lucinda	432	Thomas, Susie	128
Porter, James Summer-		Thomas, Nora	242
field	7	Thomas, Grant	261
Porter, Jemima	281	Thomas, Minnie Harris	495
Posey, Ruth Lucile	22	Thompson, Martha	393
Posey, Charles Kenneth	40	Thompson, Simon Pearcy	426
Post, Thomas Jr.	28	Tiger, John Washington	120
Price, Nora Nellie Marie	104	Tiger, Annie	121
Price, Mary Lucile	221	Tiger, Edna	155
Price, Mamie	228	Tiger, Louise	156
Randall, Sandy	244	Tiger, Lapsy	184
Reed, Robert	361	Tiger, Melissa	282
Rentie, Gracie	140	Tiger, Oda	292
Reynolds, Addie Lee	71	Tiger, Lindy	400
Reynolds, Napoleon	132	Tiger, Toche	409
Reynolds, Miles C.	232	Tiger, William Henry	457
Richard, Velva	16	Tilley, John Willis	304
Richard, Lesslie	431	Tobler, Benjamin	202
Richard, Rina	472	Tolleson, Alfred	
Roberson, Joe T.	369	Washington	15
Roberts, Liley	203	Trent, Ned Richard	211

Name.	Roll No.	Name.	Roll No.
Tuffer, Hettie	420	Williams, Haddie	101
Vowell, Earl Lafayette	78	Williams, Ada	285
Wa-co-che, Jane	344	Wills, Jack Harbert	125
Walker, Joseph	163	Wilson, Jack Elton	110
Wallace, Laura C.	335	Wilson, John Wesley	462
Washington, Frank	55	Wilson, Hubbard	463
Washington, Alice	56	Wilson, Howard	464
Watashe, James	316	Wilson, Zana	465
Watson, Chancy Lee	85	Wilson, Stephen	466
Watson, Mehaley	143	Wind, Charlie	118
Wayman, Clyde		Winn, Richard E.	435
McCausland	4	Winn, Henry O.	436
Weaver, Thelma	296	Winn, Tabbie	437
Wesley, Rose Etta	75	Winn, Prebble	438
Wesley, Lillie	131	Winn, Valley	439
Wesley, Bettie	142	Winn, Urceil	440
Wesley, Lizzie	195	Winters, Grace	24
West, Nora	322	Wisener, Oyama	178
West, Eliza	403	Woodward, James H.	289
Whetstone, Verma C.	44	Wright, Eugene M.	367
Whetstone, Dorothea		Yahola, Martha	185
Cleo	207	Yahola, Mary	469
White, Raymond	337	Yarhola, Nellie	305
Wildcat, Rhoda	421	Yarhola, Mary	371
Wiley, Virgina Dorothy	402	Yellowhead, Samuel	295
Williams, Monroe	66		

INDEX TO
CREEK FREEDMEN

Name.	Roll No.	Name.	Roll No.
Asbury, Primus	1954	Barnett, Phillip	613
Asbury, Rose	1955	Barnett, Lucy	614
Asbury, James	1956	Barnett, Jeannetta	1184
Asbury, Jenmes	1957	Barnett, Blanche	1185
Asbury, Tommy	1958	Barnett, Lucy	1327
Asbury, Joseph J.	1959	Barnett, Pearly May	1328
Asbury, Lizzie	1960	Barnett, Daisy	1329
Asbury, Affa	1961	Barnett, Billy	1389
Atkins, Roman	4509	Barnett, George	1390
Austin, Mahaley	2320	Barnett, Samuel	1391
Austin, Sam	2321	Barnett, Mabel	1392
Austin, Tildy	2322	Barnett, Izona	1393
Austin, James	2323	Barnett, Melton	1394
Austin, William	2324	Barnett, Joseph	1741
Austin, Sarah	2325	Barnett, Henry	1742
Austin, Alice	3471	Barnett, Samuel	1743
Austin, Sabra	3661	Barnett, Trump	1847
Austin, Jimmie	3663	Barnett, Charles	1886
Austin, Rena	3664	Barnett, Lillie	1887
Austin, Ruben	3665	Barnett, Mamie	1888
Bailey, Pearl	2450	Barnett, Sarah	1889
Bailey, Eliza	3115	Barnett, Wesley	1890
Bailey, Edna	3116	Barnett, Cully	1891
Baker, Sallie	4614	Barnett, Albert	1892
Baker, Ella	4615	Barnett, Andy	2045
Baker, Martha	4616	Barnett, Sam	2051
Baker, Jesse	4617	Barnett, Winnie	2052
Baker, Lola	4618	Barnett, Joe	2097
Baker, George	4619	Barnett, Mennes W.	2174
Baker, Fred	4620	Barnett, Nancy	2175
Ballard, Dollie	1287	Barnett, Ketch	2318
Ballard, Mariah	1288	Barnett, James	2935
Ballard, Alfred	1289	Barnett, Malinda	2936
Ballard, Mary	2708	Barnett, Joe	2937
Ballard, Jones	2709	Barnett, Frances	2938
Ballard, Doctor	2710	Barnett, Washington	3037
Banks, William	1548	Barnett, Emma	3038
Banks, Lettie	1549	Barnett, Arthur	3039
Banks, Walter	1550	Barnett, Jackson	3040
Banks, Hettie	1551	Barnett, Lewis	3041
Banks, Annie	3121	Barnett, Fred Lee	3042
Banks, Daisy	3122	Barnett, Josh	3096
Banks, John	3123	Barnett, Jinsey	3097
Banks, Pleasant L.	3125	Barnett, Lulu	3098
Banks, Mary A.	5097	Barnett, Peter	3099
Barber, Lulu	4411	Barnett, Robert	3100
Barber, Roxy Anna	4412	Barnett, Katie	3101
Barber, Lewis	4413	Barnett, Fanny	3102
Barber, Lawrence	5466	Barnett, Judy	3103
Barker, Elizabeth	1319	Barnett, Nelson	3106
Barker, Isabelle	3621	Barnett, Mary	3107
Barnes, Louisa	2088	Barnett, Alice	3108
Barnes, Julia	2467	Barnett, Will	3109
Barnes, Mathew	2468	Barnett, Emma	3110
Barnes, Luther	2469	Barnett, Amos	3383
Barnes, Lee	5096	Barnett, Simon	3439
Barnett, Benj.	87	Barnett, Sarah	3440
Barnett, Dinah	88	Barnett, Dick	3454
Barnett, Thomas	89	Barnett, Lizzie	3455
Barnett, Stephen	90	Barnett, Monday	3722
Barnett, George	91	Barnett, Alfred	3723
Barnett, Lilly	93	Barnett, Leoda	3724
Barnett, Cleveland	94	Barnett, Martin	3809
Barnett, Julia	95	Barnett, Annie	3810
Barnett, Benjamin, Jr.	96	Barnett, Ada	3811
Barnett, Samuel	104	Barnett, Cudjoe	3812
Barnett, Joseph	105	Barnett, Tate	4094
Barnett, Maria	106	Barnett, Garfield	4095
Barnett, Dora	152	Barnett, Thomas	4096
Barnett, Paro	174	Barnett, Harper	4097
Barnett, Thomas	250	Barnett, Creek	4098
Barnett, Affie	251	Barnett, Art	4099
Barnett, Fulton	252	Barnett, Birdie	4100
Barnett, Nellie	399	Barnett, Joe	4147
Barnett, Dick	397	Barnett, James	4224
Barnett, Polly	398	Barnett, John	4231
Barnett, Andrew	400	Barnett, Sallie	4298
Barnett, Hannah	401	Barnett, Miley	4299
Barnett, Sam'l	576	Barnett, Sarah	4300
Barnett, Louisa	577	Barnett, Doctor	4309
Barnett, Tom	610	Barnett, Wicey	4603
Barnett, Hagar	611	Barnett, Phyllis	4604

Name.	Roll No.	Name.	Roll No.
Barnett, Jack	4652	Blackburn, Priscilla	4277
Barnett, Jincy	4693	Blackburn, Willie	4278
Barnett, Mary	4694	Blackburn, Frank	4279
Barnett, William	4696	Blackburn, Charity	4280
Barnett, Eddie	4713	Blackburn, Josephine	4281
Barnett, Lucy	4714	Blackman, Earnest	3171
Barnett, Rena	4796	Blackstone, Alex	3321
Barnett, Clarence	4797	Blackwell, Rose	1099
Barnett, Jim	4832	Blackwell, Stepney	1100
Barnett, Roxana	4833	Bodry, Jesse	903
Barnettt, Elnora	4834	Bogy, Joanna	5642
Barnett, Abigail	4835	Bogy, Annie	5643
Barnett, Morris	4836	Bogy, Lillie	5644
Barnett, Melisha	4864	Bogy, Bertha	5645
Barnett, Lena	5105	Bogy, Wagner	5646
Barnett, Lilly	5118	Bogy, Fred	5647
Barnett, Emma	5126	Boon, Peter	4848
Barnett, Boston	5204	Boone, Thomas L.	2696
Barnett, Ben	5222	Bowleg, Edmond	5373
Barnett, Joe	5283	Bowlegs, Lessie	6
Barnett, Monday	5284	Bowlegs, Johnie	7
Barnett, Leroy	5285	Bowlegs, Jimmie	8
Barnett, Susie	5286	Bowlegs, Stella	9
Barnett, Emma	5287	Bowlegs, Daisy	12
Barnett, Joe	5344	Bowlegs, Synda	50
Barnett, Samantha	5365	Bowlegs, August	51
Barnett, Susie	5457	Bowlegs, Robert	52
Barnett, Lucy	5537	Bowlegs, Louisa	53
Barnette, Ben	641	Bowlegs, Angeline	54
Barnette, Willie	642	Bowlegs, Sherman	55
Barnette, Annie	643	Bowlegs, Eliza	220
Barnette, Sonny	644	Bowlegs, Lula	237
Barnette, Maria	5412	Bowlegs, Cato	690
Bartlett, Betsey	1240	Bowman, James	1652
Bartlett, Dalcy	1241	Bowman, Mary	1653
Bartlett, Ned	1242	Bowman, Robert	1654
Bartlett, Toby	1243	Bowman, George	1655
Bartlett, Mary	1244	Boyd, Elmira	5394
Bartlett, Grayson	1245	Boyd, Lena	5395
Bartlett, Nathan	1246	Boyd, George	5396
Bartlett, Adie	1247	Bowman, Sophie	5397
Bartlett, Lydie	1248	Bowman, Mulsie	5398
Bates, Mary	3631	Boyd, Julie	5399
Bates, Irene	3632	Boyd, Fannie	5400
Bates, Squire	3633	Boyd, Joseph	5401
Bates, Mary Magdalene	3634	Boyd, Mary	5402
Batts, Henrietta	566	Bradberry, Ellen	4884
Batts, Godfrey	569	Bradbury, Willie	5052
Batts, Reed	5351	Bradbury, Josie	5053
Batts, Johnny	5582	Bradford, Willie	4201
Beams, Gracie	1034	Bradford, Emma	4202
Beams, Anna	1315	Bradford, Abbie	4203
Bean, Patsey	493	Bradford, Rais	4204
Bean, Thomas	4731	Bradford, Ruthy	4205
Bean, Beatrice	4732	Bradford, Lamy	4206
Bear, Rebecca	734	Bradford, George	4207
Beaver, Julia	4504	Bradford, Annie	4208
Beaver, Vicey	4505	Bradford, Lulu	5069
Bell, Hager	3072	Brady, Adam	3534
Bell, Novella	3077	Brady, John	4830
Bell, Robert Terry	3078	Brewer, Nick	2079
Bell, Sallie	4163	Brewer, Mattie	2080
Benjamin, Ella	4878	Brewer, Emmett	2081
Berry, Ella	3676	Brewster, Joanna	3229
Berry, Margurite	3677	Brewster, Ruthie	3231
Berry, Adee	3678	Brinkley, Nealer	4580
Berry, Dereaner	3679	Bristor, Jim	5498
Berryhill, Aaron	2118	Bristor, Ben	5499
Berryhill, Eliza	2119	Broadnax, Cago	5358
Berryhill, Rose	2405	Brooks, Johnny	1316
Berryhill, Nancy	3118	Brooks, Barbary	4985
Billy, Louvina	594	Brown, Rose	107
Birney, Polly	1087	Brown, Rachael	108
Birney, Rena	1088	Brown, Amanda	141
Birney, Susie	1162	Brown, Albert	142
Birney, Henry	2732	Brown, Washington	143
Birney, Richard	2733	Brown, Maggie	144
Birney, Ada	2734	Brown, Seborn	145
Birney, Joseph	2735	Brown, Ollie	364
Bishop, Alex	3461	Brown, Albert	536
Bishop, Almeta	3462	Brown, Edna	638
Bishop, Anna	3463	Brown, Dan	808
Bishop, Joseph	5673		

Name.	Roll No.	Name.	Roll No.
Brown, Billy	809	Brown, Robert	4749
Brown, Robert	810	Brown, George	4799
Brown, Sarah E.	939	Brown, Georgia	4895
Brown, Clara	942	Brown, Fred	4901
Brown, Julia	965	Brown, Suton	4911
Brown, Mary	1015	Brown, Lemmy	4914
Brown, Jane	1143	Brown, Silas	4984
Brown, Johnny	1144	Brown, Emanuel	5002
Brown, Wallace	1145	Brown, Rivanna	5041
Brown, Nellie	1146	Brown, Duval	5042
Brown, Edward	1147	Brown, Hettie	5043
Brown, Russell	1148	Brown, Andrew	5054
Brown, Harry	1149	Brown, Ethel	5129
Brown, William	1373	Brown, Frank	5352
Brown, Willie	1374	Brown, Ben	5354
Brown, Jimmie	1375	Brown, Cy	5439
Brown, Lillie	1376	Brown, Agnes	5441
Brown, Jacob S.	1436	Brown, Rebella	5657
Brown, Clara	1437	Brown, John	5658
Brown, George	1438	Brown, Paul	5687
Brown, Harry	1439	Bruner, Paro	1
Brown, Linnie	1440	Bruner, Aggie	2
Brown, Edith	1441	Bruner, Rayford	3
Brown, Lizzie	1442	Bruner, Dinkey	4
Brown, Frank	1443	Bruner, Spainey	5
Brown, Simon	1444	Bruner, Comanche	49
Brown, Benjamin	1445	Bruner, William	56
Brown, Hannah	1446	Bruner, Hagar	57
Brown, Bertha	1447	Bruner, William	58
Brown, Pearlie	1448	Bruner, Davis	59
Brown, Frances	1788	Bruner, Susan	60
Brown, Sam	1789	Bruner, Mary	61
Brown, Annie	1790	Bruner, John	62
Brown, Sarah	1863	Bruner, Estella	63
Brown, Bertha	2128	Bruner, Addie	64
Brown, Harry	2129	Bruner, Annie	99
Brown, Amos	2130	Bruner, Rena	100
Brown, Ben	2476	Bruner, Eliza	101
Brown, Annie	2477	Bruner, Rachael	102
Brown, Harriet	2478	Bruner, George	103
Brown, Jeneva	2479	Bruner, Rose	157
Brown, Minerva	2480	Bruner, Bertha	158
Brown, Lucy	2481	Bruner, Ned	161
Brown, Tecumseh	2482	Bruner, Rogers	177
Brown, Dora	2483	Bruner, Lizzie	236
Brown, Lottie	2484	Bruner, Benjamin	238
Brown, Jane	2485	Bruner, Frank	239
Brown, Ruthie	2506	Bruner, Willie	240
Brown, Emma L.	2568	Brunner, Peyton	241
Brown, Willie Lee	2569	Bruner, Ruth	242
Brown, Alexander D.	2570	Bruner, Cora	243
Brown, Shellie	2988	Bruner, Richard	244
Brown, Castella	2989	Bruner, George	245
Brown, Georgie	2990	Bruner, Josie	254
Brown, Henrietta	2991	Bruner, Columbia	255
Brown, James	3035	Bruner, Rose	256
Brown, Gracie	3036	Bruner, Ellen N.	278
Brown, Sampson	3732	Bruner, Ella Pearl	279
Brown, Sam	3923	Bruner, Ivory Ann	280
Brown, Julia	3935	Bruner, Leona Belle	281
Brown, John	3953	Bruner, Edna Irene	282
Brown, David	3993	Bruner, Emma	293
Brown, Benjamin	3994	Bruner, Willie	330
Brown, Rachel	3995	Bruner, Jake	499
Brown, Coy	3996	Bruner, Eddie	500
Brown, Jeff	4074	Bruner, Clander	501
Brown, Charlotte	4109	Bruner, Mariah	502
Brown, Creasie	4251	Bruner, Alice	637
Brown, William	4252	Bruner, Dinah	764
Brown, Lethie	4253	Bruner, Fred	769
Brown, Henry	4254	Bruner, John	832
Brown, John	4255	Bruner, Carrie	833
Brown, Della	4256	Bruner, Annie	834
Brown, Mary	4257	Bruner, Judy	1098
Brown, Mary	4453	Bruner, Mahala	1269
Brown, Robert	4454	Bruner, Susan	1534
Brown, John	4464	Bruner, Harriet	1619
Brown, Lura	4538	Bruner, Creacy	1638
Brown, Frazier	4539	Bruner, Lewis	1639
Brown, Beulah	4562	Bruner, Jim	1640
Brown, Ada	4563	Bruner, Benny	1641
Brown, Polly	4685	Bruner, Grace	1837
Brown, Winey	4748	Bruner, Nancy	1936

Name.	Roll No.	Name.	Roll No.
Bruner, John W.	1953	Bruner, Osceola	5099
Bruner, Sarah	2021	Bruner, Ellis	5211
Bruner, Caroline	2046	Bruner, Floyd McKinley	5219
Bruner, George	2048	Bruner, Charity	5341
Bruner, Lula	2049	Bruner, Mary Ann	5346
Bruner, Elijah	2050	Bruner, Gracie	5347
Bruner, Lewis	2058	Bruner, Gertie	5382
Bruner, Liley	2059	Bruner, Clayton	5384
Bruner, Eliza	2060	Bruner, Craven	5403
Bruner, Hattie	2061	Bruner, Pearly	5406
Bruner, Washington	2062	Bruner, Caroline	5407
Bruner, Warner	2251	Bruner, Joe	5497
Bruner, Judy	2252	Bruner, Ida	5656
Bruner, Sarah	2253	Bruner, Davis	5680
Bruner, Hackless	2254	Bryant, Israel	4397
Bruner, Freedman	2255	Buckner, Isadora	761
Bruner, Alf	2256	Buffington, Jane	978
Bruner, Allie	2257	Buffington, Arthur	3685
Bruner, Rella	2258	Buffington, Charlie	3686
Bruner, Mary	2259	Bullocks, Serena	5694
Bruner, Bettie	2263	Bullocks, Lou Willie	5697
Bruner, Edward	2264	Bumpus, Fannie	2219
Bruner, Rachel	2279	Bumpus, Alice	2220
Bruner, Mollie	2487	Bumpus, George	2221
Bruner, Menus	2575	Bunn, Louisa	4374
Bruner, Leah	2576	Bunn, Ethel	4594
Bruner, Jeffry	2577	Burgess, Georgia	4750
Bruner, Louisa	2578	Burgess, Howard	4751
Bruner, Davis	2579	Burnett, Lena	4239
Bruner, Joe	2580	Burnett, Bennie	4240
Bruner, John	2581	Burnett, Jennie	4241
Bruner, Jacob	2778	Burnett, Bessie	4242
Bruner, Sarah	2779	Burney, Neosho	3373
Bruner, Rena	2780	Burney, Alice	3374
Bruner, Mattie	2781	Burney, Annie	3375
Bruner, Alex	2782	Burney, Emma	3376
Bruner, Hester	2783	Burney, Mable	3377
Bruner, Sukie	2784	Burney, Rebecca	3378
Bruner, Etha	2785	Burney, Albert	3379
Bruner, Hagar	3200	Burney, Lennie	3380
Bruner, Joe	3403	Burney, Hester	4698
Bruner, Rina	3721	Burton, Lutitia	2190
Bruner, Charlie	3737	Burton, Ludie	3055
Bruner, Sibbie	3738	Burton, Johnnie	3056
Bruner, Fannie	3739	Burton, Nettie	3057
Bruner, Warrior	3757	Burton, Millie	3978
Bruner, Mary	3758	Burton, Johnny	3979
Bruner, Ned	3759	Butler, Elvira	2041
Bruner, Joseph	3760	Byrd, Mima	537
Bruner, David	3761	Byrd, Alice R.	538
Bruner, Viola	3762	Byrd, Jimmie	5081
Bruner, Thomas	3763	Byrd, Martha	5305
Bruner, Lewis	3764	Caesar, Freddy	1864
Bruner, Joe	3802	Caesar, Eliza	1865
Bruner, John D.	3814	Caesar, Bobby	1866
Bruner, Rose	3815	Calloway, Mary	5608
Bruner, Ella	3817	Calloway, Josie	5609
Bruner, Robert	3952	Calloway, Sip	5610
Bruner, Sanguer	4016	Calloway, Henry	5611
Bruner, Cornelius	4017	Calloway, Benjamin	5612
Bruner, Ada	4018	Canard, Nelson	784
Bruner, Georgie	4019	Canard, Elijah	786
Bruner, Lilla	4026	Canard, James	787
Bruner, Rayford	4078	Canard, Jimmie	788
Bruner, Susie	4532	Canard, Johnie	789
Bruner, Robert	4583	Canard, Jerry	2166
Bruner, John Jackson	4632	Canard, Tilda	2265
Bruner, Samuel	4642	Canard, Lawrence	3137
Bruner, Lou	4643	Canard, Henry	3840
Bruner, Mary	4644	Canard, Joe	3841
Bruner, Liza	4645	Canard, Henry	5121
Bruner, Meadle	4646	Canard, Hope	5392
Bruner, Tommy	4647	Canard, Mary	5648
Bruner, Edward	4648	Canada, Louis	686
Bruner, Davis	4649	Canada, David	687
Bruner, Billy	4650	Canada, Lafierce	688
Bruner, Lou Ethel	4678	Cannon, Lizzie	15
Bruner, A. W.	4800	Capps, Annie A.	5511
Bruner, Hagar	4801	Carlina, Scott	1693
Bruner, Engle	4802	Carlina, Frank	4992
Bruner, Wash	4868	Carlina, Tilda	4993
Bruner, Ida	5074	Carlina, Solomon	4994

Name.	Roll No.	Name.	Roll No.
Carlina, Carrie	4995	Ceasar, Tommy	2432
Carlina, Thomas	4996	Ceasar, Ned	2433
Carlina, Rosie	4997	Ceasar, Annie	2434
Carlina, Neda	4998	Ceasar, Abraham	3706
Carlina, Manda	4999	Ceasar, Ransom	3813
Carlina, Eva	5000	Ceasar, Joe H.	3825
Carlina, Rush	5001	Ceasar, Phillip R.	4605
Carliner, Susan	4798	Ceasar, Parsena	5348
Canard, Ketch	3888	Chambers, Annie	616
Carolina, Phillis	201	Chambers, Bettie	1457
Carolina, James	202	Chambers, Shelly	1462
Carolina, Isaac	203	Chambers, Jimmy	1463
Carolina, Robert	204	Chambers, Minnie	1464
Carolina, Lizzie	205	Chambers, Pearl	1465
Carolina, Polly Ann	206	Charles, Lizzie	184
Carolina, Tony	210	Charles, Freddie	593
Carolina, Jane	211	Charles, Washington	948
Carolina, Ruthan	212	Charles, Lucinda	949
Carolina, Quash	750	Charles, Adaline	950
Carolina, Rose	751	Charles, Alex	951
Carolina, Josie	752	Charles, Charley	952
Carolina, Mont	753	Charles, Jimmy	953
Carolina, Sarah	754	Charles, Mary Jane	954
Carolina, Roxana	801	Charles, Willie	955
Carolina, Ellen	806	Charles, Lu Anna	956
Carolina, James	4872	Charles, Lu-Ella	957
Carolina, William	5056	Charles, Joseph	958
Carolina, Cornelia	5057	Charles, Mattie	959
Carolina, Davis	5058	Charles, Albert	1543
Carolina, Bankston	5600	Charles, Jennie	1544
Carolina, Eddie	5601	Charles, Sadie	1545
Carolina, Frank	5602	Charles, Sango	1555
Carolina, Lee Heddie	5603	Charles, Tamar	1556
Carolina, Billy	5675	Charles, Mary	1558
Carolina, Leora	5682	Charles, Nero	3355
Carr, Mary	714	Charles, Abram	3714
Carr, Dick	2240	Charles, Florence	5111
Carr, Mattie	2241	Charles, Willie	5371
Carr, Lewis	2242	Charles, Julia E.	918
Carr, Coy	2243	Charles, Hannah	920
Carson, Lennie	1976	Charles, Rhina	2018
Carson, Dollie	1977	Checotah, Hepsey	922
Carter, Betsy	792	Cherry, Sarah	1153
Carter, Lena	793	Cherry, Bob	1154
Carter, Elizabeth	794	Cherry, Alice	1155
Carter, Willis	795	Cherry, Frank	1156
Carter, Mattie	796	Cherry, Joanna	1157
Carter, Henry	797	Cherry, Lizzie	1158
Carter, Mary	798	Cherry, Eddie	1159
Carter, Creasie	869	Cherry, George	1160
Carter, Mabel	870	Cherry, Susan	1301
Carter, Bertha	871	Cherry, Albert	1302
Carter, Mollie	981	Cherry, Joseph	1303
Carter, George	982	Cherry, Ressie	1304
Carter, Henry	983	Cherry, Martha	1305
Carter, Robert	984	Cherry, Willie	1306
Carter, William	985	Cherry, Ellis	1307
Carter, Doss	986	Cherry, Rosa	1308
Carter, Mary	987	Cherry, Sarah	1309
Carter, Junius	988	Cherry, Lula	1310
Carter, Rosella	989	Cherry, Allen	1569
Carter, Nelson	990	Cherry, John	3516
Carter, Ressie	991	Cherry, Eliza	3517
Carter, Leora	992	Cherry, Ida	3518
Carter, Carrie A.	2188	Cherry, Mary	5082
Carter, Mable	2191	Cherry, Elmore	5581
Carter, Annie	2192	Childers, Rose	3430
Carter, John	3028	Childers, Gertrude	4610
Carter, Annie	3029	Childers, Nora	4611
Carter, Josh	3030	Childers, Arlena	4612
Carter, Belle	3031	Childers, Lucy	4730
Carter, Rina	4323	Childs, Johnny	5264
Carter, Dicey	4324	Childers, Isabel	5265
Carter, Martha Jane	5141	Childs, Pearlie	5266
Caesar, Wm.	1822	Choteau, Sarah	3176
Ceasar, Rose	2424	Choteau, Jenetta	3177
Ceasar, Jimmie	2425	Choteau, Jane	3178
Ceasar, Mary	2426	Choteau, Mary	3179
Ceasar, Peggy	2427	Choteau, Viola	5107
Ceasar, John	2428	Clanton, William	5669
Ceasar, Priscilla	2429	Clanton, Mabel	5670
Ceasar, Henry	2430	Clark, Fanny	2038

Name.	Roll No.	Name.	Roll No.
Clark, Albert	2040	Colbert, Fannie	3648
Clark, Tennessee	2285	Colbert, George	3649
Clark, Alex	2286	Colbert, Mack	3650
Clark, Neil	2287	Colbert, Cora	3651
Clark, Fred	2288	Colbert, Sam	4116
Clark, George	2289	Colbert, Jane	4117
Clark, Eddie	2290	Colbert, Jennie	5261
Clark, Mariah	3361	Colbert, Jennie	5271
Clark, Willie	4399	Colbert, Amanda	5272
Clark, Roy	5120	Colbert, Hamilton J.	5327
Clayton, McKinly	819	Colbert, Louiza	5639
Clinton, J. D.	5154	Colbert, Garfield	5640
Coats, Alex	3255	Colbert, Nancy	5641
Cobb, Mollie	267	Cole, Sarah	554
Cobb, Morris	539	Cole, Mabel	555
Cobb, Jim	540	Cole, Lizzie	2489
Cobb, Levi J.	596	Cole, Ina	2495
Cobb, Hardie	597	Cole, Helen	2496
Cobb, Evaline	598	Cole, Gus	2497
Cobb, Noble	599	Cole, Bessie	4546
Cobb, Bessie	600	Cole, Daniel	4547
Cobb, Amos	715	Cole Carrie	4548
Cobb, Dolly	716	Cole, Willie	5182
Cobb, Tom	717	Cole, Jesse	5183
Cobb, Coody	718	Coleman, Eva	321
Cobb, Elsie	2574	Coleman, John	323
Cobb, John	4900	Coleman, Jessie	376
Cobb, Mollie	5425	Coleman, Elvira	377
Cobb, Celia	5458	Coleman, Martha	378
Cobb, Sam	5494	Coleman, Gracie	379
Cobbrey, Rosie	3132	Coleman, March	380
Cobbrey, Priscilla	3666	Coleman, Prince	381
Cohee, Mandy	4659	Coleman, Ellen	383
Cohee, Mary Ellen	4660	Coleman, Peter	457
Cohee, America	4661	Coleman, Beckey	458
Cohee, Lafayette	4662	Coleman, James	459
Colbert, George	650	Coleman, Mandy	460
Colbert, Peter	1235	Coleman, Jesse	461
Colbert, Adline	1236	Coleman, Mary	1996
Colbert, Sofa	1237	Coleman, William	1997
Colbert, Emma	1238	Coleman, Emma	1998
Colbert, Stephen	1495	Coleman, Delila	1999
Colbert, Rachel	1524	Coleman, David	2000
Colbert, Lizzie	1560	Coleman, Mary Alice	2001
Colbert, Henry	1685	Coleman, Walter, Jr.	2002
Colbert, Betty	1776	Coleman, Thadeus William	2003
Colbert, Viola	1777	liam	2003
Colbert, Zella	1778	Coleman, Lucy	4710
Colbert, Lemuel E.	1779	Colling, Mary	2870
Colbert, Annanias	2074	Colling, Malinda	2875
Colbert, Fred	2075	Collins. Charles	2282
Colbert, Lizzie	2076	Colly, Sam	578
Colbert, Jenetta	2077	Conner, Hannah	1251
Colbert, Dora	2078	Conner, John	1252
Colbert, Stephen	2082	Conner, Liddle	3400
Colbert, Mary Jane	2083	Connor, Betsey	682
Colbert, Sarah Ann	2084	Connor, Oliver	685
Colbert, Bethena	2085	Connor, Bully	3104
Colbert, Jesse	2086	Connor, Mary Ann	3105
Colbert, Henry	2103	Coody, Joseph	964
Colbert, Charles	2120	Cooks, Rhoda	3772
Colbert, Hannah	2121	Cooks, Daisy	3773
Colbert, Elzora	2122	Cooks, Lulu	4398
Colbert, Rosy	2123	Cooks, Polly	4492
Colbert, Perry	2309	Cooks, Charlie	4493
Colbert, Grant	2376	Cooks, Geneva	5587
Colbert, Harriet	2377	Coon, Lula	3924
Colbert, Sarah	2378	Corbray, Emma	1271
Colbert, Jim	2645	Corbray, James	1496
Colbert, Bank	3450	Corbray, Nancy	1497
Colbert, Betty	3459	Corbray, Charley	1642
Colbert, Harriet	3546	Corbray, Dollie	1643
Colbert, Willie	3547	Corbray, Nellie	1644
Colbert, Ephriam	3548	Corbray, Katie	1645
Colbert, Joseph	3549	Corbray, Morris	1646
Colbert, Hattie	3550	Corbray, Rachael	1647
Colbert, Tom	3551	Corbray, Harry	1671
Colbert, Richard	3552	Corbray, Grace	1672
Colbert, David	3553	Corbray, Hagar	1674
Colbert, Dicey	3644	Corbray, Luvilla	1675
Colbert, Davis	3646	Corbray, Hackless	1676
Colbert, John	3647	Corbray, Sarah	1677

Name.	Roll No.	Name.	Roll No.
Corbray, Hattie	1678	Daniels, May Jane	2902
Corbray, Roy	1679	Daniels, Sam	2963
Corbray, Agnes	1680	Daniels, Willie	5093
Corbray, Aleck	1681	Davis, Wilson	76
Corbray, Asa	1682	Davis, Dicey	77
Corbray, Mona Jean	1683	Davis, Aleck	78
Corbray, Elijah	1893	Davis, Jennie	79
Corbray, L. Belle	1894	Davis, Winnie	160
Corbray, Mary	2930	Davis, Charity	322
Corbray, Gracie	5189	Davis, Mary	763
Corbray, Henry	5249	Davis, George	1032
Corbray, Charlotte	5250	Davis, Charles	1033
Corbray, Eva	5381	Davis, Ollie	1449
Corbray, Irene	5567	Davis, Peggy	1450
Cousins, Jack	601	Davis, Lula	1452
Cousins, Nelly	602	Davis, Turner	1453
Cousins, Georgia	603	Davis, Willie	1454
Cousins, Millie	604	Davis, Ada	1622
Cousins, Celia	605	Davis, Diana	1624
Cousins, Francis	606	Davis, Willie C.	1698
Cousins, Raford	607	Davis, Mary	1699
Cousins, Tom	608	Davis, Clifford	1700
Cousins, Joseph	609	Davis, Rosa	1701
Cousins, Jupiter	4400	Davis, Herbert	1702
Cowans, Emma	4522	Davis, Dewitt	1704
Cowans, Linda	4525	Davis, Izella	1705
Cox, Joe B.	127	Davis, Josephine	2830
Cox, Mary	128	Davis, Rufus	2831
Cox, Edward	129	Davis, Chloe E.	3085
Crabtree, Willie L. B.	5507	Davis, Robert	3150
Crabtree, Clementine Isa-		Davis, Joe	3151
belle	5515	Davis, Anderson	3234
Craig, Emma	3346	Davis, Lucinda	3235
Craig, Lawrence	3352	Davis, Hayman	3236
Crane, Flora	4526	Davis, Serena	3237
Crane, Elvira	4528	Davis, Adam	3238
Crane, Willie	5551	Davis, Josephine	3239
Craw, Maudesta L.	4961	Davis, Belle	3240
Crawford, Lillie	5404	Davis, Minnie	3241
Crittenden, Allie	5277	Davis, Rebecca	3242
Crossley, Cynda	3052	Davis, Linnie	3243
Crossley, Abraham	3053	Davis, Anderson Jr.	3244
Crosslin, Lucy	4414	Davis, Henry	3247
Crosslin, Sallie	4982	Davis, Clarence	3725
Crosslin, Abe	5635	Davis, Jackson	3824
Cruel, Emma	2268	Davis, Pearson	3859
Cruel, Ed	2269	Davis, Maggie	3861
Cruel, Maria	2270	Davis, Malinda	3862
Cruel, John	2271	Davis, Sammie	3863
Cruel, Tom	2420	Davis, James	3864
Cruel, Stephen	2421	Davis, Henry	3865
Cruel, Louis	2422	Davis, Raford	3886
Cruel, Eli	4600	Davis, Cooper	3931
Cruel, Irene	5661	Davis, Cato	3941
Cudjo, Joshua	826	Davis, Sallie	4053
Cudjo, Mary	4716	Davis, Redmond	4842
Cudjoe, John	3630	Davis, Izora	4874
Cudjoe, Mandy	5308	Davis, Fredie	5062
Cuff, Sam	556	Davis, Nancy	5068
Cuff, Lear	557	Davis, Mattie	5691
Cuff, Isabelle	559	Davison, Joseph P.	2004
Cuff, James	560	Davison, George W.	2005
Cuff, Alice	561	Dean, Elias	3850
Cully, Arthur	3984	Dean, John	3851
Cully, Willis	4651	Dean, Minnie	3852
Curns, Lucy	827	Dean, James	3853
Curns, Samuel	2857	Dean, Lou	3854
Curtis, Minerva	3944	Dean, Jesse	3855
Curtis, Lula	3945	Dean, Floyd	3856
Curtis, Nancy	5230	Dean, Nelson	3857
Cyrus, Agnes	762	Dean, Jack	3938
Dan, George	288	Dean, Joanna	4349
Dan, Mary	289	Dean, Bud	4415
Dan, William	290	Dean, Silas	4543
Dan, Matilda	291	Dean, Viola	4544
Dan, Joanna	292	Dean, John	4585
Dan, Sampson	4575	Dean, Harris	4586
Dan, Maria	5520	Dean, Mary Annie	5089
Daniel, Margaret	1054	Dean, Leo	5666
Daniels, Bob	692	Dean, Lucinda	3527
Daniels, Annie	2435	Dean, LeRoy	5671
Daniels, Rufus	2436	Deer, August	1169
Daniels, Minnie	2837	Deer, Sophia	1170

Name.	Roll No.	Name.	Roll No.
Delony, Bennie	1467	Drew, Charley	5240
Delony, Leroy	5169	Drew, Sam	5241
Dennis, Ida	4889	Drew, Jessie	5242
Dennis, Sarah	4927	Drew, Fred	5243
Derisaw, Mary Jane	3566	Drew, Savanna	5244
Dindy, Susan	21	Drew, Odessa	5245
Dindy, Wilson	22	Drew, Stephen	5477
Dindy, Dollie	23	Duff, Eveline	4339
Dindy, Cora	24	Duff, Jesse C.	4340
Dixon, Joshua	1352	Duff, Edith J.	4341
Dixon, Fred	1353	Duff, Harold A.	4342
Dixon, Kizzie	1354	Duff, Bina B.	4343
Dixon, Lennie	1355	Dunbar, Nancy	680
Dixon, Johnie	1356	Durant, William	301
Dixon, Edwin	1357	Durant, Ralph	302
Dixon, David	2628	Durant, Edward	585
Dixon, Jimmie	2629	Durant, Ben	586
Dixon, Edna	5112	Durant, Susan	938
Doil, Julia	562	Durant, Philip H.	1172
Dolman, Elizabeth Jane	2932	Durant, Monday	1273
Dolman, Henry	2933	Durant, Jim	1274
Douglas, Perry	3977	Durant, Stephen	1275
Douglass, Granville	4534	Durant, Jesse	1276
Douglass, Lura May	5500	Durant, Augusta	1277
Douglass, Theodore R.	5501	Durant, Lucinda	1278
Douglass, Barney	5502	Durant, Roxie	1279
Douglass, Billy	3493	Durant, Alberty	1280
Douglass, Jimmie	4535	Durant, Edna	1283
Douglass, Rachael	4536	Durant, Edith	1284
Douglass, Clay	4537	Durant, William	1468
Downs, Stella	5415	Durant, Elnora	1469
Doyle, Miley	1017	Durant, Georgia Ann	1470
Doyle, Frank	1527	Durant, Israel	1471
Doyle, Millie	1528	Durant, Nancy	2445
Doyle, Willie	1530	Durant, Stephen	2694
Doyle, Susie	1531	Durant, Julia	2695
Doyle, Adam	2541	Durant, Faith	3169
Doyle, Susan	2542	Durant, Katie	3193
Doyle, Eddie	2543	Durant, Sarah	3303
Drake, Nettie	2143	Durant, Fred	3304
Drake, Rosa.	2144	Durant, Minerva	3305
Drake, Hattie	2145	Durant, Peter	4050
Drake, Sheridan	2146	Durant, Hannah	4051
Drake, Sarah	2147	Durant, Squire	4052
Drake, Pearly	2148	Durant, Nelson E.	4148
Draper, Addie	2801	Durant, George	4149
Draper, Ida	2802	Durant, Clarence	4150
Draper, Rosevelt	5356	Durant, Milford	4151
Drew, Nick	677	Durant, Unip	4190
Drew, William	1249	Durant, Lewis	4384
Drew, Rose	1250	Durant, Wilson	4737
Drew, John	1416	Durant, Alice	4738
Drew, Peggy	1417	Durant, Nellie	4739
Drew, John, Jr.	1418	Durant, Hannah	4740
Drew, Elizabeth	1419	Durant, Willie	4754
Drew, David	1420	Durant, Maggie	4755
Drew, Tobe	1474	Durant, Ben	4756
Drew, Ludie	1621	Durant, Dicey	4915
Drew, Hattie	2116	Durant, Cora	4916
Drew, Nero	2200	Durant, Maria	4917
Drew, Rachael	2559	Durant, Ben	4918
Drew, Andy	2560	Durant, Hayward	5127
Drew, Jack	2561	Durant, Elnora	5186
Drew, Susie	2823	Durant, Jesse	5367
Drew, Flora	2824	Durant, Edmund	5591
Drew, Polly	2825	Durant, Nelson	5592
Drew, Robert	2854	Dyle, Hannah	812
Drew, Susie	2855	Dyle, Elsie	814
Drew, Alice S.	2856	Dyle, Dave	817
Drew, Abe	3082	Easley, Dinah	1732
Drew, Roxanna	3083	Eastman, Rosanna	5256
Drew, Josephine	3084	Eastman, Joe	5257
Drew, Jason	3917	Eastman, Lena	5258
Drew, Nathaniel	3918	Easup, Nettie	159
Drew, Arthur	3919	Edwards, Eddie	590
Drew, Henrietta	3920	Edwards, Alice	683
Drew, Georgia Ann	3921	Edwards, Jessie	684
Drew, Joe	4321	Edwards, Frank	1575
Drew, Washington	4330	Edwards, Melinda	1576
Drew, Ellis	4331	Edwards, Ruthie	1577
Drew, Roxanna	4332	Edwards, Pleas	1578
Drew, Robert	4746	Edwards, Jackson	2389
Drew, Joe	4747		

Name.	Roll No.	Name.	Roll No.
Edwards, Malinda	2390	Fieds, Tina	5568
Edwards, Robert	2391	Fields, Garfield	5569
Edwards, Willie	2392	Fields, Sylvester	5570
Edwards, Laura	2393	Fields, Varene	5571
Edwards, Jackson, Jr.	2394	Fields, Jessie	5692
Edwards, Eddie	2395	Fife, Loney	2247
Edwards, Eva	2396	Fife, Mollie	2248
Edwards, Rose	3316	Fife, Bossey	2249
Edwards, Ella	3317	Fife, Alice	2250
Edwards, Ben	3318	Fife, Sampson	2537
Edwards, Josie	3319	Fife, Hannah	2538
Edwards, Peter	3829	Fife, Hannah	2539
Edwards, Phyllis	3830	Fife, Aleck	2540
Edwards, Richard	3831	Fife, Lizzie	5045
Edwards, Ned	3832	Fife, Jim	5339
Edwards, Louisa	3833	Fink, Sarah	4416
Edwards, Jackson	3834	Fink, Jennie	4417
Edwards, Ethel	3835	Fink, Susie	4418
Edwards, Ella	4022	Fink, Mintie	4419
Edwards, Clifford	4023	Fisher, Josiah	3482
Edards, Josie	4959	Fisher, Lizzie	3483
Edwards, Elsie	5003	Fisher, Lizzie	3806
Edwards, Viola	5083	Fisher, Mose	3807
Edwards, Leona	5627	Fisher, Josiah	3808
Edwards, Beatrice	5663	Fisher, Moses A.	4907
Epperson, Eva	4164	Fisher, Willie	4986
Epperson, Roy	4165	Fisher, Aurilla	5493
Eperson, Zelma	4166	Flannagan, Caldonia	5080
Escoe, Walter	1466	Flannagan, George	
Escoe, Eddie	2684	Henry	2042
Evans, John	779	Flannigan, Sophia	2039
Evans, Phillis	2213	Fleming, Edgar	1311
Evans, Frank	2214	Fleming, Temple	1313
Evans, Maud	2215	Flint, Thomas	3142
Evans, Nettie	2216	Flint, James	3143
Evans, Bessie	2217	Flint, Polly	3144
Evans, Viola	2218	Flint, Jennie	3145
Evans, John, Jr.	5194	Flint, Nora	3146
Everett, Rina	1905	Flint, Cora	3147
Everett, Mymie	3748	Flint, Polly	3148
Eubank, Caroline	4420	Flint, Amanda	3149
Eubanks, Cora	4421	Flowers, Rosie	2871
Eubanks, James Edmund		Flowers, Silas	2872
G.	4422	Flowers, Fee	2873
Eubanks, Kittie	4423	Flowers, Thurman	2874
Eubanks, Lula	4424	Flynn, Belle	4356
Eubanks, Frances Eve-		Flynn, Louisa	4357
lene	4425	Flynn, Ella	4358
Eubanks, William	5247	Folsom, Willie	2934
Factor, Manda	4937	Ford, Joanna	2838
Faster, Carlina	5150	Ford, Nancy	2839
Favorite, Nettie H.	589	Ford, Charley	2840
Fee, Coody	3535	Ford, Paulina	2841
Fee, Nancy	3536	Ford, Ezekiel	2842
Fee, Jim	3537	Ford, Oliver	2843
Fee, Lizzie	3538	Ford, Kittie H.	3426
Fee, Rosella	3539	Ford, Florida	5085
Fee, Annie	5184	Ford, Florence	5086
Fields, Hattie	1706	Foreman, Amanda	2403
Fields, Sarah	1707	Foreman, Henry	4578
Fields, Benjamin	1728	Foreman, Daisy	4579
Fields, Lizzie	1729	Foster, Sarah	176
Fields, Lizzie	2722	Foster, Alice	179
Fields, John	2723	Foster, Rebecca	649
Fields, Tom	2724	Foster, Kasena	3223
Fields, Nellie	2725	Foster, Lucinda	3581
Fields, George	2726	Foster, Jim	3582
Fields, Elzora	3081	Foster, Onie	3583
Fields, Flora	4196	Foster, Martha	4726
Fields, Dinah	4301	Foster, Louvina	5434
Fields, Ella	4302	Foster, Phyllis	5547
Fields, Walter	4303	Fox, Joseph	4223
Fields, Arrilla	4304	Frances, Geo.	4061
Fields, Florence	4305	Francis, Sarah	4595
Fieds, Leora	4306	Francis, Jacob	4596
Fields, Myrtle	4307	Franklin, Rentie	229
Fields, Osa	4308	Franklin, Bettie	395
Fields, Lydia	4930	Franklin, Philip	396
Fields, Willie	4931	Franklin, Fred	660
Fields, Dick	4932	Franklin, Ross	661
Fields, Clifford	5168	Franklin, Tobe	662
Fields, Luvina	5375	Franklin, Dilsie	663
		Franklin, Louis	664

Name.	Roll No.	Name.	Roll No.
Franklin, Rebecca	665	Garrett, Ben	3224
Franklin, Re-anna	666	Garrett, Charles W.	4761
Franklin, Flanchie	667	Garrett, Cyril	4762
Franklin, Robert	668	Garrett, Alfred T.	4763
Franklin, Arlene	921	Garrett, William H.	4764
Franklin, Thomas	1422	Garrett, Letta E.	4765
Franklin, Glennie	1423	Garrett, Edna M.	4766
Franklin, Mary	1424	Garrett, William C.	5237
Franklin, John	1425	Garrett, Ethel	5238
Franklin, Ammon	1426	Garrett, Arlene M.	5239
Franklin, Toby	1427	Garrett, Castella	5460
Franklin, Zante	1428	Garrett, Hellen	5625
Franklin, Rebecca	1429	Gates, Sarah	1994
Franklin, Fred	1510	Gaskine, Alice	5562
Franklin, Richard	1562	Gaskine, Fred	5563
Franklin, Fanny	1563	Gaskine, Jake	5564
Franklin, Louisa	1564	Gaskine, Wiley	5565
Franklin, John	1565	Gaylord, Julia	5059
Franklin, Edward	1566	Geary, Lillie	495
Franklin, Jesse	1567	Gentry, James Ellis	831
Franklin, James	1568	Gentry, Willie	4169
Franklin, Stephen	1585	Gibson, Edmond	2834
Franklin, Solomon	2443	Gilbert, Kate	207
Franklin, Nancy	2444	Gilbert, Reecy	208
Franklin, Ben	2821	Gilbert, Isabelle	209
Franklin, Jane	2822	Glass, Kid	5683
Franklin, Silla	3154	Glover, Phoebe	2109
Franklin, Stephen	3155	Glover, Rafield	2117
Franklin, Phillis	3251	Glover, Emma	3324
Franklin, Sissie	3254	Golden, Tena	4344
Franklin, Willie	3860	Gooden, Alice	5019
Franklin, Mattie	4700	Gooden, Missouri	5506
Franklin, Aurella	5377	Goodnow, Nancy	1343
Franklin, Irene	5378	Gordon, George	439
Franklin, Bush	5577	Gordan, Lizzie	2457
Frazier, Wallace	4972	Gordon, Henry	2458
Frazier, Nannie	5262	Gordn, Herbert	2459
Frazier, Legus	5263	Gossett, Mollie	1208
Friday, Jack	1182	Gouge, Doctor	1084
Friday, David	1187	Gouge, Sally	1085
Friday, Peggie	1188	Graham, Rose	318
Friday, Berry	1189	Graham, Creasy	944
Friday, Rebecca	1190	Graham, Ida May	945
Friday, Jack	1191	Graham, Amelia	946
Friday, Bennie	1192	Graham, Weeda	947
Friday, Julia	1193	Grant, Louisa	2470
Friday, Edward	1194	Grant, Eddie	2471
Friday, Katie	1195	Grant, Julia	2472
Friday, Billy	1196	Grant, Luvena	2473
Friday, Annie	1197	Grant, Mason	2474
Friday, Jo	4904	Grant, Blance	2475
Froe, Celia	2091	Gray, Polly	3340
Froe, Fred	2092	Gray, Jane	3925
Froe, Georgia Ann	2093	Gray, Ethel	3926
Froe, Henry	5325	Gray, Lillie	3927
Fryday, Lewis	4862	Gray, Ruth	3928
Fulsom, Albert	1458	Gray, George	3929
Fulsom, Jane	1459	Gray, Samuel	3930
Fulsom, Willie	1460	Gray, Sallie	4510
Fulsom, Lula	1461	Gray, Lena	4511
Fulsom, Walter	4439	Gray, Marchie	4512
Fulsom, Harry	4440	Gray, George	5215
Fulsoom, Pearl	4441	Grayson, John	112
Fulsom, David	4445	Grayson, Island	116
Fulsom, Georgia	4446	Grayson, Sylla	117
Fulsom, Gracie A.	4447	Grayson, Warrior	118
Fulsom, Bettie	4448	Grayson, Alice	119
Fulsom, Louis	4449	Grayson, Herbert	120
Fulsom, Thomas	4587	Grayson, Louviney	122
Fulsom, Lenard A.	5060	Grayson, Dan	181
Fulsom, Riley	5411	Grayson, Aaron	214
Gains, Jessie	3175	Grayson, Sam	230
Gardner, Ida	1128	Grayson, Tommy	257
Garmon, Amy	13	Grayson, Samuel	298
Garmon, Jimmie	16	Grayson, Thomas	441
Garman, Louisa	17	Grayson, Hettie	442
Garmon, Pearlie	5550	Grayson, Ellis	443
Garnett, Phillip	940	Grayson, George	445
Garrett, Phillip	453	Grayson, George	446
Garrett, Mattie	454	Grayson, Sherman	496
Garrett, Benjamin	1508	Grayson, Dick	505
Garrett, Walter Scott	2180	Grayson, Mymie	506
Garrett, Sallie	3197		

Name.	Roll No.	Name.	Roll No.
Grayson, Hannah	507	Grayson, Louisa	1686
Grayson, Jack	508	Grayson, Sam	1687
Grayson, Eliza	549	Grayson, Alice	1688
Grayson, Johnson	550	Grayson, Rose	1689
Grayson, Cinda	551	Grayson, Raford	1690
Grayson, Dollie	552	Grayson, Jno.	1735
Grayson, Aurella	553	Grayson, Silvey	1736
Grayson, Tackey	591	Grayson, Cook	1737
Grayson, Sally	592	Grayson, Willie	1738
Grayson, Jennie	595	Grayson, Isaac	1739
Grayson, Annie	689	Grayson, Jane	1745
Grayson, Robt.	711	Grayson, Moses	1746
Grayson, Patience	712	Grayson, Joseph	1747
Grayson, Cleveland	713	Grayson, William	1815
Grayson, Warrior	748	Grayson, Sally	1816
Grayson, Elijah	765	Grayson, John	1817
Grayson, Eddie	766	Grayson, Janatta	1818
Grayson, Bettie	767	Grayson, Willie	1819
Grayson, Israel	768	Grayson, Rachael	1820
Grayson, Robt.	770	Grayson, Leona	1821
Grayson, Steve	771	Grayson, Sunny	1906
Grayson, Sharper	772	Grayson, Betty	1907
Grayson, Rosie	773	Grayson, Joe	1908
Grayson, Willie	774	Grayson, Phoebe	1909
Grayson, Caesar	802	Grayson, Emma	1910
Grayson, Paulina	803	Grayson, Gracie	1911
Grayson, Alice	804	Grayson, Misey	1912
Grayson, Bertha	805	Grayson, Stephen	1913
Grayson, Isom	807	Grayson, William	1934
Grayson, Emeline	896	Grayson, Adam	1935
Grayson, George	897	Grayson, Eddie	2530
Grayson, Louisa	898	Grayson, Rachael	2562
Grayson, Liza	899	Grayson, Rose	2642
Grayson, Catherine	900	Grayson, Roger	2680
Grayson, Mary	909	Grayson, Virey	2681
Grayson, Silla	976	Grayson, Susie	2682
Grayson, Amanda	979	Grayson, Jim	3013
Grayson, Henry	980	Grayson, Mary	3014
Grayson, Abraham	999	Grayson, Mollie	3015
Grayson, Mary	1000	Grayson, Tackey	3016
Grayson, Robt.	1001	Grayson, Arthur	3017
Grayson, General	1002	Grayson, Herbert	3018
Grayson, Bettie	1003	Grayson, Florence	3019
Grayson, Sikey	1004	Grayson, Peter	3032
Grayson, Edmund	1005	Grayson, Georgia	3033
Grayson, Leora	1006	Grayson, Beulah	3034
Grayson, Amanda	1007	Grayson, Tom	3043
Grayson, Sharper	1008	Grayson, Rose	3044
Grayson, Martha	1009	Grayson, Dinah	3045
Grayson, Tobe	1024	Grayson, Rachael	3269
Grayson, Jane	1025	Grayson, Palina	3270
Grayson, Allie	1026	Grayson, Lizzie	3271
Grayson, Jakey	1027	Grayson, Hagar	3272
Grayson, Leora	1028	Grayson, Lizzie	3273
Grayson, Onie Belle	1029	Grayson, Alice	3302
Grayson, Peter	1058	Grayson, Daniel	3418
Grayson, Mary	1059	Grayson, Curtis	3419
Grayson, Herbert	1062	Grayson, Hattie	3420
Grayson, Lena	1063	Grayson, Pearl	3421
Grayson, McKinley	1064	Grayson, Hannah	3431
Grayson, Joe	1065	Grayson, Hulen	3434
Grayson, Anthony	1101	Grayson, Millie	3435
Grayson, Annie	1102	Grayson, Irene	3436
Grayson, Stella V.	1103	Grayson, Benjamin	3437
Grayson, Deella Ann	1104	Grayson, Mitchell	3530
Grayson, Maggie	1227	Grayson, Robert	3531
Grayson, Dora	1347	Grayson, Ben	3532
Grayson, Hannah	1401	Grayson, Charlie	3533
Grayson, Willie	1402	Grayson, Will	3766
Grayson, Emma	1403	Grayson, Judy	3767
Grayson, Estella	1518	Grayson, Aaron	3842
Grayson, Peter	1519	Grayson, Mose	3843
Grayson, Sunny	1586	Grayson, Alice	3844
Grayson, Peggy	1587	Grayson, George	3845
Grayson, Freeland	1588	Grayson, Albert	3846
Grayson, Julia	1589	Grayson, Katie	3847
Grayson, Hetty	1590	Grayson, Willie James	3848
Grayson, Frank	1591	Grayson, Rosella	3849
Grayson, Lucy	1592	Grayson, Polly	3903
Grayson, Charlotte	1593	Grayson, Pompey	3904
Grayson, Amos	1594	Grayson, Jim	3905
Grayson, Mose	1650	Grayson, William	4214
Grayson, Lucy	1651	Grayson, Leah	4215

Name.	Roll No.	Name.	Roll No.
Grayson, Floyd	4216	Green, Gertie	2280
Grayson, Bill	4225	Green, Julia A.	3369
Grayson, Sam	4227	Green, Eddie	3458
Grayson, Mollie	4228	Green, Davis	4574
Grayson, Addie	4229	Green, Sammie	5117
Grayson, Mary	4359	Green, Wesley	5605
Grayson, Louella	4360	Green, Minerva	5606
Grayson, Jenetta	4361	Green, Jim	5607
Grayson, Walter	4362	Gregory, Melissa	2728
Grayson, Pleasant	4363	Greyson, Richard	510
Grayson, Evaline	4364	Greyson, Caroline	511
Grayson, Samuel	4365	Greyson, Sam	512
Grayson, Precilla	4366	Greyson, Henry	513
Grayson, Julia	4367	Greyson, Ella	514
Grayson, Katie	4368	Greyson, Annie	515
Grayson, Sandy	4373	Greyson, Jennie	516
Grayson, Louvina	4458	Greyson, Catherine	517
Grayson, Joe	4459	Greyson, Abraham	1234
Grayson, Minerva	4472	Greyson, Jim	518
Grayson, Albert	4473	Greyson, Polly	519
Grayson, Lucinda	4474	Greyson, Anthony	520
Grayson, Eli	4475	Greyson, Julia	2446
Grayson, Mark	4476	Greyson, Robert	2447
Grayson, Ollie	4477	Greyson, Hector	2448
Grayson, Lula	4478	Greyson, Zadie	5192
Grayson, Doctor	4479	Griffin, Dinah	2353
Grayson, Alfred	4576	Griffin, Amanda	5018
Grayson, David	4633	Griffin, Robert	5020
Grayson, Bertha	4672	Griffin, Mollie	5021
Grayson, Adam	4688	Griffin, Laura	5022
Grayson, Daniel	4924	Griffin, Clarence	5023
Grayson, Colbert	4926	Griffin, Elijah	5024
Grayson, James	4951	Griggs, Nancy	887
Grayson, Thomas	4952	Griggs, Ruth	888
Grayson, Boss	4953	Griggs, Warrior	3086
Grayson, William	4960	Griggs, Adeline	3087
Grayson, Mary	4971	Griggs, Jim	3088
Grayson, Willie	5123	Griggs, Walter	3089
Grayson, Jennie	5136	Griggs, Mattie	3090
Grayson, Pleasant	5147	Grimett, William	3195
Grayson, David	5148	Grimett, Lucy	3196
Grayson, Milam	5156	Grimett, Rose	3199
Grayson, Everett,	5160	Grimett, Nathan W.	3201
Grayson, Ellen	5299	Grimmett, William	5474
Grayson, Alice	5300	Guess, Amy	3785
Grayson, Ben	5329	Gwin, Ida	4623
Grayson, Angeline	5343	Gwin, Myrtle Velma	4624
Grayson, Sam	5369	Gwin, John Paul	5122
Grayson, Melinda	5419	Haggerty, Martha	5593
Grayson, Zack	5427	Haggerty, Rilda	5594
Grayson, Gertie	5428	Haggerty, Thomas	5595
Grayson, Polly	5429	Haggerty, Ora	5596
Grayson, Louisa	5430	Hall, Fannie	2565
Grayson, Richard	5435	Hall, Amanda	3565
Grayson, Daniel	5455	Halls, Delilah	1430
Grayson, Adolphus	5456	Halls, Emma	1432
Grayson, Joe	5464	Halls, Nancy	1433
Grayson, Cornelius	5523	Hamilton, Nannie	1668
Grayson, Izora	5545	Hamilton, Fannie	1669
Grayson, Susie	5660	Hamilton, Effie Ottawa	1670
Grayson, Gertrude	5684	Hamilton, Rosie	2232
Grayson, Edwin	5689	Hamilton, Kitty	2233
Green, Flem	324	Hamilton, Ada	5064
Green, Fleming	532	Hammonds, Bennie	2745
Green, Bettie	533	Hammonds, Irene	5157
Green, Martha	534	Hampton, Matilda	4803
Green, Susie	535	Hampton, Ophelia	4804
Green, Betsey	743	Hampton, Oynsby	5217
Green, Curley	744	Hardgray, Floyd	5131
Green, Tumba	745	Hardridge, Lester C.	2412
Green, Jacob	901	Hardridge, Sarah	2413
Green, Nannie	902	Hardridge, Tommy	2414
Green, Joe	904	Hardridge, Gertrude	2415
Green, Parthenia	905	Hardridge, Ralph	2416
Green, Amanda	906	Hardridge, Alvin	2417
Green, Katie	907	Hardridge, Annie	2418
Green, Dave	933	Hardridge, Emma	2419
Green, Dora	934	Hardridge, Katy	2976
Green, Esther	935	Hardridge, Eddie	2981
Green, Bettie	936	Hardridge, Monday	3046
Green, William	937	Hardridge, Charity	3047
Green, Salina	2155	Hardridge, Stroy	3048
Green, Leone	2156		

Name.	Roll No.	Name.	Roll No.
Hardridge, Nero	3049	Harrison, Evaline	2799
Hardridge, Ivey	3051	Harrison, Elizabeth	2800
Hardridge, Adam	3838	Harrison, Rachael	2803
Hardridge, Sam	3957	Harrison, Martha	2804
Hardridge, Rose	3958	Harrison, Edward	2805
Hardridge, Irene	3959	Harrison, Sarah	2806
Hardridge, Charity	5092	Harrison, Annie	2807
Hardridge, Lillie Bell	5124	Harrison, Dick	3387
Harper, Lizzie	1786	Harrison, Nellie	3388
Harris, Martha	709	Harrison, Lennie	3389
Harris, David	1875	Harrison, Harry	3390
Harris, Adeline	1876	Harrison, Emma	3391
Harirs, Annie	1880	Harrison, James	3392
Harris, Dilsey	1974	Harrison, Mattie	3393
Harris, Robert	1975	Harrison, Albert	3394
Harris, Albert	2126	Harrison, Charlie	3395
Harris, John	2127	Harrison, Jesse	3396
Harris, John	2582	Harrison, Annie	3397
Harris, Frank	2583	Harrison, Effie	3398
Harris, George	2584	Harrison, Jeff	3414
Harris, Willie	2624	Harrison, Pearlie	3652
Harris, Sarah	2625	Harrison, Stella	3749
Harris, Jennetta	2626	Harrison, Amanda	4294
Harris, Jim	2627	Harrison, Prince	4775
Harris, Betsey	2731	Harrison, Sarah	4776
Harris, Nina	3639	Harrison, Leona	4777
Harris, Jo	4198	Harrison, Lilly	5012
Harris, Samuel	4199	Harrison, Eva	5137
Harris, Mary	4520	Harrison, Castella	5321
Harris, Edgar B.	4521	Harrison, Prince	5672
Harris, Minnie	4808	Harred, Mary	175
Harris, Abram	4896	Harred, Richard	182
Harris, Manuel	5335	Harred, Lizzie	183
Harris, Ben	5543	Harred, Benus	2397
Harris, Bessie	5695	Harred, Toney	2452
Harrison, Rina	319	Harred, Mary	2453
Harrison, Nora	326	Harred, Mack	2454
Harrison, Harry	867	Harred, Annie	2455
Harrison, Stella	868	Harred, Morris	2466
Harrison, Lillie	1060	Harred, Willie	5476
Harrison, Nelson	1061	Harrod, Amanda	4347
Harrison, Chief	1176	Harrod, Rogers	5662
Harrison, Ellen	1177	Harry, Martha	1966
Harrison, Bertha	1178	Harry, George	1968
Harrison, Emma	1179	Harry, Rebecca	4897
Harrison, Anna	1180	Harry, Ruthie	4898
Harrison, Willie	1181	Harry, Frazier	4899
Harrison, Thomas	1385	Harry, William	5166
Harrison, Sarah	1386	Harvey, Lizzie	3667
Harirson, Emma	1387	Hawes, Agnes	4545
Harrison, Arthur	1529	Hawkins, Ellen	18
Harrison, William	1791	Hawkins, Clarence	20
Harrison, John	1848	Hawkins, Susie	134
Harrison, Laura	1849	Hawkins, Andrew	135
Harrison, Sylvia	1850	Hawkins, Lizzie	136
Harrison, Ella	1851	Hawkins, Wrotton	137
Harrison, Phoenix	1825	Hawkins, Elvira	138
Harrison, Cudie	1853	Hawkins, Emma	156
Harrison, Nettie	1854	Hawkins, James	565
Harrison, Washington	1855	Hawkins, Hector	567
Harrison, Dewey	1856	Hawkins, Harry	568
Harrison, Jake	1938	Hawkins, William	646
Harrison, George	2026	Hawkins, Sallie	647
Harrison, Linda	2712	Hawkins, Cora	1014
Harrison, Annie	2714	Hawkins, Fannie	1211
Harrison, Dora	2715	Hawkins, Robert C.	1978
Harrison, Mattie	2716	Hawkins, Joseph	2222
Harrison, Ribbie	2717	Hawkins, Leah	2223
Harrison, Lula	2718	Hawkins, Sambo	2224
Harrison, Jeanetta	2719	Hawkins, Peter	2225
Harrison, Cleveland	2720	Hawkins, Misa	2226
Harrison, Benjamin	2721	Hawkins, David	2227
Harrison, David	2788	Hawkins, Robert	2228
Harrison, Amanda	2789	Hawkins, Joseph, Jr.	2229
Harrison, Manuel	2790	Hawkins, William	2230
Harrison, Frank	2791	Hawkins, Mack	2231
Harrison, Ada	2792	Hawkins, Warrior	2317
Harrison, Patsy	2793	Hawkins, Martha	329
Harrison, Alice	2794	Hawkins, Lula	2327
Harrison, Charles	2795	Hawkins, Gabriel	2330
Harrison, Mollie	2797	Hawkins, Silla	2331
Harrison, Martha	2798	Hawkins, Joe	2346

Name.	Roll No.	Name.	Roll No.
Hawkins, Lettie	2347	Hawkins, Lee	5302
Hawkins, Letha	2348	Hawkins, Dan	5303
Hawkins, Freddy	2349	Hawkins, Hattie	5304
Hawkins, Lenny	2350	Hawkins, Julia	5313
Hawkins, Joe, Jr.	2351	Hawkins, Frank	5314
Hawkins, George	2352	Hawkins, Benjamin	5315
Hawkins, Nellie	2507	Hawkins, Jennie	5316
Hawkins, Bill	2508	Hawkins, Resser	5319
Hawkins, Jake	2409	Hawkins, Denes	5350
Hawkins, Eliza	2510	Hawkins, Isaac	5393
Hawkins, Saul	2511	Hawkins, George	5443
Hawkins, Lot	2512	Hawkins, Johnnie	5446
Hawkins, Bettie	2513	Hawkins, Millie	5448
Hawkins, Rosy	2514	Hawkins, James	5451
Hawkins, Thomas	2564	Hawkins, Mitchell	5452
Hawkins, Hettie	2661	Hawkins, Ross	5465
Hawkins, Emma	2662	Hawkins, Lurena	5538
Hawkins, Rina	2663	Hawkins, Jack	5572
Hawkins, Phillip	2880	Hawkins, Frank	5573
Hawkins, Susie	2881	Hawkins, Taylor	5574
Hawkins, Lewis	2882	Hawkins, Letta Ann	5575
Hawkins, Jeff	2919	Hayes, Mittie	2385
Hawkins, Celia	2920	Hayes, Jennetta	4217
Hawkins, Georgia	2921	Haynes, Henry	3417
Hawkins, Israel J.	2923	Haynes, Gertie	4826
Hawkins, Gracie	2931	Haynes, Mack	4827
Hawkins, Rap	3280	Haynes, William	4828
Hawkins, Clora Ann	3281	Haynes, John	4829
Hawkins, Dora	3307	Hemmitt, Charlotte	5664
Hawkins, Fred	3308	Hemmitt, Clara	5665
Hawkins, Mary	3311	Henderson, Peter	125
Hawkins, Samuel	3572	Henderson, Julia	126
Hawkins, Aleck	3602	Henderson, Sanders	960
Hawkins, Dembo	3946	Henderson, Ned	1493
Hawkins, Winnie	3947	Henderson, Charlotta	1583
Hawkins, Joseph	3948	Henderson, Rena	1656
Hawkins, Clora	3949	Henderson, John	2260
Hawkins, Walker	4073	Henderson, Lou Critty	2261
Hawkins, Bustin	4084	Henderson, Katie	2262
Hawkins, Jack	4125	Henry, Jane	4757
Hawkins, Jane	4126	Henry, Creasy	4758
Hawkins, Lucy	4209	Henry, Lucile	4759
Hawkins, Manuel	4210	Henry, Silla	4760
Hawkins, Pink	4211	Herod, Lewis	4613
Hawkins, Sam	4212	Herod, Leroy	5431
Hawkins, Ben	4213	Herod, Rena	5432
Hawkins, Eddie	4295	Herrod, Cyrus	3091
Hawkins, Annie	4320	Herrod, Thomas	5047
Hawkins, Lula	4533	Herrod, Millie	435
Hawkins, Edmond	4634	Herrod, Rose	437
Hawkins, Fannie	4635	Hershey, Julia	4310
Hawkins, Laura	4636	Hickles, Hubert	3353
Hawkins, Robert	4637	Higginbottom, Bettie	5383
Hawkins, Kellop	4638	Hill, Henry	5535
Hawkins, Clarence	4639	Hill, Cobbry	335
Hawkins, Willie	4640	Hill, Richard	336
Hawkins, Annie	4641	Hill, Semon	337
Hawkins, Cora	4663	Hill, Sandy	338
Hawkins, Buzze	4680	Hill, Frank	473
Hawkins, John	4681	Hill, Linda	474
Hawkins, Jamous	4682	Hill, Tom	475
Hawkins, Stidham	4787	Hill, Henry	476
Hawkins, Ellen	4788	Hill, Rutha	2009
Hawkins, Arthur	4789	Hill, Pearly	2010
Hawkins, Wash	4790	Hill, George	2011
Hawkins, Ivery	4791	Hill, Flora	2104
Hawkins, Israel	4950	Hill, Bessie	2105
Hawkins, Willie	4987	Hill, Lenny	2106
Hawkins, Mollie	5006	Hill, Eddy	2107
Hawkins, Sarah	5007	Hills, Rosa	146
Hawkins, James	5008	Hills, Gustus	147
Hawkins, Thomas	5009	Hills, Neal	148
Hawkins, Dora	5010	Hobbs, Emma	3942
Hawkins, Minnie	5115	Hobbs, Viralene	3943
Hawkins, Babe	5200	Hodge, Sallie	5366
Hawkins, Tom	5288	Hollins, Elzora	4657
Hawkins, Moses	5289	Holloway, Sarah	4741
Hawkins, Richard	5291	Holloway, Tommy	4742
Hawkins, Hannah	5292	Holloway, Lucinda	4743
Hawkins, Lourena	5293	Holloway, Robert	4744
Hawkins, Phillis	5294	Holloway, Sarah	4745
Hawkins, George	5301	Holmes, Nellie	234

Name.	Roll No.	Name.	Roll No.
Holmes, Redmond	235	Hutton, Jane	4134
Holmes, Andrew	385	Hutton, Etha	4135
Holmes, Jacob	386	Hutton, Paul	4136
Holmes, Willie	387	Hutton, Julia Lousia	4137
Holmes, Lee	388	Hutton, James	4170
Holmes, John	724	Hutton, Agnes	4171
Holmes, Bennie	725	Hutton, Walter	4172
Holmes, Neal	726	Hutton, James, Jr.	4173
Holmes, Monday	821	Hutton, Alex	4174
Holmes, Nellie	822	Hutton, Everett	4175
Holmes, Henry	823	Hutton, Delilah	4176
Holmes, Miley	824	Hutton, Ferdinand	4177
Holmes, Sarah	825	Hutton, Mary	4178
Holmes, Lemuel	4180	Hutton, Pilot	4179
Holmes, Thomas	4181	Hutton, Joe, Jr.	4715
Holmes, Ned	4182	Hutton, Leonard	5175
Holmes, Red	4184	Hutton, Everett, Jr.	5176
Holmes, Ada	4185	Hutton, Roy	5214
Holmes, Edward	4186	Hutton, Susan	5297
Holmes, Roxanna	4187	Hutton, Laura	5298
Holmes, Rena	4188	Hymes, Laura	3790
Holmes, Jack	4598	Irving, John	2588
Holmes, Hattie	4599	Irving, Mary	4679
Holmes, Francis	4752	Irving, Edward	4683
Holmes, Ellis	5202	Irving, Eliza	4684
Holmes, Sango	5306	Irving, Barney B.	4686
Holmes, Jane	5307	Isaac, John	1636
Holmes, Susie	5328	Isaac, Amy	1637
Holmes, Lucy	5345	Isaac, Caroline	2906
Holmes, Caesar	4695	Isaac, Ophelia	2907
Holmes, Clarence	5583	Isaac, Katy	2908
Homer, Annie	1795	Isaac, Della	2909
Homer, Emmett	1797	Isaac, Sarah Jane	2910
Homer, Victoria	1798	Isaac, Annie Belle	2911
Homer, Edward	1799	Isaac, Maggie	2912
Hope, James	527	Isaac, Lewis	5638
Hope, Hettie	528	Isaacs, Mary	3707
Hope, Jeff	529	Island, Eve	886
Hope, Lula	530	Island, Hattie	889
Hope, Dilsey	3792	Island, Bill	1388
Hope, Frank	3793	Island, Necey	1395
Hope, Lena	3794	Island, Amy	2008
Hope, Emma	3795	Island, Amy	2964
Hope, Paulina	3796	Island, Harry	2965
Hope, Salina	3797	Island, Gus	2966
Hope, Dinah	3798	Island, Ben	2967
Hope, Dick	3799	Island, Mack	2968
Hope, Rose	3800	Island, Delilah	2969
Hope, Mary	3801	Island, Martha	2970
Hope, Edmond	4866	Island, Jim	3124
Hope, Martha	5548	Island, George	3185
Horn, Sampson	571	Island, Cora	3186
Houston, Lucy	4168	Island, Jane	3804
Howard, Catherine	1473	Island, Annie	4905
Howard, Sarah	1881	Island, Sorrow	4935
Howard, Joseph	1882	Island, Lucy	4936
Howard, Liddie	1883	Island, Bill, Jr.	5178
Howard, Annie	1884	Island, Ed	5338
Howard, Georgia	1885	Jack, Johnnie	424
Howard, Joseph	2571	Jackson, Likey Lee	419
Howard, Jane	2572	Jackson, Ivey	420
Howard, Jane	2904	Jackson, Lemuel	678
Howard, Liley	3939	Jackson, Julia	679
Howard, Theodore	3940	Jackson, Green	701
Howard, Jackson	4088	Jackson, Angeline	702
Howard, Rebecca	4089	Jackson, Oliver	703
Howard, Jessie	4090	Jackson, Laura	704
Howard, John	4091	Jackson, Lizzie	705
Howard, Dan	4725	Jackson, Stella	706
Howard, LeRoy	5326	Jackson, Willie	967
Huddelston, Lonzo	5534	Jackson, Joseph	1209
Hudson, Sally	1719	Jackson, George	1210
Hughes, Eliza	2997	Jackson, Samuel	1212
Hunley, Rose	4717	Jackson, Mack	1213
Hutton, Henry	427	Jackson, Daisy	1214
Hutton, Joe	835	Jackson, Lizzie	1215
Hutton, Amelia	836	Jackson, Lena	1216
Hutton, John	837	Jackson, Nettie	1217
Hutton, Lewis	838	Jackson, Roselle	1221
Hutton, Dave	839	Jackson, Mary	1628
Hutton, Della	840	Jackson, Grant	1769
Hutton, Dock	4133	Jackson, Hagar	1796

Name.	Roll No.	Name.	Roll No.
Jackson, Katy	2073	James, George	2151
Jackson, York	2613	James, Rozella	2152
Jackson, Amy	2614	James, Nancy	4701
Jackson, Jack	2615	James, Georgie	4702
Jackson, Rose	2616	James, Jesse	4703
Jackson, Joe	2618	James, Frank	4704
Jackson, Freddie	2619	James, Katie	4705
Jackson, Silvia	3253	James, Gertie	5193
Jackson, Robert	3585	James, Simon	5251
Jackson, William	3586	James, Samuel	5252
Jackson, Charlie	3603	James, Johnnie	5253
Jackson, Lizzie	3604	James, Marietta	5254
Jackson, Joanna	3605	James, Lydia	5260
Jackson, Alice	3606	James, Jesse	5459
Jackson, Mary	3607	Jameson, Gabriel	2300
Jackson, Jane	3608	Jameson, 'Fanny	2301
Jackson, Hattie	3609	Jameson, Kaiser	2302
Jackson, Arthur	3662	Jameson, Jesse	2303
Jackson, Maria	3727	Jameson, Clavin	2304
Jackson, Sarah	4601	Jameson, Pauline	2305
Jackson, Clinton	4819	Jameson, Silas	2306
Jackson, Stepney	4881	Jameson, Dan	2307
Jackson, William	4882	Jameson, Floyd	2308
Jackson, Henry	4883	Jameson, Monday	2869
Jackson, Julia	4973	Jameson, Mose	3381
Jackson, Mary	4974	Jameson, Mima	3382
Jackson, William	4975	Jameson, Silla	3877
Jackson, Rennie	4976	Jameson, Budd	3980
Jackson, Edna	4977	Jameson, Lewis	3988
Jackson, George	5051	Jameson, Garfield	4015
Jackson, Mary F.	5109	Jameson, Jennie	5113
Jackson, Earler	5218	Jameson, Isom	5334
Jackson, Serena	5462	Jamison, Osane	2110
Jackson, Belle	5468	Jamison, Kizzia	2210
Jackson, Queen Victoria	5674	Jamison, Nero	2211
Jacob, Smart	5444	Jamison, Monday	2679
Jacobs, Scott	492	Jamison, Maria	2826
Jacobs, Sarah	719	Jamison, Josephine	5004
Jacobs, Dollie	720	Jefferson, Caesar	165
Jacobs, Peter	721	Jeffson, Hattie	16?
Jacobs, Nancy	722	Jefferson, Joe	1?
Jacobs, Mariah	723	Jefferson, Douglass	168
Jacobs, Flora	1571	Jefferson, George	169
Jacobs, George	1584	Jefferson, Jane	423
Jacobs, Henry	1939	Jefferson, Sampson	426
Jacobs, Becky	1940	Jefferson, Sarah	541
Jacobs, Emma	1941	Jefferson, Tooka	735
Jacobs, Eli	1942	Jefferson, Eva	856
Jacobs, Cully	1943	Jefferson, Jesse	857
Jacobs, Leo	1944	Jefferson, Rethy	961
Jacobs, Thomas	1945	Jefferson, John	1018
Jacobs, John	2291	Jefferson, Linda	1019
Jacobs, Lizzie	2292	Jefferson, Elizabeth	1020
Jacobs, Gracie	2293	Jefferson, Lula	1021
Jacobs, Mary	2294	Jefferson, James	1022
Jacobs, Mariah	2295	Jefferson, John J. Jr.	1045
Jacobs, Jane	2329	Jefferson, Mary Alice	1046
Jacobs, Eli S.	4035	Jefferson, Kitty C.	1047
Jacobs, Frank	4036	Jefferson, Mattie R.	1048
Jacobs, Millie	4037	Jefferson, Grant N.	1049
Jacobs, Noble	4817	Jefferson, Peggy Ann	1050
Jacobs, Charity	4818	Jefferson, Thurman T.	1051
Jacobs, Rachel	4820	Jefferson, Rebecca	1052
Jacobs, Charlie	1127	Jefferson, Willie Noland	1053
Jacobs, John	4821	Jefferson, Andy	1055
Jacobs, Osborn	4822	Jefferson, Sally	1056
Jacobs, Clarence	5496	Jefferson, Pride	1057
Jacobs, Alice	5686	Jefferson, James	1116
James, Rebecca	29	Jefferson, Amy	1117
James, Jimmie	30	Jefferson, Rose	1118
James, Mattie	31	Jefferson, Mary	1119
James, Sammie	32	Jefferson, Lizzie	1120
James, Clydie	33	Jefferson, John	1121
James, Josephine	34	Jefferson, Nathan	1122
James, Retha	35	Jefferson, Rolly	1123
James, Caesar	36	Jefferson, Georgia Ann	1124
James, Rosie	37	Jefferson, Polly	1125
James, Perry	38	Jefferson, Edmond	1126
James, Henrietta	39	Jefferson, Mary	1225
James, Sampson	40	Jefferson, Dick	1657
James, Ellen	674	Jefferson, Sam	1760
James, Hannah	2149	Jefferson, Thomas	1761

Name.	Roll No.	Name.	Roll No.
Jefferson, Jane	1762	Johnson, Polly	3354
Jeffeson, Rolly	1763	Johnson, Rachael	3449
Jefferson, Willie	1784	Johnson, Rose	3470
Jefferson, Arthur	1785	Johnson, Sid	3589
Jefferson, Edmund	1867	Johnson, Grant	3598
Jefferson, Sarah	1868	Johnson, Katie	3599
Jefferson, Bertha	1869	Johnson, Freeland	3600
Jefferson, Emma	1870	Johnson, Washington	3601
Jefferson, Edmund	1871	Johnson, Johnnie	4131
Jefferson, Minnie	1872	Johnson, Hettie	4218
Jefferson, Ada	1873	Johnson, Georgie	4219
Jefferson, Mariah	1874	Johnson, Samuel	4220
Jefferson, Morris	1930	Johnson, Jim	4221
Jefferson, Mollie	1931	Johnson, Katy	4480
Jefferson, Abraham	2370	Johnson, Lizzie	4588
Jefferson, John	3133	Johnson, Joe	4589
Jefferson, Ben	3401	Johnson, Hackless	4697
Jefferson, Jim	3402	Johnson, James Coody	4978
Jefferson, Isabel	3729	Johnson, Robert	4979
Jefferson, Albert	4753	Johnson, Elizabeth	4990
Jefferson, Tobe	4847	Johnson, Tom	5172
Jefferson, Cora	4894	Johnson, Rocksy	5190
Jefferson, Jennie	4928	Johnson, Ellis	5236
Jefferson, Dollie	5119	Johnson, Joe	5270
Jefferson, Gus	5140	Johnson, Artie	5417
Jefferson, Madison	5208	Johnson, George	5433
Jefferson, Joe	5337	Johnson, Ruthie	5467
Jefferson, Isabelle	5542	Johnson, Purlie	5503
Jefferson, LeRoy	5579	Jonas, Winnie	2235
Jenkins, Hattie	4160	Jonas, Frances	2236
Jenkins, Drucilla	4159	Jonas, Henrietta	2237
Jimmerson, Hattie	5101	Jonas, Viola	5688
Joans, Eliza	4465	Jones, Billy	173
Joans, Mary Ann	4466	Jones, Stella	425
Job, Dollie	2623	Jones, Austin	818
Johnson, Martha L.	170	Jones, Edward	893
Johnson, Joe	171	Jones, Rachael	993
Johnson, Ben	172	Jones, Sophrona	1461
Johnson, Jack	215	Jones, David	1925
Johnson, Rhoda	216	Jones, Lucy	1926
Johnson, Sandy	217	Jones, George	1927
Johnson, Coody	218	Jones, Mary	1928
Johnson, Quash	219	Jones, Albert	2108
Johnson, Dollie	325	Jones, Lewis	2549
Johnson, Cora	327	Jones, Mary Ann	2550
Johnson, Fred	328	Jones, Luther	2551
Johnson, Sarah	410	Jones, Gracie	2552
Johnson, Phillis	413	Jones, Robert	2553
Johnson, Lu Ann	414	Jones, Wyatt	2554
Johnson, Charlie	415	Jones, Alice	2555
Johnson, Silas	469	Jones, Martha	2751
Johnson, Tyra	491	Jones, Sammie	3027
Johnson, Lucinda	503	Jones, Martha	3114
Johnson, Pompey	579	Jones, Richard	3230
Johnson, Paro	673	Jones, Mattie	3312
Johnson, Andrew	785	Jones, Laura	3313
Johnson, Cloey	885	Jones, Louie	3314
Johnson, Israel	1806	Jones, Raford	3315
Johnson, Aaron	1807	Jones, Lillie	3507
Johnson, Miley	1825	Jones, Etta	3508
Johnson, Edmund	1826	Jones, Frank	3509
Johnson, Clara	1827	Jones, Israel	3981
Johnson, Nancy	1828	Jones, Louisa	3982
Johnson, Elmina	1829	Jones, Isaac	4145
Johnson, David	1830	Jones, Lurena	4389
Johnson, Hattie	1831	Jones, Blanche	4390
Johnson, George	1832	Jones, Xenophon	5110
Johnson, Nicey	1833	Jones, Willie	5360
Johnson, Rachael	1834	Jones, Alberta	5361
Johnson, Grant	1835	Jones, Carrie	5362
Johnson, Clara	1970	Jones, Henry	5363
Johnson, Grace	1971	Jones, Wilburn	5385
Johnson, Joseph	2007	Jones, Jennetta	5386
Johnson, Willie E.	2345	Jones, Emmet	5424
Johnson, Jesse	2544	Jones, Gertha	5478
Johnson, Lucy	2545	Kanard, Jim	4824
Johnson, Etta	2746	Kell, Dean	5380
Johnson, Leona	2752	Kelley, Ned	2929
Johnson, Dinah	2849	Kelly, Lucinda	521
Johnson, Ida	2850	Kelly, Ruthus	526
Johnson, Rebecca	2998	Kemp, John	2384
Johnson, Nellie	3092	Kennard, Bess	1086
Johnson, Judy	3252	Kennard, Hettie	1089

Name.	Roll No.	Name.	Roll No.
Kennedy, Annie	303	Lee, David A.	1494
Kernal, Sid	659	Lee, Dick	1498
Kernal, Abe	3202	Lee, Aggie	1499
Kernal, Mima	3203	Lee, John	1500
Kernal, Willie	3204	Lee, Henry	1501
Kernal, James	4063	Lee, Annie	1502
Kernal, Margaret	4064	Lee, Pleas	1503
Kernel, Nancy	286	Lee, David	1504
Kernel, Rentie	1914	Lee, Ross	1505
Kernel, Sally	1915	Lee, Amos	1506
Kernel, Thomas	1916	Lee, Ellis	1507
Kernel, Emanuel	1917	Lee, Mollie	1509
Kernel, Janatta	1918	Lee, Anna	4770
Kernel, Nancy	1919	Lee, Lucy	5309
Kernel, Cynda	1920	Lee, Dewit	5679
Kernel, Eva	1921	Leffard, Freddy	433
Kernel, Elizabeth	1922	Leffard, Arthur	434
Kernel, Lewis	3205	Lester, Zamon	2024
Kernel, Kizzie	3206	Lester, Lucy	2025
Kernel, Nannie	3207	Lester, Lizzie	2027
Kernel, Diana	3620	Lester, Sampson	2028
Kernel, Manuel	4494	Lewis, George	1602
Kernel, Ellis C.	5084	Lewis, Sarah Ann	1603
Kernel, Eddie	5087	Lewis, Henry	213
Keyes, Siney	3290	Lewis, Tally	305
Keyes, Malcomb	3294	Lewis, Philip	406
Keyes, Eva	3295	Lewis, Elzora	407
Keyes, Ruthie	3296	Lewis, Edna	408
Keyes, Rufus	3297	Lewis, Melvina	409
Keys, Nicey	4024	Lewis, Angeline	1226
Kidd, Silvey	3208	Lewis, Josephine	1231
Kidd, Myrtle	3209	Lewis, Amanda	1232
Kidd, Jessie	3210	Lewis, Eddie	1372
Kidd, Herbert	3211	Lewis, Douglass	1404
Kidd, Ella	3212	Lewis, Polly	1405
Kidd, Henrietta	3213	Lewis, Evaline	1406
Kidd, Lottie	3214	Lewis, Ben	1407
King, Emily	339	Lewis, Ellen	1408
King, Frank	340	Lewis, Gertie	1409
King, Carson	341	Lewis, Birdie	1410
King, Laura	342	Lewis, Prince	1411
King, Jennetta	343	Lewis, Lecta	1412
King, Eddie	344	Lewis, Martha	1434
King, Charlie	345	Lewis, Ellis	1879
King, Samuel	346	Lewis, Thomas	2015
King, Walter	347	Lewis, Jesse	2016
King, Patsy	2683	Lewis, Charlotte	2017
King, Irvin	4450	Lewis, Elvira	2019
King, Eula	4451	Lewis, Ben	2020
King, Frederick	4452	Lewis, John H.	2310
King, Lou	4877	Lewis, Elsie	2311
King, Ruth Ella	4955	Lewis, Sampson	2312
King, Hannah	5032	Lewis, Georgia Ann	2313
King, Falby	5436	Lewis, Hubert	2314
King, Angeline	5463	Lewis, Monday	2315
King, John	5521	Lewis, James	2316
Knowles, Hattie	4954	Lewis, Herbert	2328
Knowles, Joseph	5482	Lewis, Lillian	2431
Krooms, Katie	3232	Lewis, Harriet	2486
Lacy, Lucinda T.	2995	Lewis, Jimmy	2488
Lacy, Willie	2996	Lewis, Robert	2835
Lacy, Rebecca	4481	Lewis, Hettie	2836
Landrum, Lavina	729	Lewis, Chloe	2858
Landrum, Josie	730	Lewis, Ellis	2861
Landrum, Phillis	731	Lewis, Frances	2891
Landrum, Scipio	732	Lewis, Smart	2944
Landrum, Clydie	4157	Lewis, Betsey	2945
Landrum, Travis	4158	Lewis, Mary	2946
Landrum, Hattie	4814	Lewis, Robert	2947
Lampkins, Ellis	1596	Lewis, Johnson	2948
Lampkins, Sam	5517	Lewis, Dora	2949
Lampkins, Erie	5518	Lewis, Ira Belle	2950
Lampkins, Olene	5519	Lewis, Bee	2951
Larry, Nettie	3342	Lewis, Freeland	2952
Laslie, Lizzie	910	Lewis, Roy	2955
Lawrence, Polly	2536	Lewis, Morris	3071
Lee, Johnson	580	Lewis, Cully	3233
Lee, Sally	581	Lewis, General	3334
Lee, Bob	582	Lewis, Mary	3335
Lee, Rose	583	Lewis, Hannah	3336
Lee, Fred	584	Lewis, Johnson	3337
Lee, Ida May	919	Lewis, Tobie	3338
Lee, Rosa	1492	Lewis, Millie	3339

Name.	Roll No.	Name.	Roll No.
Lewis, Tilda	3432	Love, Eddie	2135
Lewis, Charlotte	3433	Love, Elvira	2196
Lewis, Isabel	3438	Love, Idell	2197
Lewis, Sudie	3693	Love, Fannie	3327
Lewis, Sallie	3696	Love, Josephine	3328
Lewis, Sadie	3697	Love, Ellis	3329
Lewis, Lucy	3698	Love, Sam	3330
Lewis, Joe	3705	Love, Eda	3331
Lewis, William	3736	Love, Susie	5282
Lewis, Charlie	3743	Lovett, Sam	284
Lewis, Amy	3744	Lovett, Miley	285
Lewis, Jesse	3745	Lovett, Samuel Jr.	287
Lewis, Leona	3746	Lovett, Abraham	468
Lewis, Willie	3747	Lovett, Bennie	522
Lewis, William	3750	Lovett, Sammie	523
Lewis, Lila	3751	Lovett, Pearl	524
Lewis, Elmore	3752	Lovett, Cato	525
Lewis, Katie	3753	Lovett, Cato	531
Lewis, Sarah	3754	Lovett, Bob	691
Lewis, Jesse	3755	Lovett, Mary	693
Lewis, Robert	3756	Lovett, Necey	1173
Lewis, Sarah	3922	Lovett, Bettie Ann	1174
Lewis, John	3954	Lovett, Nancy	4590
Lewis, Lee	3955	Lovett, Necey	5533
Lewis, Lucy	3956	Low, Robert	548
Lewis, Jackson	4065	Low, Polly	3298
Lewis, Frank	4066	Lowe, Washington	656
Lewis, Luanna	4067	Lowe, Theodrea	5146
Lewis, Edward	4068	Lowery, Tennessee	1673
Lewis, Fred	4069	Lowery, Steve	1684
Lewis, Jesse	4070	Lowery, Prince	1538
Lewis, Jane	4152	Lowery, Julia	1539
Lewis, Joe H.	4409	Lowery, Bud	2131
Lewis, Harriet	4460	Lowery, Pinkie	2132
Lewis, Hackless	4560	Lowery, Mary	3452
Lewis, Georgia	4885	Lowery, Jane	5580
Lewis, Boysie	4886	Luckey, Floyd	736
Lewis, Clarence	4887	Luckey, Lewis	737
Lewis, Lottie	4888	Luckey, Thomas	1932
Lewis, Howard	5049	Luckey, Sarah	1933
Lewis, Flossie	5073	Luckey, Daniel	2332
Lewis, Bettie Ann	5278	Luckey, Judy	2333
Lewis, Rayford	5376	Luckey, Freeland	2334
Lincoln, Lizzie	178	Luckey, Gertie	2335
Lincoln, Dan	2808	Luckey, Grace	2336
Lincoln, Cornelius	2809	Luckey, Daniel, Jr.	2337
Lincoln, Monday	4602	Luckey, Jane	2796
Little, Elnora	1595	Luckey, Charley	2845
Logan, Unuch	756	Luckey, Buss	2846
London, Abbey	975	Luckey, Frank	2959
London, Jack	1613	Luckey, George	2960
London, Silas	1614	Luckey, Fibby	2961
London, Clarence	1615	Luckey, Jim	3111
London, Stella	1616	Luckey, Leah	3112
London, Lillie	1617	Luckey, Spencer	3113
London, Chloe	1937	Luckey, Jimmie	3514
London, Elijah	1979	Luckey, Dick	3544
London, Chloe	1980	Luckey, Ludie	3545
London, Ellis	1981	Luckey, Israel	5104
London, Enos	1982	Luckey, Joseph	5142
London, Herbert	1983	Lunnon, Abe	4101
London, Burgess	4092	Lunnon, Kate	4102
London, Viney	4456	Lunnon, Sam	4103
London, Jesse	5231	Lunnon, Rosey	4104
London, Frank	5554	Lunnon, Sallie	4105
London, Mary	5555	Lunnon, William	4106
London, Bettie	5556	Lunnon, Henry	4107
London, Emma	5557	Lunnon, Tena	4108
Loneon, Hattie	2774	Luster, Andrew	2380
Loneon, Lutie	2775	Luster, Rose	2381
Loneon, Rufus	2776	Luster, Lottie	2382
Loneon, Jeff	2922	Luster, Willie	2383
Long, Caroline	3765	Luster, Lula	5420
Love, Dorcas	1295	Lyons, Lewis	2125
Love, Sallie	1296	Lyons, John	2647
Love, Jimmy	1297	Lyons, Rina	2648
Love, Willie	1298	Lyons, Pearl	2649
Love, Stella	1299	Lyons, Israel	2650
Love, Albert	1300	Lyons, Ethel May	2651
Love, Freddie	1897	Lyons, Bruce	4891
Love, Julia	1898	Lyons, Artie	4892
Love, Gertie	1899	Lyons, Laura	4893
Love, Ella	2134		

Name.	Roll No.	Name.	Roll No.
Lyons, Hettie May	5065	Manuel, Maxey	3301
Mackey, Ada	1611	Manuel, Rachel	3310
Mackey, Lizzie	2189	Manuel, Lizzie	3900
Mackey, John	2556	Manuel, Thos. W.	4162
Mackey, Lillie	2557	Manuel, Hardy	4322
Mackey, Eliza	2558	Manuel, Centennial	4338
Mackey, Leo	2862	Manuel, Raymond	5281
Mackey, Lovely	4118	Manuel, Daniel	5379
Mackey, LaPaz	4119	Manuel, Lilly	5387
Mackey, Pleas	4120	Manuel, Mary	5438
Mackey, Myrtle	4121	Manuel, Eliza	5505
Mackey, Louisa	4122	Manuel, Delila	5614
Mackey, Mary	4123	Marshall, Luke	130
Mackey, Phillip	5188	Marshall, Vina	131
Mackey, Leroy	5388	Marshall, Siah	436
Mackey, Floyd	5389	Marshall, Lucinda	438
Mackey, Nerlie	5390	Marshall, Dave	440
Mahardy, Babe	3936	Marshall, Lennus	629
Mahardy, Lizzie	3937	Marshall, Kathleen	695
Makins, Manerva	4200	Marshall, Agnes	1727
Malvern, Georgie	890	Marshall, Dennis	1984
Malvern, Clarence	891	Marshall, Dollie	1985
Malvern, Albert	894	Marshall, Ellen	1986
Malvern, John	1720	Marshall, Dave	1987
Malvern, Mary	1721	Marshall, Charlotte	1988
Malvern, Luanna	1722	Marshall, Lizzie	1989
Malvern, George	2925	Marshall, Tom	1990
Malvern, Mary	2926	Marshall, Clifford	1991
Malvern, Robert	2927	Marshall, Eddie	1992
Malvern, George	2928	Marshall, Viola	1993
Malvern, Arthur	3094	Marshall, Grace	2022
Malvern, Julia	3152	Marshall, Mack	2029
Malvern, Jesse	3153	Marshall, Peggy	2030
Malvern, Harry	4077	Marshall, Mariah	2031
Malvern, Tressie	5339	Marshall, Allie	2032
Malvern, Etta	3823	Marshall, Willie	2033
Manac, Mary	5536	Marshall, Arthur	2034
Manuel, Dinah	121	Marshall, Serena	2035
Manuel, Jennetta	123	Marshall, Snow	2036
Manuel, Isaac	283	Marshall, Harry	2095
Manuel, Robert J.	304	Marshall, Lilly	2168
Manuel, Emma	333	Marshall, Bill	2677
Manuel, Mary	350	Marshall, Susan	2678
Manuel, Kittie	351	Marshall, Dinah	2761
Manuel, Sophie	352	Marshall, Jimmie	2762
Manuel, Man	353	Marshall, Joseph	2763
Manuel, Adalee	354	Marshall, Ben	2764
Manuel, Tally	355	Marshall, Jeff	2765
Manual, Douglass	356	Marshall, Amy	3413
Manual, Cornelius	357	Marshall, Abednego	3497
Manual, Ellen	358	Marshall, Harriet	3506
Manuel, Bob	359	Marshall, Bennie	3741
Manuel, Nelson	360	Marshall, Bertha	3742
Manuel, Gertie	361	Marshall, Sam	3872
Manuel, Edna	362	Marshall, William	3960
Manuel, Robert	402	Marshall, Clarence	3961
Manuel, Sally	403	Marshall, Lewis	3962
Manuel, Lu Ethel	404	Marshall, Benjamin	3963
Manuel, Floyd	405	Marshall, Willieann	3964
Manuel, Morris	417	Marshall, Judey	3965
Manuel, Joe	681	Marshall, Betsey	4085
Manuel, Adam	1199	Marshall, Noah	4410
Manuel, Mulcey	1200	Marshall, Robert	4442
Manuel, Pearl	1201	Marshall, Miley	4443
Manuel, Gertie	1202	Marshall, Susie	4444
Manuel, Hannah	1203	Marshall, George	4470
Manuel, Willie	1204	Marshall, Robert	4523
Manuel, Herbert	1205	Marshall, Sarah	4524
Manuel, Sam	1206	Marshall, Fanny	4571
Manuel, Rafield	1207	Marshall, Osie	4582
Manuel, Tina	1559	Marshall, Budkin	4597
Manuel, Sam	2620	Marshall, George	4607
Manuel, Ellis	2621	Marshall, Reann	4608
Manuel, Stella	2622	Marshall, Charley	4783
Manuel, Viney	2750	Marshall, Willie	4810
Manuel, Linda	2753	Marshall, Eliza	4963
Manuel, Judy	2756	Marshall, Nina	4964
Manuel, Jim	2757	Marshall, Hubert	5125
Manuel, Katie	2758	Marshall, Vera C.	5171
Manuel, Isaac	2759	Marshall, Lillie	5450
Manuel, Phillis	2760	Marshall, Annie	5685
Manuel, Louisa	3093	Martin, Annie	1286

Name.	Roll No.	Name.	Roll No.
Martin, Eddie	1291	Moore, Gabe	4554
Martin, Jesse	1292	Moore, Rebecca	4555
Martin, Elzora	1293	Moore, Beulah	4556
Martin, Vera	1294	Moore, Jennie	4557
Martin, Sarah	3126	Moore, Margurete	4558
Martin, Arthur	3128	Moore, Willie	5559
Martin, Florence	3127	Moore, Zeke	5626
Martin, Joseph	5540	Morey, Tinnie	2972
Matawy, Sarah	1946	Morey, Jackson	2973
Mathews, Robert	2918	Morey, Pinkey	2974
Mathews, Viola	3008	Morey, Isaac	2975
Mathews, Dovey	3009	Morey, Mary	2977
Mathews, Lena	3010	Morey, Levi	2978
Mathews, Rena	3011	Morey, Earnest	2979
Mathews, John Andrew	3012	Morey, Ray	2980
Mayberry, Henry	5584	Morey, Fred	2982
Mayes, Rose	2828	Morey, Rosie	2983
Mayfield, Nancy	3522	Morgan, Fannie	2524
Mayfield, Freddie	3523	Morgan, Gertry	2525
Mayfield, Etta	3524	Morgan, Jesse	2526
Mayfield, Markham	3525	Morgan, Fannie	2527
Mayfield, Maudie	3526	Morgan, Roby	2528
Mayfield, George Jr.	5063	Morgan, Billy	2529
Mayson, Bettie	3680	Morgan, Lucy	3332
Mayson, Lillie	3681	Morgan, Cilla	3333
Mayson, Ralph	3682	Morgan, Bessie	4919
Mayson, Charity	3683	Morgan, Kempney	5416
Meriwether, Susie	1511	Morrill, Fannie	2423
Meriwether, Irene	1512	Morris, William	858
Meriwether, Minerva	1513	Morris, Nellie	859
Meriwether, Paul	1514	Morris, Rayford	860
Meriwether, Harry	1515	Morris, Thomas	861
Mike, Alex H.	3300	Morris, Molly	862
Miles, Lucy	558	Morris, Rebecca	863
Miller, Morris	2169	Morris, Jerry	864
Miller, Fanny	2170	Morris, Susan	2096
Miller, Annie	2171	Morris, Jane	2341
Miller, Nancy	2172	Morris, Austin	2958
Miller, Laura	2460	Morris, Lena	4156
Miller, Adeline	2461	Morris, Robert Dewey	4161
Miller, Jane	2462	Morris, Mitchell	4345
Miller, Melvin	2463	Morris, Joseph	5179
Miller, Beatrice	2464	Morris, Johnny	2343
Miller, Easter	2465	Morris, Lurena	2344
Miller, Frank	2466	Morrison, John	1750
Miller, Telifey	2736	Morrison, Julia	1751
Miller, Silla	4850	Morrison, Myra	1752
Miller, Willie	4851	Morrison, Manuel	1753
Miller, Annie	4852	Morrison, Diana	1754
Miller, Martha	4853	Morrison, Ceasar A.	1755
Miller, George	4854	Morrison, Phyllis	1756
Miller, Johnson	4855	Morrison, Tamar	1757
Miller, Parthenia V.	5132	Morrison, Johnson	1758
Millett, James	246	Morrison, Leona	1759
Minnis, Louisa	2153	Morrison, Joseph E.	1764
Minus, Alice	2278	Morrison, Sam	2585
Minus, Vance	2281	Morrison, Vina	2586
Minus, Arthur	5066	Morrison, Stephen	2589
Monday, Manuel	671	Morrison, Levi	2590
Monday, Berry	672	Morrison, Abe	3022
Monday, Isabell	1610	Morrison, Rebecca	3023
Monday, John	2984	Morrison, Reuben	3062
Monday, Caroline	2985	Morrison, Julia	3063
Monday, Tommy	2986	Morrison, Benjamin	3064
Monday, Henderson	4482	Morrison, James	3065
Monday, Ruthie	4483	Morrison, Raford	3066
Monday, Manuel, No. 2	4484	Morrison, Herbert	3067
Monday, Berry	4490	Morrison, Dora	3068
Monroe, Rosie	4319	Morrison, Josephine	3069
Monroe, Richard C.	4795	Morrison, Nick	3070
Moody, Angeline	3653	Morrison, Warrior	3299
Moody, Jordan	3654	Morrison, Joseph	4082
Moody, George	3656	Morrison, Simon	4527
Moody, Miles	3657	Mosely, Jane	3645
Moody, Alfred	3658	Mosely, Joe	5558
Moody, Alex	3659	Mullen, Annie	2876
Moore, Stella	4386	Mure, Julia	3498
Moore, Grant	4387	Mure, Georgia	3499
Moore, Mamie	4388	Mure, Josie	3500
Moore, Ezekiel	4391	Mure, Robert	3501
Moore, Gertrude	4392	Mure, Attie	3502
Moore, Will	4517	Mure, Sarah	3503
Moore, Sarah	4540		

Name.	Roll No.	Name.	Roll No.
Mure, Andrew	3504	McGilbray, Joe	1648
Mure, Hubbard	3505	McGilbray, Nancy	2646
Murphy, Mary E.	132	McGilbray, Monday	3399
Murphy, Hester	630	McGilbray, Ben	4863
Murphy, Fannie	631	McGilbray, William	4912
Murphy, Fred	632	McGilbray, Sampson	5637
Murphy, Ruth	633	McGilbray, Mollie	4913
Murphy, Walter	634	McGilbray, William	5667
Murray, Patsey	4401	McGirt, Eli	221
Murray, Henry	4402	McGirt, Katy	222
Murrell, Fannie	2354	McGirt, Tamer	223
Murrell, Alex	2546	McGirt, Sandy	224
Murrell, Eliza Jane	2547	McGirt, William	225
Murrell, Christie	2548	McHenry, Ella	3215
Murrell, Henry	2766	McHenry, Tommy Bea-	
Murrell, Josephine	2767	trice	3217
Murrell, Prisilla	2768	McHenry, Eula	3218
Murrell, Rena	3058	McHenry, Mary	3839
Murrell, Ellen	3059	McHenry, Floidie	5044
Murrell, Rebecca	3060	McIntosh, Sherman	72
Murrell, Thomas	3061	McIntosh, Susan	231
Murrell, Mattie	3095	McIntosh, Ned	587
Murrell, Kellop	3285	McIntosh, Wisey	588
Murrell, Annie	3286	McIntosh, Susie	627
Murrell, Kellop	3357	McIntosh, Alice	628
Murrell, Sally	3358	McIntosh, Mike	783
Murrell, David	3359	McIntosh, Wilford	791
Murrell, Goliah	3360	McIntosh, Earnest	790
Murrell, Bell	3362	McIntosh, Nancy	1183
Murrell, Paulina	3363	McIntosh, Wesley	1282
Murrell, Louvina	3364	McIntosh, Phoebe	1435
Murrell, Douglass	3365	McIntosh, Nicey	1731
Murrell, Florence	3366	McIntosh, Raford	1962
Murrell, Georgia	3367	McIntosh, Polly	1963
Murrell, Nancy	3368	McIntosh, Mary	1964
Murrell, Andy	3427	McIntosh, Minnie	1965
Murrell, Rebecca	3428	McIntosh, Lula	1967
Murrell, Sally	3429	McIntosh, Jennie	2150
Murrell, Calhoun	3460	McIntosh, Jimmie	2198
Murrell, Rufus	5469	McIntosh, Laura	2199
Murrell, Hannah	2326	McIntosh, Taylor	2246
Murrill, Beckey	1620	McIntosh, Adam	2338
Myers, Nero	615	McIntosh, Dicey	2339
Myers, Dave	1734	McIntosh, John	2340
Myers, Lewis	4010	McIntosh, Louisa	2358
Myers, Ellen	4011	McIntosh, Robt.	2360
Myers, John A.	4039	McIntosh, Ella	2361
Myers, Hagar	4040	McIntosh, Amanda	2362
Myers, Henry	4041	McIntosh, Jesse J.	2363
Myers, Johnnie	4042	McIntosh, Pompey	2364
Myles, Rina	504	McIntosh, Lulu	2365
McClain, Georgie	2111	McIntosh, Sampson	2366
McClain, Pearline	2112	McIntosh, Pearl	2367
McClain, Lena	2113	McIntosh, Goliah	2368
McClain, Mack	5076	McIntosh, Nan	2369
McCray, Maud	3699	McIntosh, Tobe	2371
McDaniel, Harriet	3591	McIntosh, Eveline	2372
McDaniel, Sherman	3592	McIntosh, Adias	2373
McDaniel, Ellis	3593	McIntosh, Myrtle	2374
McDaniel, Grover	3594	McIntosh, Hattie	2375
McDaniel, Gerthie	3595	McIntosh, John	2379
McDaniel, Rhoda	3596	McIntosh, Flora	2386
McDaniel, Dennis	3597	McIntosh, Anderson	2398
McGee, Nellie	728	McIntosh, Sally	2399
McGee, Augusta	1862	McIntosh, Shadrick	2400
McGee, Grant	5320	McIntosh, Ellis	2401
McGilbra, Lou	4857	McIntosh, Rena	2402
McGilbra, Patty	4858	McIntosh, Rosetta	2451
McGilbra, Willie	4859	McIntosh, Cuffy	2531
McGilbray, Quash	124	McIntosh, Amanda	2532
McGilbray, George	349	McIntosh, Willie	2533
McGilbray, Nancy	811	McIntosh, Sarah	2534
McGilbray, Daniel	847	McIntosh, Fanny	2644
McGilbray, Jennie	848	McIntosh, Hesther	2737
McGilbray, Rebecca	849	McIntosh, Willie	2738
McGilbray, Timmey	850	McIntosh, Amanda	2739
McGilbray, Betsey	851	McIntosh, Sophia	2740
McGilbray, Clarence	852	McIntosh, Lizzie	2741
McGilbray, Israel	853	McIntosh, Bennie	2742
McGilbray, Belle	854	McIntosh, Dido	2769
McGilbray, Dave	1142	McIntosh, Rosela	2770
McGilbray, James A.	1272	McIntosh, Joshua	2771

Name.	Roll No.	Name.	Roll No.
McIntosh, Stella	2772	McKellop, Mulcey	2069
McIntosh, Cornelius	2773	McKellop, James	2070
McIntosh, Daisy	2777	McKellop, John	2071
McIntosh, Judy	2971	McKellop, Dollie	2072
McIntosh, Elsie	2999	McKellop, Sam	2640
McIntosh, Patsey	3117	McKellop, Mary	2641
McIntosh, Gertie Fay	3174	McKellop, Annie	2643
McIntosh, Douglass	3187	McKellop, Katie	2705
McIntosh, Sally	3188	McKellop, James	2706
McIntosh, Willie	3245	McKellop, Florence	2707
McIntosh, Patience	3306	McKellop, Ben	3933
McIntosh, Betsy	3345	McKellop, Martha	5164
McIntosh, Lilly	3351	McKellop, Clara	5177
McIntosh, Laura	3384	McNac, Jennetta	3950
McIntosh, Jackson	3422	McNac, Austin	3951
McIntosh, Susie	3423	McNac, Robison	4577
McIntosh, Nancy	3424	McNac, Fred	4811
McIntosh, Sunny Milton	3425	McNac, Edward	4812
McIntosh, Rina	3447	McNac, Billie W.	4813
McIntosh, Tamie	3448	McNac, Samuel	4845
McIntosh, Gabriel	3473	McNac, Luanna	5098
McIntosh, Rochie	3474	McNack, Adam	2141
McIntosh, Ellis	3475	McNack, Silas	3881
McIntosh, Georgia	3476	McNac, Rena	4902
McIntosh, Sam	3477	McQueen, Wash	1075
McIntosh, Cynthia	3478	McQueen, Tommy	1371
McIntosh, Roy	3479	McQueen, Ella	1552
McIntosh, William	3480	McQueen, Sam	3356
McIntosh, Edna	3481	McSims, Rosa	3901
McIntosh, George	3492	Nail, Julia	3778
McIntosh, Rena	3494	Mail, Major	3779
McIntosh, Georgiana	3495	Nail, Doffey	3780
McIntosh, John	3496	Nail, Nahoma	3781
McIntosh, Joseph	3587	Nail, Walter	3782
McIntosh, Jennetta	3588	Nail, Jessie	3783
McIntosh, Benny	3590	Nail, Willie	3784
McIntosh, William	3668	Nash, Evaline	3867
McIntosh, Scott W.	3670	Nash, Arthur Ray	3870
McIntosh, Seigel E.	3671	Nave, Charles	3791
McIntosh, Neal	3672	Nave, Rachel	2181
McIntosh, Queen	3673	Nave, Cora	2182
McIntosh, Joseph	3674	Nave, Fannie Matilda	2183
McIntosh, Philip	3675	Nave, Dewitt	2184
McIntosh, Jerry	3700	Nave, Martha	2185
McIntosh, Katie	3701	Nave, Clyde	2186
McIntosh, Mary	3702	Nave, Mollie	2187
McIntosh, Roy	3703	Neal, Lula	800
McIntosh, Roxyann	3704	Nealey, Lottie	4327
McIntosh, Mary	3822	Nero, Belle	1312
McIntosh, August	3878	Nero, Cora	1598
McIntosh, Emma	3879	Nero, Tommy	1599
McIntosh, George	3884	Nero, Easy	1600
McIntosh, Mabel	3885	Nero, Lizzie	1601
McIntosh, William	3985	Nero, Louis E.	1839
McIntosh, Robert	3986	Nero, Babe	1840
McIntosh, Douglass	3987	Nero, Willie	1841
McIntosh, Rentie	3989	Nero, Robert	1842
McIntosh, Louis	3990	Nero, Molly	2173
McIntosh, Edward	3991	Nero, A. L. (or Abe)	2234
McIntosh, May	3992	Nero, Richard	2238
McIntosh, Thos.	4081	Nero, Mitchell	2697
McIntosh, Sarah	4234	Nero, Mattie	2698
McIntosh, Wiley Jr.	4297	Nero, Jimmie	2699
McIntosh, Rachel	4334	Nero, Adline	2700
McIntosh, Josephine	4335	Nero, Souda	2701
McIntosh, Esther Lee	4336	Nero, Leona	2702
McIntosh, Mabel	4337	Nero, Mary	2703
McIntosh, Simon	4938	Nero, David	3246
McIntosh, Wiley	4962	Nero, Freddie	3407
McIntosh, Etta	5043	Nero, Charley	3444
McIntosh, Jim	5102	Nero, John	5234
McIntosh, Laura	5209	Nevins, Nero	28
McIntosh, Thomas, Jr.	5340	Nevins, Ab	651
McIntosh, Silvia	5619	Nevins, Mary	652
McIntosh, Jacky	5620	Nevins, Luke	653
McIntosh, John	5621	Nevins, Joe	654
McIntosh, Harriet Beecher	5622	Nevins, Morris	655
McIntosh, George	5623	Nevins, Katy	2006
McIntosh, Coody	5624	Nevins, Mary	3000
McKinney, Fannie	1730	Nevins, Victoria	5273
McKinney, Belle	2827	Newell, Willie	3786
McKinney, Robt.	4060	Newman, Alex	1630
		Newman, Cal	1631

Name.	Roll No.	Name.	Roll No.
Newman, Martha	1632	Pea, Maggie	2957
Newman, Bertha	1633	Pea, Louisa	4564
Newman, Tom	1634	Pea, Sam	4565
Nichols, Lizzie	253	Pea, Benjamin	4566
Nichols, Rena	4111	Pea, Clem	4567
Nix, Bettie	3472	Pea, Cowee	4568
Noble, George	4920	Pea, Cora	4569
Noble, Maria	4929	Perkins, Annie	4541
Noble, Manuel	4933	Perkins, Leora	4542
Noble, Whister	4934	Perry, Polly	1808
Noble, Simon	4939	Perry, Sam	1809
Noble, Stephen	5659	Perry, Leonard	1810
Nomman, Rose	3248	Perry, Delila	1811
Nomman, Fred	3249	Perry, Lige	1812
Nomman, Jake	3250	Perry, Manda	1813
Norfer, Jane	3561	Perry, Washington	1814
Norfer, Jacob	3562	Perry, Hannah	3129
Norfer, Aggie	3563	Perry, Nettie	3130
Norfer, John	3567	Perry, Ester Lee	3131
Norfer, Hettie	3568	Perry, Lucy	4530
Norfer, Millie	3569	Perry, Julius A.	5143
Norfer, Thomas	3570	Perryman, Eveline	429
Norris, Jessie	3783	Perryman, Bob	430
Norris, Oliver	5187	Perryman, Adeline	431
Norwood, Frances	4393	Perryman, Rosy	432
Nunn, Mary	5629	Perryman, Alex S.	1546
Nunn, Corrie	5630	Perryman, Ellis	1547
Nunn, Blanche	5631	Perryman, Nellie	1691
Nunn, Marilda Lee	5632	Perryman, Sally	1824
Nunn, Matilda Dee	5633	Perryman, Allie	2754
Olden, Cora	187	Perryman, Clyde	2755
Olden, James	189	Perryman, Charles	2924
Olden, Douglass	190	Perryman, Lizzie	3054
Olden, Grather	192	Perryman, Alex	3198
Olden, Louisa	4673	Perryman, Randolph	3309
Olden, Agnes	4674	Perryman, Grant	3405
Olden, Osborn	4675	Perryman, Roy	3406
Olden, Ellen	4676	Perryman, Nick	3623
Olden, John	4871	Perryman, Mattie	3624
Oldham, Tamer	92	Perryman, Bertie	3625
Oldham, Annie	97	Perryman, George	
Oldham, Aaron	98	Leonard	3626
Osborn, Annie	4112	Perryman, Jackson	3635
Osborn, Clara	4113	Perryman, Minta	3636
Osborn, Irene	4114	Perryman, Letha	3637
Osborne, Julia	3610	Perryman, Louis	3638
Osborne, Isabelle	3611	Perryman, Sandy	3641
Osborne, Frank	3612	Perryman, Davis	3642
Osborne, Vivian W.	5207	Perryman, Herbert	3643
Overton, George	2342	Perryman, Hughey	3694
Overton, Patsy	2847	Perryman, Lizzie	3695
Overton, Ellis	2848	Perryman, John	3715
Overton, Robert	4767	Perryman, Julia	3716
Overton, Rebecca	4768	Perryman, Tom	3717
Overton, Dave	4769	Perryman, Louis	3718
Overton, David	5495	Perryman, Johnson	3719
Owen, Lizzie	3887	Perryman, Fredrick	3720
Owens, Ellen	3385	Perryman, Douglass	3966
Owens, Herbert	3386	Perryman, Julia	3967
Parker, James	10	Perryman, Jannie	3968
Parker, Minnie	11	Perryman, Stephen	3969
Parlor, Mulcey	3519	Perryman, Lou	3970
Parlor, Gus	3520	Perryman, Hector	3971
Parlor, Jennie	3521	Perryman, Bell	3972
Paro, Corrine	14	Perryman, Josie	3973
Paro, William	3189	Perryman, Dora May	3974
Paro, Hettie	3190	Perryman, Lewis	3975
Paro, Annie Jane	4772	Perryman, Jennetta	3976
Patrick, Betsey	4980	Perryman, Jacob	4086
Patrick, Abe Lincoln	4981	Perryman, Mollie	4087
Patrick, Susanna	5213	Perryman, Melvina	4189
Patterson, Isaac	1281	Perryman, Sarah	4455
Patterson, James E.	3803	Perryman, Liza	4457
Patterson, Malinda	4837	Perryman, Pompey	4921
Patterson, John	4838	Perryman, Peggy	4922
Patterson, James Jr.	5235	Perryman, Albert	4923
Payne, Angeline	25	Perryman, John	4988
Payne, Amanda	26	Perryman, Jack	4989
Payne, Nettie	27	Perryman, Jessie	5312
Payne, Amanda	4840	Perryman, Sarah	5364
Payne, Angeline	4841	Perryman, Belle	5481
Payne, Burnice	5229	Perryman, James	5508
Pea, Dave	2956	Perryman, Johnnie	5597

Name.	Roll No.	Name.	Roll No.
Peter, Clora	676	Porter, Sarah Ann	1749
Peter, Wm.	1535	Porter, Elvin	4127
Peter, Fred	1536	Porter, Rena	5050
Peter, Tommy	1537	Porter, Charley	5197
Peter, Richard	2047	Post, Mattie	4273
Peter, Levi	2692	Post, Ellie	4274
Peter, Sallie	2693	Postoak, Polly	494
Peter, Simon	4438	Postoak, Charley	707
Peters, Andrew	619	Potts, Eliza	2124
Peters, Dorcas	620	Pouncil, Katie	997
Peters, Eliza	621	Pouncil, Mary Ann	998
Peters, Minnie	622	Pouncil, Amanda	1013
Peters, Hattie	623	Pouncil, Sarah	1016
Peters, Jane	624	Pratt, Rochey	694
Peters, Sarah	625	Pratt, Leona	5108
Peters, Johnnie	626	Price, Jake	4570
Peters, Lucinda	708	Price, Jennie	4880
Peters, Mary	710	Primmer, Mary	3787
Peters, Ed	1186	Primmer, Simmie	3788
Peters, Mary	1579	Primmer, Viola	3789
Peters, Sandy	1580	Primmer, Mamie	5116
Peters, Ben	1581	Primous, Joe	4075
Peters, Henry	1582	Primous, Betsey	4076
Peters, Sarah	3258	Primus, Arthur	3571
Peters, Lee	3554	Prince, Abraham	1522
Peters, Maria	3555	Prince, Nellie	1523
Peters, Daisy	3556	Prince, Ben	1525
Peters, Willie	3557	Prince, Eddie	1526
Peters, Eugene	3640	Prince, Willie	2573
Peters, John	4406	Prince, Rufus	3325
Peters, Julia	4407	Prince, Susan	3932
Peters, Lemmie	4408	Prince, Bobby	3934
Peterson, Sallie	4226	Prince, Tom	4559
Pettitt, Eliza	4115	Prince, Andy	4591
Philips, James	294	Prince, Lucy	4592
Phillips, Pompey	696	Prince, Willie	4593
Phillips, Peggy	697	Prince, Luella	5114
Phillips, Robert	698	Prince, Johnny	5409
Phillips, Lu Anna	699	Prince, Emma	5410
Phillips, Johnny	700	Pyles, Jim	4311
Pierce, Mattie	4394	Quabner, James	4956
Pierce, Pinkie	4395	Quabner, Robert	4957
Pierce, Emma	4396	Quabner, Pilot	4958
Pippin, Eliza	2962	Quinn, Laura	5484
Poldo, Katie	258	Quinn, Bertha	5485
Poldo, Charlotte	259	Quinn, Florence	5487
Poldo, Leah	260	Quinn, Leo	5488
Poldo, Beckey	261	Quinn, Alvin	5489
Poldo, Sam	262	Quinn, Otto	5490
Poldo, Ishmael	263	Quinn, Isaac	5491
Poldo, Maggie	264	Quinn, Millard	5492
Poldo, Jeffrey	265	Ragan, Frank	3216
Poldo, Eliza	266	Ragen, Susan	2747
Poldo, Charlie	268	Ragen, Rebella	2748
Pompey, George	3529	Ragen, Thomas	2749
Pompey, Isaac	5678	Ragen, Reanna	5221
Pond, Polly	2498	Ragsdale, Amelia	4968
Pond, Cudjo	2865	Ragsdale, Zelma	4969
Pond, Leah	2866	Ragsdale, Mattie	4970
Pond, Isaac	2867	Ragsdale, Georgianna	5279
Pond, Squire	2868	Ragsdale, Sanford	5437
Pond, Helen	3170	Randolph, Cynthia	5295
Pond, Maria	3740	Rector, John	1335
Ponds, Mary	1472	Rector, Bettie	1336
Ponds, Sandy	3577	Rector, Joe	1337
Ponds, Emma	3578	Rector, Frank	1338
Ponds, Joe	3579	Rector, Fred	1339
Ponds, Willie	3580	Rector, Alfred	1340
Ponds, Robert	3770	Rector, Rebecca	5134
Ponds, Fredie	3771	Rector, Mollie	5324
Ponds, Caroline	3837	Redmon, Elizzie	1290
Ponds, Charlie	3871	Redmon, William Billie	1692
Ponds, Phoebe	4021	Redmond, Willie	465
Ponds, Charley	5167	Redmouth, Mose	1481
Ponds, Jim	5280	Reed, Celia	1010
Ponds, Bob	5576	Reed, Johnson	1011
Porlar, Emma	3465	Reed, Jane	1012
Porlar, Etta	3466	Reed, Henry C.	1030
Porlar, Ethel	3467	Reed, Emaline	1031
Porlar, Earl S.	3468	Reed, Lula	1035
Porlar, Violet E.	3469	Reed, Daisy	1036
Porter, Cuffy	1748	Reed, Bob	3050

Name.	Roll No.	Name.	Roll No.
Reese, Jennetta	3880	Rentie, Lula	4192
Reese, Drucilla	4346	Rentie, Eddie	4193
Rentie, John	277	Rentie, Annie	4194
Rentie, Dicey	299	Rentie, Elizabeth	4195
Rentie, Morris	477	Rentie, Morris	4197
Rentie, Katie	478	Rentie, Willie	4312
Rentie, Lewis	479	Rentie, Hettie	4313
Rentie, Frank	480	Rentie, Mary	4314
Rentie, Sarah	481	Rentie, Stella	431b
Rentie, Scott	482	Rentie, Clifford	4316
Rentie, King Roscoe	483	Rentie, Charlie	4317
Rentie, Daniel	484	Rentie, Clarence	4318
Rentie, Delilah	485	Rentie, Moses	5135
Rentie, Laura	486	Rentie, Georgia Ann	5144
Rentie, Emma	487	Rentie, Cella	5226
Rentie, John W.	488	Rentie, Ina Victoria	5267
Rentie, Alice	489	Rentie, Leopold	
Rentie, Kate	490	Augustus	5268
Rentie, Warrior	828	Rentie, George Washing-	
Rentie, Roy Bismark	829	ton Lubiture	5269
Rentie, Caroline	830	Rice, Clander	3326
Rentie, Joe	927	Rich, Mary	1105
Rentie, Amanda	928	Rich, Elliott	1106
Rentie, Bessie	929	Rich, Jane	1107
Rentie, Evaline	930	Rich, Thomas	1108
Rentie, Emaline	931	Rich, Rayford	1109
Rentie, Thomas	994	Rich, Jenetta	1110
Rentie, Tena	995	Rich, Hattie	1111
Rentie, Leether	996	Rich, Alferd	1112
Rentie, Lewis	1072	Rich, Rosella	1113
Rentie, Fronie	1073	Rich, Addie	1114
Rentie, Ina	1074	Rich, James	1115
Rentie, Bertha	1233	Richard, Hager	612
Rentie, Herrod	1239	Richard, Jennetta	4572
Rentie, William	1532	Richard, James	4573
Rentie, Susie	1533	Richard, Elzora	5103
Rentie, Tom	1540	Richards, Sampson	295
Rentie, Rose	1541	Richards, Rina	296
Rentie, Isaac	1618	Richards, Andrew	297
Rentie, Phyllis	1708	Richards, Jennie	1270
Rentie, Solomon	1709	Richards, Doctor	3020
Rentie, Eliza	1710	Richards, Emily	3021
Rentie, Harry	1711	Richards, Austin	3024
Rentie, Lee	1712	Richards, Tommy	3025
Rentie, George	1713	Richards, McKinley	3026
Rentie, Elijah	1714	Richards, Ben H.	3906
Rentie, Pricilla	1715	Richards, Esther	3907
Rentie, Jackson	1716	Richards, Martha	3908
Rentie, Cleveland	1717	Richards, Legus P.	3909
Rentie, Freddie	1718	Richards, Wisdom	3910
Rentie, Jennie	1740	Richards, Redfield P.	3911
Rentie, Mary	1744	Richards, Parthena A.	3912
Rentie, Monday	1781	Richards, Mary	3913
Rentie, Mary	1787	Richards, Hazel	3914
Rentie, Sophie	1838	Richards, Bertha	3915
Rentie, Sam	1843	Richardson, William	5355
Rentie, Nanny	1844	Riley, Levi	113
Rentie, Tom	1845	Riley, James	114
Rentie, Alice	1846	Riley, Mayfield	115
Rentie, Stephen	2193	Riley, Minnie	188
Rentie, Luthis	2194	Riley, Lena	191
Rentie, Elvira	2195	Riley, Bertha'	4664
Rentie, Pickett	2283	Riley, Eliza	4792
Rentie, Robert	2284	Riley, Clifford	4793
Rentie, Island	2652	Riley, Ross	4794
Rentie, Benjamin	2653	Riley, Paro	5128
Rentie, Rose Anna	2654	Riley, Nancy	5130
Rentie, Warrior Jr.	2655	Riley, Elizabeth	5552
Rentie, Mattie	2656	Roane, Lydia	2053
Rentie, Carrie	2657	Roane, Gussie	2054
Rentie, William	2658	Roane, Jimmie	2055
Rentie, Ira	2659	Roane, Willie	2056
Rentie, Jimmy	2660	Roane, Leonard	2057
Rentie, Fannie	2877	Roane, Edna	5067
Rentie, Alice	2878	Robbins, Lydia	3820
Rentie, Luanna	2879	Robbins, Ed L.	3889
Rentie, James	2893	Robbins, Addie	3890
Rentie, Hannah	2894	Robbins, May Belle	3891
Rentie, Castella	2895	Robbins, Lena Navada	3892
Rentie, Solomon	3136	Robbins, Everell Edward	3893
Rentie, Isaac	3622	Robbins, Richard R.	5210
Rentie, Ned	4124	Robbins, Clarence	5349
Rentie, John	4191	Roberson, Luvinia	738

Name.	Roll No.	Name.	Roll No.
Roberson, Bob	1625	Robins, Charley	4055
Roberson, Austin	1626	Robins, Mack	4056
Roberson, Silas	1627	Robins, Phoebe	4057
Roberson, Frances	2884	Robins, Heck	4403
Roberson, Jesse	2885	Robins, Willie	4404
Roberson, David	2886	Robins, Nora	4405
Roberson, Herbert	2887	Robins, Walter	4860
Roberson, Neil	2888	Robins, Minerva	4861
Roberson, Willie		Robinson, Clifford	331
McKinley	2889	Robinson, Pompey	366
Roberson, William	3073	Robinson, Hannah	367
Roberson, Rebecca	3074	Robinson, Dave	368
Roberson, Oscar	3075	Robinson, Eddie	369
Roberson, Edmund	3076	Robinson, Mattie	370
Roberson, Ed	4609	Robinson, General	1228
Roberson, Philip	4846	Robinson, Della	1629
Roberts, Jake	657	Robinson, Nathan	1635
Roberts, Sally	658	Robinson, Parry	1694
Roberts, Cudjo	962	Robinson, Hetty	1695
Roberts, Louvina	963	Robinson, Ella	1696
Roberts, Hannah	966	Robinson, Rapoleon	1697
Roberts, Jno.	1066	Robinson, Millie	3181
Roberts, Jane	1067	Robinson, Alex	3182
Roberts, Emma	1068	Robinson, August	3183
Roberts, Ben	1069	Robinson, Lennie	3184
Roberts, Mattie	1070	Robinson, Nellie	3259
Roberts, Della	1071	Robinson, Elza	3266
Roberts, Jacob	1076	Robinson, David	3267
Roberts, Hannah	1077	Robinson, Florence	3268
Roberts, Hattie	1078	Robinson, John	3282
Roberts, Stella	1079	Robinson, Dollie	3283
Roberts, Arthur	1080	Robinson, Lee Ella	3284
Roberts, John	1081	Robinson, Meada	3836
Roberts, Watson	1082	Robinson, Zach	5075
Roberts, Leathy	1083	Robinson, Joanna	5133
Roberts, Dave	1163	Robinson, Roy	5649
Roberts, Elliott	1164	Robison, Lewis	4856
Roberts, Jenny	1165	Robison, Zach	4908
Roberts, Clayton	1166	Robison, Fannie	4909
Roberts, Pearly	1167	Rodgers, Mary	5546
Roberts, Jessie	1168	Roe, George	1482
Roberts, Rachel	1253	Roe, John	1483
Roberts, Cornelius	1254	Roe, Elizabeth	1484
Roberts, Sherman	1255	Roe, Martha	1485
Roberts, Charity	2563	Roe, Elijah	1486
Roberts, Rufus	3415	Roe, Sarah	1487
Roberts, Nancy	3416	Rogers, Mose	44
Roberts, George	3488	Rogers, Daniel	45
Roberts, Lilly	3489	Rogers, Lennie	365
Roberts, Ben	3490	Rogers, Eliza	2387
Roberts, Jewell	3491	Rogers, Emma	2388
Roberts, Lethia	3564	Rogers, Dora Ann	4720
Roberts, Jack	3613	Rogers, Anna	4721
Roberts, Louis	3614	Rogers, Hernander	4722
Roberts, John	3615	Rogers, Lutisha	4723
Roberts, Lizzie	3616	Rose, Emily	470
Roberts, Emmett	3617	Rose, Pleasure	471
Roberts, Emery	3618	Rose, Phessie	472
Roberts, Ellis	3619	Rose, Nancy	1456
Roberts, Charles	3997	Ross, Angeline	1572
Roberts, Nancy	3998	Ross, Lewis	1573
Roberts, Gertrude	3999	Ross, Kate Annette	1574
Roberts, Lilly	4000	Ross, David	2713
Roberts, Legus	4002	Ross, Eliza	3826
Roberts, Katie	4001	Ross, Clifford	3827
Roberts, Cleveland	4003	Ross, Alfred	3828
Roberts, Alice	4004	Ross, James	4235
Roberts, McKinly	4005	Ross, Jennie	4236
Roberts, Kitty	4006	Ross, Eddie	4237
Roberts, Joseph	4491	Ross, Daniel	4238
Roberts, Anderson	4784	Ross, Salina	4495
Roberts, Samuel	4890	Ross, Lugena	4496
Roberts, Pearlie	5139	Ross, Bessie	4497
Roberts, James	5159	Ross, Henry	4498
Roberts, Irene	5162	Ross, Anna Lula	4499
Roberts, Louis	2450 5840	Ross, John	4500
Robertson, Rosey	1229	Ross, Robert	4581
Robertson, Rosella	5216	Ross, Susie	4965
Robin, Thomas	941	Ross, Arthur	4966
Robins, Nancy	1314	Ross, Minnie	4967
Robins, Emanuel	1895	Ross, Betty	5149
Robins, Tom	4013	Ross, Ethel	5151
Robins, Eliza	4014		

Name.	Roll No.	Name.	Roll No.
Ross, Lula	5152	Sango, Maria	4665
Ross, Sam	5153	Sango, Susan	4666
Ross, Susan	5690	Sango, Ruthie	4691
Rowe, Charlotte	2098	Sango, Jennetta	4692
Rowe, Fannie	2099	Sango, Rebecca	4771
Rowe, Jeff	2100	Sango, Gertrude	4773
Rowe, Mary	4873	Sango, Bennie	4870
Rowe, Hattie	4991	Sango, Willie	5180
Ruffins, Nellie	2044	Sango, Beatrice	5504
Ruffins, Frank	5585	Sango, Mary	5578
Russell, Isaiah	2852	Saulsbury, Fred	1703
Sadler, Dicey	4325	Scales, Tom	2273
Sadler, Samuel	4326	Scales, Leah	2274
Samuel, Cudjo	617	Scales, Josephine	2275
Samuel, George	618	Scales, Hannah	3320
Samuel, Easter	1896	Scales, Annie	3322
Samuel, Henderson	5413	Scales, Louis	3323
Samuels, James	2603	Scales, Benj.	4110
Samuels, Nellie	2604	Scott, Bettie	428
Samuels, Johnnie	2605	Scott, Victoria	572
Samuels, Thomas	2606	Scott, Frances	573
Samuels, Willie	2607	Scott, Jim	574
Samuels, Alfred	2608	Scott, Jennie	575
Samuels, Gertie	2609	Scott, Peter	778
Samuels, Israel	2610	Scott, Sarah	1344
Samuels, Lizzie	2611	Scott, Katy	1877
Samuels, Edna	2612	Scott, Willie	1878
Samuels, Pearl	4222	Scott, Billy	2114
Samuels, Sarah J.	5173	Scott, Nellie	2115
Sanders, Amelia	3287	Scott, Butcher	2591
Sanders, Evaline	3288	Scott, Andy	2593
Sanders, Ethel Lee	3289	Scott, Josiah	2594
Sanders, (nee Wood-		Scott, Jackson	2595
ward) Sarah	4815	Scott, William	2596
Sanders, Johnie	4816	Scott, Winnie	2597
Sanders, Alice	4849	Scott, Polly	2598
Sandy, Hagar	884	Scott, Manny	2599
Sancho, John	4093	Scott, Stella	2600
Sango, Phillis	233	Scott, Hattie	2601
Sango, Mollie	306	Scott, Mattie	2602
Sango, Alex	421	Scott, Fannie	2664
Sango, Florence Abbot	422	Scott, Fred	2665
Sango, Peter	813	Scott, Leonard	2666
Sango, Steve	816	Scott, Lulu	2667
Sango, Eliza	1037	Scott, Mary	2668
Sango, Rentie	1038	Scott, Hattie	2669
Sango, Parry	1039	Scott, Walter	2670
Sango, York	1040	Scott, Georgie	2671
Sango, Phillip	1041	Scott, Dixie	2672
Sango, Grant	1042	Scott, Edward	2673
Sango, Lizzie	1043	Scott, Alex	2674
Sango, Joe	1044	Scott, Annie	2676
Sango, Ed	2810	Scott, Ellen	2729
Sango, Lu Anna	2811	Scott, Lucretia	2730
Sango, Minnie	2812	Scott, Tackey	3260
Sango, Nettie	2813	Scott, Sammie	3261
Sango, Rosabell	2814	Scott, Tom	3262
Sango, Benjamin	2815	Scott, Walter	3263
Sango, Will	2816	Scott, Letha	3264
Sango, Precilla	2817	Scott, Butcher	3265
Sango, Mary	2818	Scott, Martha	3902
Sango, Robert	2819	Scott, Arthur	5205
Sango, Clarence	2820	Scruggs, Henry	4375
Sango, Morris	3119	Scruggs, Lewis	4376
Sango, Louisa	3156	Scruggs, Susie	4519
Sango, Lewis W.	3157	Sears, Millie	4243
Sango, Polly	3158	Sears, Jerry	4245
Sango, Harry	3159	Sears, Robert	4246
Sango, Allie	3160	Sears, Louis	4247
Sango, Liddie	3161	Sears, Walter	4248
Sango, Sallie	3162	Sears, Arthur	4249
Sango, Thomas	3163	Sears, Dennis	4250
Sango, Morris	3164	Sears, Sallie	5233
Sango, Alex	4146	Seaman, Flora	3445
Sango, Ellen	4230	Segro, Eli	4507
Sango, Lewis Jr.	4467	Segro, Willie	4508
Sango, Emma	4468	Sells, Joseph	846
Sango, Sarah Ann	4469	Sells, Maria	855
Sango, Eddie	4485	Sells, Stephen	866
Sango, Cynda	4486	Sells, Hardy	968
Sango, Emma	4487	Sells, Sila	969
Sango, Sam	4488	Sells, Herbert	970
Sango, Viola	4489		

Name.	Roll No.	Name.	Roll No.
Sells, Dewey	971	Simmons, Rose	1659
Sells, Alice	1230	Simmons, Laura	1660
Sells, Snow	1995	Simmons Cora	1661
Sells, Louisa	2090	Simmons, Ray	1662
Sells, Harry	2516	Simmons, Dora	1663
Sells, Jane	2517	Simmons, Oda	1664
Sells, Joseph	2518	Simmons, Frank	1665
Sells, Lawrence	2519	Simmons, Mary Alice	1666
Sells, Jacob	2520	Simmons, John	1667
Sells, Willie	2521	Simmons, Jake Jr.	5191
Sells, Gracie	2522	Simon, Mary	777
Sells, Rose	2523	Simon, Raford	780
Sells, Lawrence	5073	Simon, Rosa	781
Sells, Stella	5560	Simon, Jeff	782
Sells, Birdie	5561	Simon, Cora	3451
Serrell, Dorcas	865	Simon, Green	3453
Sewel, Mary	75	Skeeter, Stella	4625
Sewel, Samuel	80	Skeeter, Nellie	4626
Sewel, Pinkney	81	Skiff, Susie	895
Sewel, Elizabeth	82	Skiff, Maggie	917
Sewel, Minnie	5479	Skiff, Dempsy	1285
Sewell, Billy	1358	Sloane, Malinda	5598
Sewell, Tacey	1359	Sloane, Elizabeth	5599
Sewell, Rentie	1360	Smith, Ellen C.	307
Sewell, Andrew	1361	Smith, John C.	308
Sewell, Nancy	1362	Smith, Arnett	309
Sewell, Louis	1363	Smith, Sarah C	310
Sewell, Jimmie	1364	Smith, Gussie	320
Sewell, Freddie	1365	Smith, Sarah	332
Sewell, Martha	1366	Smith, Ellen	334
Sewell, Primus	1367	Smith, Peter	456
Sewell, Tochie	1368	Smith, Jeffrey	497
Sewell, Sofa	1369	Smith, Tamer	498
Sewell, Gussie	1370	Smith, Ether	564
Sewell, Etta	5077	Smith, Jake	675
Sewell, Joseph	5359	Smith, Lee Anderson	727
Shanklin, Clew	2954	Smith, Rebecca	733
Sharper, Jno.	3256	Smith, Sarah	923
Sharper, Milley	3257	Smith, Hardy	924
Sharper, Ben	4807	Smith, David	925
Shaw, Wallace	4020	Smith, Blanche	926
Shawnee, Ethel	19	Smith, Primus	1130
Shelton, Cora	2535	Smith, Bettie	1131
Shelton, Emma	3291	Smith, Elliott	1132
Shelton, Sudie	3292	Smith, Ross	1133
Shelton, Martha	3293	Smith, Cornelius	1134
Shepard, Jane	570	Smith, Isaac	1135
Shepard, Martha	4032	Smith, Frank	1136
Shepard, Maggie	4033	Smith, Dollie	1137
Shepard, Ben	4034	Smith, Gerthie	1138
Shepard, Walter	5566	Smith, Racie	1139
Sherman, Re Anna	639*	Smith, Bernie	1140
Sherman, Sylvetta	640	Smith, Georgia	1141
Sherman, Etta	3774	Smith, Silas	1330
Sherman, Anna	3775	Smith, Emma	1331
Sherman, Lillie	3776	Smith, Ora	1332
Sherman, Tressie	3777	Smith, Sarah Ann	1333
Sherman, Vicotria	4385	Smith, Mack	1334
Sherman, Ethel	5212	Smith, Nancy	1765
Sherman, Robert	5445	Smith, Dina	1766
Shields, Alice	4561	Smith, Stella	1767
Shoals, Georgia	2939	Smith, Raford	1768
Shoals, Lou Anderson	2940	Smith, Willie	1800
Shoals, Geneva	2941	Smith, Alice	1801
Shoals, William		Smith, Robert	1823
McKinley	2942	Smith, Sallie	1969
Shoals, Cyrus L.	2943	Smith, Angeline	2023
Shobe, Rosie	5588	Smith, Andy	2087
Shobe, Viola	5589	Smith, Rose	2089
Shobe, Eugene	5590	Smith, Annie	2102
Shoto, Sarah	4286	Smith, Milley	2239
Shoto, Clarence V.	4287	Smith, Lucy	2499
Siah, Alfred	4038	Smith, Miley	2500
Sier, Jacob	3510	Smith, Frank	2501
Sier, Ellen	3511	Smith, Ella	2502
Sier, Texanna	3512	Smith, Nancy	2503
Sier, Laura	3513	Smith, Gerthey	2504
Sier, Edna	3515	Smith, Tony	2505
Sier, Emma	5091	Smith, Harry	2617
Simmons, John W.	645	Smith, Mattie	2953
Simmons, Eugene	1023	Smith, Willie	3001
Simmons, James	1175	Smith, Joanna	3002
Simmons, Jacob	1658		

Name.	Roll No.	Name.	Roll No.
Smith, Luvina	3003	Snowden, Mathew	4140
Smith, Henry	3004	Snowden, Joseph	4141
Smith, George	3005	Snowden, Riley	4142
Smith, Pearlie	3006	Snowden, Porter	4143
Smith, Alice	3191	Snowden, Horace	4144
Smith, Leander M.	3192	Solomon, Johnnie	363
Smith, Polly	3194	Solomon, Santon	466
Smith, Annie	3275	Solomon, Goliah	972
Smith, John	3276	Solomon, Luke	973
Smith, Clarence	3277	Solomon, Nellie	974
Smith, Dillard	3278	Solomon, Samuel	2157
Smith, Fanny	3341	Solomon, Emma	2158
Smith, Archer	3343	Solomon, Stella	2159
Smith, Lewis	3573	Solomon, Nellie	2160
Smith, Chaney	3574	Solomon, David	2161
Smith, Helen	3575	Solomon, Dwight	2162
Smith, Rosa	3576	Soloomn, D. Baptist	2163
Smith, Alice	3684	Solomon, Allen	2164
Smith, Mamie	3687	Solomon, Mary	2165
Smith, Nelson	3688	Solomon, Nancy	2711
Smith, Edna	3689	Sookey, Sallie	4809
Smith, Jessie	3690	Sparks, Phoebe	85
Smith, Bertha	3691	Spencer, Minerva	2566
Smith, Robert	3692	Spencer, Sallie	2567
Smith, Frank	3882	Spencer, Sarah	4529
Smith, Thomas	3883	Spring, Nathan	5471
Smith, Sandy	3916	Spring, Ellen	5472
Smith, Isaac	4058	Stanford, Sarah	3726
Smith, Dora	4155	Stanford, Lucinda	5440
Smith, Jackson	4426	Stanford, Floyd	3728
Smith, Eddy	4427	Starr, John	1150
Smith, Jesse	4428	Starr, Mary	1151
Smith, Mattie	4429	Starr, Denvet	1152
Smith, Nina	4430	Starr, Henry	1161
Smith, Walter	4431	Starr, Marie	1455
Smith, Luvina	4433	Starr, Elmira	1733
Smith, Willie	4434	Starr, Louisa	4606
Smith, Bennie	4435	Staten, Gertie	4471
Smith, Thomas	4436	Steadham, Jennie	73
Smith, Allie	4437	Steadham, Joe	86
Smith, Hannah	4506	Steadham, Morris	374
Smith, Lizzie	4518	Steadham, Dolly	375
Smith, Denisha	4629	Steadham, Hardy	844
Smith, Ida Rutha	4630	Steadham, Rachel	845
Smith, Robert	4631	Steadham, Peter	2319
Smith, Island	4706	Steadham, Sarah	3412
Smith, Rachel	4707	Stephens, Joseph	635
Smith, Cora	4708	Stephens, Ida	1623
Smith, Georgiana	4709	Stephens, Robert Morris	1923
Smith, Viola	4724	Stephens, Rose	1924
Smith, Susie	4843	Stephens, Charlie	3730
Smith, Nicey	4844	Stephens, Winnie	3731
Smith, Thomas	4943	Stepney, Jonas	226
Smith, Herman	4944	Stepney, Noah	227
Smith, Ray	4945	Stepney, Jeff	228
Smith, Mary	4946	Stepney, Soloman	3708
Smith, Martha	4947	Stepney, Hepsey	3709
Smith, Bessie	4948	Stepney, Wallace	3710
Smith, Elvira	5070	Stepney, Willie	3711
Smith, Gertrude	5079	Stepney, Lillie	3712
Smith, Louana	5161	Stepney, Elizabeth	3713
Smith, Edna	5165	Stevens, Hattie	1929
Smith, Madison	5195	Stevens, Georgia	2133
Smith, Helen	5246	Stevens, Bennie	2136
Smith, Martha	5255	Stevens, William	2137
Smith, Emily	5342	Stevens, Dewey	2138
Smith, Millie A.	5510	Stevens, Millie	2139
Smith, Bessie Julia	5512	Stevens, Isparhecher	2140
Smith, Joseph B. Jr.	5513	Stevenson, Leah	1836
Smith, Guy	5514	Stewart, Ola	66
Smith, Chicago	5516	Stewart, Eddie	269
Smith, Julia	5634	Stewart, Mary	4501
Smith, Ed	5676	Stewart, Nathaniel	4502
Smith, Jesse	5677	Stewart, Nettie	4503
Smith, Solomon	5681	Stidham, Isabel	908
Sneed, Roxana	4513	Stidham, Tom	1091
Sneed, James	4514	Stidham, Silla	1092
Sneed, Artra, Jr.	4515	Stidham, Ollie	1093
Sneed, Roman	4516	Stidham, Gertrude	1094
Sneed, Theodore	5220	Stidham, Matilda	1095
Sneed, Julius	5544	Stidham, Lona	1096
Snowden, Bettie	4138	Stidham, Lena	1097
Snowden, Charles	4139		

Name.	Roll No.	Name.	Roll No.
Stidham, Peter	1972	Taylor, Squire	5275
Stidham, Bina	1973	Taylor, Benjamin	5276
Stidham, Prince	2704	Taylor, Fannie	5323
Stidham, Jack	4940	Taylor, Maggie	5461
Stidham, Adeline	4941	Tecumseh, John	5031
Stidham, Katie	4942	Tecumseh, Tena	5034
Stidham, Zadie	5405	Tecumseh, Tecumsey	5035
Street, Lizzie	270	Tecumseh, Marchum	5036
Street, Parlina	271	Tecumseh, Mattie	5037
Street, Nora	272	Tecumseh, Sarah	5038
Street, Garfield	273	Tecumseh, Sampson	5039
Street, Lester	274	Tecumseh, Lutitia	5040
Street, Alfred	275	Thomas, Edie	311
Street, Tom	276	Thomas, Cora	312
Street, Pearl	5374	Thomas, Jennie	313
Stroy, Nero	4059	Thomas, Leola	314
Stroy, Lila	5336	Thomas, Ambrose	315
Sugar, George	1802	Thomas, Annie	316
Sugar, Betsey	1803	Thomas, James Jr.	317
Sugar, Rena	1804	Thomas, David	1171
Sugar, Julia	1805	Thomas, Bobbrey	1649
Sugar, Harry	2245	Thomas, Sandy	2359
Sugar, Jimmie	5030	Thomas, Amelia	4045
Sugar, George Emmett	5248	Thomas, Flora	4046
Sullivan, Tina	977	Thomas, Fred	4047
Sullivan, Andrew	1341	Thomas, Frank	4048
Sullivan, Sarah	1342	Thomas, Mahaley	4049
Tab, Paul	5310	Thomas, Ada	4621
Tab, Silas	5311	Thomas, Millie	4622
Tanner, Lizzie	4153	Thomas, Wesley	4831
Taylor, Joseph	67	Thomas, Grant	5317
Taylor, Charlie	68	Thomas, Robert	5318
Taylor, Daisy	69	Thomas, Minnie	5613
Taylor, Ralph	70	Thompson, Warrior	133
Taylor, Emma	71	Thompson, Joseph	739
Taylor, Robert	149	Thompson, Matilda	740
Taylor, Lucy	150	Thompson, Lou	741
Taylor, Martin	151	Thompson, James	742
Taylor, John M.	193	Thompson, Boston	872
Taylor, Harriett	194	Thompson, Rebecca	873
Taylor, Polly	195	Thompson, Jeannetta	874
Taylor, Annie	196	Thompson, Annie	875
Taylor, Fross James	197	Thompson, Malinda	876
Taylor, Minnie	198	Thompson, Helen	877
Taylor, Harriett	199	Thompson, John	878
Taylor, Lucinda	200	Thompson, Charlie	879
Taylor, Jackson	447	Thompson, Nick	880
Taylor, Jane	448	Thompson, Henry	881
Taylor, Crawford	449	Thompson, Silva	882
Taylor, George	450	Thompson, Tommy	883
Taylor, John	451	Thompson, Fred	1345
Taylor, Gracie	452	Thompson, Luke	1723
Taylor, Sherman	455	Thompson, Ellen	1724
Taylor, Mary	749	Thompson, Molly	1725
Taylor, Kitty	1346	Thompson, Betsey	2685
Taylor, Georgia	1348	Thompson, Winnie	2686
Taylor, Johnny	1349	Thompson, Silas	2687
Taylor, Albert	1350	Thompson, Simon	2688
Taylor, George H.	1771	Thompson, Millie	2689
Taylor, Alice	1772	Thompson, Hager	2690
Taylor, Ivy	1773	Thompson, Fannie	2691
Taylor, George H. Jr.	1774	Thompson, Lilly	2786
Taylor, Blanche	1775	Thompson, John H.	2787
Taylor, Lizzie	1792	Thompson, Fanny	2851
Taylor, Malussa	1793	Thompson, Eliza	2853
Taylor, John	1794	Thompson, Walter	2859
Taylor, Amanda	3584	Thompson, Jordan	2860
Taylor, French	3821	Thompson, Ned	3138
Taylor, Tina	4288	Thompson, Leah	3139
Taylor, Sanford	4289	Thompson, Nettie	3140
Taylor, Dave	4290	Thompson, Katie	3141
Taylor, John	4291	Thompson, Sally	3484
Taylor, Jesse	4292	Thompson, Charlie	3485
Taylor, Laura	4293	Thompson, Bertha	3486
Taylor, Mary	4328	Thompson, James	3487
Taylor, Rachael	4377	Thompson, Clifford	3858
Taylor, Mariah	4378	Thompson, Lizzie	4699
Taylor, Adaline	4379	Thompson, Anna	5061
Taylor, Annie	4380	Thompson, Doney	5072
Taylor, Emily	4381	Thompson, Ruthy	5198
Taylor, Griffin	4382	Thompson, Mark	5203
Taylor, Sarah	4383	Thompson, Edward	5442
Taylor, Frances	5274	Thompson, Wesley	5522

Name.	Roll No.	Name.	Roll No.
Thornton, Rachael	65	Tucker, Robert	1264
Thursday, Dick	2832	Tucker, Rafield	1265
Thursday, Mary Jane	2833	Tucker, Richard	1396
Tiger, Jenetta	411	Tucker, Fannie	1397
Tiger, Alfred	412	Tucker, Walter	1398
Tiger, George	932	Tucker, Alvin	1399
Tiger, Henrietta	2178	Tucker, Dora	1400
Tiger, Annie	2179	Tucker, Polly	2101
Tiger, Nellie	2244	Tucker, Mary	2176
Tiger, Dick	2266	Tucker, Hattie	2177
Tiger, Martha	2267	Tucker, Puss	2296
Tiger, Viola	2272	Tucker, Rufus	2297
Tiger, Annie	4062	Tucker, Fred	2298
Tiger, Hagar	4733	Tucker, Myrtle	2299
Tiger, Annie	4734	Tucker, Douglass	2903
Tiger, Scott	4735	Tucker, Grant	3219
Tiger, Nicey	4736	Tucker, Ethel	3220
Tiger, Lydia	4782	Tucker, Mabel	3221
Tiger, Joe H.	4879	Tucker, Forrest	3222
Tiger, Nancy	5145	Tucker, Lonie	3279
Tipton, Arizona	4432	Tucker, Jim	3446
Tittle, Bessie	2890	Tucker, Jimmy	3558
Tittle, Julia	2892	Tucker, Frank	3559
Tobey, Fred	2437	Tucker, Ananias	3560
Tobey, Tina	2438	Tucker, Sandy	3627
Tobey, Coody	2439	Tucker, Phoebe	3628
Tobey, Josie	2440	Tucker, Christina	3629
Tobey, Malinda	2441	Tucker, Sam	3733
Tobey, James	2442	Tucker, Julia	3734
Tobler, Bettie	153	Tucker, Royal	3735
Tobler, Alice	154	Tucker, Sam	3768
Tobler, Lula	155	Tucker, Sammy	3769
Tobler, Ben	382	Tucker, Washington	4054
Tobler, Sandy	389	Tucker, Gabriel	4083
Tobler, Fred	390	Tucker, Fannie	4167
Tobler, Alex	391	Tucker, Isaac	4232
Tobler, Dick	393	Tucker, August	4925
Tobler, Sofa	392	Tucker, Harris	5155
Tobler, Josh.	467	Tucker, Dorine	5206
Tobler, Izonia	3983	Tucker, Hattie	5296
Tobler, Aaron	4244	Turner, Sarah	3370
Tobler, Samuel	4258	Turner, Catherine	3371
Tobler, Sallie	4259	Turner, Lilly	3372
Tobler, George	4260	Turner, Rachael	4549
Tobler, Elizabeth	4261	Turner, Annie	4550
Tobler, Charles	4262	Turner, Frances	4551
Tobler, Thomas	4263	Turner, Clarence	4552
Tobler, Minnie	4264	Turner, Jerry	4553
Tobler, Robert	4265	Tyler, Eliza	3540
Tobler, Georgianna	4266	Tyler, Pearlie	3541
Tobler, Floyd	4267	Tyler, Lucy	3542
Tobler, Julian	4268	Tyler, Gertie	3543
Tobler, Eddie	4269	Vann, Millie	162
Tobler, Samuel	4270	Vann, Mary	163
Tobler, Rufus	4271	Vann, Sarah	164
Tobler, Senora	4272	Vann, Mary	300
Tobler, Judie	4275	Vann, Jim	815
Tobler, Emma	4276	Vann, Sally	1780
Tobler, Bob	4584	Vann, Catherine	1782
Tobler, Wallace	4805	Vann, Pearl	1783
Toliver, Della	5486	Vann, Rina	2094
Tolliver, Cynthia J.	2987	Vann, Fanny	2142
Tolliver, Birtanna	2992	Vann, Summer	4027
Tolliver, Lucile	2993	Vann, Pauline	4028
Tolliver, Ivey	2994	Vann, Sadie	4029
Tom, Jimmie	4044	Vann, Hannah	4030
Tom, Nathan	5693	Vann, Josephine	4031
Toney, Jesse	1421	Vann, Carrie	4282
Toney, Jacob	1431	Vann, William	4668
Toney, Dave	5227	Vann, Lizzie	4669
Trotter, Rose	2012	Vann, Leander	4670
Trotter, Neal	2013	Vann, Clarence W.	4671
Trotter, Frank	2014	Vann, Irena	5090
Tucker, Betty	509	Vann, Rachael	5368
Tucker, Josh	648	Vannoy, Arbell	4007
Tucker, Harrison	1256	Vannoy, Lemuel	4008
Tucker, Fanny	1257	Vannoy, Pollie	4009
Tucker, Sam	1258	Vannoy, Robert	5046
Tucker, Dave	1259	Vaughan, Rhoda	3528
Tucker, Lou	1260	Vaughn, Nellie	4785
Tucker, James	1261	Vaughn, Hattie	4786
Tucker, Albert	1262	Vaughn, Mack	5170
Tucker, Joshua	1263		

Name.	Roll No.	Name.	Roll No.
Verner, Rachael	2404	Washington, Pearly	1726
Verner, Nellie	2408	Washington, Walter	3079
Verner, Martha	2409	Watson, Aurella	1218
Verner, Lucy	2410	Watson, Robt. Henry	
Verner, Bessie	2411	Preston	1219
Vincent, Henry	4780	Watson, Pink W., Jr.	1220
Vincent, Robbin	5370	Watson, Vina	3456
Vincent, Minnie	5696	Watson, Leona	5181
Virgel, Fred	3660	Watson, Theney	5228
Wade, Sam	41	Weaver, John	943
Wade, Tina	42	Weaver, Wittson	5447
Wade, Jane	43	Webber, Chlora	4727
Wade, Caroline	46	Webber, Myrtle	4728
Wade, Charley	47	Webber, Willie	4729
Wade, Israel	48	Webber, Ola	5223
Wade, Stephen	139	Webster, Charlie	2449
Wade, Lucy	140	Welch, Ada	2154
Wade, Mary	1570	Wells, Mary	2037
Walcot, Lula	232	Welsh, Mary	4348
Walden, Alice	4825	Welsh, Sarah	4350
Walker, Ida M.	348	Welsh, Minnie	4351
Walker, Elvira	384	Welsh, Maria	4352
Walker, Elnora	775	Welsh, Eddie	4353
Walker, Clarence	776	Welsh, Frank	4354
Walker, Robert	911	Welsh, Henrietta	4355
Walker, Susie	912	West, Clifford	4910
Walker, Carrie	913	Wheat, Mollie	1490
Walker, Charlie	914	Wheat, George	1491
Walker, Bessie	915	White, Gertie	1542
Walker, Hattie	916	White, Fannie	1561
Walker, Sarah	2063	White, Nancy	1947
Walker, Dave	2064	White, Lizzie	1948
Walker, Susie	2065	White, Mattie	1949
Walker, Aurora	2066	White, Tom	1950
Walker, Cloriann	2067	White, Rufus	1951
Walker, Mary	2068	White, Cheney	1952
Walker, Rebecca	3080	White, Hager	3894
Walker, Rachael	3408	White, Jessie	3895
Walker, Jerry	3409	White, Tommy	3896
Walker, Samuel	3410	White, Jim	3897
Walker, Emma	3411	White, Rachie	3898
Walker, Peggy	3816	White, Pearlie	3899
Walker, Willie	3818	White, Mattie	4296
Walker, Cora	3819	White, Hattie	4531
Walker, Harriet	4043	Willard, Doretha A.	1198
Walker, Jennetta	4329	William, Belle	1090
Walker, Hattie	4333	Williams, Louiza	83
Walker, Renzie	5033	Williams, Dave	84
Walker, James Dutcher	5232	Williams, Hetty	109
Walker, Polly	5418	Williams, Edna	110
Walker, Tamah	5541	Williams, Allie	111
Walker, Harriet	5553	Williams, Rebecca	247
Wallace, Mollie	2863	Williams, Rachael	248
Wallace, Elizabeth	2864	Williams, Boston	249
Wallace, Edward	5071	Williams, Ben	371
Wallace, Moses	5106	Williams, Rachael	372
Wallas, Chaney	4867	Williams, Joseph	373
Walton, Sarah	2913	Williams, Creacy	755
Walton, Cynda	2914	Williams, Mary Jane	757
Walton, Lizzie	2915	Williams, James	758
Walton, Craven	2916	Williams, Al. Thurman	759
Walton, Johnnie	2917	Williams, Eva	760
Wamble, Mary	4983	Williams, Eddie	799
Ware, John	1223	Williams, Hattie	1351
Ware, Eliza	1224	Williams, Nancy	1488
Ware, Jim	1266	Williams, Jane	1489
Ware, Emma	1267	Williams, Mattie	1557
Ware, Hamilton	1268	Williams, Rose	1900
Ware, Earle	5196	Williams, Roy	1901
Ware, Luna	5668	Williams, Thedora	1902
Warner, Paul	2515	Williams, John	1903
Warrior, Isaac	841	Williams, Lorena	1904
Warrior, Renzell	842	Williams, Julia	2630
Warrior, Gracie	843	Williams, Rebecca	2632
Warrior, Emanuel	1377	Williams, Lydia	2633
Warrior, Diana	1378	Williams, Lafayette	2634
Warior, William	1413	Williams, Emeline	2635
Warrior, Dora	1414	Williams, Julia Ivery	2636
Warrior, Josephine	1415	Williams, Fredonia	2637
Warrior, Curtis	5199	Williams, Myrtle	2638
Warrior, William, Jr.	5224	Williams, David	2639
Washington, Ella	416	Williams, Tommy	2675

Name.	Roll No.	Name.	Roll No.
Williams, James	2829	Wilson, Paul	546
Williams, Annie	3225	Wilson, Sarah Ann	547
Williams, Viola	3226	Wilson, Alice	636
Williams, Gertie	3227	Wilson, Amy	1597
Williams, Clarence	3228	Wilson, James	2744
Williams, Rebecca	3457	Wilson, Easter	2743
Williams, Ned	3464	Wilson, Mollie	2896
Williams, Becky	3805	Wilson, Jane	2897
Williams, Minnie	3866	Wilson, Dola	2898
Williams, Ellis	3868	Wilson, Henry	2899
Williams, Howard	3869	Wilson, La Vena	2900
Williams, Aggie	4012	Wilson, Louisa	3344
Williams, Babe	4025	Wilson, Salina	3347
Williams, Stella	4233	Wilson, Atlee	3348
Williams, John	4283	Wilson, Pearl	3349
Williams, Ella	4284	Wilson, Earnest	3350
Williams, James	4285	Wilson, Jane	4463
Williams, Alex	4628	Wilson, Patsie	4823
Williams, Kittie	4653	Wilson, Henry	4865
Williams, Edmond	4654	Wilson, Pearl	5259
Williams, Festus	4655	Wilson, Alice	5524
Williams, Amelia Ann	4656	Wilson, Nodie	5525
Williams, Robert	4658	Wilson, Ferdinand	5526
Williams, Mary	4711	Wilson, Ellis	5527
Williams, Lula	4712	Wilson, Lafayette	5528
Williams, Jones	4718	Wisner, Henry	185
Williams, Cornelia	4778	Wisner, Mitchell	186
Williams, Mary	4779	Wofford, Clarance	5138
Williams, Emma	4781	Wollard, Fannie	3135
Williams, Annie	4806	Woodall, George	4071
Williams, Cornelius	4906	Woodall, Alice	4072
Williams, Hattie	5005	Woodard, Annie	2490
Williams, Josephine	5025	Woodard, Tommy	2491
Williams, Mary	5026	Woodard, Raford	2492
Williams, Maggie	5027	Woodard, Benny	2493
Williams, Gertrude	5028	Woodard, Mary	2494
Williams, Elmira	5029	Woodard, Ora	5100
Williams, Castella	5088	Woodard, Hamilton	5549
Williams, Iva	5095	Woodley, Amanda	3274
Williams, Carl	5185	Woodly, Luther	892
Williams, Lula	5322	Woods, Georgia	3007
Williams, Albertha	5408	Woodward, Peggy	3165
Williams, Henry	5604	Woodward, Rose	3166
Williams, George	5628	Woodward, Dick	3167
Willis, Anna	3441	Woodward, Annie	3168
Willis, Robert M.	3442	Woodward, Sammie	3172
Willis, Purlie	3443	Woodward, Viola	3173
Willis, Elnora	4667	Wright, Miley	1475
Willis, John	4689	Wright, Charles	1476
Willis, Gracie	4690	Wright, Buz	1477
Willis, Fredonia	4869	Wrightt, Luella	1478
Willis, Mable	5094	Wright, Tennessee	1479
Willis, Jimmie	5470	Young, Arthur	563
Wilson, Patsy	542	Young, Katie	1480
Wilson, George	543	Young, Bettie	2587
Wilson, Frank	544	Young, Frank J.	5201
Wilson, Charlie	545		

INDEX TO
NEW BORN CREEK FREEDMEN

Name.	Roll No.	Name.	Roll No.
Byrd, Sallie E.	463	Dickson, Leona Belle	385
Byrd, Ora	464	Douglass, Magnolia	175
Byrd, Rosanna	715	Downs, Rena	395
Canada, Clem	612	Doyle, Mary	240
Canada, Anna Belle	613	Duff, Easter	297
Card, Maria	88	Durant, Robert	419
Carlina, Colbert	500	Durant, Rosavelt	543
Carolina, Owens	450	Edwards, Lincoln	32
Carolina, Finks	597	Edwards, Edgar Joe	33
Carolina, Azell	598	Edwards; Rosabelle	35
Carr, Rose	666	Edwards, Leroy	173
Carter, Raymond	317	Edwards, Robert	260
Carter, Hellen	318	Farres, Beoma	679
Carter, Johnnie	435	Fee, Rosavelt	294
Carter, Jeanie	456	Fields, Hattie May	80
Carter, James	482	Fields, Alex	119
Carter, Ada	654	Fields, Floyd	286
Carter, Jeff Allen	727	Fields, Leeman	287
Carter, Jesse	752	Fields, Bessie	518
Carter, Hannah	777	Fife, Joe Freeman	16
Cartwright, Charley	31	Finniegan, Leola	400
Carwile, Horace Greeley	96	Fisher, Raymond	142
Charles, Beatrice	290	Fisher, Caroline	383
Charles, Emma	467	Fisher, Ellis	384
Charles, Jessie	469	Flannigan, W. C.	189
Charles, Malinda	490	Flint, Leroy	632
Charles, Elnora	515	Ford, Barbara Ella	362
Chatman, Theodore	356	Ford, Andrew	529
Childers, Eula	217	Foreman, Flossie	704
Childers, Vera	218	Foster, Leonard	347
Clark, Mamie	22	Francis, Louisa	251
Clark, John	585	Francis, Matilda	252
Clark, Fill	586	Franklin, Jacob	343
Cobb, Nancy	68	Franklin, Annie	486
Cobb, Evalina	90	Franklin, Stine	658
Colbert, Alonzo	58	Franklin, Erella	132
Colbert, Oradle	59	Franklin, Louis	526
Colbert, Jesse	60	Franklin, R. E.	753
Colbert, Julia	277	Fulsom, Walter, Jr.	28
Colbert, James	513	Fulsom, Willie	34
Colbert, Lily	514	Fulsom, James	295
Colbert, Lucy	645	Fulsom, Bettie	734
Colbert, George	646	Garrett, Rayfield	72
Colbert, Lewis	681	Garrett, Ella	73
Colbert, Arthur	781	Garrett, Johnny	79
Colbert, Emma	800	Garrett, Quentin	219
Colbert, Jenetta	801	Garrett, Walter	351
Cole, Bertha	339	Garrett, Ophelia	352
Cole, Joseph	728	Garrett, Auzie	353
Cole, Jobe	729	Gaylord, Milton	17
Collins, Clarence	103	Gaylord, Princie	18
Collins, Pearl	104	Gilbert, Edward	511
Cook, Joe	706	Gilbert, Rosevelt	512
Cooks, Mattie	746	Glover, Bob	118
Corbray, Arthur	45	Graham, Will L.	387
Corbray, Lige	46	Graham, Theodore	671
Corbray, Harry Jr.	327	Gray, Alfred	536
Corbray, Aurilla	747	Grayson, Governor	183
Cousins, Rosa	545	Grayson, Sally	202
Cowans, Charley	115	Grayson, Grant	203
Cowans, Nervy	116	Grayson, Allen	246
Cox, Mayetta	740	Grayson, Edna	247
Crabtree, Della May	546	Grayson, George	257
Crabtree, Lewis	547	Grayson, Tom, Jr.	273
Crane, Clarence	495	Grayson, Katie	274
Crosslin, Lewis	243	Grayson, Van Lee	288
Cruel, Fanny	140	Grayson, Goldie	289
Cully, Annie	481	Grayson, Robby	320
Curtis, Eli	67	Grayson, Beatrice	325
Daniels, Mary	42	Grayson, Leontine	380
Davis, Newton	2	Garyson, Henry	405
Davis, Emma	19	Grayson, Shornie	448
Davis, Cullen	180	Grayson, Rosie	508
Davis, Annie	375	Grayson, Patience	509
Davis, Carl	416	Grayson, Gracie L. E. M.	528
Davis, Lillian	417	Grayson, Beatrice	573
Davis, Russel	551	Grayson, Dora	575
Dean, Mary Edna	39	Grayson, Annie	616
Dean, Goldena	241	Grayson, Eliza	628
Dean, Fredonia	422	Grayson, Ednor	633
Dean, Mary Lou	439	Grayson, Jenett	689
Dean, David	440	Grayson, Jerry	699
Devource, Georgianna	426		

Name.	Roll No.	Name.	Roll No.
Grayson, George	700	Jackson, Sommerfield	493
Grayson, Roy	766	Jackson, James W.	657
Grayson, Caline	768	Jackson, Lee	743
Grayson, Luke	769	Jackson, George	758
Green, Clemonteen	617	Jackson, Clarance	782
Green, Olliver	678	Jacobs, Willie	36
Griffin, Jimmie	92	Jacobs, Bertha	144
Griffin, Annie	475	Jacobs, Cyntha	589
Grimett, Edcar	75	Jacobs, James	772
Gross, Jessie	236	Jacobs, Joseph	773
Hairel, Luana	532	James, Cassie	121
Haley, Lucy	74	James, McKinley	193
Hamilton, Robbie	220	James, Young	194
Hamilton, Napoleon	301	James, Luella	806
Hamilton, Virginia	302	Jefferson, Josephine	340
Hampton, Osee	313	Jefferson, Romeo Wesley	621
Hampton, Osilla	577	Jefferson, Daisy Ella	
Hanley, Cyrus	695	Zelia	622
Hardridge, Martha Eva	139	Jefferson, Silas	680
Hardridge, Monday	150	Jefferson, Clyde	726
Hardridge, Lou Birdie	151	Joans, George	101
Hardridge, Leona	184	Joans, Willie	102
Hardridge, Dora	647	Johnson, Castella	280
Hardridge, Monday	750	Johnson, Joseph	292
Harris, Robert	358	Johnson, Angeline	323
Harris, Edgar	359	Johnson, Lizzie	337
Harrison, Ferdinand	188	Johnson, Mariah	388
Harrison, Bixby	602	Johnson, George	389
Harrison, Neoma R.	687	Johnson, Willie	406
Harrison, Ora Belle	688	Johnson, Lee A.	488
Harrison, Willie Elmer	198	Johnson, Deody	580
Hawkins, Violet	136	Johnson, Clarence	583
Hawkins, Essie	191	Johnson, Nellie	584
Hawkins, Philip	250	Johnson, Maddie	670
Hawkins, Leo Bennett	283	Johnson, Georgie Anna	716
Hawkins, Frank	284	Johnson, Ester Lee	717
Hawkins, Rosie	413	Johnson, Idella	718
Hawkins, Ophelia	420	Johnson, Sydney, Jr.	722
Hawkins, Dewey	522	Johnson, Bettie	738
Hawkins, Lorena	523	Johnson, Henry	739
Hawkins, Maria	576	Johnson, Alex	765
Hawkins, Mary Ann	600	Johnson, Ceaser	767
Hawkins, Bessie	708	Jonas, Louisa	427
Hawkins, Arabella	807	Jonas, Louis William	428
Hawkins, Dee	788	Jones, Clarence	78
Hemmitt, Benjamin	37	Jones, James	345
Hemmitt, Viola	38	Jones, Nalar	346
Henderson, Sulsa	185	Jones, Algerrian	396
Henderson, Rulison	186	Jones, Charley	639
Henderson, Lois	378	Jones, Liddie	640
Henley, Mark	710	Jones, Isaac	641
Herod, Joseph	229	Jones, Ada	741
Herod, Florence	230	Jones, Maudester	762
Holmes, Viola	141	Kelly, Stella	137
Holmes, Pearlie	393	Kelly, Elizabeth	138
Holmes, Roy McKinley	471	Kernel, Abe	390
Hope, Daniel	692	Kernel, Mima	479
Hope, Ella	693	Kernel, Lucy	480
Hunter, Ellice	709	Keyes, Florena	634
Hutton, Edwin	108	Keyes, Mose	635
Hutton, Viola	109	King, Leslie	505
Hutton, Langford	162	King, Lary	506
Hutton, Walter	537	King, Essie	507
Hutton, John D.	542	King, Willie	691
Hutton, Reana	697	Knowles, James W.	100
Ingram, Leonard D.	110	Lacey, Henrietta O.	631
Irving, Lillian	483	Lee, Beatrice	487
Irving, May	484	Lee, Robert	603
Irving, Fleetwood	485	Lee, Amos	604
Island, Johnny	226	Leverett, William Sheri-	
Island, Torans A.	228	dan	610
Island, Herbert	429	Leverett, Joe	611
Island, Beatrice	430	Lewis, Buzz	8
Jackson, Irene	61	Lewis, Florence Malinda	30
Jackson, Fred Douglass	62	Lewis, Hattie	95
Jackson, Samantha	105	Lewis, Tommie	174
Jackson, Virginia	187	Lewis, Aaron	271
Jackson, Emmorene	238	Lewis, William, Jr.	272
Jackson, Clarietta	239	Lewis, Castella	291
Jackson, Cora Lee	404	Lewis, Lona Belle	331
Jackson, Gertrude	441	Lewis, Sally	553
Jackson, Clarence	492	Lewis, George	627

Name.	Roll No.	Name.	Roll No.
Lewis, Jennie	672	Murrell, Rosella	125
Lewis, May Etta	751	Murrell, Edna	332
Lewis, Mollie	799	Murrell, Jeff	470
Lincoln, Emmet	66	Murrell, Lou Daisy	665
Little, Andrew, Jr.	557	Myers, Sarah	282
Little, Lillie	558	Myers, Ada	556
Littleton, Susie	4	McClain, Charlie	9
Littleton, Maggie	5	McDaniel, William Em-	
London, Maggie L.	164	mett	344
Loring, Bertha	569	McGee, Cora	333
Loveft, Joseph	652	McHanon, Floyd	504
Lowe, Stella	719	McHenry, Rosie May	270
Lowery, Stephen, Jr.	133	McHenry, Minnie	745
Lucas, Willie	113	McIntosh, Willie	157
Lucas, Nelson	114	McIntosh, Indy	158
Luckey, Castella	348	McIntosh, Elsie	159
Luckey, Jackson	516	McIntosh, Ethel	176
Luckey, William	623	McIntosh, Wm, Henri	321
Luster, Andy	451	McIntosh, Gusteva May	322
Lyons, Sofrona	195	McIntosh, Gabe	370
Maloney, Hester Ilene	735	McIntosh, Gussie	371
Maloney, Jay Sylvester	736	McIntosh, Doc	379
Malvern, Paulina	15	McIntosh, Lizzie	533
Manuel, Sherman	13	McKinney, Isabelle	128
Manuel, Raymond	14	McKinney, Tina Julia	129
Manuel, Addie	145	McNac, Robert	87
Manuel, Luanna	146	McNac, John Jr.	676
Manuel, Richard	147	Nero, Earnestine	732
Manuel, Luther	312	Nero, Hillard	733
Manuel, Silla	774	Nero, Sadie	794
Manuel, Bennie	775	Nero, Curtis	795
Manuel, Floridy	811	Newby, Almond	705
Marshall, James	328	Nivens, Isabelle	85
Marshall, Mary	329	Nivens, Julia	86
Marshall, Gracie	407	Noble, Simon	618
Marshall, Benny	408	Noble, Maxie Donia	619
Marshall, Rentie	409	Olden, Willie	415
Marshall, Gustava	421	Olden, Rubessa	418
Marshall, Julia.	548	Olden, Lemus	527
Marshall, Mizetta	643	Olden, Eather	674
Marshall, Philip	644	Oliver, Cinda	269
Martin, Castela	594	Oliver, Elwin Lee	360
Martin, Wooster	595	Osborn, Amzi A.	373
Mason, Ethel	120	Parlor, Chubby	363
Mathews, Mattie Anita	531	Patrick, Rhoda	682
Mathews, Cynthia		Payne, Rosie	181
Frances	696	Payne, Susie	601
Mayberry, Lillian	460	Payne, Evaline	756
Mayberry, Ellis	461	Perry, Catharine	574
Mayfield, Georgia	355	Perryman, Alex	56
Meriwether, Rosetta	724	Perryman, Sudie	57
Meriwether, Lillian Mary	725	Perryman, Lucus	71
Mike, Rosa	731	Perryman, Jackson, Jr.	77
Miller, Beatrice	196	Perryman, Nick, Jr.	285
Miller, Elias T.	349	Perryman, Ollie May	303
Miller, Theodore R.	350	Perryman, Grant	304
Miller, Josephine	477	Perryman, Mary	501
Miller, Sampson	605	Perryman, Bob	786
Milner, Dock	540	Peters, Leora	55
Monday, Clayton	165	Peters, Lily	473
Monday, Jesse	166	Peters, Lucy	510
Monday, Morris	498	Ponds, Hannah	234
Monday, Isaac	499	Ponds, Ruthie	235
Moore, Crawford	310	Ponds, Rhoda	559
Morgan, Jane	91	Ponds, Eddie	560
Morgan, Sanford	154	Ponds, Beatrice	561
Morgan, Gusteva	155	Porlar, Richard	76
Morgan, Daisy	156	Porter, Wisdom	503
Morris, Juanita	12	Potts, Nancy	564
Morris, Burnice	209	Pouncil, Rayford	253
Morris, Alice Edwinnie	210	Pouncil, St.	254
Morris, Spencer	626	Price, Birdie	365
Morrison, Charley	319	Price, Harry	366
Morrison, Nathaniel	412	Price, Harvy	367
Morrison, Emmet Theo-		Prince, Emma	89
dore	494	Prince, Hannah	177
Morrison, Leroy	677	Prince, Rebecca	178
Moses, Monroe,	335	Prince, Susan	179
Moses, Clinton	336	Ragen, Fred	650
Murrell, Pearlie	82	Ragen, Uen	651
Murrell, Fred	83	Rector, Sarah	261
Murrell, Ellis	124	Rector, Joseph, Jr.	262

Name.	Roll No.	Name.	Roll No.
Reed, Willie	684	Smith, Everett	97
Reed, Katie	778	Smith, Henrietta	163
Rentie, Rosevelt	47	Smith, Cherry Emer	182
Rentie, Emma	48	Smith, Lily Bell	248
Rentie, Oscar Alexander	258	Smith, Willie Ann	249
Rentie, Fannie	259	Smith, Tommy	266
Rentie, Henrietta	381	Smith, Maceo	267
Rentie, May Tina Fanella	423	Smith, Airbirdie	268
Rentie, Picket, Jr.	496	Smith, Theodore	368
Rentie, Esther	497	Smith, Gracie	369
Rentie, Ether	538	Smith, Theodore Roose-	
Rentie, Mozell Lee	609	velt	432
Rentie, Loyis Eugene	730	Smith, Lusealie	582
Rentie, Maud	744	Smith, Henrietta	636
Rentie, Irena	749	Smith, English	637
Rentie, Frances	763	Smith, Beatrice	638
Rentie, Florence	764	Smith, Annie	720
Richard, Gertie	152	Smith, Fannie May	721
Richards, Shelby C.	305	Smith, Onezah	742
Richards, Rosa	698	Smith, Alma	810
Richardson, John Davis	192	Sneed, Elvida	376
Richardson, Johnny D.	233	Sneed, Mathew	377
Riley, Novella	449	Sneed, Beatrice	648
Risby, Ella	111	Soloman, Hazel	711
Risby, Willie	112	Somers, Charley	714
Robbins, Leon	606	Standford, Alford	579
Robbins, Kathleen	607	Steele, Willie	106
Roberson, Manual	653	Steele, Sallie	107
Roberts, Susie C.	52	Stephens, Ida Beatrice	232
Roberts, Rosa	620	Stepney, Millie	754
Roberts, Roberta	805	Stidham, George	629
Robins, Alford	530	Stidham, Anna May	630
Robinson, Hettie	394	Stidham, Leatha	690
Robinson, Lena	642	Street, Lewis	712
Robinson, Peggie	780	Taylor, Hattie Lillian	224
Roe, Leonard	307	Taylor, Ruth Beatrice	225
Rogers, Lola	29	Taylor, James A.	552
Rogers, Earl	581	Taylor, Pearly	567
Rose, Byron	703	Taylor, Patterson	568
Ross, Ellis	1	Taylor, Aggie	713
Ross, Aderina Washing-		Taylor, Lou Ellen	723
ton	431	Teberry, Willie	797
Ross, Jess	588	Tell, Willie	40
Rosser, Rose Anna	521	Thomas, George	211
Rowe, Lyddie	314	Thomas, Tom	410
Rowe, Jess	324	Thomas, Samantha	411
Rowe, Alice	338	Thomas, Castella	489
Ruffins, Evalina	93	Thomas, Theo Rosevelt	534
Ruffins, Henrietta	94	Thomas, Rosie	761
Samuel, Henry	737	Thompson, Marie	50
Samuel, Thomas	804	Thompson, Pearlie	122
Samuels, Felix	686	Thompson, Cleophus	212
Sanders, Jimmy	43	Thompson, Lewis	341
Sanders, Lewey	44	Thompson, Alberta	342
Sanders, Myrtle	153	Thompson, Montie Mal-	
Sandridge, Leona	276	achi	590
Sango, Essey	465	Thompson, Toche	591
Sango, Mamie	535	Thompson, Edna	624
Sango, Calietta	664	Tiger, Joseph	221
Sango, Leona	760	Tiger, Willie	222
Scales, Lewis	694	Toliver, Robert	99
Scott, Dennis D.	397	Toney, Irene	255
Scott, Clarence	414	Toney, Escoe	256
Scott, Callena	673	Townsend, Robert	491
Scott, Raymond	25	Tucker, Clarence	21
Sears, Willie	539	Tucker, Dan	49
Sells, Johnnie	10	Tucker, Fred	227
Sewel, Booker T. W.	374	Tucker, Luther	245
Sewell, Peggy	27	Tucker, Sterling	771
Shawnee, John	24	Tyler, Roy	478
Shelton, Leora	452	Tyler, Roosevelt	783
Shoals, Booker T.	437	Vann, Henry Dick	615
Shoals, Melinda	438	Vaughn, Iona	562
Shoto, Katie	334	Vaughn, William W.	563
Sier, Sarina	372	Verner, Julia	20
Simmons, Vada Roxann	135	Walker, Rosella	237
Simmons, Louis Markus		Walker, Speed Smith	308
Arthur	199	Walker, Carson King	309
Simon, Herbert	776	Walker, Alex	311
Sims, Fannie	566	Walker, Elijah	398
Skinner, Joseph Theodore	41	Walker, Jermiah	399
Smith, Ora	6	Walker, Rosy Lee	784

Name.	Roll No.	Name.	Roll No.
Walker, Odell	785	Williams, Mary	200
Wallace, Harvey	51	Williams, Lenard	201
Wallas, Roosevelt	578	Williams, Amanda	242
Ward, Robert Lee	281	Williams, Martha	315
Warrior, Eddie	541	Williams, Ben	458
Warrior, Coren	544	Williams, Theodore Cecil	608
Washington, Geneva		Williams, Elizabeth	625
Marie	364	Willis, Lewis E., Jr.	215
Watley, Beechér Inman	134	Willis, Allena	216
Watson, Leo Lenard	69	Wilson, Bessie	298
Watson, Ioan V.	70	Wilson, Essie	299
Webb, Viola	524	Wilson, Ellen	649
Webb, Castella	525	Wilson, Antny	701
Welch, Jesse James	293	Wofford, George	160
Welsh, Mamie	84	Wofford, Leroy	161
White, Aurena	204	Woodfork, Lula	779
White, Floyd	748	Woodward, Thomas	424
Williams, Geraldine	3	Wright, Viola	306
Williams, Halcyon	11	Wright, Tommy	382
Williams, Ida	81	Young, William	403

INDEX TO
MINOR CREEK FREEDMEN

Name.	Roll No.	Name.	Roll No.
Haley, Edward	247	Marshall, William Arthur	78
Hamilton, John Henry	69	Marshall, Fain	287
Hampton, Oneal	246	Marshall, Andrew	309
Hardridge, Edith	57	Marshall, Coutsie	326
Hardridge, James	75	Mason, Leroy	81
Hardridge, Henry	148	Mathews, Viola Isabel	35
Harris, Steven	71	Maxfield, Castella	113
Harris, Willie	102	Maxwell, Rosella	13
Harrison, Darnella	62	Mayberry, Richard	286
Harrison, Leora	127	Mayfield, Lucinda Ada	46
Harrison, Willie	233	Mayfield, Emeline	285
Harry, Lizza	164	Millet, Alice	215
Hawkins, Edna May	9	Moody, Carl	199
Hawkins, Ethel May	119	Moore, Raymond	4
Hawkins, Robert	129	Moore, Ophelia	284
Hawkins, Beatrice	131	Moore, Andrew Roosevelt	263
Hawkins, Dora	204	Morgan, Irene	6
Hawkins, Frank	219	Morris, Livingston	207
Hawkins, Andrew	325	Morrison, Thomas	288
Hawkins, Annie	156	Morrison, Lemmie	262
Hemmett, Claud	293	Morrison, Stella	197
Hemmitt, Geraldine	305	Moses, Susan	185
Hemmitt, Eddie	306	McClain, John	85
Henderson, Savanna	111	McDaniel, Lucy	208
Hill, Ada	234	McGee, Eddie	116
Hodge, Augusta	47	McHannon, Steve	141
Hoffman, Allia	321	McIntosh, Ananias	99
Holmes, Arthur	87	McIntosh, Jacob	121
Holmes, Rebecca	314	McIntosh, Rebecca	295
Hope, Frances	58	McIntosh, Agness	298
Hopson, Tommy	251	McKellop, Hellen	118
Ingram, Margaret	28	McNac, Sam	133
Island, Sylvester	31	McQueen, Robert Henry	12
Jackson, Samuel	20	Nevins, Dollie	54
Jackson, Joseph	30	Osborne, Gracie	226
Jackson, Claude Roosevelt	48	Parker, Roy Lee	1
Jackson, Mollie	65	Payne, Pearly	240
Jackson, Davis	153	Perry, Lucile M.	8
Jackson, Lena	154	Perryman, Maud	229
Jackson, Ben	161	Perryman, Mamie May	248
Jackson, Herbert	203	Peters, Hallie	18
Jacobs, Eddie Lee	137	Peters, Earl	144
James, Eve	209	Phillips, Viola Rebecca	252
James, Freddie	316	Ponds, Myrta	128
James, Simeal	317	Porlar, Booker T. W.	152
Jameson, Frank	272	Ragen, Ransom	253
Jameson, Birdie	273	Rentie, Beatrice	169
Jefferson, Drucilla	84	Richard, Adline	228
Jefferson, Bettie	122	Richards, Fannie	146
Johnson, Felice Thelma	7	Riley, Floyd	94
Johnson, George Isaac	32	Robins, John Edward	29
Johnson, Leora	105	Robins, Earl	140
Johnson, Phillip	106	Robinson, David	42
Johnson, Phyllis	124	Roe, Johnnie	112
Johnson, George Emmet	195	Rogers, Fannie	255
Johnson, Emoline	322	Rose, Theola	59
Jones, James	135	Samuels, M. Vincent	117
Jones, Albert	223	Sancho, Llord	250
Jones, Walter	224	Sanders, Washington, Jr.	133
Jones, Freeman	237	Sanders, Robert Lee	149
Jones, Robert	280	Sango, Rayfield	64
Kernel, Fannie	222	Shelton, Lewis	175
King, Elsie	66	Sherman, Teddy	50
King, Elnita Margaret	159	Shoals, Virgil Joseph	299
Lacy, Hartle May	16	Sims, Rosa	205
Lewis, Irene	37	Skinner, Alma Dorothy	72
Lewis, Lennie	67	Smiles, Susie	311
Lewis, Vandevelt	138	Smith, Lincoln	51
Lewis, Rosella	191	Smith, Addie May	107
Lewis, Henry	254	Smith, Fannie Lee	108
Lewis, Louisa	291	Smith, Beckey	143
Littleton, Nelson	61	Smith, Ray	238
London, Willie	76	Smith, Alice	249
Love, Eearl	324	Smith, Elizabeth	282
Lowe, Ada	147	Soloman, Singleton	198
Lucas, John R.	80	Soloman, Edna	210
Luckey, Elrena	150	Stephens, Rena	110
Luckey, Nellie	264	Stephens, Legus	211
Maloney, Frank	180	Stewart, Zanona	24
Manuel, Warren	21	Taylor, Sam	304
Manuel, Cleland	270	Teal, Nettie	83
Marshall, Aguster	77	Tell, McKellop	206

Name.	Roll No.	Name.	Roll No.
Thompson, Anettie	23	White, Florence	132
Thompson, Nancy	166	White, Rosebram	189
Thompson, Tobias	290	Williams, Eugene	36
Travis, Theodore	93	Williams, Nearl	91
Tucker, Early Percy	44	Williams, Joeanna	145
Tucker, Dora May	172	Williams, Edna	183
Tucker, George	173	Williams, Frank	302
Tucker, Castella	188	Williams, Beedie	303
Turner, Edgar	157	Williams, Floyd	274
Wade, Bertha	181	Willis, Ray	232
Walker, Voal	55	Willoby, Laurence	11
Walker, Maud May	89	Wilson, Kelly	97
Wallace, Thos. Jefferson	90	Wilson, Vernilia	319
Wallace, Ellen Nora	217	Woodfork, Iserine	294
Ward, Dolly	289	Woodward, Blessed	114
Washington, Beatrice	281	Wofford, Archie Vernon	190
Watley, Beatrice	201	Wolfe, Nancy	194
Watson, Theodore	26	Wright, Lawrence	125
Webb, Roy Elbert	177		

INDEX TO
SEMINOLES BY BLOOD, AND FREEDMEN

Name.	Roll No.	Name.	Roll No.
Barnett, Rachael	2551	Brown, John F.	1793
Barnett, Wilson	2552	Brown, Liddie	2720
Barney, Ful-hoh-chee	1051	Brown, Lizzie	809
Barney, Milosey	1054	Brown, Lizzie	1105
Barney, Mollie	1055	Brown, Lucy	812
Barney, Siah	1052	Brown, Lucy	1645
Barney, Tommy	1053	Brown, Lula	885
Barricklow, Clara E.	1780	Brown, Pinkey	1187
Barricklow, Clarence	1781	Brown, Robert	2721
Bean, Mose	592	Brown, Siah	1241
Bear, Simon	1146	Brown, Simon	1401
Beard, Legus	2258	Brown, Sophie	1240
Becky	1422	Brown, Stanton	1789
Bemo, Charlie	1535	Brown, Thompson	1239
Bemo, George	1542	Brown, Willie	2722
Bemo, John	1537	Brown, Wisey	1402
Bemo, Julia	1536	Browning, Bessie	810
Bemo, Mary	1540	Browning, Joanna	811
Bemo, Milly	1541	Bruce, Jesse	2130
Bemo, Nora	1538	Bruner, Abe	2665
Bemo, Willy	1539	Bruner, Alice	1985
Bennett, Bessie	2013	Bruner, August	2273
Bennett, Davis	2014	Bruner, Ben	2705
Bennett, Dotsie (Maria)	2016	Bruner, Bufthenia	2205
Bennett, Montie	2015	Bruner, Caesar	2337
Berry, Henry	2657	Bruner, Charles	2493
Bettie,	103	Bruner, Clarence	2306
Betsy	1659	Bruner, Cleveland	2223
Billy	564	Bruner, Doran	1983
Billy	890	Bruner, Douglass	2065
Billy	1213	Bruner, Douglass	2203
Bottley, Isaac	1947	Bruner, Eddie	2754
Bowlegs, Annie	290	Bruner, Effie	2339
Bowlegs, August	1950	Bruner, Elijah	2229
Bowlegs, Billie	1294	Bruner, Eliza	2204
Bowlegs, Billy	2524	Bruner, Ellen Iona	1986
Bowlegs, Bina	289	Bruner, Ellwood	2305
Bowlegs, Bob	2263	Bruner, Eva	1987
Bowlegs, Bob	2529	Bruner, Florence	2225
Bowlegs, Bud	1951	Bruner, George Washington	1988
Bowlegs, Caesar	1900	Bruner, Grant	2260
Bowlegs, Cynda	291	Bruner, Hagar	2663
Bowlegs, Cyrus	2725	Bruner, Hall	1676
Bowlegs, David	1295	Bruner, Ida	1746
Bowlegs, Edmund	1786	Bruner, Istoche	1885
Bowlegs, George	2528	Bruner, Jack	2268
Bowlegs, Jack	1949	Bruner, Jamison	2224
Bowlegs, Jack	1949	Bruner, Jim	1528
Bowlegs, Jennie	2170	Bruner, John	1996
Bowlegs, Jennie	2680	Bruner, Kissie	1745
Bowlegs, Jimmie	2592	Bruner, Langston	2666
Bowlegs, John	1784	Bruner, Lizzie	68
Bowlegs, John	1959	Bruner, Lizzie	1884
Bowlegs, Lizzie	1293	Bruner, Lizzie	1990
Bowlegs, Lucy	2525	Bruner, Louisa	2297
Bowlegs, Mariah	2209	Bruner, Lucy	2065
Bowlegs, Mattie	2527	Bruner, Lucy	2221
Bowlegs, Pheney	1785	Bruner, Manda	1989
Bowlegs, Polly	1979	Bruner, Manuel	2267
Bowlegs, Robert	2516	Bruner, Margaret	2255
Bowlegs, Sallie	1292	Bruner, Mary Ann	1984
Bowlegs, William	1952	Bruner, Mary	2440
Bowlegs, William	2454	Bruner, Milton	2278
Bowlegs, Wisey	1296	Bruner, Mollie	2262
Bowlegs, Younger	288	Bruner, Myers	2003
Brown, Andrew J.	1795	Bruner, Myrtle	2068
Brown, Anna	1186	Bruner, Nancy	2303
Brown, Anna	1404	Bruner, Nancy	2338
Brown, Becky	1644	Bruner, Nicey	2067
Brown, Charley	1185	Bruner, Nora	2023
Brown, Charlie	133	Bruner, Ollie	2304
Brown, Cindy	1698	Bruner, Pauline	1677
Brown, David	1403	Bruner, Polly	2261
Brown, Elisha J.	631	Bruner, Rachael	2217
Brown, Fred	1981	Bruner, Rachel (Sr.)	2002
Brown, Henderson	2718	Bruner, Ramsey	1973
Brown, Henry	1184	Bruner, Richard	2740
Brown, Jamerson	2719	Bruner, Robert	2011
Brown, Jennie	1794	Bruner, Robin	2662
Brown, Jerry	2716	Bruner, Royal	2664
Brown, Jesse	2022	Bruner, Sally	1883
Brown, Jimmy	1982		
Brown, Joanna	586		

Name.	Roll No.	Name.	Roll No.
Bruner, Solomon	2562	Catchoche	1012
Bruner, Thomas	2220	Charlesey	169
Bruner, Ucum	2216	Charley	412
Bruner, Wilson	2222	Charley	1486
Bryant, Walton	2334	Charlie	234
Buck, Josey	1177	Charlie	813
Buek, Liley	1176	Charlie	1690
Buck, Susey	1179	Charty, Charley	574
Buck, Wesley	1178	Charty, Chepon	572
Buck, Yarner	1120	Charty, Cynda	575
Buddy,	841	Charty, Jesse	576
Bull, Lehman	1703	Charty, Jonah	578
Bull, Maxey	1702	Charty, Peggie	573
Bull, Peter	1706	Charty, Sam	1307
Bull, Sohma	1704	Charty, Williamse	577
Bull, Waitty	1705	Checotah, Ben	1680
Burden, Betsey	1397	Che-da-ka, Miley	710
Burden, Lincoln	1396	Che-da-ka, Simmer	709
Burgess, Aby	625	Che-da-ka, Wattie	711
Burgess, Caesar	622	Cheeska	1869
Burgess, Dicey	623	Chepaney	703
Burgess, Ida	1851	Cheparney	232
Burgess, Willie	1189	Cheparney	434
Butler, Elvira	2147	Cheparney	566
Butler, Henry	2148	Cheparney	666
Butler, Lizzie	2146	Cheparney	771
Butler, Martha	2127	Cheparney	1544
Butler, Tom	2145	Cheparney	1574
Caesar, Ada	453	Cheparney	1751
Caesar, Harpogee	454	Cheparny	313
Caesar, Iney	455	Cheparny	1304
Caesar, John	451	Cheponoska	212
Caesar, Missie	452	Chippee	160
Caesar, Zina	456	Chisholm, Jemima	1512
Canard, Betsey	1002	Chisholm, Joe	1687
Canard, Josiah	1001	Chisholm, Nozumka	1510
Canard, Minah	1718	Chisholm, Parney	1511
Canard, Susie	1719	Chisholm, Selo	1509
Canard, Willie	1614	Chochee	1047
Carbechochee	505	Choharjo, Joseph	958
Carbitcher, Cookey	540	Choharjo, Lucy	959
Carbitcher, Liza	546	Choharjo, Martin	1333
Carbitcher, Pittie	541	Choharjo, Susanna	960
Carolina, Albert	1957	Choharjo, Toge	1334
Carolina, Bess	2407	Chosey	435
Carolina, Charley	1908	Chotke,	1488
Carolina, Dee	2181	Chotke, Chepon	548
Carolina, Ella	2408	Chotke, Alma	1050
Carolina, Emma	2550	Chotkey, Fanny	1049
Carolina, Fay	2343	Chotkey, Tom	1048
Carolina, Georgie	2503	Choya	615
Carolina, Henry	2182	Chulma	1555
Carolina, Jesse	1955	Chumsey	515
Carolina, Joseph	2549	Chupco, Charlie	1416
Carolina, Nealy	2406	Chupco, Echoille	475
Carolina, Ned	1954	Chupco, Hannah	1418
Carolina, Nellie	2410	Chupco, Ina	493
Carolina, Peter	1958	Chupco, Jennie	909
Carolina, Pinkie	2409	Chupco, Jimmey	1417
Carolina, Prince	1956	Chupco, Johnny	1413
Carolina, Robert	2169	Chupco, Liley	889
Carolina, Sam	2548	Chupco, Lizzie	1415
Carpitche	230	Chupco, Lucy	492
Carpitche, Sammy	583	Chupco, Lucy	1414
Carr, Effie	1171	Chupco, Minnie	491
Carr, Maria	1169	Chupco, Moses	490
Carter, Alice	1072	Chupco, Polly	495
Carter, Becca	1937	Chupco, Sammy	494
Carter, Bud	2046	Chupco, Samsey	1844
Carter, Elsie	2700	Chupco, Tena	1412
Carter, Henry	1943	Chupco, Wiley	496
Carter, Jane	1942	Chupco, Wisey	944
Carter, Jimmy	971	Chupcogee, Billy	279
Carter, Joe	1940	Chupcogee, Ellen	281
Carter, Leah	1071	Chupcogee, Wilsey	280
Carter, Mariah	1962	Church, Agnes	194
Carter, Mary Belle	1941	Church, Anna	177
Carter, Philip	1938	Church, Fanny	196
Carter, Rachael	1939	Church, Janie	178
Carter, Wallace	2151	Church, Jesse	195
Catcher, Chinkah	334	Church, Louvina	193
Catcher, Louis	333	Church, Nancy	192

Name.	Roll No.	Name.	Roll No.
Church, Sam	191	Cowake	387
Cindy	763	Co-wok-o-chee	598
Cindy	974	Cox, Louis	1721
Clark, Anna	863	Cox, William	2290
Clark, James	864	Crain, Alexander W.	24
Clark, Jennie	861	Crain, Allen W.	27
Clark, Legus	860	Crain, Anna E.	26
Clark, Lucy	862	Crain, Ambrose M.	28
Cloud, George	1533	Crain, Gussie May Belle	2206
Cloud, Legus	632	Crain, Lucy	25
Cloud, Lizzie	1534	Crane, Wm. Alexander	1993
Cloud, Susie	633	Crow, George	1697
Cobb, Betsy	2324	Cudjo, Ada	2384
Cobb, Esop	2328	Cudjo, Amey	2376
Cobb, Hetty	2327	Cudjo, Bertha	2370
Co-e-see	580	Cudjo, Bettie	2672
Coffee, Mikey	651	Cudjo, Bobby	2386
Coffee, Susie	650	Cudjo, Budman	2314
Coker, Amanda	363	Cudjo, Carolina	2494
Coker, Benjamin	296	Cudjo, Clara	2670
Coker, Charlie	362	Cudjo, Dafney	2382
Coker, Chippy	360	Cudjo, Easter	2411
Coker, Cinda	1068	Cudjo, Elzora	2213
Coker, Cindy	1246	Cudjo, Eva	2377
Coker, Cooper	366	Cudjo, Evaline	2668
Coker, Daniel	297	Cudjo, Evary	2605
Coker, Endle	365	Cudjo, Gardner	2561
Coker, Hettie	359	Cudjo, George	2158
Coker, Jeff	1070	Cudjo, Jack	2674
Coker, John	1243	Cudjo, Jimmie	2184
Coker, Josey	383	Cudjo, Jimmie	2371
Coker, Kissie	364	Cudjo, John	2191
Coker, Litchee	295	Cudjo, John	2574
Coker, Lizzie	1245	Cudjo, Josie	2211
Coker, Lucinda	1354	Cudjo, Julia	2495
Coker, Minnie	361	Cudjo, King	2210
Coker, Pettie	1244	Cudjo, King	2381
Coker, Rinah	1242	Cudjo, Lesser	2611
Coley	673	Cudjo, Mamon	2606
Concharty	3	Cudjo, Mollie	2496
Concharty, Cumsey	532	Cudjo, Morris	2576
Concharty, Koley	533	Cudjo, Morris	2675
Condella, Mary	1798	Cudjo, Moty	2461
Condulle, Ida	316	Cudjo, Ned	2087
Condulle, Johnsey	317	Cudjo, Ned	2368
Conhecha	1441	Cudjo, Peggie	2671
Conner, Emma	217	Cudjo, Perry	2622
Conner, Jennie	218	Cudjo, Peter	2673
Conner, Lydia	214	Cudjo, Pinchy	2159
Conner, May	219	Cudjo, Randolph	2212
Conner, Rosanna	215	Cudjo, Reynold	2603
Conner, Susie	216	Cudjo, Rhoda	2086
Conner, William	213	Cudjo, Richard	2157
Co-nok-kee	728	Cudjo, Robert	2156
Contaley	1234	Cudjo, Rosa	2369
Coody	1358	Cudjo, Rose	2575
Coody, Bob	1075	Cudjo, Sadie	2256
Coody, Daniel	1038	Cudjo, Tena	2604
Coody, Dosar	2332	Cudjo, Tenney	2723
Coody, Hannah	2333	Cudjo, Willson	2462
Coody, Joseph	1157	Cudjoe, Bunny	2041
Coody, Lavina	1912	Cudjoe, Cora	1914
Coody, Tom	1156	Cudjoe, Dancer	1999
Coody, Wisey	1039	Cudjoe, Dell	1915
Cooper, Loley	1356	Cudjoe, Emma	2000
Cooper, Williamupke	1513	Cudjoe, Gertie	2044
Cornelius, Barney	1102	Cudjoe, Hettie	1916
Cornelius, Cyrus	1103	Cudjoe, Nora	2001
Cornelius, Tommy	1104	Cudjoe, Stephenson	1998
Cornelius, Winey	1101	Cudjoe, Sunday	1684
Cosar	135	Cudjoe, Titus	1913
Cosar	1147	Cudjoe, Viola	2040
Cosar, Cundy	1854	Cudjoe, William	2042
Cosar, Lopey	1852	Cudjoe, Witty	1997
Cosar, Lucy	138	Cully	522
Cosar, Munnah	137	Cully	932
Cosar, Sophrona	1853	Cully, Bessie	132
Cosar, Wisey	136	Cully, Eliza	1828
Cotcha, Hoktoche	227	Cully, James	134
Cotcha, Mulleana	228	Cully, Lizzie	407
Cotcha, Peter	226	Cully, Lotty	149
Cotcha, Sissy	229	Cully, Lucy	408

Name.	Roll No.	Name.	Roll No.
Cully, Maloche	409	Davis, Irene	1777
Cully, Maria	1827	Davis, Isaac	2443
Cully, Sarah	1288	Davis, Israel	2401
Cully, Sissy	617	Davis, Jack	2363
Cully, Wallace	148	Davis, Jackson	1779
Cully, William	144	Davis, Jacob	2450
Cumpsey	1799	Davis, James	2399
Cumseh	445	Davis, Jane	2398
Cumsey, Rhoda	1119	Davis, Jane	2683
Cunny, Louvinia	723	Davis, Jane	2692
Cunny, Nicey	722	Davis, Jenatta	2433
Cunsah	1521	Davis, Jennie	424
Cynda	665	Davis, Jennie	2471
Cynda	1873	Davis, Jesse	1772
Cyrus, Ben	2346	Davis, Jim	624
Cyrus, Chrissy	2345	Davis, Jim	1026
Cyrus, Davis	2330	Davis, Jim	1367
Cyrus, Dennis	1921	Davis, Jim	2470
Cyrus, Grant	2347	Davis, Jimmie	2617
Cyrus, Harry	1924	Davis, Joe	2676
Cyrus, Joseph	2420	Davis, John	1778
Cyrus, Lora	2678	Davis, John	2078
Cyrus, Lowine	2349	Davis, John	2616
Cyrus, Peter	2661	Davis, Joseph	2588
Cyrus, Phillip	2329	Davis, Julia	2452
Cyrus, Polly	1960	Davis, Katie	2460
Cyrus, Rose	2331	Davis, Leah	2057
Cyrus, Severs	2348	Davis, Legus	427
Cyrus, Tom	2336	Davis, Lila	2682
Daily, Tony	2335	Davis, Lilly	1369
Dandy	1505	Davis, Linda	2077
Daniel	700	Davis, Lizzie	2208
Davey	77	Davis, Lou	1850
David	701	Davis, Lucinda	2698
David	1335	Davis, Lula	428
Davis, Affie	2073	Davis, Martin	2202
Davis, Aleck	2472	Davis, Mattea	2079
Davis, Alice B.	1771	Davis, Maude	1775
Davis, Amey	2358	Davis, May	1774
Davis, Amosy	1611	Davis, Miley	2448
Davis, Anna	1371	Davis, Minnie	2686
Davis, Annie	2403	Davis, Missey	2402
Davis, Beckey	2437	Davis, Molena	2756
Davis, Bessie	1776	Davis, Mollie	2365
Davis, Billy	2702	Davis, Monday	2444
Davis, Bob	2614	Davis, Monday	2684
Davis, Bond	2681	Davis, Moses	1366
Davis, Charlie	2074	Davis, Myrtle	1773
Davis, Charlie	2451	Davis, Nancy	2076
Davis, Charlotte	2259	Davis, Nancy	2677
Davis, Charlotte	2435	Davis, Nellie	2701
Davis, Chubba	429	Davis, Nettie	2195
Davis, Clara	2583	Davis, Newton	2586
Davis, Cloe	2361	Davis, Oliver	2585
Davis, Clorinda	2541	Davis, Otie	2587
Davis, Cubby	2695	Davis, Peggy	2704
Davis, Daily	2072	Davis, Phillis	2194
Davis, Daily D.	2207	Davis, Pompey	2434
Davis, Dave	2449	Davis, Pussy	2696
Davis, Dilsey	2445	Davis, Retta	1849
Davis, Dilsey	2694	Davis, Rhoda	1368
Davis, Dollie	2590	Davis, Rhoda	2480
Davis, Dumas	2447	Davis, Richmond	2359
Davis, Easter	2699	Davis, Rina	2364
Davis, Elijah	2436	Davis, Robert	1365
Davis, Eliza	2570	Davis, Robert	2703
Davis, Eliza	2685	Davis, Sallie	2360
Davis, Elizabeth	2404	Davis, Sally	969
Davis, Elsie	2474	Davis, Sancho	2446
Davis, Emma	2584	Davis, Sarah	2591
Davis, Flora	2691	Davis, Scipio	2690
Davis, Florence	2589	Davis, Silwa	1894
Davis, Friday	2397	Davis, Sofa	2362
Davis, Galey	1266	Davis, Spelling	2473
Davis, General	2400	Davis, Stepney	2453
Davis, George	423	Davis, Stroy	2357
Davis, George	2080	Davis, Sunday	1268
Davis, Grace	2395	Davis, Susie	2476
Davis, Grant	2405	Davis, Thomas	2582
Davis, Hannah	2693	Davis, Thompson	1277
Davis, Harriett	2056	Davis, Tyra	2075
Davis, Harriett	2615	Davis, Venus	2540
Davis, Hattie	2477	Davis, Venus	2607

Name.	Roll No.	Name.	Roll No.
Davis, Wesley	205	Emarthla, Ada	1700
Davison, Sarah P.	2697	Emarthla, Carchee	1
Dean, Dick	2140	Emarthla, Markosy	2
Dean, Garfield	2138	Emarthla, Sally	1699
Dean, Ishmael	2383	Emarthoge, Echo	1752
Dean, Primus	2139	Emmy	1609
Deer, Annie	1765	Emoche	1662
Deer, Billy	1125	En-le-te-ke	705
Deer, Charlie	1123	Es-ho-po-na-ka	1818
Deer, Eliza	1126	Estachuksehoke	1623
Deer, Jack	1124	Estomethla	1043
Deer, Lizzie	1128	Eunasse	1859
Deer, Nancy	1131	Factor, Ada	254
Deer, Robert	1127	Factor, Bessie	256
Deer, Thomas	1129	Factor, Buckner	1261
Deer, Thompson	1130	Factor, Charley	125
Deer, Willie	1766	Factor, Edmond	499
Dennis, Betsy	2479	Factor, Edward	257
Dennis, Chaney	2464	Factor, Eka-larney	44
Dennis, Diana	2134	Factor, Ella	110
Dennis, Docksie	2571	Factor, Emane	124
Dennis, Eda	2572	Factor, Henrietta	1263
Dennis, Edna	2467	Factor, Ida	45
Dennis, Ettie	2463	Factor, Isaac	111
Dennis, Fleetwood	2573	Factor, Jimmey	122
Dennis, Harriett	2478	Factor, Jimmie	47
Dennis, Jack	2475	Factor, Joe	696
Dennis, John	2466	Factor, Joseph	114
Dennis, Julia	2512	Factor, Josey	500
Dennis, Lilly	2160	Factor, June,	497
Dennis, Rose	2514	Factor, Leah	113
Dennis, Sam	2468	Factor, Liley	559
Dennis, Silvester	2482	Factor, Lizzie	498
Dennis, Tackey	2469	Factor, Marchey	255
Dicey	1041	Factor, Martha	112
Dillsa	199	Factor, Martha	698
Dinah	380	Factor, Mary	253
Dinah	672	Factor, Minerva	115
Dindy, Belle	2488	Factor, Nancy	123
Dindy, Ben	2439	Factor, Nicholas	48
Dindy, Bessie	2485	Factor, Pardy	43
Dindy, Caesar	2483	Factor, Polda	1264
Dindy, Ester	2486	Factor, Salina	697
Dindy, Henry	2490	Factor, Sissy	695
Dindy, Joana	2487	Factor, Thomas	109
Dindy, Kittie	2484	Factor, Tokey	560
Dindy, Lou	2489	Factor, Toney	252
Dindy, Sue	2491	Factor, Walter	46
Dosar, Allie	2513	Factor, William	49
Dosar, Effie	2612	Factor, Winey	1262
Dosar, March	2623	Fanny	1140
Dosar, Nancy	2613	Fay, Alex	2342
Dosar, Bessie	2070	Fay, Effie	2246
Doser, Hazen	2026	Fay, Fannie	2243
Doser, Sarah	2027	Fay, Hayward	2241
Doser, Tucker	970	Fay, John	102
Doyle, Sam	1597	Fay, Lugenia	2248
Drew, George	2757	Fay, Martha	2244
Drew, Nancy	2714	Fay, Mary	2245
Dunford, Lula	58	Fay, Plenty	2238
Dunlap, Felix	2178	Fay, Rosa	2239
Dyal, Susie	2619	Fay, Rosy	2247
Dyer, Raiford	2519	Fay, Ruth Ann	2242
Echoille	1206	Fay, Thomas	2240
Edmond	524	Fekhoniye	1835
Edmond	621	Fife, Annie	1083
Edmond	762	Fife, Archie	1082
Edmond	1300	Fife, Dorsey	1077
Eliza	84	Fife, Jennie	1003
Eliza	248	Fife, Louis	1078
Eliza	1013	Fife, Lucinda	1080
Eliza	1308	Fife, Philip	1079
Eliza	1688	Fife, William	1081
Ellen	521	Fik-hith-ka	730
Ellen	907	Fish, Chili	391
Elochee, Nocos	807	Fish, Ellen	392
Elsa	518	Fish, Flora	355
Elsie	80	Fish, George	1317
Elsie	1388	Fish, Harriett	394
Elizabeth	993	Fish, Joanna	356
Emartha, Nokus	443	Fish, Lena	395
Emartha, Tinah	444	Fish, Louis	393
Emarthar, Aharle	667		

Name.	Roll No.	Name.	Roll No.
Fish, Milly	351	Grayson, Hettie	2557
Fish, Robert	396	Grayson, Ida	2667
Fixico, Ahaluk	501	Grayson, Joe	525
Fixico, Aharlock	945	Grayson, Joseph	1968
Fixico, Annie	147	Grayson, Josey	527
Fixico, Billy	1683	Grayson, Julia	2033
Fixico, Carpitcha	1514	Grayson, Lucy	1530
Fixico, Cheparney	172	Grayson, Margaret	2558
Fixico, Chiknaska	145	Grayson, Mary	2536
Fixico, Chitto	1117	Grayson, Millie	1527
Fixico, Cotser	1172	Grayson, Myrtle	2320
Fixico, Dinah	900	Grayson, Nancy	526
Fixico, Dossey	146	Grayson, Oda	1969
Fixico, Eufaula	170	Grayson, Pracilla	2556
Fixico, Hettie	1007	Grayson, Rachael	1965
Fixico, Hi-lo-gee	1118	Grayson, Rebecca	100
Fixico, Hulbutta	896	Grayson, Rebecca	2560
Fixico, Johnson	898	Grayson, Rhoda	99
Fixico, Johnson	1807	Grayson, Robert	1735
Fixico, Jonas	945	Grayson, Sam	2559
Fixico, Josie	942	Grayson, Sissy	528
Fixico, Lucinda	901	Grayson, Thomas	2250
Fixico, Lucy	1548	Greenleaf, Betty	534
Fixico, Maley	502	Greenleaf, Martha	535
Fixico, Matty	1173	Ground, Ida May	1983
Fixico, Mena	661	Ground, Janette	1890
Fixico, Nelsey	941	Ground, Leo	1892
Fixico, Oktiarche	619	Ground, Lewis S.	1891
Fixico, Parney	660	Hagie	1803
Fixico, Polly	171	Haney	1624
Fixico, Pompey	902	Haney, Luty	721
Fixico, Tokochee	897	Haney, Melissa	717
Fixico, Thomas	943	Haney, Mulley	15
Fixico, Tolof	899	Haney, Polly	716
Fixico, Watty	1106	Haney, Sam	715
Flanley, Maggie	1191	Haney, Willy	1618
Foster,	1610	Hanna	1484
Foster, Adeline	2299	Hannah	1748
Foster, Alice	2296	Hardy,	1594
Foster, Dindie	2295	Harjo, Abey	1438
Foster, Etta	2192	Harjo, Abler	1311
Foster, Jack	2294	Harjo, Ah	871
Foster, James	2276	Harjo, Aharlak	468
Foster, Lillie	1584	Harjo, Aleck	691
Foster, Mariah	2292	Harjo, Alex	182
Foster, Nelly	1652	Harjo, Alex	372
Foster, Robert	2293	Harjo, Alfah	156
Foster, Thomas	2291	Harjo, Alma	318
Foster, Wm.	2298	Harjo, Amey	157
Fox, Ellen	1175	Harjo, Anna	759
Fox, Yahmey	1174	Harjo, Arstaga	260
Freeman, Martha	1613	Harjo, Betsy	608
Freeman, Sandy	1899	Harjo, Billy	934
Fulsom, Lina	1633	Harjo, Billy	1424
Fuswa, George	1027	Harjo, Billy	1744
Fuswa, Jimmy	1029	Harjo, Caesar	1110
Fuswa, John	358	Harjo, Carchar	765
Fuswa, Leah	1028	Harjo, Charley	1552
Futcha-hoke	704	Harjo, Charley	447
Futopeche	247	Harjo, Charlie	707
Gaines, Molley	2282	Harjo, Cheloke	1733
Gano	675	Harjo, Cheparney	463
George	197	Harjo, Cheparney	1109
George	512	Harjo, Cheparney	1313
George	603	Harjo, Cheparney	1459
George	1387	Harjo, Cheparnoche	1324
George	1707	Harjo, Chisse	772
Gibbs, Waddie	1451	Harjo, China	66
Gibson, Ina	337	Harjo, Chola	607
Gibsy	1559	Harjo, Chuckaleese	331
Goat, John	1546	Harjo, Conchart	1436
Goat, Willey	1545	Harjo, Contulla	282
Gooden, John	1625	Harjo, Cowokcogee	1336
Gordon, Summer	2257	Harjo, Cuffee	739
Grant, Yanah	1247	Harjo, Daroche	64
Gray, Selo	1622	Harjo, David	868
Grayson, Alick	529	Harjo, David	1882
Grayson, Amanda	1966	Harjo, Dicey	347
Grayson, Ben	1967	Harjo, Dickey	874
Grayson, Davis	1529	Harjo, Duffie	369
Grayson, Edwood	1970	Harjo, Echoille	92
Grayson, Henry	2034	Harjo, Ellen	93

Name.	Roll No.	Name.	Roll No.
Harjo, Emma	929	Harjo, Nancy	1855
Harjo, En-wih-kee	766	Harjo, Narchey	605
Harjo, Eplumke	965	Harjo, Nocos	410
Harjo, Esparney	1731	Harjo, Oche	962
Harjo, Fanny	371	Harjo, Okchan	1225
Harjo, Fisher	689	Harjo, Okoske	814
Harjo, Fous	126	Harjo, Osana	926
Harjo, Fous	292	Harjo, Pahko	815
Harjo, Fousharsoche	610	Harjo, Parhos	1107
Harjo, Fulkah	1755	Harjo, Parhos	1455
Harjo, Fushutche	983	Harjo, Passuk	367
Harjo, George	385	Harjo, Petakee	736
Harjo, George	606	Harjo, Peter	258
Harjo, Harney	332	Harjo, Pilot	737
Harjo, Hettie	998	Harjo, Pin	204
Harjo, Hillie	1759	Harjo, Pin	249
Harjo, Hillis	685	Harjo, Polly	127
Harjo, Hillis	1283	Harjo, Polly	1376
Harjo, Hully	1556	Harjo, Roman	273
Harjo, Ikey	1439	Harjo, Rosana	449
Harjo, Ima	637	Harjo, Sadie	767
Harjo, Ishitchee	819	Harjo, Salina	251
Harjo, Katie	106	Harjo, Sallie	994
Harjo, Katy	487	Harjo, Sally	1425
Harjo, Katy	758	Harjo, Sam	1393
Harjo, Katy	1856	Harjo, Sampson	1881
Harjo, Jacob	1758	Harjo, Samsoche	1112
Harjo, Jemima	108	Harjo, Sarah	1857
Harjo, Jemima	450	Harjo, Selba	1337
Harjo, Jennie	368	Harjo, Seley	183
Harjo, Jennie	873	Harjo, Seluma	483
Harjo, Jennie	1456	Harjo, Siah	374
Harjo, Jim	384	Harjo, Silby	609
Harjo, Jimka	1458	Harjo, Sim-met-hoh-ye	1461
Harjo, Jimmie	688	Harjo, Sinhichke	611
Harjo, Jimmie	1314	Harjo, Sunday	738
Harjo, Jimmy	933	Harjo, Susey	448
Harjo, Jimsey	376	Harjo, Susie	687
Harjo, Jimsey	872	Harjo, Takootska	293
Harjo, John	485	Harjo, Temothle	294
Harjo, Johnnie	1557	Harjo, Thlahitchee	686
Harjo, Judy	963	Harjo, Thle	346
Harjo, Juffey	284	Harjo, Thotho	274
Harjo, Lehomate	604	Harjo, Tima	930
Harjo, Lima	471	Harjo, Timmy	1864
Harjo, Lina	320	Harjo, Toge	259
Harjo, Linda	350	Harjo, Tolof	935
Harjo, Lithey	928	Harjo, Tommy	184
Harjo, Lizzie	1460	Harjo, Totkus	482
Harjo, Losoche	1227	Harjo, Tusekia	105
Harjo, Losotka	411	Harjo, Wannie	375
Harjo, Louis	173	Harjo, Webster	370
Harjo, Louis	964	Harjo, Wesley	486
Harjo, Louis	1760	Harjo, Wiley	936
Harjo, Louisa	488	Harjo, Willea	1457
Harjo, Louisa	1108	Harjo, Willie	278
Harjo, Lousanna	174	Harjo, Winey	690
Harjo, Lousanna	740	Harjo, Wisey	1312
Harjo, Lousanna	768	Harjo, Wotka	636
Harjo, Lousanna	995	Harjo, Woxie	349
Harjo, Lowiza	927	Harjo, Yaha	62
Harjo, Lucinda	65	Harjo, Yaha	735
Harjo, Lucinda	996	Harjo, Yarna	999
Harjo, Lucy	158	Harjoche, Catcher	1841
Harjo, Lucy	1743	Harjoche, Chittoe	1166
Harjo, Lucy	1756	Harjoche, Cora	1352
Harjo, Lumsey	277	Harjoche, Cumseh	988
Harjo, Lumsey	484	Harjoche, Eliza	1351
Harjo, Mahale	1437	Harjoche, Foas	1158
Harjo, Maley	937	Harjoche, Fous	986
Harjo, Mariah	63	Harjoche, Frank	990
Harjo, Martha	1226	Harjoche, Hannah	987
Harjo, Mary	757	Harjoche, Iney	1161
Harjo, Mary Anna	1111	Harjoche, Jimmy	1162
Harjo, Miney	938	Harjoche, Johney	1160
Harjo, Mollea	612	Harjoche, Leah	1167
Harjo, Mollie	470	Harjoche, Louisa	989
Harjo, Molly	386	Harjoche, Louisa	1163
Harjo, Molly Anna	966	Harjoche, Putty	1159
Harjo, Monaohega	283	Harjochee, Liddy	186
Harjo, Nancy	773	Harjochee, Meko	373
Harjo, Nancy	1757	Harjochee, Parsuk	185

Name.	Roll No.	Name.	Roll No.
Harjochee, Tony	187	Ishmael, Dean	1946
Harjochee, Wannie	188	Ishmael, Dinah	2621
Harjoge, Carcher	1473	Island, Cindy	1926
Harjoge, Neha	1265	Island, Easter	1930
Harjoge, Nocos	668	Island, Gus	1936
Harrison, Cindy	1350	Island, Harry	1934
Harrison, Jacob	29	Island, Henry	1933
Harrison, Jefferson	35	Island, Joseph	1932
Harrison, Katie	32	Island, Laura	2418
Harrison, Lydia	1349	Island, Mat	2419
Harrison, Rosanna	30	Island, Millie	2688
Harrison, Sampson	34	Island, Ned	1931
Harrison, Thomas	8	Island, Pilot	1935
Harrison, Willie	33	Island, Rentie	2417
Harrison, Willie	1348	Jacksey	754
Hatty	1800	Jacksey	1044
Hawkins, Benny	2043	Jackson, Aaron	2287
Hawkins, Delilah	2710	Jackson, Gloine	2442
Hawkins, Eliza	1405	Jackson, Davis	2315
Hawkins, Frank	2712	Jackson, Dickson	1904
Hawkins, Lizzie	1407	Jackson, Douglass	1903
Hawkins, Mary	1406	Jackson, Eliza	1902
Hawkins, Mary	2713	Jackson, Felix	2289
Hawkins, Thomas	1375	Jackson, Inman	2288
Hawkins, William	1408	Jackson, Maria	1963
Hawkins, Willie	2711	Jackson, Mary	2367
Hayecha, John	1445	Jackson, Peggie	2366
Hayes, Willie	724	Jackson, Rachel	2137
Henne-ho-chee	601	Jackson, Rhina	2286
Henny	431	Jasksy	1194
Henny	1097	Jasksy	680
Henry	839	Jacob	743
Hepsey	473	Jacob	1363
Hepsey	1096	Jakey	652
Hesahoka	1518	James	210
Hill, James	2325	James, Annie E.	2510
Hilly	676	James, Annie E.	2517
Hilly	1695	James, Bessie	2132
Hochifke	1207	James, Jane	2131
Hoktochee	240	James, Robert	2110
Hoktoke	341	Janey	83
Holata, John	1205	Janey	1442
Holatka, Cotcha	220	Jannati	556
Holatka, Hulley	222	Jefferson, Charlie	298
Holatka, Parnosky	221	Jefferson, Chippie	300
Hollins, Alice	2375	Jefferson, Ben	2219
Hollins, Laura	2372	Jefferson, Benny	336
Holmes, Franklin	2618	Jefferson, Lena	1395
Holmes, Lizzie	2553	Jefferson, John	1419
Holmes, Richmond	2554	Jefferson, Mose	1232
Holmes, Sibbie	2555	Jefferson, Sarah	335
Hopoille	207	Jefferson, Selina	299
Hotulke, Chepon	235	Jefferson, Sissy	1394
Hotulke, Daniel	237	Jefferson, Thomas	239
Hotulke, Hepsey	238	Jefferson, Thomas	2162
Hotulke, Louisa	236	Jefferson, William	2326
Hulbutta, George	865	Jemima	808
Hulbutta, Katie	866	Jemima	1443
Hulbutta, Maloche	867	Jemima	1632
Hulbutta, Thomas	1372	Jennetta	1302
Hulhoke	1737	Jennie	246
Hulhoke	1845	Jennie	339
Hulleah	1386	Jennie	618
Hully	9	Jennie	1197
Hully	714	Jennie	1339
Hully	769	Jennie	1497
Hully, Esop	1328	Jesse	155
Hully, Harry	895	Jesse	1907
Hully, Lizzie	1327	Jessie	848
Hully, Mitta	1329	Jimmey	1224
Hully, Nora	1326	Jimmie	664
Hully, Robert	894	Jimmie	1802
Hully, Watty	1325	Jimmy	1689
Hulwa, John	1768	Jimpka	1034
Hulwa, Joseph	1000	Jimpsey	1829
Hulwa, Sally	1769	Jimsey	1554
Hutke, Eliza	714	Joanna	236
Hutke, Lisoche	1021	Jo-co-chee	1506
Hutke, Saleh	1030	Joe, Big	855
Hutche, Thomas	1675	Joe, Horace	859
Ida	1860	Joe, John	858
Iley	142	Joe, Johnsey	857

Name.	Roll No.	Name.	Roll No.
Joe, Nicey	856	Jones, Thomas	1867
John, Esta	1508	Jones, Victoria	2394
John, Lizie	1507	Joney	1483
John, Roley	1898	Josey	842
Johnie	746	Josey	852
Johnie	1042	Josey	1362
Johnoche	73	Josey	1482
Johnsey	272	Joseph	1321
Johnson, Ada	1183	Joseph, Alice	1008
Johnson, Bettie	95	Joseph, Cindy	796
Johnson, Billy	891	Joseph, Jacob	1501
Johnson, Bob	2543	Joseph, Mary	1500
Johnson, Cho-carty	982	Joseph, Medisse	1499
Johnson, David	1379	Joseph, Salta	1502
Johnson, Dickie	189	Joseph, Sandy	798
Johnson, Dinah	2281	Joseph, Stella	1004
Johnson, Dinah	2547	Joseph, W. L.	1498
Johnson, Eli	2755	Joseph, Winey	797
Johnson, Esop	2284	Joshua	1466
Johnson, Fannie	2142	Judy	476
Johnson, Frank	1250	Judy	1754
Johnson, George	1252	July, Ben	1953
Johnson, Gilbert	1134	Jumper, Lizzie	131
Johnson, Gilbert	1377	June, Hagar	2050
Johnson, Henry	2518	Kamabe	1836
Johnson, Ida	98	Kane, Eddie	571
Johnson, James	94	Kane, Nancy	569
Johnson, Jane	2143	Kane, Nellie	570
Johnson, Jemima	57	Kane, Sulpa	568
Johnson, Jimmie	2546	Kaney	1040
Johnson, John	97	Katie	1259
Johnson, John	1256	Katy	42
Johnson, John	1382	Kenah	520
Johnson, Leah	1133	Keno	1870
Johnson, Lizzie	947	Ke-pa-ya	616
Johnson, Lizzie	892	Key, Joseph	1330
Johnson, Lizzie	1331	King, Rina	2509
Johnson, Lola	1138	Kinnona	620
Johnson, Lowine	1249	Kissie	627
Johnson, Martie	946	Kissie	1423
Johnson, Mary	1380	Kith-lee	752
Johnson, Misselder	893	Kotska	150
Johnson, Molly	1378	Lanego	179
Johnson, Nora	1253	Larney, Amanda	980
Johnson, Paul	1255	Larney, Anna	12
Johnson, Peter	190	Larney, Barney	798
Johnson, Peter	2283	Larney, Betsey	1142
Johnson, Rhoda	1351	Larney, Billie	977
Johnson, Rhoda	1397	Larney, Chotkee	824
Johnson, Robert	1254	Larney, Edward	829
Johnson, Sam	1995	Larney, Eliza	175
Johnson, Sarah	3144	Larney, Eliza	275
Johnson, Silas	1248	Larney, Iste	11
Johnson, Thomas	1466	Larney, Janatta	826
Johnson, Willeya	1583	Larney, Jimka	1023
Johnson, William	2323	Larney, Joe	725
Johnson, Willie	681	Larney, John	1009
Johnson, Willie	1383	Larney, Johnson	1021
Johnson, Winnie	2542	Larney, Judie	979
Johnson, Young	2545	Larney, Lilly	276
Jonah	56	Larney, Louisa	828
Jonah	437	Larney, Lucy	1010
Jonasse	1553	Larney, Mariah	845
Jones, Annie	791	Larney, Martha	14
Jones, Arthur	410	Larney, Mollie	846
Jones, Caesar	377	Larney, Mose	726
Jones, Eddy	2385	Larney, Mose	1141
Jones, Edward	1868	Larney, Nellie	981
Jones, Everett	2333	Larney, Nicey	976
Jones, Fannie	2389	Larney, Panoche	727
Jones, George	375	Larney, Rhoda	943
Jones, Gibson,	1198	Larney, Robert	13
Jones, Harry	789	Larney, Solomon	1011
Jones, Isaac	787	Larney, Susie	825
Jones, Joe	1391	Larney, Winey	1022
Jones, Lena	1866	Larney, Wisey	827
Jones, Liddie	2390	Larney, Yama	975
Jones, Lizzie	376	Lasley, Benarus	835
Jones, Lizzie	2392	Lasley, Colbert	834
Jones, Nannie	705	Lasley, Jennie	833
Jones, Rhoda	2387	Lasley, Siyah	836
Jones, Sammy	790	Lasley, Susey	831
Jones, Selder	439		

Name.	Roll No.	Name.	Roll No.
Lasley, Winey	832	Louisa	1691
Leader, Jimmy	1682	Louisa	1740
Leah	1713	Lousanna	87
Lelusse	674	Lousanna	706
Lena	1712	Lovett, Ella	2526
Lena, Betty	1233	Lovett, Hettie	2537
Lena, Charley	1230	Lovett, Silas	2538
Lena, Effie	1181	Lovett, Tennessee	2539
Lena, Lillie	1229	Lowe, Tom	1595
Lena, Martha	1231	Lowery, John	1267
Lena, Willie	1228	Lowesa	1290
Letka, Apler	54	Lowine	1710
Letka, Dick	1192	Lowine	1658
Letka, Eliza	55	Lowiney	1741
Letka, Malinda	50	Lozana	1361
Letka, Maney	52	Lucinda	1523
Letka, Porter	56	Lucinda	1874
Letka, Solomon	53	Lucy	40
Letka, Watty	51	Lucy	206
Lewis, Fie	2270	Lucy	208
Lewis, Henrietta	2535	Lucy	853
Lewis, Kith-hoya	203	Lucy	1193
Lewis, Lester	2272	Lucy	1237
Lewis, Miller	997	Lucy	1281
Lewis, Thomas	202	Lucy	1448
Lewis, Thomas	2271	Lucy	1563
Liley	90	Lucy	1661
Liley	678	Lucy	1694
Liley	1651	Lula	908
Lina	5	Lumba	713
Lina	1489	Lumsey	75
Lincoln, Eliza	1909	Lumsey	1211
Lincoln, Everett	2218	Lundo	1347
Lincoln, Fannie	2252	Lusoche	1696
Lincoln, George	2253	Lustey, Ned	426
Lincoln, Houston	1911	Lustey, Thomas	425
Lincoln, Peter	2251	McCoy, Eliza	639
Lincoln, Philip	1910	McCoy, Epsie	642
Lincoln, Silvey	2254	McCoy, Johnsey	640
Lincoln, Washington	2344	McCoy, Loska	641
Lindsey, Hetty	1180	McCulla	1144
Lindsey, Thomas	1182	McCulla, Rosanna	1145
Litka, Albert	1808	McGeisey, James	1477
Litka, Lizzie	1809	McGeisey, Martha	931
Litka, Senecha	1810	McGeisey, Mollosey	1476
Little, Buddy	1621	McGeisey, Thomas	1475
Little, Molly	1620	McGeisey, Willie	1479
Little, Thomas	1619	McGeisy, Nora	1478
Lizzie	702	McGirt, Chiley	1219
Lizzie	760	McGirt, Elsie	1214
Lizzie	906	McGirt, Hettie	1218
Lizzie	1524	McGirt, Jennah	1216
Lizzie	1834	McGirt, Jimmy	1215
Loasta	1739	McGirt, Mollea	1217
Lodie	1833	McIntosh, Dave	2608
London, Lizzie	1648	McIntosh, Hester	2610
London, Miney	1646	McIntosh, Mary	2609
London ,Sally	1647	McNac, Joe	1720
Lopka	1737	McNac, Pauline	1099
Lottie, Affie	2152	McNac, Polly	1098
Lottie, Betsey	2425	McNac, Seeker	1100
Lottie, Cleveland	2430	Mahale	1656
Lottie, Dindy	2438	Mahardy, Betsey	2739
Lottie, Douglass	2427	Mahardy, Lyman	2742
Lottie, Isabel	2432	Mahrady, Samuel	2741
Lottie, Jonas	2431	Malinda	69
Lottie, Manuel	2426	Mandy	1504
Lottie, Mollie	2428	Maney	567
Lottie, Perry	2429	Manuel, Franklin	2730
Lottie, Stepney	2424	Manuel, Leora	2729
Lotty, Classy	2188	Manuel, Martha	2727
Lotty, Dolly	2269	Manuel, Rose	2717
Lotty, Isora	2187	Manuel, Willie	2728
Lotty, Louis	2190	Marcus	1341
Lotty, Phoebe	2189	Marcy, Sallie	1135
Lotty, Pussy	2179	Maria	314
Lotty, Rose	2180	Marks, Amos	957
Louie	561	Marks, Bobby	954
Louisa	287	Marks, John	950
Louisa,	755	Marks, Lila	953
Louisa	770	Marks, Lucy	939
Louisa	1200	Marks, Mary	956

Name.	Roll No.	Name.	Roll No.
Marks, Sissy	121	Minda	684
Marks, Titus	952	Mingo, Billy	321
Marks, Tookey	951	Mingo, Jennie	322
Marks, Wiley	955	Misselda	1389
Marpiyecher, Josie	1895	Missena	481
Marpiyecher, Wilson	1896	Missey	507
Marpiyecher, Yahnah	1897	Missie	581
Marshal, Maggie C.	2530	Mitchell, Legus	20
Marshal, Adkins	2534	Mitchell, Liddy	21
Marshall, Izora	2465	Mitchell, Meloche	23
Marshall, Lowine	36	Mitchell, Sally	19
Martha	1196	Mitchell, Salmah	22
Martha	1472	Mitchell, Wm.	18
Martha	1520	Mitchile	377
Martha	1562	Mokoyike	1480
Martha	1643	Moleya	718
Marthla, Ahale	1426	Mollie	311
Marthla, Emma	1428	Molly	504
Marthla, Hully	1430	Molly	1208
Marthla, Peachey	1427	Molly	1762
Marthlæ, Polly	1429	Monacheke	1832
Martin	579	Monday, Sibbie	310
Martin, Annie	961	Monkah	38
Marty, Nathan	128	Mooney	671
Mary	1198	Moore, Eliza	2379
Mary	1209	Moore, Katie	2378
Mary Jane	1434	Moore, Louella	2380
Matuth-hoke	1360	Moppin, Alice	1992
Maude	1282	Moppin, George	1964
Mecco, Hulbutta	1035	Moppin, Lucy	1848
Mecco, Sohathle	1036	Moppin, Minerva	1991
Meley	4	Morgan, Dave	415
Meliskoche	1615	Morgan, Edmond	419
Melisse	1037	Morgan, Ella	421
Melo	1291	Morgan, Fosta	416
Melogee	1064	Morgan, Hayga	418
Meney	517	Morgan, John	422
Mesale	480	Morgan, Wesley	420
Mesaley	79	Morgan, Willeya	417
Metetakee	878	Morris, Eliza	880
Micco, Billy	587	Morris, Fanny	882
Micco, Esale	589	Morris, Jimmey	881
Micco, Hannah	1603	Morris, Maley	879
Micco, Hempsey	536	Morris, Sally	884
Micco, Jimsey	537	Morris, Selbey	883
Micco, Lucy	591	Morrison, Flora	1925
Micco, Martha	1602	Mosar	477
Micco, Mullenana	1599	Moses, Chepon	31
Micco, Mussey	1601	Mot-hoh-ye	1257
Micco, Nelly	588	Mulcussey	1338
Micco, Peter	1600	Mulcussy	1435
Micco, Selina	590	Mulcy	231
Micco, Susey	1392	Mulgesse	200
Micco, Tallahasse	1598	Mulleah	1496
Miley	446	Mundy, Davis	2154
Miller, Clarence O.	1783	Mundy, Leitha	2153
Miller, Jackson	821	Mundy, Toney	2155
Miller, Josey	816	Mungo, Silla	2129
Miller, Katy	1067	Munnah	1066
Miller, Liddie	819	Munnah	1865
Miller, Louisa	818	Muthoye	712
Miller, Lucinda	822	Nancy	89
Miller, Nora	823	Nancy	1709
Miller, Nora F.	1782	Nannie	1303
Miller, Nussey	1069	Nannie	1905
Miller, Peter	820	Napoeche	1065
Miller, Salina	817	Narcome, Cheparny	306
Miller, Willie	949	Narcome, Maggie	305
Milley	1842	Narcome, Sallie	307
Millie	244	Narcome, Silla	309
Mills, Eke	1978	Narcome, Toney	308
Mills, Fay	1976	Natukse, Rhoda	555
Mills, Sendly	2497	Natukse, Sukey	554
Mills, Susie	1977	Nellie	1299
Mills, Tyra	1974	Nellsie	1139
Milly	523	Nelly	1235
Milly	1532	Nelly	1522
Milly	719	Nelly	1701
Milsey	922	Nelsey	1742
Mimey	1346	Ne-ma	628
Mimey	1421	Nero, Amos	544
Mina	1749	Nero, Willsie	545

Name.	Roll No.	Name.	Roll No.
Nevins, Eliza	2735	Payne, Annie	2631
Nevins, Grant	2734	Payne, Caesar	2150
Nevins, Julia	2731	Payne, Eddie	2200
Nevins, Katie	2128	Payne, Emma	1961
Nevins, Tom	2732	Payne, Frank	2052
Nevins, Webster	2733	Payne, Gibson	2149
Nevins, Wesley	2737	Payne, Grace	2632
Nicey	78	Payne, Henry	2374
Nicey	1485	Payne, Joe	2636
Nicey	1657	Payne, John	2633
Nitchey	1561	Payne, Katie	2069
Nitey	1446	Payne, Laura	2637
Nitey,	1564	Payne, Lawrence	2531
Noble, Albert	779	Payne, Lee	2635
Noble, Ben	1806	Payne, Matt	2230
Noble, Benjamin	2007	Payne, Myrtle	2634
Noble, Cindy	784	Payne, Ophelia	2227
Noble, Delia	2004	Payne, Shake	2005
Noble, Dixon	782	Payne, Tom	2630
Noble, Dora	2510	Payne, Zylphia	2201
Noble, Ebetta	2010	Pennose	842
Noble, Logan	785	Perryman, James	1585
Noble, Louisa	1980	Perryman, Wallace	1608
Noble, Lousianna	780	Peter	6
Noble, Lyman	2009	Peter	923
Noble, Mary	2726	Peter	1060
Noble, Nero	870	Peter	1210
Noble, Rinah	968	Peter	1220
Noble, Robert	2008	Peter	1830
Noble, Scipio	2133	Peter, Fanny	1566
Noble, Tom	2045	Peter, Jennatti	1567
Noble, Tommy	781	Peter, Tochee	1565
Noble, Wasutke	984	Peters, Sampson	397
Noble, William	783	Phena	312
Noble, William	2006	Phenie	924
Noble, William	2141	Philip	1440
Nokoche	1558	Phillip, Asalene	2457
Nokoseka	1155	Phillips, Flora	2456
Nokoseloche	1729	Phillips, Mary Ann	2458
Nokusile	37	Phillips, Pompey	2455
Nora	593	Phillips, Samuel	2423
Noska	549	Phoebe	139
Noska, Levi	552	Pilot	1094
Noska, Mary	550	Pilot, George	585
Noska,. Willie	551	Pilot, Mary	584
Nuksokoche	837	Pochuswa, Jim	1681
Okfuska	662	Polly	741
Okfuskey, Johnnie	343	Polly	844
Okfuskey, Mina	344	Polly	985
Okfuskey, Weatie	345	Polly	1316
Okfusky	201	Polly	1573
Omayaye	198	Polly	1738
Osborne, Lane	1994	Pompey, Alice	2311
Otheche	159	Pompey, Bessie	2185
Palmer, Betty	268	Pompey, Cora	2318
Palmer, Billie	644	Pompey, Dalton	2310
Palmer, Chunney	513	Pompey, Efford	2313
Palmer, Jim	266	Pompey, Gilbert	2312
Palmer, Kintah	465	Pompey, Hester	2319
Palmer, Legus	265	Pompey, John	2316
Palmer, Lowine	466	Pompey, Matilda	2308
Palmer, Lucy	269	Pompey, Missey	2186
Palmer, Mamie	271	Pompey, Passy	2307
Palmer, Saley	514	Pompey, Polly	2317
Palmer, Sarney	262	Pompey, Rebecca	2385
Palmer, Sepor	267	Pompey, Slavery	2309
Palmer, Sissy	643	Pompey, Stephen	2322
Palmer, Thomas	261	Ponkilla, Jimmy	869
Palmer, Willey	263	Ponluste	1519
Palmer, Wilsey	264	Pon-no-kee	338
Palmer, Yarnah	270	Porter	854
Paney	432	Porter, Billy	1494
Parney	478	Porter, Cursey	1493
Parnoche	747	Porter, George	1432
Parnosa	1645	Porter, John	1491
Par-nos-co-che	735	Porter, Minnie	1492
Parnosee	464	Porter, Samuel	1170
Parnoskey, Tena	406	Possuk, Lizzie	543
Paroah	753	Pottey	1447
Passake	1364	Powell, Charley	1612
Pa-ta-ge, Peter	645	Powell, Cheparney	440
Payne, Alfred	2373	Powell, James	438

Name.	Roll No.	Name.	Roll No.
Powell, Jennie	441	Sammah	241
Powell, Lucy	1649	Sammy	1359
Powell, Topley	1650	Samochee	1285
Powell, Willie	398	Sampson	1470
Proctor, Liley	16	Sampson, Aaron	539
Pullotka	1355	Sampson, Amoche	538
Puncho	1763	Sampson, Nelly	1168
Punka	1796	Samsoche	925
Punluste	154	Samuel	382
Punluste	1797	Sancho, Albert	2655
Putkeh	433	Sancho, Bettie	2647
Rabbit, James	1331	Sancho, Bob	2650
Raiford, Effie May	1411	Sancho, Dick	2651
Raiford, Selina	1410	Sancho, Farmer	2653
Reed, Lucy	558	Sancho, Frasier	2656
Renton, Alice	1607	Sancho, Hagar	2648
Renton, Fanny	1606	Sancho, James	2649
Renton, Johnson	1605	Sancho, July	2646
Renton, Nelly	1604	Sancho, Lucy	2654
Renty, Douglass	2117	Sancho, Sandy	2652
Renty, Eddie	2122	Sancho, Tilly	2277
Renty, George	2121	Sandridge, Augusta	2626
Renty, Jack	2124	Sandridge, Beckie	2687
Renty, Judie	2116	Sandridge, Hannah	2171
Renty, Julia	2120	Sandridge, Jenny	2629
Renty, Lucy	2123	Sanridge, Joe	2689
Renty, Mariah	2125	Sandridge, Kate	2624
Renty, Matilda	2119	Sandridge, Minerva	2625
Renty, Robert	2118	Sandridge, Tom	2627
Renty, Wilthy	2126	Sandy, Simon	2396
Rhoda	1481	Sango, Delilah	2111
Rhoda	1875	Sango, Ellen	2641
Riley, Lizzie	1825	Sango, Jack	2642
Riley, Louisa	1823	Sango, Leah	2113
Riley, Minnie	910	Sango, Leathy	2643
Riley, Polly	1820	Sango, Lucinda	2114
Riley, Selah	1822	Sango, Margaret	2638
Riley, Smitka	1821	Sango, Mary Ann	2051
Riley, Toche	1824	Sango, Mollie	2645
Riley, Tommy	1826	Sango, Samuel	2639
Riley, William	1819	Sango, Silby	2644
Ripley, George	847	Sango, Timmy	2112
Ripley, Lilly	849	Sango, Tina	2640
Ripley, Mary	848	Sango, William	101
Ripley, Nelsey	851	Sanko	1033
Ripley, Thomas	850	Sanny	565
Robert	389	Sapalpake	1092
Robert	744	Sapehunka	7
Robert	840	Sapokhohthe	508
Roberts, Andrew	2578	Sarber, Billie	547
Roberts, Caesar	2579	Sarney	1464
Roberts, Harriett	2088	Scipio	1310
Roberts, Ida	1817	Scott, Edith	1887
Roberts, Jake	2283	Scott, Ella	1888
Roberts, Lizzie	1816	Scott, George	1801
Roberts, Milfred	2579	Scott, Jim	1708
Roe, George	2091	Scott, Legusy	1626
Roe, Marshall	2090	Scott, Lizzie	1669
Rosana	557	Scott, Lucy	1886
Rosanna	1287	Scott, Natta	1121
Ross, Chilley	830	Scott, Neddie	1670
Sa-che-me-che	682	Scott, Phelan	1627
Saketheche	838	Scott, Polly	1668
Sakoeka	10	Scott, Tom	1629
Sakteke	378	Scott, Walter	1630
Saley	74	Scott, Wiley	1631
Saley	1014	Scott, Yarna	1889
Salina	630	Scott, Yeoman	1628
Salina	1693	Seeley	1195
Salinda	1467	Sefali	340
Sallie	285	Seharney	430
Sallie	1301	Sehoka	1093
Sally	141	Sehunka	489
Sally	748	Sehunka	663
Saloche	1711	Selba	1804
Salma	1871	Selda	1374
Sam, Daniel	1811	Selma	209
Sam, Lina	1674	Semissee	442
Samby, Dollie	2658	Sena, Bessie	1858
Samby, Lulu	2659	Se-ne	1462
Samby, Sampson	2660	Sentevey	1465
Samele	1761	Sigler	670

Name.	Roll No.	Name.	Roll No.
Silla	516	Stidham, Frazier	2709
Silla	1063	Stidham, George	597
Sillah	233	Stidham, John	596
Simleteke	1654	Stidham, John	1730
Simma	1575	Stidham, Lowine	1679
Silla	1750	Stidham, Mahale	594
Sim-e-di-ha-kee	388	Stidham, Polly	2706
Simena	153	Stidham, Ruthie	2708
Sim-me-te-da-kee	708	Street, Billy	2507
Simon	1315	Street, Caesar	1948
Simon, Ceasar	1901	Street, Jimmie	2506
Simon, Elsey	1764	Street, John	2504
Simon, Polly	2175	Street, Rebecca	2505
Simon, Sandy	2071	Street, Rosa	2502
Sissie	39	Street, Sadie	2508
Sissie	1320	Suc-car-see	1132
Sissy	143	Sullivan, Hagey	654
Sissy	211	Sullivan, Jacob	657
Sissy	742	Sullivan, Linda	656
Skiff, Ed	2355	Sullivan, Martha	655
Skiff, Emma	2351	Sullivan, Peter	659
Skiff, Eva	2354	Sullivan, Timmie	658
Skiff, John	2353	Sumka, Johney	1030
Skiff, Louisa	2350	Sumka, Lilly	1031
Skiff, Mike	2356	Sumpsey	629
Skiff, Nora	2352	Sunday	519
Smith, Angeline	2415	Sunny	731
Smith, Budgman	2744	Susanna	1655
Smith, Cindy	1587	Susey	76
Smith, Daniel	1588	Susey	1560
Smith, Dartie	2747	Susie	510
Smith, Earlie	2748	Susie	1332
Smith, Emmerson	2746	Suthoye	250
Smith, Hannah	2416	Su-wa-key, Eliza	1306
Smith, Henry	1591	Su-wa-key, Sallie	1305
Smith, John	1589	Tahike	792
Smith, Louis Adam	1593	Talmasey	323
Smith, Louisa	1586	Talmascy, Alfred	325
Smith, Mary	2745	Talmascy, Eliza	324
Smith, Nora	1590	Talmascy, Hoktoche	328
Smith, Rachael	1592	Talmascy, Kanate	326
Smith, Tena	2743	Talmascy, Pussy	327
Solomon	1061	Tanyan, Allie	60
Sona	677	Tanyan, Ellen	61
Sonny	1753	Tanyan, Nelia	1344
Sowanoke	613	Tanyan, Nina	1342
Sowanoke	1032	Tanyan, Sallie	1343
Sowatske	972	Tanyan, Woxie	59
Spencer, Lowila	1136	Tar-co-sar	1345
Stafey, John	1617	Tayeche	1084
Stanton	1686	Taylor, Gibson	991
Steel, Ellie	542	Taylor, Henry	774
Stephenson, Claude	2303	Taylor, Jack	904
Stephenson, Patsy	2301	Taylor, Jim	166
Stepney, Albertie	2055	Taylor, John	903
Stepney, Angeline	2172	Taylor, Judy	992
Stepney, Arthur	1918	Taylor, Lebus	168
Stepney, Benjamin	2177	Taylor, Lucinda	167
Stepney, Caesar	1922	Taylor, Molleah	887
Stepney, Classie	2173	Taylor, Sarah	776
Stepney, Daniel	2053	Taylor, Walter	778
Stepney, Fred	1919	Taylor, Washington	886
Stepney, General	2176	Taylor, Wiley	777
Stepney, George	1917	Taylor, Willie	888
Stepney, James	2174	Taylor, Yosfege	775
Stepney, Lucinda	1920	Tecumseh, Mary	2274
Stepney, Martha	2054	Tecumseh, Nick	2321
Steppe	699	Teller	1616
Stewart, Dennis	2030	Tena	1148
Stewart, Edward	2236	Te-tah-ke	602
Stewart, Grace	2237	Te-the-ke	635
Stewart, Hannah	2031	Tewe	1431
Stewart, Henry	2231	Tewee	1531
Stewart, Liddy	2235	Thahoyane	1353
Stewart, Lousanna	2136	Thasate	1357
Stewart, Mary	2232	Thlocco, Amey	1515
Stewart, Reynold	2135	Thlocco, Hannah	1879
Stewart, Tamer	2032	Thlocco, Jacob	1516
Stewart, William	1944	Thlocco, Nocosilla	1073
Stidham, Charley	595	Thlocco, Tina	1074
Stidham, Charley	1678	Thlocco, Whitlow	1517
Stidham, Emma	2707	Thocco, Emarthar	729

Name.	Roll No.	Name.	Roll No.
Thomas	1843	Tommy	1543
Thomas	1877	Toney, Betsy	2196
Thomas, Abe	2593	Toney, Gracie	2197
Thomas, Carolina	2092	Tulla	1450
Thomas, Davis	1923	Tulsay, Ellen	914
Thomas, Dennis	2094	Tulsay, Nelly	912
Thomas, Eliza	2413	Tulsay, Nora	913
Thomas, Harry	2594	Tulsay, William	911
Thomas, James	2596	Turner, Crisella	2025
Thomas, Louisa	2097	Turner, Eva	2024
Thomas, May Belle	2599	Turner, Fanny	2021
Thomas, Mily Ann	2414	Ut-tley	1062
Thomas, Mollie	2098	Vann, Rena	2115
Thomas, Nellie	2093	Wadsworth, Estella	1723
Thomas, Pearlie	2598	Wadsworth, James	1724
Thomas, Rebecca	2095	Wadsworth, John	1727
Thomas, Rebecca	2199	Wadsworth, Mary	1722
Thomas, Sam	2724	Wadsworth, Pudy	1726
Thomas, Silas	259?	Wadsworth, Tasso	1725
Thomas, Tennie	2096	Waltey	1286
Thomas, Thomas H.	2597	Wakkie, Adiah	648
Thompson	1490	Wakkie, Albussy	649
Thompson, Anna	1736	Wakkie, John	646
Thompson, Ellen	2193	Wakkie, Martha	1454
Thompson, Georgiana	2285	Wakkie, Noska	647
Thompson, Jennie	1846	Wakkie, Wiley	1452
Thompson, Sarah	2544	Wakkie, Wisey	1453
Tiger, Adam	653	Walker, Alex	1576
Tiger, Amos	1056	Walker, Belle	2017
Tiger, Anna	1190	Walker, Ben	1579
Tiger, Anne	804	Walker, Cleatwood	2751
Tiger, Anochee	801	Walker, Dinah	2012
Tiger, Bennie	1020	Walker, Edward	2241
Tiger, Black	1272	Walker, Elizabeth	2020
Tiger, Cheparney	1665	Walker, Elzora	2750
Tiger, Cheparney	1114	Walker, George	1188
Tiger, Chepon	1201	Walker, Jeff	1596
Tiger, Chotke	1547	Walker, Jimmie	1581
Tiger, Commy	472	Walker, Katie	2749
Tiger, Edmond	1323	Walker, Kissie	304
Tiger, Eliza	17	Walker, Leah	302
Tiger, George	750	Walker, Lee	2753
Tiger, George	805	Walker, Lizzie	1580
Tiger, Hully	72	Walker, Louina	1577
Tiger, Jeffrey	1666	Walker, Lucinda	303
Tiger, Jesse	802	Walker, Mattie	2018
Tiger, Jimmy	1018	Walker, Mollie	1582
Tiger, Jimpsy	1204	Walker, Peter	2752
Tiger, Joanna	1115	Walker, Sam	301
Tiger, John	1275	Walker, Seaver	1289
Tiger, John	1167	Walker, Susey	1578
Tiger, Leposey	794	Walker, Victoria	2019
Tiger, Lively	1822	Wallace	1728
Tiger, Lizzie	1113	Walter	511
Tiger, Louisa	1202	Walter	1319
Tiger, Louisa	1667	War-le-do	1058
Tiger, Lucy	1019	Warrior, Amos	2028
Tiger, Lucy	1203	Warrior, Jack	1945
Tiger, Malesa	1273	Warrior, Levi	2029
Tiger, Milly	1564	Warrior, Sarah	1861
Tiger, Miselda	751	Warrior, Stella	1862
Tiger, Molly	795	Washington, Alex	1839
Tiger, Mose	70	Washington, Annie	1838
Tiger, Nellie	1116	Washington, Eli	1840
Tiger, Nellie	1274	Washington, Eliza	2669
Tiger, Nora	806	Washington, George	413
Tiger, Peter	71	Washington, Hepsey	414
Tiger, Robert	1499	Washington, John	634
Tiger, Samsey	1563	Washington, Mandy	1837
Tiger, Susie	800	Wasutke	973
Tiger, Webster	1137	Watson, Yousta	439
Tiger, Wesley	803	Watty	600
Tikahche	1641	Weattie	615
Ti-u-na, David	1474	Webster	381
Tobie	479	Weely	764
Toche	1199	Wellington	104
Toche	1642	Wells, Ida	2279
Toche	1660	Wesley	151
Tolmochusse, John	1747	Wesley	315
Tolomka	582	West, Daniel	120
Tommy	41	West, Legus	119
Tommy	82	West, Martha	118
Tommy	1318		

Name.	Roll No.	Name.	Roll No.
West, Mary	164	Wisner, Eliza	920
West, Noah	165	Wisner, Grace	2715
West, Rebecca	117	Wisner, Henry	918
West, Sister	163	Wisner, Jenetta	917
West, Susanna	162	Wisner, Liley	915
West, Thomas	116	Wisner, Lizzie	2249
West, William	161	Wisner, Tommy	919
Wetley	245	Witlow	1831
White, Nelly	967	Wright, William	2459
Whitfield, Isaac	2082	Wyetka	1872
Whitfield, Jeffrey	2083	Wolf, Cindy	1640
Whitfield, Jennie	2081	Wolf, Copeler	1635
Whitfield, Rayno	2084	Wolf, David	1153
Whitfield, Sarah	2085	Wolf, Fannie	1046
Wildcat, Anna	402	Wolf, Fanny	354
Wildcat, Cabbichuche	399	Wolf, Hulbutta	1569
Wildcat, Eliza	405	Wolf, Hully	1398
Wildcat, Joney	401	Wolf, Ida	1151
Wildcat, Kano	403	Wolf, Jackson	756
Wildcat, Louiza	390	Wolf, Jackson	793
Wildcat, Lucy	400	Wolf, Jackson	1149
Wildcat, Maney	404	Wolf, Jennie	1059
Willea	724	Wolf, Jimmie	1814
Willea	1122	Wolf, Johnny	1223
Willea	1468	Wolf, Josie	1572
William	761	Wolf, Judie	1570
Williamkee	745	Wolf, Lena	1400
Williams, Amelia	2533	Wolf, Lucy	1568
Williams, Anna	1717	Wolf, Milla	1150
Williams, Cora	2679	Wolf, Nancy	1399
Williams, Joney	467	Wolf, Palmer	1222
Williams, Julia	2048	Wolf, Robert	1221
Williams, Lucy	1716	Wolf, Robert	1639
Williams, Mary	1715	Wolf, Sallie	1813
Williams, Sally	2047	Wolf, Sarner	1057
Williams, Shy	2049	Wolf, Silla	1637
Williamse	242	Wolf, Sissy	1638
Williamsee	1309	Wolf, Simon	749
Williamsee	1340	Wolf, Simon	1634
Willie	379	Wolf, Tawe	1636
Willie	503	Wolf, Turner	348
Willie	1692	Wolf, Tyler	1571
Willis, Ben	2234	Wolf, William	1154
Willis, Julia	2280	Wolf, Winey	1152
Wilsey	152	Wood, Jim	669
Wilson	88	Wotko, Jacksey	1685
Wilson, Billy	1673	Wotko, Jennie	562
Wilson, Doran	2036	Ya-fo-la-gee	626
Wilson, Foklotka	458	Yahola	67
Wilson, Jerry	2038	Yahola, Amey	352
Wilson, John	457	Yahola, Amey	693
Wilson, Lavina	1076	Yahola, Carpitcher	692
Wilson, Lucinda	462	Yahola, Catcher	1805
Wilson, Mary Ann	2037	Yahola, Catcher	1847
Wilson, Melissa	459	Yahola, Coo-wee-scoo-	
Wilson, Minerva	2035	wee	1271
Wilson, Mollie	460	Yahola, Davis	1370
Wilson, Morris, Jr.	2039	Yahola, Eliza	353
Wilson, Munnah	463	Yahola, Jennie	1270
Wilson, Peter	1672	Yahola, Jesse	1269
Wilson, Sam	1671	Yahola, Liley	1238
Wilson, Yarner	461	Yahola, Nokus	1863
Winey	1260	Yahola, Smitka	694
Winey	1449	Yahola, Sonak	786
Winey	1471	Yahola, Tommy	91
Winey	1653	Yakopuche	1420
Winton, Bertha	2167	Yamie, Nessie	1006
Winton, Betsy	2161	Yamie, Willie	1005
Winton, Betsy	2168	Yanah	1015
Winton, Isaiah	2165	Yarber, Mary	1025
Winton, Mary Ella	2163	Yarber, Phema	1024
Winton, Rachael	2164	Yarnah	85
Winton, Washington	2166	Yekcha, Joseph	1284
Wise, Johny	1384	Yekcha, Lousa	1279
Wise, Walter	1385	Yekcha, Marche	1278
Wisey	683	Yoney	1212
Wisey	1010	Youngs, Dinah	2620
Wisner, David	916	Yowelle	720

INDEX TO
NEW BORN SEMINOLES BY BLOOD

Name.	Roll No.	Name.	Roll No.
Ishlum	86	McMullin, Evelyn May	182
Jackie	11	McMullin, Herman L.	245
Jackson,	200	McMullin, Minnie Lorine	183
Jefferson, Hannah	48	Nancy	218
Joanna	83	Nellie	74
Johnny	172	Palmer, Barnie	240
Johnoche	6	Pon-no-kee, Martha	156
Johnson, Bennie	144	Pon-no-kee, Solomon	155
Johnson, Bessie	16	Porter, Lela	169
Johnson, Charlie	14	Powell, George	35
Johnson, Eliza	15	Renton, Lizzie	177
Johnson, Fanny	13	Renton, Minnie	176
Johnson, George	243	Renton, Robert	178
Johnson, Jenetta	151	Ripley, Bunnie	112
Johnson, Thomas	114	Ripley, Togee	111
Johnson, Thompson	150	Roberts, David	238
Jonasse, Jennie	55	Rosie	85
Jonasse, Timmie	56	Sallie	229
Jones, Louella	54	Sally	96
Jones, Nancy	105	Sewell, Emma	226
Jones, Warren	53	Sissy	113
Joseph, Fannie	170	Spain, Willie, Jr.	95
Joseph, Maney	121	Spencer, Mary	199
Joseph, Willie	207	Susey	12
Larney, Belger	10	Talmascy, Ena	52
Larney, Bunnie	120	Talmascy, Rosy	51
Larney, Charley	173	Tanyan, Wesley	152
Larney, Eliza	214	Tiger, Alice	122
Larney, Elmer	107	Tiger, Amos	139
Larney, James	119	Tiger, Ellen	123
Larney, Jimmie	174	Tiger, Julia	78
Larney, Martha	127	Tiger, Lucy	1
Larney, Rachel	213	Thompson, Herbert	115
Larney, Sally	126	Titusie	72
Larney, Sandy	110	Wakkie, Dolly	89
Leah	67	Walker, Jimmy	175
Lena, Lillie	141	Walker, Katie	101
Lena, Losenda	142	Walker, Kissie	221
Little, David	180	Walker, Stella	220
Little, Thomas, Jr.	222	Walker, Terry	100
Losanna	129	War-le-do, Simon	128
Lowe, Eliza	148	Washington, Widie	64
Lowe, Mary	147	Weitna	73
Lucy	75	West, Alice	24
Luste, Martha	189	West, Homer	25
Luste, Sele	190	Williams, Charley	219
Maley	103	Willie	124
Manana	104	Wilson, Hagar	71
Marthla, Helen	91	Wilson, Washington	70
Mary	125	Wolf, Jim	234
Micco, Katie	81	Wolf, Lucinda	134
Micco, Simma	244	Wolf, Sissy	135
Miller, Addie	109	Wood, Emmet	39
Miller, Alice	108	Wood, Fanny	37
Miller, Amosy	99	Wood, Johnnie	20
Mitchell, Lucinda	181	Wood, Julia	80
Moppin, Jimus	192	Wood, Lillie	19
Moppin, Sherman	191	Wood, Maud	38
McCulla, William	133	Wood, Susie	79
McGirt, Sallie Deer	231	Yahola, Elsie	171
McKellop, Lena	227	Yarnah	93

INDEX TO
NEW BORN SEMINOLE FREEDMEN